Gross Domestic Product, 1959–2008 (continued)
(billions of dollars, except as noted)

Year	Net Exports of Goods and Services: Net Exports	Net Exports of Goods and Services: Exports	Net Exports of Goods and Services: Imports	Government Consumption Expenditures and Gross Investment: Total	Federal: Total	Federal: National Defense	Federal: Nondefense	State and Local	Final Sales of Domestic Product	Gross Domestic Purchases[1]	Addendum: Gross National Product[2]	Percent Change from Preceding Period: Gross Domestic Product	Percent Change from Preceding Period: Gross Domestic Purchases[1]
1959	0.4	22.7	22.3	110.0	65.4	53.8	11.5	44.7	502.3	506.2	509.3	1.2	1.2
1960	4.2	27.0	22.8	111.6	64.1	53.4	10.7	47.5	519.0	522.2	529.5	1.4	1.4
1961	4.9	27.6	22.7	119.5	67.9	56.5	11.4	51.6	536.8	539.8	548.2	1.1	1.1
1962	4.1	29.1	25.0	130.1	75.3	61.1	14.2	54.9	575.4	581.5	589.7	1.4	1.3
1963	4.9	31.1	26.1	136.4	76.9	61.0	15.9	59.5	607.2	612.8	622.2	1.1	1.2
1964	6.9	35.0	28.1	143.2	78.5	60.3	18.2	64.8	651.9	656.7	668.5	1.5	1.6
1965	5.6	37.1	31.5	151.5	80.4	60.6	19.8	71.0	704.3	713.5	724.4	1.8	1.7
1966	3.9	40.9	37.1	171.8	92.5	71.7	20.8	79.2	770.3	783.9	792.9	2.8	2.8
1967	3.6	43.5	39.9	192.7	104.8	83.5	21.3	87.9	819.2	829.0	838.0	3.1	2.9
1968	1.4	47.9	46.6	209.4	111.4	89.3	22.1	98.0	899.6	908.6	916.1	4.3	4.2
1969	1.4	51.9	50.5	221.5	113.4	89.5	23.8	108.2	974.0	983.2	990.7	5.0	4.9
1970	4.0	59.7	55.8	233.8	113.5	87.6	25.8	120.3	1032.6	1034.6	1044.9	5.3	5.4
1971	0.6	63.0	62.3	246.5	113.7	84.6	29.1	132.8	1118.2	1126.5	1134.7	5.0	5.1
1972	−3.4	70.8	74.2	263.5	119.7	87.0	32.7	143.8	1232.6	1241.7	1246.8	4.3	4.5
1973	4.1	95.3	91.2	281.7	122.5	88.2	34.3	159.2	1362.7	1378.6	1395.3	5.6	5.8
1974	−0.8	126.7	127.5	317.9	134.6	95.6	39.0	183.4	1486.8	1500.8	1515.5	9.0	10.2
1975	16.0	138.7	122.7	357.7	149.1	103.9	45.1	208.7	1628.6	1622.4	1651.3	9.5	9.3
1976	−1.6	149.5	151.1	383.0	159.7	111.1	48.6	223.3	1809.8	1826.9	1842.1	5.8	5.8
1977	−23.1	159.4	182.4	414.1	175.4	120.9	54.5	238.7	2031.7	2054.0	2051.2	6.4	6.8
1978	−25.4	186.9	212.3	453.6	190.9	130.5	60.4	262.6	2294.3	2320.1	2316.3	7.0	7.1
1979	−22.5	230.1	252.7	500.8	210.6	145.2	65.4	290.2	2567.9	2585.9	2595.3	8.3	8.8
1980	−13.1	280.8	293.8	566.2	243.8	168.0	75.8	322.4	2808.9	2802.6	2823.7	9.1	10.5
1981	−12.5	305.2	317.8	627.5	280.2	196.3	84.0	347.3	3111.2	3141.0	3161.4	9.4	9.1
1982	−20.0	283.2	303.2	680.5	310.8	225.9	84.9	369.7	3289.9	3275.0	3291.5	6.1	5.7
1983	−51.7	277.0	328.6	733.5	342.9	250.7	92.3	390.5	3594.1	3588.3	3573.8	3.9	3.5
1984	−102.7	302.4	405.1	797.0	374.4	281.6	92.8	422.6	3970.5	4035.9	3969.5	3.8	3.5
1985	−115.2	302.0	417.2	879.0	412.8	311.2	101.6	466.2	4313.6	4335.5	4246.8	3.0	2.9
1986	−132.7	320.5	453.3	949.3	438.6	330.9	107.8	510.7	4589.0	4595.6	4480.6	2.2	2.3
1987	−145.2	363.9	509.1	999.5	460.1	350.0	110.0	539.4	4857.5	4884.7	4757.4	2.7	3.1
1988	−110.4	444.1	554.5	1039.0	462.3	354.9	107.4	576.7	5195.7	5214.2	5127.4	3.4	3.4
1989	−88.2	503.3	591.5	1099.1	482.2	362.2	120.0	616.9	5544.8	5572.5	5510.6	3.8	3.8
1990	−78.0	552.4	630.3	1180.2	508.3	374.0	134.3	671.9	5866.5	5881.1	5837.9	3.9	4.1
1991	−27.5	596.8	624.3	1234.4	527.7	383.2	144.5	706.7	6023.8	6023.4	6026.3	3.5	3.3
1992	−33.2	635.3	668.6	1271.0	533.9	376.9	157.0	737.0	6354.7	6371.0	6367.4	2.3	2.3
1993	−65.0	655.8	720.9	1291.2	525.2	362.9	162.4	766.0	6701.6	6722.4	6689.3	2.3	2.2
1994	−93.6	720.9	814.5	1325.5	519.1	353.7	165.5	806.3	7102.0	7165.8	7098.4	2.1	2.1
1995	−91.4	812.2	903.6	1369.2	519.2	348.7	170.5	850.0	7457.9	7489.0	7433.4	2.0	2.1
1996	−96.2	868.6	964.8	1416.0	527.4	354.6	172.8	888.6	7882.3	7913.1	7851.9	1.9	1.8
1997	−101.6	955.3	1056.9	1468.7	530.9	349.6	181.3	937.8	8333.9	8405.9	8337.3	1.7	1.4
1998	−159.9	955.9	1115.9	1518.3	530.4	345.7	184.7	987.9	8836.2	8906.9	8768.3	1.1	0.6
1999	−260.5	991.2	1251.7	1620.8	555.8	360.6	195.2	1065.0	9462.0	9528.9	9302.2	1.4	1.6
2000	−379.5	1096.3	1475.8	1721.6	578.8	370.3	208.5	1142.8	10140.0	10196.4	9855.9	2.2	2.5
2001	−367.0	1032.8	1399.8	1825.6	612.9	392.6	220.3	1212.8	10526.7	10495.0	10171.6	2.4	2.0
2002	−424.4	1005.9	1430.3	1961.1	679.7	437.1	242.5	1281.5	10457.7	10894.0	10500.2	1.7	3.8
2003	−499.4	1040.8	1540.2	2092.5	756.4	497.2	259.2	1336.0	10946.5	11460.2	11017.6	2.1	5.2
2004	−615.4	1182.4	1797.8	2216.8	825.6	550.7	274.9	1391.2	11627.3	12301.3	11762.1	2.9	4.1
2005	−713.6	1311.5	2025.1	2355.3	875.5	588.1	287.4	1479.8	12378.6	13135.5	12514.9	3.3	3.0
2006	−757.3	1480.8	2238.1	2508.1	932.2	624.1	308.0	1575.9	13129.0	13935.7	13256.6	3.2	2.6
2007	−707.8	1662.4	2370.2	2674.8	979.3	662.2	317.1	1695.5	13811.2	14515.3	13910.0	2.7	1.4
2008	−669.2	1859.4	2528.6	2882.4	1071.9	734.9	337.0	1810.4	14311.6	14933.8	14397.8	2.2	−0.3

Economics

The McGraw-Hill Series in Economics

Essentials of Economics

Brue, McConnell, and Flynn
Essentials of Economics
Second Edition

Mandel
Economics: The Basics
First Edition

Schiller
Essentials of Economics
Seventh Edition

Principles of Economics

Colander
Economics, Microeconomics, and Macroeconomics
Eighth Edition

Frank and Bernanke
Principles of Economics, Principles of Microeconomics, Principles of Macroeconomics
Fourth Edition

Frank and Bernanke
Brief Editions: Principles of Economics, Principles of Microeconomics, Principles of Macroeconomics
First Edition

McConnell, Brue, and Flynn
Economics, Microeconomics, and Macroeconomics
Eighteenth Edition

McConnell, Brue, and Flynn
Brief Editions: Microeconomics and Macroeconomics
First Edition

Miller
Principles of Microeconomics
First Edition

Samuelson and Nordhaus
Economics, Microeconomics, and Macroeconomics
Nineteenth Edition

Schiller
The Economy Today, The Micro Economy Today, and The Macro Economy Today
Twelfth Edition

Slavin
Economics, Microeconomics, and Macroeconomics
Ninth Edition

Economics of Social Issues

Guell
Issues in Economics Today
Fifth Edition

Sharp, Register, and Grimes
Economics of Social Issues
Nineteenth Edition

Econometrics

Gujarati and Porter
Basic Econometrics
Fifth Edition

Gujarati and Porter
Essentials of Econometrics
Fourth Edition

Managerial Economics

Baye
Managerial Economics and Business Strategy
Seventh Edition

Brickley, Smith, and Zimmerman
Managerial Economics and Organizational Architecture
Fifth Edition

Thomas and Maurice
Managerial Economics
Ninth Edition

Intermediate Economics

Bernheim and Whinston
Microeconomics
First Edition

Dornbusch, Fischer, and Startz
Macroeconomics
Tenth Edition

Frank
Microeconomics and Behavior
Eighth Edition

Advanced Economics

Romer
Advanced Macroeconomics
Third Edition

Money and Banking

Cecchetti
Money, Banking, and Financial Markets
Second Edition

Urban Economics

O'Sullivan
Urban Economics
Seventh Edition

Labor Economics

Borjas
Labor Economics
Fifth Edition

McConnell, Brue, and Macpherson
Contemporary Labor Economics
Ninth Edition

Public Finance

Rosen and Gayer
Public Finance
Ninth Edition

Seidman
Public Finance
First Edition

Environmental Economics

Field and Field
Environmental Economics: An Introduction
Fifth Edition

International Economics

Appleyard, Field, and Cobb
International Economics
Seventh Edition

King and King
International Economics, Globalization, and Policy: A Reader
Fifth Edition

Pugel
International Economics
Fourteenth Edition

Economics

Eighth Edition

David C. Colander

Middlebury College

McGraw-Hill Irwin

Boston Burr Ridge, IL Dubuque, IA New York San Francisco St. Louis
Bangkok Bogotá Caracas Kuala Lumpur Lisbon London Madrid Mexico City
Milan Montreal New Delhi Santiago Seoul Singapore Sydney Taipei Toronto

The McGraw-Hill Companies

McGraw-Hill Irwin

ECONOMICS
Published by McGraw-Hill/Irwin, a business unit of The McGraw-Hill Companies, Inc., 1221 Avenue of the Americas, New York, NY, 10020.

This book is printed on acid-free paper.

1 2 3 4 5 6 7 8 9 0 DOW/DOW 0 9

ISBN 978-0-07-337588-5
MHID 0-07-337588-8

Vice president and editor-in-chief: *Brent Gordon*
Publisher: *Douglas Reiner*
Director of development: *Ann Torbert*
Development editor II: *Karen L. Fisher*
Vice president and director of marketing: *Robin J. Zwettler*
Senior marketing manager: *Jennifer Lambert*
Vice president of editing, design, and production: *Sesha Bolisetty*
Senior project manager: *Susanne Riedell*
Lead production supervisor: *Carol A. Bielski*
Interior designer: *Pam Verros*
Senior photo research coordinator: *Jeremy Cheshareck*
Photo researcher: *Ira C. Roberts*
Lead media project manager: *Kerry Bowler*
Cover design: *Pam Verros*
Typeface: *10.3/12 Goudy*
Compositor: *Aptara®, Inc.*
Printer: *R. R. Donnelley*

Library of Congress Cataloging-in-Publication Data

Colander, David C.
Economics / David C. Colander. — 8th ed.
p. cm. — (The McGraw-Hill series economics)
Includes index.
ISBN-13: 978-0-07-337588-5 (alk. paper)
ISBN-10: 0-07-337588-8 (alk. paper)
1. Economics. I. Title.
HB171.5.C788 2010
330—dc22

2009021164

www.mhhe.com

Dedicated to the memory of Frank Knight and Thorstein Veblen, both of whose economics have significantly influenced the contents of this book.

About the Author

David Colander is the Christian A. Johnson Distinguished Professor of Economics at Middlebury College. He has authored, coauthored, or edited over 40 books and over 150 articles on a wide range of economic topics.

He earned his B.A. at Columbia College and his M.Phil. and Ph.D. at Columbia University. He also studied at the University of Birmingham in England and at Wilhelmsburg Gymnasium in Germany. Professor Colander has taught at Columbia University, Vassar College, and the University of Miami, as well as having been a consultant to Time-Life Films, a consultant to Congress, a Brookings Policy Fellow, and Visiting Scholar at Nuffield College, Oxford. In 2001–2002, he was the Kelley Professor of Distinguished Teaching at Princeton University.

He belongs to a variety of professional associations and has been president of both the History of Economic Thought Society and the Eastern Economics Association. He has also served on the editorial boards of the *Journal of Economic Perspectives*, *The Journal of Economic Education*, *The Journal of Economic Methodology*, *The Journal of the History of Economic Thought*, *The Journal of Socio-Economics*, and *The Eastern Economic Journal*. He has been chair of the AEA Committee on Electronic Publishing and is currently a member of the AEA Committee on Economic Education and the associate editor for content of the *Journal of Economic Education*.

He is married to a pediatrician, Patrice, who has a private practice in Middlebury, Vermont. In their spare time, the Colanders designed and built their oak post-and-beam house on a ridge overlooking the Green Mountains to the east and the Adirondacks to the west. The house is located on the site of a former drive-in movie theater. (They replaced the speaker poles with fruit trees and used the I-beams from the screen as support for the second story of the carriage house and the garage. Dave's office and library are in the former projection room.)

Preface for the Professor

"Imagine . . . a textbook that students enjoy!" That comment, from an instructor who taught at Purdue, was e-mailed to me as I was struggling to write the preface to an earlier edition. That comment still captures what I believe to be the most distinctive feature of my book. I've always felt that the books students read in their courses should speak to them and be as enjoyable as possible to read. Making the book as enjoyable to the student as possible continues to be a guiding principle for my writing.

The Book Presents Modern, Not Neoclassical, Economics

A second of my guiding principles in writing this book is to present students with the best economics I can. That means that I want to teach them *modern economics*, not neoclassical economics (or whatever else the collection of models that developed in the 1950s is called) that has developed as the standard template for all principles books.

I know the difficulties of deviating from that standard template. (After all, I'm the one who coined the 15 percent rule for textbooks.) I know and accept that if we are going to teach modern economics, it has to be done in the context of the standard textbook template, at least at this point. But recognizing the importance of the existing template is not a call for laziness and complacency in what we teach; it is a call for creativity. If we are to consider ourselves to be serious teachers of economics, we can and should be doing whatever we can to teach students modern economics, not some vestige from the past. Over the last couple of years I have been working on ways to introduce modern economics into the principles course—trying different ideas on my students and colleagues and discovering what works and what doesn't. In this edition I start to apply some of that work to this book, and start to integrate modern economics into the standard principles template.

I have discussed the difficulties of presenting modern economics with numerous colleagues, who, while most share my desire to present modern economics to students, see it as a bit of a utopian dream. One of the problems they have pointed out is that many of their students are, shall we say, less-than-perfect students.

I am not unaware of the nature of students—in fact I was one of those far-less-than-perfect students. So I am no utopian; I am a realist, who recognizes that most students could care less about how an economist thinks, and even less about how a modern economist thinks. They are taking the course because it is required, because their parents told them they had to, or because it was what fit in their schedule. That is the reality, and they are the students I'm writing for. Why am I writing for them? Because they remind me of me, and if I can excite these marginal students about economics, I will likely also excite those more perfect, self-motivated, students who professors dream of having in class. So my target student is a non-economics major who doesn't especially care what's in the book, and is much more likely to be concerned with what is going to be on the exam (and sometimes they don't even care about that). I regard this fact as liberating, not confining, which makes it even more important that we teach them modern economics, not a set of models from an outdated template. I want them to know TANSTAAFL, to know the strength of markets, the weaknesses of markets, the importance of incentives, and why economic policy is so complicated and messy.

How does a teacher excite students who are less than excited about economics? My answer to that question is that you challenge them; you talk to them, you speak a language that they can understand, and you recognize their pain. That's what I try to do in this book. I will fail with many of them, but if I don't try, then I don't deserve to be called a teacher, which in my view is the highest calling an economist can have. Research is for those who cannot teach.

Modern Economics in a Student-Friendly Colloquial Style

To reach these less-than-perfect students, I have written this book in a highly colloquial manner; the book doesn't lecture them, or talk to them in textbookese; it talks to them in conversational English. I strongly believe that most students have the ability to understand economic concepts even though on exams it often appears as if they have serious problems. In my opinion, many of their problems are not conceptual; rather, they are problems of motivation, reading, and math. The economics found in principles courses is not the student's highest priority; it certainly wasn't mine when I was 18. I'm continuously amazed at how many supposedly not-so-good students are conceptually bright. The reality is that most principles books bore this Internet generation. To teach them effectively, we've got to get their attention and hold it.

My colloquial style helps get their attention. The book talks to students and makes them feel that the textbook is a second teacher who is urging them on to study harder, and is trying to explain the material to them. That colloquial style helps with one of the biggest problems in the course—getting students to read the book. Some professors don't always like the style, but even some of them have written to me to say that they use the book anyway because their students read it. And if the students have read the book, teaching is more rewarding.

I get lots of e-mails from students—some ask me if I have sons who share my perverse sense of humor because they'd like to marry them; others tell me that I goofed somewhere in the book. Others complain about their professor—to which I answer the professor is always right. My point is not the content of the e-mails; my point is that students feel comfortable writing to me. Students hear my voice in the book. It is the only economics textbook that establishes a connection with the student. To toot my own horn (what else are prefaces for?), let me share an e-mail that the publishers received from a friend of theirs (an insider to the publishing business) and that they forwarded to me. It said:

> Dear X, My son is a freshman at The University of X. Like many kids he has grown to be less-and-less a reader until fairly recently. He is in the business school at college and he is wandering in search of an eventual major, like so many. He took the Principles Micro in the Fall and "hated" economics. On Monday he told me that his favorite course is Macro. His instructor is "not so helpful" but he is reading the book and making straight A's because the book is "so much fun to read" and he is "learning a ton of stuff." He has registered for the WSJ online and reads it every day. He is thinking of pursuing Econ as a major. It is actually the most positive review by an "end user" of a textbook that I've heard in a long time and, although it took me three days to find out the author and publisher (he didn't know; he just liked reading the book), the book is the latest edition of Colander. So: Thanks!

One of the reasons I keep working on this book is that I get a number of letters and e-mails like this one, and it boosts my admittedly already big ego, but what is life if not a big ego trip? (Yes, I recognize that that last statement is not standard textbookese, but I include it here to give you a sense of what I mean by my colloquial style, and to explain to you how I keep the students' attention as I am pounding into them the need to equate marginal cost and marginal benefits.) Numerous students tell me that they actually break a smile when they read my book, and a few tell me they crack up. Just about everyone tells me that they recognize that the person writing this book is very human—all too human in some people's view.

My colloquial style allows me greater flexibility in the material I present to students than most textbook authors have. Because I'm having a conversation with the students, I can explain to them what material is new and is to be read casually rather than to be memorized. Then, elsewhere where I am presenting material that will likely be on their exam, I can tell them that it is time to buckle down and memorize. So my colloquial style allows me to vary the presentation and I take full advantage of it in explaining to students what modern economics is.

The Meaning of Modern Economics

Modern economics can mean different things to different people, and my interpretation of modern economics includes two principles that are central to good modern economists. These two principles are that (1) institutions and history are important in policy discussions and (2) good economics is open economics—willing to deal with all ideas. The mantra of good economics is, "Tell me something I don't already know, using whatever method works." Let me discuss each of these principles briefly.

Institutions and History Are Important

If one opens up Adam Smith's *Wealth of Nations*, John Stuart Mill's *Principles of Political Economy*, or Alfred Marshall's *Principles of Economics*, one will see economic analysis placed in historical and institutional context. The modern textbook template moved away from that, and in previous editions, I have tried to return the principles of economics toward that broader template with models presented in historical and institutional context. This edition continues that emphasis on institutions and history. Modern work in game theory and strategic decision making is making it clear that the implications of economic reasoning depend on the institutional setting. To understand economics requires an understanding of existing institutions and the historical development of those institutions. In a principles course we don't have time to present much about history and institutions, but that does not preclude us from letting students know that we know that these issues are important. And that's what I try to do.

A Focus on Policy

When I say that institutions and history are important, I am talking about economic policy. As I stated above, this book is *not* written for future economics majors. Most principles students aren't going to go on in economics. Thus, this book is written for students who will probably take only one or two economics courses in their lifetime. These students are interested in policy, and what I try to present to them are the basics of modern economic reasoning as they relate to policy questions.

Because I think policy is so important, in this edition I bring a distinction made by J. N. Keynes (John Maynard Keynes' father) to the fore. That distinction is between *theorems*—the deductive conclusions of models—and *precepts*—the considered judgments of economists about the policy implications of the models. I make it clear to students that models do not tell us what to do about policy—they give us theorems. Only when we combine the model's results with our understanding of institutions, the relevance of the models given the assumptions, and normative goals, can we arrive at policy conclusions.

Openness to Various Views

While I present modern economics in the book, I present it in such a way that it is open to many different points of view. Thus, it doesn't present the material as "the truth" but simply as the conventional wisdom, the learning of which is a useful hurdle for all students to jump over. To encourage students to question conventional wisdom, there is a set of questions at the end of each chapter—Questions from Alternative Perspectives—questions written by economists from a variety of different perspectives. These include Post-Keynesian, feminist, Austrian, Radical, Institutionalist, and religious questions. The Radical questions come from the Dollars and Sense Collective, a group with whom I've worked to coordinate their readers (www.dollarsandsense.org/bookstore.html) with this text. I also often integrate Austrian ideas into my class; I find that *The Free Market* (www.mises.org/freemarket.asp) is a provocative resource.

I often pair an article in *The Free Market* with one in *Dollars and Sense* in my assignments to students for supplementary reading. Having students read both radical and Austrian views, and then integrate those views into their own, generally middle-of-the-road, views is, for me, a perfect way of teaching the principles course. (If I have radicals and libertarians in the class, I argue in favor of middle-of-the-road views.) If you like to teach the course emphasizing alternative views, you might want to assign the brief survey of different approaches to economics in the "Preface for the Student" close to the beginning of the course, and then have the students answer the alternative perspective questions at the end of each chapter.

The Evolution of a Standard Economics Textbook to a Modern Economics Textbook

My goal in writing this principles book has always been to teach students modern economics, so in a way my goal has not changed from previous editions. What has changed is my understanding of what works in a principles book and what doesn't. After years of exploration, I believe that I have found a way to introduce students to modern economics while still keeping the standard textbook template, so that they can also learn the important lessons of timeless economics. The key is to recognize that it is the modeling approach, not the specific models, that is central to economics.

Robert Solow nicely captured the importance of modeling to modern economics when he said that, for better or worse, economics is a modeling science. This means that an important aspect of teaching students modern economics involves introducing them to the modeling approach to understanding the world. The old principles textbook template to that modeling approach was to teach students the supply and demand model and how to apply it to economic problems. The problem with this approach is that supply and demand is just one model, which isn't necessarily the best model for many issues. Modern economics has kept the modeling method but has gone beyond supply and demand. I try to make that clear to students, while still teaching them to use the supply and demand model in those places where it is appropriate.

In doing so, I see myself following in the tradition of Alfred Marshall, who is most responsible for introducing the supply and demand model to principles. But his principles book, which I keep on my shelf and refer to often, made it clear to the reader that supply/demand was a shorthand method—an example of his one-thing-at-a-time method—not the end method. He emphasized that economics was an approach to problems, not a body of confirmed truths. In my view, *it is the modeling method, not the models*, that is most important to teach our students. In my presentation of models, I carefully try to guide students in the modeling method, rather than having them memorize truths from models. I carefully emphasize the limitations of the models and the assumptions that underlie them, and am constantly urging students to think beyond the models. This approach pushes the students a bit harder than the alternative, but it is, in my view, the best pedagogical approach.

Following up on that approach led me to work on a chapter on thinking like a modern economist, which I sent out to reviewers. Unlike what they had said about my earlier attempts (you don't want to hear the words they used, but let me assure you, the reviews of previous attempts didn't do much for my ego), the responses this time were highly positive, not only from reviewers, but from the top modern economists. For example, here is a comment from a former chair of a major graduate department:

> Dear Dave: Your chapter is, and I hardly ever say such a thing, magnificent. Would that students have a chance to have a teacher who can make this come alive!

Here is another from a top economic theorist:

> Dave, This chapter does a great job in explaining what economists do! Indeed I think it is so good that I wish you could publish it in some prominent place so that the public and other scientists would digest it. The public at large and many of the Nats (natural scientists) that I hang with would benefit greatly from reading this.

The reviews from the teachers were similarly positive; they said my approach works; they loved the chapter and could teach it.

At that point, I decided to go for it—to really try to present introductory students to modern economics within the standard textbook template. To do it, I kept the core of the book the same, but added three chapters dealing with modern economics in such a way that they are separable, so professors who don't want to teach them, or don't have time to teach them, don't have to do so. The three new chapters are "Thinking Like a Modern Economist," which is a new chapter in the introductory section; "Behavioral Economics and Modern Economic Policy," which is a new chapter in the micro section; and "Thinking Like a Modern Macroeconomist," which is a new chapter in the macro section of the book.

These three chapters, along with a new set of boxes, "Thinking Like a Modern Economist," which are integrated throughout the other chapters, allow me to introduce students to modern economics while still presenting them with the standard models. But in the modern presentation, the standard models are presented to students as examples of modern economists' approach, not as the modern economic approach. In recognition of the central role that game theory plays in modern economic thinking, I modified the game theory chapter significantly and moved it earlier in the text. In addition, I also added a fourth new chapter dealing with the financial crisis that hit the economy in 2008.

As I said, I have been working on these ideas for a long time, and in working on those ideas I had begun collaborating with a young colleague of mine, Casey Rothschild, who graduated from, and who is currently teaching at, MIT. Casey shares my vision of economics and also shares my passion for teaching economics. We are working on a book and some articles on modern economics, and portions of the three chapters come from that work. (Those portions are used with permission.) Our collaboration was sufficiently close that I asked him to work on some of the chapters with me, and I liked what I saw. I'm happy to say that he has agreed to become more involved with the book in the coming years.

Auto Gradable End-of-Chapter Questions

It isn't only the content of the book that has been modernized. In the last edition, McGraw-Hill introduced a new system called *Connect*™ that allowed some end-of-chapter questions to be computer graded. In this edition, I pushed the envelope further and redesigned the questions at the end of the chapter so that *all* the questions and problems (except for the "Issues to Ponder" and "Questions from Alternative Perspectives" sections) are auto gradable. This means that they can be assigned to students either as problem sets (which can be graded automatically) or as practice exercises (with immediate feedback to students). I see this as an enormous advance in pedagogy. It was a huge project to modify all the questions so that they were auto gradable, but I think it was worth it. Now, even professors in large lecture classes can assign the questions and exercises at the end of the chapters and get feedback to the students about whether they are on the right track. It is an enormous advance, and I hope that you will take advantage of it.

Summary of the Changes

Let me conclude this preface with a brief summary of the major changes in this edition.

- *Three new chapters on modern economics*. These chapters introduce students to modern economics and its policy implications. They can be skipped, or can be simply assigned to the students but not lectured on because they are self-contained. In addition, the game theory chapter has been moved up in the book and made independent of the oligopoly chapter to let students know its central importance to modern economics.

- The micro chapters are reorganized to put more policy up front and to better fit modern economics. Specifically, the game theory chapter has been developed as a separate chapter and moved up to immediately follow the logic of individual choice chapter, and the international policy chapter has been moved up to follow the taxation policy chapter.
- *Chapter on financial crisis*. A new chapter on the financial crisis brings the students up to date on what's happening with the financial crisis that hit the economy in late 2008. This chapter relates those current events with the models and policy discussion of earlier chapters.
- *Auto-gradable end-of-chapter questions*. The end-of-chapter questions and exercises have been made auto gradable, so that they can be assigned and graded either as homework or as problem sets, without the professor having to do the grading.

In-Depth Chapter-by-Chapter Discussion of Changes

Changes Common to All Chapters

- Data has been updated.
- More difficult questions at the end of the chapter have been moved to a new section, "Issues to Ponder."
- Remaining questions at the end of the chapter are revised and reorganized into one section, "Questions and Exercises."
- Web questions at the end of the chapter have been deleted.

Chapter 1, Economics and Economic Reasoning

- New section "Modern Economics" introduces methods of economic reasoning and the variety of ways modern economists develop models based on observed data. Modern economics uses a combination of inductive and deductive reasoning to gain insight into the economy. The combination of these two methods is called *abduction*.
- Two particular new terms introduced in this chapter are important to note: theorems and precepts. Theorems are propositions that are logically true based on the assumptions of a model. Precepts are policy rules that are based on theorems but also include empirical facts and goals of society. Two economists might agree on theorems, but disagree about precepts based on those theorems.
- New key terms: deduction, induction, and abduction; experimental economics; natural experiments; theorems; precepts.

Chapter 2, The Production Possibility Model, Trade, and Globalization

- Explains that laissez-faire is not a theorem, but a precept.

Chapter 3, Economic Institutions

- New short subsection "Other Roles of Households" lists ways in which households are the driving force for much of the economy.
- New subsection "Choice Architecture" within the section on government discusses policy and introduces "nudge policy." How a question is framed often affects the decision. Government can use this observation to change how choices are framed and thus influence choices. An example is the default option bias.

Chapter 4, Supply and Demand

- Some material reorganized within the chapter.

Chapter 5, Using Supply and Demand

- Replaced example of shifting demand and supply (coffee beans) with a more recent example (edible oils).

Chapter 6, Thinking Like a Modern Economist (new chapter)

This chapter introduces students to thinking like a modern economist in a fun way. It argues that the glue that holds modern economics together is its modeling approach, and presents students with a number of modern economic models. It distinguishes modern traditional economics from modern behavioral economics. It tells students how modern economics is empirical and describes how modern economists use data and theory to arrive at results.

Chapter 7, Describing Supply and Demand: Elasticities

- This is Chapter 6 from the seventh edition.
- New "Thinking Like a Modern Economist" box titled "Why Do So Many Prices End in 99 Cents?"

Chapter 8, Taxation and Government Intervention

- This is Chapter 7 from the seventh edition.
- New "Thinking Like a Modern Economist" box titled "How to Get Students to Be Responsible."

Chapter 9, International Trade Policy, Comparative Advantage, and Outsourcing

- This is Chapter 21 from the seventh edition. It has been moved up to encourage a fuller discussion of policy early in the semester.

Chapter 10, The Logic of Individual Choice: The Foundation of Supply and Demand

- This is Chapter 8 from the seventh edition.
- New "Thinking Like a Modern Economist" box titled "The Traditional Models as Stepping Stones."
- Added a new example of the status quo bias (Sweden's privatization of Social Security set one portfolio as default).

Chapter 11, Game Theory, Strategic Decision Making, and Behavioral Economics

- This is Chapter 14 from the seventh edition. It now ties in more directly with behavioral economics.
- Moved the discussion of game theory relative to oligopoly to Chapter 16.
- New "A Reminder" box titled "The Austan Goolsbee *Check-a-Box* Method for Finding Dominant Strategies and Nash Equilibria," which gives students a mechanical way to find solutions to games.
- Added new section, "Real-World Applications of Informal Game Theory," that illustrates how the TV show *Survivor* and Warren Buffett's proposal for campaign finance reform can be analyzed using game theory.
- Replaced existing example of loss aversion.

Chapter 12, Production and Cost Analysis I

- This is Chapter 9 from the seventh edition.
- Replaced the example in the box "Spin-offs, Mergers, and Transaction Costs" with a more recent example.
- New "Thinking Like a Modern Economist" box titled "What 'Goods' Do Firms Produce: The Cost of Producing Image."

Chapter 13, Production and Cost Analysis II

- This is Chapter 10 from the seventh edition.
- New "Thinking Like a Modern Economist" box titled "Social Norms and Production."

Chapter 14, Perfect Competition

- This is Chapter 11 from the seventh edition.

Chapter 15, Monopoly

- This is Chapter 12 from the seventh edition.

Chapter 16, Monopolistic Competition and Oligopoly

- This is Chapter 13 from the seventh edition.

Chapter 17, Real-World Competition and Technology

- This is Chapter 15 from the seventh edition.
- Sections moved from Chapter 14 include "Prisoner's Dilemma and a Duopoly Example," "Duopoly and a Payoff Matrix," and "Low Price Guarantees: The Advantage of Rules or Precommitment."

Chapter 18, Antitrust Policy and Regulation

- This is Chapter 16 from the seventh edition.
- Added an additional competitive force facing Microsoft—software on the Internet.
- Updated Microsoft antitrust issue with the EU.
- Updated guidelines Justice Department uses for reviewing horizontal mergers. Based on the Herfindahl index.
- Added section "Sovereign Wealth Funds" discussing investment funds held by governments that give sovereign nations a potential controlling interest in foreign companies.
- Revised assessment of deregulation from largely positive to mixed.

Chapter 19, Work and the Labor Market

- This is Chapter 17 from the seventh edition.

Chapter 20, Who Gets What? The Distribution of Income

- This is Chapter 18 from the seventh edition.
- Food stamps program has been replaced with Supplemental Nutritional Assistance Program (SNAP).

Chapter 21, Market Failure versus Government Failure

- This is Chapter 19 from the seventh edition.

Chapter 22, Behavioral Economics and Modern Economic Policy (new chapter)

This is a new chapter that looks at the policy implication of behavioral economics. It explains to students how the acceptance of behavioral economics assumptions undermines formal welfare economics' policy prescription, and presents the difficulties of drawing policy implications from behavioral economics. It introduces students to modern work in mechanism design and choice architecture and contrasts nudge policy with push policy.

Chapter 23, Microeconomics Policy, Economic Reasoning, and Beyond

- This is Chapter 20 from the seventh edition.
- Replaced value of human life estimates.

Chapter 24, Economic Growth, Business Cycles, Unemployment, and Inflation

- This is Chapter 22 from the seventh edition.
- Discussion of inflation includes price shock in mid-2008 and reversal in late 2008.

Chapter 25, Measuring the Aggregate Economy

- This is Chapter 23 from the seventh edition.
- Added discussion of the distinction between real and nominal wealth. Nominal wealth rises because of asset inflation and an increase in the productive capacity of real wealth. Distinguishing between the two is difficult. Increases in nominal wealth up until mid-2008 could perhaps largely reflect asset inflation, not increases in productive capacity.
- New key terms: real wealth, nominal wealth, asset inflation.

Chapter 26, Growth, Productivity, and the Wealth of Nations

- This is Chapter 24 from the seventh edition.
- Added discussion of the significant rise in oil prices in 2007 and part of 2008 and its effect on developing alternative fuel sources.

Chapter 27, The Aggregate Demand/Aggregate Supply Model

- This is Chapter 25 from the seventh edition.
- Revisions to this chapter prepare students for the new chapter (Chapter 29), "Thinking Like a Modern Macroeconomist."
- Additional discussion of the historical development of the *AS/AD* model.
- Emphasizes that the *AS/AD* model does not highlight dynamic feedback effects.
- Wealth effect is now more narrowly defined as the "money wealth effect." That is, when price level rises, one feels poorer because the money one holds becomes less valuable. This excludes other financial assets. The money wealth effect is now listed as the third in a list of three effects.
- Adds explanation for why one might expect the *AD* curve to be vertical.
- Adds new section "Dynamic Price Level Adjustment Feedback Effects" that explains how feedback effects from a changing price level (will shift aggregate demand curve) can overwhelm the standard effects (will change quantity of aggregate demand) and destabilize the economy. (See especially Figure 27-8.)
- Adds discussion about the feedback effect of a falling price level (reduces expected growth, reduces aggregate expenditures, undermines the financial system) under complications of the *AS/AD* model.
- Revised key term: wealth effect now called the "money wealth effect."
- New key terms: deflation and paradox of thrift.

Chapter 28, The Multiplier Model

- This is Chapter 26 from the seventh edition.
- Introduction now emphasizes that while the *AS/AD* model downplays dynamic feedback effects, the multiplier model makes them central. Suggests that the *AS/AD* model is better when economic fluctuations are minimal and the multiplier model is better when fluctuations are greater.
- Figure depicting *AS/AD* model when prices are fixed is deleted.
- Adds example of worldwide recession of 2008 into 2009.
- Discusses how the multiplier model overestimates effects of small shocks to the economy but underestimates large shocks.

- Introduces the multiplier-accelerator model in which changes in output are accelerated because changes in investment depend on changes in income.
- New key term: multiplier-accelerator model.

Chapter 29, Thinking Like a Modern Macroeconomist (new chapter)

This is a new chapter that introduces students to the modern macro DSGE model (in a fun way) and distinguishes that model from the standard macro models that they learn in the text. The DSGE model is described as a scientific model and the standard model is described as an engineering model. It also introduces students to the ultramodern complexity approach to macroeconomics and distinguishes the three approaches in terms of assumptions about the dynamics of the assumed learning process.

Chapter 30, The Financial Sector and the Economy

- This is Chapter 27 from the seventh edition.
- Revisions to this chapter focus on the financial crisis that began in 2007/2008.
- The chapter begins with a discussion of derivatives, securitization, and systemic risk.
- New section "Endogenous Money and Credit" explains how reserves and the money supply are mutually determined. The Fed targets an interest rate; the money multiplier determines the amount of reserves needed to achieve that rate.
- Discusses the increased importance of credit to the economy.
- Appendix A: Discussion of financial institutions and financial transactions cut.
- Appendix B (Creation of Money Using T-Accounts) eliminated.

Chapter 31, Monetary Policy

- This is Chapter 28 from the seventh edition.
- Incorporates the Fed's response to the financial crisis in 2008.
- Updated material to include fact that the Fed began to pay interest on reserves.
- New Figure 31-5, "Federal Funds Rate and the Taylor Rule," illustrates how, until 2006, the Fed kept the Fed funds rate lower than the Taylor Rule would suggest. May have contributed to the housing bubble.
- New section, "Quantitative Easing," discusses how the Fed uses tools other than the standard tools to try to expand the economy. Quantitative easing tools include buying bonds even when the Fed funds rate is already zero and buying other financial assets such as money market funds, corporate bonds, or mortgage-backed securities.
- Appendix A (The Effect of Monetary Policy Using T-Accounts) eliminated.
- New key term: quantitative easing.

Chapter 32, Financial Crises, Panics, and Macroeconomic Policy (new chapter)

This is a new chapter that explains why the financial crisis that hit the U.S. economy in 2008 was so scary and outlines the policy response that the government has undertaken to deal with the crisis. It divides the policy response to the crisis into three stages—triage, treatment, and rehabilitation—and compares the recent policy response with the response in the 1930s depression. In the process, it introduces students to how extrapolative expectations can lead to bubbles and depressions, and the problems that systemic risk poses for the aggregate economy.

Chapter 33, Inflation and the Phillips Curve

- This is Chapter 29 from the seventh edition.
- New example of oil and food price shocks in early 2008.
- New discussion of deflation.
- New key term: deflation.

Chapter 34, Deficits and Debt

- This is Chapter 31 from the seventh edition.
- Updated data.
- Section "Social Security, Medicare, and Lockboxes" moved to an appendix to this chapter.
- New section, "The Deficit, the Debt, and the Crisis of 2008," discusses the economic situation in late 2008 and early 2009.

Chapter 35, The Modern Fiscal Policy Dilemma

- This is Chapter 30 from the seventh edition with a *significant* revision. The chapter begins with a discussion of the evolution of fiscal policy and continues with current fiscal policy problems facing policy makers.
- Two main policy approaches are retained—functional finance (active policy when facing depression or hyperinflation) and sound finance (balance the budget).

- The discussion draws on the new concepts—precept and theorem—presented earlier in the text.
- Section on "New Classical" economics has been replaced with a section about "Fiscal Policy in 2009 and Beyond" that discusses the financial bailout and stimulus package to address the recession.
- Deleted key terms: New Classical macroeconomics (now in Chapter 29) and public finance.

Chapter 36, International Financial Policy

- This is Chapter 32 from the seventh edition.

Chapter 37, Macro Policy in a Global Setting

- This is Chapter 33 from the seventh edition.
- Mentions the 2008 global monetary crisis and recent appreciation of the dollar.

Chapter 38, Macro Policies in Developing Countries

- This is Chapter 34 from the seventh edition.
- Table showing annual inflation rates for selected years replaced with line chart of inflation by regions.

Ancillaries

McGraw-Hill has established a strong history of top-rate supplements to accompany this book, and this eighth edition strives to carry on the tradition of excellence.

Study Guide

The study guide—written by myself and Jenifer Gamber—provides a review of the concepts from each chapter. It gives students options to match a variety of learning styles: short-answer questions, matching terms with definitions, problems and applications, multiple-choice questions, brainteasers, and potential essay questions. To make the guide a true study tool, each answer includes an explanation of why it is correct. In addition, the answers to the even-numbered end-of-chapter textbook questions can be found in the study guide.

Instructor's Manual

This book boasts one of the strongest Instructor's Manuals on the market, and Paul Fisher of Henry Ford Community College has worked incredibly hard to maintain the high standard set in previous editions. Elements include:

- Learning Objectives: Lists the learning objectives for each chapter for a quick overview.
- Teaching Objectives: Alerts new professors to common student difficulties with the material and provides help for addressing them.
- Changes to the Eighth Edition: Summarizes the ways in which each chapter has been updated since the seventh edition for professors used to teaching from the previous edition.
- For Professors New to Colander: Notes some of the names, notations, definitions, or symbols that Colander uses as compared to other books to help professors new to Colander transition into the book.
- Chapter Outline: Outlines and summarizes what students are reading in this chapter in the text, both in terms of concepts and examples. Headings and subheadings are tagged with the number of the learning objective (LO) to which the material in that section most closely relates and the associated PowerPoint slide numbers, so you may also use this to help you outline your lecture.
- Additional Textbook Material: Briefly summarizes the content of various boxed material found throughout this chapter of the textbook.
- Check for Understanding: Can be assigned as short writing assignments, used for group activities, or incorporated into a lecture. The questions are labeled with the learning objective they test.
- Problem Sets: Present 5–8 questions for each chapter. They are designed to be photocopied and distributed for student use. Answers to the problem sets appear in the Instructor's Manual and online.

The Instructor's Manual also includes an essay about how to meet the unique challenges of teaching large classes. The Instructor's Manual is available on the instructor's portion of the book's Web site, www.mhhe.com/colander8e.

Test Banks

The test bank contains over 5,600 unique, quality questions for instructors to draw from in their classrooms—a great resource for all professors, and especially for departments with multiple sections. Brian Lynch of Lakeland Community College and Timothy Terrell of Wofford College worked diligently for months to make sure that this revised version is clear and useful. Each question is categorized by chapter learning objective, level of difficulty (easy, medium, hard), and economic concept. Multiple-choice items have also been identified by the

AACSB and Bloom's Taxonomy skill they cover for ease of use.

Questions were reviewed by professors and students alike to make sure that each one was effective for classroom use, and each new question was reviewed by Jenifer Gamber for accuracy, clarity, and consistency with the textbook.

An additional essay-only test bank, also revised by Paul Fisher, now consists of approximately 600 short-answer questions, essay questions, and graphical and mathematical problems. Questions vary in level of difficulty and type of skill being tested. This essay test bank is available on the instructor's side of the book's Online Learning Center, www.mhhe.com/colander8e.

Both test banks are also available in print form upon request and in the EZ Test electronic test-generator on the Instructor's side of the Online Learning Center.

McGraw-Hill *Connect Economics*

Less Managing. More Teaching. Greater Learning.

Connect Economics is an online assignment and assessment solution that offers a number of powerful tools and features to make managing assignments easier so faculty can spend more time teaching. With *Connect Economics*, students can engage with their coursework anytime and anywhere, making the learning process more accessible and efficient.

Simple assignment management

With *Connect Economics*, creating assignments is easier than ever, so you can spend more time teaching and less time managing. The assignment management function enables you to:

- Create and deliver assignments easily with selectable end-of-chapter questions and test bank items.
- Streamline lesson planning, student progress reporting, and assignment grading to make classroom management more efficient than ever.
- Go paperless with the eBook and online submission and grading of student assignments.

Smart grading

Connect Economics helps students learn more efficiently by providing feedback and practice material when they need it, where they need it. The grading function in *Connect Economics* also enables instructors to:

- Score assignments automatically, giving students immediate feedback on their work and side-by-side comparisons with correct answers.
- Access and review each response; manually change grades or leave comments for students to review.
- Reinforce classroom concepts with practice tests and instant quizzes.

Student study center

The *Connect Economics* Student Study Center is the place for students to access additional resources. The Student Study Center:

- Offers students quick access to lectures, practice materials, eBooks, and more.
- Provides instant practice material and study questions, easily accessible on the go.
- Gives students access to the Personalized Learning Plan (described below).

Personalized Learning Plan

The Personalized Learning Plan (PLP) connects each student to the learning resources needed for success in the course. For each chapter, students:

- Take a practice test to initiate the Personalized Learning Plan.
- See how their performance compares to the major concepts within each chapter.
- Receive a Personalized Learning Plan that recommends specific readings from the text, supplemental study material, and practice work that will improve their understanding of each concept.

Diagnostic and adaptive learning of concepts: LearnSmart

The LearnSmart adaptive self-study technology within *Connect Economics* provides students with a seamless combination of practice, assessment, and remediation for every concept in the textbook. LearnSmart's intelligent software adapts to every student response and automatically delivers concepts that advance the student's understanding while reducing time devoted to the concepts already mastered. LearnSmart:

- Applies an intelligent concept engine to identify the relationships between concepts and to serve new concepts to each student only when he or she is ready.
- Adapts automatically to each student, so students spend less time on the topics they understand and more on those they have yet to master.
- Provides continual reinforcement and remediation, but gives only as much guidance as students need.
- Enables you to assess which concepts students have efficiently learned on their own, thus freeing class time for more applications and discussion.

Student progress tracking
Connect Economics keeps instructors informed about how each student, section, and class is performing, allowing for more productive use of lecture and office hours. The progress-tracking function enables you to:

- View scored work immediately and track individual or group performance with assignment and grade reports.
- Access an instant view of student or class performance relative to learning objectives.
- Collect data and generate reports required by many accreditation organizations like AACSB.

McGraw-Hill *Connect Plus Economics*
McGraw-Hill reinvents the textbook learning experience for the modern student with *Connect Plus Economics*. A seamless integration of an eBook and *Connect Economics*, *Connect Plus Economics* provides all of the *Connect Economics* features plus the following:

- An integrated eBook, allowing for anytime, anywhere access to the textbook.
- Dynamic links between the problems or questions you assign to your students and the location in the eBook where that problem or question is covered.
- A powerful search function to pinpoint and connect key concepts in a snap.

In short, *Connect Economics* offers you and your students powerful tools and features that optimize your time and energies, enabling you to focus on course content, teaching, and student learning. *Connect Economics* also offers a wealth of content resources for both instructors and students. This state-of-the-art, thoroughly tested system supports you in preparing students for the world that awaits.

For more information about Connect, go to
www.mcgrawhillconnect.com
or contact your local McGraw-Hill sales representative.

McGraw-Hill Customer Care Contact Information

At McGraw-Hill, we understand that getting the most from new technology can be challenging. That's why our services don't stop after you purchase our products. You can e-mail our Product Specialists 24 hours a day to get product-training online. Or you can search our knowledge bank of Frequently Asked Questions on our support Website. For Customer Support, call **800-331-5094,** e-mail **hmsupport@mcgraw-hill.com,** or visit **www.mhhe.com/support.** One of our Technical Support Analysts will be able to assist you in a timely fashion.

CourseSmart

CourseSmart is a new way for faculty to find and review eTextbooks. It's also a great option for students who are interested in accessing their course materials digitally. CourseSmart offers thousands of the most commonly adopted textbooks across hundreds of courses from a wide variety of higher education publishers. It is the only place for faculty to review and compare the full text of a textbook online. At CourseSmart, students can save up to 50% off the cost of a print book, reduce their impact on the environment, and gain access to powerful web tools for learning including full text search, notes and highlighting, and email tools for sharing notes between classmates. Complete tech support is also included with each title.

Finding your eBook is easy. Visit **www.CourseSmart.com** and search by title, author, or ISBN.

PowerPoint Presentations

Karen Gebhardt of Colorado State University has worked tirelessly to reinvent the PowerPoint slide program from scratch, animating graphs and emphasizing important concepts. Each chapter has been scrutinized to ensure an accurate, direct connection to the textbook. This presentation is available on the instructor's side of the Online Learning Center, and an abbreviated presentation is available to students on the student's side of the Online Learning Center.

Dollars and Sense Readers

While not directly an ancillary to the book, the *Dollars and Sense* readers are annotated to fit with chapters of this book for professors who want to supplement the text with a radical perspective. Contact your McGraw-Hill representative for more information.

Package Pricing

To help lower costs of using ancillaries, McGraw-Hill has developed a variety of separate packages in which the book can be bought together with the ancillaries for a price that is close to the price of the book alone. Each of these packages has a separate ISBN number. For information on these packages, contact your McGraw-Hill sales representative.

www.mhhe.com/economics/colander8e

The Online Learning Center to accompany Colander's eighth edition is a Web site that follows the text chapter by chapter and provides a number of useful study tools:

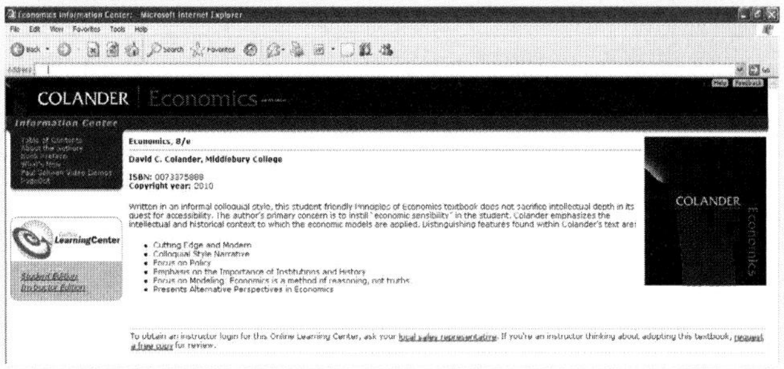

- Learning Objectives provide an at-a-glance list of what concepts students need to master.
- Chapter Summaries give an overview of the chapter.
- Quizzes help students assess areas for further study.
- Interactive graphs provide students with additional practice working with graphical material in the chapter.
- PowerPoint Presentations, now with narration, are another great way to review the chapter material.
- Web Notes bring the chapter alive. These are keyed to the Web Note symbol in the margin of the text.
- Premium content, available for a nominal fee, gives students access to audio podcasts, Solman videos, and other study tools.

Web Note

Web Notes

Michele Villinski of DePauw University has updated the Web Notes from the book; this feature extends the text discussion onto the Web. Web Notes are flagged in the margin and links are on the book's Web site.

On the book's Web site, instructors will find downloadable PowerPoints, the Instructor's Manual, and a link to Dave Colander's own Web site. The entire Web site content also can be delivered through PageOut or within a course management system (i.e., WebCT, Desire2Learn, or Blackboard).

Podcasts

Written and recorded by Robert Guell of Indiana State University, over 50 three- to five-minute audio clips delve deeper into the concepts. The audio clips (and summaries) occur throughout the book wherever you see the iPod™ icon in the margin. The Podcasts can be found on the book's Online Learning Center, under Premium Content.

Assurance of Learning Ready

Assurance of learning is an important element of many accreditation standards. *Economics*, 8e is designed specifically to support your assurance of learning initiatives. Each chapter in the book begins with a list of numbered learning objectives that appear throughout the chapter, as well as in the end-of-chapter problems and exercises. Every test bank question is also linked to one of these objectives, in addition to level of difficulty, topic area, Bloom's Taxonomy level, and AACSB skill area. *EZ Test*, McGraw-Hill's easy-to-use test bank software, can search the test bank by these and other categories, providing an engine for targeted Assurance of Learning analysis and assessment.

AACSB Statement

The McGraw-Hill Companies is a proud corporate member of AACSB International. Understanding the importance and value of AACSB Accreditation, *Economics*, 8e has sought to recognize the curricula guidelines detailed in the AACSB standards for business accreditation by connecting selected questions in the test bank to the general knowledge and skill guidelines found in the AACSB standards.

The statements contained in *Economics*, 8e are provided only as a guide for the users of this text. The AACSB leaves content coverage and assessment within the purview of individual schools, the mission of the school, and the faculty. While *Economics*, 8e and the teaching package make no claim of any specific AACSB qualification or evaluation, we have, within the test bank, labeled selected questions according to the six general knowledge and skills areas.

People to Thank

Let me conclude this preface by thanking the hundreds of people who have offered suggestions, comments, kudos, and criticism on this project since its inception. This book would not be what it is without their input. So many people have contributed to this text in so many ways that I cannot thank everyone. So, to all the people who helped—many, many thanks. I specifically want to thank the eighth edition reviewers, whose insightful comments kept me on track. Reviewers include:

John Abell
Randolph College

Randall Bennett
Gonzaga University

Tami Bertelsen
Arapahoe Community College

Gerald Bialka
University of North Florida

John Blair
Wright State University

John Boschen
College of William & Mary

Taggert Brooks
University of Wisconsin–La Crosse

Keith Brouhle
Grinnell College

Neil Browne
Bowling Green State University

Joan Buccino
Florida Southern College

Douglas Bunn
Blackburn College

Eric Burns
Herbert W. Armstrong College

Colleen Callahan
American University

Darian Chin
Corinthian College

Lisa Citron
Cascadia Community College

Jennifer Clark
Roosevelt University

George Darko
Tusculum College

Gregory DeFreitas
Hofstra University

Diana Denison
Red Rocks Community College

Liang Ding
Macalester College

Justin Dubas
Texas Lutheran University

Sarah Estelle
Rhodes College

Doug Fain
Regis University

Christine Farrell
University of the Ozarks

Lucia Farriss
Saint Leo University Center for Online Learning

Fadi Fawaz
Texas Tech University

Shelby Frost
Georgia State University

Karen Gebhardt
Colorado State University

Scott Gilbert
Southern Illinois University–Carbondale

Robert Gitter
Ohio Wesleyan University

Nicholas Gomersall
Luther College

Michael Goode
Central Piedmont Community College

Kevin Henrickson
Gonzaga University

Kermelle Hensley
Columbus Technical College

Elizabeth Hickman
Oakland City University–Bedford

Jannett Highfill
Bradley University

Reza Hossain
Mount Saint Mary College

Jack Hou
California State University–Long Beach

Chris Inama
Golden Gate University

Miren Ivankovic
Anderson University

Donna Rue Jenkins
National University

Paul Jones
National University

Lillian Kamal
University of Hartford

Logan Kelly
Bryant University

Judy Klein
Mary Baldwin College

Rachel Kreier
Deanza College

Paul Kubik
DePaul University

Simon Yuexing Lan
Auburn University–Montgomery

Anthony Laramie
Merrimack College

Mark Lautzenheiser
Earlham College

Samuel Liu
West Valley College

Christine Lloyd
Western Illinois University

Ann Mari May
University of Nebraska–Lincoln

Warren Mazek
U.S. Merchant Marine Academy

Chris McNamara
Finger Lakes Community College

Lewis Metcalf
Parkland College

Peter Mikek
Wabash College

Garrett Milam
University of Puget Sound

William Milberg
The New School for Social Research

Frannie Miller
Texas A&M University–Commerce

Daniel Mizak
Frostburg State University

Muhammad Mustafa
South Carolina State University

Ronald Nate
Brigham Young University–Idaho

Nasrin Nazemzadeh
Lone Star College–Tomball

Brendan O'Flaherty
Columbia University

Peter Paluch
State University of New York–Delhi

Nathan Perry
University of Utah–Salt Lake

Liz Peterson
Eastern Washington University

Brennan Platt
Brigham Young University–Provo

Roxanna Postolache
Capital University–Columbus

Ayman Reda
Grand Valley State University

Jonathan Sandy
University of San Diego

Richard Schatz
Whitworth University

Carol Schwartz
New York Institute of Technology

Robert Shoffner
Central Piedmont Community College

Jeffrey Silman
Paul Smith's College

Kevin Simmons
Austin College

John Somers
Portland Community College–Sylvania

Robert Sonora
Fort Lewis College

Della Sue
Marist College

Eric Taylor
Central Piedmont Community College

Zdravka Todorova
Wright State University

Dossee Toulaboe
Fort Hays State University

Stephen Tubene
University of Maryland–East Shore

Don-Joseph Uy-Barreta
Deanza College

Ramya Vijaya
Richard Stockton College of New Jersey

Randy Wade
Rogue Community College

Lynn Wallis
Clackamas Community College

Katherine Whitman
Mount St. Mary's College–Doheny

Van Wigginton
San Jacinto College–Pasadena

Andrew Williams
Delaware Tech Community College–Dover

In addition to the comments of the formal reviewers listed above, I have received helpful suggestions, encouragement, and assistance from innumerable individuals via e-mails, letters, symposia, and focus groups. Their help made this edition even stronger than its predecessor. They include James Wetzel, Virginia Commonwealth University; Dmitry Shishkin, Georgia State University; Amy Cramer, Pima Community College–West; Andrea Terzi, Franklin College; Shelby Frost, Georgia State University; Doris Geide-Stevenson, Weber State University; James Chasey, Advanced Placement Economics Teaching Consultant and Homewood-Flossmoor High School (ret.); David Tufte, Southern Utah University; Eric Sarpong, Georgia State University; Jim Ciecka, DePaul University; Fran Bradley, George School; Ron Olive, University of Massachusetts–Lowell; and Rachel Kreier, Hofstra University.

I want to give a special thank-you to the supplements authors. Jenifer Gamber expertly guided the ancillary team of Karen Gebhardt, Colorado State University; Michele Villinski, DePauw University; Timothy Terrell, Wofford College; Brian Lynch, Lakeland Community College; and Paul Aaron Fisher, Henry Ford Community College. They all did an outstanding job.

I'd also like to thank the economists who wrote the alternative perspective questions. These include Ann Mari May of the University of Nebraska–Lincoln, John Miller of Wheaton College, Dan Underwood of Peninsula College, Ric Holt of Southern Oregon University, and Bridget Butkevich of George Mason University. I enjoyed working with each of them, and while their views often differed substantially, they were all united in wanting questions that showed economics as a pluralist field that encourages students to question the text from all perspectives.

I have hired numerous students to check aspects of the book, to read over my questions and answers to questions, and to help proofread. These include Andrew Chong, Zach Colander, Kent Diep, Eric Elderbrock, Felix Forster, Stephen Jones, Sam Carson Parnell, Tim Yale, and Jing Zhuang. I thank them all.

A special thank-you for this edition goes to two people. The first is Jenifer Gamber, whose role in the book cannot be overestimated. She helped me clarify its vision by providing research, critiquing expositions and often improving them, guiding the ancillaries, and being a good friend. She has an amazing set of skills, and I thank her for using them to improve the book. The second is Karen Fisher, who came into this project and with her hard work, dedication, and superb ability made it possible to get the book done on time, even during a period of turmoil. She and Jenifer are two amazing women.

Next, I want to thank the entire McGraw-Hill team, including Douglas Reiner, the publisher; Susanne Riedell, the senior project manager; Pam Verros, the designer; Kerry Bowler, the lead media project manager; Carol Bielski, the production supervisor; and Jennifer Lambert, the senior marketing manager. All of them have done a superb job, for which I thank them sincerely.

Finally, I want to thank Pat, my wife, and my sons, Kasey and Zach, for helping me keep my work in perspective, and for providing a loving environment in which to work.

Preface for the Student: Alternative Perspectives

This book is written for you, the student. It's meant to give you a sense of what economics is, how economists think, and how they approach policy problems. There's only so much that an introductory text can cover, which means that much is left out. That includes much of the subtlety of economic thinking. So if you have a problem swallowing some of the ideas, and you believe that there's more to the issue than is presented in the text, rest assured; generally you're right. Hard choices have to be made for pedagogical purposes—issues have to be simplified and presentations curtailed. Otherwise this would be a 1,600-page book and much too heavy to carry around in a backpack.

Economics as a Method of Reasoning, Not the Truth

This book is what would be called mainstream (it presents the conventional wisdom of economists) both because I'm mainstream and because most economists are as well. But pedagogically, I also believe that students learn by questioning—to say, no, that's not right, that's not the way I see things, and then to compare their way of thinking with the conventional way. Despite my being mainstream, I'm by nature also a skeptic, and in terms of pedagogy often find myself in sympathy with Joan Robinson, a famous economist, who argued that "the purpose of studying economics is not to acquire a set of ready-made answers to economic questions, but to learn how to avoid being deceived by economists." So, to encourage questioning everything, I don't present models and insights of economists as the truth (the field of economics is far too complicated to have arrived at a single truth) but as a set of technical hurdles, reasoning processes, and arguments that students should know, and that will help prepare them to deal with economic issues. Economics primarily teaches you how to approach problems; it does not provide definitive answers about what is right and what is wrong. It is a method, not a set of truths.

Alternative Perspectives in Economics

One of the pedagogical choices I made in writing the book was to concentrate almost exclusively on the mainstream view. I strongly believe that focusing on that view is the best way to teach the course. However, I also believe that students should be aware of the diversity in economics and know that the mainstream view is not the only view out there. In fact, there are probably as many views out there as there are economists. Still, for a majority of economists, the concepts presented in this book are an acceptable pedagogical simplification of the myriad views held by economists.

Some economists, however, don't find aspects of what is presented in this text to be an acceptable simplification. They wouldn't necessarily say that the presentation is wrong; they are more likely to see it as misleading, or as diverting the discussion away from other, more relevant, issues. These economists are generally called nonmainstream or heterodox economists. A heterodox economist is *one who doesn't accept the basic underlying model used by a majority of economists as the most useful model for analyzing the economy.*

In this preface, I will briefly introduce six heterodox economic approaches to give you a sense of how their analyses differ from the mainstream analyses presented in this book. The six heterodox approaches are Austrian, Post-Keynesian, Institutionalist, Radical, feminist, and religious. Below are brief descriptions of each group, written with the help of the team of alternative-perspective economists.

Austrian Economists

Austrian economists believe in methodological individualism, by which they mean that social goals are best met through voluntary, mutually beneficial interactions. Lack of information and unsolvable incentive problems undermine the ability of government to plan, making the market the best method for coordinating economic activity. Austrian economists oppose state intrusion into private property and private activities. They are not economists from Austria; rather, they are economists from anywhere who follow the ideas of Ludwig von Mises and Friedrich von Hayek, two economists who were from Austria.

Austrian economists are sometimes classified as conservative, but they are more appropriately classified as libertarians, who believe in liberty of individuals first and in other social goals second. Consistent with their views, they are often willing to support what are sometimes considered radical ideas, such as legalizing addictive drugs or eliminating our current monetary system—ideas that most mainstream economists would oppose. Austrian economists emphasize the uncertainty in the economy and the inability of a government controlled by self-interested politicians to undertake socially beneficial policy.

One proposal of Austrian economists will give you a flavor of their approach. That proposal is to eliminate the Federal Reserve System and to establish a free market in money—a policy that would leave people free to use any money they want and that would significantly reduce banking regulation. In a sense, their proposal carries the Classical argument in favor of laissez-faire to its logical conclusions. Why should the government have a monopoly of the money supply? Why shouldn't people be free to use whatever money they desire, denominated in whatever unit they want? Why don't we rely upon competition to prevent inflation? Why don't we have a free market in money? Well-known Austrian economists include Peter Boettke, Veronique de Rugy, Mario Rizzo, David Gordon, Israel Kirzner, Peter Leeson, Chris Coyne, Steve Horwitz, Roger Garrison, and Roger Koppl.

Institutionalist Economists

Institutionalist economists argue that any economic analysis must involve specific considerations of institutions. The lineage of Institutionalist economics begins with the pioneering work of Thorstein Veblen, John R. Commons, and Wesley C. Mitchell. Veblen employed evolutionary analysis to explore the role of institutions in directing and retarding the economic process. He saw human behavior driven by cultural norms and conveyed the way in which they were with sardonic wit and penetrating insight, leaving us with enduring metaphors such as the leisure class and conspicuous consumption. Commons argued that institutions are social constructs that could improve general welfare. Accordingly, he established cooperative investigative programs to support pragmatic changes in the legal structure of government. Mitchell was a leader in developing economics as an empirical study; he was a keen observer of the business cycle and argued that theory must be informed by systematic attention to empirical data, or it was useless.

Contemporary Institutionalists employ the founders' "trilogy"—empirically informed evolutionary analysis directed toward pragmatic alteration of institutions shaping economic outcomes—in their policy approach. Examples include indicative planning—a macroeconomic policy in which the government sets up an overall plan for various industries and selectively directs credit to certain industries; and income support programs, including those assuring employment for all willing. Well-known Institutionalists include Greg Hayden, Geoff Hodgson, Anne Mayhew, James Peach, and Ronnie Phillips.

Radical Economists

Radical economists believe substantial equality-preferring institutional changes should be implemented in our economic system. Radical economists evolved out of Marxian economics. In their analysis, they focus on the lack of equity in our current economic system and on institutional changes that might bring about a more equitable system. Specifically, they see the current economic system as one in which a few people—capitalists and high-level managers—benefit enormously at the expense of many people who struggle to make ends meet in jobs that are unfulfilling or who even go without work at times. They see the fundamental instability and irrationality of the capitalist system at the root of a wide array of social ills that range from pervasive inequality to alienation, racism, sexism, and imperialism. Radical economists often use a class-oriented analysis to address these issues and are much more willing to talk about social conflict and tensions in our society than are mainstream economists.

A policy favored by many Radicals is the establishment of worker cooperatives to replace the corporation. Radicals argue that such worker cooperatives would see that the income of the firm is more equitably allocated. Likewise, Radical theorists endorse policies such as universal health care insurance that conform to the ethic of "putting people before profits."

There are a number of centers of Radical thought, including The Political Economy Research Institute, The New School for Social Research, and some campuses of the University of Massachusetts. A good place to find Radical views is the *Dollars & Sense* magazine. Well-known Radical economists include Lourdes Beneria, Sam Bowles, Arthur MacEwan, Robert Pollin, Gerald Epstein, Anwar Shaik, Michael Reich, Richard Wolff, and Stephen Resnick, as well as a number of feminist economists who would be considered both Radicals and feminists.

Feminist Economists

Feminist economics offers a substantive challenge to the content, scope, and methodology of mainstream economics. Feminist economists question the boundaries of what we consider economics to be and examine social arrangements surrounding provisioning. Feminist economists have many different views, but all believe that in some way traditional economic analysis misses many important issues pertaining to women.

Feminist economists study issues such as how the institutional structure tends to direct women into certain types of jobs (generally low-paying jobs) and away from other types of jobs (generally high-paying jobs). They draw our attention to the unpaid labor performed by women throughout the world and ask, "What would GDP look like if women's work were given a value and included?" They argue for an expansion in the content of economics to include "women as practitioners and as objects of study" and for the elimination of the masculine bias in mainstream economics. Is there such a bias? To see it, simply compare the relative number of women in your economics class to the relative number of women at your school. It is highly likely that your class has relatively more men. Feminist economists want you to ask why that is, and whether anything should be done about it.

The historical roots of feminist economics can be found in the work of such authors as Mary Wollstonecraft, John Stuart Mill, Harriet Taylor Mill, and Charlotte Perkins Gilman. Feminist economics has expanded significantly in the past 15 years and has emerged as an influential body of thought. Well-known feminist economists include Myra Strober, Diana Strassmann, Barbara Bergmann, Julie Nelson, Jane Humphries, Marianne Ferber, Randy Albelda, Nancy Folbre, and Heidi Hartmann.

Religious Economists

Religion is the oldest and, arguably, the most influential institution in the world—be it Christianity, Islam, Judaism, Buddhism, Hinduism, or any of the many other religions in the world. Modern science, of which economics is a part, emphasizes the rational elements of thought. It attempts to separate faith and normative issues from rational analysis in ways that some religiously oriented economists find questionable. The line between a religious and nonreligious economist is not hard and fast; all economists bring elements of their ethical considerations into their analysis. But those we call "religious economists" integrate the ethical and normative issues into economic analysis in more complex ways than the ways presented in the text.

Religiously oriented economists have a diversity of views; some believe that their views can be integrated reasonably well into standard economics, while others see the need for the development of a distinctive faith-based methodology that focuses on a particular group of normative concerns centered on issues such as human dignity and caring for the poor.

One religious perspective that is represented by a defined group in the U.S. economics profession is Christianity, and a number of Christian economists have joined together in the Association of Christian Economists (ACE). Its stated goal is "to encourage Christian scholars to explore and communicate the relationship between their faith and the discipline of economics, and to promote interaction and communication among Christian economists." Centers of ACE are Pepperdine University, Calvin College, and Gordon College. Leading Christian economists include Kurt Schaefer, Andrew Yuengert, and Stephen Smith.

Many of the religious alternative perspective questions that we provide in the text are from the Judeo-Christian perspective, the perspective most familiar to U.S. students. However, we intersperse some questions from other religious perspectives, both to show the similarity of views and to encourage students to think in a multicultural framework.

Post-Keynesian Economists

Post-Keynesian economists believe that uncertainty is a central issue in economics. They follow J. M. Keynes's approach more so than do mainstream economists in emphasizing institutional imperfections in the economy and the importance of fundamental uncertainty that rationality cannot deal with. They agree with Institutionalists that the study of economics must emphasize and incorporate the importance of social and political structure in determining market outcomes.

While their view about the importance of uncertainty is similar to the Austrian view, their policy response to that uncertainty is quite different. They do not see uncertainty as eliminating much of government's role in the economy; instead, they see it leading to policies in which government takes a larger role in guiding the economy.

One of their policy proposals that gives you a flavor of their approach is tax-based income policies—policies in which the government tries to directly affect the nominal wage- and price-setting institutions. Under a tax-based income policy, any firm raising its wage or price would be subject to a tax, and any firm lowering its wage or price would get a subsidy. Such a plan, they argue, would reduce the upward pressure on the nominal price level and reduce the rate of unemployment necessary to hold down inflation. Well-known Post-Keynesian economists include Paul Davidson, Jamie Galbraith, Barkley Rosser, John Cornwall, Shelia Dow, Malcolm Sawyer, Philip Arestis, Victoria Chick, Jan Kregel, and Geof Harcourt.

Consistency of the Various Approaches

A characteristic of almost all heterodox economists of all types is that their analyses tend to be less formal than mainstream analysis. *Less formal* doesn't mean better or worse. There are advantages and disadvantages to formality, but *less formal* does mean that there's more potential for ambiguity in interpretation. It's easy to say whether the logic in a formal model is right or wrong. It's much harder to say whether the logic in an informal model is right or wrong because it's often hard to see precisely what the logic is. The advantage of an informal model is that it can include many more variables and can be made more realistic, so you can discuss real-world problems more easily with that model. Nonmainstream economists often want to talk about the real world, which is why they use informal models.

Often, after I discuss the mainstream and heterodox approaches, some student asks which is right. I respond with a story told by a former colleague of mine, Abba Lerner:

> "But look," the rabbi's wife remonstrated, "when one party to the dispute presented their case to you, you said, 'You are quite right,' and then when the other party presented their case you again said, 'You are quite right.' Surely they cannot both be right?" To which the Rabbi answered, "My dear, you are quite right!"

The moral of the story is that there's nothing necessarily inconsistent among mainstream and heterodox economists' approaches. Their approaches are simply different ways of looking at the same event. Which approach is most useful depends on what issues and events you are analyzing. The class analysis used by radicals is often more appropriate to developing countries than it is to the United States, and, in analyzing developing countries, many mainstream economists also include class fights in their approach. Similarly, Austrian analysis provides more insight into the role of the entrepreneur and individual in the economy than does mainstream analysis, while Post-Keynesian and Institutionalist analyses are useful when considering major institutional changes.

The distinctions between heterodox and mainstream economists can be overdone. One economist may well fall into two or three different groupings and use a combination of various analyses.

I follow the work of heterodox economists carefully. Their writing is often more interesting than mainstream writing, which can often get rather technical and boring. But in this book, I present primarily mainstream views. I do that because that's what I see as the job of the principles of economics course. My goal, however, is to present those views to you, not to indoctrinate you with those views, and throughout the text I include some challenges to the standard views. At the end of each chapter, I also include some questions that challenge the view presented in the chapter. These questions are written by representatives of different heterodox groups. I also encourage you to look for these other views in your outside reading. The *Dollars and Sense* companion to the book has radical critiques and *Free Market*, an Austrian newsletter found at www.mises.org/freemarket.asp, has Austrian critiques. There are many other sources and Web sites for heterodox groups. Exploring these sites and learning about the many different views that are competing in the marketplace for ideas make your economics course more interesting.

A Concluding Thought

There are many ways to explore economics, and in your exploration, the textbook is only a map. You and your professor determine what you discuss and learn and what path you will take. Ultimately, that's the way it has to be. Most of you are in this course for the grade—college is a way of progressing up the ladder. That's how it was for me. But the process also can be transforming; it can change how you look at issues, how you think, and who you are. The economics courses I took were especially important in determining who I have become.

Much of the principles course is what I call hurdle jumping—calisthenics of the mind. It is a set of mind-strengthening exercises. Separately, each is not especially relevant, but combined, they help turn your weak cranial muscle into a strong muscle better able to handle the problems that life throws at you. So, do the work, even if it seems boring; follow your professor's reasoning, even if you don't agree with what he or she is arguing; and keep thinking. Read newspapers and try to apply the lessons, deciding when they apply and when they don't. But, in the process, be happy—enjoy the moment because that moment will never be again.

Brief Contents

Contents

3 Economic Institutions 55

4 Supply and Demand 83

5 Using Supply and Demand 106

11 Game Theory, Strategic Decision Making, and Behavioral Economics 255

Section III Production and Cost Analysis

12 Production and Cost Analysis I 276

13 Production and Cost Analysis II 295

Section IV Market Structure

14 Perfect Competition 317

Section V
Real-World Competition

Section VI
Factor Markets

19 Work and the Labor Market 430

19W Nonwage and Asset Income: Rents, Profits, and Interest 459 and 19W-1

20 Who Gets What? The Distribution of Income 460

Section VII
Applying Economic Reasoning to Policy

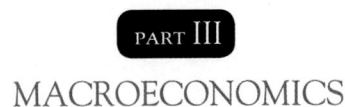

Section IV
Taxes, Budgets, and Fiscal Policy

Section V
International Policy Issues

List of Boxes

REAL-WORLD APPLICATION

ADDED DIMENSION

(continued)

A REMINDER

(continued)

THINKING LIKE A MODERN ECONOMIST

PART I

Introduction: Thinking Like an Economist

Part I is an introduction, and an introduction to an introduction seems a little funny. But other sections have introductions, so it seemed a little funny not to have an introduction to Part I; and besides, as you will see, I'm a little funny myself (which, in turn, has two interpretations; I'm sure you will decide which of the two is appropriate). It will, however, be a very brief introduction, consisting of questions you may have had and some answers to those questions.

Some Questions and Answers

Why study economics?

Because it's neat and interesting and helps provide insight into events that are constantly going on around you.

Why is this book so big?

Because there's a lot of important information in it and because the book is designed so your teacher can pick and choose. You'll likely not be required to read all of it, especially if you're on the quarter system. But once you start it, you'll probably read it all anyhow. (Would you believe?)

Why does this book cost so much?

To answer this question, you'll have to read the book.

Will this book make me rich?

No.

Will this book make me happy?

It depends.

This book doesn't seem to be written in a normal textbook style. Is this book really written by a professor?

Yes, but he is different. He misspent his youth working on cars; he married his high school sweetheart after they met again at their 20th high school reunion. Twenty-five years after graduating from high school, his wife went back to medical school and got her MD because she was tired of being treated poorly by doctors. Their five kids make sure he doesn't get carried away in the professorial cloud.

Will the entire book be like this?

No, the introduction is just trying to rope you in. Much of the book will be hard going. Learning happens to be a difficult process: no pain, no gain. But the author isn't a sadist; he tries to make learning as pleasantly painful as possible.

What do the author's students think of him?

Weird, definitely weird—and hard. But fair, interesting, and sincerely interested in getting us to learn. (Answer written by his students.)

So there you have it. Answers to the questions that you might never have thought of if they hadn't been put in front of you. I hope they give you a sense of me and the approach I'll use in the book. There are some neat ideas in it. Let's now briefly consider what's in the first six chapters.

A Survey of the First Six Chapters

This first section is really an introduction to the rest of the book. It gives you the background necessary so that the later chapters make sense. Chapter 1 gives you an overview of the entire field of economics as well as an introduction to my style. Chapter 2 focuses on the production possibility curve, comparative advantage, and trade. It explains how trade increases production possibilities but also why, in the real world, free trade and no government regulation may not be the best policy. Chapter 3 gives you some history of economic systems and introduces you to the institutions of the U.S. economy. Chapters 4 and 5 introduce you to supply and demand, and show you not only the power of those two concepts but also the limitations. Modern economics is much more than supply and demand. It involves a modeling approach. You develop a model and use that model to understand reality. Chapter 6 introduces you to economists' modeling approach and what it means to think like a modern economist.

Now let's get on with the show.

Economics and Economic Reasoning

In my vacations, I visited the poorest quarters of several cities and walked through one street after another, looking at the faces of the poorest people. Next I resolved to make as thorough a study as I could of Political Economy.

—Alfred Marshall

AFTER READING THIS CHAPTER, YOU SHOULD BE ABLE TO:

1. Define economics and explain how economists develop models.
2. Explain how to make decisions by comparing marginal costs and marginal benefits.
3. Define opportunity cost and explain its relationship to economic reasoning.
4. Explain real-world events in terms of economic forces, social forces, and political forces.
5. Differentiate between microeconomics and macroeconomics.
6. Distinguish among positive economics, normative economics, and the art of economics.

When an artist looks at the world, he sees color. When a musician looks at the world, she hears music. When an economist looks at the world, she sees a symphony of costs and benefits. The economist's world might not be as colorful or as melodic as the others' worlds, but it's more practical. If you want to understand what's going on in the world that's really out there, you need to know economics.

I hardly have to convince you of this fact if you keep up with the news. Unemployment is down; the price of gas is up; interest rates are down; businesses are going bankrupt . . . The list is endless. So let's say you grant me that economics is important. That still doesn't mean that it's worth studying. The real question then is: How much will you learn? Most of what you learn depends on you, but part depends on the teacher and another part depends on the textbook. On both these counts, you're in luck; since your teacher chose this book for your course, you must have a super teacher.[1]

What Economics Is

Economics is *the study of how human beings coordinate their wants and desires, given the decision-making mechanisms, social customs, and political realities of the society.* One of the key words in the definition of the term "economics" is *coordination.* Coordination

[1]This book is written by a person, not a machine. That means that I have my quirks, my odd sense of humor, and my biases. All textbook writers do. Most textbooks have the quirks and eccentricities edited out so that all the books read and sound alike—professional but dull. I choose to sound like me—sometimes professional, sometimes playful, and sometimes stubborn. In my view, that makes the book more human and less dull. So forgive me my quirks—don't always take me too seriously—and I'll try to keep you awake when you're reading this book at 3 a.m. the day of the exam. If you think it's a killer to read a book this long, you ought to try writing one.

can mean many things. In the study of economics, coordination refers to how the three central problems facing any economy are solved. These central problems are

1. What, and how much, to produce.
2. How to produce it.
3. For whom to produce it.

Three central coordination problems any economy must solve are what to produce, how to produce it, and for whom to produce it.

How hard is it to make the three decisions? Imagine for a moment the problem of living in a family: the fights, arguments, and questions that come up. "Do I have to do the dishes?" "Why can't I have piano lessons?" "Bobby got a new sweater. How come I didn't?" "Mom likes you best." Now multiply the size of the family by millions. The same fights, the same arguments, the same questions—only for society the questions are millions of times more complicated. In answering these questions, economies find that inevitably individuals want more than is available, given how much they're willing to work. That means that in our economy there is a problem of **scarcity**—*the goods available are too few to satisfy individuals' desires*.

The coordination questions faced by society are complicated.

Scarcity

Scarcity has two elements: our wants and our means of fulfilling those wants. These can be interrelated since wants are changeable and partially determined by society. The way we fulfill wants can affect those wants. For example, if you work on Wall Street, you will probably want upscale and trendy clothes. Up here in Vermont, I am quite happy wearing Levi's and flannel.

The degree of scarcity is constantly changing. The quantity of goods, services, and usable resources depends on technology and human action, which underlie production. Individuals' imagination, innovativeness, and willingness to do what needs to be done can greatly increase available goods and resources. Who knows what technologies are in our future—nannites or micromachines that change atoms into whatever we want could conceivably eliminate scarcity of goods we currently consume. But they would not eliminate scarcity entirely since new wants are constantly developing.

The quantity of goods, services, and usable resources depends on technology and human action.

So, how does an economy deal with scarcity? The answer is coercion. In all known economies, coordination has involved some type of coercion—limiting people's wants and increasing the amount of work individuals are willing to do to fulfill those wants. The reality is that many people would rather play than help solve society's problems. So the basic economic problem involves inspiring people to do things that other people want them to do, and not to do things that other people don't want them to do. Thus, an alternative definition of economics is that it is the study of how to get people to do things they're not wild about doing (such as studying) and not to do things they are wild about doing (such as eating all the lobster they like), so that the things some people want to do are consistent with the things other people want to do.

Modern Economics

Economics, like any field of study, evolves and changes. As technology and analytic techniques change and as new evidence is discovered, the approach that economists use to study problems changes. In early times, economics was primarily based on **deduction**—*a method of reasoning in which one deduces a theory based on a set of almost self-evident principles*. Theory consists of logical deductions based on those principles. The traditional principles upon which economic theories were built are the assumptions that people are rational and self-interested. There were, of course, enormous debates about how to interpret rationality and self-interest, but these remained theoretical debates since economists had no good way to test which interpretation was more accurate.

Modern economics is no longer solely a deductive science. Modern economics is based on both deduction and **induction**—*a method of reasoning in which one develops general principles by looking for patterns in the data.* Modern behavioral economists, for example, will do a lab experiment to see how people behave, and then build their models on the behavior that they observe. One of the reasons induction has become more important in modern economics is that computing technology has improved, lowering the cost of using inductive methods. Economists can now analyze large data sets and find patterns through the use of statistical methods. Such analysis was impossible 50 years ago and was much more difficult to do even 10 or 20 years ago. In Chapter 6 we explore these changes in more detail.

A Guide to Economic Reasoning

People trained in economics think in a certain way. They analyze everything critically; they compare the costs and the benefits of every issue and make decisions based on those costs and benefits. For example, say you're trying to decide whether a policy to eliminate terrorist attacks on airlines is a good idea. Economists are trained to put their emotions aside and ask: What are the costs of the policy, and what are the benefits? Thus, they are open to the argument that security measures, such as conducting body searches of every passenger or scanning all baggage with bomb-detecting machinery, might not be the appropriate policy because the costs might exceed the benefits. To think like an economist involves addressing almost all issues using a cost/benefit approach. Economic reasoning also involves abstracting from the "unimportant" elements of a question and focusing on the "important" ones by creating a simple model that captures the essence of the issue or problem. How do you know whether the model has captured the important elements? By collecting empirical evidence and "testing" the model—matching the predictions of the model with the empirical evidence—to see if it fits. Economic reasoning—how to think like a modern economist, making decisions on the basis of costs and benefits—is the most important lesson you'll learn from this book.

Economic reasoning is making decisions on the basis of costs and benefits.

The book *Freakonomics* gives examples of the economist's approach. It describes a number of studies by University of Chicago economist Steve Levitt that unlock seemingly mysterious observations with basic economic reasoning. For example, Levitt asks the question: Why do drug dealers on the street tend to live with their mothers? The answer he arrives at is that it is because they can't afford to live on their own; most earn less than $5 an hour. Why, then, are they dealing drugs and not working a legal job that, even for a minimum-wage job, pays over $7.00 an hour? The answer to that is determined through cost/benefit analysis. While their current income is low, their potential income as a drug dealer is much higher since, given their background and current U.S. institutions, they are more likely to move up to a high position in the local drug business (and *Freakonomics* describes how it is a business) and earn a six-figure income than they are to move up from working as a Taco Bell technician to an executive earning a six-figure income in corporate America. Levitt's model is a very simple one—people do what is in their best interest financially—and it assumes that people rely on a cost/benefit analysis to make decisions. Finally, he supports his argument through careful empirical work, collecting and organizing the data to see if they fit the model. His work is a good example of "thinking like a modern economist" in action.

Economic reasoning, once learned, is infectious. If you're susceptible, being exposed to it will change your life. It will influence your analysis of everything, including issues normally considered outside the scope of economics. For example, you will likely use economic reasoning to decide the possibility of getting a date for Saturday night, and

ADDED DIMENSION

Economic Knowledge in One Sentence: TANSTAAFL

Once upon a time, Tanstaafl was made king of all the lands. His first act was to call his economic advisers and tell them to write up all the economic knowledge the society possessed. After years of work, they presented their monumental effort: 25 volumes, each about 400 pages long. But in the interim, King Tanstaafl had become a very busy man, what with running a kingdom of all the lands and all. Looking at the lengthy volumes, he told his advisers to summarize their findings in one volume.

Despondently, the economists returned to their desks, wondering how they could summarize what they'd been so careful to spell out. After many more years of rewriting, they were finally satisfied with their one-volume effort, and tried to make an appointment to see the king. Unfortunately, affairs of state had become even more pressing than before, and the king couldn't take the time to see them. Instead he sent word to them that he couldn't be bothered with a whole volume, and ordered them, under threat of death (for he had become a tyrant), to reduce the work to one sentence.

The economists returned to their desks, shivering in their sandals and pondering their impossible task. Thinking about their fate if they were not successful, they decided to send out for one last meal. Unfortunately, when they were collecting money to pay for the meal, they discovered they were broke. The disgusted delivery man took the last meal back to the restaurant, and the economists started down the path to the beheading station. On the way, the delivery man's parting words echoed in their ears. They looked at each other and suddenly they realized the truth. "We're saved!" they screamed. "That's it! That's economic knowledge in one sentence!" They wrote the sentence down and presented it to the king, who thereafter fully understood all economic problems. (He also gave them a good meal.) The sentence?

There **A**in't **N**o **S**uch **T**hing **A**s **A** **F**ree **L**unch—**TANSTAAFL**

who will pay for dinner. You will likely use it to decide whether to read this book, whether to attend class, whom to marry, and what kind of work to go into after you graduate. This is not to say that economic reasoning will provide all the answers. As you will see throughout this book, real-world questions are inevitably complicated, and economic reasoning simply provides a framework within which to approach a question. In the economic way of thinking, every choice has costs and benefits, and decisions are made by comparing them.

Marginal Costs and Marginal Benefits

The relevant costs and relevant benefits to economic reasoning are the expected *incremental*, or additional, costs incurred and the expected *incremental* benefits that result from a decision. Economists use the term *marginal* when referring to additional or incremental. Marginal costs and marginal benefits are key concepts.

Web Note 1.1
Costs and Benefits

A **marginal cost** is *the additional cost to you over and above the costs you have already incurred.* That means not counting **sunk costs**—*costs that have already been incurred and cannot be recovered*—in the relevant costs when making a decision. Consider, for example, attending class. You've already paid your tuition; it is a sunk cost. So the marginal (or additional) cost of going to class does not include tuition.

Similarly with marginal benefit. A **marginal benefit** is *the additional benefit above what you've already derived.* The marginal benefit of reading this chapter is the *additional* knowledge you get from reading it. If you already knew everything in this chapter before you picked up the book, the marginal benefit of reading it now is zero. The marginal benefit is not zero if by reading the chapter you learn that you are prepared for class; before, you might only have suspected you were prepared.

Marginal Cost and Marginal Benefit

Comparing marginal (additional) costs with marginal (additional) benefits will often tell you how you should adjust your activities to be as well off as possible. Just follow the **economic decision rule:**

If the marginal benefits of doing something exceed the marginal costs, do it. If the marginal costs of doing something exceed the marginal benefits, don't do it.

If the marginal benefits of doing something exceed the marginal costs, do it.

If the marginal costs of doing something exceed the marginal benefits, don't do it.

As an example, let's consider a discussion I might have with a student who tells me that she is too busy to attend my classes. I respond, "Think about the tuition you've spent for this class—it works out to about $40 a lecture." She answers that the book she reads for class is a book that I wrote, and that I wrote it so clearly she fully understands everything. She goes on:

Q-1 Say you bought a share of Sun Microsystems for $100 and a share of Cisco for $10. The price of each is currently $15. Assuming taxes are not an issue, which would you sell if you need $15?

> I've already paid the tuition and whether I go to class or not, I can't get any of the tuition back, so the tuition is a sunk cost and doesn't enter into my decision. The marginal cost to me is what I could be doing with the hour instead of spending it in class. I value my time at $75 an hour [people who understand everything value their time highly], and even though I've heard that your lectures are super, I estimate that the marginal benefit of your class is only $50. The marginal cost, $75, exceeds the marginal benefit, $50, so I don't attend class.

I congratulate her on her diplomacy and her economic reasoning, but tell her that I give a quiz every week, that students who miss a quiz fail the quiz, that those who fail all the quizzes fail the course, and that those who fail the course do not graduate. In short, she is underestimating the marginal benefits of attending my classes. Correctly estimated, the marginal benefits of attending my class exceed the marginal costs. So she should attend my class.

Economics and Passion

Web Note 1.2
Blogonomics

Recognizing that everything has a cost is reasonable, but it's a reasonableness that many people don't like. It takes some of the passion out of life. It leads you to consider possibilities like these:

- Saving some people's lives with liver transplants might not be worth the additional cost. The money might be better spent on nutritional programs that would save 20 lives for every 2 lives you might save with transplants.
- Maybe we shouldn't try to eliminate all pollution because the additional cost of doing so may be too high. To eliminate all pollution might be to forgo too much of some other worthwhile activity.
- Providing a guaranteed job for every person who wants one might not be a worthwhile policy goal if it means that doing so will reduce the ability of an economy to adapt to new technologies.
- It might make sense for the automobile industry to save $12 per car by not installing a safety device, even though without the safety device some people will be killed.

Economic reasoning is based on the premise that everything has a cost.

You get the idea. This kind of reasonableness is often criticized for being coldhearted. But, not surprisingly, economists disagree; they argue that their reasoning leads to a better society for the majority of people.

Q-2 Can you think of a reason why a cost/benefit approach to a problem might be inappropriate? Can you give an example?

Economists' reasonableness isn't universally appreciated. Businesses love the result; others aren't so sure, as I discovered some years back when my then-girlfriend told me she was leaving me. "Why?" I asked. "Because," she responded, "you're so, so . . . reasonable." It took me many years after she left to learn what she already knew: There are many types of reasonableness, and not everyone thinks an economist's reasonableness is a virtue. I'll discuss such issues later; for now, let me simply warn you that, for better or worse, studying economics will lead you to view questions in a cost/benefit framework.

Opportunity costs have always made choice difficult, as we see in the early-19th-century engraving, "One or the Other."

Opportunity Cost

Putting economists' cost/benefit rules into practice isn't easy. To do so, you have to be able to choose and measure the costs and benefits correctly. Economists have devised the concept of opportunity cost to help you do that. **Opportunity cost** is *the benefit that you might have gained from choosing the next-best alternative*. To obtain the benefit of something, you must give up (forgo) something else—namely, the next-best alternative. The opportunity cost is the value of that next-best alternative; that is a cost because in choosing one thing, you are precluding an alternative choice. The TANSTAAFL story in the box on page 7 embodies the opportunity cost concept because it tells us that there is a cost to everything; that cost is the next-best forgone alternative.

Opportunity cost is the basis of cost/benefit economic reasoning; it is the benefit that you might have gained from choosing the next-best alternative.

Opportunity Cost

Let's consider some examples. The opportunity cost of going out once with Natalie (or Nathaniel), the most beautiful woman (attractive man) in the world, is the benefit you'd get from going out with your solid steady, Margo (Mike). The opportunity cost of cleaning up the environment might be a reduction in the money available to assist low-income individuals. The opportunity cost of having a child might be two boats, three cars, and a two-week vacation each year for five years, which are what you could have had if you hadn't had the child. (Kids really are this expensive.)

Examples are endless, but let's consider two that are particularly relevant to you: what courses to take and how much to study. Let's say you're a full-time student and at the beginning of the term you had to choose five courses. Taking one precludes taking some other, and the opportunity cost of taking an economics course may well be not taking a course on theater. Similarly with studying: You have a limited amount of time to spend studying economics, studying some other subject, sleeping, or partying. The more time you spend on one activity, the less time you have for another. That's opportunity cost.

Notice how neatly the opportunity cost concept takes into account costs and benefits of all other options, and converts these alternative benefits into costs of the decision you're now making.

Web Note 1.3
Opportunity Cost

The relevance of opportunity cost isn't limited to your individual decisions. Opportunity costs are also relevant to government's decisions, which affect everyone in society. A common example is what is called the guns-versus-butter debate. The resources that a society has are limited; therefore, its decision to use those resources to have more guns (more weapons) means that it will have less butter (fewer consumer goods). Thus, when society decides to spend \$50 billion more on an improved health care system, the opportunity cost of that decision is \$50 billion not spent on helping the homeless, paying off some of the national debt, or providing for national defense.

The opportunity cost concept has endless implications. It can even be turned upon itself. For instance, it takes time to think about alternatives; that means that there's a cost to being reasonable, so it's only reasonable to be somewhat unreasonable. If you followed that argument, you've caught the economic bug. If you didn't, don't worry. Just remember the opportunity cost concept for now; I'll infect you with economic thinking in the rest of the book.

Q-3 John, your study partner, has just said that the opportunity cost of studying this chapter is about 1/38 the price you paid for this book, since the chapter is about 1/38 of the book. Is he right? Why or why not?

ADDED DIMENSION

Economics in Perspective

All too often, students study economics out of context. They're presented with sterile analysis and boring facts to memorize, and are never shown how economics fits into the larger scheme of things. That's bad; it makes economics seem boring—but economics is not boring. Every so often throughout this book, sometimes in the appendixes and sometimes in these boxes, I'll step back and put the analysis in perspective, giving you an idea from whence the analysis sprang and its historical context. In educational jargon, this is called *enrichment*.

I begin here with economics itself.

First, its history: In the 1500s there were few universities. Those that existed taught religion, Latin, Greek, philosophy, history, and mathematics. No economics. Then came the *Enlightenment* (about 1700), in which reasoning replaced God as the explanation of why things were the way they were. Pre-Enlightenment thinkers would answer the question "Why am I poor?" with "Because God wills it." Enlightenment scholars looked for a different explanation. "Because of the nature of land ownership" is one answer they found.

Such reasoned explanations required more knowledge of the way things were, and the amount of information expanded so rapidly that it had to be divided or categorized for an individual to have hope of knowing a subject. Soon philosophy was subdivided into science and philosophy. In the 1700s, the sciences were split into natural sciences and social sciences. The amount of knowledge kept increasing, and in the late 1800s and early 1900s social science itself split into subdivisions: economics, political science, history, geography, sociology, anthropology, and psychology. Many of the insights about how the economic system worked were codified in Adam Smith's *The Wealth of Nations*, written in 1776. Notice that this is before economics as a subdiscipline developed, and Adam Smith could also be classified as an anthropologist, a sociologist, a political scientist, and a social philosopher.

Throughout the 18th and 19th centuries, economists such as Adam Smith, Thomas Malthus, John Stuart Mill, David Ricardo, and Karl Marx were more than economists; they were social philosophers who covered all aspects of social science. These writers were subsequently called *classical economists*. Alfred Marshall continued in that classical tradition, and his book, *Principles of Economics*, published in the late 1800s, was written with the other social sciences much in evidence. But Marshall also changed the questions economists ask; he focused on those questions that could be asked in a graphical supply/demand framework.

This book falls solidly in the Marshallian tradition. It presents economics as a way of thinking—as an engine of analysis used to understand real-world phenomena. But it goes beyond Marshall, and introduces you to a wider variety of models and thinking than the supply and demand models that Marshall used.

Marshallian economics is primarily about policy, not theory. It sees institutions as well as political and social dimensions of reality as important, and it shows you how economics ties in to those dimensions.

Economic and Market Forces

Q-4 Ali, your study partner, states that rationing health care is immoral—that health care should be freely available to all individuals in society. How would you respond?

The opportunity cost concept applies to all aspects of life and is fundamental to understanding how society reacts to scarcity. When goods are scarce, those goods must be rationed. That is, a mechanism must be chosen to determine who gets what.

Let's consider some specific real-world rationing mechanisms. Dormitory rooms are often rationed by lottery, and permission to register in popular classes is often rationed by a first-come, first-registered rule. Food in the United States, however, is generally rationed by price. If price did not ration food, there wouldn't be enough food to go around. All scarce goods must be rationed in some fashion. These rationing mechanisms are examples of **economic forces,** *the necessary reactions to scarcity*.

When an economic force operates through the market, it becomes a market force.

One of the important choices that a society must make is whether to allow these economic forces to operate freely and openly or to try to rein them in. A **market force** is *an economic force that is given relatively free rein by society to work through the market*. Market forces ration by changing prices. When there's a shortage, the price goes up. When there's a surplus, the price goes down. Much of this book will be devoted to analyzing how the market works like an invisible hand, guiding economic forces to coordinate individual actions and allocate scarce resources. The **invisible hand** is *the price mechanism, the rise and fall of prices that guides our actions in a market.*

Economic reality is controlled by three forces:

1. Economic forces (the invisible hand).
2. Social and cultural forces.
3. Political and legal forces.

Societies can't choose whether or not to allow economic forces to operate—economic forces are always operating. However, societies can choose whether to allow market forces to predominate. Social, cultural, and political forces play a major role in deciding whether to let market forces operate. Economic reality is determined by a contest among these various forces.

Social, cultural, and political forces can play a significant role in the economy.

Let's consider an example in which social forces prevent an economic force from becoming a market force: the problem of getting a date for Saturday night. If a school (or a society) has significantly more people of one gender than the other (let's say more men than women), some men may well find themselves without a date—that is, men will be in excess supply—and will have to find something else to do, say study or go to a movie by themselves. An "excess supply" person could solve the problem by paying someone to go out with him or her, but that would probably change the nature of the date in unacceptable ways. It would be revolting to the person who offered payment and to the person who was offered payment. That unacceptability is an example of the complex social and cultural norms that guide and limit our activities. People don't try to buy dates because social forces prevent them from doing so.

Q-5 Your study partner, Joan, states that market forces are always operative. Is she right? Why or why not?

Now let's consider another example in which political and legal influences stop economic forces from becoming market forces. Say you decide that you can make some money delivering mail in your neighborhood. You try to establish a small business, but suddenly you are confronted with the law. The U.S. Postal Service has a legal exclusive right to deliver regular mail, so you'll be prohibited from delivering regular mail in competition with the post office. Economic forces—the desire to make money—led you to want to enter the business, but in this case political forces squash the invisible hand.

Often political and social forces work together against the invisible hand. For example, in the United States there aren't enough babies to satisfy all the couples who desire them. Babies born to particular sets of parents are rationed—by luck. Consider a group of parents, all of whom want babies. Those who can, have a baby; those who can't have one, but want one, try to adopt. Adoption agencies ration the available babies. Who gets a baby depends on whom people know at the adoption agency and on the desires of the birth mother, who can often specify the socioeconomic background (and many other characteristics) of the family in which she wants her baby to grow up. That's the economic force in action; it gives more power to the supplier of something that's in short supply.

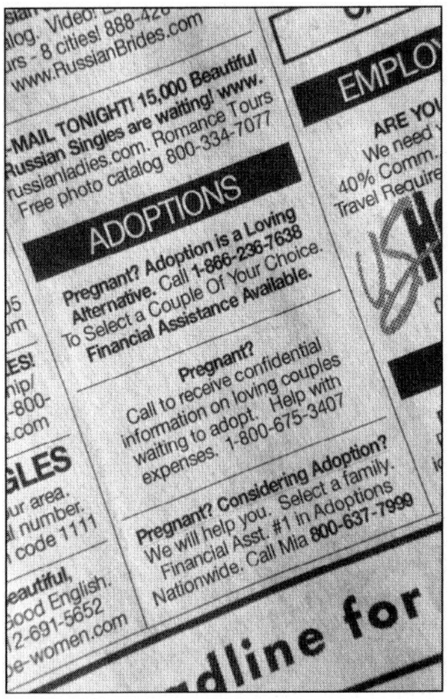

If our society allowed individuals to buy and sell babies, that economic force would be translated into a market force. The invisible hand would see to it that the quantity of babies supplied would equal the quantity of babies demanded at some price. The market, not the adoption agencies, would do the rationing.[2]

Most people, including me, find the idea of selling babies repugnant. But why? It's the strength of social forces reinforced by political forces.

What is and isn't allowable differs from one society to another. For example, in Cuba and North Korea, many private businesses are against the law, so not many people start their own businesses. In the United States, until the 1970s, it was against the law

[2]Even though it's against the law, some babies are nonetheless "sold" on a semilegal market, also called a gray market. At the turn of the century, the "market price" for a healthy baby was about $30,000. If it were legal to sell babies (and if people didn't find it morally repugnant to have babies in order to sell them), the price would be much lower because there would be a larger supply of babies. (It was not against the law to sell human eggs in the early 2000s, and one human egg was sold for $50,000. The average price was much lower; it varied with donor characteristics such as SAT scores and athletic accomplishments.)

Economic forces are always operative; society may allow market forces to operate.

to hold gold except in jewelry and for certain limited uses such as dental supplies, so most people refrained from holding gold. Ultimately a country's laws and social norms determine whether the invisible hand will be allowed to work.

Social and political forces are active in all parts of your life. You don't practice medicine without a license; you don't sell body parts or certain addictive drugs. These actions are against the law. But many people do sell alcohol; that's not against the law if you have a permit. You don't charge your friends interest to borrow money (you'd lose friends); you don't charge your children for their food (parents are supposed to feed their children); many sports and media stars don't sell their autographs (some do, but many consider the practice tacky); you don't lower the wage you'll accept in order to take a job away from someone else (you're no scab). The list is long. You cannot understand economics without understanding the limitations that political and social forces place on economic actions.

What happens in society can be seen as a reaction to, and interaction of, economic forces with other forces.

In summary, what happens in a society can be seen as the reaction to, and interaction of, these three forces: economic forces, political and legal forces, and social and historical forces. Economics has a role to play in sociology, history, and politics, just as sociology, history, and politics have roles to play in economics.

Economic Terminology

Web Note 1.4
Hip Hop Economics

Economic terminology needs little discussion. It simply needs learning. As terms come up, you'll begin to recognize them. Soon you'll begin to understand them, and finally you'll begin to feel comfortable using them. In this book, I'm trying to describe how economics works in the real world, so I introduce you to many of the terms that occur in business and in discussions of the economy. Whenever possible I'll integrate the introduction of new terms into the discussion so that learning them will seem painless. In fact I've already introduced you to a number of economic terms: *opportunity cost, the invisible hand, market forces, economic forces,* just to name a few. By the end of the book, I'll have introduced you to hundreds more.

Economic Insights

Economists have thought about the economy for a long time, so it's not surprising that they've developed some insights into the way it works. As I stated above, modern economists use a combination of both induction and deduction in arriving at insights. That combination is called *abduction*. **Abduction** is *a method of analysis that uses a combination of inductive methods and deductive methods*. Modern economics is an abductive science.

In this book I will introduce you to economic theories and models. Theories and models tie together economists' terminology and knowledge about economic institutions. Theories are inevitably too abstract to apply in specific cases, and thus a theory is often embodied in an **economic model**—*a framework that places the generalized insights of the theory in a more specific contextual setting*—or in an **economic principle**—*a commonly held economic insight stated as a law or general assumption*. To see the importance of principles, think back to when you learned to add. You didn't memorize the sum of 147 and 138; instead, you learned a principle of addition. The principle says that when adding 147 and 138, you first add 7 + 8, which you memorized was 15. You write down the 5 and carry the 1, which you add to 4 + 3 to get 8. Then add 1 + 1 = 2. So the answer is 285. When you know just one principle, you know how to add millions of combinations of numbers.

Theories, models, and principles are continually "brought to the data" to see if the predictions of the model match the data. Increases in computing power and new statistical techniques have given modern economists a far more rigorous set of procedures to determine how well the predictions fit the data than was the case for earlier economists. This has led to a greater emphasis on inductive methods, and modern economics is characterized by its strong reliance on quantitative empirical methods.

Modern empirical work takes a variety of forms. In certain instances, economists study questions by running controlled laboratory experiments. That branch of economics is called **experimental economics**—*a branch of economics that studies the economy through controlled laboratory experiments.* Where laboratory experiments are not possible, economists carefully observe the economy and try to figure out what is affecting what. To do so they look for **natural experiments**—*naturally occurring events that approximate a controlled experiment where something has changed in one place but has not changed somewhere else.* Economists can then compare the results in the two cases. An example of a natural experiment was when New Jersey raised its minimum wage and neighboring state Pennsylvania did not. Economists Alan Kruger and David Card compared the effects on unemployment in both states and found that increases in the minimum wage in New Jersey did not significantly affect employment. This led to a debate about what the empirical evidence was telling us. The reason is that in such natural experiments, it is impossible to hold "other things constant," as is done in laboratory experiments, and thus the empirical results in economics are often subject to dispute.

As I stated above, modern economics uses a combination of inductive and deductive methods to gain insight into the economy in a method called abduction. Abduction recognizes our inability to determine a final Truth with a capital T, meaning that it is true beyond any doubt, and instead looks for truth with a lowercase t. It's the best truth we have at the moment. That's the extent of truth that we will be striving for in this book.

While economic models are less general than theories, they are still usually too general to apply in specific cases. Models lead to **theorems** (*propositions that are logically true based on the assumptions in a model*). To arrive at policy **precepts** (*policy rules that conclude that a particular course of action is preferable*), these theorems must be combined with knowledge of real-world economic institutions and value judgments determining the goals for which one is striving. In discussing policy implications of theories and models, it is important to distinguish precepts from theorems.

Theories, models, and principles must be combined with a knowledge of real-world economic institutions to arrive at specific policy recommendations.

The Invisible Hand Theorem

Knowing a theory gives you insight into a wide variety of economic phenomena even though you don't know the particulars of each phenomenon. For example, much of economic theory deals with the *pricing mechanism* and how the market operates to coordinate *individuals' decisions*. Economists have come to the following theorems:

> When the quantity supplied is greater than the quantity demanded, price has a tendency to fall.
>
> When the quantity demanded is greater than the quantity supplied, price has a tendency to rise.

Q-6 There has been a superb growing season and the quantity of tomatoes supplied exceeds the quantity demanded. What is likely to happen to the price of tomatoes?

Using these generalized theorems, economists have developed a theory of markets that leads to the further theorem that, under certain conditions, markets are efficient. That is, the market will coordinate individuals' decisions, allocating scarce resources to their best possible use. **Efficiency** means *achieving a goal as cheaply as possible.* Economists call this theorem the **invisible hand theorem**—*a market economy, through the price mechanism, will tend to allocate resources efficiently.*

Theories, and the models used to represent them, are enormously efficient methods of conveying information, but they're also necessarily abstract. They rely on simplifying assumptions, and *if you don't know the assumptions, you don't know the theory*. The result of forgetting assumptions could be similar to what happens if you forget that you're

REAL-WORLD APPLICATION

Winston Churchill and Lady Astor

Lady Astor

There are many stories about Nancy Astor, the first woman elected to Britain's Parliament. A vivacious, fearless American woman, she married into the English aristocracy and, during the 1930s and 1940s, became a bright light on the English social and political scenes, which were already quite bright.

One story told about Lady Astor is that she and Winston Churchill, the unorthodox genius who had a long and distinguished political career and who was Britain's prime minister during World War II, were sitting in a pub having a theoretical discussion about morality. Churchill suggested that as a thought experiment Lady Astor ponder the following question: If a man were to promise her a huge amount of money—say a million pounds—for the privilege, would she sleep with him? Lady Astor did ponder the question for a while and finally answered, yes, she would, if the money were guaranteed. Churchill then asked her if she would sleep with him for five pounds. Her response was sharp: "Of course not. What do you think I am—a prostitute?" Churchill responded, "We have already established that fact; we are now simply negotiating about price."

One moral that economists might draw from this story is that economic incentives, if high enough, can have a powerful influence on behavior. But an equally important moral of the story is that noneconomic incentives also can be very strong. Why do most people feel it's wrong to sell sex for money, even if they might be willing to do so if the price were high enough? Keeping this second moral in mind will significantly increase your economic understanding of real-world events.

supposed to add numbers in columns. Forgetting that, yet remembering all the steps, can lead to a wildly incorrect answer. For example,

$$\begin{array}{r} 147 \\ +\ 138 \\ \hline 1{,}608 \end{array}$$ is wrong.

Knowing the assumptions of theories and models allows you to progress beyond gut reaction and better understand the strengths and weaknesses of various economic theories and models. Let's consider a central economic assumption: the assumption that individuals behave rationally—that what they choose reflects what makes them happiest, given the constraints. If that assumption doesn't hold, the invisible hand theorem doesn't hold. I find it useful to distinguish two types of modern economists: modern traditional economists and modern behavioral economists. Modern traditional economists use models that focus on traditional assumptions of rationality and self-interest; modern behavioral economists modify these assumptions, and are working on models that incorporate some predictably irrational behavior. Yet another group of modern economists deemphasizes deductive models almost completely and develops empirical models that are primarily based on statistical patterns they discover in data.

Presenting the invisible hand theorem in its full beauty is an important part of any economics course. Presenting the assumptions on which it is based and the limitations of the invisible hand is likewise an important part of the course. I'll do both throughout the book.

Economic Theory and Stories

Theory is a shorthand way of telling a story.

Economic theory, and the models in which that theory is presented, often developed as a shorthand way of telling a story. These stories are important; they make the theory come alive and convey the insights that give economic theory its power. In this book I present plenty of theories and models, but they're accompanied by stories that provide the context that makes them relevant.

At times, because there are many new terms, discussing theories takes up much of the presentation time and becomes a bit oppressive. That's the nature of the beast. As Albert Einstein said, "Theories should be as simple as possible, but not more so." When a theory becomes oppressive, pause and think about the underlying story that the theory is meant to convey. That story should make sense and be concrete. If you can't translate the theory into a story, you don't understand the theory.

Microeconomics and Macroeconomics

Economic theory is divided into two parts: microeconomic theory and macroeconomic theory. Microeconomic theory considers economic reasoning from the viewpoint of individuals and firms and builds up to an analysis of the whole economy. **Microeconomics** is *the study of individual choice, and how that choice is influenced by economic forces.* Microeconomics studies such things as the pricing policies of firms, households' decisions on what to buy, and how markets allocate resources among alternative ends. Our discussion of opportunity cost was based on microeconomic theory. The invisible hand theorem comes from microeconomics.

Microeconomics is the study of how individual choice is influenced by economic forces.

As we build up from microeconomic analysis to an analysis of the entire economy, everything gets rather complicated. Many economists try to uncomplicate matters by taking a different approach—a macroeconomic approach—first looking at the aggregate, or whole, and then breaking it down into components. **Macroeconomics** is *the study of the economy as a whole.* It considers the problems of inflation, unemployment, business cycles, and growth. Macroeconomics focuses on aggregate relationships such as how household consumption is related to income and how government policies can affect growth.

Macroeconomics is the study of the economy as a whole. It considers the problems of inflation, unemployment, business cycles, and growth.

Consider an analogy to the human body. A micro approach analyzes a person by looking first at each individual cell and then builds up. A macro approach starts with the person and then goes on to his or her components—arms, legs, fingernails, feelings, and so on. Put simply, microeconomics analyzes from the parts to the whole; macroeconomics analyzes from the whole to the parts.

Microeconomics and macroeconomics are very much interrelated. What happens in the economy as a whole is based on individual decisions, but individual decisions are made within an economy and can be understood only within that context. For example, whether a firm decides to expand production capacity will depend on what the owners expect will happen to the demand for their products. Those expectations are determined by macroeconomic conditions. Because microeconomics focuses on the individual and macroeconomics focuses on the whole economy, traditionally microeconomics and macroeconomics are taught separately, even though they are interrelated.

Q-7 Classify the following topics as macroeconomic or microeconomic:

1. The impact of a tax increase on aggregate output.
2. The relationship between two competing firms' pricing behavior.
3. A farmer's decision to plant soy or wheat.
4. The effect of trade on economic growth.

Economic Institutions

To know whether you can apply economic theory to reality, you must know about economic institutions—laws, common practices, and organizations in a society that affect the economy. Corporations, governments, and cultural norms are all examples of economic institutions. Many economic institutions have social, political, and religious dimensions. For example, your job often influences your social standing. In addition, many social institutions, such as the family, have economic functions. I include any institution that significantly affects economic decisions as an economic institution because you must understand that institution if you are to understand how the economy functions.

To apply economic theory to reality, you've got to have a sense of economic institutions.

Economic institutions differ significantly among countries. For example, in Germany banks are allowed to own companies; in the United States they cannot. This helps

REAL-WORLD APPLICATION

Economists and Market Solutions

Economic reasoning is playing an increasing role in government policy. Consider the regulation of pollution. Pollution became a policy concern in the 1960s as books such as Rachel Carson's *Silent Spring* were published. In 1970, in response to concerns about the environment, the Clean Air Act was passed. It capped the amount of pollutants (such as sulfur dioxide, carbon monoxide, nitrogen dioxides, lead, and hydrocarbons) that firms could emit. This was a "command-and-control" approach to regulation, which brought about a reduction in pollution, but also brought about lots of complaints by firms that either found the limits costly to meet or couldn't afford to meet them and were forced to close.

Enter economists. They proposed an alternative approach, called cap-and-trade, that achieved the same overall reduction in pollution but at a lower overall cost. In the plan they proposed, government still set a pollution cap that firms had to meet, but it gave individual firms some flexibility. Firms that reduced emissions by less than the required limit could buy pollution permits from other firms that reduced their emissions by more than their limit. The price of the permits would be determined in an "emissions permit market." Thus, firms that had a low cost of reducing pollution would have a strong incentive to reduce pollution by more than their limit in order to sell these permits, or rights to pollute, to firms that had a high cost of reducing pollution and therefore reduced their pollution by less than what was required. The net reduction was the same, but the reduction was achieved at a lower cost.

In 1990 Congress adopted economists' proposal and the Clean Air Act was amended to include tradable emissions permits. An active market in emissions permits developed and it is estimated that the tradable permit program has lowered the cost of reducing sulfur dioxide emissions by $1 billion a year. Economists used this same argument to promote an incentive-based solution to world pollution in an agreement among some countries to reduce world pollution known as the Kyoto Protocol. In 2008 this became the central idea in a policy proposal to reduce carbon emissions, with the U.S. government creating a law that would require firms to keep carbon emissions at some initial level but allow firms that reduce carbon emissions to "sell" their reduced emissions to other firms that could then increase their emissions by an offsetting amount. You can read more about the current state of tradable emissions at epa.gov/airmarkets.

explain why investment decisions are made differently in Germany as compared to the United States. Alternatively, in the Netherlands workers are highly unionized, while in the United States they are not. Unions in the Netherlands therefore have the power to agree to keep wages lower in exchange for more jobs. This means that government policies to control inflation might differ in these two countries.

Economic institutions sometimes seem to operate in ways quite different than economic theory predicts. For example, economic theory says that prices are determined by supply and demand. However, businesses say that they set prices by rules of thumb—often by what are called cost-plus-markup rules. That is, a firm determines what its costs are, multiplies by 1.4 or 1.5, and the result is the price it sets. Economic theory says that supply and demand determine who's hired; experience suggests that hiring is often done on the basis of whom you know, not by market forces.

These apparent contradictions have two complementary explanations. First, economic theory abstracts from many issues. These issues may account for the differences. Second, there's no contradiction; economic principles often affect decisions from behind the scenes. For instance, supply and demand pressures determine what the price markup over cost will be. In all cases, however, to apply economic theory to reality—to gain the full value of economic insights—you've got to have a sense of economic institutions.

Economic Policy Options

Economic policies are *actions (or inaction) taken by government to influence economic actions.* The final goal of the course is to present the economic policy options facing our society today. For example, should the government restrict mergers between firms? Should it run a budget deficit? Should it do something about the international trade deficit? Should it decrease taxes?

I saved this discussion for last because there's no sense talking about policy options unless you know some economic terminology, some economic theory, and something about economic institutions. Once you know something about them, you're in a position to consider the policy options available for dealing with the economic problems our society faces.

Policies operate within institutions, but policies also can influence the institutions within which they operate. Let's consider an example: welfare policy and the institution of the two-parent family. In the 1960s, the United States developed a variety of policy initiatives designed to eliminate poverty. These initiatives provided income to single parents with children, and assumed that family structure would be unchanged by these policies. But family structure changed substantially, and, very likely, these policies played a role in increasing the number of single-parent families. The result was the programs failed to eliminate poverty. Now this is not to say that we should not have programs to eliminate poverty, nor that two-parent families are always preferable to one-parent families; it is only to say that we must build into our policies their effect on institutions.

To carry out economic policy effectively, one must understand how institutions might change as a result of the economic policy.

Some policies are designed to change institutions directly. While these policies are much more difficult to implement than policies that don't, they also offer the largest potential for gain. Let's consider an example. In the 1990s, a number of Eastern European countries replaced central planning with market economies and private ownership. The result: Output in those countries fell enormously as the old institutions fell apart. While most Eastern European economies have rebounded from their initial losses, some countries of the former Soviet Union have yet to do so. The hardships these countries continue to experience show the enormous difficulty of implementing policies involving major institutional changes.

Q-8 True or false? Economists should focus their policy analysis on institutional changes because such policies offer the largest gains.

Objective Policy Analysis

Good economic policy analysis is objective; that is, it keeps the analyst's value judgments separate from the analysis. Objective analysis does not say, "This is the way things should be," reflecting a goal established by the analyst. That would be subjective analysis because it would reflect the analyst's view of how things should be. Instead, objective analysis says, "This is the way the economy works, and if society (or the individual or firm for whom you're doing the analysis) wants to achieve a particular goal, this is how it might go about doing so." Objective analysis keeps, or at least tries to keep, subjective views—value judgments—separate.

Q-9 John, your study partner, is a free market advocate. He argues that the invisible hand theorem tells us that the government should not interfere with the economy. Do you agree? Why or why not?

To make clear the distinction between objective and subjective analysis, economists have divided economics into three categories: *positive economics*, *normative economics*, and the *art of economics*. **Positive economics** is *the study of what is, and how the economy works.* It explores the pure theory of economics, and it discovers agreed-upon empirical regularities. These empirical regularities are often called empirical facts—for example, large price fluctuations in financial markets tend to be followed by additional large price fluctuations. Economic theorists then relate their theories to those facts. Positive economics asks such questions as: How does the market for hog bellies work? How do price restrictions affect market forces? These questions fall under the heading of economic theory.

Positive economics is the study of what is, and how the economy works.

As I stated above, economic theory does not provide definitive policy recommendations. It is too abstract and makes too many assumptions that don't match observed behavior. In positive economic theory, one looks for empirical facts and develops *theorems*—propositions that logically follow from the assumptions of one's model. Theorems and agreed-upon empirical facts are almost by definition beyond dispute and serve as the foundation for economic science. But these theorems don't tell us what policies should be followed.

Normative economics is the study of what the goals of the economy should be.

Policies are built on two other branches of economics: normative economics and political economy or the art of economics. **Normative economics** is *the study of what the goals of the economy should be*. Normative economics asks such questions as: What should the distribution of income be? What should tax policy be designed to achieve? In discussing such questions, economists must carefully delineate whose goals they are discussing. One cannot simply assume that one's own goals for society are society's goals. For example, let's consider a debate that is currently ongoing in economics. Some economists are worried about global warming; they believe that high consumption in rich societies is causing global warming and that the high consumption is a result of interdependent wants—people want something only because other people have it—but having it isn't necessarily making people happier. These economists argue that society's normative goal should include a much greater focus on the implications of economic activities for global warming, and the distribution of income, than is currently the case. Discussion of these goals falls under the category of normative economics.

The art of economics is the application of the knowledge learned in positive economics to the achievement of the goals determined in normative economics.

The **art of economics**, also called political economy, is *the application of the knowledge learned in positive economics to the achievement of the goals one has determined in normative economics*. It looks at such questions as: To achieve the goals that society wants to achieve, how would you go about it, given the way the economy works?[3] Most policy discussions fall under the art of economics. The art of economics branch is specifically about policy; it is designed to arrive at *precepts* or guides for policy. Precepts are based on theorems and empirical facts developed in positive economics and goals developed in normative economics. The art of economics requires economists to assess the appropriateness of theorems to achieving the normative goals in the real world. Whereas once the assumptions are agreed upon, theorems derived from models are not debatable, precepts are debatable, and economists that use the same theorems can hold different precepts. For example, a model may tell us that rent controls will cause a shortage of housing. That does not mean that rent controls are necessarily bad policies since rent controls may also have some desirable effects. The precept that rent controls are bad policy is based upon a judgment about the importance of those other effects, and one's normative judgments about the benefits and costs of the policy. In this book, when I say that economists tend to favor a policy, I am talking about precepts, which means that alternative perspectives are possible even among economists.

Q-10 Tell whether the following five statements belong in positive economics, normative economics, or the art of economics.

NE 1. We should support the market because it is efficient.

2. Given certain conditions, the market achieves efficient results.

NE 3. Based on past experience and our understanding of markets, if one wants a reasonably efficient result, markets should probably be relied on.

NE 4. The distribution of income should be left to markets.

5. Markets allocate income according to contributions of factors of production.

In each of these three branches of economics, economists separate their own value judgments from their objective analysis as much as possible. The qualifier "as much as possible" is important, since some value judgments inevitably sneak in. We are products of our environment, and the questions we ask, the framework we use, and the way we interpret the evidence all involve value judgments and reflect our backgrounds.

Maintaining objectivity is easiest in positive economics, where you are working with abstract models to understand how the economy works. Maintaining objectivity

[3]This three-part distinction was made back in 1891 by a famous economist, John Neville Keynes, father of John Maynard Keynes, the economist who developed macroeconomics. This distinction was instilled into modern economics by Milton Friedman and Richard Lipsey in the 1950s. They, however, downplayed the art of economics, which J. N. Keynes had seen as central to understanding the economist's role in policy. In his discussion of the scope and method of economics, Lionel Robbins used the term "political economy" rather than Keynes' term "the art of economics."

REAL-WORLD APPLICATION

Economics and Global Warming

A good example of the central role that economics plays in policy debates is the debate about global warming. Almost all scientists are now convinced that global warming is occurring and that human activity such as the burning of fossil fuel is the cause. The policy question is what to do about it. To answer that question, most governments have turned to economists. The first part of the question that economists have considered is whether it is worth doing anything, and in a well-publicized report commissioned by the British government, economist Nicholas Stern argued that, based upon his cost/benefit analysis, yes it is worth doing something. The reason: because the costs of not doing anything would likely reduce output by 20 percent in the future, and that those costs (appropriately weighted for when they occur) are less than the benefits of policies that can be implemented.

The second part of the question is: what policies to implement? The policies he recommended were policies that changed incentives—specifically, policies that raised the costs of emitting greenhouse gases and decreased the cost of other forms of production. Those recommended policies reflected the economist's opportunity cost framework in action: if you want to change the result, change the incentives that individuals face.

There is considerable debate about Stern's analysis—both with the way he conducted the cost/benefit analysis and with his policy recommendations. Such debates are inevitable when the data are incomplete and numerous judgments need to be made. I suspect that these debates will continue over the coming years with economists on various sides of the debate. Economists are generally not united in their views about complicated policy issues since they differ in their normative views and in their assessment of the problem and of what politically can be achieved; that's because policy is part of the art of economics, not part of positive economics. But the framework of the policy debate about global warming is the economic framework. Thus, even though political forces will ultimately choose what policy is followed, you must understand the economic framework to take part in the debate.

is harder in normative economics. You must always be objective about whose normative values you are using. It's easy to assume that all of society shares your values, but that assumption is often wrong.

It's hardest to maintain objectivity in the art of economics because it can suffer from the problems of both positive and normative economics. Because noneconomic forces affect policy, to practice the art of economics we must make judgments about how these noneconomic forces work. These judgments are likely to reflect our own value judgments. So we must be exceedingly careful to be as objective as possible in practicing the art of economics.

Web Note 1.5
The Art of Economics

Policy and Social and Political Forces

When you think about the policy options facing society, you'll quickly discover that the choice of policy options depends on much more than economic theory. Politicians, not economists, determine economic policy. To understand what policies are chosen, you must take into account historical precedent plus social, cultural, and political forces. In an economics course, I don't have time to analyze these forces in as much depth as I'd like. That's one reason there are separate history, political science, sociology, and anthropology courses.

While it is true that these other forces play significant roles in policy decisions, specialization is necessary. In economics, we focus the analysis on the invisible hand, and much of economic theory is devoted to considering how the economy would operate if the invisible hand were the only force operating. But as soon as we apply theory to reality and policy, we must take into account political and social forces as well.

An example will make my point more concrete. Most economists agree that holding down or eliminating tariffs (taxes on imports) and quotas (numerical limitations on imports) makes good economic sense. They strongly advise governments to follow a policy of free trade. Do governments follow free trade policies? Almost invariably they do not. Politics leads society in a different direction. If you're advising a policy maker, you need to point out that these other forces must be taken into account, and how other forces should (if they should) and can (if they can) be integrated with your recommendations.

Conclusion

There are tons more that could be said by way of introducing you to economics, but an introduction must remain an introduction. As it is, this chapter should have

1. Introduced you to economic reasoning.
2. Surveyed what we're going to cover in this book.
3. Given you an idea of my writing style and approach.

We'll be spending long hours together over the coming term, and before entering into such a commitment it's best to know your partner. While I won't know you, by the end of this book you'll know me. Maybe you won't love me as my mother does, but you'll know me.

This introduction was my opening line. I hope it also conveyed the importance and relevance that belong to economics. If it did, it has served its intended purpose. Economics is tough, but tough can be fun.

Summary

- The three coordination problems any economy must solve are what to produce, how to produce it, and for whom to produce it. In solving these problems, societies have found that there is a problem of scarcity.
- Deduction begins with almost self-evident principles and develops models and conclusions based on those principles. Induction looks at empirical evidence first and infers principles from those observations. Abduction is a combination of deduction and induction.
- Economic reasoning structures all questions in a cost/benefit framework: If the marginal benefits of doing something exceed the marginal costs, do it. If the marginal costs exceed the marginal benefits, don't do it.
- Sunk costs are not relevant in the economic decision rule.
- The opportunity cost of undertaking an activity is the benefit you might have gained from choosing the next-best alternative.
- "There ain't no such thing as a free lunch" (TANSTAAFL) embodies the opportunity cost concept.
- Economic forces, the forces of scarcity, are always working. Market forces, which ration by changing prices, are not always allowed to work.
- Economic reality is controlled and directed by three types of forces: economic forces, political forces, and social forces.
- Under certain conditions, the market, through its price mechanism, will allocate scarce resources efficiently.
- Economics can be divided into microeconomics and macroeconomics. Microeconomics is the study of individual choice and how that choice is influenced by economic forces. Macroeconomics is the study of the economy as a whole. It considers problems such as inflation, unemployment, business cycles, and growth.

- Economics can be subdivided into positive economics, normative economics, and the art of economics. Positive economics is the study of what is, normative economics is the study of what should be, and the art of economics relates positive to normative economics.
- Theorems are propositions that follow from the assumptions of a model; precepts are the guides for policies based on theorems, normative judgments, and empirical observations about how the real world differs from the model.

Key Terms

abduction *(12)*
art of economics *(18)*
deduction *(5)*
economic decision rule *(8)*
economic force *(10)*
economic model *(12)*
economic policy *(17)*
economic principle *(12)*
economics *(4)*
efficiency *(13)*
experimental economics *(13)*
induction *(6)*
invisible hand *(11)*
invisible hand theorem *(13)*
macroeconomics *(15)*
marginal benefit *(7)*
marginal cost *(7)*
market force *(10)*
microeconomics *(15)*
natural experiment *(13)*
normative economics *(18)*
opportunity cost *(9)*
positive economics *(17)*
precepts *(13)*
scarcity *(5)*
sunk cost *(7)*
theorem *(13)*

Questions and Exercises

1. Why does the textbook author focus on coordination rather than on scarcity when defining economics? LO1
2. Define deduction and give an example of deductive reasoning. LO1
3. Define induction and give an example of inductive reasoning. LO1
4. Your study partner has suggested that deductive reasoning is much more accurate than inductive reasoning. How would you respond? LO1
5. State whether the following is an example of deductive, inductive, or abductive reasoning:
   a. The number of rings inside a tree is the age of a tree. This tree has 10 rings. *Conclusion:* This tree is 10 years old.
   b. People spend 80 percent of their income. Susan will earn $60,000 this year. *Conclusion:* Susan will spend $48,000.
   c. Ten college students are standing in a line to choose either an economics course or an English course. The first student chooses economics. The second student chooses economics and so does the third. *Conclusion:* All college students prefer economics over English.
   d. Ten college students are standing in a line to choose either an economics course or an English course. The first student chooses economics. The second student chooses economics and so does the third. *Conclusion:* All college students prefer economics over English. The fourth student in line chooses English. The first three students were women; the fourth was a man. *Revised conclusion:* Male college students prefer English. Female college students prefer economics. LO1
6. List one recent choice you made and explain why you made the choice in terms of marginal benefits and marginal costs. LO2
7. You rent a car for $29.95. The first 150 miles are free, but each mile thereafter costs 15 cents. You plan to drive it 200 miles. What is the marginal cost of driving the car? LO2
8. Economists Henry Saffer of Kean University, Frank J. Chaloupka of the University of Illinois at Chicago, and Dhaval Dave of Bentley College estimated that the government must spend $4,170 on drug control to deter one person from using drugs and the cost that one drug user imposes on society is $897. Based on this information alone, should the government spend the money on drug control? LO2
9. What is the opportunity cost of buying a $20,000 car? LO3
10. Suppose you currently earn $30,000 a year. You are considering a job that will increase your lifetime earnings by $300,000 but that requires an MBA. The job will mean also attending business school for two years at an annual cost of $25,000. You already have a bachelor's degree, for which you spent $80,000 in tuition and books. Which of the above information is relevant to your decision whether to take the job? LO3
11. Suppose your college has been given $5 million. You have been asked to decide how to spend it to improve your college. Explain how you would use the economic decision rule and the concept of opportunity costs to decide how to spend it. LO2, LO3

12. Calculate, using the best estimates you can:
    a. Your opportunity cost of attending college.
    b. Your opportunity cost of taking this course.
    c. Your opportunity cost of attending yesterday's lecture in this course. LO3
13. In 1999 Royal Philips Electronics paid $180 million to buy 20-year naming rights of the Atlanta, Georgia, stadium, home of NBA's Atlanta Hawks. University of Massachusetts Professor Timothy D. DeSchriver and Drexel University Professor Paul E. Jensen analyzed naming rights. In their study, what was the likely impact of each of the following on a corporation's willingness to pay to name a stadium? (Difficult)
    a. An existing team is relocating to the stadium.
    b. The stadium is in a highly populated area.
    c. The stadium's current name is the Staples Center and has had that name for 20 years. LO3
14. Give two examples of social forces and explain how they keep economic forces from becoming market forces. LO4
15. Give two examples of political or legal forces and explain how they might interact with economic forces. LO4
16. Individuals have two kidneys, but most of us need only one. People who have lost both kidneys through accident or disease must be hooked up to a dialysis machine, which cleanses waste from their bodies. Say a person who has two good kidneys offers to sell one of them to someone whose kidney function has been totally destroyed. The seller asks $30,000 for the kidney, and the person who has lost both kidneys accepts the offer.
    a. Who benefits from the deal?
    b. Who is hurt?
    c. Should a society allow such market transactions? Why? LO4
17. State whether the following are primarily microeconomic or macroeconomic policy issues:
    a. Should U.S. interest rates be lowered to decrease the amount of unemployment?
    b. Will the fact that more and more doctors are selling their practices to managed care networks increase the efficiency of medical providers?
    c. Should the current federal income tax be lowered to reduce unemployment?
    d. Should the federal minimum wage be raised?
    e. Should Sprint and Verizon both be allowed to build local phone networks?
    f. Should commercial banks be required to provide loans in all areas of the territory from which they accept deposits? LO5
18. List two microeconomic and two macroeconomic problems. LO5
19. What is an economic model? What besides a model do economists need to make policy recommendations? LO1, LO6
20. Does economic theory prove that the free market system is best? Why? (Difficult) LO6
21. State whether the following statements belong in positive economics, normative economics, or the art of economics.
    a. In a market, when quantity supplied exceeds quantity demanded, price tends to fall.
    b. When determining tax rates, the government should take into account the income needs of individuals.
    c. What society feels is fair is determined largely by cultural norms.
    d. When deciding which rationing mechanism is best (lottery, price, first-come/first-served), one must take into account the goals of society.
    e. California currently rations water to farmers at subsidized prices. Once California allows the trading of water rights, it will allow economic forces to be a market force. LO6
22. Distinguish between theorems and precepts. Is it possible for two economists to agree about theorems but disagree about precepts? Why or why not? LO6

Questions from Alternative Perspectives

1. Is it possible to use objective economic analysis as a basis for government planning? (Austrian)
2. In "Rational Choice with Passion: Virtue in a Model of Rational Addiction," Andrew M. Yuengert of Pepperdine University argues that there is a conflict between reason and passion.
    a. What might that conflict be?
    b. What implications does it have for applying the economic model? (Religious)
3. Economic institutions are "habits of thought" that organize society.
    a. In what way might patriarchy be an *institution* and how might it influence the labor market?
    b. Does the free market or patriarchy better explain why 98 percent of secretaries are women and 98 percent of automobile mechanics are men? (Feminist)
4. In October of 2004, the supply of flu vaccine fell by over 50 percent. The result was that the vaccine had to be

rationed, with a priority schedule established: young children, people with weakened immunity, those over 65, etc., taking priority.
   a. Compare and contrast this allocation outcome with a free market outcome.
   b. Which alternative is more just? (Institutionalist)
5. The textbook model assumes that individuals have enough knowledge to follow the economic decision rule.
   a. How did you decide what college you would attend?
   b. Did you have enough knowledge to follow the economic decision rule?
   c. For what type of decisions do you not use the economic decision rule?
   d. What are the implications for economic analysis if most people don't follow the economic decision rule in many aspects of their decisions? (Post-Keynesian)
6. Radical economists believe that all of economics, like all theorizing or storytelling, is value-laden. Theories and stories reflect the values of those who compose them and tell them. For instance, Radicals offer a different analysis than most economists of how capitalism works and what ought to be done about its most plaguing problems: inequality, periodic economic crises with large-scale unemployment, and the alienation of the workers.
   a. What does the radical position imply about the distinction between positive economics and normative economics that the text makes?
   b. Is economics value-laden or objective and is the distinction between positive and normative economics tenable or untenable? (Radical)

Issues to Ponder

1. At times we all regret decisions. Does this necessarily mean we did not use the economic decision rule when making the decision? (Difficult) LO2
2. Economist Steven Landsburg argues that if one believes in the death penalty for murderers because of its deterrent effect, using cost/benefit analysis we should execute computer hackers—the creators of worms and viruses—because the deterrent effect in cost saving would be greater than the deterrent effect in saving lives. Estimates are that each execution deters eight murders, which, if one valued each life at about $7 million, saves about $56 million; he estimates that executing hackers would save more than that per execution, and thus would be the economic thing to do. (Difficult)
   a. Do you agree or disagree with Landsburg's argument? Why?
   b. Can you extend cost/benefit analysis to other areas? LO2
3. Adam Smith, who wrote *The Wealth of Nations*, and who is seen as the father of modern economics, also wrote *The Theory of Moral Sentiments*. In it he argued that society would be better off if people weren't so selfish and were more considerate of others. How does this view fit with the discussion of economic reasoning presented in the chapter? LO3
4. A *Wall Street Journal* article recently asked readers the following questions. What's your answer?
   a. An accident has caused deadly fumes to enter the school ventilation system where it will kill five children. You can stop it by throwing a switch, but doing so will kill one child in another room. Do you throw the switch?
   b. Say that a doctor can save five patients with an organ transplant that would end the life of a patient who is sick, but not yet dead. Does she do it?
   c. What is the difference between the two situations described in *a* and *b*?
   d. How important are opportunity costs in your decisions? LO3
5. Economics is about strategic thinking, and the strategies can get very complicated. Suppose you kiss someone and ask whether the person liked it. You'd like the person to answer "yes" and you'd like that answer to be truthful. But they know that, and if they like you, they may well say that they liked the kiss even if they didn't. But you know that, and thus might not really believe that they liked the kiss; they're just saying "yes" because that's what you want to hear. But they know that you know that, so sometimes they have to convey a sense that they didn't like it, so that you will believe them when they say that they did like it. But you know that . . . You get the picture. Economists have studied such issues; you can find a discussion of similar issues on George Mason University Economist Tyler Cowen's Web site (www.gmu.edu/jbc/Tyler). (Difficult)
   a. Should you always be honest, even when it hurts someone?
   b. What strategies can you figure out to avoid the problem of not believing the other person? LO3
6. Go to two stores: a supermarket and a convenience store.
   a. Write down the cost of a gallon of milk in each.
   b. The prices are most likely different. Using the terminology used in this chapter, explain why that is

the case and why anyone would buy milk in the store with the higher price.

c. Do the same exercise with shirts or dresses in Wal-Mart (or its equivalent) and Saks (or its equivalent). LO4

7. About 90,000 individuals in the United States are waiting for organ transplants, and at an appropriate price many individuals would be willing to supply organs. Given those facts, should human organs be allowed to be bought and sold? LO4
8. Name an economic institution and explain how it affects economic decision making or how its actions reflect economic principles. LO4
9. Tyler Cowen, an economist at George Mason University, presents an interesting case that pits the market against legal and social forces. The case involves payola—the payment of money to disk jockeys for playing a songwriter's songs. He reports that Chuck Berry was having a hard time getting his music played because of racism. To counter this, he offered a well-known disk jockey, Alan Freed, partial songwriting credits, along with partial royalties, on any Chuck Berry song of his choice. He chose *Maybellene*, which he played and promoted. It went on to be a hit, Chuck Berry went on to be a star, and Freed's estate continues to receive royalties.
   a. Should such payments be allowed? Why?
   b. How did Freed's incentives from the royalty payment differ from Freed's incentives if Chuck Berry had just offered him a flat payment?
   c. Name two other examples of similar activities—one that is legal and one that is not. LO4
10. Name three ways a limited number of dormitory rooms could be rationed. How would economic forces determine individual behavior in each? How would social or legal forces determine whether those economic forces become market forces? LO4
11. Prospect theory suggests that people are hurt more by losses than they are uplifted by gains of a corresponding size. If that is true, what implications would it have for economic policy? (Difficult) LO6
12. Is a good economist always objective? Why? LO6

Answers to Margin Questions

The numbers in parentheses refer to the page number of each margin question.

1. Since the price of both stocks is now $15, it doesn't matter which one you sell (assuming no differential capital gains taxation). The price you bought them for doesn't matter; it's a sunk cost. Marginal analysis refers to the future gain, so what you expect to happen to future prices of the stocks—not past prices—should determine which stock you decide to sell. *(8)*
2. A cost/benefit analysis requires that you put a value on a good, and placing a value on a good can be seen as demeaning it. Consider love. Try telling an acquaintance that you'd like to buy his or her spiritual love, and see what response you get. *(8)*
3. John is wrong. The opportunity cost of reading the chapter is primarily the time you spend reading it. Reading the book prevents you from doing other things. Assuming that you already paid for the book, the original price is no longer part of the opportunity cost; it is a sunk cost. Bygones are bygones. *(9)*
4. Whenever there is scarcity, the scarce good must be rationed by some means. Free health care has an opportunity cost in other resources. So if health care is not rationed, to get the resources to supply that care, other goods would have to be more tightly rationed than they currently are. It is likely that the opportunity cost of supplying free health care would be larger than most societies would be willing to pay. *(10)*
5. Joan is wrong. Economic forces are always operative; market forces are not. *(11)*
6. According to the invisible hand theorem, the price of tomatoes will likely fall. *(13)*
7. (1) Macroeconomics; (2) Microeconomics; (3) Microeconomics; (4) Macroeconomics. *(15)*
8. False. While such changes have the largest gain, they also may have the largest cost. The policies economists should focus on are those that offer the largest net gain—benefits minus costs—to society. *(17)*
9. He is wrong. The invisible hand theorem is a positive theorem and does not tell us anything about policy. To do so would be to violate Hume's dictum that a "should" cannot be derived from an "is." This is not to say that government should or should not interfere; whether government should interfere is a very difficult question. *(17)*
10. (1) Normative; (2) Positive; (3) Art; (4) Normative; (5) Positive. *(18)*

The Production Possibility Model, Trade, and Globalization

No one ever saw a dog make a fair and deliberate exchange of one bone for another with another dog.

—*Adam Smith*

Every economy must solve three main coordination problems:

1. What, and how much, to produce.
2. How to produce it.
3. For whom to produce it.

In Chapter 1, I suggested that you can boil down all economic knowledge into the single phrase "There ain't no such thing as a free lunch." There's obviously more to economics than that, but it's not a bad summary of the core of economic reasoning—it's relevant for an individual, for nonprofit organizations, for governments, and for nations. Oh, it's true that once in a while you can snitch a sandwich, but what economics tells you is that if you're offered something that approaches free-lunch status, you should also be on the lookout for some hidden cost.

A key element in getting people to recognize that lunches aren't free is the concept of opportunity cost—every decision has a cost in forgone opportunities—which I introduced you to in Chapter 1. Economists have a model, the production possibility model, that conveys the concept of opportunity costs both numerically and graphically. This model is important for understanding not only opportunity cost but also why people specialize in what they do and trade for the goods they need. Through specialization and trade, individuals, firms, and countries can achieve greater levels of production than they could otherwise achieve.

AFTER READING THIS CHAPTER, YOU SHOULD BE ABLE TO:

1. Demonstrate opportunity cost with a production possibility curve.
2. State the principle of increasing marginal opportunity cost.
3. Relate the concept of comparative advantage to the production possibility curve.
4. State how, through comparative advantage and trade, countries can consume beyond their production possibilities.
5. Explain how globalization and outsourcing are part of a global process guided by the law of one price.

The Production Possibilities Model

The production possibilities model can be presented both in a table and in a graph. (Appendix A has a discussion of graphs in economics.) I'll start with the table and then move from that to the graph. Opportunity cost can be seen numerically with a **production possibility table**—*a table that lists a choice's opportunity costs by summarizing what alternative outputs you can achieve with your*

Q-1 In the graph below, what is the opportunity cost of producing an extra unit of good *X* in terms of good *Y*?

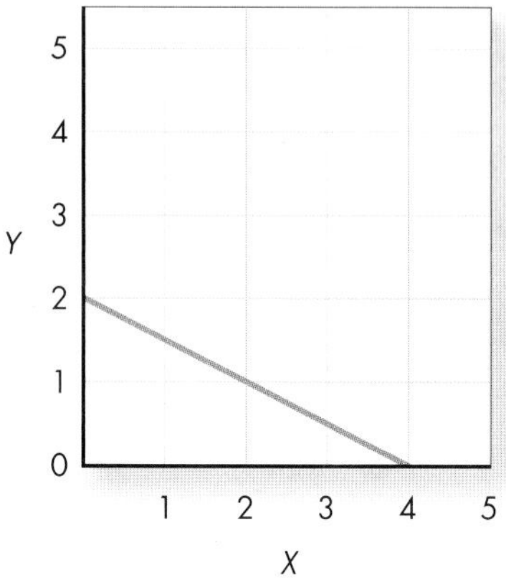

inputs. An **output** is simply *a result of an activity*, and an **input** is *what you put into a production process to achieve an output*. For example, your grade in a course is an output and your study time is an input.

A Production Possibility Curve for an Individual

Let's consider the study-time/grades example. Say you have exactly 20 hours a week to devote to two courses: economics and history. (So maybe I'm a bit optimistic.) Grades are given numerically and you know that the following relationships exist: If you study 20 hours in economics, you'll get a grade of 100; 18 hours, 94; and so forth.[1]

Let's say that the best you can do in history is a 98 with 20 hours of study a week; 19 hours of study guarantees a 96, and so on. The production possibility table in Figure 2-1(a) shows the highest combination of grades you can get with various allocations of the 20 hours available for studying the two subjects. One possibility is getting 70 in economics and 78 in history.

Notice that the opportunity cost of studying one subject rather than the other is embodied in the production possibility table. The information in the table comes from experience: We are assuming that you've discovered that if you transfer an hour of study from economics to history, you'll lose 3 points on your grade in economics and gain 2 points in history. Thus, the opportunity cost of a 2-point rise in your history grade is a 3-point decrease in your economics grade.

The production possibility curve is a curve measuring the maximum combination of outputs that can be obtained from a given number of inputs.

The information in the production possibility table also can be presented graphically in a diagram called a production possibility curve. A **production possibility curve (PPC)** is *a curve measuring the maximum combination of outputs that can be obtained from a given number of inputs*. It is a graphical presentation of the opportunity cost concept.

A production possibility curve is created from a production possibility table by mapping the table in a two-dimensional graph. I've taken the information from the table in Figure 2-1(a) and mapped it into Figure 2-1(b). The history grade is mapped, or plotted, on the horizontal axis; the economics grade is on the vertical axis.

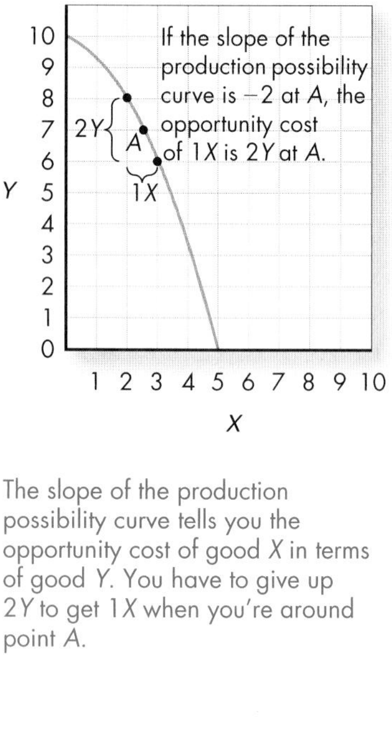

The slope of the production possibility curve tells you the opportunity cost of good *X* in terms of good *Y*. You have to give up 2*Y* to get 1*X* when you're around point *A*.

As you can see from the bottom row of Figure 2-1(a), if you study economics for all 20 hours and study history for 0 hours, you'll get grades of 100 in economics and 58 in history. Point *A* in Figure 2-1(b) represents that choice. If you study history for all 20 hours and study economics for 0 hours, you'll get a 98 in history and a 40 in economics. Point *E* represents that choice. Points *B*, *C*, and *D* represent three possible choices between these two extremes.

Notice that the production possibility curve slopes downward from left to right. That means that there is an inverse relationship (a trade-off) between grades in economics and grades in history. The better the grade in economics, the worse the grade in history, and vice versa. That downward slope represents the opportunity cost concept: you get more of one benefit only if you get less of another benefit.

The production possibility curve not only represents the opportunity cost concept but also measures the opportunity cost. For example, in Figure 2-1(b), say you want to raise your grade in history from a 94 to a 98 (move from point *D* to point *E*). The

[1]Throughout the book I'll be presenting numerical examples to help you understand the concepts. The numbers I choose are often arbitrary. After all, you have to choose something. As an exercise, you might choose different numbers than I did, numbers that apply to your own life, and work out the argument using those numbers.

FIGURE 2-1 (A AND B) **A Production Possibility Table and Curve for Grades in Economics and History**

The production possibility table (a) shows the highest combination of grades you can get with only 20 hours available for studying economics and history. The information in the production possibility table in (a) can be plotted on a graph, as is done in (b). The grade received in economics is on the vertical axis, and the grade received in history is on the horizontal axis.

Hours of Study in History	Grade in History	Hours of Study in Economics	Grade in Economics
20	98	0	40
19	96	1	43
18	94	2	46
17	92	3	49
16	90	4	52
15	88	5	55
14	86	6	58
13	84	7	61
12	82	8	64
11	80	9	67
10	78	10	70
9	76	11	73
8	74	12	76
7	72	13	79
6	70	14	82
5	68	15	85
4	66	16	88
3	64	17	91
2	62	18	94
1	60	19	97
0	58	20	100

(a) Production Possibility Table

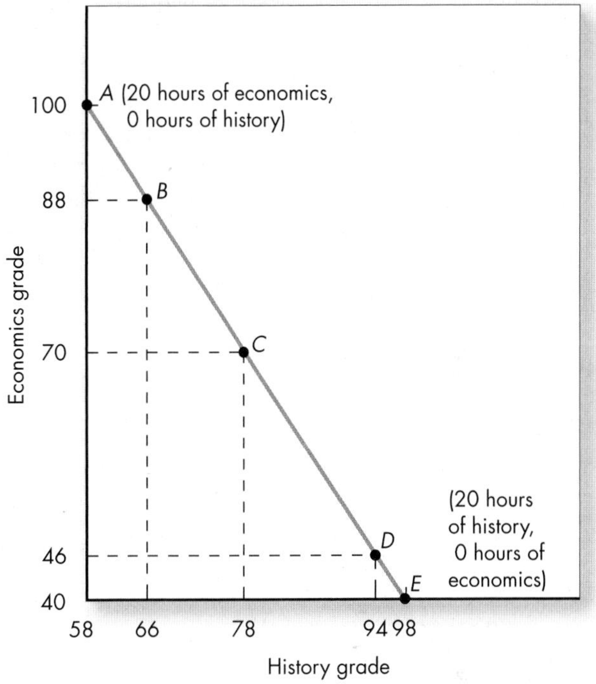

(b) Production Possibility Curve

opportunity cost of that 4-point increase would be a 6-point decrease in your economics grade, from 46 to 40.

To summarize, the production possibility curve demonstrates that

1. There is a limit to what you can achieve, given the existing institutions, resources, and technology.
2. Every choice you make has an opportunity cost. You can get more of something only by giving up something else.

Production Possibilities Curve

Increasing Marginal Opportunity Cost

In the study-time/grade example, the opportunity cost of trade remained constant; you could always trade two points on your history grade for three points on your economics grade. This assumption of an unchanging opportunity cost made the production possibility curve a straight line. Although this made the example easier, is it realistic? Probably not, especially if we are using the PPC to describe the choices that a society makes. For many of the choices society must make, opportunity costs tend to increase as we choose more and more of an item. Such a phenomenon is so common, in fact,

The principle of increasing marginal opportunity cost tells us that opportunity costs increase the more you concentrate on the activity.

that it has acquired a name: the **principle of increasing marginal opportunity cost.** That principle states:

In order to get more of something, one must give up ever-increasing quantities of something else.

In other words, initially the opportunity costs of an activity are low, but they increase the more we concentrate on that activity.

A production possibility curve that exhibits increasing marginal opportunity costs is bowed outward, as in Figure 2-2(b).

Why are production possibility curves typically bowed outward? Because some resources are better suited for the production of certain kinds of goods than other kinds of goods. To understand what that means, let's talk about the graph in Figure 2-2(b), which is derived from the table in Figure 2-2(a). This curve represents society's choice between defense spending (guns) and spending on domestic needs (butter).

Suppose society is producing only butter (point *A*). Giving up a little butter (1 pound) initially gains us a lot of guns (4), moving us to point *B*. The next 2 pounds of butter we give up gain us slightly fewer guns (point *C*). If we continue to trade butter for guns, we find that at point *D* we gain very few guns from giving up a pound of butter. The opportunity cost of choosing guns over butter increases as we increase the production of guns.

Comparative Advantage

The reason the opportunity cost of guns increases as we produce more guns is that some resources are relatively better suited to producing guns, while others are relatively better suited to producing butter. Put in economists' terminology, some resources have a

FIGURE 2-2 (A AND B) A Production Possibility Table and Curve

The table in (**a**) contains information on the trade-off between the production of guns and butter. This information has been plotted on the graph in (**b**). Notice in (**b**) that as we move along the production possibility curve from *A* to *F*, trading butter for guns, we get fewer and fewer guns for each pound of butter given up. That is, the opportunity cost of choosing guns over butter increases as we increase the production of guns. This concept is called the principle of increasing marginal opportunity cost. The phenomenon occurs because some resources are better suited for the production of butter than for the production of guns, and we use the better ones first.

% of Resources Devoted to Production of Guns	Number of Guns	% of Resources Devoted to Production of Butter	Pounds of Butter	Row
0	0	100	15	*A*
20	4	80	14	*B*
40	7	60	12	*C*
60	9	40	9	*D*
80	11	20	5	*E*
100	12	0	0	*F*

(a) Production Possibility Table

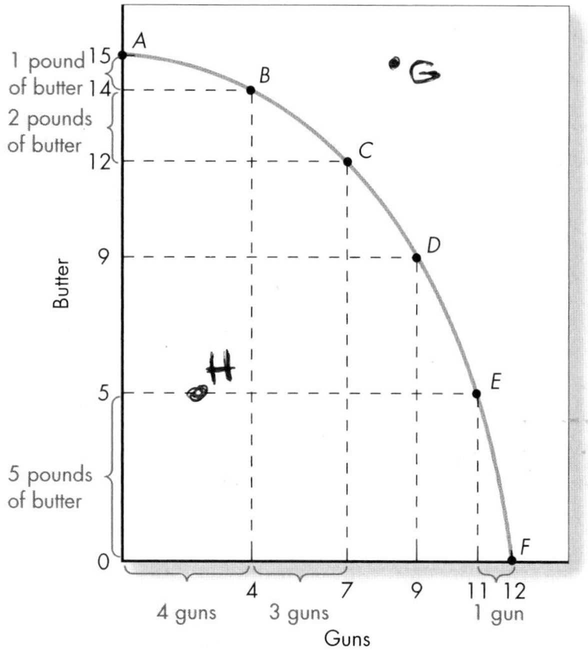

(b) Production Possibility Curve

A REMINDER ✓

Production Possibility Curves

Definition	Shape	Shifts	Points In, Out, and On
The production possibility curve is a curve that measures the maximum combination of outputs that can be obtained with a given number of inputs.	The production possibility curve is downward sloping. Most are outward bowed because of increasing marginal opportunity cost; if opportunity cost doesn't change, the production possibility curve is a straight line.	Increases in inputs or increases in the productivity of inputs shift the production possibility curve out. Decreases have the opposite effect; the production possibility curve shifts along the axis whose input is changing.	Points inside the production possibility curve are points of inefficiency; points on the production possibility curve are points of efficiency; points outside the production possibility curve are not obtainable.

comparative advantage over other resources—*the ability to be better suited to the production of one good than to the production of another good*. In this example, some resources have a comparative advantage over other resources in the production of butter, while other resources have a comparative advantage in the production of guns.

When making small amounts of guns and large amounts of butter, we first use the resources whose comparative advantage is in the production of guns to produce guns. All other resources are devoted to producing butter. Because the resources used in producing guns aren't good at producing butter, we're not giving up much butter to get those guns. As we produce more and more of a good, we must use resources whose comparative advantage is in the production of the other good—in this case, more suitable for producing butter than for producing guns. As we remove resources from the production of butter to get the same additional amount of guns, we must give up increasing amounts of butter. An alternative way of saying this is that the opportunity cost of producing guns becomes greater as the production of guns increases. As we continue to increase the production of guns, the opportunity cost of more guns becomes very high because we're using resources to produce guns that have a strong comparative advantage for producing butter.

Let's consider two more examples. Say the United States suddenly decides it needs more wheat. To get additional wheat, we must devote additional land to growing it. This land is less fertile than the land we're already using, so our additional output of wheat per acre of land devoted to wheat will be less. Alternatively, consider the use of relief pitchers in a baseball game. If only one relief pitcher is needed, the manager sends in the best; if he must send in a second one, then a third, and even a fourth, the likelihood of winning the game decreases.

Q-2 If no resource had a comparative advantage in the production of any good, what would the shape of the production possibility curve be? Why?

Comparative Advantage

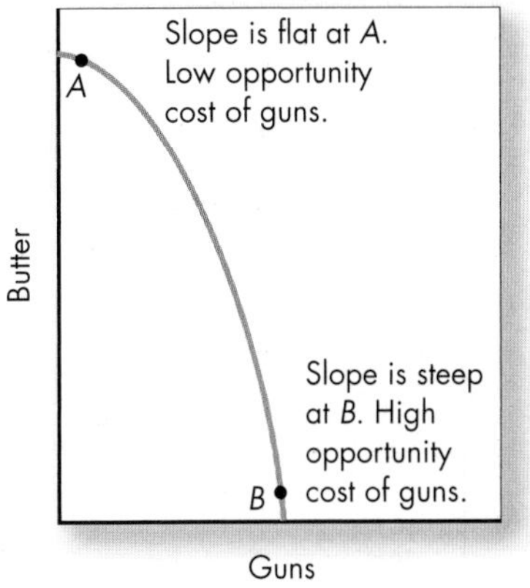

Efficiency

We would like, if possible, to get as much output as possible from a given amount of inputs or resources. That's **productive efficiency**—*achieving as much output as possible from a given amount of inputs or resources*. We would like to be efficient. The production possibility curve helps us see what is meant by productive efficiency. Consider point A

Efficiency

ADDED DIMENSION

Choices in Context

The production possibility curve presents choices without regard to time and therefore makes opportunity costs clear-cut; there are two choices, one with a higher cost and one with a lower cost. The reality is that most choices are dependent on other choices; they are made sequentially. With sequential choices, you cannot simply reverse your decision. Once you have started on a path, to take another path you have to return to the beginning. Thus, following one path often lowers the costs of options along that path, but it raises the costs of options along another path.

Such sequential decisions can best be seen within the framework of a decision tree—a visual description of sequential choices. A decision tree is shown in the accompanying figure.

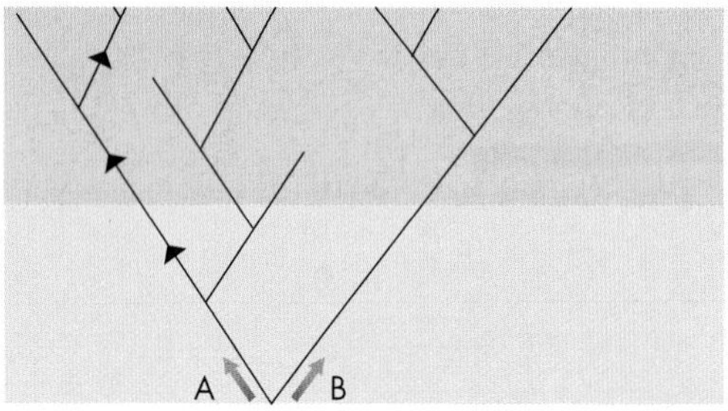

Once you make the initial decision to go on path A, the costs of path B options become higher; they include the costs of retracing your path and starting over. The decision trees of life have thousands of branches; each decision you make rules out other paths, or at least increases their costs significantly. (Remember that day you decided to blow off your homework? That decision may have changed your future life.)

Another way of putting this same point is that *all decisions are made in context:* What makes sense in one context may not make sense in another. For example, say you're answering the question "Would society be better off if students were taught literature or if they were taught agriculture?" The answer depends on the institutional context. In a developing country whose goal is large increases in material output, teaching agriculture may make sense. In a developed country, where growth in material output is less important, teaching literature may make sense.

Recognizing the contextual nature of decisions is important when interpreting the production possibility curve. Because decisions are contextual, what the production possibility curve for a particular decision looks like depends on the existing institutions, and the analysis can be applied only in institutional and historical context. The production possibility curve is not a purely technical phenomenon. The curve is an engine of analysis to make contextual choices, not a definitive tool to decide what one should do in all cases.

Q-3 Identify the point(s) of inefficiency and efficiency. What point(s) are unattainable?

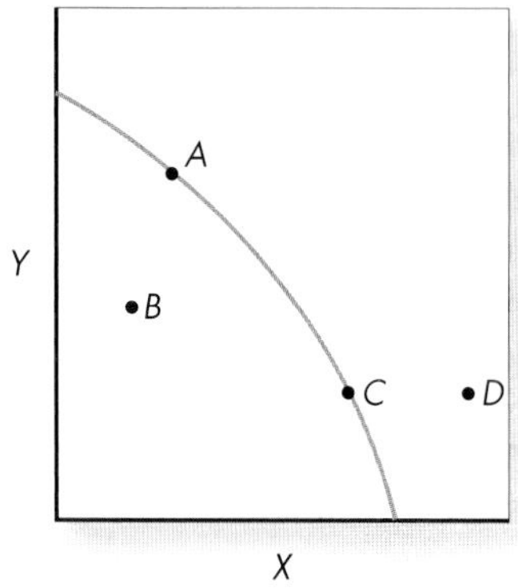

in Figure 2-3(a), which is inside the production possibility curve. If we are producing at point A, we are using all our resources to produce 6 guns and 4 pounds of butter. Point A represents **inefficiency**—*getting less output from inputs that, if devoted to some other activity, would produce more output.* That's because with the same inputs we could be getting either 8 guns and 4 pounds of butter (point *B*) or 6 pounds of butter and 6 guns (point C). As long as we prefer more to less, both points *B* and C represent **efficiency**—*achieving a goal using as few inputs as possible*. We always want to move our production out to a point on the production possibility curve.

Why not move out farther, to point *D*? If we could, we would, but by definition the production possibility curve represents the most output we can get from a certain combination of inputs. So point *D* is unattainable, given our resources and technology.

When technology improves, when more resources are discovered, or when the economic institutions get better at fulfilling our wants, we can get more output with the same inputs. What this means is that when technology or an economic institution improves, the entire production possibility curve shifts outward from *AB* to *CD* in Figure 2-3(b). How the production possibility curve shifts outward depends on how the technology improves. For example, say we become more efficient at producing

FIGURE 2-3 (A, B, AND C) Efficiency, Inefficiency, and Technological Change

The production possibility curve helps us see what is meant by efficiency. At point A, in (**a**), all inputs are used to make 4 pounds of butter and 6 guns. This is inefficient since there is a way to obtain more of one without giving up any of the other, that is, to obtain 6 pounds of butter and 6 guns (point C) or 8 guns and 4 pounds of butter (point *B*). All points inside the production possibility curve are inefficient. With existing inputs and technology, we cannot go beyond the production possibility curve. For example, point *D* is unattainable.

A technological change that improves production techniques will shift the production possibility curve outward, as shown in both (**b**) and (**c**). How the curve shifts outward depends on how technology improves. For example, if we become more efficient in the production of both guns and butter, the curve will shift out as in (**b**). If we become more efficient in producing butter, but not in producing guns, then the curve will shift as in (**c**).

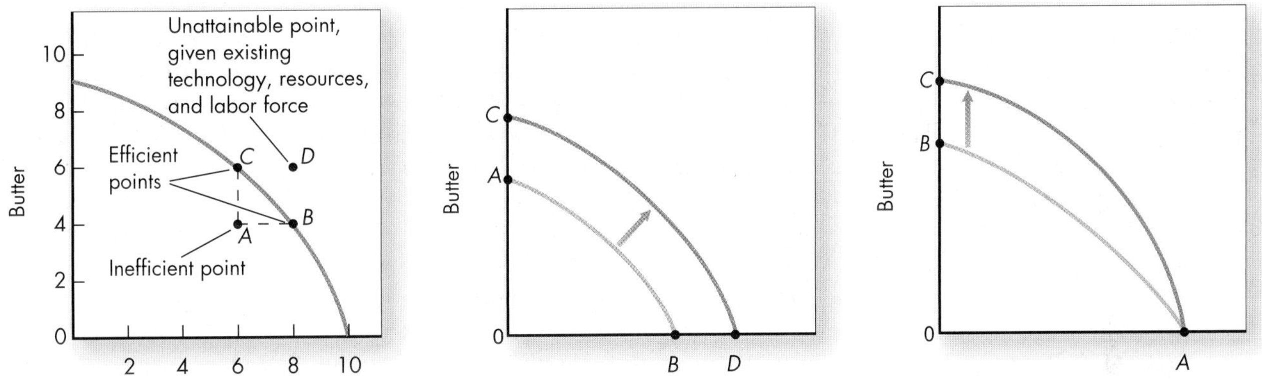

(a) Efficiency and Inefficiency **(b) Neutral Technological Change** **(c) Biased Technological Change**

butter, but not more efficient at producing guns. Then the production possibility curve shifts outward to AC in Figure 2-3(c).

Distribution and Productive Efficiency

In discussing the production possibility curve for a society, I avoided questions of distribution: Who gets what? But such questions cannot be ignored in real-world situations. Specifically, if the method of production is tied to a particular income distribution and choosing one method will help some people but hurt others, we can't say that one method of production is efficient and the other inefficient, even if one method produces more total output than the other. As I stated above, the term *efficiency* involves achieving a goal as cheaply as possible. The term has meaning only in regard to a specified goal. Say, for example, that we have a society of ascetics who believe that consumption above some minimum is immoral. For such a society, producing more for less (productive efficiency) would not be efficient since consumption is not its goal. Or say that we have a society that cares that what is produced is fairly distributed. An increase in output that goes to only one person and not to anyone else would not necessarily be efficient.

Q-4 Your firm is establishing a trucking business in Saudi Arabia. The managers have noticed that women are generally paid much less than men in Saudi Arabia, and they suggest that hiring women would be more efficient than hiring men. What should you respond?

In our society, however, most people prefer more to less, and many policies have relatively small distributional consequences. On the basis of the assumption that more is better than less, economists use their own kind of shorthand for such policies and talk about efficiency as identical to productive efficiency—increasing total output. But it's important to remember the assumption under which that shorthand is used: that the distributional effects that accompany the policy are acceptable, and that we, as a society, prefer more output.

FIGURE 2-4 (A, B, C, AND D) **Examples of Shifts in Production Possibility Curves**

Each of these curves reflects a different type of shift. (The axes are left unlabeled on purpose. Manufactured and agricultural goods may be placed on either axis.) Your assignment is to match these shifts with the situations given in the text.

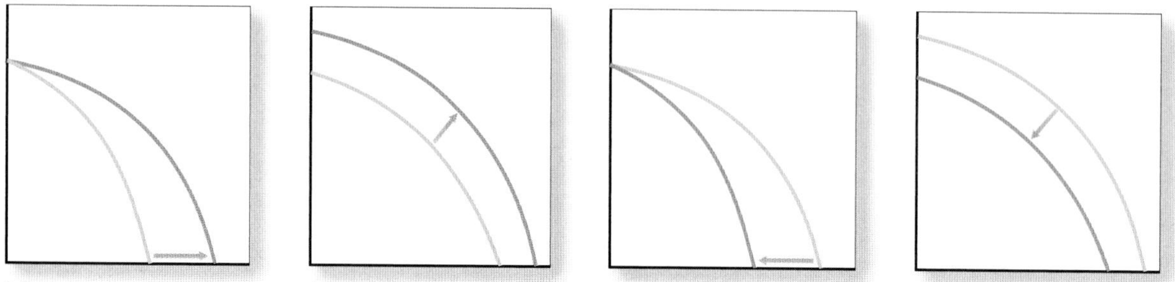

(a) (b) (c) (d)

Examples of Shifts in the PPC

To see whether you understand the production possibility curve, let us now consider some situations that can be shown with it. Below, I list four situations. To test your understanding of the curve, match each situation to one of the curves in Figure 2-4.

Q-5 When a natural disaster hits the midwestern United States, where most of the U.S. butter is produced, what happens to the U.S. production possibility curve for guns and butter?

1. A meteor hits the world and destroys half the earth's natural resources.
2. Nanotechnology is perfected that lowers the cost of manufactured goods.
3. A new technology is discovered that doubles the speed at which all goods can be produced.
4. Global warming increases the cost of producing agricultural goods.

The correct answers are: 1–d; 2–a; 3–b; 4–c.

If you got them all right, you are well on your way to understanding the production possibility curve.

Trade and Comparative Advantage

Web Note 2.1
Wine and Cloth

Now that we have gone through the basics of the production possibility curve, let's dig a little deeper. From the above discussion, you know that production possibility curves are generally bowed outward and that the reason for this is comparative advantage. To remind you of the argument, consider Figure 2-5, which is the guns and butter production possibility example I presented earlier.

At point *A*, all resources are being used to produce butter. As more guns are produced, we take resources away from producing butter that had a comparative advantage in producing guns, so we gain a lot of guns for little butter (the opportunity cost of additional guns is low). As we continue down the curve, the comparative advantage of the resources we use changes, and as we approach *B*, we use almost all resources to produce guns, so we are using resources that aren't very good at producing guns. Thus, around point *B* we gain few guns for a lot of butter (the opportunity cost of additional guns is high).

A society wants to be on the frontier of its production possibility curve. This requires that individuals produce those goods for which they have a comparative advantage. The question for society, then, is how to direct individuals toward those activities. For a firm, the answer is easy. A manager can allocate the firm's resources to their best use. For example, he or she can assign an employee with good people skills to the human resources department and another with good research skills to

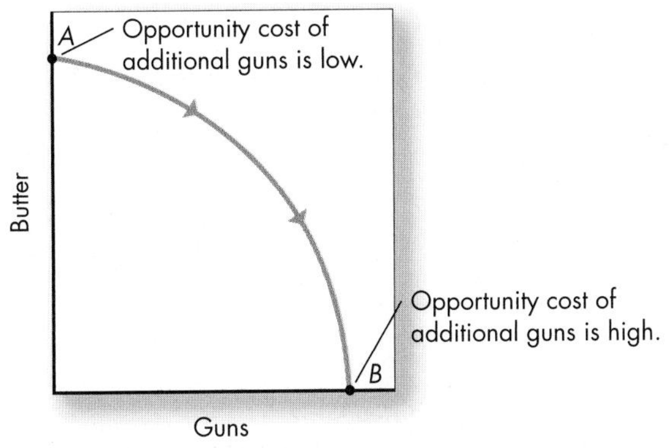

FIGURE 2-5 Comparative Advantage and the Production Possibility Curve

As we move down along the production possibility curve from point A to point B, the opportunity cost of producing guns is increasing since we are using resources less suited for gun production.

research and development. But our economy has millions of individuals, and no manager directing everyone what to do. How do we know that these individuals will be directed to do those things for which they have a comparative advantage? It was this question that was central to the British moral philosopher Adam Smith when he wrote his most famous book, *The Wealth of Nations* (1776). In it he argued that it was humankind's proclivity to trade that leads to individuals using their comparative advantage. He writes:

> This division of labour, from which so many advantages are derived, is not originally the effect of any human wisdom, which foresees and intends that general opulence to which it gives occasion. It is the necessary, though very slow and gradual consequence of a certain propensity in human nature which has in view no such extensive utility; the propensity to truck, barter, and exchange one thing for another... [This propensity] is common to all men, and to be found in no other race of animals, which seem to know neither this nor any other species of contracts... Nobody ever saw a dog make a fair and deliberate exchange of one bone for another with another dog. Nobody ever saw one animal by its gestures and natural cries signify to another, this is mine, that yours; I am willing to give this for that.

As long as people trade, Smith argues, the market will guide people, like an invisible hand, to gravitate toward those activities for which they have a comparative advantage. By specializing in the production of goods in which they have a comparative advantage, they will produce the most goods they can. They can then trade with other people who specialize in the production of other goods. For Smith, what was especially neat about this process was that it could take place without enormous amounts of government intervention. Smith writes:

Adam Smith argued that it is humankind's proclivity to trade that leads to individuals using their comparative advantage.

> Man has almost constant occasion for the help of his brethren, and it is in vain for him to expect it from their benevolence only. He will be more likely to prevail, if he can interest their self-love in his favour, and show them that it is for their own advantage to do for him what he requires of them. Whoever offers to another a bargain of any kind proposes to do this. Give me that which I want, and you shall have that which you want, is the meaning of every such offer; and it is in this manner that we obtain from one another the far greater part of those good offices which we stand in need of. It is not from the benevolence of the butcher, the brewer, or the baker, that we expect our dinner, but from their regard to their own interest. We address ourselves, not to their humanity but to their self-love, and never talk to them of our own necessities but of their advantages.

It is not from the benevolence of the butcher, the brewer, or the baker that we expect our dinner, but from their regard to their own interest.

FIGURE 2-6 Growth in the Past Two Millennia

For 1,700 years the world economy grew very slowly. Then, since the end of the 18th century with the introduction of markets and the spread of democracy, the world economy has grown at increasing rates.

Source: Angus Maddison, *Monitoring the World Economy*, OECD, 1995; Angus Maddison, "Poor until 1820," *The Wall Street Journal*, January 11, 1999; and author extrapolations.

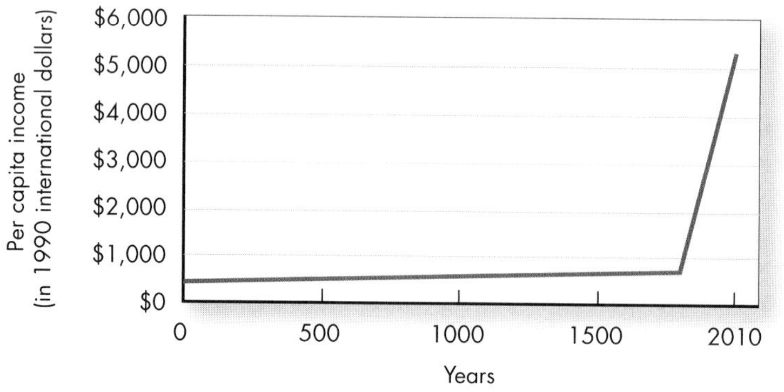

Markets, Specialization, and Growth

Markets can be very simple or very complicated.

We can see the effect of trade on our well-being empirically by considering the growth of economies. As you can see from Figure 2-6, for 1,700 years the world economy grew very slowly. Then, at the end of the 18th century, the world economy started to grow, and it has grown at a high rate since then.

What changed? The introduction of markets that facilitate trade and the spread of democracy. There's something about markets that leads to economic growth. Markets allow specialization and encourage trade. The bowing out of the production possibilities from trade is part of the story, but a minor part. As individuals compete and specialize, they learn by doing, becoming even better at what they do. Markets also foster competition, which pushes individuals to find better ways of doing things. They devise new technologies that further the growth process.

The new millennium is offering new ways for individuals to specialize and compete. More and more businesses are trading on the Internet. For example, colleges such as the University of Phoenix are providing online competition for traditional colleges. Similarly, online bookstores and drugstores are proliferating. As Internet technology becomes built into our economy, we can expect more specialization, more division of labor, and the economic growth that follows.

The Benefits of Trade

Web Note 2.2
Gains from Trade

The reasons why markets can direct people to use their comparative advantages follow from a very simple argument: When people freely enter into a trade, both parties can be expected to benefit from the trade; otherwise, why would they have traded in the first place? So when the butcher sells you meat, he's better off with the money you give him, and you're better off with the meat he gives you.

Laissez-faire is an economic policy of leaving coordination of individuals' actions to the market.

When there is competition in trading, such that individuals are able to pick the best trades available to them, each individual drives the best bargain he or she can. The end result is that both individuals in the trade benefit as much as they possibly can, given what others are willing to trade. This argument for the benefits from trade underlies the general policy of **laissez-faire**—*an economic policy of leaving coordination of individuals' actions to the market.* (*Laissez-faire*, a French term, means "Let events take their course; leave things alone.") Laissez-faire is not a theorem in economics; it is a precept because it extends the implications of a model to reality and draws conclusions about the real world. It is based on normative judgments, judgments about the relevance of the model, and assumptions upon which the model is based.

FIGURE 2-7 (A AND B) The Gains from Trade

Trade makes those involved in the trade better off. If each country specializes and takes advantage of its comparative advantage, the combined production possibility curve becomes bowed outward. In (**a**), the gains from trade are represented by the movements of the countries from points *A* and *B* to point C. In (**b**), you can see how the combined PPC reflects the "lowest cost rules" principle.

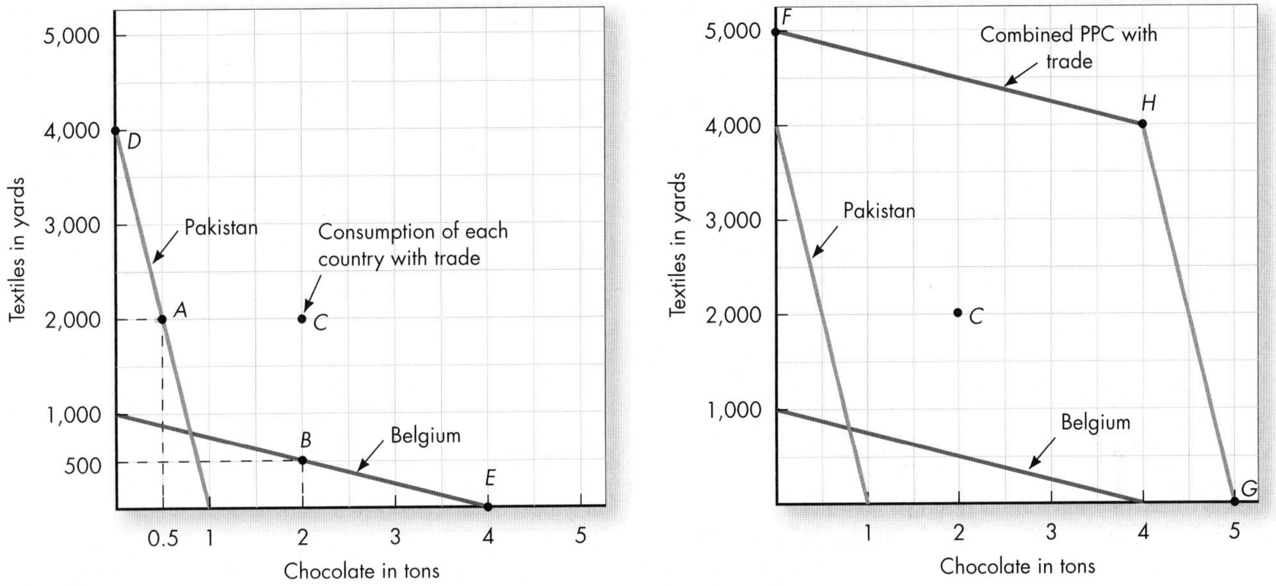

(a) Gains from Trade **(b) Combined PPC**

	Textiles	Chocolate
Pakistan	2,000 yards	0.5 ton
Belgium	500 yards	2 tons
Total	2,500 yards	2.5 tons

Let's consider a numerical example of the gains that accrue to two countries when they trade, and show how that trade increases the production possibilities, creating the bowed shape of the production possibility curve. I use an international trade example so that you can see that the argument holds for international trade as well as domestic trade.

Let's say that the two countries are Pakistan and Belgium, and that Pakistan has a comparative advantage in producing textiles, while Belgium has a comparative advantage in producing chocolate. Specifically, Pakistan can produce 4,000 yards of textiles a day, or 1 ton of chocolate a day, or any proportional combination in between. (Pakistan's opportunity cost of 1 ton of chocolate is 4,000 yards of textiles.) Pakistan's production possibility curve is shown by the orange line in Figure 2-7(a). In a given day, Belgium can produce either 1,000 yards of textiles, 4 tons of chocolate, or any proportion in between. (Belgium's opportunity cost of 1 ton of chocolate is 250 yards of textiles.) Its production possibility curve is shown by the green line in Figure 2-7(a).

In the absence of trade, the most each country can consume is some combination along its production possibility curve. Say Pakistan has chosen to produce and consume 2,000 yards of textiles and 0.5 ton of chocolate (point A), while Belgium has chosen to produce and consume 500 yards of textiles and 2 tons of chocolate (point B).

Q-6 What argument underlies the general laissez-faire policy argument?

Specialization and trade create gains that make all better off.

Let's now consider what would happen if each specialized, doing what it does best, and then traded with the other for the goods it wants. This separates the production and consumption decisions. Because Pakistan has the lower opportunity cost, it makes sense for Pakistan to specialize in textiles, producing 4,000 yards. Similarly, it makes sense for Belgium to specialize in chocolate, producing 4 tons. By specializing, the countries together produce 4 tons of chocolate and 4,000 yards of textiles. If the countries divide production so that each country gets 2,000 yards of fabric and 2 tons of chocolate, each country will be consuming at point C, even as they are producing at points *D* and *E*, respectively. Point C is beyond both countries' production possibility curves without trade, but it becomes possible with trade. This tells us an important principle about trade:

Trade lets countries consume beyond their production possibility curve.

Trade lets countries consume beyond their production possibility curve.

It is primarily these gains that lead to economists' support of free trade and their opposition to barriers to trade.

Comparative Advantage and the Combined PPC

Q-7 Steve can bake either 4 loaves of bread or 8 dozen cookies a day. Sarah can bake either 4 loaves of bread or 4 dozen cookies a day. Show, using production possibility curves, that Steve and Sarah would be better off specializing in their baking activities and then trading, rather than baking only for themselves.

Q-8 True or false? Two countries can achieve the greatest gains from trade by each producing the goods for which the opportunity costs are greatest and then trading those goods.

Constructing a production possibility curve that shows the combination of goods these two countries can produce is a useful exercise. I do so in Figure 2-7(b) by first asking how much of each good can be produced if both countries produce the same good. If both countries produce only textiles, 5,000 yards of textiles are made (point *F*). Alternatively, if they produce only chocolate, 5 tons of chocolate are produced (point G). A third possibility is that Pakistan specializes in the good in which it has a comparative advantage—textiles—and produces 4,000 yards, while Belgium specializes in the good in which it has a comparative advantage—chocolate—producing 4 tons. This combination is shown by point *H*. Since other combinations of goods are possible, connecting points *F*, *H*, and G gives us the combined production possibility curve.

Notice that this combined production possibility curve has the same slope as Belgium's from *F* to *H*, and the same slope as Pakistan's from *H* to G. That is because, when trade is allowed, *the slope of the combined production possibility curve is determined by the country with the lowest opportunity cost.* It is by producing where costs are lowest that countries can achieve gains from trade. This principle—*lowest cost rules*—gives us a sense of what happens when we expand the production possibility curve analysis to include many countries rather than just two: The production possibility curve becomes smoother as each country's comparative advantage governs a smaller portion of the shape. Eventually, as the number of countries that trade gets large, it becomes the smooth bowed curve we drew above for guns and butter.

U.S. Textile Production and Trade

When each country follows its comparative advantage, production becomes more efficient and the consumption possibilities for both countries increase. Because of these benefits, most economists support free markets and free trade. The market system gives individual firms an incentive to search for comparative advantages and to produce with lowest-cost methods at lowest-cost locations. This pressures other producers to lower their costs or get out of the business.

The pressure to find comparative advantages is never ending.

The pressure to find comparative advantages is never ending, in part because comparative advantage can change. Two hundred years ago, the United States had a comparative advantage in producing textiles. It was rich in natural resources and labor, and it had a low-cost source of power (water). As the cost of U.S. labor went up, and as trade opportunities widened, that comparative advantage disappeared. As it did, the United States moved out of the textile industry. Countries with cheaper labor, such as

Bangladesh, today have the comparative advantage in textiles. As firms have relocated textile production to Bangladesh, total costs have fallen. The gains from trade show up as higher pay for Bangladeshi workers and lower-priced cloth for U.S. consumers. Of course, trade is a two-way street. In return for Bangladesh's textiles, the United States sends computer software and airplanes, products that would be highly expensive, indeed almost impossible, for Bangladesh to produce on its own. So Bangladeshi consumers, on average, are also made better off by the trade.

Outsourcing, Trade, and Comparative Advantage

There is much more to be said about both trade and the gains from trade, and later chapters will explore trade in much more detail. But let me briefly discuss the relationship of the theory of comparative advantage to two terms that you often read about in the newspaper—*outsourcing* and *globalization*. In this book, we will use the newspaper definition of **outsourcing**—*the relocation of production once done in the United States to foreign countries*.

Outsourcing is the relocation of production once done in the United States to foreign countries.

Let's begin with outsourcing.

Outsourcing At one time, the term *outsourcing* was used in a broader context and referred to subcontracting a portion of a firm's production to another firm either within or outside the United States. However, recently, it has been used in this more narrow sense, and that is how I will use the term here. One service being outsourced today is customer support. More and more, customer support calls are routed to call centers in India, rather than in the United States. By outsourcing call services, the United States imports the service "assistance." Before recent developments in telecommunications, support call services could not be imported.

To put outsourcing in its proper perspective, you should think of it in relation to *insourcing*—the relocation of production done abroad to the United States. Outsourcing only becomes an important policy issue to the degree that it significantly exceeds insourcing. While the actual numbers on both are difficult to collect and interpret, there is a general sense that in recent years not only has outsourcing been increasing, insourcing has been decreasing, and hence insourcing is being overwhelmed by outsourcing.

Q-9 Is it likely that all U.S. jobs will one day be outsourced? Why or Why not?

Outsourcing scares many people in the United States because, with wages so much lower in many developing countries than in the United States, they wonder whether all jobs will move offshore: Will the United States be left producing anything? Economists' answer is: Of course it will. Comparative advantage, by definition, means that if one country has a comparative advantage in producing one set of goods, the other country has to have a comparative advantage in the other set of goods. The real questions are: In what goods will the United States have comparative advantages? and: How will those comparative advantages come about?

WWW Web Note 2.3
Trade and Wages

One reason people have a hard time thinking of goods in which the United States has a comparative advantage is that they are thinking in terms of labor costs. They ask: Since wages are lower in China, isn't it cheaper to produce all goods in China? The answer is no; production requires many more inputs than just "labor." Technology, institutional structure, specialized types of knowledge, and entrepreneurial know-how are also needed to produce goods, and the United States has significant advantages in these other factors. It is these advantages that result in higher U.S. wages compared to other countries.

Globalization The term *globalization* is broader than outsourcing. **Globalization** *is the increasing integration of economies, cultures, and institutions across the world*. In a globalized economy, firms think of production and sales at a global level. They produce

REAL-WORLD APPLICATION

Made in China?

Barbie and her companion Ken are as American as apple pie, and considering their origins gives us some insight into the modern U.S. economy and its interconnection with other countries. Barbie and Ken are not produced in the United States; they never were. When Barbie first came out in 1959, she was produced in Japan. Today, it is unclear where Barbie and Ken are produced. If you look at the box they come in, it says "Made in China," but looking deeper we find that Barbie and Ken are actually made in five different countries, each focusing on an aspect of production that reflects its comparative advantage. Japan produces the nylon hair. China provides much of what is normally considered manufacturing—factory spaces, labor, and energy for assembly—but it imports many of the components. The oil for the plastic comes from Saudi Arabia, which is refined into plastic pellets in Taiwan. The United States even provides some of the raw materials that go into the manufacturing process—it provides the cardboard, packing, paint pigments, and the mold.

The diversification of parts that go into the manufacturing of Barbie and Ken is typical of many goods today. As the world economy has become more integrated, the process of supplying components of manufacturing has become more and more spread out, as firms have divided up the manufacturing process in search of the least-cost location for each component.

But the global diversity in manufacturing and supply of components is only half the story of modern production. The other half is the shrinking of the relative importance of that manufacturing, and it is this other half that explains how the United States maintains its position in the world when so much of the manufacturing takes place elsewhere. It does so by maintaining its control over the distribution and marketing of the goods. In fact, of the $15 retail cost of a Barbie or Ken, $12 can be accounted for by activities not associated with manufacturing—design, transportation, merchandising, and advertising. And, luckily for the United States, many of these activities are still done in the United States, allowing the country to maintain its high living standard even as manufacturing spreads around the globe.

where costs are lowest, and sell across the world at the highest price they can get. A globalized world is a world in which economies of the world are highly integrated. Globalization has two effects on firms. The first is positive; because the world economy is so much larger than the domestic economy, the rewards for winning globally are much larger than the rewards for winning domestically. The second effect is negative; it is much harder to win, or even to stay in business, competing in a global market. A company may be the low-cost producer in a particular country yet may face foreign competitors that can undersell it. The global economy increases the number of competitors for the firm. Consider the automobile industry. Three companies are headquartered in the United States, but more than 20 automobile companies operate worldwide. U.S. automakers face stiff competition from foreign automakers; unless they meet that competition, they will not survive.

The global economy increases the number of competitors for the firm.

These two effects are, of course, related. When you compete in a larger market, you have to be better to survive, but if you do survive the rewards are greater.

Globalization increases competition by allowing greater specialization and division of labor, which, as Adam Smith first observed in *The Wealth of Nations*, increases growth and improves the standard of living for everyone. Thus, in many ways globalization is

REAL-WORLD APPLICATION

Insourcing into the United States

In a global economy, a company will locate its operations to wherever it makes most sense to produce. Generally, this means that it will locate where the costs are lowest, or where the company can get some unique benefit. When you think of costs, you should think of all costs, not just labor costs. The same with benefits. Doing so, you can see why companies insource production into the United States—as well as outsource production out of the United States.

Consider Novartis, a global pharmaceutical company, which recently moved its global research headquarters from Switzerland to Cambridge, Massachusetts. It chose the United States because Cambridge had a strong concentration of academic biomedical research facilities, making it a great place for collaborations. In this case, the United States' primary cost advantage was that it had some unique benefits that couldn't be duplicated elsewhere.

Another example of insourcing is Toyota's moving of portions of their car production from Japan to the United States. It did so to reduce transportation costs and reduce the political pressure by the U.S. Congress to institute tariffs on cars produced by foreign-owned companies. Relocating also reduced overall costs relative to Japan since Japanese workers are more expensive than the U.S. workers Toyota hires, although not relative to China, where it also has production facilities.

Even Indian and Chinese firms are establishing branches here in the United States, which is a type of insourcing. For example, Lenovo, the Chinese computer maker, acquired IBM's personal computer division and established sales offices in the United States. Other non-U.S.-based global companies are establishing research and marketing divisions in the United States to take advantage of the creative workforce, and to establish a presence in the United States.

simply another name for increased specialization. Globalization allows (indeed, forces) companies to move operations to countries with a comparative advantage. As they do so, they lower costs of production. Globalization leads to companies specializing in smaller portions of the production process because the potential market is not just one country but the world. Such specialization can lead to increased productivity as firms learn from doing.

Q-10 How does globalization reduce the costs of production?

U.S. Comparative Advantage Today and Tomorrow The United States has excelled particularly in goods that require creativity and innovation. The United States has remained the leader of the world economy and has kept a comparative advantage in many goods even with its high relative wages, in part because of continual innovation. For example, the Internet started in the United States, which is why the United States is the location of so many information technology firms. The United States also has led the way in biotechnology innovation. Similarly, the creative industries, such as film, art, and advertising, have flourished in the United States. These industries are dynamic, high-profit, high-wage industries. (One of the reasons insourcing occurs is that the United States has such a great comparative advantage in these other aspects of production.) As long as U.S. production maintains a comparative advantage in innovation, the United States will be able to specialize in goods that allow firms to pay higher wages.

The real concern about outsourcing involves what happens in the evolution and development of industries. The natural progression is that, as an industry matures, its technology and specialized knowledge spread, which allows more and more of that industry's production to be outsourced. This means that slowly over time the United States can be expected to lose its comparative advantage in currently "new" industries, such as information technology, just as has happened with other industries in the past.

ADDED DIMENSION

The Developing Country's Perspective on Outsourcing

This book is written from a U.S. point of view. From that perspective, the relevant question is: Can the United States maintain its high wages relative to the low wages in China, India, and other developing countries? I suspect that most U.S. readers hope that it can. From a developing country's perspective, I suspect that the hope is that it cannot; their hope is that their wage rates catch up with U.S. wage rates. Judged from a developing country's perspective, the question is: Is it fair that U.S. workers don't work as hard as we do but earn much more?

The market does not directly take fairness into account. The market is interested only in who can produce a good or service at the lowest cost. This means that in a competitive economy, the United States can maintain its high wages only to the degree that it can produce sufficient goods and services cheaper than low-wage countries can at the market exchange rate. It must keep the trade balance roughly equal.

Developing countries recognize that, in the past, the United States has had a comparative advantage in creativity and innovation, and they are doing everything they can to compete on these levels as well as on basic production levels. They are actively trying to develop such skills in their population and to compete with the United States not only in manufacturing and low-tech jobs but also in research, development, finance, organizational activities, artistic activities, and high-tech jobs. Right now companies in China and India are working to challenge U.S. dominance in all high-tech and creativity fields. (For example, they too are working on nanotechnology.) To do this, they are trying to entice top scientists and engineers to stay in their country, or to return home if they have been studying or working in the United States. Since more than 50 percent of all PhD's given in science, engineering, and economics go to non-U.S. citizens (in economics, it is more than 70 percent), many observers believe that the United States cannot assume its past dominance in the innovative and high-tech fields will continue forever. The competitive front that will determine whether the United States can maintain much higher wages than developing countries is not the competition in current industries, but competition in industries of the future.

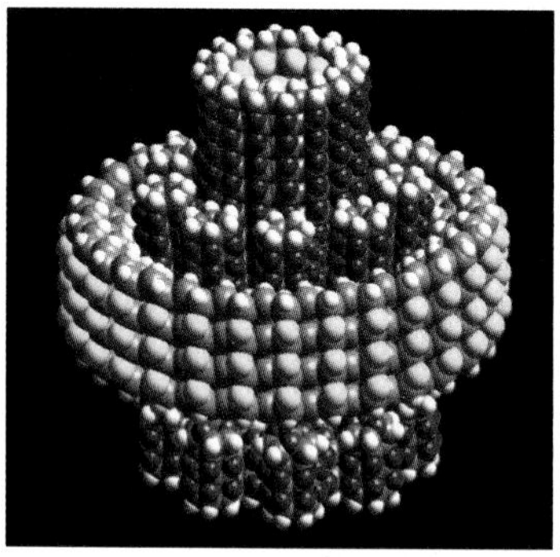

Nanotechnology—dynamic industry of the future?

However, as long as the United States remains as creative and innovative as it has in the past, the outsourcing of maturing industries can be replaced with industries that don't even exist today, just as information technology replaced many areas of manufacturing in the 1990s. One industry that some economists believe the United States is on the edge of developing is nanotechnology (machining at an atomic or molecular level, less than a thousandth the thickness of one hair). The point is that with sufficient creativity and innovation, the U.S. economic future can be quite bright.

Exchange Rates and Comparative Advantage There is, however, reason to be concerned. If innovation and creativity don't develop new industries in which the United States has a comparative advantage fast enough, as the current dynamic industries mature and move to low-wage areas, *at current exchange rates* (the value of a currency relative to the value of foreign currencies), the United States will not maintain comparative advantages in sufficient industries to warrant the relative wage differentials that exist today. In that case, U.S. demand for foreign goods and services will be higher than foreign demand for U.S. goods and services. To bring them into equilibrium, the U.S. wage premium will have to decline to regain our comparative advantages. Since nominal wages (the wages that you see in your paycheck) in the United States are unlikely to fall, this will most likely occur through a decline in the U.S. exchange rate, large increases in foreign wages, or both. Either of these will make foreign products imported into the United States more expensive and U.S. products cheaper for foreigners, and eventually will balance the comparative advantages.

Law of One Price Many Americans do not like the "exchange rate answer," but in terms of policy, it is probably the best the United States can hope for. If the United States tries to prevent outsourcing with trade restrictions, U.S.-based companies will find that they can no longer compete internationally, and the United States will be in worse shape than if it had allowed outsourcing. The reality is that competition, combined with transferable technology and similar institutions, drives wages and prices of similar factors and goods toward equality. This reality often goes by the name of the **law of one price**—*the wages of workers in one country will not differ significantly from the wages of (equal) workers in another institutionally similar country.* As we will discuss in a later chapter, the debate is about what an "equal" worker is and what an equivalent institutional structure is.

The law of one price states that wages of workers in one country will not differ significantly from the wages of (equal) workers in another institutionally similar country.

Because of a variety of historical circumstances, the United States has been able to avoid the law of one price in wages since World War I. One factor has been the desire of foreigners to increase their holding of U.S. financial assets by trillions of dollars, which has let the United States consume more goods than it produces. Another is that the United States' institutional structure, technology, entrepreneurial labor force, and nonlabor inputs have given the United States sufficiently strong comparative advantages to offset the higher U.S. wage rates. The passage of time and modern technological changes have been eroding the United States' comparative advantages based on institutional structure and technology. To the degree that this continues to happen, to maintain a balance in the comparative advantages of various countries, the wages of workers in other countries such as India and China will have to move closer to the wages of U.S. workers.

Globalization and the Timing of Benefits of Trade One final comment about outsourcing, globalization, and the U.S. economy is in order. None of the above discussion contradicts the proposition that trade makes both countries better off. Thus, the discussion does not support the position taken by some opponents to trade and globalization that outsourcing is hurting the United States and that the United States can be made better off by limiting outsourcing. Instead, the discussion is about the timing of the benefits of trade. Many of the benefits of trade already have been consumed by the United States during the years that the United States has been running trade deficits (importing more than it is exporting). The reality is that the United States has been living better than it could have otherwise precisely because of trade and outsourcing. It also has been living much better than it otherwise could because it is paying for some of its imports with IOUs promising payment in the future instead of with exports. But there is no free lunch, and when these IOUs are presented for payment, the United States will have to pay for some of the benefits that it already has consumed.

The reality is that the United States has been living better than it could have otherwise precisely because of trade and outsourcing.

Conclusion

While the production possibility curve model does not give unambiguous answers as to what government's role should be in regulating trade, it does serve a very important purpose. It is a geometric tool that summarizes a number of ideas in economics: opportunity cost, comparative advantage, efficiency, and how trade leads to efficiency. These ideas are all essential to economists' conversations. They provide the framework within which those conversations take place. Thinking of the production possibility curve (and picturing the economy as being on it) directs you to think of the trade-offs involved in every decision.

Look at questions such as: Should we save the spotted owl or should we allow logging in the western forests? Should we expand the government health care system or should we strengthen our national defense system? Should we emphasize policies that

The production possibility curve represents the tough choices society must make.

allow more consumption now or should we emphasize policies that allow more consumption in the future? Such choices involve difficult trade-offs that can be pictured by the production possibility curve.

Not everyone recognizes these trade-offs. For example, politicians often talk as if the production possibility curve were nonexistent. They promise voters the world, telling them, "If you elect me, you can have more of everything." When they say that, they obscure the hard choices and increase their probability of getting elected.

Economists continually point out that seemingly free lunches often involve significant hidden costs.

Economists do the opposite. They promise little except that life is tough, and they continually point out that seemingly free lunches often involve significant hidden costs. Alas, political candidates who exhibit such reasonableness seldom get elected. Economists' reasonableness has earned economics the nickname *the dismal science*.

Summary

- The production possibility curve measures the maximum combination of outputs that can be obtained from a given number of inputs. It embodies the opportunity cost concept.
- In general, in order to get more and more of something, we must give up ever-increasing quantities of something else. This is the principle of increasing marginal opportunity cost.
- Trade allows people to use their comparative advantage and shift out society's production possibility curve.
- The rise of markets coincided with significant increases in output. Specialization, trade, and competition have all contributed to the increase.
- Points inside the production possibility curve are inefficient, points along the production possibility curve are efficient, and points outside are unattainable.
- By specializing in producing those goods for which one has a comparative advantage (lowest opportunity cost), one can produce the greatest amount of goods with which to trade. Doing so, countries can increase consumption. The effects of specialization and trade also can be shown by a shift of the production possibility curve out.
- The typical outward bow of the production possibility curve is the result of comparative advantage and trade.
- Because many goods are cheaper to produce in countries such as China and India, production that formerly took place in the United States is being outsourced to foreign countries.
- If the United States can maintain its strong comparative advantage in goods using new technologies and innovation, the jobs lost by outsourcing can be replaced with other high-paying jobs. If it does not, then some adjustments in relative wage rates or exchange rates must occur.
- Outsourcing is a product of the law of one price, which reflects business's tendency to shift production to countries where it is cheapest to produce.
- Globalization is the increasing integration of economies, cultures, and institutions across the world.

Key Terms

comparative advantage *(29)*
efficiency *(30)*
globalization *(37)*
inefficiency *(30)*
input *(26)*
laissez-faire *(34)*
law of one price *(41)*
output *(26)*
outsourcing *(37)*
principle of increasing marginal opportunity cost *(28)*
production possibility curve (PPC) *(26)*
production possibility table *(25)*
productive efficiency *(29)*

Questions and Exercises

1. Show how a production possibility curve would shift if a society became more productive in its output of widgets but less productive in its output of wadgets. LO1
2. Show how a production possibility curve would shift if a society became more productive in the output of both widgets and wadgets. LO1
3. Design a grade production possibility table and curve that embody the principle of increasing marginal opportunity cost. LO2
4. How does the theory of comparative advantage relate to production possibility curves? LO3
5. A country has the following production possibility table:

Resources Devoted to Clothing	Output of Clothing	Resources Devoted to Food	Output of Food
100%	20	0%	0
80	16	20	5
60	12	40	9
40	8	60	12
20	4	80	14
0	0	100	15

   a. Draw the country's production possibility curve.
   b. What's happening to marginal opportunity costs as output of food increases?
   c. Say the country gets better at the production of food. What will happen to the production possibility curve?
   d. Say the country gets equally better at producing both food and clothing. What will happen to the production possibility curve? LO1, LO2
6. If neither of two countries has a comparative advantage in either of two goods, what are the gains from trade? LO4
7. Does the fact that the production possibilities model tells us that trade is good mean that in the real world free trade is necessarily the best policy? Explain. LO4
8. Suppose the United States and Japan have the following production possibility tables:

Japan		United States	
Bolts of Cloth	Tons of Wheat	Bolts of Cloth	Tons of Wheat
1,000	0	500	0
800	100	400	200
600	200	300	400
400	300	200	600
200	400	100	800
0	500	0	1,000

   a. Draw each country's production possibility curve.
   b. In what good does the United States have a comparative advantage?
   c. Is there a possible trade that benefits both countries?
   d. Draw their combined production possibility curve. LO4
9. Assume the United States can produce Toyotas at the cost of $18,000 per car and Chevrolets at $16,000 per car. In Japan, Toyotas can be produced at 1,000,000 yen and Chevrolets at 500,000 yen.
   a. In terms of Chevrolets, what is the opportunity cost of producing Toyotas in each country?
   b. Who has the comparative advantage in producing Chevrolets?
   c. Assume Americans purchase 500,000 Chevrolets and 300,000 Toyotas each year and that the Japanese purchase far fewer of each. Using productive efficiency as the guide, which country should produce Chevrolets and which should produce Toyotas? LO4
10. What effect has globalization had on the ability of firms to specialize? How has this affected the competitive process? LO5
11. If workers in China and India become as productive as U.S. workers, what adjustments will allow the United States to regain its competitiveness? LO5
12. How can exchange rates change to reduce wage differences between countries? LO5
13. How is outsourcing related to the law of one price? LO5

Questions from Alternative Perspectives

1. Why might government be less capable than the market to do good? (Austrian)
2. The text makes it look as if maximizing output is the goal of society.
   a. Is maximizing output the goal of society?
   b. If the country is a Christian country, should it be?
   c. If not, what should it be? (Religious)

3. It has been said that "capitalism robs us of our sexuality and sells it back to us."
   a. Does sex sell?
   b. Is sex used to sell goods from Land Rovers to tissue paper?
   c. Who, if anyone, is exploited in the use of sex to sell commodities?
   d. Are both men and women exploited in the same ways? (Feminist)
4. Thorstein Veblen, one economist to whom this book is dedicated, wrote that *vested interests* are those seeking "something for nothing." In this chapter, you learned how technological bias shapes the economy's production possibilities over time so that a country becomes increasingly good at producing a subset of goods.
   a. In what ways have vested interests used their influence to bias the U.S. economy toward the production of military goods at the expense of consumer goods?
   b. What are the short-term and long-term consequences of that bias for human welfare, in the United States and abroad? (Institutionalist)
5. Writing in 1776, Adam Smith was concerned not only with the profound effects of the division of labor on productivity (as your textbook notes) but also its stultifying effect on the human capacity. In *The Wealth of Nations*, Smith warned that performing a few simple operations over and over again could render any worker, no matter his or her native intelligence, "stupid and ignorant."
   a. Does the division of labor in today's economy continue to have both these effects?
   b. What are the policy implications? (Radical)

Issues to Ponder

1. When all people use economic reasoning, inefficiency is impossible because if the benefit of reducing that inefficiency were greater than the cost, the inefficiency would be eliminated. Thus, if people use economic reasoning, it's impossible to be on the interior of a production possibility curve. Is this statement true or false? Why? (Difficult) LO1
2. If income distribution is tied to a particular production technique, how might that change one's view of alternative production techniques? LO1
3. Research shows that after-school jobs are highly correlated with decreases in grade point averages. Those who work 1 to 10 hours get a 3.0 GPA and those who work 21 hours or more have a 2.7 GPA. Higher GPAs are, however, highly correlated with higher lifetime earnings. Assume that a person earns $8,000 per year for working part-time in college, and that the return to a 0.1 increase in GPA gives one a 10 percent increase in one's lifetime earnings with a present value of $80,000.
   a. What would be the argument for working rather than studying harder?
   b. Is the assumption that there is a trade-off between working and grades reasonable? LO1
4. What would the production possibility curve look like if there were decreasing marginal opportunity costs? Explain. What is an example of decreasing marginal opportunity costs? LO2
5. Lawns produce no crops but occupy more land (25 million acres) in the United States than any single crop, such as corn. This means that the United States is operating inefficiently and hence is at a point inside the production possibility curve. Right? If not, what does it mean? LO1
6. Groucho Marx is reported to have said, "The secret of success is honesty and fair dealing. If you can fake those, you've got it made." What would likely happen to society's production possibility curve if everyone could fake honesty? Why? (Hint: Remember that society's production possibility curve reflects more than just technical relationships.) (Difficult) LO1
7. In 2007 the hourly cost to employers per German industrial worker was $51. The hourly cost to employers per U.S. industrial worker was $31, while the average cost per Taiwanese industrial worker was $8.
   a. Give three reasons why firms produce in Germany rather than in a lower-wage country.
   b. Germany has just entered into an agreement with other EU countries that allows people in any EU country, including Greece and Italy, which have lower wage rates, to travel and work in any EU country, including high-wage countries. Would you expect a significant movement of workers from Greece and Italy to Germany right away? Why or why not?
   c. Workers in Thailand are paid significantly less than workers in Taiwan. If you were a company CEO, what other information would you want before you decided where to establish a new production facility? LO5

Answers to Margin Questions

1. You must give up 2 units of good Y to produce 4 units of good X, so the opportunity cost of X is ½ Y. (26)
2. If no resource had a comparative advantage, the production possibility curve would be a straight line connecting the points of maximum production of each product as in the graph below.

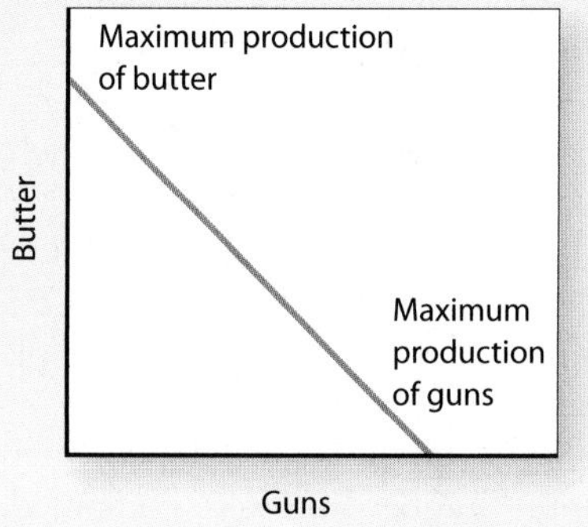

At all points along this curve, the opportunity cost of producing guns and butter is equal. (29)

3. Points A and C are along the production possibility curve, so they are points of efficiency. Point B is inside the production possibility curve, so it is a point of inefficiency. Point D is to the right of the production possibility curve, so it is unattainable. (30)
4. I remind them of the importance of cultural forces. In Saudi Arabia, women are not allowed to drive. (31)
5. The production possibility curve shifts in along the butter axis as in the graph below. (32)

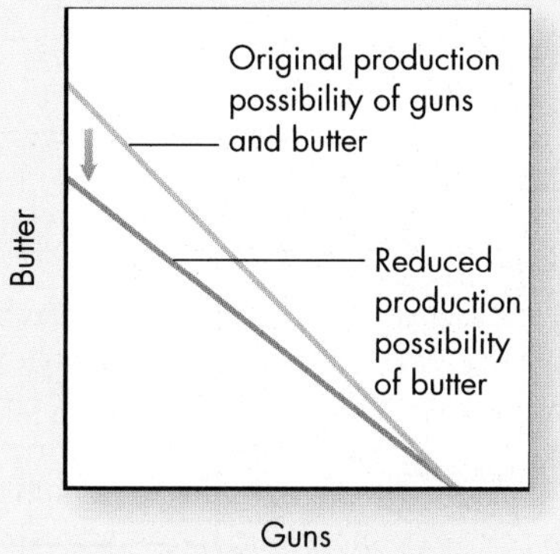

6. The argument that underlies the general laissez-faire policy argument is that when there is competition in trade, individuals are able to pick the best trades available to them and the end result is that both parties to the trade benefit as much as they possibly can. (35)
7. Steve's and Sarah's production possibility curves are shown in the figure below. If they specialize, they can, combined, produce 4 loaves of bread and 8 dozen cookies, which they can split up. Say that Steve gets 2 loaves of bread and 5 dozen cookies (point A). This puts him beyond his original production possibility curve, and thus is an improvement for him. That leaves 2 loaves of bread and 3 dozen cookies for Sarah (point B), which is beyond her original production possibility curve, which is an improvement for her. Both are better off than they would have been. (36)

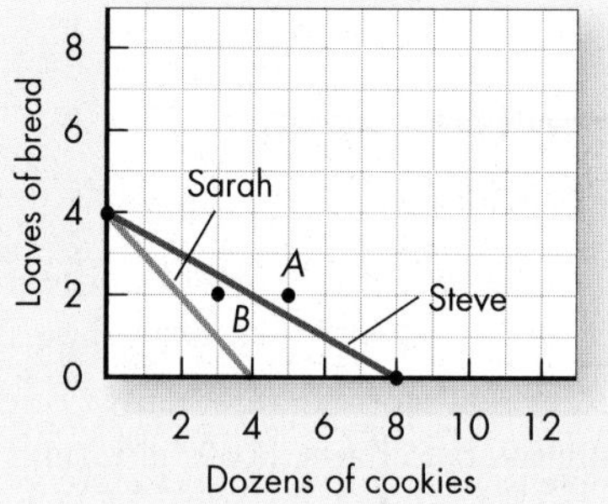

8. False. By producing the good for which it has a comparative advantage (lowest opportunity cost), a country will have the greatest amount of goods with which to trade and will reap the greatest gains from trade. (36)
9. No. By definition, if one country has a comparative advantage in producing one set of goods, the other country has a comparative advantage in the production in the other set. Jobs will be needed to support this production. Additionally, many jobs cannot be outsourced effectively because they require physical proximity to the point of sale. (37)
10. Globalization allows more trade and specialization. That specialization lowers costs of production since it allows the lowest-cost producer to produce each good. (39)

APPENDIX A

Graphish: The Language of Graphs

A picture is worth 1,000 words. Economists, being efficient, like to present ideas in **graphs,** *pictures of points in a coordinate system in which points denote relationships between numbers.* But a graph is worth 1,000 words only if the person looking at the graph knows the graphical language: *Graphish*, we'll call it. (It's a bit like English.) Graphish is usually written on graph paper. If the person doesn't know Graphish, the picture isn't worth any words and Graphish can be babble.

I have enormous sympathy for students who don't understand Graphish. A number of my students get thrown for a loop by graphs. They understand the idea, but Graphish confuses them. This appendix is for them, and for those of you like them. It's a primer in Graphish.

Two Ways to Use Graphs

In this book I use graphs in two ways:

1. To present an economic model or theory visually, showing how two variables interrelate.
2. To present real-world data visually. To do this, I use primarily bar charts, line charts, and pie charts.

Actually, these two ways of using graphs are related. They are both ways of presenting visually the *relationship* between two things.

Graphs are built around a number line, or axis, like the one in Figure A2-1(a). The numbers are generally placed in order, equal distances from one another. That number line allows us to represent a number at an appropriate point on the line. For example, point A represents the number 4.

The number line in Figure A2-1(a) is drawn horizontally, but it doesn't have to be; it also can be drawn vertically, as in Figure A2-1(b).

How we divide our axes, or number lines, into intervals is up to us. In Figure A2-1(a), I called each interval 1; in Figure A2-1(b), I called each interval 10. Point A appears after 4 intervals of 1 (starting at 0 and reading from left to right), so it represents 4. In Figure A2-1(b), where each interval represents 10, to represent 5, I place point B halfway in the interval between 0 and 10.

So far, so good. Graphish developed when a vertical and a horizontal number line were combined, as in Figure A2-1(c). When the horizontal and vertical number lines are put together, they're called *axes*. (Each line is an axis. *Axes* is the plural of *axis*.) I now have a **coordinate system**—*a two-dimensional space in which one point represents two numbers*. For example, point A in Figure A2-1(c) represents the numbers (4, 5)—4 on the horizontal number line and 5 on the vertical number line. Point *B* represents the numbers (1, 20). (By convention, the horizontal numbers are written first.)

Being able to represent two numbers with one point is neat because it allows the relationships between two numbers to be presented visually instead of having to be expressed verbally, which is often cumbersome. For example, say the cost of producing 6 units of something is $4 per unit

FIGURE A2-1 (A, B, AND C) Horizontal and Vertical Number Lines and a Coordinate System

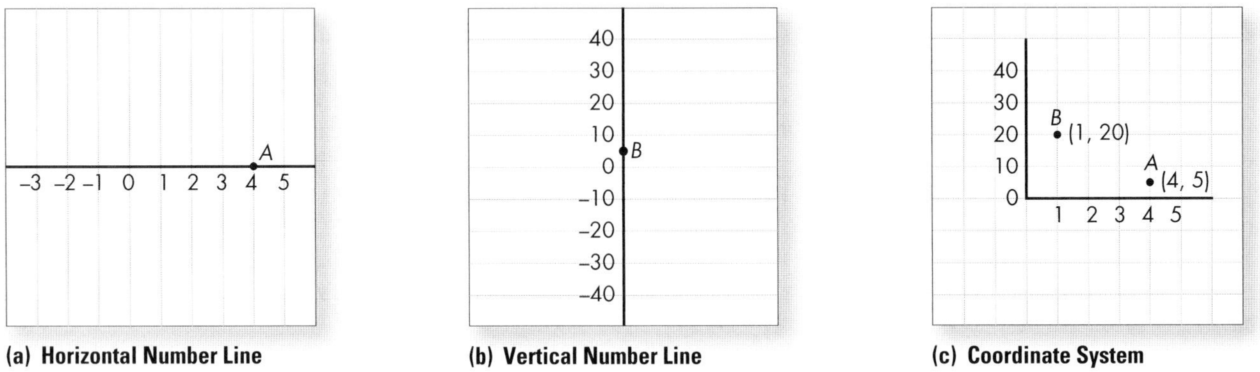

FIGURE A2-2 (A, B, C, AND D) A Table and Graphs Showing the Relationships between Price and Quantity

	Price per Pen	Quantity of Pens Bought per Day
A	$3.00	4
B	2.50	5
C	2.00	6
D	1.50	7
E	1.00	8

(a) Price Quantity Table

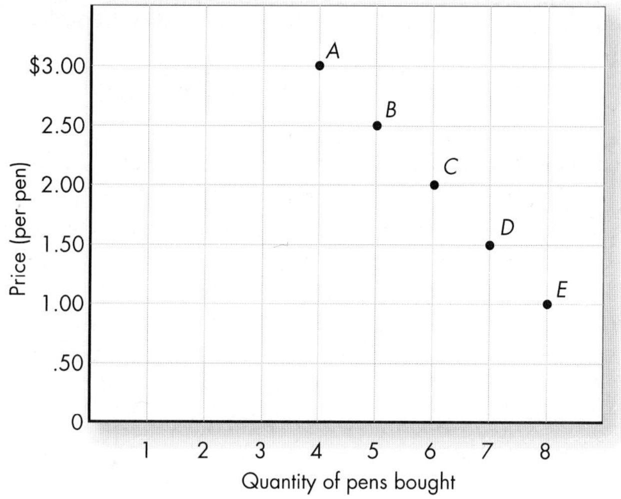

(b) From a Table to a Graph (1)

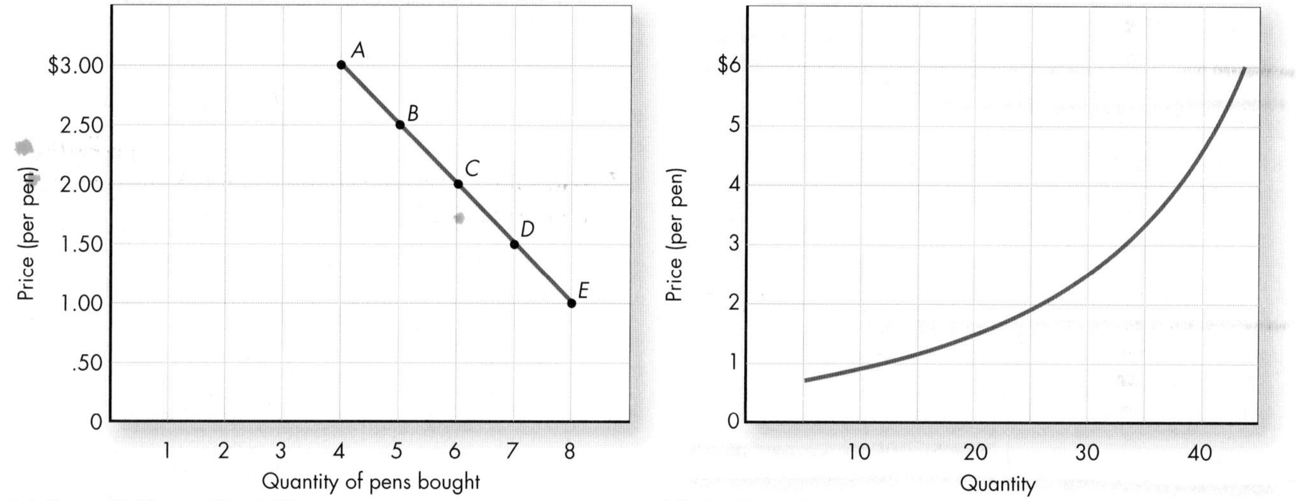

(c) From a Table to a Graph (2)

(d) Nonlinear Curve

and the cost of producing 10 units is $3 per unit. By putting both these points on a graph, we can visually see that producing 10 costs less per unit than does producing 6.

Another way to use graphs to present real-world data visually is to use the horizontal line to represent time. Say that we let each horizontal interval equal a year, and each vertical interval equal $100 in income. By graphing your income each year, you can obtain a visual representation of how your income has changed over time.

Using Graphs in Economic Modeling

I use graphs throughout the book as I present economic models, or simplifications of reality. A few terms are often used in describing these graphs, and we'll now go over them. Consider Figure A2-2(a), which lists the number of pens bought per day (column 2) at various prices (column 1).

We can present the table's information in a graph by combining the pairs of numbers in the two columns of the table and representing, or plotting, them on two axes. I do that in Figure A2-2(b).

By convention, when graphing a relationship between price and quantity, economists place price on the vertical axis and quantity on the horizontal axis.

I can now connect the points, producing a line like the one in Figure A2-2(c). With this line, I interpolate the numbers between the points (which makes for a nice

A REMINDER

Inverse and Direct Relationships

Inverse relationship:
When *X* goes up, *Y* goes down.
When *X* goes down, *Y* goes up.

Direct relationship:
When *X* goes up, *Y* goes up.
When *X* goes down, *Y* goes down.

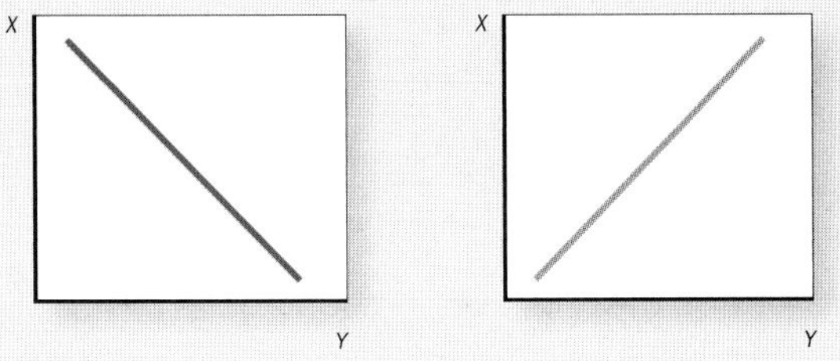

visual presentation). That is, I make the **interpolation assumption**—*the assumption that the relationship between variables is the same between points as it is at the points.* The interpolation assumption allows us to think of a line as a collection of points and therefore to connect the points into a line.

Even though the line in Figure A2-2(c) is straight, economists call any such line drawn on a graph a *curve*. Because it's straight, the curve in A2-2(c) is called a **linear curve**—*a curve that is drawn as a straight line.* Notice that this curve starts high on the left-hand side and goes down to the right. Economists say that any curve that looks like that is *downward-sloping*. They also say that a downward-sloping curve represents an **inverse relationship**—*a relationship between two variables in which when one goes up, the other goes down.* In this example, the line demonstrates an inverse relationship between price and quantity—that is, when the price of pens goes up, the quantity bought goes down.

Figure A2-2(d) presents a **nonlinear curve**—*a curve that is drawn as a curved line.* This curve, which really is curved, starts low on the left-hand side and goes up to the right. Economists say any curve that goes up to the right is *upward-sloping*. An upward-sloping curve represents a **direct relationship**—*a relationship in which when one variable goes up, the other goes up too.* The direct relationship I'm talking about here is the one between the two variables (what's measured on the horizontal and vertical lines). *Downward-sloping* and *upward-sloping* are terms you need to memorize if you want to read, write, and speak Graphish, keeping graphically in your mind the image of the relationships they represent.

Slope

One can, of course, be far more explicit about how much the curve is sloping upward or downward by defining it in terms of **slope**—*the change in the value on the vertical axis divided by the change in the value on the horizontal axis.* Sometimes the slope is presented as "rise over run":

$$\text{Slope} = \frac{\text{Rise}}{\text{Run}} = \frac{\text{Change in value on vertical axis}}{\text{Change in value on horizontal axis}}$$

Slopes of Linear Curves

In Figure A2-3, I present five linear curves and measures of their slopes. Let's go through an example to show how we can measure slope. To do so, we must pick two points. Let's use points *A* (6, 8) and *B* (7, 4) on curve *a*. Looking at these points, we see that as we move from 6 to 7 on the horizontal axis, we move from 8 to 4 on the vertical axis. So when the number on the vertical axis falls by 4, the number on the horizontal axis increases by 1. That means the slope is -4 divided by 1, or -4.

Notice that the inverse relationships represented by the two downward-sloping curves, *a* and *b*, have negative slopes, and that the direct relationships represented by the two upward-sloping curves, *c* and *d*, have positive slopes. Notice also that the flatter the curve, the smaller the numerical value of the slope; and the more vertical, or steeper, the curve, the larger the numerical value of the slope. There are two extreme cases:

1. When the curve is horizontal (flat), the slope is zero.
2. When the curve is vertical (straight up and down), the slope is infinite (larger than large).

Knowing the term *slope* and how it's measured lets us describe verbally the pictures we see visually. For example, if I say a curve has a slope of zero, you should picture in your mind a flat line; if I say "a curve with a slope of minus one," you should picture a falling line that makes a 45° angle with the horizontal and vertical axes. (It's the hypotenuse of an isosceles right triangle with the axes as the other two sides.)

Slopes of Nonlinear Curves

The preceding examples were of *linear (straight) curves*. With *nonlinear curves*—the ones that really do curve—the slope of the curve is constantly changing. As a result, we must talk about the slope of the curve at a particular point, rather than the slope of the whole curve. How can a point have a slope? Well, it can't really, but it can almost, and if that's good enough for mathematicians, it's good enough for us.

FIGURE A2-3 Slopes of Curves

The slope of a curve is determined by rise over run. The slope of curve *a* is shown in the graph. The rest are shown below:

	Rise	÷	Run	=	Slope
b	−1		+2		−.5
c	1		1		1
d	4		1		4
e	1		1		1

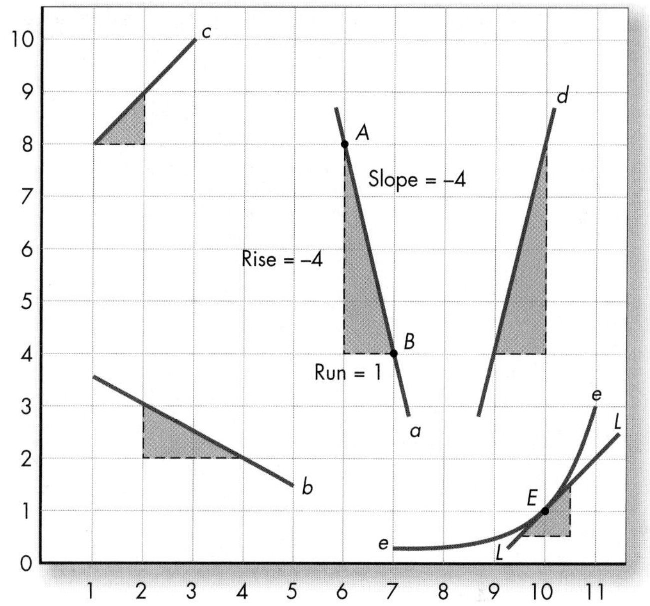

Defining the slope of a nonlinear curve is a bit more difficult. The slope at a given point on a nonlinear curve is determined by the slope of a linear (or straight) line that's tangent to that curve. (A line that's tangent to a curve is a line that just touches the curve, and touches it only at one point in the immediate vicinity of the given point.) In Figure A2-3, the line *LL* is tangent to the curve *ee* at point *E*. The slope of that line, and hence the slope of the curve at the one point where the line touches the curve, is +1.

Maximum and Minimum Points

Two points on a nonlinear curve deserve special mention. These points are the ones for which the slope of the curve is zero. I demonstrate those in Figure A2-4(a) and (b). At point *A* we're at the top of the curve, so it's at a maximum point; at point *B* we're at the bottom of the curve, so it's at a minimum point. These maximum and minimum points are often referred to by economists, and it's important to realize that the value of the slope of the curve at each of these points is zero.

There are, of course, many other types of curves, and much more can be said about the curves I've talked about. I won't do so because, for purposes of this course, we won't need to get into those refinements. I've presented as much Graphish as you need to know for this book.

FIGURE A2-4 (A AND B) A Maximum and a Minimum Point

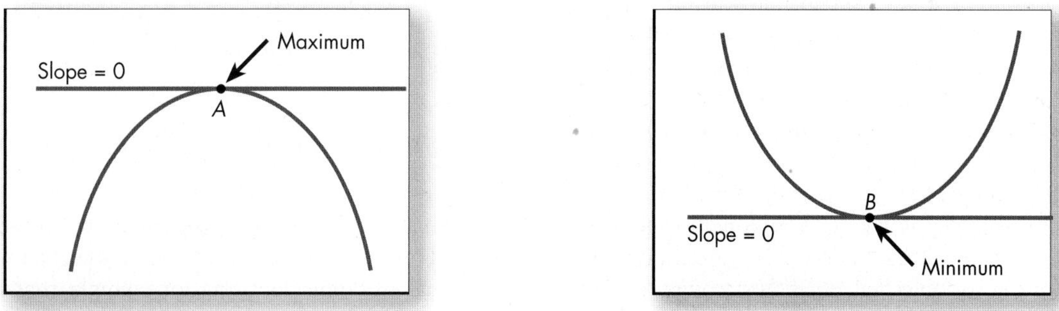

(a) Maximum Point **(b) Minimum Point**

FIGURE A2-5 (A, B, AND C) **A Shifting Curve versus a Movement along a Curve**

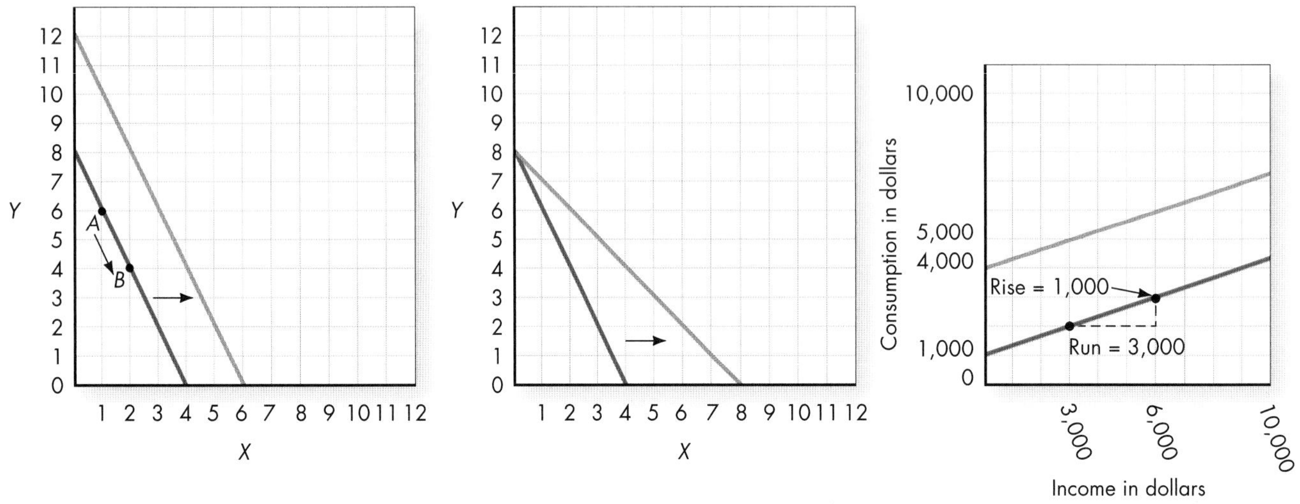

(a) Shifting Curve **(b) Changing Slope** **(c) An Example**

Equations and Graphs

Sometimes economists depict the relationships shown in graphs using equations. Since I present material algebraically in the appendixes to a few chapters, let me briefly discuss how to translate a linear curve into an equation. Linear curves are relatively easy to translate because all linear curves follow a particular mathematical form: $y = mx + b$, where y is the variable on the vertical axis, x is the variable on the horizontal axis, m is the slope of the line, and b is the vertical-axis intercept. To write the equation of a curve, look at that curve, plug in the values for the slope and vertical-axis intercept, and you've got the equation.

For example, consider the blue curve in Figure A2-5(a). The slope (rise over run) is -2 and the number where the curve intercepts the vertical axis is 8, so the equation that depicts this curve is $y = -2x + 8$. It's best to choose variables that correspond to what you're measuring on each axis, so if price is on the vertical axis and quantity is on the horizontal axis, the equation would be $p = -2q + 8$. This equation is true for any point along this line. Take point A (1, 6), for example. Substituting 1 for x and 6 for y into the equation, you see that $6 = -2(1) + 8$, or $6 = 6$. At point B, the equation is still true: $4 = -2(2) + 8$. A move from point A to point B is called a *movement along a curve*. A movement along a curve does not change the relationship of the variables; rather, it shows how a change in one variable affects the other.

Sometimes the relationship between variables will change. The curve will either shift, change slope, or both shift and change slope. These changes are reflected in changes to the m and b variables in the equation. Suppose the vertical-axis intercept rises from 8 to 12, while the slope remains the same. The equation becomes $y = -2x + 12$; for every value of y, x has increased by 4. Plotting the new equation, we can see that the curve has *shifted* to the right, as shown by the orange line in Figure A2-5(a). If instead the slope changes from -2 to -1, while the vertical-axis intercept remains at 8, the equation becomes $y = -x + 8$. Figure A2-5(b) shows this change graphically. The original blue line stays anchored at 8 and rotates out along the horizontal axis to the new orange line.

Here's an example for you to try. The lines in Figure A2-5(c) show two relationships between consumption and income. Write the equation for the blue line.

The answer is $C = \frac{1}{3}Y + \$1,000$. Remember, to write the equation you need to know two things: the vertical-axis intercept (\$1,000) and the slope ($\frac{1}{3}$). If the intercept changes to \$4,000, the curve will shift up to the orange line as shown.

Presenting Real-World Data in Graphs

The previous discussion treated the Graphish terms that economists use in presenting models that focus on hypothetical relationships. Economists also use graphs in presenting actual economic data. Say, for example, that you want to show how exports have changed over time. Then you would place years on the horizontal axis (by convention) and exports on the vertical axis, as in Figure A2-6(a) and (b).

FIGURE A2-6 (A, B, AND C) **Presenting Information Visually**

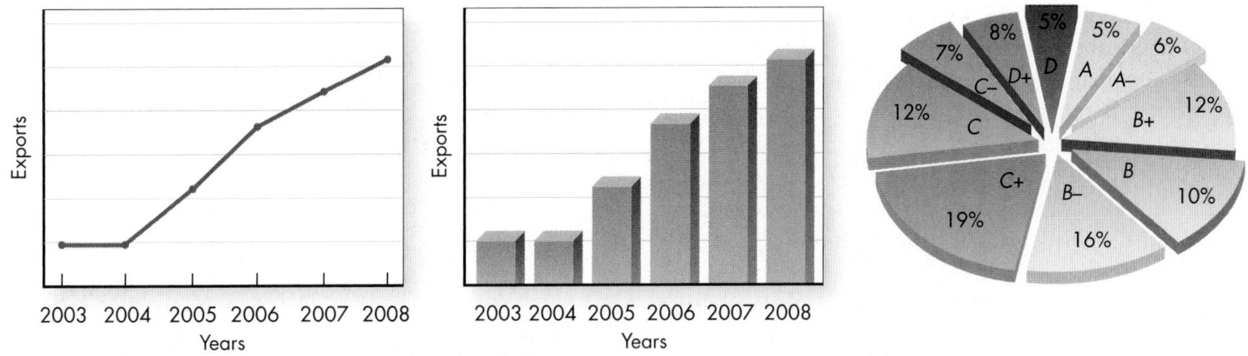

(a) Line Graph **(b) Bar Graph** **(c) Pie Chart**

Having done so, you have a couple of choices: you can draw a **line graph**—*a graph where the data are connected by a continuous line;* or you can make a **bar graph**—*a graph where the area under each point is filled in to look like a bar.* Figure A2-6(a) shows a line graph and Figure A2-6(b) shows a bar graph.

Another type of graph is a **pie chart**—*a circle divided into "pie pieces," where the undivided pie represents the total amount and the pie pieces reflect the percentage of the whole pie that the various components make up.* This type of graph is useful in visually presenting how a total amount is divided. Figure A2-6(c) shows a pie chart, which happens to represent the division of grades on a test I gave. Notice that 5 percent of the students got As.

There are other types of graphs, but they're all variations on line and bar graphs and pie charts. Once you understand these three basic types of graphs, you shouldn't have any trouble understanding the other types.

Interpreting Graphs about the Real World

Understanding Graphish is important because, if you don't, you can easily misinterpret the meaning of graphs. For example, consider the two graphs in Figure A2-7(a) and (b). Which graph demonstrates the larger rise in income? If you said (a), you're wrong. The intervals in the vertical axes differ, and if you look carefully you'll see that the curves in both graphs represent the same combination of points. So when considering graphs, always make sure you understand the markings on the axes. Only then can you interpret the graph.

FIGURE A2-7 (A AND B) **The Importance of Scales**

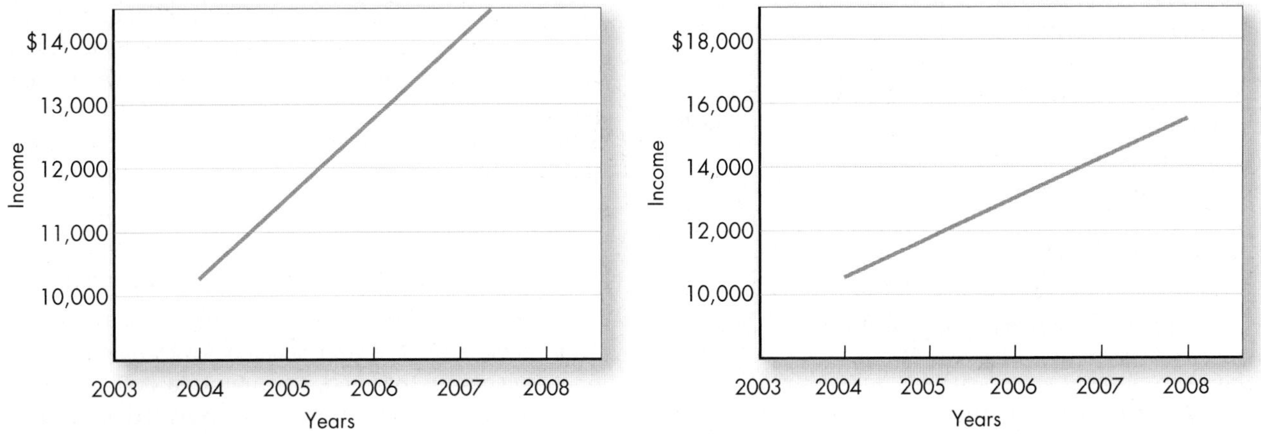

(a) Income over Time (1) **(b) Income over Time (2)**

Quantitative Literacy: Avoiding Stupid Math Mistakes

The data of economics are often presented in graphs and tables. Numerical data are compared by the use of percentages, visual comparisons, and simple relationships based on quantitative differences. Economists who have studied the learning process of their students have found that some very bright students have some trouble with these presentations. Students sometimes mix up percentage changes with level changes, draw incorrect implications from visual comparisons, and calculate quantitative differences incorrectly. This is not necessarily a math problem—at least in the sense that most economists think of math. The mistakes are in relatively simple stuff—the kind of stuff learned in fifth, sixth, and seventh grades. Specifically, as reported in "Student Quantitative Literacy: Is the Glass Half-full or Half-empty?" (Robert Burns, Kim Marie McGoldrick, Jerry L. Petr, and Peter Schuhmann, 2002 University of North Carolina at Wilmington Working Paper), when the professors gave a test to students at a variety of schools, they found that a majority of students missed the following questions.

1. What is 25 percent of 400?
   a. 25 b. 50 c. 100
   d. 400 e. none of the above
2. Consider Figure A2-8 where U.S oil consumption and U.S. oil imports are plotted for 1990–2000. Fill in the blanks to construct a true statement: U.S. domestic oil consumption has been steady while imports have been ______________; therefore U.S. domestic oil production has been ______________.
   a. rising; rising b. falling; falling
   c. rising; falling d. falling; rising
3. Refer to the following table to select the true statement.

Economic Growth in Poland
Percent Increase in GDP, 1990–1994

1990	1991	1992	1993	1994
−11.7	−7.8	−1.5	4.0	3.5

   a. GDP in Poland was larger in 1992 than in 1991.
   b. GDP in Poland was larger in 1994 than in 1993.
   c. GDP in Poland was larger in 1991 than in 1992.
   d. GDP in Poland was larger in 1993 than in 1994.
   e. Both b and c are true.

FIGURE A2-8

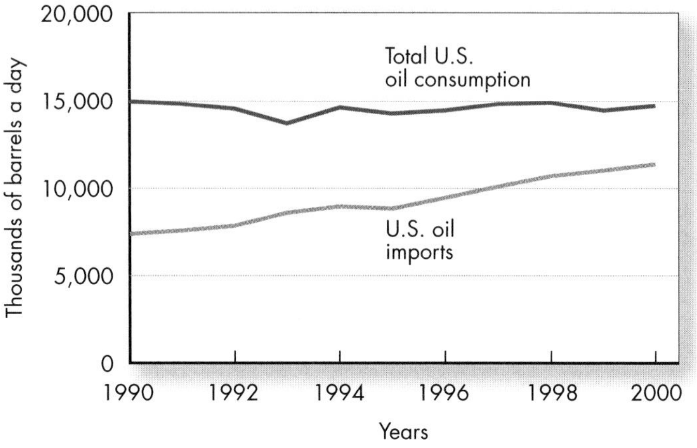

4. If U.S. production of corn was 60 million bushels in 2002 and 100 million bushels in 2003, what was the percentage change in corn production from 2002 to 2003?
   a. 40 b. 60 c. 66.67
   d. 100 e. 200

The reason students got these questions wrong is unknown. Many of them had had higher-level math courses, including calculus, so it is not that they weren't trained in math. I suspect that many students missed the questions because of carelessness: the students didn't think about the question carefully before they wrote down the answer.

Throughout this book we will be discussing issues assuming a quantitative literacy sufficient to answer these questions. Moreover, questions using similar reasoning will be on exams. So it is useful for you to see whether or not you fall in the majority. So please answer the four questions given above now if you haven't done so already.

Now that you've answered them, I give you the correct answers upside-down in the footnote at the bottom of the page.[1]

If you got all four questions right, great! You can stop reading this appendix now. If you missed one or more, read the explanations of the correct answers carefully.

1. The correct answer is c. To calculate a percentage, you multiply the percentage times the number. Thus, 25 percent of 400 is 100.
2. The correct answer is c. To answer it you had to recognize that U.S. consumption of oil comes from U.S. imports and U.S. production. Thus,

[1] 1-c; 2-c; 3-e; 4-c.

the distance between the two lines represents U.S. production, which is clearly getting smaller from 1990 to 2000.

3. The correct answer is e. The numbers given to you are percentage changes, and the question is about levels. If the percentage change is positive, as it is in 1993 and 1994, the level is increasing. Thus, 1994 is greater (by 3.5 percent) than 1993, even though the percentage change is smaller than in 1993. If the percentage change is negative, as it is in 1992, the level is falling. Because income fell in 1992, the level of income in 1991 is greater than the level of income in 1992.
4. The correct answer is c. To calculate percentage change, you first need to calculate the change, which in this case is 100 − 60, or 40. So corn production started at a base of 60 and rose by 40. To calculate the percentage change that this represents, you divide the amount of the rise, 40, by the base, 60. Doing so gives us 40/60 = 2/3 = .6667, which is 66.67 percent.

Now that I've given you the answers, I suspect that most of you will recognize that they are the right answers. If, after reading the explanations, you still don't follow the reasoning, you should look into getting some extra help in the course either from your teacher, from your TA, or from some program the college has. If, after reading the explanations, you follow them and believe that if you had really thought about them you would have gotten them right, then the next time you see a chart or a table of numbers being compared *really think about them*. Be a bit slower in drawing inferences since they are the building blocks of economic discussions. If you want to do well on exams, it probably makes sense to practice some similar questions to make sure that you have concepts down.

A Review

Let's now review what we've covered.

- A graph is a picture of points on a coordinate system in which the points denote relationships between numbers.
- A downward-sloping line represents an inverse relationship or a negative slope.
- An upward-sloping line represents a direct relationship or a positive slope.
- Slope is measured by rise over run, or a change of y (the number measured on the vertical axis) over a change in x (the number measured on the horizontal axis).
- The slope of a point on a nonlinear curve is measured by the rise over the run of a line tangent to that point.
- At the maximum and minimum points of a nonlinear curve, the value of the slope is zero.
- A linear curve has the form $y = mx + b$.
- A shift in a linear curve is reflected by a change in the b variable in the equation $y = mx + b$.
- A change in the slope of a linear curve is reflected by a change in the m variable in the equation $y = mx + b$.
- In reading graphs, one must be careful to understand what's being measured on the vertical and horizontal axes.

Key Terms

bar graph *(51)*
coordinate system *(46)*
direct relationship *(48)*
graph *(46)*
interpolation assumption *(48)*
inverse relationship *(48)*
line graph *(51)*
linear curve *(48)*
nonlinear curve *(48)*
pie chart *(51)*
slope *(48)*

Questions and Exercises

1. Create a coordinate space on graph paper and label the following points:
   a. (0, 5) b. (−5, −5)
   c. (2, −3) d. (−1, 1)

2. Graph the following costs per unit, and answer the questions that follow.

Horizontal Axis: Output	Vertical Axis: Cost per Unit
1	$30
2	20
3	12
4	6
5	2
6	6
7	12
8	20
9	30

   a. Is the relationship between cost per unit and output linear or nonlinear? Why?
   b. In what range in output is the relationship inverse? In what range in output is the relationship direct?
   c. In what range in output is the slope negative? In what range in output is the slope positive?
   d. What is the slope between 1 and 2 units?

3. Within a coordinate space, draw a line with
   a. Zero slope.
   b. Infinite slope.
   c. Positive slope.
   d. Negative slope.

4. Calculate the slope of lines *a* through *e* in the following coordinate system.

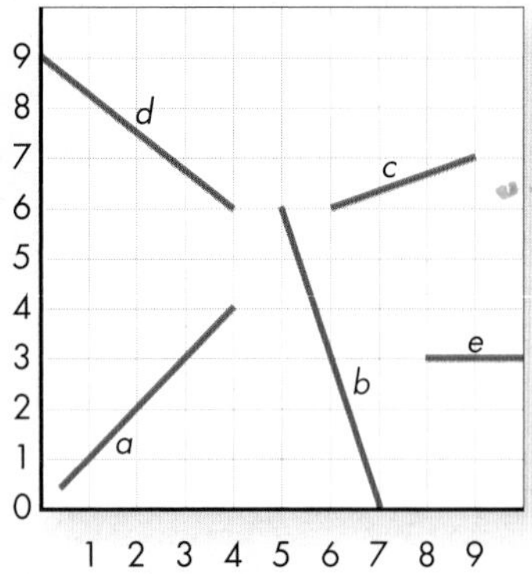

5. Given the following nonlinear curve, answer the following questions:

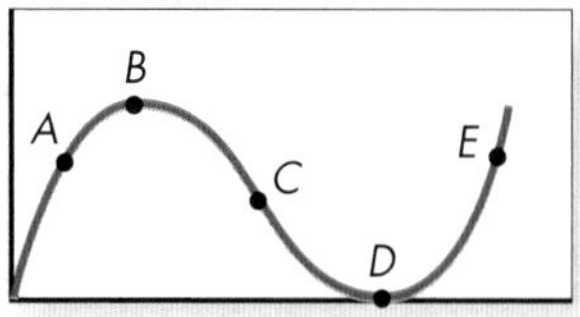

   a. At what point(s) is the slope negative?
   b. At what point(s) is the slope positive?
   c. At what point(s) is the slope zero?
   d. What point is the maximum? What point is the minimum?

6. Draw the graphs that correspond to the following equations:
   a. $y = 3x - 8$
   b. $y = 12 - x$
   c. $y = 4x + 2$

7. Using the equation $y = 3x + 1{,}000$, demonstrate the following:
   a. The slope of the curve changes to 5.
   b. The curve shifts up by 500.

8. State what type of graph or chart you might use to show the following real-world data:
   a. Interest rates from 1929 to 2005.
   b. Median income levels of various ethnic groups in the United States.
   c. Total federal expenditures by selected categories.
   d. Total costs of producing between 100 and 800 shoes.

Economic Institutions

Nobody can be a great economist who is only an economist—and I am even tempted to add that the economist who is only an economist is likely to become a nuisance if not a positive danger.

—F. Hayek

The powerful U.S. economy generates a high standard of living and sense of economic well-being (compared to most other countries) for almost all those living in the United States. The reason why is often attributed to its use of markets, and to the wonders of a market economy. To some degree, that's true, but simply saying markets are the reason for the strength of the U.S. economy obscures as much information as it conveys. First, it misses the point that other countries have markets too, but many of those have much lower standards of living. Second, it conveys a sense that markets exist independently of social and cultural institutions, and that's just not correct. Markets are highly developed social constructs that are part of a country's social and economic institutions. Markets are based on **institutions,** which Nobel Prize winning economist Douglass North defines as "*the formal and informal rules that constrain human economic behavior.*" Institutions include laws that protect ownership of property, and the legal system to enforce and interpret laws. They also include political institutions that develop those laws, the cultural traits of society that guide people's tastes and behaviors, and the many organizational structures such as corporations, banks, and nonprofit organizations that make up our economy. To understand markets, you need to understand institutions. In a principles course, we don't have time to develop a full analysis of institutions, but what we can do is to provide an overview of U.S. economic institutions, and a brief discussion of why they are important. That's what we do in this chapter.

We begin by looking at the U.S. economic system in historical perspective, considering how it evolved and how it relates to other historical economic systems. Then we consider some of the central institutions of the modern U.S. economy and how they influence the way in which the economy works.

AFTER READING THIS CHAPTER, YOU SHOULD BE ABLE TO:

1. Define *market economy.*
2. Compare and contrast socialism with capitalism.
3. Describe how businesses, households, and government interact in a market economy.
4. Summarize briefly the advantages and disadvantages of various types of businesses.
5. Explain why, even though households have the ultimate power, much of the economic decision making is done by business and government.
6. State six roles of government.
7. Explain why global policy issues differ from national policy issues.

The U.S. Economy in Historical Perspective

A market economy is an economic system based on private property and the market. It gives private property rights to individuals and relies on market forces to coordinate economic activity.

The U.S. economy is a **market economy**—*an economic system based on private property and the market in which, in principle, individuals decide how, what, and for whom to produce.* In a market economy, individuals follow their own self-interest, while market forces of supply and demand are relied on to coordinate those individual pursuits. Businesses, guided by prices in the market, produce goods and services that they believe people want and that will earn a profit for the business. Prices in the market guide businesses in deciding what to produce. Distribution of goods is to each individual according to his or her ability, effort, inherited property, and luck.

Reliance on market forces doesn't mean that political, social, and historical forces play no role in coordinating economic decisions. These other forces do influence how the market works. For example, for a market to exist, government must allocate and defend **private property rights**—*the control a private individual or firm has over an asset.* The concept of private ownership must exist and must be accepted by individuals in society. When you say, "This car is mine," it means that it is unlawful for someone else to take it without your permission. If someone takes it without your permission, he or she is subject to punishment through the legal system.

Q-1 John, your study partner, is telling you that the best way to allocate property rights is through the market. How do you respond?

How Markets Work

Markets work through a system of rewards and payments. If you do something, you get paid for doing that something; if you take something, you pay for that something. How much you get is determined by how much you give. This relationship seems fair to most people. But there are instances when it doesn't seem fair. Say someone is unable to work. Should that person get nothing? How about Joe down the street, who was given $10 million by his parents? Is it fair that he gets lots of toys, like Corvettes and skiing trips to Aspen, and doesn't have to work, while the rest of us have to work 40 hours a week and maybe go to school at night?

I'll put those questions about fairness off at this point—they are very difficult questions. For now, all I want to present is the concept of fairness that underlies a market economy: "Them that works, gets; them that don't, starve."[1] In a market economy, individuals are encouraged to follow their own self-interest.

In market economies, individuals are free to do whatever they want as long as it's legal. The market is relied on to see that what people want to get, and want to do, is consistent with what's available. Price is the mechanism through which people's desires are coordinated and goods are rationed. If there's not enough of something to go around, its price goes up; if more of something needs to get done, the price given to individuals willing to do it goes up. If something isn't wanted or doesn't need to be done, its price goes down. In a market economy, fluctuations in prices play a central role in coordinating individuals' wants.

Fluctuations in prices play a central role in coordinating individuals' wants in a market economy.

---

[1]How come the professor gets to use rotten grammar but screams when he sees rotten grammar in your papers? Well, that's fairness for you. Actually, I should say a bit more about writing style. All writers are expected to know correct grammar; if they don't, they don't deserve to be called writers. Once you know grammar, you can individualize your writing style, breaking the rules of grammar where the meter and flow of the writing require it. In college you're still proving that you know grammar, so in papers handed in to your teacher, you shouldn't break the rules of grammar until you've proved to the teacher that you know them. Me, I've done lots of books, so my editors give me a bit more leeway than your teachers will give you.

What's Good about the Market?

Web Note 3.1
What Are Markets?

Is the market a good way to coordinate individuals' activities? Much of this book will be devoted to answering that question. The answer that I, and most U.S. economists, come to is: Yes, it is a reasonable way. True, it has problems; the market can be unfair, mean, and arbitrary, and sometimes it is downright awful. Why then do economists support it? For the same reason that Oliver Wendell Holmes supported democracy—it is a lousy system, but, based on experience with alternatives, it is better than all the others we've thought of.

The primary debate among economists is not about using markets; it is about how markets should be structured, and whether they should be modified and adjusted by government regulation. Those are much harder questions, and on these questions, opinions differ enormously.

The primary debate among economists is not about using markets but about how markets are structured.

Capitalism and Socialism

The view that markets are a reasonable way to organize society has not always been shared by all economists. Throughout history strong philosophical and practical arguments have been made against markets. The philosophical argument against the market is that it brings out the worst in people—it glorifies greed. It encourages people to beat out others rather than to be cooperative. As an alternative some economists have supported socialism. In theory, **socialism** is *an economic system based on individuals' goodwill toward others, not on their own self-interest, and in which, in principle, society decides what, how, and for whom to produce.* The concept of socialism developed in the 1800s as a description of a hypothetical economic system to be contrasted with the predominant market-based economic system of the time, which was called capitalism. **Capitalism** is defined as *an economic system based on the market in which the ownership of the means of production resides with a small group of individuals called capitalists.*

Q-2 Which would be more likely to attempt to foster individualism: socialism or capitalism?

You can best understand the idea behind theoretical socialism by thinking about how decisions are made in a family. In most families, benevolent parents decide who gets what, based on the needs of each member of the family. When Sabin gets a new coat and his sister Sally doesn't, it's because Sabin needs a coat while Sally already has two coats that fit her and are in good condition. Victor may be slow as molasses, but from his family he still gets as much as his superefficient brother Jerry gets. In fact, Victor may get more than Jerry because he needs extra help.

Q-3 Are there any activities in a family that you believe should be allocated by a market? What characteristics do those activities have?

Markets have little role in most families. In my family, when food is placed on the table, we don't bid on what we want, with the highest bidder getting the food. In my family, every person can eat all he or she wants, although if one child eats more than a fair share, that child gets a lecture from me on the importance of sharing. "Be thoughtful; be considerate. Think of others first" are lessons that many families try to teach.

In theory, socialism was an economic system that tried to organize society in the same way as most families are organized, trying to see that individuals get what they need. Socialism tried to take other people's needs into account and adjust people's own wants in accordance with what's available. In socialist economies, individuals were urged to look out for the other person; if individuals' inherent goodness does not make them consider the general good, government would make them. In contrast, a capitalist economy expected people to be selfish; it relied on markets and competition to direct that selfishness to the general good.[2]

Socialism is, in theory, an economic system that tries to organize society in the same way as most families are organized—all people contribute what they can and get what they need.

[2]As you probably surmised, the above distinction is too sharp. Even capitalist societies wanted people to be selfless, but not too selfless. Children in capitalist societies were generally taught to be selfless at least in dealing with friends and family. The difficulty parents and societies face is finding a balance between the two positions: selfless but not too selfless; selfish but not too selfish.

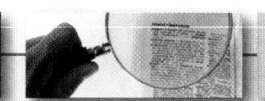

ADDED DIMENSION

Tradition and Today's Economy

In a tradition-based society, the social and cultural forces create an inertia (a tendency to resist change) that predominates over economic and political forces.

"Why did you do it that way?"

"Because that's the way we've always done it."

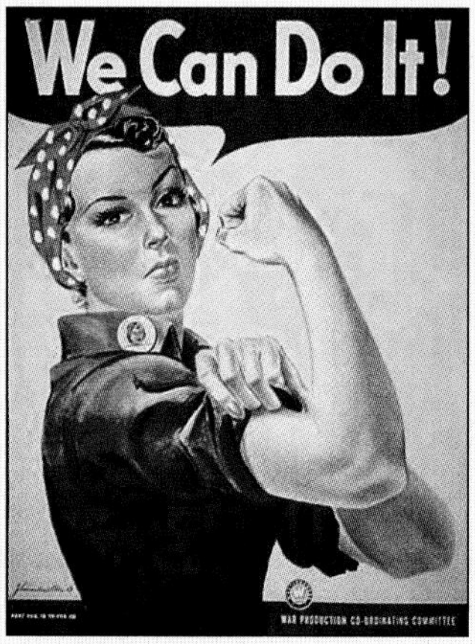

Tradition-based societies had markets, but they were peripheral, not central, to economic life. In feudal times, what was produced, how it was produced, and for whom it was produced were primarily decided by tradition.

In today's U.S. economy, the market plays the central role in economic decisions. But that doesn't mean that tradition is dead. As I said in Chapter 1, tradition still plays a significant role in today's society, and, in many aspects of society, tradition still overwhelms the invisible hand. Consider the following:

1. The persistent view that women should be homemakers rather than factory workers, consumers rather than producers.

We Can Do It!

WAR PRODUCTION CO-ORDINATING COMMITTEE

2. The raised eyebrows when a man is introduced as a nurse, secretary, homemaker, or member of any other profession conventionally identified as women's work.
3. Society's unwillingness to permit the sale of individuals or body organs.
4. Parents' willingness to care for their children without financial compensation.

Each of these tendencies reflects tradition's influence in Western society. Some are so deeply rooted that we see them as self-evident. Some of tradition's effects we like; others we don't—but we often take them for granted. Economic forces may work against these traditions, but the fact that they're still around indicates the continued strength of tradition in our market economy.

As I stated above, the term *socialism* originally developed as a description of a hypothetical, not an actual, economic system. Actual socialist economies came into being only in the early 1900s, and when they developed they differed enormously from the hypothetical socialist economies that writers had described earlier.

Q-4 What is the difference between socialism in theory and socialism in practice?

In practice socialist governments had to take a strong role in guiding the economy. Socialism became known as an economic system based on government ownership of the means of production, with economic activity governed by central planning. In a centrally planned socialist economy, sometimes called a command economy, government planning boards set society's goals and then directed individuals and firms as to how to achieve those goals.

For example, if government planning boards decided that whole-wheat bread was good for people, they directed firms to produce large quantities and priced it exceptionally low. Planners, not prices, coordinated people's actions. The results were often not quite what the planners desired. Bread prices were so low that pig farmers fed bread to their pigs even though pig feed would have been better for the pigs and bread was more costly to produce. At the low price, the quantity of bread demanded was so high that there were bread shortages; consumers had to stand in long lines to buy bread for their families.

As is often the case, over time the meaning of the word *socialism* expanded and evolved further. It was used to describe the market economies of Western Europe, which by the 1960s had evolved into economies that had major welfare support systems and governments that were very much involved in their market economies. For example, Sweden, even though it relied on markets as its central coordinating institution, was called a socialist economy because its taxes were high and it provided a cradle-to-grave welfare system.

When the Union of Soviet Socialist Republics (USSR) broke apart, Russia and the countries that evolved out of the USSR adopted a market economy as their organizing framework. China, which is ruled by the Communist Party, also adopted many market institutions. As they did, the terms *capitalism* and *socialism* fell out of favor. People today talk little about the differences in economic systems such as capitalism and socialism; instead they talk about the differences in institutions. Most economies today are differentiated primarily by the degree to which their economies rely on markets, not whether they are a market, capitalist, or socialist economy.

People today talk little about differences in economic systems; instead they talk about differences in institutions.

The term *socialism*, however, still shows up in the news. China, for example, continues to call itself a socialist country, even though it is relying more and more heavily on markets to organize production, and is sometimes seen as more capitalistic than many Western economies. Another example of the interest in socialism can be found in the rhetoric of Venezuelan President Hugo Chavez, who is attempting to transform Venezuela into what he calls "21st century socialism." He defines 21st century socialism as government ownership, or at least control, of major resources, and an economy dominated by business cooperatives owned and operated by workers supported by government loans and contracts. President Chavez argues that this "21st century socialism" will serve as a new economic model of egalitarianism for the entire world. To date, the Venezuelan economy has been growing, and the approach seems to be successful. But some of that success is due to the large oil revenues that the Venezuelan government began collecting after Chavez took over the oil companies. What will happen to the Venezuelan economy when that oil money ends is yet to be seen.

Evolving Economic Systems[3]

An important lesson of the above discussion is that economic systems and the institutions that make them up are constantly evolving, and will likely continue to evolve. Let's consider that evolution briefly. What became known as capitalism came into widespread existence in the mid-1700s; socialism came into existence in the early 1900s. Before capitalism and socialism, other forms of economic systems existed, including **feudalism**—*an economic system in which traditions rule*. In feudalism if your parents were serfs (small farmers who lived on a manor), you would be a serf. Feudalism dominated the Western world from about the 8th century to the 15th century.

Feudalism is an economic system in which traditions rule.

Throughout the feudalistic period, merchants and artisans (small manufacturers who produced goods by hand) grew in importance and wealth, and eventually their increased importance led to a change in the economic system from feudalism to **mercantilism**—*an economic system in which government determines the what, how, and for whom decisions by doling out the rights to undertake certain economic activities*.

Mercantilism is an economic system in which government doles out the rights to undertake economic activities.

Mercantilism remained the dominant economic system until the 1700s, when the **Industrial Revolution**—*a time when technology and machines rapidly modernized industrial production and mass-produced goods replaced handmade goods*—led to a decrease in power of small producers, an increase in power of capitalists, and eventually a revolution instituting capitalism as the dominant economic system.

I mention feudalism and mercantilism because aspects of both continue in economies today. For example, governments in Japan and Korea play significant roles in directing their economies. Their economic systems are sometimes referred to as *neomercantilist economies*.

[3]The appendix to this chapter traces the development of economic systems from feudalism to mercantilism to capitalism to socialism to modern-day forms of market economies in a bit more detail.

Revolutionary shifts that give rise to new economic systems are not the only way economic systems change. Systems also evolve internally, as I discussed above. For example, the U.S. economy is and has always been a market economy, but it has changed over the years, evolving with changes in social customs, political forces, and the strength of markets. In the 1930s, during the Great Depression, the U.S. economy integrated a number of what might be called socialist institutions into its existing institutions. Distribution of goods was no longer, even in theory, only according to ability; need also played a role. Governments began to play a larger role in the economy, taking control over some of the *how, what,* and *for whom* decisions. Since the 1980s, the process has been reversed. The United States became even more market oriented and the government tried to pull back its involvement in the market in favor of private enterprise. Whether that movement will continue remains to be seen, but we can expect institutions to continue to change.

The U.S. Economy

Q-5 Into what three sectors are market economies generally broken up?

Now that we have put the U.S. economic system in historical perspective, let's consider some of its main components. The U.S. economy can be divided up into three sectors: businesses, households, and government, as Figure 3-1 shows. Households supply labor and other factors of production to businesses and are paid by businesses for doing so. The market where this interaction takes place is called a *factor market.* Businesses produce goods and services and sell them to households and government. The market where this interaction takes place is called the *goods market.*

Each of the three sectors is interconnected; moreover, the entire U.S. economy is interconnected with the world economy. Notice also the arrows going out to and coming in from both business and households. Those arrows represent the connection of an economy to the world economy. It consists of interrelated flows of goods (exports and imports) and money (capital flows). Finally, consider the arrows connecting government

FIGURE 3-1 Diagrammatic Representation of a Market Economy

This circular-flow diagram of the economy is a good way to organize your thinking about the aggregate economy. As you can see, the three sectors—households, government, and business—interact in a variety of ways.

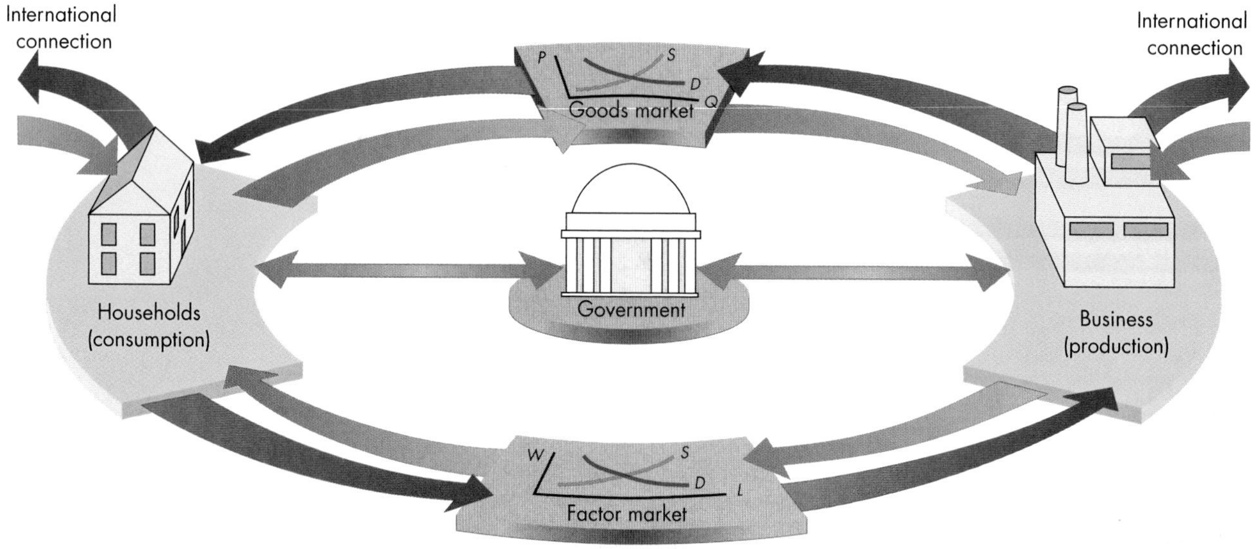

with households and business. Government taxes business and households. It buys goods and services from business and buys labor services from households. Then, with some of its tax revenue, it provides services (for example, roads, education) to both business and households and gives some of its tax revenue directly back to individuals. In doing so, it redistributes income. But government also serves a second function. It oversees the interaction of business and households in the goods and factor markets. Government, of course, is not independent. The United States, for instance, is a democracy, so households vote to determine who shall govern. Similarly, governments are limited not only by what voters want but also by their relationships with other countries. They are part of an international community of countries, and they must keep up relations with other countries in the world. For example, the United States is a member of many international organizations and has signed international treaties in which it has agreed to limit its domestic actions, such as its ability to tax imports.

Now let's look briefly at the individual components.

Business

Web Note 3.2
Starting a Business

President Calvin Coolidge once said, "The business of America is business." That's a bit of an overstatement, but business is responsible for over 85 percent of U.S. production. (Government is responsible for the other 15 percent.) In fact, anytime a household decides to produce something, it becomes a business. **Business** is simply the name given to *private producing units in our society*.

Businesses in the United States decide *what* to produce, *how* much to produce, and *for whom* to produce it.

Businesses in the United States decide *what* to produce, *how* much to produce, and *for whom* to produce it. They make these central economic decisions on the basis of their own self-interest, which is influenced by market incentives. Anyone who wants to can start a business, provided he or she can come up with the required cash and meet the necessary regulatory requirements. Each year, about 700,000 businesses are started.

Don't think of business as something other than people. Businesses are ultimately made up of a group of people organized together to accomplish some end. Although corporations account for about 90 percent of all sales, in terms of numbers of businesses, most are one- or two-person operations. Home-based businesses are easy to start. All you have to do is say you're in business, and you are. However, some businesses require licenses, permits, and approvals from various government agencies. That's one reason why **entrepreneurship** (*the ability to organize and get something done*) is an important part of business.

What Do U.S. Firms Produce? Producing physical goods is only one of society's economic tasks. Another task is to provide services (activities done for others). Services do not involve producing a physical good. When you get your hair cut, you buy a service, not a good. Much of the cost of the physical goods we buy actually is not a cost of producing the good, but is a cost of one of the most important services: distribution, which includes payments associated with having the good where you want it when you want it. After a good is produced, it has to be transported to consumers, either indirectly through retailers or directly to consumers. If the good isn't at the right place at the right time, it can often be useless.

Let's consider an example: hot dogs at a baseball game. How many of us have been irked that a hot dog that costs 40 cents to fix at home costs $5.00 at a baseball game? The reason why the price can differ so much is that a hotdog at home isn't the same as a hot dog at a game and you are willing to pay the extra $4.60 to have the hot dog when and where you want it. *Distribution*—getting goods where you want them when you want them—is as important as production and is a central component of a service economy.

The importance of the service economy can be seen in modern technology companies. They provide information and methods of handling information, not physical goods. Computer operating systems such as Linux and Windows can be supplied over the Internet; no physical production is necessary. As the U.S. economy has evolved, the relative importance of services has increased. Today, services make up approximately 85 percent of the U.S. economy, compared to 20 percent in 1947, and services are likely to continue to rise in importance in the future.

Although businesses decide what to produce, they are guided by consumer sovereignty.

Consumer Sovereignty and Business To say that businesses decide what to produce isn't to say that **consumer sovereignty** (*the consumer's wishes determine what's produced*) doesn't reign in the United States. Businesses decide what to produce based on what they believe will sell. A key question a person in the United States generally asks about starting a business is: Can I make a profit from it? **Profit** is *what's left over from total revenues after all the appropriate costs have been subtracted.* Businesses that guess correctly what the consumer wants generally make a profit. Businesses that guess wrong generally operate at a loss.

Q-6 In the United States, the invisible hand ensures that only socially valuable businesses are started. True or false? Why?

People are free to start businesses for whatever purposes they want. No one asks them: "What's the social value of your term paper assistance business, your Twinkies business, your pornography business, or your textbook publishing business?" In the United States we rely on the market to channel individuals' desire to make a profit into the general good of society. That's the invisible hand at work. As long as the business violates no law and conforms to regulations, people in the United States are free to start whatever business they want, if they can get the money to finance it.

Q-7 Are most businesses in the United States corporations? If not, what are most businesses?

Forms of Business The three primary forms of business are sole proprietorships, partnerships, and corporations. Of the 29 million businesses in the United States, approximately 71 percent are sole proprietorships, 10 percent are partnerships, and 19 percent are corporations, as we see in Figure 3-2(a). In terms of total receipts, however, we get a quite different picture, with corporations far surpassing all other business forms, as Figure 3-2(b) shows.

Sole proprietorships—*businesses that have only one owner*—are the easiest to start and have the fewest bureaucratic hassles. **Partnerships**—*businesses with two or more owners*—create possibilities for sharing the burden, but they also create unlimited liability for each of the partners. **Corporations**—*businesses that are treated as a person, and*

FIGURE 3-2 (A AND B) **Forms of Business**

The charts divide firms by the type of ownership. Approximately 71 percent of businesses in the United States are sole proprietorships (**a**). In terms of annual receipts, however, corporations surpass all other forms (**b**).

Source: *Statistics of Income*, IRS, Summer 2008 (www.irs.ustreas.gov/taxstats).

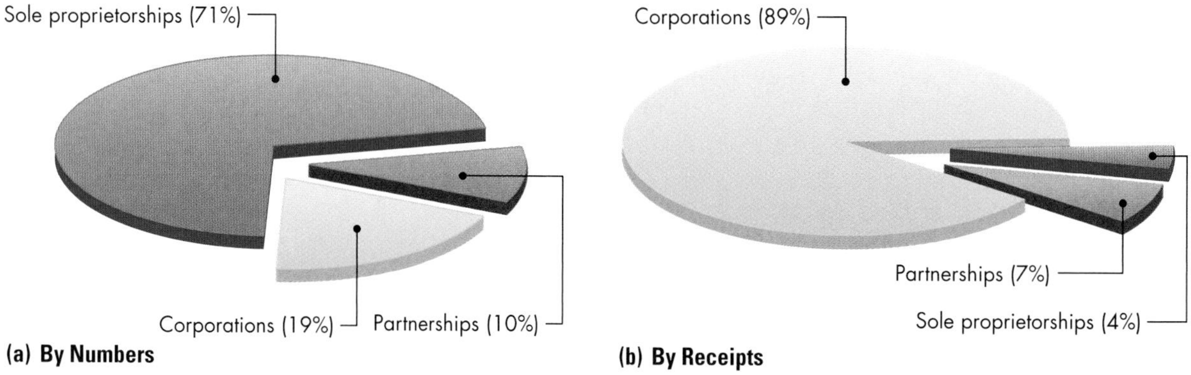

are legally owned by their stockholders, who are not liable for the actions of the corporate "person"—are the largest form of business when measured in terms of receipts. In corporations, ownership is separated from control of the firm. When a corporation is formed, it issues **stock** (*certificates of ownership in a company*), which is sold or given to individuals. Proceeds from the sale of that stock make up what is called the *equity capital* of a company.

Corporations were initially developed as institutions to make it easier for company owners (i.e., stockholders) to be separated from company management, but today many corporations exist because they offer tax and legal advantages to their owners. A corporation provides the owners with **limited liability**—*the stockholder's liability is limited to the amount the stockholder has invested in the company.* With the other two forms of business, owners can lose everything they possess even if they have only a small amount invested in the company, but in a corporation the owners can lose only what they have invested in that corporation. If you've invested $100, you can lose only $100. In the other kinds of business, even if you've invested only $100, you could lose everything; the business's losses must be covered by the individual owners. Corporations' limited liability makes it easier for them to attract investment capital. Corporations pay taxes, but they also offer their individual owners ways of legally avoiding taxes.[4]

A corporation provides the owner with limited liability.

The advantages and disadvantages of each form of business are summarized in the following table:

Advantages and Disadvantages of Various Forms of For-Profit Businesses

	Sole Proprietorship	Partnership	Corporation
Advantages	1. Minimum bureaucratic hassle 2. Direct control by owner	1. Ability to share work and risks 2. Relatively easy to form	1. No personal liability 2. Increasing ability to get funds 3. Ability to avoid personal income taxes
Disadvantages	1. Limited ability to get funds 2. Unlimited personal liability	1. Unlimited personal liability (even for partner's blunder) 2. Limited ability to get funds	1. Legal hassle to organize 2. Possible double taxation of income 3. Monitoring problems

Finance and Business Much of what you hear in the news about business concerns financial assets—assets that acquire value from an obligation of someone else to pay. Stocks are one example of a financial asset; bonds are another. Financial assets are traded in markets such as the New York Stock Exchange. Trading in financial markets can make people rich (or poor) quickly. Stocks and bonds also can provide a means through which corporations can finance expansions and new investments.

Trading in financial markets can make people rich (or poor) quickly.

An important tool investors use to decide where to invest is the accounting statements firms provide. From these, individuals judge how profitable firms are, and how profitable they are likely to be in the future. In the early 2000s, investors' trust in firms

[4]As laws have evolved, the sharp distinctions among forms of businesses have blurred. Today there are many types of corporations and types of partnerships that have varying degrees of limited liabilities.

was shattered by a series of accounting frauds, which led government to increase the regulatory control of business accounting practices.

E-Commerce and the Digital Economy Stocks were particularly important in the late 1990s to the development and expansion of new ".com" (read: dot-com) companies based on **e-commerce** (*buying and selling over the Internet*). E-commerce comes in a variety of forms, depending on who is buying and selling from whom. The following diagram provides the standard classifications. (The *B* refers to businesses and the C consumers.)

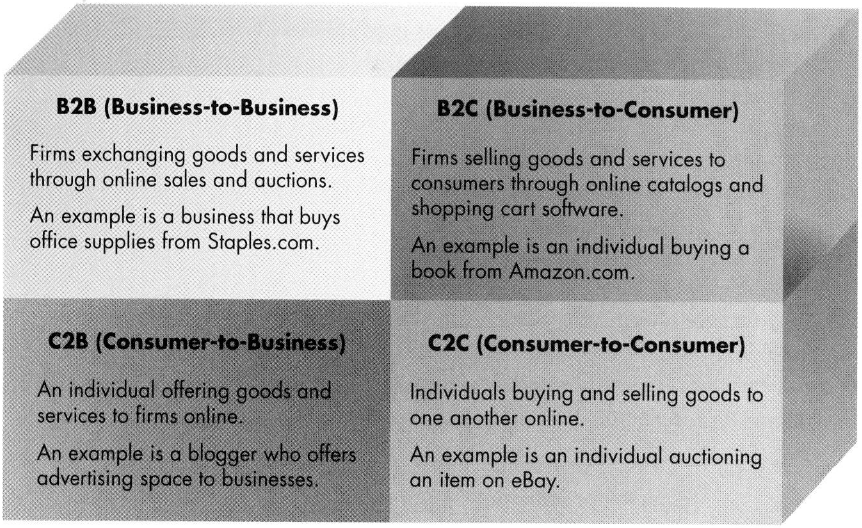

B2B (Business-to-Business)
Firms exchanging goods and services through online sales and auctions.
An example is a business that buys office supplies from Staples.com.
B2C (Business-to-Consumer)
Firms selling goods and services to consumers through online catalogs and shopping cart software.
An example is an individual buying a book from Amazon.com.
C2B (Consumer-to-Business)
An individual offering goods and services to firms online.
An example is a blogger who offers advertising space to businesses.
C2C (Consumer-to-Consumer)
Individuals buying and selling goods to one another online.
An example is an individual auctioning an item on eBay.

Notice that e-commerce includes business selling to business (B2B), business selling to consumers (B2C), consumers selling to business (C2B), and consumers selling to consumers (C2C). Although most of you see the influence of e-commerce in the B2C and C2C areas (Amazon.com and eBay are examples), B2B is the most important; it represents about 90 percent of e-commerce sales. With increasing frequency, companies are advertising specifications for needed parts and are accepting bids from a variety of new companies all over the world. The result is increased competition for existing suppliers, lower prices, and increased productivity—more output coming out of a given amount of inputs.

E-commerce is growing in importance.

E-commerce is growing in importance in the other areas too. More and more individuals are buying cars, books, and prescription drugs on the Internet. Even when they don't buy on the Internet, they will often compare prices on the Internet before making a purchase. Traditional "brick-and-mortar" firms that don't adapt to this new reality will not stay competitive and will be forced out of business. Car dealers, for example, now face consumers who have researched dealer prices and dealer costs on the Internet. Similarly, local bookstores must compete with Amazon.com, which they do by both reducing their prices and providing services that can be provided only on-site, such as book groups and cafés to enhance the shopping experience. Other brick-and-mortar companies are starting their own Internet divisions, and will combine with Internet providers, becoming "bricks-and-clicks" firms. For example, Sears bought Lands' End, and the combined company offers goods in Sears stores, over the Internet, and by catalog.

The impact of e-commerce is just beginning. The government, in fact, began to collect data about e-commerce only in 1999. Although e-commerce is growing 10 to 20 percent a year, just over 3 percent of purchases by consumers are made on the Internet. Sales among businesses on the Internet amount to over 25 percent of all business-to-business transactions, and are growing about 7 percent a year. The potential impact of e-commerce is enormous.

E-commerce brings people together at a low cost in a virtual marketplace where geographic location doesn't matter. By reducing the importance of location, e-commerce broadens the potential marketplace. No longer is Main Street, USA, or The Mall the market; the market can be as wide as the world.

E-commerce brings people together at a low cost in a virtual marketplace where geographic location doesn't matter.

For companies where location isn't important, e-commerce reduces the need for buildings, shelving, or a large retail staff, lowering the cost of starting up a new business and continuing to do business. Today, building a storefront can be as easy as registering a domain name and designing a home page. Because e-commerce creates a market without geographic boundaries, companies can search for the lowest-cost labor, hiring employees as far away as India, and sell goods to customers thousands of miles away.

Consumers can search for the lowest price from hundreds of virtual stores and, with a single click of a button, buy it. E-commerce allows small specialty firms to compete in niche markets, where previously they could not. For example, in my small Vermont town, a company exists that sells bow ties (Beau Ties Ltd.) all over the world, even though probably a total of five people in Middlebury wear bow ties. (I'm definitely not one of them.) By broadening the market and increasing the amount of information available, e-commerce places greater competitive pressure on firms. As e-commerce continues to evolve, existing firms will face greater pressure to lower their costs, lower their prices, and redefine their business models. E-commerce's long-run effect on the U.S. economy is uncertain, but what is not uncertain is that it will have an impact. To understand our economy is to understand that it has always been evolving and will continue to evolve in the future.

Households

The second classification we'll consider in this overview of U.S. economic institutions is households. **Households** (*groups of individuals living together and making joint decisions*) are the most powerful economic institution. They ultimately control government and business, the other two economic institutions. Households' votes in the political arena determine government policy; their decisions about supplying labor and capital determine what businesses will have available to work with; and their spending decisions or expenditures (the "votes" they cast with their dollars) determine what business will be able to sell.

In the economy, households vote with their dollars.

The Power of Households While the ultimate power does in principle reside with the people and households, we, the people, have assigned much of that power to representatives. As I discussed above, corporations are only partially responsive to owners of their stocks, and much of that ownership is once-removed from individuals. Ownership of 1,000 shares in a company with a total of 2 million shares isn't going to get you any influence over the corporation's activities. As a stockholder, you simply accept what the corporation does.

A major decision that corporations make independently of their stockholders concerns what to produce. True, ultimately we, the people, decide whether we will buy what business produces, but business spends a lot of money telling us what services we want, what products make us "with it," what books we want to read, and the like. Most economists believe that consumer sovereignty reigns—that we are not fooled or controlled by advertising. Still, it is an open question in some economists' minds whether we, the people, control business or the business representatives control people.

Consumer sovereignty reigns, but it works indirectly by influencing businesses.

Because of this assignment of power to other institutions, in many spheres of the economy households are not active producers of output but merely passive recipients of income, primarily in their role as suppliers of labor.

Suppliers of Labor The largest source of household income is wages and salaries (the income households get from labor). Households supply the labor with which businesses produce and government governs. The total U.S. labor force is about 154 million people, about 5.8 percent (9 million) of whom were unemployed in 2008. The average U.S. workweek is 44.1 hours for males and 41.1 hours for females. The average pay in the United States was $766 per week for males and $614 for females, which translates to $17.37 per hour for males and $14.94 for females. Of course, that average represents enormous variability and depends on the occupation and region of the country where one is employed. For example, lawyers often earn $100,000 per year; physicians earn about $150,000 per year; and CEOs of large corporations often make $2 million per year or more. A beginning McDonald's employee generally makes about $13,000 per year.

The table below shows predicted growth rates of certain jobs. Notice that many of the fastest-growing jobs are in service industries; many of the fastest declining are in manufacturing and agriculture. This is not surprising, since the United States has become largely a service economy.

Fastest-Growing Jobs*	Fastest-Declining Jobs*
Network systems and data communications analysis (53%)	Photographic processing (−50%)
Home health aides (51%)	File clerks (−41%)
Computer software engineers (49%)	Sewing machine operators (−27%)
Veterinary technologists (45%)	Electrical and electronic equipment assemblers (−27%)

*Projection through 2016, based on moderate growth assumptions.

Source: *Employment and Earnings*, Bureau of Labor Statistics, and *Occupational Outlook Handbook*, 2008–2009 (http://stats.bls.gov).

Other Roles of Households Besides being suppliers of labor, households make a significant number of the decisions in the economy. For example, households decide how much schooling to get and what to buy. They control most housing investment and the housing stock, which is half the capital stock of the country. In the aggregate, households are the driving force for much of the economy.

Government

The third major U.S. economic institution I'll consider is government. Government plays two general roles in the economy. It's both a referee (setting the rules that determine relations between business and households) and an actor (collecting money in taxes and spending that money on projects such as defense and education). Let's first consider government's role as an actor.

Web Note 3.3
Government Web Sites

Government as an Actor The United States has a federal government system, which means we have various levels of government (federal, state, and local), each with its own powers. Together they consume about 15 percent of the country's total output and employ over 22 million individuals. The various levels of government also have a number of programs that redistribute income through taxation and social welfare and assistance programs designed to help specific groups.

State and local governments employ over 19 million people and spend about $2.5 trillion a year. As you can see in Figure 3-3(a), state and local governments get much of their income from taxes: property taxes, sales taxes, and state and local income taxes. They

FIGURE 3-3 (A AND B) **Income and Expenditures of State and Local Governments**

The charts give you a sense of the importance of state and local governments—where they get (**a**) and where they spend (**b**) their revenues.

Source: *State and Local Government Finance Estimates*, Bureau of the Census (www.census.gov).

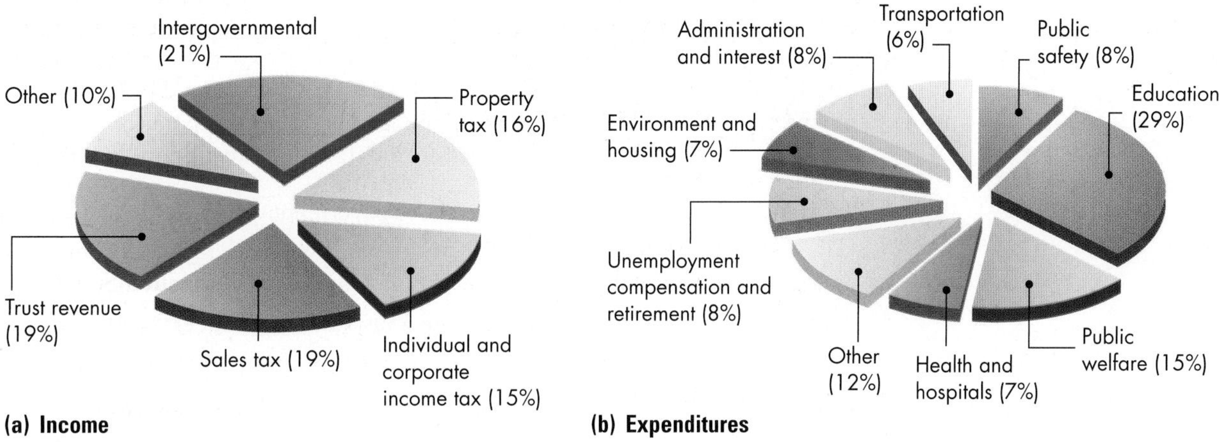

spend their tax revenues on public welfare, administration, education (education through high school is available free in U.S. public schools), and roads, as Figure 3-3(b) shows.

Q-8 The largest percentage of federal expenditures is in what general category?

Probably the best way to get an initial feel for the federal government and its size is to look at the various categories of its tax revenues and expenditures in Figure 3-4(a). Notice income taxes make up about 44 percent of the federal government's revenue, and Social Security taxes make up about 36 percent. That's 80 percent of the federal government's revenues, most of which show up as a deduction from your paycheck. In Figure 3-4(b), notice that the federal government's two largest categories of spending are income security and health and education, with expenditures on national defense close behind.

FIGURE 3-4 (A AND B) **Income and Expenditures of the Federal Government**

The pie charts show the sources and uses of federal government revenue. It is important to note that, when the government runs a deficit, expenditures exceed income and the difference is made up by borrowing, so the size of the income and expenditure pies may not be equal.

Source: *Survey of Current Business*, 2008, Bureau of Economic Analysis (www.bea.doc.gov).

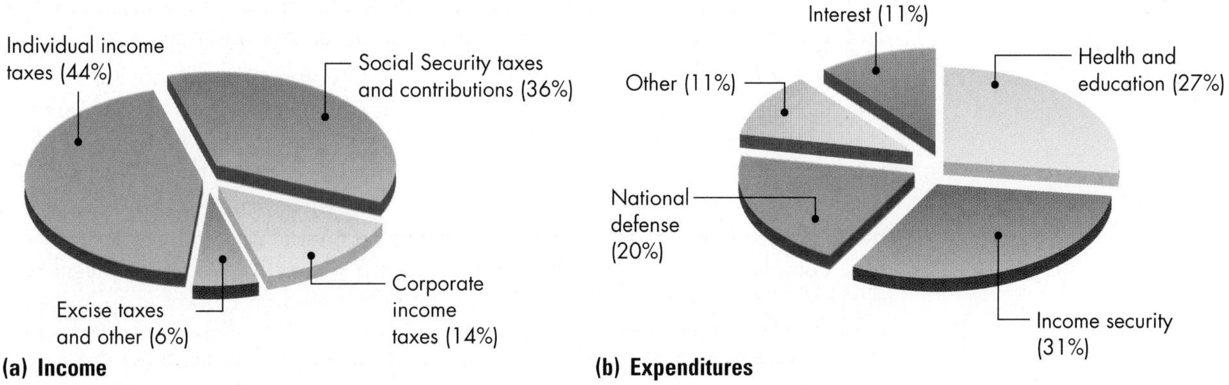

Government as a Referee Even if government spending made up only a small proportion of total expenditures, government would still be central to the study of economics. The reason is that, in a market economy, government sets the rules of interaction between households and businesses, and acts as a referee, changing the rules when it sees fit. Government decides whether economic forces will be allowed to operate freely.

Some examples of U.S. laws regulating the interaction between households and businesses today are

1. Businesses are not free to hire and fire whomever they want. They must comply with equal opportunity and labor laws. Even closing a plant requires 60 days' notice for many kinds of firms.
2. Many working conditions are subject to government regulation: safety rules, wage rules, overtime rules, hours-of-work rules, and the like.
3. Businesses cannot meet with other businesses to agree on prices they will charge.
4. In some businesses, workers must join a union to work at certain jobs.

Most of these laws evolved over time. Up until the 1930s, household members, in their roles as workers and consumers, had few rights. Businesses were free to hire and fire at will and, if they chose, to deceive and take advantage of consumers.

Over time, new laws to curb business abuses have been passed, and government agencies have been formed to enforce these laws. Many people think the pendulum has swung too far the other way. They believe businesses are saddled with too many regulatory burdens.

One big question that I'll address throughout this book is: What referee role should the government play in an economy? For example, should government use its taxing powers to redistribute income from the rich to the poor? Should it allow mergers between companies? Should it regulate air traffic? Should it regulate prices? Should it attempt to stabilize fluctuations of aggregate income?

In its role as both an actor and a referee, government plays a variety of specific roles in the economy. These include

1. Providing a stable set of institutions and rules.
2. Promoting effective and workable competition.
3. Correcting for externalities.
4. Ensuring economic stability and growth.
5. Providing public goods.
6. Adjusting for undesirable market results.

Provide a Stable Set of Institutions and Rules A basic role of government is to provide a stable institutional framework that includes the set of laws specifying what can and cannot be done as well as a mechanism to enforce those laws. For example, if someone doesn't pay you, you can't go take what you are owed; you have to go through the government court system. The government restricts individuals from enforcing contracts; it retains that role for itself. Before people conduct business, they need to know the rules of the game and have a reasonable belief about what those rules will be in the future. These rules can initially develop spontaneously, but as society becomes more complex, the rules must be formalized into written laws within a legal system; enforcement mechanisms must be established. The modern market economy requires enforceable complex contractual arrangements among individuals. Where governments don't provide a stable institutional framework, as often happens in developing and transitional countries, economic activity is difficult; usually such economies are stagnant. Zimbabwe in the early 2000s is an example. As various groups fought for political control, the Zimbabwe economy stagnated.

Promote Effective and Workable Competition In a market economy, the pressure to monopolize—for one firm to try to control the market—and competition are always in conflict, and the government must decide what role it is to play in protecting or promoting competition. Thus, when Microsoft gained a monopolistic control of the computer operating system market with Windows, the U.S. government took the company to court and challenged that monopoly.

Historically, U.S. sentiment runs against **monopoly power**—*the ability of individuals or firms currently in business to prevent other individuals or firms from entering the same kind of business.* Monopoly power gives existing firms and individuals the ability to raise their prices. Similarly, individuals' or firms' ability to enter freely into business activities is generally seen as good. Government's job is to promote competition and prevent excess monopoly power from limiting competition.

What makes this a difficult function for government is that most individuals and firms believe that competition is far better for the other guy than it is for themselves, that their own monopolies are necessary monopolies, and that competition facing them is unfair competition. For example, most farmers support competition, but these same farmers also support government farm subsidies (payments by government to producers based on production levels) and import restrictions. Likewise, most firms support competition, but these same firms also support tariffs, which protect them from foreign competition. Most professionals, such as architects and engineers, support competition, but they also support professional licensing, which limits the number of competitors who can enter their field. Now, as you will see when reading the newspapers, there are always arguments for limiting entry into fields. The job of the government is to determine whether these arguments are strong enough to overcome the negative effects those limitations have on competition.

Correct for Externalities When two people freely enter into a trade or agreement, they both believe that they will benefit from the trade. But unless they're required to do so, traders are unlikely to take into account any effect that an action may have on a third party. Economists call *the effect of a decision on a third party not taken into account by the decision maker* an **externality.** An externality can be positive (in which case society as a whole benefits from the trade between the two parties) or negative (in which case society as a whole is harmed by the trade between the two parties).

An example of a positive externality is education. When someone educates herself or himself, all society benefits, since better-educated people usually make better citizens and are better equipped to figure out new approaches to solving problems—approaches that benefit society as a whole. An example of a negative externality is pollution. Air conditioners emit a small amount of chlorofluorocarbons into the earth's atmosphere and contribute to the destruction of the ozone layer. Since the ozone layer protects all living things by filtering some of the sun's harmful ultraviolet light rays, a thinner layer of ozone can contribute to cancer and other harmful or fatal conditions. Neither the firms that produce the air conditioners nor the consumers who buy them take those effects into account. This means that the destruction of the ozone layer is an externality—the result of an effect that is not taken into account by market participants.

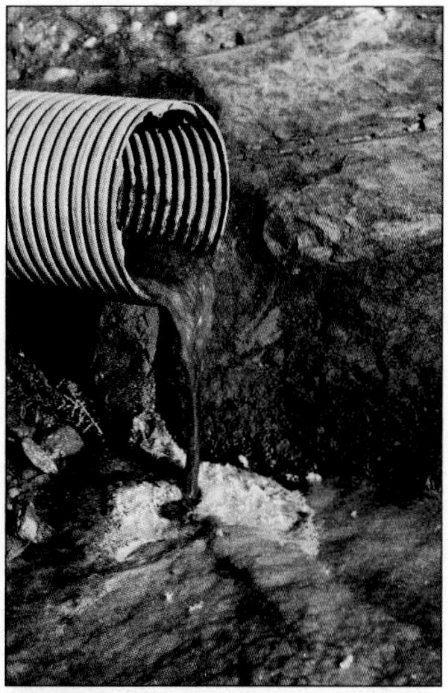

The government may be able to help correct for externalities.

When there are externalities, there is a potential role for government to adjust the market result. If one's goal is to benefit society as much as possible, actions with positive externalities should be encouraged and actions with negative externalities should be discouraged. Governments can step in and change the rules so that the actors must take into account the effect of their actions on society as a whole. I emphasize that the role is a potential one for two reasons. The first is that government often has difficulty dealing with externalities in such a way that society gains. For example, even if the U.S. government totally banned products that emit chlorofluorocarbons, other countries might not do the same and the ozone layer would continue to be destroyed. The second reason is that government is an institution that reflects, and is often guided by, politics and vested interests. It's not clear that, given the political realities, government intervention to correct externalities would improve the situation. In later chapters I'll have a lot more to say about government's role in correcting for externalities.

Ensure Economic Stability and Growth In addition to providing general stability, government has the potential role of providing economic stability. Most people would agree that if it's possible, government should prevent large fluctuations in the level of economic activity, maintain a relatively constant price level, and provide an economic environment conducive to economic growth. These aims, which became the goals of the U.S. government in 1946 when the Employment Act was passed, are generally considered macroeconomic goals. They're justified as appropriate aims for government to pursue because they involve **macroeconomic externalities** (*externalities that affect the levels of unemployment, inflation, or growth in the economy as a whole*).

A macroeconomic externality is the effect of an individual decision that affects the levels of unemployment, inflation, or growth in an economy as a whole but is not taken into account by the individual decision maker.

Here's how a macro externality could occur. When individuals decide how much to spend, they don't take into account the effects of their decision on others; thus, there may be too much or too little spending. Too little spending often leads to unemployment. But in making their spending decision, people don't take into account the fact that spending less might create unemployment. So their spending decisions can involve a macro externality. Similarly, when people raise their price and don't consider the effect on inflation, they too might be creating a macro externality.

Provide Public Goods Another role for government is to supply public goods. A **public good** is *a good that if supplied to one person must be supplied to all and whose consumption by one individual does not prevent its consumption by another individual*. In contrast, a **private good** is *a good that, when consumed by one individual, cannot be consumed by another individual*. An example of a private good is an apple; once I eat that apple, no one else can consume it. An example of a public good is national defense, which, if supplied to one, will also protect others. In order to supply defense, governments must force people to pay for it with taxes, rather than leaving it to the market to supply it.

There are very few pure public goods, but many goods have public good aspects to them, and, in general, economists use the term *public good* to describe goods that are most efficiently provided collectively rather than privately. Parks, playgrounds, roads, and (as noted above) national defense are examples. Let's consider national defense more closely. For technological reasons, national defense must protect all individuals in an area; a missile system cannot protect some houses in an area without protecting others nearby.

Everyone agrees that national defense is needed, but not everyone takes part in it. If someone else defends the country, you're defended for free; you can be a **free rider**—*a person who gets a benefit but does not contribute to paying for the cost of that benefit*. Because self-interested people would like to enjoy the benefits of national defense while letting someone else pay for it, everyone has an incentive to be a free rider. But if everyone tries to be a free rider, there won't be any national defense. In such cases, government can step in and require that everyone pay part of the cost of national defense, reducing the free rider problem.

Adjust for Undesirable Market Results A controversial role for government is to adjust the results of the market when those market results are seen as socially undesirable. Government redistributes income, taking it away from some individuals and giving it to others whom it sees as more deserving or more in need. In doing so, it attempts to see that the outcomes of trades are fair. Determining what's fair is a difficult philosophical question that economists can't answer. That question is for the people, through the government, to decide.

An example of this role involves having government decide what's best for people, independently of their desires. The market allows individuals to decide. But what if people don't know what's best for themselves? Or what if they do know but don't act on that knowledge? For example, people might know that addictive drugs are bad for them, but because of peer pressure, or because they just don't care, they may take drugs anyway. Government action prohibiting such activities through laws or high taxes may then be warranted. *Goods or activities that government believes are bad for people even though they choose to use the goods or engage in the activities* are called **demerit goods or activities.** Illegal drugs are a demerit good and using addictive drugs is a demerit activity.

Alternatively, there are some activities that government believes are good for people, even if people may not choose to engage in them. For example, government may believe that going to the opera or contributing to charity is a good activity. But in the United States only a small percentage of people go to the opera, and not everyone in the United States contributes to charity. Similarly, government may believe that whole-wheat bread is more nutritious than white bread. But many consumers prefer white bread. Goods like whole-wheat bread and activities like contributing to charity are known as **merit goods or activities**—*goods and activities that government believes are good for you even though you may not choose to engage in the activities or to consume the goods*. Government sometimes provides support for them through subsidies or tax benefits.

With merit and demerit goods, individuals are assumed to be doing what is not in their self-interest.

Choice Architecture Economists are hesitant to have government (or anyone) tell people what is best for them, but behavioral economists argue that government might be able to "nudge" people's choices in a positive way. What they have found is that how choices are presented to people affects the choices people make. Consider choosing whether your homework will count 10 or 20 percent of your final grade. Which option do students prefer? Behavioral economists have found that the answer is unclear. If students are told that their homework will count 10 percent unless they e-mail their professor and ask it to count 20 percent, most students choose the 10 percent option. But if that same professor had told students that homework would count 20 percent unless a student e-mails the professor and asks it to count 10 percent, most students will choose the 20 percent option. This is an example of what is called the *default option bias*: people tend to choose whatever is presented as the default option. Behavioral economists argue that by structuring the default option for choices that people make in a "positive" way, people's choices can be positively influenced. At a minimum they argue that economic policy should take into account the structure of choices people face.

Market Failures and Government Failures The reasons for government intervention are often summed up in the phrase *market failure*. **Market failures** are *situations in which the market does not lead to a desired result*. In the real world, market failures are pervasive—the market is always failing in one way or another. But the fact that there are market failures does not mean that government intervention will improve the situation. There are also **government failures**—*situations in which the government*

Q-9 If there is an externality, does that mean that the government should intervene in the market to adjust for that externality?

ADDED DIMENSION

Our International Competitors

The world economy is often divided into three main areas or trading blocs: the Americas, Europe and Africa, and East Asia. These trading blocs are shown in the map below.

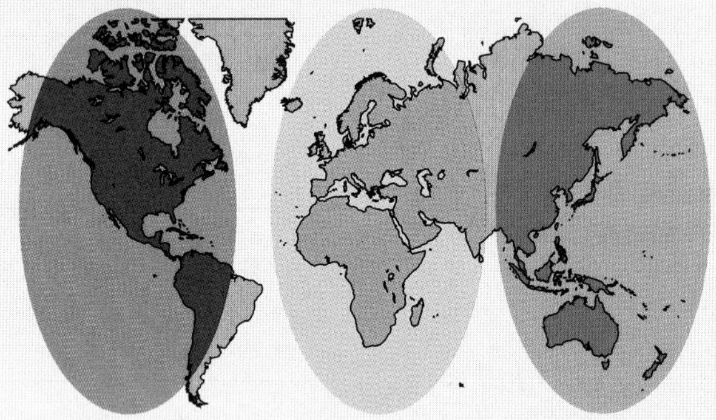

Each area has a major currency. In the Americas, it is the dollar; in Europe, it is the euro, a currency recently created by the European Union; and in East Asia, it is the Japanese yen. These areas are continually changing; the EU recently expanded to 27 countries, incorporating many of the countries of Eastern Europe. China's economy has been growing fast and, given the size of its population, is likely to overtake Japan as the key Asian economy in the coming decades.

The accompanying table gives you a sense of the similarities and differences in the economies of the United States, China, and the European Union.

	United States	China	European Union
Area (square miles)	3,537,438	3,705,407	1,535,286
Population	304 million	1.3 billion	491 million
GDP, 2008*	$13.8 trillion	$7 trillion	$14.4 trillion
Percentage of world output	21%	11%	22%
GDP per capita	$45,800	$7,690	$32,300
Natural resources	Coal, copper, lead, and others	Coal, iron ore	Coal, iron ore, natural gas, fish, and others
Exports as a percentage of GDP	8%	17%	9%
Imports as a percentage of GDP	14%	13%	10%
Currency Value (as of April 2009)	Dollar ($1 = $1)	Yuan (¥6.84 = $1)	Euro (€0.74 = $1)

*Calculated using purchasing power parity.

Source: *CIA World Factbook 2009* (www.cia.gov); and current exchange rate tables. Currency changes can affect GDP figures. GDP updated by the author.

intervenes and makes things worse. Government failures are pervasive in the government—the government is always failing in one way or another. So real-world policy makers usually end up choosing which failure—market failure or government failure—will be least problematic.

Global Institutions

What we've done so far in this chapter is to put the U.S. economy in historical and institutional perspective. In this last section, we briefly put it into perspective relative to the world economy. By doing so, we gain a number of insights into the U.S. economy. The U.S. economy makes up 21 percent of world output and consumption, a percentage that is much larger than its relative size by geographic area (6 percent of the world's land mass) or by population (less than 5 percent of the world population). Second, it is becoming more integrated; it is impossible to talk about U.S. economic institutions without considering how those institutions integrate with the world economy.

Global Corporations

Consider corporations. Most large corporations today are not U.S., German, or Japanese corporations; they are **global corporations** (*corporations with substantial operations on both the production and sales sides in more than one country*). Just because a car has a Japanese or German name doesn't mean that it was produced abroad. Many Japanese and German companies now have manufacturing plants in the United States, and many U.S. firms have manufacturing plants abroad. Others, such as Chrysler and Daimler Benz, merged and then split up again. When goods are produced by global corporations, corporate names don't always tell much about where a good is produced. As global corporations' importance has grown, most manufacturing decisions are made in reference to the international market, not the U.S. domestic market. This means that the consumer sovereignty that guides decisions of firms is becoming less and less U.S. consumer sovereignty, and more and more global consumer sovereignty.

Global corporations are corporations with substantial operations on both the production and sales sides in more than one country.

Global corporations offer enormous benefits for countries. They create jobs; they bring new ideas and new technologies to a country; and they provide competition for domestic companies, keeping them on their toes. But global corporations also pose a number of problems for governments. One is their implication for domestic and international policy. A domestic corporation exists within a country and can be dealt with using policy measures within that country. A global corporation exists within many countries and there is no global government to regulate or control it. If it doesn't like the policies in one country—say taxes are too high or regulations too tight—it can shift its operations to other countries.

WWW Web Note 3.4
Global 500

Coordinating Global Issues

Global economic issues differ from national economic issues because national economies have governments to referee disputes among players in the economy; global economies do not; no international government exists. Some argue that we need a global government to oversee global businesses. But no such government exists. The closest institution there is to a world government is the United Nations (UN), which, according to critics, is simply a debating society. It has no ability to tax and no ability to impose its will separate from the political and military power of its members. When the United States opposes a UN mandate, it can, and often does, ignore it. Hence, international problems must be dealt with through negotiation, consensus, bullying, and concessions.

Governments, however, have developed a variety of international institutions to promote negotiations and coordinate economic relations among countries. Besides the United Nations, these include the World Bank, the World Court, and the International Monetary Fund (IMF). These organizations have a variety of goals. For example, the World Bank, a multinational, international financial institution, works with developing countries to secure low-interest loans, channeling such loans to them to foster economic growth. The International Monetary Fund (IMF), a multinational, international financial institution, is concerned primarily with monetary issues. It deals with international financial arrangements. When developing countries encountered financial problems in the 1980s and had large international debts that they could not pay, the IMF helped work on repayment plans.

Governments have developed international institutions to promote negotiations and coordinate economic relations among countries. Some are:
- the UN
- the World Bank
- the World Court
- the International Monetary Fund.

Countries also have developed global and regional organizations whose job it is to coordinate trade among countries and reduce trade barriers. On the international level, the World Trade Organization (WTO) works to reduce trade barriers among countries. On the regional level, there are the European Union (EU), which is an organization of European countries that developed out of a trade association devoted to reducing trade barriers among member countries; the North American Free Trade Agreement (NAFTA),

Countries have developed global and regional organizations to coordinate trade and reduce trade barriers. Some are:
- the WTO
- the EU
- NAFTA.

an organization devoted to reducing trade barriers between the United States, Mexico, and Canada; and Mercosur, an organization devoted to reducing trade barriers among North, Central, and South American countries.

In addition to these formal institutions, there are informal meetings of various countries. These include the Group of Five, which meets to promote negotiations and to coordinate economic relations among countries. The Five are Japan, Germany, Britain, France, and the United States. The Group of Eight also meets to promote negotiations and coordinate economic relations among countries. The Eight are the five countries just named plus Canada, Italy, and Russia.

Since governmental membership in international organizations is voluntary, their power is limited.

Since governmental membership in international organizations is voluntary, their power is limited. When the United States doesn't like a World Court ruling, it simply states that it isn't going to follow the ruling. When the United States is unhappy with what the United Nations is doing, it withholds some of its dues. Other countries do the same from time to time. Other member countries complain but can do little to force compliance. It doesn't work that way domestically. If you decide you don't like U.S. policy and refuse to pay your taxes, you'll wind up in jail.

Q-10 If the United States chooses not to follow a World Court decision, what are the consequences?

What keeps nations somewhat in line when it comes to international rules is a moral tradition: Countries want to (or at least want to look as if they want to) do what's "right." Countries will sometimes follow international rules to keep international opinion favorable to them. But perceived national self-interest often overrides international scruples.

Conclusion

This has been a whirlwind introduction to economic institutions and their role in the economy. Each of them—business, households, and government—is important, and to understand what happens in the economy, one must have a sense of how these institutions work and the role they play. In the remainder of the book we won't discuss institutions much as we concentrate on presenting economic analysis. I rely upon you to integrate the analysis with institutions, as you apply the economic analysis and reasoning that you learn to the real world.

Summary

- A market economy is an economic system based on private property and the market. It gives private property rights to individuals and relies on market forces to solve the *what, how,* and *for whom* problems.
- In a market economy, price is the mechanism through which people's desires are coordinated and goods are rationed. The U.S. economy today is a market economy.
- In principle, under socialism society solves the *what, how,* and *for whom* problems in the best interest of the individuals in society. It is based on individuals' goodwill toward one another.
- In practice, socialism is an economic system based on government ownership of the means of production, with economic activity governed by central planning. Socialism in practice is sometimes called a command economy.
- The predominant market-based system during the early 1900s was capitalism, an economic system based on the market in which the ownership of production resided with a small group of individuals called capitalists.
- In feudalism, tradition rules; in mercantilism, the government rules; in capitalism, the market rules.

- Economic systems are in a constant state of evolution.
- A diagram of the U.S. market economy shows the connections among businesses, households, and government. It also shows the U.S. economic connection to other countries.
- In the United States, businesses make the *what, how,* and *for whom* decisions.
- Although businesses decide what to produce, they succeed or fail depending on their ability to meet consumers' desires. That's consumer sovereignty.
- The three main forms of business are corporations, sole proprietorships, and partnerships. Each has its advantages and disadvantages.
- Although households are the most powerful economic institution, they have assigned much of their power to government and business. Economics focuses on households' role as the supplier of labor.
- Government plays two general roles in the economy: (1) as a referee and (2) as an actor.
- Six roles of government are to (1) provide a stable set of institutions and rules, (2) promote effective and workable competition, (3) correct for externalities, (4) ensure economic stability and growth, (5) provide public goods, and (6) adjust for undesirable market results.
- To understand the U.S. economy, one must understand its role in the world economy.
- Global corporations are corporations with significant operations in more than one country. They are increasing in importance.
- Global economic issues differ from national economic issues because national economies have governments. The global economy does not.

Key Terms

business *(61)*
capitalism *(57)*
consumer sovereignty *(62)*
corporation *(62)*
demerit good or activity *(71)*
e-commerce *(64)*
entrepreneurship *(61)*
externality *(69)*
feudalism *(59)*
free rider *(70)*
global corporation *(73)*
government failure *(71)*
households *(65)*
Industrial Revolution *(59)*
institutions *(55)*
limited liability *(63)*
macroeconomic externality *(70)*
market economy *(56)*
market failure *(71)*
mercantilism *(59)*
merit good or activity *(71)*
monopoly power *(69)*
partnership *(62)*
private good *(70)*
private property right *(56)*
profit *(62)*
public good *(70)*
socialism *(57)*
sole proprietorship *(62)*
stock *(63)*

Questions and Exercises

Connect ECONOMICS

1. In a market economy, what is the central coordinating mechanism? LO1, LO2
2. In a centrally planned socialist economy, what is the central coordinating mechanism? LO2
3. How does a market economy solve the what, how, and for whom to produce problems? LO2
4. How does a centrally planned socialist economy solve the what, how, and for whom to produce problems? LO2
5. Is capitalism or socialism the better economic system? Why? LO2
6. True or false? As economic systems have evolved, there has been less need for planning. LO2
7. Why does an economy's strength ultimately reside in its people? LO3
8. What are the qualities of the Internet that have put competitive pressures on businesses? LO4
9. Why is entrepreneurship a central part of any business? LO4
10. You're starting a software company in which you plan to sell software to your fellow students. What form of business organization would you choose? Why? LO4
11. What are the two largest categories of federal government expenditures? LO6

12. A good measure of a country's importance to the world economy is its area and population. True or false? Why? LO7
13. What are the six roles of government listed in the text? LO6
14. You've set up the rules for a game and started the game but now realize that the rules are unfair. Should you change the rules? LO6
15. Say the government establishes rights to pollute so that without a pollution permit you aren't allowed to emit pollutants into the air, water, or soil. Firms are allowed to buy and sell these rights. In what way will this correct for an externality? LO6
16. Give an example of a merit good, a demerit good, a public good, and a good that involves an externality. LO6
17. What are two organizations that countries can use to coordinate economic relations and reduce trade barriers? LO7
18. Why are international organizations limited in their effectiveness? LO7

Questions from Alternative Perspectives

1. Friedrich Hayek, the man quoted at the start of the chapter, is an Austrian economist who won a Nobel Prize in economics. He argued that government intervention is difficult to contain. Suppose central planners have decided to financially support all children with food vouchers, free day care, and public school.
   a. What problems might this create?
   b. How might this lead to further interference by central planners into family choices? (Austrian)
2. In his *The Social Contract*, Jean-Jacques Rousseau argued that "no State has ever been founded without a religious basis [but] the law of Christianity at bottom does more harm by weakening than good by strengthening the constitution of the State." What does he mean by that, and is he correct? (Religious)
3. In economics, a household is defined as a group of individuals making joint decisions as though acting as one person.
   a. How do you think decisions are actually made about things like consumption and allocation of time within the household?
   b. Does bargaining take place?
   c. If so, what gives an individual power to bargain effectively for his or her preferences?
   d. Do individuals act cooperatively within the family and competitively everywhere else?
   e. Does this make sense? (Feminist)
4. This chapter emphasized the importance of the relationship between how the economic system is organized and value systems. Knowing that how I raise my child will greatly shape how he or she will ultimately fit into the social and economic process, should I raise my child to be selfless, compassionate, and dedicated to advancing the well-being of others, knowing she will probably be poor; or shall I raise her to be self-centered, uncaring, and greedy to increase her chances to acquire personal fortune? Which decision is just and why? (Institutionalist)
5. The text discusses consumer sovereignty and suggests that it guides the market choices.
   a. Is consumer sovereignty a myth or reality in today's consumer culture?
   b. Do consumers "direct" the economy as suggested by the text, or has invention become the mother of necessity, as Thorstein Veblen once quipped?
   c. If the consumer is not sovereign, then who is and what does that imply for economics? (Radical)

Issues to Ponder

1. What arguments can you give for supporting a socialist organization of a family and a market-based organization of the economy? LO2
2. Economists Edward Lazear and Robert Michael have calculated that the average family spends two and a half times as much on each adult as they do on each child.
   a. Does this mean that children are deprived and that the distribution is unfair?
   b. Do you think these percentages change with family income? If so, how?
   c. Do you think that the allocation would be different in a family in a command economy than in a capitalist economy? Why? LO2
3. One of the specific problems socialist economies had was keeping up with capitalist countries technologically. (Difficult)
   a. Can you think of any reason inherent in a centrally planned economy that would make innovation difficult?
   b. Can you think of any reason inherent in a capitalist country that would foster innovation?

c. Joseph Schumpeter, a famous Harvard economist of the 1930s, predicted that as firms in capitalist societies grew in size, they would innovate less. Can you suggest what his argument might have been?
d. Schumpeter's prediction did not come true. Modern capitalist economies have had enormous innovations. Can you provide explanations as to why? LO2

4. Tom Rollins heads a company called Teaching Co. He has taped lectures at the top universities, packaged the lectures on DVD and CD, and sells them for $90 and $150 per eight-hour series.
    a. Discuss whether such an idea could be expanded to include college courses that one could take at home.
    b. What are the technical, social, and economic issues involved?
    c. If it is technically possible and cost-effective, will the new venture be a success? LO3, LO4
5. Go to a store in your community.
    a. Ask what limitations the owners faced in starting their business.
    b. Were these limitations necessary?
    c. Should there have been more or fewer limitations?
    d. Under what heading of reasons for government intervention would you put each of the limitations?
    e. Ask what kinds of taxes the business pays and what benefits it believes it gets for those taxes.
    f. Is it satisfied with the existing situation? Why? What would it change? LO4
6. A market system is often said to be based on consumer sovereignty—the consumer determines what's to be produced. Yet business decides what's to be produced. Can these two views be reconciled? How? If not, why? LO5
7. How might individuals disagree about the government's role in intervening in the market for merit, demerit, and public goods? LO6
8. Discuss the concepts of market failure and government failure in relation to operas. LO6
9. In trade talks with Australia, the United States proposed that Australia cannot regulate the amount of foreign content on new media without first consulting the United States. Actress Bridie Carter of *McLeod's Daughters* argued against adopting the trade agreement, arguing the agreement trades away Australia's cultural identity. This highlights one of the effects of globalization: the loss of variety based on cultural differences. How important should such cultural identity issues be in trade negotiations? LO7

Answers to Margin Questions

1. He is wrong. Property rights are required for a market to operate. Once property rights are allocated, the market will allocate goods, but the market cannot distribute the property rights that are required for the market to operate. *(56)*
2. Capitalism places much more emphasis on fostering individualism. Socialism tries to develop a system in which the individual's needs are placed second to society's needs. *(57)*
3. Most families allocate basic needs through control and command. The parents do (or try to do) the controlling and commanding. Generally parents are well-intentioned, trying to meet their perception of their children's needs. However, some family activities that are not basic needs might be allocated through the market. For example, if one child wants a go-cart and is willing to do extra work at home in order to get it, go-carts might be allocated through the market, with the child earning chits that can be used for such nonessentials. *(57)*
4. In theory, socialism is an economic system based upon individuals' goodwill. In practice, socialism followed the Soviet model and involved central planning and government ownership of the primary means of production. *(58)*
5. Market economies are generally broken up into businesses, households, and government. *(60)*
6. False. In the United States, individuals are free to start any type of business they want, provided it doesn't violate the law. The invisible hand sees to it that only those businesses that customers want earn a profit. The others lose money and eventually go out of business, so in that sense only businesses that customers want stay in business. *(62)*
7. As can be seen in Figure 3-2, most businesses in the United States are sole proprietorships, not corporations. Corporations, however, generate the most revenue. *(62)*
8. The largest percentage of federal expenditures is for income security. *(67)*
9. Not necessarily. The existence of an externality creates the possibility that government intervention might help. But there are also government failures in which the government intervenes and makes things worse. *(71)*
10. The World Court has no enforcement mechanism. Thus, when a country refuses to follow the court's decisions, the country cannot be directly punished except through indirect international pressures. *(74)*

APPENDIX A

The History of Economic Systems

In the text I made the distinction between market and economic forces: Economic forces have always existed—they operate in all aspects of our lives—but market forces have not always existed. Markets are social creations societies use to coordinate individuals' actions. Markets developed, sometimes spontaneously, sometimes by design, because they offered a better life for at least some—and usually a large majority of—individuals in a society.

To understand why markets developed, it is helpful to look briefly at the history of the economic systems from which our own system descended.

Feudal Society: Rule of Tradition

Let's go back in time to the year 1000 when Europe had no nation-states as we now know them. (Ideally, we would have gone back further and explained other economic systems, but, given the limited space, I had to draw the line somewhere—an example of a trade-off.) The predominant economic system at that time was feudalism. There was no coordinated central government, no unified system of law, no national patriotism, no national defense, although a strong religious institution simply called the Church fulfilled some of these roles. There were few towns; most individuals lived in walled manors, or "estates." These manors "belonged to" the "lord of the manor." (Occasionally the "lord" was a lady, but not often.) I say "belonged to" rather than "were owned by" because most of the empires or federations at that time were not formal nation-states that could organize, administer, and regulate ownership. No documents or deeds gave ownership of the land to an individual. Instead, tradition ruled, and in normal times nobody questioned the lord's right to the land. The land "belonged to" the lord because the land "belonged to" him—that's the way it was.

Without a central nation-state, the manor served many functions a nation-state would have served had it existed. The lord provided protection, often within a walled area surrounding the manor house or, if the manor was large enough, a castle. He provided administration and decided disputes. He also decided *what* would be done, *how* it would be done, and *who* would get what, but these decisions were limited. In the same way that the land belonged to the lord because that's the way it always had been, what people did and how they did it were determined by what they always had done. Tradition ruled the manor more than the lord did.

Problems of a Tradition-Based Society

Feudalism developed about the 8th and 9th centuries and lasted until about the 15th century, though in isolated countries such as Russia it continued well into the 19th century, and in all European countries its influence lingered for hundreds of years (as late as about 140 years ago in some parts of Germany). Such a long-lived system must have done some things right, and feudalism did: It solved the *what*, *how*, and *for whom* problems in an acceptable way.

But a tradition-based society has problems. In a traditional society, because someone's father was a baker, the son also must be a baker, and because a woman was a homemaker, she wouldn't be allowed to be anything but a homemaker. But what if Joe Blacksmith Jr., the son of Joe Blacksmith Sr., is a lousy blacksmith and longs to knead dough, while Joe Baker Jr. would be a superb blacksmith but hates making pastry? Tough. Tradition dictated who did what. In fact, tradition probably arranged things so that we will never know whether Joe Blacksmith Jr. would have made a superb baker.

As long as a society doesn't change too much, tradition operates reasonably well, although not especially efficiently, in holding the society together. However, when a society must undergo change, tradition does not work. Change means that the things that were done before no longer need to be done, while new things do need to get done. But if no one has traditionally done these new things, then they don't get done. If the change is important but a society can't figure out some way for the new things to get done, the society falls apart. That's what happened to feudal society. It didn't change when change was required.

The life of individuals living on the land, called *serfs*, was difficult, and feudalism was designed to benefit the lord. Some individuals in feudal society just couldn't take life on the manor, and they set off on their own. Because there was no organized police force, they were unlikely to be caught and forced to return to the manor. Going hungry, being killed, or both, however, were frequent fates of an escaped serf. One place to which serfs could safely escape, though, was a town or city—the remains of what in Roman times had been thriving and active cities. These cities, which had been decimated by plagues, plundering bands, and starvation in the preceding centuries, nevertheless remained an escape hatch for runaway serfs because they relied far less on tradition than did manors. City dwellers had to live by their wits; many became merchants who lived predominantly by trading. They were middlemen; they would buy from one group and sell to another.

Trading in towns was an alternative to the traditional feudal order because trading allowed people to have an income independent of the traditional social structure. Markets broke down tradition. Initially merchants traded using barter (exchange of one kind of good for another): silk and spices from the Orient for wheat, flour, and artisan products in Europe. But soon a generalized purchasing power (money) developed as a medium of exchange. Money greatly expanded the possibilities of trading because its use meant that goods no longer needed to be bartered. They could be sold for money, which could then be spent to buy other goods.

In the beginning, land was not traded, but soon the feudal lord who just had to have a silk robe but had no money was saying, "Why not? I'll sell you a small piece of land so I can buy a shipment of silk." Once land became tradable, the traditional base of the feudal society was undermined. Tradition that can be bought and sold is no longer tradition—it's just another commodity.

From Feudalism to Mercantilism

Toward the end of the Middle Ages (mid-15th century), markets went from being a sideshow, a fair that spiced up people's lives, to being the main event. Over time, some traders and merchants started to amass fortunes that dwarfed those of the feudal lords. Rich traders settled down; existing towns and cities expanded and new towns were formed. As towns grew and as fortunes shifted from feudal lords to merchants, power in society shifted to the towns. And with that shift came a change in society's political and economic structure.

As these traders became stronger politically and economically, they threw their support behind a king (the strongest lord) in the hope that the king would expand their ability to trade. In doing so, they made the king even stronger. Eventually, the king became so powerful that his will prevailed over the will of the other lords and even over the will of the Church. As the king consolidated his power, nation-states as we know them today evolved. *The government became an active influence on economic decision making.*

As markets grew, feudalism evolved into mercantilism. The evolution of feudal systems into mercantilism occurred in the following way: As cities and their markets grew in size and power relative to the feudal manors and the traditional economy, a whole new variety of possible economic activities developed. It was only natural that individuals began to look to a king to establish a new tradition that would determine who would do what. Individuals in particular occupations organized into groups called *guilds*, which were similar to strong labor unions today. These guilds, many of which had financed and supported the king, now expected the king and his government to protect their interests.

As new economic activities, such as trading companies, developed, individuals involved in these activities similarly depended on the king for the right to trade and for help in financing and organizing their activities. For example, in 1492, when Christopher Columbus had the wild idea that by sailing west he could get to the East Indies and trade for their riches, he went to Spain's Queen Isabella and King Ferdinand for financial support.

Since many traders had played and continued to play important roles in financing, establishing, and supporting the king, the king was usually happy to protect their interests. The government doled out the rights to undertake a variety of economic activities. By the late 1400s, western Europe had evolved from a feudal to a mercantilist economy.

The mercantilist period was marked by the increased role of government, which could be classified in two ways: by the way it encouraged growth and by the way it limited growth. Government legitimized and financed a variety of activities, thus encouraging growth. But government also limited economic activity in order to protect the monopolies of those it favored, thus limiting growth. So mercantilism allowed the market to operate, but it kept the market under its control. The market was not allowed to respond freely to the laws of supply and demand.

From Mercantilism to Capitalism

Mercantilism provided the source for major growth in western Europe, but mercantilism also unleashed new tensions within society. Like feudalism, mercantilism limited entry into economic activities. It used a different form of limitation—politics rather than social and cultural tradition—but individuals who were excluded still felt unfairly treated.

The most significant source of tension was the different roles played by craft guilds and owners of new businesses, who were called industrialists or capitalists (businesspeople who have acquired large amounts of money and use it to invest in businesses). Craft guild members were artists in their own crafts: pottery, shoemaking, and the like. New business owners destroyed the art of production by devising machines to replace hand production. Machines produced goods cheaper and faster than craftsmen.[1] The result was an increase in supply and a downward pressure on the price, which was set by the government. Craftsmen didn't want to be replaced by machines. They argued that machine-manufactured goods didn't have the same quality as hand-crafted goods, and that the new machines would disrupt the economic and social life of the community.

Industrialists were the outsiders with a vested interest in changing the existing system. They wanted the freedom to conduct business as they saw fit. Because of the enormous cost advantage of manufactured goods over crafted goods, a few industrialists overcame government opposition and succeeded within the mercantilist system. They earned their fortunes and became an independent political power.

Once again, the economic power base shifted, and two groups competed with each other for power—this time, the guilds and the industrialists. The government had to decide whether to support the industrialists (who wanted government to loosen its power over the country's economic affairs) or the craftsmen and guilds (who argued for strong government limitations and for maintaining traditional values of workmanship). This struggle raged in the 1700s and 1800s. But during this time, governments themselves were changing. This was the Age of Revolutions, and the kings' powers were being limited by democratic reform movements—revolutions supported and financed in large part by the industrialists.

The Need for Coordination in an Economy

Craftsmen argued that coordination of the economy was necessary, and the government had to be involved. If government wasn't going to coordinate economic activity, who would? To answer that question, a British moral philosopher named Adam Smith developed the concept of the invisible hand, in his famous book *The Wealth of Nations* (1776), and used it to explain how markets could coordinate the economy without the active involvement of government.

As stated in Chapter 2, Smith argued that the market's invisible hand would guide suppliers' actions toward the general good. No government coordination was necessary.

With the help of economists such as Adam Smith, the industrialists' view won out. Government pulled back from its role in guiding the economy and adopted a laissez-faire policy.

The Industrial Revolution

The invisible hand worked; capitalism thrived. Beginning about 1750 and continuing through the late 1800s, machine production increased enormously, almost totally replacing hand production. This phenomenon has been given a name, the Industrial Revolution. The economy grew faster than ever before. Society was forever transformed. New inventions changed all aspects of life. James Watt's steam engine (1769) made manufacturing and travel easier. Eli Whitney's cotton gin (1793) changed the way cotton was processed. James Kay's flying shuttle (1733),[2] James Hargreaves' spinning jenny (1765), and Richard Arkwright's power loom (1769), combined with the steam engine, changed the way cloth was processed and the clothes people wore.

The need to mine vast amounts of coal to provide power to run the machines changed the economic and physical landscapes. The repeating rifle changed the nature of warfare. Modern economic institutions replaced guilds. Stock markets, insurance companies, and corporations all became important. Trading was no longer financed by government; it was privately financed (although government policies, such as colonial policies giving certain companies monopoly trading rights with a country's colonies, helped in that trading). The Industrial Revolution, democracy, and capitalism all arose in the middle and late 1700s. By the 1800s, they were part of the institutional landscape of Western society. Capitalism had arrived.

Welfare Capitalism

From Capitalism to ~~Socialism~~

Capitalism was marked by significant economic growth in the Western world. But it was also marked by human abuses—18-hour workdays; low wages; children as young as five years old slaving long hours in dirty, dangerous factories and mines—to produce enormous wealth for an elite few. Such conditions and inequalities led to criticism of the capitalist or market economic system.

Marx's Analysis

The best-known critic of this system was Karl Marx, a German philosopher, economist, and sociologist who wrote in the 1800s and who developed an analysis of the

[1]Throughout this section I use *men* to emphasize that these societies were strongly male-dominated. There were almost no businesswomen. In fact, a woman had to turn over her property to a man upon her marriage, and the marriage contract was written as if she were owned by her husband!

[2]The invention of the flying shuttle frustrated the textile industry because it enabled workers to weave so much cloth that the spinners of thread from which the cloth was woven couldn't keep up. This challenge to the textile industry was met by offering a prize to anyone who could invent something to increase the thread spinners' productivity. The prize was won when the spinning jenny was invented.

dynamics of change in economic systems. Marx argued that economic systems are in a constant state of change, and that capitalism would not last. Workers would revolt, and capitalism would be replaced by a socialist economic system.

Marx saw an economy marked by tensions among economic classes. He saw capitalism as an economic system controlled by the capitalist class (businessmen). His class analysis was that capitalist society is divided into capitalist and worker classes. He said constant tension between these economic classes causes changes in the system. The capitalist class made large profits by exploiting the proletariat class—the working class—and extracting what he called surplus value from workers who, according to Marx's labor theory of value, produced all the value inherent in goods. Surplus value was the additional profit, rent, or interest that, according to Marx's normative views, capitalists added to the price of goods. What standard economic analysis sees as recognizing a need that society has and fulfilling it, Marx saw as exploitation.

Marx argued that this exploitation would increase as production facilities became larger and larger and as competition among capitalists decreased. At some point, he believed, exploitation would lead to a revolt by the proletariat, who would overthrow their capitalist exploiters.

By the late 1800s, some of what Marx predicted had occurred, although not in the way that he thought it would. Production moved from small to large factories. Corporations developed, and classes became more distinct from one another. Workers were significantly differentiated from owners. Small firms merged and were organized into monopolies and trusts (large combinations of firms). The trusts developed ways to prevent competition among themselves and ways to limit entry of new competitors into the market. Marx was right in his predictions about these developments, but he was wrong in his prediction about society's response to them.

The Revolution That Did Not Occur

Western society's response to the problems of capitalism was not a revolt by the workers. Instead, governments stepped in to stop the worst abuses of capitalism. The hard edges of capitalism were softened.

Evolution, not revolution, was capitalism's destiny. The democratic state did not act, as Marx argued it would, as a mere representative of the capitalist class. Competing pressure groups developed; workers gained political power that offset the economic power of businesses.

In the late 1930s and the 1940s, workers dominated the political agenda. During this time, capitalist economies developed an economic safety net that included government-funded programs, such as public welfare and unemployment insurance, and established an extensive set of regulations affecting all aspects of the economy. Today, depressions are met with direct government policy. Antitrust laws, regulatory agencies, and social programs of government softened the hard edges of capitalism. Laws were passed prohibiting child labor, mandating a certain minimum wage, and limiting the hours of work. Capitalism became what is sometimes called welfare capitalism.

Due to these developments, government spending now accounts for about a fifth of all spending in the United States, and for more than half in some European countries. Were an economist from the late 1800s to return from the grave, he'd probably say socialism, not capitalism, exists in Western societies. Most modern-day economists wouldn't go that far, but they would agree that our economy today is better described as a welfare capitalist economy than as a capitalist, or even a market, economy. Because of these changes, the U.S. and Western European economies are a far cry from the competitive "capitalist" economy that Karl Marx criticized. Markets operate, but they are constrained by the government.

The concept *capitalism* developed to denote a market system controlled by one group in society, the capitalists. Looking at Western societies today, we see that domination by one group no longer characterizes Western economies. Although in theory capitalists control corporations through their ownership of shares of stock, in practice corporations are controlled in large part by managers. There remains an elite group who control business, but *capitalist* is not a good term to describe them. Managers, not capitalists, exercise primary control over business, and even their control is limited by laws or the fear of laws being passed by governments.

Governments, in turn, are controlled by a variety of pressure groups. Sometimes one group is in control; at other times, another. Government policies similarly fluctuate. Sometimes they are proworker, sometimes proindustrialist, sometimes progovernment, and sometimes prosociety.

From Feudalism to Socialism

You probably noticed that I crossed out *Socialism* in the previous section's heading and replaced it with *Welfare Capitalism*. That's because capitalism did not evolve to socialism as Karl Marx predicted it would. Instead, Marx's socialist ideas took root in feudalist Russia, a society that the Industrial Revolution had in large part bypassed. Since socialism arrived at a different place and a different time than Marx predicted it would, you shouldn't be surprised to read that socialism arrived in a different way than Marx predicted. The proletariat did not revolt to establish socialism. Instead, World War I, which the Russians were losing, crippled Russia's feudal economy and government. A small group of socialists overthrew the czar (Russia's king) and took over the government in 1917. They quickly pulled Russia out of the war, and then set out to organize a socialist society and economy.

Russian socialists tried to adhere to Marx's ideas, but they found that Marx had concentrated on how capitalist economies operate, not on how a socialist economy should be run. Thus, Russian socialists faced a huge task with little guidance. Their most immediate problem was how to increase production so that the economy could emerge from feudalism into the modern industrial world. In Marx's analysis, capitalism was a necessary stage in the evolution toward the ideal state for a very practical reason. The capitalists exploit the workers, but in doing so capitalists extract the necessary surplus—an amount of production in excess of what is consumed. That surplus had to be extracted in order to provide the factories and machinery upon which a socialist economic system would be built. But since capitalism did not exist in Russia, a true socialist state could not be established immediately. Instead, the socialists created *state socialism*—an economic system in which government sees to it that people work for the common good until they can be relied upon to do that on their own.

Socialists saw state socialism as a transition stage to pure socialism. This transition stage still exploited the workers; when Joseph Stalin took power in Russia in the late 1920s, he took the peasants' and small farmers' land and turned it into collective farms. The government then paid farmers low prices for their produce. When farmers balked at the low prices, millions of them were killed.

Simultaneously, Stalin created central planning agencies that directed individuals what to produce and how to produce it, and determined for whom things would be produced. During this period, *socialism* became synonymous with *central economic planning*, and Soviet-style socialism became the model of socialism in practice.

Also during this time, Russia took control of a number of neighboring states and established the Union of Soviet Socialist Republics (USSR), the formal name of the Soviet Union. The Soviet Union also installed Soviet-dominated governments in a number of Eastern European countries. In 1949 most of China, under the rule of Mao Zedong, adopted Soviet-style socialist principles.

Since the late 1980s, the Soviet socialist economic and political structure has fallen apart. The Soviet Union as a political state broke up, and its former republics became autonomous. Eastern European countries were released from Soviet control. Now they faced a new problem: transition from socialism to a market economy. Why did the Soviet socialist economy fall apart? Because workers lacked incentives to work; production was inefficient; consumer goods were either unavailable or of poor quality; and high Soviet officials were exploiting their positions, keeping the best jobs for themselves and moving themselves up in the waiting lists for consumer goods. In short, the parents of the socialist family (the Communist party) were no longer acting benevolently; they were taking many of the benefits for themselves.

These political and economic upheavals in Eastern Europe and the former Soviet Union suggest the kind of socialism these societies tried did not work. However, that failure does not mean that socialist goals are bad; nor does it mean that no type of socialism can ever work. The point is that all systems have problems, and it is likely that the political winds of change will lead to new forms of economic organization being tried as the problems of the existing system lead to political demands for change. Venezuela's recent attempt to establish a new form of socialism is an example. Given past experience with socialist systems, however, most economists believe that any future workable "new socialist" system will include important elements of market institutions.

Supply and Demand

Teach a parrot the terms supply and demand and you've got an economist.

—Thomas Carlyle

Supply and demand. Supply and demand. Roll the phrase around in your mouth; savor it like a good wine. *Supply* and *demand* are the most-used words in economics. And for good reason. They provide a good off-the-cuff answer for any economic question. Try it.

Why are bacon and oranges so expensive this winter? *Supply and demand.*

Why are interest rates falling? *Supply and demand.*

Why can't I find decent wool socks anymore? *Supply and demand.*

The importance of the interplay of supply and demand makes it only natural that, early in any economics course, you must learn about supply and demand. Let's start with demand.

AFTER READING THIS CHAPTER, YOU SHOULD BE ABLE TO:

1. State the law of demand and draw a demand curve from a demand table.
2. Explain the importance of substitution to the laws of supply and demand.
3. Distinguish shifts in demand from movements along a demand curve.
4. State the law of supply and draw a supply curve from a supply table.
5. Distinguish shifts in supply from movements along a supply curve.
6. Explain how the law of demand and the law of supply interact to bring about equilibrium.
7. Show the effect of a shift in demand and supply on equilibrium price and quantity.
8. State the limitations of demand and supply analysis.

Demand

People want lots of things; they "demand" much less than they want because demand means a willingness and ability to pay. Unless you are willing and able to pay for it, you may *want* it, but you don't *demand* it. For example, I want to own a Ferrari. But, I must admit, I'm not willing to do what's necessary to own one. If I really wanted one, I'd mortgage everything I own, increase my income by doubling the number of hours I work, not buy anything else, and get that car. But I don't do any of those things, so at the going price, $650,000, I do not demand a Ferrari. Sure, I'd buy one if it cost $30,000, but from my actions it's clear that, at $650,000, I don't demand it. This points to an important aspect of demand: The quantity you demand at a low price differs from the quantity you demand at a high price. Specifically, the quantity you demand varies inversely—in the opposite direction—with price.

Prices are the tool by which the market coordinates individuals' desires and limits how much people demand. When goods become scarce, the market reduces the quantity people demand; as their prices go up, people buy fewer goods. As goods become abundant, their prices go down, and people buy more of them.

The invisible hand—the price mechanism—sees to it that what people demand (do what's necessary to get) matches what's available.

The Law of Demand

The law of demand states that the quantity of a good demanded is inversely related to the good's price.

The ideas expressed above are the foundation of the **law of demand:**

Quantity demanded rises as price falls, other things constant.

Or alternatively:

Quantity demanded falls as price rises, other things constant.

This law is fundamental to the invisible hand's ability to coordinate individuals' desires: as prices change, people change how much they're willing to buy.

Web Note 4.1
Markets without Money

What accounts for the law of demand? If the price of something goes up, people will tend to buy less of it and buy something else instead. They will *substitute* other goods for goods whose relative price has gone up. If the price of MP3 files from the Internet rises, but the price of CDs stays the same, you're more likely to buy that new Coldplay recording on CD than to download it from the Internet.

When price goes up, quantity demanded goes down. When price goes down, quantity demanded goes up.

To see that the law of demand makes intuitive sense, just think of something you'd really like but can't afford. If the price is cut in half, you—and other consumers—become more likely to buy it. Quantity demanded goes up as price goes down.

Just to be sure you've got it, let's consider a real-world example: demand for vanity—specifically, vanity license plates. When the North Carolina state legislature increased the vanity plates' price from $30 to $40, the quantity demanded fell from 60,334 to 31,122. Assuming other things remained constant, that is the law of demand in action.

The Demand Curve

Q-1 Why does the demand curve slope downward?

A **demand curve** is *the graphic representation of the relationship between price and quantity demanded.* Figure 4-1 shows a demand curve.

As you can see, the demand curve slopes downward. That's because of the law of demand: as the price goes up, the quantity demanded goes down, other things constant. In other words, price and quantity demanded are inversely related.

FIGURE 4-1 A Sample Demand Curve

The law of demand states that the quantity demanded of a good is inversely related to the price of that good, other things constant. As the price of a good goes up, the quantity demanded goes down, so the demand curve is downward-sloping.

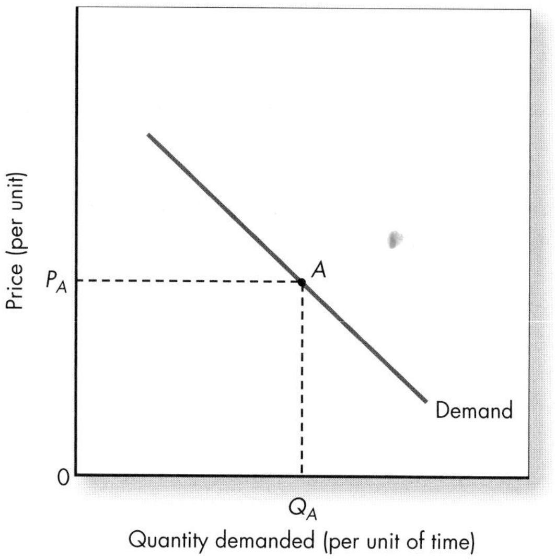

Notice that in stating the law of demand, I put in the qualification "other things constant." That's three extra words, and unless they were important I wouldn't have included them. But what does "other things constant" mean? Say that over two years, both the price of cars and the number of cars purchased rise. That seems to violate the law of demand, since the number of cars purchased should have fallen in response to the rise in price. Looking at the data more closely, however, we see that individuals' income has increased. Other things didn't remain the same.

"Other things constant" places a limitation on the application of the law of demand.

The increase in price works as the law of demand states—it decreases the number of cars bought. But the rise in income increases the demand for cars at every price. That increase in demand outweighs the decrease in quantity demanded that results from a rise in price, so ultimately more cars are sold. If you want to study the effect of price alone—which is what the law of demand refers to—you must make adjustments to hold income constant. Because other things besides price affect demand, the qualifying phrase "other things constant" is an important part of the law of demand.

The other things that are held constant include individuals' tastes, prices of other goods, and even the weather. Those other factors must remain constant if you're to make a valid study of the effect of an increase in the price of a good on the quantity demanded. In practice, it's impossible to keep all other things constant, so you have to be careful when you say that when price goes up, quantity demanded goes down. It's likely to go down, but it's always possible that something besides price has changed.

Shifts in Demand versus Movements along a Demand Curve

Shifts in Demand versus Movements along a Demand Curve

To distinguish between the effects of price and the effects of other factors on how much of a good is demanded, economists have developed the following precise terminology—terminology that inevitably shows up on exams. The first distinction is between demand and quantity demanded.

- **Demand** refers to *a schedule of quantities of a good that will be bought per unit of time at various prices, other things constant.*
- **Quantity demanded** refers to *a specific amount that will be demanded per unit of time at a specific price, other things constant.*

In graphical terms, the term *demand* refers to the entire demand curve. Demand tells us how much will be bought *at various prices*. *Quantity demanded* tells us how much will be bought at a specific price; it refers to a point on a demand curve, such as point A in Figure 4-1. This terminology allows us to distinguish between *changes in quantity demanded* and *shifts in demand.* A change in price changes the quantity demanded. It refers to a **movement along a demand curve**—*the graphical representation of the effect of a change in price on the quantity demanded.* A change in anything other than price that affects demand changes the entire demand curve. A shift factor of demand causes a **shift in demand,** *the graphical representation of the effect of anything other than price on demand*.

Q-2 The uncertainty caused by the terrorist attacks of September 11, 2001, made consumers reluctant to spend on luxury items. This reduced ________. Should the missing words be *demand for luxury goods* or *quantity of luxury goods demanded*?

To make sure you understand the difference between a movement along a demand curve and a shift in demand, let's consider an example. Singapore has one of the world's highest number of cars per mile of road. This means that congestion is considerable. Singapore adopted two policies to reduce road use: It increased the fee charged to use roads and it provided an expanded public transportation system. Both policies reduced congestion. Figure 4-2(a) shows that increasing the toll charged to use roads from $1 to $2 per 50 miles of road reduces quantity demanded from 200 to 100 cars per mile every hour (a movement along the demand curve). Figure 4-2(b) shows that providing alternative methods of transportation such as buses and subways shifts the demand curve for roads in to the left so that at every price, demand drops by 25 cars per mile every hour.

Change in price causes a movement along a demand curve; a change in a shift factor causes a shift in demand.

FIGURE 4-2 (A AND B) **Shift in Demand versus a Change in Quantity Demanded**

A rise in a good's price results in a reduction in quantity demanded and is shown by a movement up along a demand curve from point *A* to point *B* in (**a**). A change in any other factor besides price that affects demand leads to a shift in the entire demand curve, as shown in (**b**).

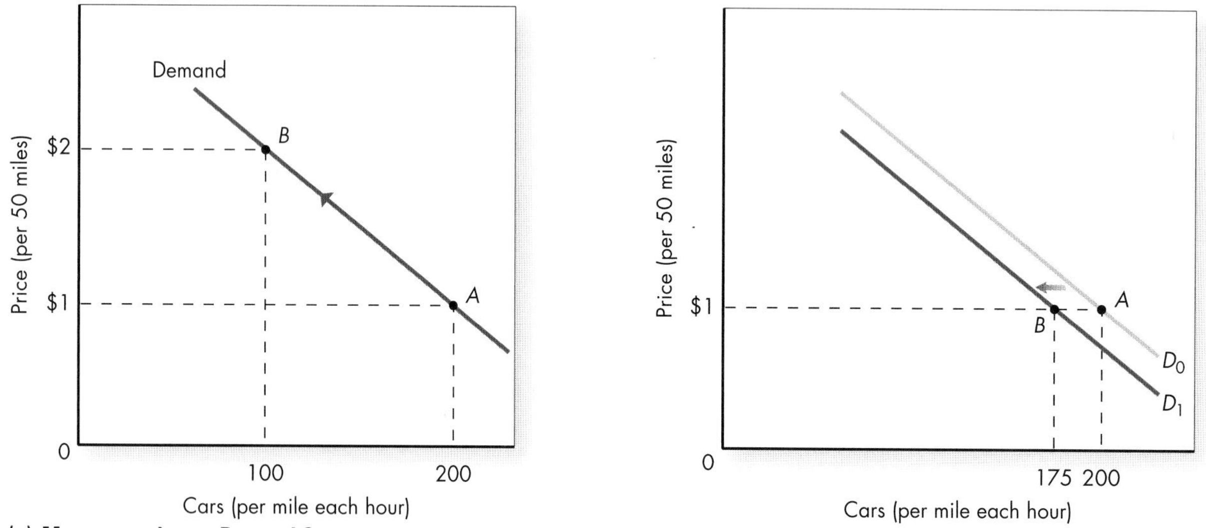

(a) Movement along a Demand Curve **(b) Shift in Demand**

Shift Factors of Demand

Important shift factors of demand include

1. Society's income.
2. The prices of other goods.
3. Tastes.
4. Expectations.
5. Taxes on and subsidies to consumers.

Web Note 4.2
Influencing Demand

Income From our example above of the "other things constant" qualification, we saw that a rise in income increases the demand for goods. For most goods this is true. As individuals' income rises, they can afford more of the goods they want, such as steaks, computers, or clothing. These are normal goods. For other goods, called inferior goods, an increase in income reduces demand. An example is urban mass transit. A person whose income has risen tends to stop riding the bus to work because she can afford to buy a car and rent a parking space.

Price of Other Goods Because people make their buying decisions based on the price of related goods, demand will be affected by the prices of other goods. Suppose the price of jeans rises from $25 to $35, but the price of khakis remains at $25. Next time you need pants, you're apt to try khakis instead of jeans. They are substitutes. When the price of a substitute rises, demand for the good whose price has remained the same will rise. Or consider another example. Suppose the price of movie tickets falls. What will happen to the demand for popcorn? You're likely to increase the number of times you go to the movies, so you'll also likely increase the amount of popcorn you purchase. The lower cost of a movie ticket increases the demand for popcorn because popcorn and movies are complements. When the price of a good declines, the demand for its complement rises.

Tastes An old saying goes: "There's no accounting for taste." Of course, many advertisers believe otherwise. Changes in taste can affect the demand for a good without a change in price. As you become older, you may find that your taste for rock concerts has changed to a taste for an evening sitting at home watching TV.

Q-3 Explain the effect of each of the following on the demand for new computers:

1. The price of computers falls by 30 percent.
2. Total income in the economy rises.

Expectations Expectations will also affect demand. Expectations can cover a lot. If you expect your income to rise in the future, you're bound to start spending some of it today. If you expect the price of computers to fall soon, you may put off buying one until later.

Taxes and Subsidies Taxes levied on consumers increase the cost of goods to consumers and therefore reduce demand for those goods. Subsidies to consumers have the opposite effect. When states host tax-free weeks during August's back-to-school shopping season, consumers load up on products to avoid sales taxes. Demand for retail goods rises during the tax holiday.

These aren't the only shift factors. In fact anything—except the price of the good itself—that affects demand (and many things do) is a shift factor. While economists agree these shift factors are important, they believe that no shift factor influences how much of a good people buy as consistently as its price. That's why economists make the law of demand central to their analysis.

A Review

Let's test your understanding: What happens to your demand curve for CDs in the following examples: First, let's say you buy an MP3 player. Next, let's say that the price of CDs falls; and finally, say that you won $1 million in a lottery. What happens to the demand for CDs in each case? If you answered: It shifts in to the left; it remains unchanged; and it shifts out to the right—you've got it.

WWW Web Note 4.3
Shifting Demand

The Demand Table

As I emphasized in Chapter 2, introductory economics depends heavily on graphs and graphical analysis—translating ideas into graphs and back into words. So let's graph the demand curve.

Figure 4-3(a), a demand table, describes Alice's demand for renting DVDs. For example, at a price of $2, Alice will rent (buy the use of) six DVDs per week, and at a price of 50 cents she will rent nine.

Four points about the relationship between the number of DVDs Alice rents and the price of renting them are worth mentioning. First, the relationship follows the law of demand: As the rental price rises, quantity demanded decreases. Second, quantity demanded has a specific *time dimension* to it. In this example, demand refers to the number of DVD rentals per week. Without the time dimension, the table wouldn't provide us with any useful information. Nine DVD rentals per year is quite different from nine DVD rentals per week. Third, the analysis assumes that Alice's DVD rentals are interchangeable—the ninth DVD rental doesn't significantly differ from the first, third, or any other DVD rental. The fourth point is already familiar to you: The analysis assumes that everything else is held constant.

FIGURE 4-3 (A AND B) From a Demand Table to a Demand Curve
The demand table in (**a**) is translated into a demand curve in (**b**). Each combination of price and quantity in the table corresponds to a point on the curve. For example, point A on the graph represents row A in the table: Alice demands nine DVD rentals at a price of 50 cents. A demand curve is constructed by plotting all points from the demand table and connecting the points with a line.

	Price per DVD	DVD Rentals Demanded per Week
A	$0.50	9
B	1.00	8
C	2.00	6
D	3.00	4
E	4.00	2

(a) A Demand Table

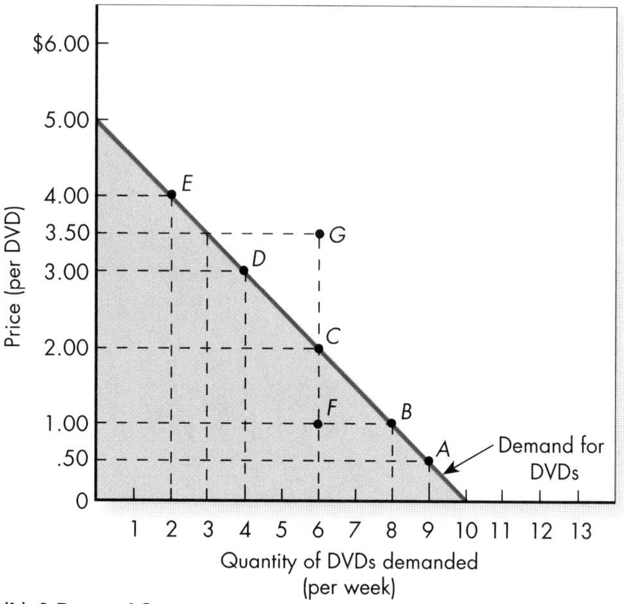

(b) A Demand Curve

From a Demand Table to a Demand Curve

Figure 4-3(b) translates the demand table in Figure 4-3(a) into a demand curve. Point A (quantity = 9, price = $.50) is graphed first at the (9, $.50) coordinates. Next we plot points *B*, *C*, *D*, and *E* in the same manner and connect the resulting dots with a solid line. The result is the demand curve, which graphically conveys the same information that's in the demand table. Notice that the demand curve is downward sloping, indicating that the law of demand holds.

The demand curve represents the maximum price that an individual will pay.

The demand curve represents the *maximum price* that an individual will pay for various quantities of a good; the individual will happily pay less. For example, say Netflix offers Alice six DVD rentals at a price of $1 each (point *F* of Figure 4-3(b)). Will she accept? Sure; she'll pay any price within the shaded area to the left of the demand curve. But if Netflix offers her six rentals at $3.50 each (point G), she won't accept. At a price of $3.50 apiece, she's willing to rent only three DVDs.

Q-4 Derive a market demand curve from the following two individual demand curves:

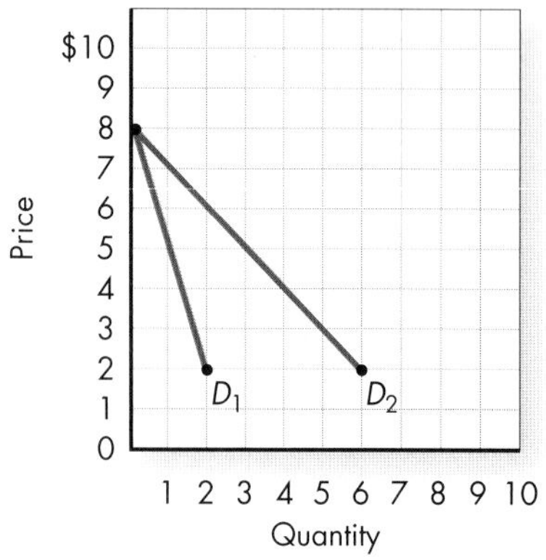

Individual and Market Demand Curves

Normally, economists talk about market demand curves rather than individual demand curves. A **market demand curve** is *the horizontal sum of all individual demand curves*. Firms don't care whether individual A or individual B buys their goods; they only care that *someone* buys their goods.

It's a good graphical exercise to add individual demand curves together to create a market demand curve. I do that in Figure 4-4. In it I assume that the market consists of three buyers, Alice, Bruce, and Carmen, whose demand tables are given in Figure 4-4(a). Alice and Bruce have demand tables similar to the demand tables discussed previously. At a price of $3 each, Alice rents four DVDs; at a price of $2, she rents six. Carmen is an all-or-nothing individual. She rents one DVD as long as the price is equal to or less than $1; otherwise she rents nothing. If you plot Carmen's demand curve, it's a vertical line. However, the law of demand still holds: As price increases, quantity demanded decreases.

FIGURE 4-4 (A AND B) **From Individual Demands to a Market Demand Curve**

The table (**a**) shows the demand schedules for Alice, Bruce, and Carmen. Together they make up the market for DVD rentals. Their total quantity demanded (market demand) for DVD rentals at each price is given in column 5. As you can see in (**b**), Alice's, Bruce's, and Carmen's demand curves can be added together to get the total market demand curve. For example, at a price of $2, Carmen demands 0, Bruce demands 3, and Alice demands 6, for a market demand of 9 (point *D*).

	(1) Price (per DVD)	(2) Alice's Demand	(3) Bruce's Demand	(4) Carmen's Demand	(5) Market Demand
A	$0.50	9	6	1	16
B	1.00	8	5	1	14
C	1.50	7	4	0	11
D	2.00	6	3	0	9
E	2.50	5	2	0	7
F	3.00	4	1	0	5
G	3.50	3	0	0	3
H	4.00	2	0	0	2

(a) A Demand Table

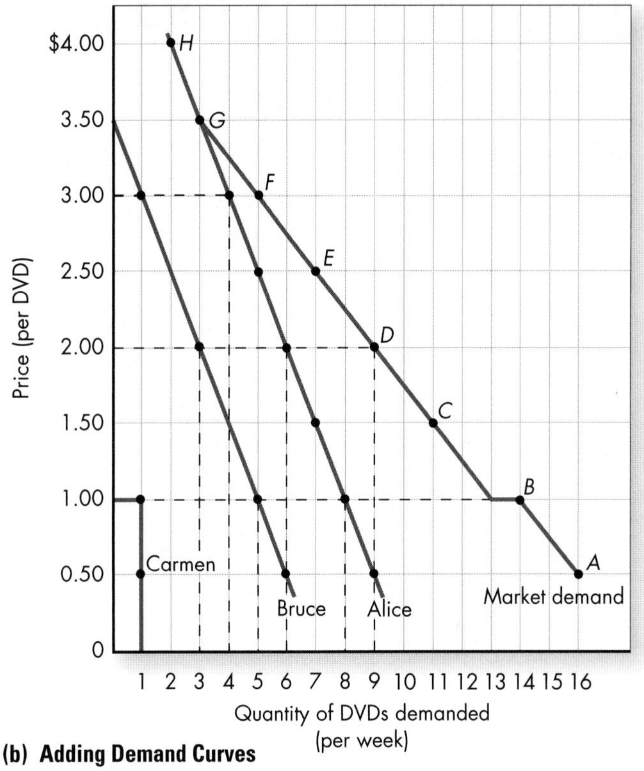

(b) Adding Demand Curves

The quantity demanded by each consumer is listed in columns 2, 3, and 4 of Figure 4-4(a). Column 5 shows total market demand; each entry is the horizontal sum of the entries in columns 2, 3, and 4. For example, at a price of $3 apiece (row *F*), Alice demands four DVD rentals, Bruce demands one, and Carmen demands zero, for a total market demand of five DVD rentals.

Figure 4-4(b) shows three demand curves: one each for Alice, Bruce, and Carmen. The market, or total, demand curve is the horizontal sum of the individual demand curves. To see that this is the case, notice that if we take the quantity demanded at $1 by Alice (8), Bruce (5), and Carmen (1), they sum to 14, which is point *B* (14, $1) on the market demand curve. We can do that for each price. Alternatively, we can simply add the individual quantities demanded, given in the demand tables, prior to graphing (which we do in column 5 of Figure 4-4(a)), and graph that total in relation to price. Not surprisingly, we get the same total market demand curve.

Individual and Market Demand Curves

In practice, of course, firms don't measure individual demand curves, so they don't sum them up in this fashion. Instead, they statistically estimate market demand. Still, summing up individual demand curves is a useful exercise because it shows you how the market demand curve is the sum (the horizontal sum, graphically speaking) of the individual demand curves, and it gives you a good sense of where market demand curves come from. It also shows you that, even if individuals don't respond to small changes in price, the market demand curve can still be smooth and downward sloping. That's because, for the market, the law of demand is based on two phenomena:

1. At lower prices, existing demanders buy more.
2. At lower prices, new demanders (some all-or-nothing demanders like Carmen) enter the market.

For the market, the law of demand is based on two phenomena:
1. At lower prices, existing demanders buy more.
2. At lower prices, new demanders enter the market.

A REMINDER

Six Things to Remember about a Demand Curve

- A demand curve follows the law of demand: When price rises, quantity demanded falls, and vice versa.
- The horizontal axis—quantity—has a time dimension.
- The quality of each unit is the same.
- The vertical axis—price—assumes all other prices remain the same.
- The curve assumes everything else is held constant.
- Effects of price changes are shown by movements along the demand curve. Effects of anything else on demand (shift factors) are shown by shifts of the entire demand curve.

Supply

In one sense, supply is the mirror image of demand. Individuals control the factors of production—inputs, or resources, necessary to produce goods. Individuals' supply of these factors to the market mirrors other individuals' demand for those factors. For example, say you decide you want to rest rather than weed your garden. You hire someone to do the weeding; you demand labor. Someone else decides she would prefer more income instead of more rest; she supplies labor to you. You trade money for labor; she trades labor for money. Her supply is the mirror image of your demand.

For a large number of goods and services, however, the supply process is more complicated than demand. For many goods there's an intermediate step: individuals supply factors of production to firms.

Let's consider a simple example. Say you're a taco technician. You supply your labor to the factor market. The taco company demands your labor (hires you). The taco company combines your labor with other inputs such as meat, cheese, beans, and tables, and produces tacos (production), which it supplies to customers in the goods market. For produced goods, supply depends not only on individuals' decisions to supply factors of production but also on firms' ability to transform those factors of production into usable goods.

The supply process of produced goods is generally complicated. Often there are many layers of firms—production firms, wholesale firms, distribution firms, and retailing firms—each of which passes on in-process goods to the next layer of firms. Real-world production and supply of produced goods is a multistage process.

Supply of produced goods involves a much more complicated process than demand and is divided into analysis of factors of production and the transformation of those factors into goods.

The supply of nonproduced goods is more direct. Individuals supply their labor in the form of services directly to the goods market. For example, an independent contractor may repair your washing machine. That contractor supplies his labor directly to you.

Thus, the analysis of the supply of produced goods has two parts: an analysis of the supply of factors of production to households and to firms and an analysis of the process by which firms transform those factors of production into usable goods and services.

The Law of Supply

There's a law of supply that corresponds to the law of demand. The **law of supply** states:

Quantity supplied rises as price rises, other things constant.

Or alternatively:

Quantity supplied falls as price falls, other things constant.

Price determines quantity supplied just as it determines quantity demanded. Like the law of demand, the law of supply is fundamental to the invisible hand's (the market's) ability to coordinate individuals' actions.

The law of supply is based on substitution and the expectation of profits.

The law of supply is based on a firm's ability to switch from producing one good to another, that is, to substitute. When the price of a good a person or firm supplies rises, individuals and firms can rearrange their activities in order to supply more of that good to the market. They want to supply more because the opportunity cost of *not* supplying the good rises as its price rises. For example, if the price of corn rises and the price of soybeans has not changed, farmers will grow less soybeans and more corn, other things constant.

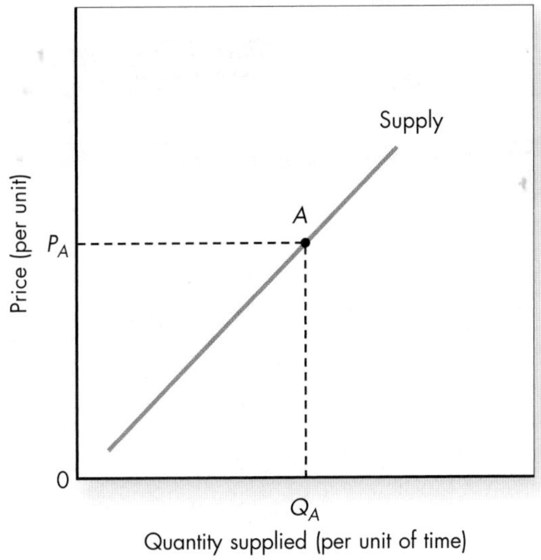

FIGURE 4-5 A Sample Supply Curve

The supply curve demonstrates graphically the law of supply, which states that the quantity supplied of a good is directly related to that good's price, other things constant. As the price of a good goes up, the quantity supplied also goes up, so the supply curve is upward-sloping.

With firms, there's a second explanation of the law of supply. Assuming firms' costs are constant, a higher price means higher profits (the difference between a firm's revenues and its costs). The expectation of those higher profits leads it to increase output as price rises, which is what the law of supply states.

The Supply Curve

A **supply curve** is *the graphical representation of the relationship between price and quantity supplied.* A supply curve is shown in Figure 4-5.

Notice how the supply curve slopes upward to the right. That upward slope captures the law of supply. It tells us that the quantity supplied varies *directly*—in the same direction—with the price.

As with the law of demand, the law of supply assumes other things are held constant. If the price of soybeans rises and quantity supplied falls, you'll look for something else that changed—for example, a drought might have caused a drop in supply. Your explanation would go as follows: Had there been no drought, the quantity supplied would have increased in response to the rise in price, but because there was a drought, the supply decreased, which caused prices to rise.

As with the law of demand, the law of supply represents economists' off-the-cuff response to the question "What happens to quantity supplied if price rises?" If the law seems to be violated, economists search for some other variable that has changed. As was the case with demand, these other variables that might change are called shift factors.

Shifts in Supply versus Movements along a Supply Curve

The same distinctions in terms made for demand apply to supply.

> **Supply** refers to *a schedule of quantities a seller is willing to sell per unit of time at various prices, other things constant.*
>
> **Quantity supplied** refers to *a specific amount that will be supplied at a specific price.*

In graphical terms, supply refers to the entire supply curve because a supply curve tells us how much will be offered for sale at various prices. "Quantity supplied" refers to a point on a supply curve, such as point A in Figure 4-5.

Shifts in Supply versus Movements along a Supply Curve

Q-5 In the early 2000s the price of gasoline rose, causing the demand for hybrid cars to rise. As a result, the price of hybrid cars rose. This made _______ rise. Should the missing words be *the supply* or *the quantity supplied*?

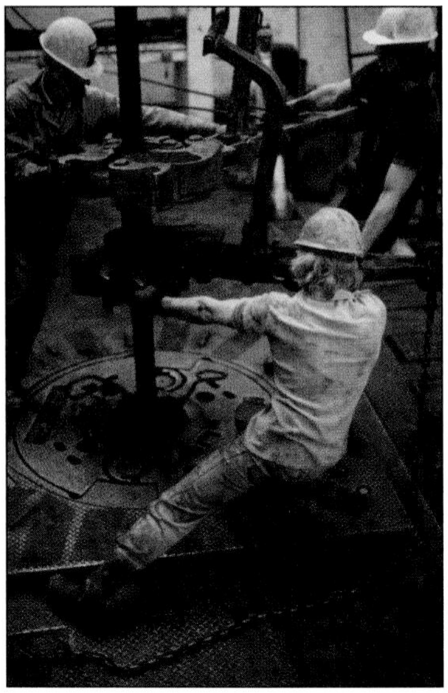

The second distinction that is important to make is between the effects of a change in price and the effects of shift factors on how much is supplied. Changes in price cause changes in quantity supplied; such changes are represented by a **movement along a supply curve**—*the graphical representation of the effect of a change in price on the quantity supplied.* If the amount supplied is affected by anything other than price, that is, by a shift factor of supply, there will be a **shift in supply**—*the graphical representation of the effect of a change in a factor other than price on supply*.

To make that distinction clear, let's consider an example: the supply of oil. In September 2005, Hurricane Katrina hit the Gulf Coast region of the United States and disrupted oil supply lines and production in the United States. U.S. production of oil declined from 4.6 to 4.1 million barrels each day at a $50 price. This disruption reduced the amount of oil U.S. producers were offering for sale *at every price*, thereby shifting the supply of U.S. oil to the left from S_0 to S_1, and the quantity of oil supplied at the $50 price fell from point A to point B in Figure 4-6. But the price did not stay at $50. It rose to $80. In response to the higher price, other areas in the United States increased their quantity supplied (from point B to point C in Figure 4-6). That increase *due to the higher price* is called a movement along the supply curve. So if a change in quantity supplied occurs because of a higher price, it is called a *movement along the supply curve;* if a change in supply occurs because of one of the shift factors (i.e., for any reason other than a change in price), it is called a *shift in supply*.

Shift Factors of Supply

Other factors besides price that affect how much will be supplied include the price of inputs used in production, technology, expectations, and taxes and subsidies. Let's see how.

Price of Inputs Firms produce to earn a profit. Since their profit is tied to costs, it's no surprise that costs will affect how much a firm is willing to supply. If costs rise, profits will decline, and a firm has less incentive to supply. Supply falls when the price of inputs rises. If costs rise substantially, a firm might even shut down.

FIGURE 4-6 Shifts in Supply versus Movement along a Supply Curve

A *shift in supply* results when the shift is due to any cause other than a change in price. It is a shift in the entire supply curve (see the arrow from A to B). A *movement along a supply curve* is due to a change in price only (see the arrow from B to C). To differentiate the two, movements caused by changes in price are called *changes in the quantity supplied,* not changes in supply.

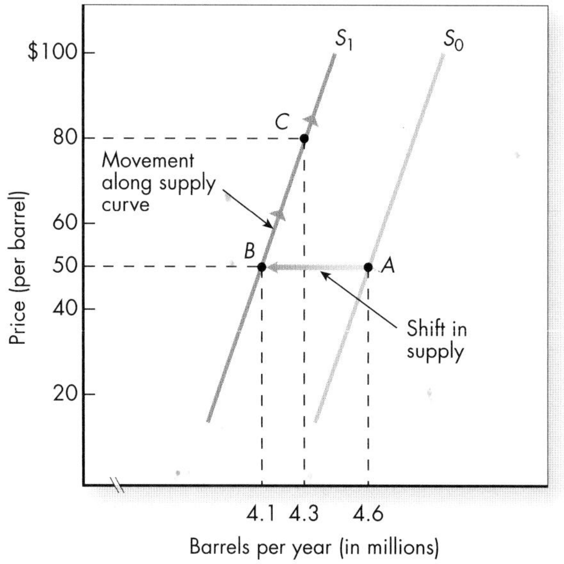

Technology Advances in technology change the production process, reducing the number of inputs needed to produce a good, and thereby reducing its cost of production. A reduction in the cost of production increases profits and leads suppliers to increase production. Advances in technology increase supply.

Expectations Supplier expectations are an important factor in the production decision. If a supplier expects the price of her good to rise at some time in the future, she may store some of today's output in order to sell it later and reap higher profits, decreasing supply now and increasing it later.

Taxes and Subsidies Taxes on suppliers increase the cost of production by requiring a firm to pay the government a portion of the income from products or services sold. Because taxes increase the cost of production, profit declines and suppliers will reduce supply. The opposite is true for subsidies. Subsidies to suppliers are payments by the government to produce goods; they reduce the cost of production. Subsidies increase supply. Taxes on suppliers reduce supply.

Q-6 Explain the effect of each of the following on the supply of romance novels:

1. The price of paper rises by 20 percent.
2. Government provides a 10 percent subsidy to book producers.

These aren't the only shift factors. As was the case with demand, a shift factor of supply is anything other than its price that affects supply.

A Review

To be sure you understand shifts in supply, explain what is likely to happen to your supply curve for labor in the following cases: (1) You suddenly decide that you absolutely need a new car. (2) You win a million dollars in the lottery. And finally, (3) the wage you earn doubles. If you came up with the answers: shift out to the right, shift in to the left, and no change—you've got it down. If not, it's time for a review.

Do we see such shifts in the supply curve often? Yes. A good example is computers. For the past 30 years, technological changes have continually shifted the supply curve for computers out to the right.

The Supply Table

Remember Figure 4-4(a)'s demand table for DVD rentals? In Figure 4-7(a), we follow the same reasoning to construct a supply table for three hypothetical DVD suppliers. Each supplier follows the law of supply: When price rises, each supplies more, or at least as much as each did at a lower price.

From a Supply Table to a Supply Curve

Figure 4-7(b) takes the information in Figure 4-7(a)'s supply table and translates it into a graph of each supplier's supply curve. For instance, point C_A on Ann's supply curve corresponds to the information in columns 1 and 2, row C. Point C_A is at a price of \$1 per DVD and a quantity of two DVDs per week. Notice that Ann's supply curve is upward sloping, meaning that price is positively related to quantity. Charlie's and Barry's supply curves are similarly derived.

The supply curve represents the set of *minimum* prices an individual seller will accept for various quantities of a good. The market's invisible hand stops suppliers from charging more than the market price. If suppliers could escape the market's invisible hand and charge a higher price, they would gladly do so. Unfortunately for them, and fortunately for consumers, a higher price encourages other suppliers to begin selling DVDs. Competing suppliers' entry into the market sets a limit on the price any supplier can charge.

FIGURE 4-7 (A AND B) From Individual Supplies to a Market Supply

As with market demand, market supply is determined by adding all quantities supplied at a given price. Three suppliers—Ann, Barry, and Charlie—make up the market of DVD suppliers. The total market supply is the sum of their individual supplies at each price, shown in column 5 of (**a**).

Each of the individual supply curves and the market supply curve have been plotted in (**b**). Notice how the market supply curve is the horizontal sum of the individual supply curves.

Quantities Supplied	(1) Price (per DVD)	(2) Ann's Supply	(3) Barry's Supply	(4) Charlie's Supply	(5) Market Supply
A	$0.00	0	0	0	0
B	0.50	1	0	0	1
C	1.00	2	1	0	3
D	1.50	3	2	0	5
E	2.00	4	3	0	7
F	2.50	5	4	0	9
G	3.00	6	5	0	11
H	3.50	7	5	2	14
I	4.00	8	5	2	15

(a) A Supply Table

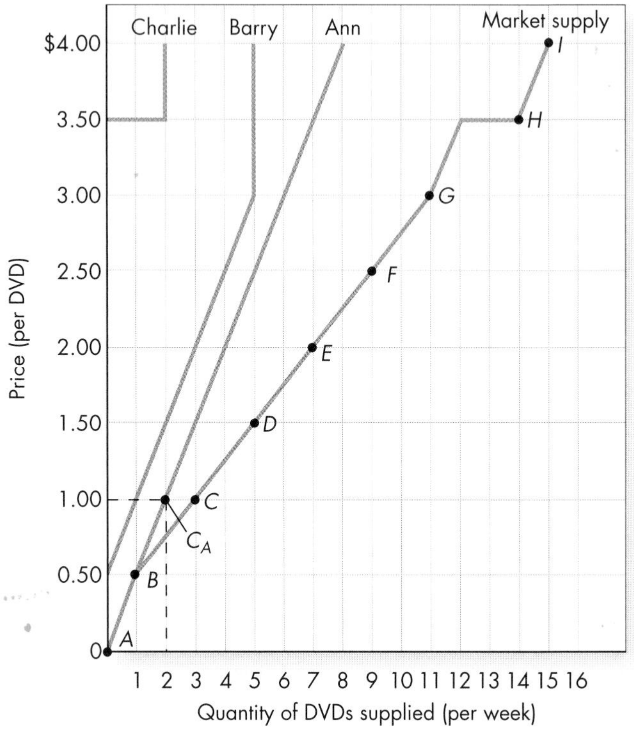

(b) Adding Supply Curves

Individual and Market Supply Curves

The market supply curve is derived from individual supply curves in precisely the same way that the market demand curve was. To emphasize the symmetry, I've made the three suppliers quite similar to the three demanders. Ann (column 2) will supply two at $1; if price goes up to $2, she increases her supply to four. Barry (column 3) begins supplying at $1, and at $3 supplies five, the most he'll supply regardless of how high price rises. Charlie (column 4) has only two units to supply. At a price of $3.50 he'll supply that quantity, but higher prices won't get him to supply any more.

Individual and Market Supply Curves

The **market supply curve** is *the horizontal sum of all individual supply curves*. In Figure 4-7(a) (column 5), we add together Ann's, Barry's, and Charlie's supplies to arrive at the market supply curve, which is graphed in Figure 4-7(b). Notice that each point corresponds to the information in columns 1 and 5 for each row. For example, point *H* corresponds to a price of $3.50 and a quantity of 14.

The law of supply is based on two phenomena:

1. At higher prices, existing suppliers supply more.
2. At higher prices, new suppliers enter the market.

The market supply curve's upward slope is determined by two different sources: as price rises, existing suppliers supply more and new suppliers enter the market. Sometimes existing suppliers may not be willing to increase their quantity supplied in response to an increase in prices, but a rise in price often brings brand-new suppliers into the market. For example, a rise in teachers' salaries will have little effect on the number of hours current teachers teach, but it will increase the number of people choosing to be teachers.

The Interaction of Supply and Demand

Thomas Carlyle, the English historian who dubbed economics "the dismal science," also wrote this chapter's introductory tidbit. "Teach a parrot the terms *supply* and *demand* and you've got an economist." In earlier chapters, I tried to convince you that economics is *not* dismal. In the rest of this chapter, I hope to convince you that, while supply and demand are important to economics, parrots don't make good economists. If students think that when they've learned the terms *supply* and *demand* they've learned economics, they're mistaken. Those terms are just labels for the ideas behind supply and demand, and it's the ideas that are important. What matters about supply and demand isn't the labels but how the concepts interact. For instance, what happens if a freeze kills the blossoms on the orange trees? If price doesn't change, the quantity of oranges supplied isn't expected to equal the quantity demanded. But in the real world, prices do change, often before the frost hits, as expectations of the frost lead people to adjust. It's in understanding the interaction of supply and demand that economics becomes interesting and relevant.

A REMINDER

Six Things to Remember about a Supply Curve

- A supply curve follows the law of supply. When price rises, quantity supplied increases, and vice versa.
- The horizontal axis—quantity—has a time dimension.
- The quality of each unit is the same.
- The vertical axis—price—assumes all other prices remain constant.
- The curve assumes everything else is constant.
- Effects of price changes are shown by movements along the supply curve. Effects of nonprice determinants of supply are shown by shifts of the entire supply curve.

Equilibrium

When you have a market in which neither suppliers nor consumers collude and in which prices are free to move up and down, the forces of supply and demand interact to arrive at an equilibrium. The concept of equilibrium comes from physics—classical mechanics. **Equilibrium** is *a concept in which opposing dynamic forces cancel each other out*. For example, a hot-air balloon is in equilibrium when the upward force exerted by the hot air in the balloon equals the downward pressure exerted on the balloon by gravity. In supply/demand analysis, equilibrium means that the upward pressure on price is exactly offset by the downward pressure on price. **Equilibrium quantity** is *the amount bought and sold at the equilibrium price*. **Equilibrium price** is *the price toward which the invisible hand drives the market*. At the equilibrium price, quantity demanded equals quantity supplied.

What happens if the market is not in equilibrium—if quantity supplied doesn't equal quantity demanded? You get either excess supply or excess demand, and a tendency for prices to change.

Excess Supply If there is **excess supply** (a surplus), *quantity supplied is greater than quantity demanded*, and some suppliers won't be able to sell all their goods. Each supplier will think: "Gee, if I offer to sell it for a bit less, I'll be the lucky one who sells my goods; someone else will be stuck with goods they can't sell." But because all suppliers with excess goods will be thinking the same thing, the price in the market will fall. As that happens, consumers will increase their quantity demanded. So the movement toward equilibrium caused by excess supply is on both the supply and demand sides.

Bargain hunters can get a deal when there is excess supply.

Excess Demand The reverse is also true. Say that instead of excess supply, there's **excess demand** (a shortage)—*quantity demanded is greater than quantity supplied*. There are more consumers who want the good than there are suppliers selling the good. Let's consider what's likely to go through demanders' minds. They'll likely call long-lost friends who just happen to be sellers of that good and tell them it's good to talk to them and, by the way, don't they want to sell that . . . ? Suppliers will be rather pleased that so many of their old friends have remembered them, but they'll also likely see the connection between excess demand and their friends' thoughtfulness. To stop their phones from ringing all the time, they'll likely raise their price. The reverse is true for excess supply. It's amazing how friendly suppliers become to potential consumers when there's excess supply.

Price Adjusts This tendency for prices to rise when the quantity demanded exceeds the quantity supplied and for prices to fall when the quantity supplied exceeds the quantity demanded is a central element to understanding supply and demand. So remember:

Prices tend to rise when there is excess demand and fall when there is excess supply.

When quantity demanded is greater than quantity supplied, prices tend to rise.

When quantity supplied is greater than quantity demanded, prices tend to fall.

Two other things to note about supply and demand are (1) the greater the difference between quantity supplied and quantity demanded, the more pressure there is for prices to rise or fall, and (2) when quantity demanded equals quantity supplied, the market is in equilibrium.

Price Adjustment and Equilibrium

People's tendencies to change prices exist as long as quantity supplied and quantity demanded differ. But the change in price brings the laws of supply and demand into play. As price falls, quantity supplied decreases as some suppliers leave the business (the law of supply). And as some people who originally weren't really interested in buying the good think, "Well, at this low price, maybe I do want to buy," quantity demanded increases (the law of demand). Similarly, when price rises, quantity supplied will increase (the law of supply) and quantity demanded will decrease (the law of demand).

Whenever quantity supplied and quantity demanded are unequal, price tends to change. If, however, quantity supplied and quantity demanded are equal, price will stay the same because no one will have an incentive to change.

The Graphical Interaction of Supply and Demand Figure 4-8 shows supply and demand curves for DVD rentals and demonstrates the force of the invisible hand. Let's consider what will happen to the price of DVDs in three cases:

1. When the price is $3.50 each.
2. When the price is $1.50 each.
3. When the price is $2.50 each.

1. When price is $3.50, quantity supplied is seven and quantity demanded is only three. Excess supply is four. Individual consumers can get all they want, but most suppliers can't sell all they wish; they'll be stuck with DVDs that they'd like to rent. Suppliers will tend to offer their goods at a lower price and demanders, who see plenty of suppliers out there, will bargain harder for an even lower price. Both these forces will push the price as indicated by the down arrows in Figure 4-8.

Now let's start from the other side.

2. Say price is $1.50. The situation is now reversed. Quantity supplied is three and quantity demanded is seven. Excess demand is four. Now it's consumers who can't get what they want and suppliers who are in the strong bargaining position. The pressures will be on price to rise in the direction of the up arrows in Figure 4-8.
3. At $2.50, price is at its equilibrium: quantity supplied equals quantity demanded. Suppliers offer to sell five and consumers want to buy five, so there's no pressure on price to rise or fall. Price will tend to remain where it is (point *E* in Figure 4-8). Notice that the equilibrium price is where the supply and demand curves intersect.

What Equilibrium Isn't

It is important to remember two points about equilibrium. First, equilibrium isn't a state of the world. It's a characteristic of the model—the framework you use to look at the world. The same situation could be seen as an equilibrium in one framework and as a

FIGURE 4-8 The Interaction of Supply and Demand

Combining Ann's supply from Figure 4-7 and Alice's demand from Figure 4-4, let's see the force of the invisible hand. When there is excess demand, there is upward pressure on price. When there is excess supply, there is downward pressure on price. Understanding these pressures is essential to understanding how to apply economics to reality.

Price (per DVD)	Quantity Supplied	Quantity Demanded	Surplus (+)/ Shortage (−)
$3.50	7	3	+4
$2.50	5	5	0
$1.50	3	7	−4

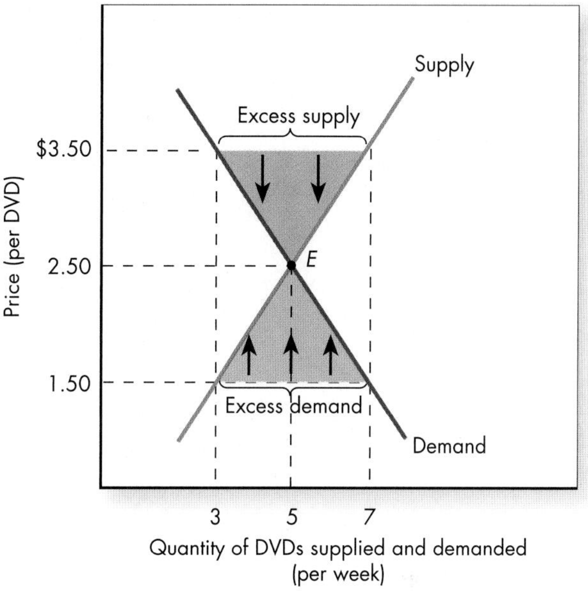

disequilibrium in another. Say you're describing a car that's speeding along at 100 miles an hour. That car is changing position relative to objects on the ground. Its movement could be, and generally is, described as if it were in disequilibrium. However, if you consider this car relative to another car going 100 miles an hour, the cars could be modeled as being in equilibrium because their positions relative to each other aren't changing.

Second, equilibrium isn't inherently good or bad. It's simply a state in which dynamic pressures offset each other. Some equilibria are good—a market in competitive equilibrium is one in which people can buy the goods they really want at the best possible price. Other equilibria are awful. Say two countries are engaged in a nuclear war against each other and both sides are blown away. An equilibrium will have been reached, but there's nothing good about it.

Equilibrium is not inherently good or bad.

Political and Social Forces and Equilibrium

Understanding that equilibrium is a characteristic of the model, not of the real world, is important in applying economic models to reality. For example, in the preceding description, I said equilibrium occurs where quantity supplied equals quantity demanded. In a model where economic forces were the only forces operating, that's true. In the real world, however, other forces—political and social forces—are operating. These will likely push price away from that supply/demand equilibrium. Were we to consider a model that included all these forces—political, social, and economic—equilibrium would be likely to exist where quantity supplied isn't equal to quantity demanded. For example:

- Farmers use political pressure to obtain prices that are higher than supply/demand equilibrium prices.
- Social pressures often offset economic pressures and prevent unemployed individuals from accepting work at lower wages than currently employed workers receive.
- Existing firms conspire to limit new competition by lobbying Congress to pass restrictive regulations and by devising pricing strategies to scare off new entrants.
- Renters often organize to pressure local government to set caps on the rental price of apartments.

FIGURE 4-9 (A AND B) Shifts in Supply and Demand

If demand increases from D_0 to D_1, as shown in (**a**), the quantity of DVD rentals that was demanded at a price of \$2.25, 8, increases to 10, but the quantity supplied remains at 8. This excess demand tends to cause prices to rise. Eventually, a new equilibrium is reached at the price of \$2.50, where the quantity supplied and the quantity demanded are 9 (point *B*).

If supply of DVD rentals decreases, then the entire supply curve shifts inward to the left, as shown in (**b**), from S_0 to S_1. At the price of \$2.25, the quantity supplied has now decreased to 6 DVDs, but the quantity demanded has remained at 8 DVDs. The excess demand tends to force the price upward. Eventually, an equilibrium is reached at the price of \$2.50 and quantity 7 (point C).

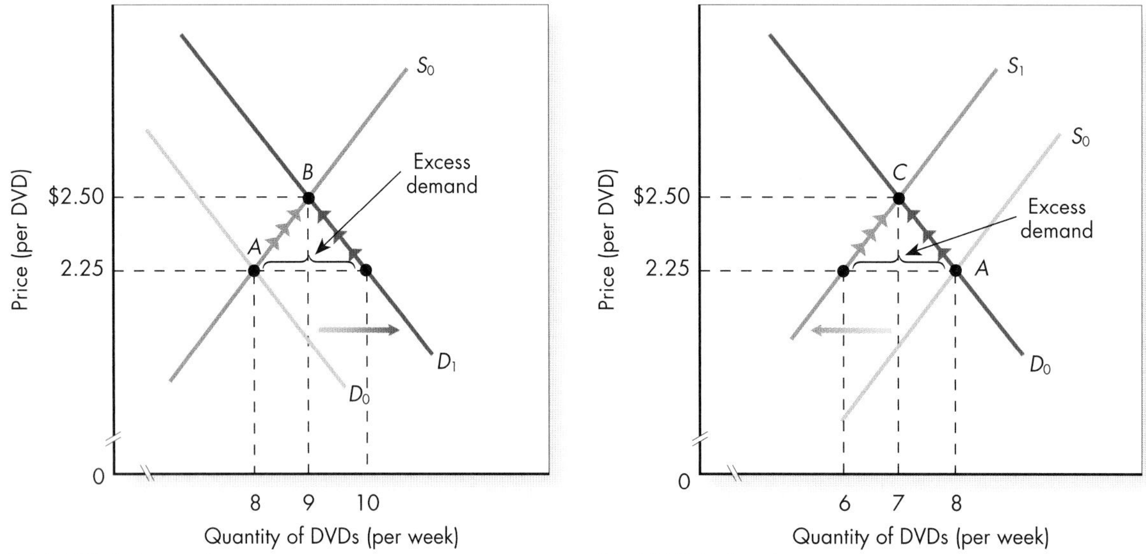

(a) A Shift in Demand **(b) A Shift in Supply**

If social and political forces were included in the analysis, they'd provide a counter–pressure to the dynamic forces of supply and demand. The result would be an equilibrium with continual excess supply or excess demand if the market were considered only in reference to economic forces. Economic forces pushing toward a supply/demand equilibrium would be thwarted by social and political forces pushing in the other direction.

Shifts in Supply and Demand

Supply and demand are most useful when trying to figure out what will happen to equilibrium price and quantity if either supply or demand shifts. Figure 4-9(a) deals with an increase in demand. Figure 4-9(b) deals with a decrease in supply.

Q-7 Demonstrate graphically the effect of a heavy frost in Florida on the equilibrium quantity and price of oranges.

Let's consider again the supply and demand for DVD rentals. In Figure 4-9(a), the supply is S_0 and initial demand is D_0. They meet at an equilibrium price of \$2.25 per DVD and an equilibrium quantity of 8 DVDs per week (point *A*). Now say that the demand for DVD rentals increases from D_0 to D_1. At a price of \$2.25, the quantity of DVD rentals supplied will be 8 and the quantity demanded will be 10; excess demand of 2 exists.

Web Note 4.4
Changes in Equilibrium

The excess demand pushes prices upward in the direction of the small arrows, decreasing the quantity demanded and increasing the quantity supplied. As it does so, movement takes place along both the supply curve and the demand curve.

The upward push on price decreases the gap between the quantity supplied and the quantity demanded. As the gap decreases, the upward pressure decreases, but as long as that gap exists at all, price will be pushed upward until the new equilibrium price (\$2.50) and new quantity (9) are reached (point *B*). At point *B*, quantity supplied

ADDED DIMENSION

The Supply and Demand for Children

In Chapter 1, I distinguished between an economic force and a market force. Economic forces are operative in all aspects of our lives; market forces are economic forces that are allowed to be expressed through a market. My examples in this chapter are of market forces—of goods sold in a market—but supply and demand also can be used to analyze situations in which economic, but not market, forces operate. An economist who is adept at this is Gary Becker of the University of Chicago. He has applied supply and demand analysis to a wide range of issues, even the supply and demand for children.

Becker doesn't argue that children should be bought and sold. But he does argue that economic considerations play a large role in people's decisions on how many children to have. In farming communities, children can be productive early in life; by age six or seven, they can work on a farm. In an advanced industrial community, children provide pleasure but generally don't contribute productively to family income. Even getting them to help around the house can be difficult.

Becker argues that since the price of having children is lower for a farming society than for an industrial society, farming societies will have more children per family. Quantity of children demanded will be larger. And that's what we find. Developing countries that rely primarily on farming often have three, four, or more children per family. Industrial societies average fewer than two children per family.

equals quantity demanded. So the market is in equilibrium. Notice that the adjustment is twofold: The higher price brings about equilibrium by both increasing the quantity supplied (from 8 to 9) and decreasing the quantity demanded (from 10 to 9).

Figure 4-9(b) begins with the same situation that we started with in Figure 4-9(a); the initial equilibrium quantity and price are eight DVDs per week and $2.25 per DVD (point A). In this example, however, instead of demand increasing, let's assume supply decreases—say because some suppliers change what they like to do and decide they will no longer supply DVDs. That means that the entire supply curve shifts inward to the left (from S_0 to S_1). At the initial equilibrium price of $2.25, the quantity demanded is greater than the quantity supplied. Two more DVDs are demanded than are supplied. (Excess demand = 2.)

This excess demand exerts upward pressure on price. Price is pushed in the direction of the small arrows. As the price rises, the upward pressure on price is reduced but will still exist until the new equilibrium price, $2.50, and new quantity, seven, are reached. At $2.50, the quantity supplied equals the quantity demanded. The adjustment has involved a movement along the demand curve and the new supply curve. As price rises, quantity supplied is adjusted upward and quantity demanded is adjusted downward until quantity supplied equals quantity demanded where the new supply curve intersects the demand curve at point C, an equilibrium of seven and $2.50.

Q-8 Demonstrate graphically the likely effect of an increase in the price of gas on the equilibrium quantity and price of hybrid cars.

Here is an exercise for you to try. Demonstrate graphically how the price of computers could have fallen dramatically in the past 10 years, even as demand increased. (Hint: Supply has increased even more, so even at lower prices, far more computers have been supplied than were being supplied 10 years ago.)

The Limitations of Supply/Demand Analysis

Supply and demand are tools, and, like most tools, they help us enormously when used appropriately. Used inappropriately, however, they can be misleading. Throughout the book I'll introduce you to the limitations of the tools, but let me discuss an important one here.

Q-9 When determining the effect of a shift factor on price and quantity, in which of the following markets could you likely assume that other things will remain constant?

1. Market for eggs.
2. Labor market.
3. World oil market.
4. Market for luxury boats.

In supply/demand analysis, other things are assumed constant. If other things change, then one cannot directly apply supply/demand analysis. Sometimes supply and demand are interconnected, making it impossible to hold other things constant. Let's take an example. Say we are considering the effect of a fall in the wage rate on unemployment. In supply/demand analysis, you would look at the effect that fall would have on workers' decisions to supply labor, and on business's decision to hire workers. But there are also other effects. For instance, the fall in the wage lowers people's income and thereby reduces demand. That reduction may feed back to firms and reduce the demand for their goods, which might reduce the firms' demand for workers. If these effects do occur, and are important enough to affect the result, they have to be added for the analysis to be complete. A complete analysis always includes the relevant feedback effects.

There is no single answer to the question of which ripples must be included, and much debate among economists involves which ripple effects to include. But there are some general rules. Supply/demand analysis, used without adjustment, is most appropriate for questions where the goods are a small percentage of the entire economy. That is when the other-things-constant assumption will most likely hold. As soon as one starts analyzing goods that are a large percentage of the entire economy, the other-things-constant assumption is likely not to hold true. The reason is found in the **fallacy of composition**—*the false assumption that what is true for a part will also be true for the whole*.

The fallacy of composition is the false assumption that what is true for a part will also be true for the whole.

Consider a lone supplier who lowers the price of his or her good. People will substitute that good for other goods, and the quantity of the good demanded will increase. But what if all suppliers lower their prices? Since all prices have gone down, why should consumers switch? The substitution story can't be used in the aggregate. There are many such examples.

Q-10 Why is the fallacy of composition relevant for macroeconomic issues?

An understanding of the fallacy of composition is of central relevance to macroeconomics. In the aggregate, whenever firms produce (whenever they supply), they create income (demand for their goods). So in macro, when supply changes, demand changes. This interdependence is one of the primary reasons we have a separate macroeconomics. In macroeconomics, the other-things-constant assumption central to microeconomic supply/demand analysis cannot hold.

It is to account for interdependency between aggregate supply decisions and aggregate demand decisions that we have a separate micro analysis and a separate macro analysis.

It is to account for these interdependencies that we separate macro analysis from micro analysis. In macro we use curves whose underlying foundations are much more complicated than the supply and demand curves we use in micro and in modern economics there is an active debate about how more complex structural models can extend our understanding of how markets operate.

One final comment: The fact that supply and demand may be interdependent does not mean that you can't use supply/demand analysis; it simply means that you must modify its results with the interdependency that, if you've done the analysis correctly, you've kept in the back of your head. Using supply and demand analysis is generally a step in any good economic analysis, but you must remember that it may be only a step.

Conclusion

Throughout the book, I'll be presenting examples of supply and demand. So I'll end this chapter here because its intended purposes have been served. What were those intended purposes? First, I exposed you to enough economic terminology and economic thinking to allow you to proceed to my more complicated examples. Second, I have set your mind to work putting the events around you into a supply/demand framework. Doing that will give you new insights into the events that shape all our lives. Once you incorporate the supply/demand framework into your way of looking at the world, you will have made an important step toward thinking like an economist.

Summary

- The law of demand states that quantity demanded rises as price falls, other things constant.
- The law of supply states that quantity supplied rises as price rises, other things constant.
- Factors that affect supply and demand other than price are called shift factors. Shift factors of demand include income, prices of other goods, tastes, expectations, and taxes on and subsidies to consumers. Shift factors of supply include the price of inputs, technology, expectations, and taxes on and subsidies to producers.
- A change in quantity demanded (supplied) is a movement along the demand (supply) curve. A change in demand (supply) is a shift of the entire demand (supply) curve.
- The laws of supply and demand hold true because individuals can substitute.
- A market demand (supply) curve is the horizontal sum of all individual demand (supply) curves.
- When quantity supplied equals quantity demanded, prices have no tendency to change. This is equilibrium.
- When quantity demanded is greater than quantity supplied, prices tend to rise. When quantity supplied is greater than quantity demanded, prices tend to fall.
- When the demand curve shifts to the right (left), equilibrium price rises (declines) and equilibrium quantity rises (falls).
- When the supply curve shifts to the right (left), equilibrium price declines (rises) and equilibrium quantity rises (falls).
- In the real world, you must add political and social forces to the supply/demand model. When you do, equilibrium is likely not going to be where quantity demanded equals quantity supplied.
- In macro, small side effects that can be assumed away in micro are multiplied enormously and can significantly change the results. To ignore them is to fall into the fallacy of composition.

Key Terms

demand *(85)*
demand curve *(84)*
equilibrium *(95)*
equilibrium price *(95)*
equilibrium quantity *(95)*
excess demand *(95)*
excess supply *(95)*
fallacy of composition *(100)*
law of demand *(84)*
law of supply *(90)*
market demand curve *(88)*
market supply curve *(94)*
movement along a demand curve *(85)*
movement along a supply curve *(92)*
quantity demanded *(85)*
quantity supplied *(91)*
shift in demand *(85)*
shift in supply *(92)*
supply *(91)*
supply curve *(91)*

Questions and Exercises

connect ECONOMICS

1. State the law of demand. Why is price inversely related to quantity demanded? LO1, LO2
2. You're given the following individual demand tables for comic books.

Price	John	Liz	Alex
$ 2	4	36	24
4	4	32	20
6	0	28	16
8	0	24	12
10	0	20	8
12	0	16	4
14	0	12	0
16	0	8	0

   a. Determine the market demand table.
   b. Graph the individual and market demand curves.
   c. If the current market price is $4, what's total market demand? What happens to total market demand if price rises to $8?
   d. Say that an advertising campaign increases demand by 50 percent. What will happen to the individual and market demand curves? LO1
3. List four shift factors of demand and explain how each affects demand. LO3
4. Distinguish the effect of a shift factor of demand on the demand curve from the effect of a change in price on the demand curve. LO3
5. State the law of supply. Why is price directly related to quantity supplied? LO4
6. Mary has just stated that normally, as price rises, supply will increase. Her teacher grimaces. Why? LO4
7. List four shift factors of supply and explain how each affects supply. LO5
8. Derive the market supply curve from the following two individual supply curves. LO5

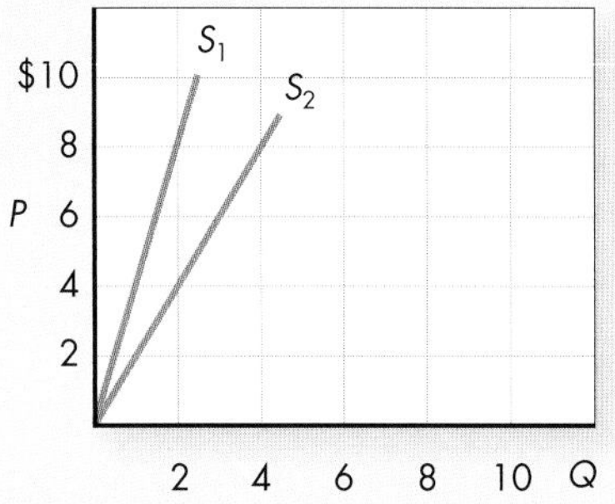

9. You're given the following demand and supply tables:

P	Demand D_1	Demand D_2	Demand D_3
$30	20	5	10
40	15	3	7
50	10	0	5
60	5	0	0

P	Supply S_1	Supply S_2	Supply S_3
$30	0	4	11
40	0	8	17
50	10	12	18
60	10	15	20

   a. Draw the market demand and market supply curves.
   b. What is excess supply/demand at price $30? Price $60?
   c. Label equilibrium price and quantity. LO6
10. It has just been reported that eating red meat is bad for your health. Using supply and demand curves, demonstrate the report's likely effect on the equilibrium price and quantity of steak sold in the market. LO7
11. Why does the price of airline tickets rise during the summer months? Demonstrate your answer graphically. LO7
12. Why does sales volume rise during weeks when states suspend taxes on sales by retailers? Demonstrate your answer graphically. LO7
13. What is the expected impact of increased security measures imposed by the federal government on airlines on fares and volume of travel? Demonstrate your answer graphically. (Difficult) LO7
14. Explain what a sudden popularity of "Economics Professor" brand casual wear would likely do to prices of that brand. LO7
15. In a flood, usable water supplies ironically tend to decline because the pumps and water lines are damaged. What will a flood likely do to prices of bottled water? LO7
16. The price of gas shot up significantly in 2008 to over $4.00 a gallon. What effect did this likely have on the demand for diesel cars that get better mileage than the typical car? LO7
17. OPEC announces it will increase oil production by 20 percent. What is the effect on the price of oil? Demonstrate your answer graphically. LO7

18. Draw hypothetical supply and demand curves for tea. Show how the equilibrium price and quantity will be affected by each of the following occurrences:
    a. Bad weather wreaks havoc with the tea crop.
    b. A medical report implying tea is bad for your health is published.
    c. A technological innovation lowers the cost of producing tea.
    d. Consumers' income falls. (Assume tea is a normal good.) LO7
19. You're a commodity trader and you've just heard a report that the winter wheat harvest will be 2.09 billion bushels, a 44 percent jump, rather than an expected 35 percent jump to 1.96 billion bushels. (Difficult)
    a. What would you expect would happen to wheat prices?
    b. Demonstrate graphically the effect you suggested in *a*. LO7
20. In the United States, say gasoline costs consumers about $2.50 per gallon. In Italy, say it costs consumers about $6 per gallon. What effect does this price differential likely have on
    a. The size of cars in the United States and in Italy?
    b. The use of public transportation in the United States and in Italy?
    c. The fuel efficiency of cars in the United States and in Italy?
    d. What would be the effect of raising the price of gasoline in the United States to $4 per gallon? LO7
21. In 2004, Argentina imposed a 20 percent tax on natural gas exports.
    a. Demonstrate the likely effect of that tax on gas exports using supply and demand curves.
    b. What did it likely do to the price of natural gas in Argentina? LO7
22. In most developing countries, there are long lines of taxis at airports, and these taxis often wait two or three hours. What does this tell you about the price in that market? Demonstrate with supply and demand analysis. LO7
23. Define the fallacy of composition. How does it affect the supply/demand model? LO8
24. In which of the following three markets are there likely to be the greatest feedback effects: market for housing, market for wheat, market for manufactured goods? LO8
25. State whether supply/demand analysis used without significant modification is suitable to assess the following:
    a. The impact of an increase in the demand for pencils on the price of pencils.
    b. The impact of an increase in the supply of labor on the quantity of labor demanded.
    c. The impact of an increase in aggregate savings on aggregate expenditures.
    d. The impact of a new method of producing CDs on the price of CDs. LO8

Questions from Alternative Perspectives

1. In a centrally planned economy, how might central planners estimate supply or demand? (Austrian)
2. In the late 19th century, Washington Gladden said, "He who battles for the Christianization of society, will find their strongest foe in the field of economics. Economics is indeed the dismal science because of the selfishness of its maxims and the inhumanity of its conclusions."
    a. Evaluate this statement.
    b. Is there a conflict between the ideology of capitalism and the precepts of Christianity?
    c. Would a society that emphasized a capitalist mode of production benefit by a moral framework that emphasized selflessness rather than selfishness? (Religious)
3. Economics is often referred to as the study of choice.
    a. In U.S. history, have men and women been equally free to choose the amount of education they receive even within the same family?
    b. What other areas can you see where men and women have not been equally free to choose?
    c. If you agree that men and women have not had equal rights to choose, what implications does that have about the objectivity of economic analysis? (Feminist)
4. Knowledge is derived from a tautology when something is true because you assume it is true. In this chapter, you have learned the conditions under which supply and demand explain outcomes. Yet, as your text author cautions, these conditions may not hold. How can you be sure if they ever hold? (Institutionalist)
5. Do you think consumers make purchasing decisions based on general rules of thumb instead of price?
    a. Why would consumers do this?
    b. What implication might this have for the conclusions drawn about markets? (Post-Keynesian)
6. Some economists believe that imposing international labor standards would cost jobs. In support of this argument, one economist said, "Either you believe labor demand curves are downward sloping, or you don't." Of course, not to believe that demand curves are negatively sloped would be tantamount to declaring yourself an economic illiterate. What else about the nature of labor demand curves might help a policy maker design policies that could counteract the negative effects of labor standards employment? (Radical)

Issues to Ponder

1. Oftentimes, to be considered for a job, you have to know someone in the firm. What does this observation tell you about the wage paid for that job? (Difficult) LO6
2. In the early 2000s, the demand for housing increased substantially as low interest rates increased the number of people who could afford homes.
   a. What was the likely effect of this on housing prices? Demonstrate graphically.
   b. In 2005, mortgage rates began increasing. What was the likely effect of this increase on housing prices? Demonstrate graphically.
   c. In a period of increasing demand for housing, would you expect housing prices to rise more in Miami suburbs, which had room for expansion and fairly loose laws about subdivisions, or in a city such as San Francisco, which had limited land and tight subdivision restrictions? LO7
3. In 1994, the U.S. postal service put a picture of rodeo rider Ben Pickett, not the rodeo star, Bill Pickett, whom it meant to honor, on a stamp. It printed 150,000 sheets. Recognizing its error, it recalled the stamp, but it found that 183 sheets had already been sold. (Difficult)
   a. What would the recall likely do to the price of the 183 sheets that were sold?
   b. When the government recognized that it could not recall all the stamps, it decided to issue the remaining ones. What would that decision likely do?
   c. What would the holders of the misprinted sheet likely do when they heard of the government's decision? LO7
4. What would be the effect of a 75 percent tax on lawsuit punitive awards that was proposed by California Governor Arnold Schwarzenegger in 2004 on: (Difficult)
   a. The number of punitive awards. Demonstrate your answer using supply and demand curves.
   b. The number of pretrial settlements. LO7
5. Why is a supply/demand analysis that includes only economic forces likely to be incomplete? LO8

Answers to Margin Questions

1. The demand curve slopes downward because price and quantity demanded are inversely related. As the price of a good rises, people switch to purchasing other goods whose prices have not risen by as much. *(84)*
2. *Demand for luxury goods.* The other possibility, *quantity of luxury goods demanded,* is used to refer to movements along (not shifts of) the demand curve. *(85)*
3. (1) The decline in price will increase the quantity of computers demanded (movement down along the demand curve); (2) With more income, demand for computers will rise (shift of the demand curve out to the right). *(87)*
4. When adding two demand curves, you sum them horizontally, as in the accompanying diagram. *(88)*

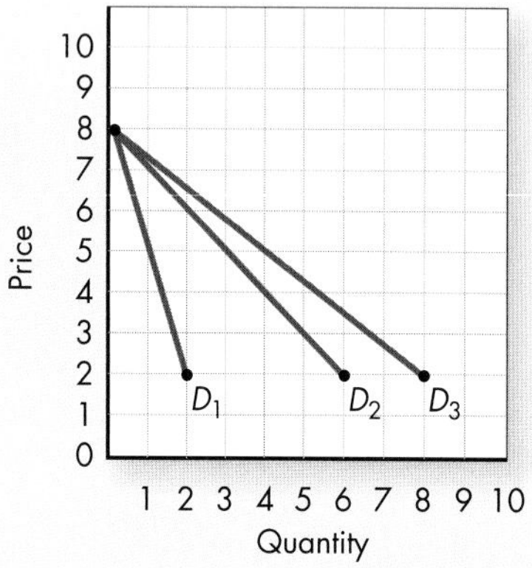

5. *The quantity supplied* rose because there was a movement along the supply curve. The supply curve itself remained unchanged. *(91)*
6. (1) The supply of romance novels declines since paper is an input to production (supply shifts in to the left); (2) the supply of romance novels rises since the subsidy decreases the cost to the producer (supply shifts out to the right). *(93)*
7. A heavy frost in Florida will decrease the supply of oranges, increasing the price and decreasing the quantity demanded, as in the accompanying graph. *(98)*

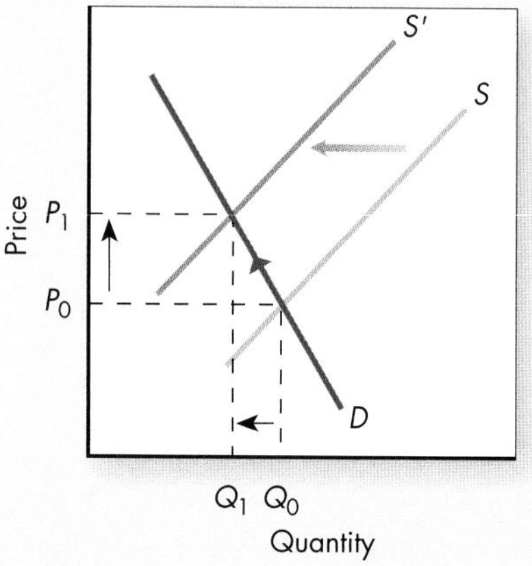

8. An increase in the price of gas will likely increase the demand for hybrid cars, increasing their price and increasing the quantity supplied, as in the accompanying graph. *(99)*

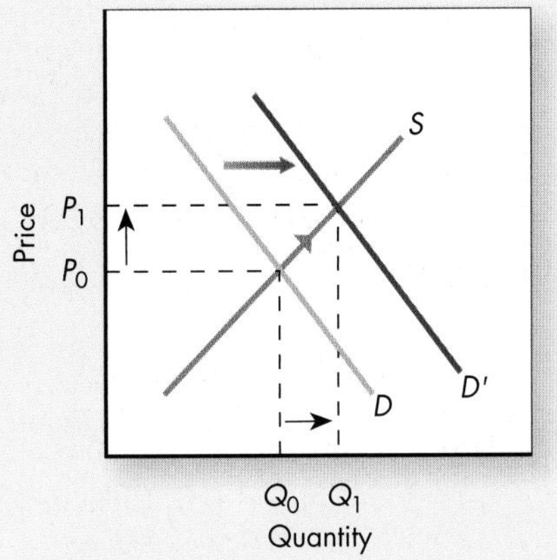

9. Other things are most likely to remain constant in the egg and luxury boat markets because each is a small percentage of the whole economy. Factors that affect the world oil market and the labor market will have ripple effects that must be taken into account in any analysis. *(100)*
10. The fallacy of composition is relevant for macroeconomic issues because it reminds us that, in the aggregate, small effects that are immaterial for micro issues can add up and be material. *(100)*

CHAPTER 5

Using Supply and Demand

It is by invisible hands that we are bent and tortured worst.

—*Nietzsche*

Supply and demand give you a lens through which to view the economy. That lens brings into focus issues that would otherwise seem like a muddle. In this chapter, we use the supply/demand lens to consider real-world events.

AFTER READING THIS CHAPTER, YOU SHOULD BE ABLE TO:

1. Explain real-world events using supply and demand.
2. Discuss how exchange rates are determined using supply and demand.
3. Demonstrate the effect of a price ceiling and a price floor on a market.
4. Explain the effect of excise taxes and tariffs on equilibrium price and quantity.
5. Explain the effect of a third-party-payer system on equilibrium price and quantity.

Real-World Supply and Demand Applications

Let's begin by giving you an opportunity to apply supply/demand analysis to real-world events. Below are three events. After reading each, try your hand at explaining what happened, using supply and demand curves. To help you in the process Figure 5-1 provides some diagrams. *Before* reading my explanation, try to match the shifts to the examples. In each, be careful to explain which curve, or curves, shifted and how those shifts affected equilibrium price and quantity.

1. In the spring of 2006, Cyclone Larry tore through key growing regions of Australia with 180-miles-per-hour winds wiping out 80 percent of Australia's banana crop. Banana prices rose overnight from $1.00 to $2.00 a pound, where they were expected to remain for some time. Market: Bananas in Australia.
2. When the price of gas rose so that it cost as much as $100 to fill a tank of gas, Americans switched from SUVs to more fuel-efficient cars. The number of people shopping for used SUVs fell over 30 percent in 2006 and 2007 and the price of used SUVs fell an average of 10 percent. Market: Used SUVs in the United States.
3. A growing middle class in China and India has increased the demand for many food products, particularly edible oils such as soy and palm. At the same time, to meet the increasing demand for ethanol, U.S. farmers have chosen to grow less soy (from which soy oil is made) and more corn. The result? Dramatic increases in the price of edible oil worldwide. Market: Global edible oils.

Now that you've matched them, let's see if your analysis matches mine.

FIGURE 5-1 (A, B, AND C)
In this exhibit, three shifts of supply and demand are shown. Your task is to match them with the events listed in the text.

Answers: 1–b; 2–a; 3–c.

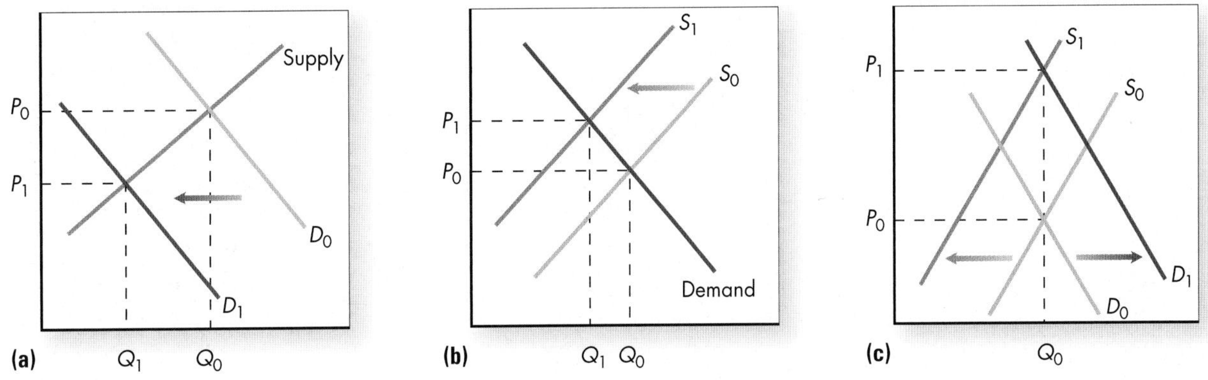

Cyclone Larry Weather is a shift factor of supply. The cyclone shifted the supply curve for bananas from Australia to the left, as shown in Figure 5-1(b). At the original price, \$1 a pound (shown by P_0), quantity demanded exceeded quantity supplied and the invisible hand of the market pressured the price to rise until quantity demanded equaled quantity supplied at \$2 a pound (shown by P_1).

Q-1 True or false? If supply rises, price will rise.

Sales of SUVs Gas is a significant cost of driving a car. To reduce their automotive gas bills, Americans reduced their demand for gas-guzzling SUVs, both new and used. Figure 5-1(a) shows that the demand curve for SUVs in the used-car market shifted from D_0 to D_1. At the original price P_0, sellers were unable to sell the SUVs they wanted to sell and began to lower their price. Buyers of used SUVs were able to purchase them at a 10 percent lower price, shown by P_1.

Edible Oils Increases in the size of the middle class in developing countries such as China and India have increased the demand for food and edible oils used to prepare those foods. This is represented by a shift in the demand for edible oils out to the right from D_0 to D_1. At the same time, increases in the price of crude oil have led U.S. farmers to grow less soy and more corn, which has shifted the supply curve from S_0 to S_1. The result has been a dramatic increase in the price of edible oils, shown in Figure 5-1(c) as an increase from P_0 to P_1.

WWW Web Note 5.1
Fair Trade Coffee

Now that we've been through some straightforward examples, let's get more adventurous and apply supply/demand analysis to a case where you really have to be careful about what price you are talking about—the demand and supply for euros, the common currency in Europe.

The Price of a Foreign Currency

The market for foreign currencies is called the foreign exchange (forex) market. It is this market that determines the **exchange rates**—*the price of one country's currency in terms of another's currency*—that newspapers report daily in tables such as the table on the next page that shows the cost of various currencies in terms of dollars and dollars in

Q-2 You are going to Chile and plan to exchange $100. According to the foreign exchange rate table in the text, how many Chilean pesos will you receive?

Currencies

April 3, 2009

U.S.-dollar foreign-exchange rates in late New York trading

Country/currency	Fri in US$	Fri per US$	US$ vs. YTD chg (%)
Americas			
Argentina peso*	0.2709	3.6914	**6.9**
Brazil real	0.4528	2.2085	**4.6**
Canada dollar	0.8128	1.2303	**1.1**
1-mos forward	0.8128	1.2303	**1.1**
3-mos forward	0.8135	1.2293	**1.0**
6-mos forward	0.8146	1.2276	**1.0**
Chile peso	0.001727	579.04	**−9.3**
Colombia peso	0.0004141	2414.88	**7.4**
Ecuador US dollar	1	1	**unch**
Mexico peso*	0.0738	13.5520	**−1.3**
Peru new sol	0.3214	3.1114	**−0.7**
Uruguay peso†	0.04170	23.98	**−1.7**
Venezuela b. fuerte	0.46570111	2.1473	**unch**
Asia-Pacific			
Australian dollar	0.7157	1.3972	**−0.6**
China yuan	0.1463	6.8348	**0.2**
Hong Kong dollar	0.1290	7.7500	**unch**
India rupee	0.02004	49.9002	**2.6**
Indonesia rupiah	0.0000872	11468	**5.2**
Japan yen	0.009973	100.27	**10.5**
1-mos forward	0.009977	100.23	**10.5**
3-mos forward	0.009988	100.12	**10.6**
6-mos forward	0.010009	99.91	**10.6**
Malaysia ringgits§	0.2793	3.5804	**3.7**
New Zealand dollar	0.5859	1.7068	**0.1**
Pakistan rupee	0.01244	80.386	**1.6**
Philippines peso	0.0210	47.733	**0.6**
Singapore dollar	0.6645	1.5049	**5.1**
South Korea won	0.0007479	1337.08	**5.9**
Taiwan dollar	0.03000	33.333	**1.7**
Thailand baht	0.02834	35.286	**1.4**
Vietnam dong	0.00006	17779	**1.7**

Country/currency	Fri in US$	Fri per US$	US$ vs. YTD chg (%)
Europe			
Czech Rep. koruna**	0.05095	19.627	**2.1**
Denmark krone	0.1811	5.5218	**3.6**
Euro area euro	1.3488	0.7414	**3.6**
Hungary forint	0.004551	219.73	**15.6**
Norway krone	0.1531	6.5317	**−6.1**
Poland zloty	0.3032	3.2982	**11.1**
Romania leu	0.3239	3.0871	**6.9**
Russia ruble‡	0.03003	33.300	**9.1**
Sweden krona	0.1257	7.9554	**1.7**
Switzerland franc	0.8842	1.1310	**6.0**
1-mos forward	0.8847	1.1303	**5.9**
3-mos forward	0.8858	1.1289	**5.9**
6-mos forward	0.8879	1.1263	**6.0**
Turkey lira**	0.6323	1.5815	**2.7**
UK pound	1.4828	0.6744	**−1.6**
1-mos forward	1.4828	0.6744	**−1.7**
3-mos forward	1.4830	0.6743	**−1.8**
6-mos forward	1.4836	0.6740	**−1.8**
Middle East/Africa			
Bahrain dollar	2.6527	0.3770	**unch**
Egypt pound*	0.1776	5.6294	**2.4**
Israel shekel	0.2400	4.1667	**10.3**
Jordan dinar	1.4129	0.7078	**−0.1**
Kenya shilling	0.01252	79.875	**2.1**
Kuwait dinar	3.4376	0.2909	**5.3**
Lebanon pound	0.0006634	1507.39	**unch**
Saudia Arabia riyal	0.2666	3.7509	**−0.1**
South Africa rand	0.1105	9.0498	**−8.7**
UAE dirham	0.2722	3.6738	**unch**
SDR††	1.5001	0.6666	**2.7**

* Floating rate †Financial §Government rate ‡Russian Central Bank rate ** Commercial rate
††Special Drawing Rights (SDR); from the International Monetary Fund; based on exchange rates for U.S., British and Japanese currencies.
Note: Based on trading among banks of $1 million and more, as quoted at 4 p.m. ET by Thomas Reuters.

terms of other currencies. From it you can see that on April 3, 2009, one riyal cost about 27 cents and one rand cost 11 cents. (If you are wondering which countries have riyals and rands for currencies, look at the table.)

People demand currencies of other countries to buy those countries' goods and assets.

Unless you collect currencies, the reason you want the currency of another country is that you want to buy something that country produces or an existing asset of that country. Say you want to buy a Hyundai car that costs 12.793 million South Korean won. Looking at the table, you see that 1 won costs $0.0007479. This means that 12.793 million won will cost you $9,567.88. So before you can buy the Hyundai, somebody must go to a forex market with $9,567.88 and exchange those dollars for 12.793 million won. Only then can the car be bought in the United States. Most final buyers don't do this; the importer does it for them. But whenever a foreign good is bought, someone must trade currencies.

The determination of exchange rates is the same as the determination of price. A currency is just another good.

To see what determines exchange rates, let's consider the price of the **euro**—*the currency used by 16 of the members of the European Union*. In 2001, one euro sold for $0.85. It rose as high as $1.50 in the early 2000s. What caused this rise? Supply and demand. Once you recognize that a currency is just another good, what may appear to be a hard subject (the determination of exchange rates) becomes an easy subject (what determines a good's price). All you have to do is to replace the good I used in Chapter 4 (DVDs) with euros, and apply the same reasoning process we've used so far to determine the equilibrium price of the euro.

A REMINDER

Supply and Demand in Action

Sorting out the effects of the shifts of supply or demand or both can be confusing. Here are some helpful hints to keep things straight:

- Draw the initial demand and supply curves and label them. The equilibrium price and quantity is where these curves intersect. Label them.
- If only price has changed, no curves will shift and a shortage or surplus will result.
- If a nonprice factor affects demand, determine the direction demand has shifted and add the new demand curve. Do the same for supply.
- Equilibrium price and quantity is where the new demand and supply curves intersect. Label them.
- Compare the initial equilibrium price and quantity to the new equilibrium price and quantity.

See if you can describe what happened in the three graphs below.

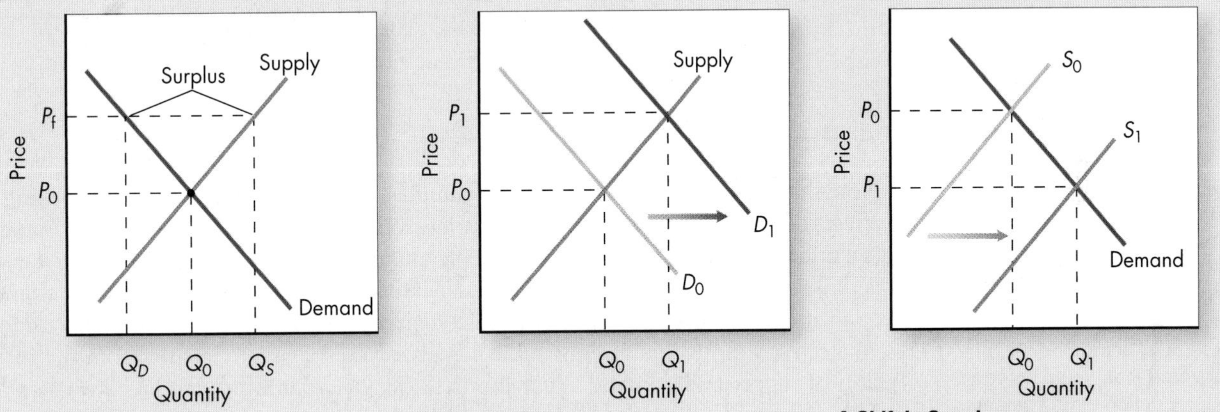

A Change in Price **A Shift in Demand** **A Shift in Supply**

Figure 5-2 shows supply and demand curves for the euro. As with any good, the supply of euros represents those people who are selling euros and the demand for the euro represents those people who are buying euros. Sellers of euros are Europeans who want to buy U.S. goods and assets. Buyers of euros are U.S. citizens who want to buy European goods and assets. (For simplicity, we assume that the only countries that exist are the United States and European countries that use the euro as their currency.)

The rise in the value of the euro in the early 2000s occurred for a number of reasons. The one we will focus on here is the recession and falling interest rates in the United States. We begin with demand D_0 and supply S_0 for euros, resulting in an equilibrium price of $0.85 in 2001. Because the U.S. economy entered a recession, and because U.S. interest rates fell, Europeans bought fewer U.S. financial assets such as stocks and bonds. That meant they supplied fewer euros because they needed to buy fewer U.S. dollars. The supply of euros fell from S_0 to S_1. At the same time, Americans also decided to buy more European stocks and bonds because European interest rates were relatively higher. In addition, the Chinese and Japanese governments increased their demand for European assets. Because they needed to pay for these European assets with euros, the demand for euros rose from D_0 to D_1. Combined, the two shifts led to a rise in the price of the euro as shown in Figure 5-2, increasing the price to $1.35 in 2005, where it remained into 2009.

Foreign Exchange

There is more to the determination of exchange rates than this, but as is often the case, supply/demand analysis gives you a good first entry into what is otherwise a potentially confusing issue.

FIGURE 5-2 The Market for Euros

The price of the euro increased as American investors increased their demand for euros to buy European goods and invest in the European stock market, while Europeans bought fewer U.S. goods and fewer American stocks, decreasing Americans' supply of euros. The combined effect was a rise in the dollar price of euros.

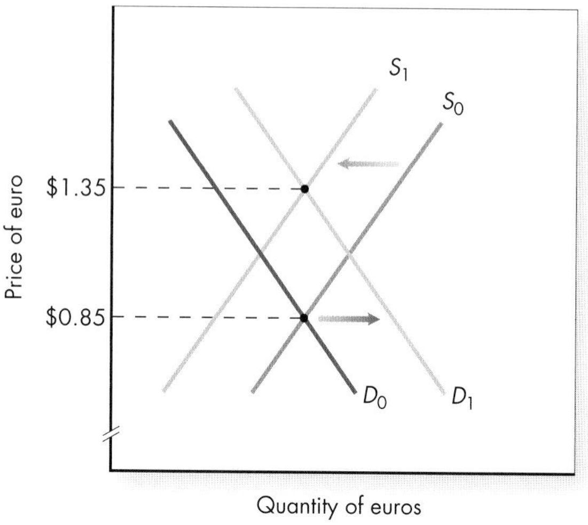

A Review

Anything other than price that affects demand or supply will shift the curves.

Now that we've been through some examples, let's review. Remember: Anything that affects demand and supply other than price of the good will shift the curves. Changes in the price of the good result in movements along the curves. Another thing to recognize is that when both curves are shifting, you can get a change in price but little change in quantity, or a change in quantity but little change in price.

Q-3 Say a hormone has been discovered that increases cows' milk production by 20 percent. Demonstrate graphically what effect this discovery would have on the price and quantity of milk sold in a market.

To test your understanding Table 5-1 gives you six generic results from the interaction of supply and demand. Your job is to decide what shifts produced those results. This exercise is a variation of the one with which I began the chapter. It goes over the same issues, but this time without the graphs. On the left-hand side of Table 5-1, I list combinations of movements of observed prices and quantities, labeling them 1–6. On the right I give six shifts in supply and demand, labeling them *a*–*f*.

If you don't confuse your "shifts of" with your "movements along," supply and demand provide good off-the-cuff answers for many economic questions.

TABLE 5-1

Price and Quantity Changes			Shifts in Supply and Demand
1.	P↑	Q↑	*a.* Supply shifts in. No change in demand.
2.	P↑	Q↓	*b.* Demand shifts out. Supply shifts in.
3.	P↑	Q?	*c.* Demand shifts in. No change in supply.
4.	P↓	Q?	*d.* Demand shifts out. Supply shifts out.
5.	P?	Q↑	*e.* Demand shifts out. No change in supply.
6.	P↓	Q↓	*f.* Demand shifts in. Supply shifts out.

You are to match the shifts with the price and quantity movements that best fit each described shift, using each shift and movement only once. My recommendation to you is to draw the graphs that are described in *a*–*f*, decide what happens to price and quantity, and then find the match in 1–6.

Q-4 If both demand and supply shift in to the left, what happens to price and quantity?

Now that you've worked them, let me give you the answers I came up with. They are: 1–*e*; 2–*a*; 3–*b*; 4–*f*; 5–*d*; 6–*c*. How did I come up with the answers? I did what I suggested you do—took each of the scenarios on the right and predicted what happens to price and quantity. For case *a*, supply shifts in to the left and there is a movement up along the demand curve. Since the demand curve is downward-sloping, the price rises

TABLE 5-2 Diagram of Effects of Shifts of Demand and Supply on Price and Quantity

This table provides a summary of the effects of shifts in supply and demand on equilibrium price and equilibrium quantity. Notice that when both curves shift, the effect on either price or quantity depends on the relative size of the shifts.

	No change in supply.	Supply shifts out.	Supply shifts in.
No change in demand.	No change.	P↓ Q↑ Price declines and quantity rises.	P↑ Q↓ Price rises. Quantity declines.
Demand shifts out.	P↑ Q↑ Price rises. Quantity rises.	P? Q↑ Quantity rises. Price could be higher or lower depending upon relative size of shifts.	P↑ Q? Price rises. Quantity could rise or fall depending upon relative size of shifts.
Demand shifts in.	P↓ Q↓ Price declines. Quantity declines.	P↓ Q? Price declines. Quantity could rise or fall depending upon relative size of shifts.	P? Q↓ Quantity declines. Price rises or falls depending upon relative size of shifts.

and quantity declines. This matches number *2* on the left. For case *b*, demand shifts out to the right. Along the original supply curve, price and quantity would rise. But supply shifts in to the left, leading to even higher prices but lower quantity. What happens to quantity is unclear, so the match must be number 3. For case *c*, demand shifts in to the left. There is movement down along the supply curve with lower price and lower quantity. This matches number 6. For case *d*, demand shifts out and supply shifts out. As demand shifts out, we move along the supply curve to the right and price and quantity rise. But supply shifts out too, and we move out along the new demand curve. Price declines, erasing the previous rise, and the quantity rises even more. This matches number 5.

I'll leave it up to you to confirm my answers to *e* and *f*. Notice that when supply and demand both shift, the change in either price or quantity is uncertain—it depends on the relative size of the shifts. As a summary, I present a diagrammatic of the combinations in Table 5-2.

Q-5 If price and quantity both fell, what would you say was the most likely cause?

Government Intervention in the Market

People don't always like the market-determined price. If the invisible hand were the only factor that determined prices, people would have to accept it. But it isn't; social and political forces also determine price. For example, when prices fall, sellers look to government for ways to hold prices up; when prices rise, buyers look to government for ways to hold prices down. Let's now consider the effect of such actions in the supply/demand model.[1] Let's start with an example of the price being held down.

---

[1] As I will discuss in Chapter 6, economists use many different models. No model precisely fits reality, and when we discuss a real-world market as fitting a model, we are using pedagogical license. As I have emphasized in previous chapters, the propositions that come out of a model are theorems–logical conclusions given the assumptions. To extend the theorem to a policy precept requires considering which assumptions of the model fit the situation one is describing.

FIGURE 5-3 Rent Control in Paris

A price ceiling imposed on housing rent in Paris during World War II created a shortage of housing when World War II ended and veterans returned home. The shortage would have been eliminated if rents had been allowed to rise to $17 per month.

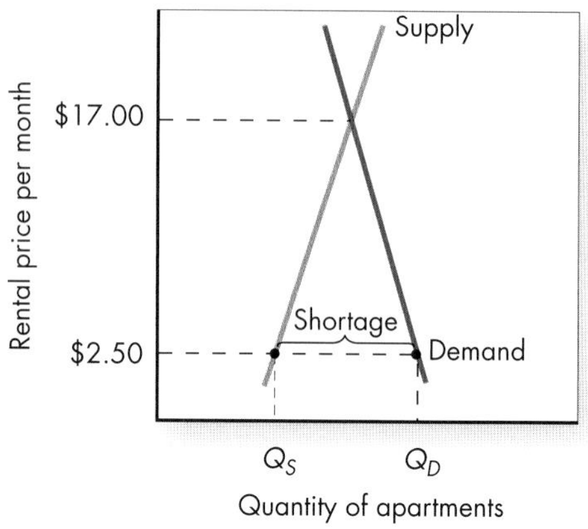

Price Ceilings

When government wants to hold prices down, it imposes a **price ceiling**—*a government-imposed limit on how high a price can be charged*. That limit is generally below the equilibrium price. (A price ceiling that is above the equilibrium price will not have any effect at all.) From Chapter 4, you already know the effect of a price that is below the equilibrium price—quantity demanded will exceed quantity supplied and there will be excess demand. Let's now look at an example of **rent control**—*a price ceiling on rents, set by government*—and see how that excess demand shows up in the real world.

Web Note 5.2 Rent Control

Rent controls exist today in a number of American cities as well as other cities throughout the world. Many of the laws governing rent were first instituted during the two world wars in the first half of the 20th century. Consider Paris, for example. In World War II, the Paris government froze rent to ease the financial burden of those families whose wage earners were sent to fight in the war. When the soldiers returned at the end of the war, the rent control was continued; removing it would have resulted in an increase in rents from $2.50 to $17 a month, and that was felt to be an unfair burden for veterans.

Price Ceilings

Figure 5-3 shows this situation. The below-market rent set by government created an enormous shortage of apartments. Initially this shortage didn't bother those renting apartments, since they got low-cost apartments. But it created severe hardships for those who didn't have apartments. Many families moved in with friends or extended families. Others couldn't find housing at all and lived on the streets. Eventually the rent controls started to cause problems even for those who did have apartments. The reason why is that owners of buildings cut back on maintenance. More than 80 percent of Parisians had no private bathrooms and 20 percent had no running water. Since rental properties weren't profitable, no new buildings were being constructed and existing buildings weren't kept in repair. It was even harder for those who didn't have apartments.

Q-6 What is the effect of the price ceiling, P_c, shown in the graph below on price and quantity?

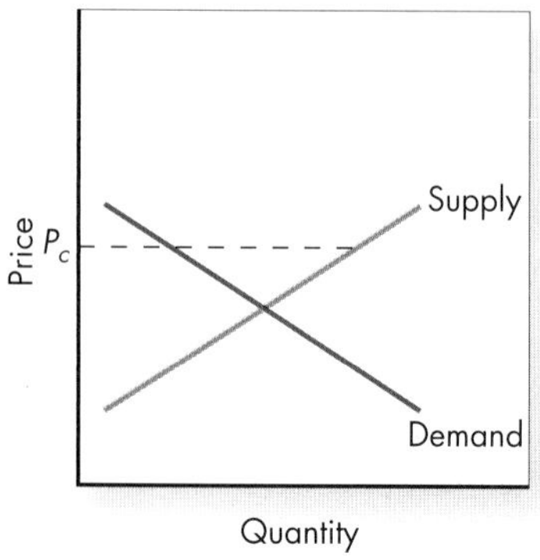

Since the market price was not allowed to ration apartments, alternative methods of rationing developed. People paid landlords bribes to get an apartment, or watched the obituaries and then simply moved in their furniture before anyone else did. Eventually the situation got so bad that rent controls were lifted.

The system of rent controls is not only of historical interest. Below I list some phenomena that existed in New York City recently.

1. A couple paid $350 a month for a two-bedroom Park Avenue apartment with a solarium and two terraces, while another individual paid $1,200 a month for a studio apartment shared with two roommates.
2. The vacancy rate for apartments in New York City was 3.5 percent. Anything under 5 percent is considered a housing emergency.

3. The actress Mia Farrow paid $2,900 a month (a fraction of the market-clearing rent) for 10 rooms on Central Park West. It was an apartment her mother first leased 60 years ago.
4. Would-be tenants made payments, called key money, to current tenants or landlords to get apartments.

Your assignment is to explain how these phenomena might have come about, and to demonstrate, with supply and demand, the situation that likely caused them. (Hint: New York City had rent control.)

Now that you have done your assignment (you have, haven't you?), let me give you my answers so that you can check them with your answers.

The situation is identical with that presented above in Figure 5-3. Take the first item. The couple lived in a rent-controlled apartment while the individual with roommates did not. If rent control were eliminated, rent on the Park Avenue apartment would rise and rent on the studio would most likely decline. Item 2: The housing emergency was a result of rent control. Below-market rent resulted in excess demand and little vacancy. Item 3: That Mia Farrow rents a rent-controlled apartment was the result of nonprice rationing. Instead of being rationed by price, other methods of rationing arose. These other methods of rationing scarce resources are called nonprice rationing. In New York City, strict rules determined the handing down of rent-controlled apartments from family member to family member. Item 4: New residents searched for a long time to find apartments to rent, and many discovered that illegal payments to landlords were the only way to obtain a rent-controlled apartment. Key money is a black market payment for a rent-controlled apartment. Because of the limited supply of apartments, individuals were willing to pay far more than the controlled price. Landlords used other methods of rationing the limited supply of apartments—instituting first-come, first-served policies, and, in practice, selecting tenants based on gender, race, or other personal characteristics, even though such discriminatory selection was illegal.

With price ceilings, existing goods are no longer rationed entirely by price. Other methods of rationing existing goods arise called nonprice rationing.

If rent controls had only the bad effects described above, no community would institute them. They are, however, implemented with good intentions—to cope with sudden increases in demand for housing that would otherwise cause rents to explode and force many poor people out of their apartments. The negative effects occur over time as buildings begin to deteriorate and the number of people looking to rent and unable to find apartments increases. As this happens, people focus less on the original renters and more on new renters excluded from the market and on the inefficiencies of price ceilings. Since politicians tend to focus on the short run, we can expect rent control to continue to be used when demand for housing suddenly increases.

Price Floors

Sometimes political forces favor suppliers, sometimes consumers. So let us now go briefly through a case when the government is trying to favor suppliers by attempting to prevent the price from falling below a certain level. **Price floors**—*government-imposed limits on how low a price can be charged*—do just this. The price floor is generally above the existing price. (A price floor below equilibrium price would have no effect.) When there is an effective price floor, quantity supplied exceeds quantity demanded and the result is excess supply.

Q-7 What is the effect of the price floor, P_f, shown in the graph below, on price and quantity?

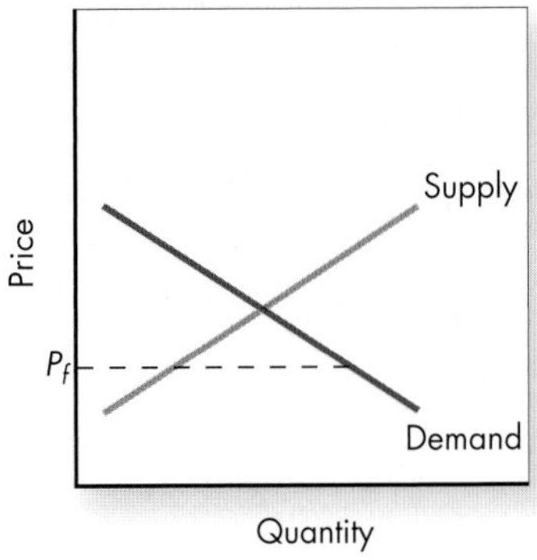

An example of a price floor is the minimum wage. Both individual states and the federal government impose **minimum wage laws**—*laws specifying the lowest wage a firm can legally pay an employee*. The U.S. federal government first instituted a minimum wage of 25 cents per hour in 1938 as part of the Fair Labor Standards Act. It has been raised many times since, and in the early 2000s the federal government voted to raise it to over $7.00 an hour. (With inflation, that's a much smaller increase than it looks.) In

FIGURE 5-4 A Minimum Wage

A minimum wage, W_{min}, above equilibrium wage, W_e, helps those who are able to find work, shown by Q_2, but hurts those who would have been employed at the equilibrium wage but can no longer find employment, shown by $Q_e - Q_2$. A minimum wage also hurts producers who have higher costs of production and consumers who may face higher product prices.

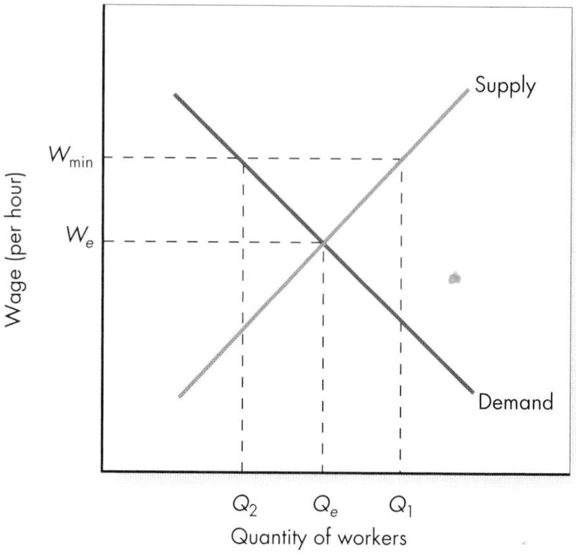

Web Note 5.3
Minimum Wage

2009 about 1.8 million hourly wage earners received the minimum wage, or about 2.2 percent of hourly paid workers, most of whom are unskilled. The market-determined equilibrium wage for skilled workers is generally above the minimum wage.

The effect of a minimum wage on the unskilled labor market is shown in Figure 5-4. The government-set minimum wage is above equilibrium, as shown by W_{min}. At the market-determined equilibrium wage W_e, the quantity of labor supplied and demanded equals Q_e. At the higher minimum wage, the quantity of labor supplied rises to Q_1 and the quantity of labor demanded declines to Q_2. There is an excess supply of workers (a shortage of jobs) represented by the difference $Q_1 - Q_2$. This represents people who are looking for work but cannot find it.

Price Floors

The minimum wage helps some people and hurts others.

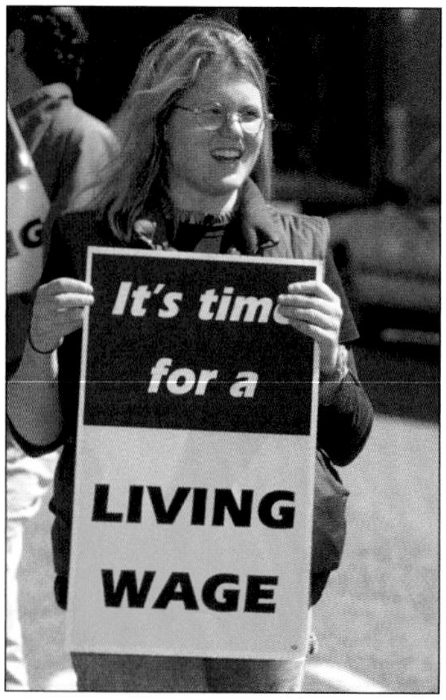

Who wins and who loses from a minimum wage? The minimum wage improves the wages of the Q_2 workers who are able to find work. Without the minimum wage, they would have earned W_e per hour. The minimum wage hurts those, however, who cannot find work at the minimum wage but who are willing to work, and would have been hired, at the market-determined wage. These workers are represented by the distance $Q_e - Q_2$ in Figure 5-4. The minimum wage also hurts firms that now must pay their workers more, increasing the cost of production, and consumers to the extent that firms are able to pass that increase in production cost on in the form of higher product prices.

All economists agree that the above analysis is logical and correct. But they disagree about whether governments should have minimum wage laws. One reason is that the empirical effects of minimum wage laws are relatively small; in fact, some studies have found them to be negligible. (There is, however, much debate about these estimates, since "other things" never remain constant.) A second reason is that some real-world labor markets are not sufficiently competitive to fit the supply/demand model. A third reason is that the minimum wage affects the economy in ways that some economists see as desirable and others see as undesirable. I point this out to remind you that the supply/demand framework is a tool to be used to analyze issues. It does not provide final answers about policy. (In microeconomics, economists explore the policy issues of interferences in markets much more carefully.)

Because the federal minimum wage is low, and not binding for most workers, a movement called the living-wage movement has begun. The living-wage movement focuses on local governments, calling on them to establish a minimum wage at a *living wage*—a wage necessary to support a family at or above the federally determined poverty line. By 2009, about 150 local governments had passed living-wage laws, with minimum wages ranging between \$7.50 an hour in Albuquerque, NM and \$14 in Manchester, CT. The analysis of these living-wage laws is the same as that for minimum wages.

Excise Taxes

Web Note 5.4
Taxing Our Sins

Let's now consider an example of a tax on goods. An **excise tax** is *a tax that is levied on a specific good*. The luxury tax on expensive cars that the United States imposed in 1991 is an example. A **tariff** is *an excise tax on an imported good.* What effect will excise taxes and tariffs have on the price and quantity in a market?

To lend some sense of reality, let's take the example from the 1990s, when the United States taxed the suppliers of expensive boats. Say the price of a boat before the luxury tax was \$60,000, and 600 boats were sold at that price. Now the government taxes suppliers \$10,000 for every luxury boat sold. What will the new price of the boat be, and how many will be sold?

A tax on suppliers shifts the supply curve up by the amount of the tax.

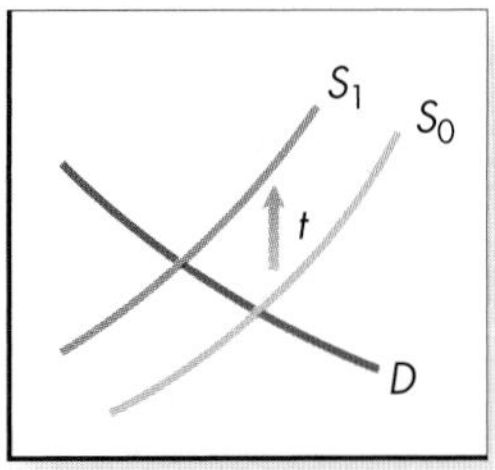

If you were about to answer "\$70,000," be careful. Ask yourself whether I would have given you that question if the answer were that easy. By looking at supply and demand curves in Figure 5-5, you can see why \$70,000 is the wrong answer.

To sell 600 boats, suppliers must be fully compensated for the tax. So the tax of \$10,000 on the supplier shifts the supply curve up from S_0 to S_1. However, at \$70,000, consumers are not willing to purchase 600 boats. They are willing to purchase only 420 boats. Quantity supplied exceeds quantity demanded at \$70,000. Suppliers lower their prices until quantity supplied equals quantity demanded at \$65,000, the new equilibrium price.

The new equilibrium price is \$65,000, not \$70,000. The reason is that at the higher price, the quantity of boats people demand is less. Some people choose not to buy boats and others find substitute vehicles or purchase their boats outside the United States. This is a movement up along a demand curve to the left. Excise taxes reduce the quantity of goods demanded. That's why boat manufacturers were up in arms after the tax was imposed and why the revenue generated from the tax was less than expected. Instead of collecting \$10,000 × 600 (\$6 million), revenue collected was only \$10,000 × 510 (\$5.1 million). (The tax was repealed three years after it was imposed.)

A tariff has the same effect on the equilibrium price and quantity as an excise tax. The difference is that only foreign producers sending goods into the United States pay the tax.

Q-8 Your study partner, Umar, has just stated that a tax on demanders of \$2 per unit will raise the equilibrium price from \$4 to \$6. How do you respond?

Excise Taxes

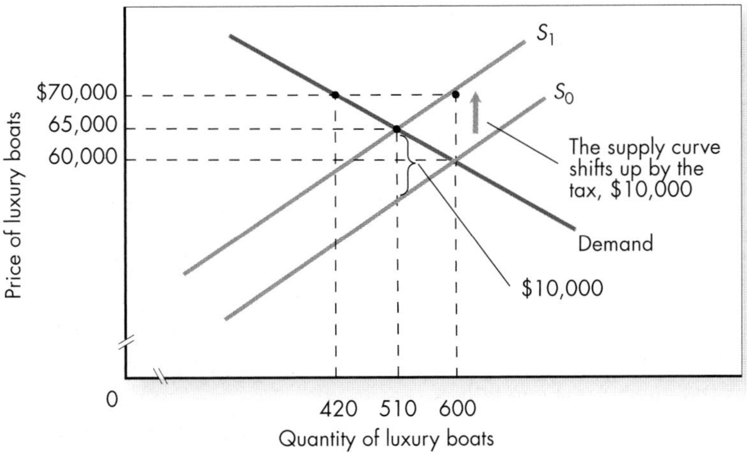

FIGURE 5-5 The Effect of an Excise Tax

An excise tax on suppliers shifts the entire supply curve up by the amount of the tax. Since at a price equal to the original price plus the tax there is excess supply, the price of the good rises by less than the tax.

An example is the 30 percent tariff imposed on steel imported into the United States in 2002. The government instituted the tariffs because U.S. steelmakers were having difficulty competing with lower-cost foreign steel. The tariff increased the price of imported steel, making U.S. steel more competitive to domestic buyers. As expected, the price of imported steel rose by over 15 percent, to about $230 a ton, and the quantity imported declined. Tariffs don't hurt just the foreign producer. Tariffs increase the cost of imported products to domestic consumers. In the case of steel, manufacturing companies such as automakers faced higher production costs. The increase in the cost of steel lowered production in those industries and increased the cost of a variety of goods to U.S. consumers.

Quantity Restrictions

Q-9 What is the effect of the quantity restrictions, Q_R, shown in the graph below, on equilibrium price and quantity?

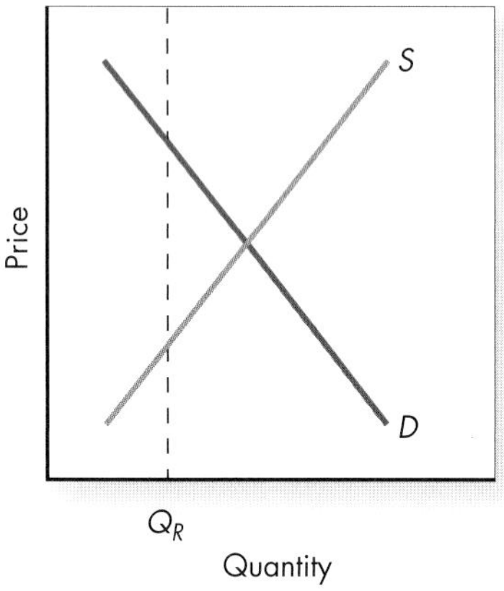

Another way in which governments often interfere with, or regulate, markets is with licenses, which limit entry into a market. For example, to be a doctor you need a license; to be a vet you need a license; and in some places to be an electrician, a financial planner, or a cosmetologist, or to fish, you need a license. There are many reasons for licenses, and we will not consider them here. Instead, we will simply consider what effect licenses have on the price and quantity of the activity being licensed. Specifically, we'll look at a case where the government issues a specific number of licenses and holds that number constant. The example we'll take is licenses to drive a taxi. In New York City, these are called taxi medallions because the license is an aluminum plate attached to the hood of a taxi. Taxi medallions were established in 1937 as a way to increase the wages of licensed taxi drivers. Wages of taxi drivers had fallen from $26 a week in 1929 to $15 a week in 1933. As wages fell, the number of taxi drivers fell from 19,000 to about 12,000. The remaining 12,000 taxi drivers successfully lobbied New York City to grant drivers with current licenses who met certain requirements permanent rights to drive taxis—medallions. (It wasn't until the early 2000s that the number of medallions was increased slightly.) The restriction had the desired effect. As the economy grew, demand for taxis grew (the demand for taxis shifted out) as shown in Figure 5-6(a) and because the supply of taxis remained at about 12,000, the wages of the taxi drivers owning medallions increased.

Issuing taxi medallions had a secondary effect. Because New York City also granted medallion owners the right to sell their medallions, a market in medallions developed. Those fortunate enough to have been granted a medallion by the city found that they had a valuable asset. A person wanting to drive a taxi, and earn those high wages, had to buy a medallion from an existing driver. This meant that while new taxi drivers

FIGURE 5-6 (A AND B)

Quantity Restrictions in the Market for Taxi Licenses

When the demand for taxi services increased, because the number of taxi licenses was limited to 12,000, wages increased to above $15 an hour, as (a) shows. Because taxi medallions were limited in supply, as demand for taxi services rose, so did the demand for medallions. Their price rose significantly, as (b) shows.

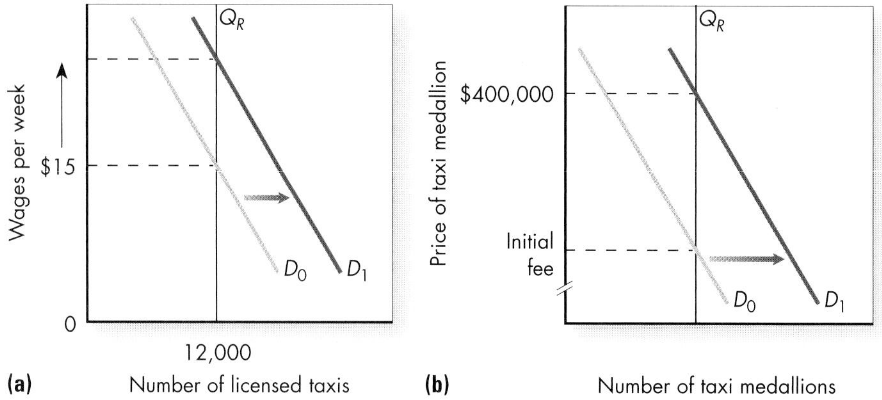

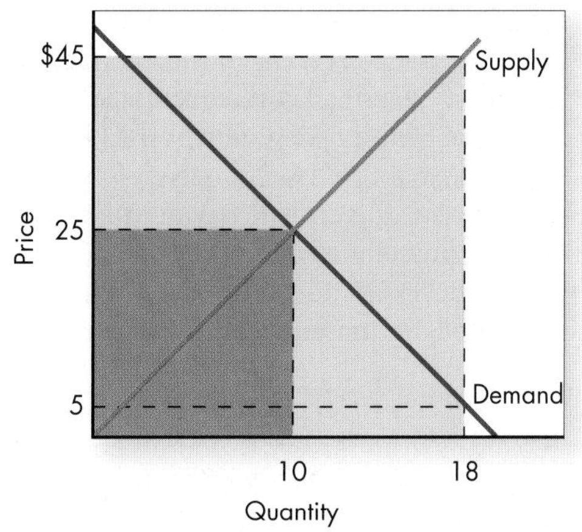

FIGURE 5-7 Third-Party-Payer Markets

In a third-party-payer system, the person who chooses the product doesn't pay the entire cost. Here, with a co-payment of $5, consumers demand 18 units. Sellers require $45 per unit for that quantity. Total expenditures, shown by the entire shaded region, are much greater compared to when the consumer pays the entire cost, shown by just the dark shaded region.

would earn a higher wage once they had bought a license, their wage after taking into account the cost of the license would be much lower.

As the demand for taxis rose, the medallions became more and more valuable. The effect on the price of medallions is shown in Figure 5-6(b). The quantity restriction, Q_R, means that any increases in demand lead only to price increases. Although the initial license fee was minimal, increases in demand for taxis quickly led to higher and higher medallion prices.

Quantity restrictions tend to increase price.

The demand for taxi medallions continues to increase each year as the New York City population grows more than the supply is increased. The result is that the price of a taxi medallion continues to rise. Even with the slight increase in the number of medallions, today taxi medallions cost about $400,000, giving anyone who has bought that license a strong reason to oppose an expansion in the number of licenses being issued.[2]

Third-Party-Payer Markets

As a final example for this chapter, let's consider third-party-payer markets. In **third-party-payer markets,** *the person who receives the good differs from the person paying for the good.* An example is the health care market where many individuals have insurance. They generally pay a co-payment for health care services and an HMO or other insurer pays the remainder. Medicare and Medicaid are both third-party payers. Figure 5-7 shows what happens in the supply/demand model when there is a third-party-payer market and a small co-payment. In the normal case, when the individual demander pays for the good, equilibrium quantity is where quantity demanded equals quantity supplied—in this case at an equilibrium price of $25 and an equilibrium quantity of 10.

Under a third-party-payer system, the person who chooses how much to purchase doesn't pay the entire cost. Because the co-payment faced by the consumer is much lower, quantity demanded is much greater. In this example with a co-payment of $5, the consumer demands 18. Given an upward-sloping supply curve, the seller requires a higher price, in this case $45 for each unit supplied to provide that quantity. Assuming the co-payment is for each unit, the consumers pay $5 of that price for a total out-of-pocket cost of $90 ($5 times 18). The third-party payer pays the remainder, $40, for a cost of $720

In third-party-payer markets, equilibrium quantity and total spending are much higher.

[2]As is usually the case, the analysis is more complicated in real life. In New York there are both individual and corporate licenses. But the general reasoning carries through: Effective quantity restrictions increase the value of a license.

($40 times 18). Total spending is $810. This compares to total spending of only $250 (25 times 10) if the consumer had to pay the entire price. Notice that with a third-party-payer system, total spending, represented by the large shaded rectangle, is much higher than total spending if the consumer paid, represented by the small darker rectangle.

The third-party-payer system describes much of the health care system in the United States today. Typically, a person with health insurance makes a fixed co-payment for an office visit, regardless of procedures and tests provided. Given this payment system, the insured patient has little incentive to limit the procedures offered by the doctor. The doctor charges the insurance company, and the insurance company pays. The rise in health care costs over the past decades can be attributed in part to the third-party-payer system.

Q-10 If the cost of textbooks were included in tuition, what would likely happen to their prices? Why?

A classic example of how third-party-payer systems can affect choices is a case where a 70-year-old man spent weeks in a hospital recovering from surgery to address abdominal bleeding. The bill, to be paid by Medicare, was nearing $275,000 and the patient wasn't recovering as quickly as expected. The doctor finally figured out that the patient's condition wasn't improving because ill-fitting dentures didn't allow him to eat properly. The doctor ordered the hospital dentist to fix the dentures, but the patient refused the treatment. Why? The patient explained: "Seventy-five dollars is a lot of money." The $75 procedure wasn't covered by Medicare.

Third-party-payer systems are not limited to health care. (Are your parents or the government paying for part of your college? If you were paying the full amount, would you be demanding as much college as you currently are?) Anytime a third-party-payer system exists, the quantity demanded will be higher than it otherwise would be. Market forces will not hold down costs as much as they would otherwise because the person using the service doesn't have an incentive to hold down costs. Of course, that doesn't mean that there are no pressures. The third-party payers—parents, employers, and government—will respond to this by trying to limit both the quantity of the good individuals consume and the amount they pay for it. For example, parents will put pressure on their kids to get through school quickly rather than lingering for five or six years, and government will place limitations on what procedures Medicare and Medicaid patients can use. The goods will be rationed through social and political means. Such effects are not unexpected; they are just another example of supply and demand in action.

Conclusion

I began this chapter by pointing out that supply and demand are the lens through which economists look at reality. It takes practice to use that lens, and this chapter gave you some practice. Focusing the lens on a number of issues highlighted certain aspects of those issues. The analysis was simple but powerful and should, if you followed it, provide you with a good foundation for understanding the economist's way of thinking about policy issues.

Summary

- By minding your *P*s and *Q*s—the shifts of and movements along curves—you can describe almost all events in terms of supply and demand.
- The determination of prices of currencies—foreign exchange rates—can be analyzed with the supply and demand model in the same way as any other good can be.
- A price ceiling is a government-imposed limit on how high a price can be charged. Price ceilings below market price create shortages.
- A price floor is a government-imposed limit on how low a price can be charged. Price floors above market price create surpluses.

- Taxes and tariffs paid by suppliers shift the supply curve up by the amount of the tax or tariff. They raise the equilibrium price (inclusive of tax) and decrease the equilibrium quantity.
- Quantity restrictions increase equilibrium price and reduce equilibrium quantity.
- In a third-party-payer market, the consumer and the one who pays the cost differ. Quantity demanded, price, and total spending are greater when a third party pays than when the consumer pays.

Key Terms

euro *(108)*
exchange rate *(107)*
excise tax *(115)*
minimum wage law *(113)*
price ceiling *(112)*
price floor *(113)*
rent control *(112)*
tariff *(115)*
third-party-payer market *(117)*

Questions and Exercises

connect ECONOMICS

1. Say that the equilibrium price and quantity both rose. What would you say was the most likely cause? LO1
2. Say that equilibrium price fell and quantity remained constant. What would you say was the most likely cause? LO1
3. The technology is now developing so that road use can be priced by computer. A computer in the surface of the road picks up a signal from your car and automatically charges you for the use of the road. How would this affect bottlenecks and rush-hour congestion? LO1
4. Demonstrate the effect on price and quantity of each of the following events:
   a. In a recent popularity test, Elmo topped Cookie Monster in popularity (this represents a trend in children's tastes). Market: cookies.
   b. The Atkins Diet that limits carbohydrates was reported to be very effective. Market: bread. LO1
5. In 2004, oil facilities in Iraq were attacked and strong economies in the United States and China boosted the demand for oil.
   a. Demonstrate graphically how these events led to increases in oil prices in June 2004. What was the effect on the equilibrium quantity of oil bought and sold?
   b. As a result of political pressure, OPEC agreed to increase the daily quota by 2 million barrels a day. What was the likely effect on equilibrium oil price and quantity? Demonstrate your answer graphically. LO1
6. Kennesaw University Professor Frank A. Adams III and Auburn University Professors A. H. Barnett and David L. Kaserman recently estimated the effect of legalizing the sale of cadaverous organs, which currently are in shortage at zero price. What are the effects of the following two possibilities on the equilibrium price and quantity of transplanted organs if their sale were to be legalized? Demonstrate your answers graphically.
   a. Many of those currently willing to donate the organs of a deceased relative at zero price are offended that organs can be bought and sold.
   b. People are willing to provide significantly more organs. LO1
7. The dollar price of the South African rand fell from 29 cents to 22 cents in 1996, the same year the country was rocked by political turmoil. Using supply/demand analysis, explain why the turmoil led to a decline in the price of the rand. LO2
8. In early 2004, following the toppling of President Aristide, the price of a 110-pound sack of rice in Haiti doubled from $22.50 to $45 because of disruptions at Haitian ports. (Eighty percent of Haiti's rice is imported.) Demonstrate graphically the effect of the import disruptions on the equilibrium price and quantity of rice purchased in Haiti. LO2
9. Demonstrate graphically the effect of an effective price ceiling. LO3
10. Demonstrate graphically why rent controls might increase the total payment that new renters pay for an apartment. LO3
11. Demonstrate graphically the effect of a price floor. LO3
12. Graphically show the effects of a minimum wage on the number of unemployed. LO3
13. Demonstrate graphically the effect of a tax on producers of $4 per unit on equilibrium price and quantity. LO4
14. Quotas, like medallions, are quantity restrictions on imported goods. Demonstrate the effect of a quota on the price of imported goods. LO4
15. The United States imposes substantial taxes on cigarettes but not on loose tobacco. When the tax went into effect, what effect did it likely have for cigarette rolling machines? (Difficult) LO4
16. In what ways is the market for public post-secondary education an example of a third-party-payer market? What's the impact of this on total educational expenditures? LO5
17. What reasons might governments have to support third-party-payer markets? (Difficult) LO5

18. You're given the following supply and demand tables:

Demand		Supply	
P	*Q*	*P*	*Q*
$0	1,200	$0	0
2	900	2	0
4	600	4	150
6	300	6	300
8	0	8	600
10	0	10	600
12	0	12	750
14	0	14	900

a. What is equilibrium price and quantity in a market system with no interferences?
b. If this were a third-party-payer market where the consumer pays $2, what is the quantity demanded? What is the price charged by the seller?
c. What is total spending in the two situations described in *a* and *b*? LO5

Questions from Alternative Perspectives

1. Some economists believe minimum wages create distortions in the labor market. If you are an employer and unable to hire the one willing and able to work for the lowest wage, how else might you choose a worker? Is this fair? Why or why not? (Austrian)
2. The book gives the example of a man who treated Medicare payments as different from his out-of-pocket payments. If you could save Medicare $100,000 by spending $20 of your own, should you? (Religious)
3. On average, women are paid less than men. What are the likely reasons for that? Should the government intervene with a law that requires firms to pay equal wages to those with comparable skills? (Feminist)
4. Biological evolution occurs very slowly; cultural evolution occurs less slowly, but still slowly compared to institutional and market evolution.
   a. Give some examples of these observations about the different speeds of adjustment.
   b. Explain the relevance of these observations to economic reasoning. (Institutionalist)
5. Most religions argue that individuals should not fully exploit market positions. For example, the text makes it sound as if allowing prices to rise to whatever level clears the market is the best policy to follow. That means that if, for example, someone were stranded in the desert and were willing to pay half his or her future income for life for a drink of water, that it would be appropriate to charge him or her that price. Is it appropriate? Why or why not? (Religious)
6. Rent control today looks far different than the rent freeze New York City enacted after World War II. Most rent controls today simply restrict annual rent increases and guarantee landlords a "fair return" in return for maintaining their properties.
   a. How would the economic effects of today's rent controls differ from the rent control programs depicted in your textbook?
   b. Do you consider them an appropriate mechanism to address the disproportionate power that landlords hold over tenants?
   c. If not, what policies would you recommend to address that inequity and the lack of affordable housing in U.S. cities? (Radical)

Issues to Ponder

1. In 1996, the television networks were given $70 billion worth of space on public airways for broadcasting high-definition television rather than auction it off. (Difficult)
   a. Why do airways have value?
   b. After the airway had been given to the network, would you expect that the broadcaster would produce high-definition television? LO1
2. About 10,000 tickets for the 2005 Men's Final Four college basketball games at the St. Louis Edward Jones Dome were to be sold in a lottery system for between $110 and $130 apiece. Typically applications exceed available tickets by 100,000. A year before the game, scalpers were already offering to sell tickets for between $200 and $2,000

depending on seat location, even though the practice is illegal. (Difficult)

a. Demonstrate the supply and demand for Final Four tickets. How do you know that there is an excess demand for tickets at $130?
b. Demonstrate the scalped price of between $200 and $2,000.
c. What would be the effect of legalizing scalping on the resale value of Final Four tickets? LO1

3. In some states and localities "scalping" is against the law, although enforcement of these laws is spotty. (Difficult)
   a. Using supply/demand analysis and words, demonstrate what a weakly enforced antiscalping law would likely do to the price of tickets.
   b. Using supply/demand analysis and words, demonstrate what a strongly enforced antiscalping law would likely do to the price of tickets. LO1
4. In 1938 Congress created a Board of Cosmetology in Washington, D.C., to license beauticians. To obtain a license, people had to attend a cosmetology school. In 1992 this law was used by the board to close down a hair-braiding salon specializing in cornrows and braids operated by unlicensed Mr. Uqdah, even though little was then taught in cosmetology schools about braiding and cornrows.
   a. What possible reason can you give for why this board exists?
   b. What options might you propose to change the system?
   c. What will be the political difficulties of implementing those options? LO1
5. In the Oregon health care plan for rationing Medicaid expenditures, therapy to slow the progression of AIDS and treatment for brain cancer were covered, while liver transplants and treatment for infectious mononucleosis were not covered.
   a. What criteria do you think were used to determine what was covered and what was not covered?
   b. Should an economist oppose the Oregon plan because it involves rationing?
   c. How does the rationing that occurs in the market differ from the rationing that occurs in the Oregon plan? LO1
6. Airlines and hotels have many frequent flyer and frequent visitor programs in which individuals who fly the airline or stay at the hotel receive bonuses that are the equivalent to discounts.
   a. Give two reasons why these companies have such programs rather than simply offering lower prices.
   b. Can you give other examples of such programs?
   c. What is a likely reason why firms whose employees receive these benefits do not require their employees to give the benefits to the firm? LO1
7. Since 1981, the U.S. government has supported the U.S. price of sugar by limiting import of sugar into the United States. Restricting imports is effective because the United States consumes more sugar than it produces.
   a. Using supply/demand analysis, demonstrate how import restrictions increase the price of domestic sugar.
   b. What other import policy could the government implement to have the same effect as the import restriction?
   c. Under the Uruguay Round of the General Agreement on Tariffs and Trade, the United States agreed to permit at least 1.25 million tons of sugar to be imported into the United States. How does this affect the U.S. sugar price support program? LO1
8. Apartments in New York City are often hard to find. One of the major reasons is rent control. (Difficult)
   a. Demonstrate graphically how rent controls could make apartments hard to find.
   b. Often one can get an apartment if one makes a side payment to the current tenant. Can you explain why?
   c. What would be the likely effect of eliminating rent controls?
   d. What is the political appeal of rent controls? LO1, LO3
9. Until recently, angora goat wool (mohair) has been designated as a strategic commodity (it used to be utilized in some military clothing). Because of that, in 1992 for every dollar's worth of mohair sold to manufacturers, ranchers received $3.60.
   a. Demonstrate graphically the effect of eliminating this designation and subsidy.
   b. Why was the program likely kept in existence for so long?
   c. Say that a politician has suggested that the government should pass a law that requires all consumers to pay a price for angora goat wool high enough so that the sellers of that wool would receive $3.60 more than the market price. Demonstrate the effect of the law graphically. Would consumers support it? How about suppliers? LO4
10. Supply/demand analysis states that equilibrium occurs where quantity supplied equals quantity demanded, but in U.S. agricultural markets quantity supplied almost always exceeds quantity demanded. How can this be? LO4
11. Nobel Prize–winning economist Bill Vickrey has suggested that automobile insurance should be paid as a tax on gas, rather than as a fixed fee per year per car. How would that change likely affect the number of automobiles that individuals own? (Difficult) LO4
12. In Japan, doctors prescribe drugs and supply the drugs to the patient, receiving a 25 percent markup. In the United States, doctors prescribe drugs, but, generally, they do not sell them. (Difficult)
    a. Which country prescribes the most drugs? Why?

b. How would a plan to limit the price of old drugs, but not new drugs to allow for innovation, likely affect the drug industry?
c. How might a drug company in the United States encourage a doctor in the United States, where doctors receive nothing for drugs, to prescribe more drugs? LO5

13. In the early 2000s, Whole Foods Market Inc. switched to a medical care plan that had a high deductible, which meant that employees were responsible for the first $1,500 of care, whereas after that they received 80 percent coverage. The firm also put about $800 in an account for each employee to use for medical care. If they did not use this money, they could carry it over to the next year.
a. What do you expect happened to medical claim costs?
b. What do you believe happened to hospital admissions?
c. Demonstrate graphically the reasons for your answers in *a* and *b*. LO5

Answers to Margin Questions

1. False. When supply rises, supply shifts out to the right. Price falls because demand slopes downward. *(107)*
2. You will receive 57,904 pesos. One U.S. dollar = 579.04 Chilean pesos. So multiplying 579.04 by 100 gives you 57,904 pesos. *(109)*
3. A discovery of a hormone that will increase cows' milk production by 20 percent will increase the supply of milk, pushing the price down and increasing the quantity demanded, as in the accompanying graph. *(110)*

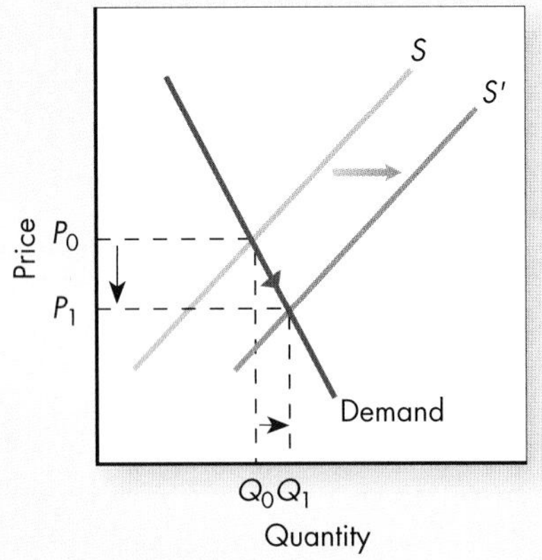

4. Quantity decreases but it is unclear what happens to price. *(110)*
5. It is likely demand shifted in and supply remained constant. *(111)*
6. Since the price ceiling is above the equilibrium price, it will have no effect on the market-determined equilibrium price and quantity. *(112)*
7. Since the price floor is below the equilibrium price, it will have no effect on the market-determined equilibrium price and quantity. *(113)*
8. I state that the tax will most likely raise the price by less than $2 since the tax will cause the quantity demanded to decrease. This will decrease quantity supplied, and hence decrease the price the suppliers receive. In the diagram below, Q falls from Q_0 to Q_1 and the price the supplier receives falls from $4 to $3, making the final price $5, not $6. *(115)*

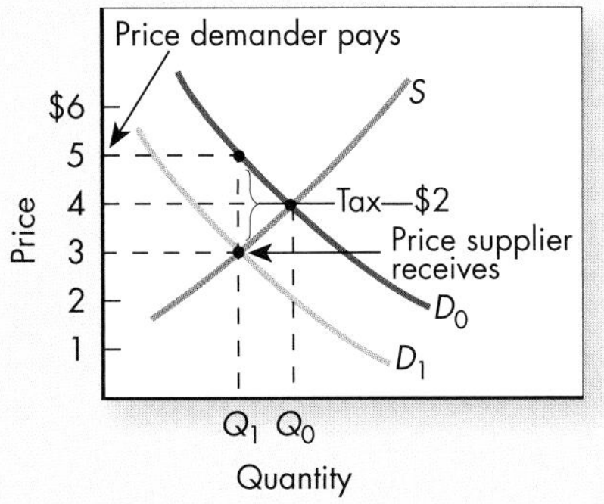

9. Given the quantity restriction, equilibrium quantity will be Q_R and equilibrium price will be P_0, which is higher than the market equilibrium price of P_e. *(116)*

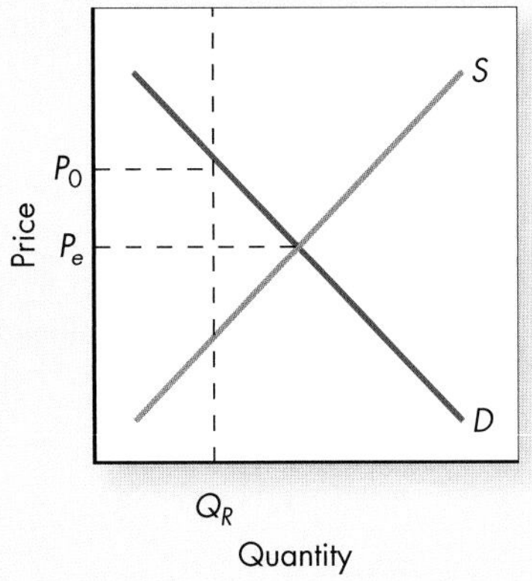

10. Universities would probably charge the high tuition they do now, but they would likely negotiate with publishers for lower textbook prices because they are both demanding and paying for the textbook. *(118)*

APPENDIX A

Algebraic Representation of Supply, Demand, and Equilibrium

In this chapter and Chapter 4, I discussed demand, supply, and the determination of equilibrium price and quantity in words and graphs. These concepts also can be presented in equations. In this appendix I do so, using straight-line supply and demand curves.

The Laws of Supply and Demand in Equations

Since the law of supply states that quantity supplied is positively related to price, the slope of an equation specifying a supply curve is positive. (The quantity intercept term is generally less than zero since suppliers are generally unwilling to supply a good at a price less than zero.) An example of a supply equation is

$$Q_S = -5 + 2P$$

where Q_S is units supplied and P is the price of each unit in dollars per unit. The law of demand states that as price rises, quantity demanded declines. Price and quantity are negatively related, so a demand curve has a negative slope. An example of a demand equation is

$$Q_D = 10 - P$$

where Q_D is units demanded and P is the price of each unit in dollars per unit.

Determination of Equilibrium

The equilibrium price and quantity can be determined in three steps using these two equations. To find the equilibrium price and quantity for these particular demand and supply curves, you must find the quantity and price that solve both equations simultaneously.

Step 1: Set the quantity demanded equal to quantity supplied:

$$Q_S = Q_D \rightarrow -5 + 2P = 10 - P$$

Step 2: Solve for the price by rearranging terms. Doing so gives:

$$3P = 15$$
$$P = \$5$$

Thus, equilibrium price is \$5.

Step 3: To find equilibrium quantity, you can substitute \$5 for P in either the demand or supply equation. Let's do it for supply: $Q_S = -5 + (2 \times 5) = 5$ units. I'll leave it to you to confirm that the quantity you obtain by substituting $P = \$5$ in the demand equation is also 5 units.

FIGURE A5-1 Supply and Demand Equilibrium

The algebra in this appendix leads to the same results as the geometry in the chapter. Equilibrium occurs where quantity supplied equals quantity demanded.

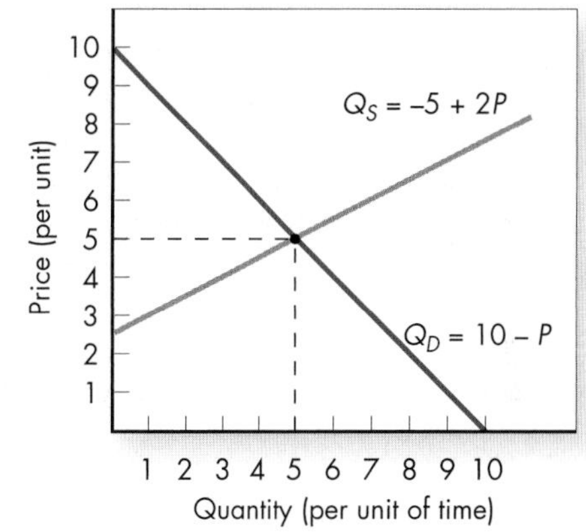

The answer could also be found graphically. The supply and demand curves specified by these equations are depicted in Figure A5-1. As you can see, demand and supply intersect; quantity demanded equals quantity supplied at a quantity of 5 units and a price of \$5.

Movements along a Demand and Supply Curve

The demand and supply curves above represent schedules of quantities demanded and supplied at various prices. Movements along each can be represented by selecting various prices and solving for quantity demanded and supplied. Let's create a supply and demand table using the above equations—supply: $Q_S = -5 + 2P$; demand: $Q_D = 10 - P$.

P	$Q_S = -5 + 2P$	$Q_D = 10 - P$
\$0	−5	10
1	−3	9
2	−1	8
3	1	7
4	3	6
5	5	5
6	7	4
7	9	3
8	11	2
9	13	1
10	15	0

As you move down the rows, you are moving up along the supply schedule, as shown by increasing quantity supplied, and moving down along the demand schedule, as shown by decreasing quantity demanded. Just to confirm your equilibrium quantity and price calculations, notice that at a price of \$5, quantity demanded equals quantity supplied.

Shifts of a Demand and Supply Schedule

What would happen if suppliers changed their expectations so that they would be willing to sell more goods at every price? This shift factor of supply would shift the entire supply curve out to the right. Let's say that at every price, quantity supplied increases by 3. Mathematically the new equation would be $Q_S = -2 + 2P$. The quantity intercept increases by 3. What would you expect to happen to equilibrium price and quantity? Let's solve the equations mathematically first.

Step 1: To determine equilibrium price, set the new quantity supplied equal to quantity demanded:

$$10 - P = -2 + 2P$$

Step 2: Solve for the equilibrium price:

$$12 = 3P$$
$$P = \$4$$

Step 3: To determine equilibrium quantity, substitute P in either the demand or supply equation:

$$Q_D = 10 - (1 \times 4) = 6 \text{ units}$$
$$Q_S = -2 + (2 \times 4) = 6 \text{ units}$$

Equilibrium price declined to \$4 and equilibrium quantity rose to 6, just as you would expect with a rightward shift in a supply curve.

Now let's suppose that demand shifts out to the right. Here we would expect both equilibrium price and equilibrium quantity to rise. We begin with our original supply and demand curves—supply: $Q_S = -5 + 2P$; demand: $Q_D = 10 - P$. Let's say at every price, the quantity demanded rises by 3. The new equation for demand would be $Q_D = 13 - P$. You may want to solve this equation for various prices to confirm that at every price, quantity demanded rises by 3. Let's solve the equations for equilibrium price and quantity.

Step 1: Set the quantities equal to one another:

$$13 - P = -5 + 2P$$

Step 2: Solve for equilibrium price:

$$18 = 3P$$
$$P = \$6$$

Step 3: Substitute P in either the demand or supply equation:

$$Q_D = 13 - (1 \times 6) = 7 \text{ units}$$
$$Q_S = -5 + (2 \times 6) = 7 \text{ units}$$

Equilibrium price rose to \$6 and equilibrium quantity rose to 7 units, just as you would expect with a rightward shift in a demand curve.

Just to make sure you've got it, I will do two more examples. First, suppose the demand and supply equations for wheat per year in the United States can be specified as follows (notice that the slope is negative for the demand curve and positive for the supply curve):

$$Q_D = 500 - 2P$$
$$Q_S = -100 + 4P$$

P is the price in dollars per thousand bushels and Q is the quantity of wheat in thousands of bushels. Remember that the units must always be stated. What are the equilibrium price and quantity?

Step 1: Set the quantities equal to one another:

$$500 - 2P = -100 + 4P$$

Step 2: Solve for equilibrium price:

$$600 = 6P$$
$$P = \$100$$

Step 3: Substitute P in either the demand or supply equation:

$$Q_D = 500 - (2 \times 100) = 300$$
$$Q_S = -100 + (4 \times 100) = 300$$

Equilibrium quantity is 300 thousand bushels.

As my final example, take a look at Alice's demand curve depicted in Figure 4-4(b) in Chapter 4. Can you write an equation that represents the demand curve in that figure? It is $Q_D = 10 - 2P$. At a price of zero, the quantity of DVD rentals Alice demands is 10, and for every increase in price of \$1, the quantity she demands falls by 2. Now look at Ann's supply curve shown in Figure 4-7(b) in Chapter 4. Ann's supply curve mathematically is $Q_S = 2P$. At a zero price, the quantity Ann supplies is zero, and for every \$1 increase in price, the quantity she supplies rises by 2. What are the equilibrium price and quantity?

Step 1: Set the quantities equal to one another:

$$10 - 2P = 2P$$

Step 2: Solve for equilibrium price:

$$4P = 10$$
$$P = \$2.5$$

Step 3: Substitute P in either the demand or supply equation:

$$Q_D = 10 - (2 \times 2.5) = 5, \text{ or}$$
$$Q_S = 2 \times 2.5 = 5 \text{ DVDs per week}$$

Ann is willing to supply five DVDs per week at $2.50 per rental and Alice demands five DVDs at $2.50 per DVD rental. Remember that in Figure 4-8 in Chapter 4, I showed you graphically the equilibrium quantity and price of Alice's demand curve and Ann's supply curve. I'll leave it up to you to check that the graphic solution in Figure 4-8 is the same as the mathematical solution we came up with here.

Price Ceilings and Price Floors

Let's now consider a price ceiling and price floor. We start with the supply and demand curves:

$$Q_S = -5 + 2P$$
$$Q_D = 10 - P$$

This gave us the solution:

$$P = 5$$
$$Q = 5$$

Now, say that a price ceiling of $4 is imposed. Would you expect a shortage or a surplus? If you said "shortage," you're doing well. If not, review the chapter before continuing with this appendix. To find out how much the shortage is, we must find out how much will be supplied and how much will be demanded at the price ceiling. Substituting $4 for price in both equations lets us see that $Q_S = 3$ units and $Q_D = 6$ units. There will be a shortage of three units. Next, let's consider a price floor of $6. To determine the surplus, we follow the same exercise. Substituting $6 into the two equations gives a quantity supplied of seven units and a quantity demanded of four units, so there is a surplus of three units.

Taxes and Subsidies

Next, let's consider the effect of a tax of $1 placed on the supplier. That tax would decrease the price received by suppliers by $1. In other words:

$$Q_S = -5 + 2(P - 1)$$

Multiplying the terms in parentheses by 2 and collecting terms results in

$$Q_S = -7 + 2P$$

This supply equation has the same slope as in the previous case, but a new intercept term—just what you'd expect. To determine the new equilibrium price and quantity, follow steps 1 to 3 discussed earlier. Setting this new equation equal to demand and solving for price gives

$$P = 5\tfrac{2}{3}$$

Substituting this price into the demand and supply equations tells us equilibrium quantity:

$$Q_S = Q_D = 4\tfrac{1}{3} \text{ units}$$

Of that price, the supplier must pay $1 in tax, so the price the supplier receives net of tax is $4⅔.

Next, let's say that the tax were put on the demander rather than on the supplier. In that case, the tax increases the price for demanders by $1 and the demand equation becomes

$$Q_D = 10 - (P + 1), \text{ or}$$
$$Q_D = 9 - P$$

Again solving for equilibrium price and quantity requires setting the demand and supply equations equal to one another and solving for price. I leave the steps to you. The result is

$$P = 4\tfrac{2}{3}$$

This is the price the supplier receives. The price demanders pay is $5⅔. The equilibrium quantity will be 4⅓ units.

These are the same results we got in the previous cases showing that, given the assumptions, it doesn't matter who actually pays the tax: The effect on equilibrium price and quantity is identical no matter who pays it.

Quotas

Finally, let's consider the effect of a quota of 4⅓ placed on the market. Since a quota limits the quantity supplied, as long as the quota is less than the market equilibrium quantity, the supply equation becomes

$$Q_S = 4\tfrac{1}{3}$$

where Q_S is the actual amount supplied. The price that the market will arrive at for this quantity is determined by the demand curve. To find that price, substitute the quantity 4⅓ into the demand equation ($Q_D = 10 - P$):

$$4\tfrac{1}{3} = 10 - P$$

and solve for P:

$$P = 5\tfrac{2}{3}$$

Since consumers are willing to pay $5⅔, this is what suppliers will receive. The price that suppliers would have been willing to accept for a quantity of $4\frac{1}{3}$ is $\$4\frac{2}{3}$. This can be found by substituting the amount of the quota in the supply equation:

$$4\tfrac{1}{3} = -5 + 2P$$

and solving for P:

$$2P = 9\tfrac{1}{3}$$
$$P = 4\tfrac{2}{3}$$

Notice that this result is very similar to the tax. For demanders it is identical; they pay $\$5\frac{2}{3}$ and receive $4\frac{1}{3}$ units. For suppliers, however, the situation is much preferable; instead of receiving a price of $\$4\frac{2}{3}$, the amount they received with the tax, they receive $5\frac{2}{3}$. With a quota, suppliers receive the "implicit tax revenue" that results from the higher price.

Questions and Exercises

1. Suppose the demand and supply for milk are described by the following equations: $Q_D = 600 - 100P$; $Q_S = -150 + 150P$, where P is price in dollars, Q_D is quantity demanded in millions of gallons per year, and Q_S is quantity supplied in millions of gallons per year.
   a. Create demand and supply tables corresponding to these equations.
   b. Graph supply and demand and determine equilibrium price and quantity.
   c. Confirm your answer to *b* by solving the equations mathematically.
2. Beginning with the equations in question 1, suppose a growth hormone is introduced that allows dairy farmers to offer 125 million more gallons of milk per year at each price.
   a. Construct new demand and supply curves reflecting this change. Describe with words what happened to the supply curve and to the demand curve.
   b. Graph the new curves and determine equilibrium price and quantity.
   c. Determine equilibrium price and quantity by solving the equations mathematically.
   d. Suppose the government set the price of milk at $3 a gallon. Demonstrate the effect of this regulation on the market for milk. What is quantity demanded? What is quantity supplied?
3. Write demand and supply equations that represent demand, D_0, and supply, S_0, in Figure A5-1 in this appendix.
   a. Solve for equilibrium price and quantity mathematically. Show your work.
   b. Rewrite the demand equation to reflect an increase in demand of 3 units. What happens to equilibrium price and quantity?
   c. Rewrite the supply equation to reflect a decrease in supply of 3 units at every price level. What happens to equilibrium price and quantity using the demand curve from *b*?
4. a. How is a shift in demand reflected in a demand equation?
   b. How is a shift in supply reflected in a supply equation?
   c. How is a movement along a demand (supply) curve reflected in a demand (supply) equation?
5. Suppose the demand and supply for wheat are described by the following equations: $Q_D = 10 - P$; $Q_S = 2 + P$, where P is the price in dollars, Q_D is quantity demanded in millions of bushels per year, and Q_S is quantity supplied in millions of bushels per year.
   a. Solve for equilibrium price and quantity of wheat.
   b. Would a government-set price of $5 create a surplus or a shortage of wheat? How much? Is $5 a price ceiling or a price floor?
6. Suppose the U.S. government imposes a $1 per gallon of milk tax on dairy farmers. Using the demand and supply equations from question 1:
   a. What is the effect of the tax on the supply equation? The demand equation?
   b. What are the new equilibrium price and quantity?
   c. How much do dairy farmers receive per gallon of milk after the tax? How much do demanders pay?
7. Repeat question 6 assuming the tax is placed on the buyers of milk. Does it matter who pays the tax?
8. Repeat question 6 assuming the government pays a subsidy of $1 per gallon of milk to farmers.
9. Suppose the demand for DVDs is represented by $Q_D = 15 - 4P$, and the supply of DVDs is represented by $Q_S = 4P - 1$. Determine if each of the following is a price floor, price ceiling, or neither. In each case, determine the shortage or surplus.
   a. $P = \$3$
   b. $P = \$1.50$
   c. $P = \$2.25$
   d. $P = \$2.50$

Thinking Like a Modern Economist

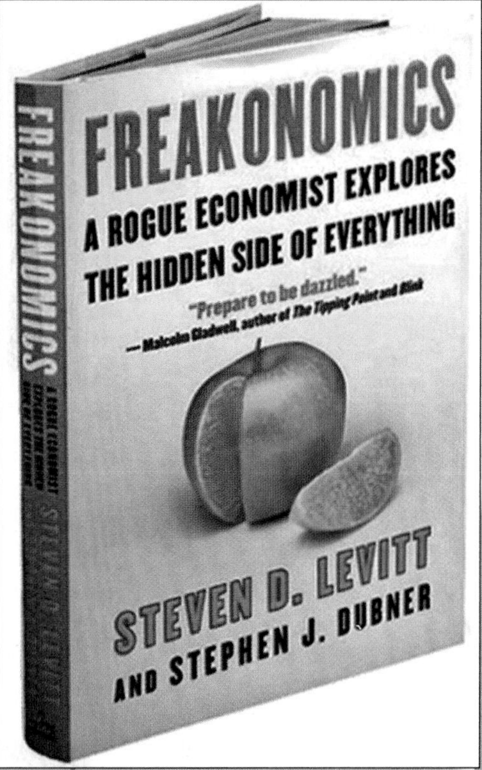

Economics is what economists do.

—*Jacob Viner*

My son doesn't think much of economists. I know that it's rather common for kids not to have high regard for their parents, but it still hurts. Recently, however, when I was attending a conference and told him that I was on a panel with Steve Levitt, my ranking moved up. In fact my son asked me, "Can you get his autograph for me? He's cool." Steve Levitt's book, *Freakonomics* (written jointly with Stephen Dubner), had hit a chord with my son, and judging from its sales, with lots of other people as well.

I raise this issue here not to sell more copies of Levitt's book (he's sold plenty), but instead to introduce you to what modern economists do, and how what modern economists do relates to the supply and demand model to which you were introduced in the last two chapters. I include this chapter to disabuse you from thinking that the supply and demand model is the holy grail of economics. Remember Carlyle's comment, "teach a parrot the words 'supply' and 'demand,' and you have an economist." He's wrong; as I stated last chapter, economists are not parrots, and to understand modern economics you have to know that modern economics uses supply and demand analysis only as a stepping stone. It's an important stepping stone, but still just a stepping stone.

Freakonomics makes the point nicely because if you look in its index, you won't find any entries under supply or demand. The reason isn't because the indexer goofed—it's because Levitt didn't use the formal supply and demand model. Instead, he applied the general ideas behind supply and demand within a variety of other models; most of his conclusions derive from his creative ability to collect data and analyze them with statistical tools. His approach is typical of how modern applied economists approach problems—they collect data, or use data collected by others, and analyze them. The purpose of this chapter is to give you a sense of what modern economists do, and how what you will learn in principles of economics relates to what modern economists do.

A key lesson of this chapter is that *supply and demand is not the glue that holds modern economics together.* Rather, modeling is the glue. When you present a problem or question to an economist, he or she will automatically attempt to reduce that question to a **model**—*a simplified representation of the problem or question that captures the essential issues*—and then work with that model and empirical evidence to understand the problem. The modeling approach is the modern economics approach.

No single model characterizes modern economic models. Modern economists are a highly diverse group of social scientists. What ties them together is their

AFTER READING THIS CHAPTER, YOU SHOULD BE ABLE TO:

1. Differentiate traditional economic building blocks from behavioral economic building blocks.
2. Explain what heuristic models are and how traditional and behavioral heuristic economic models differ.
3. Distinguish an empirical model from a formal model.
4. List two types of formal models used by modern economists.
5. Discuss how modern economics and traditional economics differ in their policy prescriptions.

Q-1 What is the glue that holds modern economics together?

training in modeling and their shared view that incentives are important, and that their models have to capture the importance of incentives.

The Nature of Economists' Models

Economists aren't the only people who use models. Most everyone does. An architect will often create on the computer or with wood a small model of a house he is building. Similarly, an engineer will test a new design with a model. So modeling alone does not distinguish an economist from other scientists and engineers. What does differentiate economists are:

1. The building blocks that economists use in their models and
2. The structure of formal models that economists find acceptable.

Building blocks refer to the assumptions of a model. The structure of a model is the form it takes—verbal, graphical, or algebraic.

By building blocks I mean the assumptions that form the basis of economic models. All economists' models hold that incentives are important, but they differ in how they picture people reacting to incentives. For example you can assume that individuals are selfish, or that individuals care about other people; the models would be different in each instance. By *structure,* I mean the form of the model—for example, a model can be verbal, graphical (for example, the supply/demand model), algebraic with simple equations (for example, $q = 4 - 2P$), or algebraic with highly complex equations[1] (for example:

$$\begin{pmatrix} \delta_t \bar{u}_k(t) \\ \delta_t \bar{v}_k(t) \end{pmatrix} = -k^2 \begin{pmatrix} D_u \bar{u}_k(t) \\ D_u \bar{v}_k(t) \end{pmatrix} + \mathbf{R}' \begin{pmatrix} \bar{u}_k(t) \\ \bar{v}_k(t) \end{pmatrix}$$

requiring mind-spinning graduate-level mathematics). The popular TV show *Numb3rs* is in many ways a description of how modern economists approach problems. In fact, many of the episodes of the show are built around models that modern economists have developed and use in their analysis.

Heuristic models are informal models expressed in words.

Models don't have to be mathematical; economists also use more informal verbal or **heuristic models**—*models that are expressed informally in words*. Models also can be made from physical components such as a small replica of a proposed house or as computer simulations such as software that models the growth of bacteria. Computer simulation models also can be interactive where individuals become part of the model. For example, SecondLife can be thought of as a model of society, and its economy can provide insight for the real-world economy. (Check out how the central authority in SecondLife changes the money supply to affect the exchange rate of SecondLife currency.) Just like these models, economic models come in many different forms with many different building blocks.

Q-2 Are modern economists more likely to use inductive models than earlier economists?

The building blocks and structures of models that economists use have evolved over time. Early economists tended to use a highly restricted set of building blocks and a narrow set of relatively simple (at least compared to their modern alternatives) formal models. **Modern economists** are *economists who are willing to use a wider range of models than did earlier economists*. For example, as discussed in Chapter 1, a major change is that modern economists use a much more inductive approach to modeling. Just to be sure you know the distinction, let's review it. An *inductive approach* is an approach to understanding a problem or question in which understanding is developed empirically from statistically analyzing what is observed in the data. Models based on an inductive approach are developed by how well they fit the data. Earlier economists were much more likely to use a *deductive approach*—an approach that begins with certain self-evident principles from which implications are deduced (logically determined).

[1]In case you were wondering, this is a reaction diffusion equation expressed in simplifying vector notation. What's a reaction diffusion equation? It's probably better not to ask.

Scientific and Engineering Models

Models can have many purposes. There are models primarily designed to provide understanding of what is happening for the sake of understanding—these are scientific models. Other models can be designed to provide insight into policy issues—these are applied-policy or engineering models. Still other models fall somewhere in between; there is no firm line distinguishing science from engineering. Most of the models you will be presented within this book fall more within the applied-policy models. They are designed to provide insight into what is happening in a way that will serve as a foundation for a discussion of policy.

Behavioral and Traditional Building Blocks

The traditional building blocks of microeconomics are the assumptions that people are rational and self-interested. What we will call **traditional economists** are *economists who study the logical implications of rationality and self-interest in relatively simple algebraic or graphical models such as the supply and demand model.* (Yes, it is true; by a mathematician's standards, supply and demand models are very simple models. But I agree with you; these simple models are often complicated enough.) Modern economists use supply and demand models, but they also use much more sophisticated models that integrate dynamics and strategic interactions into the analysis.

Traditional economists tend to use simple models based on assumptions of rationality and self-interest.

How much modern economists are willing to deviate from the traditional approach differs among modern economists. For example, some modern economists such as Nobel Prize winner Gary Becker advocate limiting economic models to these traditional building blocks. He writes: "The combined assumptions of maximizing behavior [note: maximizing behavior is how economists interpret rationality], market equilibrium, and stable preferences, used relentlessly and unflinchingly, form the heart of the economic approach." Up until the end of the 1970s, Becker's view predominated among economists. Since the 1980s, however, a group of modern economists has been edging away from these traditional building blocks.

Behavioral Economic Models

The study of models with alternative building blocks has grown so much in recent years that it has acquired a name—**behavioral economics**—*microeconomic analysis that uses a broader set of building blocks than rationality and self-interest used in traditional economics.* Instead of deductively assuming rationality and self-interest, behavioral economists inductively study people's behavior and use those behaviors in their models. Based on these inductive studies, they argue that both rationality and self-interest should be broadened somewhat. Rationality should be broadened to **purposeful behavior**—*behavior reflecting reasoned but not necessarily rational judgment*—and self-interest, to **enlightened self-interest** in which *people care about other people as well as themselves.*

Q-3 If an economist argues that people tend to be purposeful and follow their enlightened self interest, would you most likely characterize that economist as a behavioral or a traditional economist?

Behavioral economics is a leading field of research in economics today. The two important differences between traditional and behavioral building blocks are presented in Table 6-1.

TABLE 6-1 The Different Building Blocks of Traditional and Behavioral Models

Traditional Economics	Behavioral Economics
People are completely rational	People behave purposefully
People are self-interested	People follow their enlightened self-interest

Let's consider another example of behavioral economists' building blocks. Economists Matt Rabin and Ernst Fehr have developed models in which people care about fairness independently of what they themselves get. For example, they have found that when dividing up a sum of money, people try to divide the sum up fairly rather than giving it all to themselves, even though they could keep it all. In these modern models, the individuals would not be considered solely self-interested but, rather, enlightened self-interested; they care about fairness for its own sake. Economists Herbert Simon and Thomas Schelling have developed models in which people do not behave rationally, at least not in the traditional sense. For example, they have found that people will make choices based on rules of thumb such as "do what you see others doing" without rationally weighing the costs and benefits of each decision. Instead, people follow habit, which is purposeful behavior that reduces the costs of making decisions. Behavioral economists design their models accordingly.

The assumptions of a model affect the patterns that one sees in the data.

Building blocks are important: they affect how one interprets the results of an analysis; they influence the patterns one sees in a picture. For example, say you observe a firm not taking advantage of its market position. Using traditional building blocks of rationality and self-interest, this would seem very strange. You would look for some hidden reason why the firm isn't taking advantage of that position and keep searching until you find the selfish motive underlying the behavior.

Models based on behavioral building blocks, in which people and firms have goals beyond self-interest, allow researchers to consider the possibility that the firm is not taking advantage of its market position for reasons other than self-interest. Pharmaceutical companies, for example, sell AIDS drugs in African countries at prices far below market price. This could be because of political pressure, but it could also be out of a sense of fairness. A traditional economist would focus on the first; a behavioral economist would consider both possibilities and use empirical data to decide which it is. The point of this example is that an economist who is willing to use a wider set of building blocks sees different information in data than does an economist who uses the traditional building blocks. In modern economics there is a lively debate about what building blocks economists should use.

Predictable Irrationality The key to understanding the difference between behavioral economics and modern traditional economics is to recognize that behavioral economists are not just arguing that people are irrational; they are arguing that people are *predictably irrational* and that actions that traditional economists call irrational might not be irrational when considered in context.[2] For a behavioral economist, rationality comes in many forms, and what's important is that the model captures how people actually behave. Capturing this real-world nature of humans requires giving up some of the universality and power of models based on the traditional assumptions. Instead of having one model, one has a collection of models from which to choose for a variety of situations.

For behavioral economists, universality is less important than the fact that the model captures how people actually behave.

Let's consider an example of the difference. Say you are given a choice between two income streams. In the first scenario, you will earn $30,000 the first year, $27,000 the second, and $24,000 the third. In the second scenario, you will earn $24,000 the first year, $27,000 the second, and $30,000 the third. Which would you choose? A model based on traditional rationality predicts you would choose the first, since you will be able to save the additional $6,000 earned the first year, put it in the bank, and end up

---

[2]An entire book could be written on what is meant by rationality and self-interest, and in some ways, all types of behavior can be considered rational and selfish. So it can be argued that behavioral economists are not arguing that purposeful behavior includes irrational behavior, only that it includes a different type of rationality than is allowed within traditional economics.

with more than $30,000 of income in the third year. Since you get more total income with the first stream of income ($24,000 plus the $6,000 from the first year, plus two years of interest on that $6,000), it is "rationally" preferred to the second. But when economists have asked people which stream of income they preferred, economists have found that most people choose the second stream, even when it is explained that they could be better off by choosing the first.

What's going on? Behavioral economists argue that most people recognize that they don't have complete self-control; people believe that they will spend the extra $6,000 earned in the first year rather than save it. Thus, while it may be possible for people to switch the first income stream into an income stream that is preferred to the second, they don't believe that they have the discipline to do so. Thus, they actually prefer the second to the first because it precommits them to saving, and thereby constrains them from doing something they believe they will do, but which they actually don't want to do. They have developed what is called a **precommitment strategy**—*a strategy in which people consciously place limitations on their future actions, thereby limiting their choices*. The behavior is irrational because people tend to choose the stream that results in less total income; it's predictable because in experiments time and time again, people make the same choice. This seemingly irrational choice is not unique to this example but occurs in a variety of contexts.

Q-4 Can adding a constraint on people make them better off?

Are You Predictably Irrational? Economist Dan Ariely, from whose book *Predictably Irrational* many of these examples have been developed, has created a test as a fun way to introduce people to these ideas and to determine whether they exhibit predictably irrational tendencies. (You can take the full test at his book Web site, www.predictablyirrational.com.)

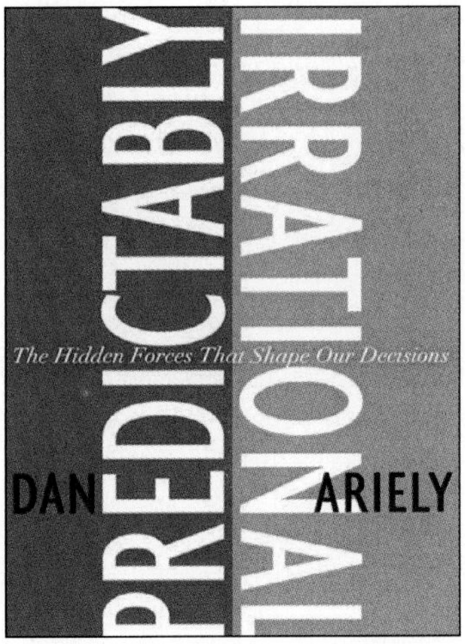

- Does how happy you are with your salary depend on how much you make relative to what your friends, family members, and neighbors make?
- When you are facing a decision to buy something, do you make your decision by considering the pleasure that this item will bring to you and contrast it with all the other possible things that you could buy for the same amount of money, now and in the future?
- How often have you watched your weight, and wanted to skip the dessert at the end of a nice meal out, but once the waiter stopped by with the dessert cart, you ended up ordering the chocolate soufflé?
- Have you ever had a romantic partner in whom you started to lose interest, but when he or she all of a sudden began to grow more distant, your interest rekindled?
- Would you be more likely to take a pencil home from work than to take 10 cents from a petty cash box?

Most people answer these questions yes, no, yes, yes, and yes. These answers are the opposite of what an economist using the traditional building blocks would predict people would answer. Behavioral economics says that we must develop additional economic models that take these predictable behaviors into account.

The Advantages and Disadvantages of Modern Traditional and Behavioral Models

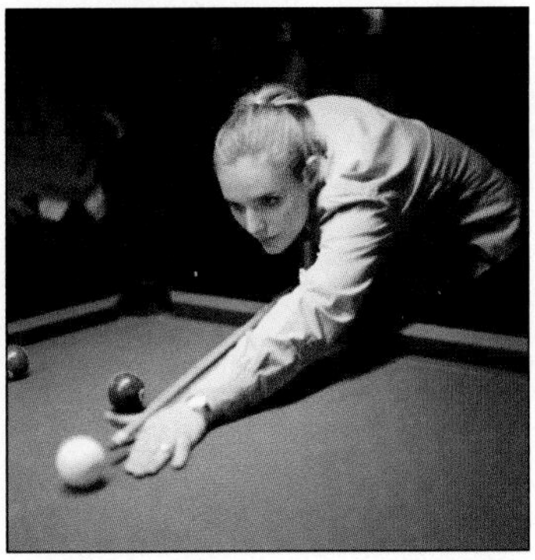

While it may seem that economists would want models that most closely reflect people's behavior, that is not so obvious—models that reflect people's actual behavior don't provide significant insight. For example, a pool player probably does not calculate the angles and spin of a ball to determine how to hit it, but it may make the most sense to assume that she does if one were modeling her behavior. The model may be easier to solve, and may be a better predictor of what will happen, than a model built on her actual behavior. Modern traditional economists emphasize the advantage of simplicity and ease of testing. Having one model means that you can test it and see if it fits reality. With many models, you have to do much more testing. For policy purposes, modern traditional economists argue that a single model that is easy to apply and test is the most useful model.

The Difficulty with Behavioral Building Blocks: Testing Modern traditional economists point out that formally moving away from the traditional building blocks is difficult because following one's enlightened self-interest rather than self-interest, and acting purposefully rather than rationally, lead to much less clear-cut models and results. By their nature, behavioral models depend on the specific context of the choices involved; so instead of a single model, there are many. This means that the broader building blocks allow many more patterns to be discerned in the data. That's both an advantage and a disadvantage because it is hard to know which pattern to focus on.

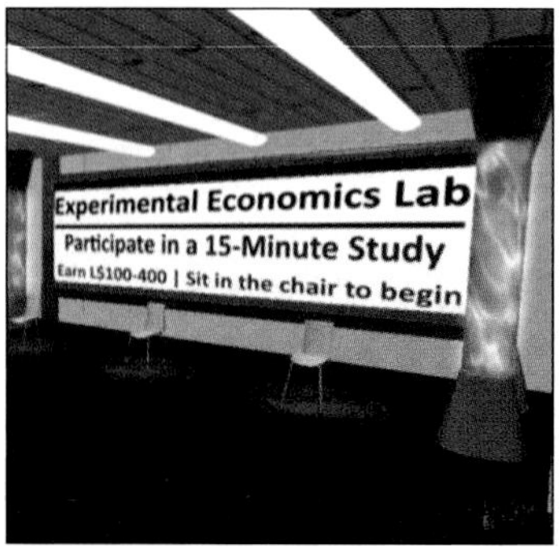

Endowment effects—the observation that what one has affects what one wants—is an example of a modern behavioral economics building block.

The behavioral economists' answer to this problem is that economists can use laboratory and field experiments, or what is called *experimental economics*, to test alternative building blocks and find those that best describe how people actually behave. Let's consider an example: In an experiment, half the participants are given a mug; the other half are given a pen, each of approximately the same value. The participants were then allowed to exchange one for the other simply by returning the first item. Since who got the pen or the mug was random, the rationality building block would suggest that about half of each group would choose to trade for the other. In fact, only 10 percent of each group chose to trade, suggesting that what one has influences what one wants—in contradiction to the traditional building block of rationality. A behavioral economist would then include **endowment effects** (*people value something more just because they have it*) in their building blocks for models. Endowment effects fit the broader "behaving purposefully" building block; they do not fit the narrower "rationality" building block.

Behavioral economists using *evolutionary models*—models of how an individual's preferences are determined on the basis of natural selection of what is useful for survival—argue that the endowment effect is hardwired into people's brains because it serves a very useful evolutionary function. It makes people happier with what they have, which decreases the social conflict over who gets what. The endowment effect probably makes it possible for parents to put up with their children, and to actually believe that they are close to perfect, even though, to an objective observer, they are far from perfect. In fact, without the endowment effect, we would probably have an online market in children, where you could trade yours for someone else's.

Traditional models provide simple and clear results, which can highlight issues that behavioral models cannot.

Traditional Models Provide Simplicity and Insight Modern traditional economists don't agree with the direction that behavioral economics is heading in terms of giving up the old building blocks; they strongly prefer staying with the narrower building blocks of rationality and self-interest. The reason is the simplicity and clarity that come from models with these traditional building blocks; these traditional models give clear-cut results that nicely highlight issues in ways that the modern building blocks do not. This view was expressed by University of Chicago economist Gary Becker when he said that traditional building blocks, used unflinchingly, are the

ADDED DIMENSION

Neuroeconomics and Microeconomics

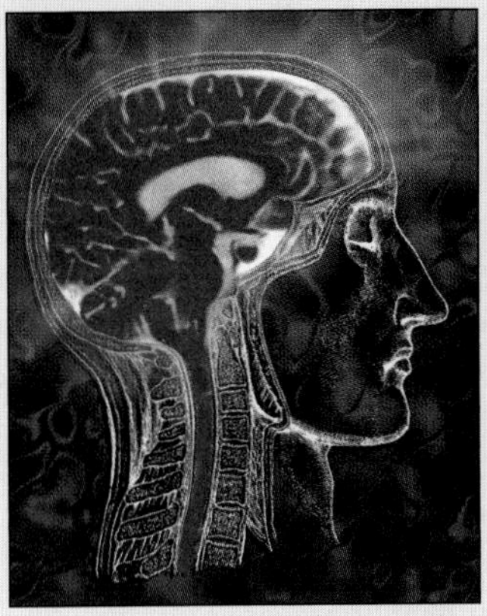

Both traditional and behavioral economics generally assume that the most basic building block of economic analysis is the individual. Where the two groups differ is in the assumptions they make about how the individual behaves. Some economists, such as Cal-Tech economist Colin Camerer and University of Zurich economist Ernst Fehr, have questioned whether economists should study building blocks more basic than the individual. They argue that individuals are made up of cells, and that behavior is the result of chemical and electrical processes in the brain. By studying these brain processes, we can better understand an individual's behavior. To do this they perform CT scans of people's brains under a variety of controlled conditions and see what part of the brain is reacting. Their work goes under the name *neuroeconomics*.

What they have found is that choice is a very complicated electrochemical phenomenon. For example, inconsistent decisions are often not the result of a mistake that would have been corrected if someone had pointed out the inconsistency, but, instead, the result of different electrochemical processes occurring in the brain. People are essentially hard-wired to be inconsistent. In a sense, more than one "you" are making decisions. There is the "emotional you" when your emotions hold sway and the "rational you" when the rational side of your brain holds sway. Depending on which "you" is being affected, the choice that "you" prefer can be quite different. And when both you's are affected, the result is often confusion. (This is a reason why advertisers appeal to both emotion and rationality simultaneously.)

This supports the behavioral economists' argument that we need to use building blocks that are different than the traditional ones. It also opens up a whole new set of possibilities about controlling behavior, such as the precommitment savings strategy discussed in the text. Another example of that precommitment strategy is not keeping dessert in the refrigerator to avoid temptation. Such precommitment strategies allow the "rational you" to win out over the "emotional you."

essence of the economic approach. He would argue that behavioral economists have flinched.[3]

Because Becker and other similarly minded economists taught at the University of Chicago, until recently, this unflinching approach was associated with what was called the *Chicago approach* to economics. Recently, however, a number of University of Chicago school economists such as Richard Thaler have begun using a broader set of building blocks, and, as I will discuss below, have been in the forefront of drawing policy implications from models based on modern building blocks.

Web Note 6.1
Predictably Irrational

Behavioral Economic Models Reflect Observed Behavior Behavioral economists' response to Becker and others who advocate sticking with the traditional building blocks is that they agree that the traditional model provides enormous insights and that *they do not advocate discarding the supply/demand model or the traditional building*

[3]Some economists, called *evolutionary economists*, believe that even this group of building blocks does not go far enough. They advocate thinking of individuals as reflecting their evolutionary tendencies and being shaped by the market into the type of individuals that more economists assume are their inherent natures. Others, called *econophysicists* because they are often trained as physicists, argue that for many aggregate issues individual behavior is irrelevant; what happens in the aggregate reflects statistical properties of interactions that are independent of agents and that are independent of the building blocks used within the model.

blocks, especially when teaching economics. Their argument is not that models built on the traditional building blocks—such as supply and demand—are irrelevant; it is simply that the traditional building blocks do not explain everything, and that attempts to use them to explain everything actually undermine our understanding of what models using the traditional building blocks do explain. Behavioral economists argue that empirical work has convincingly shown that people are predictably irrational in some of their behaviors, and modern economics must take that into account.

Q-5 Which are better—models based on traditional building blocks or models based on behavioral building blocks?

Eventually, the hope of modern economics is that economists will have a set of models that "explain" the decisions we observe, along with a guide explaining which models fit what situations. Alas, you're not going to get that guide in this book (or in any other textbook). Economists are just not there yet. In fact, we're far from it, and even those who use the new building blocks do not believe that the behavioral models are sufficiently developed to replace the traditional models as the pedagogical core of economics. That's why I focus on the traditional building blocks and the standard supply/demand model throughout the book. But that focus should not lead you to think of the supply/demand model and its assumptions as anything more than a beginning of an introduction to modern economics.

Types of Models

As I stated above, economists have many types of models—verbal, empirical, and formal models. Modern economists use all of them. Thus, to understand modern economics, you need to know the various types and their advantages and disadvantages. Let's consider each briefly.

Behavioral and Traditional Informal (Heuristic) Models

Most of the time when laypeople hear about the results of an economist's analysis, they don't see the underlying formal model. Instead, all they see is a heuristic or verbal discussion that conveys the essence of the model. But if you search deeper into the discussion, you can generally extract the model and see whether the economist is using behavioral or traditional building blocks.

To show you the difference between heuristic models based on traditional building blocks and ones based on broader behavioral building blocks, let's consider some discussions in two popular books that apply economic reasoning to everyday events. That consideration will help clarify the difference between an economist using traditional building blocks and one using behavioral building blocks.

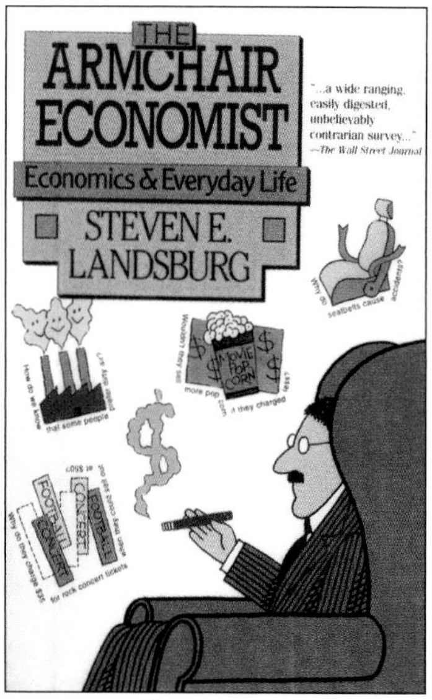

Steven Landsburg's An Armchair Economist *is a book based on heuristic models using the self-interest and rationality building blocks.*

The Armchair Economist: Heuristic Models Using Traditional Building Blocks Let's begin with a consideration of a model of University of Rochester economist Steven Landsburg. Landsburg calls himself an "armchair economist," by which he means that he provides heuristic models to explain everyday events. For the most part, Landsburg's heuristic models use traditional economic building blocks; he unflinchingly and happily pulls out unexpected implications from models built on those assumptions. Thus, Landsburg is an excellent example of a modern economist who sticks to traditional building blocks.

The particular model of his that I will consider deals with a sometimes taboo topic—sex. His model is designed to make the reader think, and to see how economic reasoning can come to counterintuitive conclusions. Coming to such highly counterintuitive ideas is seen as a strong plus for these models based on traditional building blocks. An important purpose of the traditional model is to get people to think of questions in a different way than they normally do, and in the process provide important insights.

More Sex Is Safer Sex In one of his more provocative models (available on *Slate*, www.slate.com/id/2033), Landsburg considers the problem facing Martin, "a charming and generally prudent young man with a limited sexual history, who has been gently flirting with his coworker Joan." Landsburg describes a situation in which Martin and Joan were both thinking that they might go home together after an office party that would be held the next day. However, on the way to the party, Martin notices a Center for Disease Control subway advertisement advocating the virtues of abstinence. Feeling guilty about his thoughts, he decides to stay home rather than to tempt himself. He is being virtuous.

Joan shows up at the party and, in Martin's absence, she hooks up with an "equally charming but considerably less prudent Maxwell." Maxwell is rather careless in practicing safe sex, and the end result of this hookup is that Joan ends up with AIDS—all because Martin was virtuous. (Economic models conveying these parables of the problems with being virtuous have a long history in economics, going back to Bernard Mandeville who wrote *The Fable of the Bees* back in the 1700s.)

Landsburg then argues that this story demonstrates that Martin's withdrawal from the mating game has made the mating game more dangerous for others. He argues that it follows that the world would be better off (specifically, we could slow the spread of AIDS) if "the Martins of the world would loosen up a little." He then reports some empirical estimates by a Harvard professor that if everyone with fewer than about 2.25 partners per year were to take additional partners more frequently, we could actually slow the spread of AIDS. Landsburg argues the following: "To an economist, it's crystal clear why people with limited sexual pasts choose to supply too little sex in the present: their services are underpriced."

Landsburg's model is meant to shock, which it does. But it is also meant to hone people's reasoning ability, which it also does. It captures the economic insight that when effects of one's decisions on others are not included in a person's decision-making process—that is, where there are externalities—the decision will not lead to the aggregate outcome that most people would prefer. But they are the decisions that Landsburg thinks people will make. Landsburg's model is based on the traditional building block of strong self-interest.

Decisions about sexual activity may have externalities and therefore what is best for the individuals involved may not be best for society.

Why Car Insurance Costs More Some Places Than Others While Landsburg is traditional in his building blocks, he is not always traditional in the formal models he uses, and in some of the issues he studies, he goes far beyond the simple supply/demand model. For example, in another model, he considers the issue of why car insurance costs three times as much in Philadelphia, Pennsylvania, than in Ithaca, New York, even though the theft and accident rates are not significantly different between the two cities. The model he uses is a "path-dependent tipping-point" model with two, rather than one, equilibria. In a tipping-point model, the model can arrive at quite different results depending on people's initial choice. The results are path dependent, and without knowing the path, one cannot predict the equilibrium. Tipping-point models are a type of a broader group of models called **path-dependent models**—*models in which the path to equilibrium affects the equilibrium*. Path-dependent models require a knowledge of the relevant history to reach a conclusion. Were the supply/demand model a path-dependent model, it would not lead to a unique equilibrium price.

The argument Landsburg gives is the following. In the pricing of insurance, there is a feedback effect of the initial choices people make of whether to buy insurance that affects the cost of insurance. If a few people decide not to buy insurance, the costs of insurance to others who do buy insurance will be higher since, if they have an accident with an uninsured driver, their insurance will have to pay. Because insurance costs are higher, even more people drive without insurance, further increasing

REAL-WORLD APPLICATION

Can You Explain Landsburg's Provocative Insights?

The two arguments that I present in the text are examples of Landsburg's provocative approach, which is characteristic of modern traditional economists. Below are some of his other provocative conclusions based on traditional building blocks. See if you can figure out what the implicit model is that leads to that conclusion. If you can't figure out the model, or want to check your reasoning, his arguments can be found in his book *More Sex Is Safer Sex*, and brief summaries of his reasoning can be found on the text Web site.

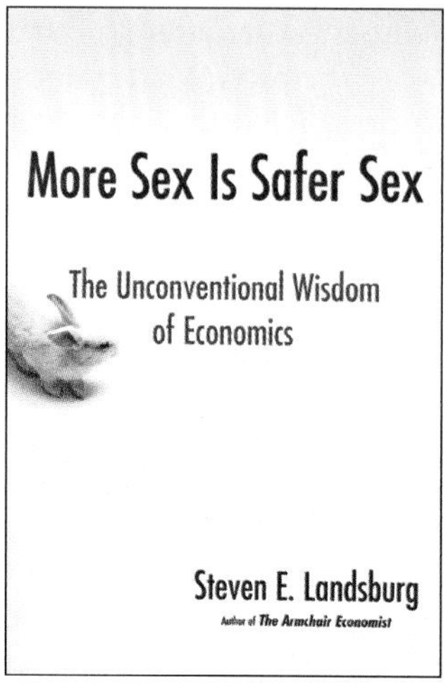

1. Daughters cause divorce.
2. A taste for revenge is healthier than a thirst for gold.
3. A ban on elephant hunting is bad news for elephants.
4. Disaster assistance is bad news for the people who receive it.
5. Malicious computer hackers should be executed.
6. The most charitable people support the fewest charities.
7. Writing books is socially irresponsible.
8. Elbowing your way to the front of the water-fountain line is socially responsible.

Many of these are presented a bit in jest (I think)—they are meant to shock and get you to think. But that is precisely how the best advocates of the traditional building blocks use their heuristic models based on traditional building blocks. The models provide you with a different view of an issue, and thereby increase your understanding of what's really going on.

the rates for those who do buy insurance. Landsburg argues that that is what happened in Philadelphia. In Ithaca, however, the situation went the other way—many initially bought insurance, which meant that insurance costs for everyone were lower, which led others to buy insurance, which led to even lower rates. Both equilibria are self-reinforcing, and, once chosen, are very difficult to change, without a major intervention by government.

Such government interventions go against Landsburg's (and most traditional economists') intuition. Traditional models based on the traditional building blocks without externalities almost inevitably lead to a laissez-faire policy. He states, "For ideological free marketers (like myself), theories (like this one) can be intellectually jarring. We are accustomed to defending free markets as the guarantors of both liberty and prosperity, but here's a case where liberty and prosperity are at odds: by forcing people to act against their own self-interest in the short run, governments can make everybody more prosperous in the long run. . . . Is it worth sacrificing a small amount of freedom for cheaper auto insurance? I am inclined to believe that the answer is yes, but the question makes me squirm a bit."

Here we see a heuristic model based on reasoning that people are rational and self-interested, as in the supply/demand model. But because it is not a supply/demand model with a single equilibrium, it leads to a quite nontraditional result of two possible equilibria. It also leads to a potential policy solution—one requiring all individuals to get insurance. The policy discussion highlighted by this model is highly relevant because it is now part of the debate about health care in the United States. Advocates of government-mandated health insurance argue that an individual's decision to go without health-care insurance increases the costs of health care for all, and this has pushed the United States to an undesirable equilibrium. They argue that mandatory insurance would switch the United States to a preferable alternative equilibrium.

The Economic Naturalist: Heuristic Models Using Behavioral Building Blocks Let's now turn to some models from another popular book, this one by Cornell economist Robert Frank, entitled *The Economic Naturalist.* Frank's approach is very similar to Landsburg's. He observes the events around him and tries to understand them using economic building blocks. The difference between Frank and Landsburg is that Frank is much more willing than Landsburg to go beyond the traditional building blocks. He assumes that people are only purposeful, not rational, and that they follow enlightened self-interest rather than being only self-interested. This allows for a much wider range of models and set of explanations, as well as a much wider range of policy interventions that follow from the model. We can see the difference by considering two of the models he presents.

Why Are People More Likely to Return Cash Than a Lampshade? The first of his models that we will consider is designed to explain why people are more likely to return cash to a store when given too much change by a cashier than to return a piece of merchandise for which they were not charged. He begins by reporting the results of a survey in which 90 percent of the respondents said they would return $20 to a store if given that amount extra in change, but only 10 percent said they would return a $20 lampshade if the cashier had neglected to charge for it. If people took only their own interests into account, they shouldn't return either.

That people return a $20 lampshade that was mistakenly not scanned less often than they will return an overpayment of $20 in change supports the assumption of purposeful behavior.

He explains this difference in behavior by arguing that people take into account *who* will be hurt by the action. In the case of the cash, the "cashier will have to pay out of her own pocket." Thus, he reasons most people will not want her to be penalized. In the case of the lampshade, it is the store, not the individual, that will suffer the loss, and people are much less worried about hurting stores than they are about hurting people. Notice the difference in Frank's assumption as compared to Landsburg's. In Frank's model, people are somewhat self-interested (they keep the $20 lampshade), but not totally self-interested (they return the $20). Using a model with traditional building blocks, the prediction would be that no one would return the money. Frank's behavioral model allows for the possibility that individuals care about the impact of their actions on others.

Why Don't More People Wear Velcro Shoes? A second model found in Frank's book deals with why people continue to wear shoes with shoelaces, even though Velcro shoes are more practical, and, according to Frank, "offer clear advantages over laces" because lace shoes can become untied, causing people to fall and trip. He argues that the reason why shoelaces are still predominant is that the very young (who don't know how to tie shoes) and the very old (who are too feeble to bend down and tie shoes) wear them, and that therefore Velcro shoes have become associated with what Frank calls "incompetence and fragility"—characteristics with which most people don't want to be associated.

Where this explanation deviates from the traditional building blocks is the rationality assumption. Using a technology that is less efficient than another (shoelaces over Velcro) is irrational, and thus doesn't make sense. The behavioral assumption in Frank's model is that people care about what other people think about them and thus take social issues, not just economic issues, into account when making their decisions. Behavioral economic models take social dimensions of problems into account; traditional economic models don't.

Behavioral models take social considerations into account; traditional models do not.

I should include an addendum (confession?) to this model; I've worn Velcro shoes for the last 20 years, much to the horror of my children, who asked me not to be seen with them when I wear them. Why do I wear them? I suspect because of my training in traditional economic models. That training has shaped me so that I value efficiency for

Q-6 Does the author's tendency to wear Velcro shoes demonstrate that he is beyond social pressures?

REAL-WORLD APPLICATION

Can You Explain Frank's Observations?

The text recounts two heuristic models that are found in Robert Frank's *The Economic Naturalist.* In his review of Frank's book, Vanderbilt economist John Siegfried listed the questions that led to 10 other models in Frank's book. Below is Siegfried's list; I leave it to you to develop the model that would explain the questions.

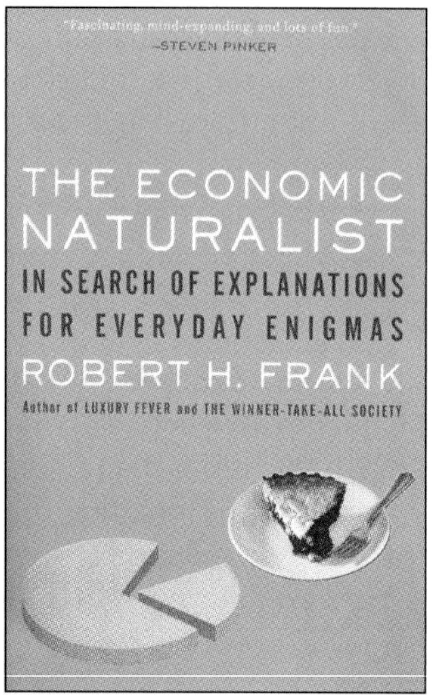

1. Why does a light come on when you open a refrigerator, but not a freezer?
2. Why do dry cleaners charge more for women's shirts than for men's?
3. Why are brown eggs more expensive than white ones?
4. Why do women endure the discomfort of high heels?
5. Why are whales in danger of extinction, but not chickens?
6. If we have Blockbuster video, why don't we have Blockbuster book?
7. Why is there so much mathematical formalism in economics?
8. Why do stores post signs saying that guide dogs are permitted inside?
9. Why do most U.S. department stores put men's fashions on the ground floor?
10. Why is it easier to find a partner when you already have one?

If you want to see the models Frank came up with, see his book *The Economic Naturalist.* Short summaries of the explanations Frank followed can be found on the textbook Web site.

its own sake. By wearing Velcro shoes I am making a statement to society (I am as much a social creature as others) that I am not driven by social norms about dressing (anyone who has seen my standard attire can attest to the fact that I am not). I consciously do it (at least in the sense of not allowing my wife to put out the clothes she wants me to wear) and, to some degree, I revel in the looks I get because it means that I am free, and efficient, allowing me to consider others slaves of some designer. I tell my kids that some day the world will follow me. They tell me, "Don't hold your breath."

My behavior represents another dimension of behavior that behavioral economists have discovered. Studying a model and using its assumptions can lead you to adopt its assumptions as your own; thus, the models you choose to use to look at the world can influence your behavior. This means that studying economics may not only provide you with insights; it also may change you.

The Limits of Heuristic Models I could go on with hundreds of these vignettes; they are entertaining, fun, and good practice for the mind. If my sole purpose were to entertain you, I'd include a lot more. But the principles course is meant to do more than entertain; it is meant to teach, and except when they are writing for laypeople, most economists see heuristic models as simply a stepping stone to a more formal model. The reason is that heuristic models are not sufficiently precise, making their validity impossible to test. Think back to the heuristic models we presented and ask yourself how convinced you were by the arguments. Each was relatively easy to modify to come to a different conclusion.

For example, what if Joan had chosen not to hook up with anyone? Or what if she had seen the same abstinence ad as had Martin? Then the argument would have been reversed. Would that mean that the Martins of the world should have less sex? Or what if Velcro shoes suddenly became "in." Would that mean that the more practical solution wins out? So, while the heuristic models embodied in the vignettes are entertaining, it is a fair question to ask whether we really know anything more about the world after learning about the models than we did before. To a scientist the answer is no, we don't, at least in a scientific sense. That's why science is not based on heuristic models.

Empirical Models

Q-7 Why are economists very hesitant to base knowledge on heuristic models?

Scientists are very hesitant to base any knowledge on anecdotes or heuristic models, even highly convincing ones. The reason is that they have found that the human mind is extremely good at creating convincing stories that make sense within its own world view or frame, but not necessarily outside of it. They have found that the human mind is what psychologists call a *fast pattern completer*. Heuristic models exploit this tendency in humans that gives people a sense of understanding, but not necessarily a true understanding. Scientists argue that to extend a heuristic model to true understanding, you have to quantify and empirically test your arguments.

The Importance of Empirical Work in Modern Economics This leads us to a second important element of modern economics: it is highly empirical. That is, modern economics is based on experiments that can be replicated, or on statistical analysis of real-world observations. While the importance of empirical work has a long history in economics, going back to William Petty in the 1600s, up until the 1940s, economics primarily concentrated on deductive, not inductive, reasoning. That occurred because of the lack of data and the lack of computational power to analyze data.

With the development of **econometrics**—*the statistical analysis of economic data*—in the 1940s, that started to change. But because of limited data and computing power, empirical work in economics did not move to the forefront in economics until the late 1980s when computer power had expanded enough to begin making such an empirical approach useful. At that point, induction started to supplement deduction as the economist's method for understanding the real world. Since the late 1980s this movement toward induction has accelerated, so that today it is fair to say that the development of computing power has fundamentally changed the way economic research is done.

Modern economics—models based on both traditional and behavioral building blocks—relies on experiments and statistical analysis of real-world observations.

The strong reliance on empirical work is true of all modern economists—both those who use traditional building blocks and those who use behavioral building blocks. Today, much empirical work in economics is not based on formal deductive models, but rather on heuristic models—relatively simple and informal models that capture a possible insight, such as those we discussed above by Frank and Landsburg.

The difference between an economic scientist's heuristic model and those of Frank and Landsburg presented above is that the economic scientist doesn't stop with the heuristic model, as did Frank and Landsburg's presentations. He or she builds an empirical model around that heuristic model and supports the argument with empirical evidence. Essentially, what he or she does is to take relationships found in the heuristic model and see if these relationships can be generalized subject to scientifically based statistical studies. Economists call this approach "letting the data speak." To let the data speak, you collect data and analyze them with statistical and econometric tools.

To analyze an issue with an **empirical model**—*a model that statistically discovers a pattern in the data*—the researcher empirically studies the relationship he or she arrived at in her heuristic model. That's what Steve Levitt has done with enormous creativity and success. He has looked at a variety of issues: Do sumo wrestlers throw matches? Do basketball teams cheat? And why do drug dealers often live with their mothers? He looks at the data, creates simple informal models and hypotheses, and uses those models to structure his empirical study. For example, he reasoned that if who won sumo wrestling matches did not involve cheating, whether a wrestler was close to winning

FIGURE 6-1 Grades versus Class Size

A regression finds a line that best fits a combination of points such as the one shown here. It appears from this scatter plot that class size affects the average grade.

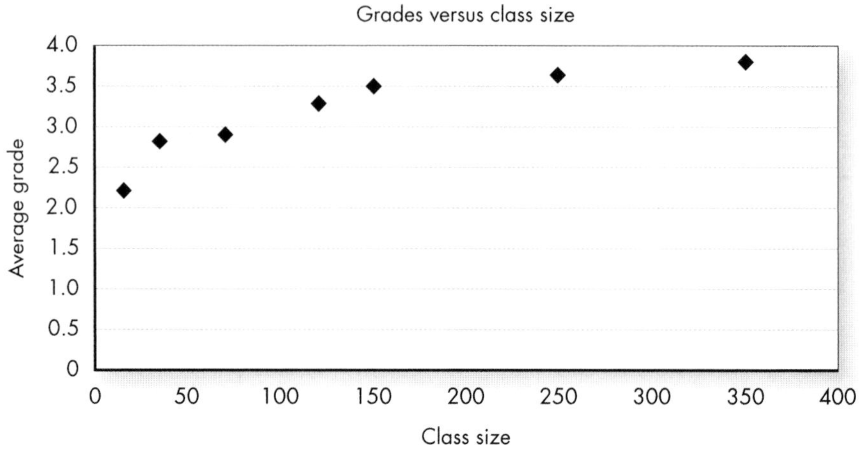

enough matches to raise his ranking would not make a difference as to whether he won a match or not. But he reasoned further that if wrestlers are self-interested and rational, they will have an incentive to agree to quid pro quo arrangements to cheat and throw a match, allowing opponents to win a match in exchange for their throwing a future match. So now he had a testable hypothesis. His hypothesis was: *the closer a wrestler is to raising his rank, the more often his opponent will intentionally lose.* He then collected and statistically analyzed the data. What he discovered was that how close a wrestler was to elimination did make a difference, which allowed him to conclude that sumo wrestlers "cheat."

A regression model is a model that statistically relates one set of variables to another.

Regression Models A primary tool of an empirical economist is a **regression model,** *an empirical model in which one statistically relates one set of variables to another*, and the statistical tools that accompany it. For example, say you are wondering if a professor giving higher grades increases the number of students in his class. You would collect data about two variables—the grades he gives and enrollment in his classes—giving you a relationship shown in Figure 6-1. Then you would "run a regression," which essentially means that you use a statistical package to find a line that "best fits" the data, where by "best fit" one means making the distances between that line and the points as small as possible. If the "best fit" line is upward-sloping, as it would be here, then the regression model's answer to the question is a tentative yes, subject to all the things that were held constant.

The "goodness of fit" between the two variables is described by the **coefficient of determination,** which is *a measure of the proportion of the variability in the data that is accounted for by the statistical model*. The larger the coefficient of determination, the better the fit, and if it is a perfect fit, then every point will be on the "best fit" line. This isn't a statistics class so I won't go into further explanation, but that short description should give you a sense of how empirical regression models work. Regression models are the workhorses of much of what applied microeconomists do, and modern economists become almost magicians at pulling information out from data.

Often economists' empirical models explore issues far from the standard domain of economics. One example recounted in Ian Ayres' book *Super Crunchers* (a book that nicely explains the importance of data analysis to modern society) is by Princeton professor Orley Ashenfelter. He developed a model that predicted whether a particular year's wine would be a good one. He hypothesized that the quality of a wine in a particular year depended on rainfall, weather, and similar elements in that year. He collected all the appropriate data, and then related those data to the price of wine by running a regression. He then developed the following relationship from his regression model:

Wine quality = 12.145 + 0.001 (Winter rainfall) + 0.06 (Average growing-season temperature) − 0.004 (Harvest rainfall)

This relationship tells us that the quality of a Bordeaux wine depends upon rainfall and temperature. He upset "wine connoisseurs" by arguing that his simple regression model does a better job at determining a good year for wine than they can through tasting. Moreover, he argued that his model can determine quality long before wine connoisseurs could even start tasting the wine. So when choosing a wine, forget about sniffing, swirling, and tasting; just get your computer out, collect the data, plug in the numbers, and solve the equation. Is he right? I'm no wine connoisseur, but the people I talk to (admittedly, they tend to be economists) believe that he is.

Another regression model has been used by baseball teams to determine how valuable a prospect is. Econometrically trained specialists collected data on young baseball recruits and ran regressions, finding how different skills are correlated with a team's success. When these specialists did this, they found that bases on balls were almost as important as hits. Thus, they argued that a person's ability to draw a walk should be one of the variables considered in choosing a recruit, something that previously wasn't done. They then used that regression model to predict which young recruit would most likely help a team win. The strategy worked, as discussed by Michael Lewis in *Moneyball*; after using the model, the Oakland Athletics won their division, despite their low payroll. Oakland's success did not go unnoticed; when the Boston Red Sox, a team with a high payroll, started using the model, they won the World Series.

Regression models can reveal all sorts of relationships from the effect of weather on the quality of wine to the contribution of a player's ability to draw a walk toward a team's season record.

These empirical models are sometimes called *data-mining models*, but I prefer to call them *pattern-finding models*. They play an important role in the modern microeconomist's tool kit and have increased in importance because of the enormous increase in computing power and statistical software. This increase in computer power allows economic researchers to find stable patterns in data much more easily than before. This pattern-finding process of modeling is itself being automated, and with sophisticated econometric software, economists can have the computer automatically find patterns and turn those patterns into models.

Summarizing: The development of computer power and these empirical models has led to an enormous change in how modern microeconomics is done. For example, when I asked top graduate students as part of an interview what differentiated an economist from another social scientist, they did *not* say that they differed from other social scientists in the building blocks they used. Instead, they said that the difference was the economist's reliance on formal empirical methods.[4]

Simple Data Models: Charts, Graphs, and Quantitative Argumentation

As a principles student, you will likely not be developing regression models, but you will be building models based on data by developing a chart or a graph that demonstrates how something is changing over time or a pattern that captures the co-movement of two variables. These charts and graphs might not have the full scientific look of a regression model, but they are often more useful. What characterizes the modern economic way of thinking is not the regression model per se, but using quantitative data to make an argument, often by presenting those data with a simple chart or graph.

[4]That may change in the future since other social sciences are becoming much more empirical as well, but for the next decade they will likely still lag behind economics.

The Role of Formal Models

Were economic modeling only a matter of data mining, empirical models would replace all other types of modeling, but it is not, and they haven't. Data, by themselves, have no meaning; they have to be interpreted and given meaning, and how one interprets the data depends on the model and the building blocks one has in one's mind. Either implicitly or explicitly, one's model guides how one organizes the data. That's why theory remains important, and an important part of this principles course is meant to give you practice in understanding the theoretical structure of economic thinking.

The same pattern can be interpreted in multiple ways. Economists rely on theoretical models to help them interpret the data.

You can see the importance of theory by thinking about a magic eye picture—as you change your focus, what you see will change. (You can see a magic eye picture at www.magiceye.com/3dfun/stwkdisp.shtml.) A simpler such example is conveyed by the figure of the old woman shown here. Did you see an "old woman"? Most of you will have because that's how I described it. But what if I had said "beautiful young woman" rather than "old woman"? If I had, I suspect you might have seen the picture in a different light. The moral: Which pattern your eye sees in pictures, and even more so in data, depends on the implicit model or frame that you bring to the picture or the data. (If you only see one, keep looking; the eye of the "old woman" is the ear of the beautiful young woman.)

I raise this issue of framing because it highlights the difficulty of pulling information from an empirical model. Two different economists may well see different results even with the same empirical model. Let's consider an example of such a recent debate in economics. The debate concerns the deterrent effect of the death penalty.

In natural science one would determine whether the death penalty has a deterrent effect by doing a controlled experiment that isolates specific variables and changing one variable to see if it causes another to change. But in economics such controlled experiments are generally impossible. An economist can't suggest that we try out the death penalty to see what its deterrent effect would be. So instead of using controlled experiments, economists need to be creative and search for what they call a **natural experiment** (*an event created by nature that can serve as an experiment*) that may help to shed light on an issue.

Doing such a study with existing data, economists Isaac Ehrlich and Joanna Shepherd have found a statistical relationship between the death penalty and the number of murders. In one statistical study, Erlich found that an increase in the number of executions by one percent is associated with a decrease in the murder rate by one-half of a percent, while Shepherd found that one execution deterred seven to eight murders. These statistical relationships have been contested by a number of economists. They pointed out that how the variables are specified and the equations mattered. For example, using the same data, John Donohue and Justin Wulfers came to quite different conclusions. They stated: "The view that the death penalty deters is still the product of belief, not evidence."

I'm not going to get into the debate here; I don't claim to know who is right. I recount it merely to give you a sense that given the limited ability economists have to conduct controlled experiments, letting the data speak will not necessarily provide the definitive answer. This means that economists, and other social scientists, must rely on their theoretical models to guide them in interpreting data and in drawing out policy implications from their work.

Q-8 True or false: Debates in modern economics will be resolved by letting the data speak.

Different Types of Formal Models That Economists Use The above discussion leads us to a third difference between earlier economics and modern economics. Earlier economics used models with relatively simple relationships among variables; the supply/demand model is an example of such a simple model. Modern economists—both modern traditional and modern behavioral economists—still use simple models, but they also use models that allow for much more complex relationships among variables than do the simple models. These analytically sophisticated models cannot be expressed

TABLE 6-2 What Characterizes a Modern Economist?

Earlier Economists	Modern Economists
Used traditional building blocks	May use traditional or behavioral building blocks
Primarily deductive methods	Much more empirical—use deductive and inductive methods
Used simple supply/demand models	Use both simple supply/demand models and more complicated models

in the two-dimensional graphs used by earlier economists. Table 6-2 summarizes the three primary differences between earlier economists and modern economists.

An example of the difference between earlier economists and modern economists can be seen by considering the "tipping point" model that Landsburg used to analyze differences in car insurance prices. As I stated earlier, that model is a path-dependent model, which technically means that any decision feeds back into the model. In a path-dependent model, you can only know what will happen if you know the path the model takes. Mathematically, specifying path-dependent models is much more complicated than specifying supply/demand models; you have to use an advanced-calculus, differential-equations model rather than a standard algebraic model, or you have to solve it computationally.

Q-9 Is the supply and demand model a path-dependent model?

The reason why formal models have evolved from simple models to more complex and highly technical mathematical models, again, is that technology has changed. In this case, the technology is mathematics. Today's economists are much better trained in mathematics than were earlier economists, which allows economists to go far beyond the interrelationships allowed in supply/demand models. With advances in mathematics, for example,

- You can have models with many equilibria, so it is difficult to know what an equilibrium is.
- You can have models in which not only are the variables related, so too are the changes in variables and the changes in changes in variables.
- You can have models in which systemic equilibrium involves enormous continual change in the parts so that even though the system is in equilibrium, the individual parts are not.
- You can have models in which relationships are nonlinear on various levels, and in which an infinitely small change can lead to drastically different results.

The potential interrelationships that can be captured in modern formal models are almost unending, and when one studies the broad range of models with all these potential interrelationships, the number of potential outcomes in the economy is awesome. There is a formal theoretical model that can arrive at just about any possible conclusion.

Which theoretical model is right? Do you choose models with more complex building blocks, as argued by behavioral economists? Or do you choose models with more limiting traditional building blocks? Do you not worry about building blocks? Or do you just worry about which model best fits the empirical evidence? Such questions are the grist of the modern economists' debates. (And you thought we were boring people; if my kids only understood how wildly interesting these questions are—would you believe?)

The Trade-off between Simplicity and Completeness One might think that one should use the most complex model with the broadest building blocks because that would give you the broadest approach. But that doesn't necessarily follow. Each new interrelationship involves adding an additional level of technical difficulty, and the more complex the model, the harder it is to arrive at a conclusion. Thus, in their modeling, economists make a continual trade-off between simplicity and completeness. At the principles level, the choice is clear: KISS (Keep It Simple Stupid) rules, which is why the graphical supply/demand model is the workhorse of principles of economics. That's why, even though modern economics goes far beyond supply and demand, the principles course focuses on supply and demand and teaches students the traditional model.[5] Almost all economists agree that for introducing principles students to economic reasoning, used appropriately with sufficient caveats, the supply/demand model is a really neat model that the profession has had lots of experience teaching. It is the perfect calisthenics of the mind for moving on to models with more complicated behavioral building blocks.

Let me give an example of where the model one uses matters: the state of the aggregate economy in 2008. The question at issue is: Should we be worried about the economy going into a depression or not? The traditional aggregate-supply/aggregate-demand model, which has become the standard textbook model, suggests we should not be concerned. In it, the economy is close to equilibrium, and policies exist to move it to equilibrium if it isn't. That isn't the case for some of the more complex formal models. In these more complex models, the aggregate economy can suddenly change depending on what people believe. You can have what is called a **self-confirming equilibrium**—*an equilibrium in a model in which people's beliefs become self-fulfilling*—so if people think the economy will go into a depression, it will. In some models, what people believe might not even matter; you can have *strange attractor models*, sometimes called **butterfly effect models**—*models in which a small change causes a large effect*. For example, a butterfly flapping its wings in China can cause the output of the U.S. economy to fall significantly. In these models, a small change could tip the economy into a low-growth, high-unemployment equilibrium that would be difficult to escape. In these models, therefore, we have reason to be seriously concerned about the U.S. economy going into a depression.

Web Note 6.2
Models in Movies

Other Formal Models There are many other types of formal models as well. For example, *set theory models* are models based only on formal logical relationships. Yet another is a **game theory model**—*a model in which one analyzes the strategic interaction of individuals when they take into account the likely response of other people to their actions*. Game theory models form the core of much of what is studied in graduate microeconomics today. Thus, the standard graduate microeconomics text has only three supply-and-demand diagrams in an entire 1,000-plus-page book.

Game theory models analyze the strategic interaction among individuals.

More complicated models often yield no analytic solution—that is, you can't solve the set of equations to discover the equilibrium in the model. These complicated analytic models were unusable for a traditional economist because a model that you can't solve analytically didn't provide any insight. That isn't the case for a modern economist. If a modern economist can't solve a model analytically, he or she will estimate the solution by simulating the model with a computer. Computational power replaces analytic elegance. Thus, computer simulation is an important tool of modern economists (both those using behavioral and those using traditional assumptions), and in his or her research a modern economist will often go from struggling with analytically solving a model to simulating it on the computer, and then back to trying to solve it analytically.

---

[5]I discuss the justification for why the textbooks focus on the supply/demand model and the traditional model, even as the economists in their research have moved from them, in *The Stories Economists Tell* and a *Journal of Economic Education* article, "What Economists Teach and What We Believe." While the supply/demand model captures these ideas, for mathematically inclined students, as Harold Kuhn, a famous mathematical economist, once told his students, the lessons can be generalized into a set of constrained optimization models assuming convex functions, and if principles students were strongly mathematically inclined, many of the models could be presented in calculus format. A brief introduction to the calculus of constrained optimization is available in the *Honors Companion* accompanying this book available on my Web site.

Economists use a number of different types of computer simulations. The one described above was a simulation designed to solve a model with a specified set of equations that can't be solved analytically. In those types of simulations, the computer is a computational assistant that can arrive at estimated solutions to complicated analytic sets of equations. This approach is widespread. A more novel approach to computer simulation is designed to deal with problems that are so difficult that you don't even know how to specify the equations. How do economists model when they can't specify the equations that describe the relationships in the model? They use the computer to guide them in specifying the model itself.

This alternative approach to modeling is called the **agent-based computational (ACE) model**—*a culture dish approach to the study of economic phenomena in which agents* (encapsulated collections of data and methods representing an entity residing in that environment on the computer) *are allowed to interact in a computationally constructed environment and the researcher observes the results of that interaction*. (For more information about ACE models, see www.econ.iastate.edu/tesfatsi/ace.htm.) ACE modeling is fundamentally different than standard modeling. It is computer based, and it has no equations that have to be solved. Instead, ACE researchers simply try to create virtual computer models that capture the essence of the interdependencies, and then observe the results. So rather than solve a model, you build a computer model with computer agents; you then run the model thousands of times and keep track of the results.

The ACE model is like a petri dish of individual economic actors deployed with specific behaviors. Economists watch and study the relationships and behaviors that develop.

This is a fascinating new approach to modeling complex systems because it allows for all types of interactions. It has the possibility of fundamentally changing the way economists model and how they understand the economy because it allows researchers to consider much more complicated interactions than they could if they had to "solve" the model on their own. For example, ACE models can allow multiple equilibria and the possibility of many levels of path dependency—complications that are beyond traditional models. Recognizing that the models may reflect path dependency, the ACE modeler doesn't run the program once; he or she runs it thousands of times and sees the range of results. So just like engineers are now using virtual computer modeling to design planes and cars, economists are now using virtual computer models to understand how the economy works and to devise policies that might make it work better.

Empirically Testing Formal Models With so many different models, one must ask the question: How do you decide which model to use? To decide, economists empirically test alternative models and try to see which one fits best. Essentially it reverses the process used in heuristic empirical modeling, where the data were collected and analyzed before the hypothesis was determined and are then used to determine the hypothesis. With empirically tested formal models, the hypothesis is formulated first—without knowledge of the data—and then the hypothesis is tested to see if the data fit the model. Obviously, formulating hypotheses without knowing the data is difficult, and thus economists try to test hypotheses on "out of sample" data—data that were not used in the formulation of the hypothesis. If they don't have such data, they try to develop the data, or something close to them, with experiments and clever observation of events.

Today, fitting the models to the data involves much of what modern economists do. "Bringing the model to the data" is a phrase you hear all the time from modern economists. Economists are continually asking questions such as: "How does the model work in 'out of sample data'?" "Do we have a natural experiment that we can use to test the model?" "Can we develop a randomized experiment that will test the model?" "Can we design a lab experiment that will test the model?" and "Can we design a field experiment to test the model?"

Such empirical testing requires precision, which means that to truly bring the model to the data, one needs a formal model where all relationships are precisely specified,

A REMINDER

Modern Traditional and Behavioral Economists

	Earlier Economics	Modern Economics	
		Modern Behavioral Economists	Modern Traditional Economists
Assumptions	Rationality Self-interest	Purposeful behavior Enlightened self-interest	Rationality Self-interest
Approach	Deduction	Induction and deduction; emphasis on experimental economics and empirical models	Induction and deduction; emphasis on empirical models
Types of models	Simple supply/demand models	All types including highly complex mathematical models and ACE models	All types including highly complex mathematical models and ACE models

rather than a heuristic model where relationships are imprecise. Thus, the "empirical models" discussed earlier are quite different from the "empirically tested formal models" that form the foundation of economic science. Empirical models based on heuristic models are fine for policy analysis, and for guiding real-world policy decisions that have to be made before one has a full scientific understanding of an issue. These models are absolutely necessary. But before one elevates the insights of the model to the level of full scientific knowledge, one needs much more precise models. As I stated at the beginning of the chapter, most of this book is concerned with engineering models, not scientific models, which is why we will not explore the intricacies of testing formal models.

The difference between the empirical models discussed earlier and the empirically tested formal models described here is a subtle, but important, difference. In a heuristic empirical model, one has only an informal model that lets the data speak first, as heard through your general worldview embodied in your building blocks. After you've heard the data, you can provide an explanation for what you have heard. That explanation will be based on your implicit formal model, *but the empirical model cannot be an explicit test of the model* since the actual model came from the data; there is no formal model to test. To empirically test a formal model or a formalized empirical model developed from a data set, the process is different. Here, one carefully develops the implications of the formal model as they relate to the issue. Then one empirically tests this model's implications against another set of data.

Application: Why Did the Price of Chocolate Rise? To see how formal models can make a difference in how one thinks about real-world problems, let's consider an example of a puzzle that economists are working on. This example gives you a sense of why modern economists have moved to these more complicated models and how the results of the two models differ—even with the same data. The puzzle is the following—the price of chocolate. From 2006 to 2008, the price of chocolate went up to $2,600 a ton from $1,500 a ton. The question is why.

You should be able to give the traditional economic analysis of what likely happened from the analysis of earlier chapters—that explanation would involve supply falling, demand rising, or a combination of the two. (A good exercise is to graph these to see why that would be the explanation.) In a principles course, that would be the right answer. For real-world researchers it is not enough. The problem is that the data don't reveal any apparent shifts in either supply or demand. So why did the price change when supply and demand did not?

Exploring the situation further, economists discovered that there was a structural change in the market. *Hedge funds*—investment funds representing rich investors that had few constraints on what they could buy—that had access to large amounts of credit were moving their investments out of real estate and into commodities over this time period. Chocolate was one of these commodities, but commodities whose prices rose also included oil and grains, both of which also experienced sudden large increases in price during this same time period. These hedge funds did not want the chocolate, and they did not buy chocolate and store it. Instead, they were buying what are called *chocolate futures*—the right to buy chocolate at a specified point in the future at a specified price—in large amounts. Specifically, they increased their demand for chocolate futures from 260 thousand tons to 706 thousand tons over a couple of years, which amounts to an increase from less than 10 percent to more than 20 percent of the total market demand.

The question that policy makers posed to economists was whether this hedge fund activity in the futures market was the cause of the rise in the price of chocolate (and other commodities), and if it were the cause, would the rise in price be permanent or temporary? The supply/demand model doesn't directly answer that question. The answer requires an analysis that includes inventories and that captures the relationship between future expected prices—the futures prices of chocolates—and the current price of chocolate. That means that you need a model of intertemporal (across time periods) equilibrium with heterogeneous agents (agents that are not exactly alike).

You also need to figure out how the new behavioral economics building blocks might be playing a role in determining the outcome. For example, one key concept of behavioral economics is anchor points. *Anchor points* are points toward which people gravitate. The existence of anchor points can lead to multiple equilibria for the model. It is possible that the hedge funds increased other participants' anchor point for chocolate prices, which in turn led them to increase their inventory of chocolate. The demand increases, and ratifies the increase in price, even though there was no need for price to increase had the anchor point not changed. (I should also point out that hedge funds pay economists large amounts of money to model the economy and to decide where they should invest their funds. So if hedge funds were doing this, it may be because they hired a modern economist who developed a model that showed them how they might do it.)

The analysis quickly becomes complicated, but what is clear is that one needs a more advanced formal model than the supply/demand model to deal with the question. As I was writing this chapter, the question was still unanswered, but the general result of the models that are reported in the press was that while the hedge fund purchases of the futures in the chocolate market could temporarily push up the price of chocolate, they were unlikely to do so permanently, unless they provoked a response by government that had feedback effects on the chocolate market.

However, that result isn't much comfort to chocoholics since the models also suggested that it might take three or four years before the system adjusts, and in the meantime, significant disruption could continue in the chocolate market. Moreover, by then it is possible that the hedge funds could have sold their positions in chocolate futures to others, pocketing their gains. As they do so, one would expect a sudden fall in the price of chocolate significantly below its long-run average. Related puzzles exist in the oil and grain markets, and economists are hard at work on them. The lesson of this example: supply and demand are just the beginning for a modern economist.

What Difference Does All This Make to Policy?

Let me now turn to a consideration of what difference these modeling considerations have for policy. The answer is: a lot. Let me briefly distinguish the differences. An economist who concentrates on a single frame tends to be more consistent in his or her policy recommendation. Generally, for traditional economists, the framework is that the market is likely the best way to deal with a problem, and that, left alone, the market will guide people toward doing the best they, and society, can, given the constraints. Steven Landsburg nicely summed up what a traditional economist expects in his discussion of the insurance markets.

Modern economists, with their multiple frames, are less sure of the conclusion that the market will solve every problem. They accept that the market has nice properties, but they also find that it has limitations. They know that there are many models where there is a potential role for public policy in dealing with those limitations. That's why *for a modern economist policy does not follow directly from a model*. As I discussed in the introductory chapter, models provide *theorems*—results that follow logically from a model—not *precepts*—general rules for public policy. Precepts are developed from theorems that follow from various models, along with knowledge of history and of limitations of the models. In this book, when discussing theorems, I will concentrate on traditional economics, but when discussing precepts, I will go beyond traditional economics and report the combined judgments of modern economists—giving you a sense of some of the differences that arise when one uses more complicated models or the broader behavioral building blocks.

Q-10 If a model tells you that price controls will reduce people's welfare, does it follow that economists will advise governments not to impose price controls?

Let's consider three examples where a modern economist's precepts might differ from a traditional economist's precepts.

How much emphasis should be given to benefits of economic growth?

The traditional economist's precept is that more is preferred to less, and that more output is generally good; thus, policies directed at achieving more growth make society better off. The behavioral economic precept is that growth should be questioned. They point out that people's happiness depends on their relative, not their absolute, income after an annual per capita income of about $15,000 is reached. That means that more growth will not necessarily benefit society, and suggests that more focus should be given to how the existing income is distributed, rather than just focusing on total income.

Should the government have done something about the rise in housing prices in the early 2000s?

The traditional precept is that no, government probably shouldn't have. The rise in prices of housing that occurred represented people's valuation of the worth of the house. They may have made a mistake in this instance, but there is no reason to believe that the government would have gotten it right, and you can only tell whether houses are overvalued after the fact, not before.

The modern precept (based on dynamic models of interacting agents) is that bubbles are possible, and that the housing market in the early 2000s had all the signs of a bubble, which means that the government might have usefully intervened. The bursting of the housing bubble was something that was predicable, and something that policy could have eliminated the need for.

Are people saving enough?

The traditional precept is that people make rational decisions and if they are choosing to save little, that reflects their desires and best estimates of their need. The behavioral economics precept is that how much people save depends on the institutional structure, and with so much of the institutional structure designed to get people to spend, people likely save far too little. But this does not mean that one has to tell people to save more. One simply has to change the institutional structure and people will save more. For example, as opposed to having to check a box to have some income devoted to savings, saving would become the default option, and people would have to check a box if they don't want to save. By changing the default option on retirement savings plans, one can significantly change the amount people choose to save, leaving people free to make their own decision in both cases.

I could give many more such examples.

Conclusion

This has been a wide-ranging survey of just what it is that economists do, and what it means to think like a modern economist. Summarizing, briefly, modern economics goes far beyond supply and demand. Modern microeconomics is open to a wider range of building blocks and models, and is highly empirical. Thinking like a modern economist means approaching problems through modeling, and then relating the results of the model to the empirical evidence. Ultimately, the choice of models is made by empirically testing those models and choosing the one that does the best job of predicting.

The distinction between modern and traditional economists can be overdone. In many ways, the difference is just in when to put real-world complications into the model. Traditional economists use the traditional building blocks, and then adjust the model to fit the more complicated real world. That has the advantage of keeping the basic model clean and as simple as possible, but has the cost of not fitting many real-world situations. Modern economists use more complicated models so that fewer adjustments need to be made. The advantage is that the models better fit more real-world situations, but the disadvantage is that the models are not as clean and clear-cut as the traditional approach.

For teaching purposes, KISS reigns, and most economists, including me, continue to emphasize the traditional micro- and macroeconomic models. Modern insights are added as addenda and modifications.

KISS reigns.

Summary

- Models are the glue that holds economics together. But economists differ in the models that they use.
- A deductive approach is to begin with principles and logically deduce the implications of those principles. An inductive approach is to develop a model based on patterns in observed data. Modern economists tend to approach models inductively, while traditional economists approach models deductively.
- Behavioral economists replace the traditional assumption of rationality with purposeful behavior and replace self-interest with enlightened self-interested behavior.
- While models based on modern building blocks often better fit observed behavior, they often do not generalize to contexts outside the one being studied.
- Heuristic models are models expressed informally in words. They can be based on either traditional building blocks like the models of Landsburg or modern building blocks like the models of Frank.
- The validity of models often is determined based on their ability to explain real-world data. Thus, models must be tested against the data. This is part of the scientific method.
- An empirical model is a model that statistically discovers a pattern in the data. For such a model to be scientifically tested, it must be tested against another set of data. A regression model is an example of an empirical model.
- Two types of models used by modern economists are game-theory models and agent-based computational models.
- Modern economists use multiple frames and carefully distinguish theorems that follow from models from precepts that rely on theorems, but also rely on judgments about history and institutions.

Key Terms

agent-based computational (ACE) model *(145)*
behavioral economics *(129)*
butterfly effect model *(144)*
coefficient of determination *(140)*
econometrics *(139)*
empirical model *(139)*
endowment effects *(132)*
enlightened self-interest *(129)*
game theory model *(144)*
heuristic model *(128)*
model *(127)*
modern economist *(128)*
natural experiment *(142)*
path-dependent model *(135)*
precommitment strategy *(131)*
purposeful behavior *(129)*
regression model *(140)*
self-confirming equilibrium *(144)*
traditional economist *(129)*

Questions and Exercises

connect ECONOMICS

1. How is a model different from the reality that it represents? Give an example. LO1
2. How does an inductive approach to economics differ from a deductive approach? LO1
3. What are the two main building blocks for traditional economists? How do they differ from the building blocks of behavioral economists? LO1
4. How does enlightened self-interest differ from self-interest? LO1
5. One rule of thumb many people follow is "eat until your plate is clean." How does this rule of thumb violate the rationality assumption? LO1
6. Name two advantages and two disadvantages of the traditional model. LO1
7. Name two advantages and two disadvantages of the behavioral model. LO1
8. Is experimental economics best seen as an inductive or deductive science? Explain your answer. LO1
9. What is a *heuristic model*? Can a heuristic model be traditional? Why or why not? LO2
10. Even though the Betamax format is believed to have been better than the VHS format, early market leadership by VHS established VHS as the dominant choice for videocassette recorders. Some argue that if Betamax had an early lead, it would have been the dominant technology. What kind of equilibrium model best fits this description and why? LO2
11. Why might government intervention make sense in a model of path-dependency but not a supply/demand model? LO2
12. According to economist Robert Frank, why are people more likely to return $20 they'd been given in error in change than a lampshade that had not been scanned at checkout? What does this say about traditional building blocks? LO2
13. Why do economists rely more on empirical evidence today than they did 100 years ago? LO3
14. What does it mean to "let the data speak"? LO3
15. What is a regression? LO3
16. What characteristics would you look for in data to use as a natural experiment? LO3
17. What are the three major differences between earlier and modern economists? LO3
18. What is a self-confirming equilibrium? Use the supply/demand model to demonstrate how the expectation of lower prices can be self-confirming. LO4
19. What is an agent-based computational model? LO4
20. Why is "out-of-sample" data important for testing inductive models? LO4
21. A student is given the option of selecting two homework schedules—one in which three five-page papers and one one-page paper are due at the end of the semester and another in which the first papers are due the third, sixth, and ninth weeks of the semester and the last paper is due at the end.
    a. Why might a student choose the first option?
    b. Why might a student choose the second option?
    c. Which is the rational choice? LO5
22. In a recent study, when asked to choose between an iPod and $100, people were more likely to choose the money. But when they were given an iPod and then asked if they would trade it for $100, they were more likely to choose the iPod.
    a. What effect does this reflect?
    b. Is this behavior rational? LO5

Questions from Alternative Perspectives

1. How might modeling itself frame an economist's analysis, making the economist unable to see basic truths about the way in which society subjugates women? (Feminist)
2. Was Mother Teresa rational? (Religious)
3. It is sometimes said that modern economists pose little questions that can be answered while sociologists pose large questions that cannot be answered. How might that description be related to the economist's modeling approach? (Radical)
4. The book talks as if modern economists have made a large break from traditional assumptions; many heterodox economists see the two as simply minor modifications of the same approach. In what way is that true? (Austrian)
5. If modern economics focuses on empirical models, does that mean that those aspects of life that cannot be quantified are shortchanged? (Institutionalist)

Issues to Ponder

1. What does it mean to assume that people are purposeful in their behavior instead of rational? LO1
2. In one study, a group of Asian-American women were asked to take a math exam. First they were divided into two groups. Before taking the test, individuals in the first group were asked their opinions about coed dorms while the second were asked their family history. Those who had been reminded by the questions that they were women performed worse than those who were reminded that they were Asian. How is this an example of predictably irrational behavior? LO1
3. Is the supply/demand model a path-dependent model? Why or why not? LO4
4. Can an economist who bases her models on traditional building blocks be a modern economist? Why or why not? LO1
5. What might an economist do if he cannot solve a model analytically? (Give up is not an option.) LO4

Answers to Margin Questions

1. Modeling, not supply and demand, is the glue that holds modern economics together. *(128)*
2. Because of technological changes in computing, modern economists are more likely to use inductive models compared to earlier economists who gave more weight to deductive models. *(128)*
3. These are both assumptions associated with behavioral economists. *(129)*
4. It depends on what model you use. In a traditional model it cannot because people choose what is best for them. Thus a constraint upon choice must make them worse off. In a behavioral model, it may make them better off because people are not assumed to have complete self-control. *(131)*
5. It depends. Both have their advantages and disadvantages, and a choice can be made only when one knows the purpose of the model. *(134)*
6. No, it simply demonstrates that he is affected by them in different ways than are other people. *(137)*
7. Economists are hesitant to base knowledge on heuristic models because they are only suggestive, and are subject to people's tendency to be fast pattern completers. Science involves slow, and precise, pattern completion. The rules of scientific models are in many ways rules designed to slow people down and make sure the patterns they complete really do fit together. *(139)*
8. False, while it would be nice if that were the case, the data speak very softly and what one hears depends upon one's frame. Thus, in economics the data seldom provide definitive answers, and economists must rely on their theoretical models to guide them. *(142)*
9. No, in a path-dependent model the path to equilibrium affects the equilibrium. The supply/demand model assumes that is not the case. *(143)*
10. No, one derives theorems (logical implications) from models; policy is based on precepts. Thus, the fact that most economists oppose price controls is based on both a model and judgments about the appropriateness of that model. (148)

PART II

Microeconomics

> In my vacations, I visited the poorest quarters of several cities and walked through one street after another, looking at the faces of the poorest people. Next I resolved to make as thorough a study as I could of Political Economy.

You may remember having already seen this quotation from Alfred Marshall. It began the first chapter. I chose this beginning for two reasons. First, it gives what I believe to be the best reason to study economics. Second, the quotation is from a hero of mine, one of the economic giants of all times. His *Principles of Economics* was the economists' bible in the late 1800s and early 1900s. How important was Marshall? It was Marshall who first used the supply and demand curves as an engine of analysis.

I repeat this quotation here because, for Marshall, economics was microeconomics, and it is his vision of economics that underlies this book's approach to microeconomics. For Marshall, economics was an art that was meant to be applied—used to explain why things were the way they were, and what we could do about them. He had little use for esoteric theory that didn't lead to a direct application to a real-world problem. Reflecting on the state of economics in 1906, Marshall wrote to a friend:

> I had a growing feeling in the later years of my work at the subject that a good mathematical theorem dealing with economic hypotheses was very unlikely to be good economics: and I went more and more on the rules—(1) Use mathematics as a shorthand language, rather than as an engine of inquiry. (2) Keep to them until you have done. (3) Translate into English. (4) Then illustrate by examples that are important in real life. (5) Burn the mathematics. (6) If you can't succeed in (4), burn (3). This last I did often. (From a letter from Marshall to A. L. Bowley, reprinted in A. C. Pigou, *Memorials of Alfred Marshall*, p. 427.)

Marshall didn't feel this way about mathematical economics because he couldn't do mathematics. He was trained as a formal mathematician, and he was a good one. But, for him, mathematics wasn't economics, and the real world was too messy to have applied to it much of the fancy mathematical economic work that some of his fellow economists were doing. Marshall recognized the influence of market, political, and social forces and believed that all three had to be taken into account in applying economic reasoning to reality.

You won't see much highfalutin mathematical economics in these microeconomic chapters. The chapters follow the Marshallian methodology and present the minimum of formal theory necessary to apply the concepts of economics to the real world, and then they do just that: start talking about real-world issues.

Section I, The Power of Traditional Economic Models (Chapters 7, 8, and 9), develops the traditional economic model and shows you how it can be used to analyze policy issues. Section II, Choice and Decision Making (Chapters 10 and 11), presents both the traditional and modern theories of choice, including the game theoretic foundations of modern economic thinking and new developments in behavioral economics. Section III, Production and Cost Analysis (Chapters 12 and 13) shows the foundation of cost analysis and how it relates to firms.

Section IV, Market Structure (Chapters 14–16), introduces you to various market structures. Section V, Real-World Competition (Chapters 17 and 18), introduces you to real-world competition and antitrust policy.

Section VI, Factor Markets (Chapters 19–20), looks at a particular set of markets—factor markets. These markets play a central role in determining the distribution of income. These chapters won't tell you how to get rich (you'll have to wait for the sequel for that), but they will give you new insights into how labor markets work.

Section VII, Applying Economic Reasoning to Policy (Chapters 21–23), provides an overview of the implications of microeconomics for policy. It includes both general overviews and analyses of specific issues.

CHAPTER 7

Describing Supply and Demand: Elasticities

The master economist must understand symbols and speak in words. He must contemplate the particular in terms of the general, and touch abstract and concrete in the same flight of thought.

—**J. M. *Keynes***

AFTER READING THIS CHAPTER, YOU SHOULD BE ABLE TO:

1. Use the terms *price elasticity of supply* and *price elasticity of demand* to describe the responsiveness of quantities to changes in price.
2. Calculate elasticity graphically and numerically.
3. Distinguish five elasticity terms that are used to differentiate varying degrees of responsiveness.
4. Explain the importance of substitution in determining elasticity of supply and demand.
5. Relate price elasticity of demand to total revenue.
6. State how other elasticity concepts are useful in describing the effect of shift factors on demand.
7. Explain how the concept of *elasticity* makes supply and demand analysis more useful.

When JetBlue entered the airline industry, it decided to set its fares about 50 percent lower than what other airlines were charging. That decision was based on the prediction that lowering price would entice a large number of travelers to switch carriers and book travel with JetBlue. That is, JetBlue was hoping that the quantity demanded was very responsive to a change in price, or, in economic terminology, that the demand for air travel was price elastic.

Information about elasticity is extremely important to firms in making their pricing decisions, and to economists in their study of the economy. That's one reason why grocery stores like shoppers to use their preferred customer cards. These cards provide them with data about shopper behavior such as how sensitive shoppers are to price changes. Whenever a firm is thinking of changing its prices, it has a strong interest in elasticity.

Price Elasticity

The most commonly used elasticity concept is price elasticity of demand and supply. **Price elasticity of demand** is *the percentage change in quantity demanded divided by the percentage change in price:*

$$E_D = \frac{\text{Percentage change in quantity demanded}}{\text{Percentage change in price}}$$

Price elasticity of supply is *the percentage change in quantity supplied divided by the percentage change in price:*

$$E_S = \frac{\text{Percentage change in quantity supplied}}{\text{Percentage change in price}}$$

Let's consider some numerical examples. Say the price of a good rises by 10 percent and, in response, quantity demanded falls by 20 percent. The price elasticity of demand is 2 (−20 percent/10 percent). Notice that I said 2, not −2. Because quantity demanded is inversely related to price, the calculation for the price elasticity of demand comes out negative. Despite this fact, economists talk about price elasticity of demand as a positive number. (Those of you who remember some math can think of elasticity as an *absolute value* of a number, rather than a simple number.) Using this convention makes it easier to remember that a *larger* number for price elasticity of demand means quantity demanded is *more responsive* to price.

Price elasticity is the percentage change in quantity divided by the percentage change in price.

Q-1 If when price rises by 4 percent, quantity supplied rises by 8 percent, what is the price elasticity of supply?

To make sure you have the idea down, let's consider two more examples. Say that when price falls by 5 percent, quantity supplied falls by 2 percent. In this case, the price elasticity of supply is 0.4 (2 percent/5 percent). And, finally, say the price goes up by 10 percent and in response the quantity demanded falls by 15 percent. Price elasticity of demand is 1.5 (15 percent/10 percent).

Price Elasticity

What Information Price Elasticity Provides

Price elasticity of demand and supply tells us exactly how quantity responds to a change in price. A price elasticity of demand of 0.3 tells us that a 10 percent rise in price will lead to a 3 percent decline in quantity demanded. If the elasticity of demand were a larger number, say 5, the same 10 percent rise in price will lead to a 50 percent decline in quantity demanded. As elasticity increases, quantity responds more to price changes.

Classifying Demand and Supply as Elastic or Inelastic

It is helpful to classify elasticities by relative responsiveness. Economists usually describe supply and demand by the terms *elastic* and *inelastic*. Formally, demand or supply is **elastic** if *the percentage change in quantity is greater than the percentage change in price* ($E > 1$). Conversely, demand or supply is **inelastic** if *the percentage change in quantity is less than the percentage change in price* ($E < 1$). In the last two examples, an elasticity of demand of 0.3 means demand is inelastic ($E_D < 1$), and an elasticity of demand of 5 means demand is elastic ($E_D > 1$).

Elastic: $E > 1$
Inelastic: $E < 1$

The commonsense interpretation of these terms is the following: An *inelastic* supply means that the quantity supplied doesn't change much with a change in price. For example, say the price of land rises. The amount of land supplied won't change much, so the supply of land is inelastic. An *elastic* supply means that quantity supplied changes by a larger percentage than the percentage change in price. For example, say the price of pencils doubles. What do you think will happen to the quantity of pencils supplied? I suspect it will more than double, which means that the supply of pencils is elastic.

Elasticity Classifications

The same terminology holds with demand. Consider a good such as a Parker ballpoint pen that has a close substitute, a PaperMate ballpoint pen. If Parker's price rises, the quantity demanded will fall a lot as people shift to the substitute (a PaperMate ballpoint pen). So the demand for Parker ballpoint pens would be highly elastic. Alternatively, consider table salt, which has no close substitute at current prices. Demand for table salt is highly inelastic. That is, a rise in the price of table salt does not result in a large decline in quantity demanded.

Q-2 If price elasticity of demand is greater than 1, what would we call demand: elastic or inelastic?

Elasticity Is Independent of Units

Before continuing, notice that elasticity measures the percentage, not the unit, change in variables. Using percentages allows us to measure responsiveness independent of units, making comparisons among different goods easier. Say a $1 increase in the price

Percentages allow us to have a measure of responsiveness that is independent of units, making comparisons of responsiveness among different goods easier.

of a $1,000 computer decreases the quantity demanded by 1, from 10 to 9. Say also that a $1 increase in the price of a pen, from $1 to $2, decreases quantity demanded by 1—from 10,000 to 9,999. Using unit changes, the $1 price increase reduced the quantities demanded for both pens and computers by 1. But such a comparison of unit changes is not very helpful. To see that, ask yourself if you were planning on raising your price, which good you'd rather be selling.

The computer price increased by 1/1,000 of its original price, a relatively small percentage increase, and quantity demanded declined by 1/10 of original sales, a large percentage decline. The percentage decline in quantity demanded exceeded the percentage rise in price, so your total revenue (Price × Quantity) would decrease. The percentage increase in price of pens was relatively large—100 percent—and the percentage decline in quantity demanded was relatively small—1/100 of 1 percent. So if you raise the price of pens, total revenue increases. Clearly, if you're raising your price in these examples, you'd rather be selling pens than computers.

By using percentages, this is made clear: With computers, a 0.1 percent increase in price decreases quantity demanded by 10 percent, so the elasticity is 100. With pens, a 100 percent increase in price decreases quantity demanded by 0.01 percent—an elasticity of 0.0001.

Calculating Elasticities

To see that you've got the analysis down, calculate price elasticity of demand or supply in the following three real-world examples:

> *Case 1:* In 2005 the City of London raised the daily toll motorists pay to drive in central London by 46 percent. The increase reduced the number of motorists driving in central London by 3 percent.
>
> *Case 2:* In the 1980s, when gasoline prices rose by 9 percent in Washington, D.C., the quantity of gasoline demanded there fell by 40 percent.
>
> *Case 3:* When the minimum wage in Vermont rose by 10 percent, the quantity of labor supplied for relevant jobs increased by about 1.8 percent.

In the first case, price elasticity of demand is 0.07. The quantity of motorists in London did not change much when the toll was increased. Elasticity was less than 1, so demand was inelastic. In the second case, price elasticity of demand is 4.4. The quantity of gas demanded in Washington, D.C., responded by a lot to a relatively small change in gas prices. Elasticity was greater than 1, so demand was elastic. The price elasticity of supply in the third case is 0.18. The quantity of labor supplied did not respond much to the change in wage. Elasticity was less than 1, so supply was inelastic.

Let's now calculate some elasticities graphically. Let's begin by determining the price elasticity of demand between points *A* and *B* in Figure 7-1(a).

The demand curve in the figure is a hypothetical demand for WolfPack Simulation Software. You can see that as the price of the software rises from $20 to $26, the quantity demanded falls from 14,000 to 10,000 units a year. To determine the price elasticity of demand, we need to determine the percentage change in quantity and the percentage change in price. In doing so, there is a small problem that is sometimes called the *endpoint problem:* The percentage change differs depending on whether you view the change as a rise or a decline. For example, say you calculate the rise in price from $20 to $26, starting from $20. That gives you a percentage increase in price of [(20 − 26)/20] × 100 = 30 percent. If, however, you calculate that same change in price, $6, as a fall in price from $26 to $20, the percentage decrease in price is [(26 − 20)/26] × 100 = 23 percent. The easiest way to solve this problem is to use the average of the two end values to calculate percentage change. In our example, instead

Economists use the average of the two end values to get around the endpoint problem.

FIGURE 7-1 (A, B, AND C) Graphs of Elasticities

In (**a**) we are calculating the elasticity of the demand curve between A and B. We essentially calculate the midpoint and use that midpoint to calculate percentage changes. This gives us a percentage change in price of 26 percent and a percentage change in quantity of 33 percent, for an elasticity of 1.27. In (**b**) the percentage change in price is 10.53 percent and the percentage change in quantity is 1.87 percent, giving an elasticity of 0.18. In (**c**), the calculations are left for you to do.

Answers to (c): $a = 4$; $b = 0.54$; $c = 0.67$

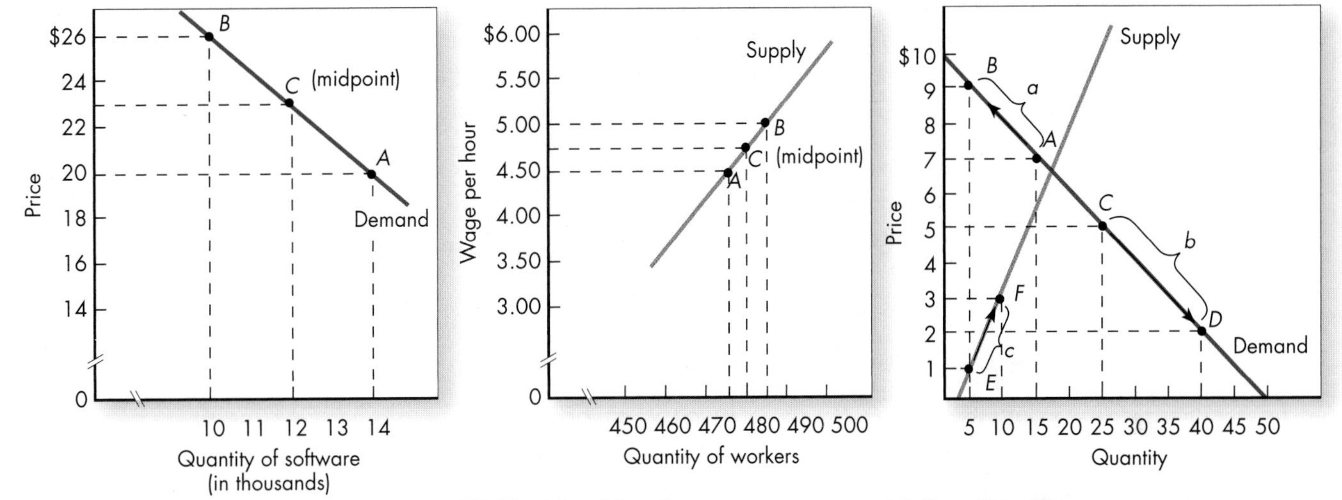

(a) Elasticity of Demand **(b) Elasticity of Supply** **(c) Some Examples**

of using 20 or 26 as a starting point, you use (20 + 26)/2, or 23. So the percentage change in price is

$$\frac{P_2 - P_1}{\frac{1}{2}(P_1 + P_2)} = \frac{(26 - 20)}{23} \times 100 = 26 \text{ percent}$$

Similarly, the percentage change in quantity is

$$\frac{Q_2 - Q_1}{\frac{1}{2}(Q_1 + Q_2)} = \frac{(10 - 14)}{12} \times 100 = -33 \text{ percent}$$

Having done this, we can calculate elasticity as usual by dividing the percentage change in quantity by the percentage change in price:

$$\text{Elasticity} = \frac{\text{Percentage change in quantity}}{\text{Percentage change in price}} = \frac{-33}{26} = 1.27^{1}$$

The elasticity of demand between points A and B is approximately 1.3. This means that a 10 percent increase in price will cause a 13 percent fall in quantity demanded. Thus, demand between A and B is elastic.

Other Examples

In Figure 7-1(b) I go through another example, this time using the supply elasticity from case 3 on p. 156. Initially, the Vermont minimum wage was $4.50 an hour; it

[1] I dropped the negative sign because, as discussed earlier, economists talk about price elasticity of demand as a positive number.

Q-3 What is the approximate elasticity between points *A* and *B* on the graph below?

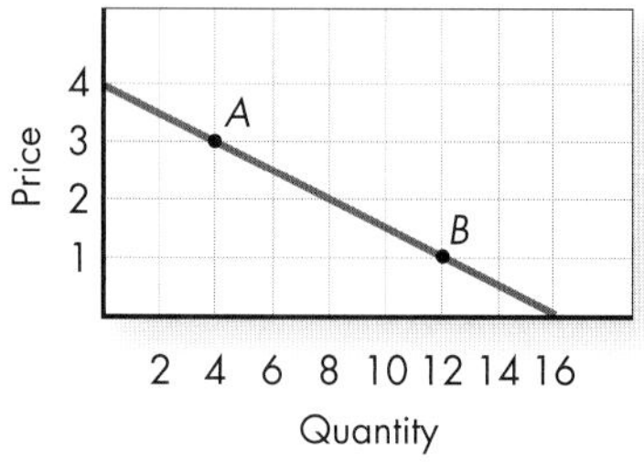

was then raised to \$5 an hour. The average of the two end points is \$4.75 and so the percentage change in price is $(0.50/4.75) \times 100 = 10.53$ percent. The initial quantity of labor supplied I estimated for my area in Vermont was 476; the rise in the minimum wage increased that number to 485, which gives us a percentage change in quantity of $(9/480.5) \times 100 = 1.87$ percent. To calculate the elasticity of supply, divide the percentage change in quantity by the percentage change in price to get $1.87/10.53 = 0.18$. A 10 percent rise in the minimum wage will bring about a 1.8 percent increase in quantity of labor supplied. The labor supply at the minimum wage in Vermont is inelastic.

Learning the mechanics of calculating elasticities takes some practice, so in Figure 7-1(c) I give you three additional examples, leaving the calculations for you.

a. Move from *A* to *B* on the demand curve.
b. Move from C to *D* on the demand curve.
c. Move from *E* to *F* on the supply curve.

Now that you've calculated them (you have, haven't you?), I'll let you know that the answers can be found upside down at the bottom of the caption for Figure 7-1.

Thinking Like a Modern Economist

Why Do So Many Prices End in 99 Cents?

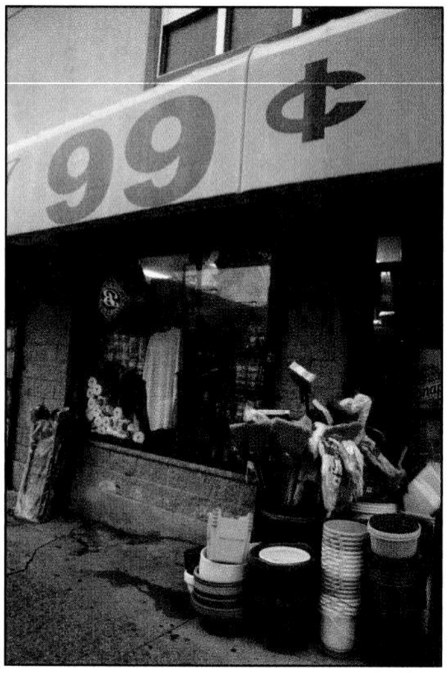

The traditional economic assumption is that a 1 percent change in price, say from \$1.01 to \$1.00, is the close equivalent to a 1 percent change in price, say from \$1.00 to 99 cents. Both should have almost identical effects. Behavioral economists have found that that is not the case; people react more to a fall in price from \$1.00 to 99 cents than they do to a fall in price from \$1.01 to \$1.00. That's why we see so many prices that end in 99 cents. People perceive a \$4.00 price as much higher than a \$3.99 price, and they buy much more at \$3.99. So the elasticity is much greater for price declines from \$1.00 to \$0.99 than from \$1.01 to \$1.00. This is a predictably irrational behavior.

Another predictably irrational behavior involves a zero price—when goods are free. People seem to react quite differently to a zero price than to other prices. In an experiment, MIT behavioral economists Kristina Shampanies, Nina Mozas, and Dan Ariely offered to sell people one of two chocolates—a ritzy Lindt Chocolate truffle for 15 cents or a Hershey kiss for 1 cent. Seventy-three percent chose the truffle and 27 percent chose the Kiss. Then they reduced the price of both chocolates by a penny—the Lindt chocolate to 14 cents and the Kiss to FREE. The effect on demand was enormous. Now only 31 percent chose the Lindt and 69 percent chose the Hershey Kiss. A zero price seems to have a big effect on the quantity demanded.

Firms know that people react to zero prices in this manner, and they try to take advantage of it all the time. For example, they offer "free" goods that aren't really free; *buy one, and get one free* sells a lot more goods than cutting price by 50 percent.

Elasticity and Supply and Demand Curves

There are two important points to remember about elasticity and supply and demand curves. The first is that elasticity is related to (but is not the same as) slope, and the second is that elasticity changes along straight-line demand and supply curves.

Elasticity Is Not the Same as Slope

Let's begin with the first point. The relationship between elasticity and slope is the following: The steeper the curve becomes at a given point, the less elastic is supply or demand. The limiting examples of this are a vertical curve (most steep), shown in Figure 7-2(a), and a horizontal (least steep) curve, shown in Figure 7-2(b).

The vertical demand curve shown in Figure 7-2(a) demonstrates how a change in price leads to no change in quantity demanded. Economists describe this curve as **perfectly inelastic**—*quantity*

FIGURE 7-2 (A–D) Elasticities and Supply and Demand Curves

In (a) and (b), two special elasticity cases are shown. A perfectly inelastic curve is vertical; a perfectly elastic curve is horizontal. In (c) and (d), I show how elasticity generally varies along both supply and demand curves. Along demand curves, it always goes from infinity at the vertical axis intercept to zero at the horizontal axis intercept. How elasticity of supply varies depends on which axis the supply curve intersects. If it intersects the vertical axis, elasticity starts at infinity and declines, and eventually approaches 1. If it intersects the horizontal axis, it starts at zero and increases, and eventually approaches 1. The one exception is when the supply curve intersects the origin. A good exercise is to determine what happens to elasticity in that case. (Hint: See the Added Dimension box on page 160.)

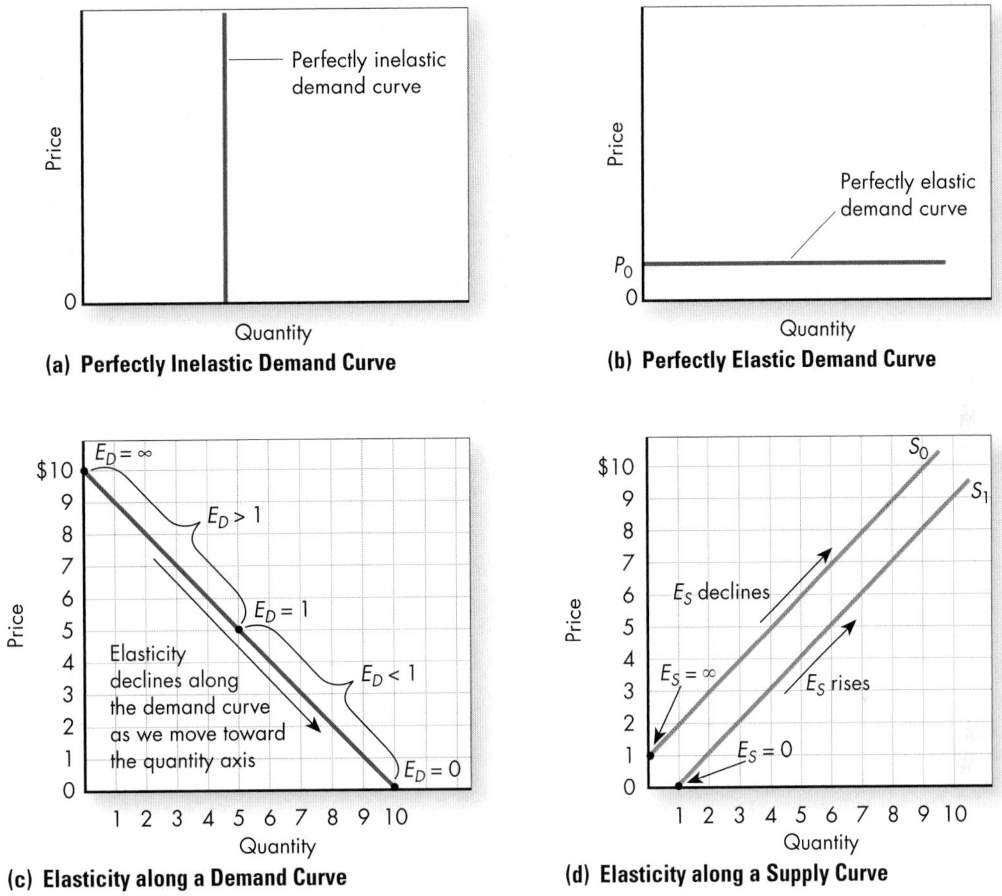

does not respond at all to changes in price ($E = 0$). Curves that are vertical are perfectly inelastic. The demand curve shown in Figure 7-2(b), in contrast, is horizontal. A change in price from above or below P_0 results in an infinitely large increase in quantity demanded. This curve is **perfectly elastic,** reflecting the fact that *quantity responds enormously to changes in price* ($E = \infty$). Horizontal curves are perfectly elastic. From these extreme cases, you can see that steeper (more vertical) curves at a given point are more *in*elastic and less steep (more horizontal) curves at a given point are more elastic. Elasticity, however, is not the same as slope. The second point illustrates this well.

Elasticity Is Not the Same as Slope

Elasticity Changes along Straight-Line Curves

On straight-line supply and demand curves, slope does not change, but elasticity does. Figure 7-2(c and d) shows how elasticity changes along demand and supply curves. At the price intercept of the demand curve in Figure 7-2(c), demand is perfectly elastic ($E_D = \infty$); elasticity becomes smaller as price declines until it becomes perfectly inelastic

Q-4 Your study partner, Nicole, has just stated that a straight-line demand curve is inelastic. How do you respond?

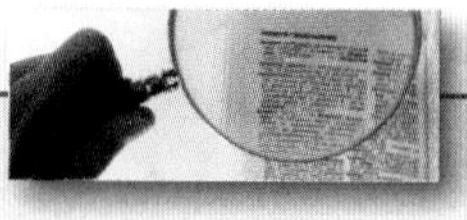

ADDED DIMENSION

Calculating Elasticity at a Point

The text explained how to calculate elasticity of a range along a demand and supply curve. But what if you're asked to calculate elasticity at a specific point and you don't know the percentage change in price and quantity? In that case, you can use the following procedure.

Say you want to determine the elasticity at point *A* in Figure (a). First create a line segment, with the point as the segment's midpoint. The segment can be of any length. In Figure (a) I have selected a segment that begins 4 units on the quantity axis before the quantity at *A* and extends 4 units beyond the quantity at *A*. Thus, the quantity extends from 20 to 28. Next, determine the price relevant for the quantities chosen. In the example, the price corresponding to the quantity 28 is $3, and the price corresponding to the quantity 20 is $5.

I've now got my line segment, so I am ready to calculate the relevant percent changes. Percentage change in quantity = $[(28 - 20)/24] \times 100 = 33$ percent. Percentage change in price = $[(5 - 3)/4] \times 100 = 50$ percent. Elasticity at point *A* is $33/50 = 0.66$.

To see that you've got the calculation down, in Figure (b) I present four points—two on a demand curve and two on a supply curve. Your assignment is to determine the elasticity of the four points on your own.

Now that you've done the calculations—you have, right?—you can look at the bottom of Figure (b), where I give you the correct answers. If you got all four right, you're in good shape. If not, it's time for a review. (And if you're taking the easy road and not calculating them on your own, it's time to get yourself in gear and start studying—remember, this stuff doesn't get into your head through osmosis.)

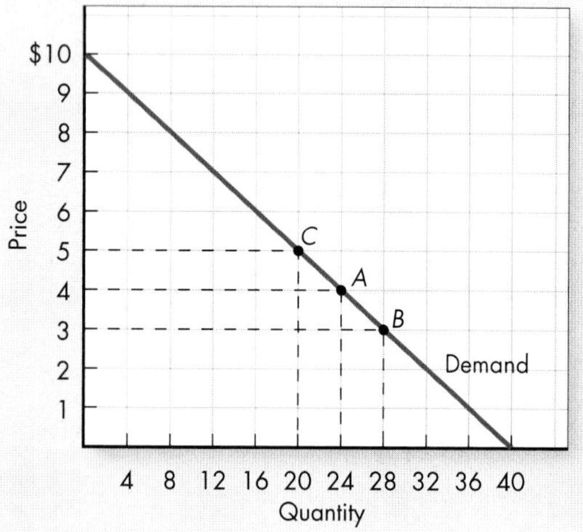

(a) Elasticity of Demand

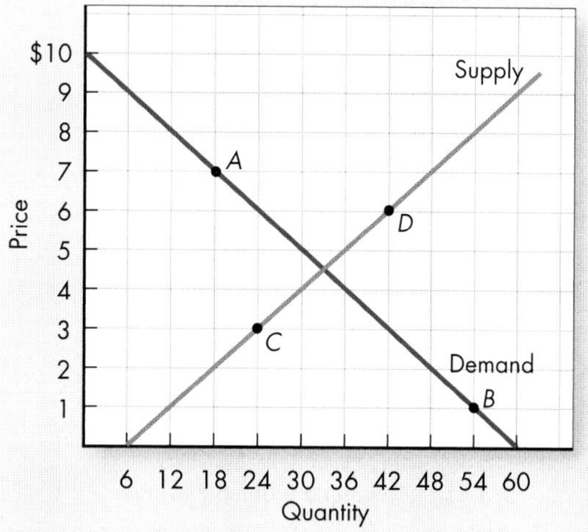

(b) Some Examples

Answers to (b): A = 2.33; B = 0.11; C = 0.75; D = 0.86.

($E_D = 0$) at the quantity intercept. At one point along the demand curve, between an elasticity of infinity and zero, demand is **unit elastic**—*the percentage change in quantity equals the percentage change in price* ($E = 1$). In Figure 7-2(c) demand is unit elastic at a price of $5. To confirm this, calculate elasticity of demand between $4 and $6. The percentage change in price is $(2/5) \times 100 = 40$ percent, and the percentage change in quantity is $(2/5) \times 100 = 40$ percent. The point at which demand is unit elastic divides the demand curve into two sections—an elastic portion ($E_D > 1$) above the point at which demand is unit elastic and an inelastic portion ($E_D < 1$) below the point at which demand is unit elastic.

ADDED DIMENSION

Geometric Tricks for Estimating Price Elasticity

There are a couple of useful tricks to determine whether a point on a straight-line supply or demand curve is elastic or inelastic. The trick with demand is the following: (1) Determine where the demand curve intersects the price and quantity axes. (2) At a point midway between the origin and the quantity line intersection, draw a vertical line back up to the demand curve. The point where it intersects the demand curve will have an elasticity of 1; it will be unit elastic; all points to the left of that line will be elastic, and all points to the right of that will be inelastic.

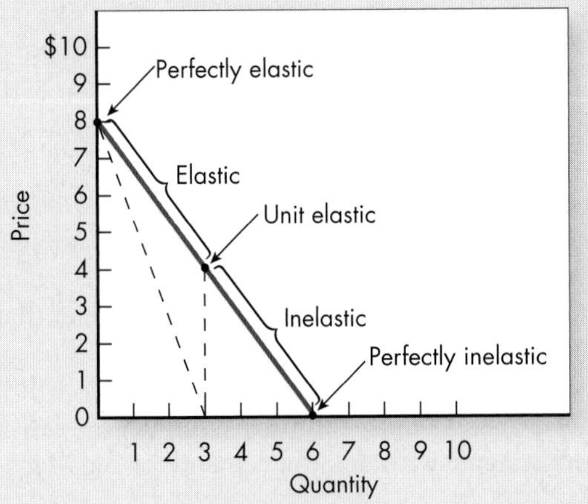

To determine whether a straight-line supply curve is elastic or inelastic you simply extend it to one of the axes, as in the following graph. The point at which this extension intersects the axes indicates the elasticity of the supply curve:

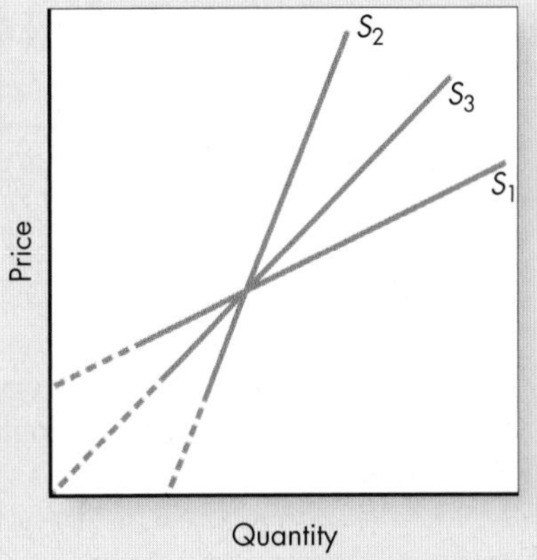

- If the extension intersects the vertical (price) axis, as does S_1, all points on the supply curve have an elasticity greater than 1; the supply curve is elastic.
- If the extension intersects the horizontal (quantity) axis, as does S_2, all points on the supply curve have an elasticity less than 1; the supply curve is inelastic.
- If the extension intersects the two axes at the origin, the supply curve has an elasticity of 1; the supply curve has unit elasticity.

If you combine these tricks with a knowledge that a perfectly elastic supply or demand curve is horizontal and crosses the price axis, and a perfectly inelastic supply or demand curve is vertical and crosses the quantity axis, you can even remember which is which. If a straight-line supply curve crosses the quantity axis, all points on it are inelastic; if it crosses the price axis, all points on it are elastic. Similarly, the top half of the demand curve (the part that crosses the price axis) is elastic; the bottom half (the part that crosses the quantity axis) is inelastic.

The change in elasticity along a supply curve is less dramatic. At the point on a straight-line supply curve that intercepts the price axis, supply is perfectly elastic ($E_S = \infty$). Points become less elastic as you move out along the supply curve. At the point on a straight-line supply curve that intercepts the quantity axis, supply is perfectly inelastic ($E_S = 0$); it becomes more elastic as you move out along the supply curve. These changes are labeled in Figure 7-2(d). I leave it to you to determine what happens to the elasticity of the supply curve if the supply curve intercepts the origin. (Hint: See the Added Dimension box "Geometric Tricks for Estimating Price Elasticity.")

Five elasticity terms are:
1. perfectly elastic ($E = \infty$);
2. elastic ($E > 1$);
3. unit elastic ($E = 1$);
4. inelastic ($E < 1$); and
5. perfectly inelastic ($E = 0$).

As a review, the five terms to describe elasticity along a curve are listed here from most to least elastic:

1. *Perfectly elastic:* Quantity responds enormously to changes in price ($E = \infty$).
2. *Elastic:* The percentage change in quantity exceeds the percentage change in price ($E > 1$).
3. *Unit elastic:* The percentage change in quantity is the same as the percentage change in price ($E = 1$).
4. *Inelastic:* The percentage change in quantity is less than the percentage change in price ($E < 1$).
5. *Perfectly inelastic:* Quantity does not respond at all to changes in price ($E = 0$).

Now that you have seen that elasticity changes along straight-line supply and demand curves, the first point—that elasticity is related to but not the same as slope—should be clear. Whereas elasticity changes along a straight-line curve, slope does not.

Substitution and Elasticity

Now that you know how to measure elasticity, let's consider some of the factors that are likely to make supply and demand more or less elastic, that is, more or less responsive to price.

The most important determinant of price elasticity of demand is the number of substitutes for the good.

How responsive quantity demanded and quantity supplied will be to changes in price can be summed up in one word: substitution. As a general rule, the more substitutes a good has, the more elastic is its supply or demand.

The reasoning is as follows: If a good has substitutes, a rise in the price of that good will cause the consumer to shift consumption to those substitute goods. Put another way, when a satisfactory substitute is available, a rise in that good's price will have a large effect on the quantity demanded. For example, I think a Whopper is a satisfactory substitute for a Big Mac. If most people agree with me, the demand for Big Macs would be very elastic.

Factors that affect a good's substitutability of demand differ from factors that affect a good's substitutability of supply. So I will consider each separately. I begin with demand.

Substitution and Demand

The number of substitutes a good has is affected by several factors. Four of the most important are

1. The time period being considered.
2. The degree to which a good is a luxury.
3. The market definition.
4. The importance of the good in one's budget.

These four reasons are derivatives of the substitution factor. Let's consider each to see why.

The more substitutes, the more elastic the demand and the more elastic the supply.

1. *The time period being considered.* The larger the time interval considered, or the longer the run, the more elastic is the good's demand. There are more substitutes in the long run than in the short run. That's because the long run provides more alternatives. Consider when the price of rubber went up considerably during World War II. In the short run, rubber had few substitutes; the demand for rubber was inelastic. In the long run, however, the rise in the price of rubber stimulated research for alternatives.

Today automobile tires, which were made of all rubber when World War II broke out, are made from almost entirely synthetic materials. In the long run, demand was very elastic.

2. *The degree to which a good is a luxury.* The less a good is a necessity, the more elastic is its demand. Because by definition one cannot do without necessities, they tend to have fewer substitutes than do luxuries. Insulin for a diabetic is a necessity; the demand is highly inelastic. Chocolate Ecstasy cake, however, is a luxury. A variety of other luxuries can be substituted for it (for example, cheesecake or a ball game).

3. *The market definition.* As the definition of a good becomes more specific, demand becomes more elastic. If the good we're talking about is broadly defined (say, transportation), there aren't many substitutes and demand will be inelastic. If you want to get from A to B, you need transportation. If the definition of the good is narrowed—say, to "transportation by bus"—there are more substitutes. Instead of taking a bus, you can walk, ride your bicycle, or drive your car. In that case, demand is more elastic.

Q-5 What are four important factors affecting the number of substitutes a good has?

4. *The importance of the good in one's budget.* Demand for goods that represent a large proportion of one's budget is more elastic than demand for goods that represent a small proportion of one's budget. Goods that cost very little relative to your total expenditures aren't worth spending a lot of time figuring out whether there's a good substitute. An example is pencils. Their low price means most people would buy just as many even if their price doubled. Their demand is inelastic. It is, however, worth spending lots of time looking for substitutes for goods that take a large portion of one's income. The demand for such goods tends to be more elastic. Many colleges have discovered this as they tried to raise tuition when other colleges did not. The demand curve they faced was elastic.

Substitution and Supply

The same general issues involving substitution are relevant when considering determinants of the elasticity of supply. But when it comes to supply, economists focus on time rather than on other factors because time plays such a central role in determining supply elasticity. The general rule is: The longer the time period considered, the more elastic is supply. The reasoning is the same as with demand; in the long run, there are more alternatives, so it is easier (less costly) for suppliers to change and produce other goods.

The longer the time period considered, the more elastic the supply.

To emphasize the importance of time, economists distinguish three time periods relevant to supply:

1. In the instantaneous period, quantity supplied is fixed, so supply is perfectly inelastic. This supply is sometimes called the momentary supply.
2. In the short run, some substitution is possible, so short-run supply is somewhat elastic.
3. In the long run, significant substitution is possible; supply becomes very elastic.

Q-6 Is supply generally more elastic in the short run or in the long run?

In determining the elasticity of supply, one must, however, remember an additional factor: Many supplied goods are produced, so we must take into account how easy it is to increase production of those same goods. For example, if the cost per unit of producing a good is constant, its supply is likely highly elastic.

How Substitution Factors Affect Specific Decisions

Let's consider how some of the substitution factors affect a specific decision. Let's say you've been hired by two governments (the city of Washington, D.C., and the

U.S. government) to advise them about the effect that raising the gas tax by 10 percent will have on tax revenues. You look at the three factors that affect elasticity of demand.

In your report to the two governments, you would point out that in the short run demand is less elastic than in the long run, since people aren't going to trade in their gas-guzzling cars for fuel-efficient cars immediately in response to a 10 percent rise in gas taxes—partly because they can't afford to, partly because they don't want to, and partly because not that many fuel-efficient cars are available to buy at the moment. When the time comes, however, that they would ordinarily purchase a new car, they're likely to switch to cars that are more fuel-efficient than their old cars, and to switch as much as they can to forms of transportation that are more fuel-efficient than cars. In the long run the demand will be far more elastic.

In the long run, demand generally becomes more elastic.

The second point you'd note is that gasoline is generally considered a necessity, although not all driving is necessary. However, since gasoline is only a small part of what it costs to drive a car, demand will probably tend to be inelastic.

As for the third factor (how specifically the good is defined), you have to be careful. It makes your recommendations for the government of the city of Washington, D.C., and the U.S. government quite different from each other. For the U.S. government, which is interested in the demand for gasoline in the entire United States, gasoline has a relatively inelastic demand. The general rule of thumb is that a 1-cent rise in tax will raise tax revenues by $1 billion. That inelasticity can't be carried over to the demand for gasoline in a city such as Washington, D.C. Because of the city's size and location, people in Washington have a choice. A large proportion of the people who buy gas in Washington could as easily buy gas in the adjacent states of Maryland or Virginia. Gasoline in Washington is a narrowly defined good and therefore has a quite elastic demand. A rise in price will mean a large fall in the quantity of gas demanded.

I mention this point because someone forgot about it when the city of Washington, D.C., raised the tax on a gallon of gasoline by 8 cents, a rise at that time of about 9 percent (this was case 2 in our discussion of calculating elasticities on p. 156). In response, monthly gasoline sales in Washington fell from 16 million gallons to less than 11 million gallons, a 40 percent decrease! The demand for gas in Washington was not inelastic, as it was for the United States as a whole; it was very elastic ($E_D = 4.4$). Washingtonians went elsewhere to buy gas.

The fact that smaller geographic areas have more elastic demands limits how highly state and local governments can tax goods relative to their neighboring localities or states. Where there are tax differences, new stores open all along the border and existing stores expand to entice people to come over that border and save on taxes. For example, the liquor tax is higher in Vermont than in New Hampshire, so it isn't surprising that right across the border from Vermont, New Hampshire has a large number of liquor stores. Here's one final example: If you look at license plates in Janzen Beach, Oregon (right across the Washington state border), you'll see a whole lot of Washington license plates. Why? If you answered that it likely has something to do with differential sales taxes in Washington and Oregon, you've got the idea.

Empirical Estimates of Elasticities of Demand and Supply

Web Note 7.1
Price Elasticity of Gas Demand

The table below presents empirical estimates of elasticity of demand. Notice that, as expected, long-run elasticities are greater than short-run elasticities for each good. Also notice that the estimates are for the entire United States; estimates for a specific region in the United States could be expected to show more elasticity.

Product	Price Elasticity Short-Run	Long-Run
Movies/motion pictures	0.87	3.67
Tobacco products	0.46	1.89
Electricity (for household consumption)	0.13	1.89
Foreign travel by U.S. residents	0.14	1.77
Air travel	0.80	—
Rail transit	0.62	1.59
Beer	0.56	1.39
Toys (nondurable)	0.30	1.02
Health services	0.20	0.92
Wine	0.68	0.84
Gasoline	0.03	0.53
University tuition	0.52	—

Sources: Hendrik S. Houthakker and Lester D. Taylor, *Consumer Demand in the United States: Analyses and Projections*, 2nd ed. (Cambridge, MA: Harvard University Press, 1970); W. S. Comanor and T. A. Wilson, *Advertising and Market Power* (Cambridge, MA: Harvard University Press, 1974); Shermon Folland, Allen C. Goodman, and Miron Stano, *The Economics of Health Care* (New York: Macmillan, 1993); Yu Hsing and Hui S. Chang, "Testing Increasing Sensitivity of Enrollment at Private Institutions to Tuition and Other Costs," *The American Economist* 41, no. 1 (Spring 1996); Richard Voith, "The Long-Run Elasticity of Demand for Commuter Rail Transportation," *Journal of Urban Economics* 30 (1991); Jonathan E. Hughes, Christopher R. Knittel, and Daniel Sperling, "Evidence of a Shift in Short-Run Price Elasticity of Gasoline Demand," UC Davis Working Paper (2006); Department of Energy, Office of Policy and International Affairs, *Policies and Measures for Reducing Energy-Related Greenhouse Gas Emissions: Lessons from Recent Literature* (July 1996); Bureau of Transportation Statistics, 2003.

Taking an example from the table, notice that the long-run demand for movies is elastic. If movie theaters raise their prices, it's relatively easy for individuals simply to stay home and watch television. Movies have close substitutes, so we would expect the demand to be relatively elastic.

As a second example, in the short run, the demand for gasoline is highly inelastic. People do not change their driving behavior much in response to a change in gas prices. Thus, when the price of gasoline rose from $3.00 to more than $4.00 in mid 2008, initially the quantity demanded only decreased slightly. In the long run, however, it becomes less inelastic since people can shift to using other methods of transportation, and can buy more energy-efficient vehicles. That shift began in earnest in late 2008, even when the price of gasoline fell somewhat. Sales of gas-guzzling SUVs declined by more than 30 percent from the previous year, while sales of fuel-efficient hybrids rose over 20 percent and ridership on mass transit rose by double digits.

There are many fewer empirical measurements of supply than there are of demand. The reason concerns the structure of markets for produced goods, and the complicated nature of production. Most retail markets have seller-set or posted prices—you go to the store and pay the listed price of toothpaste. You can buy as much as you want at that price, so in a sense, the supply of toothpaste (and most retail goods) is perfectly elastic until the store runs out, whereupon the supply becomes perfectly inelastic. But, in another sense, there is no supply curve since the selling price is determined by the seller's pricing strategy, not by the market. I will hold off discussion of such issues until after we discuss costs, production, and various market structures.

We do find empirical measurements of supply in factor markets, such as the market for labor services. For example, economist David Blau has estimated that the supply of child care labor is elastic—it may be as high as 1.9—which means that a 10 percent rise in the wages paid to child care workers will lead to a 19 percent increase in the quantity of child care workers. More generally, economists have estimated that the labor supply elasticity of heads of households is about 0.1, and for secondary workers is about 1.1. A good test of whether you intuitively understand elasticities is whether you can explain why the latter is more elastic.

Other areas in which elasticities of supply are estimated are agricultural and raw materials markets. Estimating supply elasticities here is possible because these goods are often sold in auction markets where price is directly determined by supply and demand, rather than in posted-price markets such as toothpaste sold in grocery stores. In these markets, economists have generally found that short-run supplies are highly inelastic and long-run supplies are highly elastic.

Elasticity, Total Revenue, and Demand

Knowing elasticity of demand is useful to firms because from it they can tell whether the total revenue will go up or down when they raise or lower their prices. The total revenue a supplier receives is the price he or she charges times the quantity he or she sells. (Total revenue equals total quantity sold multiplied by the price of the good.) Elasticity tells sellers what will happen to total revenue if their price changes. Specifically:

- If demand is elastic ($E_D > 1$), a rise in price lowers total revenue. (Price and total revenue move in opposite directions.)
- If demand is unit elastic ($E_D = 1$), a rise in price leaves total revenue unchanged.
- If demand is inelastic ($E_D < 1$), a rise in price increases total revenue. (Price and total revenue move in the same direction.)

Q-7 If demand is inelastic and a firm raises price, what happens to total revenue?

The relationship between elasticity and total revenue is no mystery. There's a very logical reason why they are related, which can be seen most neatly by recognizing that total revenue ($P \times Q$) is represented by the area under the demand curve at that price and quantity. For example, at point *E* on the demand curve in Figure 7-3(a), the

FIGURE 7-3 (A, B, AND C) Elasticity and Total Revenue

Total revenue is measured by the rectangle produced by extending lines from the demand curve to the price and quantity axes. The change in total revenue resulting from a change in price can be estimated by comparing the sizes of the before and after rectangles. If price is being raised, total revenue increases by rectangle C and decreases by rectangle B. As you can see, the effect of a price rise on total revenue differs significantly at different points on a demand curve; (**a**) shows an almost unitary elastic range, (**b**) shows an inelastic range, and (**c**) shows an elastic range.

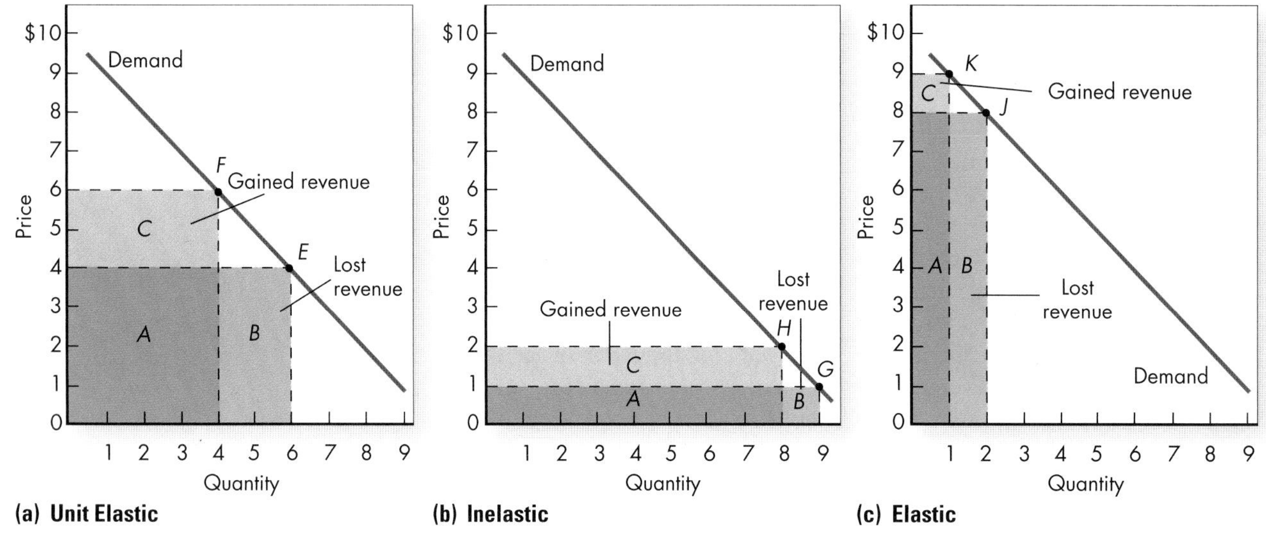

total revenue at price \$4 and quantity 6 is the area designated by the *A* and *B* rectangles, \$24.

If we increase price to \$6, quantity demanded decreases to 4, so total revenue is still \$24. Total revenue has remained constant, so the demand curve from point *E* to point *F* is unit elastic. The new total revenue is represented by the *A* and *C* rectangles. The difference between the old total revenue (*A* and *B*) and the new total revenue (*A* and C) is the difference between the rectangles *B* and C. Comparing these rectangles provides us with a visual method of estimating elasticities.

Elasticity and the Total Revenue Rule

Figure 7-3(b) shows an inelastic range; Figure 7-3(c) shows a highly elastic range. While in Figure 7-3(b) the slope of the demand curve is the same as in Figure 7-3(a), we begin at a different point on the demand curve (point G). If we raise our price from \$1 to \$2, quantity demanded falls from 9 to 8. The gained area (rectangle C) is much greater than the lost area (rectangle B). In other words, total revenue increases significantly, so the demand curve between points *H* and G is highly inelastic.

In Figure 7-3(c) the demand curve is again the same, but we begin at still another point, *J*. If we raise our price from \$8 to \$9, quantity demanded falls from 2 to 1. The gained area (rectangle C) is much smaller than the lost area (rectangle B). In other words, total revenue decreases significantly, so the demand curve from points *J* to *K* is highly elastic.

Total Revenue along a Demand Curve

The way in which elasticity changes along a demand curve and its relationship to total revenue can be seen in Figure 7-4. When output is zero, total revenue is zero; similarly, when price is zero, total revenue is zero. That accounts for the two endpoints of the total

With elastic demands, a rise in price decreases total revenue. With inelastic demands, a rise in price increases total revenue.

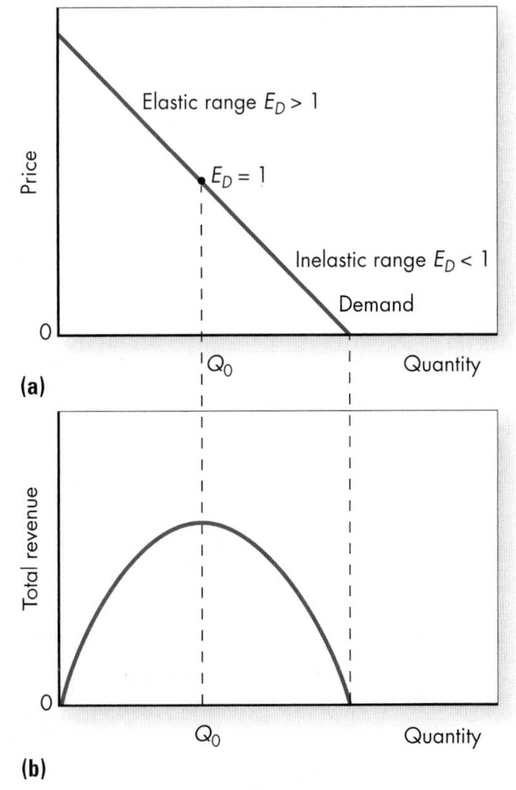

FIGURE 7-4 (A AND B) **How Total Revenue Changes**

Total revenue is at a maximum when elasticity equals 1, as you can see in (**a**) and (**b**). When demand is elastic, total revenue decreases with an increase in price. When demand is inelastic, total revenue increases with an increase in price.

Relationship between Elasticity (*E*) and Total Revenue (*TR*)

	Price Rise	Price Decline
Elastic ($E_D > 1$)	*TR* ↓	*TR* ↑
Unit Elastic ($E_D = 1$)	*TR* constant	*TR* constant
Inelastic ($E_D < 1$)	*TR* ↑	*TR* ↓

revenue curve in Figure 7-4(b). Let's say we start at a price of zero, where demand is perfectly inelastic. As we increase price (decrease quantity demanded), total revenue increases significantly. As we continue to do so, the increases in total revenue become smaller until finally, after output of Q_0, total revenue actually starts decreasing. It continues decreasing at a faster and faster rate until finally, at zero output, total revenue is zero.

Web Note 7.2
Elasticity and Cartels

As an example of where such calculations might come in handy, recall the vanity license plates that we used to illustrate the law of demand in Chapter 4. A rise in the price of vanity plates of about 29 percent, from \$30 to \$40, decreased the quantity demanded about 64 percent, from 60,334 to 31,122, so the price elasticity of demand was about 0.64/0.29 = 2.2. Since demand was elastic, total revenue fell. Specifically, total revenue fell from \$1,810,020 (\$30 × 60,334) to \$1,244,880 (\$40 × 31,122).

Elasticity of Individual and Market Demand

In thinking about elasticity of demand, keep in mind the point made in Chapter 4: The market demand curve is the horizontal summation of individual demand curves; some individuals have highly inelastic demands and others have highly elastic demands. A slight rise in the price of a good will cause some people to stop buying the good; the slight increase won't affect other people's quantity demanded for the good at all. Market demand elasticity is influenced both by how many people drop out totally and by how much an existing consumer marginally changes his or her quantity demanded.

Firms have a strong incentive to separate out people with less elastic demand and charge them a higher price.

If a firm can somehow separate the people with less elastic demand from those with more elastic demand, it can charge more to the individuals with inelastic demands and less to individuals with elastic demands. Economists call this *price discrimination*. We see firms throughout the economy trying to use price discrimination. Let's consider three examples:

1. Airlines' Saturday stay-over specials. If you stay over a Saturday night, usually you can get a much lower airline fare than if you don't. The reason is that businesspeople have inelastic demands and don't like to stay over Saturday nights, while pleasure travelers have more elastic demands. By requiring individuals to stay over Saturday night, airlines can separate out businesspeople and charge them more.
2. The phenomenon of selling new cars. Most new cars don't sell at the listed price. They sell at a discount. Salespeople are trained to separate out comparison shoppers (who have more elastic demands) from impulse buyers (who have inelastic demands). By not listing the selling price of cars so that the discount can be worked out in individual negotiations, salespeople can charge more to customers who have inelastic demands.
3. The almost-continual-sale phenomenon. Some items, such as washing machines, go on sale rather often. Why don't suppliers sell them at a low price all the time? Because some buyers whose washing machines break down have inelastic demands. They can't wait, so they'll pay the "unreduced" price. Others have elastic demands; they can wait for the sale. By running sales (even though they're frequent sales), sellers can separate consumers with inelastic demand curves from consumers with elastic demand curves.

Other Elasticity Concepts

Other Elasticities

There are many other elasticity concepts besides the price elasticity of demand and the price elasticity of supply. Since these other elasticities can be useful in specifying the effects of shift factors on the demand for a good, I will introduce you to two of them: income elasticity of demand and cross-price elasticity of demand.

REAL-WORLD APPLICATION

Empirically Measuring Elasticities

Where do firms get the information they need to calculate elasticities? Think of the grocery store where you can get a special buyer's card; the checkout clerk scans it and you get all the discounts. And the card is free! Those grocery stores are not just being nice. When the clerk scans your purchases, the store gets information that is forwarded to a central processing unit that can see how people react to different prices. This information allows firms to fine-tune their pricing—raising prices on goods for which the demand is inelastic and lowering prices on goods for which the demand is elastic.

Alternatively, think of the warranty cards that you send in when you buy a new computer or a new TV. The information goes into the firms' databases and is used by their economists in future price-setting decisions.

How do stores use this information? One way is that they develop user profiles, and run promotions on items such as laundry products, carbonated soft drinks, cereal, and several other items for which consumers are most responsive to price (i.e., the demand is elastic). This attracts shoppers to their store. Then, the stores place high-profit novelty items that consumers generally do not compare across stores, but for which demand is inelastic, in prominent in-store displays. It's not quite a bait-and-switch strategy, but it is a strategy to lure shoppers into a store for a "deal" but still end up selling higher-priced products than their competitors. Another way stores calculate the elasticity of demand for goods is to initially charge different prices in different stores, and then, once they have determined the elasticity, they choose a price that maximizes total profit.

The definition of these concepts is straightforward. **Income elasticity of demand** is defined as *the percentage change in demand divided by the percentage change in income*. Put another way,

$$\text{Income elasticity of demand} = \frac{\text{Percentage change in demand}}{\text{Percentage change in income}}$$

It tells us the responsiveness of demand to changes in income. (Notice I used *demand*, not *quantity demanded*, to emphasize that in response to a change in anything but the price of that good, the entire demand curve shifts; there's no movement along the demand curve.) **Cross-price elasticity of demand** is defined as *the percentage change in demand divided by the percentage change in the price of a related good*. Put another way,

Income elasticity of demand shows the responsiveness of demand to changes in income.

$$\text{Cross-price elasticity of demand} = \frac{\text{Percentage change in demand}}{\text{Percentage change in price of a related good}}$$

These other elasticity concepts tell you how much the demand curve will shift when there is a change in a shift factor. Let's consider each separately.

Cross-price elasticity of demand shows the responsiveness of demand to changes in prices of related goods.

Income Elasticity of Demand

The most commonly used of the elasticity terms introduced above is *income elasticity of demand*. Income elasticity of demand tells us how much demand will change with a change in income. An increase in income generally increases one's consumption of almost all goods, although the increase may be greater for some goods than for others. **Normal goods**—*goods whose consumption increases with an increase in income*—have income elasticities greater than zero.

Q-8 If a good's consumption increases with an increase in income, what type of good would you call it?

Normal goods are sometimes divided into luxuries and necessities. **Luxuries** are *goods that have an income elasticity greater than 1*—their percentage increase in demand is greater than the percentage increase in income. For example, say your income goes up 10 percent and you buy 20 percent more songs from iTunes. The income elasticity of iTunes music is 2; thus, iTunes music is a luxury good. Alternatively, say your income goes up by 100 percent and your demand for shoes goes up by 50 percent. Your income elasticity for shoes would be 0.5. Shoes are a **necessity**—*a good that has an income elasticity between 0 and 1*. The consumption of a necessity rises by a smaller proportion than the rise in income.

Web Note 7.3
Inferior Goods

It is even possible that an increase in income can cause a *decrease* in the consumption of a particular good. These goods have a negative income elasticity of demand. The term applied to such goods is **inferior goods**—*goods whose consumption decreases when income increases*. In some circumstances, potatoes could be an example of an inferior good. As income goes up, people might so significantly shift their consumption toward meat and away from potatoes that their total consumption of potatoes decreases. A recent study by a Stanford economist found tortillas to be an inferior good in Mexico.

The table below presents income elasticities measured for some groups of goods.

	Income Elasticity	
Commodity	**Short-Run**	**Long-Run**
Motion pictures	0.81	3.41
Foreign travel	0.24	3.09
Hard liquor	—	2.50
Jewelry and watches	1.00	1.64
Dental services	—	1.60
Private university tuition	—	1.10
Tobacco products	0.21	0.86
Beer	—	0.84
Health care	—	0.82
Furniture	2.60	0.53
Food produced and consumed on farms	−0.61	—

Sources: Hendrik S. Houthakker and Lester D. Taylor, *Consumer Demand in the United States: Analyses and Projections*, 2nd ed. (Cambridge, MA: Harvard University Press, 1970); E. A. Selvanthan, "Cross-Country Alcohol Consumption: An Application of the Rotterdam Demand System," *Applied Economics* 23 (1991); Shermon Folland, Allen C. Goodman, and Miron Stano, *The Economics of Health Care* (New York: Macmillan, 1993); Yu Hsing and Hui S. Chang, "Testing Increasing Sensitivity of Enrollment at Private Institutions to Tuition and Other Costs," *The American Economist* 41, no. 1 (Spring 1996); Donald E. Freeman, "Is Health Care a Necessity or a Luxury?" *Applied Economics* (March 2003).

Notice a few things about this table. In the short run, people often save high proportions of their increases in income, so most goods, other than impulse goods, such as furniture, have low short-run income elasticities. To avoid this problem, economists generally focus on long-run income elasticities. Notice which goods are necessities (the ones with long-run income elasticities less than 1). Notice also which goods are luxuries (the ones with elasticities greater than 1). Finally, notice the one good with a negative income elasticity—food produced and consumed on farms. As mentioned above, such goods are called inferior goods. As income rises, people buy proportionately less of such goods.

Cross-Price Elasticity of Demand

Cross-price elasticity of demand is another frequently used elasticity concept. Let's consider an example. Say the price of Apple iPhones rises. What is likely to happen to the demand for Sprint's Instinet? It is likely to rise, so the cross-price elasticity between the two is positive. Positive cross-price elasticities of demand mean the goods are

substitutes—*goods that can be used in place of one another*. When the price of a good goes up, the demand for the substitute goes up.

Most goods have substitutes, so most cross-price elasticities are positive. But not all. To see that, let's consider another example: Say the price of hot dogs rises; what is likely to happen to the demand for ketchup? If you're like me and use lots of ketchup on your hot dogs, as you cut your consumption of hot dogs, you will also cut your consumption of ketchup. Ketchup and hot dogs are not substitutes but rather complements. **Complements** are *goods that are used in conjunction with other goods*. A fall in the price of a good will increase the demand for its complement. The cross-price elasticity of complements is negative.

WWW Web Note 7.4

Substitutes have positive cross-price elasticities; complements have negative cross-price elasticities.

Some estimates of cross-price elasticities of demand are shown in the table below.

Commodities	Cross-Price Elasticity
Beef in response to price changes in pork	0.11
Beef in response to price changes in chicken	0.02
U.S. automobiles in response to price changes in European and Asian automobiles	0.28
European automobiles in response to price changes in U.S. and Asian automobiles	0.61
Beer in response to price changes in wine	0.23
Hard liquor in response to price changes in beer	−0.11

Sources: J. A. Johnson and E. H. Oksanen, "Socioeconomic Determinants of the Consumption of Alcoholic Beverages," *Applied Economics* (1974); Patrick S. McCarthy, "Market Price and Income Elasticities of New Vehicle Demand," *Review of Economics and Statistics* (August 1996); Kuo S. Huang, "Nutrient Elasticities in a Complete Food Demand System," *American Journal of Agricultural Economics* (February 1996).

You can see that the strongest substitutes are European autos for U.S. and Asian autos. A 10 percent fall in the price of U.S. and Asian autos leads to a 6 percent fall in the demand for European autos. Hard liquor and beer are complements. If the price of beer falls by 10 percent, the demand for hard liquor increases by 1.1 percent.

Some Examples

To make sure you've got these concepts down, see Figure 7-5, which demonstrates two examples. In Figure 7-5(a), income has risen by 20 percent, increasing demand at price

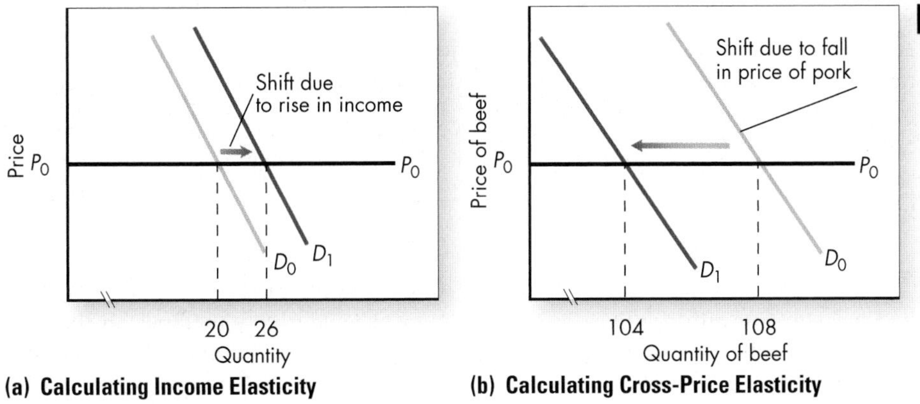

FIGURE 7-5 (A AND B)
Calculating Elasticities

Shift factors, such as income or price of another good, shift the entire demand curve. To calculate these elasticities, we see how much demand will shift at a constant price and then calculate the relevant elasticities.

A REMINDER

A Review of the Alternative Elasticity Terms

Income elasticity of demand is defined as *the percentage change in demand divided by the percentage change in income.*

$$\text{Income elasticity of demand} = \frac{\text{Percentage change in demand}}{\text{Percentage change in income}}$$

Cross-price elasticity of demand is defined as *the percentage change in demand divided by the percentage change in the price of a related good.*

$$\text{Cross-price elasticity of demand} = \frac{\text{Percentage change in demand}}{\text{Percentage change in price of a related good}}$$

Complement: Cross-price elasticity of demand is negative.

Substitute: Cross-price elasticity of demand is positive.

Normal good: Income elasticity of demand is positive.

Luxury: Income elasticity is greater than 1.

Necessity: Income elasticity is less than 1.

Inferior good: Income elasticity of demand is negative.

P_0 from 20 to 26. To determine the income elasticity, we must first determine the percentage change in demand. We calculate the percentage demand to be $6/[(20 + 26)/2] = (6/23) \times 100 = 26$ percent. The percentage change in income is 20, so the income elasticity is 26/20, or 1.3.

In Figure 7-5(b), a 33 percent fall in the price of pork has caused the demand for beef to fall by 3.8 percent—from 108 to 104 at a price of P_0. The cross-price elasticity of demand is $3.8/33 = 0.12$.

The Power of Supply/Demand Analysis

Now that you've got the elasticity terms down, let's consider some examples that demonstrate the power of supply/demand analysis when it is combined with the concept of elasticity. Let's start with some easy cases.

When Should a Supplier Not Raise Price?

First, let's say a firm is trying to increase its profits and hires you to tell it whether it should raise or lower its price. The firm knows that it faces an inelastic demand. Should it raise its price?

I hope your answer was: Definitely yes. How can I be so sure the correct answer is yes? Because I remembered the discussion of the relationship between price elasticity of demand with total revenue. With an inelastic demand, the percentage change in quantity is less than the percentage change in price, so total revenue must increase with an increase in price. Total costs also will decrease, so profits—total revenues minus total costs—also must increase.

Along those same lines, consider a university president thinking of raising tuition. Say that raising tuition by 10 percent will decrease the number of students by 1 percent. What's the price elasticity? The percentage change in quantity is 1 percent; the percentage change in price is 10. Dividing the percentage change in quantity by the percentage change in price, we have an elasticity of 0.1. That's an inelastic demand ($E_D < 1$), so raising tuition will increase the university's total revenue.

But if a 10 percent rise in tuition will decrease the enrollment by 25 percent, the elasticity will be large (2.5). In response to an increase in tuition, the university's total revenue will decrease significantly. When you have an elastic demand, you should hesitate to increase price. To make sure you're following the argument, explain the likely effect an elastic demand will have on lowering tuition. (Your argument should involve the *possibility* of increasing profit.) If you're not following the argument, go back to the section on elasticity and total revenue, especially Figure 7-3.

When the long-run and short-run elasticities differ, the analysis becomes somewhat more complicated. Consider the case of a local transit authority that, faced with a budget crisis, increased its fares from \$1.50 to \$1.75. The rise in revenue during the first year helped the authority balance its books. But in the two years following, ridership declined so much that total revenue fell. What happened? In the short-run, commuters had few substitutes to taking the bus—demand was relatively inelastic so that total revenue rose when fares were increased. But, as time went on, commuters found alternative ways to get to work. Long-run demand was more elastic in this case, so much so that total revenue declined.

Q-9 A firm faces an elastic demand for its product. It has come to an economist to advise it on whether to lower its price. The answer she gives is: Maybe. Why is this the right answer?

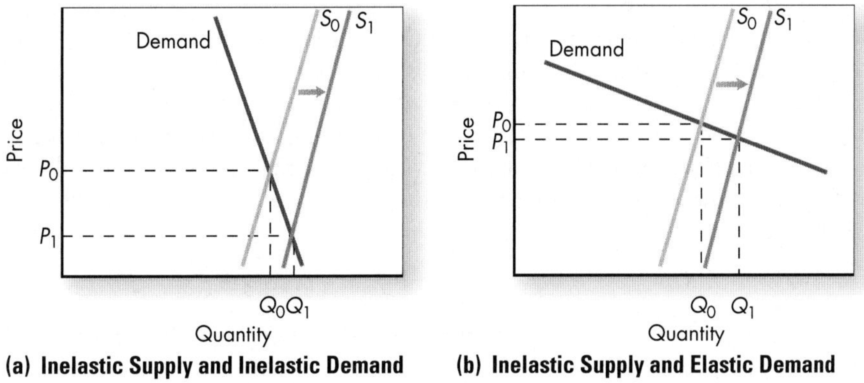

FIGURE 7-6 (A AND B)
Effects of Shifts in Supply on Price and Quantity

In (**a**), supply intersects demand where demand is inelastic and the quantity effects are relatively small. In (**b**), demand is more elastic and the quantity effects are much larger. In general the effects of shifts in supply on equilibrium quantity and price are determined by the elasticity of demand.

Elasticity and Shifting Supply and Demand

Let's now turn to shifts in supply and demand. Knowing the elasticity of the supply and demand curves allows us to be more specific about the effects of shifts in supply and demand.

Figure 7-6 demonstrates the relative effects of supply shifts on equilibrium price and quantity under different assumptions about elasticity. As you can see, the more elastic the demand, the greater the effect of a supply shift on quantity, and the smaller the effect on price. Going through a similar exercise for demand shifts with various supply elasticities is also a useful exercise. If you do so, you will see that the more elastic the supply, the greater the effect of a demand shift on quantity, and the smaller the effect on price.

We can be even more precise with regard to the percentage change in price. Specifically, when demand shifts,

$$\text{Percentage change in price} = \frac{\text{Percentage change in demand}}{E_D + E_S}$$

When supply shifts,

$$\text{Percentage change in price} = \frac{\text{Percentage change in supply}}{E_D + E_S}$$

Q-10 The elasticity of supply is 1 and the elasticity of demand is 2. If demand increases by 10 percent, by what percentage will price change?

Let's consider two examples. Suppose demand shifts out to the right by 5 percent, the elasticity of demand is 0.8, and the elasticity of supply is 2. Price will rise by 5/2.8, or 1.8 percent. Alternatively, if supply shifts out to the right by 33 percent and the elasticity of demand and supply are both 1, price will fall by 33/2, or 16.5 percent. In general, the more elastic supply and demand, the less price will change for a given percentage change in either demand or supply.

To be sure that you have understood elasticity, consider the following three observations about price and quantity and match them with the three descriptions of supply and demand:

a. Price rises significantly; quantity hardly changes at all.
b. Price remains almost constant; quantity increases enormously.
c. Price falls significantly; quantity hardly changes at all.

1. Demand is highly elastic; supply shifts out.
2. Supply is highly inelastic; demand shifts out.
3. Demand is highly inelastic; supply shifts out.

The answers are a–2; b–1; c–3.

Conclusion

I'll stop the exercises here. As you can see, the elasticity concept is important. Economists use it all the time when discussing supply and demand.

However, the elasticity concept is not easy to remember, or to calculate, so working with it takes some practice. It becomes a bit less forbidding if you remember that elasticity is what your shorts lose when they've been through the washer and drier too many times. If a relationship is elastic, price (for price elasticity) exerts a strong pull on quantity. If it's inelastic, there's little pull on quantity.

Summary

- Elasticity is defined as percentage change in quantity divided by percentage change in some variable that affects demand (or supply) or quantity demanded (or supplied). The most common elasticity concept used is price elasticity.

$$E_D = \frac{\text{Percentage change in quantity demanded}}{\text{Percentage change in price}}$$

$$E_S = \frac{\text{Percentage change in quantity supplied}}{\text{Percentage change in price}}$$

- Elasticity is a better descriptor than is slope because it is independent of units of measurement.
- To calculate percentage changes in prices and quantities, use the average of the end values.
- Five elasticity terms are: *elastic* ($E > 1$); *inelastic* ($E < 1$); *unit elastic* ($E = 1$); *perfectly inelastic* ($E = 0$); and *perfectly elastic* ($E = \infty$).
- The more substitutes a good has, the greater its elasticity.
- Factors affecting the number of substitutes in demand are (1) time period considered, (2) the degree to which the good is a luxury, (3) the market definition, and (4) the importance of the good in one's budget.
- The most important factor affecting the number of substitutes in supply is time. As the time interval lengthens, supply becomes more elastic.
- Elasticity changes along straight-line demand and supply curves. Demand becomes less elastic as we move down along a demand curve.
- When a supplier raises price, if demand is inelastic, total revenue increases; if demand is elastic, total revenue decreases; if demand is unit elastic, total revenue remains constant.
- Other important elasticity concepts are income elasticity and cross-price elasticity of demand.

$$\text{Income elasticity of demand} = \frac{\text{Percentage change in demand}}{\text{Percentage change in income}}$$

$$\text{Cross-price elasticity of demand} = \frac{\text{Percentage change in demand}}{\text{Percentage change in price of a related good}}$$

- Knowing elasticities allows us to be more precise about the qualitative effects that shifts in demand and supply have on prices and quantities.
- When demand shifts,

$$\text{Percentage change in price} = \frac{\text{Percentage change in demand}}{E_D + E_S}$$

- When supply shifts,

$$\text{Percentage change in price} = \frac{\text{Percentage change in supply}}{E_D + E_S}$$

Key Terms

complement *(171)*
cross-price elasticity of demand *(169)*
elastic *(155)*
income elasticity of demand *(169)*
inelastic *(155)*
inferior good *(170)*
luxury *(169)*
necessity *(170)*
normal good *(169)*
perfectly elastic *(159)*
perfectly inelastic *(158)*
price elasticity of demand *(154)*
price elasticity of supply *(154)*
substitute *(171)*
unit elastic *(160)*

Questions and Exercises

1. Determine the price elasticity of demand if, in response to an increase in price of 10 percent, quantity demanded decreases by 20 percent. Is demand elastic or inelastic? LO2, LO3
2. A firm has just increased its price by 5 percent over last year's price, and it found that quantity sold remained the same.
   a. The firm comes to you and wants to know its price elasticity of demand.
   b. How would you calculate it?
   c. What additional information would you search for before you did your calculation? LO2
3. When tolls on the Dulles Airport Greenway were reduced from $1.75 to $1.00, traffic increased from 10,000 to 26,000 trips a day. Assuming all changes in quantity were due to the change in price, what is the price elasticity of demand for the Dulles Airport Greenway? LO2
4. One football season Domino's Pizza, a corporate sponsor of the Washington Redskins (a football team), offered to reduce the price of its medium-size pizza by $1 for every touchdown scored by the Redskins during the previous week. Until that year, the Redskins weren't scoring many touchdowns. Much to the surprise of Domino's, in one week in 1999, the Redskins scored six touchdowns. (Maybe they like pizza.) Domino's pizzas were selling for $2 a pie! The quantity of pizzas demanded soared the following week from 1 pie an hour to 100 pies an hour. What was price elasticity of demand for Domino's pizza? LO2
5. Which has greater elasticity: a supply curve that goes through the origin with slope of 1 or a supply curve that goes through the origin with slope of 4? LO2
6. Why would an economist be more hesitant about making an elasticity estimate of the effect of an increase in price of 1 percent rather than an increase in price of 50 percent? LO2
7. A major cereal producer decides to lower price from $3.60 to $3 per 15-ounce box. (Difficult)
   a. If quantity demanded increases by 18 percent, what is the price elasticity of demand?
   b. If, instead of lowering its price, the cereal producer had increased the size of the box from 15 to 17.8 ounces, what would you expect that the response would have been? Why? LO2
8. Federal Reserve Bank of Chicago economist William Hunter and G-7 Group economist Mary Rosenbaum estimated the demand elasticity for motor fuel to be between 0.4 and 0.85.
   a. If the price rises 10 percent and the initial quantity sold is 10 million gallons, what is the range of estimates of the new quantity demanded?
   b. In carrying out their estimates, they came up with different elasticity estimates for rises in price than for falls in price, with an increase in price having a larger elasticity than a decrease in price. What hypothesis might you propose for their findings? LO2
9. Calculate the price elasticities of the designated points on the following graph. (Reread the box "Calculating Elasticity at a Point.") LO2

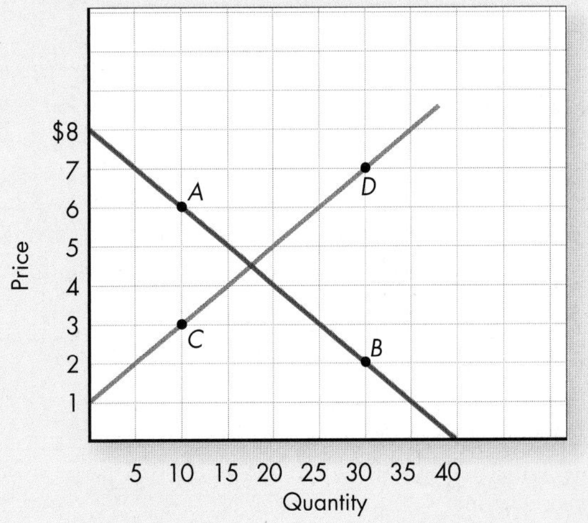

10. Calculate the elasticity of the designated ranges of supply and demand curves on the following graph. LO2

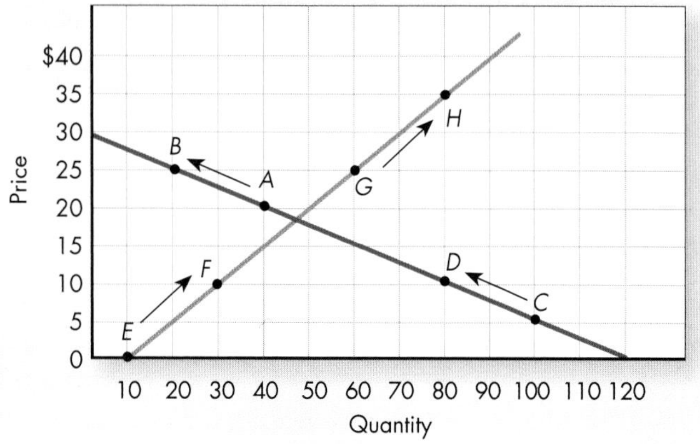

11. Which of the pairs of goods would you expect to have a greater price elasticity of demand?
    a. Cars, transportation.
    b. Housing, leisure travel.
    c. Rubber during World War II, rubber during the entire 20th century. LO4
12. For each of the following goods, state whether it is a normal good, a luxury, a necessity, or an inferior good. Explain your answers. LO4
    a. Vodka.
    b. Table salt.
    c. Furniture.
    d. Perfume.
    e. Beer.
    f. Sugar.
13. Economists have estimated the following transportation elasticities. For each pair, explain possible reasons why the elasticities differ.
    a. Elasticity of demand for buses is 0.23 during peak hours and 0.42 during off-peak hours.
    b. Elasticity of demand for buses is 0.7 in the short run and 1.5 in the long run.
    c. Elasticity of demand for toll roads is 4.7 for low-income commuters and 0.63 for high-income commuters. LO4
14. Kean University Professor Henry Saffer and Wharton School of Business Professor Dave Dhaval estimated that if the alcohol industry increased the prices of alcoholic beverages by 100 percent underage drinking would fall by 28 percent and underage binge drinking would fall by 51 percent.
    a. What is the elasticity of demand of underage drinking and binge drinking?
    b. What might explain the difference in elasticities? LO4
15. A newspaper recently lowered its price from 50 cents to 30 cents. As it did, the number of newspapers sold increased from 240,000 to 280,000.
    a. What was the newspaper's elasticity of demand?
    b. Given that elasticity, did it make sense for the newspaper to lower its price?
    c. What would your answer be if much of the firm's revenue came from advertising and the higher the circulation, the more it could charge for advertising? LO2, LO5
16. Once a book has been written, would an author facing an inelastic demand curve for the book prefer to raise or lower the book's price? Why? LO5
17. University of Richmond Professor Erik Craft analyzed the states' pricing of vanity plates. He found that in California, where vanity plates cost $28.75, the elasticity of demand was 0.52. In Massachusetts, where vanity plates cost $50, the elasticity of demand was 3.52.
    a. Assuming vanity plates have zero production cost and his estimates are correct, was each state collecting the maximum revenue it could from vanity plates? Explain your reasoning.
    b. What recommendation would you have for each state to maximize revenue?
    c. If these estimates are correct, which state was most likely to be following a politically unsupportable policy?
    d. Assuming the demand curves were linear, graphically demonstrate your reasoning in *a* and *b*. LO5
18. Which of the following producers would you expect to support a tax on beer? Which would not? Explain your answer by referring to the estimates in the table on page 171.
    a. Producers of hard liquor.
    b. Producers of wine. LO5, LO7
19. In the discussion of elasticity and raising and lowering prices, the text states that if you have an elastic demand, you should hesitate to raise your price, and that lowering price can *possibly* increase profits (total revenue minus total cost). Why is the word *possibly* used? (Difficult) LO5
20. How is elasticity related to the revenue from a sales tax? LO5
21. Calculate the income elasticities of demand for the following:
    a. Income rises by 20 percent; demand rises by 10 percent.
    b. Income rises from $30,000 to $40,000; demand increases (at a constant price) from 16 to 19. LO6
22. According to Exhibitor Relations Co., in 2006 average movie ticket prices were $6.55 and attendance was 1.4 billion; in 2007 ticket prices were $6.88 and attendance was 1.41 billion. (Difficult)
    a. What happened to total revenue from 2006 to 2007?
    b. If you were to estimate elasticity from these figures, what would your estimate be?
    c. What provisos would you offer about your estimate of elasticity? LO6
23. In 2004, Congress allocated over $20 billion to fight illegal drugs. About 60 percent of the funds was directed at reducing the supply of drugs through domestic law enforcement and interdiction. Some critics of this approach

argue that supply-side approaches to reduce the drug supply actually help drug producers. (Difficult)

a. Demonstrate graphically the effect of supply-side measures on the market for illegal drugs.
b. Explain how these measures affect drug producers. (Hint: Consider the elasticity of demand.)
c. Demonstrate the effect of demand-side measures such as treatment and prevention on the market for illegal drugs.
d. How does the shift in demand affect the profitability of producers? LO6

24. For each of the following pairs of goods, state whether the cross-price elasticity is likely positive, negative, or zero. Explain your answers. LO6
    a. Lettuce, carrots.
    b. Housing, furniture.
    c. Nike sneakers, Puma sneakers.
    d. Jeans, formal suits.

25. When the price of ketchup rises by 15 percent, the demand for hot dogs falls by 1 percent.
    a. Calculate the cross-price elasticity of demand.
    b. Are the goods complements or substitutes?
    c. In the original scenario, what would have to happen to the demand for hot dogs for us to conclude that hot dogs and ketchup are substitutes? LO6

26. The short-run elasticity of demand for gasoline sold at gas stations is 0.20 and elasticity of supply is 1. If terrorism reduces supply by 5 percent, and gas were selling for $1.75 before terrorism, what would you predict would happen to the price of gas? LO7

27. What will be the percentage change in price in the following instances?
    a. Demand shifts to the right by 10 percent, elasticity of demand is 1, elasticity of supply is 2.
    b. Demand shifts to the right by 10 percent, elasticity of demand is 0.2, elasticity of supply is 0.5.
    c. Supply shifts to the right by 25 percent, elasticity of demand is 3, elasticity of supply is 2. LO7

Questions from Alternative Perspectives

1. The text tells us that there are long-run elasticities and short-run elasticities.
   a. How long is the long run and how long is the short run?
   b. What meaning do the elasticity measures have if you don't know those lengths? (Austrian)

2. In this chapter, we learn that most new cars aren't sold at their list price but are sold at a discount and that this allows dealerships to charge more to customers with inelastic demand. At the same time, studies have shown that retail car dealerships systematically offer substantially better prices on identical cars to white men than they do to blacks or women. (Source: Ian Ayres, "Fair Driving: Gender and Race Discrimination in Retail Car Negotiations," *Harvard Law Review* 104 (1991): 817–72.)
   a. Why do you think this happens?
   b. In this example, does the existence of price discrimination allow for racial or sexual discrimination? (Feminist)

3. Early economists made a distinction between needs and wants. Needs were economists' concern; wants were of far less importance.
   a. Is such a distinction useful?
   b. Would making such a distinction change the nature of economic analysis?
   c. Does the fact that the book makes no distinction between luxuries and necessities other than in their elasticity of demand reflect a bias of economic analysis? (Religious)

4. In the chapter, you saw that an increase in Vermont's minimum wage stimulated a small quantity response.
   a. What does this tell you about the nature of the labor market in Vermont? (Hint: Think carefully and critically about the conditions shaping worker options and their responses to changes in wages.)
   b. What policy implications does your answer to *a* suggest? (Institutionalist)

5. If elasticities are constantly changing as the time period gets longer, how do managers use a measure of elasticity of demand to determine the price they charge? If they don't use elasticities, how do they set price? (Post-Keynesian)

6. Price elasticity is not just a technical economic concept. It also reflects the distribution of economic power—the bargaining power and economic opportunities of buyers and sellers.
   a. When suppliers (for example, landlords or energy companies) hold disproportionate power over buyers, or consumers (for example, employers in low-wage labor markets) hold disproportionate power over sellers, what meaning do elasticities have?
   b. Should anything be done about those inequities? (Radical)

Issues to Ponder

1. In the box "Geometric Tricks for Estimating Price Elasticity," there are three statements about the elasticities of straight-line supply curves. One of those statements is that supply curves intersecting the quantity axis are inelastic. Can you prove that that is true by algebraic manipulation of the elasticity formula? LO2
2. In the 1960s, coffee came in 1-pound cans. Today, most coffee comes in 11-ounce cans. (Difficult)
   a. Can you think of an explanation why?
   b. Can you think of other products besides coffee whose standard size has shrunk? (Often the standard size is supplemented by a "super-size" alternative.) LO4
3. Demand for "prestige" college education is generally considered to be highly inelastic. What does this suggest about tuition increases at prestige schools in the future? Why don't colleges raise tuition by amounts even greater than they already do? (Difficult) LO5
4. Colleges have increasingly used price sensitivity to formulate financial aid. The more eager the student, the less aid he or she can expect to get. Use elasticity to explain this phenomenon. Is this practice justified? (Difficult) LO5
5. If there were only two goods in the world, can you say whether they would be complements or substitutes? Explain your answer. LO6

Answers to Margin Questions

1. Price elasticity of supply = Percentage change in quantity supplied divided by percentage change in price = 8/4 = 2. *(155)*
2. If price elasticity of demand is greater than 1, by definition demand is elastic. *(155)*
3. The percentage change in quantity is 100 (8/8 × 100) and the percentage change in price is 100 (2/2 × 100). Elasticity, therefore, is approximately 1 (100/100). *(158)*
4. I tell her that she is partially right (for the bottom part of the curve), but that elasticity on a straight-line demand curve changes from perfectly elastic at the vertical axis intersection to perfectly inelastic at the horizontal axis intersection. *(159)*
5. Four factors affecting the number of substitutes in demand are (1) time period considered, (2) the degree to which the good is a luxury, (3) the market definition, and (4) importance of the good in one's budget. *(163)*
6. Supply is generally more elastic in the long run because there are more alternative goods and services for producers to produce. *(163)*
7. If demand is inelastic, total revenue increases with an increase in price. *(166)*
8. If consumption increases with an increase in income, the good is a normal good. *(169)*
9. With an elastic demand, lowering price will increase total revenue because it will increase sales. But producing more also will increase costs, so information about total revenue is not enough to answer the question. *(172)*
10. Price increases 3⅓ percent. Percentage change in price is the percentage change in demand (10) divided by the sum of the elasticities of supply and demand (1 + 2). *(173)*

CHAPTER 8

Taxation and Government Intervention

Collecting more taxes than is absolutely necessary is legalized robbery.

—*Calvin Coolidge*

John Baptiste Colbert, finance minister for Louis XIV, once said that the art of taxation consists of plucking the goose so as to obtain the largest amount of feathers with the least amount of squawk. In figuring out what taxes will bring about the least amount of squawk, politicians have turned to economists, who, in turn, turn to their models. Previous chapters introduced you to those models; in this chapter, we apply the models to taxation. As we do that, you'll see that when combined with the concept of elasticity, supply and demand become powerful tools. We'll see how by considering the burden of taxation and government intervention into markets.

AFTER READING THIS CHAPTER, YOU SHOULD BE ABLE TO:

1. Show how equilibrium maximizes producer and consumer surplus.
2. Demonstrate the burden of taxation to consumers and producers.
3. Explain why the person who physically pays the tax is not necessarily the person who bears the burden of the tax.
4. Demonstrate how an effective price ceiling is the equivalent of a tax on producers and a subsidy to consumers.
5. Define rent seeking and show how it is related to elasticity.
6. State the general rule of political economy.

Producer and Consumer Surplus

We begin our discussion of the effects of taxation and government intervention by looking at how economists measure the benefits of the market to consumers and producers; the benefit can be seen by considering what the supply and demand curves are telling us. Each of these curves tells us how much individuals are willing to pay (in the case of demand) or accept (in the case of supply) for a good. Thus, in Figure 8-1(a), a consumer is willing to pay \$8 each for 2 units of the good. The supplier is willing to sell 2 units for \$2 apiece.

If the consumer pays less than what he's willing to pay, he ends up with a net gain—the value of the good to him minus the price he actually paid for the good. Thus, the distance between the demand curve and the price he pays is the net gain for the consumer. Economists call this net benefit **consumer surplus**—*the value the consumer gets from buying a product less its price*. It is represented by the area underneath the demand curve and above the price that an individual pays. Thus, with the price at equilibrium (\$5), consumer surplus is represented by the blue area.

FIGURE 8-1 (A AND B) Consumer and Producer Surplus

Market equilibrium price and quantity maximize the combination of consumer surplus (shown in blue) and producer surplus (shown in brown) as demonstrated in (**a**). When price deviates from its equilibrium, as in (**b**), combined consumer and producer surplus falls. The gray shaded region shows the loss of total surplus when price is $1 higher than equilibrium price.

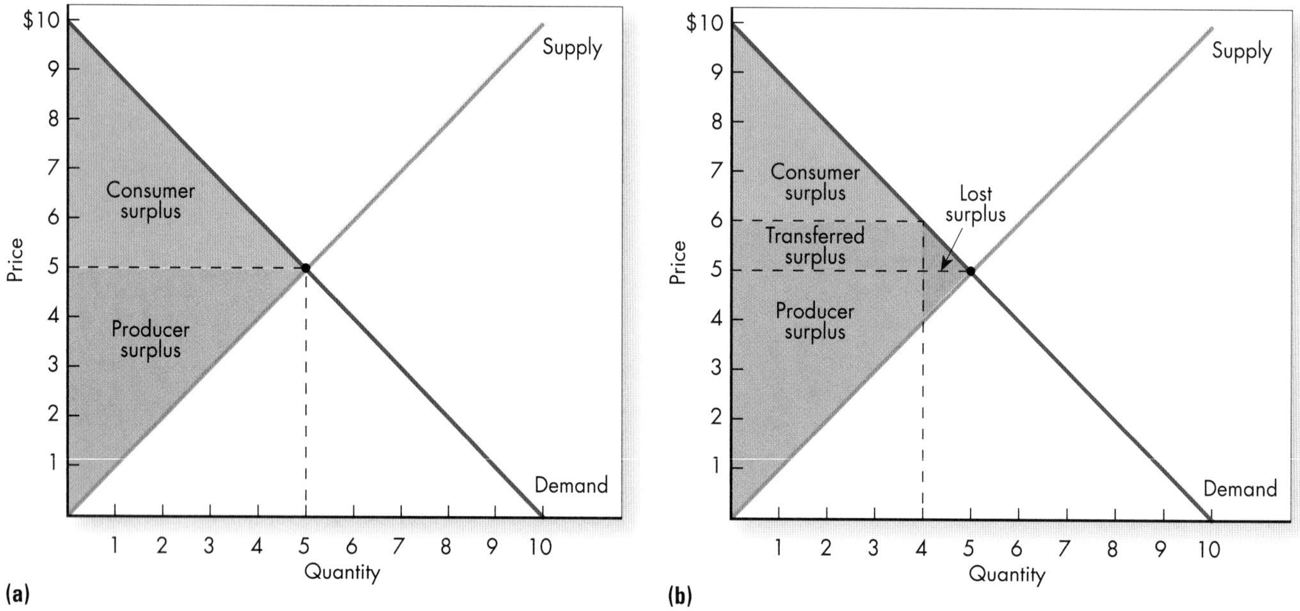

Q-1 If price moves from disequilibrium to equilibrium, what happens to the combination of producer and consumer surplus in the market?

Producer and Consumer Surplus

Similarly, if a producer receives more than the price she would be willing to sell it for, she too receives a net benefit. Economists call this gain **producer surplus**—*the price the producer sells a product for less the cost of producing it.* It is represented by the area above the supply curve but below the price the producer receives. Thus, with the price at equilibrium ($5), producer surplus is represented by the brown area.

What's good about market equilibrium is that it makes the combination of consumer and producer surpluses as large as it can be. To see this, say that for some reason the equilibrium price is held at $6. Consumers will demand only 4 units of the good, and some suppliers are not able to sell all the goods they would like. The combined producer and consumer surplus will decrease, as shown in Figure 8-1(b). The gray triangle represents lost consumer and producer surplus. In general, a deviation of price from equilibrium lowers the combination of producer and consumer surplus. This is one of the reasons economists support markets and why we teach the supply/demand model. It gives us a visual sense of what is good about markets: By allowing trade, markets maximize the combination of consumer and producer surplus.

For straight-line demand curves, the amount of surplus can be determined by calculating the area of the relevant triangle or rectangle. For example, in Figure 8-1(a), the consumer surplus triangle has a base of 5 and a height of 5 (10 − 5). Since the area of a triangle is ½ (base × height), the consumer surplus is 12.5 units. Alternatively, in Figure 8-1(b), the lost surplus from a price above equilibrium price is 1. This is calculated by determining that the height of the triangle (looked at sideways) is 1 (5 − 4) and the base is 2 (6 − 4), making the area of lost surplus ½ × 2 × 1 = 1. In this case, the consumer and producer share in the loss equally. The higher price transfers 4 units of surplus from consumer to producer, calculated by determining the area of the rectangle

ADDED DIMENSION

The Ambiguity of Total Surplus

The consumer and producer surplus concepts do not treat all wants equally. How much importance your surplus is given depends on how much income you have. People with lots of income generate lots of surplus; people with little income general little. So if Mr. Rich likes gold-plated toilets but dislikes bread, while Mr. Poor likes bread but has little money to spend on bread, it is gold-plated toilets, not bread, that will generate the most consumer surplus.

What this means is that if income were distributed differently, our measure of consumer surplus would change. Let's consider an extreme example to show the problems this can present. Say we have two individuals, Jules and Jim, and two goods, apples and oranges. Jules likes only oranges and Jim likes only apples. If Jim has all the income, only apples will provide any consumer surplus. Now, say that Jules has all the income. In that case, only oranges will provide any consumer surplus. More generally, when two individuals have different tastes, the way in which income is distributed between them can change the measure of consumer surplus.

Economists get around part of the problem theoretically either by assuming individuals have the same tastes or by assuming that income can be costlessly redistributed. This separates the issue of equity from the issue of efficiency. In practice, economists recognize that these conditions do not hold. They know that, in the real world, it is extraordinarily difficult to redistribute income. You can't go up to Bill Gates and tell him, "Hey, you need to give $10 billion to some poor people." (Although he might choose to do it on his own, as he has done.)

For this reason economists are careful to apply the producer and consumer surplus analysis only to those cases where the conditions are "reasonable" approximations of reality—where distributional and taste issues do not play a big role in a policy recommendation. Of course, economists may disagree on what are "reasonable" approximations of reality. That is why economic policy is an art, not a science.

(base × height) created by the origin and output, 4, and prices 5 and 6, which equals $(6 - 5)(4 - 0) \times 4 = 4$. This leaves the consumer with 8 units of surplus.[1]

To fix the ideas of consumer and producer surplus in your mind, let's consider a couple of real-world examples. Think about the water you drink. What does it cost? Almost nothing. Given that water is readily available, it has a low price. But since you'd die from thirst if you had no water, you are getting an enormous amount of consumer surplus from that water. Next, consider a ballet dancer who loves the ballet so much he'd dance for free. But he finds that people are willing to pay to see him and that he can receive $4,000 a performance. He is receiving producer surplus.

Burden of Taxation

Now that you have seen how market equilibrium can provide benefits to producers and consumers, as measured by producer and consumer surplus, let's see how taxes affect that surplus. You already know that taxes on suppliers shift the supply curve up. In most cases, equilibrium price rises and equilibrium quantity declines. Taxes on consumers shift the demand curve up, also raising equilibrium price and reducing equilibrium quantity. In both cases, taxes reduce, or limit, trade. Economists often talk about the limitations that taxes place on trade as the *burden of taxation*. Figure 8-2 provides the basic framework for understanding the burden of taxation. For a given good, a per-unit tax t paid by the supplier increases the price at which suppliers are willing to sell that

A tax paid by the supplier shifts the supply curve up by the amount of the tax.

[1]Additional explanations of how to calculate consumer and producer surplus can be found on the Web at www.mhhe.com/colander8e.

FIGURE 8-2 The Costs of Taxation

A per-unit tax t paid by the supplier shifts the supply curve up from S_0 to S_1. Equilibrium price rises from P_0 to P_1, and equilibrium quantity falls from Q_0 to Q_1. Consumer surplus is represented by areas A, B, and C before the tax and area A after the tax. Producer surplus is represented by areas D, E, and F before the tax and area F after the tax. Government collects tax shown by areas B and D. The tax imposes a deadweight loss, represented by the welfare loss triangle of areas C and E.

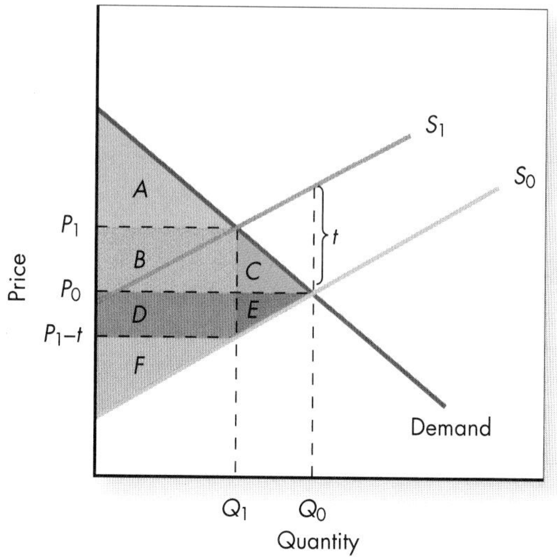

Costs and Incidence of Taxation

good. The effect of the tax is shown by a shift upward of the supply curve from S_0 to S_1. The equilibrium price of the good rises and the quantity sold declines.

Before the tax, consumers pay P_0 and producers keep P_0. Consumer surplus is represented by areas $A + B + C$, and producer surplus is represented by areas $D + E + F$. With the tax t, equilibrium price rises to P_1 and equilibrium quantity falls to Q_1. Consumers now pay a higher price P_1, but producers keep less, only $P_1 - t$. Tax revenue paid equals the tax t times equilibrium quantity Q_1, or areas B and D.

Q-2 Demonstrate the welfare loss of a tax when the supply is highly elastic and the demand is highly inelastic.

The total cost to consumers and producers is taxes they pay *plus* lost surplus because of fewer trades. Consumers pay area B in tax revenue and lose area C in consumer surplus. Producers pay area D in tax revenue and lose area E in producer surplus. The triangular area $C + E$ represents a cost of taxation over and above the taxes paid to government. It is lost consumer and producer surplus that is not gained by government. *The loss of consumer and producer surplus from a tax* is known as **deadweight loss.** Deadweight loss is shown graphically by the **welfare loss triangle**—*a geometric representation of the welfare cost in terms of misallocated resources caused by a deviation from a supply/demand equilibrium*. Keep in mind that with the tax, quantity sold declines. The loss of welfare, therefore, represents a loss for those consumers and producers who, because of the tax, no longer buy or sell goods.

Mansard roofs

The deadweight loss from taxes shows up in a variety of other ways. Say the government establishes a property tax that increases with the number of floors a building has, as Paris did in the 1700s. A three-story building was taxed a third higher than a two-story building. That will lead people to build in a way to minimize the number of measured floors, with large roofs that hide an extra floor. The Mansard roof—as shown in the photo in the margin—does this, and such roofs can be found throughout Paris. They are building in a style that is less efficient (in terms of the building's function) than they would build without the tax. Building in a style that is less efficient in terms of function is another consequence of a tax, and is a type of deadweight loss.[2]

The cost of taxation includes the direct cost of revenue paid, lost surplus, and administrative cost.

The costs of taxation don't end there. Resources must be devoted by government to administer the tax code and by individuals to comply with it. Firms and individuals

[2]Interestingly, in terms of aesthetics, people have come to like the style of Paris roofs; it is one of the many things that makes Paris distinct. Including aesthetics complicates the analysis enormously. Economic reasoning is based on the architectural view that form follows function.

A REMINDER

What Goods Should Be Taxed?

What goods should be taxed depends on the goal of government. If the goal is to fund a program with as little loss as possible in consumer and producer surplus, then the government should tax a good whose supply or demand is inelastic. If the goal is to change behavior, taxes will be most effective if demand or supply is elastic. As a quick review, use the following table:

Goal of Government	Most Effective When
Raise revenue, limit deadweight loss	Demand or supply is inelastic
Change behavior	Demand or supply is elastic

Distributional issues also must be considered when determining what goods are to be taxed. In general, the group with the relatively more inelastic supply or demand will bear a greater portion of the tax. The following table reviews these conclusions:

Elasticity	Who Bears the Burden?
Demand inelastic and supply elastic	Consumers
Supply inelastic and demand elastic	Producers
Both supply and demand elastic	Shared; but the group whose supply or demand is more inelastic pays more

either spend hours filling out income tax forms or pay others to do so. Firms hire accountants and lawyers to take full advantage of any tax-code allowances. Administration costs are often as much as 5 percent or more of the total tax revenue paid to government. Like the tax itself, these costs increase the price at which producers are willing to sell their goods, reducing quantity sold and further increasing welfare loss.

Who Bears the Burden of a Tax?

Taxes are like hot potatoes: Everyone wants to pass them on to someone else. Nobody wants to pay taxes, and there are usually large political fights about whom government should tax. For example, should the Social Security tax (mandated by the Federal Insurance Contributions Act, or FICA) be placed on workers or on the company that hires them? The supply/demand framework gives an unexpected answer to this question.

Burden Depends on Relative Elasticity Let's consider the issue of who bears the burden of a tax by looking at the example involving excise taxes introduced in Chapter 5. There I defined an **excise tax** as *a tax levied on a specific good* and gave the example of a luxury tax on expensive boats that the United States imposed in 1990. An excise tax can be levied on (physically paid by) the consumer or the seller.

The person who physically pays the tax is not necessarily the person who bears the burden of the tax.

The person who *physically pays* the tax, however, is not necessarily the person who *bears the burden* of the tax. Who bears the burden of the tax (also known as tax incidence) depends on who is best able to change his or her behavior in response to the tax,

FIGURE 8-3 (A, B, AND C) **Who Bears the Burden of a Tax?**

In the general case, the burden of a tax is determined by the relative elasticities of supply and demand. The blue shaded area shows the burden on the consumer; the brown shaded area shows the burden on the supplier. This split occurs regardless of who actually pays the tax, as can be seen by noticing that the burden of the tax is equal in (**a**), where the supplier pays the tax, and in (**c**), where the consumer pays the tax. In (**b**) you can see how consumers with an inelastic demand bear a greater burden of the tax.

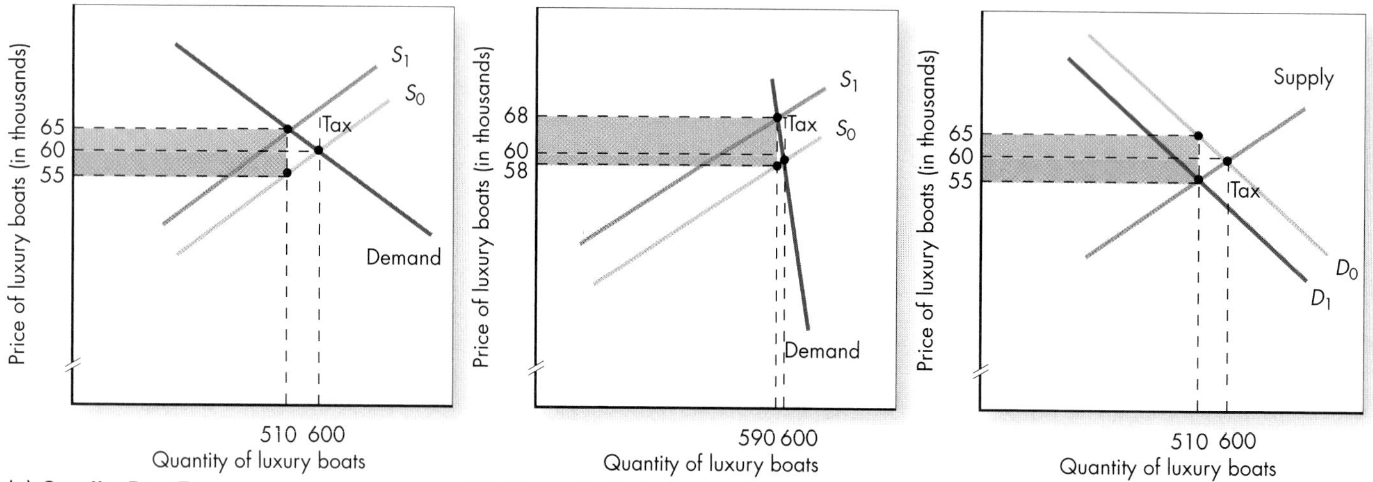

(a) Supplier Pays Tax **(b) Demand Is Inelastic** **(c) Consumer Pays Tax**

Q-3 If a person has a highly elastic demand, will he likely bear a large or small percentage of the burden of a tax?

or who has the greater elasticity. Elasticity and supply/demand analysis let us answer the question "Who will end up bearing the burden of the tax?" (More technically: "What is the incidence of the tax?")

Figure 8-3(a) shows the case I considered in Chapter 5. A $10,000 per-unit tax levied on the supplier shifts the supply curve up from S_0 to S_1. That reduces quantity supplied and quantity demanded by 90—from 600 to 510. The equilibrium price rises from $60,000 to $65,000. Suppliers are able to shift $5,000 of the total $10,000 per-unit tax onto consumers, leaving the suppliers the burden of the remaining $5,000.

Had we known elasticities at the market equilibrium, we could have stated, without additional calculations, that the tax burden would be shared equally. Specifically, suppliers sold and consumers purchased 90 fewer boats, an approximate 15 percent reduction. The suppliers' price fell by about 8 percent while the consumers' price rose by about 8 percent, meaning the elasticity of both supply and demand was approximately 1.9.[3] With equal elasticities, the tax burden will be divided equally.

In reality, the tax burden is rarely shared equally because elasticities are rarely equal. The relative burden of the tax follows this general rule: *The more inelastic one's relative supply and demand, the larger the burden of the tax one will bear.* If demand were more inelastic, sellers would have been able to sell the boats at a higher price and could have passed more of the tax along to the buyers.

Tax burden is allocated by relative elasticities.

Figure 8-3(b) shows what the divisions would have been had the demand curve been highly inelastic. In this case, the price would rise more, the supplier would pay a lower proportion of the tax (the brown area), and the consumer would pay a much larger proportion (the blue area). The general rule about elasticities and the tax burden is this: If demand is more inelastic than supply, consumers will pay a higher percentage

[3]There will be slight variations in the measured elasticities depending on how they are calculated. The precise equality holds only for point elasticities. (See the previous chapter.)

of the tax; if supply is more inelastic than demand, suppliers will pay a higher share. This rule makes sense—*elasticity is a measure of how easy it is for the supplier and consumer to change behavior and substitute another good.*

More specifically, we can calculate the fraction of the tax actually borne by the demander by dividing the price elasticity of supply by the sum of the price elasticities of supply and demand:

$$\text{Fraction of tax borne by demander} = \frac{E_S}{E_D + E_S}$$

Similarly, we can calculate the fraction of the tax borne by the supplier by dividing the price elasticity of demand by the sum of the price elasticities of supply and demand:

Q-4 How much of a $100 tax would a consumer pay if elasticity of demand is .2 and price elasticity of supply is 1.8?

$$\text{Fraction of tax borne by supplier} = \frac{E_D}{E_D + E_S}$$

For example, say the price elasticity of supply is 4 and the price elasticity of demand is 1. In that case, the supplier will pay one-fifth [1/(1 + 4)] of the tax and the consumer will pay four-fifths [4/(1 + 4)] of the tax. This situation is shown in Figure 8-3(b).

The rule about the elasticities and the tax burden can lead to some unexpected consequences of taxation. For example, the U.S. luxury tax on boats was initially implemented as a way to tax the wealthy. It turned out, however, that the wealthy found substitutes for American-made boats; their demand was relatively elastic. They either purchased other luxury items or purchased their boats from foreign firms. U.S. boat manufacturers, however, couldn't easily switch to producing other products. Their supply was inelastic. As a result, when they tried to pass on the cost increase to consumers, their sales plummeted. They had to lower their price by almost as much as the tax, which meant that they were bearing most of the burden of the tax. As noted in Chapter 5, pressured by boat manufacturers, the government repealed the luxury tax on boats three years after it was instituted.

Who Pays a Tax Is Not Necessarily Who Bears the Burden The allocation of tax burden by relative elasticity means that it doesn't matter who actually pays the tax and that, as I said earlier, the person who bears the burden can differ from the person who pays. To assure yourself that it doesn't matter who pays the tax, ask yourself how your answer would have differed if the tax of $10,000 had been paid by the consumer. Figure 8-3(c) shows this case. Because the tax is paid by the consumer, the demand curve shifts down by the amount of the tax. As you can see, the results of the tax are identical. The percentage of the tax paid by the supplier and the consumer, after adjusting for the changes in supply and demand price, is independent of who actually makes the physical payment of the tax.

The burden is independent of who physically pays the tax.

Tax Incidence and Current Policy Debates

Now let's consider two policy questions in relation to what we have learned about tax incidence.

Social Security Taxes The first policy question concerns the Social Security (or payroll) tax, which accounts for 36 percent of federal government revenue. In 2009, the Social Security and Medicare tax rate was 12.4 percent on wages up to an annual maximum wage of $106,500, and another 2.9 percent on all wages, no matter how high. As a political compromise, half of Social Security taxes are placed on the employee and half on the employer. But the fact that the law places the tax equally on both does not mean that the burden of the tax is shared equally between employees and employers.

Q-5 If Social Security taxes were paid only by employees, what would likely happen to workers' pretax pay?

REAL-WORLD APPLICATION

College Newspaper Editors Should Take More Economics

In almost all towns and counties, nearly every year property taxes rise. College and university towns are no different. In 2006, the Orange County Board of Commissioners imposed a 7-cent property tax increase per $100 assessed value on properties in Orange County, the county where the University of North Carolina is located. UNC's student newspaper, the *Daily Tar Heel,* covered the story and suggested that off-campus rents would surely rise.

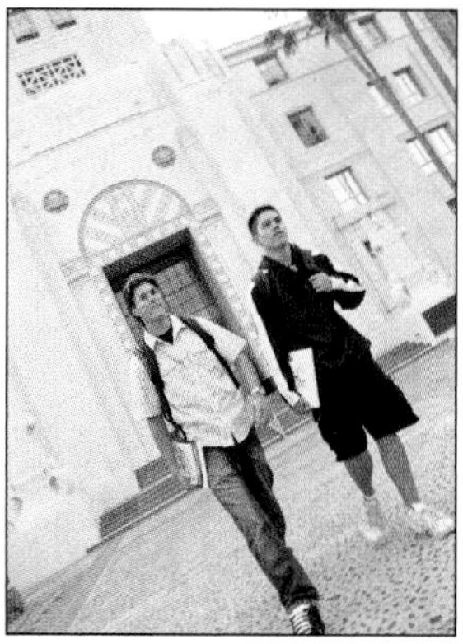

Based on the tools you've learned in this chapter, you know that the answer to that is not "surely" but is, rather, that the answer depends on elasticities. In the short run, the supply of housing tends to be very inelastic. The demand for housing by students, however, is generally quite elastic; they just haven't got much money, and often can choose to live on campus in a dorm. So who will likely pay almost all the property tax? The owner of the house, which means that rents are unlikely to be significantly affected by the tax. To put some numbers on it, economists who study the tax incidence of property taxes have found that for every $1 increase in property taxes, about 85 cents is paid by landlords and 15 cents is paid by renters, which means that the renter's share of the 7-cent per $100 tax increase on an apartment valued at $100,000 amounts to about 85 cents a month.

On average, labor supply tends to be less elastic than labor demand. This means that the Social Security tax burden is primarily on the employees, even though employees see only their own statutory portion of the Social Security tax on their pay stub.

Web Note 8.1
Debating Social Security

Now, let's say that you are advising a person running for Congress who has come up with the idea to place the entire tax on the employer and eliminate the tax on the employee. What will the effect of that be? Our tax incidence analysis tells us that, ultimately, it will have no effect. Wages paid to employees will fall to compensate employers for the cost of the tax. This example shows that who is assessed the tax can be quite different than who actually bears the burden, or incidence, of the tax. The burden will be borne by those with the most inelastic supply or demand because they are less able to get out of paying the tax by substitution.

So what do you tell the candidate? Is the idea a good one or not? Although economically it will not make a difference who pays the tax, politically it may be a popular proposal because individuals generally look at statutory assessment, not incidence. The candidate may gain significant support from workers, since they would no longer see a Social Security tax on their pay stub. The moral, then, is this: Politics often focuses on surface appearance; economics tries to get under the surface, and what is good economics is not always good politics.

What makes sense politically is not always what makes sense economically.

Sales Taxes Our second policy question concerns sales taxes paid by retailers on the basis of their sales revenue. In my state, the general sales tax is 6 cents on the dollar. Since sales taxes are broadly defined, consumers have little ability to substitute. Demand is inelastic and consumers bear the greater burden of the tax. Although stores could simply incorporate the tax into the price of their goods, most stores add the tax onto the bill after the initial sale is calculated, to make you aware of the tax. Again, it doesn't matter whether the tax is assessed on the store or on you.

Recently, however, the Internet has given consumers a substitute to shopping at actual retail stores. Retail sales over the Internet are over $140 billion annually and are continuing to grow. States have found it very difficult to tax Internet sales because the supplier has no retail address. The point of sale is in cyberspace. Technically in these cases, the buyer is required to pay the tax to the state where he or she lives, but in practice that seldom happens. How to tax Internet sales will be heavily debated over the next few years. The federal government currently has placed a moratorium on new Internet sales taxes. As Internet sales grow, states will lose more and more sales tax revenue and retail shops will bear a larger portion of the tax levied on their sales, which together will invite strong pressure to end the moratorium, and to establish procedures in which the tax on Internet sales is automatically assessed and paid.

Government Intervention

Taxes are not the only way government affects our lives. For example, government establishes laws that dictate what we can do, what prices we can charge for goods, and what working conditions are and are not acceptable. This second part of the chapter continues the discussion of such issues, which began in Chapter 5. I show how the elasticity concept can help us talk about such interventions and how, using the producer and consumer surplus framework, such interventions can be seen as a combination tax and subsidy that does not show up on government books.

Government Intervention as Implicit Taxation

To see how government intervention in the market can be viewed as a combination tax and subsidy, let's first consider the two types of price controls mentioned in Chapter 5: price ceilings and price floors.

Price Ceilings and Floors As I discussed in Chapter 5, an effective **price ceiling** is *a government-set price below the market equilibrium price*. It is in essence an implicit tax on producers and an implicit subsidy to consumers. Consider the effect of a price ceiling on producer and consumer surplus, shown in Figure 8-4(a).

If the price were at the market equilibrium price, the total surplus would be the combination of the areas A through F. But with an effective price ceiling P_1, the quantity supplied falls from Q_0 to Q_1. The combined producer and consumer surplus is reduced by triangles C and E. The loss of surplus represents those individuals who

Q-6 Demonstrate the effect of an effective price ceiling on producer and consumer surplus when both supply and demand are highly inelastic.

FIGURE 8-4 (A AND B) **Effect of Price Controls on Consumer and Producer Surplus**

Price floors and price ceilings create deadweight loss just as taxes do. In (**a**) we see how a price ceiling, P_1, transfers surplus *D* from producers to consumers. Price ceilings are equivalent to a tax on producers and a subsidy to consumers. In (**b**) we see how a price floor, P_2, transfers surplus *B* from consumers to producers. With either a price floor or a price ceiling, areas C and E represent the welfare loss triangle.

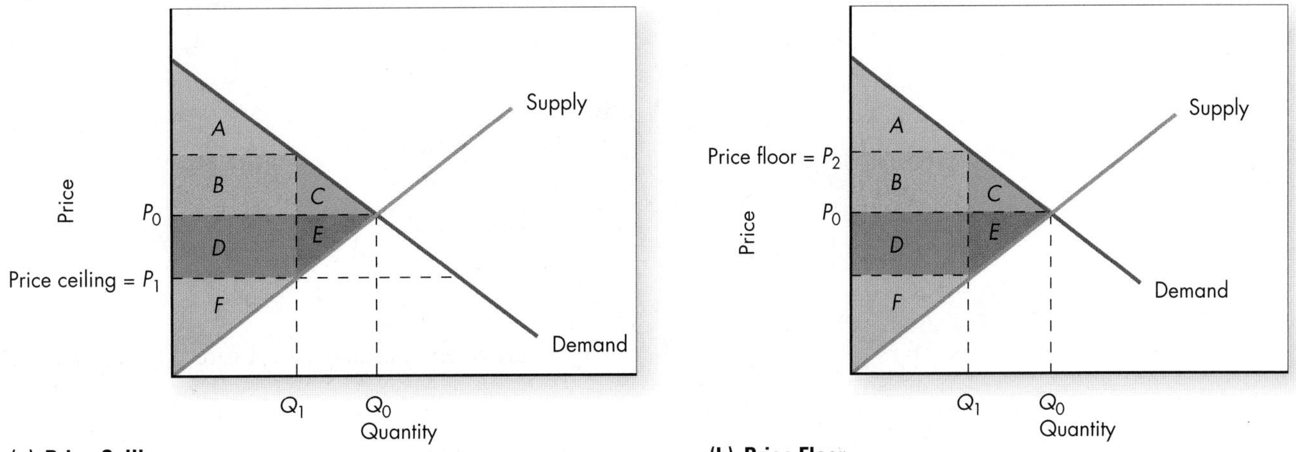

(a) Price Ceiling **(b) Price Floor**

would like to make trades—the individuals represented by the demand and supply curves between Q_1 and Q_0—but cannot do so because of the price ceiling.

A price ceiling is a combination implicit tax on suppliers and implicit subsidy to consumers.

This loss of consumer and producer surplus is identical to the welfare loss from taxation.[4] That is not a coincidence. The price ceiling is a combination implicit tax on suppliers, shown by area *D*, and implicit subsidy to consumers of that same area. It is as if government places a tax on suppliers when they sell the good, and then gives that tax revenue to consumers when they purchase the good.

Price floors have the opposite effect on the distribution of consumer and producer surplus. Effective **price floors**—*government-set prices above equilibrium price*—transfer consumer surplus to producers. They can be seen as a tax on consumers of area *B* and a subsidy to producers of that same area, as shown in Figure 8-4(b). Price floors also impose a deadweight loss, shown by the welfare loss triangle, areas *C* and *E*.

Price ceilings create shortages; taxes do not.

The Difference between Taxes and Price Controls While the effects of taxation and controls are similar, there is an important difference: *Price ceilings create shortages; taxes do not.* The reason is that taxes leave people free to choose how much they want to supply and consume as long as they pay the tax. Taxes create a wedge between the price the consumers pay and the price the suppliers receive just large enough to equate quantity demanded with quantity supplied.

Web Note 8.2
Sin Taxes

Since with price ceilings the price consumers pay is the same as the price suppliers receive, as long as the price ceiling is below equilibrium price, the desired quantity demanded will exceed the quantity supplied. Some method of rationing—limiting the demand or increasing the supply in the case of price ceilings, and limiting the supply or increasing the demand in the case of price floors—must be found. Because so far we have assumed that suppliers can choose how much or how little they want to supply, there are shortages. Such shortages create black markets—markets in which individuals buy or sell illegally. (Taxes also may create black markets if buyers and sellers attempt to evade the tax.)

Rent Seeking, Politics, and Elasticities

If price controls reduce total producer and consumer surplus, why do governments institute them? The answer is that *people care more about their own surplus than they do about total surplus*. As we have seen, price ceilings redistribute surplus from producers to consumers, so if the consumers have the political power, there will be strong pressures to create price ceilings. Alternatively, if the suppliers have the political power, there will be strong pressures to create price floors.

The possibility of transferring surplus from one set of individuals to another causes people to spend time and resources on doing so. For example, if criminals know that $1 million ransoms are commonly paid for executives, it will be worthwhile for them to figure out ways to kidnap executives—which happens in some developing and transitional economies. (That's why all countries state that they will never pay ransoms; however, not all countries follow their stated policies.)

The possibility of kidnapping, in turn, causes executives to hire bodyguards, which in turn causes kidnappers to think of ingenious ways to kidnap (which in turn . . .). The result is that, as one group attempts to appropriate surplus from another group, enormous amounts of resources are spent on activities that benefit no one.

Web Note 8.3
Lobbying for Rent

The same reasoning holds for lobbying government. Individuals have an incentive to spend resources to lobby government to institute policies that increase their own surplus. Others have an incentive to spend money to counteract those lobbying efforts.

[4]As I will discuss below, for price controls the welfare triangle provides a minimum amount of loss in consumer and producer surplus; the actual loss may be greater.

REAL-WORLD APPLICATION

The Excess Burden of a Draft

One way to deal with shortages is to require by law that suppliers supply all the goods demanded at the ceiling price. The military draft is an example. A draft is a law that requires some people to serve a set period in the armed forces at whatever pay the government chooses. It has often been used as a way of meeting the military's need for soldiers. The draft is a price ceiling combined with forced supply.

The effects of a draft are shown in the graph. A draft must be imposed when the wage offered by the army is below equilibrium because the quantity of soldiers demanded exceeds the quantity supplied. In the graph, the offered wage W_0 is below the equilibrium wage W_e. The market answer to the shortage would be to increase the wage to W_e, which would both reduce the quantity of soldiers demanded by government and increase the quantity of people willing to become soldiers. How much the wage would need to be increased to bring about equilibrium depends on the elasticity of supply and demand. If both supply and demand are inelastic, then the pay will need to be increased enormously; if both are elastic, the pay will need to be increased only slightly.

The people who are proposing the draft suspect that both supply and demand are inelastic, in which case the market solution would be very expensive to the government, requiring large increases in taxes. They argue that a draft is much cheaper, and requires lower taxes.

Our supply/demand analysis reveals the fallacy in that reasoning. It's true that with a draft the government does not have to collect as much revenue as it would have to if it raised the wage to a market-clearing wage. But that doesn't mean it's costless because the draft places an implicit hidden tax on the draftees. By paying a lower-than-equilibrium wage and instituting a draft, which requires draftees to serve in the military whether they want to or not, the supply curve effectively becomes the horizontal line at W_0. Individuals drafted are implicitly taxed by the difference between the wage they would have received, W_e, in their alternative private employment and the military wage, W_0. For example, when Elvis Presley was drafted, he gave up a wage of over a million dollars a year for a wage of about $5,000 a year. That is a large implicit tax on him. So, the draft imposes an implicit tax on draftees that doesn't show up on the government books.

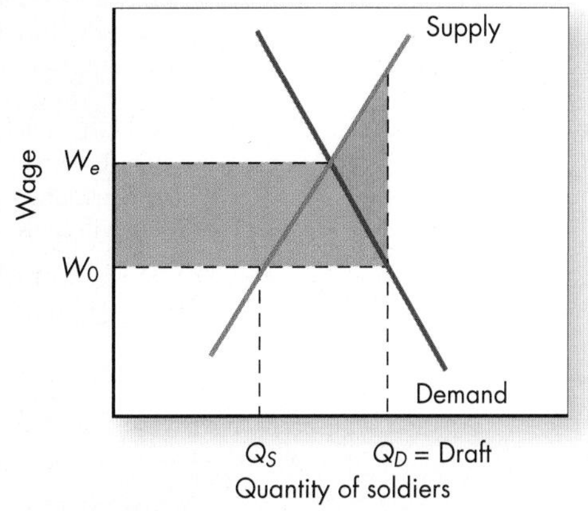

Who, you ask, gets the proceeds of the tax? Those proceeds are implicitly given to those who consume defense services. Specifically, in the graph, the brown shaded area is transferred from suppliers to consumers of national defense. In this case, the welfare loss triangle is the shaded triangle to the right of the market equilibrium. It represents the opportunities that the suppliers lose but that the demanders do not receive.

The welfare loss triangle shows only the minimum loss that the ceiling will create. The analysis assumes that the individuals drafted will be those whose opportunity cost of being drafted is lowest. In fact, that is not the case. The actual amount of loss depends on how the draft selects individuals. If it selects individuals totally randomly (which, in principle, is how drafts are structured), it will draft some into the armed forces who would not consider serving even at the equilibrium wage (Elvis Presley, for example). Thus, the welfare loss is larger for interferences in the market such as the draft than it is for an equivalent tax, although it is difficult to specify how much larger.

Activities designed to transfer surplus from one group to another are called **rent-seeking activities.** Rent-seeking activities require resources, and the net result is unproductive. **Public choice economists**—*economists who integrate an economic analysis of politics with their analysis of the economy*—argue that rent seeking through government is significant, and that much of the transfer of surplus that occurs through government intervention creates an enormous waste of resources. They argue that the taxes and the benefits of government programs offset each other and do not help society significantly, but they

Q-7 Would a firm's research and development expenditures be classified as rent seeking?

FIGURE 8-5 Inelastic Demand and the Incentive to Restrict Supply

When demand is inelastic, increases in productivity that shift the supply curve to the right result in lower revenue for suppliers. Although suppliers gain area *B*, they lose the much larger area *A*. Suppliers have an incentive to restrict supply when demand is inelastic because, by doing so, they will increase their revenues.

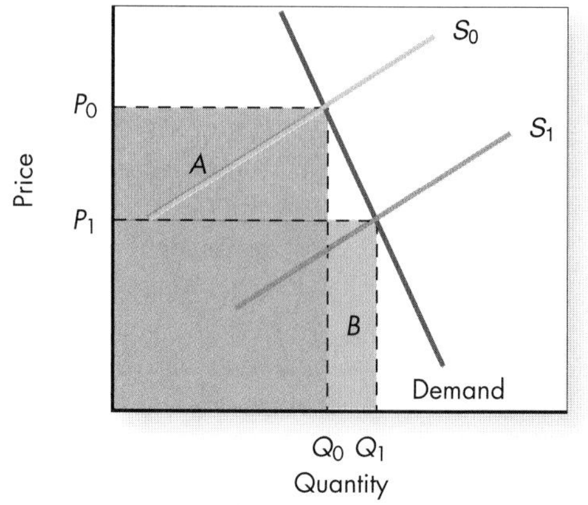

do cost resources. These economists point out that much of the redistribution through government is from one group of the middle class to another group of the middle class.

Inelastic Demand and Incentives to Restrict Supply To understand the rent-seeking process a bit better, let's look more carefully at the incentives that consumers and producers have to lobby government to intervene in the market. We'll begin with suppliers. A classic example of the political pressures to limit supply is found in agricultural markets. Within the past century, new machinery, new methods of farming, and hybrid seeds have increased the productivity of farmers tremendously. You might think that because farmers can now produce more at a lower cost, they'd be better off. But if you think that, you're ignoring the interaction of supply and demand. As advances in productivity increase supply, they do increase the quantity sold, but they also result in lower prices. Farmers sell more but they get less for each unit they sell. Because food is a necessity and has few substitutes, the demand for many agricultural goods is inelastic. Since demand is inelastic, the price declines by a greater proportion than the rise in quantity sold, meaning that total revenue declines and the farmers are actually worse off. The situation is shown in Figure 8-5.

Q-8 How can an increase in productivity harm suppliers?

Because of the increase in supply, price declines from P_0 to P_1 and quantity sold increases from Q_0 to Q_1. The farmer's revenue rises by area *B* but also falls by the larger area *A*. To counteract this trend, farmers have an incentive to get government to restrict supply or create a price floor, thereby raising their revenue. In fact, that's what they did in the 1930s. Farmers then were instrumental in getting the government to establish the Farm Board, a federal agency whose job was to manage productivity of agricultural goods. The benefits of limiting competition are greatest for suppliers when demand is inelastic because price will rise proportionately more than quantity will fall.

Farmers have been very successful in lobbying government to restrict the supply of agricultural goods. Public choice economists have suggested that the reasons for farm groups' success involve the nature of the benefits and costs. The groups that are hurt by agricultural subsidies are large, but the negative effect on each individual in that group is relatively small. Large groups that experience small costs per individual don't provide a strong political opposition to a small group that experiences large gains. This seems to reflect a **general rule of political economy** in a democracy: *When small groups are helped by a government action and large groups are hurt by that same action, the small group tends to lobby far more effectively than the large group; thus, policies tend to reflect the small group's interest, not the interest of the large group.*

The general rule of political economy states that small groups that are significantly affected by a government policy will lobby more effectively than large groups that are equally affected by that same policy.

This simple example provides us with an important insight about how markets work and how the politics of government intervention work. Inelastic demand creates an enormous incentive for suppliers either to pressure government to limit the quantity supplied or to get together and look for other ways to limit the quantity supplied. The more inelastic demand is, the more suppliers have to gain by restricting supply.

Sometimes sellers can get government to limit quantity supplied through licensing; other times they can limit supply by force. A well-placed threat ("If you enter this market, I will blow up your store") is often effective. In some developing economies, such threats are common. What stops existing suppliers from making good on such threats? Government. But the government also creates opportunities for individuals to prevent others from entering the market. Therein lies a central problem of political economy. You need government to see that competition works—to ensure that existing suppliers don't prevent others from entering the market—but government can also be used to prevent competition and protect existing suppliers. Government is part of both the problem and the solution.

WWW Web Note 8.4 Professional Licensing

The central problem of political economy is that you need government to ensure that competition works, but government also can be used to prevent competition.

Inelastic Supplies and Incentives to Restrict Prices Firms aren't the only ones who can lobby government to intervene. Consider consumers. When supply is inelastic, consumers can face significant price increases if their demand increases. Thus, when the supply of a good is inelastic and the demand for that good rises, prices will rise significantly and consumers will scream for price controls.

This is what happened in the New York City rent-control example (price ceilings imposed on apartments) in Chapter 5. During World War II, an influx of short-term workers into New York City increased demand for apartments. Because supply was inelastic, rents rose tremendously. To keep apartments affordable, the city capped rents.

Q-9 If supply is perfectly inelastic, will price controls cause a large shortage?

Such controls are not costless. One of the results of rent control is an ongoing shortage of apartments. As we noted earlier, effective price ceilings will cause a shortage unless suppliers are forced to supply a market-clearing quantity. With the knowledge of elasticities, you also know whether a large or small shortage will develop with a price ceiling and whether a large or small surplus will develop with a price floor.

To make sure you understand how elasticity can tell you the relative size of a surplus or shortage when there are price controls, look at Figure 8-6, which shows three cases of price floors, each with different elasticities of supply and demand.

FIGURE 8-6 (A, B, AND C) Price Floors and Elasticity of Demand and Supply

A price floor above equilibrium market price will always create a surplus. The extent of the surplus created depends on the elasticity of the curves. With elastic curves, a large surplus is created by price controls; with inelastic curves, a small surplus is created. Thus, in (**a**) the intersection of supply and demand occurs where the curves are most elastic and the result is the largest surplus. In (**b**) demand and supply intersect where the demand curve is less elastic and the surplus declines. In (**c**) demand and supply intersect where supply and demand are most inelastic and the result is the smallest surplus.

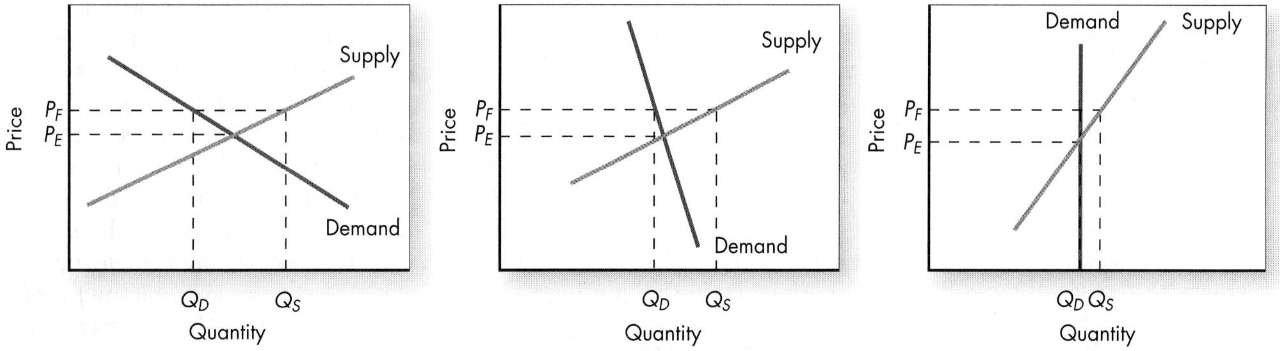

(a) Price Floor with Elastic Supply and Demand

(b) Price Floor with Elastic Supply and Inelastic Demand

(c) Price Floor with Inelastic Supply and Demand

The more elastic supply and demand, the larger the surplus or shortage created by price controls.

As you can see, all three cases create excess supply—surpluses—but the proportional amount of excess supply depends on the elasticity. In Figure 8-6(a), supply and demand intersect at P_E, where they are relatively elastic. There, the price floor, P_F, leads to a relatively large surplus. Figure 8-6(b) represents an intermediate case: The intersection is where supply is elastic and demand is highly inelastic, and a relatively smaller surplus is created by the price floor. In Figure 8-6(c), where the demand and supply curves intersect at relatively inelastic portions, the surplus created by the price floor is relatively small. A good exercise is to go through the same analysis for price ceilings.

The Long-Run/Short-Run Problem of Price Controls Now let's combine our analysis of price controls with another insight from the elasticity chapter—that in the long run, supply tends to be much more elastic than in the short run. This means that price controls will cause only relatively small shortages or surpluses in the short run, but large ones in the long run. Let's consider how this would play out in our rent-control example—see Figure 8-7. In the short run, supply is inelastic; thus, if demand shifts from D_0 to D_1, and the government allows landlords to charge the price they want, they will raise their price significantly, from P_0 to P_1.

In the long run, however, additional apartments will be built and other existing buildings will be converted into apartments. Supply becomes more elastic, rotating from S_0 to S_1. Faced with additional competition, landlords will lower their price to P_2 In the long run, price will fall and the number of apartments rented will increase.

Herein lies another political policy problem. In large part, it is the rise in price that brings in new competitors and increases in output. But if the government imposes price controls, keeping prices at P_0, the long-run incentives for competitors to enter the market will be eliminated. Landlords would not build additional apartments, and the shortage resulting from the price controls ($Q_3 - Q_0$) would remain. The political problems arise because politics generally responds to short-run pressures. In the short run, demand and supply are generally inelastic, making it

Thinking Like a Modern Economist

How to Get Students to Be Responsible

Traditional economic policy focuses on getting the incentives right. If you want people to do less of something, raise its price. Behavioral economists take a broader view of policy and argue that economists' policy should go beyond incentives. For example, they point out that at times being in a state of high emotion "makes" people act irrationally (at least when compared to the choices they would make when not emotional). To demonstrate this tendency, Duke economist Dan Ariely tested people's reactions under different emotional states. In one experiment, students answered the following questions in two different states: a normal state of calm and an emotionally excited state. (To get them into an emotional state, he showed students erotic photos.)

- Could you enjoy sex with someone you hate?
- Would you slip a person a drug to increase the chance that he or she would have sex with you?
- Would you always use a condom?

He found that students in an emotional state were often twice as likely to answer "yes, yes, and no" than when they were calm and collected. Behavioral economists argue that these and similar results suggest that policies designed around rational responses to incentives in situations that involve emotion likely will not work. Instead, policy makers must design policies that take into account people's emotional self, which is far less likely to respond to incentives. Dan Ariely writes, "If we don't teach our young people how to deal with sex when they are half out of their minds, we are not only fooling them; we are fooling ourselves as well."

Policy makers include not only governments. They also include parents. And emotions don't affect just sexual decisions, they affect other high-risk behavior such as driving. To help parents deal with situations where their teenagers' emotions lead them to drive too quickly, Ariely suggests that if parents provide their teenagers with cars, those cars should be equipped with a radio that automatically switches from playing 2Pac to Schumann's Second Symphony (and a phone that automatically calls his or her parents) whenever the student exceeds 65 miles an hour. I leave it to you to figure out if the policy makes sense, and whether some similar plan could be designed to get teenagers to abstain from sex, or at least practice safe sex.

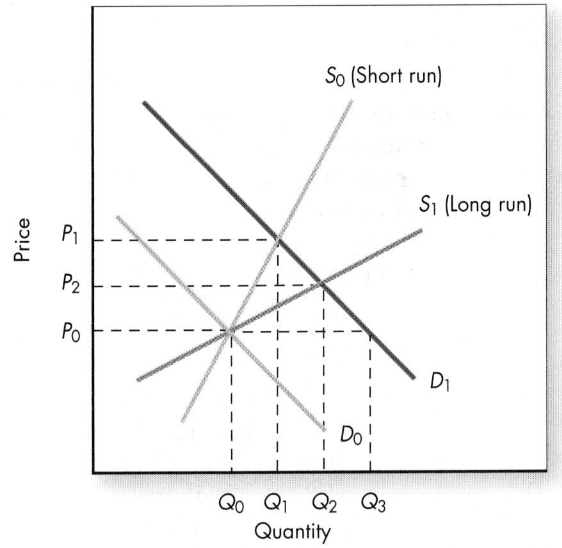

FIGURE 8-7
Long-Run and Short-Run Effects of Price Controls

This exhibit shows how lower long-run elasticities result in smaller price increases when demand increases. Price ceilings keep the long-run supply from lowering price impacts of shocks to housing markets.

look as if the price ceiling will not create significant problems. But in the long run, supply is usually elastic. Price controls that might alleviate the short-run problem cause fewer new apartments to be built. In the long run, the shortage becomes even more severe. As we noted in Chapter 5, the rent-control laws in New York City were initially written to be effective whenever the vacancy rate was below 5 percent, which was the vacancy rate at the time. But the rent controls stopped new apartments from being built and old ones from being maintained. Today, the vacancy rate is less than 4 percent and many rent-controlled apartments have deteriorated. The government's imposition of a price ceiling prevents the market from achieving a more desirable long-run equilibrium, at which output has expanded and price has fallen from its initially high level.

Q-10 Why do price controls tend to create ongoing shortages or surpluses in the long run?

Conclusion

Government is a part of our life and, therefore, so too are taxes. Economic theory doesn't say government should or shouldn't play any particular role in the economy or what the taxes should be. Those decisions depend on normative judgments and the relevant costs and benefits. What economic theory does is to help point out the costs and benefits. For example, in the case of taxes, economists can show that the cost of taxation in terms of lost surplus is independent of who physically pays the tax.

In thinking about taxes and government involvement, the public often perceives economic theory and economists as suggesting the best policy is one of laissez-faire, or government noninvolvement in the economy. Many economists do suggest a laissez-faire policy, but that suggestion is based on empirical observations of government's role in the past, not on economic theory.

Economists' suggestions for laissez-faire policy are based on empirical observations of government's role in the past, not on economic theory.

Still, economists as a group generally favor less government involvement than does the general public. I suspect this is because economists are taught to look below the surface at the long-run effect of government actions. They've discovered that the effects often aren't the intended effects, and that programs frequently have long-run consequences that make the problems worse, not better. Economists, both liberal and conservative, speak in the voice of reason: "Look at all the costs; look at all the benefits. Then decide whether government should or should not intervene." The supply/demand framework and the elasticity concept are extremely useful tools in making those assessments.

Summary

- Equilibrium maximizes the combination of consumer surplus and producer surplus. Consumer surplus is the net benefit a consumer gets from purchasing a good, while producer surplus is the net benefit a producer gets from selling a good.
- Government taxes firms and individuals in order to carry out its six roles in a market economy. A government will maximize benefits to society only if it chooses to tax when the marginal benefit of the goods and services provided with the revenue of the tax exceeds the cost of the tax.
- Taxes create a loss of consumer and producer surplus known as deadweight loss, which graphically is represented by the welfare loss triangle.
- The cost of taxation to consumers and producers includes the actual tax paid, the deadweight loss, and the costs of administering the tax.
- Who bears the burden of the tax depends on the relative elasticities of demand and supply. The more inelastic one's relative supply and demand, the larger the burden of the tax one will bear.
- Price ceilings and price floors, like taxes, result in loss of consumer and producer surplus.
- Price ceilings transfer producer surplus to consumers and therefore are equivalent to a tax on producers and a subsidy to consumers. Price floors have the opposite effect; they are a tax on consumers and a subsidy to producers.
- Rent-seeking activities are designed to transfer surplus from one group to another. Producers facing inelastic demand for their product will benefit more from rent-seeking activities than producers facing elastic demand. Consumers facing inelastic supply for a product benefit more from rent-seeking activities such as lobbying for price ceilings than consumers facing an elastic supply.
- The more elastic supply and/or demand is, the greater the surplus is with an effective price floor and the greater the shortage is with an effective price ceiling.
- The general rule of political economy is that policies tend to reflect small groups' interests, not the interests of large groups.
- The negative aspects of price controls worsen as the length of time considered rises because elasticity rises as time progresses.

Key Terms

consumer surplus *(179)*
deadweight loss *(182)*
excise tax *(183)*
general rule of political economy *(190)*
price ceiling *(187)*
price floor *(188)*
producer surplus *(180)*
public choice economist *(189)*
rent-seeking activity *(189)*
welfare loss triangle *(182)*

Questions and Exercises

connect ECONOMICS

1. Explain why the combination of consumer and producer surplus is not maximized if there is either excess demand or supply. LO1
2. Use economic reasoning to explain why nearly every purchase you make provides you with consumer surplus. LO1
3. How is elasticity related to the revenue from a sales tax? LO2
4. Minneapolis Federal Reserve Bank economist Edward Prescott estimates the elasticity of the U.S. labor supply to be 3. Given this elasticity, what would be the impact of funding the Social Security program with tax increases

on the number of hours worked and on the amount of taxes collected to fund Social Security? LO2

5. The president of Lebanon Valley College proposed the following tuition program: provide a 50 percent tuition reduction for those graduating in the top 10 percent of their high school class, 33 percent reduction for those in the top 20 percent, and 25 percent reduction for those in the top 30 percent. All scholarship recipients were also required to maintain a minimum GPA. The comptroller estimated that the elasticity of demand for these students was greater than 1. (Difficult)
   a. Economics Professor Paul Heise recommended that the president institute the program, arguing that it would increase revenues. What was his argument?
   b. Why did the program distinguish among top-performing students?
   c. Why didn't the president reduce tuition for all students? LO2
6. Demonstrate the welfare loss of
   a. A restriction on output when supply is perfectly elastic.
   b. A tax *t* placed on suppliers.
   c. A subsidy *s* given to suppliers.
   d. A restriction on output when demand is perfectly elastic. LO2
7. Use the graph below that shows the effect of a $4 per-unit tax on suppliers to answer the following questions:

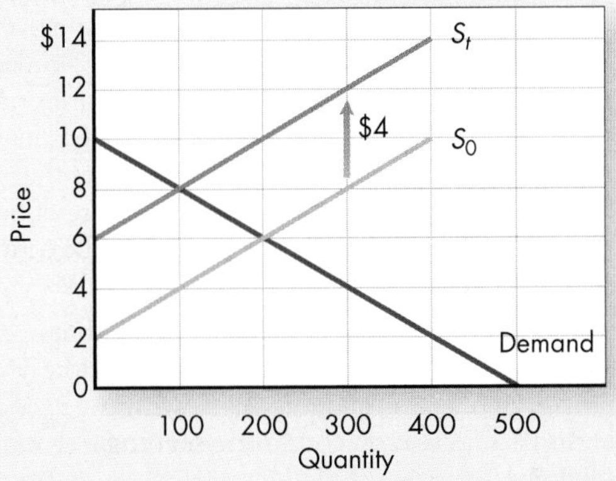

   a. What are equilibrium price and quantity before the tax? After the tax?
   b. What is producer surplus when the market is in equilibrium before the tax? After the tax?
   c. What is consumer surplus when the market is in equilibrium before the tax? After the tax?
   d. What is total tax revenue collected after the tax is implemented? LO1, LO2
8. If the federal government wanted to tax a good and suppliers were strong lobbyists, but consumers were not, would government prefer supply or demand to be more inelastic? Why? LO3
9. What types of goods would you recommend that the government tax if it wants the tax to result in no welfare loss? Name a few examples. LO3
10. Suppose demand for cigarettes is inelastic and the supply of cigarettes is elastic. Who would bear the larger share of the burden of a tax placed on cigarettes? LO3
11. If the demand for a good is perfectly elastic and the supply is elastic, who will bear the larger share of the burden of a tax on the good where the tax is paid by consumers? LO3
12. What percent of a tax will the demander pay if price elasticity of supply is 0.3 and price elasticity of demand is 0.7? What percent will the supplier pay? LO3
13. Which good would an economist normally recommend taxing if government wanted to minimize welfare loss and maximize revenue: a good with an elastic or inelastic supply? Why? LO3
14. Should tenants who rent apartments worry that increases in property taxes will increase their rent? Does your answer change when considering the long run? LO3
15. In 2004, the University of California education system drastically cut enrollment due to significant state budget cuts and asked 7,600 applicants to defer enrollment for two years after completing two years at a community college. Tuition costs remained fixed by the state. (Difficult)
   a. Demonstrate the situation described in 2004 with supply and demand curves, carefully labeling any excess supply or demand for college admissions.
   b. What is the market solution to the excess demand for college?
   c. What is a possible reason the market solution was not pursued? LO3
16. Calculate the percent of the tax borne by the demander and supplier in each of the following cases:
   a. $E_D = 0.3, E_S = 1.2$
   b. $E_D = 3, E_S = 2$
   c. $E_D = 0.5, E_S = 1$
   d. $E_D = 0.5, E_S = 0.5$
   e. Summarize your findings regarding relative elasticity and tax burden. LO3
17. In which case would the shortage resulting from a price ceiling be greater: when supply is inelastic or elastic? Explain your answer. LO4
18. Demonstrate how a price floor is like a tax on consumers and a subsidy to suppliers. Label the following: tax on consumers, transfer of surplus to suppliers, and welfare loss.
   a. Who gets the revenue in the case of a tax?
   b. Who gets the revenue in the case of a price floor? LO4
19. Suppose government imposed a minimum wage above equilibrium wage.
   a. Assuming nothing else changes, what do you expect to happen to the resulting shortage of jobs as time progresses?
   b. What do you expect to happen to the producer surplus transferred to minimum wage earners as time progresses? LO4

20. Use the graph below to answer the following questions:

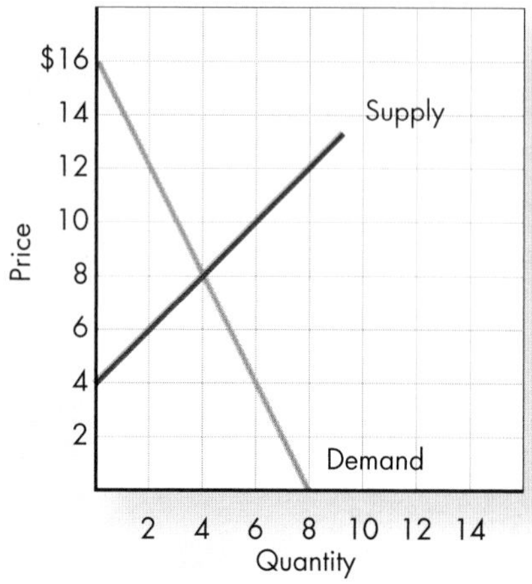

   a. What are equilibrium price and quantity?
   b. What is producer surplus when the market is in equilibrium?
   c. What is consumer surplus when the market is in equilibrium?
   d. If price were held at $12 a unit, what are consumer and producer surplus? LO1, LO4

21. A political leader comes to you and wonders from whom she will get the most complaints if she institutes a price ceiling when demand is inelastic and supply is elastic.
   a. How do you respond?
   b. Demonstrate why your answer is correct. LO4

22. Define rent seeking. Do firms have a greater incentive to engage in rent-seeking behavior when demand is elastic or when it is inelastic? LO5

23. What is the general rule of political economy? Give an example from the real world. LO6

Questions from Alternative Perspectives

1. The quotation from Calvin Coolidge at the beginning of the chapter equates taxation to robbery.
   a. Is that a reasonable position to take?
   b. What alternatives to taxation could a country consider to collect the revenue it needs to operate? (Austrian)
2. The chapter frames the issue of the effects of taxation in terms of its effects on producer and consumer surplus.
   a. What does that framework leave out of the analysis?
   b. How might one frame the analysis differently?
   c. If women are discriminated against and receive less income than men on average, do they get less weight than men in consumer surplus? (Feminist)
3. Do Pierre, a software engineer earning $200,000 a year, and Sally, a single mother whose welfare benefits are about to expire, get equal weight in the measure of consumer surplus? (Institutionalist)
4. The elasticity of the supply of labor in part determines who bears the burden of Social Security taxes. Those taxes are levied in matching 6.2 percent shares on workers' wages and wages paid out by employers. Economists treat the two shares as one tax and then consider two cases. In competitive labor markets, the supply of labor is taken to be totally inelastic. In noncompetitive labor markets, workers' bargaining power matches that of employers and the supply and demand curves for labor have similar elasticities. Who bears the burden of Social Security taxes in each case? Illustrate your answer with two labor market diagrams. (Hint: Empirical evidence indicates that in the noncompetitive case, the employer's share of Social Security taxes is passed on to consumers in the form of higher prices.) (Radical)
5. God sees all individuals as equal, and that what one does to the least of his children, one does to all. How does that approach to thinking about issues fit with the economic analysis that focuses on consumer and producer surplus? (Religious)

Issues to Ponder

1. Many of the buildings in Paris have Mansard roofs, such as those shown in the photograph on page 182.
   a. What property tax structure would bring this about?
   b. Could you imagine a change in the property tax that would reduce the number of Mansard roofs built?
   c. Can you think of other design elements that reflect tax structure? LO2
2. Because of the negative incentive effect that taxes have on goods with elastic supply, in the late 1980s Margaret Thatcher (then prime minister of Great Britain) changed the property tax to a poll tax (a tax at a set rate that every individual must pay).
   a. Show why the poll tax is preferable to a property tax in terms of consumer and producer surplus.
   b. What do you think the real-life consequences of the poll tax were? LO2

3. Can you suggest a tax system that led to this building style, which was common in old Eastern European cities? (Difficult) LO3

4. The Pure Food and Drug Act of 1906 is known as "Dr. Wiley's Law." It is generally regarded by non-economic historians as representing the triumph of consumer interests over producer interests. (Difficult)
   a. Why might an economist likely be somewhat wary of this interpretation?
   b. What evidence would a skeptical economist likely look for to determine the motives behind the passage of this law?
   c. What would be the significance of the fact that the Pure Food and Drug Act was passed in 1906, right when urbanization and technological change were fostering new products that competed significantly with existing producers' interests? LO6

Answers to Margin Questions

1. The combination of consumer and producer surplus will increase since there will be no lost surplus at the equilibrium price. *(180)*
2. Welfare loss when supply is highly elastic and demand is highly inelastic is shown by the shaded triangle in the graph below. The supply curve shifts up by the amount of the tax. Since equilibrium quantity changes very little, from Q_0 to Q_1, welfare loss is very small. *(182)*

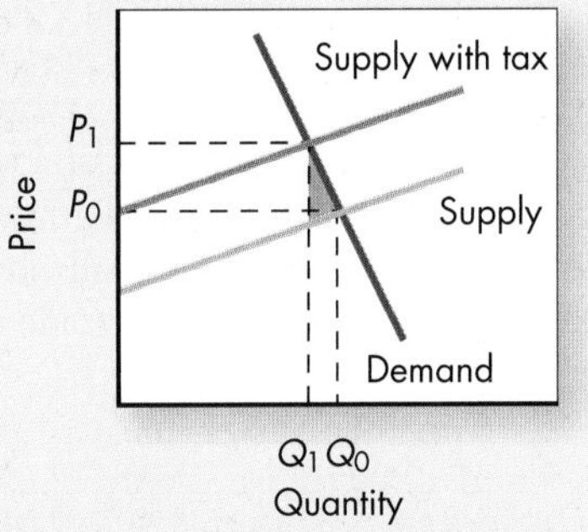

3. If a person's demand is highly elastic, he would bear a small percentage of the burden of a tax. *(184)*
4. The percentage of the tax borne by the consumer equals price elasticity of supply divided by the sum of the price elasticities of demand and supply, or

$$\frac{1.8}{(0.2 + 1.8)} = 0.9.$$

   The consumer pays $90 of the tax. *(185)*
5. If the entire amount of the tax were levied on employees, their before-tax income would rise because employers would have to compensate their employees for the increased taxes they would have to physically pay. The burden of the taxation does not depend on who pays the tax. It depends on relative elasticities. *(185)*
6. The effect of a price ceiling below equilibrium price when demand and supply are inelastic is shown in the following graph. Quantity demanded exceeds quantity supplied, but because demand and supply are both inelastic, the shortage is not big. Likewise, the welfare loss triangle, shown by the shaded area in the graph, is not large. *(187)*

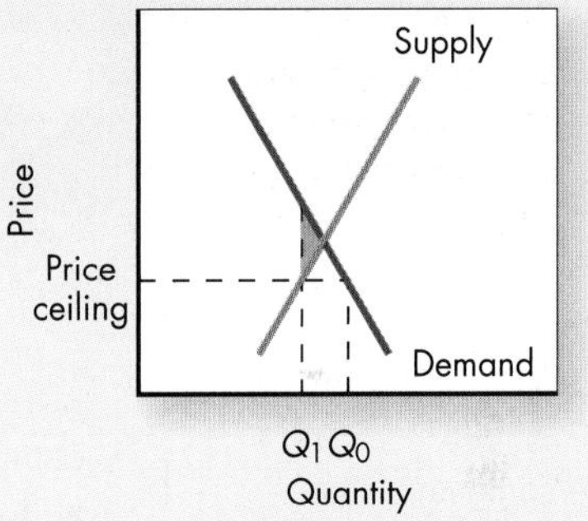

7. No. Research and development expenditures are an effort to increase technology to either lower production costs or discover a new product that can be marketed. If the firm can get a patent on that new product, the firm will have a monopoly and be able to restrict supply, transferring surplus from consumers to itself, but this is not rent seeking. Rent-seeking activities are designed to transfer surplus from one group to another given current technology. They are unproductive. *(189)*
8. If suppliers are selling a product for which demand is inelastic, increases in productivity would result in a drop in price that would be proportionately greater than the rise in equilibrium quantity. Total revenue would decline for suppliers. *(190)*
9. With a perfectly inelastic supply, price controls will cause a smaller shortage compared to other supply elasticities. *(191)*
10. Price controls tend to create ongoing shortages and surpluses in the long run because they prevent market forces from working. *(193)*

International Trade Policy, Comparative Advantage, and Outsourcing

One of the purest fallacies is that trade follows the flag. Trade follows the lowest price current. If a dealer in any colony wished to buy Union Jacks, he would order them from Britain's worst foe if he could save a sixpence.

—***Andrew Carnegie***

AFTER READING THIS CHAPTER, YOU SHOULD BE ABLE TO:

1. Summarize some important data of trade.
2. Explain the principle of comparative advantage.
3. List three determinants of the terms of trade.
4. Explain why economists' and laypeople's views of trade differ.
5. Distinguish between inherent and transferable comparative advantages.
6. Explain three policies countries use to restrict trade.
7. Summarize why economists generally oppose trade restrictions.
8. Explain how free trade associations both help and hinder international trade.

If economists had a mantra, it would be "Trade is good." Trade allows specialization and division of labor and thereby promotes economic growth. Consistent with that mantra, most economists oppose trade restrictions. Not everyone agrees with economists; almost every day we hear calls from some sector of the economy to restrict foreign imports to save U.S. jobs and protect U.S. workers from unfair competition. In this chapter we consider why economists generally favor free trade, and why, despite what economists tell them, countries impose trade restrictions.

Patterns of Trade

Before I consider these issues, let's look at some numbers to get a sense of the nature and dimensions of international trade.

Increasing but Fluctuating World Trade

In 1928, total world trade was about $635 billion (in today's dollars). U.S. gross domestic product (GDP) was about $1,060 billion, so world trade as a percentage of U.S. GDP was almost 60 percent. In 1935, that ratio had fallen to less than 30 percent. In 1950 it was 20 percent. Then it started rising. Today it is about 280 percent, with world trade amounting to about $41 trillion. As you can see, international trade has been growing, but with significant fluctuations in that growth. Sometimes international trade has grown rapidly; at other times it has grown slowly or has even fallen.

In part, fluctuations in world trade result from fluctuations in world output. When output rises, international trade rises; when output falls, international trade falls. Fluctuations in world trade are also in part explained by trade restrictions that countries have imposed from time to time. For example, decreases in world income during the Depression of the 1930s caused a large decrease in trade, but that decrease was exacerbated by a worldwide increase in trade restrictions.

Differences in the Importance of Trade

The importance of international trade to countries' economies differs widely, as we can see in the table below, which presents the importance of the shares of exports—the value of goods and services sold abroad—and imports—the value of goods and services purchased abroad—for various countries.

	Total Output*	Export Ratio	Import Ratio
Netherlands	$ 754	74%	66%
Germany	3,297	45	40
Canada	1,326	38	34
Italy	2,107	28	29
France	2,562	27	28
United Kingdom	3,280	29	33
Japan	4,377	14	13
United States	14,264	11	16

*Numbers in billions.

Source: *World Development Indicators*, 2008, The World Bank.

Among the countries listed, the Netherlands has the highest amount of exports compared to total output; the United States has the lowest.

The Netherlands' imports are also the highest as a percentage of total output. Japan's are the lowest. The relationship between a country's imports and its exports is no coincidence. For most countries, imports and exports roughly equal one another, though in any particular year that equality can be rough indeed. For the United States in recent years, imports have generally significantly exceeded exports. But that situation can't continue forever, as I'll discuss.

Total trade figures provide us with only part of the international trade picture. We must also look at what types of goods are traded and with whom that trade is conducted.

What and with Whom the United States Trades

The majority of U.S. exports and imports involve significant amounts of manufactured goods. This isn't unusual, since much of international trade is in manufactured goods.

Figure 9-1 shows the regions with which the United States trades. Exports to Canada and Mexico made up the largest percentage of total U.S. exports to individual countries in 2008. The largest regions to whom the U.S. exports are the Pacific Rim and the European Union. Countries from which the United States imports major quantities include Canada and Mexico and the regions of the European Union and the Pacific Rim. Thus, the countries we export to are also the countries we import from.

The primary trading partners of the United States are Canada, Mexico, the European Union, and the Pacific Rim countries.

The Changing Nature of Trade The nature of trade is continually changing, both in terms of the countries with which the United States trades and the goods and services traded. For example, U.S. imports from China, India, and other East Asian countries have increased substantially in recent years. In the late 1980s goods from China accounted for 2.5 percent of all U.S. merchandise imports. Today they account for 16 percent. Imports from India have increased tenfold over that time—from 0.1 percent to 1 percent of all goods imported.

FIGURE 9-1 (A AND B) U.S. Exports and Imports by Region

Major regions that trade with the United States include Canada, Mexico, the European Union, and the Pacific Rim.

Source: FT900 U.S. International Trade in Goods and Services 2009, U.S. Census Bureau (www.census.gov).

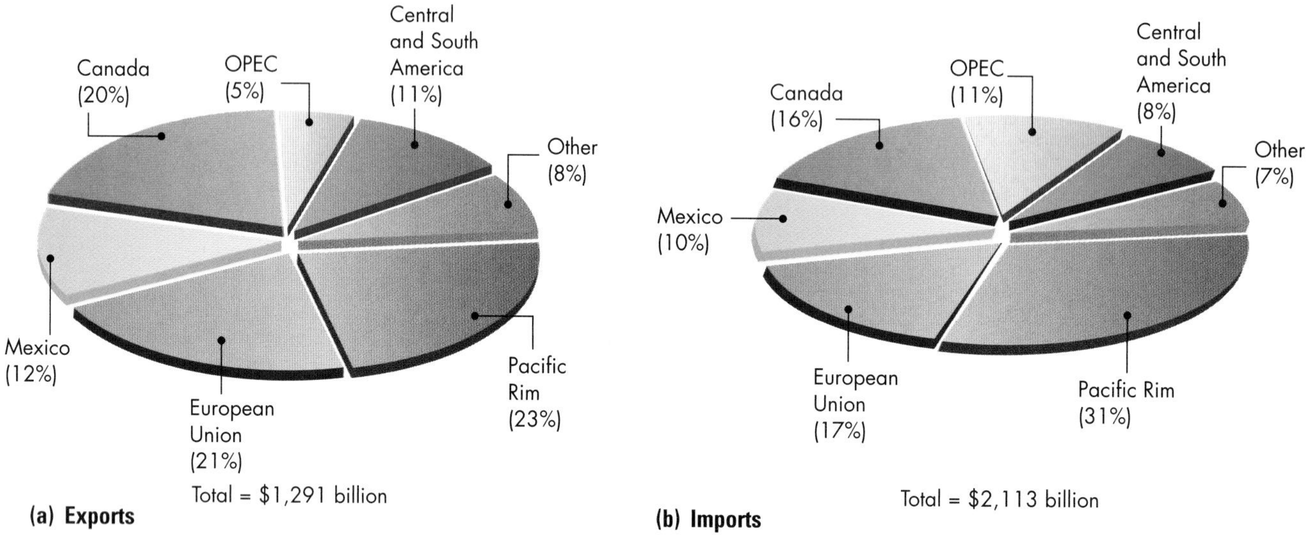

Q-1 How has the nature of U.S. imports from China changed in recent years?

The kind of goods and services the United States imports also has changed. Thirty years ago, the goods the United States imported from China and India were primarily basic manufacturing goods and raw commodities. Technologically advanced goods were produced here in the United States. That is changing. Today we are importing high-tech manufactured goods from these countries, and they are even developing their own new products that require significant research and development.

The change in the nature of the goods that a country produces and exports up the technological ladder is typical for developing countries. It characterized Japan, Korea, and Singapore in the post–World War II era, and today characterizes China and India. As this movement up the technological ladder occurs, foreign companies that had been subcontractors for U.S. companies become direct competitors of the U.S. companies. For example, the automaker Kia and the electronics producer Samsung have developed into major global firms, and in the future you can expect numerous Chinese companies to become household names.

We can expect the nature of trade to change even more in the future as numerous technological changes in telecommunications continue to reduce the cost of both voice and data communications throughout the world and expand the range of services that can be provided by foreign countries. Production no longer needs to occur in the geographic area where the goods are consumed. For example, financial accounting, compositing (typesetting) of texts, and research can now be done almost anywhere, and transferred with the click of a mouse. Even the customer service calls for a U.S. company can be answered almost anywhere at the same phone costs as if they were answered in the United States. (India, which has a sizeable well-educated, English-speaking population, even trains its employees to speak with a Midwest U.S. accent to make it less apparent to customers that the call is being answered in India.) This trade in services is what the press often refers to as *outsourcing*, but it is important to remember that outsourcing is simply a description of some aspects of trade.

Is Chinese and Indian Outsourcing Different From Previous Outsourcing?

There has been a lot of discussion about outsourcing to China and India recently, and thus it is worthwhile to consider what is, and what is not, different about trade with China and India. First, what isn't new is trade. Manufacturers have used overseas suppliers for years. What is different about outsourcing to China and India today compared to earlier outsourcing to Japan, Singapore, and Korea in the 1980s and 1990s is the potential size of that outsourcing. China and India have a combined population of 2.5 billion people, a sizable number of whom are well educated and willing to work for much lower wages than U.S. workers. As technology opens up more areas to trade, and as India and China move up the technology chain, U.S.-based firms will likely experience much more competition than they have experienced to date. How U.S. companies deal with this competition will likely be the defining economic policy issue for the next decade. If they develop new technologies and new industries in which the United States has comparative advantages, then the United States' future can be bright. If they don't, significant, difficult adjustment will need to occur.

How U.S. companies deal with new high-tech competition will likely be the defining economic policy issue for the next decade.

The rising competitiveness of Asian economies with the U.S. economy is manifested in the large deficit the United States is running on its **balance of trade**—*the difference between the value of exports and the value of imports*—as is shown in Figure 9-2(a). A trade deficit means that U.S. imports exceed U.S. exports. The United States has been running trade deficits since the 1970s, and in 2008 the U.S. trade deficit reached over $820 billion. The trade deficit looks a little less threatening when considered as a percentage of GDP, as is shown in Figure 9-2(b), but it is still of concern. This means that the United States is consuming a lot more than it is producing, and paying for current consumption with promises to pay in the future.

FIGURE 9-2 (A AND B) The U.S. Trade Balance

The United States has been running trade deficits since the 1970s. Panel (**a**) shows the trade deficit in billions of dollars. As (**b**) shows, the trade deficit looks slightly less threatening when considered as a percent of GDP.

Source: U.S. Department of Commerce: Bureau of Economic Analysis (www.bea.gov).

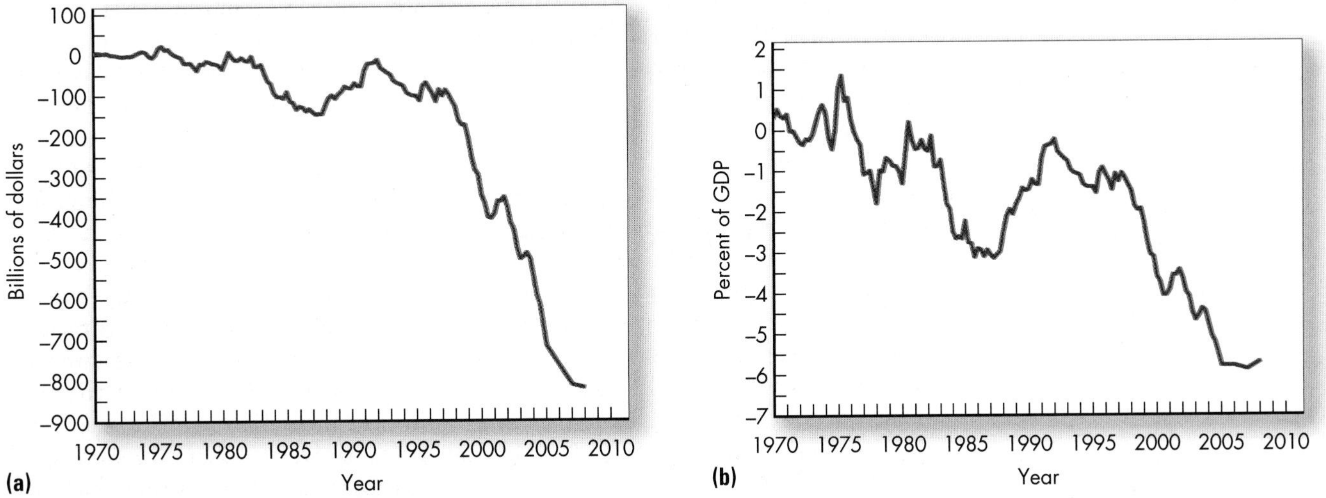

ADDED DIMENSION

International Issues in Perspective

Since the 1970s, international issues have become increasingly important for the U.S. economy. That statement would be correct even if the reference period went back as far as the late 1800s. From the late 1800s through the first 40 years of the 1900s, the United States was in an isolationist period in which the country turned inward in both economic and foreign policies.

The statement would not be correct if the reference period were earlier than the late 1800s. In the 1600s, 1700s, and most of the 1800s, international trade was vital to the American economy—even more vital than now. The American nation grew from colonial possessions of England, France, and Spain. These "new world" colonial possessions were valued for their gold, agricultural produce, and natural resources. From a European standpoint, international trade was the colonies' reason for being.*

A large portion of the U.S. government's income during much of the 1800s came from tariffs. Our technology was imported from abroad, and international issues played a central role in wars fought here. (Many historians believe that the most important cause of the U.S. Civil War was the difference of views about tariffs on manufactured goods. The South opposed them because it wanted cheap manufactured goods, while the North favored them because it wanted to protect its manufacturing industries.) Up until the 1900s, no one would have studied the U.S. economy independently of international issues. Not only was there significant international trade; there was also significant immigration. The United States is a country of immigrants.

Only in the late 1800s did the United States adopt an isolationist philosophy in both politics and trade. So in reference to that isolationist period, the U.S. economy has become more integrated with the world economy. However, in a broader historical perspective, that isolationist period was an anomaly, and today's economy is simply returning international issues to the key role they've usually played.

Another important insight is that international trade has social and cultural dimensions. While much of the chapter deals with specifically economic issues, we must also remember the cultural and social implications of trade.

Let's consider an example from history. In the Middle Ages, Greek ideas and philosophy were lost to Europe when hordes of barbarians swept over the continent. These ideas and that philosophy were rediscovered in the Renaissance only as a by-product of trade between the Italian merchant cities and the Middle East. (The Greek ideas that had spread to the Middle East were protected from European upheavals.) *Renaissance* means rebirth: a rebirth in Europe of Greek learning. Many of our traditions and sensibilities are based on those of the Renaissance, and that Renaissance was caused, or at least significantly influenced, by international trade. Had there been no trade, our entire philosophy of life might have been different.

In economics courses we do not focus on these broader cultural issues but instead focus on relatively technical issues such as the reasons for trade and the implications of tariffs. But keep in the back of your mind these broader implications as you go through the various components of international economics. They add a dimension to the story that otherwise might be forgotten.

*The Native American standpoint was, I suspect, somewhat different.

Debtor and Creditor Nations

Running a trade deficit isn't necessarily bad.

Running a trade deficit isn't necessarily bad. In fact, while you're doing it, it's rather nice. If you were a country, you probably would be running a trade deficit now since, most likely, you're consuming (importing) more than you're producing (exporting). How can you do that? By living off past savings, getting support from your parents or a spouse, or borrowing.

Countries have the same options. They can live off foreign aid, past savings, or loans. The U.S. economy is currently financing its trade deficit by selling off assets—financial assets such as stocks and bonds, or real assets such as real estate and corporations. Since the assets of the United States total many trillions of dollars, it can continue to run trade deficits of a similar size for years to come, but in doing so it is reducing its wealth each year.

The United States has not always run a trade deficit. Following World War II it ran trade surpluses—an excess of exports over imports—with other countries, so it was an international lender. Thus, it acquired large amounts of foreign assets. Because of the large trade deficits the United States has run since the 1980s, now the United States is a large debtor nation. The United States has borrowed more from abroad than it has lent abroad.

Q-2 Will a debtor nation necessarily be running a trade deficit?

As the United States has gone from being a large creditor nation to being the world's biggest debtor, international considerations have been forced on the nation. The cushion of being a creditor—of having a flow of interest income—has been replaced by the trials of being a debtor and having to pay out interest every year without currently getting anything for it when they pay that interest. Eventually, the United States will have to deal with this issue. Before we consider how it might do so, let's review the principle of comparative advantage, which is central to economists' understanding of trade.

The Principle of Comparative Advantage

The reason two countries trade is that trade can make both countries better off. The reason that this is true is the principle of comparative advantage to which you were introduced in Chapter 2. It is, however, important enough to warrant an in-depth review. The basic idea of the principle of **comparative advantage** is that *as long as the relative opportunity costs of producing goods (what must be given up in one good in order to get another good) differ among countries, then there are potential gains from trade*. Let's review this principle by considering the story of I.T., an imaginary international trader, who convinces two countries to enter into trades by giving both countries some of the advantages of trade; he keeps the rest for himself.

The principle of comparative advantage states that as long as the relative opportunity costs of producing goods differ among countries, then there are potential gains from trade.

The Gains from Trade

Here's the situation. On his trips to the United States and Saudi Arabia, I.T. noticed that the two countries did not trade. He also noticed that the opportunity cost of producing a ton of food in Saudi Arabia was 10 barrels of oil and that the opportunity cost for the United States of producing a ton of food was 1/10 of a barrel of oil. At the time, the United States' production was 60 barrels of oil and 400 tons of food, while Saudi Arabia's production was 400 barrels of oil and 60 tons of food.

Q-3 If the opportunity cost of oil for food were the same for both the United States and Saudi Arabia, what should I.T. do?

The choices for the United States can be seen in Figure 9-3(a), and the choices for Saudi Arabia can be seen in Figure 9-3(b). The tables give the numerical choices and the figures translate those numerical choices into graphs.

These graphs represent the two countries' production possibility curves. Each combination of numbers in the table corresponds to a point on the curve. For example, point *B* in each graph corresponds to the entries in row *B*, columns 2 and 3, in the relevant table.

Let's assume that the United States has chosen point C (production of 60 barrels of oil and 400 tons of food) and Saudi Arabia has chosen point *D* (production of 400 barrels of oil and 60 tons of food).

FIGURE 9-3 (A AND B) Comparative Advantage: The United States and Saudi Arabia

Looking at tables (a) and (b), you can see that if Saudi Arabia devotes all its resources to oil, it can produce 1,000 barrels of oil, but if it devotes all of its resources to food, it can produce only 100 tons of food. For the United States, the story is the opposite: Devoting all of its resources to oil, the United States can only produce 100 barrels of oil—10 times less than Saudi Arabia—but if it devotes all of its resources to food, it can produce 1,000 tons of food—10 times more than Saudi Arabia. Assuming resources are comparable, Saudi Arabia has a comparative advantage in the production of oil, and the United States has a comparative advantage in the production of food. The information in the tables is presented graphically below each table. These are the countries' production possibility curves. Each point on each country's curve corresponds to a row on that country's table.

Percentage of Resources Devoted to Oil	Oil Produced (barrels)	Food Produced (tons)	Row
100%	100	0	*A*
80	80	200	*B*
60	60	400	*C*
40	40	600	*D*
20	20	800	*E*
0	0	1,000	*F*

United States' Production Possibility Table

Percentage of Resources Devoted to Oil	Oil Produced (barrels)	Food Produced (tons)	Row
100%	1,000	0	*A*
80	800	20	*B*
60	600	40	*C*
40	400	60	*D*
20	200	80	*E*
0	0	100	*F*

Saudi Arabia's Production Possibility Table

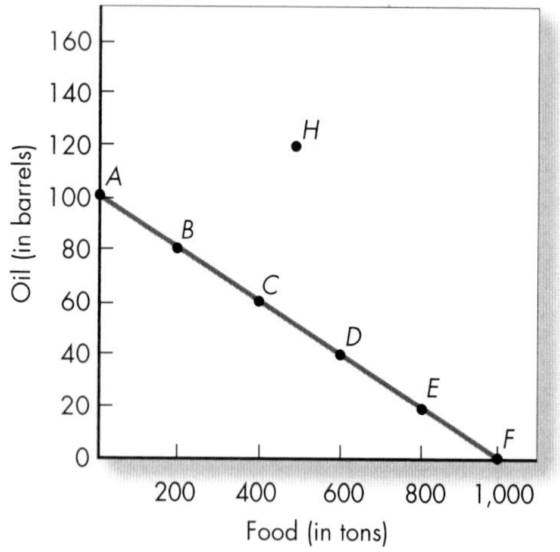

(a) United States' Production Possibility Curve

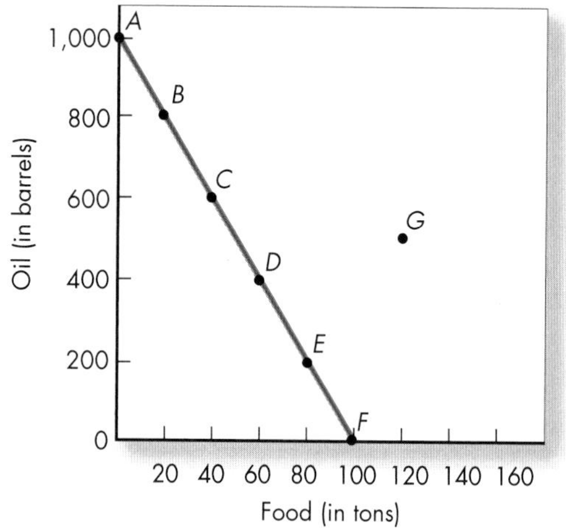

(b) Saudi Arabia's Production Possibility Curve

Now I.T., who understands the principle of comparative advantage, comes along and offers the following deal to the United States:

> If you produce 1,000 tons of food and no oil (point *F* in Figure 9-3(a)) and give me 500 tons of food while keeping 500 tons for yourself, I'll guarantee you 120 barrels of oil, double the amount you're now getting. I'll put you on point *H*, which is totally above your current production possibility curve. You'll get more oil and have more food. It's an offer you can't refuse.

I.T. then flies off to Saudi Arabia, to whom he makes the following offer:

> If you produce 1,000 barrels of oil and no food (point *A* in Figure 9-3(b)) and give me 500 barrels of oil while keeping 500 barrels for yourself, I guarantee you 120 tons of food, double the amount of food you're now getting. I'll put you on

point G, which is totally above your current production possibility curve. You'll get more oil and more food. It's an offer you can't refuse.

Both countries accept; they'd be foolish not to. So the two countries' final consumption positions are as follows:

	Oil (barrels)	Food (tons)
Total production	1,000	1,000
U.S. consumption	120	500
U.S. gain in consumption	+60	+100
Saudi consumption	500	120
Saudi gain in consumption	+100	+60
I.T.'s profit	380	380

For arranging the trade, I.T. makes a handsome profit of 380 tons of food and 380 barrels of oil. I.T. has become rich because he understands the principle of comparative advantage.

Now obviously this hypothetical example significantly overemphasizes the gains a trader makes. Generally the person arranging the trade must compete with other traders and offer both countries a better deal than the one presented here. But the person who first recognizes a trading opportunity often makes a sizable fortune. The second and third persons who recognize the opportunity make smaller fortunes. Once the insight is generally recognized, the possibility of making a fortune is gone. Traders still make their normal returns, but the instantaneous fortunes are not to be made without new insight. In the long run, benefits of trade go to the producers and consumers in the trading countries, not the traders.

Dividing Up the Gains from Trade

As the above story suggests, when countries avail themselves of comparative advantage, there are high gains of trade to be made. Who gets these gains is unclear. The principle of comparative advantage doesn't determine how those gains of trade will be divided up among the countries involved and among traders who make the trade possible. While there are no definitive laws determining how real-world gains from trade will be apportioned, economists have developed some insights into how those gains are likely to be divided up. The first insight concerns how much the trader gets. The general rule is

> The more competition that exists among traders, the less likely it is that the trader gets big gains of trade; more of the gains from trade will go to the citizens in the two countries, and less will go to the traders.

Three determinants of the terms of trade are

1. The more competition, the less the trader gets.
2. Smaller countries get a larger proportion of the gain than larger countries.
3. Countries producing goods with economies of scale get a larger gain from trade.

What this insight means is that where entry into trade is unimpaired, most of the gains of trade will pass from the trader to the countries. Thus, the trader's big gains from trade occur in markets that are newly opened.

This insight isn't lost on trading companies. Numerous import/export companies exist whose business is discovering possibilities for international trade in newly opened markets. Individuals representing trading companies go around hawking projects or goods to countries. For example, at the end of the 1999 NATO bombing campaign in Kosovo, what the business world calls the *import/export contingent* flew to Kosovo with offers of goods and services to sell. Many of these same individuals had been in Iraq and

Iran in the early 1990s, in Saudi Arabia when oil prices rose in the 1970s, and in the Far East when China opened its doors to international trade in the 1980s.

A second insight is

> Once competition prevails, smaller countries tend to get a larger percentage of the gains of trade than do larger countries.

The reason, briefly, is that more opportunities are opened up for smaller countries by trade than for larger countries. The more opportunities, the larger the relative gains. Say, for instance, that the United States begins trade with Mali, a small country in Africa. Enormous new consumption possibilities are opened up for Mali—prices of all types of goods will fall. Assuming Mali has a comparative advantage in fish, before international trade began, cars were probably extraordinarily expensive in Mali, while fish was cheap. With international trade, the price of cars in Mali falls substantially, so Mali gets the gains. Because the U.S. economy is so large compared to Mali's, the U.S. price of fish doesn't change noticeably. Mali's fish are just a drop in the bucket. The price ratio of cars to fish doesn't change much for the United States, so it doesn't get much of the gains of trade. Mali gets almost all the gains from trade.

There's an important catch to this gains-from-trade argument. The argument holds only if competition among traders prevails. That means that Mali residents are sold cars at the same price (plus shipping costs) as U.S. residents. International traders in small countries often have little competition from other traders and keep large shares of the gains from trade for themselves. In the earlier food/oil example, the United States and Saudi Arabia didn't get a large share of the benefits. It was I.T. who got most of the benefits. Since the traders often come from the larger country, the smaller country doesn't get this share of the gains from trade; the larger country's international traders do.

A third insight is

> Gains from trade go to the countries producing goods that exhibit economies of scale.

Q-4 In what circumstances would a small country not get the larger percentage of the gains from trade?

Trade allows an increase in production. If there are economies of scale, that increase can lower the average cost of production of a good. Hence, an increase in production can lower the price of the good in the producing country. The country producing the good with the larger economies of scale has its costs reduced by more, and hence gains more from trade than does its trading partner.

Comparative Advantage in Today's Economy

The comparative advantage model conveys a story with the theme, "trade is good"; trade benefits both parties to the trade. This story doesn't fit much of the lay public's view of trade, nor the fears of outsourcing discussed above. If trade is good, why do so many people oppose it, and what accounts for the difference between economists' view of trade and the lay public's view? I suggest three reasons.

Gains from trade are often stealth gains.

One reason for the difference is that laypeople often do not recognize the gains of trade—the gains are often stealth gains such as a decline in prices—while they easily identify the loss of jobs caused by the trade adjustments as countries shift production to take advantage of trade. For example, consider the price of clothing: A shirt today costs far less in real terms (in terms of the number of hours you have to work to buy it) than it did a decade or two ago. Much of the reason for that is trade. But how many people attribute that fall in price of shirts to trade? Not many; they just take it for granted. But the reality is that much of our current lifestyle in the United States has been made possible by trade.

Much of our current lifestyle is made possible by trade.

Another reason for the difference between the lay view of trade and economists' view is that the lay public often believes that since countries such as China have lower wages, they must have a comparative advantage in just about everything, so that if we allow free trade, eventually we will lose all U.S. jobs. This belief is an internal logical contradiction; by definition comparative advantage refers to relative opportunity cost. If one country has a comparative advantage in one set of goods, the other country must have a comparative advantage in another set.

That said, economists also must admit that the lay public does have a point. The comparative advantage model assumes that a country's imports and exports are equal. As we saw above, U.S. imports and exports are not equal. Currently, the United States imports much more than it exports, and foreign countries are accepting our IOUs in exchange for those imports. As long as foreign countries are willing to accept those promises of the United States to pay some time in the future, they can have a comparative advantage in the production of many more goods than the United States.[1] Currently, people in other countries finance the U.S. trade deficit by buying U.S. assets. Once the other countries decide that it is no longer in their interests to finance the U.S. trade deficit, economic forces such as the adjustment of exchange rates will be set in motion to restore a more equal division of comparative advantages.

The comparative advantage model assumes that a country's imports and exports are equal.

A third reason accounting for the difference between the lay view of trade and the economists' view is that laypeople often think of trade as trade in just manufactured goods. Trade is much broader, and includes the services that traders provide. Countries can have comparative advantages in trade itself, and the gains the trader makes can account for the seeming differences in countries' comparative advantages.

Q-5 What are three reasons for the difference between laypeople's and economists' views of trade?

Notice in my example that the international traders who brought the trade about benefited significantly from trade. I included traders because trade does not take place on its own—markets and trade require entrepreneurs. The market is not about abstract forces; it is about real people operating to improve their position. Many of the gains from trade do not go to the countries producing or consuming the good but rather to the trader. And the gains that traders get can be enormous.

Consider, for example, the high-priced sneakers ($200) that many "with-it" students wear. Those sneakers are likely made in China, costing about $8 to make. So much of the benefits of trade do not go to the producer or the consumer; they go to the trader. However, not all of the difference is profit. The trader has other costs; there are, for example, costs of transportation and advertising—someone has to convince you that you need those "with-it" sneakers. (Just do it, right?) A portion of the benefits of the trade is accruing to U.S. advertising firms, which can pay more to creative people who think up those crazy ads.

The United States currently has a large comparative advantage in facilitating trade. Many of the firms that specialize in the role as trader are U.S.-based companies, and these companies buy many of the goods and services that support trade from their home country—the United States. Therefore, trade with China and India has been generating jobs in the United States. These are jobs that laypeople often do not associate with trade—jobs in research, management, advertising, and distribution of goods. What this means is that goods manufactured in China, India, and other Asian countries are creating demand for advertising, management, and distribution, and are therefore creating jobs and income in the United States. That's one reason for the large increase in service jobs in the U.S. economy.

Trade with China and India has been generating jobs in the United States.

[1]One could make the model fit reality if one thinks of the United States as having a comparative advantage in producing IOUs.

A final consideration to keep in mind is that trade increases income and wealth abroad, thereby creating additional demand for U.S. goods. Two billion consumers whose incomes are increasing offer many new growth opportunities for U.S. firms. Trade expands the total pie, and even when a country gets a smaller proportion of the new total pie, the absolute amount it gets can increase.

When one adds these considerations to the initial layperson's reaction to trade, a much more nuanced view emerges that makes trade look much better. This does not mean that trade presents no problems. One big policy problem is that the benefits of trade are quite uneven. The people whose jobs are outsourced are significantly hurt by trade and are very visible. The benefits of trade in lower prices and jobs created by trade are spread throughout the economy and are much less visible. It is the concentrated nature of the costs of trade and dispersed nature of the benefits that will continue to present a challenge to policy makers when dealing with the effects of trade.

The concentrated nature of the costs of trade and the dispersed nature of the benefits present a challenge for policy makers.

Other Sources of U.S. Comparative Advantage

When thinking about how the theory of comparative advantage relates to the current debate about outsourcing—what jobs are outsourced and what jobs are created in the United States—it is important to remember that comparative advantage is not determined by wages alone. Many other factors enter into comparative advantage and these other factors give the United States a comparative advantage in a variety of goods and services. Some of those other sources of U.S. comparative advantage include

1. *Skills of the U.S. labor force.* Our educational system and experience in production (learning by doing) have created a U.S. workforce that is highly productive, which means that it can be paid more and still be competitive.
2. *U.S. governmental institutions.* The United States has a stable, relatively noncorrupt government, which is required for effective production. These institutions give firms based in the United States a major comparative advantage.
3. *U.S. physical and technological infrastructure.* The United States has probably the best infrastructure for production in the world. This infrastructure includes extensive road systems, telecommunications networks, and power grids.
4. *English is the international language of business.* U.S. citizens learn English from birth. Chinese and Indian citizens must learn it as a second language. One is seldom as comfortable or productive working in one's second language as in one's first language.
5. *Wealth from past production.* The United States is extraordinarily wealthy, which means that the United States is the world's largest consumer. Production that supports many aspects of consumption cannot be easily transferred geographically, and thus the United States will maintain a comparative advantage in producing these nontransferable aspects of consumption.
6. *U.S. natural resources.* The United States is endowed with many resources: rich farmland, a pleasant and varied climate, beautiful scenery for tourism, minerals, and water. These give it comparative advantages in a number of areas.
7. *Cachet.* The United States continues to be a cultural trendsetter. People all over the world want to watch U.S. movies, want to have U.S. goods, and are influenced by U.S. advertising agencies to favor U.S. goods. As long as that is the case, the United States will have a comparative advantage in goods tied to that cachet.
8. *Inertia.* It takes time and costs money to change production. Companies will not move production to another country for a small cost differential. The difference has to be large, it has to be expected to continue for a long time, and it

must be large enough to offset the risk of the unknown. Thus, the current place of production has an advantage over other potential places for production simply because the current location is known.

9. *U.S. intellectual property rights*. Currently, U.S. companies and individuals hold a large number of intellectual property rights, which require other countries that use their patented goods or methods to pay U.S. patent holders. Every time someone (legally) buys the Windows operating system for his or her computer, a portion of the purchase price covers a payment to a U.S. company. America's culture of embracing new ideas and questioning authority cultivates an environment of innovation that will likely continue to generate new intellectual property rights.
10. *A relatively open immigration policy*. Many of the brightest, most entrepreneurial students of developing countries immigrate and settle in the United States. They create jobs and help maintain U.S. comparative advantages in a number of fields, especially high-technology fields. More than 50 percent of the engineering degrees, for example, go to foreign students, many of whom remain in the United States.

The United States has numerous sources of comparative advantage.

Combined, these other sources of comparative advantage will maintain the United States' competitiveness in a variety of types of production for the coming decades.

Some Concerns about the Future

The above discussion of the sources of U.S. comparative advantage should have made those of you who are U.S. citizens feel a bit better about the future of the U.S. economy; the United States is not about to lose all its jobs to outsourcing. But that does not mean that there are not real issues of concern. The typical layperson's concern that the comparative advantage story does not capture what is going on with trade and outsourcing has some real foundations, and deserves to be considered seriously.

Inherent and Transferable Sources of Comparative Advantages When David Ricardo first made the comparative advantage argument in the early 1800s, he was talking about an economic environment that was quite different than today's. His example was Britain and Portugal, with Britain producing wool and Portugal producing wine. What caused their differing costs of production was climate; Britain's climate was far less conducive to growing grapes than Portugal's but more conducive to raising sheep. Differing technologies or labor skills in the countries did not play a key role in their comparative advantages, and it was highly unlikely that the climates, and therefore comparative advantages, of the countries could change. Put another way, both countries have inherent sources of comparative advantages, which we will call **inherent comparative advantages**—*comparative advantages that are based on factors that are relatively unchangeable*, rather than transferable sources of comparative advantages, which we will call **transferable comparative advantages**—*comparative advantages based on factors that can change relatively easily*.

As the theory of comparative advantage developed, economists applied it to a much broader range of goods whose sources of comparative advantage were not due to climate. For example, some countries had land, specific resources, capital, types of labor, or technology as sources of comparative advantage. Extending the analysis to these other sources of comparative advantage makes sense, but it is important to keep in mind that only some of these comparative advantages are inherent; others are transferable. Comparative advantages due to resources or climate are unlikely to change; comparative advantages that depend on capital, technology, or education, however, can change. In fact, we would expect them to change.

The Law of One Price Whether a country can maintain a much higher standard of living than another country in the long run depends in part on whether its sources of comparative advantage are transferable or inherent. Saudi Arabia will maintain its comparative advantage in producing oil, but the United States' comparative advantage based on better education is likely to be more fleeting. In cases where sources of comparative advantage are not inherent, economic forces will push to eliminate that comparative advantage. The reason is the law of one price: in a competitive market, there will be pressure for equal factors to be priced equally. If factor prices aren't equal, firms can reduce costs by redirecting production to countries where factors are priced lower. The tendency of economic forces to eliminate transferable comparative advantage is sometimes called the *convergence hypothesis*. Even seemingly inherent comparative advantages can be changed by technology. Consider oil. The development of cost-effective fuel cells may leave Saudi Arabia with a comparative advantage in oil but not necessarily with a comparative advantage in producing energy.

Law of one price: in a competitive market, there will be pressure for equal factors to be priced equally.

When markets are working, any country with a comparative advantage due only to transferable capital and technology will lose that comparative advantage as capital and technology spread to other countries. Ultimately, in the case of transferable comparative advantage, production will shift to the lower-wage country that has equivalent institutional structures. This is the law of one price in action: The same good—including equivalent labor—must sell for the same price, unless trade is restricted or other differences exist. That is what's happening now with the United States and outsourcing. Skills needed to do information technology work, for example, are transferable. Because an information technology professional with three to five years' experience earns about $75,000 in the United States and only $26,000 in India, those jobs are moving abroad. As long as wages differ, and the workers' productivities in countries are comparable, transferable comparative advantages of U.S. production will continue to erode, and as they erode, production and jobs will be moved abroad.

Transferable comparative advantages will tend to erode over time.

The question, therefore, is not: Why is outsourcing to China and India occurring today? The questions are: Why didn't it happen long ago, and how did U.S. productivity, and hence its standard of living, come to so exceed China's and India's productivity, and hence their standards of living? Or alternatively: How did the United States get in its current high-wage position, and is it likely to maintain that position into the indefinite future?

How the United States Gained and Is Now Losing Sources of Comparative Advantage To better understand the current U.S. position, let's look at it historically. The United States developed its highly favorable position from the 1920s until the late 1940s when the two world wars directed production toward the United States. Those wars, the entrepreneurial spirit of the U.S. population, U.S. institutions conducive to production, and the flow of technology and capital into the United States gave the United States a big boost both during the two world wars and after. Coming out of World War II, at the then-existing exchange rates, the United States had a major cost advantage in producing a large majority of goods, just as China has a cost advantage in producing the large majority of goods today.

Such cost advantages in a majority of areas of production are not sustainable because the balance of trade will be highly imbalanced. In the absence of specific policy by governments, or large private flows of capital, eventually that imbalance will right itself. After World War II, the trade balance that favored the United States was maintained temporarily by U.S. companies, which invested heavily in Europe, and by the U.S. government, which transferred funds to Europe with programs such as the Marshall Plan. These flows of capital financed Europe's trade deficits and allowed the United States to run large trade surpluses, just as current flows of investment into the United States from

In the absence of specific policy by governments, or large private flows of capital, eventually any large trade imbalance will right itself.

a variety of countries, and the explicit policy of buying U.S. bonds by Chinese and Japanese central banks, are financing the U.S. trade deficits now, and allowing large Chinese trade surpluses with the United States.

Methods of Equalizing Trade Balances Capital flows that sustain trade imbalances eventually stop, and when they do, adjustments in sources of comparative advantages must take place so that the trade surplus countries—such as China today—become less competitive (lose sources of comparative advantage) and the trade deficit countries—in this case, the United States—become more competitive (gain sources of comparative advantage). This adjustment can occur in a number of ways. The two most likely adjustments today are that wages in China rise relative to wages in the United States or the U.S. exchange rate falls. Both adjustments will make Chinese goods relatively more expensive and U.S. goods relatively cheaper, just as these adjustments did with countries such as Japan, Taiwan, and Korea in previous decades. Neither of these is especially pleasant for us, which is why we will likely hear continued calls for trade restrictions in the coming decade.

Q-6 What are two likely adjustments that will reduce the wage gap between China and the United States?

Unfortunately, as I will discuss below, the trade restriction policies that governments can undertake will generally make things worse. In a globalized free-trade economy, the U.S. wage advantage can only be maintained to the degree that total cost of production of a good in the United States (with all the associated costs) is no more expensive than the total cost of producing that same good abroad (with all the associated costs). The degree to which production shifts because of lower wages abroad depends on how transferable are the U.S. comparative advantages that we listed above. Some of them are generally nontransferable, and thus will support sustained higher relative U.S. wages. English as the language of business; the enormous wealth of the United States gained earlier; inertia; and U.S. political, social, and capital infrastructure will keep much production in the United States, and will maintain a comparative advantage for U.S. production even with significantly higher U.S. wages.

The U.S. wage advantage can only be maintained to the degree that total cost of production of a good in the United States is no more than the total cost of that same good abroad.

But in the coming decades, we can expect a narrowing of the wage gap between the United States and China and India. Given these strong market forces that cannot be prevented without undermining the entire international trading system, about the only available realistic strategy for the United States is to adapt to this new situation. Its best strategy is to work toward maintaining existing comparative advantages through investment in education and infrastructure, while continuing to provide an environment conducive to innovation so that we develop comparative advantages in new industries.

Trade Balances and a Global Recession In 2009 the world economy entered into a deep global recession. As U.S. income fell, imports fell, which meant that exports of other countries fell. (Remember, one country's imports are another country's exports.) As countries tried to stimulate their economies through increasing government spending, there was strong pressure to direct that spending to domestically produced goods, not to imports. For example, the U.S. government instituted a "Buy American" requirement for its stimulus package so that the money had to go toward buying American goods rather than imports. The problem is that such policies will likely lead to retaliation, making all economies worse off, and in 2009 there was serious concern among economists that a global trade war might break out.

Varieties of Trade Restrictions

The policies countries can use to restrict trade include tariffs and quotas, voluntary restraint agreements, embargoes, regulatory trade restrictions, and nationalistic appeals. I'll consider each in turn and also review the geometric analysis of each.

FIGURE 9-4 (A AND B) Selected Tariff Rates

The tariff rates in **(a)** will be continually changing as the changes negotiated by the World Trade Organization come into effect. In **(b)** you see tariff rates for the United States since 1920.

Source: General Agreement on Tariffs and Trade (GATT) and the World Bank (www.worldbank.org).

Country	%	Country	%
Argentina	5.2	Norway	1.9
Australia	3.1	Peru	8.7
Canada	1.5	Philippines	3.1
Colombia	9.6	Poland	2.0
Czech Rep.	2.0	Singapore	0
European Union	2.5	South Africa	5.4
Hungary	2.0	Sri Lanka	7.7
India	14.5	Thailand	4.9
Indonesia	6.0	United States	1.6
Japan	2.5	Venezuela	12.7
Mexico	3.0	Zimbabwe	7.3

(a) Tariff Rates by Country

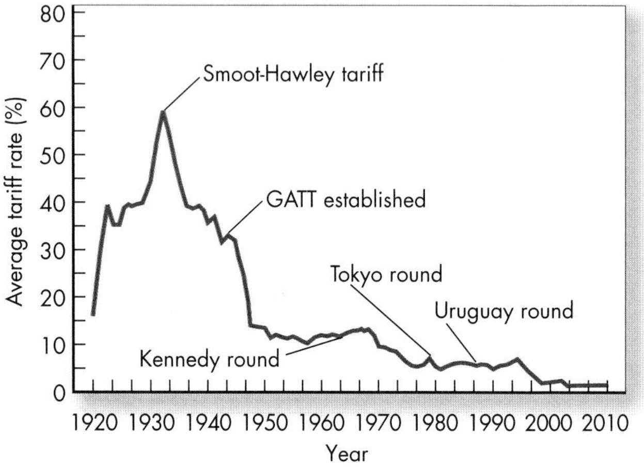

(b) U.S. Tariff Rates since 1920

Tariffs and Quotas

Three policies used to restrict trade are
1. Tariffs (taxes on internationally traded goods).
2. Quotas (quantity limits placed on imports).
3. Regulatory trade restrictions (government-imposed procedural rules that limit imports).

Tariffs and Quotas

Tariffs are *taxes governments place on internationally traded goods*—generally imports. (Tariffs are also called *customs duties.*) Tariffs are the most-used and most-familiar type of trade restriction. Tariffs operate in the same way a tax does: They make imported goods relatively more expensive than they otherwise would have been, and thereby encourage the consumption of domestically produced goods. On average, U.S. tariffs raise the price of imported goods by less than 3 percent. Figure 9-4(a) presents average tariff rates for industrial goods for a number of countries and the European Union, and Figure 9-4(b) shows the tariff rates imposed by the United States since 1920.

Probably the most infamous tariff in U.S. history is the Smoot-Hawley Tariff of 1930, which raised tariffs on imported goods to an average of 60 percent. It was passed at the height of the Great Depression in the United States in the hope of protecting American jobs. It didn't work. Other countries responded with similar tariffs. As a result of these trade wars, international trade plummeted from $60 billion in 1928 to $25 billion in 1938, unemployment worsened, and the international depression deepened. These effects of the tariff convinced many, if not most, economists that free trade is preferable to trade restrictions.

The dismal failure of the Smoot-Hawley Tariff was the main reason the **General Agreement on Tariffs and Trade (GATT),** *a regular international conference to reduce trade barriers*, was established in 1947 immediately following World War II. In 1995 GATT was replaced by the **World Trade Organization (WTO),** *an organization whose functions are generally the same as GATT's were—to promote free and fair trade among countries*. Unlike GATT, the WTO is a permanent organization with an enforcement system (albeit weak). Since its formation, rounds of negotiations have resulted in a decline in worldwide tariffs.

Quotas are *quantity limits placed on imports*. They have the same effect on equilibrium price and quantity as the quantity restrictions discussed in Chapter 5, and their effect in limiting trade is similar to the effect of a tariff. Both increase price and reduce quantity. Tariffs, like all taxes on suppliers, shift the supply curve up by the amount of the tax, as Figure 9-5 shows. A tariff, T, raises equilibrium price from P_0 to P_1 by an amount that is less than the tariff, and equilibrium quantity declines from Q_0 to Q_1. With a quota, Q_1, the equilibrium price also rises to P_1.

There is, however, a difference between tariffs and quotas. In the case of the tariff, the government collects tariff revenue represented by the shaded region. In the case of a quota, the government collects no revenue. The benefit of the increase in price goes to the importer as additional corporate revenue. So which of the two do you think import companies favor? The quota, of course—it means more profits as long as your company is the one to receive the rights to fill those quotas. In fact, once quotas are instituted, firms compete intensely to get them.

Tariffs affect trade patterns. For example, as of 2009 the United States imposes a tariff on light trucks from Japan, so the United States imports few light trucks from Japan. You will see Japanese-named trucks, but most of these are produced in the United States. Many similar examples exist, and by following the tariff structure, you can gain a lot of insight into patterns of trade.

The issues involved with tariffs and quotas can be seen in a slightly different way by assuming that the country being considered is small relative to the world economy and that imports compete with domestic producers. The small-country assumption means that the supply from the world to this country is perfectly elastic at the world price, \$2, as in Figure 9-6(a).

The world price of the good is unaffected by this country's demand. This assumption allows us to distinguish the world supply from domestic supply. In the absence of any trade restrictions, the world price of \$2 would be the domestic price. Domestic low-cost suppliers would supply 100 units of the good at \$2. The remaining 100 units demanded are being imported.

FIGURE 9-5 **The Effects of Tariffs and Quotas**

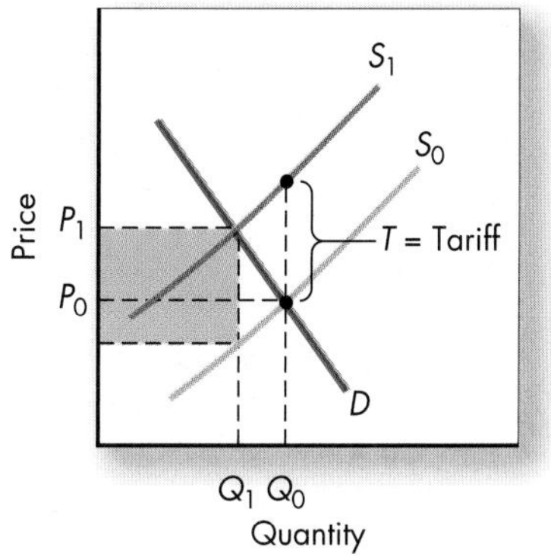

FIGURE 9-6 (A AND B) **Tariffs and Quotas When the Domestic Country Is Small**

This exhibit shows the effects of a tariff in (**a**) and of a quota in (**b**) when the domestic country is small. The small-country assumption means that the world supply is perfectly elastic, in this case at \$2.00 a unit. With a tariff of 50 cents, world supply shifts up by 50 cents. Domestic quantity demanded falls to 175 and domestic quantity supplied rises to 125. Foreign suppliers are left supplying the difference, 50 units. The domestic government collects revenue shown in the shaded area. The figure in (**b**) shows how the same result can be achieved with a quota of 50. Equilibrium price rises to \$2.50. Domestic firms produce 125 units and consumers demand 175 units. The difference between the tariff and the quota is that, with a tariff, the domestic government collects the revenue from the higher price. With a quota, the benefits of the higher price accrue to the foreign and domestic producers.

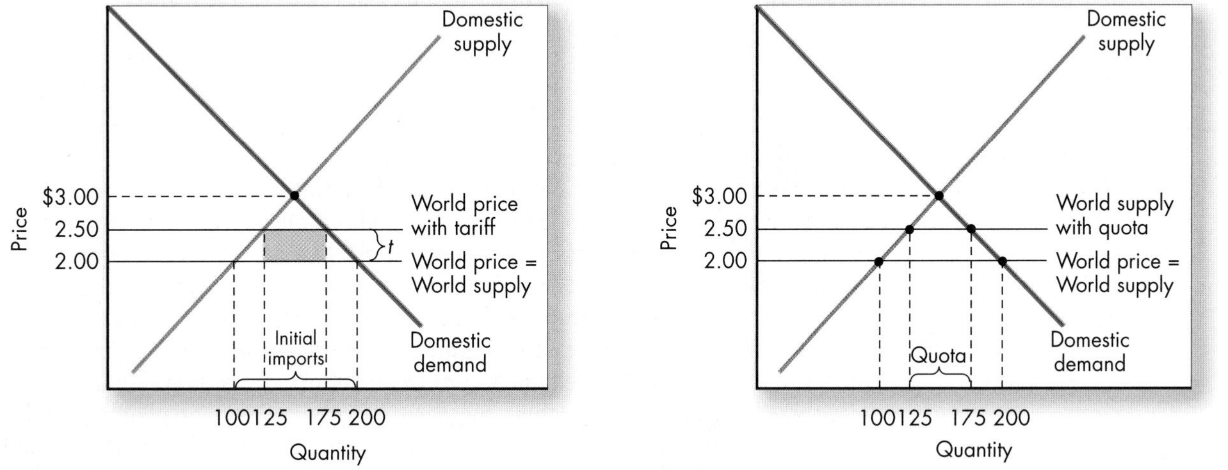

(a) With a Tariff **(b) With a Quota**

In Figure 9-6(a) I show the effect of a tariff of 50 cents placed on all imports. Since the world supply curve is perfectly elastic, all of this tax, shown by the shaded region, is borne by domestic consumers. Price rises to $2.50 and quantity demanded falls to 175. With a tariff, the rise in price will increase domestic quantity supplied from 100 to 125 and will reduce imports to 50. Now let's compare this situation with a quota of 50, shown in Figure 9-6(b). Under a quota of 50, the final price would be the same, but higher revenue would accrue to foreign and domestic producers rather than to the government. One final difference: Any increase in demand under a quota would result in higher prices because it would have to be filled by domestic producers. Under a tariff, any increase in demand would not affect price.

Voluntary Restraint Agreements

Voluntary restraint agreements are often not all that voluntary.

Imposing new tariffs and quotas is specifically ruled out by the WTO, but foreign countries know that WTO rules are voluntary and that, if a domestic industry brought sufficient political pressure on its government, the WTO rules would be forgotten. To avoid the imposition of new tariffs on their goods, countries often voluntarily restrict their exports. That's why Japan has agreed informally to limit the number of cars it exports to the United States.

The effect of such voluntary restraint agreements is similar to the effect of quotas: They directly limit the quantity of imports, increasing the price of the good and helping domestic producers. For example, when the United States encouraged Japan to impose "voluntary" quotas on exports of its cars to the United States, Toyota benefited from the quotas because it could price its limited supply of cars higher than it could if it sent in a large number of cars, so profit per car would be high. Since they faced less competition, U.S. car companies also benefited. They could increase their prices because Toyota had done so.

Embargoes

An embargo is a total restriction on import or export of a good.

An **embargo** is *a total restriction on the import or export of a good*. Embargoes are usually established for international political reasons rather than for primarily economic reasons.

An example was the U.S. embargo of trade with Iraq prior to the U.S. invasion. The U.S. government hoped that the embargo would so severely affect Iraq's economy that Saddam Hussein would lose political power. It did make life difficult for Iraqis, but it did not bring about the downfall of the Hussein government. The United States has also imposed embargoes on Cuba, Iran, and Libya.

Regulatory Trade Restrictions

Web Note 9.1
Sugar Regulation

Tariffs, quotas, and embargoes are the primary *direct* methods to restrict international trade. There are also indirect methods that restrict trade in not-so-obvious ways; these are called **regulatory trade restrictions** (*government-imposed procedural rules that limit imports*). One type of regulatory trade restriction has to do with protecting the health and safety of a country's residents. For example, a country might restrict imports of all vegetables grown where certain pesticides are used, knowing full well that all other countries use those pesticides. The effect of such a regulation would be to halt the import of vegetables. Another example involves building codes. U.S. building codes require that plywood have fewer than, say, three flaws per sheet. Canadian building codes require that plywood have fewer than, say, five flaws per sheet. The different building codes are a nontariff barrier that makes trade in building materials between the United States and Canada difficult.

A second type of regulatory restriction involves making import and customs procedures so intricate and time-consuming that importers simply give up. For example, at one time France required all imported VCRs to be individually inspected in Toulouse. Since Toulouse is a provincial city, far from any port and outside the normal route for imports after they enter France, the inspection process took months.

Q-7 How might a country benefit from having an inefficient customs agency?

Some regulatory restrictions are imposed for legitimate reasons; others are designed simply to make importing more difficult and hence protect domestic producers from international competition. It's often hard to tell the difference. A good example of this difficulty began in 1988, when the EU disallowed all imports of meat from animals that had been fed growth-inducing hormones. As the box "Hormones and Economics" on the next page details, the debate continues.

Some regulatory restrictions are imposed for legitimate reasons; others are designed simply to make importing more difficult.

Nationalistic Appeals and "Buy Domestic" Requirements

Finally, nationalistic appeals can help to restrict international trade. "Buy American" campaigns and Japanese xenophobia[2] are examples. Many Americans, given two products of equal appeal except that one is made in the United States and one is made in a foreign country, would buy the U.S. product. To get around this tendency, foreign and U.S. companies often go to great lengths to get a MADE IN THE U.S.A. classification on goods they sell in the United States. For example, components for many autos are made in Japan but shipped to the United States and assembled in Ohio or Tennessee so that the finished car can be called an American product. These "Buy American" policies can even be requirements. For example, the U.S. government stimulus package of 2009 included a "Buy American" clause that required recipients to spend the money they received on American, not foreign, goods.

WWW Web Note 9.2
Buy American

Reasons for Trade Restrictions

Let's now turn to a different question: If trade is beneficial, as it is in our example of I.T., why do countries restrict trade?

Unequal Internal Distribution of the Gains from Trade

One reason is that the gains of trade are not equally distributed. In the example of the argument for trade discussed at the beginning of the chapter, I.T. persuaded Saudi Arabia to specialize in the production of oil rather than food, and persuaded the United States to produce more food than oil. That means, of course, that some U.S. oil workers will have to become farmers, and in Saudi Arabia some farmers will have to become oil producers.

Often people don't want to make radical changes in the kind of work they do—they want to keep on producing what they're already producing. So when these people see the same kinds of goods that they produce coming into their country from abroad, they lobby to prevent the foreign competition.

Had I.T. been open about the difficulties of trading, he would have warned the countries that change is hard. It has very real costs that I.T. didn't point out when he made his offers. But these costs of change are relatively small compared to the gains from trade. Moreover, they're short-run, temporary costs, whereas gains from trade are permanent, long-run gains. Once the adjustment has been made, the costs will be gone but the benefits will still be there.

For most goods, the benefits for the large majority of the population so outweigh the small costs to some individuals that, decided on a strict cost/benefit basis, international

[2]*Xenophobia* is a Greek word meaning "fear of foreigners." Pronounce the *x* like *z*.

REAL-WORLD APPLICATION

Hormones and Economics

Trade restrictions, in practice, are often much more complicated than they seem in textbooks. Seldom does a country say, "We're limiting imports to protect our home producers." Instead the country explains the restrictions in a more politically acceptable way. Consider the fight between the European Union (EU) and the United States over U.S. meat exports. In 1988 the EU, in line with Union-wide internal requirements, banned imports of any meat from animals treated with growth-inducing hormones, which U.S. meat producers use extensively. The result: the EU banned the meat exported from the United States.

The EU claimed that it had imposed the ban only because of public health concerns. The United States claimed that the ban was actually a trade restriction, pointing out that its own residents ate this kind of meat with confidence because a U.S. government agency had certified that the levels of hormones in the meat were far below any danger level.

The United States retaliated against the EU by imposing 100 percent tariffs on Danish and West German hams, Italian tomatoes, and certain other foods produced by EU member nations. The EU threatened to respond by placing 100 percent tariffs on $100 million worth of U.S. walnuts and dried fruits, but instead entered into bilateral meetings with the United States. Those meetings allowed untreated meats into the EU for human consumption and treated meats that would be used as dog food. In response, the United States removed its retaliatory tariff on hams and tomato sauce, but retained its tariffs on many other goods. In the 1990s, Europe's dog population seemed to be growing exponentially as Europe's imports of "dog food" increased by leaps and bounds. In 1996 the United States asked the WTO to review the EU ban. It did so in 1997, finding in favor of the United States. The EU appealed and in 1999 the WTO stood by its earlier ruling and the United States reimposed the 100 percent tariffs. Since then, the EU has stood firm and has conducted studies that, it says, show the use of growth hormones to be unsafe, but the WTO continues to rule that they are safe. In 2004, the EU replaced its ban on U.S. beef with a provisional ban until it collects more information, and argued that this provisional ban met the WTO rules. The United States disagreed and continued its retaliatory tariffs. In January 2009, for example, the U.S. government placed a 300 percent tariff on Roquefort cheese as one of its retaliatory measures. So the dispute continues more than 25 years after it started.

Which side is right in this dispute? The answer is far from obvious. Both the United States and the EU have potentially justifiable positions. As I said, trade restrictions are more complicated in reality than in textbooks.

trade is still a deal you can't refuse. The table below lists economists' estimates of the cost to consumers of saving a job in some industries through trade restrictions.

Industry	Cost of Production (per job saved)
Footwear	$505,000
Sugar	213,000
Apparel	181,000
Dairy	167,000
Canned tuna	43,000

Source: *Economic Effects of Significant Import Restraints*, 2007, U.S. International Trade Commission (www.usitc.gov).

With benefits so outweighing costs, it would seem that transition costs could be forgotten. But they can't.

Benefits of trade are generally widely scattered among the entire population. In contrast, costs of free trade often fall on small groups of people who loudly oppose the particular free trade that hurts them. This creates a political push against free trade.

Benefits of trade are generally widely scattered among the entire population. In contrast, costs of free trade often fall on specific small groups.

It isn't only in the United States that the push for trade restrictions focuses on the small costs and not on the large benefits. For example, the European Union (EU) places large restrictions on food imports from nonmember nations. If the EU were to remove those barriers, food prices in EU countries would decline significantly—it is estimated that meat prices alone would fall by about 65 percent. Consumers would benefit, but farmers would be hurt. The farmers, however, have the political clout to see that the costs are considered and the benefits aren't. The result: The EU places high duties on foreign agricultural products.

The cost to society of relaxing trade restrictions has led to a number of programs to assist those who are hurt. Such programs are called **trade adjustment assistance programs**—*programs designed to compensate losers for reductions in trade restrictions*.

Governments have tried to use trade adjustment assistance to facilitate free trade, but they've found that it's enormously difficult to limit the adjustment assistance to those who are actually hurt by international trade. As soon as people find that there's assistance for people injured by trade, they're likely to try to show that they too have been hurt and deserve assistance. Losses from free trade become exaggerated and magnified. Instead of only a small portion of the gains from trade being needed for trade adjustment assistance, much more is demanded—often even more than the gains.

Telling people who claim to be hurt that they aren't really being hurt isn't good politics. That's why offering trade adjustment assistance as a way to relieve the pressure to restrict trade is a deal many governments can refuse.

Telling people who claim to be hurt that they aren't really being hurt isn't good politics.

Haggling by Companies over the Gains from Trade

Many naturally advantageous bargains aren't consummated because each side is pushing for a larger share of the gains from trade than the other side thinks should be allotted.

To see how companies haggling over the gains of trade can restrict trade, let's reconsider the original deal that I.T. proposed. I.T. got 380 tons of food and 380 barrels of oil. The United States got an additional 100 tons of food and 60 barrels of oil. Saudi Arabia got an additional 100 barrels of oil and 60 tons of food.

Suppose the Saudis had said, "Why should we be getting only 100 barrels of oil and 60 tons of food when I.T. is getting 380 barrels of oil and 380 tons of food? We want an additional 300 tons of food and another 300 barrels of oil, and we won't deal unless we get them." Similarly the United States might have said, "We want an additional 300 tons of food and an additional 300 barrels of oil, and we won't go through with the deal unless we get them." If either the U.S. or the Saudi Arabian company that was involved in the trade for its country (or both) takes this position, I.T. might just walk—no deal. Tough bargaining positions can make it almost impossible to achieve gains from trade.

Strategic bargaining can lead to higher gains from trade for the side that drives the hardest bargain, but it also can make the deal fall through.

The side that drives the hardest bargain gets the most gains from the bargain, but it also risks making the deal fall through. Such strategic bargaining goes on all the time. **Strategic bargaining** means *demanding a larger share of the gains from trade than you can reasonably expect*. If you're successful, you get the lion's share; if you're not successful, the deal falls apart and everyone is worse off.

Haggling by Countries over Trade Restrictions

Another type of trade bargaining that often limits trade is bargaining between countries. Trade restrictions and the threat of trade restrictions play an important role in that kind of haggling. Sometimes countries must go through with trade restrictions that they really don't want to impose, just to make their threats credible.

Once one country has imposed trade restrictions, other countries attempt to get those restrictions reduced by threatening to increase their own restrictions. Again, to make the threat credible, sometimes countries must impose or increase trade restrictions simply to show they're willing to do so. For example, in the mid-1990s China was allowing significant illegal copying of U.S. software without paying royalties. The United States exerted pressure to stop such copying but felt that China was not responding effectively. To force compliance, the United States made a list of Chinese goods that it threatened with 100 percent tariffs unless China complied. The United States did not want to put on these restrictions but felt that it would have more strategic bargaining power if it threatened to do so. Hence the name **strategic trade policies**—*threatening to implement tariffs to bring about a reduction in tariffs or some other concession from the other country*.

Q-8 In strategic trade bargaining, it is sometimes reasonable to be unreasonable. True or false? Explain.

Strategic trade policies are threats to implement tariffs to bring about a reduction in tariffs or some other concession from the other country.

Ultimately, strategic bargaining power depends on negotiators' skills and the underlying gains from trade that a country would receive. A country that would receive only a small portion of the gains from trade is in a much stronger bargaining position than a country that would receive significant gains. It's easier for the former to walk away from trade.

The potential problem with strategic trade policies is that they can backfire. One rule of strategic bargaining is that the other side must believe that you'll go through with your threat. Thus, strategic trade policy can lead a country that actually supports free trade to impose trade restrictions, just to show how strongly it believes in free trade.

Specialized Production

My discussion of comparative advantage took it as a given that one country was inherently more productive than another country in producing certain goods. But when one looks at trading patterns, it's often not at all clear why particular countries have a productive advantage in certain goods. There's no inherent reason for Switzerland to specialize in the production of watches or for South Korea to specialize in the production of cars. Much in trade cannot be explained by inherent resource endowments. If they don't have inherent advantages, why are countries and places often so good at producing what they specialize in? Two important explanations are that they *learn by doing* and that *economies of scale* exist.

Learning by doing means becoming better at a task the more you perform it.

Learning by Doing **Learning by doing** means *becoming better at a task the more often you perform it*. Take watches in Switzerland. Initially production of watches in Switzerland may have been a coincidence; the person who started the watch business happened to live there. But then people in the area became skilled in producing watches. Their skill made it attractive for other watch companies to start up. As additional companies moved in, more and more members of the labor force became skilled at watchmaking and word went out that Swiss watches were the best in the world. That reputation attracted even more producers, so Switzerland became the watchmaking capital of the world. Had the initial watch production occurred in Austria, not Switzerland, Austria might be the watch capital of the world.

When there's learning by doing, it's much harder to attribute inherent comparative advantage to a country. One must always ask: Does country A have an inherent comparative advantage, or does it simply have more experience? Once country B gets the experience, will country A's comparative advantage disappear? If it will, then country B has a strong reason to limit trade with country A in order to give its own workers time to catch up as they learn by doing.

REAL-WORLD APPLICATION

The Antiglobalization Forces

Often when the World Trade Organization or a similar type organization promoting free trade hosts a meeting, protests (sometimes violent ones) are held by a loosely organized collection of groups opposing globalization. The goals of these groups are varied. Some argue that trade hurts developed countries such as the United States; others argue that it hurts developing countries by exploiting poor workers so that Westerners can get luxuries cheaply. Still others argue against a more subtle Western economic imperialism in which globalization spreads Western cultural values and undermines developing countries' social structures.

Each of these arguments has some appeal, although making the first two simultaneously is difficult because it says that voluntary trade hurts both parties to the trade. But the arguments have had little impact on the views of most policy makers and economists.

Supporting free trade does not mean that globalization does not have costs. It does have costs, but many of the costs associated with free trade are really the result of technological changes. The reality is that technological developments, such as those in telecommunications and transportation, are pushing countries closer together and will involve difficult social and cultural changes, regardless of whether trade is free or not. Restricting trade might temporarily slow these changes but is unlikely to stop them.

Most empirical studies have found that, with regard to material goods, the workers in developing countries involved in trade are generally better off than those not involved in trade. That's why most developing countries work hard to encourage companies to move production facilities into their countries. From a worker's perspective, earning \$4 a day can look quite good when the alternative is earning \$3 a day. Would the worker rather earn \$10 a day? Of course, but the higher the wages in a given country, the less likely it is that firms are going to locate production there.

Many economists are sympathetic to various antiglobalization arguments, but they often become frustrated at the lack of clarity of the antiglobalization groups' views. To oppose something is not enough; to effect positive change, one must not only understand how the thing one opposes works but also have a realistic plan for a better alternative.

Economies of Scale In determining whether an inherent comparative advantage exists, a second complication is **economies of scale**—*the situation in which costs per unit of output fall as output increases*. Many manufacturing industries (such as steel and autos) exhibit economies of scale. The existence of significant economies of scale means that it makes sense (that is, it lowers costs) for one country to specialize in one good and another country to specialize in another good. But who should specialize in what is unclear. Producers in a country can, and generally do, argue that if only the government will establish barriers, they'll be able to lower their costs per unit and eventually sell at lower costs than foreign producers.

In economies of scale, costs per unit of output go down as output increases.

Q-9 Is it efficient for a country to maintain a trade barrier in an industry that exhibits economies of scale?

Most countries recognize the importance of learning by doing and economies of scale. A variety of trade restrictions are based on these two phenomena. The most common expression of the learning-by-doing and economies-of-scale insights is the **infant industry argument,** which is that *with initial protection, an industry will be able to become competitive*. Countries use this argument to justify many trade restrictions. They argue, "You may now have a comparative advantage, but that's simply because you've been at it longer, or are experiencing significant economies of scale. We need trade restrictions on our _____ industry to give it a chance to catch up. Once an infant industry grows up, then we can talk about eliminating the restrictions."

The infant industry argument says that with initial protection, an industry will be able to become competitive.

Macroeconomic Aspects of Trade

The comparative advantage argument for free trade assumes that a country's resources are fully utilized. When countries don't have full employment, imports can decrease domestic aggregate demand and increase unemployment. Exports can stimulate domestic aggregate demand and decrease unemployment. Thus, when an economy is in a recession, there is a strong macroeconomic reason to limit imports and encourage exports. These macroeconomic effects of free trade play an important role in the public's view of imports and exports. When a country is in a recession, pressure to impose trade restrictions increases substantially. We saw this in 2009 when, faced with the job losses due to the serious recession, there was serious pressure to design programs to keep spending in the United States where it would create jobs and not be spent on imports that would create jobs for other countries.

National Security

Countries often justify trade restrictions on grounds of national security. These restrictions take two forms:

1. Export restrictions on strategic materials and defense-related goods.
2. Import restrictions on defense-related goods. For example, in a war we don't want to be dependent on oil from abroad.

Reasons for restricting trade include

1. Unequal internal distribution of the gains from trade.
2. Haggling by companies over the gains from trade.
3. Haggling by countries over trade restrictions.
4. Specialized production: learning by doing and economies of scale.
5. Macroeconomic aspects of trade.
6. National security.
7. International politics.
8. Increased revenue brought in by tariffs.

For a number of goods, national security considerations make sense. For example, the United States restricts the sale of certain military items to countries that may be fighting the United States someday. The problem is where to draw the line about goods having a national security consideration. Should countries protect domestic agriculture? All high-technology items, since they might be useful in weapons? All chemicals? Steel? When a country makes a national security argument for trade, we must be careful to consider whether a domestic political reason may be lurking behind that argument.

International Politics

International politics frequently provides another reason for trade restrictions. Over the past decades, the United States restricted trade with Cuba to punish that country for trying to extend its Marxist political and economic policies to other Latin American countries. The United States also has trade restrictions on Iran for its position on nuclear power plants. The list can be extended, but you get the argument: Trade helps you, so we'll hurt you by stopping trade until you do what we want. So what if it hurts us too? It'll hurt you more than it hurts us.

Increased Revenue Brought in by Tariffs

A final argument made for one particular type of trade restriction—a tariff—is that tariffs bring in revenues. In the 19th century, tariffs were the U.S. government's primary source of revenue. They are less important as a source of revenue today for many developed countries because those countries have instituted other forms of taxes. However, tariffs remain a primary source of revenue for many developing countries. They're relatively easy to collect and are paid by people rich enough to afford imports. These countries justify many of their tariffs with the argument that they need the revenues.

Why Economists Generally Oppose Trade Restrictions

Each of the preceding arguments for trade restrictions has some validity, but most economists discount them and support free trade. The reason is that, in their considered judgment, the harm done by trade restrictions outweighs the benefits. This is true, even though, from the U.S. perspective, transferable comparative advantages are likely to place significant pressures on jobs to leave the United States, and hold down U.S. wages in the coming decades. Most economists believe that the United States will be better off if it allows free trade than it would be if it did not.

Economists generally oppose trade restrictions because

1. From a global perspective, free trade increases total output.
2. International trade provides competition for domestic companies.
3. Restrictions based on national security are often abused or evaded.
4. Trade restrictions are addictive.

Free Trade Increases Total Output

Economists' first argument for free trade is that, viewed from a global perspective, free trade increases total output. From a national perspective, economists agree that particular instances of trade restrictions may actually help one nation, even as most other nations are hurt. But they argue that the country imposing trade restrictions can benefit *only if the other country doesn't retaliate* with trade restrictions of its own. Retaliation is the rule, not the exception, however, and when there is retaliation, trade restrictions cause both countries to lose. Thus, if the United States were to place a tariff on goods from China, those aspects of production that depend on Chinese goods would be hurt, and, as I discussed above, there are many such goods. Moreover, China would likely place tariffs on goods from the United States, hurting both countries. Such tariffs would cut overall production, making both countries worse off.

International Trade Provides Competition

A second reason most economists support free trade is that trade restrictions reduce international competition. International competition is desirable because it forces domestic companies to stay on their toes. If trade restrictions on imports are imposed, domestic companies don't work as hard and therefore become less efficient.

For example, in the 1950s and 1960s, the United States imposed restrictions on imported steel. U.S. steel industries responded to this protection by raising their prices and channeling profits from their steel production into other activities. By the 1970s, the U.S. steel industry was using outdated equipment to produce overpriced steel. Instead of making the steel industry stronger, restrictions made it a flabby, uncompetitive industry.

In the 1980s and 1990s, the U.S. steel industry became less and less profitable. Larger mills closed or consolidated, while nonunion minimills, which made new steel out of scrap steel, did well. By the late 1990s, minimills accounted for 45 percent of total U.S. steel production. In 2002 it looked as if a number of larger mills were going to declare bankruptcy, and enormous pressure was placed on the federal government to bail them out by taking over their pension debt and instituting tariffs. The U.S. government responded by imposing 20–30 percent tariffs on foreign steel imports. Most economists opposed the tariffs and pointed out that they were unlikely to lead to a rebuilding of the U.S. steel industry because other countries had a comparative advantage in steel production. Moreover, other countries would retaliate with tariffs on U.S. goods. Despite their opposition, the tariffs were instituted. Major U.S. trading partners—including EU countries, Japan, and China—responded by threatening to implement tariffs on U.S. goods worth about $335 million, and in 2003, the U.S. government withdrew the tariffs.

Very few of the infant industries protected by trade restrictions have ever grown up.

Web Note 9.3
Thumbs Up or Down?

The benefits of international competition are not restricted to mature industries like steel; they can also accrue to young industries wherever they appear. Economists dispose of the infant industry argument by reference to the historical record. In theory the argument makes sense. But very few of the infant industries protected by trade restrictions have ever grown up. What tends to happen instead is that infant industries become dependent on the trade restrictions and use political pressure to keep that protection. As a result, they often remain immature and internationally uncompetitive. Most economists would support the infant industry argument only if the trade restrictions included definite conditions under which the restrictions would end.

Restrictions Based on National Security Are Often Abused or Evaded

Most economists agree with the national security argument for export restrictions on goods that are directly war related. Selling bombs to Iran, whom the United States has called a member of the Axis of Evil, doesn't make much sense. Economists point out that the argument is often carried far beyond goods directly related to national security. For example, in the 1980s the United States restricted exports of sugar-coated cereals to the Soviet Union purportedly for reasons of national security. Sugar-frosted flakes may be great, but they were unlikely to help the Soviet Union in a war.

Another argument that economists give against the national security rationale is that trade restrictions on military sales can often be evaded. Countries simply have another country buy the goods for them. Such third-party sales—called *transshipments*—are common in international trade and limit the effectiveness of any absolute trade restrictions for national security purposes.

Economists also argue that by fostering international cooperation, international trade makes war less likely—a significant contribution to national security.

Trade Restrictions Are Addictive

Yes, some restrictions might benefit a country, but almost no country can limit its restrictions to the beneficial ones.

Economists' final argument against trade restrictions is: Yes, some restrictions might benefit a country, but almost no country can limit its restrictions to the beneficial ones. Trade restrictions are addictive—the more you have, the more you want. Thus, a majority of economists take the position that the best response to such addictive policies is "Just say no."

Institutions Supporting Free Trade

Web Note 9.4
Promoting Trade

As I have stated throughout the text, economists generally like markets and favor trade being as free as possible. They argue that trade allows specialization and the division of labor. When each country follows its comparative advantage, production is more efficient and the production possibility curve shifts out. These views mean that most economists, liberal and conservative alike, generally oppose international trade restrictions.

Despite political pressures to restrict trade, governments have generally tried to follow economists' advice and have entered into a variety of international agreements and organizations. The most important is the World Trade Organization (WTO), which has about 150 members, and is the successor to the General Agreement on Tariffs and Trade (GATT). You will still occasionally see references to GATT, even though the WTO has taken its place. One of the differences between the WTO and GATT is that the WTO includes some enforcement mechanisms.

Important international economic organizations include the WTO, which took the place of GATT.

Achieving agreement on trade barrier reductions is politically difficult, as is demonstrated by the latest WTO negotiations, called the Doha Development Round. Begun in 2001, it was meant to lead to fairer trade rules for developing countries, especially in

ADDED DIMENSION

Dumping

The WTO allows countries to impose trade restrictions on imports if they can show that the goods are being dumped. *Dumping* is selling a good in a foreign country at a lower price than in the country where it's produced. On the face of it, who could complain about someone who wants to sell you a good cheaply? Why not just take advantage of the bargain price? The first objection is the learning-by-doing argument. To stay competitive, a country must keep on producing. Dumping by another country can force domestic producers out of business. Having eliminated the competition, the foreign producer has the field to itself and can raise the price. Thus, dumping can be a form of predatory pricing.

The second argument against dumping involves the short-term macroeconomic and political effects it can have on the importing country. Even if one believes that dumping is not a preliminary to predatory pricing, it can displace workers in the importing country, causing political pressure on that government to institute trade restrictions. If that country's economy is in a recession, the resulting unemployment will have substantial macroeconomic repercussions, so pressure for trade restrictions will be amplified.

agriculture. The Round did not go well; the United States and Europe were unwilling to eliminate subsidies to their farmers that the developing countries said made it impossible for them to compete fairly, and hence would not reduce their tariffs on manufactured goods. As of 2009, there was still no agreement.

The push for free trade has a geographic dimension, which includes **free trade associations**—*groups of countries that have reduced or eliminated trade barriers among themselves*. The European Union (EU) is the most famous free trade association. All barriers to trade among the EU's member countries were removed in 1992. In the coming decade, more European countries can be expected to join the EU. In 1993, the United States and Canada agreed to enter into a similar free trade union, and they, together with Mexico, created the North American Free Trade Association (NAFTA). Under NAFTA, tariffs and other trade barriers among these countries are being gradually reduced. Some other trading associations include Mercosur (among South American countries) and ASEAN (among Southeast Asian countries).

A free trade association is a group of countries that allows free trade among its members and puts up common barriers against all other countries' goods.

Economists have mixed reactions to free trade associations. They see free trade as beneficial, but they are concerned about the possibility that these regional free trade associations will impose significant trade restrictions on nonmember countries. They also believe that bilateral negotiations between member nations will replace multilateral efforts among members and nonmembers. Whether the net effect of these bilateral negotiations is positive or negative remains to be seen.

Q-10 What is economists' view of limited free trade associations such as the EU or NAFTA?

Groups of other countries have loose trading relationships because of cultural or historical reasons. These loose trading relationships are sometimes called trading zones. For example, many European countries maintain close trading ties with many of their former colonies in Africa where they fit into a number of overlapping trading zones. European companies tend to see that central area as their turf. The United States has close ties in Latin America, making the Western hemisphere another trading zone. Another example of a trading zone is that of Japan and its economic ties with other Far East countries; Japanese companies often see that area as their commercial domain.

These trading zones overlap, sometimes on many levels. For instance, Australia and England, Portugal and Brazil, and the United States and Saudi Arabia are tied together for historical or political reasons, and those ties lead to increased trade between them that seems to deviate from the above trading zones. Similarly, as companies become more and more global, it is harder and harder to associate companies with particular countries. Let me give an example: Do you know who the largest exporters of cars from the United States are? The answer is: Japanese automobile companies!

Thus, there is no hard-and-fast specification of trading zones, and knowing history and politics is important to understanding many of the relationships.

A most-favored nation is a country that will pay as low a tariff on its exports as will any other country.

One way countries strengthen trading relationships among groups of countries is through a most-favored-nation status. The term **most-favored nation** refers to *a country that will be charged as low a tariff on its exports as any other country*. Thus, if the United States lowers tariffs on goods imported from Japan, which has most-favored-nation status with the United States, it must lower tariffs on those same types of goods imported from any other country with most-favored-nation status.

Conclusion

International trade, and changing comparative advantages, will become more and more important for the United States in the coming decades. With international transportation and communication becoming easier and faster, and with other countries' economies growing, the U.S. economy will inevitably become more interdependent with the other economies of the world. As international trade becomes more important, the push for trade restrictions will likely increase. Various countries' strategic trade policies will likely conflict, and the world could find itself on the verge of an international trade war that would benefit no one.

Concern about that possibility leads most economists to favor free trade. As often happens, economists advise politicians to follow a politically unpopular policy—to take the hard course of action. Whether politicians follow economists' advice or whether they follow the politically popular policy will play a key role in determining the course of the U.S. economy in the 2000s.

Summary

- The nature of trade is continually changing. The United States is importing more and more high-tech goods and services from India and China and other East Asian countries.
- Outsourcing is a type of trade. Outsourcing is a larger phenomenon today compared to 30 years ago because China and India are so large, enormous outsourcing is possible.
- According to the principle of comparative advantage, as long as the relative opportunity costs of producing goods (what must be given up in one good in order to get another good) differ among countries, there are potential gains from trade.
- Three insights into the terms of trade include
    1. The more competition exists in international trade, the less the trader gets and the more the involved countries get.
    2. Once competition prevails, smaller countries tend to get a larger percentage of the gains from trade than do larger countries.
    3. Gains from trade go to countries that produce goods that exhibit economies of scale.
- The gains from trade in the form of low consumer prices tend to be widespread and not easily recognized, while the costs in jobs lost tend to be concentrated and readily identifiable.
- The United States has comparative advantages based on its skilled workforce, its institutions, and its language, among other things.
- Inherent comparative advantages are based on factors that are relatively unchangeable. They are not subject to the law of one price.

- Transferable comparative advantages are based on factors that can change relatively easily. The law of one price can eliminate these comparative advantages.
- Trade restrictions include tariffs and quotas, embargoes, voluntary restraint agreements, regulatory trade restrictions, and nationalistic appeals.
- Reasons that countries impose trade restrictions include unequal internal distribution of the gains from trade, haggling by companies over the gains from trade, haggling by countries over trade restrictions, learning by doing and economies of scale, macroeconomic aspects of trade, national security, international political reasons, and increased revenue brought in by tariffs.
- Economists generally oppose trade restrictions because of the history of trade restrictions and their understanding of the advantages of free trade.
- The World Trade Organization is an international organization committed to reducing trade barriers.
- Free trade associations help trade by reducing barriers to trade among member nations. Free trade associations could hinder trade by building up barriers to trade with nations outside the association; negotiations among members could replace multilateral efforts to reduce trade restrictions among members and nonmembers.

Key Terms

balance of trade *(201)*
comparative advantage *(203)*
economies of scale *(219)*
embargo *(214)*
free trade association *(223)*
General Agreement on Tariffs and Trade (GATT) *(212)*
infant industry argument *(219)*
inherent comparative advantage *(209)*
learning by doing *(218)*
most-favored nation *(224)*
quota *(212)*
regulatory trade restriction *(214)*
strategic bargaining *(217)*
strategic trade policy *(218)*
tariff *(212)*
trade adjustment assistance program *(217)*
transferable comparative advantage *(209)*
World Trade Organization (WTO) *(212)*

Questions and Exercises

1. Will a country do better importing or exporting a good for which it has a comparative advantage? Why? LO1
2. Widgetland has 60 workers. Each worker can produce 4 widgets or 4 wadgets. Each resident in Widgetland currently consumes 2 widgets and 2 wadgets. Wadgetland also has 60 workers. Each can produce 3 widgets or 12 wadgets. Wadgetland's residents consume 1 widget and 9 wadgets. Is there a basis for trade? If so, offer the countries a deal they can't refuse. LO2
3. Suppose there are two states that do not trade: Iowa and Nebraska. Each state produces the same two goods: corn and wheat. For Iowa the opportunity cost of producing 1 bushel of wheat is 3 bushels of corn. For Nebraska the opportunity cost of producing 1 bushel of corn is 3 bushels of wheat. At present, Iowa produces 20 million bushels of wheat and 120 million bushels of corn, while Nebraska produces 20 million bushels of corn and 120 million bushels of wheat.
   a. Explain how, with trade, Nebraska can end up with 40 million bushels of wheat and 120 million bushels of corn while Iowa can end up with 40 million bushels of corn and 120 million bushels of wheat.
   b. If the states ended up with the numbers given in *a*, how much would the trader get? LO2

4. Suppose that two countries, Machineland and Farmland, have the following production possibility curves.

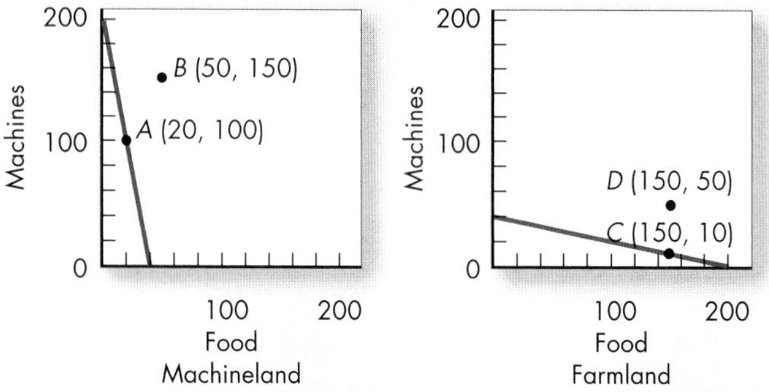

a. Explain how these two countries can move from points *A* and *C*, where they currently are, to points *B* and *D*.
b. If possible, state by how much total production for the two countries has risen.
c. If you were a trader, how much of the gains from trade would you deserve for discovering this trade?
d. If there were economies of scale in the production of both goods, how would your analysis change? LO2

5. Suppose there are two countries, Busytown and Lazyasiwannabe, with the following production possibility tables:

Busytown

% of Resources Devoted to Cars	Cars Produced (thousands)	Gourmet Meals Produced (thousands)
100%	60	0
80	48	10
60	36	20
40	24	30
20	12	40
0	0	50

Lazyasiwannabe

% of Resources Devoted to Cars	Cars Produced (thousands)	Gourmet Meals Produced (thousands)
100%	50	0
80	40	10
60	30	20
40	20	30
20	10	40
0	0	50

a. Draw the production possibility curves for each country.
b. Which country has the comparative advantage in producing cars? In producing gourmet meals?
c. Suppose each country specializes in the production of one good. Explain how Busytown can end up with 36,000 cars and 22,000 meals and Lazyasiwannabe can end up with 28,000 meals and 24,000 cars. LO2

6. Why does competition among traders affect how much of the gains from trade are given to the countries involved in the trade? LO3
7. Why do smaller countries usually get most of the gains from trade? LO3
8. What are some reasons why a small country might not get the gains of trade? LO3
9. Which country will get the larger gain from trade: a country with economies of scale or diseconomies of scale? Explain your answer. LO3
10. Country A can produce, at most, 40 olives or 20 pickles, or some combination of olives and pickles such as the 20 olives and 10 pickles it is currently producing. Country B can produce, at most, 120 olives or 60 pickles, or some combination of olives and pickles such as the 100 olives and 50 pickles it is currently producing.
    a. Is there a basis for trade? If so, offer the two countries a deal they can't refuse.
    b. How would your answer to *a* change if you knew that there were economies of scale in the production of pickles and olives rather than the production possibilities described in the question? Why? If your answer is yes, which country would you have produce which good? LO2, LO3
11. What are three reasons why economists' and laypeople's view of trade differ? LO4
12. List at least three sources of comparative advantage that the United States has and will likely maintain over the coming decade. LO5
13. How do inherent comparative advantages differ from transferable comparative advantages? LO5
14. From the standpoint of adjustment costs to trade, which would a country prefer—inherent or transferable comparative advantage? Why? LO5
15. What is the law of one price? LO5
16. Why is the law of one price important to any discussion of the future of the U.S. economy? LO5
17. Which is the law of one price likely to eliminate: a transferable or an inherent comparative advantage? Explain your answer. LO5
18. What are two methods by which the wage gap between Chinese and U.S. workers will likely narrow? LO5
19. Demonstrate graphically how the effects of a tariff differ from the effects of a quota. LO6
20. How do the effects of voluntary restraint agreements differ from the effects of a tariff? LO6

21. The world price of textiles is P_w, as in the accompanying figure of the domestic supply and demand for textiles.

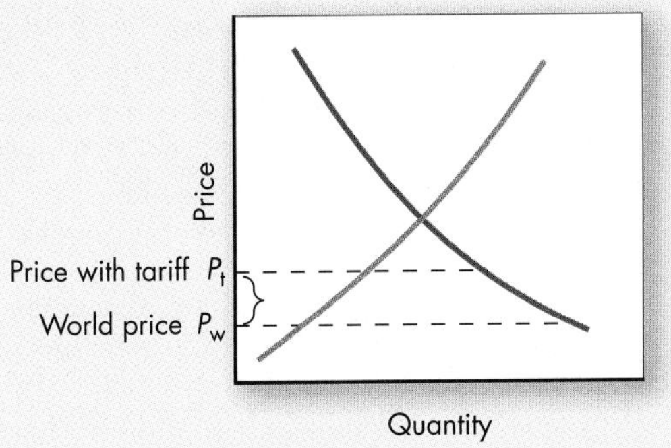

The government imposes a tariff t, to protect the domestic producers. For this tariff:
a. Label the revenue gains to domestic producers.
b. Label the revenue to government.
c. Label the costs to domestic producers.
d. Are the gains to domestic producers greater than the costs? Why? LO6

22. If you were economic adviser to a country that was following your advice about trade restrictions and that country fell into a recession, would you change your advice? Why, or why not? (Difficult) LO7

23. What are two reasons economists support free trade? LO7

24. On January 1, 2005, quotas on clothing imports to the United States first instituted in the 1960s to protect the U.S. garment industry were eliminated.
a. Demonstrate graphically how this change affected equilibrium price and quantity of imported garments.
b. Demonstrate graphically how U.S. consumers benefited from the end of the quota system.
c. What was the likely effect on profits of foreign companies that sold clothing in the U.S. market? LO6, LO7

25. What is the relationship between GATT and WTO? LO8

Questions from Alternative Perspectives

1. Evaluate the following statement: Comparative advantage will benefit all people because everyone has a comparative advantage in something. Therefore, trade based on comparative advantage should be facilitated without undue government intervention. (Austrian)

2. In the 10th century B.C., King Solomon brought the Israelites into great economic wealth through specialization and trade. It was difficult when faced with the practices and beliefs of their trading partners, however, for Israel to maintain its identity as a people of one God. King Solomon, for example, provided a place for each of his wives to worship the gods of her own people. If such syncretism (adoption of foreign practices and beliefs) is inevitable with increased globalization, should trade be encouraged, even today? (Religious)

3. Global outsourcing has cost the U.S. economy far over one million jobs since 2001, or somewhere between 15 and 35 percent of the total decline in employment since the onset of the 2001 recession.
a. How does outsourcing affect the bargaining power of U.S. workers and the bargaining power of U.S. employers?
b. What will it likely do to the overall level of U.S. workers' wages?
c. What will it likely do to lawyers' wages?
d. If you stated that it affected lawyers' wages differently, do you believe that the U.S. policy response to outsourcing would be different? (Post-Keynesian)

4. In David Ricardo's original example of comparative advantage in his *Principles of Political Economy*, written in 1817, Portugal possesses an absolute advantage in both the production of cloth and the production of wine. But England has a comparative advantage in the production of cloth, while Portugal's comparative advantage is in wine production. According to Ricardo, an English political economist, England should specialize in the production of cloth and Portugal in wine making.
a. Was Ricardo's advice self-serving?
b. Knowing that light manufacturing, such as clothing and textile production, has led most industrialization processes, would you have advised 19th century Portugal to specialize in wine making? (Radical)

5. The text presents free trade as advantageous for developing countries. However, in its period of most rapid development, the half century following the Civil War, the United States imposed tariffs on imports that averaged around 40 percent, a level higher than those in all but one of today's developing economies.
a. Why did so many of today's industrialized countries not follow those policies as they were developing?
b. What does this insight into economic history suggest about the doctrine of free trade and whose interests it serves? (Radical)

Issues to Ponder

1. How is outsourcing to China and India today different than U.S. outsourcing in the past? LO4
2. One of the basic economic laws is "the law of one price." It says that given certain assumptions one would expect that if free trade is allowed, the price of goods in countries should converge.
   a. Can you list what three of those assumptions likely are?
   b. Should the law of one price hold for labor also? Why or why not?
   c. Should it hold for capital more so or less so than for labor? Why? LO5
3. Suggest an equitable method of funding trade adjustment assistance programs.
   a. Why is it equitable?
   b. What problems might a politician have in implementing such a method? LO6
4. When the United States placed a temporary price floor on tomatoes imported from Mexico, U.S. trade representative Mickey Kantor said, "The agreement will provide strong relief to the tomato growers in Florida and other states, and help preserve jobs in the industry." What costs did Americans bear from the price floor? (Difficult) LO6
5. Mexico exports many vegetables to the United States. These vegetables are grown using chemicals that are not allowed in U.S. vegetable agriculture. Should the United States restrict imports of Mexican vegetables? Why or why not? (Difficult) LO6, LO7
6. The U.S. government taxes U.S. companies for their overseas profits, but it allows them to deduct from their U.S. taxable income the taxes that they pay abroad and interest on loans funding operations abroad, with no limits on the amount deducted. (Difficult)
   a. Is it possible that the overseas profit tax produces no net revenue?
   b. What would you suggest to the government about this tax if its desire were to increase corporate income tax revenue?
   c. Why might the government keep this tax even if it were not collecting any net revenue? LO6, LO7
7. In the 1930s Clair Wilcox of Swarthmore College organized a petition by economists "that any measure which provided for a general upward revision of tariff rates be denied passage by Congress, or if passed, be vetoed." It was signed by one-third of all economists in the United States at the time, of all political persuasions. A month later, the Smoot-Hawley Tariff was passed.
   a. Why did economists oppose the tariff?
   b. Demonstrate the effect of the tariff on the price of goods.
   c. How would the tariff help the economy if other countries did not institute a retaliatory tariff?
   d. What would be the effect on the macroeconomy if other countries did institute a retaliatory tariff? LO6, LO7

Answers to Margin Questions

1. The type of goods being imported has changed from primarily low-tech goods to technologically advanced goods. *(200)*
2. A debtor nation will not necessarily be running a trade deficit. *Debt* refers to accumulated past deficits. If a country had accumulated large deficits in the past, it could run a surplus now but still be a debtor nation. *(203)*
3. He should walk away because there is no basis for trade. *(203)*
4. The percentage of gains from trade that goes to a country depends upon the change in the price of the goods being traded. If trade led to no change in prices in a small country, then that small country would get no gains from trade. Another case in which a small country gets a small percentage of the gains from trade would occur when its larger trading partner was producing a good with economies of scale and the small country was not. A third case is when the traders who extracted most of the surplus or gains from trade come from the larger country; then the smaller country would end up with few of the gains from trade. *(206)*
5. Three reasons for the difference are (1) gains from trade are often stealth gains, (2) comparative advantage is determined by more than wages, and (3) nations trade more than just manufactured goods. *(207)*
6. Two likely adjustments that will reduce the wage gap are a fall in the value of the dollar (U.S. exchange rate) and a rise in Chinese wages relative to U.S. wages. *(211)*
7. An inefficient customs agency can operate with the same effect as a trade restriction, and if trade restrictions would help the country, then it is possible that an inefficient customs agency could also help the country. *(215)*
8. True. In strategic trade bargaining it is sometimes reasonable to be unreasonable. The belief of the other bargainer

that you will be unreasonable leads you to be able to extract larger gains from trade. Of course, this leads to the logical paradox that if "unreasonable" is "reasonable," unreasonable really is reasonable, so it is only reasonable to be reasonable. Sorting out that last statement can be left for a philosophy or logic class. *(218)*

9. Whether or not it is efficient for a country to maintain barriers to trade in an industry that exhibits economies of scale depends upon the marginal costs and marginal benefits of maintaining those barriers. Having significant economies of scale does mean that average costs of production will be lower at higher levels of production; however, trade restrictions might mean that the industry might be able to inflate its costs. *(219)*

10. Most economists have a mixed view of limited free trade associations such as NAFTA or the EU. While they see free trade as beneficial, they are concerned about the possibility that these limited trade associations will impose trade restrictions on nonmember countries. Whether the net effect of these will be positive or negative is a complicated issue. *(223)*

CHAPTER 10

The Logic of Individual Choice: The Foundation of Supply and Demand

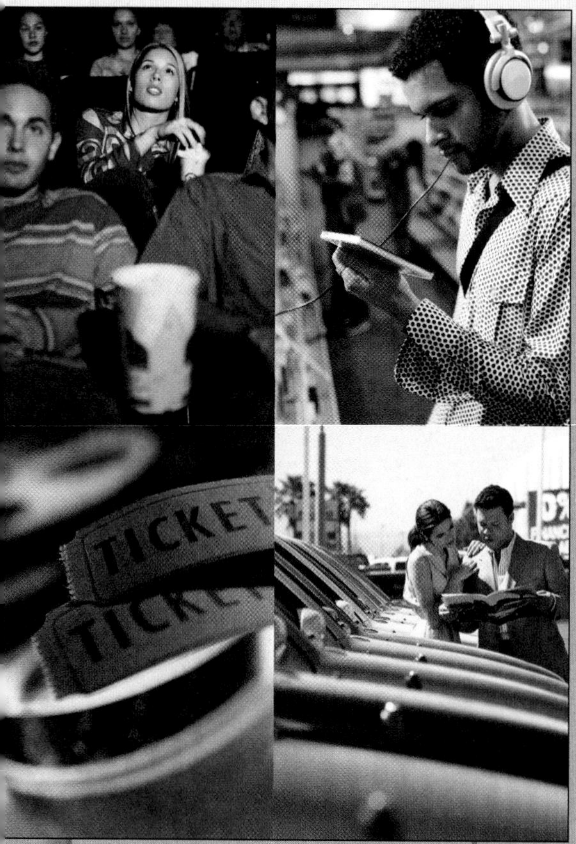

The theory of economics must begin with a correct theory of consumption.

—*Stanley Jevons*

It's Friday night and you've managed to scrimp and save $50 to take a break from classes and buy two tickets, one for yourself and one for a friend, to see the rock concert at the field house. But then you think about it; maybe going to a movie and having a hot fudge sundae after for the two of you would make more sense. Or maybe a big steak dinner just for yourself. Or maybe ordering Chinese. Or maybe studying and giving the money to the homeless shelter. Choices, choices; they are around you all the time.

How individuals make choices is central to microeconomics. It is the foundation of economic reasoning and it gives economics much of its power. The first part of this chapter shows you that foundation and leads you through some exercises to make sure you understand the reasoning. The second part of the chapter relates that analysis to the real world, giving you a sense of when the model is useful and when it's not.

As you go through this chapter, think back to Chapter 1, which set out the goals for this book. One goal was to get you to think like an economist. This chapter, which formally develops the reasoning process behind economists' cost/benefit approach to problems, examines the underpinnings of how to think like an economist.

AFTER READING THIS CHAPTER, YOU SHOULD BE ABLE TO:

1. Discuss the principle of diminishing marginal utility.
2. Summarize the principle of rational choice.
3. Explain the relationship between marginal utility and price when a consumer is maximizing total utility.
4. Explain how the principle of rational choice accounts for the laws of demand and supply.
5. Name three assumptions of the theory of choice and discuss why they may not reflect reality.
6. Give an example of how behavioral economists change the assumption of utility maximization.

Utility Theory and Individual Choice

Different sciences have various explanations for why people do what they do. For example, Freudian psychology tells us we do what we do because of an internal fight between the id, ego, and superego plus some hangups we have about our bodies. Other psychologists tell us it's a search for approval by our peers; we want to be OK. Economists agree that these are important reasons but argue that if we want an analysis that's simple enough to apply to policy problems, these heavy psychological explanations are likely to get us all mixed up. At least to start with, we need an easier underlying psychological foundation. And economists have one—self-interest. People do what they do because it's in their self-interest.

Economists' traditional analysis of individual choice doesn't deny that most of us have our quirks. That's obvious in what we buy. On certain items we're pennypinchers; on others we're big spenders. For example, how many of you or your parents clip coupons to save 40 cents on cereal but then spend $40 on a haircut? How many save 50 cents a pound by buying a low grade of meat but then spend $20 on a bottle of wine, $75 on dinner at a restaurant, or $60 for a concert ticket?

But through it all comes a certain rationality. Much of what people do reflects their rational self-interest. That's why economists start their analysis of individual choice with a relatively simple, but powerful, underlying psychological foundation.

Using that simple theory, two things determine what people do: **utility**—*the pleasure or satisfaction people get from doing or consuming something*, and the price of doing or consuming that something. Price is the tool the market uses to bring the quantity supplied equal to the quantity demanded. Changes in price provide incentives for people to change what they're doing. Through those incentives, the invisible hand guides us all. To understand economics, you must understand how price affects our choices. That's why we focus on the effect of price on the quantity demanded. We want to understand the way in which a change in price will affect what we do.

In summary, economists' theory of rational choice is a simple, but powerful, theory that shows how these two things—pleasure and price—are related.

Thinking Like a Modern Economist

The Traditional Models as Stepping Stones

As I discussed in Chapter 6, behavioral economists are beginning to explore consistent deviations from rationality and self-interest, and in doing so they are expanding the building blocks of economics. But doing so has a cost—it complicates the model enormously, and a more complicated model is much more difficult to use. The advantage of using traditional building blocks is that it comes to black-and-white conclusions—and then lets you decide whether the model is or is not applicable.

Behavioral economists recognize the cost and are trying to characterize types of decisions that fit the traditional model and types of decisions that don't. Unfortunately, the work is still in an early stage and they have a long way to go. That's why, at this point in time, when it comes to teaching economics, almost all economists—including behavioral economists—agree that the best place to start is with models based on the traditional building blocks. That's why this book is structured like it is—it focuses on models with the traditional building blocks, but lets you know that, in their research, modern economists are going beyond the traditional models.

Web Note 10.1
Utility and Pleasure

Utility is the pleasure or satisfaction that people get from doing or consuming something.

Total Utility and Marginal Utility

In thinking about utility, it's important to distinguish between *total utility* and *marginal utility*. **Total utility** refers to *the total satisfaction one gets from consuming a product*. **Marginal utility** refers to *the satisfaction one gets from consuming one additional unit of a product above and beyond what one has consumed up to that point*. For example, eating a whole pound of Beluga caviar might give you 4,700 units of utility.[1] Consuming the first 15 ounces may have given you 4,697 units of utility. Consuming the last ounce of caviar might give you an additional 3 units of utility. The 4,700 is total utility; the 3 is the marginal utility of eating that last ounce of caviar.

It is important to distinguish between marginal and total utility.

An example of the relationship between total utility and marginal utility is given in Figure 10-1. Let's say that the marginal utility of the 1st slice of pizza is 14, and since

[1]Throughout the book I choose specific numbers to make the examples more understandable and to make the points I want to make. Economists don't use actual numbers to discuss utility. At the principles level, they use such numbers to make the presentation easier. A useful exercise is for you to choose different numbers and reason your way through the same analysis. In Appendix A, I go through the same analysis without using actual numbers.

FIGURE 10-1 (A, B, AND C) Marginal and Total Utility

Marginal utility tends to decrease as consumption of a good increases. Notice how the information in the table (a) can be presented graphically in two different ways. The two different ways are, however, related. The downward slope of the marginal utility curve (c) is reflected in the total utility curve bowed downward in (b). Notice that marginal utility relates to changes in quantity so the marginal utility line is graphed at the halfway point. For example, in (c), between 7 and 8, marginal utility becomes zero.

Number of Pizza Slices	Total Utility	Marginal Utility
0	0	
1	14	14
2	26	12
3	36	10
4	44	8
5	50	6
6	54	4
7	56	2
8	56	0
9	54	−2

(a) Utility Table

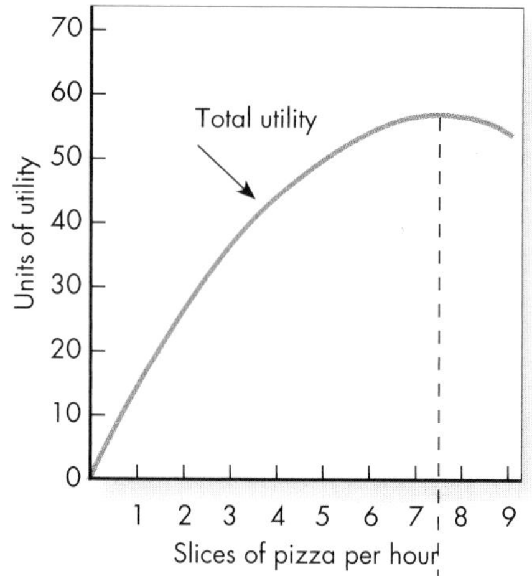

(b) Total Utility

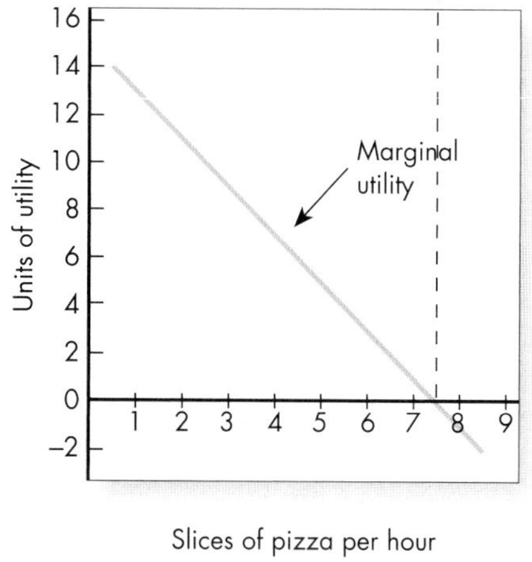

(c) Marginal Utility

Eating contests are proof that, at some point, utility becomes zero.

Q-1 If the total utility curve is a straight line—that is, does not exhibit diminishing marginal utility—what will the marginal utility curve look like?

you've eaten only 1 slice, the total utility is also 14. Let's also say that the marginal utility of the 2nd slice of pizza is 12, which means that the total utility of 2 slices of pizza is 26 (14 + 12). Similarly for the 3rd, 4th, and 5th slices of pizza, whose marginal utilities are 10, 8, and 6, respectively. The total utility of your eating those 5 pieces of pizza is the sum of the marginal utilities you get from eating each of the 5 slices. The sixth row of column 2 of Figure 10-1(a) shows that sum.

Notice that marginal utility shows up between the lines. That's because it is the utility of *changing* consumption levels. For example, the marginal utility of changing from 1 to 2 slices of pizza is 12. The relationship between total and marginal utility also can be seen graphically. In Figure 10-1(b), we graph total utility (column 2 of the utility table) on the vertical axis and the number of slices of pizza (column 1 of the utility table) on the horizontal axis. As you can see, total utility increases up to 7 slices of pizza; after 8 slices it starts decreasing—after 8 pieces of pizza, you're so stuffed that you can't stand to look at another slice.

In Figure 10-1(c), we graph marginal utility (column 3 of the utility table) on the vertical axis and slices of pizza (column 1) on the horizontal axis. Notice how marginal utility decreases while total utility increases. When total utility stops increasing (between 7 and

8 slices), marginal utility is zero. Beyond this point, total utility decreases and marginal utility is negative. An additional slice of pizza will actually make you worse off.

Diminishing Marginal Utility

Now let's consider the shapes of these curves a bit more carefully: What are they telling us about people's choices? As we've drawn the curves, the marginal utility that a person gets from each additional slice of pizza decreases with each slice of pizza eaten. Economists believe that the shape of these curves is generally a reasonable description of the pattern of people's enjoyment. They call that pattern the **principle of diminishing marginal utility:**

> *As you consume more of a good, after some point, the marginal utility received from each additional unit of a good decreases with each additional unit consumed, other things equal.*

The principle of diminishing marginal utility states that, after some point, the marginal utility received from each additional unit of a good decreases with each additional unit consumed, other things equal.

As individuals increase their consumption of a good, at some point, consuming another unit of the product will simply not yield as much additional pleasure as did consuming the preceding unit.

Consider, for example, that late-night craving for a double-cheese-and-pepperoni pizza. You order one and bite into it. Ah, pleasure! But if you've ordered a large pizza and you're eating it all by yourself, eventually you'll get less additional enjoyment from eating additional slices. In other words, the marginal utility you get is going to decrease with each additional slice of pizza you consume. That's the principle of diminishing marginal utility.

Diminishing Marginal Utility

Notice that the principle of diminishing marginal utility does not say that you don't enjoy consuming more of a good; it simply states that as you consume more of the good, you enjoy the additional units less than you did the initial units. A fourth slice of pizza still tastes good, but it doesn't match the taste of the third slice. At some point, however, marginal utility can become negative. Say you had two large pizzas and only two hours in which to eat them. Eating the last slice could be pure torture. But in most situations, you have the option *not* to consume any more of a good. When consuming a good becomes torture (meaning its utility is negative), you simply don't consume any more of it. If you eat a slice of pizza (or consume an additional unit of a good), that's a good indication that its marginal utility is still positive.

Q-2 Consuming more of a good generally increases its marginal utility. True or false? Why?

WWW Web Note 10.2 Diminishing Marginal Utility

Rational Choice and Marginal Utility

The analysis of rational choice is the analysis of how individuals choose goods within their budget in order to maximize total utility, and how maximizing total utility can be accomplished by considering marginal utility. That analysis begins with the premise that rational individuals want as much satisfaction as they can get from their available resources. The term *rational* in economics means, specifically, that people prefer more to less and will make choices that give them as much satisfaction as possible. The problem is that people face a budget constraint. They must choose among the alternatives. How do they do that?

Because people face a budget constraint, they must choose among alternatives.

Some Choices

Let's start by considering three choices. (Answer each choice as you read it.)[2]

Choice 1: Between spending another dollar on a slice of pizza that gives you an additional 41 units of utility, or spending another dollar on a hero sandwich that gives you an additional 30 units of utility.

[2]To keep the analysis simple in this example, I consider either/or decisions. Below, I show how to extend the analysis to marginal choices.

Choice 2: Between reading an additional chapter in this book that gives you an additional 200 units of utility at a cost of one hour of your time, or reading an additional chapter in psychology that gives you an additional 100 units of utility at a cost of 40 minutes of your time.

Choice 3: Between having your next date with that awesome guy Jerry, which gives you an additional 2,000 units of utility and costs you $70, or taking out plain Jeff on your next date, which gives you an additional 200 units of utility and costs you $10.

The correct choices, in terms of marginal utility, are (1) the pizza, (2) a chapter of this book, and (3) Jerry.

If you answered all three correctly, either you're lucky or you have a good intuitive understanding of the principle of rational choice. Now let's explore the principle of rational choice more thoroughly by considering each of the three examples.

Choice 1 Since the slice of pizza and the hero sandwich both cost $1, and the pizza gives you more units of utility than the hero, the pizza is the rational choice. If you spend $1 on the hero rather than the pizza, you're losing 11 units of utility and not making yourself as happy as you could be. You're being irrational. Any choice (for the same amount of money) that doesn't give you as much utility as possible is an irrational choice.

But now let's say that the price of heroes falls to 50 cents so that you can buy two heroes for the same price you previously had to pay for only one. Let's also say that two heroes would give you 56 units of utility (not $2 \times 30 = 60$—remember the principle of diminishing marginal utility). Which would now be the more rational choice? The two heroes, because their 56 units of utility are 15 more than you would get from that dollar spent on one slice of pizza.

Another way of thinking about your choice is to recognize that essentially what you're doing is buying units of utility. Obviously you want to get the most for your money, so you choose goods that have the highest units of utility per unit of cost. Let's see how this way of thinking about a decision works by considering our second choice.

Q-3 Which is the rational choice: watching one hour of MTV that gives you 20 units of utility or watching a two-hour movie that gives you 30 units of utility?

Choice 2 Here the two alternatives have a cost in time, not money. The analysis, however, is the same. You calculate the marginal utility (additional units of utility) of the choice facing you and divide that by the costs of the activity; that gives you the marginal utility per unit of cost. Then choose the activity that has the higher marginal utility per unit of cost or lower cost per unit of utility. When you do that, you see that this chapter gives you 3⅓ units of utility per minute (200/60 = 3⅓), while the psychology chapter gives you 2⅓ units of utility per minute. So you choose to read another chapter in this book.[3]

Choice 3 Taking out Jerry gives you 28½ units of utility per dollar (2,000/$70), while taking out Jeff gives you 20 units of utility per dollar (200/$10). So you choose to take out Jerry.[4]

[3]As I've pointed out before, I choose the numbers to make the points I want to make. A good exercise for you is to choose different numbers that reflect your estimate of the marginal utility you get from a choice, and see what your rational choices are.

[4]In these examples, I am implicitly assuming that the "goods" are divisible. Technically, this assumption is needed for marginal utilities to be fully specified.

The Principle of Rational Choice

The **principle of rational choice** is as follows: *Spend your money on those goods that give you the most marginal utility (MU) per dollar.* The principle of rational choice is important enough for us to restate.

The principle of rational choice tells us to spend our money on those goods that give us the most marginal utility per dollar.

If $\frac{MU_x}{P_x} > \frac{MU_y}{P_y}$, choose to consume an additional unit of good *x*.

If $\frac{MU_x}{P_x} < \frac{MU_y}{P_y}$, choose to consume an additional unit of good *y*.

By substituting the marginal utilities and prices of goods into these formulas, you can always decide which good it makes more sense to consume. Consume the one with the highest marginal utility per dollar.

Web Note 10.3
Maximizing Utility

Simultaneous Decisions

So far in discussing our examples, we've considered the choices separately. But in real life, choices aren't so neatly separated. Say you were presented with all three choices simultaneously. If you make all three of the decisions given in the examples, are you being rational? The answer is no. Why? The pizza gives you 41 units of utility per dollar; taking out Jerry gives you 28½ units of utility per dollar. You aren't being rational; you aren't maximizing your utility. It would clearly make sense to eat more pizza, paying for it by cutting the date with Jerry short. (Skip the coffee at the end of the meal.)

But what about the other choice: studying psychology or economics? We can't compare the costs of studying to the costs of the other goods because, as I noted earlier, the costs of both studying alternatives are expressed in terms of time, not money. If we can assign a money value to the time, however, we can make the comparison. Let's say you can earn $6 per hour, so the value of your time is 10 cents per minute. This allows us to think about both alternatives in terms of dollars and cents. Since a chapter in economics takes an hour to read, the cost in money of reading a chapter is 60 minutes × 10 cents = $6. Similarly, the cost of the 40 minutes you'd take to read the psychology chapter is $4.

With these values, we can compare our studying decisions with our other decisions. The value in units of utility per dollar of reading a chapter of this book is

$$\frac{200}{\$6} = 33\tfrac{1}{3} \text{ units of utility per dollar}$$

Q-4 True or false? You are maximizing total utility only when the marginal utility of all goods is zero. Explain your answer.

So forget about dating Jerry with its 28½ units of utility per dollar. Your rational choice is to study this chapter while stuffing yourself with pizza.

But wait. Remember that, according to the principle of diminishing marginal utility, as you consume more of something, the marginal utility you get from it falls. So as you consume more pizza and spend more time reading this book, the marginal utilities of these activities will fall. Thus, as you vary your consumption, the marginal utilities you get from the goods are changing.

Maximizing Utility and Equilibrium

When do you stop changing your consumption? The principle of rational choice says you should keep adjusting your spending within your budget if the marginal utility per dollar (*MU/P*) of two goods differs. The only time you don't adjust your spending is

The utility-maximizing rule:

$\frac{MU_x}{P_x} = \frac{MU_y}{P_y}$

when there is no clear winner. *When the ratios of the marginal utility to price of the two goods are equal*, you're maximizing utility; this is the **utility-maximizing rule:**

$$\textit{If } \frac{MU_x}{P_x} = \frac{MU_y}{P_y}, \textit{ you're maximizing utility.}$$

When you're maximizing utility, you're in equilibrium. To understand how, by adjusting your spending, you can achieve equilibrium, it's important to remember the principle of diminishing marginal utility. As we consume more of an item, the marginal utility we get from the last unit consumed decreases. Conversely, as we consume *less* of an item, the marginal utility we get from the last unit consumed *increases*. (The principle of diminishing marginal utility operates in reverse.)

Achieving equilibrium by maximizing utility (juggling your choices, adding a bit more of one and choosing a bit less of another) requires more information than I've so far presented. We need to know the marginal utility of alternative amounts of consumption for each choice and how much we have to spend on all those items. With that information, we can choose among alternatives, given our available resources.

An Example of Maximizing Utility

Table 10-1 offers an example in which we have the necessary information to make simultaneous decisions and maximize utility. In this example, we have $7 to spend on ice cream cones and Big Macs. The choice is between ice cream at $1 a cone and Big Macs at $2 apiece. In the table, you can see the principle of diminishing marginal utility in action. The marginal utility (*MU*) we get from either good decreases as we consume more of it. *MU* becomes negative after 5 Big Macs or 6 ice cream cones.

The key columns for your decision are the *MU/P* columns. They tell you the *MU* per dollar spent on each of the items. By following the rule that we choose the good with the higher marginal utility per dollar, we can quickly determine the optimal choice.

Let's start by considering what we'd do with our first $2. Clearly we'd only eat ice cream. Doing so would give us 29 + 17 = 46 units of utility, compared to 20 units of utility if we spent the $2 on a Big Mac. How about our next $2? Again the choice is clear; the 10 units of utility per dollar from the Big Mac are plainly better than the 7 units of utility per dollar we can get from ice cream cones. So we buy 1 Big Mac and 2 ice cream cones with our first $4.

TABLE 10-1 Maximizing Utility

This table provides the information needed to make simultaneous decisions. Notice that the marginal utility we get from another good declines as we consume more of it. To maximize utility, adjust your choices until the marginal utility of all goods is equal.

	Big Macs (*P* = $2)				Ice Cream (*P* = $1)		
Q	***TU***	***MU***	***MU/P***	***Q***	***TU***	***MU***	***MU/P***
0	0			0	0		
1	20	20	10	1	29	29	29
2	34	14	7	2	46	17	17
3	44	10	5	3	53	7	7
4	47	3	1.5	4	55	2	2
5	47	0	0	5	56	1	1
6	42	−5	−2.5	6	56	0	0
7	32	−10	−5	7	52	−4	−4

Now let's consider our fifth and sixth dollars. The *MU/P* for a second Big Mac is 7. The *MU/P* for a third ice cream cone is also 7, so we could spend the fifth dollar on either—if McDonald's will sell us half a Big Mac. We ask them if they will, and they tell us no, so we must make a choice between either two additional ice cream cones or another Big Mac for our fifth and sixth dollars. Since the marginal utility per dollar of the fourth ice cream cone is only 2, it makes sense to spend our fifth and sixth dollars on another Big Mac. So now we're up to 2 Big Macs and 2 ice cream cones and we have one more dollar to spend.

Now how about our last dollar? If we spend it on a third ice cream cone, we get 7 additional units of utility. If McDonald's maintains its position and only sells whole Big Macs, this is our sole choice since we only have a dollar and Big Macs sell for $2. But let's say that McDonald's wants the sale and this time offers to sell us half a Big Mac for $1. Would we take it? The answer is no. One-half of the next Big Mac gives us only 5 units of utility per dollar, whereas the third ice cream cone gives us 7 units of utility per dollar. So we spend the seventh dollar on a third ice cream cone.

With these choices and $7 to spend, we've arrived at equilibrium—the marginal utilities per dollar are the same for both goods and we're maximizing total utility. Our total utility is 34 from 2 Big Macs and 53 units of utility from the 3 ice cream cones, making a total utility of 87.

Why do these two choices make sense? Because they give us the most total utility for the $7 we have to spend. We've followed the utility-maximizing rule: Maximize utility by adjusting your choices until the marginal utilities per dollar are the same. These choices make the marginal utility per dollar between the last Big Mac and the last ice cream cone equal. The marginal utility per dollar we get from our last Big Mac is

$$\frac{MU}{P} = \frac{14}{\$2} = 7$$

The marginal utility per dollar we get from our last ice cream cone is

$$\frac{MU}{P} = \frac{7}{\$1} = 7$$

The marginal utility per dollar of each choice is equal, so we know we can't do any better. For any other choice, we would get less total utility, so we could increase our total utility by switching to one of these two choices.

Extending the Principle of Rational Choice

Our example involved only two goods, but the reasoning can be extended to the choice among many goods. Our analysis has shown us that the principle of rational choice among many goods is simply an extension of the principle of rational choice applied to two goods. That general principle of rational choice is to consume more of the good that provides a higher marginal utility per dollar.

The Principle of Rational Choice and Utility Maximization

$$\text{When } \frac{MU_x}{P_x} > \frac{MU_z}{P_z}, \text{ consume more of good } x.$$

$$\text{When } \frac{MU_y}{P_y} > \frac{MU_z}{P_z}, \text{ consume more of good } y.$$

Stop adjusting your consumption when the marginal utilities per dollar are equal.

So the general utility-maximizing rule is that you are maximizing utility when the marginal utilities per dollar of the goods consumed are equal.

$$\text{When } \frac{MU_x}{P_x} = \frac{MU_y}{P_y} = \frac{MU_z}{P_z}, \text{ you are maximizing utility.}$$

A REMINDER

Choices at the Margin

Remember that an individual is maximizing utility if the marginal utilities per dollar for each good are equal:

$$\frac{MU_x}{P_x} = \frac{MU_y}{P_y}$$

If $MU_x/P_x < MU_y/P_y$, then good *X* isn't providing enough marginal utility to be in equilibrium, so reduce the amount of good *X* and increase the amount of good *Y*. Because of diminishing marginal utility, doing this will raise the marginal utility of *X* and lower the marginal utility of *Y*.

If $MU_x/P_x = MU_y/P_y$, but then the price of good *X* rises, good *X* will no longer provide enough marginal utility to be in equilibrium. MU_y/P_y will exceed MU_x/P_x. So again, reduce the amount of good *X* and increase the amount of good *Y* to return to equilibrium.

When this rule is met, the consumer is in equilibrium; the cost per additional unit of utility is equal for all goods and the consumer is as well off as it is possible to be.

Notice that the rule does not say that the rational consumer should consume a good until its marginal utility reaches zero. The reason is that consumers don't have enough money to buy all they want. They face a budget constraint and do the best they can under that constraint—that is, they maximize utility. To buy more goods, a person has to work more, so she should work until the marginal utility of another dollar earned just equals the marginal utility of goods purchased with another dollar. According to economists' analysis of rational choice, a person's choice of how much to work is made simultaneously with the person's decision of how much to consume. So when you say you want a Porsche but can't afford one, economists ask whether you're working two jobs and saving all your money to buy a Porsche. If you aren't, you're demonstrating that you don't really want a Porsche, given what you would have to do to get it.

Rational Choice and the Laws of Demand and Supply

Now that you know the rule for maximizing utility, let's see how it relates to the laws of demand and supply. We begin with demand. The law of demand says that quantity demanded is inversely related to price. That is, when the price of a good goes up, the quantity we consume of it goes down.

The Law of Demand

Now let's consider the law of demand in relation to our principle of rational choice. When the price of a good goes up, the marginal utility *per dollar* we get from that good goes down. So when the price of a good goes up, if we were initially in equilibrium, we no longer are. Therefore, we choose to consume less of that good. The principle of rational choice shows us formally that following the law of demand is the rational thing to do.

According to the principle of rational choice, if there is diminishing marginal utility and the price of a good goes up, we consume less of that good. Hence, the principle of rational choice leads to the law of demand.

Let's see how. If

$$\frac{MU_x}{P_x} = \frac{MU_y}{P_y}$$

and the price of good *y* goes up, then

$$\frac{MU_x}{P_x} > \frac{MU_y}{P_y}$$

Our utility-maximizing rule is no longer satisfied. Consider the preceding example, in which we were in equilibrium with 87 units of utility (34 from 2 Big Macs and 53 from 3 ice cream cones) with the utility-maximizing rule fulfilled:

$$\underset{\text{Big Mac}}{\frac{14 \text{ units of utility}}{\$2}} = \underset{\text{Ice cream}}{\frac{7 \text{ units of utility}}{\$1}} = 7$$

If the price of an ice cream cone rises from $1 to $2, the marginal utility per dollar for Big Macs (whose price hasn't changed) exceeds the marginal utility per dollar of ice cream cones:

Big Mac > Ice cream

$$\frac{14}{\$2} > \frac{7}{\$2}$$

To satisfy our utility-maximizing rule so that our choice will be rational, we must somehow raise the marginal utility we get from the good whose price has risen. Following the principle of diminishing marginal utility, we can increase marginal utility only by *decreasing* our consumption of the good whose price has risen. As we consume fewer ice cream cones and more Big Macs, the marginal utility of ice cream rises and the marginal utility of a Big Mac falls.

This example can be extended to a general rule: If the price of a good rises, you'll increase your total utility by consuming less of it. When the price of a good goes up, consumption of that good will go down. Our principle of rational choice underlies the law of demand:

Q-5 If you are initially in equilibrium and the price of one good rises, how would you adjust your consumption to return to equilibrium?

Quantity demanded rises as price falls, other things constant.

Or alternatively:

Quantity demanded falls as price rises, other things constant.

Income and Substitution Effects

So far I haven't said precisely how much the quantity demanded would decrease with an increase in the price of an ice cream cone from $1 to $2. I didn't because of a certain ambiguity that arises when one talks about changes in nominal prices. To understand the cause of this ambiguity, notice that if the price of an ice cream cone has risen to $2, with $7 we can no longer consume 2 Big Macs and 3 ice cream cones. We've got to cut back for two reasons: First, we're poorer due to the rise in price. *The reduction in quantity demanded because we're poorer* is called the **income effect.** Second, the *relative* prices have changed. The price of ice cream has risen relative to the price of Big Macs. *The reduction in quantity demanded because relative price has risen* is called a **substitution effect.** Technically the law of demand is based only on the substitution effect.

Q-6 What are two effects that generally cause the quantity demanded to fall when the price rises?

To separate the two effects, let's assume that somebody compensates us for the rise in the price of ice cream cones. Since it would cost $10 [(2 × $2 = $4) + (3 × $2 = $6)] to buy what $7 bought previously, we'll assume that someone gives us an extra $3 to compensate us for the rise in price. Since we are not any poorer because of the price change, this eliminates the income effect. We now have $10, so we can buy 2 Big Macs and the 3 ice cream cones as we did before. If we do so, our total utility is once again 87 (34 units of utility from 2 Big Macs and 53 units of utility from 3 ice cream cones.) But will we do so? We can answer that with the table.

	Big Macs (*P* = $2)				Ice Cream (*P* = $2)		
Q	*TU*	*MU*	*MU/P*	*Q*	*TU*	*MU*	*MU/P*
0	0			0	0		
		20	10			29	14.5
1	20			1	29		
		14	7			17	8.5
2	34			2	46		
		10	5			7	3.5
3	44			3	53		

We see that the second Big Mac gives us more *MU* per dollar than the third cone. What happens if we exchange an ice cream cone for an additional Big Mac, so instead of buying 3 ice cream cones and 2 Big Macs, we buy 3 Big Macs and 2 ice cream cones? The *MU* per dollar of Big Macs falls from 7 to 5 and the *MU* per dollar of the ice cream cone (whose price is now $2) rises from 3.5 to 8.5. Our total utility rises to 44 from 3 Big Macs and 46 from 2 ice cream cones, for a total of 90 units of utility rather than the previous 87. We've increased our total utility by shifting our consumption out of ice cream, the good whose price has risen. The price of ice cream went up and, even though we were given more money so we could buy the same amount as before, we did not; we bought fewer ice cream cones. That's the substitution effect in action: It tells us that when the relative price of a good goes up, the quantity purchased of that good decreases, *even if you're given money to compensate you for the rise*.

The Law of Supply

According to the principle of rational choice, if there is diminishing marginal utility and the price of supplying a good goes up, you supply more of that good.

The above discussion focused on demand and goods we consume, but this analysis of choice holds for the law of supply of factors of production, such as labor, that individuals supply to the market, as well as for demand. In supply decisions, you are giving up something—your time, land, or some other factor of production—and getting money in return. To show you how this works, let's consider one final example: how much labor you should supply to the market.

Say that working another hour at your part-time job pays you another $8 and that you currently work 20 hours per week. That additional income from the final hour of work gives you an additional 24 units of utility. Also assume that your best alternative use of that hour—studying economics—gives you another 24 units of utility. (You didn't know economics gave you so much pleasure, did you?) So what should you do when your boss asks you to work an extra hour? Tell her no, you are already satisfying the utility-maximum rule $MU_w/W = MU_s/W$.

$$\underset{\text{Studying}}{\frac{24 \text{ units of utility}}{\$8}} = \underset{\text{Working}}{\frac{24 \text{ units of utility}}{\$8}}$$

The price of studying an additional hour is also your wage per hour because that wage is the opportunity cost of studying.

Q-7 Use the principle of rational choice to explain how you would change your quantity of work supplied if your employer raised your wage by $1 per hour.

But now say that your boss offers to raise your wage to $8.50 per hour for work you do over 20 hours. That means that both your wage at work and the price of studying have increased. But now you can get more goods for working that additional hour. Let's say that those additional goods raise the marginal utility you get from an additional hour of work to 32 additional units of utility. Now the marginal utility of working an additional hour exceeds the marginal utility of studying an additional hour:

$$\underset{\text{Studying}}{\frac{24 \text{ units of utility}}{\$8.50}} < \underset{\text{Working}}{\frac{32 \text{ units of utility}}{\$8.50}}$$

So you work the extra hour.

Now say your boss comes to you and asks what it would take to get you to work five hours more per week. After running the numbers through your computer-mind, you solve the utility-maximizing rule and tell her, "$10.00 an hour for overtime work and you've got your worker." Combining these hours and wages gives you the supply curve shown in Figure 10-2, which demonstrates the law of supply. As you have seen, factor supply curves can be derived from a comparison of marginal utilities for various activities in relation to work.

FIGURE 10-2 Deriving Labor Supply from Marginal Utility

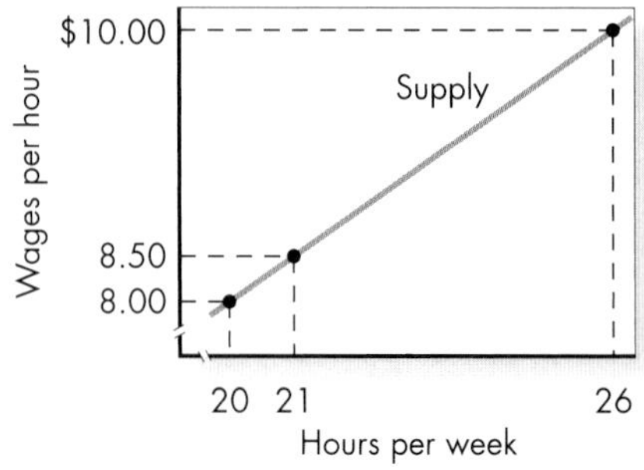

To see that you have the reasoning down, say that an exam is coming and you haven't studied. This will likely raise the marginal utility of studying sufficiently, so you will choose to work less, if you have a choice. What will that change do to the supply curve?

If you answered that it will shift it to the left, you're in good shape.

Opportunity Cost

Before we leave the principle of rational choice, let's consider how it relates to the opportunity cost concept that I presented in earlier chapters. *Opportunity cost* was the benefit forgone of the next-best alternative. Now that you've been through the principle of rational choice, you have a better sense of what is meant by opportunity cost of a forgone opportunity: It is essentially the marginal utility per dollar you forgo from the consumption of the next-best alternative.

The principle of rational choice states that, to maximize utility, choose goods until the opportunity costs of all alternatives are equal.

To say $MU_x/P_x > MU_y/P_y$ is to say that the opportunity cost of not consuming good x is greater than the opportunity cost of not consuming good y. So you consume x.

When the marginal utilities per dollar spent are equal, the opportunity cost of the alternatives are equal. In reality, people don't use the utility terminology, and, indeed, a specific measure of utility doesn't exist. But the choice based on the price of goods relative to the benefit they provide is used all the time. Instead of utility terminology, people use the "really need" terminology. They say they will work the extra hour rather than study because they *really need* the money. To say you are working because you "really need" the money is the equivalent of saying the marginal utility of working is higher than the marginal utility of other choices. So the general rule fits decisions about supply, even if most people don't use the word *utility*. The more you "really, really need" something, the higher its marginal utility.

Q-8 If the opportunity cost of consuming good x is greater than the opportunity cost of consuming good y, which good has the higher marginal utility per dollar?

Applying Economists' Theory of Choice to the Real World

Understanding a theory involves more than understanding how a theory works; it also involves understanding the limits the assumptions underlying the theory place on the use of the theory. As I've noted above, economists are questioning some of the assumptions on which traditional economists' analysis of choice is based. Let's consider some of their questions. The first assumption we'll consider is the implicit assumption that decisions can be made costlessly.

The Cost of Decision Making

The principle of rational choice makes reasonably good intuitive sense when we limit our examples to two or three choices, as I did in this chapter. But in reality, we make hundreds of thousands of choices simultaneously. It simply doesn't make intuitive sense that we're going to apply rational choice to all those choices at once. That would exceed our decision-making abilities. This cost of decision making means that it is only rational to be somewhat irrational—to do things without applying the principle of rational choice. Thinking about decisions is one of the things we all economize on.

How real-world people make decisions in real-world situations is an open question that modern economists are spending a lot of time researching. Following the work of Nobel Prize winner Herbert Simon, a number of economists have come to believe that, to make real-world decisions, most people use *bounded rationality*—rationality based on rules of thumb—rather than using the principle of rational choice. They argue that many of our decisions are made with our minds on automatic pilot. This view of rationality has significant implications for interpreting and predicting economic events. For example,

Q-9 Bounded rationality violates the principle of rational choice. True or false?

one rule of thumb is "You get what you pay for," which means that something with a high price is better than something with a low price. Put technically, we rely on price to convey information about quality. This reliance on price for information changes the inferences one can draw from the analysis, and can lead to upward-sloping demand curves.

A second rule of thumb that people sometimes use is "Follow the leader." If you don't know what to do, do what you think smart people are doing. Consider the clothes you're wearing. I suspect many of your choices of what to wear reflect this and the previous rules of thumb. Suppliers of clothing certainly think so and spend enormous amounts of money to exploit these rules of thumb. They try to steer your automatic pilot toward their goods. The suppliers emphasize these two rules ("You get what you pay for" and "Follow the leader") to convince people their product is the "in" thing to buy. If they succeed, they've got a gold mine; if they fail, they've got a flop. Advertising is designed to mine these rules of thumb.

Advertising is designed to mine rules of thumb.

In technical terms, the "Follow the leader" rule leads to *focal point equilibria,* in which a set of goods is consumed, not because the goods are objectively preferred to all other goods, but simply because, through luck, or advertising, they have become focal points to which people have gravitated. Once some people started consuming a good, others followed.

Given Tastes

A second assumption that behavioral economists are questioning is that our preferences are given and are not shaped by society. In reality, our preferences are determined not only by nature but also by our experiences—by nurture. Let's consider an example: Forty percent of major league baseball players chew tobacco, but close to zero percent of college professors chew tobacco. Why? Are major league baseball players somehow born with a tobacco-chewing gene while college professors are not? I doubt it. Tastes often are significantly influenced by society.

Conspicuous Consumption Another aspect of taste that has been described by economists is **conspicuous consumption**—*the consumption of goods not for one's direct pleasure, but simply to show off to others.* The term was created approximately 100 years ago by the famous institutional economist Thorstein Veblen. Veblen argued that, just as some animals strut around to

Thinking Like a Modern Economist

Mental Accounting

If some of the analysis in this chapter doesn't sit well with you, you're not alone. It assumes that people make decisions on the margin and are able to make mental calculations easily. Behavioral economists, over the past 10 years, have been exploring exactly how people make decisions. The chapter explores a few of them. Here's another.

Consider the following scenario. You buy a $100 ticket to a concert and lose it on the way. If you had another $100, would you buy a replacement ticket and still go to the concert? Most people answer "no." But consider this second scenario. You're on your way to buy a $100 concert ticket and you lose $100 in cash on the way. You still have enough cash to buy the ticket. Do you? Most people answer "yes."

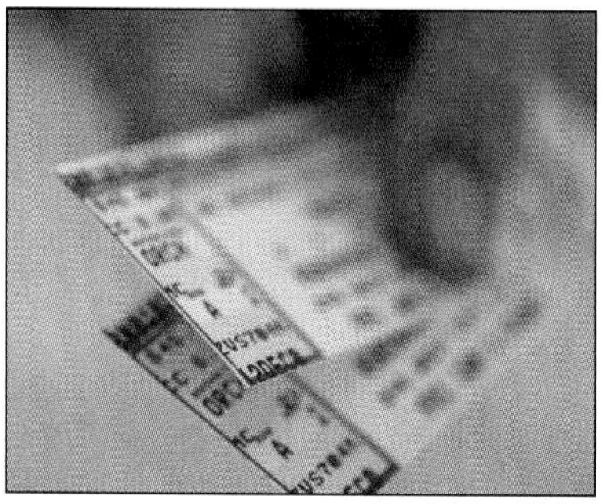

Why the difference even though the financial situation is equivalent in both situations? Behavioral economists suggest that people make choices within particular mental categories, instead of over all categories. In the first scenario, the ticket was in the "concert" category. Adding another $100 places too much in that mental category. So people decline doing so. In the second scenario, the $100 cash wasn't in the "concert" category, so spending another spare $100 doesn't add to that category. You'd already mentally allocated $100 to that category.

show their abilities, humans consume to show that they can "afford it." For Veblen, mansions, designer clothing, and $300 appetizers were all examples of conspicuous consumption. He further argued that male industrialists (which were all industrialists at the time) were so busy with business that they didn't have time to show off enough, so they married a trophy spouse whose purpose was to show off for them in the most ostentatious manner possible.

Web Note 10.4
Veblen Goods

Tastes and Individual Choice One way in which economists integrate the above insights into economics is by emphasizing that the analysis is conducted on the assumption of "given tastes." As discussed above, in reality, economists agree that often forces besides price and marginal utility play a role in determining what people demand. They fully recognize that a whole other analysis is necessary to supplement theirs—an analysis of what determines taste.

Ask yourself what you ate today. Was it health food? Pizza? Candy? Whatever it was, it was probably not the most efficient way to satisfy your nutritional needs. The most efficient way to do that would be to eat only soybean mush and vitamin supplements at a cost of about $300 per year. That's less than one-tenth of what the average individual today spends on food per year. Most of us turn up our noses at soybean mush. Why? Because tastes are important.

I emphasize this point because some economists have been guilty of forgetting their simplifying assumption. Some economists in the 1800s thought that society's economic needs eventually would be fully met and that we would enter a golden age of affluence where all our material wants would be satisfied. They thought there would be surpluses of everything. Clearly that hasn't happened. Somehow it seems that whenever a need is met, it's replaced by a want, which soon becomes another need.

Somehow, whenever a need is met, it's replaced by a want, which soon becomes another need.

There are, of course, examples of wants being temporarily satisfied, as a U.S. company on a small island in the Caribbean is reported to have discovered. Employees weren't showing up for work. The company sent in a team of efficiency experts who discovered the cause of their problem: The firm had recently raised wages, and workers had decided they could get all they wanted (warm weather, a gorgeous beach, plenty of food, and a little bit of spending money) by showing up for work once, maybe twice, a week. Such a situation was clearly not good for business, but the firm found a solution. It sent in thousands of Sears catalogs (back when Sears sent catalogs), and suddenly the workers were no longer satisfied with what they already had. They wanted more and went back to work to get it. When they were presented with new possibilities, their wants increased. Companies know that tastes aren't constant, and they spend significant amounts of money on advertising to make consumers have a taste for their goods. It works, too.

Web Note 10.5
Tastes and Choices

Tastes are also important in explaining differences in consumption between countries. For example, a Japanese person wouldn't consider having a meal without rice. Rice has a ceremonial, almost mystical value in Japan. In many parts of the United States, supper means meat and potatoes. In Germany, carp (a large goldfish) is a delicacy; in the United States, many people consider carp inedible. In the United States, corn is a desirable vegetable; in parts of Europe, until recently, it was considered pig food.

Q-10 Using the principle of rational choice, explain why a change in tastes will shift a demand curve.

To say we don't analyze tastes in the core of economic theory doesn't mean that we don't take them into account. Think back to Chapter 4, when we distinguished shifts in demand (the entire demand schedule shifts) from movements along the demand curve. Those movements along the demand curve were the effect of price. Tastes were one of the shift factors of demand. So economists do include tastes in their analysis; a change in tastes makes the demand curve shift.

Economists take into account changes in tastes as shift factors of demand.

ADDED DIMENSION

Making Stupid Decisions

It is hard to make good decisions. You need lots of training—in math, in economics, in logic. Think of kids—do five-year-olds make rational decisions? Some dyed-in-the-wool utilitarians might argue that whatever decision one makes must, by definition, be rational, but such usage makes the concept tautological—true by definition.

When applying the theory of rational choice, most economists agree that some decisions people make can be irrational. For example, they will concede that five-year-olds make a lot of what most parents would call stupid (or irrational) decisions. By a stupid decision, they mean a decision with expected consequences that, if the child had logically thought about them, would have caused the child not to make that particular decision. But five-year-olds often haven't learned how to think logically about expected consequences, so even traditional economists don't assume decisions made by five-year-olds reflect the rational choice model.

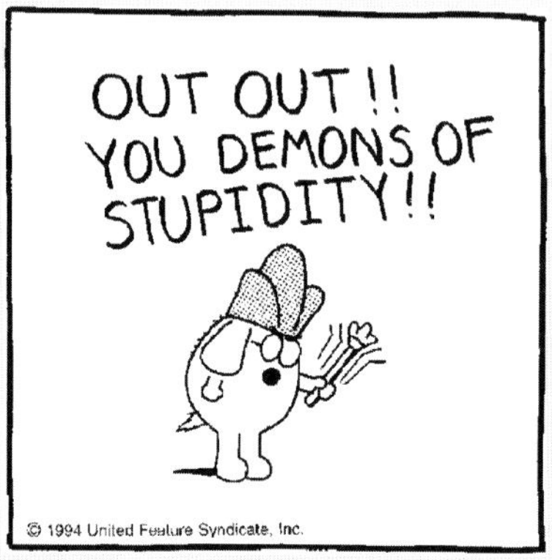

DILBERT © reprinted by permission of United Feature Syndicate, Inc.

In the real world, parents and teachers spend enormous effort to teach children what is rational, reasonable, and "appropriate." Children's decision-making process reflects that teaching. But parents and teachers teach more than a decision-making process; they also teach children a moral code that often includes the value of honor and the value of selflessness. These teachings shape their children's decision-making process (although not always in the way that parents or teachers think or hope) and modify their preferences. So our decision-making process and our preferences are, to some degree, taught to us.

Recognizing that preferences and decision-making processes are, to some degree, taught, not inherent, eliminates the fixed point by which to judge people's decisions: Are they making decisions that reflect their true needs, or are they simply reflecting what they have been taught? Eliminating that fixed point makes it difficult to draw unambiguous policy implications from economists' model of rational choice.

Utility Maximization

Behavioral economics is the study of economic choice that is based on realistic psychological foundations.

A third assumption that behavioral economists question is that individuals maximize a utility function that involves getting more for themselves. In experiments, behavioral economists have found that many people don't behave that way—at least in laboratory experiments.

Let's consider one example: the **ultimatum game.** Say that two people are given the opportunity to split $10. One person is allowed to make the decision as to how to divide it. He can keep whatever portion he wants, say $9.90, and give 10 cents to the other, or he could give a 50–50 split. But in the ultimatum game, *the first person only gets the money if the other person accepts the offer. If the second person does not accept, they both get nothing.*

From a purely selfish rationality standpoint, the first individual would keep most of the money, giving only a small amount to the other. Moreover, since the other person comes out better if he accepts even the small amount, he should accept any offer (even one cent) because it makes him better off in terms of his income. So the prediction from the standard economic model is that the first person will keep most of the $10 and the second person will accept whatever amount is offered. But, when people play this game, this is not what happens. Instead, generally the first person offers something close to 50–50, which is almost always accepted. However, in instances where the first person offers only a small amount, the offer is generally rejected. It seems that people have a sense of fairness in their decisions, and are willing to pay money (reduce their income) to enforce that sense of fairness.

In other experiments, behavioral economists have found a strong **status quo bias**—*an individual's actions are very much influenced by the current situation, even when that reasonably does not seem to be very important to the decision*. An example of this in the real world occurred when Sweden privatized its social security system in 2000. When privatizing retirement, Sweden offered its citizens 456 funds from which to choose to invest. Even though the Swedish government encouraged participants to actively choose their own portfolio, it also offered one of the funds as a default. Even with over 450 other funds from which to choose, 33 percent chose the default fund, a far higher percentage than would be expected if the fund had not been identified as the default. As we will discuss in Chapter 22, some behavioral economists have suggested that policy makers can take advantage of this status quo bias when they design policy by structuring programs so that choices are framed in ways that lead people to do what policy makers want them to do. Since individuals are freely choosing, they argue that such policy design does not violate consumer sovereignty.

There are many more such experiments and behavioral economic insights that are changing the face of modern economics. But these insights should be seen as complements to, rather than substitutes for, standard economic reasoning.

Conclusion

We began this chapter with a discussion of the simplifying nature of the economists' analysis of rational choice. Now that you've been through it, you may be wondering if it's all that simple. In any case, I'm sure most of you would agree that it's complicated enough. When we're talking about formal analysis, I'm in total agreement.

But if you're talking about informal analysis and applying the analysis to the real world, most economists also would agree that this theory of choice is in no way acceptable. Economists believe that there's more to life than maximizing utility. We believe in love, anger, and doing crazy things just for the sake of doing crazy things. We're real people.

But, we argue, simplicity has its virtue, and often people hide their selfish motivations. Few people like to go around and say, "I did this because I'm a self-interested, calculating person who cares primarily about myself." Instead they usually emphasize other motives: "Society conditioned me to do it"; "I'm doing this to achieve fairness"; "It's my upbringing." And they're probably partially right, but often they hide and obscure their self-interested motives in their psychological explanations. The beauty of the simple traditional economic psychological assumption is that it cuts through many obfuscations (that's an obfuscating word meaning "smokescreens") and, in doing so, often captures a part of reality that others miss. Let's consider a couple of examples.

Economists use their simple self-interest theory of choice because it cuts through many obfuscations, and, in doing so, often captures a part of reality that others miss.

Why does government restrict who's allowed to practice law? The typical layperson's answer is "to protect the public." The traditional economic answer is that many of the restrictions do little to protect the public. Instead their primary function is to restrict the *number* of lawyers and thereby increase the marginal utility of existing lawyers and the price they can charge.

Why do museum directors almost always want to increase the size of their collections? The layperson's (and museum directors') answer is that they're out to preserve our artistic heritage. The traditional economic answer is that it often has more to do with maximizing the utility of the museum staff. (Economist William Grampp made this argument in a book about the economics of art. He supported his argument by pointing out that more than half of museums' art is in storage and not accessible to the public. Acquiring more art will simply lead to more art going into storage.)

Approaching problems by asking the question "What's in it for the people making the decision?" is a useful approach that will give you more insight than many other approaches.

Now in no way am I claiming that the traditional economic answer based on pure self-interest is always the correct one. But I am arguing that approaching problems by asking the question "What's in it for the people making the decisions?" is a useful approach that will give you more insight into what's going on than many other approaches. It gets people to ask tough, rather than easy, questions. After you've asked the tough questions, then you can see how to modify the conclusions by looking deeply into the real-world institutions.

All too often, students think of economics and economic reasoning as establishment reasoning. That's not true. Economic reasoning can be extremely subversive to existing establishments. But whatever it is, it is not subversive in order to be subversive, or proestablishment to be proestablishment. It's simply a logical application of a simple idea—individual choice theory—to a variety of problems.

Summary

- Total utility is the satisfaction obtained from consuming a product; marginal utility is the satisfaction obtained from consuming one additional unit of a product.
- The principle of diminishing marginal utility states that after some point, the marginal utility of consuming more of the good will fall.
- The principle of rational choice is

  If $\frac{MU_x}{P_x} > \frac{MU_y}{P_y}$, choose to consume more of good x.

  If $\frac{MU_x}{P_x} < \frac{MU_y}{P_y}$, choose to consume more of good y.
- The utility-maximizing rule says:

  If $\frac{MU_x}{P_x} = \frac{MU_y}{P_y}$, you're maximizing utility; you're indifferent between good x and good y.
- Unless $MU_x/P_x = MU_y/P_y$, an individual can rearrange his or her consumption to increase total utility.
- Opportunity cost is essentially the marginal utility per dollar one forgoes from the consumption of the next-best alternative.
- The law of demand can be derived from the principle of rational choice.
- If you're in equilibrium and the price of a good rises, you'll reduce your consumption of that good to reestablish equilibrium.
- The law of demand is based on the income effect and the substitution effect. The income effect is the reduction in quantity demanded when price rises because the price rise makes one poorer. The substitution effect is the reduction in quantity demanded when price rises because you substitute a good whose price has not risen.
- The law of supply can be derived from the principle of rational choice.
- If your wage rises, the marginal utility of the goods you can buy with that wage will rise and you will work more to satisfy the utility-maximizing rule.
- To apply economists' analysis of choice to the real world, we must carefully consider, and adjust for, the underlying assumptions, such as costlessness of decision making and given tastes.
- The theory of choice assumes decision making is costless, tastes are given, and individuals maximize utility.
- Behavioral economics is the study of economic choice that is based on realistic psychological foundations.
- The ultimatum game suggests that people care about fairness as well as total income. The status quo bias suggests that actions are based on perceived norms.

Key Terms

conspicuous consumption *(242)*
income effect *(239)*
marginal utility *(231)*
principle of diminishing marginal utility *(233)*
principle of rational choice *(235)*
status quo bias *(245)*
substitution effect *(239)*
total utility *(231)*
ultimatum game *(244)*
utility *(231)*
utility-maximizing rule *(236)*

Questions and Exercises

1. Explain how marginal utility differs from total utility. LO1
2. According to the principle of diminishing marginal utility, how does marginal utility change as more of a good is consumed? As less of a good is consumed? LO1
3. What key psychological assumptions do economists make in their theory of individual choice? LO2
4. Complete the following table of Scout's utility from drinking cans of soda and answer the questions below.

Cans of Soda	Total Utility	Marginal Utility
0	–	
1	–	10
2	22	12
3	32	–
4	–	8
5	–	4
6	44	–
7	42	–

   a. At what point does marginal utility begin to fall?
   b. Will Scout consume the 7th can of soda? Explain your answer.
   c. True or false? Scout will be following the utility-maximizing rule by consuming 2 cans of soda. Explain your answer. LO2, LO3

5. The following table gives the price and total utility of three goods: A, B, and C.

		Total Utility							
Good	Price	1	2	3	4	5	6	7	8
A	$10	200	380	530	630	680	700	630	430
B	2	20	34	46	56	64	72	78	82
C	6	50	60	70	80	90	100	90	80

As closely as possible, determine how much of the three goods you would buy with $20. Explain why you chose what you did. LO2, LO3

6. The following table gives the marginal utility of John's consumption of three goods: A, B, and C.

Units of Consumption	*MU* of *A*	*MU* of *B*	*MU* of *C*
1	20	25	45
2	18	20	30
3	16	15	24
4	14	10	18
5	12	8	15
6	10	6	12

   a. Good A costs $2 per unit, good B costs $1, and good C costs $3. How many units of each should a consumer with $12 buy to maximize his or her utility?
   b. How will the answer change if the price of B rises to $2?
   c. How about if the price of C is 50 cents but the other prices are as in *a*? LO2, LO3

7. The total utility of your consumption of widgets is 40; it changes by 2 with each change in widgets consumed. The total utility of your consumption of wadgets is also 40 but changes by 3 with each change in wadgets consumed. The price of widgets is $2 and the price of wadgets is $3. How many widgets and wadgets should you consume? LO3
8. Suppose a large cheese pizza costs $10 and a calzone costs $5. You have $40 to spend. The marginal utility (*MU*) that you derive from each is as follows:

Number	*MU* of Pizza	*MU* of Calzone
0		
1	60	30
2	40	28
3	30	24
4	20	20
5	10	10

   a. How many of each would you buy?

b. Suppose the price of a calzone rises to $10. How many of each would you buy?
c. Use this to show how the principle of rational choice leads to the law of demand. LO2, LO3, LO4

9. Early Classical economists found the following "diamond/water" paradox perplexing: "Why is water, which is so useful and necessary, so cheap, when diamonds, which are so useless and unnecessary, so expensive?" Using the utility concept, explain why it is not really a paradox. (Difficult) LO3
10. State the law of demand and explain how it relates to the principle of rational choice. LO4
11. State the law of supply and explain how it relates to opportunity cost. LO4
12. If the supply curve is perfectly inelastic, what is the opportunity cost of the supplier? (Difficult) LO4
13. There is a small but growing movement known as "voluntary simplicity," which is founded on the belief in a simple life of working less and spending less. Do Americans who belong to this movement follow the principle of rational choice? (Difficult) LO4
14. Your study partner tells you that if you are compensated for the impact on your budget of a rise in the price of a good, your purchase choices won't change. Is he right? Explain. LO4
15. According to Thorstein Veblen, what is the purpose of conspicuous consumption? Does the utility derived from the consumption of these goods come from their price or functionality? Give an example of such a good. LO5, LO6
16. Say that the ultimatum game described in the chapter was changed so that the first individual could keep the money regardless of whether the offer was accepted by the second individual or not.
    a. What would you expect would likely happen to the offers?
    b. What would happen to the acceptances? LO5, LO6

Questions from Alternative Perspectives

1. The book seems to suggest that all decisions are economic decisions.
    a. Would you agree with that?
    b. How would tithing fit into the decision-making calculus? (Religious)
2. In his book *Why Perestroika Failed: The Politics and Economics of Socialist Transformation*, Austrian economist Peter Boettke argues that Soviet-style socialist countries had to fail because they could not appropriately reflect individuals' choices. What was his likely argument? (Austrian)
3. The book discusses the issue of decision making in reference to the individual, but generally households, not individuals, make decisions.
    a. How do you think decisions are actually made about issues such as consumption and allocation of time within the household?
    b. Does bargaining take place?
    c. If so, what gives an individual power to bargain effectively for his or her preferences?
    d. Do individuals act cooperatively within the family and competitively everywhere else? (Feminist)
4. Often, people buy a good to impress others and not because they want it.
    a. What implications would such actions have for the application of economic analysis?
    b. How many goods are bought because people want them and how many goods are bought because of advertising and conspicuous consumption? (Post-Keynesian)
5. Most people believe that marginal utility diminishes with each additional dollar of income (or one more dollar is worth more to a poor person than a rich one).
    a. If that is true, how would you design an income tax that imposes an equal burden in lost utility on rich and poor households?
    b. How would your answer differ if the marginal utility of income did not diminish?
    c. How would your answer differ if your goal was to leave households with equal levels of utility from their last dollar of income? (Radical)

Issues to Ponder

1. How would the world be different than it is if the principle of diminishing marginal utility seldom held true? (Difficult) LO1
2. It is sometimes said that an economist is a person who knows the price of everything but the value of nothing. Is this statement true or false? Why? (Difficult) LO2

3. Assign a measure of utility to your studying for various courses. Do your study habits follow the principle of rational choice? LO2
4. Explain your motivation for four personal decisions you have made in the past year, using economists' model of individual choice. LO2
5. Nobel Prize-winning economist George Stigler explains how the famous British economist Phillip Wicksteed decided where to live. His two loves were fresh farm eggs, which were more easily obtained the farther from London he was, and visits from friends, which decreased the farther he moved away from London. Given these two loves, describe the decision rule that you would have expected Wicksteed to follow. (Difficult) LO2
6. Although the share of Americans who say they are "very happy" hasn't changed much in the last five decades, the number of products produced and consumed per person has risen tremendously. How can this be? (Difficult) LO5
7. Give an example of a recent purchase for which you used a rule of thumb in your decision-making process. Did your decision follow the principle of rational choice? Explain. LO5, LO6
8. Economic experiments have found that individuals prefer an outcome where no one is made better off to an outcome where the welfare of only some is improved if that improvement in welfare is unequally distributed. Why do you think this is so? LO5, LO6
9. You are buying your spouse, significant other, or close friend a ring. You decide to show your reasonableness and buy a cubic zirconium ring that sells at 1/50 the cost of a mined diamond and that any normal person could not tell from a mined diamond just by looking at it. In fact, the zirconium will have more brilliance and fewer occlusions (imperfections) than a mined diamond.
   a. How will your spouse (significant other, close friend) likely react?
   b. Why?
   c. Is this reaction justified? LO5
10. Joseph Gallo, the founder of the famous wine company that bears his name, said that when he first started selling wine right after Prohibition (laws outlawing the sale of alcohol), he poured two glasses of wine from the same bottle and put a price of 10 cents a bottle on one and 5 cents a bottle on the other. He let people test both and asked them which they wanted. Most wanted the 10-cent bottle, even though they were the same wine. (Difficult)
    a. What does this tell us about people?
    b. Can you think of other areas where that may be the case?
    c. What does this suggest about pricing? LO5, LO6

Answers to Margin Questions

1. If the total utility curve is a straight line, the marginal utility curve will be flat with a slope of zero since marginal utility would not change with additional units. *(232)*
2. False. The principle of diminishing marginal utility is that as one increases consumption of a good, the good's marginal utility decreases. *(233)*
3. Given a choice between the two, the rational choice is to watch MTV for one hour since it provides the higher marginal utility per hour. *(234)*
4. False. You are maximizing total utility when the marginal utilities per dollar are the same for all goods. This does not have to be where marginal utility is zero. *(235)*
5. If I am initially in equilibrium, then $MU_x/P_x = MU_y/P_y = MU_z/P_z$ for all goods I consume. If the price of one good goes up, I will decrease my consumption of that good and increase the consumption of other goods until the equilibrium is met again where $MU_x/P_x = MU_y/P_y = MU_z/P_z$. *(239)*
6. The two effects are the income effect and the substitution effect. *(239)*
7. If offered one more dollar per hour, I would choose to substitute labor for leisure since the price of leisure (pay per hour of work) has increased. Following the principle of rational choice, I would work more to lower the marginal utility of work so that $MU_w/P_w = MU_l/P_l$. *(240)*
8. Good *y* has the higher marginal utility per dollar since the opportunity cost of consuming good *x* is the marginal utility per dollar of consuming good *y*. *(241)*
9. This could be true or false. It depends on how you interpret bounded rationality. If it is interpreted within a costless decision-making environment, it does violate the principle of rational choice since there is no reason to be less than rational. If, however, it is interpreted within a costly decision-making environment, then you can be making decisions within a range because the marginal cost of increasing the range of choices exceeds the marginal benefit of doing so, and in that case bounded rationality is consistent with the principle of rational choice. Information is not costless. *(241)*
10. If a person is in equilibrium and a change in tastes leads to an increase in the marginal utility for one good, he will increase consumption of that good to reestablish equilibrium. A change in tastes will shift a demand curve because it will cause a change in quantity consumed without a change in the good's price. *(243)*

APPENDIX A

Indifference Curve Analysis

As I stated in the chapter, analyzing individual choice using actual numbers is unnecessary. In the chapter, I asked you to make a deal with me: You'd remember that actual numbers are unnecessary and I'd use them anyway. This appendix is for those who didn't accept my deal (and for those whose professors want them to get some practice in Graphish). It presents an example of a more formal analysis of individual choice.

Sophie's Choice

Sophie is a junk food devotee. She lives on two goods: chocolate bars, which cost $1 each, and cans of soda, which sell for 50 cents apiece. Sophie is trying to get as much pleasure as possible, given her resources. Alternatively expressed, Sophie is trying to maximize her utility, given a budget constraint.

By translating this statement of Sophie's choice into graphs, I can demonstrate the principle of rational choice without ever mentioning any specific amount of utility.

The graph we'll use will have chocolate bars on the vertical axis and cans of soda on the horizontal axis, as in Figure A10-1.

Graphing the Budget Constraint

Let's begin by asking: How can we translate her budget constraint (the $10 maximum she has to spend) into Graphish? The easiest way to do that is to ask what would happen if she spends her $10 all on chocolate bars or all on cans of soda. Since a chocolate bar costs $1, if she spends it all on chocolate bars, she can get 10 bars (point *A* in Figure A10-1). If she spends it all on cans of soda, she can get 20 cans of soda (point *B*). This gives us two points.

FIGURE A10-1 Graphing the Budget Constraint

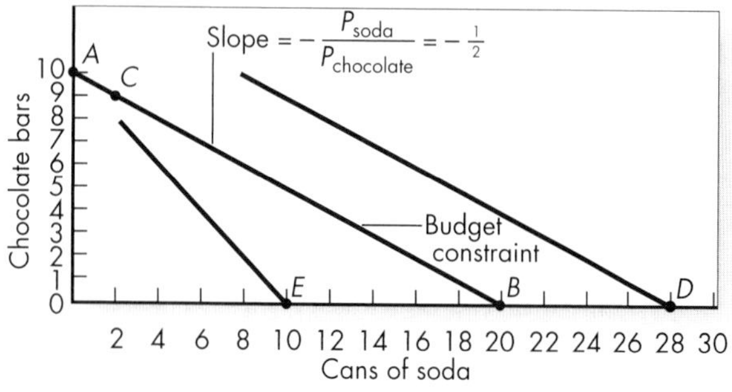

But what if she wants some combination of soda and chocolate bars? If we draw a line between points *A* and *B*, we'll have a graphical picture of her budget constraint and can answer that question because a **budget constraint** is *a curve that shows us the various combinations of goods an individual can buy with a given amount of money*. The line is her budget constraint in Graphish.

To see that it is, say Sophie is spending all her money on chocolate bars. She then decides to buy one fewer chocolate bar. That gives her $1 to spend on soda, which, since those cans cost 50 cents each, allows her to buy 2 cans. Point C (9 chocolate bars and 2 cans of soda) represents that decision. Notice how point C is on the budget constraint. Repeat this exercise from various starting points until you're comfortable with the fact that the line does indeed represent the various combinations of soda and chocolate bars Sophie can buy with the $10. It's a line with a slope of −½ and intersects the chocolate-bars axis at 10 and the cans-of-soda axis at 20.

To be sure that you've got it, ask yourself what would happen to the budget constraint if Sophie got another $4 to spend on the two goods. Going through the same reasoning should lead you to the conclusion that the budget constraint will shift to the right so that it will intersect the cans-of-soda axis at 28 (point *D*), but its slope won't change. (I started the new line for you.) Make sure you can explain why.

Now what if the price of a can of soda goes up to $1? What happens to the budget line? (This is a question many people miss.) If you said the budget line becomes steeper, shifting in along the cans-of-soda axis to point *E* while remaining anchored along the chocolate-bars axis until the slope equals −1, you've got it. If you didn't say that, go through the same reasoning we went through at first (if Sophie buys only cans of soda . . .) and then draw the new line. You'll see it becomes steeper. Put another way, the absolute value of the slope of the curve is the ratio of the price of cans of soda to the price of chocolate bars; the absolute value of the slope becomes greater with a rise in the price of cans of soda.

Graphing the Indifference Curve

Now let's consider the second part of Sophie's choice: the pleasure part. Sophie is trying to get as much pleasure as she can from her \$10. How do we deal with this in Graphish?

To see, let's go through a thought experiment. Say Sophie had 14 chocolate bars and 4 cans of soda (point A in Figure A10-2). Let's ask her, "Say you didn't know the price of either good and we took away 4 of those chocolate bars (so you had 10). How many cans of soda would we have to give you so that you would be just as happy as before we took away the 4 chocolate bars?"

Since she's got lots of chocolate bars and few cans of soda, her answer is probably, "Not too many; say, 1 can of soda." This means that she would be just as happy to have 10 chocolate bars and 5 cans of soda (point B) as she would to have 14 chocolate bars and 4 cans of soda (point A). Connect those points and you have the beginning of a "just-as-happy" curve. But that doesn't sound impressive enough, so, following economists' terminology, we'll call it an **indifference curve**—*a curve that shows combinations of goods among which an individual is indifferent*. She's indifferent between points A and B.

FIGURE A10-2 Sophie's Indifference Curve

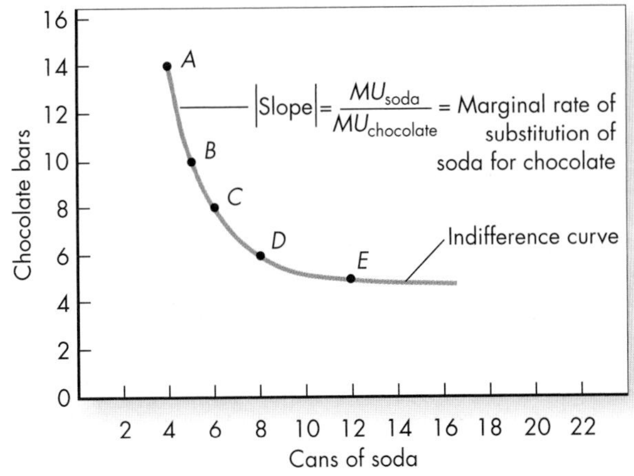

Chocolate Bars	Cans of Soda	
14	4	*A*
10	5	*B*
8	6	*C*
6	8	*D*
5	12	*E*

If you continue our thought experiment, you'll get a set of combinations of chocolate bars and cans of soda like that shown in the table in Figure A10-2.

If you plot each of these combinations of points on the graph in Figure A10-2 and connect all these points, you have one of Sophie's indifference curves: a curve representing combinations of cans of soda and chocolate bars among which Sophie is indifferent.

Let's consider the shape of this curve. First, it's downward-sloping. That's reasonable; it simply says that if you take something away from Sophie, you've got to give her something in return if you want to keep her indifferent between what she had before and what she has now. The absolute value of the slope of an indifference curve is the **marginal rate of substitution**—*the rate at which one good must be added when the other is taken away in order to keep the individual indifferent between the two combinations*.

Second, it's bowed inward. That's because as Sophie gets more and more of one good, it takes fewer and fewer of another good to compensate for the loss of the good she incurred in order to get more of the other good. The underlying reasoning is similar to that in our discussion of the law of diminishing marginal utility, but notice we haven't even mentioned utility. Technically the reasoning for the indifference curve being bowed inward is called the **law of diminishing marginal rate of substitution**—which tells us that *as you get more and more of a good, if some of that good is taken away, then the marginal addition of another good you need to keep you on your indifference curve gets less and less*.

Even more technically, we can say that the absolute value of the slope of the indifference curve equals the ratio of the marginal utility of cans of soda to the marginal utility of chocolate bars:

$$\left|\text{Slope}\right| = \frac{MU_{\text{soda}}}{MU_{\text{chocolate}}} = \text{Marginal rate of substitution}$$

That ratio equals the marginal rate of substitution of cans of soda for chocolate bars. Let's consider an example. Say that in Figure A10-2 Sophie is at point A and that the marginal utility she gets from an increase from 4 to 5 cans of soda is 10. Since we know that she was willing to give up 4 chocolate bars to get that 1 can of soda (and thereby move from point A to point B), that 10 must equal the loss of utility she gets from the loss of 4 chocolate bars out of the 14 she originally had. So the marginal rate of substitution of cans of soda for chocolate bars between points A and B must be 4. That's the absolute value of the slope of that curve. Therefore, her *MU* of a chocolate bar must be about 2.5 (10 for 4 chocolate bars).

FIGURE A10-3 A Group of Indifference Curves

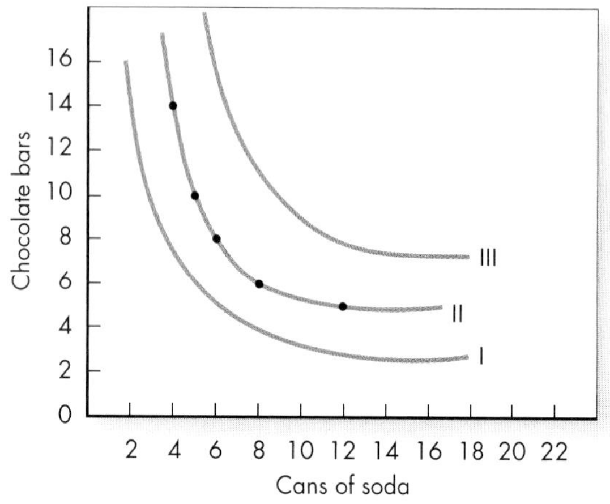

You can continue this same reasoning, starting with various combinations of goods. If you do so, you can get a whole group of indifference curves like that in Figure A10-3. Each curve represents a different level of happiness. Assuming she prefers more to less, Sophie is better off if she's on Curve II than if she's on Curve I, and even better off if she's on Curve III. Her goal in life is to get out to the furthest indifference curve she can.

To see whether you've followed the reasoning, ask yourself the following question: "Assuming Sophie prefers more of a good to less (which seems reasonable), can any two of Sophie's indifference curves cross each other as the ones in Figure A10-4 do?"

The answer is no, no, no! Why? Because they're indifference curves. If the curves were to cross, the "prefer-more-to-less" principle would be violated. Say we start at point A: Sophie has 8 chocolate bars and 6 cans of soda. We know that since *A* (8 chocolate bars and 6 sodas) and *B* (6 chocolate bars and 8 cans of soda) are on the same indifference curve, Sophie is indifferent between A and *B*. Similarly with points *B* and *C*: Sophie would just as soon have 9 chocolate bars and 7 cans of soda as she would 6 chocolate bars and 8 cans of soda.

It follows by logical deduction that point A must be indifferent to C. But consider points A and C carefully. At point C, Sophie has 7 cans of soda and 9 chocolate bars. At point A she has 6 cans of soda and 8 chocolate bars. At point C she has more of both goods than she has at point A, so to say she's indifferent between these two points violates the "prefer-more-to-less" criterion. Ergo (that's Latin, meaning "therefore"), two indifference curves cannot intersect. That's why we drew the group of indifference curves in Figure A10-3 so that they do not intersect.

FIGURE A10-4 Why Indifference Curves Cannot Cross

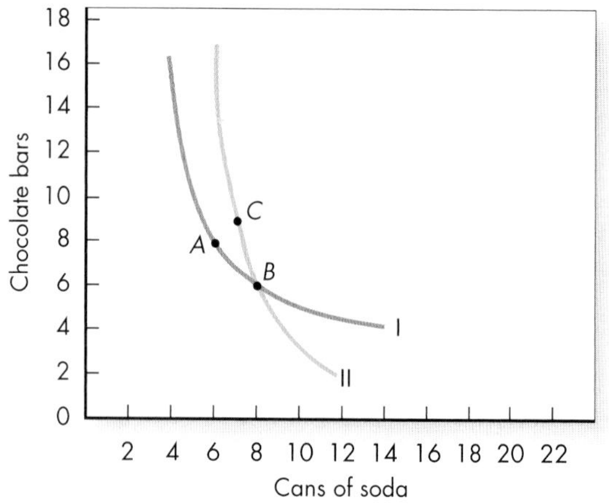

Combining Indifference Curves and Budget Constraints

Now let's put the budget constraint and the indifference curves together and ask how many chocolate bars and cans of soda Sophie will buy if she has $10, given the psychological makeup described by the indifference curves in Figure A10-3.

To answer that question, we must put the budget line of Figure A10-1 and the indifference curves of Figure A10-3 together, as we do in Figure A10-5.

FIGURE A10-5 Combining Indifference Curves and Budget Constraint

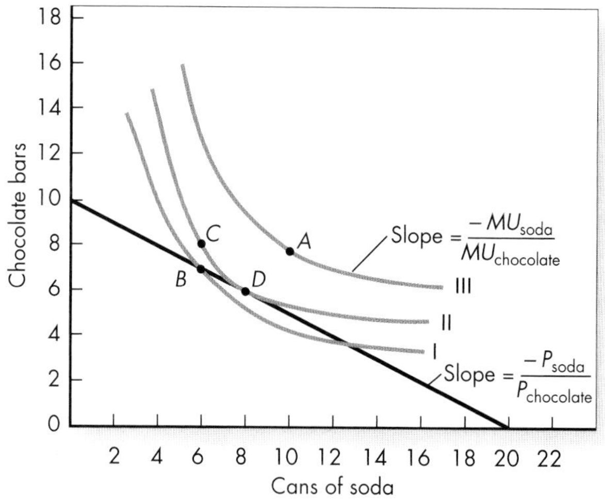

As we discussed, Sophie's problem is to get to as high an indifference curve as possible, given her budget constraint. Let's first ask if she should move to point A (8 chocolate bars and 10 cans of soda). That looks like a good point. But you should quickly recognize that she can't get to point A; her budget line won't let her. (She doesn't have enough money.) Well then, how about point *B* (7 chocolate bars and 6 cans of soda)? She can afford that combination; it's on her budget constraint. The problem with point *B* is the following: She'd rather be at point C since point C has more chocolate bars and the same amount of soda (8 chocolate bars and 6 cans of soda). But, you say, she can't reach point C. Yes, that's true, but she can reach point *D*. And, by the definition of indifference curve, she's indifferent between point C and point *D*, so point *D* (6 chocolate bars and 8 cans of soda), which she can reach given her budget constraint, is preferred to point *B*.

The same reasoning holds for all other points. The reason is that the combination of chocolate bars and cans of soda represented by point *D* is the best she can do. It is the point where the indifference curve and the budget line are tangent—the point at which the slope of the budget line $(-P_s/P_c)$ equals the slope of the indifference curve $(-MU_s/MU_c)$. Equating those slopes gives $(-P_s/P_c) = (MU_s/MU_c)$, or

$$MU_c/P_c = MU_s/P_s$$

This equation, you may remember from the chapter, is the equilibrium condition of our principle of rational choice. So by our Graphish analysis we arrived at the same conclusion we arrived at in the chapter, only this time we did it without using actual numbers. This means that even without a utilometer, economists' principle of rational choice is internally logical.

FIGURE A10-6 (A AND B)
From Indifference Curves to Demand Curves

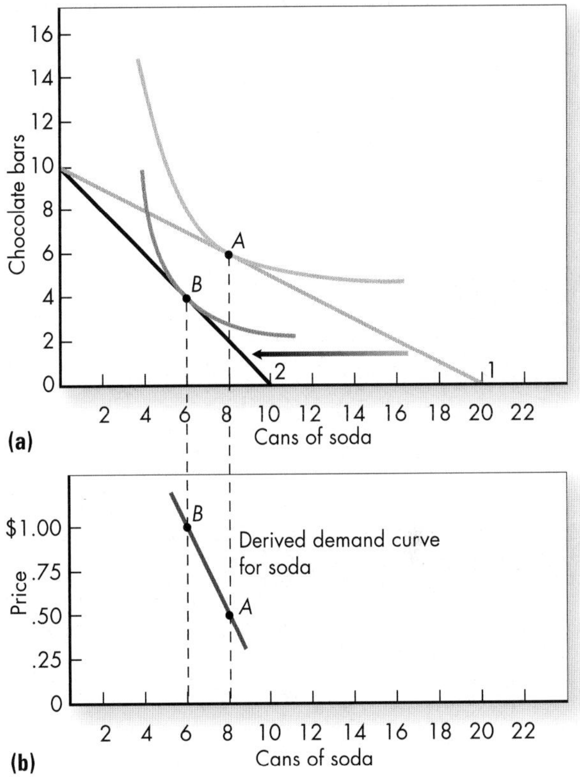

Deriving a Demand Curve from the Indifference Curve

Not only can we derive the principle of rational choice with indifference curve/budget line analysis, we also can derive a demand curve. To do so, ask yourself what a demand curve is. It's the quantity of a good that a person will buy at various prices. Since the budget line gives us the relative price of a good, and the point of tangency of the indifference curve gives us the quantity that a person would buy at that price, we can derive a demand curve from the indifference curves and budget lines. To derive a demand curve, we go through a set of thought experiments asking how many cans of soda Sophie would buy at various prices. We'll go through one of those experiments.

We start with the analysis we used before when Sophie started with $10 and chose to buy 8 cans of soda when the price of a can of soda was 50 cents (point A in Figure A10-6(a)). That analysis provides us with one point on the demand curve. I represent that by point A in Figure A10-6(b). At a price of 50 cents, Sophie buys 8 cans of soda.

Now say the price of a can of soda rises to $1. That rotates the budget line in, from budget line 1 to budget line 2 as in Figure A10-6(a). She can't buy as much as she could before. But we can determine how much she'll buy by the same reasoning we used previously. She'll choose a point at which her lower indifference curve is tangent to her new budget line. As you can see, she'll choose point *B*, which means that she buys 6 cans of soda when the price of a can of soda is $1. Graphing that point (6 cans of soda at $1 each) on our price/quantity axis in Figure A10-6(b), we have another point on our demand curve, point *B*. Connect these two together and you can see we're getting a downward-sloping demand curve, just as the law of demand said we would. To make sure you understand, continue the analysis for a couple of additional price changes.

You'll see that the demand curve you derive will be downward-sloping.

There's much more we can do with indifference curves. We can distinguish income effects and substitution effects. (Remember, when the price of a can of soda rose, Sophie was worse off. So to be as well off as before, as is required by the substitution effect, she'd have to be compensated for that rise in price by an offsetting fall in the price of chocolate bars.) But let's make a deal. You tentatively believe me when I say that all kinds of stuff can be done with indifference curves and budget constraints, and I'll leave the further demonstration and the proofs for you to experience in the intermediate microeconomics courses.

Key Terms

budget constraint *(250)*
indifference curve *(251)*
law of diminishing marginal rate of substitution *(251)*
marginal rate of substitution *(251)*

Questions and Exercises

1. Zachary has \$5 to spend on two goods: video games and hot dogs. Hot dogs cost \$1 apiece while video games cost 50 cents apiece.
   a. Draw a graph of Zachary's budget constraint, placing video games on the Y axis.
   b. Suppose the price of hot dogs falls to 50 cents apiece. Draw the new budget constraint.
   c. Suppose Zachary now has \$8 to spend. Draw the new budget constraint using the prices from *b*.
2. Zachary's indifference curves are shown in the following graph. Determine on which indifference curve Zachary will be, given the budget constraints and prices in *a*, *b*, and *c* from problem 1.

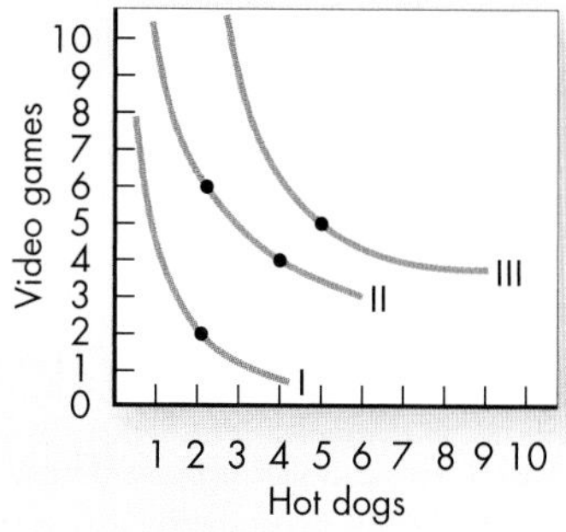

   a. Given a choice, which budget constraint would Zachary prefer most? Least?
   b. What is the marginal rate of substitution of hot dogs for video games at each of the combinations chosen with budget constraints *a*, *b*, and *c* in problem 1?
3. What would an indifference curve look like if the marginal rate of substitution were zero? If it were constant?
4. What might an indifference curve look like if the law of diminishing marginal utility did not hold?

Game Theory, Strategic Decision Making, and Behavioral Economics

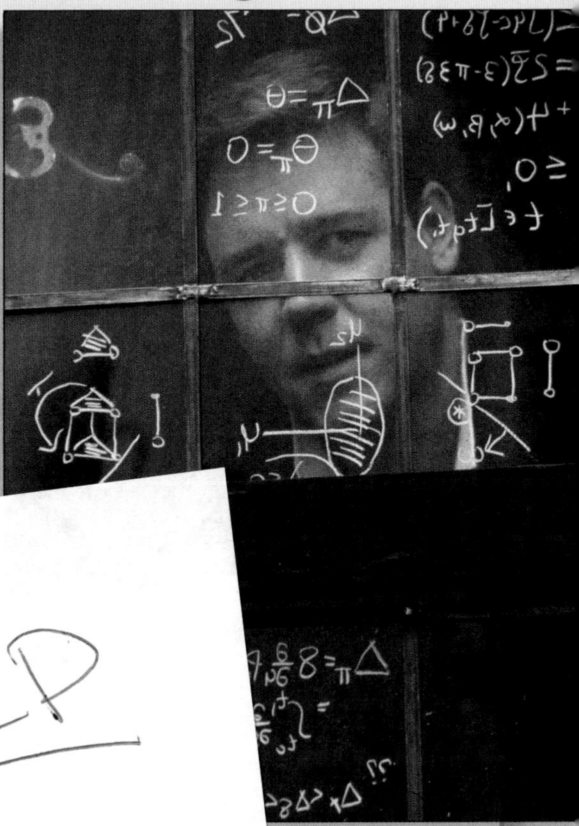

All men can see the tactics whereby I conquer, but what none can see is the strategy out of which victory is evolved.

—Sun Tzu

In the movie *A Beautiful Mind*, John Nash and some friends walk into a bar with the idea of meeting some women. They see some wo… whom is blond, and discuss their strategy to … friends that if each were to approach the proble… initially go for the blond (whom they conside… so it's a bit clichéish—movies generally are). N…

> If everyone competes for the blond, we blo… one gets her. So then we all go for her frien… cold shoulder, because no one likes to be se… winner. But what if none of us go for the bl… each other's way; we don't insult the other g… way we win. That's the only way we all get a… *Mind: The Shooting Script*, Akiva Goldsman, …

In the movie this is Nash's eureka moment: Each … best interest, will not necessarily arrive at the best … Smith is wrong.

Game Theory and the Economi… Way of Thinking

The general reasoning process that Nash is portrayed as using captures a central element of the modern economic way of thinking.[2] That central element is *strategic thinking*. Whenever the decisions being analyzed involve interdependent

…G THIS CHAPTER, …E ABLE TO:

…me theory is more …ndard models of …r.

2. …ovide an example of a prisoner's dilemma game.
3. Explain what is meant by Nash equilibrium.
4. Distinguish between a dominant strategy and a mixed strategy.
5. Give two examples of seemingly irrational behavior that behavioral economists are attempting to explain and include in their economic models.
6. Explain why economists' traditional models remain relevant even if the findings of behavioral economists are true for many, and even most, individuals.

---

[1]I am only reporting, not condoning, the portrayal in the movie. I fully agree that Nash's EQ (emotional quotient) and sense of what is socially appropriate can be questioned. If you saw the movie, you probably agree, too.

[2]The reasoning attributed to Nash in the film can also be questioned. (Economists have pointed out that the movie gets the reasoning about the men's best strategy mixed up. Chalk these inaccuracies up to artistic license; it made for a better scene, so they didn't care about its being wrong. Their reasoning was probably: Except for economists and mathematicians, no one will notice or care.)

SKIP

problems 1, 3, 5, 7, 9, pg. 102

decisions, the decision makers' strategy needs to be considered. Since all types of decisions are interdependent, the study of such interdependent decision-making processes is central to modern economics. In fact, in recent years an entire theory of strategic thinking, called **game theory**—*formal economic reasoning applied to situations in which decisions are interdependent*—has developed.

Game theory is formal economic reasoning applied to situations in which decisions are interdependent.

Game theory is a broad-based approach to understanding human interaction, and is not solely a tool used by economists. All social scientists—political scientists, sociologists, and anthropologists as well as economists—are using game theory more and more as a tool of analysis. Thus, you can see political scientists discussing war strategy and sociologists discussing social relationships in game theoretic terms. In many ways, game theory is the underlying model of the social sciences.

The Flexibility of Game Theory

More and more, game theory is becoming the basic tool of modern economics, in many cases replacing supply and demand as economists' core model of choice. Today, when graduate students study microeconomics, they spend more time learning game theory than they spend learning the intricacies of supply and demand models. Game theory has become so important because it is a highly flexible tool that can be applied to many situations without making the restrictive assumptions of the supply/demand model.

Game theory is a highly flexible tool.

Q-1 True or false? Game theory is inconsistent with supply/demand analysis. Explain your answer.

Game Theory and Economic Modeling

Before we analyze some specific games, let's step back and reflect on modern economists' modeling method—their way of thinking—and consider where game theory fits within that method. Nobel Prize–winning economist Bob Solow has nicely summarized economists' way of thinking as follows: "You look at a problem; you create a simple model that captures its essence; you empirically test how well that model fits the data, and if it fits, you use that model as a guide to understanding the problem and devising a solution." As I discussed in Chapter 6, this method sometimes gets lost as introductory students learn how to apply the models that have already been developed, rather than learning how to develop their own models.

I suspect that oftentimes when you have learned a model, you sensed that it was a stretch to make the model fit real-world situations. Economists share that concern, and are continually tweaking the existing models and developing other models that help us understand real-world problems and issues. That's why game theory developed; it offers a new set of models with which to approach economic issues. Game theory models can be better tailored to fit the actual problem, and thus are more flexible than the standard models. The cost of that flexibility is that individual game theory models are not as broad as the standard models. A different game theory model must be developed for each different situation and for each different set of assumptions. So rather than having a single model with a single equilibrium solution, in game theory there are many models that often have multiple equilibrium solutions. Hence, game theory is really a framework—a method—rather than a finished set of models to mechanistically use in understanding real-world events.

Game theory models are more flexible than the standard economic models.

The Game Theory Framework

To introduce you to the game theory framework, let's consider a variation of a story told by Avinash Dixit and Susan Skeath in their excellent book on game theory, *Games of Strategy*. In it, four students, who all had A averages, had partied the night before the exam (yes, partying happens) and had slept through the exam. Since they were "A" students, and they felt the professor liked them, they decided to make up a sad sob story and convince her that they should be allowed to take the exam late. So they went to the professor all apologetic, explaining how they had meant to come to the exam, but when they were returning from visiting a sick brother of one of them (who lived 100 miles away), they had had a flat tire. Unfortunately, there was no spare, and it took them five hours to get the flat fixed, making them late for the exam. They knew it wasn't the best story but they figured it was worth a try.

To their surprise the professor agreed with no problem to let them take the exam two days later. So they studied hard, figuring they were a shoo-in for As. The professor put them each in separate rooms and gave them the exam. The first page, worth 10 points, was an easy question, which they all were sure they aced. The second page, however, had just one question, but it was worth 90 points. The question was: "Which tire?"

This is an example of a screening question, which is meant to reveal strategic information about the person who answers. A **screening question** is *a question structured in a way to reveal strategic information about the person who answers*. If they had actually had a flat, the question would be easy to answer, and they would get their As. But if they didn't have a flat (and didn't coordinate their stories beforehand), it is highly unlikely that they would all pick the same answer, and the professor would know that they were lying. Of course, if they had been bright, or had studied game theory, they would have expected that the professor would use such a screening device and would have figured out which tire to say went flat before they went in. But of course, if the professor had taught them game theory, or knew they were even better-than-"A" students, she would have assumed that they would have coordinated their stories about which tire, and she would have worked out an even more elaborate testing strategy to get them to reveal the truth. Game theory studies such issues. Devising such strategies and understanding the strategic interaction of individuals when they take into account the expected reaction of others are the essence of game theory.

A screening question is a question structured in such a way as to reveal strategic information about the person who answers.

You have already seen some of the games that comprise game theory—for example, the ultimatum game in the earlier chapter on individual choice. In the remainder of the chapter, we introduce you to some other games and game theory concepts. The goal of the chapter is not to make you game theorists, but to give you a sense of the way in which economists think and try to understand the many puzzles that are out there.

The Prisoner's Dilemma

Let's begin with the most famous of all games—the **prisoner's dilemma,** *a well-known two-person game that demonstrates the difficulty of cooperative behavior in certain circumstances*. The standard prisoner's dilemma can be seen in the following example: Two people suspected of committing a crime are brought into the police station and interrogated separately. They know that if neither of them confesses, the police have only enough evidence to charge each with a minor crime for which each will serve 6 months. The police know that too, but they also know that the criminals are guilty of a more serious felony. The police, however, have insufficient evidence to prosecute for the more serious crime. In order to make their case, the police offer each prisoner the following deal if he confesses to the more serious crime:

WWW Web Note 11.1
The Prisoner's Dilemma

> "If both you and the other prisoner confess, instead of being sentenced to the maximum 10 years in prison, the two of you will each serve only 5 years in jail. Further, if you confess but the other prisoner doesn't confess, in exchange for your serving as a witness for the prosecution, we will drop the charges for the lesser felony, and

FIGURE 11-1
Prisoner's Dilemma

This payoff matrix illustrates the prisoner's dilemma. If the prisoners could agree not to confess, each would get a light sentence. But each prisoner is offered the chance to go free if he confesses to the crime and agrees to serve as a witness against the other prisoner. With this incentive, both will likely confess and each will be sentenced to 5 years in jail.

	B Confesses	**B** Does not confess
A Confesses	Prisoner **A**: 5 years / Prisoner **B**: 5 years	Prisoner **A**: Goes free / Prisoner **B**: 10 years
A Does not confess	Prisoner **A**: 10 years / Prisoner **B**: Goes free	Prisoner **A**: 6 months / Prisoner **B**: 6 months

you will be set free. If, however, you don't confess and the other suspect does, you will be sentenced to the maximum 10 years in prison. If neither confesses, both will be charged with the lesser felony and serve 6 months."

A payoff matrix is a table that shows the outcome of every choice by every player, given the possible choices of all other players.

The choice each suspect faces is: Do I confess or not confess? The outcome of each choice can be presented in what is called a **payoff matrix**—*a table that shows the outcome of every choice by every player, given the possible choices of all other players*—shown in Figure 11-1. The payoff matrix shows the three elements of any game: the *players* (in this case, two of them, A and B), their possible *strategies* (in this case, to confess or not confess), and the contingent *payoffs* (in this case, their sentences) for each possible outcome.

What strategy will each choose? The combined best option for them, if they could coordinate their actions, is most likely for neither to confess; each gets a short sentence of 6 months. But will they choose that option if they use strategic reasoning? To see whether they do, consider the possibilities each faces. Prisoner A's choices are shown in the rows of Figure 11-1. The blue triangle shows Prisoner A's punishment and the green triangle shows Prisoner B's punishment for each possible outcome. Say that Prisoner A does not confess, putting us in the bottom row of the payoff matrix. He now uses the pay-off matrix to consider what options Prisoner B faces. If Prisoner B also does not confess, they both get 6 months in jail (the bottom right corner of the matrix). But if Prisoner B confesses while Prisoner A has not confessed, then Prisoner B will go free. So Prisoner B's best strategy, if Prisoner A does not confess, is to confess; instead of serving a 6-month sentence, he goes free.

Q-2 In the payoff matrix in Figure 11-1, what is B's best strategy if A confesses?

Now say that Prisoner A confesses, putting us in the top row of the payoff matrix. In this case, if Prisoner B does not confess, Prisoner B gets 10 years, and if he confesses, 5 years. Again, confessing is Prisoner B's best strategy. Prisoner A concludes that regardless of what he does, Prisoner B's best strategy is to confess, so Prisoner A has to assume that if Prisoner B is following his best options, Prisoner B will confess.

Q-3 In the payoff matrix in Figure 11-1, what is B's best strategy if A does not confess?

The same reasoning holds for Prisoner B, so each of their optimal strategies (the ones that maximize the expected benefits) is to confess, placing them in the upper left corner of the matrix. Since neither can count on the other *not* to confess, which would lead to the combined best outcome for them, the optimal strategy will be for each to confess because each must assume the other will do the same. Confessing is the rational thing for each prisoner to do. That's why it's called the *prisoner's dilemma*.

Let's consider the reasoning and assumptions of game theory that led us to the outcome. First, we assumed that the prison sentences capture all the relevant costs and benefits of their decisions. Second, we assumed that no cooperation was possible. The prisoner's dilemma is an example of what is called a **noncooperative game**—*a game in which each player is out for him- or herself and agreements are either not possible or not enforceable.* If the prisoners could have trusted each other to choose the action that helps them both jointly, not only themselves, the optimal strategy is "not to confess," and they both get only a light sentence. Thus, if people's utility functions are interdependent so that each cares about the other person and him- or herself equally, or if the two of them can enter into binding contracts to act that way before they are questioned, then they can escape the dilemma. The "Code of Silence" that is often attributed to the Mafia is an example of such a binding contract; they know that they must do what is in the best interest of the group, or they will be "taken out."

Q-4 If Prisoners A and B are in love and care for each other as they care for themselves, what is the expected outcome of the prisoner's dilemma game?

Such binding contracts are seldom possible, which makes the dilemma real for many prisoners, and for many individuals and firms. What is possible is what economists call **cheap talk**—*communication that occurs before the game is played that carries no cost and is backed up only by trust, and not any enforceable agreement.* If standard game theory assumptions hold, cheap talk does not influence the results, since the players cannot trust the other players to follow through on what they say. As producer Samuel Goldwyn said, and baseball coach Yogi Berra is famous for repeating, "A verbal contract isn't worth the paper it's written on." But economists have shown that cheap talk might not be so cheap. In many experiments, cheap talk does influence the outcome of a game, especially ones where players have significant difficulty figuring out their optimal strategy. These empirical findings suggest that, to some degree, people do have interdependent utility functions, where each person cares about others as well as him- or herself.

Q-5 In formal game theory, should cheap talk influence the results?

Web Note 11.2
Cheap Talk

Dominant Strategies and Nash Equilibrium

In analyzing the prisoner's dilemma, notice that the analysis is based on the assumption that the players figure out the other player's best strategy and build into his or her decision the assumption that the other player will choose that best strategy, while taking into account the fact that the first player is doing the same analysis in reverse. In this prisoner's dilemma case, each player has a single best strategy. *A strategy that is preferred by a player regardless of the opponent's move* is called a **dominant strategy.**

A key concept in analyzing games is a concept called a Nash equilibrium, in honor of John Nash, who first proposed it as a solution concept for strategic games. Specifically, a **Nash equilibrium** is *a set of strategies for each player in the game in which no player can improve his or her payoff by changing strategy unilaterally.*[3] A Nash equilibrium is the predicted outcome of a non-cooperative game if each player follows his best strategy and assumes that the other players are following their best strategies. The solution to the prisoner's dilemma is a Nash equilibrium.

A Nash equilibrium is a set of strategies for each player in the game in which no player can improve his or her payoff by changing strategy unilaterally.

Notice that the Nash equilibrium doesn't have to be the solution that is jointly best for all players. The solution that is jointly best for both prisoners in the prisoner's dilemma is that neither prisoner confesses. But without the possibility of enforceable cooperation, "not confessing" independently is not the best strategy for either prisoner.

[3]The concept of a Nash equilibrium has a long history and goes back to August Cournot, a French economist in the 1800s, and is sometimes called a Cournot Nash equilibrium. Nash's specific contribution was to prove that all finite games have such equilibria.

A REMINDER ✓

The Austan Goolsbee *Check-a-Box* Method for Finding Dominant Strategies and Nash Equilibria

Getting used to thinking in terms of pay-off matrices is hard for some students, and economist Austan Goolsbee has pointed out a neat way of finding both *dominant strategies* and *Nash equilibria.* It works by marking the best strategies for each player. Here's how you do it:

1. Put a check mark for each of B's best strategies.
2. Put an *x* for each of A's best strategies.
3. Compare checks and *x*'s:
   a. A row with two check marks or two *x*'s is a dominant strategy.
   b. A box with a check mark and an *x* is a Nash equilibrium.

Let's see how it works with an example. Start by looking at the choices facing individual A—confess or not confess—and ask yourself: What is her best strategy if B confesses? What is her best strategy if B does not confess?

- If B confesses, we are in column 1, and A's best strategy is to confess. Put an *x* in the upper-left-hand box.
- If B does not confess (column 2), then A's best strategy is to confess, so put an *x* in the upper-right-hand box.

Continue by asking the same questions for individual B.

- If A confesses, we are in the top row, and B's best strategy is to confess, so put a check mark in the upper-left-hand box.
- If A does not confess (bottom row), B's best strategy is to confess. So put a check mark in the lower-left-hand box.

	B Confesses	**B** Does not confess
A Confesses	X ✓ Prisoner **A**: 5 years; Prisoner **B**: 5 years	X Prisoner **A**: Goes free; Prisoner **B**: 10 years
A Does not confess	✓ Prisoner **A**: 10 years; Prisoner **B**: Goes free	Prisoner **A**: 6 months; Prisoner **B**: 6 months

By looking at the pattern of check marks and *x*'s, you can make the following conclusions:

- Do any rows have two *x*'s? *Yes. Confessing is a dominant strategy for A.*
- Do any columns have two check marks? *Yes. Confessing is a dominant strategy for B.*
- Do any boxes have both a check mark and an *x*? *Yes. Both A and B confessing is a Nash equilibrium.*

An Overview of Game Theory as a Tool in Studying Strategic Interaction

There are many different assumptions that can be made about the nature of the strategic interaction, and in formal game theory, different assumptions about the nature of those interactions lead to different kinds of games. For example, in the prisoner's dilemma game discussion, we were careful to point out that cooperation was not allowed. In many real-world situations, cooperation is possible, so economists have also developed an analysis of **cooperative games**—*games in which players can form coalitions and can enforce the will of the coalition on its members.* The possibility for cooperation is often greater when a game will be repeated. Because players have the opportunity to communicate, reward, and punish one another in a repeated game, the outcome of a repeated game can often be different than the outcome of a game played just once.

Yet another assumption relates to the order in which players make their decisions. In **sequential games,** *players make decisions one after another, so one player responds to* *the known decisions of other players*. Sequential games stand in contrast to **simultaneous move games,** *where players make their decisions at the same time as other players without knowing what choices the other players have made*. Tic-tac-toe is an example of a sequential game; the prisoner's dilemma and rock-paper-scissors are examples of simultaneous move games.

Often in sequential games, the order makes a big difference. For example, some games have first mover advantage; tic-tac-toe, for instance. Other games have second mover advantage. Say Todd and Jenifer both attend the same school. Todd isn't wild about Jenifer, but Jenifer is wild about Todd. They both eat in the same dining hall, which has two tables. If Todd is the first mover, then he ends up sitting with Jenifer since she will always sit at the table with him. If Jenifer is the first mover and chooses a table, Todd will always sit at another table. In this game, the second mover has the advantage.

Some Specific Games

Let's now discuss how game theory can be used as a tool in studying strategic interactions by looking at specific games. Let's start with an easy game—tic-tac-toe. Tic-tac-toe is not a very interesting strategic game because it has a clear-cut answer that, I suspect, most of you know. Assuming people want to win and that they behave rationally—that is, they play a strategy that gives them the best chance of winning—tic-tac-toe will always end in a tie.

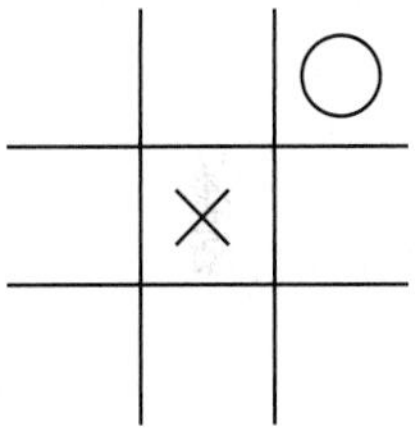

Tic-tac-toe often ends in a tie.

Formal game theory predicts any tic-tac-toe game (or similar game) will end in a tie because formal game theory assumes all players (1) are fully forward looking, (2) always behave in a manner that gives them the highest payoff, and (3) expect all other players to behave in that same manner. This is what we mean when we say that players are rational.

It is this assumption of rationality that allows us to give precise answers to game theoretic situations. Of course, people aren't always rational, and it is important to remember that formal game theory only provides a prediction about the outcome of a game. Actual behavior may deviate from the formal game theoretic predictions and modern behavioral economists use games in their experiments to discover where people's behavior is predictably irrational.

Behavioral economics examines the deviations between formal game theoretical predictions and actual outcomes of games.

To compare the theoretical and empirical results, the real-world games that provide the empirical results must correspond to the assumptions of the theoretical model. Unfortunately, real-world games seldom do, which is why economists are turning more and more toward controlled experiments to test the predictions of games. These controlled experiments—either in the field, seeing what actually happens in real life when the games are played under various circumstances, or in the laboratory—where the game is structured to match the assumptions of the theory—are increasing, and the *experimental economics* branch of economics is increasing in importance. (Two economists, Vernon Smith and Danny Kahneman, received the Nobel Prize for their work in experimental economics in 2002.) There is much debate about how much we can rely on such experiments since the controls are never, and often far from, perfect.

Strategies of Players

The analysis of games is often conducted by using a method called **backward induction,** where *you begin with a desired outcome and then determine the decisions that could have led you to that outcome*. With sequential decisions, you continue the backward induction until you arrive at the best strategy for your first move. The tic-tac-toe game is easy to analyze because it is a sequential game with a complete set of choices that can be determined by working backwards from the desired outcome (winning the game) to the

In backward induction, you begin with a desired outcome and then determine the decisions that will lead you to that outcome.

ADDED DIMENSION

Game Theory and Experimental Economics

Game theory has offered significant insight into the structure of economic problems but arrives at the conclusion that a number of alternative solutions are possible. A new branch of economics—experimental economics—has developed that offers insight into which outcome will be forthcoming. Let's consider an example.

When game theorists have done experiments, they have found that people believe that the others in the game will work toward a cooperative solution. Thus, when the gains from cheating are not too great, often people do not choose the individual profit-maximizing position but instead choose a more cooperative strategy, at least initially. Such cooperative solutions tend to break down, however, as the benefits of cheating become larger. Additionally, as the number of participants gets larger, the less likely it is that the cooperative solution will be chosen and the more likely it is that competitive solutions will be chosen.

Experimental economists also have found that the structure of the game plays an important role in deciding the solution. For example, posted-price markets, in which the prices are explicitly announced, are more likely to reach a collusive result than are nonposted- or uncertain-price markets, where actual sale prices are not known. Experiments in game theory are used extensively in designing auctions for allocating such things as telecom licenses or oil leases. Seeing how these auctions were designed gives you a good sense of how game theory, experiments, and real-world experience are combined to design policy.

The policy makers started with the results of the formal game and integrated those into the regulations of the actual bidding process. Then, game theorists pointed out how bidders could exploit loopholes in the regulations. Policy makers then modified the regulations and went through the process again, with game theorists pointing out potential loopholes. Eventually policy makers arrived at the best regulations they could design; then they turned to experimental economists who ran experimental auctions to see if the designs worked—much like airplane designs are tested in wind tunnels before they are actually built. Then the auctions were redesigned, and reconsidered by the game theorists, and, eventually, used as the regulations in the auctions for the telecom licenses and oil rights.

---

initial decision of where to place your X or O. Sometimes backward induction leads you to an optimal rollback strategy. *Optimal rollback strategies* are based on assuming your opponent follows her best strategy, which is based on assuming you follow your best strategy, which . . . Optimal rollback strategies are much harder to determine in simultaneous move games because you have to figure out what the person is *likely* to do when you are making your move. (As your hand flies out in a rock-paper-scissors game, you can't base your choice on your opponent's choice in the game.)

Web Note 11.3
Sequential Games

Dominant Strategy As you saw in the prisoner's dilemma game, in some games, a player will prefer a strategy regardless of the opponent's move. No matter what choice one prisoner makes, assuming the other player is rational, the other prisoner's best strategy is to confess. As I discussed above, such a strategy is called a dominant strategy. So, even though the prisoner's dilemma is a simultaneous game, there is a dominant strategy, with both players "knowing" (given the assumptions of the model) what the other person will do.

A dominant strategy is a strategy that is preferred by a player regardless of the opponent's move.

Mixed Strategy Many simultaneous games don't have a single dominant strategy. Again, consider rock-paper-scissors. Whether you choose rock, paper, or scissors depends on what your opponent chooses. What you don't want to happen is for your opponent to figure out a pattern in your choices. It makes sense to vary your choices randomly so that your opponent has no pattern on which to base his strategy. This strategy is called a **mixed strategy**—*a strategy of choosing randomly among moves*.

A mixed strategy is a strategy of choosing randomly among moves.

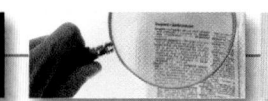

Even if a sequential game has an optimal solution, we may not be able to figure out that solution. Sequential move games can involve so many sequential moves that figuring out a rollback strategy is impossible. Chess is an example. Technically chess has a full rollback strategy—once the first move is made, if one had a sufficiently powerful and fast computing ability, that person is the winner. But our computing ability is not sufficient to compute that rollback strategy; chess grand masters have beat computers whose calculations were based on a rollback strategy. But computer chess moves do not have to be based solely on rollback strategies; they can be based on patterns ascertained by studying previous winning strategies. Computers whose strategy was based on a combination of rollback strategies *and* patterns of human play have been able to beat grand masters in chess. Most games that people play in real life are far more complicated than chess, and thus require a combination of intuition, calculation, and common sense.

Strategies in games can change dramatically with just a single change in the rules. Consider the effect of moving from a game played only once to a game played repeatedly. Say you are playing the ultimatum game, which I introduced you to in Chapter 10. In the ultimatum game, two players are offered $10 to split between the two of them, as long as they both agree to accept the money. One player is allowed to decide how to split up the $10, and the other player has the choice of accepting the deal or not accepting the deal.

In a single-play ultimatum game, the optimal strategy, assuming people are only concerned with how much money they receive, is clear. The first player's optimal strategy is to give himself almost all the money, say $9.99, offering the second player 1 cent. The second player is clearly better off receiving the 1 cent rather than nothing, so his optimal strategy is to accept. In a repeated play ultimatum game—a game that will be played a number of times with the same players—the strategy is not so clear-cut. By refusing the 1 cent, the second player can send a signal to the first player that if he wants to keep any of the money, he had better raise his offer. So repeated games offer more possibilities for implicit cooperation than do single-play games. The empirical evidence bears this out.

Q-6 In a single-play ultimatum game, what is the optimal strategy for the first player?

An Example of Strategy: The Two-Thirds Game Let's now consider another game, called the two-thirds game, that demonstrates how backward induction and rollback reasoning work. The two-thirds game is the following: you, and all members of your class, are to choose a number between 0 and 100. You win if the number you have chosen is two-thirds of the average chosen by the class. Before you proceed with reading the chapter, write down your choice.

Now, let's consider your reasoning. First, if you chose a number greater than 67, you were daydreaming rather than thinking. Even if all the other students chose 100, you would still lose, since 2/3 of 100 is 67. Now, let's say you thought a bit and assumed that people would choose randomly, which means that the average would be 50, and 2/3 of it would be 33. That would be a more likely answer, but John Nash wouldn't have thought much of it as an answer. Why? Because don't you think other people are as smart as you—and would use the same reasoning? That's the standard game theory assumption—that people will assume that others will use the best deductive reasoning possible. Making the assumption that people choose the best, we see that it makes sense to assume that people would not initially choose randomly, but instead would reason as you did—and choose 33, 2/3 of which would be 22, so it would make more sense to choose 22. However, even if you chose 22, you are still only part way toward thinking strategically.

I say part way to strategic thinking because 22 would not be the solution John Nash would have arrived at. He would have pointed out that if other people were following that same reasoning, they would have arrived at the same conclusion as you did, and would not have put down 22, but would have put down 2/3 of 22, or 14.7, so to choose any number higher than 14.7 is unreasonable. But that is not the end of the rollback reasoning. In fact, one can carry the reasoning back further and further, until finally the number you choose approaches zero. In fact, any number other than zero would lose to

Q-7 What is the Nash equilibrium in the two-thirds game?

REAL-WORLD APPLICATION

What Game Is Being Played?

In analyzing a game, it is important to know how much players know about the game being played, and whether that knowledge is symmetrical—all players have equal information—or asymmetrical—one player has more information than the others. The implications of asymmetrical knowledge can be seen by considering a game played in the movie *The Princess Bride*. The game is a battle of the wits, with the winner getting the heroine, Buttercup. In it, the hero, Wesley, offers the villain, the Sicilian, Vizzini, this challenge. Wesley places two glasses of wine on the table and states that one contains a deadly poison. The game is for Vizzini to choose a glass, and then for them both to drink. Vizzini accepts the challenge. The scene goes as follows:

> *Wesley:* All right: where is the poison? The battle of wits has begun. It ends when you decide and we both drink, and find out who is right and who is dead.

At this point, Vizzini babbles on in order to get Wesley to turn around; when Wesley does so, Vizzini switches the glasses so that what Wesley thinks is his glass is actually the glass that he thinks Vizzini is getting. By this move Vizzini figures he can win the game by changing it to a sequential game—he plans only to drink after Wesley has drunk. Since he has switched the glasses, he figures that Wesley will only drink if Wesley believes that his is not the poisoned glass. Since the glasses are switched, that decision to drink will mean that Vizzini has the nonpoisoned glass, and thus Vizzini can drink safely. (He has switched the game into an asymmetric sequential game where he has the advantage.) The scene continues as follows.

Vizzini: Let's drink—me from my glass, and you from yours. [*Allowing Wesley to drink first, he swallows his wine.*]
Wesley: You guessed wrong.
Vizzini (roaring with laughter): You only think I guessed wrong—that's what's so funny! I switched glasses when your back was turned. You fool. You fell victim to one of the classic blunders. The most famous is "Never get involved in a land war in Asia." But only slightly less well known is this: "Never go in against a Sicilian when death is on the line."
[He laughs and roars and cackles and whoops until he falls over dead.]
[At this point the heroine, Buttercup, enters the scene]
Buttercup: To think—all that time it was your cup that was poisoned.
Wesley: They were both poisoned. I spent the last few years building up an immunity to iocane powder.

The scene makes for some comic relief in the movie, but our interest is in the strategy. Given what Vizzini thought he knew, Vizzini's strategy was sound. But in this case, the game he thought he was playing was not the game he was playing. The game he was actually playing was a game in which he could only lose. This presents another lesson from game theory—often when another individual presents you with a choice, particularly one that seems especially beneficial, the choice you are making will often not be the choice you think you are making, and the game will often be rigged to your disadvantage (you don't have full information). Hence, the general rule of thumb: If it sounds too good to be true, most likely it is.

a smaller number. (This is the rollback strategy in action because the full set of choices is considered in light of the consequences for decisions of all players.) For this game, the Nash equilibrium is zero.

Informal Game Theory and Modern Behavioral Economics

Some games have no Nash equilibrium, and other games have an infinite number of them. Moreover, the probability of all people following their best strategy is highly unlikely, and thus, choosing the Nash equilibrium for the above game would almost always cause you to lose. (Actually, in first-time plays of the two-thirds game, the usual answer comes out with an average of about 30–40.) But then, if we play it again, after we have seen the answer to the first game, the average falls. Figure 11-2 shows the typical outcomes of multiple rounds of play. Initially the average guess is about 35, and it decreases with each additional time played.[4]

Notice that, as the game was played the second time, after the reasoning was explained, the average number chosen by students decreased, and hence moved toward the Nash equilibrium. These results demonstrate another aspect of game theory: players learn, which means that, in practice, repeated games often have different results than one-time games.

Even after the reasoning of the two-thirds game is fully explained to students, the average number they choose never reaches zero, so here we have an example of a game with a Nash equilibrium that, in practice, is not reached. One reason why the Nash equilibrium is not reached is that people's reasoning process is more complicated than assumed by Nash. People do not assume that all other people behave rationally; instead they are making complicated estimates of other people's behavior based on their past behavior and their sense of other people. This means that to apply game theory to real-world problems, game theory must be accompanied by a combination of reasoning, intuition, and empirical study about how people actually behave.

To apply game theory to real-world problems, game theory must be accompanied by a combination of reasoning, intuition, and empirical study about how people actually behave.

Informal Game Theory

While formal game theory can quickly become very complicated and mathematically intimidating, much of the power of game theory does not lie in its formal application, but rather in its informal application, which simply involves setting up a study of human interactions in a game theoretic or strategic framework. Informal game theory is often called *behavioral game theory* because it relies on empirical observation, not deductive logic alone, to determine the likely choices of individuals. Instead of assuming that people are high-powered calculating machines who can figure out their optimal strategy, no matter how complicated it may be (that's the Nash equilibrium), informal game theory looks at how people actually think and behave and is thus empirically

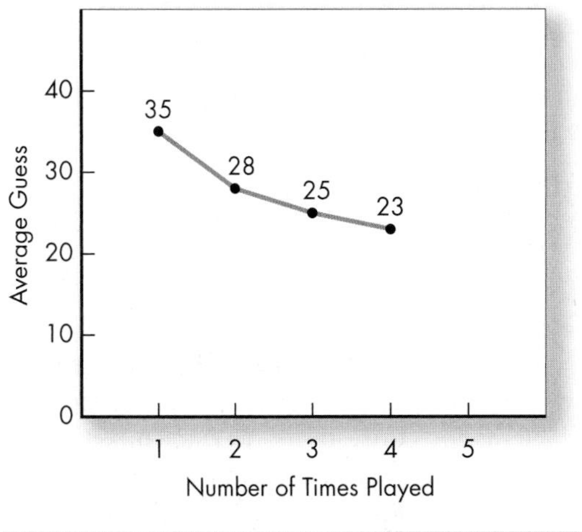

FIGURE 11-2 The Two-Thirds Game

Although when using an optimal roll-back strategy, the solution to the two-thirds game is zero, most people do not choose zero. Instead, as they play the game over and over again, their guesses fall from about 35 in the initial round to the 20s in the third, fourth, and fifth rounds as this graph illustrates.

[4]For a discussion of evidence about playing the two-thirds game, see Virtudes Alba-Fernández, Pablo Brañas-Garza, Francisca Jiménez-Jiménez, and Javier Rodero-Cosano, "Teaching Nash Equilibrium and Dominance: A Classroom Experiment on the Beauty Contest," *Journal of Economic Education* 37, no. 3 (Summer 2006), pp. 305–22.

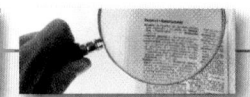

ADDED DIMENSION

The Segregation Game and Agent-Based Modeling

To see the power of Schelling's informal approach to game theory, let us consider one of his thought experiments that uses the game theory framework. In this example, the question he was interested in was why our society is so segregated when much of the population seems to have only slight tendencies toward segregation. As he was thinking of this question, he imagined a society with two types of individuals. Both types had only a slight preference for living next to individuals from their group, but that preference was not strong. His question was: Would that slight preference lead to significant segregation on the aggregate level?

To answer the question, he created a model that consists of a grid. On this grid he assumed people have a slight preference for living next to people with their same characteristics. He then went through a variety of experiments that explored what the result of that slight preference would be. What he discovered was that a slight preference on the individual level could lead to significant aggregate segregation with each group living in segregated areas. Schelling's "game" has been computerized and can be explored on the Web (www.econ.iastate.edu/tesfatsi/demos/schelling/schellhp.htm).

As you play this game, notice that although the game has no single solution, it does give you insight into the process through which segregation comes about. When Schelling first devised his game, powerful computers were still in their infancy. That has now changed. Schelling's approach has led to a whole field of economics, called agent-based modeling, in which agents are "created" in the computer and then allowed to interact. The researchers then look at the resulting patterns that are created and try to use those patterns to understand complex economic phenomena. Ultimately, agent-based computational economics (ACE) modelers hope to create virtual economies, in which one can pretest the effects of policy in the "virtual economy" before one adopts it in practice. We are a long way from that goal, but it has already had some interesting uses. For example, Disneyland has used agent-based modeling to keep its lines as short as possible.

based. Informal game theory doesn't provide definite answers; instead, it provides a framework for approaching questions.

This approach to game theory was developed by Nobel Prize winner Thomas Schelling, who argued that much of the power of game theory comes in the framework it provides for thinking about problems, rather than from formal solutions. The power of game theory comes from simply structuring a problem as a strategic interaction problem and writing down a payoff matrix. The box "The Segregation Game and Agent-Based Modeling" explores one of Schelling's informal models.

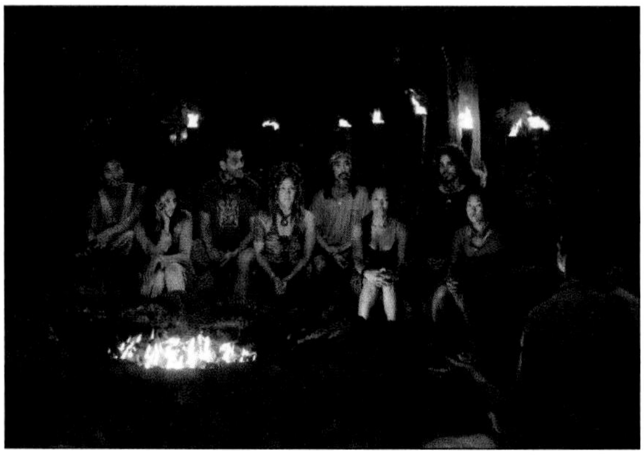

Real-World Applications of Informal Game Theory

In their book *The Art of Strategy*, Avinash Dixit and Barry Nalebuff describe a number of examples of real-world applications of informal game theory. Let's discuss a couple of them. The first involves the TV show *Survivor*—a show that gains much of its interest by creating strategic problems for contestants that are mixed with games of skill. Each week one contestant is eliminated until two are left, at which time all the eliminated contestants get to vote on who wins the grand million-dollar prize. This means that contestants must be ruthless (think about how to get other people thrown off), but also be considered fair and nice in order to get people to vote for them in the final choice. That's the show's hook.

The situation Dixit and Nalebuff describe is probably the most famous episode of the show in which eventually there were three players left: Rudy, a former Navy Seal, who was seen as honest and fair and was most people's favorite; Richard, a corporate consultant who was seen as a cold and calculating "pudgy nudist"; and Kelly, a 23-year-old river guide who was also seen as cold and calculating, although maybe a bit less than Richard, and she was definitely not pudgy. In the final challenge, the three of them had to stand on a pole with one hand on something called the immunity idol for as long as they could. The one who stayed on the longest would win the challenge and would get to decide which two went into the final.

Both Kelly and Richard knew that if Rudy made it to the final, he would win since he was the other players' favorite. So they both wanted Rudy off. The problem for Richard was that he had an alliance with Rudy, and if he won the challenge and kicked Rudy off, he would have to violate the alliance and would likely lose to Kelly in the voting. Thus, the options as seen by Richard:

- Rudy wins—he would pick Richard to continue, but Rudy would beat Richard in the final.
- Kelly wins—she would pick Richard to continue, and it is unclear who would win.
- Richard wins—he would either pick Rudy to continue, but then would lose in the final, or he would pick Kelly to continue, in which case, because he had broken his alliance with Rudy, he would almost certainly lose in the final voting.

Given these options, Dixit and Nalebuff point out that Richard has a dominant strategy—to lose, hoping that Kelly wins. Richard did precisely that—he quit the immunity challenge early; Kelly won the challenge, chose Richard to continue, and, in the final voting, Richard won the million-dollar prize. Rudy cast the deciding vote for Richard, even though Richard's losing on purpose had effectively cost Rudy the game.

A second example they give involves a proposal by Warren Buffett to get a strict campaign finance reform bill passed. In an op-ed piece in the *New York Times*, Buffett proposed a very strong campaign finance reform that would ban all types of contributions that most people believe should be banned, but that would make it more difficult for incumbents to win elections. The problem is that incumbents are the ones who vote on campaign reform bills, but they actually have little incentive to vote in effective campaign finance reform since that would make it hard for them to win elections. Thus, incumbents want to portray themselves as being in favor of campaign finance reform, but they don't really want to vote it in. To get around the problem, Buffett put forward the following suggestion:

> Well just suppose some eccentric billionaire (not me, not me!) made the following offer: If the bill was defeated, this person—the EB—would donate $1 billion in an allowable manner (soft money makes all possible) to the political party that had delivered the most votes to getting it passed. Given this diabolical application of game theory, the bill would sail through Congress and thus cost our EB nothing (establishing him as not so eccentric after all). (Warren, Buffett, "The Billionaire's Buyout Plan," *New York Times*, September 10, 2000.)

The proposal places both Democrats and Republicans in a prisoner's dilemma. Consider their options. If they vote against the bill and the bill is successful, they will deliver $1 billion to the other party, which will give the other party an enormous advantage in the next election, offsetting their advantage in fund-raising. Thus, there is no gain in opposing the bill for a party if the other party supports it. This means that the dominant strategy for both sides would be to support the bill. So the bill would pass.

As a bonus, Buffett noted that the effectiveness of the plan "would highlight the absurdity of claims that money doesn't influence Congressional votes." Unfortunately no eccentric billionaire has come forward with the offer, and with the increase in political party fund-raising, it will likely take an eccentric multibillionaire today to implement it.

There are many more applications of the ideas in informal game theory to the real world, and much of modern economic thinking involves posing problems as strategic games, analyzing the strategic decision-making problem facing both sides, and designing an institutional structure that achieves the goals one wants to achieve.

An Application of Game Theory: Auction Markets

Web Note 11.4 Online Auctions

Game theory has highlighted the importance of strategy in individuals' decision making. Looking at problems with this approach has resulted in extraordinarily powerful solutions to economic problems. Let's consider one example that was devised by Nobel Prize–winning economist William Vickrey.

He analyzed the strategies of people in a standard sealed-bid auction where participants are not aware of other bids. In a standard auction, the person who bids the highest gets the good. Let's say that you are bidding on a computer that you really want, for which you would be willing to pay $500. In this auction, if you were fully rational and Nash-like, would you bid $500? The answer is no; that's not your best strategy; your best strategy is to lower your bid enough so that it is slightly higher than what you expect the next highest bidder to bid. If you believe that to be very low, you can do much better than paying your full price.

Q-8 How does a Vickrey auction differ from a standard sealed-bid auction?

Vickrey suggested what is now called the **Vickrey auction**—*a sealed-bid auction where the highest bidder wins but pays the price bid by the next-highest bidder.* He demonstrated that this second-price auction changes the strategy of the bidders, giving them an incentive to bid their true valuation for the good since by bidding his or her true value, a bidder will win the auction without paying the higher amount.

In a highest bid auction, a bidder's strategy is to not bid the highest, but rather to bid slightly higher than the next-highest bidder. Say you would be willing to pay $500, but you think the next-highest bidder will only bid $220. You might bid $230 since if you bid $500 you would be paying $270 more than you had to pay. In a Vickrey auction, your strategy changes. Since you are not paying your bid, but rather the second-highest bid, you could bid $500, and if the second-highest bidder only bid $220, you would only pay $220.

The advantage of the Vickrey auction bid becomes more apparent when you incorrectly guessed the second-highest bidder's bid. Say that second-highest bid was $300, but you thought it was only going to be $220, so you bid $250. In the standard auction, you would not win—the other bidder would win, even though you were willing to pay more for it. In the Vickrey auction bid, the person who wants it most wins. Vickrey auctions are now often used in auctions for oil lease rights, radio spectrums, and Google's online advertisement program AddWords.

Behavioral Economics and Game Theory

While formal game theory relies upon precise definitions of rationality, informal game theory is used to explore what rationality is and the nature of individuals' utility functions. Modern behavioral economists use an approach that builds on the traditional economics that you've been presented with in earlier chapters—utility maximization, equilibrium, and efficiency—but instead of stopping there, and assuming that the theory has to be right, extends the theory to fit the observations in the real world, modifying the theory where necessary to achieve the fit. This means that instead of exploring the theoretical results of a formal model with a set of assumptions, behavioral economists use *experiments* in which people actually play the formal games to explore the validity of the assumptions in formal game theory and how they might be revised. Work in behavioral economics has led to significant advances in our understanding of the nature of preferences and choice.

For example, one of the basic assumptions of economics is that people are self-interested, and they do what benefits them. In some ways, this assumption is true by definition. One can assume that altruistic people help others because other people's welfare is a component of their utility function. Such a tautological approach to the analysis of choice is not especially helpful, since it is true by definition. Game theory allows us to explore the degree to which, and the nature in which, individuals are concerned with others.

Games and Perceptions of Fairness

Consider a variation of the ultimatum game called the trust game. As with the ultimatum game, the trust game has two players. The first player is given $10 and the choice about how to split it. The difference is that she can either keep it all for herself or "invest" some portion, which is tripled and given to the other player. The second person, called the "trustee," can either keep the now tripled amount or return some portion of it to the first person. At this point the game ends. The Nash equilibrium of this game—what would happen if people are only concerned with themselves, and are fully "rational"—is for the first player to keep the entire $10.

The rollback reasoning (beginning with the last choice) goes like this: the dominant strategy of the "trustee" is to keep any money that is shared since there is no possibility for the first player to reciprocate. Knowing that, the dominant strategy for the first person is to share nothing in the first place. No gains from cooperation are possible.

Experimental evidence shows that, on average, individuals invest about $5 and, on average, trustees return a little less than the investment. It is as if people want to trust and to reward trust. In other experiments, it has been found that people will even spend money of their own to punish others who do not respond "fairly" to offers. So, if people feel someone is being unfair, people will reduce their own income to make that person pay.

Loss Aversion and Incorrect Inference

Another example of where the empirical work suggests that people do not behave as the traditional model predicts concerns how people value things. Standard economic theory assumes that value is independent of what you have; that is, preferences are independent of endowment. To test whether this is true, Stanford neuropsychologist Brian Knutson did an experiment where he offered people either an iPod or $100. When given the opportunity to choose between the two, most people chose $100. But when participants were initially given an iPod, but then were offered $100 in exchange for the iPod, most chose to keep the iPod. That ownership increases the value of a good is even confirmed by brain scans that show increased brain activity associated with fear of loss when a good is acquired. Experiments suggest that the traditional assumptions about economic behavior do not always reflect actual behavior.

Web Note 11.5
Opting In or Opting Out?

Framing Effects

Another of the findings of behavioral economics is the importance of **framing effects**—*the tendency of people to base their choices on how the choice is presented.* The classic example of framing effects was presented by Columbia psychologist Amos Tversky and Princeton psychologist Daniel Kahneman. They asked people how they would respond in the following situations of 600 people who were threatened by a disease. Subjects were given the following two undesirable options. In the first experiment, the options were: (A) a

Framing effects are the tendency of people to base their choices on how the choice is presented.

Q-9 If a firm wants to increase the number of employees who participate in a savings plan, should the enrollment form ask whether the employee wants an automatic withdrawal from a paycheck to retirement or automatic deposit to retirement from a paycheck?

guarantee of saving 200 lives for sure but losing the others or (B) a 1/3 chance of saving all 600, but a 2/3 chance of saving no one. Most people chose A over B. Then, they offered the same people the following choices: (A) guaranteed outcome of losing 400 lives for sure but saving the others or (B) a 2/3 chance of 600 dying and a 1/3 chance of no one dying. Most people chose B over A. Now consider the two choices—they are exactly the same, but people responded differently if the choice was presented in the negative rather than the positive frame. This result has been widely duplicated and framing effects are an important part of modern economics.

Behavioral Economics and the Traditional Model

There are many more such findings, and behavioral economists are attempting to integrate those findings with traditional economic reasoning. As they do this, the methods of economics are changing. As I stated above, game theory is growing enormously in importance. Why? Because game theory allows a wider range of assumptions than does standard theory—which allows us to state the economic result more precisely. But, as we saw in the example of the two-thirds game, game theory alone does not provide answers. Thus, economists are doing much more in the way of empirical work and incorporating experimental work into their methodology.

Experimental economics is a burgeoning field. It includes laboratory experiments in which assumptions of the economic model are carefully followed, to see how subjects actually respond, and field experiments, in which the precise conditions are not as carefully controlled, but subjects are provided a more realistic setting. Behavioral economists also use computer simulations and even brain scans. One of the branches of behavioral economics is called neuroeconomics, which relies on CAT scans of individuals' brains to study individual choices.

Behavioral economics provides a more nuanced view of human behavior than does standard economics.

What comes out of behavioral economics is a much more nuanced view of humans. They are purposeful, rather than fully rational; they demonstrate enlightened self-interest rather than greed; and they are boundedly rational rather than fully "Nash-style" rational.

The Importance of the Traditional Model: Money Is Not Left on the Table

Whenever "money is left on the table," we can expect firms and individuals who understand the economic model to develop businesses and schemes to take that money off the table.

The fact that people do not act as the traditional economic model predicts does not mean that the traditional assumptions and model are irrelevant—quite the contrary. People acting differently than they would if the standard rationality assumptions hold true creates potential profit opportunities for individuals to take advantage of people's actual behavior. It means that "money is being left on the table." Whenever "money is left on the table," we can expect firms and individuals who understand the economic model to develop businesses and schemes to take that money off the table—to transfer money from those who are acting "irrationally" to those who are acting "rationally." What this means is that the findings of behavioral economics make understanding the logic of the traditional model even more important than it would be if everyone acted according to its assumptions. If you don't understand it, you can expect to lose money to those who do. The point is that the traditional economic model doesn't require everyone, or even a majority of people, to behave in accordance with its assumptions for its predictions to come true. All it takes is a few people to behave rationally because those few can develop businesses and institutions that make people pay for their "irrationality" and lack of self-interest.

Q-10 If 90 percent of people operate as behavioral economics suggests, does that mean that the standard economic model is no longer applicable?

Advertising mutual funds is an example. Those advertisements emphasize past performance, and in selling actively managed mutual funds (which have higher management fees) firms strongly emphasize past performance, even though past performance of a mutual fund often has little or no predictive power of future earnings of that mutual fund. Often investment companies have many actively managed mutual funds, some of which do well in a specific time period, and some of which do poorly, just because of random variation. With a variety of such funds, they can always have some that have done better than average. When the mutual fund salesman calls his clientele, he will push the actively managed funds that have done well, taking advantage of people's tendency to think that past history is more relevant to future behavior than it often is. Investment salesmen and fund managers make a good living selling such funds—that's the transfer of money from the unwise (in an economic sense) to the wise (in an economic sense). Most economists suggest that the way around this is to buy indexed mutual funds, which are mutual funds that contain a broad set of stocks that reflect the broader market, and are not actively managed. These index funds have much smaller fees and avoid "leaving money on the table" that can be transferred to those who understand the economic model.

Conclusion

Let me now conclude. I hope that this chapter shows you that if you had concerns about whether the traditional models learned in earlier chapters fit reality, they were legitimate concerns. Economic models don't tell you how people should behave, or how they do behave. They aren't meant to do that. Instead, they give insights into how people behave, and how to think strategically. Any economic model must be used with judgment. As Alfred Marshall, an economist whose approach I have followed, said, "The economic model is not a tool that gives answers to questions; it is an apparatus of the mind that helps its possessor come to reasonable conclusions." The overall logic of the economic model provides insight even if most people do not behave as the assumptions predict. Money is not left on the table, and when people act differently than the economic model, we can expect people and firms to figure out ways to take advantage of their behavior.

The economic model is an apparatus of the mind that helps its possessor come to reasonable conclusions.

Those concerns that you had about the relevance of the traditional economic models are also concerns that economists have, and are the basis of current research. In their research economists are pushing the boundaries of the traditional model and are developing new models to include such concerns. Don't think of economic theory as a static, unchanging theory; think of it as a dynamic theory, which is continually taking into account new discoveries and incorporating those discoveries into the model.

Summary

- Game theory is a highly flexible modeling approach that can be used to study a variety of situations in which decisions are interdependent.
- A prisoner's dilemma game is one in which both players have a dominant strategy that leads them to a jointly undesirable outcome.
- A payoff matrix provides a summary of each player's strategies and how the outcomes of their choices depend on the actions of other players.
- A Nash equilibrium is an equilibrium of a game that results from a noncooperative game when each player plays his or her best strategy. With a Nash equilibrium, no player can improve his or her payoff by changing strategy unilaterally.
- A dominant strategy is one that is preferred regardless of one's opponent's move. A mixed strategy is choosing randomly.

- Behavioral economics examines deviations between formal game theoretical predictions and actual outcomes of games.
- Loss aversion and framing effects are examples of findings in behavioral economics that challenge the traditional model's predictions.
- The traditional model remains relevant because it only takes a few people to realize that money has been left on the table for the results of the standard model to hold.

Key Terms

backward induction *(261)*
cheap talk *(259)*
cooperative game *(260)*
dominant strategy *(259)*
framing effect *(269)*
game theory *(256)*
mixed strategy *(262)*
Nash equilibrium *(259)*
noncooperative game *(259)*
payoff matrix *(258)*
prisoner's dilemma *(257)*
screening question *(257)*
sequential game *(260)*
simultaneous move game *(261)*
Vickrey auction *(268)*

Questions and Exercises

1. The chapter outlines two approaches to economics.
   a. What are those two approaches?
   b. Which approach is more likely to rely on experimental evidence?
   c. Which approach is more likely to rely on formal game theory?
   d. How might the two approaches be reconciled? LO1
2. Write down a payoff matrix different than the one presented in the text that demonstrates a prisoner's dilemma. LO2
3. Write down a payoff matrix in which players would not face the prisoner's dilemma. LO2
4. In the following payoff matrix, Player A announces that she will cooperate.

		Player **B**	
		Defect	Cooperate
Player **A**	Cooperate	**A**: −1 **B**: 2	**A**: 0.5 **B**: 1
	Defect	**A**: 0 **B**: 0.5	**A**: 1 **B**: −1

   a. How is this likely to change the outcome?
   b. What does your answer to *a* suggest about the value of cheap talk?
   c. How could Player A make her pronouncement believable? LO2
5. State whether each of the following situations is a simultaneous or sequential game. Explain your answer.
   a. A congressional vote by roll call.
   b. The ultimatum game.
   c. The Civil War.
   d. The segregation game (requires reading the box "The Segregation Game and Agent-Based Modeling" on page 266). LO2
6. Is the solution to the prisoner's dilemma game a Nash equilibrium? Why? LO3
7. If a player does not have a dominant strategy, can the game still have a Nash equilibrium? LO3
8. True or false? If a game has a Nash equilibrium, that equilibrium will be the equilibrium that we expect to observe in the real world. LO3
9. Two firms have entered an agreement to set prices. The payoff matrix on the next page shows profit for each firm in a market depending upon whether the firm cheats on the agreement by reducing its prices.
   a. What is the dominant strategy for each firm, if any?
   b. What is the Nash equilibrium, if any? LO3

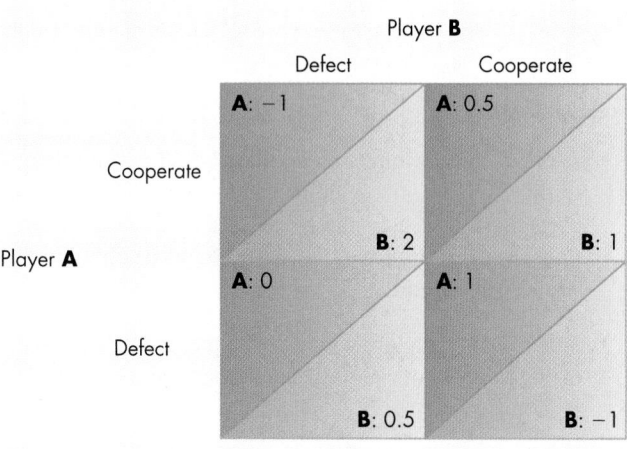

	B Cheats	**B** Does not cheat
A Cheats	Firm **A**: $0; Firm **B**: $0	Firm **A**: $100; Firm **B**: −$50
A Does not cheat	Firm **A**: −$50; Firm **B**: $100	Firm **A**: $50; Firm **B**: $50

10. Two people are arrested and charged with the same crime. Each is given the opportunity to accuse the other of the crime. The payoff matrix shows how much time each will serve depending on who rats out whom.

	B Accuses A	**B** Remains silent
A Accuses B	Prisoner **A**: 2 years; Prisoner **B**: 2 years	Prisoner **A**: Goes free; Prisoner **B**: 10 years
A Remains silent	Prisoner **A**: 10 years; Prisoner **B**: Goes free	Prisoner **A**: Goes free; Prisoner **B**: Goes free

   a. What is the dominant strategy for each, if any?
   b. What is the Nash equilibrium, if any? LO3
11. Would the results of the prisoner's dilemma game be different if it were a sequential rather than a simultaneous game? LO4
12. Can a player have a rollback strategy in a simultaneous move game? LO4
13. How is investing in the stock market similar to playing the two-thirds game? LO4
14. Why do sellers generally prefer a Vickrey auction to a regular sealed bid if sellers don't receive the highest bid in the Vickrey auction? LO4
15. For each of the following, state whether Player A and Player B have a dominant strategy and, if so, what each player's dominant strategy is. LO4

a.

Player **A** \ Player **B**	**X**	**Y**
X	**A**: 5; **B**: 5	**A**: 10; **B**: 2
Y	**A**: 2; **B**: 10	**A**: 8; **B**: 8

b.

Player **A** \ Player **B**	**X**	**Y**
X	**A**: 8; **B**: −8	**A**: 4; **B**: −4
Y	**A**: 10; **B**: −10	**A**: −5; **B**: 5

c.

Player **A** \ Player **B**	**X**	**Y**
X	**A**: −2; **B**: 1	**A**: −1; **B**: 2
Y	**A**: −1; **B**: −1	**A**: −3; **B**: 1

16. Say that you are bidding in a sealed-bid auction and that you really want the item being auctioned. Winning it would be worth $250 to you. Say you expect the next-highest bidder to bid $100.
   a. In a standard "highest-bid" auction, what bid would you make?
   b. In a Vickrey auction, what bid would you make?

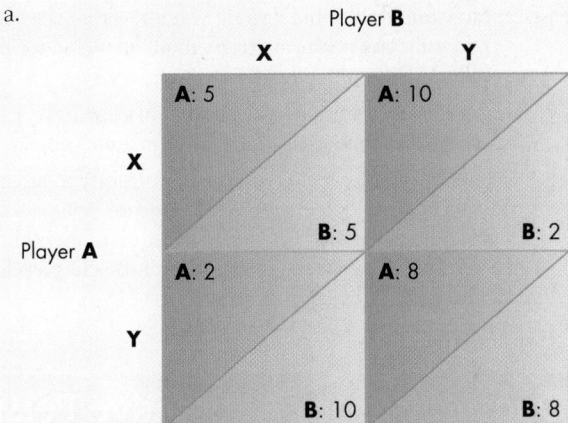

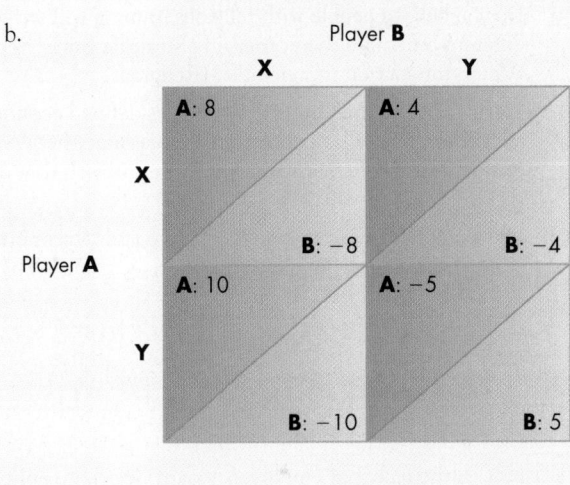

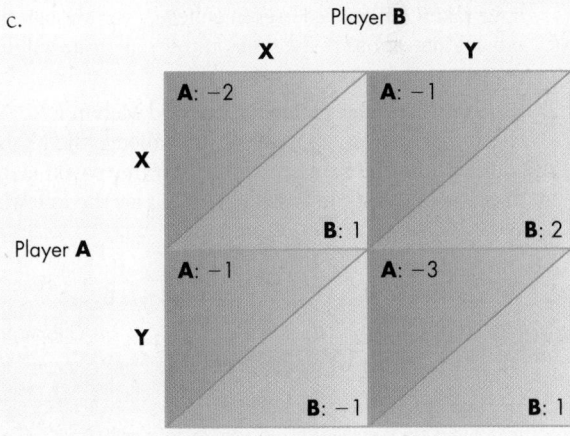

c. How might your bid differ if you knew that the seller had someone at the auction submitting a bid for the seller? (Difficult) LO4

17. Why might the multiple-play ultimatum game have a different result than the single-play ultimatum game? LO5

18. When consumers were given the opportunity to select a package of ground beef labeled "75% lean" or a package of ground beef labeled "25% fat," most consumers chose "75% lean." Why? What concept from the chapter does this illustrate? LO5

19. On your way to a concert, you lose a ticket down the subway grate. It is irretrievable. According to the standard model, would it be rational to buy a replacement ticket if one were available at the ticket box office at the same price as your lost ticket? LO5

20. Why does it take just a few people to act rationally for the standard model to hold? LO6

Questions from Alternative Perspectives

1. Do you believe people with religious training will arrive at different outcomes than others in a strategic game? Why? Which interaction is preferable? (Religious)
2. Austrian economist Ludwig von Mises defined economics as "the science of human action." Does game theory or standard supply/demand analysis better fit with that definition? Why? (Austrian)
3. Do you believe that women will arrive at different outcomes than men when playing a strategic game? Why? Which is preferable? (Feminist)
4. How does game theory demonstrate the importance of institutions? (Institutionalist)
5. In the opening to this chapter, the author describes a scene in the movie *A Beautiful Mind*. What is disturbing about that scene? Is John Nash representative of economic sensibility? (Feminist)
6. How do the findings of behavioral economics undermine the assumptions of the standard model as to the nature of human beings? (Radical)

Issues to Ponder

1. How is the fact that employers look to see that applicants have taken difficult courses in college, even though the subject matter has no bearing on the work they will likely do, an example of screening? LO1
2. In 1950, economists Merrill Flood and Melvin Dresher devised an experiment to challenge the Nash equilibrium. They presented the following payoff matrix to two economists and asked them to play the following game 100 times in succession:

		Player **B**	
		Defect	Cooperate
Player **A**	Cooperate	**A**: −1 / **B**: 2	**A**: 0.5 / **B**: 1
	Defect	**A**: 0 / **B**: 0.5	**A**: 1 / **B**: −1

   a. What is the Nash equilibrium of this payoff matrix?
   b. Is the payoff matrix symmetric? If not, who has the advantage? Do you think this affected the strategy of the players? If so, how?
   c. In 60 of the 100 games, the players cooperated. Why do you think this was so?
   d. What do you suppose the players chose for the 100th play? Why? LO2
3. In 1970 economist Martin Shubik proposed the following game. It involved auctioning off a one-dollar bill with the following rules:
   1. The highest bidder wins the dollar bill and pays his bid.
   2. The *second-highest* bidder also has to pay the amount of his last bid—and gets *nothing* in return.
   3. Each new bid has to be higher than the current high bid.
   4. The game ends when there is no new bid within a specified time limit.

   a. When the dollar was auctioned off, do you suppose that the highest bid was less than or greater than a dollar? Why?
   b. Can a rational player ever lose the auction once he has started bidding?
   c. Is it rational to begin bidding? LO4

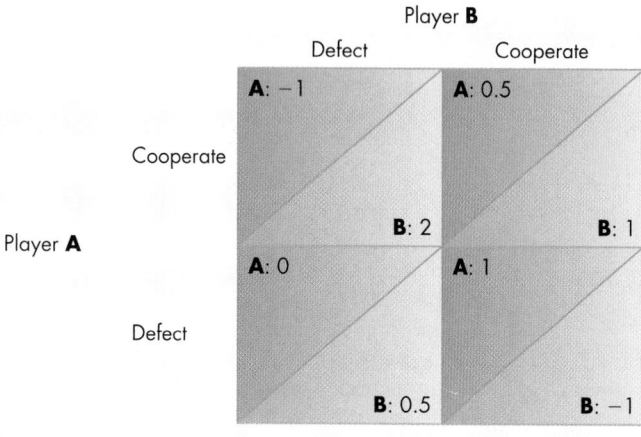

4. Suppose the two-thirds game were changed to the "average" game, so that the class had to guess a number between 0 and 100, and the person who wins is the person who guesses closest to the average number.
   a. What would the Nash equilibrium likely be?
   b. If your class played this "average" game, would you expect the equilibrium to approach the Nash equilibrium?
   c. If the equilibrium in playing the real-world game is not the Nash equilibrium, what might explain the difference? LO4

5. Say that 90 percent of the people in a market demonstrate loss aversion and 10 percent are "rational." Say that, initially, all people have equal wealth.
   a. How would you expect the wealth distribution to change over time?
   b. Would you expect the traditional model's predictions, which are based on the assumption of rationality, to be correct? Why?
   c. How might you determine the percentage of "rational" people needed for the standard model to give accurate aggregate predictions? (Difficult) LO6

Answers to Margin Questions

1. False. The two are not inconsistent. Game theory is a more flexible framework than supply/demand analysis because it can account for less restrictive assumptions compared to supply/demand analysis. *(256)*
2. If A confesses, B's best strategy is also to confess. *(258)*
3. If A does not confess, B's best strategy is to confess. *(258)*
4. Assuming that love means they trust one another, both are more likely to choose to not confess. Each person is willing to spend six months in prison to show their love and care for the other. *(259)*
5. Because cheap talk carries no cost and is unenforceable, it is not expected to influence the results of a game. *(259)*
6. The optimal strategy for the first player of a single-play ultimatum game is to offer as little as possible to the second player because the second player is better off with any amount greater than zero. *(263)*
7. The Nash equilibrium in the two-thirds game is zero. *(263)*
8. In the Vickrey auction, the highest bidder wins but pays the second-highest bid, while in a standard sealed bid, the highest bidder wins and pays the highest bid. *(268)*
9. Assuming positive framing effects, the question should be framed as a contribution to retirement rather than a withdrawal from a paycheck. *(270)*
10. No, it does not. The remaining 10 percent of rational people will develop businesses to make the remaining 90 percent pay for their irrationality and lead the overall economy to the results of the traditional model. *(270)*

CHAPTER 12

Production and Cost Analysis I

Production is not the application of tools to materials, but logic to work.

—Peter Drucker

The ability of market economies to supply material goods and services to members of their societies is one of the strongest arguments for using the market as a means of organizing society. Just consider the coordination needed to provide you a freshly brewed Starbucks latte in the morning. Trees had to be harvested and made into paper; the paper had to be processed and made into cups and printed with the Starbucks logo. Coffee beans had to be grown, picked, roasted, and ground. The espresso maker parts had to be made and the maker assembled. These ingredients were produced in 20 different countries and shipped to a Starbucks near you at the right time and in the right quantities. Finally, a barista had to be paid enough to prepare coffee when people want it—on the way to *their* jobs, in which they were producing goods that people from many other countries will end up consuming. Somehow markets are able to channel individuals' imagination, creativity, and drive into the production of material goods and services that other people want. They do this by giving people incentives to supply goods and services to the market.

Ultimately all supply comes from individuals. Individuals control the factors of production such as land, labor, and capital. Why do individuals supply these factors to the market? Because they want something in return. This means that industry's ability to supply goods depends on individuals' willingness to supply the factors of production they control. This connection was obvious in the formerly socialist countries such as Russia when consumer goods were often unavailable. People in those countries stopped working (supplying their labor). They reasoned: Why supply our labor if there's nothing to get in return?

The analysis of supply is more complicated than the analysis of demand. In the supply process, people first offer their factors of production to the market. Then the factors are transformed by firms, such as GM or IBM, into goods that consumers want. **Production** is the name given to that *transformation of factors into goods and services*.

To simplify the analysis, economists separate out the consideration of the supply of factors of production (considered in detail in later chapters) from the supply of produced goods. This allows us to assume that the prices of factors of production

AFTER READING THIS CHAPTER, YOU SHOULD BE ABLE TO:

1. Differentiate economic profit from accounting profit.
2. Distinguish between long-run and short-run production.
3. State the law of diminishing marginal productivity.
4. Calculate fixed costs, variable costs, marginal costs, total costs, average fixed costs, average variable costs, and average total costs, given the appropriate information.
5. Distinguish the various kinds of cost curves and describe the relationships among them.
6. Explain why average cost curves are U-shaped.

are constant, which simplifies the analysis of the supply of produced goods enormously. There's no problem with doing this as long as you remember that behind any produced good are individuals' factor supplies. Ultimately people, not firms, are responsible for supply.

Even with the analysis so simplified, there's still a lot to cover—so much, in fact, that we devote two chapters (this chapter and the next) to considering production, costs, and supply. In this chapter, I introduce you to the production process and short-run cost analysis. Then, in the next chapter, I focus on long-run costs and how cost analysis is used in the real world.

The Role of the Firm

With goods that already exist, such as housing and labor, the law of supply is rather intuitive. Their supply to the market depends on people's opportunity costs of keeping their houses and time for themselves and of supplying them to the market. But many of the things we buy (such as DVDs, cars, and jackets) don't automatically exist; they must be produced. The supply of such goods depends on production.

Firms:
1. Organize factors of production, and/or
2. Produce goods and services, and/or
3. Sell produced goods and services.

A key concept in production is the firm. A **firm** is *an economic institution that transforms factors of production into goods and services*. A firm (1) organizes factors of production and/or (2) produces goods and/or (3) sells produced goods to individuals, businesses, or government.

Which combination of activities a firm will undertake depends on the cost of undertaking each activity relative to the cost of subcontracting the work out to another firm. Some firms are what might be called *virtual firms*. They don't "produce" anything; they simply subcontract out all production. An example is Perdue chickens. Perdue does not grow any chickens itself. It hires farmers to grow chickens. It provides the farmers with chicks and a detailed set of directions about how to raise them into chickens. Perdue then hires another company to pick up the adult chickens for slaughter, puts its label on the processed chickens, and ships them to supermarkets. While most firms are not totally virtual, more and more of the organizational structures of businesses are being separated from the production process. As cost structures change because of technological advances such as the Internet, an increasing number of well-known firms will likely concentrate on organizational instead of production activities.

WWW Web Note 12.1 Virtual Firms

More and more of the organizational structures of business are being separated from the production process.

Firms Maximize Profit

The firm plays the same role in the theory of supply that the individual does in the theory of demand. The difference is that whereas individuals maximize utility, firms maximize profit. Profit is defined as follows:

Profit = *Total revenue* − *Total cost*

In accounting, total revenue equals total sales times price; if a firm sells 1,000 pairs of earrings at $5 each, its total revenue is $5,000. For an accountant, total costs are the wages paid to labor, rent paid to owners of capital, interest paid to lenders, and actual payments to other factors of production. If the firm paid $2,000 to employees to make the earrings and $1,000 for the materials, rent, and interest, total cost is $3,000.

In determining what to include in total revenue and total costs, accountants focus on such explicit revenues and explicit costs. That's because they must have quantifiable measures that go into a firm's income statement. For this reason, you can think of *accounting profit* as explicit revenue less explicit cost. The accounting profit for the earring firm described above is $2,000.

REAL-WORLD APPLICATION

Spin-Offs, Mergers, and Transaction Costs

In Chapter 3, we discussed the types of firms that exist in real life, and explained how they are one of the most important of the economic institutions. They are the organizations that translate factors of production into consumer goods. Types of real-world firms include sole proprietorships, partnerships, corporations, for-profit firms, nonprofit firms, and cooperatives. Each type has its own problems, and organizational theory is a key area of research in economics. One of those areas of research considers why the nature of firms changes over time.

Much of the research in organizational theory is based upon the work of Chicago economist Ronald Coase who pointed out that in order to understand the firm, one must understand that how activities are organized in firms depends on the transaction costs (costs of undertaking trades through the market) it faces. Production internal to the firm reduces transaction costs but also can increase costs since internal-to-the-firm production involves command and control and is not subject to the competition of the market. (Coase won a Nobel Prize for his work in 1991.)

To see how transactions costs affect the nature of firms, let's consider a change in the structure of Time Warner. In 2008, Time Warner, Inc. spun off its cable division, which means that it divided into two firms. What previously was done by one firm is now done by two firms, and Time Warner, Inc. entered into a market transaction to sell media content to the new cable company, Time Warner Cable, which distributes the content. One of the reasons Time Warner, Inc. spun off Time Warner Cable was that the two companies faced different cost structures and they believed that the reduction in costs from separating would more than offset an increase in transaction cost of Time Warner Cable having to buy content from Time Warner, Inc.

The introduction of the Internet has significantly lowered the transaction costs of buying many components of production, which means that more and more firms are finding it advantageous to reduce their in-house production and outsource aspects of production. For example, firms now outsource bookkeeping and computer services work. Publishers are also outsourcing the technical aspect of the production of books to specialty firms in order to take advantage of market competition. The key point to remember is that as transaction costs change, the efficient structure of firms changes, which brings about a change in the nature of firms.

Economists have different measures of revenues and costs and hence have a different measure of profit. Economists include in revenue and costs both explicit and implicit costs and revenues. Their measure of profit is both explicit and implicit revenue less both explicit and implicit costs.

Accounting focuses on explicit costs and revenues; economics focuses on both explicit and implicit costs and revenues.

Implicit costs include the opportunity costs of the factors of production provided by the owners of the business. Say that the owner of our earring firm could have earned \$1,500 working elsewhere if she did not own the earring firm. The opportunity cost of working in her own business is \$1,500. It is an implicit cost of doing business and would be included as a cost. For economists, **total cost** is *explicit payments to the factors of production plus the opportunity cost of the factors provided by the owners of the firm*. Total cost of the earring firm is \$3,000 in explicit cost and \$1,500 in implicit cost, or \$4,500. Generally, implicit costs must be estimated and are not directly measurable, which is why accountants do not include them.

Implicit revenues include the increase in the value of assets. Say the earring firm owns a kiosk whose market value rises from \$10,000 to \$11,000. The economic concept of revenue would include the \$1,000 increase in the value of the kiosk as part of total revenue. For economists, **total revenue** is *the amount a firm receives for selling its product or service plus any increase in the value of the assets owned by the firm*. Total revenue of the earring firm is \$5,000 in explicit revenue plus \$1,000 in implicit revenue, or \$6,000. For economists,

Web Note 12.2
Economic vs
Accounting Costs

Economic profit = (*Explicit and implicit revenue*) − (*Explicit and implicit cost*)

So in this case, economic profit is (\$5,000 + \$1,000) − (\$3,000 + \$1,500) = \$1,500. The difference really has to do with measurability. Implicit costs must be estimated, and

ADDED DIMENSION

Value Added and the Calculation of Total Production

This book (like all economics textbooks) treats production as if it were a one-stage process—as if a single firm transforms a factor of production into a consumer good. Economists write like that to keep the analysis manageable. (Believe me, it's complicated enough.) But you should keep in mind that reality is more complicated. Most goods go through a variety of stages of production.

For example, consider the production of desks. One firm transforms raw materials into usable raw materials (iron ore into steel); another firm transforms usable raw materials into more usable inputs (steel into steel rods, bolts, and nuts); another firm transforms those inputs into desks, which it sells wholesale to a general distributor, which then sells them to a retailer, which sells them to consumers. Many goods go through five or six stages of production and distribution. As a result, if you added up all the sales of all the firms, you would overstate how much total production was taking place.

To figure out how much total production is actually taking place, economists use the concept *value added.* Value added is the contribution that each stage of production makes to the final value of a good. A firm's value added is the firm's total output less the cost of the inputs bought from other firms. For example, if a desk assembly firm spends $4,000 on component parts and sells its output for $6,000, its value added is $2,000, or 33⅓ percent of its revenue.

When you add up all the stages of production, the value added of all the firms involved must equal 100 percent, and no more, of the total output. When I discuss "a firm's" production of a good in this book, to relate that discussion to reality, you should think of that firm as a composite of all the firms contributing to the production and distribution of that product.

Why is it important to remember that there are various stages of production? Because it brings home to you how complicated producing a good is. If any one stage gets messed up, the good doesn't get to the consumer. Producing a better mousetrap isn't enough. The firm also must be able to get it out to consumers and let them know that it's a better mousetrap. The traditional economic model doesn't bring home this point. But if you're ever planning to go into business for yourself, you'd better remember it. Many people's dreams of supplying a better product to the market have been squashed by this reality.

the estimations can sometimes be inexact. General accounting rules do not permit such inexactness because it might allow firms to misstate their profit, something accounting rules are designed to avoid.

The Production Process

As I stated at the beginning of the chapter, supply is the key to the market's ability to provide the goods people want. Underlying supply is production; firms are important because they control the production process.

The Long Run and the Short Run

The production process is generally divided into a *long-run* planning decision, in which a firm chooses the least expensive method of producing from among all possible methods, and a *short-run* adjustment decision, in which a firm adjusts its long-run planning decision to reflect new information.

A long-run decision is a decision in which the firm can choose among all possible production techniques.

A short-run decision is a decision in which the firm is constrained in regard to what production decisions it can make.

In a **long-run decision,** *a firm chooses among all possible production techniques*. This means that it can choose the size of the plant it wants, the type of machines it wants, and the location it wants. The firm has fewer options in a **short-run decision,** in which *the firm is constrained in regard to what production decisions it can make*.

The terms *long run* and *short run* do not necessarily refer to specific periods of time independent of the nature of the production process. They refer to the degree of flexibility the firm has in changing the level of output. In the long run, by definition, the firm can vary the inputs as much as it wants. In the short run, some of the flexibility that existed in the long run no longer exists. In the short run, some inputs are so costly to adjust that they are treated as fixed. *So in the long run, all inputs are variable; in the short run, some inputs are fixed.*

Production Tables and Production Functions

How a firm combines factors of production to produce goods and services can be presented in a **production table** (*a table showing the output resulting from various combinations of factors of production or inputs*).

Real-world production tables are complicated. They often involve hundreds of inputs, hundreds of outputs, and millions of possible combinations of inputs and outputs. Studying these various combinations and determining which is best requires expertise and experience. Business schools devote entire courses to it (operations research and production analysis); engineering schools devote entire specialties to it (industrial engineering).

Studying the problems and answering the questions that surround production is much of what a firm does: What combination of outputs should it produce? What combination of inputs should it use? What combination of techniques should it use? What new techniques should it explore? To answer these questions, the managers of a firm look at a production table.

Production tables are so complicated that in introductory economics we concentrate on short-run production analysis in which one of the factors is fixed. Doing so allows us to capture some important technical relationships of production without getting too tied up in numbers. The relevant part of a production table of earrings appears in Figure 12-1(c). In it the number of the assumed fixed inputs (machines) has already been determined. Columns 1 and 2 of the table tell us how output of earrings varies as the variable input (the number of workers) changes. For example, you can see that with 3 workers the firm can produce 17 pairs of earrings. Column 3 tells us workers' **marginal product** (*the additional output that will be forthcoming from an additional worker, other inputs constant*). Column 4 tells us workers' **average product** (*output per worker*).

The marginal product is the additional output forthcoming from an additional input, other inputs constant; the average product is the total output divided by the quantity of the input.

It is important to distinguish marginal product from average product. Workers' average product is the total output divided by the number of workers. For example, let's consider the case of 5 workers. Total output is 28, so average product is 5.6 (28 divided by 5). To find the marginal product, we must ask how much additional output will be forthcoming if we change the number of workers. For example, if we change from 4 to 5 workers, the additional worker's marginal product will be 5; if we change from 5 to 6, the additional worker's marginal product will be 3. That's why the marginal products are written between each level of output.

The information in a production table is often summarized in a production function. A **production function** is *the relationship between the inputs (factors of production) and outputs*. Specifically, the production function tells the maximum amount of output that can be derived from a given number of inputs. Figure 12-1(a) is the production function

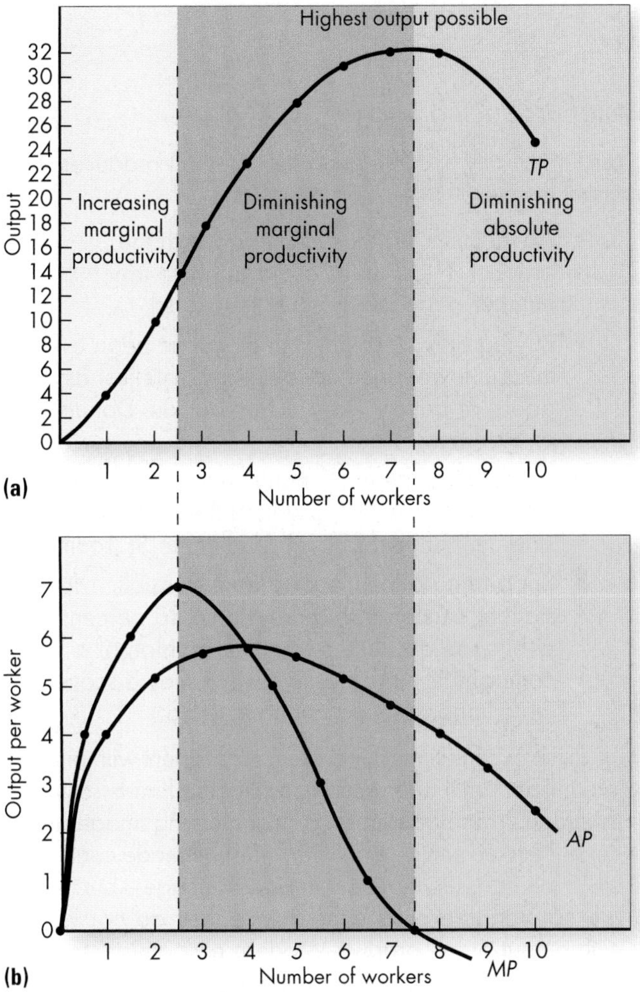

FIGURE 12-1 (A, B, AND C)

A Production Table and Production Function

The production function in (**a**) is a graph of the production table in (**c**). Its shape reflects the underlying production technology. The graph in (**b**) shows the marginal and average product. Notice that when marginal product is increasing, the production function is bowed upward; when marginal product is decreasing, the production function is bowed downward; when marginal product is zero, the production function is at its highest point. Firms are interested in producing where both average product and marginal product are positive and falling, which starts at 4 workers and ends at 7.5 workers.

Number of Workers	Total Output	Marginal Product (Change in Total Output)	Average Product (Total Product/ Number of Workers)	
1	4	4	4	Increasing marginal productivity
2	10	6	5	
3	17	7	5.7	Diminishing marginal productivity
4	23	6	5.8	
5	28	5	5.6	
6	31	3	5.2	
7	32	1	4.6	
8	32	0	4.0	Diminishing absolute productivity
9	30	−2	3.3	
10	25	−5	2.5	

(c)

that displays the information in the production table in Figure 12-1(c). The number of workers is on the horizontal axis and the output of earrings is on the vertical axis.

The Law of Diminishing Marginal Productivity

Figure 12-1(b) graphs the workers' average and marginal productivities from the production function in Figure 12-1(a). (Alternatively you can determine those graphs by plotting columns 3 and 4 from the table in Figure 12-1(c).) Notice that both marginal and average productivities are initially increasing, but that eventually they both decrease. Between 7 and 8 workers, the marginal productivity of workers actually becomes negative.

Marginal Product and the Law of Diminishing Marginal Productivity

This means that initially this production function exhibits increasing marginal productivity and then it exhibits *diminishing marginal productivity*. Eventually it exhibits negative marginal productivity.

The same information can be gathered from Figure 12-1(a), but it's a bit harder to interpret.[1] Notice that initially the production function is bowed upward. Where it's bowed upward there is increasing marginal productivity, as you can see if you extend a line

Q-1 What are the normal shapes of marginal productivity and average productivity curves?

[1]Technically the marginal productivity curve is a graph of the slope of the total product curve.

Thinking Like a Modern Economist

What "Goods" Do Firms Produce: The Costs of Producing Image

The textbook economic models are implicitly structured around the production of physical goods that require physical inputs. Such physical goods have become less important in the modern economy. In today's economy, many of the goods that firms produce involve intangibles such as image and perception. For example, Starbucks is not only producing coffee; it is also producing an image of luxury, so when you buy a Frappucino, you are actually buying something that makes you feel good about yourself—you see yourself as a quality person. Or when you buy a car—you are not just buying a car—you are buying an image for yourself. Modern firms spend enormous time and effort trying to associate whatever they are selling with an image that people want to associate with themselves.

Image is real, and has real effects. For example, experimental economists have shown that people respond better to medicine with a high price than to that same medicine with a low price. (This is a variation of the well-known placebo effect in medicine; people get better from taking a sugar pill if they think it is a medicine that is going to help them.)

Producing "image" rather than physical products affects both the structure of costs and how costs are analyzed. Specifically, producing image tends to require large expenditures not directly related to production of any specific good that the firm produces. It might involve

- Advertising that has little to do with the product. ("Just do it" could apply to any number of goods, not just sneakers.)
- Buying only the highest-price coffee bean even though lower-price coffee might taste just as good, or better. (Do you buy Dunkin' Donuts or Starbucks brand?)
- Associating the firm's name with something positive, that is, underwriting the cost of a stadium. (Think of Busch Stadium in St. Louis.)
- Supporting a local sports team or public radio station. (According to one study, 88 percent of public radio listeners say their opinion of a company is more positive when they discover the company supports public radio.)

These expenditures might seem inconsistent with profit maximizing until one recognizes that the firm is selling its image. These nondirect costs of creating image are not quite fixed costs—since they must be made continually if the firm is to maintain its good's image—but they are not variable costs either, since they do not vary with output of the product. Modern economists' more advanced models of costs capture these distinctions.

down to Figure 12-1(b). Then, between 2.5 and 7.5 workers, the production function is bowed downward but is still rising. In this range, there's diminishing marginal productivity, as you can see by extending a line down to Figure 12-1(b). Finally marginal productivity is negative.

The most important area of these relationships is the area of diminishing marginal productivity and falling average product (between 4 and 7.5 workers). Why? Because a firm is most likely to operate in that area. If it's in the first range and marginal productivity is increasing, a firm can increase its existing workers' output by hiring more workers; it will have a strong incentive to do so and get out of that range. Similarly, if hiring an additional worker actually cuts total output (as it does when marginal productivity is negative), the firm would be crazy to hire that worker. So it stays out of that range.

This range of the relationship between fixed and variable inputs is so important that economists have formulated a law that describes what happens in production processes when firms reach this range—when more and more of one input is added to a fixed amount of another input. The **law of diminishing marginal productivity** states that *as more and more of a variable input is added to an existing fixed input, eventually the additional output one gets from that additional input is going to fall.*

The law of diminishing marginal productivity is sometimes called the *flowerpot law* because if it didn't hold true, the world's entire food supply could be grown in one flowerpot. In the absence of diminishing marginal productivity, we could take a flowerpot and keep adding seeds to it, getting more and more food per seed until we had enough to feed the world. In reality, however, a given flowerpot is capable of producing only so much food no matter how many seeds we add to it. At some point, as we add more and more seeds, each additional seed will produce less food than did the seed before it. That's the law of diminishing marginal productivity in action. Eventually the pot reaches a stage of diminishing absolute productivity, in which the total output, not simply the output per unit of input, decreases as inputs are increased.

Q-2 Firms are likely to operate on what portion of the marginal productivity curve?

The law of diminishing marginal productivity states that as more and more of a variable input is added to an existing fixed input, after some point the additional output one gets from the additional input will fall.

The Costs of Production

In any given firm, owners and managers probably discuss costs far more than anything else. Invariably costs are too high and the firm is trying to figure out ways to lower them. But the concept *costs* is ambiguous; there are many different types of costs and it's important to know what they are. Let's consider some of the most important categories of costs in reference to Table 12-1, which shows costs associated with making between 3 and 32 pairs of earrings.

Fixed Costs, Variable Costs, and Total Costs

Fixed costs are *costs that are spent and cannot be changed in the period of time under consideration*. There are no fixed costs in the long run since all inputs are variable and hence their costs are variable. In the short run, however, a number of costs will be fixed. For example, say you make earrings. You buy a machine for working with silver, but suddenly

Web Note 12.3
What's Fixed?
What's Variable?

TABLE 12-1 **The Cost of Producing Earrings**

1	2	3	4	5	6	7	8
Output	Fixed Costs (*FC*)	Variable Costs (*VC*)	Total Costs (*TC*) (*FC* + *VC*)	Marginal Costs (*MC*) (Change in Total Costs/ Change in Output)	Average Fixed Costs (*AFC*) (*FC*/Output)	Average Variable Costs (*AVC*) (*VC*/Output)	Average Total Costs (*ATC*) (*AFC* + *AVC*)
3	$50	$ 38	$ 88		$16.67	$12.66	$29.33
				$12			
4	50	50	100		12.50	12.50	25.00
9	50	100	150		5.56	11.11	16.67
				8			
10	50	108	158		5.00	10.80	15.80
16	50	150	200		3.13	9.38	12.51
				7			
17	50	157	207		2.94	9.24	12.18
22	50	200	250		2.27	9.09	11.36
				10			
23	50	210	260		2.17	9.13	11.30
27	50	255	305		1.85	9.44	11.29
				15			
28	50	270	320		1.79	9.64	11.43
32	50	400	450		1.56	12.50	14.06

there's no demand for silver earrings. Assuming that machine can't be modified and used for other purposes, the money you spent on it is a fixed cost. So within this model, all fixed costs are assumed to be sunk costs.

Fixed costs are shown in column 2 of Table 12-1. Notice that fixed costs remain the same ($50) regardless of the level of production. As you can see, it doesn't matter whether output is 3 or 32; fixed costs are always $50.

Besides buying the machine, the silversmith must also hire workers. These workers are the earring firm's **variable costs**—*costs that change as output changes.* The earring firm's variable costs are shown in column 3. Notice that as output increases, variable costs increase. For example, when the firm produces 9 pairs of earrings, variable costs are $100; when it produces 10, variable costs rise to $108.

All costs are either fixed or variable in the standard model, so the *total cost* is the sum of the fixed and variable costs:

TC = FC + VC

$$TC = FC + VC$$

The earring firm's total costs are presented in column 4. Each entry in column 4 is the sum of the entries in columns 2 and 3 in the same row. For example, to produce 16 pairs of earrings, fixed costs are $50 and variable costs are $150, so total cost is $200.

Average Total Cost, Average Fixed Cost, and Average Variable Cost

Total cost, fixed cost, and variable cost are important, but much of a firm's discussion is about average cost. So the next distinction we want to make is between total cost and average cost. To arrive at the earring firm's average cost, we simply divide the total amount of whatever cost we're talking about by the quantity produced. Each of the three costs we've discussed has a corresponding average cost.

Average cost equals total cost divided by quantity.

For example, **average total cost** (often called average cost) equals *total cost divided by the quantity produced.* Thus:

$$ATC = TC/Q$$

Average fixed cost equals *fixed cost divided by quantity produced:*

$$AFC = FC/Q$$

Average variable cost equals *variable cost divided by quantity produced:*

$$AVC = VC/Q$$

Q-3 If total costs are $400, fixed costs are 0, and output is 10, what are average variable costs?

Average fixed cost and average variable cost are shown in columns 6 and 7 of Table 12-1. The most important average cost concept, average total cost, is shown in column 8. Average total cost also can be thought of as the sum of average fixed cost and average variable cost:

$$ATC = AFC + AVC$$

As you can see, the average total cost of producing 16 pairs of earrings is $12.50. It can be calculated by dividing total cost ($200) by output (16).

Marginal Cost

All these costs are important to our earring firm, but they are not the most important costs it considers when deciding how many pairs of earrings to produce. That distinction goes to marginal cost, which appears in column 5.[2] **Marginal cost** is *the*

[2]Since only selected output levels are shown, not all entries have marginal costs. For a marginal cost to exist, there must be a marginal change, a change by only one unit.

increase (decrease) in total cost from increasing (decreasing) the level of output by one unit. Let's find marginal cost by considering what happens if our earring firm increases production by one unit—from 9 to 10. Looking again at Table 12-1, we see that the total cost rises from \$150 to \$158. In this case, the marginal cost of producing the 10th unit is \$8.

Average Total Cost, Average Variable Cost, and Marginal Cost

Graphing Cost Curves

Let's say that the owner of the earring firm sees things better in pictures and asks you (an economic consultant) to show her what all those numbers in Table 12-1 mean. To do so, you first draw a graph, putting quantity on the horizontal axis and a dollar measure of various costs on the vertical axis.

Total Cost Curves

Web Note 12.4
Short-run Cost Curves

Figure 12-2(a) graphs the total cost, total fixed cost, and total variable costs of all the levels of output given in Table 12-1.[3] The total cost curve is determined by plotting the entries in column 1 and the corresponding entries in column 4. For example, point *L* corresponds to a quantity of 10 and a total cost of \$158. Notice that the curve is upward-sloping: Increasing output increases total cost.

The total fixed cost curve is determined by plotting column 1 and column 2 on the graph. The total variable cost curve is determined by plotting column 1 and column 3.

As you can see, the total variable cost curve has the same shape as the total cost curve: Increasing output increases variable cost. This isn't surprising, since the total cost curve is the vertical summation of total fixed cost and total variable cost. For

FIGURE 12-2 (A AND B) Total and Per-Unit Output Cost Curves

Total fixed costs, shown in (**a**), are always constant; they don't change with output. All other total costs increase with output. As output gets high, the rate of increase has a tendency to increase. The average fixed cost curve, shown in (**b**), is downward-sloping; the average variable cost curve and average total cost curve are U-shaped. The U-shaped *MC* curve goes through the minimum points of the *AVC* and *ATC* curves. (The *AFC* curve is often not drawn since *AFC* is also represented by the distance between the *AVC* and *ATC*.)

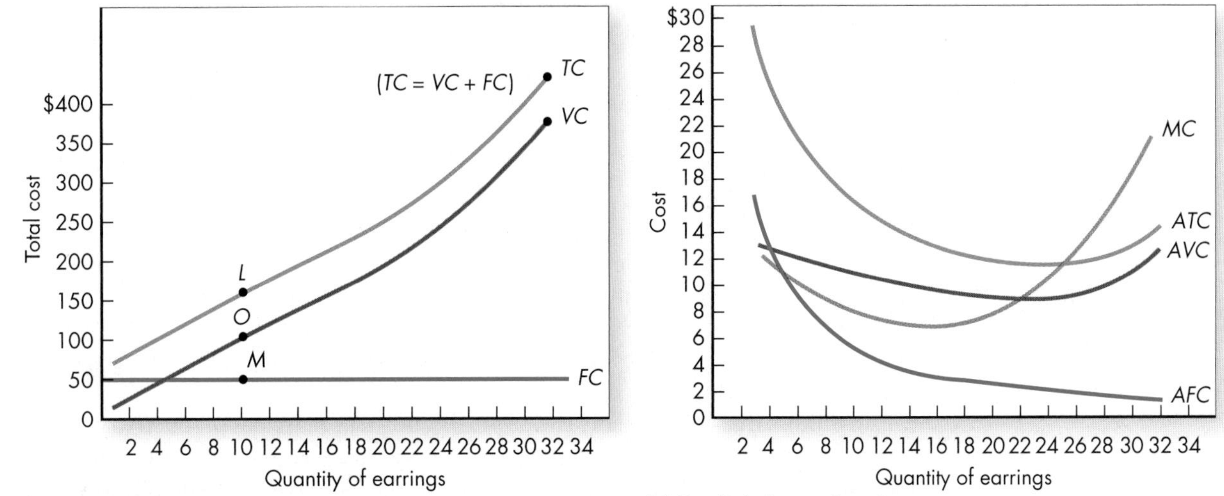

(a) Total Cost Curves **(b) Per Unit Output Cost Curves**

[3]To keep the presentation simple, we focus only on the most important part of the total cost curve, that part that follows the simplest rules. Other areas of the total cost curve can be bowed downward rather than bowed upward.

example, at output 10, total fixed cost equals \$50 (point M); total variable cost equals \$108 (point O); and total cost equals \$158 (point *L*).

Average and Marginal Cost Curves

The marginal cost curve goes through the minimum point of the average total cost curve and average variable cost curve; each of these curves is U-shaped. The average fixed cost curve slopes down continuously.

Figure 12-2(b) presents the average fixed cost curve, average total cost curve (or average cost curve, as it's generally called), average variable cost curve, and marginal cost curve associated with the cost figures in Table 12-1. Each point on the four curves represents a combination of two corresponding entries in Table 12-1. Points on the average variable cost curve are determined by plotting the entries in column 1 and the corresponding entries in column 7. Points on the average fixed cost curve are determined by entries in column 1 and the corresponding entries in column 6. Points on the average total cost curve are determined by entries in column 1 and the corresponding entries in column 8. Finally, the marginal cost curve is determined by plotting the entries in column 1 and the corresponding entries in column 5. As was the case with the total cost curves, all the firm's owner need do is look at this graph to find the various costs associated with different levels of output, since the graphical visualization of cost curves provides a good sense of what happens to costs as we change output.

Downward-Sloping Shape of the Average Fixed Cost Curve

Let's start our consideration with average fixed cost. Average fixed cost is decreasing throughout. The average fixed cost curve looks like a child's slide: It starts out with a steep decline; then it becomes flatter and flatter. What this tells us about production is straightforward: As output increases, the same fixed cost can be spread over a wider range of output, so average fixed cost falls. Average fixed cost initially falls quickly but then falls more and more slowly. As the denominator gets bigger while the numerator stays the same, the increase has a smaller and smaller effect.

The U Shape of the Average Cost Curves

Q-4 Draw a graph of both the marginal cost curve and the average cost curve.

Let's now move on to the average cost curves. Why do they have the shapes they do? Or, expressed another way, how does our analysis of production relate to our analysis of costs? You may have already gotten an idea of how production and costs relate if you remembered Figure 12-1 and recognized the output numbers that we presented were similar output numbers to those that we used in the cost analysis. Cost analysis is simply another way of considering production analysis. The laws governing costs are the same laws governing productivity.

As more and more of a variable input are added to a fixed input, the law of diminishing marginal productivity causes marginal and average productivities to fall. As these fall, marginal and average costs rise.

In the short run, output can be raised only by increasing the variable input. But as more and more of a variable input are added to a fixed input, the law of diminishing marginal productivity enters in. Marginal and average productivities fall. The key insight here is that when marginal productivity falls, marginal cost must rise, and when average productivity falls, average variable cost must rise. So to say that productivity falls is equivalent to saying that cost rises.

It follows that if eventually the law of diminishing marginal productivity holds true, then eventually both the marginal cost curve and the average cost curve must be upward-sloping. And, indeed, in our examples they are. It's also generally assumed that at low levels of production, marginal and average productivities are increasing. This means that marginal cost and average variable cost are initially falling. If they're falling initially and rising eventually, at some point they must be neither rising nor falling. This means that both the marginal cost curve and the average variable cost curve are U-shaped.

As you can see in Figure 12-2(b), the average total cost curve has the same general U shape as the average variable cost curve. It has the same U shape because it is the vertical summation of the average fixed cost curve and the average variable cost curve. Its minimum, however, is to the right of the minimum of the average variable cost curve. We'll discuss why after we cover the shape of the average variable cost curve.

Q-5 What determines the distance between the average total cost and the average variable cost?

Average total cost initially falls faster and then rises more slowly than average variable cost. If we increased output enormously, the average variable cost curve and the average total cost curve would almost meet. Average total cost is of key importance to the firm's owner. She wants to keep it low.

Q-6 If you increase output enormously, what two cost curves would almost meet?

The Relationship between the Marginal Productivity and Marginal Cost Curves

Let's now consider the relationship between marginal product and marginal cost. In Figure 12-3(a), I draw a marginal cost curve and average variable cost curve. Notice

FIGURE 12-3 (A AND B) **The Relationship between Productivity and Costs**

The shapes of the cost curves are mirror-image reflections of the shapes of the corresponding productivity curves. (The corresponding productivity curve is an implicit function in which marginal productivity is related to output rather than inputs. At each output there is an implicit number of workers who would supply that output.) When one is increasing, the other is decreasing; when one is at a minimum, the other is at a maximum.

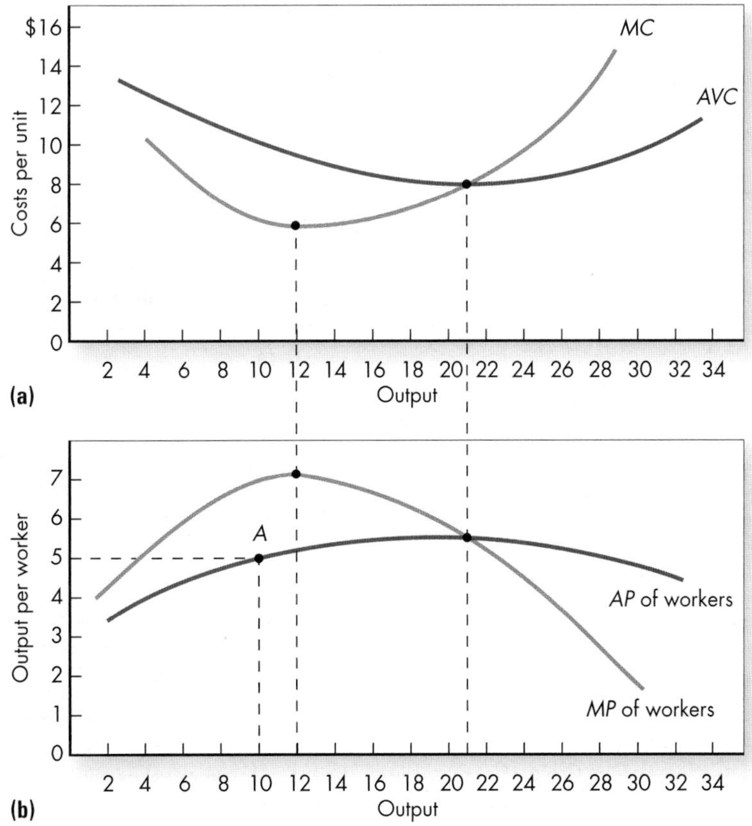

When marginal cost exceeds average cost, average cost must be rising. When marginal cost is less than average cost, average cost must be falling. This relationship explains why marginal cost curves always intersect the average cost curve at the minimum of the average cost curve.

their U shape. Initially costs are falling. Then there's some minimum point. After that, costs are rising.

If $MP > AP$, then AP is rising. If $MP < AP$, then AP is falling.

In Figure 12-3(b), I graph the average and marginal productivity curves similar to those that I presented in Figure 12-1(b), although this time I relate average and marginal productivities to output, rather than to the number of workers. This allows us to relate output per worker and output. Say, for example, that we know that the average product of 2 workers is 5, and that 2 workers can produce an output of 10. This means that when output is 10, the workers' average productivity is 5. By continuing this reasoning, we can construct the curves. Point A corresponds to an output of 10 and average productivity of 5.

Q-7 When the marginal cost equals the minimum point of the average variable cost, what is true about the average productivity and marginal productivity of workers?

Now let's compare the graphs in Figure 12-3 (a and b). If you look at the two graphs carefully, you'll see that one is simply the mirror image of the other. The minimum point of the average variable cost curve (output = 21) is at the same level of output as the maximum point of the average productivity curve; the minimum point of the marginal cost curve (output = 12) is at the same level of output as the maximum point on the marginal productivity curve. When the productivity curves are falling, the corresponding cost curves are rising. Why is that the case? Because as productivity falls, costs per unit increase; and as productivity increases, costs per unit decrease.

When the productivity curves are falling, the corresponding cost curves are rising.

The Relationship between the Marginal Cost and Average Cost Curves

Web Note 12.5 Marginal Costs in the Information Economy

Now that we've considered the shapes of each cost curve, let's consider some of the important relationships among them—specifically the relationships between the marginal cost curve on the one hand and the average variable cost and average total cost curves on the other. These relationships are shown graphically for a different production process in Figure 12-4.

FIGURE 12-4

The Relationship of Marginal Cost Curve to Average Variable Cost and Average Total Cost Curves

The marginal cost curve goes through the minimum points of both the average variable cost curve and the average total cost curve. Thus, there is a small range where average total costs are falling and average variable costs are rising.

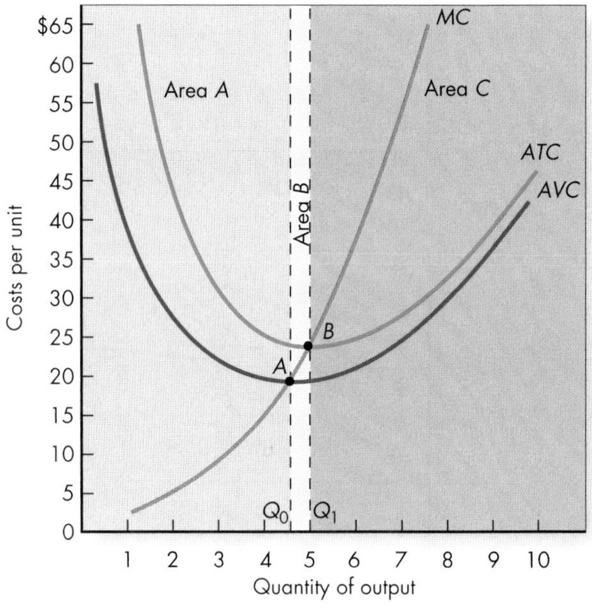

Let's first look at the relationship between marginal cost and average total cost. In the green shaded and yellow shaded areas (areas A and B) at output below 5, even though marginal cost is rising, average total cost is falling. Why? Because, in areas A and B, the marginal cost curve is below the average total cost curve. At point B, where average total cost is at its lowest, the marginal cost curve intersects the average total cost curve. In area C, above output 5, where average total cost is rising, the marginal cost curve is above the *ATC* curve.

The positioning of the marginal cost curve is not happenstance. The position of marginal cost relative to average total cost tells us whether average total cost is rising or falling.

If MC > *ATC*, then *ATC* is rising.

If MC = *ATC*, then *ATC* is at its low point.

If MC < *ATC*, then *ATC* is falling.

To understand why this is, think of it in terms of your grade point average. If you have a B average and you get a C on the next test (that is, your marginal grade is a C), your grade point average will fall below a B. Your marginal grade is below your average grade, so your average grade is falling. If you get a C+ on the next exam (that is, your marginal grade is a C+), *even though your marginal grade has risen from a* C *to a* C+, your grade point average will fall. Why? Because your marginal grade is still below your average grade. To make sure you understand the concept, explain the next two cases:

Q-8 If marginal costs are increasing, what is happening to average total costs?

1. If your marginal grade is above your average grade, your average grade will rise.
2. If your marginal grade and average grade are equal, the average grade will remain unchanged.

Q-9 If marginal costs are decreasing, what must be happening to average variable costs?

Marginal and average reflect a general relationship that also holds for marginal cost and average variable cost.

Q-10 Why does the marginal cost curve intersect the average total cost curve at the minimum point?

If MC > *AVC*, then *AVC* is rising.

If MC = *AVC*, then *AVC* is at its low point.

If MC < *AVC*, then *AVC* is falling.

This relationship is best seen in the yellow shaded area (area *B*) of Figure 12-4, when output is between Q_0 and Q_1. In this area, the marginal cost curve is above the average variable cost curve, so average variable cost is rising; but the MC curve is below the average total cost curve, so average total cost is falling. The intuitive explanation for the relationship in this area is that average total cost includes average variable cost, but it also includes average fixed cost, which is falling. As long as short-run marginal cost is only slightly above average variable cost, the average total cost will continue to fall. Put another way: Once marginal cost is above average variable cost, as long as average variable cost doesn't rise by more than average fixed cost falls, average total cost will still fall.

Intermission

At this point I'm going to cut off the chapter, not because we're finished with the subject, but because there's only so much that anyone can absorb in one chapter. It's time for a break.

A REMINDER

Review of Costs

Term	Definition	Equation
Marginal cost	The additional cost resulting from a one-unit increase in output.	$MC = \Delta TC$
Total cost	The sum of all costs of inputs used by a firm in production.	$TC = FC + VC$
Average total cost	Total cost per unit of production.	$ATC = AFC + AVC = TC/Q$
Fixed cost	Cost that is already spent and cannot be recovered. It exists only in the short run.	FC
Average fixed cost	Fixed costs per unit of production.	$AFC = FC/Q$
Variable cost	Costs that vary with production.	VC
Average variable cost	Variable costs per unit of production.	$AVC = VC/Q$

Dr. Seuss books are often more interesting than economics books.

Those of you with significant others, go out and do something significant. Those of you with parents bearing the cost of this education, give them a call and tell them that you appreciate their expenditure on your education. Think of the opportunity cost of that education to them; it's not peanuts. Those of you who are married should go out and give your spouse a big kiss; tell him or her that the opportunity cost of being away for another minute was so high that you couldn't control yourself. Those of you with kids, go out and read them a Dr. Seuss book. (My favorite is about Horton.) Let's face it—Seuss is a better writer than I, and if you've been conscientious about this course, you may not have paid your kids enough attention. We'll return to the grind in the next chapter.

Summary

- Accounting profit is explicit revenue less explicit cost. Economists include implicit revenue and cost in their determination of profit.
- Implicit revenue includes the increases in the value of assets owned by the firm. Implicit costs include opportunity cost of time and capital provided by the owners of the firm.
- In the long run, a firm can choose among all possible production techniques; in the short run, the firm is constrained in its choices.
- The law of diminishing marginal productivity states that as more and more of a variable input is added to a fixed input, the additional output the firm gets will eventually be decreasing.
- Costs are generally divided into fixed costs, variable costs, and total costs.
- $TC = FC + VC$; MC = change in TC; $AFC = FC/Q$; $AVC = VC/Q$; $ATC = AFC + AVC$.
- The average variable cost curve and marginal cost curve are mirror images of the average product curve and the marginal product curve, respectively.
- The law of diminishing marginal productivity causes marginal and average costs to rise.
- If $MC > ATC$, then ATC is rising.
  If $MC = ATC$, then ATC is constant.
  If $MC < ATC$, then ATC is falling.
- The marginal cost curve goes through the minimum points of the average variable cost curve and average total cost curve.

Key Terms

average fixed cost *(284)*
average product *(280)*
average total cost *(284)*
average variable cost *(284)*
economic profit *(278)*
firm *(277)*
fixed cost *(283)*
law of diminishing marginal productivity *(282)*
long-run decision *(280)*
marginal cost *(284)*
marginal product *(280)*
production *(276)*
production function *(280)*
production table *(280)*
profit *(277)*
short-run decision *(280)*
total cost *(278)*
total revenue *(278)*
variable cost *(284)*

Questions and Exercises

connect ECONOMICS

1. What costs and revenues do economists include when calculating profit that accountants don't include? Give an example of each. LO1
2. Peggy-Sue's cookies are the best in the world, or so I hear. She has been offered a job by Cookie Monster, Inc., to come to work for them at \$125,000 per year. Currently, she is producing her own cookies, and she has revenues of \$260,000 per year. Her costs are \$40,000 for labor, \$10,000 for rent, \$35,000 for ingredients, and \$5,000 for utilities. She has \$100,000 of her own money invested in the operation, which, if she leaves, can be sold for \$40,000 that she can invest at 10 percent per year.
   a. Calculate her accounting and economic profits.
   b. Advise her as to what she should do. LO1
3. Economan has been infected by the free enterprise bug. He sets up a firm on extraterrestrial affairs. The rent of the building is \$4,000, the cost of the two secretaries is \$40,000, and the cost of electricity and gas comes to \$5,000. There's a great demand for his information, and his total revenue amounts to \$100,000. By working in the firm, though, Economan forfeits the \$50,000 he could earn by working for the Friendly Space Agency and the \$4,000 he could have earned as interest had he saved his funds instead of putting them in this business.
   a. What is profit or loss by an accountant's definitions?
   b. What is profit or loss by an economist's definitions? LO1

4. What is the difference between marginal product and average product? LO3
5. Explain how studying for an exam is subject to the law of diminishing marginal productivity. LO3
6. If average product is falling, what is happening to short-run average variable cost? LO4
7. Find and graph the *TC*, *AFC*, *AVC*, *AC*, and MC from the following table. LO4

Units	*FC*	*VC*
0	$100	$ 0
1	100	40
2	100	60
3	100	70
4	100	85
5	100	130

8. Explain how each of the following will affect the average fixed cost, average variable cost, average total cost, and marginal cost curves faced by a steel manufacturer:
   a. New union agreement increases hourly pay.
   b. Local government imposes an annual lump-sum tax per plant.
   c. Federal government imposes a "stack tax" on emission of air pollutants by steel mills.
   d. New steel-making technology increases productivity of every worker. LO4
9. The following cell-phone offer by Sprint is typical of what one can get on a cell phone plan: 4,000 free minutes for $39.99 a month. The fine print says that only 350 of those minutes are anytime minutes; the remaining are restricted to evening and weekend usage. If you go over your allotted time, you are charged 35 cents per minute for any additional minutes.
   a. What is your marginal cost? Graph it.
   b. What would your average variable cost curve for peak time usage look like?
   c. If you do not keep track of your usage, how would you figure your marginal cost?
   d. Why do firms offer such confusing plans?
   e. Were firms that charged this way in favor of or against portability of phone numbers? LO4
10. If marginal cost is increasing, what do we know about average cost? LO5
11. If machines are variable and labor fixed, how will the general shapes of the short-run average cost curve and marginal cost curve change? (Difficult) LO5
12. A firm has fixed costs of $100 and variable costs of the following:

Output	1	2	3	4	5	6	7	8	9
Variable costs	$35	75	110	140	175	215	260	315	390

   a. Show *AFC*, *ATC*, *AVC*, and MC in a table.
   b. Graph the *AFC*, *ATC*, *AVC*, and MC curves.
   c. Explain the relationship between the MC curve and the *AVC* and *ATC* curves.
   d. Say fixed costs dropped to $50. Which curves shifted? Why? LO5
13. If average productivity falls, will marginal cost necessarily rise? How about average cost? LO6
14. An economic consultant is presented with the following total product table and asked to derive a table for average variable costs. The price of labor is $15 per hour.

Labor	*TP*
1	5
2	15
3	30
4	36
5	40

   a. Help him do so.
   b. Show that the graph of the average productivity curve and average variable cost curve are mirror images of each other.
   c. Show the marginal productivity curve for labor inputs between 1 and 5.
   d. Show that the marginal productivity curve and marginal cost curve are mirror images of each other. LO3, LO4, LO6
15. Say that a firm has fixed costs of $100 and constant average variable costs of $25.
   a. Show *AFC*, *VC*, *AVC*, and MC in a table.
   b. Graph the *AFC*, *ATC*, *AVC*, and MC curves.
   c. Explain why the curves have the shapes they do.
   d. What law is not operative for this firm? LO3, LO4, LO5
16. Say a firm has $100 in fixed costs and average variable costs increase by $5 for each unit, so that the cost of 1 is $25, the cost of 2 is $30, the cost of 3 is $35, and so on.
   a. Show *VC*, *AFC*, *AVC*, and MC in a table.
   b. Graph the *AFC*, *ATC*, *AVC*, and MC curves associated with these costs.
   c. Explain how costs would have to increase in order for the curves to have the "normal" shapes of the curves presented in the text. LO3, LO4, LO5

Questions from Alternative Perspectives

1. The text presents very detailed cost tables when it considers the decisions of firms.
   a. Do entrepreneurs have such cost tables available to them when they enter a business?
   b. If not, how do they gather such information?
   c. If such information is gathered through trial and error, what implications does that have for government intervention in the marketplace? (Austrian)
2. Say that a drug firm could increase its profit by marketing a drug that it knows might have serious side effects. Say also that it knows that it can never be prosecuted for doing so.
   a. Would it?
   b. Should it? (Religious)
3. The analysis in the book suggests that firms hire inputs so that they hold costs as low as possible. Yet, as Gloria Steinem has pointed out, looking at reality one sees men selling refrigerators and women selling men's underwear.
   a. Do you believe that that allocation of jobs reflects firms trying to minimize costs because of the relative expertise of women and men?
   b. If not, what does it reflect? (Feminist)
4. The text does not emphasize firms' role in shaping the tastes and preferences of consumers even though this is a very important role with firms spending more than $200 billion a year on advertising. If it is true that firms are shaping consumer preferences, whose welfare are people maximizing when they make consumption decisions? (Institutionalist)
5. Wal-Mart, the nation's largest retailer, has perfected a "just in time competitive strategy." This retail giant relies on barcodes for instant inventory, distribution centers that purchase supplies at the last minute and deliver only when needed, a small core of suppliers that Wal-Mart can pressure for large discounts, routinized work that requires on average seven hours of training, and part-time workers who often work full-time hours without getting corresponding benefits. How does this "just-in-time" approach change the mix of fixed and variable costs to the advantage of Wal-Mart? (Radical)

Issues to Ponder

1. "There is no long run; there are only short and shorter runs." Evaluate that statement. (Difficult) LO2
2. If you increase production to an infinitely large level, the average variable cost and the average total cost will merge. Why? (Difficult) LO5
3. Say that neither labor nor machines are fixed but that there is a 50 percent quick-order premium paid to both workers and machines for delivery of them in the short run. Once you buy them, they cannot be returned, however. What do your short-run marginal cost and short-run average total cost curves look like? (Difficult) LO6

Answers to Margin Questions

1. Normally the marginal productivity curve and average productivity curve are both inverted U shapes. *(281)*
2. Firms are likely to operate on the downward-sloping portion of the marginal productivity curve because on the upward-sloping portion, firms could increase workers' output by hiring more workers. It will continue to hire more workers at least to the point where diminishing marginal productivity sets in. *(283)*
3. Average variable costs would be $40. *(284)*
4. As you can see in the graph, both these curves are U-shaped and the marginal cost curve goes through the average cost curve at the minimum point of the average cost curve. *(286)*

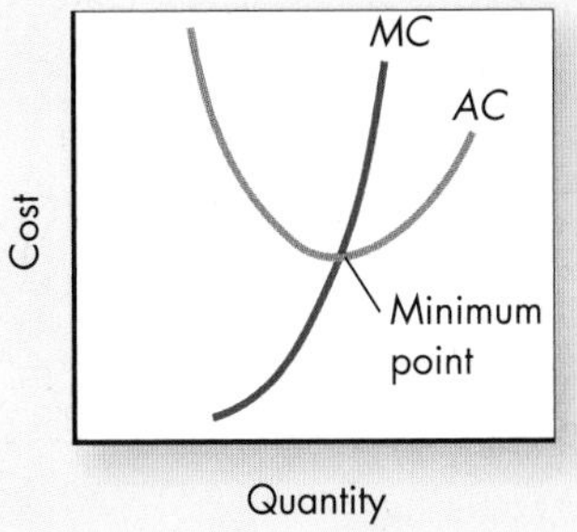

5. The distance between the average total cost and the average variable cost is determined by the average fixed cost at that quantity. As quantity increases, the average fixed cost decreases, so the two curves get closer and closer together. *(287)*
6. As output increases, the average total costs and average variable costs come closer and closer together. *(287)*
7. Since the average productivity and marginal productivity of workers are the mirror images of average costs and marginal costs, and when the marginal costs and average costs intersect the two are equal, it follows that the average productivity and marginal productivity of workers must be equal at that point. *(288)*
8. It is impossible to say what is happening to average total costs on the basis of what is happening to marginal costs. It is the magnitude of marginal costs relative to average total costs that is important. *(289)*
9. It is impossible to say because it is the magnitude of marginal cost relative to average variable cost that determines what is happening to average variable cost. *(289)*
10. The marginal cost curve intersects the average total cost curve at the minimum point because once the marginal cost exceeds average total costs, the average total costs must necessarily begin to rise, and vice versa. *(289)*

Production and Cost Analysis II

Economic efficiency consists of making things that are worth more than they cost.

—*J. M. Clark*

Welcome back from your intermission. I hope you've reestablished your relationship with the real world and are ready to return, with renewed vigor, to the world of economics. When we took our intermission last chapter, we had worked our way through the various short-run costs. That short run is a time period in which some inputs are fixed. In the first part of this chapter, we consider firms' long-run decisions and the determinants of the long-run cost curves. Then, in the second part, we'll talk about applying cost analysis to the real world.

AFTER READING THIS CHAPTER, YOU SHOULD BE ABLE TO:

1. Distinguish technical efficiency from economic efficiency.
2. Explain how economies and diseconomies of scale influence the shape of long-run cost curves.
3. State the envelope relationship between short-run cost curves and long-run cost curves.
4. Explain the role of the entrepreneur in translating cost of production to supply.
5. Discuss some of the problems of using cost analysis in the real world.

Making Long-Run Production Decisions

Firms have many more options in the long run than they do in the short run. They can change any input they want. Plant size is not given; neither is the technology available given.

To make their long-run decisions, firms look at the costs of the various inputs and the technologies available for combining those inputs, and then decide which combination offers the lowest cost.

Say you're opening a hamburger stand. One decision you'll have to make is what type of stove to buy. You'll quickly discover that many different types are available. Some use more gas than others but cost less to buy; some are electric; some are self-cleaning and hence use less labor; some are big; some are little; some use microwaves; some use convection. Some have long-term guarantees; some have no guarantees. Each has a colorful brochure telling you how wonderful it is. After studying the various detailed specifications and aspects of the production technology, you choose the stove that has the combination of characteristics that you believe best fits your needs.

Next you decide on workers. Do you want bilingual workers, college-educated workers, part-time workers, experienced workers . . . ? You get the idea: Even simple production decisions involve complicated questions. These decisions are made on the basis of the expected costs, and expected usefulness, of inputs.

Technical Efficiency and Economic Efficiency

When choosing among existing technologies in the long run, firms are interested in the lowest cost, or most economically efficient, methods of production. They consider all technically efficient methods and compare their costs. The terms *economically efficient* and *technically efficient* differ in meaning. Here's how: **Technical efficiency** in production means that *as few inputs as possible are used to produce a given output.*

Web Note 13.1
Cheap Labor

Many different production processes can be technically efficient. For example, say you know that to produce 100 tons of wheat, you can use 10 workers and 1 acre or 1 worker and 100 acres. Which of these two production techniques is more efficient? Both can be technically efficient since neither involves more of both inputs. But that doesn't mean that both are equally economically efficient. That question can't be answered unless you know the relative costs of the two inputs. If an acre of land rents for $1 million and each worker costs $10 a day, our answer likely will be different than if land rents for $40 an acre and each worker costs $100 a day. The **economically efficient** method of production is *the method that produces a given level of output at the lowest possible cost.*

Q-1 True or false? If a process is economically efficient, it is also technically efficient. Explain your answer.

In long-run production decisions, firms will look at all available production technologies and choose the technology that, given the available inputs and their prices, is the economically efficient way to produce. These choices will reflect the prices of the various factors of production. Those prices, in turn, will reflect the factors' relative scarcities.

Consider the use of land by firms in the United States and in Japan. The United States has large amounts of land (8 acres) per person, so the price of land is lower than in Japan, which has only 0.73 acre per person. An acre of rural land in the United States might cost about $1,300; in Japan it costs over $10,000. Because of this difference in the price of inputs, production techniques use land much more intensively in Japan than in the United States. Similarly with China: Labor is more abundant and capital is scarcer, so production techniques in China use capital much more intensively than it is used in the United States. Whereas China would use hundreds of workers and very little machinery to build a road, the United States would use three or four people along with three machines. Both countries are being economically efficient, but because costs of inputs differ, the economically efficient method of production differs. Thus, the economically efficient method of production is the technically efficient method of production that has the lowest cost. (For a further, graphical analysis of economic efficiency, see Appendix A.)

Q-2 Why does China use production techniques that require more workers per acre of land than does the United States?

Determinants of the Shape of the Long-Run Cost Curve

In the last chapter, we saw that the law of diminishing marginal productivity accounted for the shape of the short-run average cost curve. The firm was adding more of a variable input to a fixed input. The law of diminishing marginal productivity doesn't apply to the long run since, in the long run, all inputs are variable. The most important determinants of what is economically efficient in the long run are economies and diseconomies of scale. Let's consider each of these in turn and see what effect they will have on the shape of the long-run average cost curve.

The shape of the long-run cost curve is due to the existence of economies and diseconomies of scale.

Economies of Scale

We say that production exhibits **economies of scale** *when long-run average total costs decrease as output increases.* For example, if producing 40,000 DVD players costs a firm

REAL-WORLD APPLICATION

Changing Technology in Automobile Production

In the late 1980s, the normal production run of a U.S. automaker was 200,000 units. Why was it so high? Because of indivisible setup costs of the then-current production technology. In order to reduce those indivisible setup costs to an acceptable level, the production level per year had to equal at least 200,000, or the car was considered an economic failure. Small-sports-car sales did not meet that sales level, and so, in the 1980s, small, low-cost sports cars faded from the scene. For example, the Pontiac Fiero, a small American sports car, was dropped in 1988.

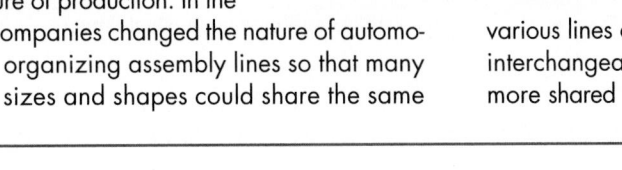

But what is an indivisible setup cost depends on the structure of production. In the 1980s, Japanese companies changed the nature of automobile production by organizing assembly lines so that many cars with different sizes and shapes could share the same assembly line, allowing economies of scope (discussed later in the chapter). This redesign lowered the indivisible setup costs for each type of car, and made the Japanese companies' minimum profitable production level 30,000, not 200,000. The Mazda Miata was one of the first cars developed using this new assembly-line approach, and it was a big success. In response to the challenge, other car companies switched their assembly lines to this alternative, and, over the past 20 years, there has been an enormous increase in the number of reasonably priced sporty two-seaters.

These changes are ongoing, with Toyota leading the way as it designs its various lines of cars so that the components of one are more interchangeable with the components of another, allowing more shared assembly lines and lower indivisible setup costs.

$16 million ($400 each), but producing 200,000 costs the firm $40 million ($200 each), between 40,000 and 200,000 units, production exhibits significant economies of scale. One can also say that there are increasing returns to scale.

In real-world production processes, at low levels of production, economies of scale are extremely important because many production techniques require a certain minimum level of output to be useful. For example, say you want to produce a pound of steel. You can't just build a mini blast furnace, stick in some coke and iron ore, and come out with a single pound of steel. The smallest technically efficient blast furnaces have a production capacity measured in tons per hour, not pounds per year. The cost of the blast furnace is said to be an **indivisible setup cost** (*the cost of an indivisible input for which a certain minimum amount of production must be undertaken before the input becomes economically feasible to use*).

Web Note 13.2
Economies of Scale

In the production of steel, the cost of a blast furnace is an indivisible setup cost that requires a minimum level of production to be economically feasible.

Indivisible setup costs are important because they create many real-world economies of scale: As output increases, the costs per unit of output decrease. As an example, consider this book. Setting the type for it is an indivisible setup cost; it is a cost that must be incurred if any production is to take place, but it is not a cost that increases with the number of books produced. That means that the more copies of the book that are produced, the lower the typesetting cost per book. That's why it costs more per book to produce a textbook for an upper-level, low-enrollment course than it does for a lower-level, high-enrollment course. The same amount of work goes into both (both need to be written, edited, and set into type), and the printing costs differ only slightly. The actual print-run costs of printing a book are only about $3 to $8 per book. The other costs are indivisible setup costs. Prices of produced goods, including books, reflect their costs of production. As you move to upper-level academic courses, where print runs are smaller, you'll likely discover that the books are smaller and less colorful but are priced the same as, or more than, this introductory text.

Q-3 Why are larger production runs often cheaper per unit than smaller production runs?

FIGURE 13-1 (A AND B) **A Typical Long-Run Average Total Cost Table and Curve**

In the long run, average costs initially fall because of economies of scale; then they are constant for a while, and finally they tend to rise due to diseconomies of scale.

Quantity	Total Costs of Labor	Total Costs of Machines	Total Costs = $TC_L + TC_M$	Average Total Costs = TC/Q
11	$381	$254	$ 635	$58
12	390	260	650	54
13	402	268	670	52
14	420	280	700	50
15	450	300	750	50
16	480	320	800	50
17	510	340	850	50
18	549	366	915	51
19	600	400	1,000	53
20	666	444	1,110	56

(a) Long-Run Production Table

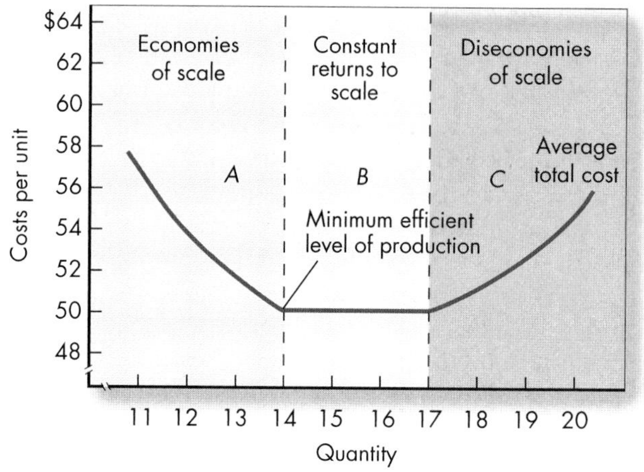

(b) Long-Run Average Cost Curve

In the long-run planning decisions about the cost of producing this book, the expected number of copies to be sold was an important element. That figure influenced the number of books produced, which in turn affected the expected cost per unit. This will be the case any time there are economies of scale. With economies of scale, cost per unit of a small production run is higher than cost per unit of a large production run.

In the longer run, all inputs are variable, so only economies of scale can influence the shape of the long-run cost curve.

Figure 13-1(a) demonstrates a long-run production table; Figure 13-1(b) shows the related typical shape of a long-run average cost curve. (Notice that there are no fixed costs. Because we're in the long run, all costs are variable.) Economies of scale account for the downward-sloping part. Cost per unit of output is decreasing.

Because of the importance of economies of scale, businesspeople often talk of a minimum efficient level of production. What they mean by minimum efficient level of production is that, given the price at which they expect to be able to sell a good, the indivisible setup costs are so high that production runs of less than a certain size don't make economic sense. Thus, the **minimum efficient level of production** is *the amount of production that spreads setup costs out sufficiently for a firm to undertake production profitably*. At this point, the market has expanded to a size large enough for firms to take advantage of all economies of scale. The minimum efficient level of production is where the average total costs are at a minimum.

Diseconomies of Scale

Diminishing marginal productivity refers to the decline in productivity caused by increasing units of a variable input being added to a fixed input. Diseconomies of scale refer to the decreases in productivity that occur when there are equal percentage increases of all inputs (no input is fixed).

Notice that on the right side of Figure 13-1(b) the long-run average cost curve is upward-sloping. Average cost is increasing. We say that production exhibits **diseconomies of scale** *when long-run average total costs increase as output increases*. For example, if producing 200,000 DVD players costs the firm $40 million ($200 each) and producing 400,000 DVD players costs the firm $100 million ($250 each), there are diseconomies of scale associated with choosing to produce 400,000 rather than 200,000. One also can say there are decreasing returns to scale. Diseconomies of scale usually, but not always, start occurring as firms get large.

REAL-WORLD APPLICATION

Travels of a T-Shirt and Economies of Scale

The T-shirt said "MADE IN CHINA," but when economist Pietra Rivoli, in her delightful book *The Travels of a T-Shirt in the Global Economy*, tracked down the process of making the T-shirt that she bought in Florida, she discovered that it's a lot more complicated than that. True, the company that sewed the shirt was in Shanghai, China. But guess where the cotton for the shirt came from? West Texas, USA, at a farm like the Reinsch family farm that is highlighted in Rivoli's book.

Now here's an exam question for you: Why, if China's labor cost is 1/20th that of U.S. labor costs, is the cotton for a T-shirt grown in the United States, shipped across the ocean to China to be woven and sewn into a T-shirt, and shipped back again to the United States to be sold?

Answer: Economies of scale (and some U.S. subsidies, but you aren't expected to know that yet). In fact, the United States leads the world in the production of cotton, and has done so for over 200 years. Farms in Africa average 8 acres and in China average less than 1 acre. The Reinsch's farm is 1,000 acres and can produce about 500,000 pounds of cotton, enough for 1.3 million T-shirts. Size makes a difference; cotton farmers outside the United States almost exclusively handpick their cotton. Because U.S. farmers have such large farms, they can use large machinery to do all the picking, and thereby take advantage of economies of scale, countering the much higher labor costs in the United States.

Diseconomies of scale could not occur if production relationships were only technical relationships. If that were the case, the same technical process could be used over and over again at the same per-unit cost. In reality, however, production relationships have social dimensions, which introduce the potential for important diseconomies of scale into the production process in two ways:

1. As the size of the firm increases, monitoring costs generally increase.
2. As the size of the firm increases, team spirit or morale generally decreases.

Q-4 If production involved only technical relationships and had no social dimension, what would the long-run average total cost curve look like?

Monitoring costs are *the costs incurred by the organizer of production in seeing to it that the employees do what they're supposed to do*. If you're producing something yourself, the job gets done the way you want it done; monitoring costs are zero. However, as the scale of production increases, you have to hire people to help you produce. This means that if the job is to be done the way you want it done, you have to monitor (supervise) your employees' performance. The cost of monitoring can increase significantly as output increases; it's a major contributor to diseconomies of scale. Most big firms have several layers of bureaucracy devoted simply to monitoring employees. The job of middle managers is, to a large extent, monitoring.

As firms become larger, monitoring costs increase and achieving team spirit is more difficult.

The other social dimension that can contribute to diseconomies of scale is the loss of **team spirit** (*the feelings of friendship and being part of a team that bring out people's best efforts*). Most types of production are highly dependent on team spirit. When the team spirit or morale is lost, production slows considerably. The larger the firm is, the more difficult it is to maintain team spirit.

An important reason diseconomies of scale can come about is that the bigger things get, the more checks and balances are needed to ensure that the right hand and the left hand are coordinated. The larger the organization, the more checks and balances and the more paperwork.

Some large firms manage to solve these problems and avoid diseconomies of scale. But problems of monitoring and loss of team spirit often limit the size of firms. They

A REMINDER

Distinguishing Diseconomies of Scale from Diminishing Marginal Productivity

As pointed out in the text, the shapes of the short-run average cost curve and the long-run average cost curve are similar. But the reasons underlying those shapes are quite different. It is important to reemphasize that difference. In the short run, some inputs are fixed; in the long run, all inputs vary.

Let's first review why the short-run average cost curve is U-shaped. What accounts for its shape is what's happening to marginal productivity of each additional unit of input *keeping all other inputs fixed.* Since costs are based on inputs, how much an input contributes to output directly affects the costs of production. Average total costs in the short run fall initially because of the assumption of increasing marginal productivity: Additional inputs are able to produce increasing increments of output. An example is a 5 percent increase in the quantity of labor, holding capital constant, leading to a 10 percent increase in output.

Eventually, marginal productivity falls and the short-run average cost curve slopes upward. Adding more of *one* factor of production, holding the others constant, contributes less and less to output, causing marginal costs, and eventually average costs, to rise. An example of diminishing marginal productivity is a 5 percent increase in the quantity of labor, holding capital constant, leading to a 2 percent increase in output. The assumption of initially increasing marginal productivity and eventually diminishing marginal productivity leads to the U shape of the short-run average cost curve.

Now consider the long-run average cost curve. Its shape is determined by what's happening to returns to scale. Returns to scale are not about how changes in one input affect output. Instead, they involve changing *all inputs proportionately*. If there are economies of scale, increasing all factors of production equally, say by 5 percent, leads to a greater than 5 percent increase in output.

The assumption economists make in the long run is that initially economies of scale cause the long-run average total cost curve to slope downward. Eventually, however, there are diseconomies of scale. That is, increasing all inputs equally, say by 5 percent, leads to a smaller increase in output, say by 3 percent. Diseconomies of scale cause average total costs to rise and the long-run average total cost curve to slope upward. If there are neither economies of scale nor diseconomies of scale, the average total cost curve is flat because inputs and output both are changing by equal proportions. An example is a 5 percent increase in all inputs leading to a 5 percent increase in output. With constant returns to scale, average costs do not change.

The assumption we make about production in the long run is that there are first increasing, then constant, and finally decreasing returns to scale. That assumption about returns to scale accounts for the U shape of the long-run average cost curve.

underlie diseconomies of scale in which less additional output is produced for a given increase in inputs, so that per-unit costs of output increase.

Constant Returns to Scale

Sometimes in a range of output, a firm does not experience either economies of scale or diseconomies of scale. In this range, there are **constant returns to scale** *where long-run average total costs do not change with an increase in output*. Constant returns to scale are shown by the flat portion of the average total cost curve in Figure 13-1(b). Constant returns to scale occur when production techniques can be replicated again and again to increase output. This occurs before monitoring costs rise and team spirit is lost.

Q-5 Why is the short-run average cost curve a U-shaped curve?

The long-run and the short-run average cost curves have similar U shapes. But it's important to remember that the reasons why they have this U shape are quite different. The assumption of initially increasing and then eventually diminishing marginal productivity (as a variable input is added to a fixed input) accounts for the shape of the short-run average cost curve. Economies and diseconomies of scale account for the shape of the long-run average total cost curve. (See the box "Distinguishing Diseconomies of Scale from Diminishing Marginal Productivity" for a review of why.)

Q-6 Why is the long-run average total cost curve generally considered to be a U-shaped curve?

The Importance of Economies and Diseconomies of Scale

Economies and diseconomies of scale play important roles in real-world long-run production decisions. Economies of scale are an important reason why firms attempt to expand their markets either at home or abroad. If they can make and sell more at lower per-unit costs, they will make more profits. Diseconomies of scale prevent a firm from expanding and can lead corporate raiders to buy the firm and break it up in the hope that the smaller production units will be more efficient, thus eliminating some of the diseconomies of scale.

Economies and diseconomies of scale play important roles in real-world long-run production decisions.

Envelope Relationship

Since in the long run all inputs are flexible, while in the short run some inputs are not flexible, long-run cost will always be less than or equal to short-run cost at the same level of output. To see this, let's consider a firm that had planned to produce 100 units but now adjusts its plan to produce more than 100. We know that in the long run the firm chooses the lowest-cost method of production. In the short run, it faces an additional constraint: All expansion must be done by increasing only the variable input. That constraint must increase average cost (or at least not decrease it) compared to what average cost would have been had the firm planned to produce that level to begin with. If it didn't, the firm would have chosen that new combination of inputs in the long run. Additional constraints increase cost. The *envelope relationship* is the relationship between long-run and short-run average total costs. It is shown in Figure 13-2.

The envelope relationship is the relationship explaining that, at the planned output level, short-run average total cost equals long-run average total cost, but at all other levels of output, short-run average total cost is higher than long-run average total cost.

Why it is called an envelope relationship should be clear from the figure. Each short-run average total cost curve touches (is tangent to) the long-run average total cost curve at one, and only one, output level; at all other output levels, short-run average cost exceeds long-run average cost. The long-run average total cost curve is an envelope of short-run average total cost curves.

The intuitive reason why the short-run average total cost curves always lie above or tangent to the long-run average cost curve is simple. In the short run, you have chosen a plant; that plant is fixed, and its costs for that period are part of your average fixed costs. Changes must be made within the confines of that plant. In the long run, you can change everything, choosing the combination of inputs in the most efficient

More on the Envelope Relationship

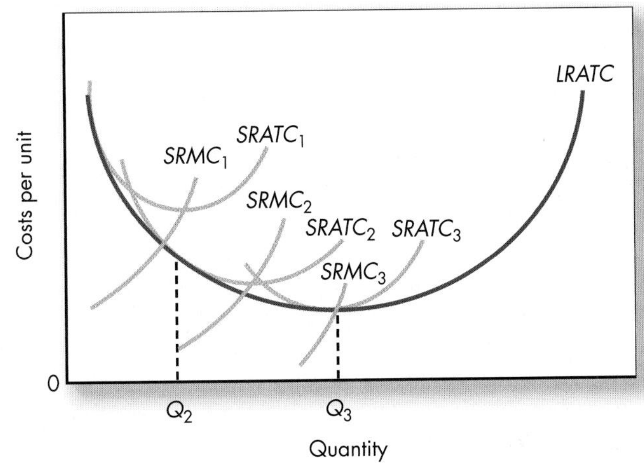

FIGURE 13-2
Envelope of Short-Run Average Total Cost Curves

The long-run average total cost curve is an envelope of the short-run average total cost curves. Each short-run average total cost curve touches the long-run average total cost curve at only one point. (*SR* stands for short run; *LR* stands for long run.)

REAL-WORLD APPLICATION

Why Are Textbooks So Long?

Understanding costs and their structure will help you understand why intro economics textbooks are so long—and why their length is to your advantage.

The majority of the costs of a book are fixed costs in relation to the length of the book. The initial costs in terms of length are about 20 percent of the total price of the book. So increasing the length of the book increases costs slightly. But the longer length allows the writer to include more issues that some professors want and many professors require to even consider using the book. That means that greater length can allow publishers to sell more books, allowing the fixed costs to be divided over more output. This decrease in fixed cost per unit can lower average total cost more than increasing the length of the book increases average total costs per unit. So if the added length increases the number of users, the additional length can lower the average cost of the book.

Length does lower the costs of the book—up to a point. Textbook publishers are continually looking for that point. They direct authors to shorten their books but also to include almost all issues that various groups want. The latter direction—in favor of inclusion—often takes precedence, which is why textbooks are so long. This doesn't mean that textbooks will always be longer. Recently, economics textbooks have become smaller because students began to complain that the texts were getting too heavy to carry. There has also been technological change; books are now placing some of the less-used chapters on the Web. (This book has two Web chapters.)

manner. The more options you have to choose from, the lower the costs of production. Put another way: Constraints always raise costs (or at least won't lower them). So in the long run, costs must be the same or lower.

Another insight to note about this envelope relationship is the following: When there are economies of scale and you have chosen an efficient plant size for a given output, your short-run average costs will fall as you increase production. Technically, this must be the case because the short-run marginal cost (*SRMC*) curve goes through the minimum point of the short-run average total cost (*SRATC*) curve, and the minimum point of the *SRATC* curve is to the right of the efficient level of production in the long run. That means that at output Q_2, $SRMC_2$ has to be below $SRATC_2$ and short-run average total cost has to be falling. Intuitively, what's happening is that at output Q_2, your fixed costs are high. Now demand increases and you increase production. Your average fixed costs are high; your marginal costs are low; and initially the fall in average fixed costs more than offsets the increased marginal cost. Once marginal cost exceeds *SRATC*, that no longer is the case.[1]

Only when the firm is at the minimum point of the long-run average total cost (*LRATC*) curve (at output Q_3) is the $SRATC_3$ curve tangent to the *LRATC* curve at a point where the *SRMC* curve intersects both the curves. For large markets, this point is the least-cost production level of a firm.

[1]The above reasoning depends on the curves being smooth (i.e., having no kinks), a standard assumption of the model. If we give up the smoothness assumption, the *SRATC* curve could be kinked and the *SRMC* curve could be discontinuous. In that case, the *SRATC* curve might be tangent to the *LRATC* curve from the left, but not from the right, and it might not decrease. This would make movement from the long to the short run a discrete jump, whereas the existing model and smoothness assumption make it a smooth continuous movement. So if your intuition doesn't lead you to understand the model, you are probably thinking of a model with different assumptions. You'll be in good company, too. When an economist by the name of Jacob Viner first created this model, his intuition led him to a different result because his intuition was basing the analysis on different assumptions than he was using in his formal model.

Entrepreneurial Activity and the Supply Decision

In this chapter and the preceding one, we have discussed the technical nature of costs and production. In the next chapter, we will formally relate costs of production to the supply of goods. As a bridge between the two chapters, let's consider the entrepreneur, who establishes the relationship between costs and the supply decision, and discuss some of the problems of using cost analysis in the real world.

In thinking about the connection between cost and supply, one fundamental insight is that the revenue received for a good must be greater than the planned cost of producing it. Otherwise why would anyone supply it? The difference between the expected price of a good and the expected average total cost of producing it is the supplier's expected economic profit per unit. It's profit that underlies the dynamics of production in a market economy.

The expected price must exceed the opportunity cost of supplying the good for a good to be supplied.

Cost curves do not become supply curves through some magic process. To move from cost to supply, entrepreneurial initiative is needed. An **entrepreneur** is *an individual who sees an opportunity to sell an item at a price higher than the average cost of producing it*. The entrepreneur is the organizer of production and the one who visualizes the demand and convinces the individuals who own the factors of production that they want to produce that good. Businesses work hard at maintaining the entrepreneurial spirit in their employees. The greater the difference between price and average total cost, the greater the entrepreneur's incentive to tackle the organizational problems and supply the good.

WWW Web Note 13.3
Entrepreneurship

Q-7 Why is the role of the entrepreneur central to the production process in the economy?

Using Cost Analysis in the Real World

All too often, students walk away from an introductory economics course thinking that cost analysis is a relatively easy topic. Memorize the names, shapes, and relationships of the curves, and you're home free. In the textbook model, that's right. In real life, it's not because actual production processes are marked by economies of scope, learning by doing and technological change, many dimensions, unmeasured costs, joint costs, indivisible costs, uncertainty, asymmetries, and multiple planning and adjustment periods with many different short runs. And this is the short list!

Economies of Scope

The cost of production of one product often depends on what other products a firm is producing. Economists say that in the production of two goods, there are **economies of scope** *when the costs of producing products are interdependent so that it's less costly for a firm to produce one good when it's already producing another*. For example, once a firm has set up a large marketing department to sell cereal, the department might be able to use its expertise in marketing a different

Thinking Like a Modern Economist

Social Norms and Production

The traditional economic model presents the production decision as a cost-based decision. The firm calculates the cost of inputs and chooses the lowest-price input. Modern economists believe that these costs are important, but they also believe that a number of other elements come into play. They are working to devise models that incorporate them. One of the most important of those other elements is social norms, and the choices a firm makes so that they fit the social norms of society. Behavioral economist Dan Ariely argues that social norms play a far greater role in a firm's decisions than the traditional economic model includes. He argues both that firms should include social norms in their decision making and that economists should develop new models of the firms that incorporate social norms in their decision process. He writes:

> If corporations started thinking in terms of social norms, they would realize that these norms build loyalty and—more important—make people want to extend themselves to the degree that corporations need today: to be flexible, concerned, and willing to pitch in. That's what a social relationship delivers.

Web Note 13.4
Increasing the Scope

Q-8 What is the difference between an economy of scope and an economy of scale?

product—say, dog food. A firm that sells gasoline can simultaneously use its gas station attendants to sell soda, milk, and incidentals. The minimarts so common along our highways and neighborhood streets developed because gasoline companies became aware of economies of scope.

Economies of scope play an important role in firms' decisions about what combination of goods to produce. They look for both economies of scope and economies of scale. When you read about firms' mergers, think about whether the combination of their products will generate economies of scope. Many otherwise unexplainable mergers between seemingly incompatible firms can be explained by economies of scope.

Economies of Scale and Economies of Scope

By allowing firms to segment the production process, globalization has made economies of scope even more important to firms in their production decisions. Low-cost labor in other countries has led U.S. firms to locate their manufacturing processes in those countries and to concentrate domestic activities on other aspects of production. As I have stressed throughout this book, production is more than simply manufacturing; the costs of marketing, advertising, and distribution are often larger components of the cost of a good than are manufacturing costs. Each of these involves special knowledge and expertise, and U.S. companies are specializing in the marketing, advertising, and distribution aspects of the production process. By concentrating on those aspects, and by making themselves highly competitive by taking advantage of low-cost manufacturing elsewhere, U.S. firms become more competitive and expand, increasing demand for U.S. labor. Often they expand into new areas, taking advantage of economies of scope in distribution and marketing.

Consider Nike—it produces shoes, right? Wrong. It is a U.S. marketing and distribution company; it outsources all its production to affiliate companies. Nike is expanding, but not in the production of shoes. It is expanding into leisure clothing, where it hopes economies of scope in its marketing and distribution specialties will bring it success.

Nike is only one of many examples. The large wage differentials in the global economy are causing firms to continually reinvent themselves—to shed aspects of their

Production then: The nature of production has changed considerably in the last 70 years. This picture shows a 1933 production line in which people did the work as the goods moved along the line.

business where they do not have a comparative advantage, and to add new businesses where their abilities can achieve synergies and economies of scope.

Learning by Doing and Technological Change

The production terminology that we've been discussing is central to the standard economic models. In the real world, however, other terms and concepts are also important. The production techniques available to real-world firms are constantly changing because of *learning by doing* and *technological change*. These changes occur over time and cannot be accurately predicted.

Unlike events in the standard economic model, all events in the real world are influenced by the past; people learn by doing. But to keep the model simple, learning by doing isn't a part of the traditional economic model. **Learning by doing** simply means that *as we do something, we learn what works and what doesn't, and over time we become more proficient at it*. Practice may not make perfect, but it certainly makes better and more efficient. Many firms estimate that output per unit of input will increase by 1 or 2 percent a year, even if inputs or technologies do not change, as employees learn by doing.

Q-9 Does learning by doing cause the cost curve to be downward-sloping?

Many firms estimate worker productivity to grow 1 to 2 percent a year because of learning by doing.

The concept of learning by doing emphasizes the importance of the past in trying to predict performance. Let's say a firm is deciding between two applicants for the job of managing its restaurant. One was a highly successful student but has never run a restaurant; the other was an OK student who has run a restaurant that failed. Which one does the firm hire? The answer is unclear. The first applicant may be brighter, but the lack of experience will likely mean that the person won't be hired. Businesses give enormous weight to experience. So this firm may reason that in failing, the second applicant will have learned lessons that make her the better candidate. U.S. firms faced such a choice when they were invited to expand into the new market economies of Eastern Europe in the early 1990s. Should they hire the former communist managers who had failed to produce efficiently, or should they hire the reformers? (Generally they decided on the former communist managers, hoping they had learned by failing.)

Production now: The nature of production has changed considerably in the last 70 years. This picture shows a modern production line. Robots do much of the work.

Technological change is *an increase in the range of production techniques that leads to more efficient ways of producing goods as well as the production of new and better goods*. That is, technological change offers an increase in the known range of production. For example, at one point automobile tires were made from rubber, clothing was made from cotton and wool, and buildings were made of wood. As a result of technological change, many tires are now made from petroleum distillates, much clothing is made from synthetic fibers (which in turn are made from petroleum distillates), and many buildings are constructed from steel.

Technological change can fundamentally alter the nature of production costs.

The standard long-run model takes technology as a given. From our experience, we know that technological change affects firms' decisions and production. Technological change can fundamentally alter the nature of production costs.

Web Note 13.5
Moore's Law

In some industries, technological change is occurring so fast that it overwhelms all other cost issues. The computer industry is a good example. The expectation of technological change has been built into the plans of firms in that industry. The industry has followed Moore's law, which states that the cost of computing will fall by half every 18 months. Indeed, that has happened since the computer was first offered to the mass retail market. With costs falling that fast because of learning by doing and technological change, all other cost components are overwhelmed, and, instead of costs increasing as output rises significantly, as might be predicted because of diseconomies of scale, costs keep going down.

The fall in the cost of computer chips has affected other industries as well. All types of household goods that use computer technology—including telephones, refrigerators, automobiles, TVs and VCRs, and compact disc players—are undergoing enormous change. For instance, VCRs are now almost extinct; they have been replaced by DVD players—where all images are transmitted digitally. Another change is that mass-stamped CDs are being replaced by individual CDs created by downloading files from the Internet using MP3 technology. In a few years, CDs may not be used at all—music can now be stored in music memory banks and computer hard drives. Computer technology has also revolutionized automobiles, making them more reliable and of much higher quality per dollar spent. In the 1960s, I could work on my own car, changing the points or modifying the carburetor. Modern cars have no such parts; they have been replaced by electronic parts. When a car isn't running right, its owner must now take it to a garage. My point is that automobiles have fundamentally changed; they are much more efficient and reliable and their price has fallen because of the introduction of computer technology. Technological change drives costs down, and can overwhelm diseconomies of scale, causing prices to fall more and more.

Technological change occurs in all industries, not only high-tech industries.

Don't think of technological change as occurring only in high-tech industries. Consider chicken production. The price of chickens has fallen enormously over the past 50 years. Why? Because of technological change. At one time, chickens were raised in farmyards. They walked around, ate scraps and feed, and generally led a chicken's life. Walking around had definite drawbacks—it took space (which cost money); it made standardization (a requirement of taking advantage of economies of scale) difficult, which prevented lowering costs; it used energy, which meant more feed per pound of chicken; and sometimes it led to disease, since chickens walked in their own manure.

The technological change was to put the chickens in wire cages so that the manure falls through to a conveyor belt and is transferred outside. Another conveyor belt feeds the chickens food laced with antibiotics to prevent disease. Soft music is played to keep them calm (they burn fewer calories). Once they reach the proper weight, they are slaughtered in a similar automated process. How the chickens feel about this technological change is not clear. (When I asked them, all they had to say was *cluck*.)

This method of raising chickens will likely be replaced in the next couple of decades by another technological change—genetic engineering that will allow chicken parts to be produced directly from single cells. Only the breasts and drumsticks will be produced (and wings if you live in Buffalo). All low-efficiency, low-profit-margin parts such as necks, feet, and heads will be eliminated.

In many businesses, the effect of learning by doing and technological change on prices is built into the firm's pricing structure. If they expect their costs to fall with more experience, or if they expect technological advances to lower costs in the future, they might bid low for a big order to give themselves the chance to lower their costs through learning by doing or technological change.

Technological change and learning by doing are intricately related. The efficient chicken production we now have did not come about overnight. It occurred over a 20-year period as firms learned how to do it. Chickens respond to Mozart better than to hip-hop. That had to be learned. Similarly, genetic reproduction of chicken parts will evolve as scientists and firms learn more about cloning and DNA.

Technological change and learning by doing are intricately related.

Many Dimensions

The only dimension of output in the standard model is how much to produce. Many, if not most, decisions that firms make are not the one-dimensional decisions of the traditional model, such as "Should we produce more or less?" They're multi-dimensional questions such as "Should we change the quality? Should we change the wrapper? Should we improve our shipping speed? Should we increase our inventory?" Each of these questions relates to a different dimension of the production decision and each has its own marginal costs. Thus, there isn't just one marginal cost; there are 10 or 20 of them. Good economic decisions take all relevant margins into account.

Good economic decisions take all relevant margins into account.

The reason that the traditional model is important is that each of these questions can be analyzed by applying the same reasoning used in the traditional model. But you must remember, *in applying the analysis, it's the reasoning, not the specific model, that's important.*

Unmeasured Costs

If asked, "In what area of decision making do businesses most often fail to use economic insights?" most economists would say costs. The relevant costs are generally not the costs you'll find in a firm's accounts.

Why the difference? Economists operate conceptually; they include in costs exactly what their theory says they should. They include all opportunity costs. Accountants who have to measure firms' costs in practice and provide the actual dollar figures take a much more pragmatic approach; their concepts of costs must reflect only explicit costs—those costs that are reasonably precisely measurable.

To highlight the distinction, let me review the difference between explicit and implicit costs (discussed in the previous chapter) and introduce another difference—how economists and accountants measure depreciation of capital.

Economists Include Opportunity Cost First, say that a business produces 1,000 widgets[2] that sell at $4 each for a total revenue of $4,000. To produce these widgets, the business had to buy $1,200 worth of widgetgoo, which the owner has hand-shaped into widgets. An accountant would say that the total cost of producing 1,000 widgets was $1,200 and that the firm's profit was $2,800. That's because an accountant uses explicit costs that can be measured.

[2]What's a widget? It's a wonderful little gadget that's the opposite of a wadget. (No one knows what they look like or what they are used for.) Why discuss widgets? For the same reason that scientists discuss fruit flies—their production process is simple, unlike most real-world production processes.

Q-10 As the owner of the firm, Jim pays himself $1,000. All other expenses of the firm add up to $2,000. What would an economist say are the total costs for Jim's firm?

Economic profit is different. An economist, looking at that same example, would point out that the accountant's calculation doesn't take into account the time and effort that the owner put into making the widgets. While a person's time involves no explicit cost in money, it does involve an opportunity cost, the forgone income that the owner could have made by spending that time working in another job. If the business takes 400 hours of the person's time and the person could have earned $8 an hour working for someone else, then the person is forgoing $3,200 in income. Economists include that implicit cost in their concept of cost. When that implicit cost is included, what looks like a $2,800 profit becomes a $400 economic loss.

Economic Depreciation versus Accounting Depreciation **Depreciation** is *a measure of the decline in value of an asset that occurs over time*. Say a firm buys a machine for $10,000 that's meant to last 10 years. After 1 year, machines like that become in short supply, so instead of falling, its value rises to $12,000. An accountant, looking at the firm's costs that year, would use historical cost (what the machine cost in terms of money actually spent) depreciated at, say, 10 percent per year, so the machine's depreciation for each of its 10 years of existence would be $1,000. An economist would say that since the value of the machine is rising, the machine has no depreciation; it has appreciation and provides a revenue of $2,000 to the firm. The standard model avoids such messy, real-world issues of measuring depreciation costs and instead assumes that all costs are measurable in a single time period.

The Standard Model as a Framework

Despite its limitations, the standard model provides a good framework for cost analysis.

The standard model can be expanded to include these real-world complications. Modern production is data intensive and, as computing and information processing costs fall, cost accounting and production decisions are becoming more and more integrated with the economist's analysis. Just about every industry has industry-specific software that tailors economic analysis to its particular needs. For example, Robert Kaplan of the Harvard Business School argues that cost accounting systems based on traditional concepts of fixed and variable costs lead firms consistently to make the wrong decisions. He argues that in today's manufacturing, direct labor costs have fallen substantially—in many industries to only 2 or 3 percent of the total cost—and overhead costs have risen substantially. This change in costs facing firms requires a much more careful division among types of overhead costs, and a recognition that what should and should not be assigned as a cost to a particular product differs with each decision.

I don't discuss these real-world complications because I suspect that even with its simplifications, the standard model has been more than enough to learn in an introductory course. Learning the standard model, however, provides you with only the rudiments of cost analysis, in the same way that learning the rules of mechanics provides you with only the basics of mechanical engineering. In addition to a knowledge of the laws of mechanics, building a machine requires years of experience. Similarly for economics and cost analysis. Introductory economics provides you with a superb framework for starting to think about real-world cost measurement, but it can't make you an expert cost analyst.

Conclusion and a Look Ahead

We've come to the end of our discussion of production, cost, and supply. The two chapters we spent on them weren't easy; there's tons of material here, and, quite frankly, it will likely require at least two or three reads and careful attention to your professor's lecture before your mind can absorb it. So if you're planning to sleep through a lecture, the ones on these chapters aren't the ones for that.

These chapters, in combination with our discussion of individual choice and game theory, will provide the framework for most of the later chapters, which really do get into interesting real-world issues. But you've got to know the basics to truly understand those issues. So, now that you've come to the end of these two chapters, unless you really feel comfortable with the analysis, it's probably time to review them from the beginning. (Sorry, but remember, there ain't no such thing as a free lunch.)

Summary

- An economically efficient production process must be technically efficient, but a technically efficient process need not be economically efficient.
- The long-run average total cost curve is U-shaped. Economies of scale initially cause average total cost to decrease; diseconomies eventually cause average total cost to increase.
- Production is a social, as well as a technical, phenomenon; that's why concepts like team spirit are important—and that's why diseconomies of scale occur.
- The marginal cost and short-run average cost curves slope upward because of diminishing marginal productivity. The long-run average cost curve slopes upward because of diseconomies of scale.
- There is an envelope relationship between short-run average cost curves and long-run average cost curves. The short-run average cost curves are always above the long-run average cost curve.
- An entrepreneur is an individual who sees an opportunity to sell an item at a price higher than the average cost of producing it.
- Once we start applying cost analysis to the real world, we must include a variety of other dimensions of costs that the traditional model does not cover.
- Costs in the real world are affected by economies of scope, learning by doing and technological change, the many dimensions to output, and unmeasured costs such as opportunity costs.

Key Terms

constant returns to scale *(300)*
depreciation *(308)*
diseconomies of scale *(298)*
economically efficient *(296)*
economies of scale *(296)*
economies of scope *(303)*
entrepreneur *(303)*
indivisible setup cost *(297)*
learning by doing *(305)*
minimum efficient level of production *(298)*
monitoring cost *(299)*
team spirit *(299)*
technical efficiency *(296)*
technological change *(306)*

Questions and Exercises

1. What is the difference between technical efficiency and economic efficiency? LO1
2. One farmer can grow 1,000 bushels of corn on 1 acre of land with 200 hours of labor and 20 pounds of seed. Another farmer can grow 1,000 bushels of corn on 1 acre of land with 100 hours of labor and 20 pounds of seed.
   a. Could both methods be technically efficient?
   b. Is it possible that both of these production processes are economically efficient? LO1
3. A dressmaker can sew 800 garments with 160 bolts of fabric and 3,000 hours of labor. Another dressmaker can sew 800 garments with 200 bolts of fabric and 2,000 hours of identical labor. Fabric costs $100 a bolt and labor costs $10 an hour.
   a. Is it possible for both methods to be technically efficient? Why or why not?
   b. Is it possible for both methods to be economically efficient? Why or why not? LO1

4. A student has just written on an exam that, in the long run, fixed cost will make the average total cost curve slope downward. Why will the professor mark it incorrect? LO2
5. What inputs do you use in studying this book? What would the long-run average total cost and marginal cost curves for studying look like? Why? LO2
6. Why could diseconomies of scale never occur if production relationships were only technical relationships? LO2
7. There are large economies of scale in making flat-screen TVs, and there are also important elements of learning by doing, as with most technologies.
   a. Given that information, what would you expect to happen to the price of flat-screen TVs as the industry matures?
   b. In 2007, increasing the supply of flat-screen TVs was difficult, and the demand for flat-screen TVs increased faster than the supply. Given this information, what would you have predicted about the price of flat-screen TVs in 2008?
   c. In 2008, a number of new plants for producing flat-screen TVs began production. What likely happened to prices of flat-screen TVs in 2009? LO2
8. In the early 2000s car makers began to design vehicles' chassis, engine, and transmissions so that different models could be produced on the same assembly line. Within the first year of implementing the plan, Ford cut production costs by $240 per car.
   a. What cost concept was Ford taking advantage of to produce its savings?
   b. What effect did the plan likely have on Ford's short-run average total cost curve? LO2
9. Draw a long-run average total cost curve.
   a. Why does it slope downward initially?
   b. Why does it eventually slope upward?
   c. How would your answers to *a* and *b* differ if you had drawn a short-run cost curve?
   d. How large is the fixed-cost component of the long-run cost curve?
   e. If there were constant returns to scale everywhere, what would the long-run cost curve look like? LO2
10. Sea lions have been depleting the stock of steelhead trout. One idea to scare sea lions off the Washington state coast was to launch fake killer whales, predators of sea lions. The cost of making the first whale is $16,000—$5,000 for materials and $11,000 for the mold. The mold can be reused to make additional whales, so additional whales would cost $5,000 apiece. (Difficult)
    a. Make a table showing the total cost and average total cost of producing 1 to 10 fake killer whales.
    b. Does production of fake whales exhibit diseconomies of scale, economies of scale, or constant returns to scale?
    c. What is the fixed cost of producing fake whales?
    d. What is the variable cost of producing fake whales? LO2
11. What is the role of the entrepreneur in translating cost of production into supply? LO4
12. Your average total cost is $40; the price you receive for the good is $12. Should you keep on producing the good? Why? LO4
13. A student has just written on an exam that technological change will mean that the cost curve is downward-sloping. Why did the teacher mark it wrong? LO5
14. If you were describing the marginal cost of an additional car driving on a road, what costs would you look at? What is the likely shape of the marginal cost curve? LO5

Questions from Alternative Perspectives

1. The text presents costs as if a firm could look them up in a book.
   a. How do you believe a firm's true costs are revealed?
   b. Is this an optimal method of finding out costs? (Austrian)
2. The chapter points out that "businesses give enormous weight to experience" or learning by doing. Empirical evidence suggests that, in surveys and applications, women tend to report in far less detail the nature of their jobs as compared with men.
   a. How might this contribute to differences in "experience" between men and women?
   b. In what other ways might women's real-world experiences be undervalued when they go to look for jobs? (Feminist)
3. Adam Smith argued that at birth most people were similarly talented, and that differences in individual abilities, and hence productivity, are largely the effect of the division of labor, not its cause. What implications does that insight have for economic policy, and for the way we should treat others who receive less income than we do? (Religious)
4. Firms have an incentive to "externalize" their costs, that is, to make others face the opportunity costs of their actions while firms reduce their own accounting costs.
   a. Give some examples of firms doing this.
   b. What implications for policy does it have? (Institutionalist)

5. A major survey conducted by economists David Levine and Laura Tyson found that "In most reported cases the introduction of substantive shop floor participation (job redesign and participatory work groups) leads to some combination of an increase in satisfaction, commitment, quality and productivity, and a reduction in turnover and absenteeism." Despite that evidence of real cost savings of participatory work groups, only a few U.S. corporate employers (for instance, Xerox and Scott Paper) have taken this high road to labor relations, while many continue to pursue the low road Wal-Mart-like approach to cost saving. Why is that? (Radical)

Issues to Ponder

1. A pair of shoes that wholesales for $28.79 has approximately the following costs:

Manufacturing labor	$ 2.25
Materials	4.95
Factory overhead, operating expenses, and profit	8.50
Sales costs	4.50
Advertising	2.93
Research and development	2.00
Interest	.33
Net income to producer	3.33
Total	$28.79

   a. Which of these costs would likely be a variable cost?
   b. Which would likely be a fixed cost?
   c. If output were to rise, what would likely happen to average total costs? Why? LO2

2. A major issue of contention at many colleges concerns the cost of meals that is rebated when a student does not sign up for the meal plan. The administration usually says that it should rebate only the marginal cost of the food alone, which it calculates at, say, $1.25 per meal. Students say that the marginal cost should include more costs, such as the saved space from fewer students using the facilities and the reduced labor expenses on food preparation. This can raise the marginal cost to $6.00. (Difficult)
   a. Who is correct, the administration or the students?
   b. How might your answer to *a* differ if this argument were being conducted in the planning stage, before the dining hall is built?
   c. If you accept the $1.25 figure of a person not eating, how could you justify using a higher figure of about $6.00 for the cost of feeding a guest at the dining hall, as many schools do? LO2

3. When economist Jacob Viner first developed the envelope relationship, he told his draftsman to make sure that all the marginal cost curves went through both (1) the minimum point of the short-run average cost curve and (2) the point where the short-run average total cost curve was tangent to the long-run average total cost curve. The draftsman told him it couldn't be done. Viner told him to do it anyhow. Why was the draftsman right? (Difficult) LO3

4. The cost of setting up a steel mill is enormous. For example, a Gary, Indiana, hot-strip mill would cost an estimated $1.5 billion to build. Using this information and the cost concepts from the chapter, explain the following quotation: "To make operations even marginally profitable, big steelmakers must run full-out. It's like a car that is more efficient at 55 miles an hour than in stop-and-go traffic at 25." (Difficult) LO3

Answers to Margin Questions

1. True. Since an economically efficient method of production is that method that produces a given level of output at the lowest possible cost, it also must use as few inputs as possible. It is also technically efficient. *(296)*

2. China uses more labor-intensive techniques than does the United States because the price of labor is much lower in China relative to the United States. Both countries are producing economically efficiently. *(296)*

3. Larger production runs are generally cheaper per unit than smaller production runs because of indivisible setup costs, which do not vary with the size of the run. *(297)*

4. Because the same technical process could be used over and over again at the same cost, the long-run average cost curve would never become upward-sloping. *(299)*

5. The short-run average cost curve initially slopes downward because of increasing marginal productivity and large average fixed costs, then begins sloping upward because of diminishing marginal productivity, giving it a U shape. *(300)*

6. The long-run average total cost curve is generally considered to be U-shaped because initially there are economies

of scale and, for large amounts of production, there are diseconomies of scale. *(301)*

7. Economic activity does not just happen. Some dynamic, driven individual must instigate production. That dynamic individual is called an entrepreneur. *(303)*
8. Economies of scale are economies that occur because of increases in the amount of one good a firm is producing. Economies of scope occur when producing different types of goods lowers the cost of each of those goods. *(304)*
9. Learning by doing causes a shift in the cost curve because it is a change in the technical characteristics of production. It does not cause the cost curve to be downward-sloping—it causes it to shift downward. *(305)*
10. An economist would say that he doesn't know what total cost is without knowing what Jim could have earned if he had undertaken another activity besides running his business. Just because he paid himself $1,000 doesn't mean that $1,000 is his opportunity cost. *(308)*

APPENDIX A

Isocost/Isoquant Analysis

In the long run, a firm can vary more than one factor of production. One of the decisions firms face in this long run is which combination of factors of production to use. Economic efficiency involves choosing those factors to minimize the cost of production.

In analyzing this choice of which combination of factors to use, economists have developed a graphical technique called *isocost/isoquant analysis*. In this technique, the analyst creates a graph placing one factor of production, say labor, on one axis and another factor, say machines, on the other axis, as I have done in Figure A13-1. Any point on that graph represents a combination of machines and labor that can produce a certain amount of output, say 8 pairs of earrings. For example, point A represents 3 machines and 4 units of labor being used to produce 8 pairs of earrings. Any point in the blue shaded area represents more of one or both factors and any point in the brown shaded area represents less of one or both factors.

FIGURE A13-1 The Isocost/Isoquant Graph

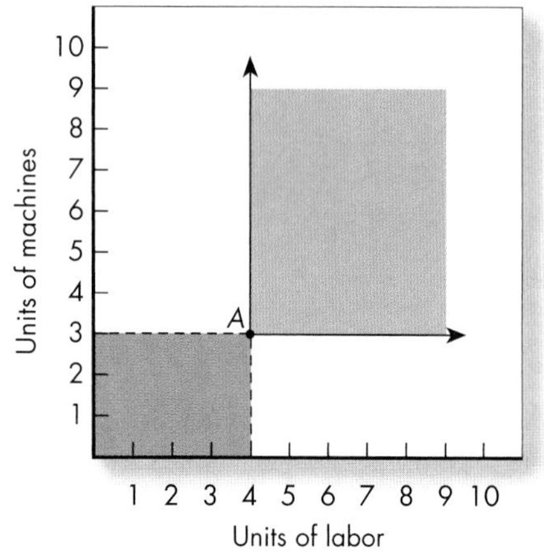

The Isoquant Curve

The firm's problem is to figure out how to produce its output—let's say it has chosen an output of 60 pairs of earrings—at as low a cost as possible. That means somehow we must show graphically the combinations of machines and labor that can produce 60 pairs of earrings as cheaply as possible. We do so with what is called an isoquant curve. An **isoquant curve** is *a curve that represents combinations of factors of production that result in equal amounts of output*. (*Isoquant* is a big name for an "equal quantity.") At all points on an isoquant curve, the firm can produce the same amount of output. So, given a level of output, a firm can find out what combinations of the factors of production will produce that output. Suppose a firm can produce 60 pairs of earrings with the following combination of labor and machines:

	Labor	Machines	Pairs of Earrings
A	3	20	60
B	4	15	60
C	6	10	60
D	10	6	60
E	15	4	60
F	20	3	60

This table shows the technical limits of production. It shows that the firm can use, for example, 3 units of labor and 20 machines or 20 units of labor and 3 machines to produce 60 pairs of earrings. The isoquant curve is a graphical representation of the table. I show the isoquant curve for producing 60 pairs in Figure A13-2. Points A to F represent rows A to F in the table.

To be sure you understand it, let's consider some points on the curve. Let's start at point A. At point A, the firm is producing 60 pairs of earrings using 20 machines and 3 workers. If the firm wants to reduce the number of machines by 5, it must increase the number of units of labor by 1 to keep output constant. Doing so moves the firm to point B. At point B, the firm is also producing 60 pairs of earrings, but is doing it with 15 machines and 4 workers. Alternatively, if the firm were at point D, and it wants to reduce the number of machines from 6 to 4, it must increase the number of units of labor from 10 to 15 to keep output constant at 60. At any point on this isoquant curve, the firm is being technically efficient—it is using as few resources as possible to produce 60 pairs of earrings. It would never want to produce 60 at a point like G because that point uses more inputs. It is a technically inefficient method of production.

The numbers in the production table and the shape of the curve were not chosen randomly. They were chosen to be consistent with the law of diminishing marginal productivity, which means the curve is bowed inward. That is because as the firm increases the use of one factor more and more, it must use fewer and fewer units of the other factor to keep output constant. This reflects the technical considerations embodied in the law of diminishing marginal productivity. Thus, the chosen numbers tell us that if a firm wants to keep output constant, as it adds more and more of one factor (and less of the other factor), it has to use relatively more of that factor. For example, initially it might add 1 machine to replace 1 worker, holding output constant. If it continues, it will have to use 1.5 machines, then 2 machines, and so on.

The rate at which one factor must be added to compensate for the loss of another factor, to keep output constant, is called the **marginal rate of substitution.** To say that there is diminishing marginal productivity is to say that there is a diminishing marginal rate of substitution. It is because the table assumes a diminishing marginal rate of substitution that the isoquant curve is bowed inward.

Graphically, the slope of the isoquant curve is the marginal rate of substitution. To be exact, the absolute value of the slope at a point on the isoquant curve equals the ratio of the marginal productivity of labor to the marginal productivity of machines:

$$|\text{Slope}| = \frac{MP_{\text{labor}}}{MP_{\text{machines}}} = \begin{array}{c}\text{Marginal}\\ \text{rate of}\\ \text{substitution}\end{array}$$

With this equation, you can really see why the isoquant is downward-sloping. As the firm moves from point A to point F, it is using more labor and fewer machines. Because of the law of diminishing marginal productivity, as the firm moves from A to F, the marginal productivity of labor decreases and the marginal productivity of machines increases. The slope of the isoquant falls since the marginal rate of substitution is decreasing.

Let's consider a specific example. Say in Figure A13-2 the firm is producing at point B. If it cuts its input by 5 machines but also wants to keep output constant, it must increase labor by 2 (move from point B to point C). So the marginal rate of substitution of labor for machines between points B and C must be 5/2 or 2.5.

The firm can complete this exercise for many different levels of output. Doing so will result in an **isoquant map,** *a set of isoquant curves that shows technically efficient combinations of inputs that can produce different levels of output.* Such a map for output levels of 40, 60, and 100 is shown in Figure A13-3.

Each curve represents a different level of output. Isoquant I is the lowest level of output, 40, and isoquant III is the highest level of output. When a firm chooses an output level, it is choosing one of those isoquants. The chosen isoquant represents the technically efficient combinations of resources that can produce the desired output.

FIGURE A13-2 **Isoquant Curve for 60 Pairs of Earrings**

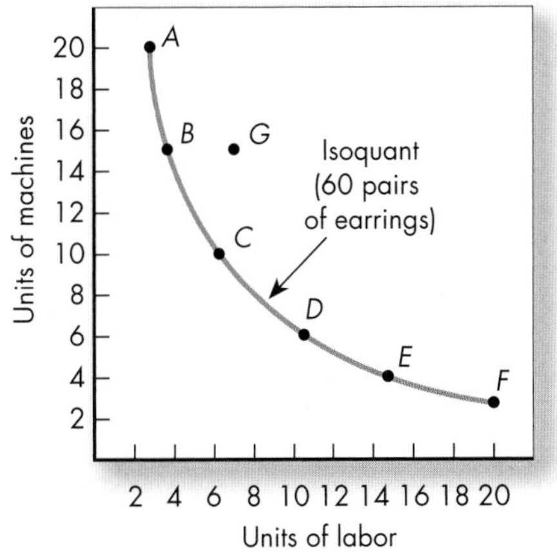

FIGURE A13-3 An Isoquant Map

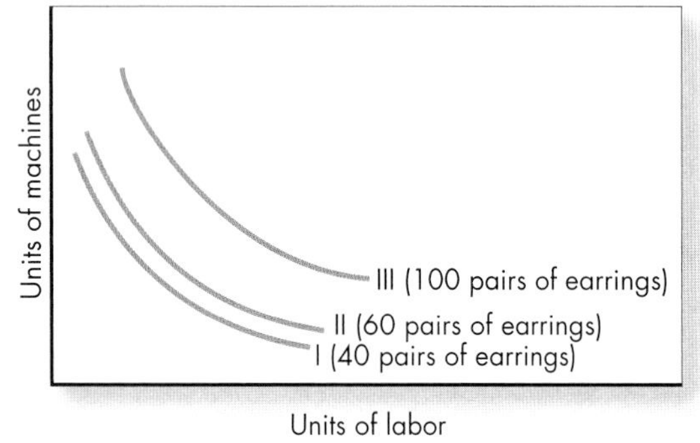

The Isocost Line

So far I have only talked about technical efficiency. To move to economic efficiency, we have to bring in the costs of production. We do so with the **isocost line**—*a line that represents alternative combinations of factors of production that have the same costs*. (*Isocost* is a fancy name for "equal cost.") Each point on the isocost line represents a combination of factors of production that, in total, cost the firm an equal amount.

To draw the isocost line, you must know the cost per unit of each input as well as the amount the firm has chosen to spend on production. Say labor costs $5 a unit, machinery costs $3 a unit, and the firm has chosen to spend $60. What is the greatest number of earrings it can produce with that $60? To answer that question, we need to create a curve representing the various amounts of inputs a firm can get with that $60. We do so in the following manner. Say the firm decides to spend the entire $60 on labor. Since labor costs $5 a unit, it can buy 12 units of labor. This alternative is represented by point A in Figure A13-4.

Alternatively, since machines cost $3 a unit, if the firm chooses to spend all of the $60 on machines, it can buy 20 machines (point B in Figure A13-4). This gives us two points on the isocost curve. Of course, the assumption of diminishing marginal rates of substitution makes it highly unlikely that the firm would want to produce at either of these points. Instead, it would likely use some combination of inputs. But these extreme points are useful nonetheless because by connecting them (the line that goes from A to B in Figure A13-4), we can see the various combinations of inputs that also cost $60.

To see that this is indeed the case, say the firm starts with 20 machines and no labor. If the firm wants to use some combination of labor and machinery, it can give up some machines and use the money it saves by using fewer machines to purchase units of labor. Let's say it gives up 5 machines, leaving it with 15. That means it has $15 to spend on labor, for which it can buy 3 units of labor. That means 15 machines and 3 units of labor is another combination of labor and machines that cost the firm $60. This means that point C is also a point on the isocost line. You can continue with this exercise to prove to yourself that the line connecting points A and B does represent various combinations of labor and machinery the firm can buy with $60. Thus, the line connecting A and B is the $60 isocost line.

To see that you understand the isocost line, it is useful to go through a couple of examples that would make it shift. For example, what would happen to the isocost line if the firm chooses to increase its spending on production to $90? To see the effect, we go through the same exercise as before: If it spent it all on labor, it could buy 18 units of labor. If it spent it all on machines, it could buy 30 units of machinery. Connecting these points will give us a curve to the right of and parallel to the original curve. It has the same slope because the relative prices of the factors of production, which determine the slope, have not changed.

Now ask yourself, What happens to the isocost line if the price of labor rises to $10 a unit? If you said the isocost curve becomes steeper, shifting along the labor axis to point *D* while remaining anchored along the machinery axis until the slope is −10/3, you've got it. In general, the absolute value of the slope of the isocost curve is the ratio of the price of the factor of production on the *x*-axis to the

FIGURE A13-4 Isocost Curves

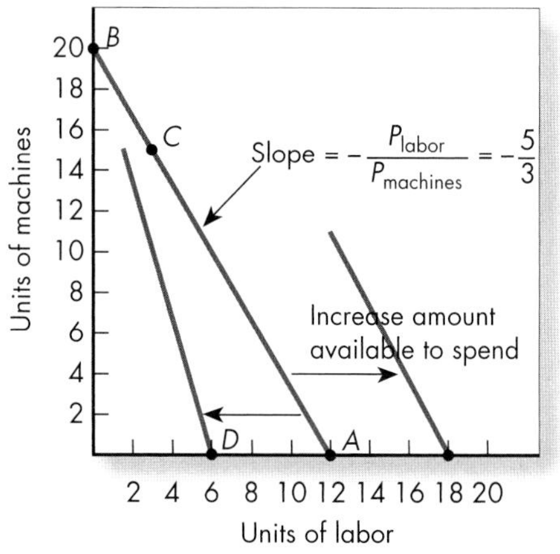

price of the factor of production on the y-axis. That means that as the price of a factor rises, the end point of the isocost curve shifts in on the axis on which that factor is measured.

Choosing the Economically Efficient Point of Production

Now let's move on to a consideration of the economically efficient combination of resources to produce 60 pairs of earrings with $60. To do that, we must put the isoquant cost curve from Figure A13-2 and the isocost curve from Figure A13-4 together. We do so in Figure A13-5.

The problem for the firm is to produce as many pairs of earrings as possible with the $60 it has to spend. Or, put another way, given a level of production it has chosen, it wants to produce at the least-cost combination of the factors of production.

Let's now find the least-cost combination of inputs to produce 60 pairs of earrings. Let's say that, initially, the firm chooses point A on its isoquant curve—that's at 15 machines and 4 workers. That produces 60 pairs of earrings, but has a cost of $45 + $20 = $65. The firm can't produce 60 pairs of earrings unless it is willing to spend more than $60. If it fires a worker to bring its cost in line, moving it to point *B*, it moves down to a lower isoquant—it is producing only 40 pairs.

If the firm has a less-than-competent manager, that manager will conclude that you can't produce 60 for $60. But say the firm has an efficient manager—one who has

FIGURE A13-5 Combining Isoquant and Isocost Curves

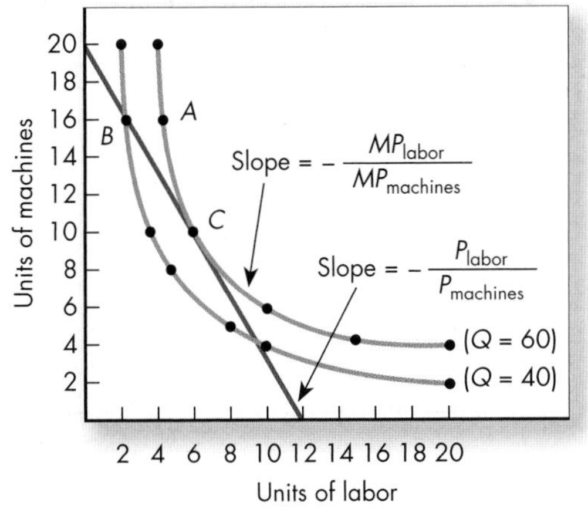

taken introductory economics. As opposed to *reducing* the number of workers as the other manager did, she *increases* the number of workers to 6 and reduces the number of machines to 10. Doing so still produces 60 pairs of earrings, since C is a point on the isoquant curve, but the strategy reduces the cost from $65 at point A to $60 (10 machines at $3 = $30 and 6 workers at $5 = $30). So she is producing 60 pairs of earrings at a cost of $60. She is operating at the economically efficient point—point C.

Let's talk about the characteristics of point C. Point C is the point where the isoquant curve is tangent to the isocost curve—the point at which the slope of the isoquant curve ($-MP_L/MP_M$) equals the slope of the isocost curve ($-P_L/P_M$). That is, $-MP_L/MP_M = -P_L/P_M$. This can be rewritten as:

$$MP_L/P_L = MP_M/P_M$$

What this equation says is that when the additional output per dollar spent on labor equals the additional output per dollar spent on machines, the firm is operating efficiently. It makes sense. If the additional output per dollar spent on labor exceeded the additional output per dollar spent on machines, the firm would do better by increasing its use of labor and decreasing its use of machines.

Point C represents the combination of labor and machines that will result in the highest output given the isocost curve facing the firm. To put it in technical terms, the firm is operating at an economically efficient point where marginal rate of substitution equals the ratio of the factor prices. Any point other than C on the isocost curve will cost $60 but produce fewer than 60 pairs of earrings. Any other point than C on the isoquant curve will produce 60 pairs of earrings but cost more than $60. Only C is the economically efficient point given the factor costs.

To see that you understand the analysis, say that the price of labor falls to $3 and you still want to produce 60. What will happen to the amount of labor and machines you hire? Alternatively, say that the price of machines rises to $5 and you want to spend only $60. What will happen to the amount of labor and machines you hire?

If your answers are (1) you hire more workers and fewer machines and (2) you reduce production using fewer machines and, maybe, less labor, you've got the analyses down. If you didn't give those answers, I suggest rereading this appendix, if it is to be on the exam, and working through the questions and exercises.

Key Terms

isocost line *(314)*
isoquant curve *(312)*
isoquant map *(313)*
marginal rate of substitution *(313)*

Questions and Exercises

1. What happens to the marginal rate of substitution as a firm increases the use of one input, keeping output constant? What accounts for this?
2. Draw an isocost curve for a firm that has $100 to spend on producing jeans. Input includes labor and materials. Labor costs $8 and materials cost $4 a unit. How does each of the following affect the isocost curve? Show your answer graphically.
   a. Production budget doubles.
   b. Cost of materials rises to $10 a unit.
   c. Cost of labor and materials each rises by 25 percent.
3. Show, using isocost/isoquant analysis, how firms in the United States use relatively less labor and relatively more land than Japan for the production of similar goods, yet both are behaving economically efficiently.
4. Demonstrate the difference between economic efficiency and technical efficiency, using the isocost/isoquant analysis.
5. Draw a hypothetical isocost curve and an isoquant curve tangent to the isocost curve. Label the combination of inputs that represents an economically efficient use of resources.
   a. How does a technological innovation affect your analysis?
   b. How does the increase in the price of the input on the *x*-axis affect your analysis?
6. Show graphically the analysis of the example in Figure A13-5 if the price of labor falls to $3. Demonstrate that the firm can increase production given the same budget.
7. Show graphically the analysis of the example in Figure A13-5 if the price of machines rises to $5. Demonstrate that the firm must reduce production if it keeps the same budget.

Perfect Competition

There's no resting place for an enterprise in a competitive economy.

—Alfred P. Sloan

The concept *competition* is used in two ways in economics. One way is as a process. *Competition as a process* is a rivalry among firms and is prevalent throughout our economy. It involves one firm trying to figure out how to take away market share from another firm. An example is my publishing firm giving me a contract to write a great book like this in order for the firm to take market share away from other publishing firms that are also selling economics textbooks. The other use of *competition* is as a *perfectly competitive market structure*. It is this use that is the subject of this chapter. Although perfect competition has highly restrictive assumptions, it provides us with a reference point for thinking about various market structures and competitive processes. Why is such a reference point important? Think of the following analogy.

In physics when you study the laws of gravity, you initially study what would happen in a vacuum. Perfect vacuums don't exist, but talking about what would happen if you dropped an object in a perfect vacuum makes the analysis easier. So too with economics. Our equivalent of a perfect vacuum is perfect competition. In perfect competition, the invisible hand of the market operates unimpeded. In this chapter, we'll consider how perfectly competitive markets work and see how to apply the cost analysis developed in the previous two chapters.

AFTER READING THIS CHAPTER, YOU SHOULD BE ABLE TO:

1. List the six conditions for a perfectly competitive market.
2. Explain why producing an output at which marginal cost equals price maximizes total profit for a perfect competitor.
3. Demonstrate why the marginal cost curve is the supply curve for a perfectly competitive firm.
4. Determine the output and profit of a perfect competitor graphically and numerically.
5. Construct a market supply curve by adding together individual firms' marginal cost curves.
6. Explain why perfectly competitive firms make zero economic profit in the long run.
7. Explain the adjustment process from short-run equilibrium to long-run equilibrium.

A Perfectly Competitive Market

A **perfectly competitive market** is *a market in which economic forces operate unimpeded*. For a market to be called *perfectly competitive*, it must meet some stringent conditions:

1. Both buyers and sellers are price takers.
2. The number of firms is large.
3. There are no barriers to entry.
4. Firms' products are identical.
5. There is complete information.
6. Selling firms are profit-maximizing entrepreneurial firms.

These conditions are needed to ensure that economic forces operate instantaneously and are unimpeded by political and social forces. For example, if there weren't a large number of firms, the few firms in the industry would have an incentive to get together and limit output so they could get a higher price. They would stop the invisible hand from working. Similarly for the other conditions, although the reasoning why they're necessary can get rather complicated.

The Necessary Conditions for Perfect Competition

To give you a sense of these conditions, let's consider each a bit more carefully.

1. *Both buyers and sellers are price takers.* A **price taker** is *a firm or individual who takes the price determined by market supply and demand as given.* When you buy, say, toothpaste, you go to the store and find that the price of toothpaste is, say, \$2.33 for the medium-size tube; you're a price taker. The firm, however, is a price maker since it set the price at \$2.33. So even though the toothpaste industry is highly competitive, it's not a perfectly competitive market. In a perfectly competitive market, market supply and demand determine the price; both firms and consumers take the market price as given.
2. *The number of firms is large.* This is almost self-explanatory. *Large* means sufficiently large so that any one firm's output compared to the market output is imperceptible, and what one firm does has no influence on what other firms do.

Q-1 Why is the assumption of no barriers to entry necessary for the existence of perfect competition?

Web Note 14.1
Barriers to Entry

3. *There are no barriers to entry.* **Barriers to entry** are *social, political, or economic impediments that prevent firms from entering a market.* They might be legal barriers such as exist when firms acquire a patent to produce a certain product. Barriers might be technological, such as when the minimum efficient level of production allows only one firm to produce at the lowest average total cost. Or barriers might be created by social forces, such as when bankers will lend only to individuals with specific racial characteristics. Perfect competition can have no barriers to entry.
4. *Firms' products are identical.* This requirement means that each firm's output is indistinguishable from any other firm's output. Corn bought by the bushel is relatively homogeneous. One kernel is indistinguishable from any other kernel. In contrast, you can buy 30 different brands of many goods—soft drinks, for instance: Pepsi, Coke, 7UP, and so on. They are all slightly different from one another and thus not identical.
5. *There is complete information.* In a perfectly competitive market, firms and consumers know all there is to know about the market—prices, products, and available technology, to name a few aspects. If any firm experiences a technological breakthrough, all firms know about it and are able to use the same technology instantaneously. No firm or consumer has a competitive edge over another.
6. *Selling firms are profit-maximizing entrepreneurial firms.* Firms can have many goals and be organized in a variety of ways. For perfect competition to exist, firms must seek maximum profit and only profit, and the people who make the decisions must receive only profits and no other form of income from the firms.

The Definition of Supply and Perfect Competition

These are enormously strong conditions and are seldom met simultaneously. But they are necessary for a perfectly competitive market to exist. Combined, they create an environment in which each firm, following its own self-interest, will offer goods to the

REAL-WORLD APPLICATION

The Internet and the Perfectly Competitive Model

Recent technological developments are making the perfectly competitive model more directly relevant to our economy. Specifically, the Internet has eliminated the spatial dimension of competition (except for shipping), allowing individuals to compete globally rather than locally. When you see a bid on the Internet, you don't care where the supplier is (as long as you do not have to pay shipping fees). Because it allows access to so many buyers and sellers, the Internet reduces the number of seller-set posted price markets (such as found in retail stores), and replaces them with auction markets.

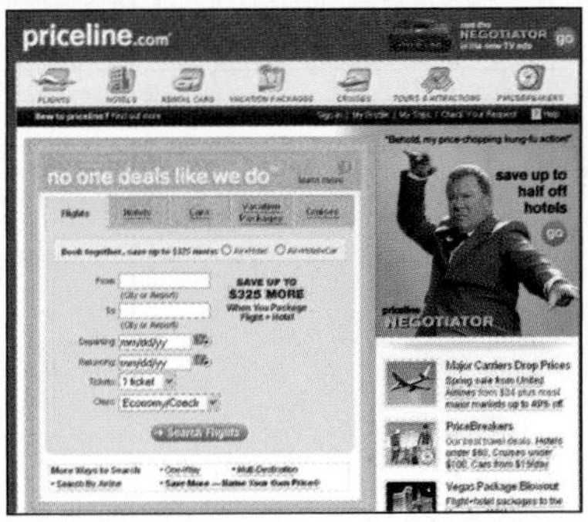

The Internet has had its biggest impact in firms' buying practices. Today, when firms want to buy standardized products, they will often post their technical requirements for desired components on the Net and allow suppliers from all over the world to bid to fill their orders. Firms have found that buying in this fashion over the Internet has, on average, lowered the prices they pay by over 10 percent.

Similar changes are occurring in consumer markets. With sites like Priceline.com, individuals can set the price they are willing to pay for goods and services (such as hotel rooms and airline tickets) and see if anyone wants to supply them. (Recently, I successfully bid $150 for a $460 retail price hotel room in New York City.) With sites such as eBay, you can buy and sell almost anything. The Internet even has its own payment systems, such as PayPal.

In short, with the Internet, entry and exit are much easier than in traditional brick-and-mortar business, and that makes the market more like a perfectly competitive market. As Internet search engines become better designed for commerce, and as more people become Internet savvy, the economy will more and more closely resemble the perfectly competitive model.

market in a predictable way. If these conditions hold, we can talk formally about the supply of a produced good and how it relates to costs. This follows from the definition of supply we gave in Chapter 4:

> *Supply* is a schedule of quantities of goods that will be offered to the market at various prices.

Web Note 14.2
Supply in Perfect Competition

This definition requires the supplier to be a price taker (our first condition). In almost all other market structures (frameworks within which firms interact economically), firms are not price takers; they are price makers. They don't ask, "How much should I supply, given the market price?" Instead they ask, "Given a demand curve, how much should I produce and what price should I charge?" In other market structures, the supplier sets the quantity and price, based on costs, at whatever level is best for it.[1]

The second condition—that the number of firms is large—is necessary so that firms have no ability to *collude* (to operate in concert so that they can get more for themselves). Conditions 3 through 5 are closely related to the first two; they make it impossible for any firm to forget about the hundreds of other firms out there just waiting to replace their supply. Condition 6 tells us a firm's goals. If we didn't know the goals, we wouldn't know how firms would react when faced with the given price.

[1]A firm's ability to set price doesn't mean that it can choose just any price it pleases. Other market structures can be highly competitive, so the range of prices a firm can charge and still stay in business is often limited. Such highly competitive firms are not perfectly competitive—they still set price rather than supply a certain quantity and accept whatever price they get.

FIGURE 14-1 (A AND B) **Market Demand Curve versus Individual Firm Demand Curve**

Even though the demand curve for the market is downward-sloping, the perceived demand curve of an individual firm is perfectly elastic because each firm is so small relative to the market.

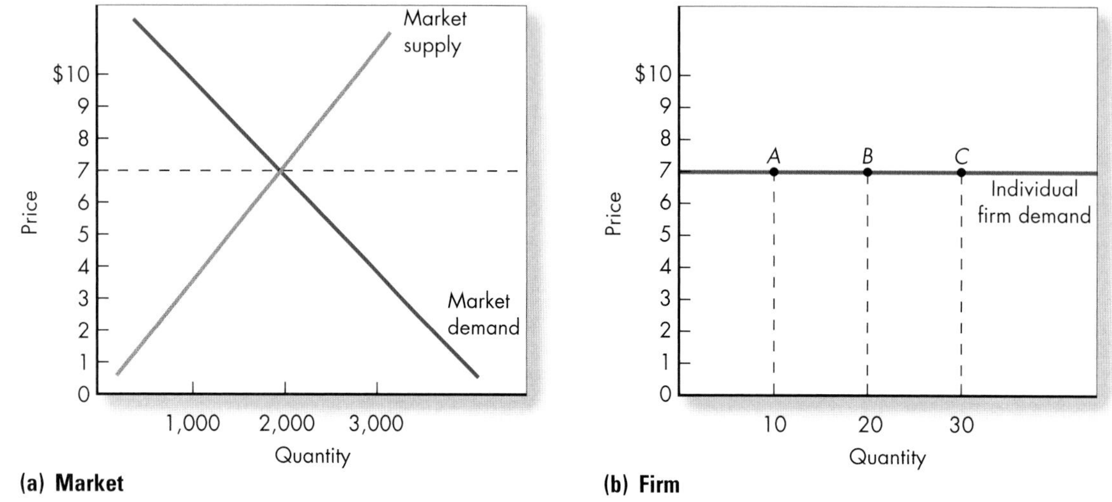

What's nice about these conditions is that they allow us to formally relate supply to a cost concept that we developed in the two previous chapters: marginal cost. If the conditions hold, a firm's supply curve will be that portion of the firm's short-run marginal cost curve above the average variable cost curve, as we'll see shortly.

If the conditions for perfect competition aren't met, then we can't use our formal concept of supply and how it relates to cost; we can, however, still talk informally about the supply of produced goods and cost conditions. That's what most economists do, keeping in the back of their minds which conditions aren't met and modifying the analysis accordingly. Even if the conditions for perfect competition don't fully exist, supply forces are still strong and many of the insights of the competitive model can be applied to firm behavior in other market structures.

Even if we can't technically specify a supply curve, supply forces are still strong and many of the insights of the competitive model carry over.

Demand Curves for the Firm and the Industry

Now that we've considered the competitive supply curve for the firm, let's turn our attention to the competitive demand curve for the firm. Here we must recognize that the demand curve for the industry is downward-sloping as in Figure 14-1(a), but the perceived demand curve for the firm is horizontal (perfectly elastic), as in Figure 14-1(b).

Q-2 How can the demand curve for the market be downward-sloping but the demand curve for a competitive firm be perfectly elastic?

Why the difference? It's a difference in perception. Each firm in a competitive industry is so small that it perceives that its actions will not affect the price it can get for its product. Price is the same no matter how much the firm produces. Think of an individual firm's actions as removing one piece of sand from a beach. Does that lower the level of the beach? For all practical, and even most impractical, purposes, we can assume it doesn't. Similarly for a perfectly competitive firm. That is why we consider the demand curve facing the firm to be horizontal.

The price the firm can get is determined by the market supply and demand curves shown in Figure 14-1(a). Market price is $7, and the firm represented in Figure 14-1(b) will get $7 for each unit of its product whether it produces 10 units (point A), 20 units (point B), or 30 units (point C). Its demand curve is perfectly elastic even though the demand curve for the market is downward-sloping.

Market vs. Firm Demand

FIGURE 14-2 (A AND B) Marginal Cost, Marginal Revenue, and Price

The profit-maximizing output for a firm occurs where marginal cost equals marginal revenue. Since for a competitive firm $P = MR$, its profit-maximizing output is where $MC = P$. At any other output, it is forgoing profit.

Price = *MR*	Quantity Produced	Marginal Costs
$35.00	0	
		$28.00
35.00	1	
		20.00
35.00	2	
		16.00
35.00	3	
		14.00
35.00	4	
		12.00
35.00	5	
		17.00
35.00	6	
		22.00
35.00	7	
		30.00
35.00	8	
		40.00
35.00	9	
		54.00
35.00	10	

(a) *MC*/Price Table

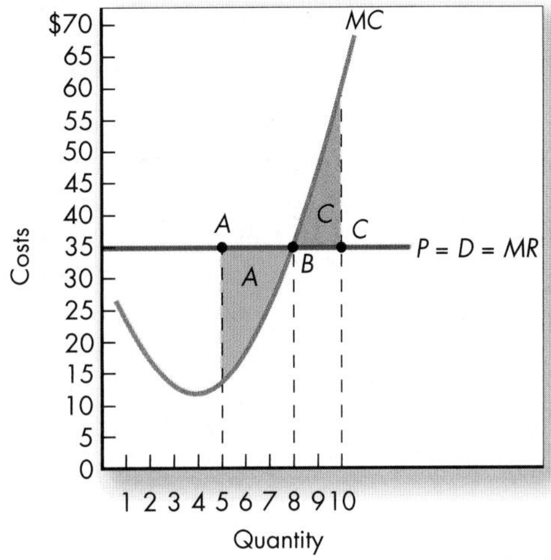

(b) *MC*/Price Graph

This difference in perception is extremely important. It means that firms will increase their output in response to an increase in market demand even though that increase in output will cause price to fall and can make all firms collectively worse off. But since, by the assumptions of perfect competition, they don't act collectively, each firm follows its self-interest. Let's now consider that self-interest in more detail.

The Profit-Maximizing Level of Output

The goal of a firm is to maximize profits—to get as much for itself as possible. So when it decides what quantity to produce, it will continually ask the question "What will changes in how much I produce do to profit?" Since profit is the difference between total revenue and total cost, what happens to profit in response to a change in output is determined by **marginal revenue (*MR*),** *the change in total revenue associated with a change in quantity*, and **marginal cost (MC),** *the change in total cost associated with a change in quantity*. That's why marginal revenue and marginal cost are key concepts in determining the profit-maximizing or loss-minimizing level of output of any firm.

To determine the profit-maximizing output, all you need to know is *MC* and *MR*.

To emphasize the importance of *MR* and MC, those are the only cost and revenue figures shown in Figure 14-2. Notice that we don't illustrate profit at all. We'll calculate profit later. All we want to determine now is the profit-maximizing level of output. To do this, you need only know MC and *MR*. Specifically, a firm maximizes profit when MC = *MR*. To see why, let's first look at MC and *MR* more closely.

Marginal Revenue

Let's first consider marginal revenue. Since a perfect competitor accepts the market price as given, marginal revenue is simply the market price. In the example shown in Figure 14-2, if the firm increases output from 2 to 3, its revenue rises by $35 (from $70 to $105). So its marginal revenue is $35, the price of the good. Since at a price of $35 it can sell as much as it wants, for a competitive firm, *MR* = *P*.

For a competitive firm, *MR* = *P*.

Marginal revenue is given in column 1 of Figure 14-2(a). As you can see, *MR* equals $35 for all levels of output. But that's what we saw in Figure 14-1, which showed that the demand curve for a perfect competitor is perfectly elastic at the market price. For a perfect competitor, the marginal revenue curve and demand curve it faces are the same.

Marginal Cost

Now let's move on to marginal cost. I'll be brief since I discussed marginal cost in detail in an earlier chapter. Marginal cost is the change in total cost that accompanies a change in output. Figure 14-2(a) shows marginal cost in column 3. Notice that initially in this example, marginal cost is falling, but by the fifth unit of output, it's increasing. This is consistent with our discussion in earlier chapters.

Notice also that the marginal cost figures are given for movements from one quantity to another. That's because marginal concepts tell us what happens when there's a change in something, so marginal concepts are best defined between numbers. The numbers in column 3 are the marginal costs. So the marginal cost of increasing output from 1 to 2 is $20, and the marginal cost of increasing output from 2 to 3 is $16. The marginal cost right at 2 (which the marginal cost graph shows) would be between $20 and $16, at approximately $18.

Profit Maximization: MC = *MR*

As I noted above, to maximize profit, a firm should produce where marginal cost equals marginal revenue. Looking at Figure 14-2(b), we see that a firm following that rule will produce at an output of 8, where MC = *MR* = $35. Now let me try to convince you that 8 is indeed the profit-maximizing output. To do so, let's consider three different possible quantities the firm might look at.

Q-3 What are the two things you must know to determine the profit-maximizing output?

Let's say that initially the firm decides to produce 5 widgets, placing it at point *A* in Figure 14-2(b). At output *A*, the firm gets $35 for each widget, but its marginal cost of increasing output is $17. We don't yet know the firm's total profit, but we do know how changing output will affect profit. For example, say the firm increases production from 5 to 6. Its revenue will rise by $35. (In other words, its marginal revenue is $35.) Its marginal cost of increasing output is $17. Since profit increases by $18 (the difference between *MR*, $35, and MC, $17), it makes sense (meaning the firm can increase its profit) to increase output from 5 to 6 units. It makes sense to increase output as long as the marginal cost is below the marginal revenue. The blue shaded area (*A*) represents the entire increase in profit the firm can get by increasing output.

Now let's say that the firm decides to produce 10 widgets, placing it at point C. Here the firm gets $35 for each widget. The marginal cost of producing that 10th unit is $54. So, MC > *MR*. If the firm decreases production by one unit, its cost decreases by $54 and its revenue decreases by $35. Profit increases by $19 ($54 − $35 = $19), so at point C, it makes sense to decrease output. This reasoning holds true as long as the marginal cost is above the marginal revenue. The brown shaded area (C) represents the increase in profits the firm can get by decreasing output.

At point *B* (output = 8) the firm gets $35 for each widget, and its marginal cost is $35, as you can see in Figure 14-2(b). The marginal cost of increasing output by one unit is $40 and the marginal revenue of selling one more unit is $35, so its profit falls by $5. If the firm decreases output by one unit, its MC is $30 and its *MR* is $35, so its profit falls by $5. Either increasing or decreasing production will decrease profit, so at point *B*, an output of 8, the firm is maximizing profit.

Profit-maximizing condition for a competitive firm: *MC* = *MR* = *P*.

Since *MR* is just market price, we can state the **profit-maximizing condition** of a competitive firm as MC = *MR* = *P*.

You should commit this profit-maximizing condition to memory. You should also be sure that you understand the intuition behind it. If marginal revenue isn't equal to marginal cost, a firm obviously can increase profit by changing output. If that isn't obvious, the marginal benefit of an additional hour of thinking about this condition will exceed the marginal cost (whatever it is), meaning that you should . . . right, you guessed it . . . study some more.

If marginal revenue does not equal marginal cost, a firm can increase profit by changing output.

The Marginal Cost Curve Is the Supply Curve

Now let's consider again the definition of the supply curve as a schedule of quantities of goods that will be offered to the market at various prices. Notice that the upward-sloping portion of the marginal cost curve fits that definition. It tells how much the firm will supply at a given price. Figure 14-3 shows the various quantities the firm will supply at different market prices beginning at the upward-sloping portion at point A. If the price is $35, we showed that the firm would supply 8 (point C). If the price had been $19.50, the firm would have supplied 6 (point B); if the price had been $61, the firm would have supplied 10 (point D). Because the marginal cost curve tells us how much of a produced good a firm will supply at a given price, *the marginal cost curve is the firm's supply curve*. The MC curve tells the competitive firm how much it should produce at a given price. (As you'll see later, there's an addendum to this statement. Specifically, the marginal cost curve is the firm's supply curve only if price exceeds average variable cost.)

Because the marginal cost curve tells us how much of a produced good a firm will supply at a given price, the marginal cost curve is the firm's supply curve.

Firms Maximize Total Profit

Notice that when you talk about maximizing profit, you're talking about maximizing *total profit*, not profit per unit. Profit per unit would be maximized at a much lower output level than is total profit. Profit-maximizing firms don't care about profit per unit; as long as an increase in output will increase total profits, a profit-maximizing firm should increase output. That's difficult to grasp, so let's consider a concrete example.

Q-4 Why do firms maximize total profit rather than profit per unit?

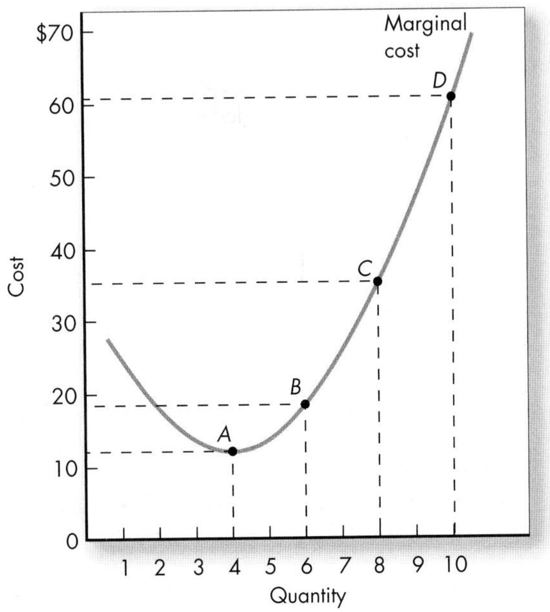

FIGURE 14-3 The Marginal Cost Curve Is a Firm's Supply Curve

Since the marginal cost curve tells the firm how much to produce, the marginal cost curve is the perfectly competitive firm's supply curve. This exhibit shows four points on a firm's supply curve; as you can see, the quantity the firm chooses to supply depends on the price. For example, if market price is $19.50, the firm produces 6 units.

Say two people are selling T-shirts that cost \$4 each. One sells 2 T-shirts at a price of \$6 each and makes a profit per shirt of \$2. His total profit is \$4. The second person sells 8 T-shirts at \$5 each, making a profit per unit of only \$1 but selling 8. Her total profit is \$8, twice as much as the fellow who had the \$2 profit per unit. In this case, \$5 (the price with the lower profit per unit), not \$6, yields more total profit.

Profit Maximization Using Total Revenue and Total Cost

An alternative method of determining the profit-maximizing level of output is to look at the total revenue and total cost curves directly. Figure 14-4 shows total cost and total revenue for the firm we're considering so far. The table in Figure 14-4(a) shows total revenue in column 2, which is just the number of units sold times market price. Total cost is in column 3. Total cost is the cumulative sum of the marginal costs from Figure 14-2(a) plus a fixed cost of \$40. Total profit (column 4) is the difference between total revenue and total cost. Looking down column 4 of Figure 14-4(a), you can quickly see that the profit-maximizing level of output is 8, as it was using the $MR = MC$ rule, since total profit is highest at an output of 8.

In Figure 14-4(b) we plot the firm's total revenue and total cost curves from the table in Figure 14-4(a). The total revenue curve is a straight line; each additional unit sold increases revenue by the same amount, \$35. The total cost curve is bowed upward at most quantities, reflecting the increasing marginal cost at different levels of output. The firm's profit is represented by the distance between the total revenue curve and the total cost curve. For example, at output 5, the firm makes \$45 in profit.

Total profit is maximized where the vertical distance between total revenue and total cost is greatest. In this example, total profit is maximized at output 8, just as in the

FIGURE 14-4 (A AND B) Determination of Profits by Total Cost and Total Revenue Curves

The profit-maximizing output level also can be seen by considering the total cost curve and the total revenue curve. Profit is maximized at the output where total revenue exceeds total cost by the largest amount. This occurs at an output of 8.

Quantity	Total Revenue	Total Cost	Total Profit
0	\$ 0	\$ 40	\$−40
1	35	68	−33
2	70	88	−18
3	105	104	1
4	140	118	22
5	175	130	45
6	210	147	63
7	245	169	76
8	280	199	81
9	315	239	76
10	350	293	57

(a) Total Revenue and Total Cost Table

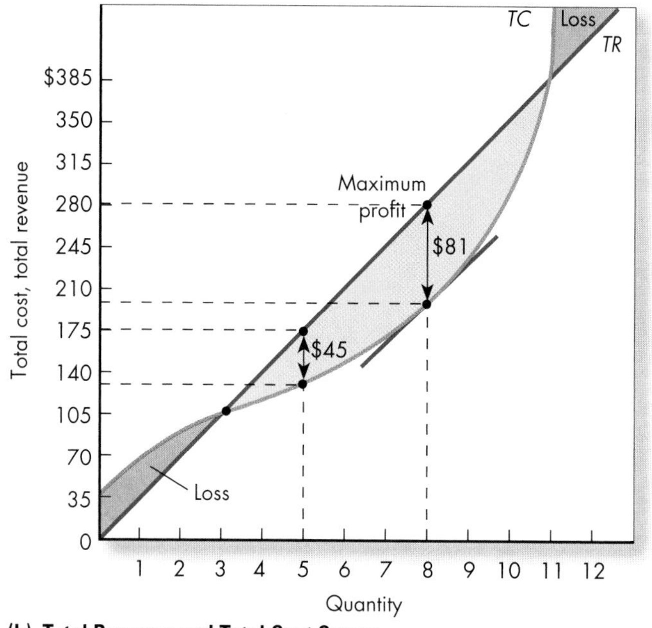

(b) Total Revenue and Total Cost Curves

alternative approach. At that output, marginal revenue (the slope of the total revenue curve) and marginal cost (the slope of the total cost curve) are equal.

Total Profit at the Profit-Maximizing Level of Output

In the initial discussion of the firm's choice of output, given price, I carefully presented only marginal cost and price. We talked about maximizing profit, but nowhere did I mention what profit, average total cost, average variable cost, or average fixed cost is. I mentioned only marginal cost and price, to emphasize that marginal cost is all that's needed to determine a competitive firm's supply curve (and a competitive firm is the only firm that has a supply curve) and to determine the output that will maximize profit. Now that you know that, let's turn our attention more closely to profit.

Marginal cost is all that is needed to determine a competitive firm's supply curve.

Determining Profit from a Table of Costs and Revenue

The $P = MR = MC$ condition tells us how much output a competitive firm should produce to maximize profit. It does not tell us the profit the firm makes. *Profit is determined by total revenue minus total cost.* Table 14-1 expands Figure 14-2(a) and presents a table of all the costs relevant to the firm. Going through the columns and reminding yourself of the definition of each is a good review of the two previous chapters. If the definitions don't come to mind immediately, you need a review. If you don't know the definitions of *MC*, *AVC*, *ATC*, *FC*, and *AFC*, go back and reread those chapters.

The firm is interested in maximizing profit. Looking at Table 14-1, you can quickly see that the profit-maximizing position is 8, as it was before, since at an output of 8, total profit is highest.

Using the $MC = MR = P$ rule, you can also see that the profit-maximizing level of output is 8. Increasing output from 7 to 8 has a marginal cost of \$30, which is less than \$35, so it makes sense to do so. Increasing output from 8 to 9 has a marginal cost of \$40, which is more than \$35, so it does not make sense to do so. The output 8 is the profit-maximizing output. At that profit-maximizing level of output, the profit the firm earns is \$81, which is calculated by subtracting total cost of \$199 from total revenue of \$280. Notice also that average total cost is lowest at an output of about 7, and the average

TABLE 14-1 Costs Relevant to a Firm

Price = Marginal Revenue	1 Quantity Produced	2 Total Fixed Cost	3 Average Fixed Cost	4 Total Variable Cost	5 Average Variable Cost	6 Total Cost	7 Marginal Cost	8 Average Total Cost	9 Total Revenue	10 Total Profit
\$35.00	0	\$40.00	—	0	—	\$ 40.00		—	0	\$−40.00
35.00	1	40.00	\$40.00	\$28.00	\$28.00	68.00	\$28.00	\$68.00	\$ 35.00	−33.00
35.00	2	40.00	20.00	48.00	24.00	88.00	20.00	44.00	70.00	−18.00
35.00	3	40.00	13.33	64.00	21.33	104.00	16.00	34.67	105.00	1.00
35.00	4	40.00	10.00	78.00	19.50	118.00	14.00	29.50	140.00	22.00
35.00	5	40.00	8.00	90.00	18.00	130.00	12.00	26.00	175.00	45.00
35.00	6	40.00	6.67	107.00	17.83	147.00	17.00	24.50	210.00	63.00
35.00	7	40.00	5.71	129.00	18.43	169.00	22.00	24.14	245.00	76.00
35.00	8	40.00	5.00	159.00	19.88	199.00	30.00	24.88	280.00	81.00
35.00	9	40.00	4.44	199.00	22.11	239.00	40.00	26.56	315.00	76.00
35.00	10	40.00	4.00	253.00	25.30	293.00	54.00	29.30	350.00	57.00

FIGURE 14-5 (A, B, AND C) Determining Profits Graphically

The profit-maximizing output depends *only* on where the MC and MR curves intersect. The total amount of profit or loss that a firm makes depends on the price it receives and its average total cost of producing the profit-maximizing output. This exhibit shows the case of (**a**) a profit, (**b**) zero profit, and (**c**) a loss.

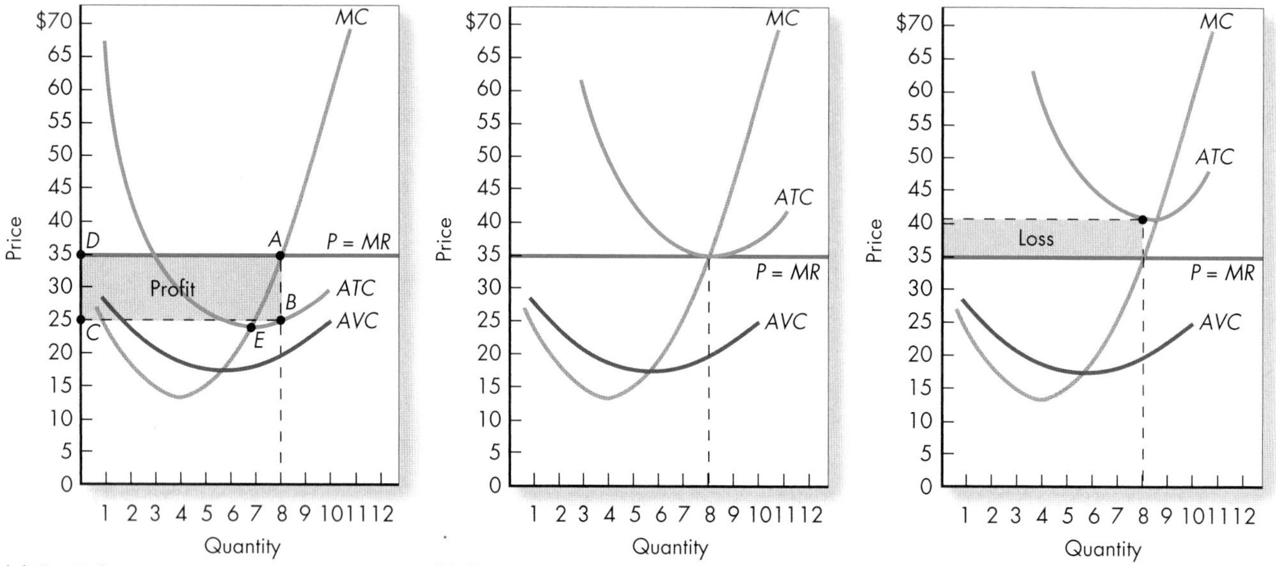

(a) Profit Case **(b) Zero Profit Case** **(c) Loss Case**

variable cost is lowest at an output of about 6.[2] Thus, the profit-maximizing position (which is 8) is *not* necessarily a position that minimizes either average variable cost or average total cost. It is only the position that maximizes total profit.

Determining Profit from a Graph

The profit-maximizing output can be determined in a table (as in Table 14-1) or in a graph (as in Figure 14-5).

These relationships can be seen in a graph. In Figure 14-5(a) I add the average total cost and average variable cost curves to the graph of marginal cost and price first presented in Figure 14-2. Notice that the marginal cost curve goes through the lowest points of both average cost curves. (If you don't know why, it would be a good idea to go back and review the previous chapters.)

Q-5 If the firm described in Figure 14-5 is producing 4 units, what would you advise it to do, and why?

Find Output Where MC = MR The way you find profit graphically is first to find the point where MC = *MR* (point A). That intersection determines the quantity the firm will produce if it wants to maximize profit. Why? Because the vertical distance between a point on the marginal cost curve and a point on the marginal revenue curve represents the additional profit the firm can make by changing output. For example, if it increases production from 6 to 7, its marginal cost is $22 and its marginal revenue is $35. By increasing output it can increase profit by $13 (from $63 to $76). The same reasoning holds true for any output less than 8. For outputs higher than 8, the opposite reasoning holds true. Marginal cost exceeds marginal revenue, so it pays to decrease output. So, to maximize profit, the firm must see that there is no distance between the two curves—it must see where they intersect.

[2]I say "about 6" and "about 7" because the table gives only whole numbers. The actual minimum point occurs at 5.55 for average variable cost and 6.55 for average total cost. The nearest whole numbers to these are 6 and 7.

***Find Profit per Unit Where* MC = MR** After having determined the profit-maximizing quantity, drop a vertical line down to the horizontal axis and see what average total cost is at that output level (point *B*). Next extend a line back to the vertical axis (point C). That tells us that the average total costs per unit are $25. Next go up the price axis to the price that the firm receives (point *D*). For a competitive firm, that price is the marginal revenue as well as its average revenue, since the price is constant. The difference between this price and average cost is profit per unit. Connecting these points gives us the shaded rectangle, *ABCD*, which is the total profit earned by the firm (the total quantity times the profit per unit).

Notice that at the profit-maximizing position, the profit per unit isn't at its highest because average total cost is *not* at its minimum point. Profit per unit of output would be highest at point *E*. A common mistake that students make is to draw a line up from point *E* when they are finding profits. That is wrong. It is important to remember: *To determine maximum profit, you must first determine what output the firm will choose to produce by seeing where* MC *equals* MR *and then determine the average total cost at that quantity by dropping a line down to the* ATC *curve*. Only then can you determine what maximum profit will be.

Thinking Like a Modern Economist

Profit Maximization and Real-World Firms

Most real-world firms do not have profit as their only goal. The reason is that, in the real world, the decision maker's income is part of the cost of production. For example, a paid manager has an incentive to hold down costs but has little incentive to hold down his income, which, for the firm, is a cost. Alternatively, say that a firm is a worker-managed firm. If workers receive a share of the profits, they'll push for higher profits, but they'll also see to it that in the process of maximizing profits they don't hurt their own interest—maximizing their wages.

A manager-managed firm will push for high profits but will see to it that it doesn't achieve those profits by hurting the manager's interests. Managers' pay will be high. In short, real-world firms will hold down the costs of factors of production *except* the cost of the decision maker.

In real life, this problem of the lack of incentives to hold down costs is important. For example, firms' managerial expenses often balloon even as firms are cutting "costs." Similarly, CEOs and other high-ranking officers of the firm often have enormously high salaries. How and why the lack of incentives to hold down costs affects the economy is best seen by first considering the nature of an economy with incentives to hold down all costs. That's why we use as our standard model the traditional profit-maximizing firm. (*Standard model* means the model that economists use as our basis of reasoning; from it, we branch out.) Using game theory models, modern economists work with firms to devise incentive-compatible contracts that align the goals of decision makers in the firm with the goals of the owners of firms.

***Zero Profit or Loss Where* MC = MR** Notice also that as the curves in Figure 14-5(a) are drawn, *ATC* at the profit-maximizing position is below the price, and the firm makes a profit per unit of a little over $10. The choice of short-run average total cost curves was arbitrary and doesn't affect the firm's profit-maximizing condition: MC = *MR*. It could have been assumed that fixed cost was higher, which would have shifted the *ATC* curve up. In Figure 14-5(b) it's assumed that fixed cost is $81 higher than in Figure 14-5(a). Instead of $40, it's $121. The appropriate average total cost curve for a fixed cost of $121 is drawn in Figure 14-5(b). Notice that in this case economic profit is zero and the marginal cost curve intersects the minimum point of the average total cost curve at an output of 8 and a price of $35. In this case, the firm is making zero economic profit. (Remember from the last chapter that even though economic profit is zero, all resources, including entrepreneurs, are being paid their opportunity cost.)

When the *ATC* curve is below the marginal revenue curve, the firm makes a profit. When the *ATC* curve is above the marginal revenue curve, the firm incurs a loss.

To determine maximum profit, you must first determine what output the firm will choose to produce by seeing where *MC* equals *MR*, and then extending a line to the *ATC* curve.

Q-6 What is wrong with the following diagram?

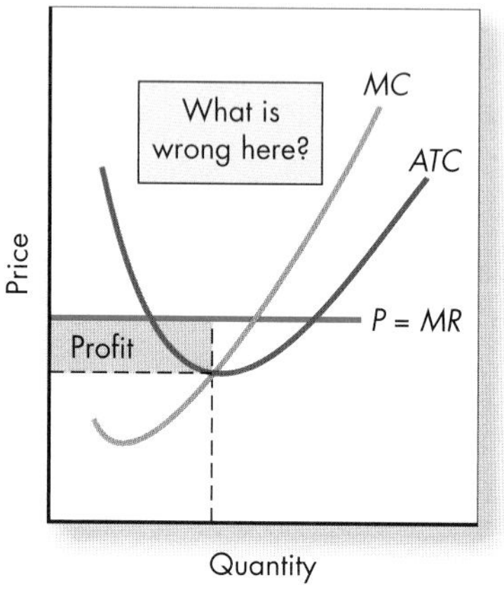

Q-7 In the early 2000s, many airlines were making losses, yet they continued to operate. Why?

In Figure 14-5(c), fixed cost is much higher—$169. Profit-maximizing output is still 8, but now at an output of 8, the firm is making an economic loss of $6 on each unit sold, since its average total cost is $41. The loss is given by the shaded rectangle. In this case, the profit-maximizing condition is actually a loss-minimizing condition. So $MC = MR = P$ is both a *profit-maximizing condition* and a *loss-minimizing condition.*

I draw these three cases to emphasize to you that determining the profit-maximizing output level doesn't depend on fixed cost or average total cost. It depends only on where marginal cost equals price.

The Shutdown Point

Earlier I stated the supply curve of a competitive firm is its marginal cost curve. More specifically, the supply curve is the part of the marginal cost curve that is above the average variable cost curve. Considering why this is the case should help the analysis stick in your mind.

Let's consider Figure 14-6(a)—a reproduction of Figure 14-5(c)—and the firm's decision at various prices. At a price of $35, it's incurring a loss of $6 per unit. If it's making a loss, why doesn't it shut down? The answer lies in the fixed costs. There's no use crying over spilt milk. In the short run, a firm knows these fixed costs are sunk costs; it must pay them regardless of whether or not it produces. The firm considers only the costs it can save by stopping production, and those costs are its variable costs. As long as a firm is covering its variable costs, it pays to keep on producing. By producing, its loss is $48; if it stopped producing, its loss would be all the fixed costs ($169). So it makes a smaller loss by producing.

The shutdown point is the point below which the firm will be better off if it shuts down than it will if it stays in business.

If $P >$ minimum of AVC, the firm will continue to produce in the short run. If $P <$ minimum of AVC, the firm will shut down.

However, once the price falls below average variable costs (below $17.80), it will pay to shut down (point *A* in Figure 14-6(a)). In that case, the firm's loss from producing would be more than $169, and it would do better to simply stop producing temporarily and avoid paying the variable cost. Thus, the point at which price equals *AVC* is the **shutdown point** (*that point below which the firm will be better off if it temporarily shuts down than it will if it stays in business*). When price falls below the shutdown point, the average variable costs the firm can avoid paying by shutting down exceed the price it would get for selling the good. When price is above average variable cost, in the short run a firm should keep on producing even though it's making a loss. As long as a firm's total revenue is covering its total variable cost, temporarily producing at a loss is the firm's best strategy because it's making a smaller loss than it would make if it were to shut down.

Short-Run Market Supply and Demand

Most of the preceding discussion has focused on supply and demand analysis of a firm. Now let's consider supply and demand in an industry. We've already discussed industry demand. Even though the demand curve faced by the firm is perfectly elastic, the industry demand curve is downward-sloping.

The market supply curve is the horizontal sum of all the firms' marginal cost curves, taking account of any changes in input prices that might occur.

How about the industry supply curve? We previously demonstrated that the supply curve for a competitive firm is that portion of a firm's marginal cost curve that is above the average variable cost curve. To discuss the industry supply curve, we must use a market supply curve. In the short run when the number of firms in the market is fixed, the **market supply curve** is just the *horizontal sum of all the firms' marginal cost curves, taking account of any changes in input prices that might occur.* To move from individual firms' marginal cost curves or supply curves to the market supply curve, we add the quantities all firms will supply at each possible price. Since all firms in a competitive market have identical marginal cost curves, a quick way of summing the quantities is to

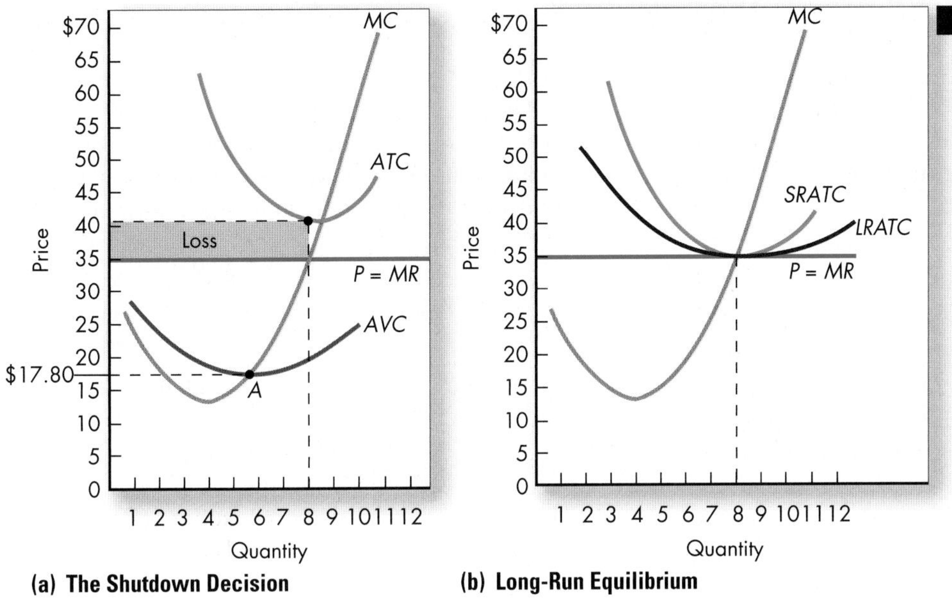

FIGURE 14-6 The Shutdown Decision and Long-Run Equilibrium

A firm should continue to produce as long as price exceeds average variable cost. Once price falls below that, it will do better by temporarily shutting down and saving the variable costs. This occurs at point A in (**a**). In (**b**), the long-run equilibrium position for a firm in a competitive industry is shown. In that long-run equilibrium, only normal profits are made.

multiply the quantities from the marginal cost curve of a representative firm at each price by the number of firms in the market. As the short run evolves into the long run, the number of firms in the market can change. As more firms enter the market, the market supply curve shifts to the right because more firms are supplying the quantity indicated by the representative marginal cost curve. Likewise, as the number of firms in the market declines, the market supply curve shifts to the left. Knowing how the number of firms in the market affects the market supply curve is important to understanding long-run equilibrium in perfectly competitive markets.

Long-Run Competitive Equilibrium

The analysis of the competitive firm consists of two parts: the short-run analysis just presented and the long-run analysis. In the short run, the number of firms is fixed and the firm can either earn economic profit or incur economic loss. In the long run, firms enter and exit the market and neither economic profits nor economic losses are possible. In the long run, firms make zero economic profit. Thus, in the long run, only the zero profit equilibrium shown in Figure 14-6(b) is possible. As you can see, at that long-run equilibrium, the firm is at the minimum of both the short-run and the long-run average total cost curves.

Why can't firms earn economic profit or make economic losses in the long run? Because of the entry and exit of firms: If there are economic profits, firms will enter the market, shifting the market supply curve to the right. As market supply increases, the market price will decline and reduce profits for each firm. Firms will continue to enter the market and the market price will continue to decline until the incentive of economic profits is eliminated. At that price, all firms are earning zero profit. Similarly, if the price is lower than the price necessary to earn a profit, firms incurring losses will leave the market and the market supply curve will shift to the left. As market supply shifts to the left, market price will rise. Firms will continue to exit the market and

Since profits create incentives for new firms to enter, output will increase, and the price will fall until zero profits are being made.

Web Note 14.3
Shutdown and Exit

A REMINDER

Finding Output, Price, and Profit

To find a competitive firm's price, level of output, and profit given a firm's marginal cost curve and average total cost curve, use the following four steps:

1. Determine the market price at which market supply and demand curves intersect. This is the price the competitive firm accepts for its products.
2. Draw the horizontal marginal revenue (*MR*) curve at the market price.
3. Determine the profit-maximizing level of output by finding the level of output where the *MR* and *MC* curves intersect.
4. Determine profit by subtracting average total costs at the profit-maximizing level of output from the price and multiplying by the firm's output.

If you are demonstrating profit graphically, find the point at which $MC = MR$. Extend a line down to the *ATC* curve. Extend a line from this point to the vertical axis. To complete the box indicating profit, go up the vertical axis to the market price.

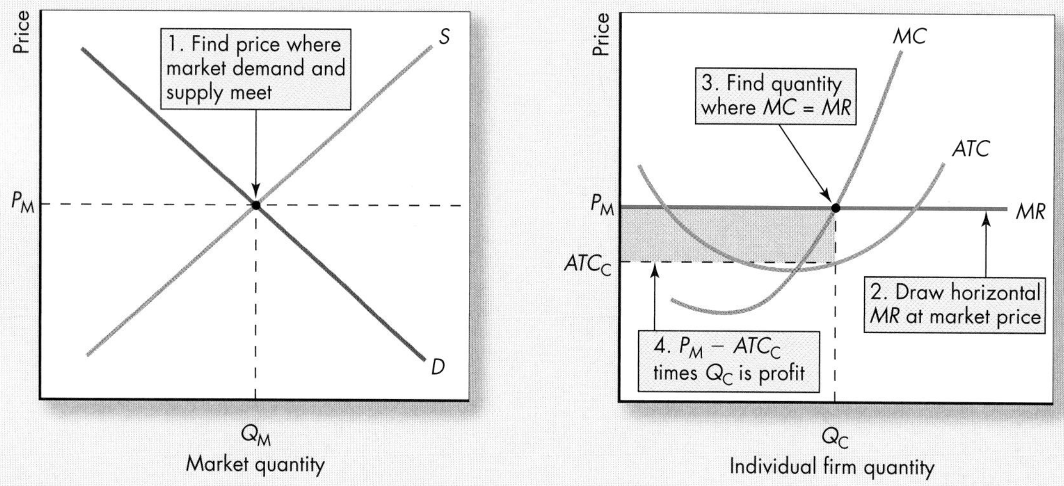

market price will continue to rise until all remaining firms no longer incur losses and earn zero profit. Only at zero profit do entry and exit stop.

Zero profit does not mean that entrepreneurs don't get anything for their efforts. The entrepreneur is an input to production just like any other factor of production. In order to stay in the business, the entrepreneur must receive the opportunity cost, or **normal profit** (*the amount the owners of business would have received in the next-best alternative*). That normal profit is built into the costs of the firm; economic profits are profits above normal profits.

Q-8 If a competitive firm makes zero profit, why does it stay in business?

Another aspect of the zero profit position deserves mentioning. What if one firm has superefficient workers or machinery? Won't the firm make a profit in the long run? The answer is, again, no. In a long-run competitive market, other firms will see the value of those workers and machines and will compete to get them for themselves. As firms compete for the superefficient factors of production, the prices of those specialized inputs will rise until all profits are eliminated. Those factors will receive what are called

REAL-WORLD APPLICATION

The Shutdown Decision and the Relevant Costs

The previous two chapters emphasized that it is vital to choose the relevant costs to the decision at hand. Discussing the shutdown decision gives us a chance to demonstrate the importance of those choices. Say the firm leases a large computer it needs to operate. The rental cost of that computer is a fixed cost for most decisions, if, as long as the firm keeps the computer, the rent must be paid whether or not the computer is used. However, if the firm can end the rental contract at any time, and thereby save the rental cost, the computer is not a fixed cost. But neither is it your normal variable cost. Since the firm can end the rental contract and save the cost only if it shuts down, that rental cost of the computer is an *indivisible setup cost.* For the shutdown decision, the computer cost is a variable cost. For other decisions about changing quantity, it's a fixed cost.

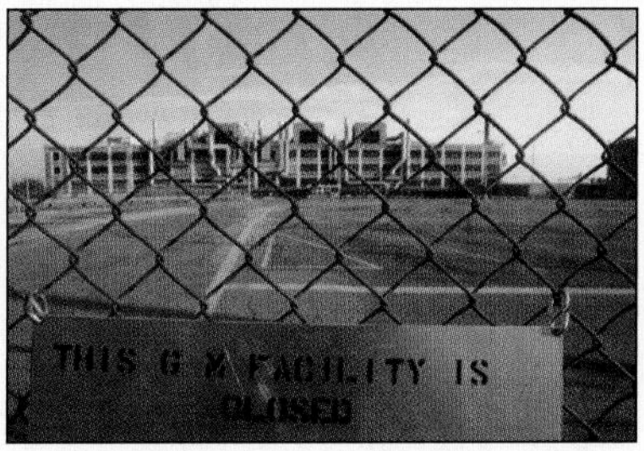

The moral: The relevant cost can change with the decision at hand, so when you apply the analysis to real-world situations, be sure to think carefully about what the *relevant cost* is.

Consider the problem facing GM and other U.S. auto producers. In their contracts with their workers, they have agreed to pay their workers whether they work or not, making labor costs, in large part, fixed. This means that GM actually saves much less when cutting production than it would if it did not have to pay idle workers. The implication of these contracts is that when demand falls, GM has a strong incentive to keep on producing, and then to sell the cars at a loss. Why sell at a loss? Because the loss is less than if GM had shut down production. GM is currently trying to restructure its contracts, and many economists believe that the continued survival of GM depends on its ability to restructure its labor contracts and change many of its fixed costs to variable costs, so that its production can respond more quickly to changes in demand.

rents to their specialized ability. For example, say the average worker receives $400 per week, but Sarah, because she's such a good worker, receives $600. So $200 of the $600 she receives is a rent to her specialized ability. Either her existing firm matches that $600 wage or she will change employment.

The zero profit condition is enormously powerful; it makes the analysis of competitive markets far more applicable to the real world than can a strict application of the assumption of perfect competition. If economic profit is being made, firms will enter and compete that profit away. Price will be pushed down to the average total cost of production as long as there are no barriers to entry. As we'll see in later chapters, in their analysis of whether markets are competitive, many economists focus primarily on whether barriers to entry exist.

The zero profit condition is enormously powerful; it makes the analysis of competitive markets far more applicable to the real world than would otherwise be the case.

Adjustment from the Short Run to the Long Run

Now that we've been through the basics of the perfectly competitive supply and demand curves, we're ready to consider the two together and to see how the adjustment to long-run equilibrium will likely take place for the firm and in the market.

An Increase in Demand

First, in Figure 14-7(a and b), let's consider a market that's in equilibrium but that suddenly experiences an increase in demand. Figure 14-7(a) shows the market reaction. Figure 14-7(b) shows a representative firm's reaction. Originally market equilibrium occurs at a price of $7 and market quantity supplied of 700 thousand units (point A in

FIGURE 14-7 (A AND B) Market Response to an Increase in Demand

Faced with an increase in demand, which it sees as an increase in price and hence profits, a competitive firm will respond by increasing output (from *A* to *B*) in order to maximize profit. The market response is shown in (**a**); the firm's response is shown in (**b**). As all firms increase output and as new firms enter, price will fall until all profit is competed away. Thus, the long-run market supply curve will be perfectly elastic, as is S_{LR} in (**a**). The final equilibrium will be the original price but a higher output. The original firms return to their original output (*A*), but since there are more firms in the market, the market output increases to *C*.

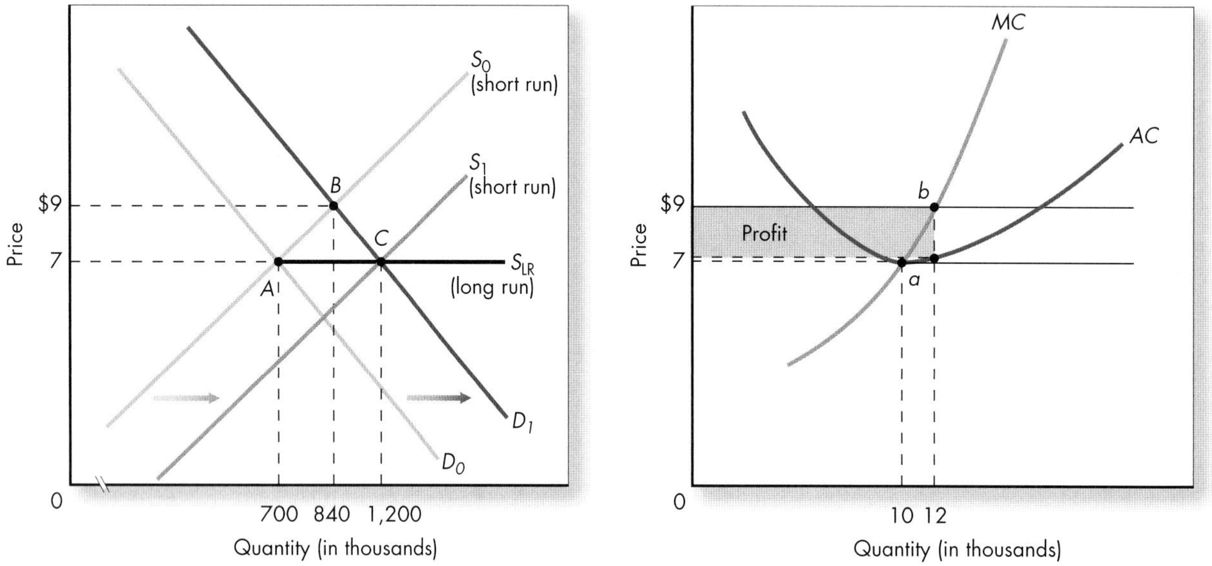

(a) Market **(b) Firm**

(a)), with each of 70 firms producing 10 thousand units (point *a* in (b)). Firms are making zero profit because they're in long-run equilibrium. If demand increases from D_0 to D_1, the firms will see the market price increasing and will increase their output until they're once again at a position where MC = *P*. This occurs at point *B* at a market output of 840 thousand units in (a) and at point *b* at a firm output of 12 thousand in (b). In the short run, the 70 existing firms each makes an economic profit (the shaded area in Figure 14-7(b)). Price has risen to $9, but average cost is only $7.10, so if the price remains $9, each firm is making a profit of $1.90 per unit. But price cannot remain at $9 since new firms will have an incentive to enter the market.

Q-9 If berets suddenly became the "in" thing to wear, what would you expect to happen to the price in the short run? In the long run?

As new firms enter, if input prices remain constant, the short-run market supply curve shifts from S_0 to S_1 and the market price returns to $7. The entry of 50 new firms provides the additional output in this example, bringing market output to 1.2 million units sold for $7 apiece. The final equilibrium will be at a higher market output but at the same price.

Long-Run Market Supply

In the long run, firms earn zero profits.

The long-run market supply curve is a schedule of quantities supplied when firms are no longer entering or exiting the market. This occurs when firms are earning zero profit. In this case, the long-run supply curve is created by extending to the right the line connecting points A and C. Since equilibrium price remains at $7, the long-run supply curve is perfectly elastic. The long-run supply curve is horizontal because factor prices are constant and there are constant returns to scale. That is, factor prices do not increase as industry output increases. Economists call this market a *constant-cost industry*. Two other possibilities exist: an *increasing-cost industry* (in which factor prices rise as more firms enter the market and existing firms expand production) and a *decreasing-cost industry* (in which factor prices fall as industry output expands).

Factor prices are likely to rise when industry output increases if the factors of production are specialized. An increase in the demand for the factors of production that accompanies an increase in output, in this case, will bid up factor prices. The effect on long-run supply is the following: The rise in factor prices forces costs up for each individual firm and increases the price at which firms earn zero profit. Firms will stop entering the market and expanding production at a higher equilibrium price since the price at which zero profit is made has risen. Therefore, in increasing-cost industries, the long-run supply curve is upward-sloping. In the extreme case, in which all firms in an industry are competitively supplying a perfectly inelastic resource or factor input, the long-run market supply curve is perfectly inelastic (vertical). Any increase in demand would increase the price of that factor. Costs would rise in response to the increase in demand; output would not. Input costs would also rise if there are diseconomies of scale in the input-supplying industry. In both cases, the long-run equilibrium price would have been higher and output would have been lower than if input prices remained constant.[3]

The other possibility is a decreasing-cost industry. If factor prices decline when industry output expands, individual firms' cost curves shift down. As they do, the price at which the zero profit condition falls and the price at which firms cease to enter the market also falls. In this case, the long-run market supply curve is downward-sloping. Factor prices may decline as output rises when new entrants make it more cost-effective for other firms to provide services to all firms in the area. The supply of factors of production expands and reduces the price of inputs to production.

Notice that in the long-run equilibrium, once again zero profit is being made. Long-run equilibrium is defined by zero economic profit. Notice also that the long-run supply curve is more elastic than the short-run supply curve. That's because output changes are much less costly in the long run than in the short run. *In the short run, the price does more of the adjusting. In the long run, more of the adjustment is done by quantity.*

A REMINDER

A Summary of a Perfectly Competitive Industry

Four things to remember when considering a perfectly competitive industry are

1. The profit-maximizing condition for perfectly competitive firms is $MC = MR = P$.
2. To determine profit or loss at the profit-maximizing level of output, subtract the average total cost at that level of output from the price and multiply the result by the output level.
3. Firms will shut down production if price falls below the minimum of their average variable costs.
4. A perfectly competitive firm is in long-run equilibrium only when it is earning zero economic profit, or when price equals the minimum of long-run average total costs.

Q-10 In the early 2000s, demand for burkhas (the garment the Taliban had required Afghani women to wear) declined when the Taliban were ousted. In the short run, what would you expect to happen to the price of burkhas? How about in the long run?

An Example in the Real World

The perfectly competitive model and the reasoning underlying it are extremely powerful. With them you have a simple model to use as a first approach to predict the effect of an event, or to explain why an event occurred. For example, consider the decision of the owners of the Kmart chain of department stores to close nearly 300 stores after experiencing two years of losses.

Web Note 14.4
Is It Perfect Competition or Not?

Figure 14-8 shows what happened. Initially, Kmart saw the losses it was suffering as temporary. In the two years prior to the shutdown decision, Kmart's cost curves looked

[3] To check your understanding, ask yourself the following question: What if there had been economies of scale? If you answered, "There couldn't have been," you're really into economic thinking. (For those of you who aren't all that heavily into economic thinking, the reason is that if there had been economies of scale, the market structure would not have been perfectly competitive. One firm would have kept expanding and expanding and, as it did, its costs would have kept falling.)

FIGURE 14-8 A Real-World Example: A Shutdown Decision

Supply/demand analysis can be applied to a wide variety of real-world examples. This exhibit shows one, but there are many more. As you experience life today, a good exercise is to put on your supply/demand glasses and interpret everything you see in a supply/demand framework.

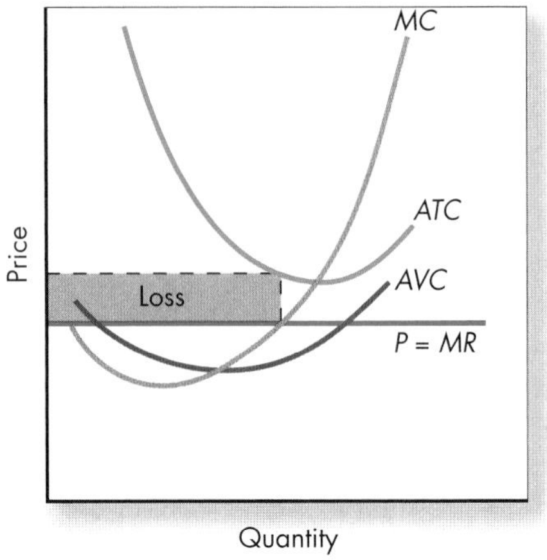

like those in Figure 14-8. Since price exceeded average variable cost, Kmart continued to produce even though it was making a loss.

But after two years of losses, Kmart's perspective changed. The company moved from the short run to the long run. Kmart began to believe that the demand wasn't temporarily low but rather permanently low. It began to ask: What costs are truly fixed and what costs are simply indivisible costs that we can save if we close down completely, selling our buildings and reducing our overhead? Since in the long run all costs are variable, the *ATC* became its relevant *AVC*. Kmart recognized that prices had fallen below these long-run average costs. At that point, it shut down those stores for which $P < AVC$.

There are hundreds of other real-world examples to which the perfectly competitive model adds insight. That's one reason why it's important to keep it in the back of your mind.

Conclusion

We've come to the end of the presentation of perfect competition. It was tough going, but if you went through it carefully, it will serve you well, both as a basis for later chapters and as a reference point for how real-world economies work. But like many good things, a complete understanding of the chapter doesn't come easy.

Summary

- The necessary conditions for perfect competition are that buyers and sellers be price takers, the number of firms be large, there be no barriers to entry, firms' products be identical, there be complete information, and sellers be profit-maximizing entrepreneurial firms.
- The profit-maximizing position of a competitive firm is where marginal revenue equals marginal cost.
- The supply curve of a competitive firm is its marginal cost curve. Only competitive firms have supply curves.

- To find the profit-maximizing level of output for a perfect competitor, find that level of output where $MC = MR$. Profit is price less average total cost times output at the profit-maximizing level of output.
- In the short run, competitive firms can make a profit or loss. In the long run, they make zero profits.
- The shutdown price for a perfectly competitive firm is a price below average variable cost.
- The short-run market supply curve is the horizontal summation of the marginal cost curves for all firms in the market. An increase in the number of firms in the market shifts the market supply curve to the right, while a decrease shifts it to the left.
- Perfectly competitive firms make zero profit in the long run because if profit were being made, new firms would enter and the market price would decline, eliminating the profit. If losses were being made, firms would exit and the market price would rise.
- The long-run supply curve is a schedule of quantities supplied where firms are making zero profit.
- The slope of the long-run supply curve depends on what happens to factor prices when output increases.
- Constant-cost industries have horizontal long-run supply curves. Increasing-cost industries have upward-sloping long-run supply curves, and decreasing-cost industries have downward-sloping long-run supply curves.

Key Terms

barriers to entry *(318)*
marginal cost (MC) *(321)*
marginal revenue (MR) *(321)*
market supply curve *(328)*
normal profit *(330)*
perfectly competitive market *(317)*
price taker *(318)*
profit-maximizing condition *(322)*
shutdown point *(328)*

Questions and Exercises

1. Why must buyers and sellers be price takers for a market to be perfectly competitive? LO1
2. Draw marginal cost, marginal revenue, and average total cost curves for a typical perfectly competitive firm and indicate the profit-maximizing level of output and total profit for that firm. Is the firm in long-run equilibrium? Why or why not? LO4, LO6
3. Draw marginal cost, marginal revenue, and average total cost curves for a typical perfectly competitive firm in long-run equilibrium and indicate the profit-maximizing level of output and total profit for that firm. LO6
4. What portion of the marginal cost curve is the firm's supply curve? LO3
5. What will be the effect of a technological development that reduces marginal costs in a competitive market on short-run price, quantity, and profit? LO3, LO4
6. You're thinking of buying one of two firms. One has a profit margin of \$8 per unit; the other has a profit margin of \$4 per unit. Which should you buy? Why? (Difficult) LO4
7. A perfectly competitive firm sells its good for \$20. If marginal cost is four times the quantity produced, how much does the firm produce? Why? (Difficult) LO4
8. State what is *wrong* with each of the graphs. LO4

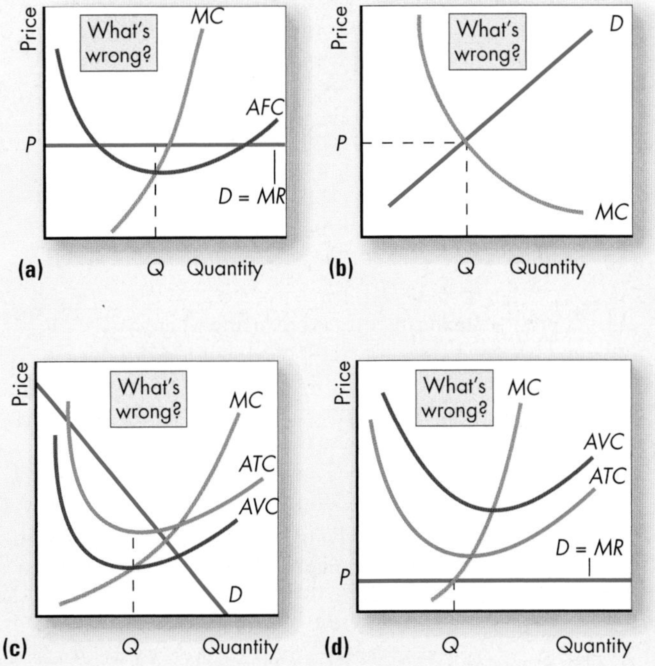

9. Graphically demonstrate the quantity and price of a perfectly competitive firm.
   a. Why is a slightly larger quantity not preferred?
   b. Why is a slightly lower quantity not preferred?
   c. Label the shutdown point in your diagram.
   d. You have just discovered that shutting down means that you would lose your land zoning permit, which is required to start operating again. How does that change your answer to *c*? LO4
10. How is a firm's marginal cost curve related to the market supply curve? LO5
11. Draw the *ATC*, *AVC*, and *MC* curves for a typical firm. Label the price at which the firm would shut down temporarily and the price at which the firm would exit the market in the long run. LO6
12. Under what cost condition is the shutdown point the same as the point at which a firm exits the market? LO6
13. a. Based on the following table, what is the profit-maximizing output?

Output	Price	Total Costs
0	$10	$ 31
1	10	40
2	10	45
3	10	48
4	10	55
5	10	65
6	10	80
7	10	100
8	10	140
9	10	220
10	10	340

   b. How would your answer change if, in response to an increase in demand, the price of the good increased to $15? LO2, LO4
14. A profit-maximizing firm is producing where *MR* = MC and has an average total cost of $4, but it gets a price of $3 for each good it sells.
   a. What would you advise the firm to do?
   b. What would you advise the firm to do if you knew average variable costs were $3.50? LO2, LO4, LO6
15. Each of 10 firms in a given industry has the costs given in the left-hand table. The market demand schedule is given in the right-hand table.

Quantity	Total Cost
0	12
1	24
2	27
3	31
4	39
5	53
6	73
7	99

Price	Quantity Demanded
2	110
4	100
6	90
8	80
10	70
12	60
14	50
16	40

   a. What is the market equilibrium price and the price each firm gets for its product?
   b. What is the equilibrium market quantity and the quantity each firm produces?
   c. What profit is each firm making?
   d. Below what price will firms begin to exit the market? LO4, LO6
16. Why is the long-run market supply curve upward-sloping in an increasing-cost industry? LO7
17. Why is the long-run market supply curve downward-sloping in a decreasing-cost industry? LO7
18. Why is the long-run market supply curve horizontal in a constant-cost industry? LO7
19. A farmer is producing where MC = *MR*. Say that half of the cost of producing wheat is the rental cost of land (a fixed cost) and half is the cost of labor and machines (a variable cost). If the average total cost of producing wheat is $8 and the price of wheat is $6, what would you advise the farmer to do? ("Grow something else" is not allowed.) (Difficult) LO2, LO4, LO6
20. Use the accompanying graph, which shows the marginal cost and average total cost curves for the shoe store Zapateria, a perfectly competitive firm.
   a. How many pairs of shoes will Zapateria produce if the market price of shoes is $70 a pair?
   b. What is the total profit Zapateria will earn if the market price of shoes is $70 a pair?
   c. Should Zapateria expect more shoe stores to enter this market? Why or why not?
   d. What is the long-run equilibrium price in the shoe market assuming it is a constant-cost industry? LO4, LO7

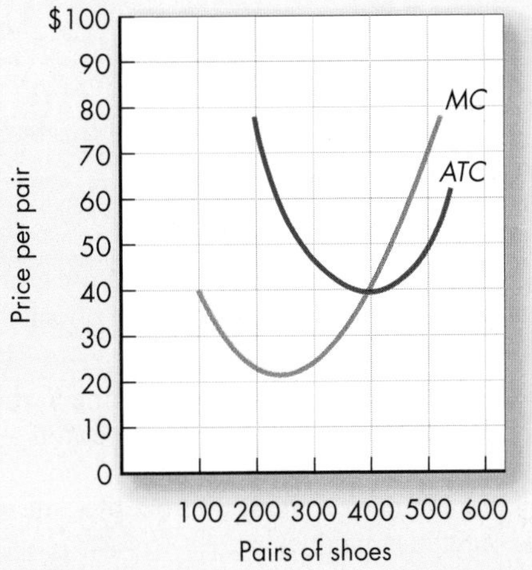

21. Suppose an increasing-cost industry is in both long-run and short-run equilibrium. Explain what will happen to the following in the long run if the demand for that product declines:
    a. Price.
    b. Quantity.
    c. Number of firms in the market.
    d. Profit. LO7
22. A *Wall Street Journal* headline states: "A Nation of Snackers Snubs Old Favorite: The Beloved Cookie." As U.S. consumers adopted more carbohydrate-conscious diets, the number of cookie boxes sold declined 5.4 percent that year, the third consecutive year of decline.
    a. Assuming the cookie industry is perfectly competitive, demonstrate using market supply and demand curves the effect of this decline in demand on equilibrium price and quantity in the short run.
    b. Assuming a cookie firm was in equilibrium before the change in demand, and that it is a constant-cost industry, demonstrate the effect of the decline on equilibrium price for an individual cookie firm in the short run.
    c. How might your answer to *a* change if you are considering the long run? LO7
23. Demonstrate the effect of the following on demand and supply in the short run and the long run.
    a. In 2005 a decades-old textile quota expired, reducing demand for textiles imported from Mexico under the quota-free North American Free Trade Agreement. The biggest competition Mexico faces is from the Chinese textile market. Market: Mexican textile market. (Assume this is an increasing-cost industry.)
    b. In the 1990s the European Union harmonized all taxes, which raised taxes on French restaurants. Assume restaurants are a constant-cost industry. LO7

Questions from Alternative Perspectives

1. The book presents the perfectly competitive model as the foundation for economic analysis.
    a. How well does the theory of perfect competition reflect the real world?
    b. What role, if any, does the government have in promoting perfectly competitive markets?
    c. What is the danger in the government's intervening to promote competitive markets? (Austrian)
2. This chapter discusses perfect competition as a benchmark to think about the economy.
    a. Can labor market discrimination—hiring someone on the basis of race or gender rather than capability—exist in a perfectly competitive industry?
    b. Can the elimination of discrimination increase efficiency? (Feminist)
3. Perfect competition is analytically elegant.
    a. What percent of an economy's total production do you think is provided by perfectly competitive firms?
    b. Based on your answer to *a*, why does the text spend so much time on perfect competition? (Institutionalist)
4. The perfectly competitive model assumes that firms know when marginal revenue equals marginal costs.
    a. If a firm doesn't have this information, can it produce at the profit-maximizing level of output?
    b. If firms don't have such knowledge, how might the theory of perfect competition be changed to better reflect reality? (Post-Keynesian)
5. As the chapter points out, the Internet has made the U.S. economy more competitive by lowering barriers to entry and exit from industries.
    a. To what extent is the Internet itself competitive?
    b. Can competitive conditions develop from information technology, a techology that was created initially by centralized planning, that depends on agreed-upon rules to conduct business, and that has notoriously low marginal costs? (Think of the cost of burning a CD off the Internet.) (Radical)

Issues to Ponder

1. If a firm is owned by its workers but otherwise meets all the qualifications for a perfectly competitive firm, will its price and output decisions differ from the price and output decisions of a perfectly competitive firm? Why? (Difficult) LO4
2. The milk industry has a number of interesting aspects. Provide economic explanations for the following: (Difficult)
   a. Fluid milk is 87 percent water. It can be dried and reconstituted so that it is almost indistinguishable from fresh milk. What is a likely reason that such reconstituted milk is not produced?
   b. The United States has regional milk-marketing regulations whose goals are to make each of the regions self-sufficient in milk. What is a likely reason for this?
   c. A U.S. senator from a milk-producing state has been quoted as saying, "I am absolutely convinced . . . that simply bringing down dairy price supports is not a way to cut production." Is it likely that he is correct? What is a probable reason for his statement? LO4
3. A California biotechnology firm submitted a tomato that will not rot for weeks to the U.S. Food and Drug Administration. It designed such a fruit by changing the genetic structure of the tomato. What effect will this technological change have on (Difficult)
   a. The price of tomatoes?
   b. Farmers who grow tomatoes?
   c. The geographic areas where tomatoes are grown?
   d. Where tomatoes are generally placed on salad bars in winter? LO4
4. Hundreds of music stores have been closing in the face of stagnant demand for CDs and new competitors—online music vendors and discount retailers.
   a. How would price competition from these new sources cause a retail store to close.
   b. In the long run, what effect will new entrants have on the price of CDs? LO7
5. In 2004 FAO Schwartz closed its 89 Zany Brainy stores.
   a. Demonstrate graphically the relationship between *ATC*, *AVC*, and price faced by Zany Brainy stores when they decided to close.
   b. Assuming the market is perfectly competitive and is a constant-cost industry, what will happen in this market in the long run? Demonstrate with market supply and demand curves. LO7

Answers to Margin Questions

1. Without the assumption of no barriers to entry, firms could make a profit by raising price; hence, their demand curve would not be perfectly elastic and, hence, perfect competition would not exist. *(318)*
2. The competitive firm is such a small portion of the total market that it can have no effect on price. Consequently it takes the price as given, and, hence, its perceived demand curve is perfectly elastic. *(320)*
3. To determine the profit-maximizing output of a competitive firm, you must know price and marginal cost. *(322)*
4. Firms are interested in getting as much for themselves as they possibly can. Maximizing total profit does this. Maximizing profit per unit might yield very small total profits. *(323)*
5. If the firm in Figure 14-5 were producing 4 units, I would explain to it that the marginal cost of increasing output is only $12 and the marginal revenue is $35, so it should significantly expand output until 8, where the marginal cost equals the marginal revenue, or price. *(326)*
6. The diagram is drawn with the wrong profit-maximizing output and, hence, the wrong profit. Output is determined where marginal cost equals price and profit is the difference between the average total cost and price at that output, not at the output where marginal cost equals average total cost. The correct diagram is shown here. *(328)*

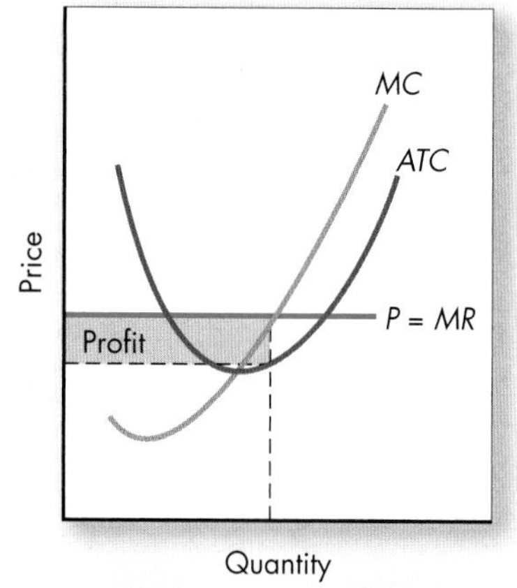

7. The marginal cost for airlines is significantly below average total cost. Since they're recovering their average variable cost, they continue to operate. In the long run, if this continues, some airlines will be forced out of business. *(328)*
8. The costs for a firm include the normal costs, which in turn include a return for all factors of production. Thus, it is worthwhile for a competitive firm to stay in business, since it is doing better than, or at least as well as, it could in any other activity. *(330)*
9. Suddenly becoming the "in" thing to wear would cause the demand for berets to shift out to the right, pushing the price up in the short run. In the long run, the market is probably not perfectly competitive and it would likely push the price down because there probably are considerable economies of scale in the production of berets. *(332)*
10. A decline in demand pushed the short-run price of these burkhas down. In the long run, however, once a number of burkha makers go out of business, the price of burkhas should eventually move back to approximately where it was before the decline, assuming constant input prices. *(333)*

CHAPTER 15

Monopoly

Monopoly is business at the end of its journey.

—Henry Demarest Lloyd

In the last chapter we considered perfect competition. We now move to the other end of the spectrum: monopoly. **Monopoly** is *a market structure in which one firm makes up the entire market*. It is the polar opposite to competition. It is a market structure in which the firm faces no competitive pressure from other firms.

Monopolies exist because of barriers to entry into a market that prevent competition. These can be legal barriers (as in the case where a firm has a patent that prevents other firms from entering), sociological barriers where entry is prevented by custom or tradition, natural barriers where the firm has a unique ability to produce what other firms can't duplicate, or technological barriers where the size of the market can support only one firm.

AFTER READING THIS CHAPTER, YOU SHOULD BE ABLE TO:

1. Summarize how and why the decisions facing a monopolist differ from the collective decisions of competing firms.
2. Explain why $MC = MR$ maximizes total profit for a monopolist.
3. Determine a monopolist's price, output, and profit graphically and numerically.
4. Show graphically the welfare loss from monopoly.
5. Explain why a price-discriminating monopolist will earn more profit than a normal monopolist.
6. Explain why there would be no monopoly without barriers to entry.
7. List three normative arguments against monopoly.

The Key Difference between a Monopolist and a Perfect Competitor

A key question we want to answer in this chapter is: How does a monopolist's decision differ from the collective decision of competing firms (i.e., from the competitive solution)? Answering that question brings out a key difference between a competitive firm and a monopoly. Since a competitive firm is too small to affect the price, it does not take into account the effect of its output decision on the price it receives. A competitive firm's marginal revenue (the additional revenue it receives from selling an additional unit of output) is the given market price. A monopolistic firm takes into account that its output decision can affect price; its marginal revenue is not its price. A monopolistic firm will reason: "If I increase production, the price I can get for each unit sold will fall, so I had better be careful about how much I increase production."

Let's consider an example. Say your drawings in the margins of this book are seen by a traveling art critic who decides you're the greatest thing since Rembrandt, or at least since Andy Warhol. Carefully he tears each page out of the book, mounts them on special paper, and numbers them: Doodle Number 1

(Doodle While Contemplating Demand), Doodle Number 2 (Doodle While Contemplating Production), and so on.

All told, he has 100. He figures, with the right advertising and if you're a hit on the art circuit, he'll have a monopoly in your doodles. He plans to sell them for $20,000 each: He gets 50 percent, you get 50 percent. That's $1 million for you. You tell him, "Hey, man! I can doodle my way through the entire book. I'll get you 500 doodles. Then I get $5 million and you get $5 million."

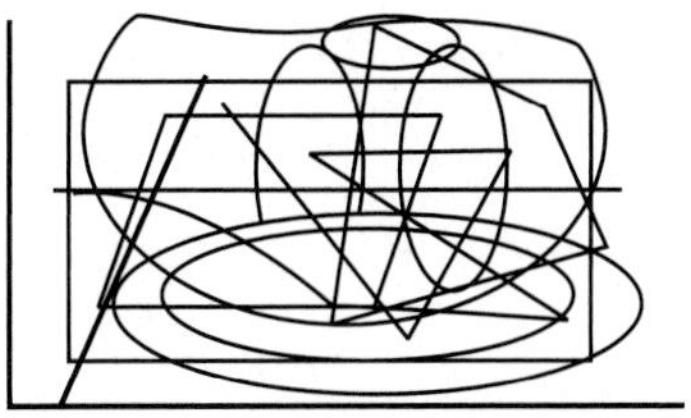

Doodle Number 27: Contemplating Costs

The art critic has a pained look on his face. He says, "You've been doodling when you should have been studying. Your doodles are worth $20,000 each only if they're rare. If there are 500, they're worth $1,000 each. And if it becomes known that you can turn them out that fast, they'll be worth nothing. I won't be able to limit quantity at all, and my monopoly will be lost. So obviously we must figure out some way that you won't doodle anymore—and study instead. Oh, by the way, did you know that the price of an artist's work goes up significantly when he or she dies? Hmm?" At that point you decide to forget doodling and to start studying, and to remember always that increasing production doesn't necessarily make suppliers better off.

Q-1 Why should you study rather than doodle?

As we saw in the last chapter, competitive firms do not take advantage of that insight. Each individual competitive firm, responding to its self-interest, is not doing what is in the interest of the firms collectively. In competitive markets, as one supplier is pitted against another, consumers benefit. In monopolistic markets, the firm faces no competitors and does what is in its best interest. Monopolists can see to it that the monopolists, not the consumers, benefit; perfectly competitive firms cannot.

Monopolists see to it that monopolists, not consumers, benefit.

A Model of Monopoly

How much should the monopolistic firm choose to produce if it wants to maximize profit? To answer that we have to consider more carefully the effect that changing output has on the total profit of the monopolist. That's what we do in this section. First, we consider a numerical example; then we consider that same example graphically. The relevant information for our example is presented in Table 15-1.

Determining the Monopolist's Price and Output Numerically

Table 15-1 shows the price, total revenue, marginal revenue, total cost, marginal cost, average total cost, and profit at various levels of production. It's similar to the table in

TABLE 15-1 Monopolistic Profit Maximization

1 Quantity	2 Price	3 Total Revenue	4 Marginal Revenue	5 Total Cost	6 Marginal Cost	7 Average Total Cost	8 Profit
0	$36	$ 0		$ 47			$−47
			$33		$ 1		
1	33	33		48		$48.00	−15
			27		2		
2	30	60		50		25.00	10
			21		4		
3	27	81		54		18.00	27
			15		8		
4	24	96		62		15.50	34
			9		16		
5	21	105		78		15.60	27
			3		24		
6	18	108		102		17.00	6
			−3		40		
7	15	105		142		20.29	−37
			−9		56		
8	12	96		198		24.75	−102
			−15		80		
9	9	81		278		30.89	−197

the last chapter where we determined a competitive firm's output. The big difference is that marginal revenue changes as output changes and is not equal to the price. Why?

First, let's remember the definition of marginal revenue: Marginal revenue is the change in total revenue associated with a change in quantity. In this example, if a monopolist increases output from 4 to 5, the price it can charge falls from \$24 to \$21 and its revenue increases from \$96 to \$105, so marginal revenue is \$9. Marginal revenue of increasing output from 4 to 5 for the monopolist reflects two changes: a \$21 gain in revenue from selling the 5th unit and a \$12 decline in revenue because the monopolist must lower the price on the previous 4 units it produces by \$3 a unit, from \$24 to \$21. This highlights the key characteristic of a monopolist—its output decision affects its price. Because an increase in output lowers the price on all previous units, a monopolist's marginal revenue is always below its price. Comparing columns 2 and 4, you can confirm that this is true.

A monopolist's marginal revenue is always below its price.

Now let's see if the monopolist will increase production from 4 to 5 units. The marginal revenue of increasing output from 4 to 5 is \$9, and the marginal cost of doing so is \$16. Since marginal cost exceeds marginal revenue, increasing production from 4 to 5 will reduce total profit and the monopolist will not increase production. If it decreases output from 4 to 3, where MC < *MR*, the revenue it loses (\$15) exceeds the reduction in costs (\$8). It will not reduce output from 4 to 3. Since it cannot increase total profit by increasing output to 5 or decreasing output to 3, it is maximizing profit at 4 units.

Q-2 In Table 15-1, explain why 4 is the profit-maximizing output.

As you can tell from the table, profits are highest (\$34) at 4 units of output and a price of \$24. At 3 units of output and a price of \$27, the firm has total revenue of \$81 and total cost of \$54, yielding a profit of \$27. At 5 units of output and a price of \$21, the firm has a total revenue of \$105 and a total cost of \$78, also for a profit of \$27. The highest profit it can make is \$34, which the firm earns when it produces 4 units. This is its profit-maximizing level.

Determining the Monopolist's Price and Output Graphically

The monopolist's output decision also can be seen graphically. Figure 15-1 graphs the table's information into a demand curve, a marginal revenue curve, and a marginal cost

FIGURE 15-1

Determining the Monopolist's Price and Output Graphically

The profit-maximizing output is determined where the MC curve intersects the *MR* curve. To determine the price (at which MC = *MR*) that would be charged if this industry were a monopolist with the same cost structure as that of firms in a competitive market, we first find that output and then extend a line to the demand curve, in this case finding a price of \$24. This price is higher than the competitive price, \$20.50, and the quantity, 4, is lower than the competitor's quantity, 5.17.

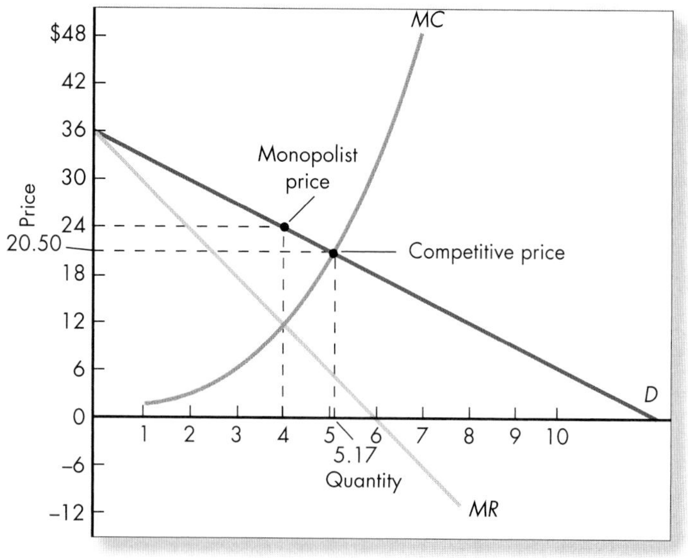

ADDED DIMENSION

A Trick in Graphing the Marginal Revenue Curve

Here's a trick to help you graph the marginal revenue curve. The *MR* line starts at the same point on the price axis as does a linear demand curve, but it intersects the quantity axis at a point half the distance from where the demand curve intersects the quantity axis. (If the demand curve isn't linear, you can use the same trick if you use lines tangent to the curved demand curve.) So you can extend the demand curve to the two axes and measure halfway on the quantity axis (3 in the graph on the right). Then draw a line from where the demand curve intersects the price axis to that halfway mark. That line is the marginal revenue curve.

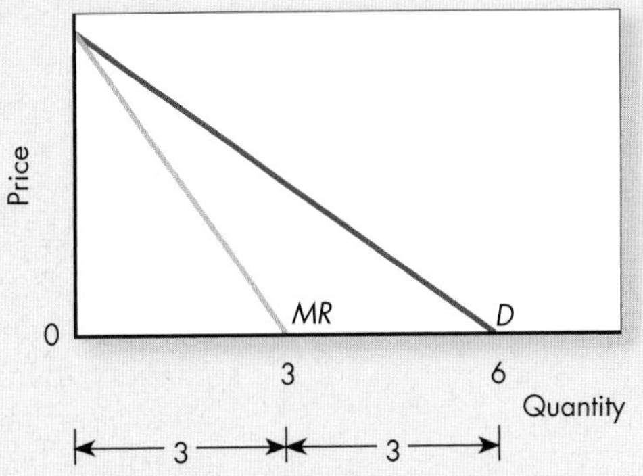

curve. The marginal cost curve is a graph of the change in the firm's total cost as it changes output. It's the same curve as we saw in our discussion of perfect competition. The marginal revenue curve tells us the change in total revenue when quantity changes. It is graphed by plotting and connecting the points given by quantity and marginal revenue in Table 15-1.

The marginal revenue curve for a monopolist is new, so let's consider it a bit more carefully. It tells us the additional revenue the firm will get by expanding output. It is a downward-sloping curve that begins at the same point as the demand curve but has a steeper slope. In this example, marginal revenue is positive up until the firm produces 6 units. Then marginal revenue is negative; after 6 units the firm's total revenue decreases when it increases output.

Notice specifically the relationship between the demand curve (which is the average revenue curve) and the marginal revenue curve. Since the demand curve is downward-sloping, the marginal revenue curve is below the average revenue curve. (Remember, if the average curve is falling, the marginal curve must be below it.)

Having plotted these curves, let's ask the same questions as we did before: What output should the monopolist produce, and what price can it charge? In answering those questions, the key curves to look at are the marginal cost curve and the marginal revenue curve.

Q-3 In the graph below, indicate the monopolist's profit-maximizing level of output and the price it would charge.

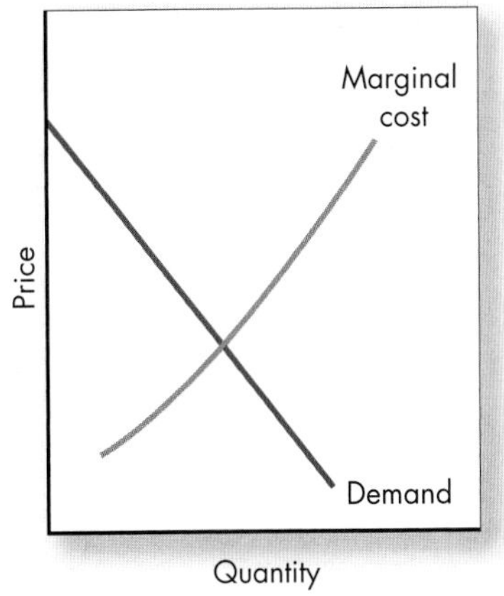

MR = MC *Determines the Profit-Maximizing Output* The monopolist uses the general rule that any firm must follow to maximize profit: Produce the quantity at which MC = MR. If you think about it, it makes sense that the point where marginal revenue equals marginal cost determines the profit-maximizing output. If the marginal revenue is below the marginal cost, it makes sense to reduce production. Doing so decreases marginal cost and increases marginal revenue. When MR < MC, reducing output increases total profit. If marginal cost is below marginal revenue, you should increase production because total profit will rise. If the marginal revenue is equal to marginal cost, it does not make sense to increase or reduce production. So the monopolist should produce at the output level where MC = MR. As you can see, the output

MR and Profit Maximization in Monopoly

the monopolist chooses is 4 units, the same output that we determined numerically.[1] This leads to the following insights:

The general rule that any firm must follow to maximize profit is: Produce at an output level at which $MC = MR$.

If $MR > MC$, the monopolist gains profit by increasing output.

If $MR < MC$, the monopolist gains profit by decreasing output.

If $MC = MR$, the monopolist is maximizing profit.

Thus, $MR = MC$ is the profit-maximizing rule for a monopolist.

The Price a Monopolist Will Charge The $MR = MC$ condition determines the quantity a monopolist produces; in turn, that quantity determines the price the firm will charge. A monopolist will charge the maximum price consumers are willing to pay for that quantity. Since the demand curve tells us what consumers will pay for a given quantity, to find the price a monopolist will charge, you must extend the quantity line up to the demand curve. We do so in Figure 15-1 and see that the profit-maximizing output level of 4 allows a monopolist to charge a price of $24.

Comparing Monopoly and Perfect Competition

Q-4 Why does a monopolist produce less output than would perfectly competitive firms in the same industry?

For a competitive industry, the horizontal summation of firms' marginal cost curves is the market supply curve.[2] Output for a perfectly competitive industry would be 5.17, and price would be $20.50, as Figure 15-1 shows. The monopolist's output was 4 and its price was $24. So, if a competitive market is made into a monopoly, you can see that output would be lower and price would be higher. The reason is that the monopolist takes into account the effect that restricting output has on price.

Equilibrium output for the monopolist, like equilibrium output for the competitor, is determined by the $MC = MR$ condition, but because the monopolist's marginal revenue is below its price, its equilibrium output is different from a competitive market.

An Example of Finding Output and Price

We've covered a lot of material quickly, so it's probably helpful to go through an example slowly and carefully review the reasoning process. Here's the problem:

> Say that a monopolist with marginal cost curve MC faces a demand curve *D* in Figure 15-2(a). Determine the price and output the monopolist would choose.

The first step is to draw the marginal revenue curve, since we know that a monopolist's profit-maximizing output level is determined where $MC = MR$. We do that in Figure 15-2(b), remembering the trick in the box on page 343 of extending our demand curve back to the vertical and horizontal axes and then bisecting the horizontal axis.

The second step is to determine where $MC = MR$. Having found that point, we extend a line up to the demand curve and down to the quantity axis to determine the output the monopolist chooses, Q_M. We do this in Figure 15-2(c). Finally we see where the quantity line intersects the demand curve. Then we extend a horizontal line from that point to the price axis, as in Figure 15-2(d). This determines the price the monopolist will charge, P_M.

---

[1]This could not be seen precisely in Table 15-1 since the table is for discrete jumps and does not tell us the marginal cost and marginal revenue exactly at 4; it only tells us the marginal cost and marginal revenue ($8 and $15, respectively) of moving from 3 to 4 and the marginal cost and marginal revenue ($16 and $9, respectively) of moving from 4 to 5. If small adjustments (1/100 of a unit or so) were possible, the marginal cost and marginal revenue precisely at 4 would be $12.

[2]The above statement has some qualifications best left to intermediate classes.

FIGURE 15-2 (A, B, C, AND D) Finding the Monopolist's Price and Output

Determining a monopolist's price and output can be tricky. The text discusses the steps shown in this figure. To make sure you understand, try to go through the steps on your own, and then check your work with the text.

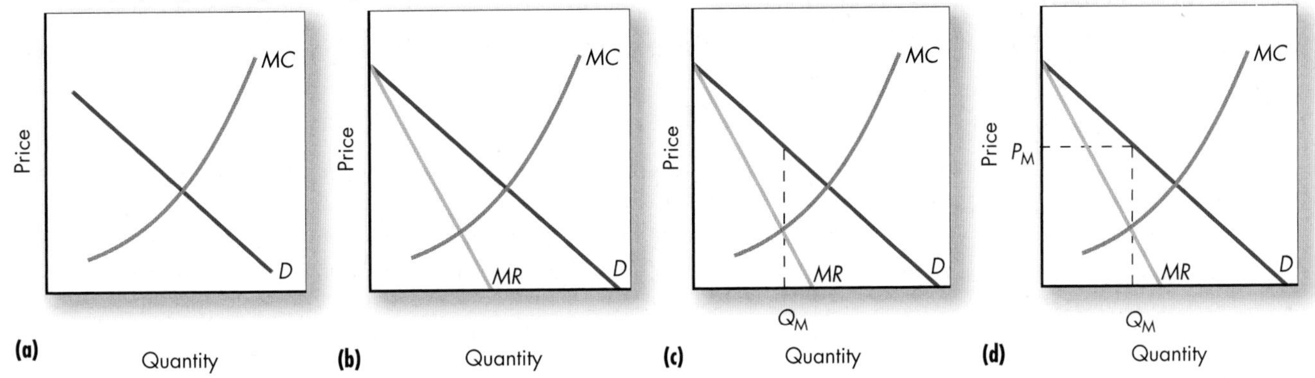

Profits and Monopoly

The monopolist's profit can be determined only by comparing average total cost to price. So before we can determine profit, we need to add another curve: the average total cost curve. As we saw with a perfect competitor, it's important to follow the correct sequence when finding profit:

- First, draw the firm's marginal revenue curve.
- Second, determine the output the monopolist will produce by the intersection of the marginal cost and marginal revenue curves.
- Third, determine the price the monopolist will charge for that output. (Remember, the price it will charge depends on the demand curve.)
- Fourth, determine the monopolist's profit (loss) by subtracting average total cost from average revenue (*P*) at that level of output and multiplying by the chosen output.

If price exceeds average total cost at the output it chooses, the monopolist will make a profit. If price equals average total cost, the monopolist will make no profit (but it will make a normal return). If price is less than average cost, the monopolist will incur a loss: Total cost exceeds total revenue.

Q-5 Indicate the profit that the monopolist shown in the graph below earns.

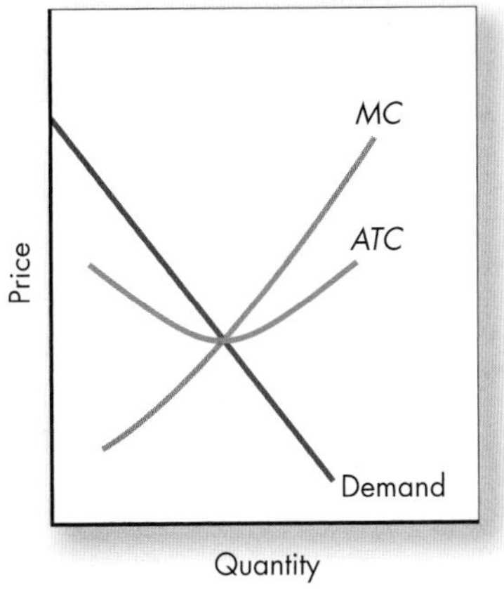

A Monopolist Making a Profit

I consider the case of a monopolist making a profit in Figure 15-3, going through the steps slowly. The monopolist's demand, marginal cost, and average total cost curves are presented in Figure 15-3(a). Our first step is to draw the marginal revenue curve, which has been added in Figure 15-3(b). The second step is to find the output level at which marginal cost equals marginal revenue. From that point, draw a vertical line to the horizontal (quantity) axis. That intersection tells us the monopolist's output, Q_M in Figure 15-3(b). The third step is to find what price the monopolist will charge at that output. We do so by extending the vertical line to the demand curve (point A) and then extending a horizontal line over to the price axis. Doing so gives price, P_M. Our fourth step is to determine the average total cost at that quantity. We do so by seeing where our vertical line at the chosen output intersects the

A REMINDER

Finding a Monopolist's Output, Price, and Profit

To find a monopolist's level of output, price, and profit, follow these four steps:

1. Draw the marginal revenue curve.
2. Determine the output the monopolist will produce: The profit-maximizing level of output is where the *MR* and *MC* curves intersect.
3. Determine the price the monopolist will charge: Extend a line from where *MR* = *MC* up to the demand curve. Where this line intersects the demand curve is the monopolist's price.
4. Determine the profit the monopolist will earn: Subtract the *ATC* from price at the profit-maximizing level of output to get profit per unit. Multiply profit per unit by quantity of output to get total profit.

average total cost curve (point *B*). That tells us the monopolist's average cost at its chosen output.

To determine profit, we extend lines from where the quantity line intersects the demand curve (point *A*) and the average total cost curve (point *B*) to the price axis in Figure 15-3(c). The resulting shaded rectangle in Figure 15-3(c) represents the monopolist's profit.

A Monopolist Breaking Even and Making a Loss

In Figure 15-4 we consider two other average total cost curves to show you that a monopolist may make a loss or no profit as well as an economic profit. In Figure 15-4(a) the monopolist is making zero profit; in Figure 15-4(b) it's making a loss. Whether a firm is making a profit, zero profit, or a loss depends on average total costs relative to price. So clearly, in the short run, a monopolist can be making either a profit or a loss, or it can be breaking even.

Most of you, if you've been paying attention, will say, "Sure, in the model monopolists might not make a profit, but in the real world monopolists are making a killing." And it is true that numerous monopolists make a killing. But many more monopolists just break even or lose money. Each year the U.S. Patent Office issues nearly 500,000 patents. A **patent** is *legal protection of a technical innovation that gives the person holding it sole right to use that innovation*—in other words, it gives the holder a monopoly to produce a good. Most patented goods make a loss; in fact, the cost of getting the patent often exceeds the revenues from selling the product.

Each year the Home Shopping Network (HSN) considers thousands of products, and only a very few actually make it onto the network. Let's consider an example—the self-stirring pot. It was a pot with a battery-operated stirrer attached to its lid. The stirrer was designed to prevent the bottom of the pot from burning. Unfortunately for the inventor, HSN considered the cost (even after economies of scale were taken into account) far

FIGURE 15-3 (A, B, AND C) **Determining Profit for a Monopolist**

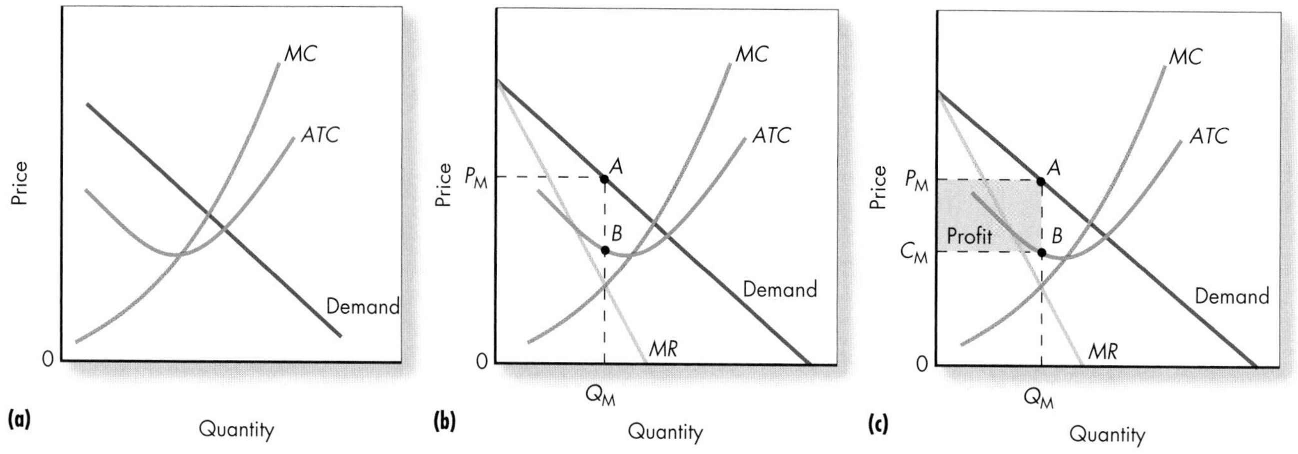

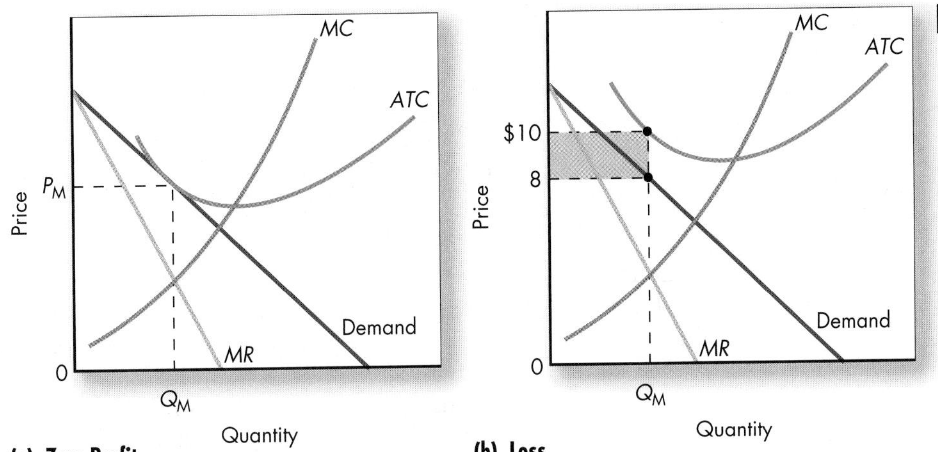

(a) Zero Profit **(b) Loss**

FIGURE 15-4 (A AND B)
Other Monopoly Cases

Depending on where the *ATC* curve falls, a monopolist can make a profit, break even (as in (**a**)), or make a loss (as in (**b**)) in the short run. In the long run, a monopolist who is making a loss will get out of business.

more than what people would be willing to pay and therefore decided not to include the pot in its offerings. The inventor had a monopoly on the production and sale of the self-stirring pot, but only a loss to show for it. Examples like this can be multiplied by the thousands. The reality for many monopolies is that their costs exceed their revenues, so they make a loss.

The Welfare Loss from Monopoly

As we saw above, monopolists aren't guaranteed a profit. Thus, profits can't be the primary reason that the economic model we're using sees monopoly as bad. If not because of profits, then what standard is the economic model using to conclude that monopoly is undesirable?

One reason can be seen by reconsidering graphically the normal monopolist equilibrium and perfectly competitive equilibrium in reference to producer and consumer surplus. This we do in Figure 15-5. In a competitive equilibrium, the total consumer and producer surplus is the area between the demand curve and the marginal cost curve up to market equilibrium quantity Q_C. The monopolist reduces output to Q_M and raises price to P_M. The benefit lost to society from reducing output from Q_C to Q_M is measured by the area under the demand curve between output levels Q_C and Q_M. That area is represented by the shaded areas labeled *A*, *B*, and *D*. Area *A*, however, is regained by society. Society gains the opportunity cost of the resources that are freed up from reducing production—the value of the resources in their next-best use indicated by the shaded area *A*. So the net cost to society of decreasing output from Q_C to Q_M is represented by areas *B* and *D*. (Area *C* simply represents a transfer of surplus from consumers to the monopolist. It is neither a gain nor a loss to society. Since both monopolist and consumer are members of society, the gain and loss net out.) The triangular areas *B* and *D* are the net cost to society from the existence of monopoly.

The welfare loss from monopoly is a triangle, as in the graph below. It is not the loss that most people consider. They are often interested in normative losses that the graph does not capture.

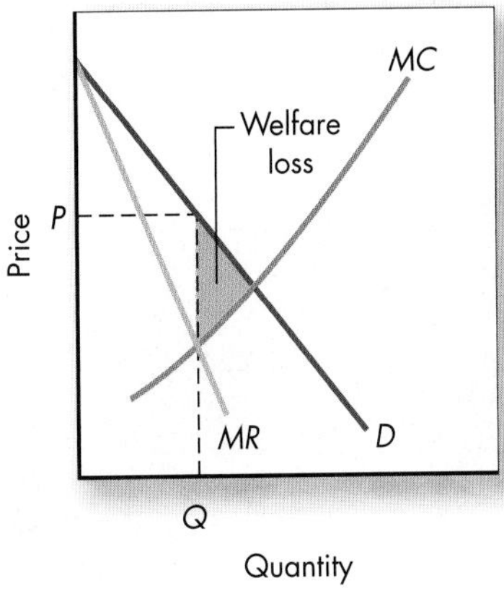

As discussed in an earlier chapter, the area designated by *B* and *D* is often called the *deadweight loss* or *welfare loss triangle*. That welfare cost of monopoly is one of the reasons economists oppose monopoly. That cost can be summarized as follows: Because monopolies charge a price that is higher than marginal cost, people's decisions don't reflect the true cost to society. Price exceeds marginal cost. Because price exceeds marginal cost,

FIGURE 15-5
The Welfare Loss from Monopoly

The welfare loss from a monopoly is represented by the triangles *B* and *D*. The rectangle C is a transfer from consumer surplus to the monopolist. The area *A* represents the opportunity cost of diverted resources. This is not a loss to society since the resources will be used in producing other goods.

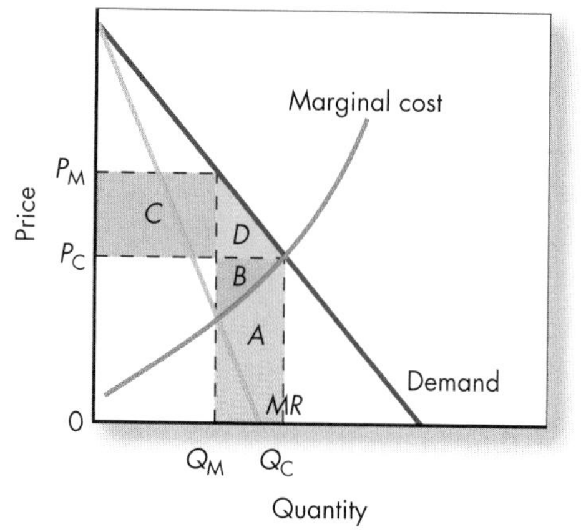

Q-6 Why is area C in Figure 15-5 not considered a loss from monopoly?

people's choices are distorted; they choose to consume less of the monopolist's output and more of some other output than they would if markets were competitive. That distinction means that the marginal cost of increasing output is lower than the marginal benefit of increasing output, so there's a welfare loss.

The Price-Discriminating Monopolist

When a monopolist price-discriminates, it charges individuals high up on the demand curve higher prices and those low on the demand curve lower prices.

So far we've considered monopolists that charge the same price to all consumers. Let's consider what would happen if our monopolist suddenly gained the ability to **price-discriminate**—*to charge different prices to different individuals or groups of individuals* (for example, students as compared to businesspeople). If a monopolist can identify groups of customers who have different elasticities of demand, separate them in some way, and limit their ability to resell its product between groups, it can charge each group a different price. Specifically, it could charge consumers with less elastic demands a higher price and individuals with more elastic demands a lower price. By doing so, it will increase total profit. Suppose, for instance, Megamovie knew that at $10 it would sell 1,000 movie tickets and at $5 a ticket it would sell 1,500 tickets. Assuming Megamovie could show the film without cost, it would maximize profits by charging $10 to 1,000 moviegoers, earning a total profit of $10,000. If, however, it could somehow attract the additional 500 viewers at $5 a ticket without reducing the price to the first 1,000 moviegoers, it could raise its profit by $2,500, to $12,500. As you can see, a price-discriminating monopolist increases its profit.

Web Note 15.1
Divide and Conquer

We see many examples of price discrimination in the real world:

1. *Movie theaters give discounts to senior citizens and children.* Movie theaters charge senior citizens and children a lower price because they have a more elastic demand for movies.
2. *Airline Super Saver fares include Saturday-night stayovers.* This is a method of price discrimination. Businesspeople who have highly inelastic demands generally aren't willing to stay over a Saturday night, so they're charged a high price while tourists and leisure travelers who have far more elastic demands and who are willing to stay over a Saturday night are charged a lower price.
3. *Automobiles are seldom sold at list price.* Once again we have an example of price discrimination. Salespeople can size up the customer and determine the customer's elasticity. People who haven't done the research and don't know that

Automobiles are seldom sold at list price.

selling at 10 percent off list is normal (that is, people with inelastic demands) pay higher prices than people who search out all the alternatives (people with elastic demand).

4. *Tracking consumer information and pricing accordingly*. Two people buying something on the Internet are not necessarily presented with the same price. Firms collect data about individuals with tracking devices called cookies, which are deposited on buyers' computer hard drives, and offer prices according to their estimated elasticity of demand. Thus, when you are searching the Internet for something to buy, you might be presented with a different price than someone else visiting the same site.

To see whether you are following the reasoning, try to provide a price-discrimination explanation for the following:

1. Theaters have special rates on Monday and Tuesday nights.
2. Retail tire companies run special sales about half the time.
3. Restaurants generally make most of their profit on alcoholic drinks and just break even on food.
4. College-town stores often give students discounts.

Q-7 Why does a price-discriminating monopolist make a higher profit than a normal monopolist?

Now that you've answered those, see if you can extend your understanding by listing the central characteristics of markets that make them highly susceptible to price discrimination.

If you answered, "The market demand is made up of distinguishable individuals who have different demand elasticities," you've got it.

Barriers to Entry and Monopoly

Web Note 15.2
Diamonds Are Forever

The standard model of monopoly just presented is simple, but, like many things simple, it hides some issues. One issue the standard model of monopoly hides is in this question: What prevents other firms from entering the monopolist's market? You should be able to answer that question relatively quickly. If a monopolist exists, it must exist due to some type of barrier to entry (a social, political, or economic impediment that prevents firms from entering the market). Three important barriers to entry are natural ability, economies of scale, and government restrictions. In the absence of barriers to entry, the monopoly would face competition from other firms, which would erode its monopoly. Studying how these barriers to entry are established enriches the standard model and lets us distinguish different types of monopoly.

If there were no barriers to entry, profit-maximizing firms would always compete away monopoly profits.

Natural Ability

A barrier to entry that might exist is that a firm is better at producing a good than anyone else. It has unique abilities that make it more efficient than all other firms. The barrier to entry in such a case is the firm's natural ability. The defense attorneys in the Microsoft antitrust case argued that it was Microsoft's superior products that led to its capture of 90 percent of the market.

Monopolies based on ability usually don't provoke the public's ire. Often in the public's mind such monopolies are "just monopolies." The standard economic model doesn't distinguish between a "just" and an "unjust" monopoly. The just/unjust distinction raises the question of whether a firm has acquired a monopoly based on its ability or on certain unfair tactics such as initially pricing low to force competitive companies out of business but then pricing high. Many public debates over monopoly focus on such normative issues, about which the economists' standard model has nothing to say.

ADDED DIMENSION

Can Price Controls Increase Output and Lower Market Price?

In an earlier chapter, you learned how effective price ceilings increase market price, reduce output, and reduce the welfare of society. With any type of price control in a competitive market, some trades that individuals would like to have made are prevented. Thus, with competitive markets, price controls of any type are seen as generally bad (though they might have some desirable income distribution effects).

When there is monopoly, the argument is not so simple. The monopoly price is higher than the marginal cost and society loses out; monopolies create their own deadweight loss. In the monopoly case, price controls can actually lower price, increase output, and reduce deadweight loss. Going through the reasoning why provides a good review of the tools.

The figure below shows you the argument.

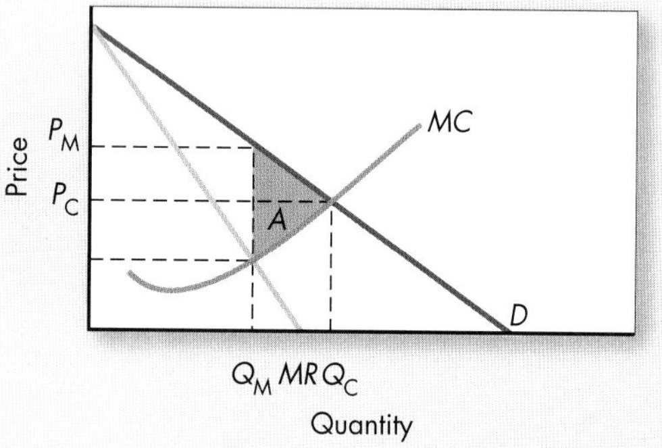

The monopoly sets its quantity where $MR = MC$. Output is Q_M and price is P_M; the welfare loss is the blue shaded triangle A. Now say that the government comes in and places a price ceiling on the monopolist at the competitive price, P_C. Since the monopolist is compelled by law to charge price P_C, it no longer has an incentive to restrict output. Put another way, the price ceiling—the dashed line P_C—becomes the monopolist's demand curve and marginal revenue curve. (Remember, when the demand curve is horizontal, the marginal revenue curve is identical to the demand curve.) Given the law, the monopolist's best option still is to produce where $MC = MR$, but that means charging price P_C and increasing output to Q_C. As you can see from the figure, the price ceiling causes output to rise and price to fall.

If, when there is monopoly, price controls can increase efficiency, why don't economists advocate price controls more than they do? Let's review four reasons why.

1. For price controls to increase output and lower price, the price has to be set within the right price range—below the monopolist's price and above the price where the monopolist's marginal cost and marginal revenue curves intersect. It is unclear politically that such a price will be chosen. Even if regulators could pick the right price initially, markets may change. Demand may increase or decrease, putting the controlled price outside the desired range.
2. All markets are dynamic. The very existence of monopoly profits will encourage other firms in other industries to try to break into that market, keeping the existing monopolist on its toes. Because of this dynamic element, in some sense no market is ever a pure textbook monopoly.
3. Price controls create their own deadweight loss in the form of rent seeking. Price controls do not eliminate monopoly pressures. The monopolist has a big incentive to regain its ability to set its own price and will lobby hard to remove price controls. Economists see resources spent to regain their monopoly price as socially wasteful.
4. Economists distrust government. Governments have their own political agendas—there is no general belief among economists that governments will try to set the price at the competitive level. Once one opens up the price control gates in cases of monopoly, it will be difficult to stop government from using price controls in competitive markets.

The arguments are, of course, more complicated, and will be discussed in more detail, but this should give you a good preview of some of the policy arguments to come in later chapters.

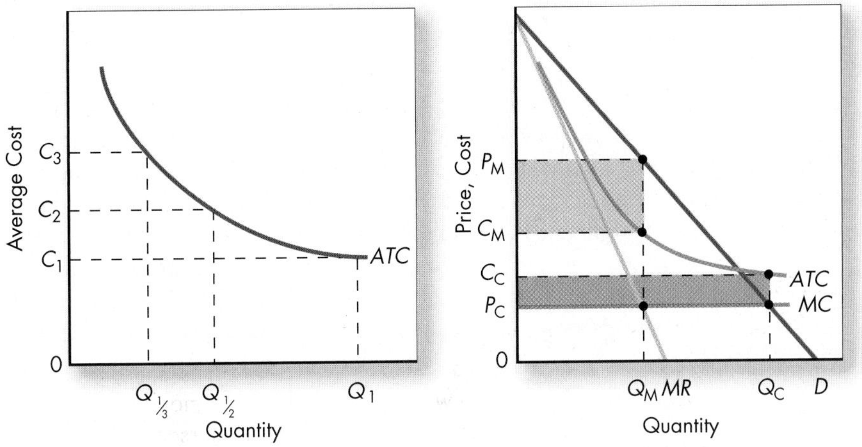

(a) Average Cost for Natural Monopolist

(b) Profit of Natural Monopolist

FIGURE 15-6 (A AND B)
A Natural Monopolist

The graph in (**a**) shows the average cost curve for a natural monopoly. One firm producing Q_1 would have a lower average cost than a combination of firms would have. For example, if three firms each produced $Q_{1/3}$, the average cost for each would be C_3.

The graph in (**b**) shows that a natural monopolist would produce Q_M and charge a price P_M. It will earn a profit shown by the orange shaded box. If the monopolist were required to charge a price equal to marginal cost, P_C, it would incur a loss shown by the blue shaded box.

Economies of Scale

An alternative reason why a barrier to entry might exist is that there are significant economies of scale. If sufficiently large economies of scale exist, it would be inefficient to have two producers since if each produced half of the output, neither could take advantage of the economies of scale. Such industries are called natural monopolies. A **natural monopoly** is *an industry in which a single firm can produce at a lower cost than can two or more firms*. A natural monopoly will occur when the technology is such that indivisible setup costs are so large that average total costs fall within the range of possible outputs. I demonstrate that case in Figure 15-6(a).

In a natural monopoly, a single firm can produce at a lower cost than can two or more firms.

If one firm produces Q_1, its cost per unit is C_1. If two firms each produces half that amount, $Q_{1/2}$, so that their total production is Q_1, the cost per unit will be C_2, which is significantly higher than C_1. In cases of natural monopoly, as the number of firms in the industry increases, the average total cost of producing a fixed number of units increases. For example, if each of three firms in an industry had a third of the market, each firm would have an average cost of C_3.

Q-8 Why is the competitive price impossible for an industry that exhibits strong economies of scale?

Until the 1990s local telephone service was a real-world example of such a natural monopoly. It made little sense to have two sets of telephone lines going into people's houses. I say "until recently" because technology changes and now, with wireless communications and cable connections, the technical conditions that made local telephone service a natural monopoly are changing. Such change is typical; natural monopolies are only natural given a technology.

A natural monopoly also can occur when a single industry standard is more efficient than multiple standards, even when that standard is owned by one firm. An example is the operating system for computers. A single standard is much more efficient than multiple standards because the communication among computer users is easier.

From a welfare standpoint, natural monopolies are different from other types of monopolies. In the case of a natural monopoly, even if a single firm makes some monopoly profit, the price it charges may still be lower than the price two firms making normal profit would charge because its average total costs will be lower. In the case of a natural monopoly, not only is there no welfare loss from monopoly, but there can actually be a welfare gain since a single firm producing is so much more efficient than many firms producing. Such natural monopolies are often organized as public

REAL-WORLD APPLICATION

Monopolizing Monopoly

Have you ever played Monopoly? Probably you have. And in the process, you have made money for Parker Brothers, the firm that has the monopoly on Monopoly. How they got it is an interesting story of actual events following games and vice versa. The beginnings of the Monopoly game go back to a Quaker woman named Lizzie Magie, who was part of the one-tax movement of populist economist Henry George. That movement, which was a central populist idea in the late 1800s, wanted to put a tax on all land rent to finance government. George argued that there would be no need for an income tax; the tax on the land monopoly would finance it all. Lizzie Magie created a game, called the Landlord's Game, as a way of teaching George's ideas, and showing how monopoly caused problems. She patented the game in 1904.

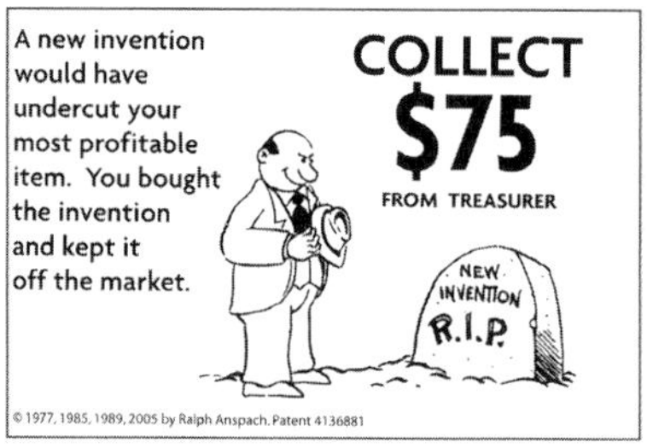

Despite the patent, people copied the game with her approval, since her desire was to spread George's ideas. As the game spread, it kept changing form and rules, and eventually acquired the property names associated with Atlantic City, which the game now uses, and came to be called Monopoly. A number of variations of the game developed.

In the 1930s Charles Darrow was taught the game and had some friends write up the rules, which they copyrighted. (They couldn't patent the game because they didn't invent it.) In 1935 Darrow made an agreement with Parker Brothers, a firm that sold games, that gave them the right to produce this monopoly game, paying a royalty. As Parker Brothers discovered the history of the monopoly game and of the particular games that preceded it, Parker Brothers bought the right to the previous games so that they would secure their full rights to Monopoly. It paid the various people between $500 and $10,000 for those rights. In 1974, an economics professor, Ralph Anspach, created an "Anti-Monopoly" game that pitted monopolists against competitors. That game led to suits and countersuits between Anspach and General Mills Fun Group, which had bought Parker Brothers in the interim, as they attempted to protect their monopoly.

utilities. For example, most towns have a single water department supplying water to residents.

Figure 15-6(b) shows the profit-maximizing level of output and price that a natural monopolist would choose. To show the profit-maximizing level of output, I've added a marginal cost curve that is below the average total cost curve. (If you don't know why this must be the case, a review of costs is in order.) A natural monopolist uses the same $MC = MR$ rule that a monopolist uses to determine output. The monopolist will produce Q_M and charge a price P_M. Average total costs are C_M and the natural monopolist earns a profit shown by the orange shaded box.

Where a natural monopoly exists, the perfectly competitive solution is impossible, since average total costs are not covered where $MC = P$. A monopolist required by government to charge the competitive price P_C, where $P = MC$, will incur a loss shown by the blue shaded box because marginal cost is always below average total cost. Either a government subsidy or some output restriction is necessary in order for production to be feasible. In such cases, monopolies are often preferred by the public as long as they are regulated by government. I will discuss the issues of regulating natural monopolies in the chapter on real-world competition.

Web Note 15.3
The Best Monopoly in America

Government-Created Monopolies

A third reason monopolies can exist is that they're created by government. The support of laissez-faire by Classical economists such as Adam Smith and their opposition to monopoly arose in large part in reaction to those government-created monopolies, not in reaction to any formal analysis of welfare loss from monopoly.

Normative Views of Monopoly

Many laypeople's views of government-created monopoly reflect the same normative judgments that Classical economists made. Classical economists considered, and much of the lay public considers, such monopolies unfair and inconsistent with liberty. Monopolies prevent people from being free to enter whatever business they want and are undesirable on normative grounds. In this view, government-created monopolies are simply wrong.

This normative argument against government-created monopoly doesn't extend to all types of government-created monopolies. The public accepts certain types of government-created monopoly that it believes have overriding social value. An example is patents. To encourage research and development of new products, government gives out patents for a wide variety of innovations, such as genetic engineering, Xerox machines, and cans that can be opened without a can opener.

Q-9 If a patent is a monopoly, why does the government give out patents?

A second normative argument against monopoly is that the public doesn't like the income distributional effects of monopoly. Although, as we saw in our discussion of monopoly, monopolists do not always earn an economic profit, they often do, which means that the monopoly might transfer income in a way that the public (whose normative views help determine society's policy toward monopoly) doesn't like. This distributional effect of monopoly based on normative views of who deserves income is another reason many laypeople oppose monopoly: They believe it transfers income from "deserving" consumers to "undeserving" monopolists.

A third normative reason people oppose government-created monopoly that isn't captured by the standard model of monopoly is that the possibility of government-created monopoly encourages people to spend a lot of their time in political pursuits trying to get the government to favor them with a monopoly, and less time doing "productive" things. It causes *rent-seeking* activities in which people spend resources to gain monopolies for themselves.

Possible economic profits from monopoly lead potential monopolists to spend money to get government to give them a monopoly.

Each of these arguments probably plays a role in the public's dislike of monopoly. As you can see, these real-world arguments blend normative judgments with objective analysis, making it difficult to arrive at definite conclusions. Most real-world problems require this blending, making applied economic analysis difficult. The economist must interpret the normative judgments about what people want to achieve and explain how public policy can be designed to achieve those desired ends.

Government Policy and Monopoly: AIDS Drugs

Let's now consider how economic theory might be used to analyze monopoly and to suggest how government might deal with that monopoly. Specifically, let's consider the problem of acquired immune deficiency syndrome (AIDS) and the combination of medicinal drugs to fight AIDS. These drugs were developed by a small group of pharmaceutical companies, which own patents on them, giving them a monopoly. Patents are given on medicine to encourage firms to find cures for various diseases. The monopoly the patent gives them lets them charge a high price so that the firms can expect to make a profit from their research. Whether such patents are in the public interest isn't an issue, since the patent has already been granted.

Q-10 The medicinal drug tetracycline sold for animals costs about $^1/_{20}$ as much as the same drug sold for human beings. What is the likely explanation?

The issue is what to do about these drugs. Currently demand for them is highly inelastic, so the price pharmaceutical companies can charge is high even though their marginal cost of producing them is low. Whether they are making a profit depends on their cost of development. But since that cost is already spent, that's irrelevant to the current marginal cost; development cost affects their *ATC* curve, not their marginal cost curve. Thus, the pharmaceutical companies are charging an enormously high price for drugs that may help save people's lives and that cost the companies a very small amount to produce.

What, if anything, should the government do? Some people have suggested that the government regulate the price of the drugs, requiring the firms to charge only their marginal cost. This would make society better off. But most economists point out that doing so will significantly reduce the incentives for drug companies to research new drugs. One reason drug companies spend billions of dollars for drug research is their expectation that they'll be able to make large profits if they're successful. If drug companies expect the government to come in and take away their monopoly when they're successful, they won't search for cures. So forcing these pharmaceutical companies to charge a low price for their drugs would help AIDS victims, but it would hurt people suffering from diseases that are currently being researched and that might be researched in the future. So there's a strong argument not to regulate.

But the thought of people dying when a cheap cure—or at least a partially effective treatment—is available is repulsive to me and to many others. In the 1990s Sub-Saharan African countries, which account for more than 75 percent of all AIDS deaths in the world, threatened to license production of these drugs to local manufacturers and make the drugs available at cost. U.S. pharmaceutical companies initially pressured the United States to cut off foreign aid if the African countries carried out their threat, but because of the bad public relations that the drug firms were getting, they stopped enforcing their patents in developing countries, making drugs for AIDS available to AIDS patients in poor nations at a much lower price than they do to others (an example of price discrimination).

An alternative policy suggested by economic theory to deal with such drug problems is for the government to buy the patents and allow anyone to make the drugs so their price would approach their marginal cost. Admittedly, this would be expensive. It would cause negative incentive effects because the government would have to increase taxes to cover the buyout's costs. But this approach would avoid the problem of the regulatory approach and achieve the same ends. However, it also would introduce new problems, such as determining which patents the government should buy.

Whether such a buyout policy makes sense remains to be seen, but in debating such issues the power of the simple monopoly model becomes apparent.

Conclusion

We've come to the end of the presentation of the formal models of perfect competition and monopoly. Working through the models takes a lot of effort, but it's effort well spent. In Chapter 1, I quoted Einstein: "A theory should be as simple as possible, but not more so." This chapter's analysis isn't simple; it takes repetition, working through models, and doing thought experiments to get it down pat. But it's as simple as possible. Even so, it's extremely easy to make a foolish mistake, as I did in my Ph.D. oral examination when I was outlining an argument on the blackboard. ["*What* did you say the output would be for this monopolist, Mr. Colander?"] As I learned then, it takes long hours of working through the models again and again to get them right.

Summary

- The price a monopolist charges is higher than that of a competitive market due to the restriction of output; a monopolist can make a profit in the long run.
- A monopolist's profit-maximizing output is where marginal revenue equals marginal cost.
- A monopolist can charge the maximum price consumers are willing to pay for the quantity the monopolist produces.
- To determine a monopolist's profit, first determine its output (where MC = *MR*). Then determine its price and average total cost at that output level. The difference between price and average total cost at the profit-maximizing level of output is profit per unit. Multiply this by output to find total profit.
- Because monopolists reduce output and charge a price that is higher than marginal cost, monopolies create a welfare loss to society.
- If a monopolist can (1) identify groups of customers who have different elasticities of demand, (2) separate them in some way, and (3) limit their ability to resell its product between groups, it can price-discriminate.
- A price-discriminating monopolist earns more profit than a normal monopolist because it can charge a higher price to those with less elastic demands and a lower price to those with more elastic demands.
- Three important barriers to entry are natural ability, economies of scale, and government restrictions.
- Natural monopolies exist in industries with strong economies of scale. Because their average total costs are always falling, it is more efficient for one firm to produce all the output.
- The competitive price is impossible in a natural monopoly because marginal cost is always below average total cost. No firm would enter an industry where not even normal (zero economic) profit can be made.
- Normative arguments against monopoly include the following: (1) monopolies are inconsistent with freedom, (2) the distributional effects of monopoly are unfair, and (3) monopolies encourage people to waste time and money trying to get monopolies.

Key Terms

monopoly *(340)*
natural monopoly *(351)*
patent *(346)*
price-discriminate *(348)*

Questions and Exercises

Connect ECONOMICS

1. Demonstrate graphically the profit-maximizing positions for a perfect competitor and a monopolist. How do they differ? LO1
2. Monopolists differ from perfect competitors because monopolists make a profit. True or false? Why? LO1
3. Why is marginal revenue below average revenue for a monopolist? LO1
4. Say you place a lump-sum tax (a tax that is treated as a fixed cost) on a monopolist. How will that affect her output and pricing decisions? LO3
5. A monopolist is selling fish. But if the fish don't sell, they rot. What will be the likely elasticity at the point on the demand curve at which the monopolist sets the price? (Difficult) LO3
6. A monopolist with a straight-line demand curve finds that it can sell two units at $12 each or 12 units at $2 each. Its fixed cost is $20 and its marginal cost is constant at $3 per unit.
   a. Draw the MC, *ATC*, *MR*, and demand curves for this monopolist.
   b. At what output level would the monopolist produce?
   c. At what output level would a perfectly competitive firm produce? LO3

7. State what's wrong with the following graphs: LO3

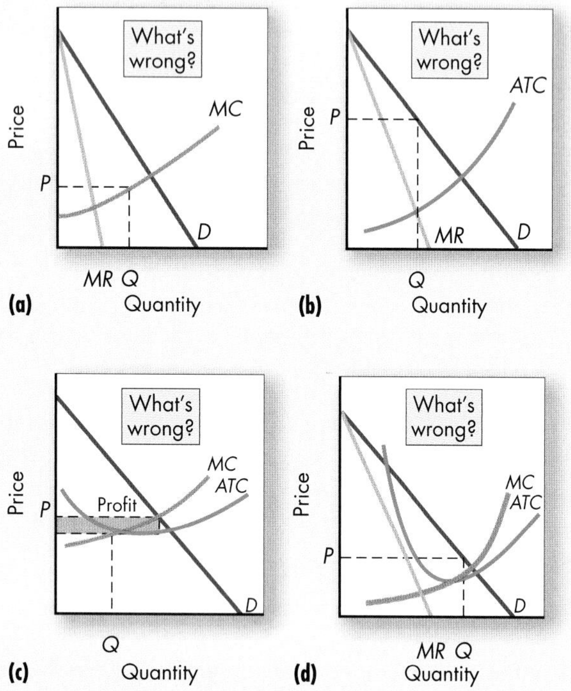

8. Demonstrate the welfare loss created by a monopoly. LO4
9. Will the welfare loss from a monopolist with a perfectly elastic marginal cost curve be greater or less than the welfare loss from a monopolist with an upward-sloping marginal cost curve? LO4
10. During the 2001 anthrax seare, the U.S. government threatened to disregard Bayer's patent of ciprofloxacin, the most effective drug to fight anthrax, and license the production of the drug to American drug companies to stockpile the drug in case of an anthrax epidemic. While the policy would lower costs to the U.S. government of stockpiling the drug, it also would have other costs. What are those costs? (Difficult) LO3, LO4
11. What three things must a firm be able to do to price-discriminate? LO5
12. Best-selling horror, *Duma Key* by Stephen King, was sold in hardback for $28 when it was released on July 15, 2003. One year later, the publisher issued a soft-cover edition for $9.99. What accounts for the difference in price? (Note: The marginal cost of printing a book with a soft cover is not much less than the cost of a hardcover book.) LO5
13. Econocompany is under investigation by the U.S. Department of Justice for violating antitrust laws. The government decides that Econocompany has a natural monopoly and that, if it is to keep the government's business, it must sell at a price equal to marginal cost. Econocompany says that it can't do that and hires you to explain to the government why it can't.
    a. You do so in reference to the following graph.
    b. What price would it charge if it were unregulated?
    c. What price would you advise that it should be allowed to charge? LO6

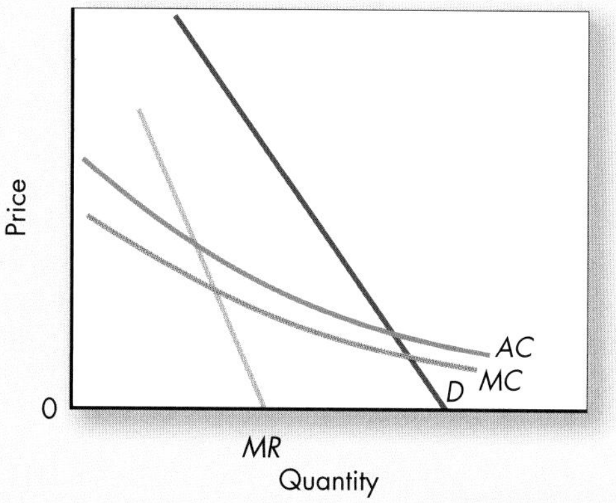

14. In the late 1990s, the Government Accounting Office reported that airlines block new carriers at major airports.
    a. What effect does this have on fares and the number of flights at those airports?
    b. How much are airlines willing to spend to control the use of gates to block new carriers? LO6
15. How is efficiency related to the number of firms in an industry characterized by strong economies of scale? LO6

Questions from Alternative Perspectives

1. Austrian economists observe that most lasting monopolies are the result of government and that any attempt to make government strong enough to control monopolies may result in an abuse of government power to protect and create more monopolies. What cautionary advice could we draw from this observation? (Austrian)
2. Do men have a monopoly over the best jobs in the United States? If so, how is that monopoly protected? (Feminist)
3. When analyzing the conduct of "modern" industry, Thorstein Veblen argued that captains of industry

succeeded by eliminating their rivals through predatory exploitation and thus sabotaging production efficiency for personal fortune.

a. How does John D. Rockefeller's late 19th-century view that he liked to give competitors "a good sweating" and Bill Gates's "We will crush them" approach to Java fit into Veblen's argument?

b. What are the policy implications of predatory exploitation? (Institutionalist)

4. Large pharmaceutical firms use monopoly power granted by patents to sell drugs at prices that far exceed marginal costs. Evidence from countries without effective patent protections suggests that these drugs could sell for as little as 25 percent of their patent-protected prices. That difference cost U.S. consumers (including the government) about $80 billion in the year 2000, nearly four times what pharmaceutical corporations spent on research that year.

a. How should we deal with these disturbing abuses of the patent system?

b. Should the government buy back patents as your textbook discusses, or should it not issue them in the first place?

c. Should patents be granted in some industries but not others?

d. If so, how should we encourage research in areas with no patent protection? (Radical)

5. The original language for patent law comes from Thomas Jefferson. He wrote that patents can be obtained for "any new and useful art, machine, manufacture, or composition of matter, or any new or useful improvement thereof." These words remain at the core of U.S. patent law.

a. Do they allow life forms to be patented?

b. Should they?

c. If humans can create life forms, does that undermine the existence of God? (Religious)

Issues to Ponder

1. Explain the effects on college education of the development of a teaching machine that you plug into a student's brain and that makes the student understand everything. How would your answer differ if a college could monopolize production of this machine? (Difficult) LO3

2. Assume your city government has been contracting with a single garbage collection firm that has been granted an exclusive franchise, the sole right, to pick up trash within the entire city limits. However, it has been proposed that companies be allowed to compete for business with residents on an individual basis. The city government has estimated the price residents are willing to pay for various numbers of garbage collections per month and the total costs facing the garbage collector per resident as shown in the following table.

Pickup (*Q*)	Price per Pickup (Demand)	Total Revenue (*TR*)	Marginal Revenue (*MR*)	Total Cost (*TC*)	Marginal Cost (*MC*)	Average Total Cost (*ATC*)
0	$4.20	0	—	$ 3.20	—	—
1	3.80	___	___	4.20	___	___
2	3.40	___	___	5.60	___	___
3	3.00	___	___	7.80	___	___
4	2.60	___	___	10.40	___	___
5	2.20	___	___	13.40	___	___
6	1.90	___	___	16.80	___	___

a. What are the fixed costs per month of garbage collection per resident?

b. Considering that the current garbage collection firm the city has contracted with has a monopoly in garbage collection services, what is the current number of collections residents receive per month and the price charged residents for each collection? What is the economic profit received from each resident by the monopoly firm?

c. If competitive bidding were allowed and therefore a competitive market for garbage collection services developed, what would be the number of collections per month and the price charged residents per collection? What is the economic profit received from each resident by the competitive firms?

d. Based on the above analysis, should the city government allow competitive bidding? Why? Would you expect there to be any quality differences between the monopolistic and competitive trash collection firms? LO1, LO3

3. When you buy a cheap computer printer or home fax, you can sometimes get it for free after the rebate. Why would a firm sell you something for a zero price? (The answer isn't that it wants to be nice.) LO4

4. Provide a price-discrimination argument for the existence of the four unexplained examples of price discrimination in the text. LO5

5. Oftentimes, gas stations a couple of miles apart will differ in prices by as much as 5 to 10 cents per gallon

because oil companies use a pricing system called zone pricing. For example, gas is sold wholesale to stations in Pleasanton, California, at about a 13 percent discount from the wholesale price in nearby Palo Alto. (Difficult)
   a. Why might oil companies do this?
   b. The FTC has been reviewing the practice. What policies might you suggest for them to consider to stop the practice, and what are the potential problems with those policies?
   c. Would such a policy lower the overall price of gas? LO5
6. Most magazines offer enormous subscription deals for college students. For example, *Time* magazine offers a one-year subscription for $29.95, when the cover price is $3.95 per issue. This is an 85 percent discount.
   a. Why do they do this?
   b. How would your answer change if you are told that most subscribers get enormous discounts, and that *Time*'s subscription revenue does not cover its costs?
   c. What is a likely reason why magazines sell their magazines so cheaply? LO5
7. Copyrights provide authors with a monopoly.
   a. What effect would eliminating copyrights have on the price and output of textbooks?
   b. Should copyrights be eliminated? LO6

Answers to Margin Questions

1. If you doodle too much, your doodles will become worthless. Besides, if you want to pass the next test, you have to study. *(341)*
2. At output 4, the marginal cost of $12 (between $8 and $16) equals the marginal revenue of $12 (between $15 and $9), making it the profit-maximizing output. It has the highest total profit, $34. *(342)*
3. To determine the profit-maximizing price and output, one must determine where the marginal revenue curve equals marginal cost. So one must first draw the marginal revenue curve and see where it intersects marginal cost. That intersection determines the quantity, as in the graph on the right. Carrying the line up to the demand curve determines the price. *(343)*

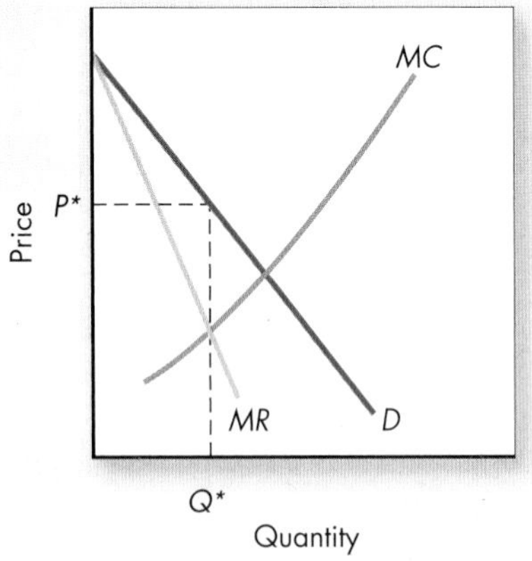

4. A monopolist produces less output than a perfectly competitive firm because a monopolist takes into account the fact that increasing output will lower the price of all previous units. *(344)*
5. To determine profit, follow the following four steps: (1) draw the marginal revenue curve, (2) find the level of output where MC = *MR* indicated in the graph below by Q*, (3) find the price the monopolist would charge indicated by *P** and extend a horizontal line from the demand curve at that price to the price axis, (4) determine the average total cost at Q* shown by C* and extend a horizontal line from the *ATC* curve at that cost to the price axis. The box created is the monopolist's profit. The profit is the shaded box shown in the graph below. *(345)*

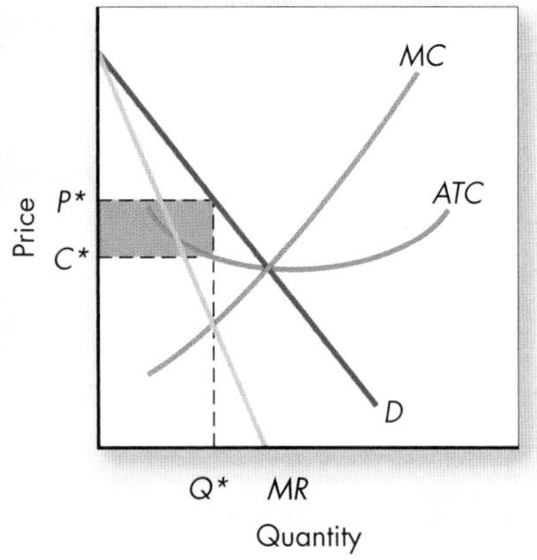

6. Area C represents the profit going to a monopolist. It is not considered a loss since, while consumers lose it, monopolists gain it. It is a redistribution of resources rather than an efficiency loss. *(348)*
7. A price-discriminating monopolist makes a greater profit than a normal monopolist because a price-discriminating monopolist is able to charge a higher price to those consumers who have less elastic demands. *(349)*

8. The marginal cost curve for an industry that exhibits strong economies of scale is always below average total costs. Therefore, the competitive price, where $P = MC$, will always result in losses for firms. Firms would not enter into such an industry and there would be no supply. *(351)*
9. The government gives out patents to encourage research and development of new products. This suggests that the public and government believe that certain monopolies have overriding social value. *(353)*
10. A likely explanation for identical medicinal drugs being sold at a much lower cost for animals than for human beings is differing elasticities of demand. The demand for drugs for human beings is highly inelastic, whereas the demand for medicinal drugs for animals is elastic. When there is a price-discriminating monopolist for these drugs, those with more inelastic demands are charged higher prices. *(354)*

APPENDIX A

The Algebra of Competitive and Monopolistic Firms

In the Appendix to Chapter 5, I presented the algebra relevant to supply and demand. To relate that algebra to competitive firms, all you must remember is that the market supply curve equals the marginal cost curve for the competitive industry. Let's review it briefly.

Say that marginal costs, and thus market supply, for the industry is given by

$$P = 2Q_S + 4$$

Let's also say that the market demand curve is

$$Q_D = 28 - \tfrac{1}{4}P$$

To determine equilibrium price and quantity in a competitive market, you must equate quantity supplied and quantity demanded and solve for price. First, rewrite the marginal cost equation with quantity supplied on the left:

$$Q_S = \tfrac{1}{2}MC - 2$$

Then set quantity demanded equal to quantity supplied and $MC = P$. Then solve for equilibrium price:

$$\begin{aligned} Q_S = Q_D \Rightarrow 28 - \tfrac{1}{4}P &= \tfrac{1}{2}P - 2 \\ 112 - P &= 2P - 8 \\ 3P &= 120 \\ P &= 40 \end{aligned}$$

Thus, the equilibrium price is \$40. Competitive firms take this price as given and produce up until their marginal cost equals price. The industry as a whole produces 18 units.

Now let's consider the algebra relevant for a monopolistic firm. In the monopolistic case, supply and demand are not enough to determine where the monopolist will produce. The monopolist will produce where marginal revenue equals marginal cost. But, for the monopolist, the industry demand curve is the demand curve, which means that in order to determine where the monopolist will produce, we must determine the marginal revenue curve that goes along with the above demand curve. There are two ways to do that.

First, if you know calculus, you can determine the marginal revenue curve in the following manner: Since marginal revenue tells us how much total revenue will change with each additional unit produced, you first specify the demand curve in terms of quantity produced.

$$P = 112 - 4Q$$

Since $TR = PQ$ we can multiply this by Q to get total revenue. Doing so gives us

$$TR = PQ = 112Q - 4Q^2$$

To find marginal revenue, take the first derivative of total revenue with respect to Q.

$$P = 112 - 8Q$$

Second, if you don't know calculus, all you need to remember is the trick shown in a box in the chapter on how to graph the marginal revenue curve. Remember, the marginal revenue curve starts at the same price as the demand curve and bisects the quantity axis at one-half the value of the quantity axis intercept of the demand curve. The marginal revenue curve, because it bisects the quantity axis at one-half the value of the quantity axis intercept of the accompanying demand curve, must fall twice as fast as the market demand curve. That is, its slope is twice the slope of the market demand curve.

Knowing that its slope is twice the market demand curve slope, you can write the marginal revenue curve with the same price axis intercept as the demand curve and a slope of two times the slope of the demand curve. (Warning: this only works with linear demand curves.) The price-axis intercept of the demand curve is the value of P where Q equals 0: 112. The quantity-axis intercept of the demand curve is the value of Q where P equals 0: 28.

So, the marginal revenue curve has a price-axis intercept at 112 and a quantity-axis intercept at 14. Mathematically, such a curve is represented by

$$P = 112 - (112/14)P$$

or

$$P = 112 - 8Q$$

Now that we've determined the monopolist's marginal revenue curve, we can determine its equilibrium quantity by setting $MR = MC$ and solving for Q. Doing so gives us

$$112 - 8Q = 2Q + 4$$
$$-10Q = -108$$
$$Q = 10.8$$

The monopolist then charges the price consumers are willing to pay for that quantity. Mathematically, substitute 10.8 into the demand equation and solve for price:

$$P = 112 - 4(10.8)$$
$$P = \$68.80$$

Comparing the price and quantity produced by a monopolist and those of a competitive industry shows that the monopolist charges a higher price and produces a lower output.

Questions and Exercises

1. The market demand curve is $Q_D = 50 - P$. The marginal cost curve is $MC = 4Q + 6$.
   a. Assuming the marginal cost curve is for a competitive industry as a whole, find the profit-maximizing level of output and price.
   b. Assuming the marginal cost curve is for only one firm that comprises the entire market, find the profit-maximizing level of output and price.
   c. Compare the two results.
2. The market demand curve is $Q_D = 160 - 4P$. A monopolist's total cost curve is $TC = 6Q^2 + 15Q + 50$.
   a. Find the profit-maximizing level of output and price for a monopolist.
   b. Find its average cost at that level of output.
   c. Find its profit at that level of output.
3. Suppose fixed costs for the monopolist in Question 2 increase by 52.
   a. Find the profit-maximizing level of output and price for a monopolist.
   b. Find its average cost at that level of output.
   c. Find its profit at that level of output.
4. The market demand curve is $Q_D = 12 - \frac{1}{3}P$. Costs do not vary with output.
   a. Find the profit-maximizing level of output and price for a monopolist.
   b. Find the profit-maximizing level of output and price for a competitive industry.

CHAPTER 16

Monopolistic Competition and Oligopoly

Competition, you know, is a lot like chastity. It is widely praised, but alas, too little practiced.

—*Carol Tucker*

Back in the 1960s, my uncle bought a Japanese car, and the town was aghast—how daring, and in many people's minds—how foolish he was. In 2009 when I mentioned to my kids that I was thinking of getting an American car—they looked at me aghast—how foolish could I be (although they have no doubt that I can be very foolish, and embarrassing). I point this out because it demonstrates (1) how market structure can change over time—how the American firms' monopoly on car production gave way to Japanese and European competition—and (2) how the market structures we discussed in the last two chapters—perfectly competitive markets and monopoly—are insufficient to describe real-world markets. The reality is that real-world market structures generally fall in between the two, and in this chapter I introduce you to two market structures in between—monopolistic competition and oligopoly.

Market structure refers to *the physical characteristics of the market within which firms interact*. It is determined by the number of firms in the market and the barriers to entry. Considering **monopolistic competition**—*a market structure in which there are many firms selling differentiated products and few barriers to entry*—and **oligopoly**—*a market structure in which there are only a few firms and firms explicitly take other firms' likely response into account*—not only provides you with a sense of how the models can apply to the real world but also helps cement in your mind the concepts introduced in the last chapter. In oligopoly, there are often significant barriers to entry.

AFTER READING THIS CHAPTER, YOU SHOULD BE ABLE TO:

1. List the four distinguishing characteristics of monopolistic competition.
2. Demonstrate graphically the equilibrium of a monopolistic competitor.
3. State the central element of oligopoly.
4. Explain why decisions in the cartel model depend on market share and decisions in the contestable market model depend on barriers to entry.
5. Describe two empirical methods of determining market structure.

Characteristics of Monopolistic Competition

The four distinguishing characteristics of monopolistic competition are

1. Many sellers.
2. Differentiated products.
3. Multiple dimensions of competition.
4. Easy entry of new firms in the long run.

Let's consider each in turn.

REAL-WORLD APPLICATION

Foreign Competitive Oligopolies

Market structures change over time. Take, for instance, the automobile industry, which has always been used as the classic oligopoly model. Starting in the 1970s, however, foreign automakers have made large inroads into, and have added new competition to, the U.S. market. Foreign companies such as Honda and Toyota have entered the U.S. market, as seen in the accompanying pie chart.

In 2008, the four-firm concentration ratio was over 70 percent, so the industry would be still classified as an oligopoly. In 2009, the auto industry went through significant upheavals with U.S. firms finding themselves in bankruptcy or in danger of falling into bankruptcy. But the industry remained an oligopoly with firms taking into account the reactions of other firms when making decisions. However, because of the increase in competition, it was becoming more monopolistically competitive.

Such change in industry structure is to be expected. Monopoly and oligopoly create the possibility that firms can make above-normal profits. Above-normal profits invite entry, and unless there are entry barriers, the result will likely be a breakdown in that monopoly or oligopoly. In the future we can expect Korean and Chinese auto firms to be entering the top four.

Market Shares in the U.S. Automotive Industry as of 2008

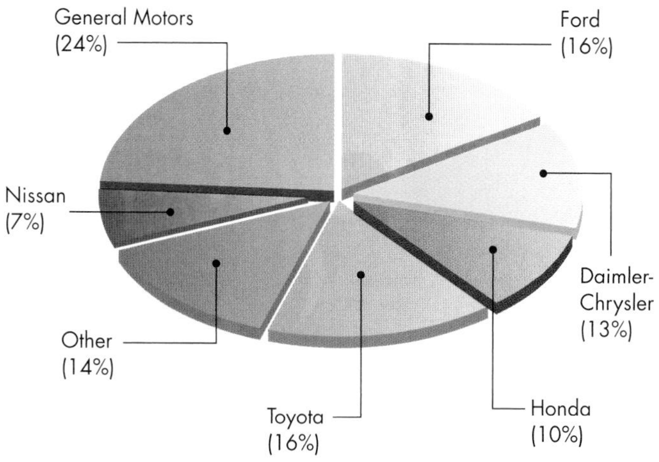

Source: *Automotive News*, 2009.

Many Sellers

When there are only a few sellers, it's reasonable to explicitly take into account your competitors' reaction to the price you set. When there are many sellers, it isn't. In monopolistic competition, firms don't take into account rivals' reactions. Here's an example. There are many types of soap: Ivory, Irish Spring, Yardley's Old English, and so on. So when Ivory decides to run a sale, it won't spend a lot of time thinking about Old English's reaction. There are so many firms that one firm can't concern itself with the reaction of any specific firm. The soap industry is characterized by monopolistic competition. In contrast, there are only a few major automobile firms, so when GM sets its price, it will explicitly consider what Ford's reaction may be. If GM raises its price, will Ford go along and also raise price? Or will it hold its price at its current level and try to sell its cars on the basis of lower prices? The automobile industry is an oligopoly.

The fact that there are many sellers in monopolistic competition also makes collusion difficult since, when there are many firms, getting all of them to act as one is difficult. In economists' models, monopolistically competitive firms are assumed to act independently.

Product Differentiation

The "many sellers" characteristic gives monopolistic competition its competitive aspect. Product differentiation gives it its monopolistic aspect. In a monopolistically competitive market, the goods that are sold aren't homogeneous, as in perfect competition; they are differentiated slightly. Irish Spring soap is slightly different from Ivory, which in turn is slightly different from Yardley's Old English.

So in one sense each firm has a monopoly in the good it sells. But that monopoly is fleeting; it is based on advertising to convince people that one firm's good is different from the goods of competitors. The good may or may not really be different. Bleach differs little from one brand to another, yet buying Clorox makes many people feel that they're getting pure bleach. I generally don't buy it; I generally buy generic bleach. Ketchup, however, while made from the same basic ingredients, differs among brands (in my view). For me, only Heinz ketchup is real ketchup. (However, recently, my wife switched and put Hunt's ketchup in a Heinz bottle, and pointed out to me that I didn't notice. She's right; I didn't notice. But I still want Heinz ketchup; it's what my mother gave me, and seeing the Heinz bottle there, and believing that there is Heinz ketchup in it, makes me feel good—so much for my economist's rationality.)

Web Note 16.1
Product Differentiation

Because a monopolistic competitor has some monopoly power, advertising to increase that monopoly power (and hence increase the firm's profits) makes sense as long as the marginal benefit of advertising exceeds the marginal cost. Despite the fact that their goods are similar but differentiated, to fit economists' monopolistically competitive model, firms must make their decisions as if they had no effect on other firms.

Multiple Dimensions of Competition

In perfect competition, price is the only dimension on which firms compete; in monopolistic competition, competition takes many forms. Product differentiation reflects firms' attempt to compete on perceived attributes; advertising is another form competition takes. Other dimensions of competition include service and distribution outlets. These multiple dimensions of competition make it much harder to analyze a specific industry, but the alternative methods of competition follow the same two general decision rules as price competition:

In monopolistic competition, competition takes many forms.

- Compare marginal costs and marginal benefits; and
- Change that dimension of competition until marginal costs equal marginal benefits.

Ease of Entry of New Firms in the Long Run

The last condition a monopolistically competitive market must meet is that entry must be relatively easy; that is, there must be no significant entry barriers. Barriers to entry create the potential for long-run economic profit and prevent competitive pressures from pushing price down to average total cost. In monopolistic competition, if there were long-run economic profits, other firms would enter until no economic profit existed.

Output, Price, and Profit of a Monopolistic Competitor

Although a full analysis of the multiple dimensions of monopolistic competition cannot be compressed into two dimensions, a good introduction can be gained by considering it within the standard two-dimensional (price, quantity) graph.

To do so we simply consider the four characteristics of monopolistic competition and see what implication they have for the analysis. First, we recognize that the firm has some monopoly power; therefore, a monopolistic competitor faces a downward-sloping demand curve. The downward-sloping demand curve means that in making decisions about output, the monopolistic competitor will, as will a monopolist, face a marginal revenue curve that is below price. At its profit-maximizing output, marginal cost will be less than price (not equal to price as it would be for a perfect competitor). We consider that case in Figure 16-1(a).

FIGURE 16-1 (A AND B)
Monopolistic Competition

In (a) you can see that a monopolistically competitive firm prices in the same manner as a monopolist. It sets quantity where marginal revenue equals marginal cost. In (b) you can see that the monopolistic competitor is not only a monopolist but also a competitor. Competition implies zero economic profit in the long run.

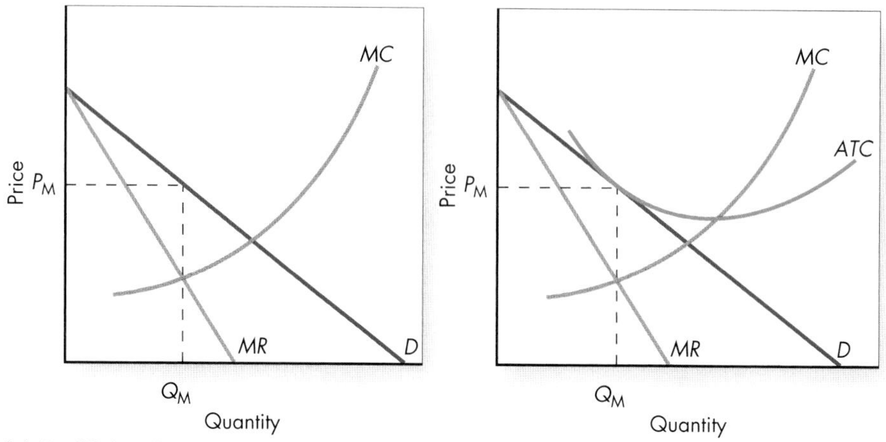

(a) Equilibrium Price and Quantity **(b) Zero Profit**

The monopolistic competitor faces the demand curve *D*, marginal revenue curve *MR*, and marginal cost curve MC. This demand curve is its portion of the total market demand curve. Using the MC = *MR* rule discussed in the last chapter, you can see that the firm will choose output level Q_M (because that's the level of output at which marginal revenue intersects marginal cost). Having determined output, we extend a dotted line up to the demand curve and see that the firm will set a price equal to P_M. This price exceeds marginal cost. So far all we've done is reproduce the monopolist's decision.

Q-1 How does the equilibrium for a monopoly differ from that for a monopolistic competitor?

Where does the competition come in? Competition implies zero economic profit in the long run. (If there's profit, a new competitor will enter the market, decreasing the existing firms' demand [shifting it to the left].) In long-run equilibrium, a perfect competitor makes only a normal profit. Economic profits are determined by *ATC*, not by MC, so the competition part of monopolistic competition tells us where the average total cost curve must be at the long-run equilibrium output. It must be equal to price, and it will be equal to price only if the *ATC* curve is tangent to the demand curve at the output the firm chooses. We add that average total cost curve to the MC, *MR*, and demand curves in Figure 16-1(b). Profit or loss, I hope you remember, is determined by the difference between price and average total cost at the quantity the firm chooses.

To give this condition a little more intuitive meaning, let's say, for instance, that the monopolistically competitive firm is making a profit. This profit would set two adjustments in motion. First, it would attract new entrants. Some of the firm's customers would then defect, and its portion of the market demand curve would decrease. Second, to try to protect its profits, the firm would likely increase expenditures on product differentiation and advertising to offset that entry. (There would be an All New, Really New, Widget campaign.) These expenditures would shift its average total cost curve up. These two adjustments would continue until the profits disappeared and the new demand curve is tangent to the new average total cost curve. A monopolistically competitive firm can make no long-run economic profit.

Comparing Monopolistic Competition with Perfect Competition

If both the monopolistic competitor and the perfect competitor make zero economic profit in the long run, it might seem that, in the long run at least, they're identical. They aren't, however. The perfect competitor perceives its demand curve as perfectly

FIGURE 16-2 (A AND B) A Comparison of Perfect and Monopolistic Competition

The perfect competitor perceives its demand curve as perfectly elastic, and zero economic profit means that it produces at the minimum of the *ATC* curve, as represented in (**a**). A monopolistic competitor, on the other hand, faces a downward-sloping demand curve and produces where marginal cost equals marginal revenue, as represented in (**b**). In long-run equilibrium, the *ATC* curve is tangent to the demand curve at that level, which is *not* at the minimum point of the *ATC* curve. The monopolistic competitor sells Q_M at price P_M. A perfect competitor with the same marginal cost curve would produce Q_C at price P_C.

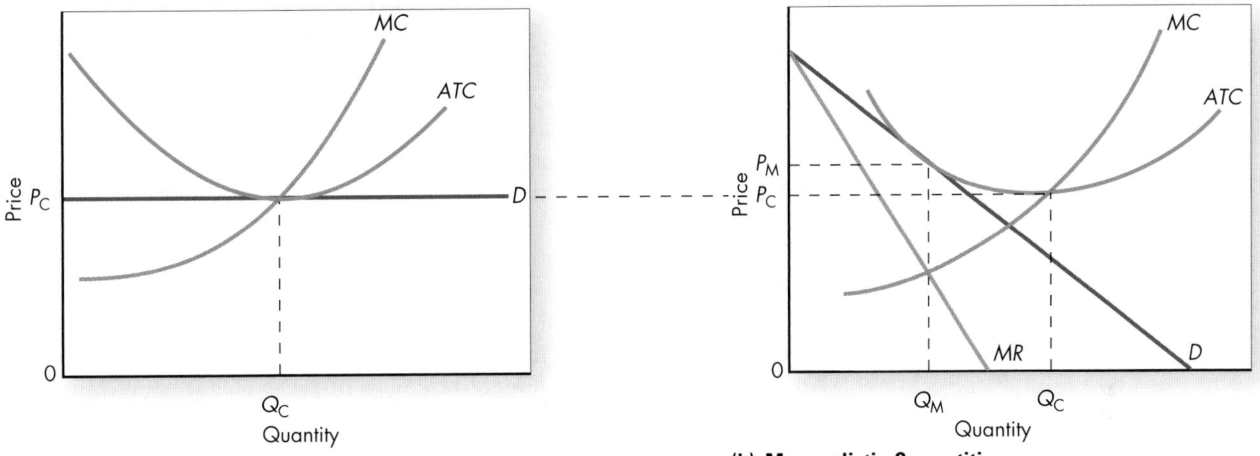

(a) Perfect Competition **(b) Monopolistic Competition**

elastic, and the zero economic profit condition means that it produces at the minimum of the average total cost curve where the marginal cost curve equals price. We demonstrate that case in Figure 16-2(a).

The monopolistic competitor faces a downward-sloping demand curve for its differentiated product. It produces where the marginal cost curve equals the marginal revenue curve, and not where MC equals price. In equilibrium, price exceeds marginal cost. The average total cost curve of a monopolistic competitor is tangent to the demand curve at that output level, which cannot be at the minimum point of the average total cost curve since the demand curve is sloping downward. The minimum point of the average total cost curve (where a perfect competitor produces) is at a higher output (Q_C) than that of the monopolistic competitor (Q_M). I demonstrate the monopolistically competitive equilibrium in Figure 16-2(b) to allow you to compare monopolistic competition with perfect competition.

The perfect competitor in long-run equilibrium produces at a point where MC = *P* = *ATC*. At that point, *ATC* is at its minimum. A monopolistic competitor produces at a point where MC = *MR*. Price is higher than marginal cost. For a monopolistic competitor in long-run equilibrium:

For a monopolistic competitor in long-run equilibrium, $(P = ATC) \geq (MC = MR)$.

$$(P = ATC) \geq (MC = MR)$$

At that point, *ATC* is *not* at its minimum.

What does this distinction between a monopolistically competitive industry and a perfectly competitive industry mean in practice? It means that for a monopolistic competitor, since increasing output lowers average cost, increasing market share is a relevant concern. If only the monopolistic competitor could expand its market, it could do better. For a perfect competitor, increasing output offers no benefit in the form of lower average cost. A perfect competitor would have no concern about market share (the firm's percentage of total sales in the market).

Comparing Monopolistic Competition with Monopoly

The difference between a monopolist and a monopolistic competitor is in the position of the average total cost curve in long-run equilibrium.

An important difference between a monopolist and a monopolistic competitor is in the position of the average total cost curve in long-run equilibrium. For a monopolist, the average total cost curve can be, but need not be, at a position below price so that the monopolist makes a long-run economic profit. In contrast, the average total cost curve for a monopolistic competitor must be tangent to the demand curve at the price and output chosen by the monopolistic competitor. No long-run economic profit is possible.

Advertising and Monopolistic Competition

While firms in a perfectly competitive market have no incentive to advertise (since they can sell all they want at the market price), monopolistic competitors have a strong incentive. That's because their products are differentiated from the others; advertising plays an important role in providing that differentiation.

Goals of advertising include shifting the firm's demand curve to the right and making it more inelastic.

Goals of Advertising Goals of advertising include shifting the firm's demand curve to the right and making it more inelastic. Advertising works by providing consumers with information about the firm's product and by making people want only a specific brand. That allows the firm to sell more, to charge a higher price, or to enjoy a combination of the two.

Q-2 Why do monopolistically competitive firms advertise and perfect competitors do not?

When many firms are advertising, the advertising might be done less to shift the demand curve out than to keep the demand curve where it is—to stop consumers from shifting to a competitor's product. In either case, firms advertise to move the demand curve further out and to make it more inelastic than it would be if the firms weren't advertising.

Advertising has another effect; it shifts the average total cost curve up. Thus, in deciding how much to advertise, a firm must consider advertising's effect on both revenue and cost. It is advantageous to the firm if the marginal revenue of advertising exceeds the marginal cost of advertising.

Does Advertising Help or Hurt Society? Our perception of products (the degree of trust we put in them) is significantly influenced by advertising. Think of the following pairs of goods:

Web Note 16.2
Brand Names

Rolex	Cheerios	Clorox bleach	Bayer
Timex	Oat Circles	generic bleach	generic aspirin

Each of these names conveys a sense of what it is and how much trust we put in the product, and that determines how much we're willing to pay for it. For example, most people would pay more for Cheerios than for Oat Circles. Each year firms in the United States spend more than $200 billion on advertising. A 30-second commercial during the Super Bowl can cost as much as $3 million. That advertising increases firms' costs but also differentiates their products.

Are we as consumers better off or worse off with differentiated products? That's difficult to say. There's a certain waste in much of the differentiation that occurs. It shows up in the graph by the fact that monopolistic competitors don't produce at the minimum point of their average total cost curve. But there's also a sense of trust that we get from buying names we know and in having goods that are slightly different from one another. I'm a sophisticated consumer who knows that there's little difference between generic aspirin and Bayer aspirin. Yet sometimes I buy Bayer aspirin even though it costs more.

Edward Chamberlin, who, together with Joan Robinson, was the originator of the description of monopolistic competition, believed that the difference between the cost of a perfect competitor and the cost of a monopolistic competitor was the cost of what he called "differentness."[1] If consumers are willing to pay that cost, then it's not a waste but, rather, it's a benefit to them.

We must be careful about drawing any implications from this analysis. Average total cost for a monopolistically competitive firm includes advertising and costs of differentiating a product. It's debatable whether we as consumers are better off with as much differentiation as we have, or whether we'd all be better off if all firms produced a generic product at a lower cost.

Characteristics of Oligopoly

The central element of oligopoly is that there are a small number of firms in an industry so that, in any decision a firm makes, it must take into account the expected reaction of other firms. Oligopolistic firms are mutually interdependent and can be collusive or noncollusive.

Oligopolistic firms are mutually interdependent.

This mutual interdependence is the big difference between monopolistic competition and oligopoly. In oligopoly, firms explicitly take other firms' actions into account. In monopolistic competition, there are so many firms that individual firms tend not to explicitly take into account rival firms' likely responses to their decisions. Collusion is difficult. In oligopoly there are fewer firms, and each firm is more likely to explicitly engage in **strategic decision making**—*taking explicit account of a rival's expected response to a decision you are making*. In oligopolies all decisions, including pricing decisions, are strategic decisions. Collusion is much easier. Thus, one distinguishes between monopolistic competition and oligopoly by whether or not firms explicitly take into account competitors' reactions to their decisions.

Oligopolies take into account the reactions of other firms; monopolistic competitors do not.

Q-3 Your study partner, Jean, has just said that monopolistic competitors use strategic decision making. How would you respond?

Why is the distinction important? Because it determines whether economists can model and predict the price and output of an industry. Nonstrategic decision making can be predicted relatively accurately if individuals behave rationally. Strategic decision making is much more difficult to predict, even if people behave rationally. What one person does depends on what he or she expects other people to do, which in turn depends on what others expect the one person to do. Consistent with this distinction, economists' model of monopolistic competition has a definite prediction. A model of monopolistic competition will tell us: Here's how much will be produced and here's how much will be charged. Economists' models of oligopoly don't have a definite prediction. There are no unique price and output decisions at which an oligopoly will rationally arrive; there are a variety of rational oligopoly decisions, and a variety of oligopoly models.

Most industries in the United States have some oligopolistic elements. If you ask almost any businessperson whether he or she directly takes into account rivals' likely response, the answer you'll get is "In certain cases, yes; in others, no."

Most retail stores that you deal with are oligopolistic in your neighborhood or town, although by national standards they may be quite competitive. For example, how many grocery stores do you shop at? Do you think they keep track of what their competitors are doing? You bet. They keep a close eye on their competitors' prices and set their own accordingly.

Models of Oligopoly Behavior

No single general model of oligopoly behavior exists. The reason is that an oligopolist can decide on pricing and output strategy in many possible ways, and there are no compelling grounds to characterize any of them as *the* oligopoly strategy. Although there

[1] Joan Robinson, a Cambridge, England, economist, called this the theory of imperfect competition, rather than the theory of monopolistic competition.

are five or six formal models, I'll focus on two informal models of oligopoly behavior that give you insight into real-world problems. The two models we'll consider are the cartel model and the contestable market model. These should give you a sense of how real-world oligopolistic pricing takes place.

Models of Oligopoly

Why, you ask, can't economists develop a simple formal model of oligopoly? The reason lies in the interdependence of oligopolists. Since there are few competitors, what one firm does specifically influences what other firms do, so an oligopolist's plan must always be a contingency or strategic plan. If my competitors act one way, I'll do X, but if they act another way, I'll do Y. Strategic interactions have a variety of potential outcomes rather than a single outcome such as in the formal models we discussed. An oligopolist spends enormous amounts of time guessing what its competitors will do, and it develops a strategy of how it will act accordingly. As discussed in Chapter 11, an entire theory called game theory has developed that considers interdependent decisions. The appendix to this chapter shows how game theory can be applied to oligopoly decisions.

The Cartel Model

If oligopolies can limit the entry of other firms and form a cartel, they increase the profits going to the combination of firms in the cartel.

A **cartel** is *a combination of firms that acts as if it were a single firm;* a cartel is a shared monopoly. If oligopolies can limit entry by other firms, they have a strong incentive to cartelize the industry and to act as a monopolist would, restricting output to a level that maximizes profit to the combination of firms. Thus, the **cartel model of oligopoly** is *a model that assumes that oligopolies act as if they were monopolists that have assigned output quotas to individual member firms of the oligopoly so that total output is consistent with joint profit maximization.* All firms follow a uniform pricing policy that serves their collective interest.

Web Note 16.3
Price-Fixing

Since a monopolist makes the most profit that can be squeezed from a market, cartelization is the best strategy for an oligopoly. It requires each oligopolist to hold its production below what would be in its own interest were it not to collude with the others. Such explicit formal collusion is against the law in the United States, but informal collusion is allowed and oligopolies have developed a variety of methods to collude implicitly. Thus, the cartel model has some relevance.

Q-4 Why is it difficult for firms in an industry to maintain a cartel?

The model has some problems, however. For example, various firms' interests often differ, so it isn't clear what the collective interest of the firms in the industry is. In many cases a single firm, often the largest or dominant firm, takes the lead in pricing and output decisions, and the other firms (which are often called *fringe firms*) follow suit, even though they might have preferred to adopt a different strategy.

This dominant-firm cartel model works only if the smaller firms face barriers to entry, or the dominant firm has significantly lower cost conditions. If that were not the case, the smaller firms would pick up an increasing share of the market, eliminating the dominant firm's monopoly. An example of such a dominant-firm market was the copier market in the 1960s and 1970s, in which Xerox set the price and other firms followed. That copier market also shows the temporary nature of such a market. As the firms became more competitive on cost and quality, Xerox's market share fell and the company lost its dominant position. The copier market is far more competitive today than it used to be.

In some cases, firms collude implicitly—they just happen to make the same pricing decisions. This is not illegal.

In other cases the various firms meet—sometimes only by happenstance, at the golf course or at a trade association gathering—and arrive at a collective decision. In the United States, meetings for this purpose are illegal, but they do occur. In yet other cases, the firms engage in **implicit collusion**—*multiple firms make the same pricing decisions even though they have not explicitly consulted with one another.* They "just happen" to come to a collective decision.

Implicit Price Collusion Implicit price collusion, in which firms just happen to charge the same price but didn't meet to discuss price strategy, isn't against the law.

Oligopolies often operate as close to the fine edge of the law as they can. For example, many oligopolistic industries allow a price leader to set the price, and then the others follow suit. The airline and steel industries take that route. Firms just happen to charge the same price or very close to the same price.

It isn't only in major industries that you see such implicit collusion. In small towns, you'll notice that most independent carpenters charge the same price. There's no explicit collusion, but were a carpenter to offer to work for less than the others, he or she would feel unwelcome at the local breakfast restaurant.

Or let's take another example: the Miami fish market, where sport fishermen sell their catch at the dock. When I lived in Miami, I often went to the docks to buy fresh fish. There were about 20 stands, all charging the same price. Price fluctuated, but it was by subtle agreement, and close to the end of the day the word would go out that the price could be reduced.

I got to know some of the sellers and asked them why they priced like that when it would be in their individual interest to set their own price. Their answer: "We like our boat and don't want it burned." They may have been talking in hyperbole, but social pressures play an important role in stabilizing prices in an oligopoly.

Cartels and Technological Change Even if all firms in the industry cooperate, other firms, unless they are prevented from doing so, can always enter the market with a technologically superior new product at the same price or with the same good at a lower price. It is important to remember that technological changes are constantly occurring, and that a successful cartel with high profits will provide incentives for significant technological change, which can eliminate demand for its monopolized product.

Why Are Prices Sticky? Informal collusion happens all the time in U.S. businesses. One characteristic of informal collusive behavior is that prices tend to be sticky—they don't change frequently. The existence of informal collusion is an important reason why prices are sticky. But it's not the only reason.

Another possible reason is that firms don't collude, but do have certain expectations of other firms' reactions, which changes their perceived demand curves. Specifically, they perceive a kinked demand curve facing them. This kinked demand curve is used especially to explain why firms often do not use lower-price strategies to increase sales.

Let's go through the reasoning behind the kinked demand curve. If a firm increases its price, and the firm believes that other firms won't go along, its perceived demand curve for increasing price will be very elastic (D_1 in Figure 16-3). It will lose lots of business to the other firms that haven't raised their price. The relevant portions of its demand curve and its marginal revenue curve are shown in blue in Figure 16-3.

If it decreased its price, however, the firm assumes that all other firms would immediately match that decrease, so it would gain very few, if any, additional sales. A large fall in price would result in only a small increase in sales, so its demand is very inelastic (D_2 in Figure 16-3). This less elastic portion of the demand curve and the corresponding marginal revenue curve are shown in orange in Figure 16-3.

Q-5 Is the demand curve as perceived by an oligopolist likely to be more or less elastic for a price increase or a price decrease?

Notice that when you put these two curves together, you get a rather strange demand curve (it's kinked) and an even stranger marginal revenue curve (one with a gap). I didn't make a mistake in drawing the curves; that's the way they come out given the assumptions. When the demand curve has a kink, the marginal revenue curve must have a gap.

When the demand curve has a kink, the marginal revenue curve must have a gap.

If firms do indeed perceive their demand curves to be kinked at the market price, we have another explanation of why prices tend to be sticky. Shifts in marginal cost (such as MC_0 to MC_1) will not change the firm's profit maximization position. A large shift in marginal cost is required before firms will change their price. Why should this be the case? The intuitive answer lies in the reason behind the kink. If the firm raises its price,

FIGURE 16-3 The Kinked Demand Curve

One explanation of why prices are sticky is that firms face a kinked demand curve. When we draw the relevant marginal revenue curve for the kinked demand, we see that the corresponding *MR* curve is discontinuous. It has a gap in it. Shifts in marginal costs between *c* and *d* will not change the price or the output that maximizes profits.

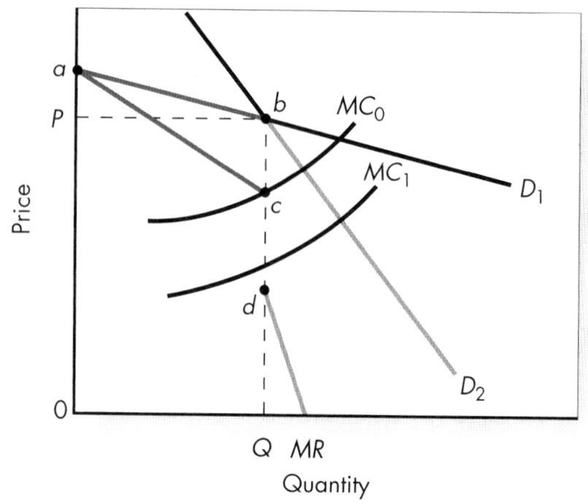

other firms won't go along, so it will lose lots of market share. However, when the firm lowers price, other firms will go along and the firm won't gain market share. Thus, the firm has strong reasons not to change its price in either direction.

I should emphasize that the kinked demand curve is not a theory of oligopoly pricing. It does not say why the original price is what it is; the kinked demand curve is simply a theory of sticky prices.

The Contestable Market Model

In the contestable market model of oligopoly, pricing and entry decisions are based only on barriers to entry and exit, not on market structure. Thus, even if the industry contains only one firm, it could still be a competitive market if entry is open.

A second model of oligopoly is the *contestable market model*. The **contestable market model** *is a model of oligopoly in which barriers to entry and barriers to exit, not the structure of the market, determine a firm's price and output decisions*. Thus, it emphasizes entry and exit conditions, and says that the price that an oligopoly will charge will exceed the cost of production only if new firms cannot exit and enter the market. The higher the barriers, the more the price exceeds cost. Without barriers to entry or exit, the price an oligopolist sets will be equivalent to the competitive price. Thus, an industry that structurally looks like an oligopoly could set competitive prices and output levels.

Comparison of the Contestable Market Model and the Cartel Model

Because of the importance of social pressures in determining strategies of oligopolies, no one "oligopolistic model" exists. Oligopolies with a stronger ability to collude (that is, more social pressures to prevent entry) are able to get closer to a monopolist solution. Equilibrium of oligopolies with weaker social pressures and less ability to prevent new entry is closer to the perfectly competitive solution. That's as explicit as we can be.

Q-6 What are the two extremes an oligopoly model can take?

An oligopoly model can take two extremes: (1) the cartel model, in which an oligopoly sets a monopoly price, and (2) the contestable market model, in which an oligopoly with no barriers to entry sets a competitive price. Thus, we can say that an oligopoly's price will be somewhere between the competitive price and the monopolistic price. Other models of oligopolies give results in between these two.

Much of what happens in oligopoly pricing is highly dependent on the specific legal structure within which firms interact. In Japan, where large firms are specifically allowed to collude, we see Japanese goods selling for a much higher price than those same Japanese goods sell for in the United States. For example, you may well pay twice as much for a Japanese television in Japan as you would in the United States. From the behavior of Japanese firms, we get a sense of what pricing strategy U.S. oligopolists would follow in the absence of the restrictions placed on them by law.

New Entry as a Limit on the Cartelization Strategy One of the things that limits oligopolies from acting as a cartel is the threat from outside competition. The threat will tend to be more effective if this outside competitor is much larger than the firms in the oligopoly.

For example, small-town banks have a tendency to collude (implicitly, of course), offering lower interest to savers and charging higher interest to borrowers than big banks charge, even though their average costs aren't significantly higher. When I ask small-town banks why this is, they tell me that my perceptions are faulty and that I should mind my own business. But if a big bank, which couldn't care less about increasing the wealth of a small-town banker, enters the town and establishes a branch office, interest rates to savers seem to go up and interest rates to borrowers seem to go down. The big bank can add significant competition—competition that couldn't come from within the town.

On a national scale, the outside competition often comes from international firms. For example, implicit collusion among U.S. automobile firms led to foreign firms' entry into the U.S. automobile market. There are many such examples of this outside competition breaking down cartels with no barriers to entry. Thus, a cartel with no barriers to entry faces a long-run demand curve that's very elastic. This means that its price will be very close to its marginal cost and average cost. This is the same prediction that came from the contestable market theory.

Price Wars With oligopolies, there's always the possibility of a price war. The reasons for such wars are varied. Since oligopolistic firms know their competitors, they can personally dislike them; sometimes a firm's goal can be simply to drive a disliked competitor out of business, even if that process hurts the firm itself. Passion and anger play roles in oligopoly pricing because interpersonal and interfirm relations are important.

Alternatively, a firm might follow a predatory pricing strategy—a strategy of pushing the price down temporarily to drive the other firm out of business to increase long-term profits. Some argue that Microsoft followed a predatory pricing strategy by virtually giving away its Office Suite on new computer systems to make its software the industry standard. If the predatory pricing strategy is successful, the firm can charge an even higher price because potential entrants know that the existing firm will drive them out if they try to enter. It's this continual possibility that strategies can change that makes oligopoly prices so hard to predict. (In an earlier chapter we discussed game theory, which is an important tool that economists use to study strategic pricing by oligopolies.)

Since we have come to the end of our presentation of the analytics of market structure, a review is in order. The box "A Comparison of Various Market Structures" provides that review. It lists the four central market structures, and the similarities and differences among them. It is worth a careful review.

Classifying Industries and Markets in Practice

Web Note 16.4
Porter's Five Forces

An industry seldom fits neatly into one category or another. Inevitably, numerous arbitrary decisions must be made as to what the appropriate market is, and whether the industry comes closest to the characteristics of one or the other market structure. So to classify actual industries, a variety of procedures and measures have been developed, and in this section we review those procedures and measures.

A REMINDER

A Comparison of Various Market Structures

Structure / Characteristics	Monopoly	Oligopoly	Monopolistic Competition	Perfect Competition
Number of Firms	One	Few	Many	Almost infinite
Barriers to Entry	Significant	Significant	Few	None
Pricing Decisions	$MC = MR$	Strategic pricing, between monopoly and perfect competition	$MC = MR$	$MC = MR = P$
Output Decisions	Most output restriction	Output somewhat restricted	Output restricted somewhat by product differentiation	No output restriction
Interdependence	Only firm in market, not concerned about competitors	Interdependent strategic pricing and output decision	Each firm acts independently	Each firm acts independently
Profit	Possibility of long-run economic profit	Some long-run economic profit possible	No long-run economic profit possible	No long-run economic profit possible
P* and *MC	$P > MC$	$P > MC$	$P > MC$	$P = MC$

To see the problems that arise in classifying industries, consider the banking industry. There are about 9,000 banks in the United States, and banking is considered reasonably competitive. However, a particular small town may have only one or two banks, so there will be a monopoly or oligopoly with respect to banks in that town. Is the United States or the town the relevant market? The same argument exists when we think of international competition. Many firms sell in international markets and, while a group of firms may compose an oligopoly in the United States, the international market might be more accurately characterized by monopolistic competition.

Another dimension of the classification problem concerns deciding what is to be included in an industry. If you define the industry as "the transportation industry," there are many firms. If you define it as "the urban transit industry," there are fewer firms; if you define it as "the commuter rail industry," there are still fewer firms.

Similarly with the geographic dimension of industry. There's more competition in the global market than in the local market. The narrower the definition, the fewer the firms.

One of the ways in which economists classify markets in practice is by cross-price elasticities (the responsiveness of the change in the demand for a good to change in the price of a related good). Industrial organization economist F. M. Sherer has suggested the following rule of thumb: When two goods have a cross-price elasticity greater than or equal to 3, they can be regarded as belonging to the same market.

The North American Industry Classification System

The **North American Industry Classification System (NAICS)** is *an industry classification that categorizes industries by type of economic activity and groups firms with like production processes*. In the NAICS, all firms are placed into 20 broadly defined two-digit sectors. These two-digit sectors are further subdivided into three-digit subsectors, four-digit industry groupings, five-digit industries, and six-digit national industry groupings. Each subgrouping becomes more and more narrowly defined. Table 16-1 lists the 20 sectors and shows the subgroupings for one sector, Information, to give you an idea of what's included in each.

Q-7 Which would have more output: the two-digit industry 21 or the four-digit industry 2111? Explain your reasoning.

When economists talk about industry structure, they generally talk about industries in the four- to six-digit subsector groupings in the United States. This is a convention. Economists are often called on to give expert testimony in court cases, and if an

TABLE 16-1 Industry Groupings in the North American Industry Classification System

Two-Digit Sectors		Three- to Six-Digit Subsectors
11	Agriculture, forestry, fishing, and hunting	
21	Mining	
22	Utilities	
23	Construction	
31–33	Manufacturing	
42	Wholesale trade	
44–45	Retail trade	
48–49	Transportation and warehousing	517 Telecommunications
51	Information	5172 Wireless telecommunications carriers (except satellite)
52	Finance and insurance	517211 Paging
53	Real estate and rental and leasing	
54	Professional, scientific, and technical services	
55	Management of companies and enterprises	
56	Administrative and support, and waste management and remediation services	
61	Education services	
62	Health care and social assistance	
71	Arts, entertainment, and recreation	
72	Accommodation and food services	
81	Other services (except public administration)	
92	Public administration	

Source: U.S. Census Bureau (www.census.gov/epcd/www/naics.html).

economist wants to argue that an industry is more competitive than its opponents say it is, he or she challenges this convention of using a four- to six-digit classification of industry, asserting that the classification is arbitrary (which it is) and that the relevant market should be the two- to three-digit classification.

Empirical Measures of Industry Structure

To empirically measure industry structure, economists use one of two methods: the concentration ratio or the Herfindahl index.

A **concentration ratio** is *the value of sales by the top firms of an industry stated as a percentage of total industry sales*. The most commonly used concentration ratio is the four-firm concentration ratio. For example, a four-firm concentration ratio of 60 percent tells you that the top four firms in the industry produce 60 percent of the industry's output. The higher the ratio, the closer the industry is to an oligopolistic or monopolistic type of market structure.

The Herfindahl index is a method used by economists to classify how competitive an industry is.

The **Herfindahl index** is *an index of market concentration calculated by adding the squared value of the individual market shares of all the firms in the industry*. For example, say that 10 firms in the industry each has 10 percent of the market:

$$\text{Herfindahl Index} = 10^2 + 10^2 + 10^2 + 10^2 + 10^2 + 10^2 + 10^2 + 10^2 + 10^2 + 10^2 = 1{,}000$$

Because it squares market shares, the Herfindahl index gives more weight to firms with large market shares than does the concentration ratio measure.

The Herfindahl index weights the largest firms in the industry more heavily than the concentration ratio because it squares market shares.

The two measures can differ because of their construction, but generally if the concentration ratio is high, so is the Herfindahl index. The table below presents the four-firm concentration ratio and the Herfindahl index of selected industries.

Industry	Four-Firm Concentration Ratio	Herfindahl Index
Poultry	46	773
Soft drinks	52	896
Breakfast cereal	78	2,999
Women's and misses' dresses	21	186
Book printing	38	492
Stationery	51	976
Soap and detergent	38	664
Men's footwear	44	734
Women's footwear	64	1,556
Pharmaceuticals	34	506
Computer and peripheral equipment	49	1,183
Radio, TV, wireless broadcasting	42	583
Burial caskets	73	2,965

Source: *Census of Manufacturers* (factfinder.census.gov).

The Herfindahl index plays an important role in government policy; it is used as a rule of thumb by the U.S. Department of Justice in determining whether an industry is sufficiently competitive to allow a merger between two large firms. If the Herfindahl index is less than 1,000, the Department of Justice generally assumes the industry is sufficiently competitive, and it doesn't look more closely at the merger. We'll discuss this in more detail in the chapter on antitrust policy.

Conglomerate Firms and Bigness

Neither the four-firm concentration ratio nor the Herfindahl index gives us a picture of corporations' bigness. That's because many corporations are conglomerates—companies that span a variety of unrelated industries. For example, a conglomerate might produce both shoes and automobiles.

To see that concentration ratios are not an index of bigness, say the entire United States had only 11 firms, each with a 9 percent share of each industry. Both indexes would classify the U.S. economy as unconcentrated, but many people would seriously doubt whether that were the case. Little work has been done on classifying conglomerates or in determining whether they affect an industry's performance.

Q-8 If the four-firm concentration ratio of an industry is 60 percent, what is the highest Herfindahl index that industry could have? What is the lowest?

Oligopoly Models and Empirical Estimates of Market Structure

To see how empirical measures of market structure relate to oligopoly models, let's consider the cartel and contestable market models of oligopoly. The cartel model fits best with these empirical measurements because it assumes that the structure of the market (the number of firms) is directly related to the price a firm charges. It predicts that oligopolies charge higher prices than do monopolistic competitors, who in turn charge higher prices than competitive firms charge.

The contestable market model gives far less weight to the empirical estimates of market structure. According to it, markets that structurally look highly oligopolistic could actually be highly competitive—much more so than markets that structurally look less competitive. This contestable market model view of judging markets by performance, not structure, has had many reincarnations. Close relatives of it have previously been called the *barriers-to-entry* model, the *stay-out pricing* model, and the *limit-pricing* model. These models provide a view of competition that doesn't depend on market structure.

Q-9 The Herfindahl index is 1,500. Using a contestable market approach, what would you conclude about this industry?

To see the implications of the contestable market approach, let's consider an oligopoly with a four-firm concentration ratio of 60 percent and a Herfindahl index of 1,500. Using the structural approach, we would say that, because of the multiplicity of oligopoly models, we're not quite sure what price firms in this industry would charge, but that it seems reasonable to assume that there would be some implicit collusion and that the price would be closer to a monopolist price than to a competitive price. If that same market had a four-firm concentration ratio of 30 percent and a Herfindahl index of 700, the industry would be more likely to have a competitive price.

Q-10 The Herfindahl index is 1,500. Using a structural analysis of markets approach, what would you conclude about this industry?

A contestable market model advocate would disagree, arguing that barriers to entry and exit are what's important. If no significant barriers to entry exist in the first case but significant barriers to entry exist in the second case, the second case would be more monopolistic than the first. An example is the Miami fish market mentioned earlier, where there were 20 sellers (none with a large percentage of the market) and significant barriers to entry (only fishers from the pier were allowed to sell fish there and the slots at the pier were limited). Because of those entry limitations, the pricing and output decisions would be close to the monopolistic price. If you took that same structure but had free entry, you'd get much closer to competitive decisions.

As I presented the two views, I emphasized the differences in order to make the distinction clear. However, I must also point out that there's a similarity in the two views. Often barriers to entry are the reason there are only a few firms in an industry. And when there are many firms, that suggests that there are few barriers to entry. In such situations, which make up the majority of cases, the two approaches come to the same conclusion.

Conclusion

As you can see, the real world gets very complicated very quickly. I'll show you just how complicated in the chapter on real-world competion and technology. But don't let the complicated real world get you down on the theories presented here. It's precisely because the real world is so complicated that we need some framework, like the one presented in this chapter. That framework lets us focus on specific issues—and hopefully the most important.

Summary

- Monopolistic competition is characterized by (1) many sellers, (2) differentiated products, (3) multiple dimensions of competition, and (4) ease of entry for new firms.
- The central characteristic of oligopoly is that there are a small number of interdependent firms.
- In monopolistic competition, firms act independently; in an oligopoly, they take account of each other's actions.
- Monopolistic competitors differ from perfect competitors in that the former face a downward-sloping demand curve.
- A monopolistic competitor differs from a monopolist in that a monopolistic competitor makes zero economic profit in long-run equilibrium.
- An oligopolist's price will be somewhere between the competitive price and the monopolistic price.
- A contestable market theory of oligopoly judges an industry's competitiveness more by performance and barriers to entry than by structure. Cartel models of oligopoly concentrate on market structure.
- Industries are classified by economic activity in the North American Industry Classification System (NAICS). Industry structures are measured by concentration ratios and Herfindahl indexes.
- A concentration ratio is the sum of the market shares of individual firms with the largest shares in an industry.
- A Herfindahl index is the sum of the squares of the individual market shares of all firms in an industry.

Key Terms

cartel *(368)*
cartel model of oligopoly *(368)*
concentration ratio *(374)*
contestable market model *(370)*
Herfindahl index *(374)*
implicit collusion *(368)*
market structure *(361)*
monopolistic competition *(361)*
North American Industry Classification System (NAICS) *(373)*
oligopoly *(361)*
strategic decision making *(367)*

Questions and Exercises

1. What are the ways in which a firm can differentiate its product from that of its competitors? What is the overriding objective of product differentiation? LO1
2. What are the "monopolistic" and the "competitive" elements of monopolistic competition? LO1

3. What are some of the barriers to entry in the restaurant industry? LO1
4. What are some of the barriers to entry in the automobile industry? LO1
5. Both a perfect competitor and a monopolistic competitor choose output where MC = *MR*, and neither makes a profit in the long run. How is it, then, that the monopolistic competitor produces less than a perfect competitor? LO2
6. If a monopolistic competitor is able to restrict output, why doesn't it earn economic profits? LO2
7. Suppose a monopolistic competitor in long-run equilibrium has a constant marginal cost of $6 and faces the demand curve given in the following table:

Q	20	18	16	14	12	10	8	6
P	$ 2	4	6	8	10	12	14	16

   a. What output will the firm choose?
   b. What will be the monopolistic competitor's average fixed cost at the output it chooses? LO2
8. You're the manager of a firm that has constant marginal cost of $6. Fixed cost is zero. The market structure is monopolistically competitive. You're faced with the following demand curve:

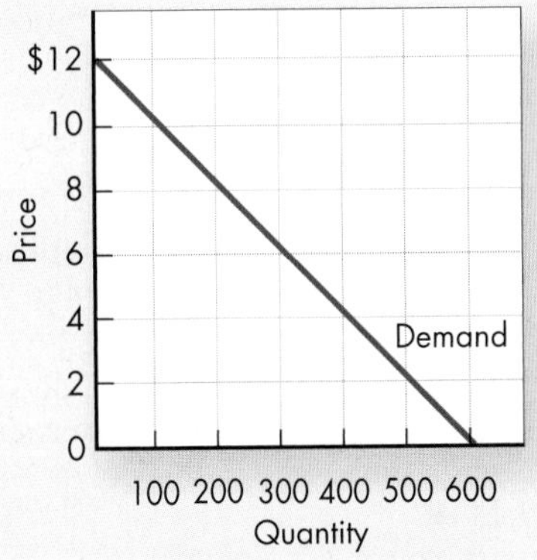

   a. Determine graphically the profit-maximizing price and output for your firm in the short run. Demonstrate what profit or loss you'll be making.
   b. What happens in the long run? LO2
9. Manufacturers often pay "slotting fees," payments to retailers to provide their product prime shelf space. These fees range from $25,000 for one item in one store to $3 million for a chain of stores. An example is placing Doritos within a football display before Super Bowl Sunday.
   a. In what type of market structure would this behavior likely be prevalent?
   b. What does this behavior accomplish for the firm? Relate your answer to the observation that a typical supermarket stocks about 30,000 products.
   c. Demonstrate the likely long-term profit in this market structure.
   d. Firms have complained to the FTC that this practice is unfair. What is their likely argument?
   e. What is an argument on the other side of that presented in *d*? LO2
10. Is an oligopolist more or less likely to engage in strategic decision making compared to a monopolistic competitor? LO3
11. What is the difference between the contestable market model and the cartel model of oligopoly? LO4
12. How are the contestable market model and the cartel model of oligopoly related? LO4
13. Is a contestable model or cartel model more likely to judge an industry by performance? Explain your answer. LO4
14. What did Adam Smith mean when he wrote, "Seldom do businessmen of the same trade get together but that it results in some detriment to the general public"? LO4
15. In 1982 Robert Crandell, CEO of American Airlines, phoned the Braniff Airways CEO and said, "Raise your fares 20 percent and I'll raise mine the next morning."
   a. Why would he do this?
   b. If you were the Braniff Airways CEO, would you have gone along?
   c. Why should Crandell not have done this? LO4
16. Which industry is more highly concentrated: one with a Herfindahl index of 1,200 or one with a four-firm concentration ratio of 55 percent? LO5
17. Kellogg's, which controls 32 percent of the breakfast cereal market, cut the prices of some of its best-selling brands of cereal to regain market share lost to Post, which controls 20 percent of the market. General Mills has 24 percent of the market. The price cuts were expected to trigger a price war. Based on this information, what market structure best characterizes the market for breakfast cereal? LO5
18. The pizza market is divided as follows:

Pizza Hut	20.7%
Domino's	17.0
Little Caesars	6.7
Pizza Inn/Pantera's	2.2
Round Table	2.0
All others	51.4

   a. How would you describe its market structure?
   b. What is the approximate Herfindahl index?
   c. What is the four-firm concentration ratio? LO5

Questions from Alternative Perspectives

1. Firms in a monopolistically competitive market depend on differentiating their products.
   a. How do firms differentiate their products?
   b. Aside from commodities such as gold and grain, how many homogeneous products can you name?
   c. What does your answer to *b* suggest about market structure in the real world?
   d. Does the existence of monopolistically competitive markets imply that government should intervene in these markets? (Austrian)
2. In which market structure would women likely be most successful? Why? (Feminist)
3. Any large grocery store carries at least seven different kinds of corn chips—baked, fried, salsa-flavored, white, yellow, blue, and lime-flavored.
   a. When is product differentiation real and when is it an illusion?
   b. Is there an objective universal answer to *a*?
   c. Are there any individually objective answers to *a* and *b*?
   d. Does your answer to *c* tell you anything about the economic implication of the benefit of markets? (Hint: Is the assumption of rational consumers with well-ordered preference functions necessary to the arguments that markets benefit society?) (Institutionalist)
4. Does market structure determine firm behavior or does firm behavior determine market structure? (Post-Keynesian)
5. Industry-to-industry concentration levels in the U.S. economy have changed little over recent decades. Corporate ownership of assets, however, has become far more concentrated. Five decades ago, the top 200 manufacturing firms accounted for 48 percent of all sales in the U.S. economy. By 1993, the 200 biggest industrial businesses controlled 65 percent of sales. At the same time, however, employment has shifted somewhat toward smaller firms.
   a. Using the report on concentration ratios in U.S. industries in your textbook and the description above, what is the level of competition in today's U.S. economy?
   b. Which model of market structures—from monopoly to perfect competition—best captures the U.S. economy? (Radical)

Issues to Ponder

1. Does the product differentiation in monopolistic competition make us better or worse off? Why? (Difficult) LO1
2. A firm is convinced that if it lowers its price, no other firm in the industry will change price; however, it believes that if it raises its price, some other firms will match its increase, making its demand curve more inelastic. The current price is $8 and its marginal cost is constant at $4. (Difficult)
   a. Sketch the general shape of the firm's *MR*, *MC*, and demand curves and show why there are two possible equilibria.
   b. If there are two equilibria, which of the two do you think the firms will arrive at? Why?
   c. If the marginal cost falls to $3, what would you predict would happen to price?
   d. If the marginal cost rises to $5, what would you predict would happen to price?
   e. Do a survey of five or six firms in your area. Ask them how they believe other firms would respond to their increasing or decreasing price. Based on that survey, discuss the relevance of this kinked demand model compared to the one presented in the book. LO2
3. Private colleges of the same caliber generally charge roughly the same tuition. Would you characterize these colleges as a cartel type of oligopoly? (Difficult) LO4
4. In the 1990s, the infant/preschool toy market four-firm concentration ratio was 72 percent. With 8 percent of the market, Mattel was the fourth largest firm in that market. Mattel proposed to buy Fisher-Price, the market leader with 27 percent.
   a. Why would Mattel want to buy Fisher-Price?
   b. What arguments can you think of in favor of allowing this acquisition?
   c. What arguments can you think of against allowing this acquisition?
   d. How do you think the four-firm concentration ratio for the entire toy industry would compare to this infant/preschool toy market concentration ratio? LO4, LO5

Answers to Margin Questions

1. Both a monopoly and a monopolistic competitor produce where marginal cost equals marginal revenue. The difference is the position of the average total cost curve. For a monopolistic competitor, the average total cost curve must be tangent to the demand curve because a monopolistic competitor makes no profits in the long run. A monopoly can make profits in the long run, so its average total cost can be below the price. *(364)*
2. Monopolistically competitive firms advertise because their products are differentiated from others. Advertising can convince people that a firm's product is better than that of other firms and increase demand for its product. Perfect competitors, in contrast, have no incentive to advertise since their products are the same as every other firm's product and they can sell all they want at the market price. *(366)*
3. I would respond that monopolistic competitors, by definition, do not take into account the expected reactions of competitors to their decisions; therefore, they cannot use strategic decision making. I would tell Jean she probably meant, "*Oligopolies* use strategic decision making." *(367)*
4. Maintaining a cartel requires firms to make decisions that are not in their individual best interests. Such decisions are hard to enforce unless there is an explicit enforcement mechanism, which is difficult in a cartel. *(368)*
5. The demand curve perceived by an oligopolist is more elastic above the current price because it believes that others will not follow price increases. If it increased price, its quantity demanded would fall by a lot. The opposite is true below the current price. The demand curve below current price is less elastic. Price declines would be matched by competitors and the oligopolist would see little change in quantity demanded with a price decline. *(369)*
6. The two extremes an oligopoly model can take are (1) a cartel model, which is the equivalent of a monopoly, and (2) a contestable market model, which, if there are no barriers to entry, is the equivalent of a competitive industry. *(370)*
7. The smaller the number of digits, the more inclusive the classification. Therefore, the two-digit industry would have significantly more output. *(373)*
8. The highest Herfindahl index for this industry would occur if one firm had the entire 60 percent, and all other firms had an infinitesimal amount, making the Herfindahl index slightly over 3,600. The lowest Herfindahl index this industry could have would occur if each of the top four firms had 15 percent of the market, yielding a Herfindahl index of 900. *(375)*
9. The contestable market approach looks at barriers to entry, not structure. Therefore, we can conclude nothing about the industry from the Herfindahl index. *(375)*
10. In a market with a Herfindahl index of 1,500, the largest firm would have, at most, slightly under 38 percent of the market. The least concentrated such an industry could be would be if seven firms each had between 14 and 15 percent of the market. In either of these two cases, the industry would probably be an oligopolistic industry and could border on monopoly. *(375)*

APPENDIX A

Game Theory and Oligopoly

In Chapter 11 I discussed game theory and its ability to shed light on a broader set of issues than the traditional model. You can see the power of game theory by applying it to oligopoly. As discussed in this chapter, oligopoly involves *strategic interaction* in which the firms take into account the decisions of the other firms. In all the other basic models—supply/demand, perfect competition, monopolistic competition, and monopoly—firms did not take into account the decisions of other firms. In those models, firms assumed that their decisions had no effect on other firms' decisions. In perfect competition and monopolistic competition, the argument justifying that assumption was that the firms were so small that their decisions didn't matter to others in the industry; in monopoly, the argument justifying that assumption was that the firm faced no competitors, so there was no other firm to consider. In oligopoly that wasn't the case, which meant that we could not develop a neat formal geometric model of firm behavior.

Game theory allows us to develop more precise models of oligopolistic markets, and of all situations that involve strategic interaction. Thus, game theory can be seen as a complement to, not a replacement for, the supply/demand model. In fact if the game is structured to reflect the assumptions of the supply/demand model, the reasoning in game theory is consistent with supply/demand analysis. Given the same assumptions, game theory comes to the same conclusions as supply/demand analysis.

Prisoner's Dilemma and a Duopoly Example

The easiest application of game theory to oligopoly involves the prisoner's dilemma. To keep the analysis easy, we will assume there are only two firms in the market, which makes the oligopoly what is called a **duopoly**—*an oligopoly with only two firms*. So let us consider the strategic decisions facing a "foam peanut" (packing material) company in a duopoly. Let us assume that the average total cost and marginal cost of producing foam peanuts are the same for both firms. These costs are shown in Figure A16-1(a).

Assume that a production facility with a minimum efficient scale of 4,000 tons is the smallest that can be built. In Figure A16-1(b), the marginal costs are summed and the industry demand curve is drawn in a way that the competitive price is $500 per ton and the competitive output is 8,000 tons. The relevant industry marginal revenue curve is also drawn.

If the firms can coordinate their actions (fully collude), they will act as a joint monopolist setting total output at 6,000 tons where *MR* = MC (3,000 tons each). As you can see in Figure A16-1(a), this gives each a price of $600 with a cost of $575 per ton, for a joint economic profit of $150,000, or $75,000 each. If the firms do not coordinate their actions, they will produce where the MC curve intersects the demand curve, setting output at 8,000 tons, producing 4,000 tons each. At this level of output, price is $500 a ton. With average costs of $500, neither earns an economic profit. The firms prefer fully colluding to the situation where they do not coordinate their actions (the competitive equilibrium), where they earn zero economic profit.

If they can ensure that they will both abide by the agreement, the monopolist output will be the joint profit-maximizing output. But the strategic reasoning doesn't end there. What if one firm reasons that it can earn more by cheating on the deal? What if one firm produces 4,000 tons (1,000 tons under the counter)? The additional 1,000 tons in output will cause the price to fall to $550 per ton. The cheating firm's average total costs fall to $500 as its output rises to 4,000, so its profit rises to $200,000. However, the noncheating firm's profit moves in the opposite direction. Its average total costs remain $575, but the price it receives falls to $550, so it loses $75,000 instead of making $75,000. The division of profits and output is shown in Figure A16-2.

In Figure A16-2(a), you can see that the firm that abides by the agreement and produces 3,000 units makes a

FIGURE A16-1 (A AND B) Firm and Industry Duopoly Cooperative Equilibrium

In (**a**) I show the marginal and average total cost curves for either firm in the duopoly. To get the average and marginal costs for the industry, you double each. In (**b**) the industry marginal cost curve (the horizontal sum of the individual firms' marginal cost curves) is combined with the industry demand and marginal revenue curves. At the competitive solution for the industry, output is 8,000 and price is $500. As you can see in (**a**), at that price economic profits are zero. At the monopolistic solution, output is 6,000 and price is $600. As you can see in (**a**), *ATC* is $575 at an industry output of 6,000 (firm output of 3,000), so each firm's profit is $25 × 3,000 = $75,000 (the shaded area in (**a**)).

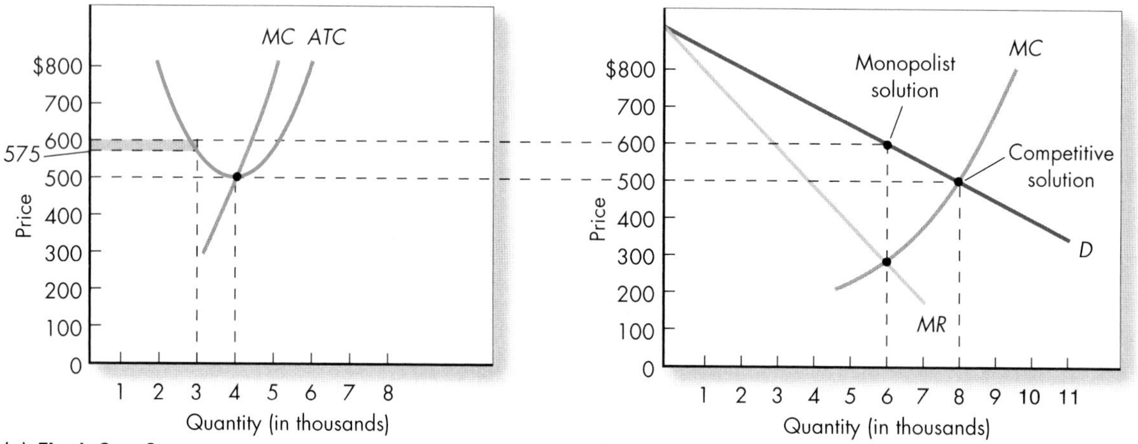

(a) Firm's Cost Curves **(b) Industry: Competitive and Monopolist Solutions**

FIGURE A16-2 (A, B, AND C) Firm and Industry Duopoly Equilibrium When One Firm Cheats

Figures (a) and (b) show the noncheating and the cheating firms' output and profit, respectively, while (c) shows the industry output and price. Say they both cheat. The price is $500 and output is 8,000 (4,000 per firm) (point A in (c)). Both firms make zero profit. If neither cheats, the industry output is 6,000, the price is $600, and their *ATC* is $575. This outcome gives them a profit of $75,000 each and would place them at point C in (c). If one firm cheats and the other does not, the output is 7,000 and the industry price is $550 (point B in (c)). The noncheating firm's $75,000 loss is shown by the shaded area in (a). The cheating firm's $200,000 profit is shown by the shaded area in (b).

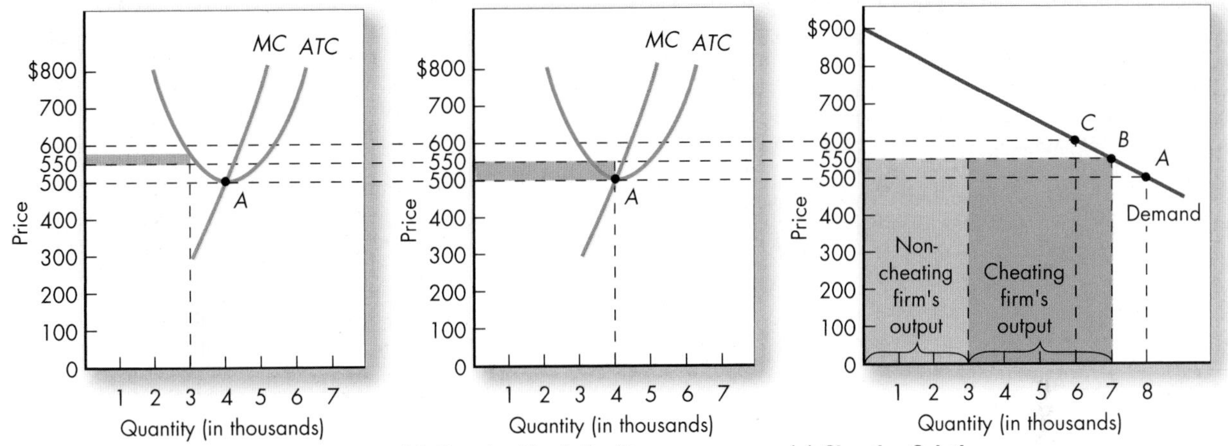

(a) Noncheating Firm's Loss **(b) Cheating Firm's Profit** **(c) Cheating Solution**

loss of $75,000; its average total costs are $575 and the price it receives is $550. In Figure A16-2(b), you can see that the cheating firm makes a profit of $200,000; its average costs are $500, so it is doing much better than when it did not cheat. The combined profit of the cheating and the noncheating firms is $125,000 ($200,000 − $75,000 = $125,000), which is lower than if they cooperated. By cheating, the firm has essentially transferred $125,000 of the other firm's profit to itself and has reduced their combined profit by $25,000. Figure A16-2(c) shows how output is split between the two firms.

Once the other firm realizes that the first firm will benefit by cheating and cannot enforce the agreement, it will do better by cheating too. By cheating, it eliminates its loss and the other firm's profit. Output moves to the competitive output, 8,000, and both of the firms make zero profit.

It is precisely to provide insight into this type of strategic situation that game theory was developed. It does so by analyzing the strategies of both firms under all circumstances and placing the combination in a payoff matrix.

Duopoly and a Payoff Matrix

The duopoly presented above is a variation of the prisoner's dilemma game. The results can also be presented in a payoff matrix that captures the essence of the prisoner's dilemma. In Figure A16-3, each square shows the payoff from a pair of decisions listed in the columns and rows.

The blue triangles show A's profit; the green triangles show B's profit. For example, if neither cheats, the result for both is shown in the lower-right square, and if they both cheat, the result is shown in the upper-left square.

Notice the dilemma they are in if cheating cannot be detected. If they can't detect whether the other one cheated and each believes the other is maximizing profit, each must expect the other one to cheat. But if firm A expects firm B to cheat, the relevant payoffs are in the first column. Given this expectation, if firm A doesn't cheat, it loses $75,000. So firm A's optimal strategy is to cheat. Similarly for firm B. If it expects firm A to cheat, its relevant payoffs are in the first row. Firm B's optimal strategy is to cheat. But if they both cheat, they end up in the upper-left square with zero profit.

In reality, of course, cheating is partially detectable, and even though explicit collusion and enforceable contracts are illegal in the United States, implicit collusive contracts are not. Moreover, in markets where similar conditions hold time after time, the cooperative solution is more likely since each firm will acquire a reputation based on its past actions, and firms can retaliate against other firms that cheat. But

FIGURE A16-3 The Payoff Matrix of Strategic Pricing Duopoly

The strategic dilemma facing each firm in a duopoly can be shown in a payoff matrix that captures the four possible outcomes. A's strategies are listed vertically; B's strategies are listed horizontally. The payoffs of the combined strategies for both firms are shown in the four boxes of the matrix, with B's payoff shown in the green shaded triangles and A's payoff shown in the blue shaded triangles. For example, if A cheats but B doesn't, A makes a profit of $200,000, but B loses $75,000.

Their combined optimal strategy is to cartelize and achieve the monopoly payoff, with both firms receiving a profit of $75,000. However, each must expect that if it doesn't cheat and the other does cheat, it will lose $75,000. To avoid losing that $75,000, both firms will cheat, which leads them to the payoff in the upper-left corner—the competitive solution with zero profit for each firm.

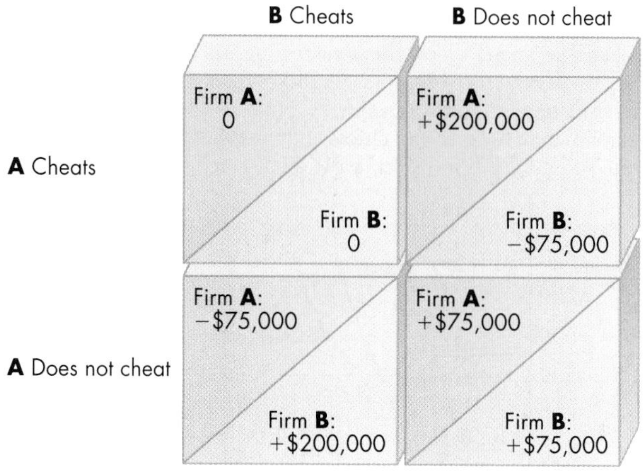

the basic dilemma remains for firms and tends to push oligopolies toward a zero-profit competitive solution.

The push toward a zero-profit equilibrium can be seen in the price war between Amazon.com and Buy.com. When Amazon.com lowered its threshold for free shipping from $99 to $49, Buy.com responded by offering free shipping on all sales the very next day and then added to that an offer to beat Amazon.com prices by 10 percent. Amazon responded by further reducing its free shipping threshold to $25. Another example is in airline pricing. When a low-fare airline enters a market, the existing airlines generally match, or even go below, the low-fare airline's fare.

Low Price Guarantees: The Advantage of Rules or Precommitment

Game theory also sheds light on institutional arrangements of oligopolistic firms. One that has now become standard practice for many oligopolistic firms is the low price guarantee, in which a store, such as Wal-Mart, states that it will guarantee that the price it charges is lower than the price at any other store in the area. To back up that guarantee, the store offers any customer who finds a lower price a "double the difference back guarantee." One's initial thought likely is that such low price guarantees are good for consumers—they guarantee consumers low prices. But when considering the low price guarantee within a game theoretic framework, that conclusion is not so clear.

Notice what the low price guarantee does for Wal-Mart; it provides information about the pricing of competing firms, and warns the other firms that Wal-Mart will have that information very quickly. Second, consider what this low price guarantee does to a competitor's, such as Kmart's, strategy. With the low price guarantee, Kmart knows that if it tries to charge a lower price than Wal-Mart, Wal-Mart will quickly and automatically reduce its price to one even lower. This changes Kmart's strategy since it now makes little sense to try to outcompete Wal-Mart on price. With the guarantee in place, both Wal-Mart's and Kmart's best strategy is not to compete on price. So, paradoxically, the net effect of the "low price guarantee" can be to raise the overall price that consumers pay.

Key Term

duopoly *(380)*

Questions and Exercises

1. Netflix and Blockbuster each expects profit to rise by $100,000 in the coming year. Netflix, thinking that it would like its net profit to rise by more, considers advertising during the Super Bowl. An advertisement on the Super Bowl will cost $80,000. If Netflix advertises, and Blockbuster does not, it expects its profit to rise by $230,000 instead of $100,000, while Blockbuster's profit will rise by only $50,000. Netflix also knows that if it does not advertise, but Blockbuster does, its profit will rise by only $50,000 while Blockbuster's profit will rise by $230,000 instead of just $100,000. If both firms advertise, their profit will rise by the same as if neither had advertised, except each will have spent $80,000 for the ad.
   a. Develop the payoff matrix for the decision facing Netflix and Blockbuster.
   b. Is there a dominant strategy?
   c. If so, what is it?

2. Two firms, TwiddleDee and TwiddleDum, make up the entire market for widgets. They have identical costs. They are currently colluding explicitly and are making $2 million each. TwiddleDee has a new CEO, Mr. Notsonice, who is considering cheating and producing more than he has agreed to produce. He has been informed by his able assistant that if he cheats, he can increase the firm's profit by $1 million at the cost of TwiddleDum losing $1 million of its profits. If both cheat, their profits are $1.5 million each. (TwiddleDum faces the same option.) You have been hired to advise Mr. Notsonice.
   a. Construct a payoff matrix for him that captures the essence of the decision.
   b. If the game is only played once, what strategy would you advise?
   c. How would your answer to *b* change if the game were to be played many times?

CHAPTER 17

Real-World Competition and Technology

It is ridiculous to call this an industry. This is rat eat rat; dog eat dog. I'll kill 'em, and I'm going to kill 'em before they kill me. You're talking about the American way of survival of the fittest.

—*Ray Kroc (founder of McDonald's)*

AFTER READING THIS CHAPTER, YOU SHOULD BE ABLE TO:

1. Define the monitoring problem and state its implications for economics.
2. Explain how corporate takeovers can limit X-inefficiency.
3. Discuss why competition should be seen as a process, not a state.
4. List two actions firms take to break down monopoly and three they take to protect monopoly.
5. Discuss why oligopoly is the best market structure for technological change.

When Microsoft was designing Zune, the Microsoft workers were sent a link to a video of Steven Jobs (the CEO of Apple) showing Jobs stating, "The only problem with Microsoft is that they have no taste—Absolutely no taste." The goal of Microsoft showing the video to Microsoft workers was to infuriate the Microsoft workers sufficiently so that they would show that not only do they have taste, but that they can bury Apple and its iPod. It was to make the competition with Apple personal. It didn't work, and Apple has gone public with its "no taste" view of Microsoft in a series of TV ads that portray Apple computer as the tasteful computer compared to a rather stodgy PC.

In earlier chapters we've seen some nice, neat models, but as we discussed in a previous chapter, often these models don't fit reality directly. Real-world markets aren't perfectly monopolistic; they aren't perfectly competitive either. They're somewhere between the two. The monopolistic competition and oligopoly models in the previous chapter come closer to reality and provide some important insights into the "in-between" markets, but, like any abstraction, they, too, fail to capture aspects of the actual nature of competition.

The earlier chapter on strategic thinking and game theory introduced you to some tools modern economists use in dealing with real-world issues. In this chapter, I build on that understanding and give you a sense of what actual firms, markets, and competition are like. This chapter also discusses an issue that is very much in the news—technology—and relates it to the models we developed earlier and shows how economists' modern models differ from the traditional textbook models.

When reading this chapter, think about the two uses of competition discussed in the chapter on perfect competition: competition as a process, the end state of which is zero profits, and competition as market structure. In this chapter the focus is on competition as a process—it is a rivalry between firms and between individuals. This competitive process is active in all market forms and is key to understanding real-world competition.

The Goals of Real-World Firms and the Monitoring Problem

Maybe the best place to start is with the assumption that firms are profit maximizers. There's a certain reasonableness to this assumption; firms definitely are concerned about profit, but are they trying to maximize profit? The answer is: It depends.

Short-Run versus Long-Run Profit

The first insight is that if firms are profit maximizers, they aren't just concerned with short-run profit; most are concerned with long-run profit. Thus, even if they can, they may not take full advantage of a potential monopolistic situation now to strengthen their long-run position. For example, many stores have liberal return policies: "If you don't like it, you can return it for a full refund." Similarly, many firms spend millions of dollars improving their reputations or building up a brand. Most firms want to be known as good citizens. Such expenditures on reputation and goodwill can increase long-run profit, even if they reduce short-run profit.

Q-1 What are two reasons why real-world firms are not pure profit maximizers?

The Problem with Profit Maximization

A second insight into how real-world firms differ from the model is that in the real world the decision makers' income is often a cost of the firm. Most real-world production doesn't take place in owner-operated businesses; it takes place in large corporations with eight or nine levels of management, thousands of stockholders whose stock is often held in trust for them, and a board of directors, chosen by management, overseeing the company by meeting two or three times a year. Signing a proxy statement is as close as most stockowners get to directing "their company" to maximize profit.

Most real-world production doesn't take place in owner-operated businesses; it takes place in large corporations.

Managers' Incentives Why is the structure of the firm important to the analysis? Because economic theory tells us that, unless someone is seeing to it that they do, self-interested decision makers have little incentive to hold down their pay. But their pay is a cost of the firm. And if their pay isn't held down, the firm's profit will be lower than otherwise. Most firms put some pressure on managers to make at least a predesignated level of profit. (If you ask managers, they'll tell you that they face enormous pressure.) So the profit motive certainly plays a role—but to say that profit plays a role is not to say that firms maximize profit. Having dealt with many companies, I'll go out on a limb and say that there are enormous wastes and inefficiencies in many U.S. businesses.

This structure presents a problem in applying the model to the real world. The textbook economic model assumes that individuals are utility maximizers—that they're motivated by self-interest. Then, in the textbook model of the firm, the assumption is made that firms, composed of self-interest-seeking individuals, are profit-seeking firms, without explaining how self-interest-seeking individuals who manage real-world corporations will find it in their interest to maximize profit for the firm. Economists recognize this problem, which was introduced in an earlier chapter. It's an example of the **monitoring problem**—*the need to oversee employees to ensure that their actions are in the best interest of the firm*.

The monitoring problem is that employees' incentives differ from the owner's incentives.

Need for Monitoring Monitoring is required because employees' incentives differ from the owner's incentives, and it's costly to see that the employee does the owner's bidding. The monitoring problem is now a central problem focused on by economists who specialize in industrial organization. They study internal structures of firms and look for a contract that managers can be given: an **incentive-compatible contract** in which *the incentives of each of the two parties to the contract are made to correspond as closely as possible*. The specific monitoring problem relevant to firm structure is that often

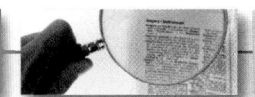

ADDED DIMENSION

Who Controls Corporations?

When a corporation is formed, it issues stock, which is sold or given to individuals. Ownership of stock entitles you to vote in the election of a corporation's directors, so in theory holders of stock control the company. In practice, however, in most large corporations, ownership is separated from control of the firm. Most stockholders have little input into the decisions a corporation makes. Instead, corporations are often controlled by their managers, who often run them for their own benefit as well as for the owners'. The reason is that the owners' control of management is limited.

A large percentage of most corporations' stock is not even controlled by the owners; instead, it is controlled by financial institutions such as mutual funds (financial institutions that invest individuals' money for them) and by pension funds (financial institutions that hold people's money for them until it is to be paid out to them upon their retirement). Thus, ownership of corporations is another step removed from individuals. Studies have shown that 80 percent of the largest 200 corporations in the United States are essentially controlled by managers and have little effective stockholder control.

Why is the question of who controls a firm important? Because economic theory assumes the goal of business owners is to maximize profits, which would be true of corporations if stockholders made the decisions. Managers don't have the same incentives to maximize profits that owners do. There's pressure on managers to maximize profits, but that pressure can often be weak or ineffective. An example of how firms deal with this problem involves stock options. Many companies give their managers stock options—rights to buy stock at a low price—to encourage them to worry about the price of their company's stock. But these stock options dilute the value of company ownership, decrease profits per share, and can give managers an incentive to overstate profits through accounting gimmicks, as happened at Enron, Xerox, and a number of other firms in the early 2000s.

Self-interested managers are interested in maximizing firm profit only if the structure of the firm requires them to do so.

owners find it too costly to monitor the managers to ensure that managers do what's in the owners' interest. And self-interested managers are interested in maximizing the firm's profit only if the structure of the firm requires them to do so.

When appropriate monitoring doesn't take place, high-level managers can pay themselves very well. As can be seen in the table of CEO compensation of selected companies below, many U.S. managers receive multimillion-dollar salaries. But are these salaries too high? That's a difficult question.

Web Note 17.1
Executive Compensation

Company	CEO Compensation in 2008
Oracle	$556,980,000
Occidental Petroleum	222,640,000
HESS	154,580,000
Ultra Petroleum	116,930,000
EOG Resources	90,470,000
WR Berkley	87,480,000
Burlington Santa Fe	68,620,000
Allegheny Energy	67,260,000
Monsanto	64,600,000
Deere & Co	61,300,000

Source: *Forbes* magazine.

REAL-WORLD APPLICATION

Why Are CEOs Paid So Much?

CEOs are paid more today than they were 25 years ago—a lot more. Today, CEO's pay at top companies is over 400 times that of what an average worker receives, while 25 years ago, CEOs received only 40 times as much. Why the change? Some have suggested that it's just that CEOs are greedy. That's probably true, but it doesn't explain why CEOs are paid so much more today than before, unless they've become a lot greedier, which is unlikely; they've always been greedy. So we have to look elsewhere for an answer.

One thing that's changed in the past 25 years is the bargaining power of workers. Worker's pay is now being held down by competition and outsourcing. (If workers ask for a raise, the company responds, "No way," and threatens to shift production to China; the workers are forced to give in to save their jobs.) But CEO's pay is not restrained by outsourcing. (At least not yet.) This means that back in the 1980s, high CEO compensation would create labor unrest; today, it does not.

Economists Xavier Gabaix of Princeton and Augustin Landier of New York University develop that line of reasoning and argue that the rise in CEO's pay is the result of supply and demand forces. They argue that, today, unconstrained supply and demand forces determine pay of CEOs, whereas back in the 1980s, the bargaining considerations of workers partially prevented supply and demand forces from fully operating.

To explain why CEOs are paid so much more today than they were earlier, they argue that the demand for top CEOs has increased significantly in recent years because there are more large firms today than there were 25 years ago, making small differences in CEO performance matter a lot. They further argue that CEO talent is in short supply, which means that the supply curve for top-rate CEOs is highly inelastic, just like the supply curve for top football players, who also get very high pay. Replacing a top CEO by a CEO ranked 250th, they calculate, would reduce a company's market value by 0.016 percent, which for a large firm they calculated to be about $60 million. This means that today large firms are competing for the highly inelastic supply of high-quality CEOs, and the high demand pushes the pay up. So their answer to the question of why CEOs are paid so much more now is that the number of large firms has increased, which has shifted out the demand for CEOs enormously.

This explanation, if correct, offers a policy suggestion for those who feel that the CEOs aren't deserving of their high pay: make the income tax more progressive. A high tax on an inelastic supply will not decrease the quantity supplied significantly, so if one makes the income tax more progressive, it will have little effect on the quantity of CEO effort supplied and thus will have minimal negative effects on efficiency.

One way to get an idea about an answer is to compare U.S. managers' salaries with those in Japan, where the control of firms is different. Banks in Japan have significant control over the operations of firms, and they closely monitor firms' performance. The result is that, in Japan, high-level managers on average earn about one-fifth of what their U.S. counterparts make, while wages of low-level workers are comparable to those of low-level workers in the United States. Given Japanese companies' success in competing with U.S. companies, this suggests that high managerial pay in the United States reflects a monitoring problem inherent in the structure of corporations common to all third-party-payer systems. There are, of course, other perspectives. Considering what some sports, film, and music stars receive places the high salaries of U.S. managers in a different light.

Q-2 Why would most economists be concerned about third-party-payer systems in which the consumer and the payer are different?

What Do Real-World Firms Maximize?

If firms don't maximize profit, what do they maximize? What are their goals? The answer again is: It depends.

Real-world firms often have a set of complicated goals that reflect the organizational structure and incentives built into the system. Clearly, profit is one of their goals. Firms spend a lot of time designing incentives to get managers to focus on profit.

Although profit is one goal of a firm, often firms focus on other intermediate goals such as cost and sales.

But often intermediate goals become the focus of firms. For example, many real-world firms focus on growth in sales; at other times they institute a cost-reduction program to increase long-run profit. At still other times they may simply take it easy and not push hard at all, enjoying the position they find themselves in—being what British economist Joan Robinson called **lazy monopolists**—*firms that do not push for efficiency, but merely enjoy the position they are already in*. This term describes many, but not all, real-world corporations. When Robinson coined the term, firms faced mostly domestic competition. Today, with firms facing more and more global competition, firms are a bit less lazy than they were—as we'll discuss later in this chapter.

The Lazy Monopolist and X-Inefficiency

Lazy monopolists are not profit maximizers; they see to it that they make enough profit so that the stockholders aren't squealing, but they don't push as hard as they could to hold their costs down. They perform as efficiently as is consistent with keeping their jobs. The result is what economists call **X-inefficiency** (*firms operating far less efficiently than they could technically*). Such firms have monopoly positions, but they don't make large monopoly profits. Instead, their costs rise because of inefficiency; they may simply make a normal level of profit or, if X-inefficiency becomes bad enough, a loss.

Q-3 Why doesn't a manager have the same incentive to hold costs down as an owner does?

The standard model avoids dealing with the monitoring problem by assuming that the owner of the firm makes all the decisions. The owners of firms who receive the profit, and only the profit, would like to see that all the firm's costs are held down. Unfortunately, very few real-world firms operate that way. In reality owners seldom make operating decisions. They hire or appoint managers to make those decisions. The managers they hire don't have that same incentive to hold costs down. Therefore, it isn't surprising to many economists that managers' pay is usually high and that high-level managers see to it that they have "perks" such as chauffeurs, jet planes, ritzy offices, and assistants to do as much of their work as possible.

The equilibrium of a lazy monopolist is presented in Figure 17-1. A monopolist would produce at price P_M and quantity Q_M. Average total cost would be C_M, so the monopolist's profit would be the entire shaded rectangle (areas *A* and *B*). The lazy monopolist would allow costs to increase until the firm reached its normal level of profit. In Figure 17-1, costs rise to C_{LM}. The profit of the lazy monopolist is area *B*. The remainder of the potential profit is eaten up in cost inefficiencies.

The competitive pressures a firm faces limit its laziness.

What places a limit on firms' laziness is the degree of competitive pressures they face. All economic institutions must have sufficient revenue coming in to cover costs, so all economic institutions have a limit on how lazy and inefficient they can get—a limit imposed by their monopoly position. They can translate the monopoly profit into X-inefficiency, thereby benefiting the managers and workers in the firm, but once they've done so, they can't be more inefficient. They would go out of business.

How Competition Limits the Lazy Monopolist

If all individuals in the industry are lazy, then laziness becomes the norm and competitive pressures don't reduce their profits. Laziness is relative, not absolute. But if a new firm comes in all gung-ho and hardworking, or if an industry is opened up to international competition, the lazy monopolists can be squeezed and must undertake

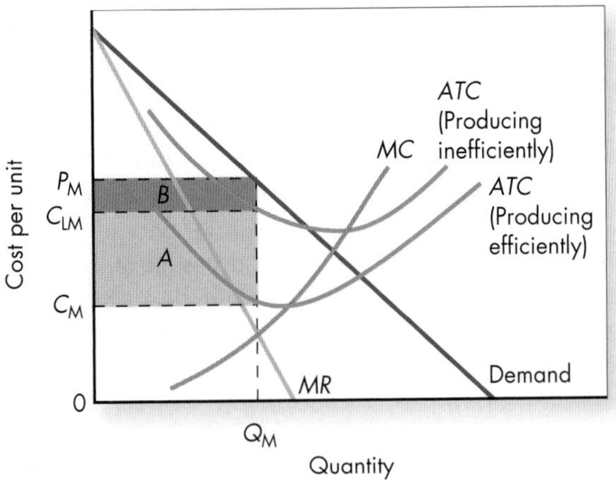

FIGURE 17-1
True Cost Efficiency and the Lazy Monopolist

A monopolist producing efficiently would have costs C_M and would produce at price P_M and quantity Q_M. A lazy monopolist, in contrast, would let costs rise until the minimum level of profit is reached—in this example at C_{LM}. Profit for the monopolist is represented by the entire shaded area, whereas profit for the lazy monopolist is squeezed down to area *B*.

massive restructuring to make themselves competitive. Many U.S. firms have been undergoing such restructuring in order to make themselves internationally competitive.

A second way in which competitive pressure is placed on a lazy monopolist is by a **corporate takeover,** in which *another firm or a group of individuals issues a tender offer (that is, offers to buy up the stock of a company) to gain control and to install its own managers*. In the last few years many of these takeovers were done by private equity firms, which are firms that are not listed on the stock exchange. Most of these private equity firms are primarily investment vehicles, whose expertise is in finance, not in production. They buy up firms that have not been performing well financially and push them to improve their financial payout by becoming more efficient. Usually such tender offers are financed by large amounts of debt, which means that if the takeover is successful, the firm will need to make large profits just to cover the interest payments on the debt.

A corporate takeover, or simply the threat of a takeover, can improve a firm's efficiency.

Managers generally don't like takeovers. A takeover may cost them their jobs and the perks that go along with those jobs, so they'll often restructure the company on their own as a preventive measure. Such restructuring frequently means incurring large amounts of debt to finance a large payment to stockholders. These payments put more pressure on management to operate efficiently. Thus, the threat of a corporate takeover places competitive pressure on firms to maximize profits.

Q-4 In what way does the threat of a corporate takeover place competitive pressures on a firm?

Were profit not a motive at all, one would expect the lazy monopolist syndrome to take precedence. In fact, it's not surprising that nonprofit organizations often display lazy monopolist tendencies. For example, some colleges, schools, libraries, jails, and nonprofit hospitals have a number of rules and ways of doing things that, upon reflection, benefit the employees of the institution rather than the customers. At most colleges, students aren't polled about what time they would prefer classes to meet; instead, the professors and administrators decide when they want to teach. I leave it to you to figure out whether your college exhibits these tendencies and whether you'd prefer that your college, library, or hospital change to a for-profit institution. Studying these incentive-compatible problems is what management courses are all about.

Web Note 17.2
Creative Destruction

Motivations for Efficiency Other Than the Profit Incentive

I'm not going to discuss management theory here other than to stimulate your thinking about the problem. However, I'd be remiss in presenting you this broad outline of the monitoring problem without mentioning that the drive for profit isn't the only drive that pushes for efficiency. Some individuals derive pleasure from efficiently-run organizations. Such individuals don't need to be monitored. Thus, if administrators are well intentioned, they'll hold down costs even if they aren't profit maximizers. In such cases, monitoring (creating an organization and structure that gives people profit incentives) can actually reduce efficiency! It's amazing to some economists how some nonprofit organizations operate as efficiently as they do—some libraries and colleges fall into that category. Their success is built on their employees' pride in their jobs, not on their profit motive.

Individuals have complicated motives; some simply have a taste for efficiency.

Most economists don't deny that such inherently efficient individuals exist, and that most people derive some pleasure from efficiency, but they believe that it's hard to maintain that push for efficiency year in, year out, when some of your colleagues are lazy monopolists enjoying the fruits of your efficiency. Most people derive some pleasure from efficiency, but, based on their observation of people's actions, economists believe that holding down costs without the profit motive takes stronger willpower than most people have.

The Fight between Competitive and Monopolistic Forces

Even if all the assumptions for perfect competition could hold true, it's unlikely that real-world markets would be perfectly competitive. The reason is that perfect competition assumes that individuals accept a competitive institutional structure, even though changing that structure could result in significant gains for sellers or buyers. The simple fact is that *self-interest-seeking individuals don't like competition for themselves* (although they do like it for others), and when competitive pressures get strong and the invisible hand's push turns to shove, individuals often shove back, using either social or political means. That's why you can understand real-world competition only if you understand how the invisible hand, social forces, and political pressures push against each other to create real-world economic institutions. Real-world competition should be seen as a process—a fight between the forces of monopolization and the forces of competition.

Competition is a process—a fight between the forces of monopolization and the forces of competition.

How Monopolistic Forces Affect Perfect Competition

Let's consider some examples. During the Depression of the 1930s, competition was pushing down prices and wages. What was the result? Individuals socially condemned firms for unfair competition, and numerous laws were passed to prevent it. Unions were strengthened politically and given monopoly powers so they could resist the pressure to push down wages. The Robinson-Patman Act was passed, which made it illegal for many firms to lower prices. Individual states passed similar laws, and in the 1990s it was under one of these that Wal-Mart lost a court case in which it was accused of charging too-low prices in its pharmacies.

The United States has myriad laws, regulations, and programs that prevent agricultural markets from working competitively.

As another example, consider agricultural markets, which have many of the conditions for almost perfect competition. To my knowledge, not one country in the world allows a competitive agricultural market to exist. The United States has myriad laws, regulations, and programs that prevent agricultural markets from working competitively. U.S. agricultural markets are characterized by price supports, acreage limitations, and quota systems. Thus, where perfectly competitive markets could exist, they aren't allowed to. An almost infinite number of other examples can be found. Our laws and social values and customs simply do not allow perfect competition to work because government emphasizes other social goals besides efficiency. When competition negatively affects these other goals (which may or may not be goals that most people in society hold), government prevents competition from operating.

Q-5 Explain, using supply and demand curves, why most agricultural markets are not perfectly competitive.

Economic Insights and Real-World Competition

The extreme rarity of perfectly competitive markets *should not* make you think that economics is irrelevant to the real world. Far from it. In fact, the movement away from perfectly competitive markets could have been predicted by economic theory.

Consider Figure 17-2. Competitive markets will exist only if suppliers or consumers don't collude. If the suppliers producing $0L$ can get together and restrict entry, preventing suppliers who would produce LM from entering the industry, the remaining suppliers can raise their price from P_M to P_L, giving them the shaded area A in additional income. If the cost of their colluding and preventing entry is less than that amount, economic theory predicts that these individuals will collude. The suppliers kept out of the market lose only area C, so they don't have much incentive to fight the restrictions on entry. Consumers lose the areas A plus B, so they have a strong incentive to fight. However, often their cost of organizing a protest is higher than the suppliers' cost of collusion, so consumers accept the restrictions.

Suppliers introducing restrictions on entry seldom claim that the reason for the restrictions is to increase their incomes. Usually they couch the argument for restrictions in terms of the general good, but, while their reasons are debatable, the net effect of restricting entry into a market is to increase suppliers' income to the detriment of consumers.

How Competitive Forces Affect Monopoly

Q-6 Why is it almost impossible for a perfect monopoly to exist?

Don't think that because perfect competition doesn't exist, competition doesn't exist. In the real world, competition is fierce; the invisible hand is no weakling. It holds its own against other forces in the economy.

Competition is so strong that it makes the other extreme (perfect monopolies) as rare as perfect competition. For a monopoly to last, other firms must be prevented from entering the market. In reality it's almost impossible to prevent entry, and therefore it's almost impossible for perfect monopoly to exist. Monopoly profits send out signals to other firms who want to get some of that profit for themselves.

Breaking Down Monopoly To get some of the profit, firms will break down a monopoly through political or economic means. If the monopoly is a legal monopoly, high profit will lead potential competitors to lobby to change the law underpinning

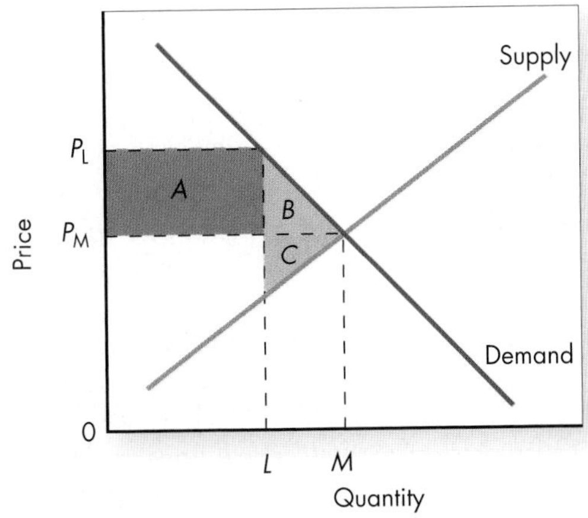

FIGURE 17-2 Movement Away from Competitive Markets

Where suppliers of $0L$ can restrict suppliers of LM from entering the market, they can raise the price of the good from P_M to P_L, giving the suppliers of $0L$ area A in additional income. The suppliers kept out of the market lose area C. The consumers, however, lose both areas A and B. Often the costs of organizing for consumers are higher than the costs for the suppliers, so consumers accept the market restrictions.

that monopoly. If the law can't be changed—say, the monopolist has a patent (which, as I discussed in the chapter on monopoly, is a legal right to be the sole supplier of a good)—potential competitors will generally get around the obstacle by developing a slightly different product or by working on a new technology that avoids the monopoly but satisfies the relevant need.

Say, for example, that you've just discovered the proverbial better mousetrap. You patent it and prepare to enjoy the life of a monopolist. But to patent your mousetrap, you must submit to the patent office the technical drawings of how your better mousetrap works. That gives all potential competitors (some of whom have better financing and already existing distribution systems) a chance to study your idea and see if they can think of a slightly different way (a way sufficiently different to avoid being accused of infringing on your patent) to achieve the same end. They often succeed—so in some cases firms don't apply for patents on new products because the information in the patent application spells out what's unique about the product. That information can help competitors more than the monopoly provided by the patent would hurt them. Instead many firms try to establish an initial presence in the market and rely on inertia to protect what little monopoly profit they can extract.

Establishing an initial presence in a market can be more effective than obtaining a patent when trying to extract monopoly profit.

Reverse Engineering Going to the patent office isn't the only way competitors gather information about competing products. One of the other ways routinely used by firms is called **reverse engineering**—*the process of a firm buying other firms' products, disassembling them, figuring out what's special about them, and then copying them within the limits of the law.*

Variations on reverse engineering go on in all industries. Consider the clothing industry. One firm I know of directs its secretaries to go to top department stores on their lunch hour and buy the latest fashions. The secretaries bring the clothes back and, that afternoon, the seamstresses and tailors dismantle each garment into its component parts, make a pattern of each part, and sew the original up again. The next day the secretary who chose that garment returns it to the department store, saying, "I don't really like it."

Meanwhile the firm has express-mailed the patterns to its Hong Kong office, and two weeks later its shipment of garments comes in—garments that are almost, but not perfectly, identical to the ones the secretaries bought. The firm sells this shipment to other department stores at half the cost of the original.

If you ask businesspeople, they'll tell you that competition is fierce and that profit opportunities are fleeting—which is a good sign that competition does indeed exist in the U.S. economy.

Competition and Natural Monopoly

The view one takes of the fight between competitive and monopolistic forces influences one's view of what government policy should be in relation to natural monopolies—industries whose average total cost is falling as output increases. We saw in the chapter on monopolies that natural monopolies can make large profits and that consequently there have been significant calls for government regulation of these monopolies to prevent their "exploitation" of the consumer.

Over the past decade, economists and policy makers have become less supportive of such regulation. They argue that even in these cases of natural monopoly, competition works in other ways. High monopoly profits lead to research on alternative ways of supplying the product, such as sending TV signals through electrical lines or sending phone messages by satellite. New technologies provide competition to existing firms. When this competition doesn't work fast enough, people direct their efforts toward

New technologies can compete with and undermine natural monopolies.

government, and political pressure is brought to bear either to control the monopoly through regulation or to break up the monopoly.

Web Note 17.3
Regulating Natural Monopolies

Regulating Natural Monopolies In the past, the pressure to regulate natural monopolies has been stronger than competitive pressure that lowers prices. Regulated natural monopolies have been given the exclusive right to operate in an industry but, in return, they've had to agree to have the price they charge and the services they provide regulated. Regulatory boards control the price that natural monopolies charge so that it will be a "fair price," which they generally define as a price that includes all costs plus a normal return on capital investment (a normal profit, but no economic profit). Most states have a number of regulatory boards.

When firms are allowed to pass on all cost increases to earn a normal profit on those costs, they have little or no incentive to hold down costs.

When firms are allowed to pass on all cost increases to earn a normal profit on those costs, they have little or no incentive to hold down costs. In such cases, X-inefficiency develops with a passion, and such monopolies look for capital-intensive projects that will increase their rate bases. To fight such tendencies, regulatory boards must screen every cost and determine which costs are appropriate and which aren't—an almost impossible job. For example, nuclear power is an extremely capital-intensive method of producing electric power, and regulated electric companies favored nuclear power plants until they were told that some nuclear power plant construction costs could not be passed on.

Q-7 What is the problem with regulations that set prices relative to costs?

Once regulation gets so specific that it's scrutinizing every cost, the regulatory process becomes extremely bureaucratic, which itself increases the cost. Moreover, to regulate effectively, the regulators must have independent information and must have a sophisticated understanding of economics, cost accounting, and engineering. Often regulatory boards are made up of volunteer laypeople who start with little expertise; they are exhausted or co-opted by the political infighting they have had to endure by the time they develop some of the expertise they need. As is often the case in economics, there's no easy answer to the problem.

It is because of the problems with regulation that more and more economists argue that even in the case of natural monopoly, no explicit regulation is desirable, and that society would be better off relying on direct competitive forces guided by broader regulatory guidelines emphasizing free entry into the industry. They argue that regulated monopolies inevitably inflate their costs so much and are so inefficient and lazy that a monopoly right should never be granted.

Deregulating Natural Monopolies In the 1980s and 1990s, such views led to the deregulation and competitive supply of both electric power and telephone services.[1] Regulators are making these markets competitive by breaking down the layers of the industry into subindustries and deregulating those subindustries that can be competitive. For example, the phone industry can be divided into the phone line industry, the caller service industry, the pay phone industry, and the directory information industry. By dividing up the industry, regulators can carve out the part that has the characteristics of a natural monopoly and open the remaining parts to competition.

Let's take a closer look at the electrical industry. It used to be that electricity was supplied by independent local firms, each providing electricity for its own local customers. Today, however, electricity is supplied through a large grid that connects many regions of the country. With this grid, electricity generated in one area can easily be sent all over the country, and suppliers can compete for customers in a variety of regions.

[1]Telephone regulation will be discussed more fully in the chapter on antitrust policy and regulation.

The grid makes competition in power supply feasible, and many states have adopted provisions to open their electricity markets to multiple providers.

Economies of scale can create natural monopolies.

The power line industry, however, is not competitive. It would be extremely costly for each company to run a separate power line into your house. That is, the power line industry exhibits *economies of scale*. Because of the economies of scale, the power line industry is the natural monopoly aspect of electrical power supply. The deregulation of electricity involves splitting off the production of electricity from the maintenance of the line—and choosing an appropriate charge for electric line maintenance. While in the newspapers you will likely read that the electrical power industry is being deregulated, that is not quite correct. Only those portions of the market where competition is likely to exist are being deregulated.

How Firms Protect Their Monopolies

The image I've presented of competition being motivated by profits is a useful one. It shows how a market economy adjusts to ever-changing technology and demands in the real world. Competition is a dynamic, not a static, force.

Firms do not sit idly by and accept competition. They fight it.

Firms do not sit idly by and accept competition. They fight it. How do monopolies fight real-world competition? By spending money on maintaining their monopoly. By advertising. By lobbying. By producing products that are difficult to copy. By not taking full advantage of their monopoly position, which means charging a low price that discourages entry. Often firms could make higher short-run profits by charging a higher price, but they forgo the short-run profits in order to strengthen their long-run position in the industry.

Cost/Benefit Analysis of Creating and Maintaining Monopolies

Q-8 What decision rule does a firm use when deciding whether to create or maintain a monopoly?

Preventing real-world competition costs money. Monopolies are expensive to create and maintain. Economic theory predicts that if firms have to spend money on creating and protecting their monopoly, they're going to "buy" less monopoly power than if it were free. How much will they buy? They will buy monopoly power until the marginal cost of such power equals the marginal benefit. Thus, they'll reason:

- Does it makes sense for us to hire a lobbyist to fight against this law that will reduce our monopoly power? Here is the probability that a lobbyist will be effective, here is the marginal cost, and here is the marginal benefit.
- Does it make sense for us to buy this machine? If we do, we'll be the only one to have it and are likely to get this much business. Here is the marginal cost, and here is the marginal benefit.
- Does it make sense for us to advertise to further our market penetration? Here are the likely various marginal benefits; here are the likely marginal costs.

Examples of firms spending money to protect or create monopolies are in the news all the time. The farm lobby fights to keep quotas and farm support programs. Drug companies spend a lot of resources to discover new drugs they can patent. A vivid example of the length to which firms will go to create a monopoly position is Owens Corning's fight to trademark its hue of pink Fiberglas. Owens Corning spent more than $200 million to advertise and promote its color "pink" and millions more in the court to protect its right to sole use of that hue. Owens Corning has weighed the costs and benefits and believes that its pink provides sufficient brand recognition to warrant spending millions to protect it.

REAL-WORLD APPLICATION

Branding

One of the important ways in which firms try to maintain a monopoly position is called *branding*. U.S. firms spend close to $400 billion to advertise their products, trying to produce brand names and create a pleasant image in the minds of consumers. Here are a few food-related brand names. I'm sure you know about most, but a couple are still in the process of forming brand recognition.

- *Coffee.* When you think of coffee, you think of Starbucks and inexpensive extravagance. You might not be able to afford a Lexus, but you can afford a Starbucks cup of coffee.
- *Chicken.* Perdue doesn't produce any chicken, but it does do a lot of advertising, and it brands the chickens it sells, so when you think of chicken, you think of Perdue. You also think Perdue when you see Kevin Harvick race because he has a big Perdue logo on his racecar.
- *Bananas.* A banana is a banana is a banana, but only if you haven't been influenced by Miss Chiquita. At its peak, the Chiquita banana jingle was played 376 times a day on radio stations across the United States.
- *Steak.* Most steaks are currently sold generically. Firms such as Omaha Steaks are trying to change that. Don't just buy a steak—buy an Omaha steak.
- *Water.* Firms take water from the tap (or possibly from a spring), run it through some filters, and sell the image of purity by creating a nice-sounding name—Dasani, Vermont Pure . . . Well, it's better for you than soda.
- *Pork.* Pork tends to be associated with pigs and does not carry a "good-for-you" image. A national association of pork producers is trying to change that image: "Pork—the other white meat."

Establishing Market Position

In winner-take-all markets, the initial competition is on establishing market position.

Some economists, such as Robert Frank at Cornell University, have argued that today's economy is becoming more and more like a monopoly economy. Modern competition, he argues, is a winner-take-all competition. In such a competition, the winner (established because of brand loyalty, patent protection, or simply consumer laziness) achieves a monopoly and can charge significantly higher prices than its costs without facing competition. The initial competition, focusing on establishing market position, is intense.

To see how important establishing a market position is in today's economy, consider the initial public offering (IPO) of the new firms that were so highly valued by Wall Street in the late 1990s. Many of these new firms had no profits and no likelihood of profits for a number of years, but they were selling at extraordinarily high stock prices. Why? The reasoning was that these companies were spending money to establish brand names. As their names became better known, they would establish a monopoly position, and eventually their monopoly positions would be so strong that they couldn't help but make a profit. With the dot-com stock market crash in the early 2000s, this argument was shown to be wrong for most of these firms. For one or two lucky firms that established their brands, it was true. The problem is that most people have no way of differentiating between the two. In 2004 Google made a well-publicized IPO, which attracted much interest. I didn't take part because, on fundamentals, the price seemed high. However, within three months after the IPO, the price of Google stock had doubled from the IPO price and in 2008, it was five times as high and the market was valuing Google at $130 billion. (So much for my focus on stock market fundamentals.)

Technology

Technological development—*the discovery of new or improved products or methods of production*—has been a driving force in the economy in recent years. As we saw in the second chapter on production and cost analysis, technological advance lowers the costs of production and makes economies more efficient—producing more output with the same number of inputs.

Technological advance is a natural outcome of specialization because it requires large investments of time and money in very specialized areas. Specialization allows producers to learn more about the particular aspects of production in which they specialize. As they learn more, they become not only more productive but also more likely to produce technological advances because they gain a deeper understanding of their specialty.

For example, instead of producing an entire line of clothing, companies might specialize in the production of certain types of carbon-based fibers and explore ways of making more useful material. The result of such specialization can be a technological advance such as Gore-Tex—a material that insulates but also "breathes" and thus keeps individuals dry and cool on warm rainy days, and dry and warm on cold rainy or snowy days. Instead of spreading resources to the entire process of making a jacket, a company can concentrate on just one aspect—fibers.

Technology, Efficiency, and Market Structure

Given the significance of technology, an important question is: What causes technology to grow? Market incentives are an important part of the answer. Before markets existed, economies grew slowly. After markets came into existence in the 1700s, technology advanced more rapidly because individuals gained incentives, in the form of profits, to discover new and cheaper ways of doing things. Globalization of our economy provides an even greater incentive to develop new technologies because the revenue that can be captured from a global market with over 6.7 billion people (world population) is much greater than the revenue that can be generated from about 300 million people (U.S. population).

Are some market structures more conducive to growth than others? The answer economists have come to is a tentative yes, and it is an answer that makes certain market structures look better than the way they were presented earlier. Let's review what we've learned about market structure. In the basic supply/demand framework, perfect competition is seen as the benchmark—it leads to efficient outcomes. All other market structures lead to some deadweight loss. But the supply/demand framework does not consider technological issues. It implicitly assumes that technology is unchanging or is unaffected by market structure. If market structure does affect technological advance, another type of efficiency must be considered. This efficiency might be called dynamic efficiency. **Dynamic efficiency** refers to *a market's ability to promote cost-reducing or product-enhancing technological change*. Market structures that best promote technological change are dynamically efficient. Oligopoly provides the best market structure for technological advance. To see why, let's look at the four market structures: perfect competition, monopolistic competition, monopoly, and oligopoly.

In considering market structures, dynamic efficiency must be considered as well as static efficiency.

Perfect Competition and Technology

Q-9 Why isn't perfect competition a good market structure for technological advance?

Perfectly competitive firms have no incentive to develop new technologies. Moreover, perfect competitors earn no profits and consequently may not be able to acquire the funds to devote to research and development that leads to technological change. Even if they did, they would gain little from it. A perfectly competitive market would quickly transfer the gains of the innovation to other firms, making it difficult for the innovating firm to recoup the costs of developing the new technology.

Monopolistic Competition and Technology

Monopolistic competition is somewhat more conducive to technological change because firms have some market power. The promise of gaining additional market power provides the incentive to fund research in new technologies. But, as we learned earlier, monopolistic competitors also lack long-run profits. Easy entry limits their ability to recoup their investment in technological innovation. Eventually, their increased market share will deteriorate and they will return to earning normal profits.

Through its support of patents, the United States does provide incentives to innovate. Patents allow the development of new products through the promise of monopoly profits for a specified period of time. Of course, a firm with a patent will change the market structure into a monopoly.

Monopoly and Technology

On the other end of the spectrum is pure monopoly. Monopolies may earn the profits needed for research and development, but they seldom have the incentive to innovate. Since a monopolist's market is protected from entry, the easiest path is the lazy monopolist path. Since many monopolies are created by government (the government gives a monopoly to a specific company), pure monopolists don't face the threat of new competitors. Until recently, European telephone companies and European domestic airlines were monopolies. These industries developed far fewer innovations than did the equivalent U.S. firms that faced more competition, and European industry prices were much higher than those in the United States.

In response to these observations, European governments have moved toward privatization and more competition. Both telecommunications and domestic airlines have been privatized, and their monopolies are slowly being removed. The result has been a fall in prices of their products and expanding new technologies in the telecommunications industries. For example, you can now fly between major European cities on airlines such as easyJet or Ryanair for as low as $25.

Oligopoly and Technology

Oligopoly tends to be most conducive to technological change.

Q-10 Why is oligopoly the best market structure for technological advance?

That leaves oligopoly. Oligopoly is the market structure that is most conducive to technological change. Since the typical oligopolist realizes ongoing economic profit, it has the funds to carry out research and development. Moreover, the belief that its competitors are innovating also forces it to do so. Oligopolists are constantly searching for ways to get an edge on competitors, so most technological advance takes place in oligopolistic industries.

The computer industry is an example of an oligopolistic market that has demonstrated tremendous innovation. Technological progress has been rapid, following *Moore's law*—every 18 months the cost of computer speed is cut by half. Another example is the telecommunications industry, which has been oligopolistic since the breakup of AT&T and which has been experiencing enormous technological change.

Some economists, especially those who favor a model in which the threat of competition is enough to keep a firm behaving competitively (a contestable market approach), argue that market structure does not matter for technological progress. It is the conditions of entry that matter. They argue that it is primarily developments in pure science that lead to technological advance. Businesses sample technological advances and develop those that have market potential. They argue that technological advances lead to the formation of oligopolies; oligopolies don't necessarily lead to technological advances. The cigarette industry and the aluminum industry are highly oligopolistic but have had little technological advance. In the steel industry, companies outside the group of existing producers started minimills that led to technological advance. The process did not originate with the oligopolistic steel companies.

Network Externalities, Standards, and Technological Lock-In

Web Note 17.4
Network Economies

In support of the view that technology determines market structure, economists have focused on those aspects of production that involve *network* externalities. An externality, as explained in Chapter 3, is an effect of a decision on a third party that is not taken into account by the decision maker. A **network externality** occurs *when greater use of a product increases the benefit of that product to everyone*. Telephones exhibit network externalities. If you were the only person in the world with a telephone, it would be pretty useless. As the number of people with telephones increases, the telephone's value to communication grows enormously. Another example of a product with network externalities is the Windows operating system. It is of much more use to you if many other people use it too, because you can then communicate with other Windows users and purchase software based on that platform.

Network externalities lead to market standards and affect market structure.

Network externalities are important to market structure because they lead to the development of industry standards. Standards become important because network externalities involve the interaction among individuals and processes. Many examples of the development of industry standards exist. Some are television broadcast standards (they differ in the United States and Europe, which is why U.S. TVs cannot be used in Europe), building standards (there is a standard size of doors), and electrical current standards (220 or 110; AC or DC).

Standards and Winner-Take-All Industries Network externalities have two implications for the economic process. First, they increase the likelihood that an industry becomes a winner-take-all industry. Early in the development of new products, there may be two or three competing standards, any one of which could be a significant improvement over what existed before. As network externalities broaden the use of a product, the need for a single standard becomes more important and eventually one standard wins out. The firm that gets its standard accepted as the industry standard gains an enormous advantage over the other firms. This firm will dominate the market. Microsoft and its Windows operating system are an example of how getting your product accepted as the standard can do wonders for the firm. Once a standard develops, even if the other firms try to enter with a better technological standard, they will have a hard time competing because everyone is already committed to the existing industry standard. Deviating from that standard will reduce the benefits of the network externality.

The first-mover advantage helps explain the high stock prices of start-up technology companies.

First-Mover Advantage Firms in an industry developing a standard will have a strong incentive to be the first to market with the product; they will be willing to incur large losses initially in their attempt to set the industry standard. The "first-mover advantage" helps explain why the stock of small technology companies sold for extremely high prices even though they were having large losses. The large losses were created because the firms were spending money to gain market share so that their products would become the industry standard. If the firm is successful in getting its product accepted as the standard, the demand for the product will rise and it will have enormous profits in the future.

Technological Lock-In The second implication of network externalities is that the market might not gravitate toward the most efficient standard. Economists debate how standards can be inefficient and yet be maintained by the first-mover advantage. Some economists argue that the inefficiency can be quite large; others argue that it is small. One aspect of the debate has centered around the QWERTY keyboard on computers. Research by Stanford economist Paul David showed that the arrangement of the keys in the QWERTY keyboard was designed to slow people's typing down so that the keys would not stick on the early mechanical typewriters. As the technology of typewriters improved, the need to slow down typing soon ended, but because the QWERTY keyboard was introduced first, it had become the standard. Other, more efficient keyboards have been proposed but not adopted. The QWERTY keyboard has remained, even with its built-in inefficiencies. David suggested that QWERTY is a metaphor for **technological lock-in**—*when prior use of a technology makes the adoption of subsequent technologies difficult.*

QWERTY is a metaphor for technological lock-in.

David's technological lock-in argument suggests that many of our institutions and technologies may be inefficient. Other economists argue that the QWERTY keyboard was not that inefficient and if it had been, other keyboards would have been adopted. I am not sure who is right in this debate, but it may soon be made obsolete by another technological development: voice recognition software, which will make keyboarding a relic of the past.

The QWERTY debate is a part of a larger debate about the competitive process and government involvement in that process. The issues are somewhat the same as they were in the earlier discussion of government regulation of natural monopolies. Many economists see government involvement as necessary to protect the economy and the consumer. They advocate what economist Brian Arthur calls "a nudging hand" approach, in which the government keeps the competition fair.

Other economists see monopoly as part of the competitive process—something that will be eliminated as competitive forces act against it. Standards will develop, but they will be temporary. If the standards are sufficiently inefficient, they will be replaced, or an entirely new product will come along that makes the old standard irrelevant. For such economists, neither natural monopoly nor technological lock-in is a reason for government interference. Government interference, even the nudging hand, would slow or stop the competitive process and make society worse off.

Modern debates about policy regarding competition take dynamic issues into account, but still leave open a debate about what the role of government should be.

Who is right? My own view leans toward the competitive process view with a nudge here or there, but one cannot be dogmatic about it; each case must be decided on its own merits. Moreover, even in those cases where explicit regulation is not called for, the government must set up appropriate rules and property rights to see that the competitive playing field is reasonably level.

An example of what I mean by setting appropriate rules can be seen in the ongoing process of ending local telephone service monopolies and allowing consumers choice in both local and long-distance carriers. Whether this process will be a success depends on the charge the local telephone firms are allowed to make for access to their phone lines into individuals' houses. Government must determine the charge and set up fair initial rules. Unless it does, the competitive process won't work properly.

Conclusion

The stories of competition and monopoly have no end. Both are continuous processes. Monopolies create competition. Out of the competitive struggle, other monopolies emerge, only to be beaten down by competition. Technology is a big part of that struggle.

Individuals and firms, motivated by self-interest, try to use the changes brought by technology to their benefit. By doing so, they change both the nature of the economy and the direction of technological change itself.

Summary

- The goals of real-world firms are many. Profit plays a role, but the actual goals depend on the incentive structure embodied in the structure of the firm.
- The monitoring problem arises because the incentives faced by managers are not always to maximize the profit of the firm. Economists have helped design incentive-compatible contracts to help alleviate the monitoring problem.
- Monopolists facing no competition can become lazy and not hold down costs as much as they are able. X-inefficiency refers to firms operating less efficiently than they could technically.
- X-inefficiency can be limited by the threat of competition or takeovers. Corporate takeovers often mean change in management.
- The competitive process involves a continual fight between monopolization and competition. Suppliers are willing to pay an amount equal to the additional profit gained from the restriction. Consumers are willing to pay an amount equal to the additional cost of products to avoid a restriction. Consumers, however, face a higher cost of organizing their efforts.
- Firms compete against patents that create monopolies by making slight modifications to existing patents and engaging in reverse engineering to copy other firms' products within the limits of the law.
- The U.S. government is deregulating natural monopolies by dividing the firms into various subindustries, carving out those parts that exhibit the characteristics of a natural monopoly, and opening the remaining parts to competition.
- Firms protect their monopolies by such means as advertising, lobbying, and producing products that are difficult for other firms to copy.
- Firms will spend money on monopolization until the marginal cost equals the marginal benefit.
- Oligopoly provides the best market structure for technological advance because oligopolists have an incentive to innovate in the form of additional profits and because they have the profits to devote to investing in the research and development of new technologies.

Key Terms

corporate takeover *(389)*
dynamic efficiency *(396)*
incentive-compatible contract *(385)*
lazy monopolist *(388)*
monitoring problem *(385)*
network externality *(398)*
reverse engineering *(392)*
technological development *(396)*
technological lock-in *(399)*
X-inefficiency *(388)*

Questions and Exercises

1. Describe the monitoring problem. How does an incentive-compatible contract address the monitoring problem? LO1
2. It is obvious that all for-profit businesses in the United States will maximize profit. True or false? Why? LO2
3. Define *X-inefficiency*. Can a perfect competitor be X-inefficient? Explain why or why not. LO2
4. Some analysts have argued that competition will eliminate X-inefficiency from firms. Will it? Why? LO2

5. Nonprofit colleges must be operating relatively efficiently. Otherwise for-profit colleges would develop and force existing colleges out of business. True or false? Why? LO3
6. If it were easier for consumers to collude than for suppliers to collude, there would often be shortages of goods. True or false? Why? LO3
7. If it were easier for consumers to collude than for suppliers to collude, the price of goods would be lower than the competitive price. True or false? Why? LO3
8. Why would a company want to sacrifice short-run profits to establish market position? LO3
9. The title of an article in *The Wall Street Journal* was "Pricing of Products Is Still an Art, Often Having Little Link to Costs." In the article, the following cases were cited:
   - Vodka pricing: All vodkas are essentially indistinguishable—colorless, tasteless, and odorless—and the cost of producing vodka is independent of brand name, yet prices differ substantially.
   - Perfume: A $100 bottle of perfume may contain $4 to $6 worth of ingredients.
   - Jeans and "alligator/animal" shirts: The "plain pocket" jeans and the Lacoste knockoffs often cost 40 percent less than the brand-name items, yet the knockoffs are essentially identical to the brand-name items.

   a. Do these differences undermine economists' analysis of pricing? Why or why not?
   b. What does each of these examples likely imply about fixed costs and variable costs?
   c. What do they likely imply about costs of production versus costs of selling?
   d. As what type of market would you characterize each of the above examples? LO3
10. Demonstrate graphically the net gain to producers and the net loss to consumers if suppliers are able to restrict their output to Q_r in the accompanying graph. Demonstrate the net deadweight loss to society. LO3

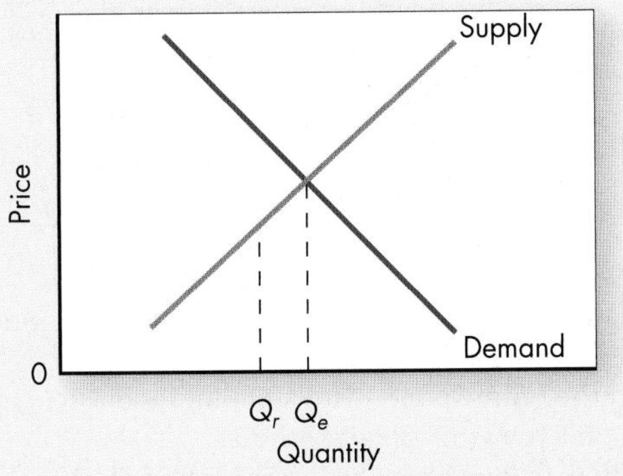

11. Up to how much is the monopolist depicted in the accompanying graph willing to spend to protect its market position? Demonstrate your answer graphically. LO3

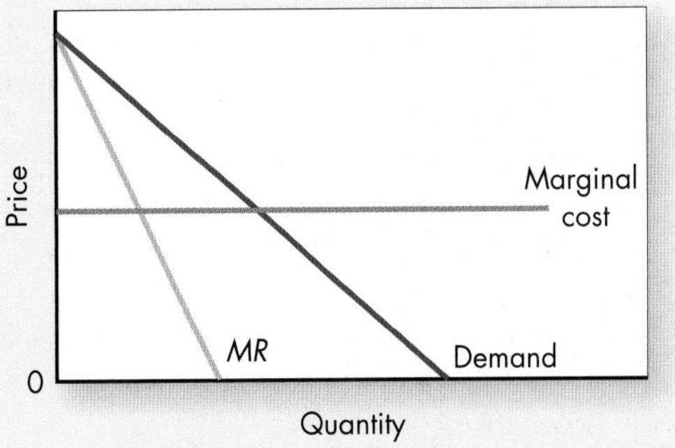

12. Discuss each of the following market structures in terms of static and dynamic efficiency.
    a. Perfect competition.
    b. Monopolistic competition.
    c. Oligopoly.
    d. Monopoly. LO3
13. Soft-drink companies pay universities for the exclusive "pouring rights" to sell their products on campus. In a recent deal, the University at Buffalo signed a contract with Pepsi for $220,000 per year limiting on-campus soft-drink sales to only Pepsi.
    a. Why would Pepsi agree to pay such a fee?
    b. What would likely happen if there were no pouring rights on campus?
    c. Is the sale of pouring rights beneficial to students or harmful to them? LO3
14. Monopolies are bad; patents give firms monopoly; therefore, patents are bad. True or false? Why? LO4
15. Natural monopolies should be broken up to improve competition. True or false? Why? LO4
16. Technically competent firms will succeed. True or false? Why? LO4
17. What two characteristics does a market structure need to have for firms in that industry to engage in technological advance? LO5
18. Taking into consideration changing technologies, why might the basic supply/demand framework not lead to the most efficient outcome? LO5
19. How do network externalities increase the winner-take-all nature of a market? LO5
20. One of the things that is slowing the development of nanotechnology is the legal morass of patents that anyone working with new ideas must deal with. Some have argued that the government should give prizes for new discoveries, such as was offered for the first private flight in space, or as was offered by Napoleon for the discovery of how to store vegetables for long periods, rather than award patents, such as are awarded to drugs.
    a. What is the advantage of prizes over patents?
    b. What is the cost? LO5

Questions from Alternative Perspectives

1. Some economists have compared managers to politicians.
   a. How do the incentives facing managers resemble those of politicians?
   b. How do they differ?
   c. What does your answer say about the relative value of each to society? (Austrian)
2. Think of the pay of various groups in society.
   a. How does the compensation awarded to heads of religious organizations compare to the salary of CEOs in profit-making organizations?
   b. What is the explanation for this difference?
   c. Should there be a difference? (Religious)
3. In the list of CEOs in the chapter, how many of the CEOs were women? (To find out, you can go to the *paywatch* source, www.paywatch.org, on the Web.) What is the likely reason for your finding? (Feminist)
4. While some assets, such as forests, can provide benefits to society in perpetuity, some firms see forests as consumable assets. One example was when corporate raider James Goldsmith forcibly acquired Crown Zellerbach in Washington State. After doing so, he cut all of Crown Zellerbach's trees, including one 12,000-acre clear-cut, and then sold off all the company's remaining assets piecemeal, a practice called "junk bond forestry." What does this suggest about the long-term environmental sustainability of free market decisions? (Institutionalist)
5. Because the future is inherently uncertain, firms often follow "rules of thumb" to make decisions such as how much capital (factories and machinery for production) to buy and how to price their products. Examples are financial ratios and mark-up pricing.
   a. Does this behavior make sense?
   b. How does uncertainty that firms face encourage firms to use "rules of thumb"?
   c. What implications for economic analysis do firms' use of rules of thumb have? (Post-Keynesian)
6. Large corporations spend tremendous sums in an effort to influence public policy. Some corporations fund "citizens'" groups to push policies that the corporations want. Giant drug companies fund scientists to prove that the companies' drugs work. Large businesses even hire economists to come up with theories that show why huge businesses and mega-mergers could be beneficial (or at least not harmful).
   a. What are some likely results if corporations control "the marketplace of ideas"?
   b. What, if anything, should be done about this control? (Radical)

Issues to Ponder

1. Airlines and hotels have many frequent-flier and frequent-visitor programs in which individuals who fly the airline or stay at the hotel receive bonuses that are the equivalent of discounts.
   a. Give two reasons why these companies have such programs rather than simply offering lower prices.
   b. Can you give other examples of such programs?
   c. What is a likely reason why firms don't monitor these programs?
   d. Should the benefits of these programs be taxable? LO1
2. Are managers and high-level company officials paid high salaries because they're worth it to the firm, or because they're simply extracting profit from the company to give to themselves? How would you tell whether you're correct? LO2
3. Author Charles Murray has argued that museums actually inhibit rather than foster the appreciation of art. He points out that the technology exists to make essentially "perfect" copies of any major art work that even the best-trained artistic eye could not differentiate from the original. (Difficult)
   a. What would the introduction of this technology do to art museums?
   b. If that is true, why do you believe that the technology is not used?
   c. How are reproductions of music symphonies handled legally?
   d. What would the prohibition of making recordings of music performances do to the demand for musicians and for symphony halls?
   e. Why are music and symphonies handled differently from art? LO3
4. Find a prescription drug that you, someone in your family, or a friend normally takes.
   a. What is the price you (they) pay for it?
   b. What is the lowest online U.S. price for that drug? (Costco is a good place to look.)
   c. If the online price (with shipping) is cheaper, why don't you (they) buy it online?
   d. Now that you have that price information, will you buy the drug online in the future?
   e. What does this process tell you about the competitiveness of the drug market? LO3

5. According to *The Wall Street Journal,* the wholesale price of the generic drug fluoxetine (the generic for Prozac) is $3.60 per 100.
   a. Given that the cost of dispensing them is about $5 to $10 per prescription, how much would you expect the drug to sell for?
   b. In 2008 a prescription for 100 tablets of fluoxetine was selling for $54 at DrugStore.com. It sold for similar prices at other pharmacies. What would you conclude about the market structure, given that information?
   c. At pharmnet.com one can buy 100 fluoxetine tablets for $26. If this is true, what can we say about drug market imperfections? LO3
6. Monsanto Corporation lost its U.S. patent protection for its highly successful herbicide Roundup in the year 2000. What do you suppose was Monsanto's strategy for Roundup in the short run? In the long run? (Difficult) LO4

Answers to Margin Questions

1. Firms are not interested in just short-run profits. They are also interested in long-run profits. So a firm might sacrifice short-run profits for higher long-run profits. Also, those making the decisions for the firm are not always those who own the firm. *(385)*
2. Most economists are concerned about third-party-payer systems because of the problems of monitoring. It is the consumers who have the strongest incentive to make sure that they are getting value for their money. Any third-party-payer system reduces the consumers' vigilance and therefore puts less pressure on holding costs down. *(387)*
3. A manager does not have the same incentive to hold costs down as an owner does because when an owner holds costs down, the owner's profits are increased, but when a manager holds costs down, the increased profits accrue to the owner, not the manager. Thus, the manager has less direct motivation to hold costs down than an owner does. This is especially true if the costs being held down are the manager's perks and pay. *(388)*
4. The threat of a corporate takeover places competitive pressures on firms because it creates the possibility that the managers will be replaced and lose all their perks and above-market-equilibrium pay. *(389)*
5. Most agricultural markets are not perfectly competitive because the gains to producers from moving away from competitive markets are fairly large and, for small deviations from competitive markets, the costs are fairly small to those suppliers and consumers who are kept out. This can be seen in the graph below.

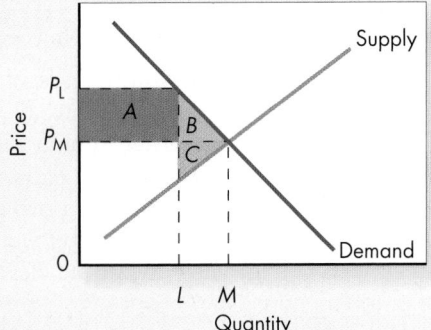

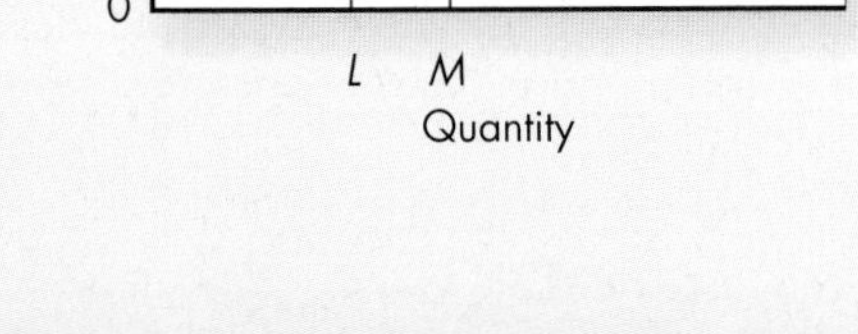

If suppliers producing 0*L* got together and limited supply to *L*, they could push the price up to P_L and could gain the rectangle A for themselves. Consumers and suppliers who are kept out of the market lose triangles *B* and C respectively, which, in the diagram, are not only each smaller than A, but also *B* and C combined are smaller than A. Of course, the area A is lost to the consumers, but the costs of organizing those consumers to fight and protect competition are often prohibitively large. *(390)*

6. It is almost impossible for perfect monopoly to exist because preventing entry is nearly impossible. Monopoly rents are a signal to potential entrants to get the barriers of entry removed. *(391)*
7. The problem with regulation that sets prices relative to costs is that this removes the incentive for firms to hold down costs and can lead to X-inefficiency. While, in theory, regulators could scrutinize every cost, in practice that is impossible—there would have to be a regulatory board duplicating the work that a firm facing direct market pressure undertakes in its normal activities. *(393)*
8. If the additional benefits of creating or maintaining a monopoly exceed the cost of doing so, do it. If they don't, don't. *(394)*
9. Perfect competition is not conducive to technological advance because firms don't earn the profits needed to invest in research and development. It also doesn't have the promise of future above-normal profits needed to motivate researchers to innovate. *(396)*
10. Oligopoly is the best market structure for technological advance because oligopolists have the profits to devote to research and development and have the incentive to innovate. Innovation may provide the oligopolist with a way to increase market share. *(397)*

CHAPTER 18

Antitrust Policy and Regulation

We have always known that heedless self-interest was bad morals; we now know that it is bad economics.

—***Franklin Delano Roosevelt***

AFTER READING THIS CHAPTER, YOU SHOULD BE ABLE TO:

1. Explain the difference between the structure and the performance methods of judging competition.
2. Give a brief history of U.S. antitrust policy.
3. State the resolution of the IBM, AT&T, and Microsoft antitrust cases.
4. Differentiate among horizontal, vertical, and conglomerate mergers.
5. List five reasons why unrelated firms would want to merge.
6. Compare U.S. antitrust policy with antitrust policy of other countries.
7. List three alternatives to antitrust policy that government can use to affect the competitive process.

In the courtroom everyone waits for the Microsoft star witness, an economist who is arguing that Microsoft does not have a monopoly. On the stand he testifies, "The market is too dynamic, too much in flux for a monopoly to exist."

"But how about the fact that Microsoft intentionally tied its Web browser to its Windows operating system in order to harm Netscape's ability to compete?" the government lawyer asks.

"Those were technical decisions," the economist answers, "necessary to make the Web browser operate efficiently."

"Yeah, right," replies the government lawyer.

The above is a paraphrase of what was said in a federal court in an antitrust case the government brought against Microsoft. It captures a very real aspect of all theoretical discussions of market structure and policy. Once theory is translated into policy, market structure and behavior play an important role in how the economy functions. One way in which theory is translated into policy is through antitrust policy and regulation. In this chapter we consider both.

Antitrust Policy: Judgment by Performance or Structure?

Antitrust policy is *the government's policy toward the competitive process*. It's the government's rulebook for carrying out its role as referee. In volleyball, for instance, the rulebook would answer such questions as: When should a foul be called? When has a person caught and thrown rather than hit the ball over the net? In business a referee is needed for such questions as: When can two companies merge? What competitive practices are legal? When is a company too big? To what extent is it fair for two companies to coordinate their pricing policies? When is a market sufficiently competitive or too monopolistic?

The United States has seen wide swings in economists' prescriptions concerning such questions, depending on which of the two views of competition has held sway. The two competing views are

1. **Judgment by performance:** *We should judge the competitiveness of markets by the performance (behavior) of firms in that market.*
2. **Judgment by structure:** *We should judge the competitiveness of markets by the structure of the industry.*

Judgment by performance is the view that competitiveness of a market should be judged by the behavior of firms in that market.

Judgment by structure is the view that competitiveness of a market should be judged by the structure of that market.

To show how the U.S. government has applied these two views of competition in promoting workable and effective competition, this chapter considers government's application of antitrust laws to regulate business. It then considers how recent structural changes in the economy are altering the government's role in refereeing the market.

History of U.S. Antitrust Laws

Although U.S. ideology has always been strongly in favor of laissez-faire and government noninvolvement in business, there has simultaneously been a populist (pro-people) sensibility that fears bigness and monopoly. These fears of bigness and monopoly burst forth in the late 1800s as many firms were merging or organizing together to form trusts or cartels. As stated in the chapter on monopolistic competition, a *cartel*—or, as I'll use the term in this chapter, a *trust*—is a combination of firms in which the firms haven't actually merged but nonetheless act essentially as a single entity. A trust sets common prices and governs the output of individual member firms. A trust can, and often does, act like a monopolist.

In the 1870s and 1880s, trusts were forming in a number of industries, including railroads, steel, tobacco, and oil. Some of these trusts' actions are typified by John D. Rockefeller's Standard Oil. Standard Oil demanded that railroads pay it kickbacks on freight rates. These payments allowed Standard Oil to set lower prices for its products than could other companies, which had to pay the railroads' full price on freight. Standard Oil thus could sell at lower prices than its competitors.

If prices had remained low, this would have had a positive effect on consumers and a negative effect on Standard Oil's competitors. But prices didn't remain low. By 1882, Standard Oil had driven many of its competitors out of business, and the writing was on the wall for those competitors that remained. At that time, Standard Oil created a trust and "invited" its few surviving competitors to join. Then Standard Oil Trust used the monopoly power it had gained to close down refineries, raise prices, and limit the production of oil. The price of oil rose from a competitive level to a monopolistic level, and the consumer ended up suffering.

The Sherman Antitrust Act

Public outrage against trusts like Standard Oil's was high. The organizers of the trusts were widely known as *robber barons* because of their exploitation of natural resources and their other unethical behavior. The trusts were seen as making enormous profits, preventing competition, and in general bullying everyone in sight. In response, the U.S. Congress passed the **Sherman Antitrust Act** of 1890—*a law designed to regulate the competitive process*.

Public outrage at the formation and activities of trusts such as Standard Oil led to the passage of the Sherman Act, the Clayton Act, and the Federal Trade Commission Act.

The Sherman Act contained two main sections:

Section 1: Every contract, combination in the form of trust or otherwise, or conspiracy, in restraint of trade or commerce among the several States, or with foreign nations, is hereby declared to be illegal.

Q-1 What were the two provisions of the Sherman Antitrust Act?

> Section 2: Every person who shall monopolize, or attempt to monopolize, or combine or conspire with any other person or persons, to monopolize any part of the trade or commerce among the several States, or with foreign nations, shall be deemed guilty of a misdemeanor, and, on conviction thereof, shall be punished by a fine not exceeding five thousand dollars, or by imprisonment not exceeding one year, or by both said punishments, at the discretion of the court.

The Sherman Act was broad and sweeping, but vague.

The Sherman Act was meant to be as sweeping and broad as its language sounds. After all, it was passed in response to a public outcry against trusts. But if you look at it carefully, in some respects it is vague and weak. For example, offenses under Section 2 were initially only misdemeanors, not felonies.[1] It's unclear what constitutes "restraint of trade." Moreover, although the act prohibits monopolization, it does not explicitly prohibit monopolies. In short, with the Sherman Act, Congress passed the buck to the courts, letting them decide U.S. antitrust policy.[2]

The following story summarizes the courts' role in antitrust policy. Three umpires are describing their job. The youngest of the three says, "I call them as I see them." The middle-aged umpire says, "No, that's not what an umpire does. An umpire calls them the way they are." The senior umpire says, "You're both wrong. They're nothing until I call them." And that's how it is with the courts and monopoly. Whether a firm is behaving monopolistically isn't known until the court makes its decision.

As Congress was passing the Sherman Act, economists too were debating the implications of trusts and whether it was in the public interest to restrict them. Part of the debate concerned whether the mergers reflected technological changes in production and expanding transportation systems that made increased economies of scale more important (in which case restricting trusts might not be in the public interest since doing so might prevent firms from taking advantage of economies of scale), or whether trusts simply represented attempts at monopolization to restrict output and generate monopoly profits (in which case restricting trusts would more likely be in the public interest since doing so would reduce monopoly).

Economists reflecting the performance viewpoint argued that competition was strong and would ultimately limit monopolies.

A second part of the debate concerned how fast economic forces would operate and how fragile competition was. Some economists argued that competition was strong and that it would limit the profit trusts and monopolies made and force them to charge the competitive price (in which case restricting trusts might not be in the public interest). These economists were reflecting the performance viewpoint—that competition should be relied on to break down the monopolies. They argued that bigness doesn't imply the absence of market competition and that the government's role should merely be to make sure that no significant barriers to entry are created.

Economists reflecting the structure viewpoint argued that trusts should be broken up by government.

Other economists, reflecting the structure viewpoint, argued that competition was fragile and required a large number of small firms. They argued that trusts and monopolies (even if they don't charge monopolistic prices) are bad, that the trusts should be broken up by government, and that laws should not allow new monopolies or trusts to be formed. However, the debate was for the courts, not economists, to settle.

The Standard Oil and American Tobacco Cases: Judging Market Competitiveness by Performance

Web Note 18.1
The Trusts

In 1911, the U.S. Supreme Court established its interpretation of the Sherman Act by handing down its opinions in cases involving Standard Oil and the American Tobacco

[1]Under federal law, a misdemeanor is any misconduct punishable by only a fine or a jail sentence of a year or less. A felony requires a sentence of more than a year.

[2]Subsequent amendments to the Sherman Act have strengthened it. For example, offenses under Section 2 are now felonies, not misdemeanors.

Company. The Court determined that both companies were structural monopolies; each company controlled 90 percent of its market. However, the Court decided that the monopolistic structure of the markets did not violate the Sherman Antitrust Act. A company's violation of the act was determined not by the structure of the industry but by the particular firm's performance—that is, by whether or not the firm engaged in "unfair business practices." This judgment by performance, not judgment by structure, is often called the *abuse theory* because a firm is legally considered a monopoly only if it commits monopolistic abuses.

Standard Oil and the American Tobacco Company were judged guilty, not because of their structure, but because of their performance.

In these two cases the distinction was academic. Both Standard Oil and American Tobacco were judged guilty (very guilty) of unfair business practices and were broken up. But the academic distinction played an important role in determining the industrial structure of the United States. It allowed structural monopolies to exist but prohibited them from using certain monopolistic practices, such as demanding kickbacks.

In 1920, this structure/performance distinction was important in a case involving U.S. Steel. Here the Supreme Court ruled that, while U.S. Steel was a structural monopoly, it was not a monopoly in performance. That is, the firm had not used unfair business practices to become a monopolist and thus was not in violation of antitrust law. Unlike Standard Oil, U.S. Steel was not required to break up into smaller companies.

Q-2 What was the resolution of the Standard Oil case?

The Clayton Act and the Federal Trade Commission Act

In an attempt to give more guidance to the courts and to provide for more vigorous enforcement of the antitrust provisions, in 1914 Congress passed the Clayton Antitrust Act and the Federal Trade Commission Act.

The **Clayton Antitrust Act** is *a law that made four specific monopolistic practices illegal* when their effect was to lessen competition:

1. Price discrimination, that is, selling identical goods to different customers at different prices.
2. Tie-in contracts, in which the buyer must agree to deal exclusively with one seller and not to purchase goods from competing sellers.
3. Interlocking directorships, in which memberships of boards of directors of two or more firms are almost identical.
4. Buying stock in a competitor's company when the purpose of buying that stock is to reduce competition.

The Clayton Antitrust Act made four specific monopolistic practices illegal:

1. Price discrimination.
2. Tie-in contracts.
3. Interlocking directorships.
4. Purchase of a competitor's stock.

In establishing the Federal Trade Commission (FTC) in 1914, Congress gave it the power to regulate competition and police markets. The **Federal Trade Commission Act** is *a law that made it illegal for firms to use "unfair methods of competition" and to engage in "unfair or deceptive acts or practices,"* whether or not those actions had any impact on competition. Other than that broad mandate, Congress gave the FTC little direction as to what rules to use to regulate trade and police markets. As a result, for more than 20 years the commission was rather ineffective. In 1938, however, it was given the job of preventing false and deceptive advertising, which remains one of its primary roles.

The ALCOA Case: Judging Market Competitiveness by Structure

Judgment by performance was the primary criterion governing U.S. antitrust policy until 1945. In 1945 the U.S. courts changed their interpretation of the law with the Aluminum Company of America (ALCOA) case. In the ALCOA case, the company was found guilty of violating the antitrust statutes even though the court did not rule that ALCOA had been guilty of unfair practices. What ALCOA had done was to use its

Q-3 What was the resolution of the ALCOA case?

Web Note 18.2
Predatory Pricing

knowledge of the market to expand its capacity before any competitors had a chance to enter the market. In addition, it had kept its prices low to prevent potential entry by competitors, an activity known as *predatory pricing*. It showed no signs of exploiting its monopoly power to charge high prices or to force competing firms out of business. Thus, on performance standards, it was not violating the law. But in the ALCOA case, the structure of the market, not the company's performance, was used to determine whether ALCOA was in violation of antitrust law.

Judging Markets by Structure and Performance: The Reality

Judgment by structure seems unfair on a gut level. After all, in economics the purpose of competition is to motivate firms to produce better goods than their competitors are producing, and to do so at lower cost. If a firm is competing so successfully that all the other firms leave the industry, the successful firm will be a monopolist, and on the basis of judgment by structure will be guilty of antitrust violations. Under the judgment-by-structure criterion, a firm is breaking the law if it does what it's supposed to be doing: producing the best product it can at the lowest possible cost.

An important reason supporting the structure criterion is practicality.

Supporters of the judgment-by-structure criterion recognize this problem but nonetheless favor the structure criterion. An important reason for this is practicality.

Contextual Judgments and the Capabilities of the Courts Judgment by performance requires that each action of a firm be analyzed on a case-by-case basis. Doing that is enormously time-consuming and expensive. In some interpretations, actions of a firm might be considered appropriate competitive behavior; in other interpretations, the same actions might be considered inappropriate. For example, say that an automobile company requires that in order for its warranty to hold, owners of its warranteed vehicles must use only the company's parts and service centers. Is this requirement of the automobile company intended to create a monopoly position for its parts and service center divisions or to ensure proper maintenance? The answer depends on the context of the action.

But judging each case contextually is beyond the courts' capabilities. There are so many firms and so many actions that the courts can't judge all industries on their performance. They must devise a way to limit the issues they look at. In order to apply the performance criterion reasonably, the Supreme Court must set out certain guidelines to tell firms in what situations the Court will take a closer look at their performance. Because the available information concerns structure, those guidelines inevitably refer to market structure, even though it is firms' performance that will ultimately be judged. So even though judging by structure may have problems, it is necessary.

It's very much like the procedure college admissions offices use in deciding which applicants to accept. They judge applicants on their "total performance," not just on their quantitative scores on standardized tests. However, they often set a certain quantitative score to reduce applications to a manageable number. Applicants below the cutoff are automatically rejected; applicants above it are considered one by one.

Another argument in favor of judging competitiveness by structure is that structure can be a predictor of future performance. Advocates of this criterion argue that a monopolist may be pricing low now, but it is, after all, a monopolist and won't price low in the future. The low price will eliminate competition now, and, once the competition is gone, the firm will not be able to resist the temptation to use its monopoly power.

Choosing the relevant market when evaluating competitiveness is difficult to do.

Determining the Relevant Market and Industry Supporters of the performance criterion admit that this standard has problems, but they point out that the structure criterion also has problems. As you saw in the chapter on monopolistic competition, it's difficult to determine the relevant market (local, national, or international)

REAL-WORLD APPLICATION

Wal-Mart, State Laws, and Competition

It isn't only the federal government that has laws regulating competition. States have a variety of laws that govern competitive practices. One such state law is Arkansas's Unfair Practices Act, which prohibits selling, or advertising for sale, items below cost "for the purpose of injuring competitors and destroying competition." In the early 1990s, three Arkansas pharmacies sued Wal-Mart for violating this law by selling its goods at "too low" a price.

Wal-Mart initially lost the suit in Arkansas; however, in 1995 the Arkansas Supreme Court overturned the lower court decision and held that Wal-Mart's pricing was not part of a strategy to price below cost over a prolonged period.

We may see more such suits, especially in the pricing of prescription pharmaceuticals, since Wal-Mart introduced a $4 price for a 30-day prescription of a variety of generic drugs (including 14 of the top 20 best-selling prescription drugs) and other discount stores followed suit. However, these suits are likely to fail for two reasons. First, Wal-Mart now takes into account state laws, and the $4 program is not available in states where its lawyers see the state laws as a potential problem. And second, the competition has changed. Back in the 1990s, Wal-Mart was competing with local drug stores that had high profit margins but low volume. Now it's competing with other chains—Kmart, Wegman's, BJ's, Costco—that have entered the prescription drug market and established their own low-cost generic programs.

All of these chains argue that when they charge a low price, they are not doing it to "destroy competition" or "injure competitors," but rather to maintain low prices for consumers. They claim that their pricing policies promote, not destroy, competition.

In principle, most economists agree with Wal-Mart and other chains; new competition, by its very nature, hurts existing businesses—that's the way the competitive process works. Those who don't sell for the lowest price lose, and those who do gain. But most economists also recognize that Wal-Mart's brand of competition can affect the social fabric of small-town economies. A new Wal-Mart store can undermine the town centers and replace them with commercial sprawl on the outskirts of these towns. Whether these externalities are a reason to limit Wal-Mart's aggressive pricing policies is a debatable question.

and the relevant industry (three-digit or five-digit NAICS code) necessary to identify the structural competitiveness of any industry.

Such questions have been the center of many antitrust court cases. For example, in the ALCOA case, the company argued that metals such as copper and steel were interchangeable with aluminum, and that therefore the relevant industry to consider was the metals industry. If the Court had chosen metals, not aluminum, as the relevant industry, ALCOA wouldn't have been found to have a monopoly. The Court decided, however, that aluminum had sufficiently unique properties to constitute its own market. Since the Court determined that ALCOA had 90 percent of the aluminum market, ALCOA was declared a monopoly and was broken up.

Q-4 What was the resolution of the Du Pont case?

The arguments in the Du Pont case (1956) again centered on the definition of *industry*. The Supreme Court found that Du Pont was innocent of monopolizing the production of cellophane even though Du Pont was the only producer of cellophane. The Court reasoned that the relevant industry was not the cellophane industry but rather the flexible wrap industry, which also included aluminum foil and wax paper. Du Pont did not have a monopoly of the flexible wrap industry and, thus, the Court said, was not in violation of the antitrust laws.

More recently, the Department of Justice opposed a merger between Gillette and Parker Pens, arguing that the combined firm would control about 40 percent of the premium-fountain-pen market. The Court, however, allowed the merger, arguing that the relevant market was much larger—the market for premium writing instruments, which also included mechanical pencils, ballpoint pens, and rollerballs. The premium-writing-instruments market had many more competitors than the premium-fountain-pen market.

Similar ambiguities exist with the decision about the relevant geographic market. In the Pabst Brewing case (1966), the definition of the market played a key role. Pabst wanted to merge with the Blatz Brewing Company. On a national scale, both companies were relatively small, accounting together for about 4.5 percent of beer sales in the United States as a whole. Pabst argued that the United States was the relevant market. The Court, however, decided that Wisconsin, where Pabst had its headquarters, was the relevant market, and since the two firms held a 24 percent share of that market, the merger was not allowed.

Both structure and performance criteria have ambiguities, and in the real world there are no definitive criteria for judging whether a firm has violated the antitrust statutes.

What should one make of debates regarding relevant markets? The bottom line is that both structure and performance criteria have ambiguities, and in the real world there are no definitive criteria for judging whether a firm has violated the antitrust statutes. A firm isn't at fault or in the clear until the courts make the call.

Recent Antitrust Enforcement

In recent years, few mergers have been challenged by the government. In 2007, for example, the Department of Justice challenged only 4 of the more than 10,000 mergers that took place among U.S. companies. Most of those challenged were settled, abandoned, or restructured. Despite the fact that few recent mergers have been challenged, antitrust law still works mainly through its deterrent effect. Many potential mergers are never even proposed because firms know they would not be allowed.

Few major antitrust cases have been brought, in part because a century of experience has taught business what the law allows, and in part because the government has been lenient in its interpretation of the antitrust laws. That leniency has three interrelated causes. The first is a change in the American ideology. Whereas in the 1950s and 1960s the prevailing ideology saw big business as "bad," by the 1980s big business was seen as a combination of good and bad. In this new ideological framework, the political pressure to push antitrust enforcement waned. Second, as the United States became more integrated into the global economy, big business faced significant international competition and hence competition created by U.S. market structure became less important. Third, as technologies became more complicated, the issues in antitrust enforcement also became more complicated for the courts to handle. By the time the legal system had resolved a case, the technology would have changed so much that the issues in that case were no longer relevant.

Since the 1980s the United States has been more lenient in antitrust cases because of a change in ideology, the globalization of the U.S. economy, and the increasing complexity of technology.

Three Modern Antitrust Cases

The modern era of antitrust policy has been marked by important cases in the computer and telecommunications markets. One such case was against IBM.

The IBM Case

In 1967 the U.S. Department of Justice sued IBM for violating the antitrust laws. The department argued that the company had a 72 percent share of the general-purpose electronic digital computing industry, and that it had acquired that market share because of unfair business practices such as bundling of hardware, software, and maintenance services at a single price (that is, requiring customers to buy all three together). If you wanted IBM equipment (hardware), you also had to take IBM service and software

REAL-WORLD APPLICATION

Nefarious Business Practices

In a secretly recorded comment during a price-fixing meeting, the former president of Archer Daniels Midland (ADM), a major supplier of food and grain, stated, "Our competitors are our friends and our customers are our enemies."

The U.S. antitrust laws concern far more than mergers and market structure; they also place legal restrictions on certain practices of businesses such as price-fixing. By law, firms are not allowed to *explicitly* collude in order to fix prices above the competitive level. A key aspect of the law is the explicit nature of the collusion that is disallowed. Airlines, gas stations, and firms in many other industries have prices that generally move in tandem—when one firm changes its price, others seem to follow. Such practices would suggest that these firms are implicitly colluding, but they are not violating the law unless there is explicit collusion.

To prove explicit collusion is difficult—there must be a smoking gun, and there is seldom sufficient evidence of explicit collusion to prosecute businesses. There are exceptions, however. In 1996, ADM was caught red-handed when one of its former officials gave prosecutors tapes of meetings in which price-fixing occurred. Meeting secretly around the world, in countries like Mexico, France, Canada, and Japan, ADM executives tried to fix prices of Lysine, a feed additive, and citric acid. One of ADM's officials, working undercover for the FBI, secretly recorded these meetings. Faced with the taped evidence against them, ADM agreed to pay $100 million in fines—the largest criminal antitrust fine in history up to that year. Since that time, fines have risen to even greater sums, with British Airways paying a fine of $547 million for price fixing.

Company	Fine (in millions)
British Airways (2007)	$547
Roche Holding (1997)	500
Samsung (2005)	300
Infineon (2005)	160
Japan Airlines (2008)	110

whether you wanted them or not. When you bought an IBM machine, you bought everything, so other companies had little chance to compete. Moreover, the department argued that IBM constantly redesigned its computers, making it impossible for other companies to keep up and compete fairly on the sale of any IBM mainframe-compatible item.

In technology industries, the market is continually changing.

IBM argued that the relevant market was broader, that it included all types of computers such as military computers, programmable calculators, and other information-processing products. It further claimed that its so-called unfair practices were simply a reflection of efficient computer technology. Fast-moving technological developments required it to continually redesign its products merely to provide its customers with the latest, best equipment. And, it said, the only way to provide the best level of service to its customers was to include its maintenance services in the price of its products. The case dragged on for years until finally, in 1982, the government withdrew its case.

The reason it did so was that the market had changed. Many of the government's objections had become moot; mainframe computers were being replaced with personal computers, a market in which Apple and DEC had become serious competitors, and the globalization of the computer industry made IBM's dominance in the United States far less important.

IBM may have won the battle in the antitrust case against it, but in doing so it may have lost the war. Here's why.

Q-5 What was the resolution of the IBM case?

About the same time as the case was at its height, IBM was negotiating with an upstart company about an operating system for a small part of its market—the personal computer (PC) market, which was just developing. Bill Gates, the president of the young company, offered to sell its disk operating system (DOS) to IBM for $75,000. IBM refused to buy it; to have bought DOS would have given IBM greater control over the PC market, and would have made a court-ordered breakup of IBM more likely. Instead, IBM left Bill Gates to license DOS to IBM and everyone else, while IBM concentrated on mainframe computers and the production of PCs.

The IBM case was dropped by the United States, but the prosecution likely led to IBM's problems in the 1990s. It won but it also lost.

By the early 1990s, the cost of that decision was clear. The mainframe market was dying, and IBM was hemorrhaging losses. Meanwhile, Bill Gates had become a multibillionaire, and his company—Microsoft—had become a controlling force in the PC market. Now the tables were turned and in 1994 it was Microsoft that was being pursued by the U.S. government for violating antitrust laws.

The losses at IBM ended in the mid-1990s and its competitive position improved as it switched from being a hardware provider to being a service provider. (It sold its PC division to Lenovo, a Chinese computer company.) Thus, ultimately it weathered the antitrust case, but its history was forever changed.

The AT&T Case

The other major antitrust case of the 1980s, the AT&T case, demonstrates another aspect of U.S. antitrust policy and shows how technological change plays an important role in competition and questions of industrial market structure.

AT&T as a Regulated Monopoly Up until 1982, AT&T was what was called a *regulated monopoly*. It had the exclusive right to provide telephone service in the United States. AT&T controlled 90 percent of the telecommunications market: long-distance and local telephone service, and the production of telephones themselves as well as other communications equipment.

A natural monopoly is an industry in which significant economies of scale make the existence of more than one firm inefficient.

Why was it given that right? Because it was felt that economies of scale and network externalities made supplying telephone service a **natural monopoly** (*an industry in which significant economies of scale make the existence of more than one firm inefficient*). Telephone service required every house to be connected with lines, which had to be buried underground or strung overhead on poles. It made little sense to have more than one company stringing competing lines. Moreover, the government decided that telephone service ought to be available to all Americans, even those living in rural and other remote areas, where service was more costly to provide, and AT&T was required to provide universal service. Unregulated companies likely would have practiced *cream skimming* (providing service to low-cost areas and avoiding high-cost areas).

In return for its monopoly, AT&T was subjected to regulatory control by the Federal Communications Commission and state utility commissions. This government regulation was designed to limit the company's profit to a fair level and prevent it from abusing its monopoly. It also restricted AT&T's business to telephone services.

Under AT&T's monopoly, phone service in the United States was the best and cheapest in the world, although some believed it could and should have been even cheaper. Some economists argued that AT&T's guarantee of a "fair" return on its investment gave it a strong incentive to act as a lazy monopolist and to invest heavily, thereby increasing costs. If a company knows it can pass its costs on to customers (and add a profit margin as well), it has little incentive to hold down costs. But even if service was more expensive than it needed to be, on the whole most agreed that the system worked well.

Technological Change and Competition In the 1970s technological changes fundamentally altered the nature of the long-distance telephone industry. Satellite transmission and fiber optics made physical line connections no longer the only option, so long-distance telephone service was no longer a natural monopoly. The FCC allowed some competition using these new technologies, and as significant competition began to develop, AT&T's new competitors claimed that they weren't being allowed reasonable access to the AT&T-controlled local telephone network. AT&T charged competing firms high fees for access to all its local lines—fees that competitors argued were unfair.

The issue was complicated by the fact that the regulatory commissions had set local charges low and long-distance rates high (implicitly subsidizing local service with AT&T's long-distance profits). As long as AT&T controlled both local and long-distance calling, its revenues were unaffected by this rule. But when competitors began to undercharge AT&T on long-distance service, AT&T grew increasingly concerned. AT&T's high access charges were an attempt to see that the competitors used some of their own profits to help subsidize local rates.

As a result of these claims and counterclaims, the Department of Justice introduced an antitrust suit against AT&T in 1974, alleging that potential competitors were not being allowed reasonable access to AT&T's local telephone network. The case had merit, but so did AT&T's defense: How could a firm provide high-cost local service at a low price with no way to pay for it? As is now usual for any contested antitrust case, the case went on and on, and no conclusion was in sight.

Resolution of the AT&T Case In January 1982, AT&T and the Department of Justice announced that they had settled the case and that AT&T had agreed to be broken up. Specifically, AT&T agreed that by January 1, 1984, it would divest itself of 22 local operating companies, which accounted for more than 75 percent of AT&T's assets. These companies quickly merged into seven local operating companies that became known as the *Baby Bells*. AT&T kept its long-distance telephone service, its manufacturing division, and its research facilities. In return, AT&T was allowed to enter any unregulated business it desired, such as data transmission and computers. The Baby Bells, alternatively, were restricted to the local telephone market.

The AT&T case was settled by AT&T agreeing to be split up into regional companies handling local service, and AT&T itself competing in the long-distance market.

The result of this settlement was an enormous upheaval in the telephone industry. Local rates for phone service went up twofold or even threefold, while long-distance rates fell substantially. Major competitors emerged, and competition for long-distance business became fierce.

Q-6 What was the resolution of the AT&T case?

Developments since the AT&T Case The breakup of AT&T was not the end of the changes. The seven Baby Bells continued merging with one another, and by 2005 only four remained: SBC Communications, Verizon, Bell South, and Qwest. In 1995, AT&T had divided itself into three companies: AT&T, Lucent Technologies, and National Cash Register. Only AT&T remained in the market for communication services, expanding its offerings into wireless communications, digital cable, cable, and long distance. In 2004, however, it withdrew from the residential local and long-distance phone markets. Then in 2005 it was taken over by one of its former parts—SBC Communications, which operated Cingular Wireless—and the combined company chose to use the AT&T name. Then in 2006, the new AT&T was taken over by Bell South, another of the former Baby Bells, and the combined company again called itself at&t (now in lowercase), making it the new, new at&t. So the name, at&t, still exists, but the company that the name is associated with is quite different from the company that was the subject of the antitrust suit, and it is a company that has twice been taken over by its former parts. Why the enormous change? Because of rapid technological change, which alters the nature of industries and introduces competition in ways that previously had not been possible.

The Microsoft Case

One of the most important antitrust cases brought in the 1990s was the Microsoft case. This is an extremely interesting case to consider both because of its similarities to the IBM case and because of the issues it raises about competition, the competitive process, and government's role in that competitive process.

Microsoft makes computer software. From the company's small start some 35 years ago, sales of Microsoft software have grown to account for about 50 percent of the world's software market. Its PC operating system, Windows, accounts for an even larger share—more than 90 percent—of the world's operating system software market.

Since all software must be compatible with an operating system, the widespread use of Windows gives Microsoft enormous power—power that competitors claim it has used to gain competitive advantage for its other divisions. Competitors' calls for action, and reports of monopolistically abusive acts by Microsoft, led the U.S. Department of Justice in 1998 to charge Microsoft with violating antitrust laws.

The government suit against Microsoft charged the company with being a monopoly and using that monopoly power in a predatory way. Specifically, it charged Microsoft with:

1. Possessing monopoly power in the market for personal computer operating systems.
2. Tying other Microsoft software products to its Windows operating system.
3. Entering into agreements that keep computer manufacturers that install Windows from offering competing software.

Microsoft had dominated the market for PC operating systems for about a decade. The U.S. Department of Justice argued that this long-standing monopoly position was the result of unfair business practices. Microsoft argued that Windows sold so well because it was a superior product. Microsoft further argued that, because it faced competition from technological change, it was not a monopolist.

Is Microsoft a Monopolist? The computer software industry is a market with barriers to entry that originate from two sources: network externalities and economies of scale. Network externalities exist because as the number of applications supported by a single platform increases, the value of the platform also increases. Economies of scale exist because the cost of developing a new platform and new software is significant, while the cost of producing it is minimal. It is a potential candidate for monopoly.

Is Microsoft a monopoly in the market for operating systems? Looking only at the market within a static framework, Microsoft, given its stable 90 percent share, almost definitely has a monopoly. Looking at the market from a dynamic perspective, the issue is much more complicated. Competing operating systems exist.

The Linux operating system is a particularly strong potential competitor because it is an "open-source" operating system. All programmers can get the code and modify it, allowing them to tailor it for their software and streamline the structure of their programs. Because its code is freely available, Linux reduces the costs of software development and leads to more efficient programs.

A second potential competitive force is the merging of software and hardware. As the power of computers increases according to Moore's law, it is becoming more and more feasible to design specific chips to do specific jobs, incorporating into a single chip aspects that were previously separated into hardware and software. Within 10 years the entire PC structure—a machine to handle a multitude of tasks—could become obsolete, and instead the market may consist of $10 or $15 machines that will perform specific tasks more efficiently than can a multipurpose machine like the PC. Already, PDAs

Whether one sees Microsoft as a monopolist depends in part on whether one views it in a static or dynamic framework.

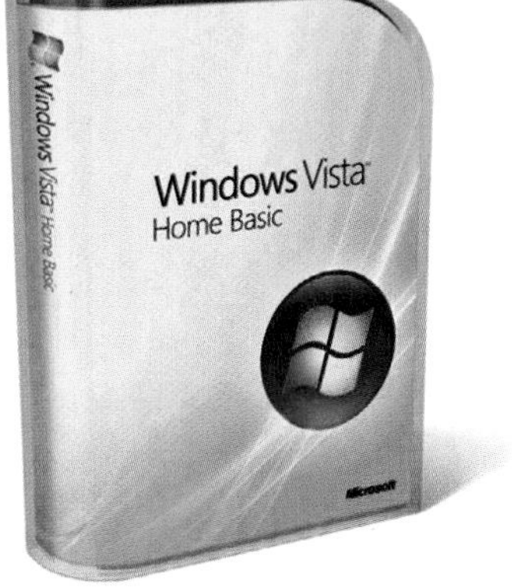

(personal digital assistants) and smart phones run software without Windows. A third potential competitive force involves the Internet. With Internet access, a person does not need a PC, or even software and an operating system. All one needs is Internet access to software providers. More and more this access is becoming easily available on the Internet. Some observers believe that this is the future of computing—all one will need is Internet access. The hardware and software that currently make up a computer will be provided more efficiently by firms that will make them available on demand. They point out that everyone doesn't carry around their own electric generator—they plug into the electric network when they need electricity. The same thing is likely to happen with computing needs.

If they are correct, the PC will become as obsolete as vinyl records, eight-track tapes, and, soon, CDs. Google's introduction of a new Internet browser, Chrome, is seen by many observers as an initial step in that direction. They argue that Google, by creating a new browser to compete with Microsoft's Explorer, is hoping to create a platform that eventually will allow them to provide software services directly to people, without the need for a PC or the Windows operating system.

Each of these changes could eliminate Microsoft's monopoly advantage. In this dynamic view of the market, Microsoft's monopoly is at best temporary, and will survive only if it outcompetes the other technologies. For example, some estimate that within a few years Windows on PCs will account for only about 60 percent of the market for devices that can run applications.

Is Microsoft a Predatory Monopolist? The U.S. Department of Justice argued that Microsoft used its monopoly in the operating systems market to gain a larger share of the software market and engaged in unfair practices against its competitors to maintain the barriers to entry in the operating systems market. Let's first look at its actions to gain market share in the software market.

Competing software companies alleged that companies like Novell (now Corel), which had the leading word-processing software, WordPerfect, were put at a significant disadvantage because Microsoft combined its software with the Windows operating system. Not surprisingly, Microsoft's Word has become the dominant word-processing system. By directing the development of new software to favor Windows, Microsoft strengthened the barrier to entry created by network externalities. Microsoft also penalized computer manufacturers that installed Windows if they installed competing software. IBM, for example, was denied Windows 95 when it decided to pre-install its PCs with Lotus, a direct competitor to Microsoft's Excel. Microsoft also was alleged to have engaged in unfair practices in how it addressed the threat of competition in the operating system market.

Resolution of the Microsoft Case So is Microsoft a monopoly? And has it been involved in anticompetitive practices? The answers the court gave were yes and yes. In 2000 a judge concluded that Microsoft violated Section 2 of the Sherman Act by attempting to maintain its monopoly power by anticompetitive means. He also ruled that Microsoft violated Section 1 of the Sherman Act by unlawfully tying its Web browser to its operating system. In a strongly worded decision he stated that "Microsoft mounted a deliberate assault upon entrepreneurial efforts that, left to rise or fall on their own merits, could well have enabled the introduction of competition into the market." As a remedy the government proposed breaking up Microsoft into two companies. Microsoft quickly appealed, and in mid-2001 the appeals court ruled that, while Microsoft was indeed a monopoly, a breakup was not necessary—instead, the case should be resolved by mediation. A result of that mediation was that Microsoft agreed not to engage in contracts that prohibited PC makers from using competing products or in practices that favored PC makers that offered only Microsoft products. It also agreed to release technical information about Windows improvements to software developers. Microsoft maintained its right to keep e-mail systems and software programs such as media players bundled with Windows. Most observers believe that these limitations do not place a serious constraint on Microsoft's domination of the software industry since, for a number of its competitors, that technical information would be provided too late. In the four years that had passed since the beginning of the case, Microsoft had already integrated its Windows operating system with Microsoft media players and had developed a head start in integrating a number of other new technologies into its Windows operating system.

Microsoft and the European Union While Microsoft was negotiating with regulators in the United States, it also faced antitrust investigation in the European Union. In 2004, the European Union found that Microsoft was guilty of two anticompetitive practices: tying its Windows Media Player to its operating system and designing its server software to give its own software an advantage over competitors. Unlike regulators in the United States who negotiated a consent decree with Microsoft, regulators in the European Union fined Microsoft and set strict conditions on how Microsoft could build and sell software. Specifically, it required Microsoft to sell a version of Windows without Windows Media Player and ordered that Microsoft share, or license, technical information about its operating system with competing software developers. After years of appeals and negotiations, Microsoft agreed to comply. However, the EU was unsatisfied with its compliance and in 2008 the EU fined Microsoft over a billion dollars for noncompliance. Then, in 2009 the EU brought a new suit against Microsoft and so the story continues.

Google, the Internet, and Microsoft

Web Note 18.3
Microsoft, Google, and Apple

By delaying the proceedings against it, Microsoft avoided being significantly affected by most of the restrictions the courts placed on its practices. By the time the restrictions were implemented, technology had changed, and Microsoft's advantage was so set that other firms could not compete effectively. However, Microsoft did not avoid competition from outside the PC industry. Technological change not only made the restrictions ineffective, it also made Microsoft's attempts at controlling the market ineffective. The real threat to Microsoft's dominating the PC industry has come from technological developments that change the way in which computers are used. By 2007, many more computers were connected to the Internet, which means that the operating system and the specific software on a PC are less important, since software can be accessed over the Internet. For example, Google offers free word processing software that does not depend on the Windows operating system; the Internet is replacing the computer. The possibility of people being able to rent computer time on the Internet with whatever software they want is currently being discussed, which, if established, will make the Windows operating system even less important. Microsoft recognized this and in 2007 introduced a new operating system, Windows Vista, which was more closely connected to the Web. Microsoft hoped Vista would effectively counter Web-based operating systems and, if adopted, would eliminate the need for a PC-based operating system. Vista was not a huge success, and in 2009 Microsoft's dominance of the computer operating system market was in decline. Thus, even though Microsoft has been able to escape the legal challenges, and maintain its dominance from those who challenge it in court, Microsoft still faces significant competition as new technologies undermine its entire business model.

Assessment of U.S. Antitrust Policy

Economic scholars' overall assessment of antitrust policy is mixed. In certain cases, such as the IBM case, most agree that antitrust prosecution went too far. But most believe that other decisions (as in the 1911 Standard Oil and American Tobacco cases) set a healthy precedent by encouraging a more competitive U.S. business environment. Almost all agree that antitrust enforcement has not reduced the size of firms below the minimally efficient level, the level at which a firm can take full advantage of economies of scale. But they are mixed in their judgments as to whether the enforcement was needed. Performance advocates generally believe that it was not, while structural advocates generally believe that it was. They are also mixed in their judgment about whether any type of antitrust action is feasible in a technologically dynamic industry such as computers or telecommunications.

Economists' judgment on antitrust is mixed.

Mergers, Acquisitions, and Takeovers

Other than the Microsoft case, major U.S. antitrust activity was minimal in the early 2000s. But industrial structure has changed significantly. The nature of those changes was treated in the second chapter on production and cost analysis, where I discussed how firms are increasingly looking for alternative ways of structuring themselves so that they can achieve economies of scope and economies of scale that go along with specialization. To do this, firms are simultaneously merging and breaking up. Firms are allowed to break up as much as they want; when they merge, however, they must see that any merger falls within the antitrust guidelines. In order to put recent merger activity into perspective, let's consider the various subcategories and types of mergers that are possible.

Acquisitions and Takeovers

Merger is a general term meaning *the act of combining two firms*. The picture it conveys is of two firms combining to form one firm. That picture isn't always appropriate, however. For example, often the firm buying another company is essentially what's called a *shell corporation*, which exists primarily to buy up other firms. A combination that is technically a merger but has distinguishing characteristics all its own is the **takeover**—*the purchase of one firm by a shell firm that then takes direct control of all the purchased firm's operations*. The term *takeover* is used to emphasize that little true merging is taking place. Takeovers change the control over the firm but do not affect market concentration.

Another kind of merger is an **acquisition**—*a transaction in which a company buys another company and the purchaser has the right of direct control over the resulting operation (but does not always exercise that right)*. It is a merger, but it is not a merger of equals, and the acquiring firm does not necessarily take over direct control of the acquired firm's operations. In a merger of equals, neither firm takes over the other, and it's not clear who'll be in charge after the merger.

Takeovers and acquisitions are said to be *friendly* or *hostile*. In a friendly takeover, one corporation is willing to be acquired by the other. A **hostile takeover** is *a merger in which the firm being taken over doesn't want to be taken over*. How can that happen?

Remember the discussion of corporations from Chapter 3. Corporations are owned by stockholders, but are managed by a different group of individuals. The two groups' interests do not necessarily coincide. When it is said that a corporation doesn't want to be taken over, that means that the corporation's managers don't want the company to be taken over. In a hostile takeover, the management of each corporation presents its side to the shareholders of both corporations. The shareholders of the corporation that is the takeover target ultimately decide whether or not to sell their shares. If enough shareholders sell, the takeover succeeds.

In a hostile takeover, the shareholders ultimately decide whether to sell their shares.

Mergers

Mergers are also classified by the types of businesses that are merging.

Horizontal mergers are companies in the same industry merging together.

Horizontal Mergers Most U.S. antitrust policy has concerned **horizontal mergers**—*the combining of two companies in the same industry*. The creation of Standard Oil is an example of a horizontal merger. The 2006 merger between AT&T and Cingular is another. Since the passage of the Celler-Kefauver Act of 1950, almost all mergers of companies with substantial market shares in the same industry have been prohibited, even though enforcement was loosened in the 1980s. For example, in 2003 the FTC blocked a proposed merger between Nestlé and Dreyers because the combined firm would have controlled 60 percent of the super-premium ice-cream market with only one other competing company, Unilever, which sells Ben & Jerry's.

The general guidelines that the Justice Department currently uses for horizontal mergers is based on the Herfindahl Index.

Herfindahl Index	Review by Justice Department
Below 1,000	Not challenged
1,000–1,800	Reviewed if the Herfindahl index increases by more than 100 points
1,800+	Reviewed if the Herfindahl index increases by more than 50 points

These are thresholds for review. The review of a proposed horizontal merger looks at whether the merger will result in the ability of the firm to "maintain prices above competitive levels for a significant period of time" (*Horizontal Merger Guidelines*, Department of Justice) by improving the firm's ability either to coordinate its actions with other firms or to unilaterally raise its prices. The Justice Department looks most closely at mergers that result in 35 percent market share, but still takes into account whether viable competitors provide sufficient alternatives to keep prices at competitive levels.

Vertical mergers are combinations of two companies, one of which supplies inputs to the other's production.

Q-7 If Ben & Jerry's, a maker of ice cream, bought a dairy farm, what type of merger would it be?

Vertical Mergers A **vertical merger** is *a combination of two companies that are involved in different phases of producing a product*, one company being a buyer of products the other company supplies. For example, a computer company buying an electronic chip company is a vertical merger. Similarly, if a clothes manufacturer buys a retail boutique, that's a vertical merger. If either of the merged firms is able to limit access of other buyers or sellers to the market, such a merger is in violation of the Clayton Act.

A famous vertical merger case is the Du Pont/General Motors case (1961), in which Du Pont was required to sell its 23 percent share of General Motors because Du Pont was a major supplier to the automobile industry. The Supreme Court felt Du Pont's ownership share of GM was restricting competition. Similarly in the Brown Shoe/Kinney Shoe case (1962), Brown Shoe, primarily a wholesaler, was forbidden to buy Kinney Shoe, which was a chain of shoe retailers.

In most of the 1980s, the U.S. government challenged any vertical merger in which the supplying firm had a 10 percent or more market share and the buyer company purchased 6 percent or more of the market. This rule was loosened some as the 1980s progressed, but specific new guidelines were not developed. Although today few vertical mergers are challenged, in 1999 a planned merger between the largest U.S. retail bookseller, Barnes & Noble, and the largest U.S. wholesale bookseller, Ingram, was dropped after the FTC raised concerns that the merger would allow Barnes & Noble to raise the costs faced by rival retailers by denying access to Ingram's books on competitive terms.

Conglomerate Mergers A third type of merger is a conglomerate merger. **Conglomerate mergers** involve *the merging of relatively unrelated businesses*. Conglomerate mergers are generally approved by the U.S. antitrust laws under the assumption that they do not significantly restrict competition. Thus, when Tyco acquired nine firms in 2001 in the health care, finance, personal care, and security industries, no antitrust action was taken to prevent the mergers because the firms were unrelated.

Why would unrelated firms want to merge? Or why would one firm want to be bought out by another? There are five general reasons:

1. *To achieve economies of scope*. Although the businesses are unrelated, some overlap is almost inevitable, so economies of scope are likely. For example, one firm's technical or marketing expertise may be helpful to the other firm, or the conglomerate's increased size may give it better bargaining power with its suppliers.
2. *To get a good buy*. Firms are always on the lookout for good buys. If a firm believes that another firm's stock is significantly undervalued, it can buy that stock at its low price and then sell it at a profit later when the stock is no longer undervalued.
3. *To diversify*. Many industries have a cyclical nature. In some parts of the business cycle they do poorly; in other parts of the business cycle they do just fine. Buying an unrelated company allows a firm to diversify and thereby to even out the cyclical fluctuation in its profits.
4. *To ward off a takeover bid*. Firms are always susceptible to being bought out by someone else. Sometimes they prevent an unwanted buyout by merging with another firm in order to become so large that they're indigestible.
5. *To strengthen their political-economic influence*. The bigger you are, the more influence you have. Individuals who run companies like to have and use influence. Merging can increase their net influence considerably.

Conglomerate mergers are combinations of unrelated businesses. Five reasons why unrelated firms merge are

1. To achieve economies of scope.
2. To get a good buy.
3. To diversify.
4. To ward off a takeover bid.
5. To strengthen their political-economic influence.

Q-8 When the long-distance phone company AT&T merged with the cellular phone company McCaw to create AT&T Wireless Services, what type of merger was it?

Recent Merger Activity and Deacquisitions

Figure 18-1 presents the number of mergers in the United States each year since 1892. As you can see, mergers rose significantly in the late 1990s and into the early 2000s.

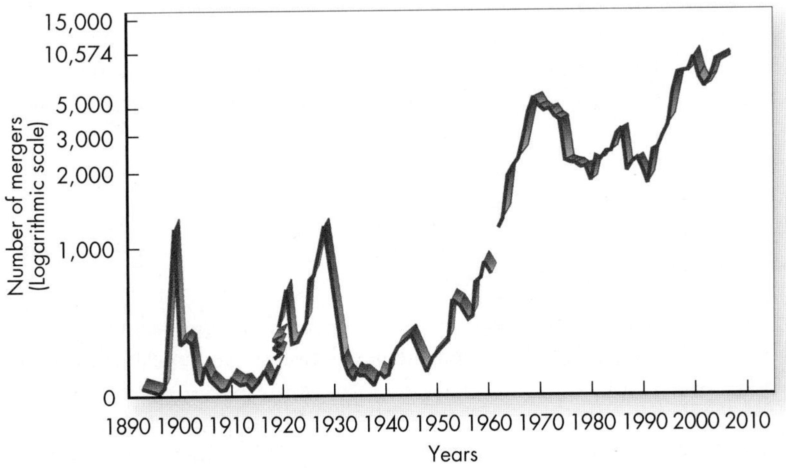

FIGURE 18-1
Mergers in the United States since 1892

The number of mergers in the United States has fluctuated substantially in the last 100 years. Source of data changed in 1962, accounting for the break in the series.

Source: Federal Trade Commission, national press, Mergerstat.com, and author extrapolations.

The primary reasons for the increase in the number of mergers are globalization, deregulation, and technological change. Globalization leads to mergers because firms can gain instant foreign distribution networks and knowledge of local markets from mergers. They also can lower costs by restructuring production to low-cost areas. Deregulation of the telecommunications, electricity, and financial industries has encouraged mergers that take advantage of economies of scale and scope. Bank mergers and phone company mergers are examples.

The acceleration of technological change in recent years is another contributor to merger activity. Firms are looking for ways to develop new technologies or take advantage of new technologies, and merging with another company is one way to acquire a new technology. The merger of America Online and Time Warner is an example of an Internet (technology) company combining with a "content" company. (Such mergers don't always achieve the desired effect; that was the case with the AOL/Time-Warner merger.)

At the same time that these mergers are taking place, firms are also engaging in **deacquisitions**—*one company's sale of either parts of another company it has bought or parts of itself.* Sometimes regulators require such deacquisitions as a condition of approving a merger. Deacquisition also occurs as firms focus on those areas where they have comparative advantage and where growth is highest, and sell off aspects of their firms that are not part of their core business. Automobile firms are breaking off their component manufacturing operations. To name just a few examples, in the 2000s AT&T broke up on its own into four parts, only to later combine with some of its parts; IBM sold off its PC unit to Lenovo, and in 2007 Mercedes spun off Chrysler Motors, which in 2009 combined with Fiat in an attempt to stay in business. There will likely be many more such changes. The motto of the 2000s is that firms have to continually reinvent themselves.

As I mentioned at the beginning of this section, voluntarily breaking up companies is becoming much more common as firms try to find their niche in the global marketplace. Companies are continually spinning off portions of their business where they do not believe they have a comparative advantage, and buying businesses where they think they do have a comparative advantage. This process is likely to continue, making the U.S. market structure a continually changing landscape.

The U.S. market structure is a continually changing landscape.

Assessment of Mergers and Acquisitions

I've introduced a lot of terms in this section and, ideally, started you thinking about the issues involved in deciding on a merger and acquisition policy. This chapter does not arrive at definite conclusions, and in this it reflects the economics profession, which has no one position on what policy the United States should follow toward mergers.

But the economics profession's failure to come to an undivided view on mergers isn't necessarily a failing of economists. Mergers have both costs and benefits, and reasonable people will assess them differently.

International Competition and Antitrust Policy in Other Countries

As I discussed in the last chapter, the nature of competition is changing in the United States. Ten or twenty years ago, when people talked about competition, they meant competition among U.S. firms. Now, however, they often mean international competition.

Because of this internationalization of competition, the political climate in the United States is changing. More and more, U.S. antitrust policy makers see the international market as the relevant market. The policy focus of government is shifting from "Is U.S. industry internally competitive so that it does not take advantage of the

REAL-WORLD APPLICATION

Accounting, Fraud, and Government Regulation

In the early 2000s, serious accounting irregularities came to light in firms such as Enron and WorldCom. These firms, and many others, had used various accounting procedures—some legal, some not—to make their profits appear higher than they actually were. When the irregularities were revealed, these companies' stock values fell precipitously. In the case of Enron and WorldCom, the decline took the companies into bankruptcy.

Why would firms lie about profits? An important reason is that higher profits lead to higher stock prices—and top managers' pay (which includes stock options) depends on the price of the stock. *Options* are rights to buy a stock at a set price regardless of what happens to the price of the stock. If the stock price rises above the option price, those who exercise their options pocket the difference. Enough options and a high enough price can amount to tens or hundreds of millions of dollars. The high reported profits drive share prices high and, assuming the managers sell the stock before the accounting irregularity is discovered, they make a fortune even as the company is left in ruins.

In response to stories like these, the U.S. government increased regulation of company accounting rules, created a new board to oversee those rules, and required CEOs to sign off on the accuracy of the accounting figures provided to investors.

Will the new laws help? Perhaps somewhat, but problems remain. For example, despite most economists' suggestion that firms report stock options on the books as a cost, which would lessen the incentive of companies to give stock options to managers, the new government regulation does not require that. So there will remain an incentive on the part of managers to overstate profits. However, the New York Stock Exchange, a private company that oversees trading of many stocks, now requires including stock options as costs for companies listed on the exchange, so we will likely see this change taking place at many large companies.

consumer?" to "Is U.S. industry internationally competitive so that it can compete effectively in the world economy?"

European Antitrust Policy

Perhaps the biggest change on the antitrust front is the emergence of a strong European antitrust policy. Before the European Union (EU) was established, most of the countries that are now members had relatively weak antitrust laws. There were a number of reasons for this: given their relatively small size, each country needed large domestic firms to achieve economies of scale; they saw the international market as the relevant market; they were less populist than the United States; and they saw government and business as partners, not antagonists. The establishment of the EU changed the situation somewhat as the **European Commission (EC),** *the EU's antitrust agency*, superceded the member-countries' relatively lenient antitrust laws.

Q-9 Are the EC's antitrust policies more or less lenient toward non-European firms than toward European firms?

One of the reasons to establish a common market was to allow corporations to become larger and take advantage of economies of scale. So, throughout the 1990s, the EC was very lenient in allowing mergers and, from 1991 to 1998, the EC disallowed only 10 mergers. In 2002, the EC actively promoted mergers but was constantly in opposition to individual governments that wanted to block certain mergers to protect domestic firms. These governments held "golden shares" which entitled them to veto mergers whenever they saw fit. In order to give the EC more power in the matter, the European Court ruled that "golden shares" would no longer entitle an individual government to block a legitimate merger. The Court ruled that mergers could only be disallowed for reasons of national security.

In the early 2000s, however, the EC started to be less lenient toward non-European firms. For example, in the early 2000s General Electric attempted to merge with

Honeywell. The merger was approved by U.S. authorities, and since both were U.S.-based companies, it seemed as if the merger would go through. The EC, however, blocked the merger because the combined revenues were more than $4.2 billion, of which about $212 million was from Europe, which meant they fell under EU as well as U.S. jurisdiction. Besides the GE case, the EC also brought separate cases against two major American companies, Microsoft and Coca-Cola, leading some observers to claim the EU was using antitrust policy as a weapon against U.S. companies.

Globalization and Antitrust in the Future

Given the ongoing globalization of markets, we can expect more and more jurisdictional legal battles in antitrust. As China and India develop stronger antitrust laws, and as their economies continue to develop and expand, their antitrust policies will become more important globally. There will likely be significant charges that the EU or the U.S. antitrust decisions are favoring their domestic companies and hindering foreign-based companies. Enormous political pressures will likely be brought to bear on these decisions as countries' different legal systems and history work toward an acceptable integration. In today's global economy, antitrust issues are, by nature, global, but a country's antitrust laws are not. This reality will continue to cause problems in antitrust, and in other areas of regulating business, in the coming decades.

Sovereign Wealth Funds

Web Note 18.4
Sovereign Wealth Funds

Another recent institutional change with important market structure effects is the establishment of **sovereign wealth funds**—*investment funds held by governments*. A number of governments with large trade and budget surpluses such as the oil-producing countries Norway, Saudi Arabia, and Russia, as well as China, are accumulating assets in several wealth funds, valued in 2009 in the trillions of dollars. Previously, government holdings of assets were limited to other government bonds, but recently that has been changing—these sovereign wealth funds are looking for higher returns by investing their money in the stock market and in other private assets. What this means is that foreign governments are buying up U.S. companies, or at least stock in U.S. companies, through these funds. If they choose to vote their shares, it is possible that they, as owners of the U.S. company, could direct the company to do what their government wants. This presents potential problems—for example, what if the Russian government gains control of IBM and decides to shut down U.S. plants, and move production to Russia? This is unlikely, but many other conflicts of a similar nature are likely.

Foreign government ownership of U.S. companies is a new problem that has not been considered by economists. Before this time, governments, except for central banks, did not hold financial assets, and central banks generally held bonds, not stocks. Globalization, and the large U.S. trade deficit, has changed that, and in the coming decade we can expect new rules being developed about what companies sovereign wealth funds can own, and what role they can play in voting the stock that they do own.

Regulation, Government Ownership, and Industrial Policies

The government also can affect the competitive process by (1) regulation, (2) government ownership, and (3) industrial policy.

Antitrust policy is not the only way in which governments affect the competitive process. Other ways include (1) regulating the activities of firms, (2) government ownership—taking charge of the firms and operating them directly, and (3) industrial policy—influencing firms with laws and taxes. While I consider these issues in other parts of the book, here I want to briefly discuss some of the central elements of these three means of affecting the competitive process.

Regulation

Regulation involves the setting of the rules that firms must follow if they are to conduct business. There are two types of regulation: price regulation and social regulation. *Price regulation* is regulation directed at industries that have natural monopoly elements. In order to allow them to take advantage of economies of scale, firms are given an exclusive right to conduct business but are subject to pricing controls. Examples of regulatory agencies include the Federal Energy Regulatory Commission (FERC), which regulates gas and oil pipelines and other energy-related areas; the Federal Communications Commission (FCC), which regulates cable television, telephones, television, and other communications areas; and the Securities and Exchange Commission (SEC), which regulates financial markets.

Two types of regulation are price regulation and social regulation.

Social regulation is concerned with the conditions under which goods and services are produced, the safety of those goods, and the side effects of production on society. Examples of social regulatory bodies include the Food and Drug Administration (FDA), the Environmental Protection Agency (EPA), and the Equal Employment Opportunity Commission (EEOC).

Price Regulation Price regulation is usually imposed in those industries where there seems to be a natural monopoly, as discussed in the chapter on monopoly. In such cases, a single producer is most efficient because two firms could not take advantage of the economies of scale. But if the firm is to have the monopoly, it will be able to charge high prices to consumers and transfer the consumer surplus into its profit. Thus, when government grants such monopolies, it also must regulate their prices. Usually this has taken the form of requiring the firm to charge its average total cost plus a profit margin.

That sounds reasonable in theory, but the practice has problems. The first is that the regulated firm does not have an incentive to hold down costs. Cost increases lead directly to price increases. X-inefficiency will exist. Regulatory boards have tried to counteract the tendency of rising costs by permitting firms to pass on only "legitimate" costs, but generally the people on the regulatory boards do not have the accounting expertise to review costs and determine whether they are legitimate or not, especially when the companies have a strong incentive to make all costs look legitimate.

Price-regulated firms often do not have an incentive to hold down costs.

The problem is worsened by the fact that the boards are often made up of individuals from the industry that is being regulated. This gives the commission necessary expertise, but it also creates a potentially unhealthy connection between the regulatory commission and the firms being regulated. Some economists have argued that the connection is so close that the regulatory board simply reflects the regulated firms' interests, and that the board protects firms from competition arising from technological change.

Another problem raised by critics is that, once established, regulation may tend to extend far beyond natural monopolies and be introduced into industries where competition could work. Still another problem is that regulation continues even after technological change has created competitive market conditions. The trucking and airline industries are examples. Often the regulatory boards simply function as a way of allowing an industry to operate as a legal cartel, holding prices up rather than keeping them down.

Problems with price regulation have led to deregulation in recent years.

The above criticisms have led to significant deregulation over the last 20 years. Trucking, airlines, finance, and aspects of phone service and electric power generation have all been deregulated. The results have been mixed. Deregulation has allowed more competition and has lowered prices, but it has also led to significant problems with the financial markets. It allowed financial firms to expand credit significantly, which led to the collapse of major Wall Street firms, and of financial markets generally. Behavioral economists argued that the excesses in credit markets were the result of individual's predictably irrational behavior, and argued that in future discussions of deregulation, behavioral economic insights should be taken into account.

***Social Regulation*[3]** Whereas most economists are skeptical of pricing regulation, they are far more divided on social regulation. Social regulation differs from pricing regulation in that

1. Social regulation applies to most firms and is not designed specifically for a natural monopoly. For example, when the Occupational Safety and Health Administration (OSHA) issues a requirement that all workers have a periodic break from work, it applies to all firms in the United States that fall under OSHA's control.
2. Social regulation affects large aspects of business: working conditions, the quality of the products, and the production processes firms are allowed to use.

Whereas pricing regulation has declined in the last 20 years, social regulation has increased substantially. Economists debate whether this is good or bad. Critics of social regulation point out that regulation has high administrative and compliance costs and that those costs hurt consumers more than the regulation benefits them. They believe that this occurs because the social regulation laws are too often poorly written and ambiguous, and put into law without knowing what is reasonable and feasible. The result is higher prices, far less technical progress, and fewer new entrants as the regulatory burdens become unbearable for small firms.

Web Note 18.5
Why Regulation Matters

Advocates of social regulation agree with some of the above but argue that the benefits of social regulation are worth the costs, and that the objections are simply a call for better regulation. They argue that social regulation has made manufacturing much safer in the United States, improved the quality of life and the environment enormously, introduced far more justice into the economy, and reduced discrimination.

Judging between these two views is difficult because measurement of both the costs and benefits is difficult if not impossible. In such cases, the economic cost/benefit framework cannot provide a definitive answer.

Government Ownership

Instead of regulation, an alternative way of dealing with the problems of natural monopolies is for the government itself to own the firms. European countries have used this approach much more often than has the United States. Instead of regulating the telephone (or other natural monopoly) industry, governments took it over and ran it with state employees. Since the 1980s most countries have been selling off

[3]Social regulation is discussed more fully in the chapter on microeconomic policy.

government-owned businesses to private owners. Why? They have found that government-owned firms did not have an incentive to hold costs down or to introduce new technology. Workers in government-owned firms, who were guaranteed jobs, used political threats to hold their wages high. Since the government firms faced little competition, they could raise prices and pass on the higher costs to consumers. The result was that European prices for telephone service, airline travel, and electricity were much higher than in the United States. Economic integration in Europe has been accompanied by privatization of many of the formerly government-owned industries, and a fall in prices in many of these industries.

Government-owned firms tend not to have an incentive to hold costs down.

Q-10 Why have European countries recently privatized many government-owned firms in the telecommunications, electricity, and airline industries?

Industrial Policies

In thinking about government's relation with business, it is important to remember that, in actual fact, the United States has always had, and always will have, a type of **industrial policy**—*a formal policy that government takes toward business*. That policy is embodied in its tax code, its laws, its regulatory structure, and the positions the government takes in international negotiations about tariffs and trade. An example is the U.S. government's strong support of international copyrights and patents, which prevent foreign firms from making "knockoffs" without paying a royalty to the U.S. firm. The policy is, however, an implicit policy of working with business, not an explicit policy of directing business.

An industrial policy is a formal policy that government takes toward business.

Many close connections between government and business have developed. For example, the military works closely with its suppliers, and the relationship between them has been called a *military-industrial complex*. This combination of business and government plays important roles in making decisions about what is produced. For example, when Congress seemed about to cut production of the B-2 Stealth bomber, Northrup, the plane's manufacturer, took out full-page newspaper ads, pointing out that parts of the B-2 were produced in 48 states and that thousands of jobs would be lost if the government canceled the contract. Congress gave in, as it has done on many other defense items that are widely regarded as nonessential to national security. Many other business-government alliances exist in the United States, and there are similar government-drug complexes, government-higher-education complexes, and government-high-tech complexes. In a democracy where politicians are dependent on business for funding their campaigns, such complexes are inevitable.

Conclusion

We've come to the end of our discussion of market structure and government policy toward the competitive process. What conclusion should we reach? That's a tough question because the problem has so many dimensions. What we can say is that market structure is important, and generally more competition is preferred to less competition. We can also say that, based on experience, government-created and protected monopolies have not been the optimal solution, especially when industries are experiencing technological change. But how government should deal with monopolies that develop as part of the competitive process is less clear. Competition has both dynamic elements and market structure elements, and often monopolies that develop as part of the competitive process are temporary—and they will be overwhelmed by other monopolies. Thus, the debate about government entering into the market to protect competition has no single answer, which makes cases like the Microsoft antitrust case difficult to resolve.

Summary

- Antitrust policy is the government's policy toward the competitive process.
- Judgment by performance means judging the competitiveness of markets by the behavior of firms in that market. Judgment by structure means judging the competitiveness of markets by how many firms operate in the industry and their market shares.
- There is a debate on whether markets should be judged on the basis of structure or on the basis of performance.
- Important antitrust laws include the Sherman Antitrust Act, the Clayton Antitrust Act, and the Federal Trade Commission Act.
- The antitrust suit against IBM filed in 1967 was withdrawn in 1982 because the computer market had changed, making the charges against IBM moot.
- The antitrust suit against AT&T ended in a settlement that required AT&T to be broken up. AT&T both divided itself and merged with other companies.
- In 2000 the courts found that Microsoft had a monopoly that was protected by barriers to entry and that Microsoft engaged in practices to maintain that monopoly power. Microsoft agreed to stop some practices.
- Three types of mergers are horizontal, vertical, and conglomerate.
- A horizontal merger is the combination of two companies in the same industry, a vertical merger is the combination of two companies in different industries, and a conglomerate merger is the combination of two companies in relatively unrelated industries.
- Five reasons that two unrelated firms would want to merge are economies of scope, a good buy, diversification, warding off of a takeover bid, and strengthening of political-economic influence.
- The increasing internationalization of the U.S. market has changed U.S. antitrust policy from looking at just domestic competition to considering international competition.
- Antitrust issues are, by nature, global, but a country's antitrust laws are not.
- Three ways other than antitrust policy that government affects the competitive process are regulation, government ownership, and industrial policy.

Key Terms

acquisition *(417)*
antitrust policy *(404)*
Clayton Antitrust Act *(407)*
conglomerate merger *(419)*
deacquisition *(420)*
European Commission (EC) *(421)*
Federal Trade Commission Act *(407)*
horizontal merger *(418)*
hostile takeover *(417)*
industrial policy *(425)*
judgment by performance *(405)*
judgment by structure *(405)*
merger *(417)*
natural monopoly *(412)*
Sherman Antitrust Act *(405)*
sovereign wealth funds *(422)*
takeover *(417)*
vertical merger *(418)*

Questions and Exercises

connect ECONOMICS

1. What is the difference between judgment by performance and judgment by structure? LO1
2. Distinguish the basis of judgment for the Standard Oil and the ALCOA cases. LO2

3. How did the Clayton Antitrust Act clarify the Sherman Antitrust Act? LO2
4. If you were an economist for a firm that wanted to merge, would you argue that the three-digit or five-digit NAICS industry is the relevant market? Why? LO2
5. Suppose you are an economist for Mattel, manufacturer of the doll Barbie, which was making an unsolicited bid to take over Hasbro, manufacturer of the doll G.I. Joe.
   a. Would you argue that the relevant market is dolls, preschool toys, or all toys including video games? Why?
   b. Would your answer change if you were working for Hasbro? LO2
6. Demonstrate graphically how regulating the price of a monopolist can both increase quantity and decrease price. (Difficult)
   a. Why did the regulation have the effect it did?
   b. How relevant to the real world do you believe this result is in the "contestable markets" view of the competitive process?
   c. How relevant to the real world do you believe this result is in the "cartel" view of the competitive process? LO2
7. How did the antitrust suit against IBM affect IBM's future business? LO3
8. In what market did Microsoft have a monopoly in the late 1990s and early 2000s? LO3
9. What technological advances threatened Microsoft's monopoly? LO3
10. Under the Department of Justice guidelines, would a merger be allowed between two firms in an industry with a Herfindahl index of 1,200? One firm has 8 percent of the market and the other firm has 11 percent of the market. LO4
11. Should the United States have a policy against conglomerate mergers? Why or why not? (Difficult) LO4
12. Discuss the effect of antitrust policy in the:
   a. monopolist competition model.
   b. cartel model of oligopoly.
   c. contestable market model of oligopoly. LO4
13. In 1993 Mattel proposed acquiring Fisher-Price for $1.2 billion. In the toy industry, Mattel is a major player with 11 percent of the market. Fisher-Price has 4 percent. The other two large firms are Tyco, with a 5 percent share, and Hasbro, with a 15 percent share. In the infant/preschool toy market, Mattel has an 8 percent share and Fisher-Price has a 27 percent share, the largest. The other two large firms are Hasbro, with a 25 percent share, and Rubbermaid, with a 12 percent share.
   a. What are the approximate Herfindahl and four-firm concentration ratios for these industries? (Assume all other firms in each industry have 1 percent of the market each.)
   b. If you were Mattel's economist, which industry definition would you suggest using in court if you were challenged by the government?
   c. Give an argument why the merger might decrease competition.
   d. Give an argument why the merger might increase competition. LO4
14. How has the globalization of the U.S. economy changed U.S. antitrust policy? LO6
15. What two methods does government have for dealing with natural monopolies? What problems are associated with each? LO7

Questions from Alternative Perspectives

1. A monopolist prices its products above marginal cost, but it also may face pressure to keep prices low.
   a. If there is open entry into the market, should there be any monopoly?
   b. Should government use high or low prices as an indication of monopoly power?
   c. If it uses high or low prices to determine whether a firm is a monopoly, how does it decide what are high and low prices? (Austrian)
2. The chapter begins with a quotation from Franklin Delano Roosevelt stating that "We have always known that heedless self-interest was bad morals; we now know that it is bad economics."
   a. In what way is "heedless self-interest" bad morals?
   b. In what way is "heedless self-interest" bad economics? (Religious)
3. In the past two chapters you have learned much about market power: how it is used, the efficiency implications, and how society has responded. Yet this power remains, albeit minimally checked from time to time. The economist Thorstein Veblen would not be surprised by this. He would argue that firms use market power because they can. How do monopolists use "power" to manipulate outcomes? (Institutionalist)
4. Alexis de Tocqueville once stated that "The Americans have applied to the sexes the great principle of political economy which governs the manufacturers of our age, by carefully dividing the duties of men from those of women, in order that the great work of society may be the better carried on …"
   a. Do you agree with his statement?
   b. What problems might his argument have? (Feminist)

5. A *BusinessWeek* magazine study of mergers and acquisitions between 1990 and 1995 found that 83 percent of these deals achieved, at best, marginal returns, and 50 percent recorded a loss.
   a. If such mergers are not especially profitable, why do they occur?
   b. U.S. antitrust policy has changed dramatically since the 1960s when the government regularly blocked mergers among companies in the same industry. Today, the federal government is much less active; it allows almost all mergers. Is this new approach justified, or has government just given in to the powers that be?
   c. What antitrust policies would work best in today's U.S. economy? (Radical)

Issues to Ponder

1. How would the U.S. economy likely differ today if Standard Oil had not been broken up? LO2
2. Colleges require that students take certain courses at that college in order to get a degree. Is that an example of a tie-in contract that limits consumers' choices? If so, should it be against the law? LO2
3. Colleges give financial aid to certain students. Is this price discrimination? If so, should it be against the law? LO2
4. Should interlocking directorships be against the law? Why or why not? (Difficult) LO2
5. In 1992 American Airlines offered a 50-percent-off sale and cut fares. In 1993 Continental Airlines and Northwest Airlines sued American Airlines over this action. (Difficult)
   a. What was the likely basis of the suit?
   b. How does the knowledge that Continental and Northwest were in serious financial trouble play a role in the suit? LO2
6. Has telephone service improved since AT&T was broken up? What does this imply about antitrust laws? LO3
7. You're working at the Department of Justice. Ms. Ecofame has just brought in a new index, the Ecofame index, which she argues is preferable to the Herfindahl index. The Ecofame index is calculated by cubing the market share of the top 10 firms in the industry.
   a. Calculate an Ecofame guideline that would correspond to the Department of Justice guidelines.
   b. State the advantages and disadvantages of the Ecofame index as compared to the Herfindahl index. LO4
8. How would you design an industrial policy to avoid the problems inherent in industrial policies? (Difficult) LO7

Answers to Margin Questions

1. The Sherman Antitrust Act contained two main sections. The first stated that every contract, combination, or conspiracy in restraint of trade was illegal. The second stated that every person who shall monopolize or attempt to monopolize shall be deemed guilty of a misdemeanor. These provisions, while sounding strong, were so broad that they were almost unenforceable, and the interpretation was left to the courts. *(406)*
2. In the Standard Oil case, the Court determined that Standard Oil controlled 90 percent of the market. It said that this monopolistic structure of the market did not necessarily violate the Sherman Antitrust Act. However, the Court also decided that Standard Oil had engaged in systematic abuse and unfair business practices, and therefore was guilty of antitrust violations and must be broken up. *(407)*
3. In the ALCOA case, the Supreme Court changed the interpretation of the law. Here it found ALCOA was not guilty of any unfair practices. It agreed that ALCOA had used its knowledge of the market to expand capacity before any competitors had a chance to enter, and had kept its price low to prevent entry. Thus, on performance standards, it was not violating the law. But the Court decided the structure of the market, not the company's performance, was the appropriate standard by which to judge cases, and, therefore, ALCOA was in violation of the antitrust law. *(407)*
4. In the 1956 Du Pont case, the Supreme Court found that Du Pont was innocent of monopolizing the production of cellophane, even though it was the only producer. The Court's reasoning was that the relevant market was the entire flexible wrap industry, not just cellophane. Since

Du Pont did not dominate the flexible wrap industry, it was not in violation of antitrust law. *(409)*

5. In the late 1960s, the Department of Justice filed suit against IBM for violating the antitrust laws. It alleged that IBM had a monopoly of the general-purpose electronic digital computing industry and that it had acquired its market share because of unfair business practices. The case dragged on for 13 years but never went to court. In 1982, the government withdrew its lawsuit. The antitrust case, however, had significant effects on IBM. It is likely that the experience caused IBM to shy away from the then-small personal computer market. This decision by IBM very likely was the beginning of the serious problems that IBM faced in the 1990s. *(411)*
6. In 1978, the Department of Justice sued AT&T, alleging that its potential competitors were not being allowed reasonable access to AT&T's local telephone network. The case was resolved in January 1982, when AT&T agreed to let itself be broken up. Specifically, AT&T divested itself of 22 operating companies and focused thereafter only on long-distance telephone service, manufacturing, and research and development. This settlement left AT&T free to enter into any unregulated business it desired, and in the 1990s AT&T expanded with fiber-optic networks. Ironically, these expansions placed it in direct competition with the still-regulated Baby Bells, which had inherited AT&T's monopoly rights. *(413)*
7. If Ben & Jerry's bought a dairy farm, it would be a vertical merger because Ben & Jerry's would be buying one of its suppliers. *(418)*
8. AT&T's merger with McCaw was a mixture of a horizontal merger and a conglomerate merger. It is a horizontal merger to the degree that one interprets the industry broadly as a "communications industry." It is a conglomerate merger if one interprets the industry narrowly and distinguishes the wireless communications industry from the wire communications industry. *(419)*
9. The EC is less lenient toward non-European firms. *(421)*
10. European countries have been privatizing firms in telecommunications, electricity, and airline industries because the government-owned firms were inefficient, resulting in higher costs for consumers and less innovation. *(425)*

CHAPTER 19

Work and the Labor Market

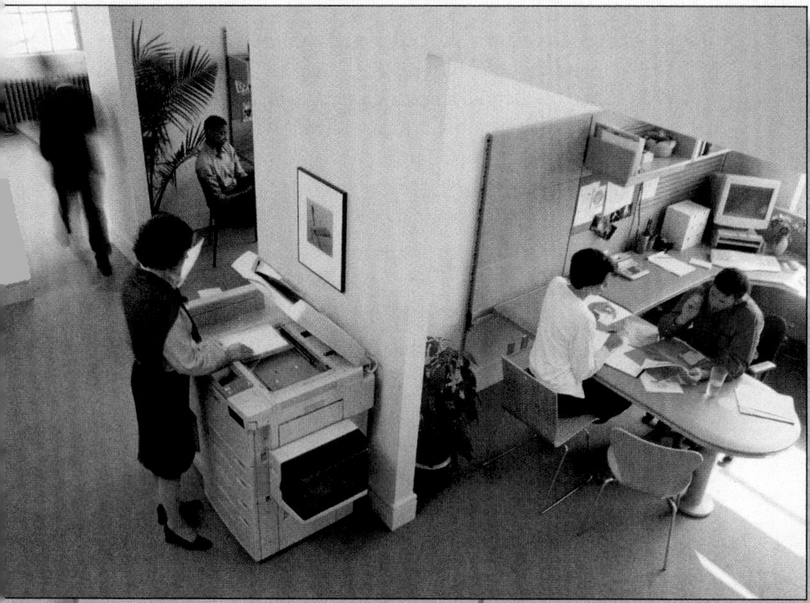

Work banishes those three great evils: boredom, vice, and poverty.

—*Voltaire*

AFTER READING THIS CHAPTER, YOU SHOULD BE ABLE TO:

1. Use the theory of rational choice to explain why an increase in the marginal tax rate is likely to reduce the quantity of labor supplied.
2. List four factors that influence the elasticity of market labor supply.
3. Explain how the demand for labor is a derived demand.
4. List four factors that influence the elasticity of market labor demand.
5. Define *monopsony* and *bilateral monopoly.*
6. Discuss real-world characteristics of labor markets in terms of market, political, and social forces.
7. List three types of discrimination.

Most of us earn our living by working. We supply labor (get a job) and get paid for doing things that other people tell us they want done. Even before we get a job, work is very much a part of our lives. We spend a large portion of our school years preparing for work. Probably many of you are taking this economics course because you've been told that it will help prepare you for a job—or that it will get you more pay than you're getting in your present job. For you, this course is investment in human capital (skills embodied in workers through experience, education, and on-the-job training). If work in the marketplace isn't already familiar to you, once you get out of school it will become so (unless you're sitting on a hefty trust fund or marry somebody who is).

Your job will likely occupy at least a third of your waking hours. To a great extent, it will define you. When someone asks, "What do you do?" you won't answer, "I clip coupons, go out on dates, visit my children . . ." Instead you'll answer, "I work for the Blank Company" or "I'm an economist" or "I'm a teacher." Defining ourselves by our work means that work is more than the way we get income. It's a part of our social and cultural makeup. If we lose our jobs, we lose part of our identity.

There's no way I can discuss all the social, political, cultural, and economic dimensions of work and labor in one chapter, but it's important to begin by at least pointing them out in order to put my discussion of labor markets in perspective. A **labor market** is *a factor market in which individuals supply labor services for wages to other individuals and to firms that need (demand) labor services*. Because social and political pressures are particularly strong in labor markets, we can understand the nature of such markets only by considering how social and political forces interact with economic forces to determine our economic situation.

If the invisible hand were the only force operating, wages would be determined entirely by supply and demand. There's more to it than that, as you'll see, but it shouldn't surprise you that my discussion of the invisible hand and the labor market is organized around the concepts of supply and demand.

ADDED DIMENSION

Other Factors of Production

The factors of production are sometimes classified as land, labor, and capital, and income from these factors are rent, wages, and interest and profits respectively. We focus on labor because it is the most important source of income for most of you, and given the limited time in a principles course, choices have to be made. (Opportunity cost rears its head. You can find a discussion of these other factors in the online Chapter 19W, "Nonwage and Asset Income: Rents, Profits, and Interest" at www.mhhe.com/colander8e.) I should, however, note a couple of issues about these other factors of production. First, land as a factor of production depends on property rights. How property rights are determined and structured plays an important role in the amount of rent and the distribution of that rent. Whereas most people would agree that people deserve the fruits of their labor, there is less agreement about rent.

Second, capital is much more difficult to analyze than labor or land. In fact, capital is one of the most difficult aspects of economics, and we do not have a good theory of the rate of interest or profits. The modern theory of capital focuses on human capital, intellectual capital, and social capital as well as financial and physical capital. A full analysis of these various elements and the income that derives from their use is far beyond an introductory course.

The Supply of Labor

The labor supply choice facing an individual (that is, the decisions of whether, how, and how much to work) can be seen as a choice between nonmarket activities and legal market activities. Nonmarket activities include sleeping, dating, studying, playing, cooking, cleaning, gardening, and black market trading. Legal market activities include taking some type of paid job or working for oneself, directly supplying products or services to consumers.

Many considerations are involved in individuals' choices of whether and how much to work and at what kind of job to work. Social background and conditioning are especially important, but the factor economists focus on is the **incentive effect** (*how much a person will change his or her hours worked in response to a change in the wage rate*). The incentive effect is determined by the value of supplying one's time to legal market activities relative to the value of supplying one's time to nonmarket activities. The normal relationship is:

Economists focus on the incentive effect when considering an individual's choice of whether and how much to work.

The higher the wage, the higher the quantity of labor supplied.

Applying rational choice theory to the supply of labor tells us that the higher the wage, the higher the quantity of labor supplied.

This relationship between the wage rate and the quantity of labor supplied is shown in Figure 19-1. The wage rate is measured on the vertical axis; the quantity of labor supplied is measured on the horizontal axis. As you can see, the supply curve's upward

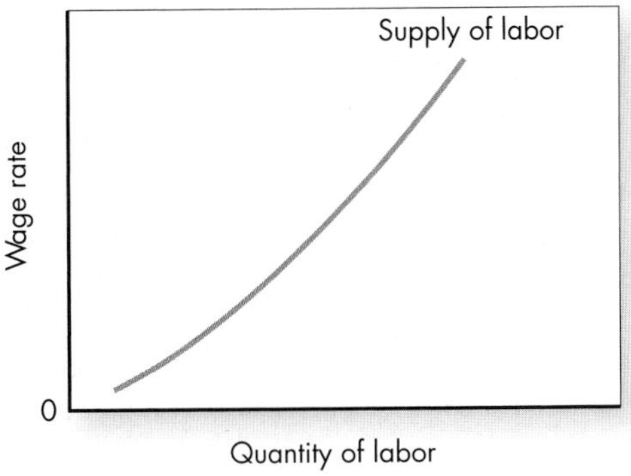

FIGURE 19-1 The Supply of Labor

The supply of labor is generally considered to be upward-sloping because the opportunity cost of not working increases as wages get higher.

slope indicates that as the wage rate increases, the quantity of labor supplied increases. Why is that the normal relationship? Because work involves opportunity cost. By working one hour more, you have one hour less to devote to nonmarket activities, which often are simply called *leisure*. Alternatively, if you devote the hour to nonmarket activities, you lose one hour's worth of income from working.

Q-1 Under the usual conditions of supply, what would you expect would happen to the amount of time you study if the wage of your part-time job rises?

Say, for example, that by working you would have made $10 per hour. If you decide to work two hours less, you'll have $20 less to spend but two hours more available for other activities (including spending the smaller amount of money). When the wage rises, say to $12 per hour, an hour of leisure has a higher opportunity cost. As the cost of leisure goes up, you buy less of it, meaning that you work more.

As I noted in my general discussions of supply and demand, the incentive effects represented by the market supply curve come from individuals' either/or decisions to enter, or leave, the labor market; and from individuals' decisions to work more, or fewer, hours. Given the institutional constraints in the labor market, which require many people to work a fixed number of hours if they work at all, much of the incentive effect of higher wages influences the either/or decisions of individuals. This affects the labor force participation rate (the number of people employed or looking for work as a percentage of people able to work) rather than adjusting the number of hours worked. For example, when wages rise, retired workers may find it worthwhile to go back to work, and many teenagers may choose to find part-time jobs.

Real Wages and the Opportunity Cost of Work

The upward-sloping supply curve of labor tells you that, other things equal, as wages go up, the quantity of labor supplied goes up. But if you look at the historical record, you will see that over the last century, real wages in the United States increased substantially, but the average number of hours worked per person fell. This difference is partly explained by the income effect. Higher incomes make people richer, and richer people can afford to choose more leisure. (See the box "Income and Substitution Effects.")

Given that people are far richer today than they were 50 or 100 years ago, it isn't surprising that they work less. What's surprising is that they work as much as they do—eight hours a day rather than the four or so hours a day that would be enough to give people the same income they had a century ago.

The explanation for why people haven't reduced their hours of work more substantially can be found in how leisure has changed. A century ago, conversation was an art. People could use their time for long, leisurely conversations. Letter writing was a skill all educated people had, and cooking dinner was a three-hour event. If today people were satisfied with leisure consisting of long conversations, whittling, and spending quality time with their families rather than skiing, golfing, or traveling, they could get by with working perhaps only four or five hours per day instead of eight hours. But that isn't the case.

Modern gadgets increase the efficiency of leisure but cost money, which means people must work more to enjoy their leisure.

Today leisurely dinners, conversations about good books, and witty letters have been replaced by "efficient" leisure: a fast-food supper, a home video, and the instant analysis of current events. Microwave ovens, frozen dinners, Pop-Tarts, cellular telephones, the Internet—the list of gadgets and products designed to save time is endless. All these gadgets that increase the "efficiency" of leisure (increase the marginal utility per hour of leisure spent) cost money, which means people today must work more to enjoy their leisure! In the United States, one reason people work hard is so that they can play hard (and expensively).

Economists do not try to answer the normative question of whether people are better off today, working hard to play hard, or simply are more harried.

The fast pace of modern society has led a number of people to question whether we, as a society, are better off working hard to play hard. Are we better off or simply more harried? Most economists don't try to answer this normative question; but they do point out that people are choosing their harried lifestyle, so to argue that people are worse off,

ADDED DIMENSION

Income and Substitution Effects

Because labor income is such an important component of most people's total income, when wages change other things often do not stay equal, and at times the effect can seem strange. For example, say that you earn $10 an hour and you decide to work eight hours per day. Suddenly demand for your services goes up and you find that you can receive $40 an hour. Will you decide to work more hours? According to the rational choice rule, you will, but you also might decide that at $40 an hour you'll work only six hours a day—$240 a day is enough; the rest of the day you want leisure time to spend your money. In such a case, a higher wage means working less, and the measured supply curve of labor would be backward bending.

Does this violate the rational choice rule? The answer is no, because other things—specifically your income—do not remain equal. The higher wage makes you decide to work more—as the rational choice rule says; but the effect of the higher wage is overwhelmed by the effect of the higher income that allows you to decide to work less.

To distinguish between these two effects, economists have given them names. The decision, based on the principle of rational choice, to work more hours when your pay goes up is called the *substitution effect.* You substitute work for leisure because the price of leisure has risen. The decision to work fewer hours when your pay goes up, based on the fact that you're richer and therefore can live a better life, is called the *income effect.*

It's possible that the income effect can exceed the substitution effect, and a wage increase can cause a person to work less, but that possibility does not violate the rational choice rule, which refers to the substitution effect only. For those of you who didn't make a deal with me in Chapter 10 on individual choice, a good exercise is to show the income and substitution effects with indifference curves and to demonstrate how it might be possible for an increase in the wage to lead to a decline in hours of work.

one must argue that people are choosing something they don't really want. That may be true, but it's a tough argument to prove.

The Supply of Labor and Nonmarket Activities

In addition to leisure, labor supply issues and market incentives play an important role in other nonmarket activities. For example, a whole set of illegal activities, such as selling illegal drugs, are alternatives to taking a legal job.

Web Note 19.1
Who Works?

Let's say that an 18-year-old street kid figures he has only two options: He can either work at a minimum wage job or deal drugs illegally. Let's say that dealing drugs risks getting arrested or shot, but it also means earning $50 or $75 an hour. Given that choice, many risk takers opt to sell drugs. When an emergency room doctor asked a shooting victim in New York City why he got involved in selling drugs, he responded, "I'm not going to work for chump change. I make $3,000 a week, tax-free. What do they pay you, sucker?" The doctor had to admit that even he wasn't making that kind of money.

As we discussed in Chapter 1, most low-level drug dealers don't earn anywhere near that pay, but dealing drugs offers a few the chance to advance and earn that and more. For middle-class individuals who have prospects for good jobs, the cost of being arrested can be high—an arrest can destroy their future prospects. For poor street kids with little chance of getting a good job, an arrest makes little difference to their future. For them the choice is heavily weighted toward selling drugs. This is especially true for the entrepreneurial types—the risk takers—the movers and shakers who might have become the business leaders of the future. I've asked myself what decision I would have made had I been in their position. And I suspect I know the answer.

Prohibiting certain drugs leads to potentially high income from selling those drugs and has significant labor market effects. The incentive effects that prohibition has on the choices of jobs facing poor teenagers is a central reason why some economists support the legalization of currently illegal drugs.

Income Taxation, Work, and Leisure

Q-2 Why do income taxes reduce your incentive to work?

It is after-tax income, not before-tax income, that determines how much you work. Why? Because after-tax income is what you give up by not working. The government, not you, forgoes what you would have paid in taxes if you had worked. This means that when the government raises your marginal tax rate (the tax you pay on an additional dollar of income), your incentive to work falls. Really high marginal tax rates—say 60 or 70 percent—can significantly reduce individuals' incentive to work and earn income.

One main reason why the U.S. government reduced marginal income tax rates in the 1980s was to reduce the negative incentive effects of high taxes. Whereas in the 1950s and 1960s the highest U.S. marginal income tax rate was 70 percent, today the highest marginal income tax rate is 35 percent. European countries, which have significantly higher marginal tax rates than the United States, are currently struggling with the problem of providing incentives for people to work.

European countries, which have relatively high marginal tax rates, are struggling with the problem of providing incentives for people to work.

Reducing the marginal tax rate in the United States hasn't completely eliminated the problem of negative incentive effects on individuals' work effort. The reason is that the amount people receive from many government redistribution programs is tied to earned income. When your earned income goes up, your benefits from these programs go down.

Say, for example, that you're getting welfare and you're deciding whether to take an $8-an-hour job. Income taxes and Social Security taxes reduce the amount you take home from the job by 20 percent, to $6.40 an hour. But you also know that the Welfare Department will reduce your welfare benefits by 50 cents for every dollar you take home. This means that you lose another $3.20 per hour, so the marginal tax rate on your $8-an-hour job isn't 20 percent; it's 60 percent. By working an hour, you've increased your net income by only $3.20. When you consider the transportation cost of getting to and from work, the expense of getting new clothes to wear to work, the cost of child care, and other job-associated expenses, the net gain in income is often minimal. Your implicit marginal tax rate is almost 100 percent! At such rates, there's an enormous incentive either not to work or to work off the books (get paid in cash so you have no recorded income that the government can easily trace).

The negative incentive effect can sometimes be even more indirect. For example, college scholarships are generally given on the basis of need. A family that earns more gets less in scholarship aid; the amount by which the scholarship is reduced as a family's income increases acts as a marginal tax on individuals' income. Why work hard to provide for yourself if a program will take care of you if you don't work hard? Hence, the irony in any need-based assistance program is that it reduces the people's incentive to prevent themselves from being needy. These negative incentive effects on labor supply that accompany any need-based program present a public policy dilemma for which there is no easy answer.

Q-3 What is the irony of any need-based program?

The Elasticity of the Supply of Labor

Elasticity of market supply depends on

1. Individuals' opportunity cost of working.
2. The type of market being discussed.
3. The elasticity of individuals' supply curves.
4. Individuals entering and leaving the labor market.

Exactly how these various incentives affect the amount of labor an individual supplies is determined by the elasticity of the individual's labor supply curve.

The elasticity of the market supply curve is determined by the elasticity of individuals' supply curves and by individuals entering and leaving the labor force. Both of these, in turn, are determined by individuals' opportunity cost of working. If a large number of people are willing to enter the labor market when wages rise, then the market labor supply will be highly elastic even if individuals' supply curves are inelastic.

The elasticity of supply also depends on the type of market being discussed. For example, the elasticity of the labor supply facing one firm of many in a small town will likely be far greater than the elasticity of the labor supply facing all firms combined in that town. If only one firm raises its wage, it will attract workers away from other firms; if all the firms in town raise their wages, any increase in labor must come from increases in labor force participation, increases in hours worked per person, or in-migration (the movement of new workers into the town's labor market).

Existing workers prefer inelastic labor supplies because that means an increase in demand for labor will raise their wage by more. Employers prefer elastic supplies because that means an increase in demand for labor doesn't require large wage increases. These preferences can be seen in news reports about U.S. immigration laws, their effects, and their enforcement. Businesses such as hotels and restaurants often oppose strict immigration laws. Their reason is that jobs such as janitor, chambermaid, and busperson are frequently filled by new immigrants or illegal aliens who have comparatively low wage expectations.

Because of the importance of the elasticity of labor supply, economists have spent a great deal of time and effort estimating it. Their best estimates of labor supply elasticities to market activities are about 0.1 for heads of households and 1.1 for secondary workers in households. These elasticity figures mean that a wage increase of 10 percent will increase the quantity of labor supplied by 1 percent for heads of households (an inelastic supply) and 11 percent for secondary workers in households (an elastic supply). Why the difference? Institutional factors. Hours of work are only slightly flexible. Since most heads of households are employed, they cannot significantly change their hours worked. Many secondary workers in households are not employed, and the higher elasticity reflects new secondary workers entering the labor market.

Immigration and the International Supply of Labor

Web Note 19.2
Leaving Home

International limitations on the flow of people, and hence on the flow of labor, play an important role in elasticities of labor supply. In many industries, wages in developing countries are 1/10 or 1/20 the wages in the United States. This large wage differential means that many people from those low-wage countries would like to move to the United States to earn the higher wages. Because they cannot always meet the legal immigration restrictions that limit the flow, many people come into the United States illegally. In addition to about one million legal immigrants per year, up until the recession of 2008, about one million people per year came illegally. Illegal immigrants take a variety of jobs at lower wages and worse conditions than U.S. citizens and legal immigrants are willing to take. The result is that the actual supply of labor is more elastic than the measured supply, especially in those jobs that cannot be easily policed.

In the early 1990s, the European Union introduced open borders among member countries. That institutional change has brought about a more open flow of individuals into higher-wage EU countries from lower-wage EU countries, although other institutionalized restrictions on flows of people, such as language and culture barriers, prevented the EU from being a unified labor market through the early 2000s.

The Derived Demand for Labor

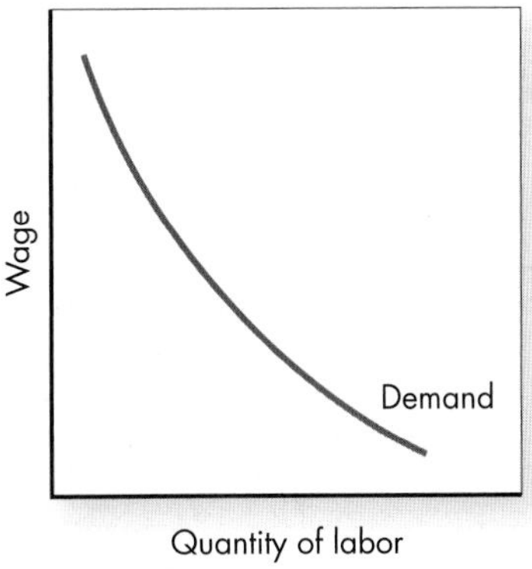

The higher the wage, the lower the quantity of labor demanded.

The demand for labor follows the basic law of demand:

The higher the wage, the lower the quantity of labor demanded.

This relationship between the wage rate and the quantity of labor demanded is shown in the graph in the margin. Its downward slope states that as the wage rate falls, the quantity of labor demanded rises. The reason for this relationship differs between the demand for labor by self-employed individuals and by firms.

When individuals are self-employed (work for themselves), the demand for their labor is the demand for the product or service they supply—be it cutting hair, shampooing rugs, or filling teeth. You have an ability to do something, you offer to do it at a certain price, and you see who calls. You determine how many hours you work, what price you charge, and what jobs you take. The income you receive depends on the demand for the good or service you supply and your decision about how much labor you want to supply. In analyzing self-employed individuals, we can move directly from demand for the product to demand for labor.

When a person is not self-employed, determining the demand for labor isn't as direct. It's a two-step process: Consumers demand products from firms; firms, in turn, demand labor and other factors of production. The demand for labor by firms is a **derived demand**—*the demand for factors of production by firms, which depends on consumers' demands*. In other words, it's derived from consumers' demand for the goods that the firm sells. Thus, you can't think of demand for a factor of production such as labor separately from demand for goods. Firms translate consumers' demands into a demand for factors of production.

Derived demand is the demand for factors of production by firms, which depends on consumers' demands.

Factors Influencing the Elasticity of Demand for Labor

Four factors that influence the elasticity of demand for labor are

1. The elasticity of demand for the firm's good.
2. The relative importance of labor in the production process.
3. The possibility, and cost, of substitution in production.
4. The degree to which marginal productivity falls with an increase in labor.

The elasticity of the derived demand for labor, or for any other input, depends on a number of factors. One of the most important is (1) *the elasticity of demand for the firm's good*. The more elastic the final demand, the more elastic the derived demand. Other factors influencing the elasticity of derived demand include (2) *the relative importance of the factor in the production process* (the more important the factor, the less elastic is the derived demand); (3) *the possibility of, and cost of, substitution in production* (the easier substitution is, the more elastic is the derived demand); and (4) *the degree to which marginal productivity falls with an increase in labor* (the faster productivity falls, the less elastic is the derived demand).

Each of these relationships follows from the definition of *elasticity* (the percentage change in quantity divided by the percentage change in price) and a knowledge of production. To be sure you understand, ask yourself the following question: If all I knew about two firms was that one was a perfect competitor and the other was a monopolist, which firm would I say is likely to have the more elastic derived demand for labor? If your answer wasn't automatically "the competitive firm" (because its demand curve is perfectly elastic and hence more elastic than a monopolist's), I would suggest that at this point you review the discussion of factors influencing demand elasticity in the chapter on elasticities and relate that to this discussion. The two discussions are similar and serve as good reviews for each other.

Q-4 Name at least two factors that influence the elasticity of a firm's derived demand for labor.

Labor as a Factor of Production

The traditional factors of production are land, labor, capital, and entrepreneurship. When economists talk of the labor market, they're talking about two of these factors: labor and entrepreneurship. **Entrepreneurship** is *labor that involves high degrees of organizational skills, concern, oversight responsibility, and creativity*. It is a type of creative labor.

Entrepreneurship is labor that involves high degrees of organizational skills, concern, oversight responsibility, and creativity.

The reason for distinguishing between labor and entrepreneurship is that an hour of work is not simply an hour of work. If high degrees of organizational skill, concern, oversight responsibility, and creativity are exerted (which is what economists mean by *entrepreneurship*), one hour of such work can be the equivalent of days, weeks, or even years of simple labor. That's one reason why pay often differs between workers doing what seems to be the same job. It's also why one of the important decisions a firm makes is what type of labor to hire. Should the firm try to hire high-wage entrepreneurial labor or low-wage nonentrepreneurial labor?

In the appendix to this chapter, I formally develop the firm's derived demand. Here in the chapter itself I will simply point out that the demand for labor follows the basic law of demand—the lower the price, the higher the quantity demanded. Figure 19-2

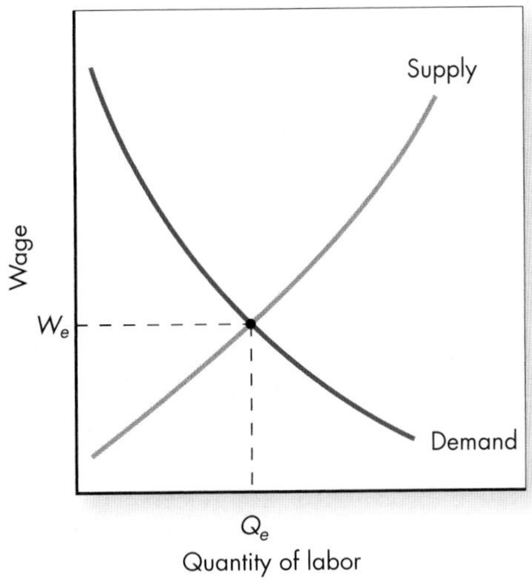

FIGURE 19-2
Equilibrium in the Labor Market

When the supply and demand curves for labor are placed on the same graph, the equilibrium wage, W_e, is where the quantity supplied equals quantity demanded. At this wage, Q_e laborers are supplied.

shows a demand-for-labor curve combined with a supply-of-labor curve. As you would expect, equilibrium is at wage W_e and quantity supplied Q_e.

Shift Factors of Demand

Factors that shift the demand curve for labor will put pressure on the equilibrium price to change. Let's consider some examples. Say the cost of a competing factor of supply, such as a machine that also could do the job, rises. That would shift the demand for this factor (labor) out to the right, and in doing so put pressure on the wage to rise.

Alternatively, say a new technology develops that requires skills different from those currently being used—for instance, requiring knowing how to use a computer rather than knowing how to use a slide rule. The demand for individuals knowing how to use slide rules will decrease, and their wage will tend to fall.

Another example: Say an industry becomes more monopolistic. What will that do to the demand for labor in that industry? Since monopolies produce less output, the answer is that it would decrease the demand for workers, since the industry would hire fewer of them. The demand for workers would shift in and wages would tend to fall.

Finally, say the demand for the firm's good increases. It's clear that the firm's demand for labor will also increase. The way in which these shift factors work is developed in more detail in the appendix to this chapter.

Q-5 What would happen to a firm's demand for labor if its product became more popular?

Technology and the Demand for Labor How will a change in technology affect the demand for labor? This question has often been debated, and it has no unambiguous answer. What economists do know is that the simple reasoning often used by laypeople when they argue that the development of new technology will decrease the demand for labor is wrong. That simple reasoning is as follows: "Technology makes it possible to replace workers with machines, so it will decrease the demand for labor." This is sometimes called *Luddite reasoning* because it's what drove the Luddites to go around smashing machines in early-19th-century England.

What's wrong with Luddite reasoning? First, look at history. Technology has increased enormously, yet the demand for labor has not decreased; instead it has increased as output has increased. In other words, Luddite reasoning doesn't take into account the fact that total output can change. A second problem with Luddite reasoning is that

Web Note 19.3
Crowdsourcing

labor is necessary for building and maintaining the machines, so increased demand for machines increases the demand for labor.

Luddite reasoning isn't *all* wrong. Technology can sometimes decrease the demand for certain skills. The computer has decreased demand for calligraphers; the automobile reduced demand for carriage makers. New technology changes the types of labor demanded. If you have the type of labor that will be made technologically obsolete, you can be hurt by technological change. However, technological change hasn't reduced the overall demand for labor; it has instead led to an increase in total output and a need for even more laborers to produce that output.

In the 21st century we're likely to see a continued increase in the use of robots to do many repetitive tasks that blue-collar workers formerly did. Thus, demand for manufacturing labor will likely continue to decline, but it will be accompanied by an increase in demand for service industry labor—designing and repairing robots and designing activities that will fill up people's free time.

International Competitiveness and a Country's Demand for Labor Many of the issues in the demand for labor concern one firm's or industry's demand for labor relative to another firm's or industry's demand. When we're talking about the demand for labor by the country as a whole—an issue fundamentally important to many of the policy issues being discussed today—we have to consider the country's overall international competitiveness. A central determinant of a country's competitiveness is the relative wage of labor in that country compared to the relative wage of labor in other countries.

Wages vary considerably among countries. For example, in 2007 workers in the manufacturing industry earned an average $30.56 an hour in the United States, $50.73 an hour in Germany, and $3.91 an hour in Mexico. Multinational corporations are continually making decisions about where to place production facilities, and labor costs—wage rates—play an important role in these decisions.

Other factors besides wages play an important role in a firm's decision where to locate.

But why produce in the United States when the hourly rate in Taiwan, for example, was only 1/4 that in the United States? Or in Mexico, where the hourly rate was only 1/10 that in the United States? The reasons are complicated, but include (1) differences in workers—U.S. workers may be more productive; (2) transportation costs—producing in the country to which you're selling keeps transportation costs down; (3) potential trade restrictions—Japan was under enormous pressure from the U.S. government to reduce its trade surplus with the United States, and producing in the United States helped it avoid future trade restrictions; and (4) compatibility of production techniques with social institutions—production techniques must fit with a society's social institutions. If they don't, production will fall significantly. Number (5) is the *focal point phenomenon*—a situation where a company chooses to move, or expand, production to another country because other companies have already moved or expanded there. A company can't consider all places, and it costs a lot of money to explore a country's potential as a possible host country. Japanese businesses know what to expect when they open a plant in the United States; they don't know in many other countries. So the United States and other countries that Japanese businesses have knowledge about become focal points. They are considered as potential sites for business, while other, possibly equally good, countries are not. Combined, these reasons lead to a "follow-the-leader" system in which countries fall in and out of global companies' production plans. The focal-point countries expand and develop; the others don't.

Q-6 Name two factors besides relative wages that determine the demand for labor in one country compared to another.

As I have discussed in a number of chapters, the outsourcing that is currently occurring is a reflection of the relative cost differential that firms calculate as they are deciding where to place production units. Initially, that cost differential included large setup costs, making U.S. production cost-effective in many industries despite lower wages elsewhere. As firms have spent the setup costs to establish production facilities abroad, that cost differential relevant to their decisions is increasing, which will mean that U.S.-based production will be experiencing strong pressure to move offshore in the coming decade. Unless offset by new jobs in other industries, the resulting increase in demand for foreign-based workers and decrease in demand for U.S.-based workers will likely put upward pressure on foreign wages and keep strong downward pressure on U.S. wages, limiting wage increases.

The Role of Other Forces in Wage Determination

Supply and demand forces strongly influence wages, but they do not fully determine wages. Real-world labor markets are filled with examples of individuals or firms who resist these supply and demand pressures through organizations such as labor unions, professional associations, and agreements among employers. But, as I've emphasized throughout the book, supply/demand analysis is a useful framework for considering such resistance.

Supply and demand forces strongly influence wages, but they do not fully determine wages.

For example, say that you're advising a firm's workers on how to raise their wages. You point out that if workers want to increase their wages, they must figure out some way either to increase the demand for their services or to limit the labor supplied to the firm. One way to limit the number of workers the firm will hire (and thus keep existing workers' wages high) is to force the firm to pay an above-equilibrium wage, as in Figure 19-3(a). Say that in their contract negotiations the workers get the firm to agree to pay a wage of W_1. At wage W_1, the quantity of labor supplied is Q_S and the quantity of labor demanded is Q_D. The difference, $Q_S - Q_D$, represents the number of people who want jobs at wage W_1 but will not be employed. In such a case, jobs must be rationed. Whom you know, where you come from, or the color of your skin may play a role in whether you get a job with that firm.

As a second example, consider what would happen if U.S. immigration laws were liberalized. If you say the supply curve of labor would shift out to the right and the wage level would drop, you're right, as shown in Figure 19-3(b). In it the supply of labor increases from S_0 to S_1. In response, the wage falls from W_0 to W_1 and the quantity of labor demanded increases from Q_0 to Q_1.

In analyzing the effect of such a major change in the labor supply, however, remember that the supply and demand framework is relevant only if the change in the supply

Q-7 How could an increase in the supply of labor lead to an increase in the demand for labor?

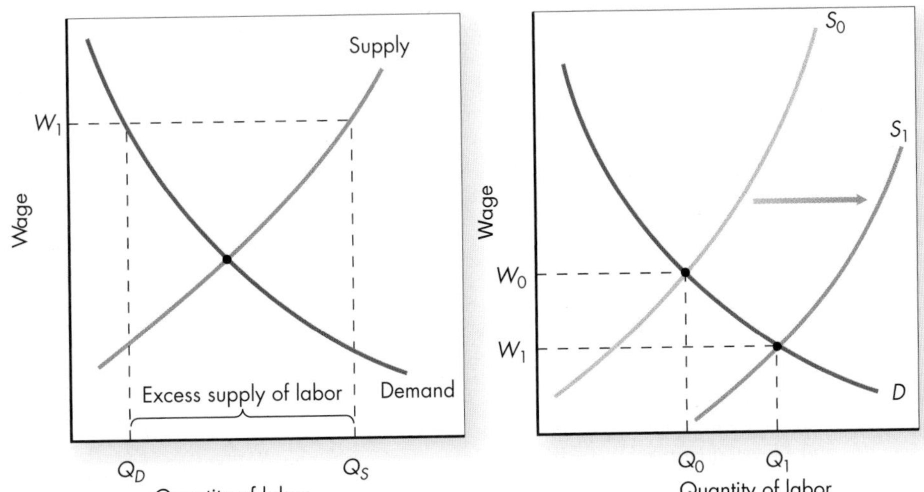

(a) Maintaining Excess Supply

(b) An Increase in Supply

FIGURE 19-3 (A AND B)
The Labor Market in Action

In **(a)** you can see the effect of an above-equilibrium wage: If workers force the firm to pay them a wage of W_1, more workers will be supplied (Q_S) than demanded (Q_D). With an excess supply of labor, jobs must be rationed. In **(b)** you can see the effect of an increase in the supply of labor. Assuming the demand for labor remains the same, the increase in the supply of labor will cause the wage level to drop from W_0 to W_1.

Looking at the overall effects of a change, rather than just the partial equilibrium effects, often makes the final result less clear-cut.

of labor doesn't also affect the demand for labor. In reality, a liberalization of U.S. immigration laws might increase the demand for products, thereby increasing the demand for labor and raising wages. When you look at the overall effect of a change, you will often find that the final result is less clear-cut. That's why it's important always to remember the assumptions behind the model you're using. Those assumptions often add qualifications to the simple "right" answer.

Imperfect Competition and the Labor Market

A monopsony is a market in which a single firm is the only buyer.

Just as product markets can be imperfectly competitive, so too can labor markets. For example, there might be a **monopsony** (*a market in which a single firm is the only buyer*). An example of a monopsony is a "company town" in which a single firm is the only employer. Whereas a monopolist takes into account the fact that if it sells more it will lower the market price, a monopsonist takes into account the fact that it will raise the market prices if it buys more. Thus, it buys less and pays less than would a market with an equivalent number of competitive buyers.

Alternatively, laborers might have organized together in a union that allows workers to operate as if there were only a single seller. In effect, the union could operate as a monopoly. Alternatively again, there might be a **bilateral monopoly** (*a market with only a single seller and a single buyer*). Let's briefly consider these three types of market imperfections.

Monopsony

A monopsonist takes into account the fact that hiring another worker will increase the wage rate it must pay all workers.

Monopsony

When there's only one buyer of labor services, it makes sense for that buyer to take into account the fact that if it hires another worker, the equilibrium wage will rise and it will have to pay more to all workers. The choice facing a monopsonist can be seen in Figure 19-4, in which the supply curve of labor is upward-sloping so that the **marginal factor cost** (*the additional cost to a firm of hiring another worker*) is above the supply curve since the monopsonist takes into account the fact that hiring another worker will increase the wage rate it must pay to all workers.

Instead of hiring Q_c workers at a wage of W_c, as would happen in a competitive labor market, the monopsonist hires Q_m workers and pays them a wage of W_m. (A good exercise to see that you understand the argument is to show that where there's a monopsonist, a minimum wage simultaneously can increase employment and raise the wage.)

FIGURE 19-4
Monopsony, Union Power, and the Labor Market

A monopsonist hires fewer workers and pays them less than would a set of competitive firms. The monopsonist determines the quantity of labor, Q_m, to hire at the point where the marginal factor cost curve intersects the demand curve. The monopsonist pays a wage of W_m. A union has a tendency to push for a higher wage, W_u, and a lower quantity of workers, Q_u.

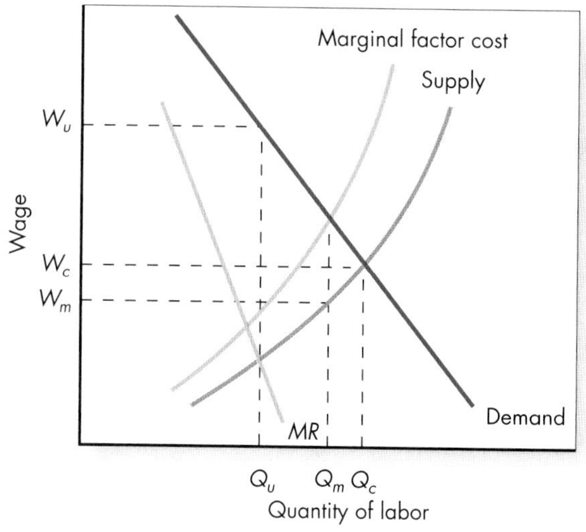

Union Monopoly Power

When a union exists, it will have an incentive to act as a monopolist, restricting supply to increase its members' wages. To do so it must have the power to restrict both supply and union membership. A union would have a strong tendency to act like a monopolist and to move to an equilibrium somewhat similar to the monopsonist case, except for one important difference. The wage the union would set wouldn't be below the competitive wage; instead, the wage would be above the competitive wage at W_u, as in Figure 19-4. Faced with a wage of W_u, competitive firms will hire Q_u workers. Thus, with union monopoly power, the benefits of restricting supply accrue to the union members, not to the firm as in the monopsonist case.

Bilateral Monopoly

As our final case, let's consider a bilateral monopoly in which a monopsonist faces a union with monopoly power. In this case, we can say that the equilibrium wage will be somewhere between the monopsonist wage W_m and the union monopoly power wage W_u. The equilibrium quantity will be somewhere between Q_u and Q_m in Figure 19-4. Where in that range the wage and equilibrium quantity will be depends on the two sides' negotiating skills and other noneconomic forces.

A bilateral monopoly is a market in which a single seller faces a single buyer.

Political and Social Forces and the Labor Market

Let's now consider some real-world characteristics of U.S. labor markets. For example:

1. English teachers are paid close to what economics teachers are paid even though the quantity of English teachers supplied significantly exceeds the quantity of English teachers demanded, while the quantity of economics teachers supplied is approximately equal to the quantity demanded.
2. On average, women earn about 85 cents for every $1 earned by men.
3. Certain types of jobs are undertaken primarily by members of a single ethnic group. For example, a large percentage of construction workers on high-rise buildings are Mohawk Indians. They have an uncanny knack for keeping their balance on high, open building frames.
4. Firms often pay higher than "market" wages.
5. Firms often don't lay off workers even when demand for their products decreases.
6. It often seems that there are two categories of jobs: dead-end jobs and jobs with potential for career advancement. Once in a dead-end job, a person finds it almost impossible to switch to a job with potential.
7. The rate of unemployment among blacks is more than twice as high as the rate among whites.

Supply/demand analysis alone doesn't explain these phenomena. Each of them can, however, be explained as the result of market, political, and social forces. Thus, to understand real-world labor markets, it is necessary to broaden the analysis of labor markets to include other forces that limit the use of the market. These include legal and social limitations on the self-interest-seeking activities of firms and individuals. Let's consider a couple of the central issues of interaction among these forces and see how they affect the labor market.

To understand real-world labor markets, one must broaden the analysis.

Fairness and the Labor Market

People generally have an underlying view of what's fair. That view isn't always consistent among individuals, but it's often strongly held. The first lesson taught in a personnel or

ADDED DIMENSION

Nonwage Income and Property Rights

The four traditional categories of income are wages, rent, profits, and interest. Wages, discussed in the text, are determined by economic factors (the forces of supply and demand), with strong influences by political and social forces, which often restrict entry or hold wages higher than what they would be in a truly competitive market.

The same holds true for nonwage income: payments for use of land (rent), capital (profit), and financial assets (interest). The forces of supply and demand also determine these forms of income. But, as we have emphasized, supply and demand are not necessarily the end of the story. Supply and demand determine price and income, given an institutional structure that includes property rights (the rights given to people to use specified property) and the contractual legal system (the set of laws that govern economic behavior of the society). If you change property rights, you change the distribution of income. Thus, in a larger sense, supply and demand don't determine the distribution of income; the distribution of property rights does.

The system of property rights and the contractual legal system that underlie the U.S. economy evolved over many years. Many people believe that property rights were unfairly distributed to begin with; if you believe that, you'll also believe that the distribution of income and the returns to those property rights are unfair. In other words, you can favor markets but object to the underlying property rights. Many political fights about income distribution concern fights over property rights, not fights over the use of markets.

Such distributional fights have been going on for a long time. In feudal times, much of the land was held communally; it belonged to everyone, or at least everyone used it. It was common land—a communally held resource. As the economy evolved into a market economy, that land was appropriated by individuals, and these individuals became landholders who could determine the use of the land and could receive rent for allowing other individuals to use that land. Supply and demand can explain how much rent will accrue to a landholder; it cannot explain the initial set of property rights.

The type of issues raised by looking at the underlying property rights are in large part academic for Western societies. The property rights that exist, and the contractual legal system under which markets operate, are given. You're not going to see somebody going out and introducing a new alternative set of property rights in which the ownership of property is transferred to someone else. The government may impose shifts at the margin; for example, new zoning laws—laws that set limits on the use of one's property—will modify property rights and create fights about whether society has the right to impose such laws. But there will be no wholesale change in property rights. That's why most economic thinking simply takes property rights as given.

But taking property rights as given isn't a reasonable assumption for the developing countries or the formerly socialist countries still in the process of establishing markets and framing up their structure of property rights. In recent years, institutional economists have redirected their analysis to look more closely at the underlying legal and philosophical basis of supply and demand. As they do so, they are extending and modifying the economic theory of income distribution.

human resources course is that people aren't machines. They're human beings with feelings and emotions. If they feel good about a job, if they feel they're part of a team, they will work hard; if they feel they're being taken advantage of, they can be highly disruptive.

On some assembly-line jobs, it is relatively easy to monitor effort, so individuals can be—and in the past often were—treated like machines. Their feelings and emotions were ignored. Productivity was determined by the speed of the assembly line; if workers couldn't or wouldn't keep up the pace, they were fired.

Efficiency Wages Most modern jobs, however, require workers to make decisions and to determine how best to do a task. Today's managers are aware that workers' emotional state is important to whether they make sound decisions and do a good job. So most firms, even if they don't really care about anything but profit, will try to keep their workers happy. It's in their own interest to do so. That might mean paying workers more than the going market wage, not laying them off even if layoffs would make sense economically, providing day care so the workers aren't worried about their children, or keeping wage differentials among workers small to limit internal rivalry. Such actions can often make long-run economic sense, even though they might cost the firm in the short run. They are common enough that they have acquired a name—**efficiency wages** *(wages paid above the going market wage to keep workers happy and productive)*.

Views of fairness also enter into wage determination through political channels. Social views of fairness influence government, which passes laws to implement those views. Minimum wage laws, comparable worth laws, and antidiscrimination laws are examples.

Q-8 Why might efficiency wages make sense in the long run?

Firms sometimes pay what's called efficiency wages to keep workers happy and productive.

Comparable Worth Laws Let's consider one of those, **comparable worth laws,** which are *laws mandating comparable pay for comparable work*—that is, mandatory "fairness." The problem in implementing these laws is in defining what is comparable. Do you define comparable work by the education it requires, by the effort the worker puts out, or by other characteristics? Similarly with pay: Compensation has many dimensions and it is not at all clear which are the relevant ones, or whether the political system will focus on the relevant ones.

Economists who favor comparable worth laws point out that social and intrafirm political issues are often the determining factors in setting pay. In fact, firms often have their own implicit or explicit comparable worth systems built into their structure. For example, seniority, not productivity, often determines pay. Bias against women and minorities and in favor of high-level management is sometimes built into firms' pay-setting institutions. In short, within firms, pay structure is influenced by, but is not determined by, supply and demand forces. Comparable worth laws are designed to affect those institutional biases and thus are not necessarily any less compatible with supply and demand forces than are current pay-setting institutions.

The federal government is not the only government agency that establishes labor laws. State and local governments also do. For example, recently a number of local governments have established "living wage" laws, which are a type of minimum wage law that requires specified employers to pay a "living wage." "Living wage" is most often defined as that wage that would allow one worker, working 40 hours a week, to support a family of four at the poverty level. The analysis of these laws is similar to that of the minimum wage.

Job Discrimination and the Labor Market

Web Note 19.4
Faculty Hiring Bias

Discrimination exists in all walks of life: On average, women are paid less than men, and blacks are often directed into lower-paying jobs. Economists have done a lot of research to understand the facts regarding discrimination and what can be done about it. The first problem is to measure the amount of discrimination and get an idea of how much discrimination is caused by what. Let's consider discrimination against women.

On average, women receive somewhere around 85 percent of the pay that men receive. That has increased from about 60 percent in the 1970s. This pay gap suggests that discrimination is occurring. The economist's job is to figure out how much of this is statistically significant and, of the portion that is caused by discrimination, what the nature of that discrimination is.

Q-9 Economic theory argues that discrimination should be eliminated. True or false? Why?

Analyzing the data, economists have found that somewhat more than half of the pay difference can be explained by causes other than discrimination, such as length of time on the job. But that still leaves a relatively large difference that can be attributed to discrimination.

Three Types of Direct Demand-Side Discrimination In analyzing discrimination, it's important to distinguish various types. The first is demand-side discrimination based on relevant individual characteristics. Firms commonly make decisions about employees based on individual characteristics that will affect job performance. For example, restaurants might discriminate against (avoid hiring) applicants with sourpuss

Three types of demand-side discrimination are

1. Discrimination based on individual characteristics that will affect job performance.
2. Discrimination based on correctly perceived statistical characteristics of the group.
3. Discrimination based on individual characteristics that don't affect job performance or are incorrectly perceived.

ADDED DIMENSION

Democracy in the Workplace

In the United States, slavery is illegal. You cannot sell yourself to someone else, even if you want to. It's an unenforceable contract. But work, which might be considered a form of partial slavery, is legal. You can sell your labor services for a specific, limited period of time.

Is there any inherent reason that such partial slavery should be seen as acceptable? The answer to that question is complicated. It deals with the rights of workers and is based on value judgments. You must answer it for yourself. I raise it because it's a good introduction to Karl Marx's analysis of the labor market (which deals with alienation) and to some recent arguments about democracy in the workplace.

Marx saw selling labor as immoral, just as slavery was immoral. He believed that capitalists exploited workers by alienating them from their labor. The best equivalent I can think of is the way most people today view the selling of sex. Most people see selling sex as wrong because it alienates a person from his or her own body. Marx saw all selling of labor that same way. A labor market makes workers see themselves as objects, not as human beings.

The underlying philosophical issues of Marx's concern are outside of economics. Most people in the United States don't agree with Marx's philosophical underpinnings. But it's nonetheless a useful exercise to think about this issue and ask yourself whether it helps explain why we treat the labor market as different from other markets and limit by law the right of employers to discriminate in the labor market.

Some of Marx's philosophical tenets are shared by the modern democracy-in-the-workplace movement. In this view, a business isn't owned by a certain group; it is an association of individuals who have come together to produce a certain product. For one group—the owners of stock—to have all the say as to how the business is run, and for another group—the regular workers—to have no say, is immoral in the same way that not having a democratic government is immoral. According to this view, work is as large a part of people's lives as is national or local politics, and a country can call itself a democracy only if it has democracy in the workplace.

As with most grandiose ideas, this one is complicated, but it's worth considering because it's reflected in certain laws. Consider, for example, the 1989 federal law that limits firms' freedom to close plants without giving notice to their workers. The view that workers have certain inalienable rights played a role in passing that law.

For those of you who say "Right on!" to the idea of increasing workers' rights, let me add a word of caution. Increasing workers' rights has a cost. It makes it less likely that firms and individuals who can think up things that need doing will do so, and thus will decrease the number of jobs available. It also will increase firms' desire to discriminate. If you know you must let a person play a role in decisions once you hire that person, you're going to be much more careful about whom you hire.

None of these considerations means that democracy in the workplace can't work. The Brazilian firm Semco is an example. There are examples of somewhat democratic "firms." Universities are run as partial democracies, with the faculty deciding what policies should be set. (There is, however, serious debate about how well universities are run.) But as soon as you add worker democracy to production, more questions come up: What about consumers? Shouldn't they, too, have a voice in decisions? What about the community within which the firm is located?

Economics can't answer such questions. Economics can, however, be used to predict and analyze some of the difficulties such changes might bring about.

personalities. Another example might be a firm hiring more young salespeople because its clients like to buy from younger rather than older employees. If that characteristic can be an identifying factor for a group of individuals, the discrimination becomes more visible.

A second type of demand-side discrimination is discrimination based on group characteristics. This occurs when firms make employment decisions about individuals because they are members of a group who on average have particular characteristics that affect job performance. A firm may correctly perceive that young people in general have a lower probability of staying on a job than do older people and therefore may discriminate against younger people.

A third type of demand-side discrimination is discrimination based on irrelevant individual characteristics. This discrimination is based either on individual characteristics that do not affect job performance or on incorrectly perceived statistical characteristics of groups. A firm might not hire people over 50 because the supervisor doesn't like working with older people, even though older people may be just as productive as, or even more productive than, younger people.

Of the three types, the third will be easiest to eliminate; it doesn't have an economic motivation. In fact, discrimination based on individual characteristics that don't affect job performance is costly to a firm. Competing firms will hire these people and be in a better competitive position because they did so. Market forces will work toward eliminating this type of discrimination.

An example of the success of a firm's policy to reduce discrimination is the decision by McDonald's to create a special program to hire workers with learning disabilities. Individuals who have learning disabilities often make good employees. They tend to have lower turnover rates and follow procedures better than do many of the more transient employees McDonald's hires. Moreover, through their advertising, McDonald's helped change some negative stereotypes about people with disabilities. So in this case market forces and political forces are working together.

Discrimination based on characteristics that affect job performance is hard to eliminate.

If the discrimination is of either of the first two types (that is, based on characteristics that do affect job performance, either directly or statistically), the discrimination will be harder to eliminate. In these cases, not discriminating can be costly to the firm, so political forces to eliminate discrimination will be working against market forces to keep discrimination.

Whenever discrimination saves the firm money, the firm will have an economic incentive to use subterfuges to get around an antidiscrimination law. These subterfuges will make the firm appear to be complying with the law, even when it isn't. An example would be a firm that finds some other reason besides age to explain why it isn't hiring an older person.

Institutional Discrimination Institutional discrimination is discrimination in which the structure of the job makes it difficult or impossible for certain groups of individuals to succeed. Institutional discrimination does not come from the demand side, but is built into the institutional structure. Consider colleges and universities. To succeed in the academic market, one must devote an enormous amount of effort during one's 20s and 30s. But these are precisely the years when, given biology and culture, many women have major family responsibilities, making it difficult for women to succeed. Were academic institutions different—say, a number of positions at universities were designed for high-level, part-time work during this period—it would be easier for women to advance their careers.

Requiring peak time commitment when women are also facing peak family responsibilities is the norm for many companies, too. Thus, women face significant institutional discrimination.

Institutions can have built-in discrimination.

Whether this institutional discrimination is embodied in the firm's structure or in the family is an open question. For example, sociologists have found that in personal relationships women tend to move to be with their partners more than men move to be with their partners. In addition, women in two-parent relationships generally do much more work around the house and take a greater responsibility for child rearing than men do even when both are employed.

How important are these sociological observations? In discussing discrimination I ask the members of my class if they expect their personal relationships with their partners to be fully equal. The usual result is the following: 80 percent of the women expect a fully equal relationship; 20 percent expect their partner's career to come first. Eighty percent of the men expect their own careers to come first; 20 percent expect an equal relationship. I then point out that somebody's expectations aren't going to be fulfilled.

Put simply, most observers believe that the institutional discrimination that occurs in interpersonal relationships is significant.

Economists have made adjustments for these sociological factors, and have found that institutional factors explain a portion of the lower pay that women receive but that other forms of workplace discrimination also explain a portion.

Whether prejudice should be allowed to affect the hiring decision is a normative question for society to settle. In answering these normative questions, our society has passed laws making it illegal for employers to discriminate on the basis of race, religion, sex, age, disability, or national origin. The reason society has made it illegal is its ethical belief in equal opportunity for all, or at least most, individuals. (Homosexuals still aren't protected by federal legislation assuring them equal opportunities.)

The Evolution of Labor Markets

Now that we've briefly considered how noneconomic forces can influence labor markets, let's turn our attention to how labor markets developed.

Labor markets as we now know them developed in the 1700s and 1800s. Given the political and social rules that operated at that time, the invisible hand was free to push wage rates down to subsistence level. Workweeks were long and working conditions were poor. Laborers began to turn to other ways—besides the market—of influencing their wage. One way was to use political power to place legal restrictions on employers in their relationship with workers. A second way was to organize together—to unionize. Let's consider each in turn.

Laws play an important role in the structure of labor markets.

Evolving Labor Laws Over the years, government has responded to workers' political pressure with numerous laws that limit what can and what cannot be done in the various labor markets. For example, in many areas of production, laws limit the number of normal hours a person can work in a day to eight. The laws also prescribe the amount

In the late 1800s, many workers worked in sweatshops; they often had quotas that required them to work 60 or more hours a week. Fines were imposed for such indiscretions as talking or smiling.

of extra pay an employee must receive when working more than the normal number of hours. (Generally it's time-and-a-half.) Similarly, the number and length of workers' breaks are defined by law (one break every four hours).

Child labor laws mandate that a person must be at least 16 years old to be hired. The safety and health conditions under which a person can work are regulated by laws. (For example, on a construction site, all workers are required to wear hard hats.) Workers can be fired only for cause, and employers must show that they had cause to fire a worker. (For example, a 55-year-old employee cannot be fired simply because he or she is getting old.) Employers must not allow sexual harassment in the workplace. (Bosses can't make sexual advances to employees and firms must make a good-faith attempt to see that employees don't sexually harass their co-workers.)

Combined, these laws play an enormously important role in the functioning of the labor market.

Web Note 19.5
Laws or Contracts?

Unions and Collective Bargaining Some of the most important labor laws concern workers' right to organize together in order to bargain collectively with employers. These laws also specify the tactics workers can use to achieve their ends. In the latter part of the 1800s, workers had few rights to organize themselves. The Knights of Labor was formed in 1869, and by 1886 it had approximately 800,000 members. But a labor riot in 1886 turned public opinion against these workers and led to the organization's breakup. In its place, the American Federation of Labor developed and began to organize strikes to achieve higher wages.

Business opposed unions' right to strike, and initially the government supported business. Police and sometimes the army were sent in to break up strikes. Under the then-existing legal structure of the economy, unions were seen as monopolistic restraints on trade and an intrusion into management rights.

In the 1930s, society's view of unions changed (in part as a backlash to the strong-arm tactics used by firms to break up unions), and laws such as the National Labor Relations Act (also called the Wagner Act) were passed guaranteeing workers the right to form unions, to strike, and to engage in collective bargaining. As Figure 19-5 shows, from 1935 to the mid-1950s unions grew significantly in size and importance and remained strong until the late 1970s.

Businesses weren't happy with unions' increasing strength, and in 1947 they managed to get the Taft-Hartley Act passed. That act placed limitations on union activities. It allowed states to pass "right-to-work" laws forbidding union membership to be made a

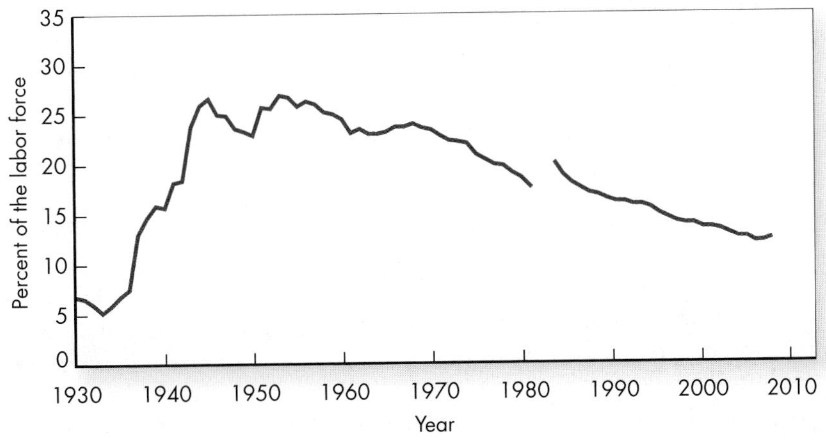

FIGURE 19-5
Change in Union Membership

The graph shows union membership from 1930. As can be seen, after the Depression in the 1930s, unions grew in importance. Since the mid-1970s the importance of unions has declined. (Note: The series from 1930 to 1981 excludes members of professional and public employee associations. The series from 1983 and beyond is from *Current Population Statistics*.)

Source: Bureau of Labor Statistics (http://www.bls.gov).

A closed shop is a firm in which the union controls hiring.

A union shop is a firm in which all workers must join the union.

requirement for continued employment. Moreover, it made **closed shops,** *firms where the union controls hiring,* illegal. Before anyone can be hired in a closed shop, he or she must be a member of the particular union. Federal law does permit **union shops**—*firms in which all workers must join the union.* Individuals are required to join a union after working for the firm for a period of time. The Taft-Hartley Act also outlawed *secondary boycotts.* In a secondary boycott, in order to strengthen its bargaining position, a union gets unions at other firms to force their firms to refuse to buy a firm's products, under threat of a strike.

Union power weakened considerably in 1981, when, in response to a strike by air traffic controllers, President Ronald Reagan fired all the controllers and refused to hire them back. Private firms similarly won the right to hire permanent replacements for striking workers. That stance significantly changed the atmosphere within which unions operate.

Part of the reason labor union membership has declined in recent years is the unions' successes.

As Figure 19-5 shows, the percent of workers who belong to unions has declined since the 1970s, as unions have lost their bargaining power. Because of that decline, unions don't have the political or economic clout they once had. Part of the reason, ironically, is their success. By pressuring the government to pass laws that protected workers, unions made themselves less necessary. Another part of the reason is the changing nature of production in the United States. Labor unions were especially strong in manufacturing industries. As the relative number of manufacturing jobs has declined in the United States and the number of service jobs has increased, the base of union membership has been reduced. Unions have somewhat compensated for this change by pushing unionization drives among government employees. Today, nearly 50 percent of union members work for the government. These unions are becoming stronger and will likely be exerting their influence.

Conclusion: The Labor Market and You

This chapter is meant to give you a sense of how the labor market works. But what does it all mean for those of you who'll soon be getting a job or are in the process of changing jobs? I'll try to answer that question in this last section.

Table 19-1 shows a variety of useful statistics about the labor market. Let's consider how some of them might affect you. For example, consider relative pay of jobs requiring a college degree compared to jobs requiring only a high school diploma. Jobs requiring a college degree pay significantly more, on average, than do jobs requiring only a high school diploma. In recent years the income gap between the two groups has noticeably increased. So the answer to the question of whether it's worthwhile to stick college out for another couple of years and get a degree is probably yes.

Advice: It pays to finish college.

Next, consider the salaries of Ph.D.s compared to the salaries of MBAs. A Ph.D. is a person who has gone to graduate school after college, usually for a number of years, and earned an advanced degree called a **D**octorate of **Ph**ilosophy—even though one can earn a Ph.D. in many subjects besides philosophy (such as economics). As you can see, Ph.D.s' starting salaries are lower than salaries of MBAs (masters of business administration) and professionals with other kinds of advanced degrees. Does this mean that Ph.D.s are discriminated against? Not necessarily. It's possible that Ph.D.s' lower pay suggests that Ph.D.s derive a "psychic income" from their work in addition to the amount of money they earn.

Q-10 Ph.D.s earn less than MBAs, so therefore one should get an MBA rather than a Ph.D. True or false? Why?

Since Ph.D.s are often quite smart, their willingness to accept psychic income as a substitute for higher pay suggests that there's much more to consider in a job than the salary. What's most important about a job isn't the wage, but whether you like what you're doing and the life that job provides. (Of course, their lower salaries also could imply that Ph.D.s really aren't so smart.)

So my suggestion to you is definitely to finish college, especially if you enjoy it. (And with books like this, how could you help but enjoy it?) But go to graduate school only if you really enjoy learning. In picking your job, first and foremost pick a job that

TABLE 19-1 (A AND B) Some Typical Starting Salaries

Occupation	Private or State
Physician assistant	$69,000
Management analyst	40,000
Budget analyst	40,000
Economist	40,000
Secondary school teacher	37,000
Flight attendant	32,000
Insurance sales	32,000
Secretary	28,000
Maintenance and repair	24,000
Retail sales (salary and commission)	18,000

Sources: Author's estimates based on *Occupational Outlook Handbook*, 2008–09 and U.S. Dept. of Labor Statistics (pay varies significantly by region) (http://www.bls.gov).

(a) Some Typical Starting Salaries of BAs

Degree	Annual Salary*
Law (3 years)	
Large firms	$125,000
Small firms	68,000
Engineering	
Bachelor's degree	60,000
Master's degree	65,000
Business	
Bachelor's degree	41,000
Master's (MBA) degree (2 years)	75,000
M.D. (4 years and 3-year internship)	120,000
Ph.D. (5 years)	
In economics	70,000
In humanities	55,000

*These figures are rough estimates based on data from the Department of Labor and informal surveys of author.

(b) Starting Salaries for Selected Professional Degrees

you enjoy (as long as it pays you enough to live on). Among jobs you like, choose a job in a field in which the supply of labor is limited, or the demand for labor is significantly increasing. Either of those trends is likely to lead to higher wages. After all, if you're doing something you like, you might as well get paid as much as possible for it.

Jobs in which the supply will likely be limited are those in which social or political forces have placed restrictions on entry or those requiring special abilities. If you have some special ability, try to find a job you enjoy in which you can use that ability. You might also look for a job in which entry is restricted, but beware: Jobs that are restricted in supply must be rationed, so while such jobs pay higher wages, you may need personal connections to obtain one of them.

I'm sure most of you are aware that your choice of jobs is one of the most important choices you'll be making in your life. So I'm sure you feel the pressure. But you should also know that a job, unlike marriage, isn't necessarily supposed to be for life. There's enormous flexibility in the U.S. labor market. Many people change jobs six or seven times in their lifetimes. So while the choice is important, a poor choice can be remedied; don't despair if the first job you take isn't perfect. Good luck.

Summary

- Incentive effects are important in labor supply decisions. The higher the wage, the higher the quantity supplied.
- Elasticity of market supply of labor depends on (1) individuals' opportunity cost of working, (2) the type of market being discussed, (3) the elasticity of individuals' supply curves, and (4) individuals entering and leaving the labor market.
- The demand for labor by firms is derived from the demand by consumers for goods and services. It follows the basic law of demand—the higher the wage, the lower the quantity demanded.

- Elasticity of market demand for labor depends on (1) the elasticity of demand for the firm's good, (2) the relative importance of labor in production, (3) the possibility and cost of substitution in production, and (4) the degree to which marginal productivity falls with an increase in labor.
- Technological advances and changes in international competitiveness shift the demand for labor. Both have reduced demand for some types of labor and increased demand for other types. The net effect has been an increase in the demand for labor.
- A monopsony is a market in which a single firm is the only buyer. A monopsonist hires fewer workers at a lower wage compared to a competitive firm.
- A bilateral monopoly is a market in which there is a single seller and a single buyer. The wage and number of workers hired in a bilateral monopoly depend on the relative strength of the union and the monopsonist.
- Firms are aware of workers' well-being and will sometimes pay efficiency wages to keep workers happy and productive.
- Views of fairness in the labor market have led to laws that mandate comparable pay for comparable work.
- Discrimination may be based on (1) relevant individual characteristics, (2) group characteristics, or (3) irrelevant individual characteristics. The easiest to eliminate is discrimination based on irrelevant individual characteristics. The other two are motivated by market incentives.
- Labor laws have evolved and will continue to evolve. Since the 1980s, labor unions have been declining in importance.

Key Terms

bilateral monopoly *(440)*
closed shops *(448)*
comparable worth laws *(443)*
derived demand *(436)*
efficiency wages *(443)*
entrepreneurship *(436)*
incentive effect *(431)*
labor market *(430)*
marginal factor cost *(440)*
monopsony *(440)*
union shops *(448)*

Questions and Exercises

1. Why are social and political forces more active in the labor market than in most other markets? LO1
2. Economist Edward Prescott observed that while Americans worked 5 percent fewer hours per week than the French in the 1970s, they worked 50 percent more hours per week in the early 2000s. He found that taxes accounted for nearly all of the difference. What was his likely argument? LO1
3. If the wage goes up 20 percent and the quantity of labor supplied increases by 5 percent, what's the elasticity of labor supply? LO2
4. A recent study by the International Labor Organization estimates that 250 million children in developing countries between the ages of 5 and 14 are working either full or part time. The estimates of the percentage of children working within particular countries is as high as 42 percent in Kenya. Among the reasons cited for the rise in child labor are population increases and poverty.
   a. Why do firms hire children as workers?
   b. Why do children work?
   c. What considerations should be taken into account by countries when deciding whether to implement an international ban on trade for products made with child labor? LO2
5. In 1997, a Dutch charity sponsored an incentive program in which teachers received prizes equal to about 30 percent of their salary if their students improved their scores on a standardized test.
   a. What effect would you expect the program to have on test scores?
   b. If not all the teachers' students were required to take the test, how would the program have to treat students who did not take the exam?
   c. What would be the most likely way in which the program would change what teachers did? LO2
6. H-1B visas allow U.S. firms to hire foreign professionals for up to a total of six years. In 2003, the cap on H-1B visas was raised from 65,000 to 195,000.
   a. Why would professional organizations, such as the American Engineering Association, oppose such an increase?

b. Why would high-tech companies support such an increase?
c. Do you support the increase? Why or why not? LO2

7. As telecommunications improve, performers can reach larger and larger audiences. In the past, one could only perform in a concert hall; today one can perform for the entire world. How might that change in technology affect the relative pay of performers? LO3

8. "Fair trade" goods are goods that are produced with labor paid "living wages" and under humane production facilities that are certified by a regulatory group. Do firms have a strong incentive to sell fair trade goods? LO3

9. Assume the law of diminishing marginal productivity holds true.
   a. If individuals emigrate from a country such as Haiti, what should happen to the wage of the remaining workers?
   b. If your answer for *a* does not match the data, what explanation might you give for it? LO3

10. The president of the United States receives an annual salary of $400,000. Derek Jeter, shortstop for the New York Yankees, receives $20.6 million annually.
   a. Based on marginal productivity theory, what does this say about their contributions to society?
   b. What qualifications to your answer might you suggest about their relative contributions, and what do your adjustments have to say about marginal productivity theory? LO3

11. University of Texas at Arlington professors Craig A. Depken II and Dennis P. Wilson have studied the pay of baseball players and discovered the following relationship between each play and team revenue (values adjusted for inflation):

Play	Change in Team Revenue
Home run	$406,143
Offensive walk	71,602
Hit	36,911
Strikeouts	−71,602

   a. Assuming the relationships hold true, and given performance below, what salary would you estimate for each player in 2006?

Player	2006 Salary	Hits	Home Runs	Offensive Walks	Strikeouts
Alex Rodriguez	$22 million	166	35	8	139
Barry Bonds	$19 million	99	26	38	51
Jeff Kent	$9.4 million	119	14	0	69

   b. If the pay of these players is higher than their marginal revenue products, how can you explain that? LO3

12. The following statement appeared in a recent article: 7½ cents of every dollar spent at retail stores in America is spent at Wal-Mart. With such market power, Wal-Mart is able to name the price at which it is willing to buy goods from suppliers.
   a. Could this be a correct statement if Wal-Mart's suppliers were operating in a perfectly competitive market?
   b. What if it were operating in an imperfectly competitive market, specifically a monopsonistic market?
   c. What would be the lower limit of the price Wal-Mart could name? LO5

13. Demonstrate graphically the effect of a minimum wage law. Does economic theory tell us such a law would be a bad idea? LO6

14. Show graphically how a minimum wage can simultaneously increase employment and raise the wage rate. LO5, LO6

15. Comparable worth laws require employers to pay the same wage scale to workers who do comparable work or have comparable training. What likely effect would these laws have on the labor market? LO6

16. Explain each of the following phenomena using the invisible hand or social or political forces:
   a. Firms often pay higher than market wages.
   b. Wages don't fluctuate much as unemployment rises.
   c. Pay among faculty in various disciplines at colleges does not vary much although market conditions among disciplines vary significantly. LO6

17. In the early 1990s a teen subminimum training wage law was passed by which employers were allowed to pay teenagers less than the minimum wage.
   a. What effect would you predict this law would have, based on standard economic theory?
   b. In analyzing the effects of the law, Professors Card and Kreuger of Princeton University found that few businesses used it and that it had little effect. Why might that have been the case? LO6

18. Economists Mark Blaug and Ruth Towse studied the market for economists in Britain and found that the quantity demanded was about 150–200 a year, and that the quantity supplied was about 300 a year.
   a. What did they predict would happen to economists' salaries?
   b. What likely happens to the excess economists?
   c. Why doesn't the price change immediately to bring the quantity supplied and the quantity demanded into equilibrium? LO6

Questions from Alternative Perspectives

1. How might the minimum wage lead to greater racial and gender discrimination in the labor market? (Austrian)
2. In his book *Forbidden Grounds*, University of Chicago Professor Richard Epstein argues that federal employment antidiscrimination laws ought to be abolished. [Hint. Reading Westmont College economist Edd Noell's paper "Racial Discrimination, Police Power and the 1964 Civil Rights Act in Richard Epstein's Forbidden Grounds: An Evaluation of The Case Against Discrimination Laws" (available on the Web at ACE, www.gordon.edu/ace) will be helpful in answering this question.]
   a. How might a Christian economist evaluate the need for federal laws prohibiting racial discrimination?
   b. Why should a Christian economist think more carefully than another economist about the relation between economic liberty and tolerance of the taste for discrimination? (Religious)
3. Gloria Steinem pointed out the following: "I've yet to be on any campus where women weren't worried about some aspect of combining marriage, children, and a career. I've yet to find one where many men were worrying about the same thing."
   a. What does this insight suggest about the working of the labor market in the United States?
   b. Does this male bias in the labor market affect the efficiency of the economy? (Feminist)
4. Table 19-1 in the text provides data about starting salaries for selected professional degrees; in it you can see that Ph.D. economists are paid less than MBAs. If economists are rational, why are they economists? (Institutionalist)
5. Radical economists argue that labor markets are governed by nonmarket forces such as discrimination as well as by the supply and demand for labor. As they see it, poverty and inequality are not aberrations but systematic labor market outcomes. They also believe that unions are much-needed equalizers that help low-wage workers.
   a. How does the radical view of the workings of labor markets and role of unions differ from that presented in your textbook?
   b. In your opinion, how fairly do labor markets operate?
   c. Do labor market outcomes need redress through collective action? (Radical)

Issues to Ponder

1. "Welfare laws are bad, not for society, but for the people they are meant to help." Discuss. (Difficult) LO1
2. Which would you choose: selling illegal drugs at $75 an hour (20 percent chance per year of being arrested) or a $6-an-hour factory job? Why? LO1
3. Some economists have argued against need-based scholarships because they work as an implicit tax on parents' salaries and hence discourage saving for college. (Difficult)
   a. If the marginal tax rate parents face is 20 percent, and 5 percent of parents' assets will be deducted from a student's financial aid each year for the four years a child is in school, what is the implicit marginal tax on that portion of income that is saved? (For simplicity assume the interest rate is zero and that the parents' contribution is paid at the time the child enters college.)
   b. How would your answer differ if parents had two children with the second entering college right after the first one graduated? (How about three?) (Remember that the assets will likely decrease with each child graduating.)
   c. When parents are divorced, how should the contribution of each parent be determined? If your school has need-based scholarships, how does it determine the expected contributions of divorced parents?
   d. Given the above, would you suggest moving to an ability-based scholarship program? Why or why not? LO1
4. According to economist Colin Camerer of the California Institute of Technology, many New York taxi drivers decide when to finish work for the day by setting an income goal for themselves. Once they reach it, they stop working. (Difficult)
   a. Is that what you would expect if the drivers are rational?
   b. Prospect theory suggests that people gain less utility from winning a certain sum of money than the utility they would lose if they lost that same sum. How can prospect theory explain the behavior of taxi drivers? LO1
5. Why might it be inappropriate to discuss the effect of immigration policy using supply and demand analysis? (Difficult) LO2, LO4
6. Why is unemployment nearly twice as high among blacks as among whites? What should be done about the situation? LO6, LO7
7. Give four reasons why women earn less than men. Which reasons do you believe are most responsible for the wage gap? LO7

8. Interview three married female and three married male professors at your college, asking them what percentage of work in the professor's household each adult household member does.
   a. Assuming your results can be extended to the population at large, what can you say about the existence of institutional discrimination?
   b. If gender-related salary data for individuals at your college are available, determine whether women or men of equal rank and experience receive higher average pay.
   c. Relate your findings in *a* and *b*. LO7

9. In an article in the *Journal of Human Resources* titled "The Economic Reality of the Beauty Myth," Lafayette Professor Susan Averett and Baruch College Professor Sanders Korenman found that family income of obese women is about 17 percent lower than that of women who are of recommended weight. The differential was less for men than for women.
   a. What conclusions can you draw from these findings?
   b. Do the findings necessarily mean that there is a "beauty" discrimination?
   c. What might explain the larger income penalty for women? LO7

Answers to Margin Questions

1. Under usual conditions of supply, one would expect that if the wage of my part-time job rises, the quantity of labor I supply in that part-time job also rises. Institutional constraints such as tax considerations or company rules might mean that the quantity of labor I supply doesn't change. However, under the usual conditions of supply, I will study less if the wage of my part-time job rises. *(432)*
2. Taxes reduce the opportunity cost, or relative price, of nonwork activities. So you will substitute leisure for labor as marginal tax rates increase. *(434)*
3. The irony of any need-based program is that such a program reduces people's incentive to prevent themselves from becoming needy. *(434)*
4. Some factors that influence the elasticity of a firm's derived demand for labor include (1) the elasticity of demand for the firm's good; (2) the relative importance of labor in the production process; (3) the possibility, and cost, of substitution in production; and (4) the degree to which marginal productivity falls with an increase in labor. *(436)*
5. The demand for laborers at that firm would shift out to the right. *(437)*
6. Differences among countries in productivity, transportation costs, trade restrictions, and social institutions all determine the relative demand for labor in one country compared to another country. *(438)*
7. If the increase in labor supply leads to an increase in the demand for products in general, the increase in labor supply also will lead to an increase in labor demand. *(439)*
8. Firms might pay workers higher-than-competitive-wages in the long run to cultivate worker loyalty and get workers to work harder. *(443)*
9. Economic theory does not argue that discrimination should be eliminated. Economic theory tries to stay positive. Discrimination is a normative issue. If one's normative views say that discrimination should be eliminated, economic theory might be useful to help do that most efficiently. *(443)*
10. There is more to life than income, so it does not necessarily follow that one should take the job that pays the highest wage. (In the author's view, a Ph.D.'s life is far more fulfilling than an MBA's life, although some MBAs may disagree with that.) Each person must decide for him- or herself how to weigh the various dimensions of a job. *(448)*

Appendix A

Derived Demand

This appendix considers the issues of derived demand in more detail. Although it focuses on the derived demand for labor, you should note that the formal analysis of the firm's derived demand for labor presented in the chapter is quite general and carries over to the derived demand for capital and for land. Firms translate consumers' demands for goods into derived demands for any and all of the factors of production. Let's start our consideration by looking at the firm's decision to hire.

The Firm's Decision to Hire

What determines a firm's decision to hire someone? The answer is simple. A profit-maximizing firm hires someone if it thinks there's money to be made by doing so. Unless there is, the firm won't hire the person. So for a firm to decide whether to hire someone, it must compare the worker's **marginal revenue product (MRP)** (*the marginal revenue it expects to earn from selling the additional worker's output*) with the wage that it expects to pay the additional worker. For a competitive firm (for which $P = MR$), that marginal revenue product equals the worker's **value of marginal product (VMP)**—the worker's **marginal physical product (MPP)** (*the additional units of output that hiring an additional worker will bring about*) times the price (P) at which the firm can sell the additional product.

Marginal revenue product = $MPP \times P$

Say, for example, that by hiring another worker a firm can produce an additional 6 widgets an hour, which it can sell at \$2 each. That means the firm can pay up to \$12 per hour and still expect to make a profit. Notice that a key question for the firm is: How much additional product will we get from hiring another worker? A competitive firm can increase its profit by hiring another worker as long as the value of the worker's marginal product (which also equals her marginal revenue product) ($MPP \times P$) is higher than her wage.

To see whether you understand the principle, consider the example in Figure A19-1(a). Column 1 shows the number of workers, all of whom are assumed to be identical. Column 2 shows the total output of those workers. Column 3 shows the marginal physical product of an additional worker. This number is determined by looking at the change in the total product due to this person's work. For example, if the firm is currently employing 30 workers and it hires one more, the firm's total product or output will rise from 294 to 300, so the marginal product of moving from 30 to 31 workers is 6.

Notice that workers' marginal product decreases as more workers are hired. Why is this? Remember the assumption of fixed capital: More and more workers are working with the same amount of capital and there is diminishing marginal productivity.

FIGURE A19-1 (A AND B) Determining How Many Workers to Hire and the Firm's Derived Demand for Labor

The marginal revenue product is any firm's demand curve for labor. Since for a competitive firm $P = MR$, a competitive firm's derived demand curve is its value of the marginal product curve ($P \times MPP$). This curve tells us the additional revenue the firm gets from having an additional worker. From the chart in **(a)** we can see that when the firm increases from 27 to 28 workers, the marginal product per hour for each worker is 9. If the product sells for \$2, then marginal revenue product is \$18, which is one point on the demand curve for labor (point A in **(b)**). When the firm increases from 34 to 35 workers, the value of the marginal product decreases to \$4. This is another point on the firm's derived demand curve (point B in **(b)**). By connecting the two points, as I have done in **(b)**, you can see that the firm's derived demand curve for labor is downward-sloping.

1 Number of Workers	2 Total Product per Hour	3 Marginal Physical Product per Hour	4 Average Product per Hour	5 Marginal Revenue Product (*MRP*)
27	270	9.00	10.00	\$18
28	279	8.00	9.96	16
29	287	7.00	9.90	14
30	294	6.00	9.80	12
31	300	5.00	9.68	10
32	305	4.00	9.53	8
33	309	3.00	9.36	6
34	312	2.00	9.18	4
35	314		8.97	

(a)

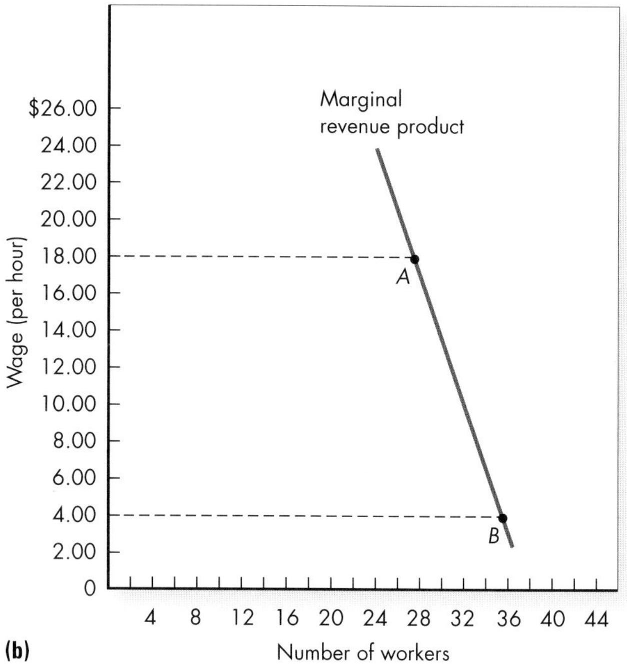

(b)

Column 4 shows **labor productivity**—*the average output per worker,* which is a statistic commonly referred to in economic reports. It's determined by dividing the total output by the number of workers. Column 5 shows the additional worker's marginal revenue product, which, since the firm is assumed to be competitive, is determined by multiplying the price the firm receives for the product it sells ($2) by the worker's marginal physical product.

Column 5, the marginal revenue product, is of central importance to the firm. It tells the firm how much additional money it will make from hiring an additional worker. That marginal revenue product represents a competitive firm's demand for labor.

Figure A19-1(b) graphs the firm's derived demand for labor, based on the data in column 5 of Figure A19-1(a). The resulting curve is the firm's **derived demand curve for labor,** which *shows the maximum amount of labor, measured in labor hours, that a firm will hire.* To see this, let's assume that the wage is $9 and that the firm is hiring 30 workers. If it hires another worker so it has 31 workers, workers' marginal revenue product of $12 exceeds their wage of $9, so the firm can increase profits by doing so. It increases output and profits since the additional revenue the firm gets from increasing workers from 30 to 31 is $12 and the additional cost the firm incurs is the wage of $9.

Now say the firm has hired 4 additional workers so it has 34 workers. As the firm hires more workers, the marginal product of workers declines. As you can see from the graph in Figure A19-1(b), the marginal revenue product of decreasing from 34 to 33 workers is $6. Since the workers' marginal revenue product of $6 is less than their wage of $9, now the firm can increase profits by laying off some workers. Doing so decreases output but increases profit because it significantly increases the average product of the remaining workers.

Only when a worker's wage of $9 equals the marginal revenue product does the firm have no incentive to change the number of employees. In this example, the wage ($9) equals workers' marginal revenue product at 32 workers. When the firm is hiring 32 workers, either hiring another worker or laying off one worker will decrease profits. Decreasing from 32 to 31 workers loses $10 in revenue, but increasing from 32 to 33 workers gains $8 in revenue, but costs $9 in wages. Since the marginal revenue product curve tells the firm, given a wage, how many workers it should hire, *the marginal revenue product curve is the firm's demand curve for labor.*

The fact that the demand curve for labor is downward-sloping means that as more workers are hired, workers' marginal product falls. This might tempt you to think that the last worker hired is inherently less productive than the first worker hired. But that simply can't be because, by assumption, the workers are identical. Thus, the marginal product of any worker must be identical to the marginal product of any other worker, given that a specified number of workers are working. What the falling marginal product means is that *when 30 rather than 25 workers are working,* the marginal product of any one of those 30 workers is less than the marginal product of any one of 25 of those workers when only 25 are working. When the other inputs are constant, hiring an additional worker lowers the marginal product not only of the last worker but also of any of the other workers.

To understand what's going on here, you must remember that when marginal product is calculated, all other inputs are held constant—so if a firm hires another worker, that worker will have to share machines or tools with other workers. When you share tools, you start running into significant bottlenecks, which cause production to fall. That's why the marginal product of workers goes down when a new worker is hired. This assumption that all other factors of production are held constant is an important one. If all other factors of production are increased, it is not at all clear that workers' productivity will fall as output increases.

Why does a firm hire another worker if doing so will lead to a fall in other workers' productivity and, possibly, a fall in the average productivity of all workers? Because the firm is interested in total profit, not productivity. As long as hiring an extra worker increases revenue by more than the worker costs, the firm's total profit increases. A profit-maximizing firm would be crazy not to hire another worker, even if by doing so it lowers the marginal product of the workers.

The economic model of labor markets assumes that marginal productivities can be determined relatively easily. In reality they can't. They require guesses and estimates that are often influenced by a worker's interaction with the person doing the guessing and estimating. Thus, social interaction plays a role in determining wages. If you get along with the manager, his estimate of your marginal productivity is likely to be higher than if you don't. And for some reason, managers' estimates of their own marginal productivity tend to be high. In part because of difficulties in estimating marginal productivities, actual pay can often differ substantially from marginal productivities.

Factors Affecting the Demand for Labor

There are many technical issues that determine how the demand for products is translated through firms into a demand for labor (and other factors of production), but we need not go into them in detail. I will, however, state three general principles:

1. Changes in the demand for a firm's product will be reflected in changes in its demand for labor.
2. The structure of a firm plays an important role in determining its demand for labor.

3. A change in the other factors of production that a firm uses will change its demand for labor.

Let's consider each of these principles in turn.

Changes in the Firm's Demand

The first principle is almost self-evident. An increase in the demand for a product leads to an increase in demand for the laborers who produce that product. The increase in demand pushes the price up, raising the marginal revenue product of labor (which, you'll remember, for a competitive firm is the price of the firm's product times the marginal physical product of labor).

The implications of this first principle, however, are not so self-evident. Often people think of firms' interests and workers' interests as being counter to one another, but this principle tells us that in many ways they are not. What benefits the firm also benefits its workers. Their interests are in conflict only when it comes to deciding how to divide up the total revenues among the owners of the firm, the workers, and the other inputs. Thus, it's not uncommon to see a firm and its workers fighting each other at the bargaining table, but also working together to prevent imports that might compete with the firm's product or to support laws that may benefit the firm.

An example of such cooperation occurred when union workers at a solar energy firm helped fight for an extension of government subsidies for solar energy. Why? Because their contract included a clause that if the solar energy subsidy bill passed, the union workers' wages would be significantly higher than if it didn't. This cooperation between workers and firms has led some economists to treat firms and workers as a single entity, out to get as much as they can as a group. These economists argue that it isn't helpful to separate out factor markets and goods markets. They argue that bargaining power models, which combine factor and goods markets, are the best way to analyze at what level wages will be set. In other words, the cost of labor to a firm should be modeled as if it is determined at the same time that its price and profitability are determined, not separately.

The Structure of the Firm and Its Demand for Labor

The way in which the demand for products is translated into a demand for labor is determined by the structure of the firm. For example, let's consider the difference between a monopolistic industry and a competitive industry. For both, the decision about whether to hire is based on whether the wage is below or above the marginal revenue product. But the firms that make up the two industries calculate their marginal revenue products differently.

The price of a competitive firm's output remains constant regardless of how many units it sells. Thus, its marginal revenue product equals the value of the marginal product. To calculate its marginal revenue product we simply multiply the price of the firm's product by the worker's marginal physical product. For a competitive firm:

Marginal revenue product of a worker =
Value of the worker's marginal product =
MPP × Price of product

The price of a monopolist's product decreases as more units are sold since the monopolist faces a downward-sloping demand curve. The monopolist takes that into account. That's why it focuses on marginal revenue rather than price. As it hires more labor and produces more output, the price it charges for its product will fall. Thus, for a monopolist:

Marginal revenue product of a worker =
MPP × Marginal revenue

Since a monopolist's marginal revenue is always less than price, a monopolist industry will always hire fewer workers than a comparable competitive industry, which is consistent with the result we discussed in the chapter on monopoly: that a monopolistic industry will always produce less than a competitive industry, other things equal.

To ensure that you understand the principle, let's consider the example in Table A19-1, a table of prices, wages, marginal revenues, marginal physical products, and

TABLE A19-1 The Effect of Monopoly and Firm Structure on the Demand for Labor

1	2	3	4	5	6	7
					Marginal Revenue Product	
Number of Workers	Wage	Price *P*	Marginal Revenue (Monopolist) *MR*	Marginal Physical Product *MPP*	Competitive (*MPP* × P)	Monopolist (*MPP* × *MR*)
5	$2.85	$1.00	$.75	5	$5.00	$3.75
6	2.85	.95	.65	3	2.85	1.95
7	2.85	.90	.55	1	.90	.55

marginal revenue products for a firm in a competitive industry and a monopolistic industry.

A firm in a competitive industry will hire up to the point where the wage equals $MPP \times P$ (columns 5×3). This occurs at 6 workers. Hiring either fewer or more workers would mean a loss in profits for a firm in a competitive industry.

Now let's compare the competitive industry with an equivalent monopolistic industry. Whereas the firm in the competitive industry did not take into account the effect an increase in output would have on prices, the monopolist will. It takes into account the fact that to sell the additional output of an additional worker, it must lower the price of the good. The relevant marginal revenue product for the monopolist appears in column 7. At 6 workers, the worker's wage rate of $2.85 exceeds the worker's marginal revenue product of $1.95, which means that the monopolist would hire fewer than 6 workers—5 full-time workers and 1 part-time worker.

As a second example of how the nature of firms affects the translation of demand for products into demand for labor, consider what would happen if workers rather than independent profit-maximizing owners controlled the firms. You saw before that whenever another worker is hired, other inputs constant, the marginal physical product of all similar workers falls. That can contribute to a reduction in existing workers' wages. The profit-maximizing firm doesn't take into account that effect on existing workers' wages. It wants to hold its costs down. If existing workers are making the decisions about hiring, they'll take that wage decline into account. If they believe that hiring more workers will lower their own wage, they have an incentive to see that new workers aren't hired. Thus, like the monopolist, a worker-controlled firm will hire fewer workers than a competitive profit-maximizing firm.

There aren't many worker-controlled firms in the United States, but a number of firms include existing workers' welfare in their decision processes. Moreover, with the growth of the team concept, in which workers are seen as part of a team with managers, existing workers' input into managerial decision making is increasing. In many U.S. firms, workers have some say in whether additional workers will be hired and at what wage they will be hired. Other firms have an implicit understanding or a written contract with existing workers that restricts hiring and firing decisions.

Why do firms consider workers' welfare? They do so to be seen as "good employers," which makes it easier for them to hire in the future. Given the strong social and legal limitations on firms' hiring and firing decisions, one cannot simply apply marginal productivity theory to the real world. One must first understand the institutional and legal structures of the labor market. However, the existence of these other forces doesn't mean that the economic forces represented by marginal productivity don't exist. Rather, it means that firms struggle to find a wage policy that accommodates both economic and social forces in their wage-setting process. For example, in 2004 the United Autoworkers Union negotiated multitier wage contracts with auto-parts suppliers Delphi and Visteon. The companies continued to pay their existing workers a higher wage, but paid new workers a lower wage, even though old and new workers were doing identical jobs. These multitier wage contracts were the result of the interactions of the social and market forces.

Changes in Other Factors of Production

A third principle determining the derived demand for labor is the amount of other factors of production that the firm has. Given a technology, an increase in other factors of production will increase the marginal physical product of existing workers. For example, let's say that a firm buys more machines so that each worker has more machines with which to work. The workers' marginal physical product increases, and the cost per unit of output for the firm decreases. The net effect on the demand for labor is unclear; it depends on how much the firm increases output, how much the firm's price is affected, and how easily one type of input can be substituted for another—or whether it must be used in conjunction with others.

While we can't say what the final effect on demand will be, we can determine the firm's **cost minimization condition**—*where the ratio of marginal product to the price of an input is equal for all inputs.*[1] When a firm is using resources as efficiently as possible, and hence is minimizing costs, the marginal product of each factor of production divided by the price of that factor must equal that of all the other factors. Specifically, the *cost minimization condition* is

$$\frac{MP_l}{w} = \frac{MP_m}{P_m} = \frac{MP_x}{P_x}$$

where

w = Wage rate
l = Labor
m = Machines
x = Any other input

If this cost minimization condition is not met, the firm could hire more of the input with the higher marginal product relative to price, and less of other inputs, and produce the same amount of output at a lower cost.

[1]This condition was explicitly discussed in terms of isocost/isoquant analysis in the appendix to the second production and cost analysis chapter.

Let's consider a numerical example. Say the marginal product of labor is 20 and the wage is $4, while the marginal product of machines is 30 and the rental price of machines is $4. You're called in to advise the firm. You say, "Fire one worker, which will decrease output by 20 and save $4; spend that $4 on machines, which will increase output by 30." Output has increased by 10 while costs have remained constant. As long as the marginal products divided by the prices of the various inputs are unequal, you can make such recommendations to lower cost.

Conclusion

Changes in these factors make demand for labor shift around a lot. This shifting introduces uncertainty into people's lives and into the economic system. Often people attempt to build up institutional barriers to reduce uncertainty—through either social or political forces. Thus, labor markets function under an enormous volume of regulations and rules. We need to remember that while economic factors often lurk behind the scenes to determine pay and hiring decisions, these are often only part of the picture.

Key Terms

cost minimization condition *(457)*
derived demand curve for labor *(455)*
labor productivity *(455)*
marginal physical product (*MPP*) *(454)*
marginal revenue product (*MRP*) *(454)*
value of marginal product (*VMP*) *(454)*

Questions and Exercises

1. Using the information in Figure A19-1, answer the following questions:
   a. If the market wage were $7 an hour, how many workers would the firm hire?
   b. If the price of the firm's product fell to $1, how would your answer to *a* change?
2. If firms were controlled by workers, would they likely hire more or fewer workers? Why?
3. In the 1980s and the 1990s farmers switched from small square bales, which they hired students on summer break to stack for them, to large round bales, which can be handled almost entirely by machines. What is the likely reason for the switch?
4. Should teachers be worried about the introduction of computer- and video-based teaching systems? Why or why not?
5. A competitive firm gets $3 per widget. A worker's average product is 4 and marginal product is 3. What is the maximum the firm should pay the worker?
6. How would your answer to Question 5 change if the firm were a monopolist?
7. Fill in the following table for a competitive firm that has a $2 price for its goods.

Number of Workers	*TP*	*MPP*	*AP*	*MRP*
1	10		____	
		____		____
2	19			
		8		____
3	____		____	
				____
4	____		8.5	
		____		$12
5	____		____	

8. Your manager comes in with three sets of proposals for a new production process. Each process uses three inputs: land, labor, and capital. Under proposal A, the firm would be producing an output where the *MPP* of land is 30, labor is 42, and capital is 36. Under proposal B, at the output produced the *MPP* would be 20 for land, 35 for labor, and 96 for capital. Under proposal C, the *MPP* would be 40 for land, 56 for labor, and 36 for capital. Inputs' cost per hour is $5 for land, $7 for labor, and $6 for capital.
   a. Which proposal would you adopt?
   b. If the price of labor rises to $14, how will your answer change?

Nonwage and Asset Income: Rents, Profits, and Interest

The first man to fence in a piece of land, saying "This is mine," and who found people simple enough to believe him, was the real founder of civil society.

—Jean-Jacques Rousseau

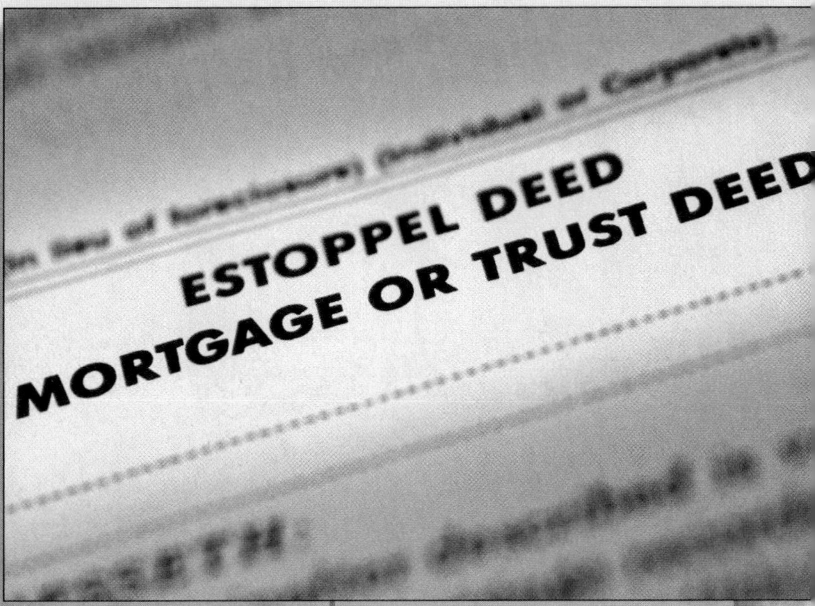

This Web chapter can be found at: www.mhhe.com/colander8e

Chapter Outline

AFTER READING THIS CHAPTER, YOU SHOULD BE ABLE TO:

1. Define *rent* and explain why landowners will bear the entire burden of a tax on land.
2. Explain rent seeking and its relationship to property rights.
3. Differentiate between normal profits and economic profits.
4. Summarize the reasons an entrepreneur searches out market niches.
5. Define *interest* and demonstrate how it is used in determining present value.
6. Use the annuity rule and the rule of 72 to determine present value.
7. Explain the marginal productivity theory of income distribution.

CHAPTER 20

Who Gets What? The Distribution of Income

"God must love the poor," said Lincoln, "or he wouldn't have made so many of them." He must love the rich, or he wouldn't divide so much mazuma among so few of them.

—H. L. Mencken

In 2008, Lawrence J. Ellison, CEO of Oracle, earned $557 million (base pay plus stock options); that's about $10.7 million per week. Assuming he worked 70 hours per week (you have to work hard to earn that kind of money), that's more than $153,022 per hour.

AFTER READING THIS CHAPTER, YOU SHOULD BE ABLE TO:

1. State what a Lorenz curve is.
2. Explain how the definition of poverty is both an absolute and a relative measure.
3. Discuss U.S. income inequality in a global context.
4. Summarize the statistical findings on income and wealth distribution.
5. State two alternative ways to describe income distribution.
6. Explain three problems in determining whether equal income distribution is fair.
7. List three side effects of redistributing income.
8. Summarize the U.S. tax and expenditure programs to redistribute income.

Today, the average doctor earns $180,000 per year; that's $3,462 per week. Assuming she works 70 hours per week (she's conscientious, makes house calls, and spends time with her hospitalized patients), that's $49 per hour.

Joe Smith, a cashier in a fast-food restaurant, earns $8 per hour. But to earn enough for his family to be able to eat, he works a lot of overtime, for which he is paid time-and-a-half, or $12 per hour. So he makes $34,000 per year, or $680 per week, by working 70 hours per week.

Minh Nguyen, a peasant in Vietnam, earns $250 a year; that's $4.80 per week. Assuming he works 70 hours per week (you have to work hard when you are truly poor just to keep from starving), that's 7 cents per hour.

Are such major differences typical of how income is distributed among people in general? Are such differences fair? And if they're unfair, what can be done about them? This chapter addresses such issues. (I should warn you, however: If you're looking for answers, this chapter won't provide them; it will simply make the assumptions on both sides clear.)

The issues addressed in these questions play a fundamentally important role in policy debates today. The reason why is that in the last 20 years the income distribution in the United States has changed considerably. Many formerly middle-income people have moved into the upper-income levels; their wealth and their control of real assets have grown considerably. But simultaneously, lower-income people's income has stagnated or fallen. This change is bringing income distribution issues to center stage in modern policy debates.

Ways of Considering the Distribution of Income

There are several different ways to look at income distribution. In the 1800s, economists were concerned with how income was divided among the owners of businesses (for whom profits were the source of income), the owners of land (who received rent), and workers (who earned wages). That concern reflected the relatively sharp distinctions among social classes that existed in capitalist societies at that time. Landowners, workers, and owners of businesses were separate groups, and few individuals moved from one group to another.

Time has changed that. Today workers, through their pension plans and investments in financial institutions, are owners of over 50 percent of all the shares issued on the New York Stock Exchange. Landowners as a group receive a relatively small portion of total income. Companies are run not by capitalists, but by managers who are, in a sense, workers. In short, the social lines have blurred.

This blurring of the lines between social classes doesn't mean that we can forget the question "Who gets what?" It simply means that our interest in who gets what has a different focus. We no longer focus on classification of income by source. Instead we look at how total income is distributed among income groups. How much income do the top 5 percent get? How much do the top 15 percent get? How much do the bottom 10 percent get? **Share distribution of income** is *the relative division of total income among income groups*.

The share distribution of income is the relative division of total income among income groups.

A second distributional issue economists are concerned with is the **socioeconomic distribution of income** (*the allocation of income among relevant socioeconomic groupings*). How much do blacks get relative to whites? How much do the old get compared to the young? How much do women get compared to men?

The socioeconomic distribution of income is the relative division or allocation of total income among relevant socioeconomic groups.

The Lorenz Curve

The U.S. share distribution of income measures aggregate family income, from the poorest segment of society to the richest. It ranks people by their income and tells how much the richest 20 percent (a quintile) and the poorest 20 percent receive. For example, the poorest 20 percent might get 5 percent of the income and the richest 20 percent might get 40 percent.

Figure 20-1(a) presents the share distribution of income for the United States in 2007. In it you can see that the 20 percent of Americans receiving the lowest level of income got 3.4 percent of the total income. The top 20 percent of Americans received 49.7 percent of the total income. The ratio of the income of the top 20 percent compared to the income of the bottom 20 percent was about 14:1.

A **Lorenz curve** is *a geometric representation of the share distribution of income among families in a given country at a given time*. It measures the cumulative percentage of *families* on the horizontal axis, arranged from poorest to richest, and the cumulative percentage of *family income* on the vertical axis. Since the figure presents cumulative percentages (all of the families with income below a certain level), both axes start at zero and end at 100 percent.

A Lorenz curve is a geometric representation of the share distribution of income among families in a given country at a given time.

A perfectly equal distribution of income would be represented by a diagonal line like the one in Figure 20-1(b). That is, the poorest 20 percent of the families would have 20 percent of the total income (point *A*); the poorest 40 percent of the families would have 40 percent of the income (point *B*); and 100 percent of the families would have 100 percent of the income (point *C*). An unequal distribution of income is represented by a Lorenz curve that's below the diagonal line. All real-world Lorenz curves are below the diagonal because in the real world income is always distributed unequally.

Q-1 When drawing a Lorenz curve, what do you put on the two axes?

The blue line in Figure 20-1(b) represents a Lorenz curve of the U.S. income distribution presented in Figure 20-1(a)'s table. From Figure 20-1(a) you know that, in

FIGURE 20-1 (A AND B) **A Lorenz Curve of U.S. Income**

If income were perfectly equally distributed, the Lorenz curve would be a diagonal line. In (**b**) we see the U.S. Lorenz curve based on the numbers in (**a**) compared to a Lorenz curve reflecting a perfectly equal distribution of income.

Source: *Current Population Reports*, U.S. Bureau of the Census, 2008 (www.census.gov).

Income Quintile	Percentage of Total Family Income	Cumulative Percentage of Total Family Income
Lowest fifth	3.4%	3.4%
Second fifth	8.7	12.1
Third fifth	14.8	26.9
Fourth fifth	23.4	50.3
Highest fifth	49.7	100.0

(a)

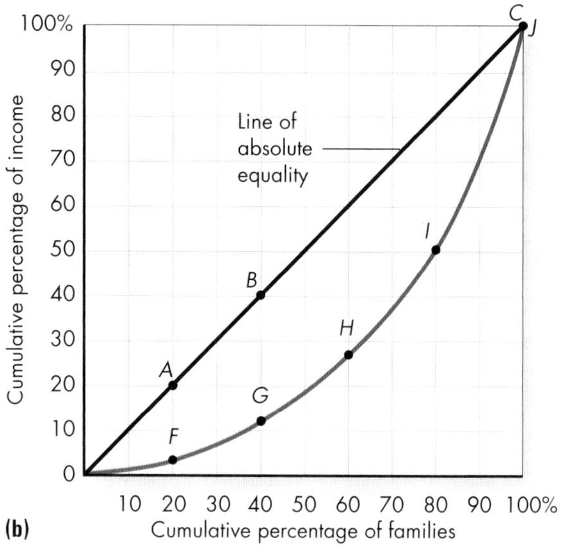

(b)

2007, the bottom 20 percent of the families in the United States received 3.4 percent of the income. Point *F* in Figure 20-1(b) represents that combination of percentages (20 percent and 3.4 percent). To find what the bottom 40 percent received, we must add the income percentage of the bottom 20 percent and the income percentage of the next 20 percent. Doing so gives us 12.1 percent (3.4 plus 8.7 percent from column 2 of Figure 20-1(a)). Point G in Figure 20-1(b) represents the combination of percentages (40 percent and 12.1 percent). Continuing this process for points *H*, *I*, and *C*, you get a Lorenz curve that shows the share distribution of income in the United States in 2007.

U.S. Income Distribution over Time

From 1929 to 1970, income inequality in the United States decreased. From 1970 to 2007, it increased.

Lorenz curves are most useful in visual comparisons of income distribution over time and between countries. Figure 20-2 presents Lorenz curves for the United States in 1929, 1970, and 2007. They show that from 1929 to 1970 the share distribution of income became more equal. (The curve for 1970 is closer to being a diagonal than the curve for 1929.) Income of the bottom fifth of families rose by a much higher proportion than did income of the top fifth. That was a continuation of a trend that had begun in the 1920s. In the 1970s that trend stopped and began to reverse. As you can see, from 1970 to 2007 income distribution became less equal. (The curve for 2007 is further from being diagonal than is the curve for 1970.) The income of the bottom fifth of families fell by over 10 percent, while the income of the top fifth rose significantly.

Important reasons for the initial increase in equality are the redistribution measures instituted by the U.S. government between the 1930s and the 1970s, including welfare programs, unemployment insurance, Social Security, progressive taxation (taxation of higher income at higher rates, lower income at lower rates), and improved macroeconomic performance of the economy.

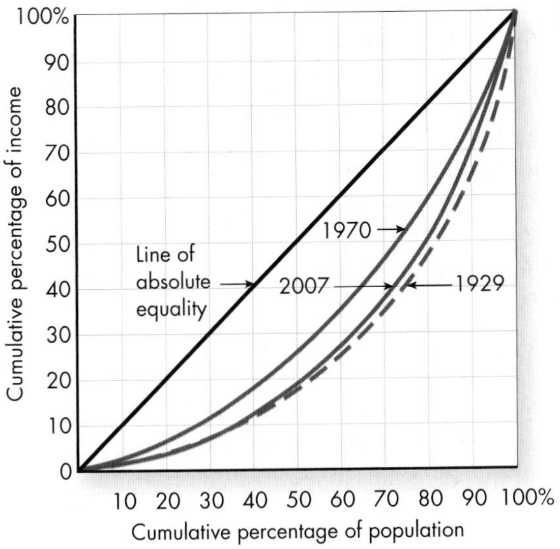

FIGURE 20-2
Lorenz Curves for the United States: 1929, 1970, and 2007

The amount of inequality of income distribution has fluctuated in the United States. Until about 1970, it decreased; since then it has increased.

Source: *Current Population Reports*, U.S. Bureau of the Census, 2008 (www.census.gov).

The trend back toward greater inequality starting in the 1970s was caused by a fall in the real income of the poor, when their wage increases didn't keep up with price increases. While wages have fluctuated with the business cycle since then, the trend toward greater inequality has continued. Taxes have become less progressive, government funding for social programs has fallen, and the wages of unskilled and medium-skilled workers have been squeezed by an influx of immigrants into the United States who are willing to work for low wages, and by global competition.

The distribution of income over time is not only affected by business cycles, government policy, and competitive pressures; it is also affected by demographic and technological factors. Many families have relatively low income in their early years, relatively higher income in their middle years, and then relatively low income again in their retirement years. The Lorenz curve reflects these differences, so even if lifetime income were equally distributed, income in any one year would not be. Moreover, when the percentages of these groups change, the Lorenz curve will change. For example, when the baby-boom generation retires and no longer works, collective income will fall. That decline in income relative to the income of the smaller number of working families will affect the Lorenz curve.

The effect of technology is a bit different; that effect is easiest to convey with an example. Before the development of radio, TV, records, tapes, CDs, and MP3 players, the number of people who could listen to a performer was limited by how many people could fit in a concert hall. Without recordings or broadcasting to satisfy the demand for entertainment, that meant lots of local singers could earn a decent, but not phenomenal, wage. As recording, broadcasting, and transportation technology progressed, the number of people who could listen to a performance was nearly unlimited and "superstars" were born. The "almost superstars" lost out and were destined to sing for low wages at weddings, bar mitzvah parties, and church recitals, while the superstars became multimillionaires. Similar changes occurred in sports and other performance activities. The point of the example is that technology can significantly influence income distribution. University of Chicago economist Kevin Murphy argues that as global competition continues to grow, and as telecommunications networks expand, the pressure for income inequality to increase will continue.

Technology has played a role in increasing income inequality.

Defining Poverty

Poverty can be defined as a relative or absolute concept.

Much of the government's concern with income distribution has centered on the poorest group—those in poverty. Defining poverty is not easy. Do we want to define it as an absolute amount of real income that does not change over time? If poverty were defined as an *absolute* amount of real income, few in the United States would be in poverty today; most of today's poor have higher real incomes than did the middle class 50 or 60 years ago. Or do we want to define it as a *relative* concept that rises as the average income in the society rises? For example, anyone with an income of less than one-fifth of the average income could be defined as being in poverty. If that relative concept of poverty were chosen, then the proportion of people classified as poor would always be the same.

The Official Definition of Poverty

Q-2 Is the U.S. definition of poverty an absolute or a relative definition?

Poverty is defined by the U.S. government as having an income equal to or less than three times an average family's minimum food expenditures as calculated by the U.S. Department of Agriculture.

The United States uses a definition of poverty that is a combination of a relative and an absolute measure. Thus, it satisfies neither those who favor an absolute measure nor those who favor a relative measure, and there are calls to increase and calls to decrease the **poverty threshold**—*the income below which a family is considered to live in poverty.* The official definition of poverty is the following:

> A family is in poverty if its income is equal to or less than three times an average family's minimum food expenditures as calculated by the U.S. Department of Agriculture.

The minimum weekly food budget includes 4 eggs, 1½ pounds of meat, 3 pounds of potatoes, about 4 pounds of vegetables, and other foods; the cost is about $33.97 per person per week. By the latest calculations, that means that for a family of four, the poverty line is $21,200.

As Table 20-1 shows, using the official poverty measure, the number of people in poverty decreased in the 1960s and then began increasing in the 1970s. In 2007, 37.3 million Americans lived below the poverty threshold.

TABLE 20-1 Number and Percentage of Persons in Poverty

	Number of People (in millions)	Percentage of Population	Poverty Income of Family of 4* (in current dollars)
1960	39.9	22.2%	$ 3,022
1970	24.4	12.6	3,986
1980	29.3	13.0	8,414
1990	33.6	13.5	13,359
2000	31.6	11.3	17,603
2001	32.9	11.7	18,100
2002	34.6	12.1	18,224
2003	35.9	12.5	18,660
2004	37.0	12.7	19,307
2005	37.0	12.6	19,971
2006	36.5	12.3	20,794
2007	37.3	12.5	21,027
2008			21,200

*Family of 4 with 2 related children.

Source: *Current Population Reports*, U.S. Bureau of the Census, 2008 (www.census.gov).

Debates about the Definition of Poverty

The minimum food budget used to determine the poverty line was determined in the 1960s and has not been recalculated to account for rising standards of living. Thus, it is in principle an absolute measure. Starting in 1969, however, the amount needed to buy that food is adjusted by the rate of inflation rather than by the rise in the price of the originally selected foods. Since food prices have risen by less than the rise in the general price level, the poverty threshold has gone up by more than it would have had food prices been used. That means the definition includes significant aspects of relativity and had a purely absolute measure been used, the poverty rate would be considerably lower.

Those who favor a relative measure of poverty argue that our current poverty measure is too low. They point out that since food is now closer to a fourth of a family's total budget, it would make sense to increase the poverty threshold by multiplying food expenditures by a number a bit less than four rather than by three. Doing so would raise the poverty threshold for a family of 4 to about $28,000 and would add millions of people to the poverty roll.

There are arguments that the poverty line is both too high and too low.

Those who favor an absolute measure of poverty argue that the current measure is too high. They point out that U.S. poverty figures do not include in-kind (noncash) transfers such as food stamps and housing assistance. Nor does the current poverty measure take into account underreporting of income, or the savings people have. (Many elderly people may have low incomes but significant wealth, which they could choose to spend.) If we make adjustments for in-kind transfers and underreporting of income, the official number of people in poverty decreases to about 60 percent of the official number. University of Texas economist Daniel Slesnick takes it further and points out that, since the price of food has increased at less than the rate of inflation, a much lower level of expenditures than the amount used to calculate the poverty threshold will provide a "nutritionally adequate diet." Slesnick calculated that when one takes the decrease in the relative price of food into account, the number of people in poverty would have fallen to one-seventh the official count.

The moral of this debate: Like most economic statistics, poverty statistics should be used with care.

Like most economic statistics, poverty statistics should be used with care.

The Costs of Poverty

Web Note 20.1
Poverty and Achievement

People who favor policies aimed at achieving equality of income argue that poverty brings significant costs to society. One is that society suffers when some of its people are in poverty, just as the entire family suffers when one member doesn't have enough to eat. Most people derive pleasure from knowing that others are not in poverty.

Another cost of poverty is that it increases incentives for crime. People with little income have little to lose. As people's incomes increase they have more to lose by committing crimes, and therefore fewer crimes are committed. Consistent with this argument, the crime rate has largely declined in the 1990s and early 2000s, as the economy grew. When the economy entered a severe recession in 2008, crime rates were expected to rise.

Those who favor equality of income argue that the increased poverty in the late 1970s and 1980s represents a failure of the economic policies of that period. Others respond that the widening gap between rich and poor is not the result of government tax and spending policies. It has more to do with demographic changes. For example, the number of single-parent families increased dramatically during this period, while rapid growth of the labor force depressed wages for young unskilled workers.

Advocates of reducing poverty respond that this argument is unconvincing. They argue that the tax cuts of the 1980s favored the rich while decreased funding for government programs hurt the poor. To compensate, they argue, free day care should be provided for children so that single parents can work full-time, and government should

ADDED DIMENSION

The Gini Coefficient

A second measure economists use to talk about the degree of income inequality is the Gini coefficient of inequality. The Gini coefficient is derived from the Lorenz curve by comparing the area between the (1) Lorenz curve and the diagonal (area *A*) and (2) the total area of the triangle below the diagonal (areas *A* and *B*). That is:

Gini coefficient = Area *A*/(Areas *A* + *B*)

A Gini coefficient of zero would be perfect equality, since area *A* is 0 if income is perfectly equally distributed. The highest the Gini coefficient can go is 1. So all Gini coefficients must be between 0 and 1. The lower the Gini coefficient, the closer the income distribution is to being equal. The Gini coefficient for the United States was 0.463 in 2007.

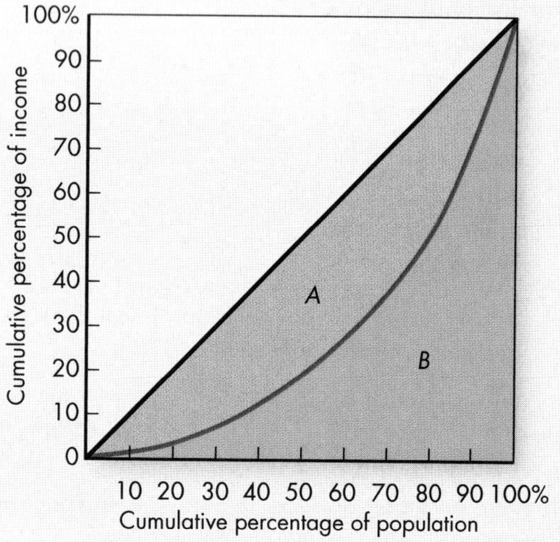

The following table gives Gini coefficients for a number of other countries. The Gini coefficients for transitional economies such as the Slovak Republic have risen over the last few years because they are now market economies and their incomes are less equally distributed.

Gini Coefficients for Selected Countries

Algeria	.353
Bangladesh	.334
Brazil	.570
Canada	.326
Czech Republic	.254
Denmark	.247
Germany	.283
Guatemala	.551
Hungary	.269
Indonesia	.343
Japan	.249
Latvia	.377
Netherlands	.309
Panama	.561
Philippines	.445
Romania	.310
Slovak Republic	.284
South Africa	.578
Thailand	.420
United Kingdom	.360
United States	.463

Source: 2007/08 *Human Development Reports* (hdrstats.undp.org).

supplement the low wages of the working poor. They argue that demographic changes are not a valid excuse for ducking a question of morality.

Social and Economic Mobility

Concern about poverty in the United States has been lessened by the belief that the United States has significant economic and social mobility. Individuals who worked hard could escape poverty, and individuals who didn't work hard would end up, or remain, in poverty. While everyone knew that the poor had it harder, and the rich easier, the United States was seen as a meritocracy, where hard work and ability were key to advancing both economically and socially. In the 1960s and 1970s, studies found that the United States had significant upward and downward mobility, confirming this belief. Recent studies, however, have questioned this view.

Specifically, a recent study by economist Bernt Bratsberg and his colleagues discovered that income mobility has significantly declined in the United States, and that now, the United States has less mobility than Europe. They determined this by ranking countries on a scale of zero to one, with zero meaning perfect mobility (a child's income bears no relation to its parent's income) and one meaning no mobility (a child's income is identical to its parent's income). They found that, for sons, Sweden scored a .2, Britain scored a .36, and the United States scored a .54, suggesting that the United States had only about half as much social mobility as did Sweden and Britain. The situation was worse at the bottom; children born to a family in the bottom fifth of the U.S. income distribution were the least likely to move up. Other studies have confirmed this finding; it is harder for people today to surpass their parents on the income scale than it was a generation ago, and it is much harder for someone in the United States compared to someone in Europe to move up the income scale.

International Dimensions of Income Inequality

When considering income distribution, we usually are looking at conditions within a single country. For example, an American among the richest 5 percent of the U.S. population gets approximately 30 times what an American who is among the poorest 20 percent of the American people gets.

Web Note 20.2
International Income Distribution Data

There are other ways to look at income. We might judge income inequality in the United States relative to income inequality in other countries. Is the U.S. distribution of income more or less equal than another country's? We could also look at how income is distributed among countries. Even if income is relatively equally distributed within countries, it may be unequally distributed among countries.

Comparing Income Distribution across Countries

Figure 20-3 gives us a sense of how the distribution of income in the United States compares to that in other countries. We see that the United States has significantly more income inequality than Sweden, but significantly less than Brazil (and many other developing and newly industrialized countries).

The United States has less income inequality than most developing countries but more income inequality than many developed countries.

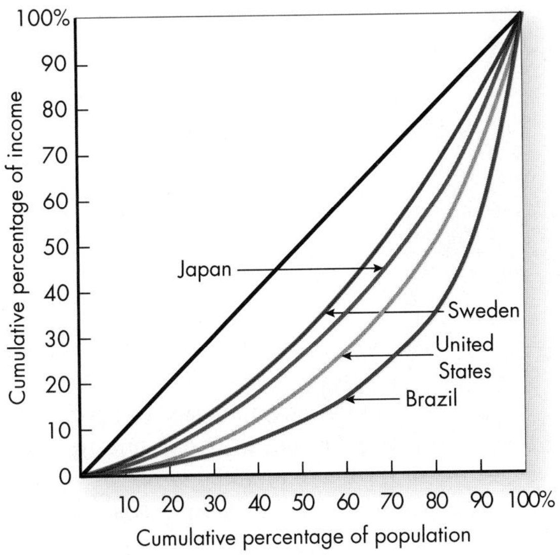

FIGURE 20-3
U.S. Income Distribution Compared to That of Other Countries

Among countries of the world, the United States has neither the most equal nor the most unequal distribution of income.

Source: *World Development Report*, The World Bank (www.worldbank.org).

Q-3 How does the income distribution in the United States compare with that in other countries?

An important reason why the United States has more income inequality than Sweden is that Sweden's tax system is more progressive. Until recently (when Sweden's socialist party lost power), the top marginal tax rate on the highest incomes in Sweden was 80 percent, compared to about 35 percent in the United States. Given this difference, it isn't surprising that Sweden has less income inequality.

Income Distribution among Countries

World income inequality is much greater than country income inequality.

When we consider the distribution of world income, the picture becomes even more unequal than the picture we see within countries. The reason is clear: Income is highly unequally distributed among countries. The average per capita income of the richest countries in the world is more than 100 times the average income of the poorest countries of the world. Thus, a Lorenz curve of world income would show much more inequality than the Lorenz curve for a particular country. Worldwide, income inequality is enormous. A minimum level of income in the United States would be a wealthy person's income in a poor country like Bangladesh.

The Total Amount of Income in Various Countries

To gain a better picture of income distribution problems, you need to consider not only the division of income but also the total amounts of income in various countries. Figure 20-4 presents per capita income (gross domestic product) for various countries. Looking at the enormous differences of income among countries, we must ask which is more important: the distribution of income or the absolute level of income. Which would you rather be: one of four members in a family that has an income of $3,000 a year, which places you in the top 10 percent of Bangladesh's income distribution, or one of four members of a family with an income of $12,000 (four times as much), which places you in the bottom 10 percent of the income earners in the United States?

FIGURE 20-4 Per Capita Income (Gross Domestic Product) in Various Countries

Income is unequally distributed among the countries of the world. These relative comparisons change considerably over time as exchange rates fluctuate. These estimates are done using the Atlas method, which averages exchange rates over adjacent years. The PPP estimates would show less inequality.

Source: *World Bank Key Development Indicators*, 2008 (www.worldbank.org).

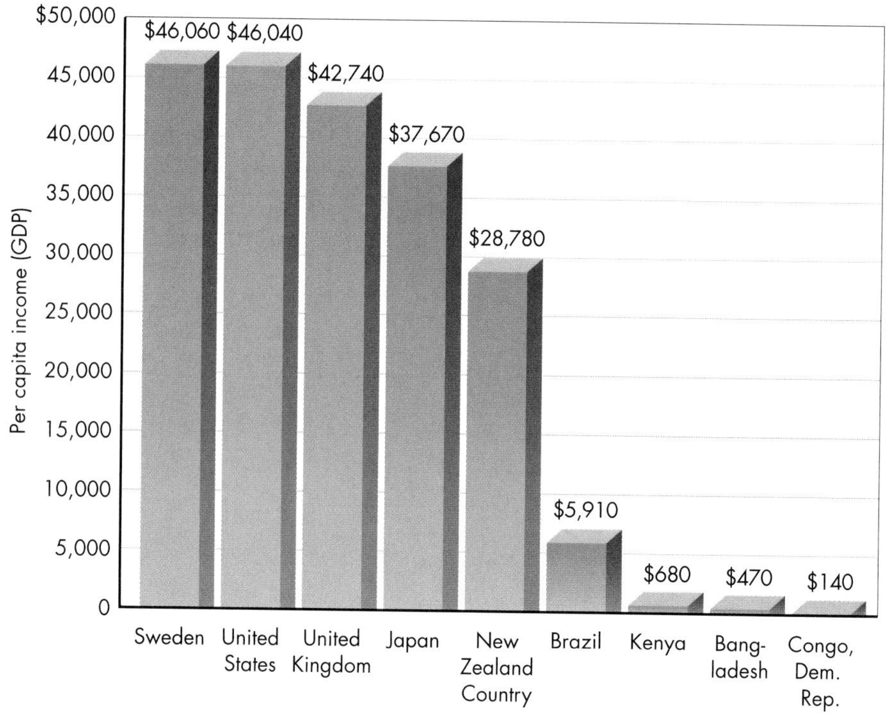

The Distribution of Wealth

In considering equality, two measures are often used: *equality of wealth* and *equality of income*. Because of space limitations, my focus will be on income, but I want to mention wealth. **Wealth** is *the value of the things individuals own less the value of what they owe*. It is a *stock* concept representing the value of assets such as houses, buildings, and machines. For example, a farmer who owns a farm with a net worth of $1 million is wealthy compared to an investment banker with a net worth of $225,000.

Wealth is the value of assets individuals own less the value of what they owe.

Income is *payments received plus or minus changes in value in a person's assets in a specified time period*. In contrast to wealth, income is a *flow* concept. It's a stream through time. That farmer might have an income of $20,000 a year while the investment banker might have an income of $80,000 a year. The farmer, with $1 million worth of assets, is wealthier than the investment banker, but the investment banker has a higher income.

Income is payments received plus or minus changes in value of a person's assets in a specified time period.

A Lorenz Curve of the Distribution of Wealth

Figure 20-5 compares the Lorenz curve for wealth in the United States with the Lorenz curve for income in the United States. You can see that wealth in the United States is more unequally distributed than income and that the bottom 40 percent of the U.S. population has close to zero wealth.

In the United States, wealth is significantly more unequally distributed than is income.

How Much Wealth Do the Wealthy Have?

Relative comparisons such as those depicted by Lorenz curves don't give you a sense of how much wealth it takes to be "wealthy." The following numbers provide you with a better sense. Bill Gates, who founded Microsoft and became the richest person in the United States, had a net worth of about $66 billion in 2008. Four of the 15 wealthiest people in the United States were from the Walton family (whose father founded Wal-Mart), each with $23 billion. Most of us have little chance of joining that group; in fact, most of us have little possibility of becoming one of the top 5 percent of the wealthholders in the United States, which would require total wealth of at least $4 million. Once there was a time when people's ultimate financial goal was to be a

Billionaires often lose a billion here, gain a billion there; sometimes they even become multibillionaires. Seldom do they become poor.

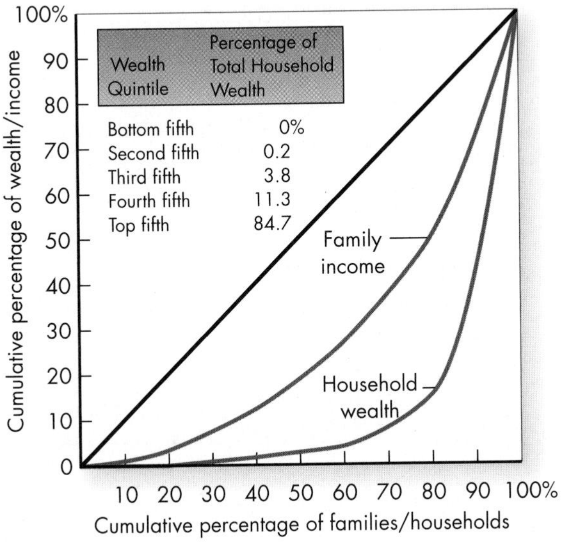

FIGURE 20-5
Wealth Distribution in the United States and Wealth Compared to Income

Wealth is much more unequally distributed than income in the United States. In fact, the lowest 40 percent of the population has 1.2 percent of the wealth; these people have borrowed nearly as much as they own.

Source: U.S. Bureau of the Census and Edward N. Wolf, New York University (with permission).

The millionaire's club is no longer highly exclusive.

millionaire. In the 2000s, the ultimate financial goal for the wealthiest people is to be a billionaire. The millionaire's club is no longer highly exclusive.

Of course, people in the club don't always stay there; the club is constantly changing. For example, a number of families who were in the club earlier are no longer in it. Many billionaires lost billions in the recent collapse of the world stock market and fell off the list of the world list of wealthiest people. Today, some of these people and families might only be multimillionaires.

Socioeconomic Dimensions of Income Inequality

The share distribution of inequality is only one of the dimensions that inequality of income and wealth can take. As I mentioned before, the distribution of income according to source of income (wages, rents, and profits) was once considered important. Today's focus is on the distribution of income based on race, ethnic background, geographic region, and other socioeconomic factors such as gender and type of job.

Income Distribution According to Socioeconomic Characteristics

Table 20-2 gives an idea of the distribution of income according to socioeconomic characteristics.

TABLE 20-2 Various Socioeconomic Income Distribution Designations

Median Income, 2007 By Occupational Category	Male	Female
Management	$71,949	$52,510
Business and Financial	64,965	46,974
Health care support	42,323	35,719
Protective service	40,266	31,997
Food preparation	21,765	18,060
Building and grounds cleaning and maintenance	26,291	19,093
Personal care	30,575	21,256
Sales	48,392	30,777
Office and administrative support	36,466	31,173
Farming, fishing, and forestry	23,117	18,564
Construction and extraction	35,771	32,011
Installation, maintenance, and repair	41,472	40,325
Production	36,565	24,722
Transportation and material moving	50,979	32,409

By Sex	Median Income 1980	1990	2000	2007
Male	$15,340	$27,866	$39,792	$45,113
Female	6,772	19,816	29,334	35,102

By Age, 2007	Median Household Income
15–24	$31,790
25–34	51,016
35–44	62,124
45–54	65,476
55–64	57,386
Over 65	28,305

By Race, 2007	Median Household Income
Asian	$66,103
White	54,920
Black	33,916
Hispanic origin	38,679

Source: *Current Population Reports*, *Consumer Income*, U.S. Bureau of the Census (www.census.gov).

You can see that income differs substantially by type of job, leading some economists to argue that a new professional/nonprofessional class distinction is arising in the United States. Substantial differences also exist between the incomes of women and men, and between whites and blacks.

Income Distribution According to Class

As I stated above, early economists focused on the distribution of income by wages, profits, and rent because that division corresponded to their class analysis of society. Landowners received rent, capitalists received profit, and workers received wages. Tensions among these classes played an important part in economists' analyses of the economy and policy.

Even though class divisions by income source have become blurred, other types of socioeconomic classes have taken their place. The United States has a kind of upper class. In fact, a company in the United States publishes the *Social Register,* containing the names and pedigrees of about 35,000 socially prominent people who might be categorized "upper class." Similarly, it is possible to further divide the U.S. population into a middle class and a lower class.

The United States has socioeconomic classes with some mobility among classes. This is not to say such classes should exist; it is only to say that they do exist.

Class divisions are no longer determined solely by income source. For example, upper-class people do not necessarily receive their income from rent and profits. CEOs of major companies are generally considered upper class, and they receive much of their income as payment for their services. Today we have "upper-class" people who derive their income from wages and "lower-class" people who derive their income from profits (usually in the form of pensions, which depend on profits from the investment of pension funds in stocks and bonds). Of course, once people become rich, they earn interest and profits on their wealth as well as income.

The Importance of the Middle Class What has made the most difference in today's class structure in the United States compared to its class structure in earlier periods and to the structure in today's developing countries is the tremendous growth in the relative size of the middle class. Economists used to see the class structure as a pyramid. From a base composed of a large lower class, the pyramid tapered upward through a medium-sized middle class to a peak occupied by the upper class (Figure 20-6(a)). The

FIGURE 20-6 (A, B, AND C) The Class System as a Pyramid, a Diamond, and a Pentagon

The class structure in developing countries is a pyramid; in the United States the class structure is more like a pentagon.

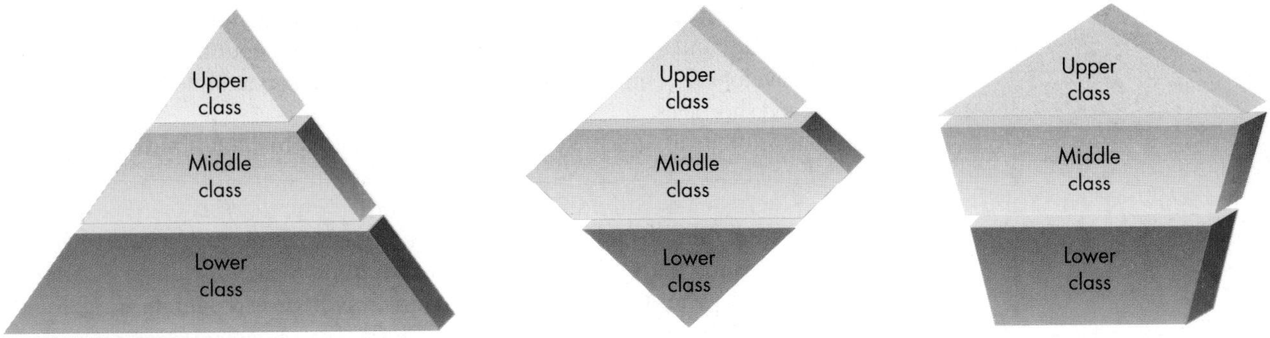

(a) A Pyramid Class Structure **(b) A Diamond Class Structure** **(c) A Pentagonal Class Structure**

In the United States, the middle class is the largest class.

class structure is still pyramidal in most developing countries. However, in the United States in the 1960s and 1970s, the middle class grew, and the geometric portrayal of the U.S. class structure changed from a pyramid in Figure 20-6(a) to the diamond shape in Figure 20-6(b) with a small upper class, a large middle class, and a small lower class. In the last 20 years, that diamond geometric portrayal has become less appropriate as some in the middle class have done well and moved into the upper middle class, while others have done poorly, expanding the number at the bottom. Today, the pentagonal shape shown in Figure 20-6(c) seems a more appropriate description of the class structure in the United States. The middle class is still relatively large, but the bottom, what some have described as an underclass—a group of people at the bottom who are just getting along and, while they may temporarily escape poverty, are always on the edge of the poverty line—has gotten larger too. This underclass includes a disproportionate percentage of blacks, and has been expanded by a significant number of illegal immigrants. With the decline of social mobility in the United States, this group of people and their children has only a slight chance of entering into the middle class.

Q-4 How have distributional fights about income changed over time?

Whatever the best geometric portrayal of the class system, the increase in the relative size of the middle class in developed countries has significantly blurred the distinction between capitalists and workers. In early capitalist society, the distributional fight (the fight over relative income shares) was largely between workers and capitalists. In modern market-based societies, the distributional fight is among various types of individuals. Union workers are pitted against nonunion workers; salaried workers are pitted against workers paid by the hour. The old are pitted against the young; women are pitted against men; blacks are pitted against Hispanics and Asians, and all three groups are pitted against whites.

Distributional Questions and Tensions in Society While mainstream economists tend to focus on the share distribution of income, nonmainstream economists tend to emphasize class and group structures in their analysis. Radical economists emphasize the control that the upper class has over the decision process and the political process. Libertarian economists emphasize the role of special interests of all types in shaping government policy. Both radical and libertarian analyses bring out the tensions among classes in society much better than does the mainstream, classless analysis.

Both radical and libertarian analyses bring out the tensions among classes in society much better than does mainstream classless analysis.

When people identify with a particular class or group, they will often work to further the interests of that class or group. They also generally have stronger feelings about inequalities among classes or groups than when they lack that sense of class or group identity. Using a classless analysis means overlooking the implications of class and group solidarity in affecting the tensions in society.

Those tensions show up every day in political disputes over the tax system, in the quiet fuming of individuals as they see someone else earning more for doing the same job, and in strikes and even riots. Such tensions exist in all countries. In some transitional and developing countries, they break out into the open as armed insurrections or riots over food shortages.

Web Note 20.3
Contrasting Analyses

Those tensions have been kept to a minimum in American society. A majority of Americans believe that income distribution is sufficiently fair for them to accept their share more or less contentedly. To remedy the unfairness that does exist, they don't demand that the entire system be replaced. Instead they work for change within the present system. They look to affirmative action laws, comparable worth laws, minimum wage laws, and social welfare programs for any improvement they perceive to be necessary or desirable. There's much debate about whether these government actions have achieved the desired ends, but the process itself reduces tensions and has worked toward maintaining the entire system.

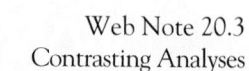

People's acceptance of the U.S. economic system is based not only on what the distribution of income is but also on what people think it should be and what they consider fair. It is to that question that we now turn.

Income Distribution and Fairness

Judgments about whether the distribution of income is fair, or should be changed, are normative ones, based on the values the analyst applies to the situation. Value judgments necessarily underlie all policy prescriptions.

Value judgments necessarily underlie all policy prescriptions.

Philosophical Debates about Equality and Fairness

Depending on one's values, any income distribution can be justified. For example, Friedrich Nietzsche, the 19th-century German philosopher, argued that society's goal should be to support its supermen—its best and brightest. Lesser individuals' duty should be to work for the well-being of these supermen. Bertrand de Juvenal, a 20th-century philosopher, has argued that a high level of income inequality is necessary to sustain the arts, beauty, education, and civilization. He and others say that a world of equally distributed income would be a world without beauty. Even if we don't personally own beautiful, expensive homes or aren't devoted opera fans, these philosophers argue, our lives are improved because some people do own such homes and because opera performances exist. Inequality creates diversity that enriches the lives of everyone.

Other philosophers disagree strongly. They argue that equality itself is the overriding goal. That view is embodied in the Declaration of Independence: "We hold these truths to be self-evident, that all men are created equal." And for many people the inherent value of equality is not open to question—it is simply self-evident.

Q-5 Is it self-evident that greater equality of income would make the society a better place to live? Why?

Believing that equality is an overriding goal does not necessarily imply that income should be equally distributed. For example, John Rawls (a Harvard University professor who believed that equality is highly desirable and that society's goal should be to maximize the welfare of the least well-off) agreed that to meet that goal some inequality is necessary. Rawls argued that if, in pursuing equality, you actually make the least well-off worse off than they otherwise would have been, then you should not pursue equality any further. For example, say under one policy there would be perfect equality and everyone would receive $10,000 per year. Under another policy, the least well-off person receives $12,000 per year and all others receive $40,000. Rawls argued that the second policy is preferable to the first even though it involves more inequality.

Economists, unlike philosophers, are not concerned about justifying any particular distribution of income. In their objective role, economists limit themselves to explaining the effects that various policies will have on the distribution of income; they let the policy makers judge whether those effects are desirable.

However, in order to judge economic policies, you, in your role as a citizen who elects policy makers, must make certain judgments about income distribution because all real-world economic policies have distribution effects. Accordingly, a brief discussion of income distribution and fairness is in order.

Fairness and Equality

The U.S. population has a strong general tendency to favor equality—equality is generally seen as fair. Most people, including me, share that view. However, in some instances equality of income is not directly related to people's view of fairness. For example, consider this distribution of income between John and Fred:

John gets $50,000 a year.

Fred gets $12,000 a year.

Q-6 You are dividing a pie among five individuals. What would be a fair distribution of that pie?

ADDED DIMENSION

What Should Be the Goal of Economic Policy?

Today, most discussions of economic policy focus on a goal of increasing income: Policies that achieve higher income are good; policies that do not are bad. Historically, that has not always been the goal. In the 1800s the economic policy focused on basic goods—distinguishing necessities from luxuries. Only policies that increased basic goods were good; the welfare implications of policies that increased luxuries were much more problematic.

The 1930s marked a major change in how economic policy was conceived. Economics began focusing much more on utility, downplaying the distinction between luxuries and basic goods. With this change, the goal of economic policy focused much more on total income, regardless of how that income was divided. The division of goods into necessities and luxuries was seen as adding a normative element to policy that was outside the purview of positive economics.

Recently, Nobel Prize–winning economist Amartya Sen has argued against that utilitarian approach, pointing out that normative elements are unavoidable in policy analysis. He argues that using income as a measure of welfare is not the best approach and has suggested replacing it with a "capabilities" measure. For Sen, the goal of economic policy should be to increase a society's capabilities, which he defines as an individual's freedom within that society to achieve a particular life. For Sen, capabilities are best measured by basic indicators such as life expectancy, literacy, and infant mortality rates—not by income. Poor ratings on such indicators impede people from leading good and happy lives. Sen's work is controversial, but it is important in reminding us that the goals of economic policy should always be kept in mind and that we should not simply accept the goal as being an increase in total income.

Think a minute. Is that fair?

The answer I'm hoping for is that you don't yet have enough information to make the decision.

Fairness has many dimensions and it is often difficult to say what is fair and what isn't.

Here's some more information. Say that John gets that $50,000 for holding down three jobs, while Fred gets his $12,000 for sitting around doing nothing. At this point, many of us would argue that it's possible John should be getting even more than $50,000 and Fred should be getting less than $12,000.

Three problems in determining whether an equal income distribution is fair are

1. People don't start from equivalent positions.
2. People's needs differ.
3. People's efforts differ.

But wait! What if we discover that Fred is an invalid and unless his income increases to $15,000 a year he will die? Most of us would change our minds again and argue that Fred deserves more, regardless of how much John works.

But wait! How about if, after further digging, we discover that Fred is an invalid because he squandered his health on alcohol, drugs, and fried foods? In that case some people would likely change their minds again as to whether Fred deserves more.

By now you should have gotten my point. Looking only at a person's income masks many dimensions that most people consider important in making value judgments about fairness.

Fairness as Equality of Opportunity

When most people talk about believing in equality of income, they often mean they believe in equality of opportunity for comparably endowed individuals to earn income. If equal opportunity of equals leads to inequality of income, then the inequality of income is fair. Unfortunately, there's enormous latitude for debate on what constitutes equal opportunity of equals.

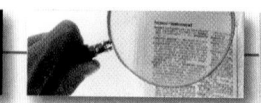

In the real world, needs differ, desires differ, and abilities differ. Should these differences be considered relevant differences in equality? You must answer that question before you can judge any economic policy because to make a judgment on whether an economic policy should or should not be adopted, you must make a judgment about whether a policy's effect on income is fair. In making those judgments, most people rely on their immediate gut reaction. I hope what you have gotten out of the discussion about John and Fred and equality of opportunity is the resolve to be cautious about trusting your gut reactions. The concept of fairness is crucial and complicated, and it deserves deeper consideration than just a gut reaction.

The concept of fairness is crucial and complicated, and it deserves deeper consideration than just a gut reaction.

The Problems of Redistributing Income

Let's now say that we have considered all the issues discussed so far in this chapter and have concluded that some redistribution of income from the rich to the poor is necessary if society is to meet our ideal of fairness. How do we go about redistributing income?

First, we must consider what programs exist and what their negative side effects might be. The side effects can be substantial and can subvert the intention of the program so that far less money is available overall for redistribution and inequality is reduced less than we might expect.

Three Important Side Effects of Redistributive Programs

Three important side effects that economists have found in programs to redistribute income are

1. A tax may result in a switch from labor to leisure.
2. People may attempt to avoid or evade taxes, leading to a decrease in measured income.
3. Redistributing money may cause people to make themselves look as if they're more needy than they really are.

Three side effects of redistribution of income are

1. The labor/leisure incentive effect.
2. The avoidance and evasion incentive effect.
3. The incentive effect to look more needy than you are.

All economists believe that people will change their behavior in response to changes in taxation and income redistribution programs. These responses, called *incentive effects of taxation*, are important and must be taken into account in policy making. But economists differ significantly in the importance they assign to incentive effects, and empirical evidence doesn't resolve the question. Some economists believe that incentive effects are so important that little taxation for redistribution should take place. They argue that when the rich do well, the total pie is increased so much that the spillover benefits to the poor are greater than the proceeds the poor would get from redistribution. For example, supporters of this view argue that the growth in capitalist economies was made possible by entrepreneurs. Because those entrepreneurs invested in new technology, income in society grew. Moreover, those entrepreneurs paid taxes. The benefits resulting from entrepreneurial action spilled over to the poor, making the poor far better off than any redistribution would. The fact that some of those entrepreneurs became rich is irrelevant because their actions made all society better off.

Q-7 When determining the effects of programs that redistribute income, can one reasonably assume that other things will remain equal?

Other economists believe that there should be significant taxation for redistribution. While they agree that sometimes the incentive effects are substantial, they see the goal of equality overriding these effects.

Politics, Income Redistribution, and Fairness

We began this discussion of income distribution and fairness by assuming that our value judgments should determine the way in which taxes are structured—that if our values led us to the conclusion that the poor deserved more income, we could institute policies that would get more to the poor. Reality doesn't necessarily work that way. Often politics, not value judgments, plays a central role in determining what taxes individuals will pay. The group that can deliver the most votes will elect lawmakers who will enact tax policies that benefit that group at the expense of groups with fewer votes.

Often politics, not value judgments, plays a central role in determining what taxes an individual will pay.

On the surface, the democratic system of one person/one vote would seem to suggest that the politics of redistribution would favor the poor, but it doesn't. One would expect that the poor would use their votes to make sure income was redistributed to them from the rich. Why don't they? The answer is complicated.

One reason is that many of the poor don't vote because they assume that one vote won't make much difference. As a result, poor people's total voting strength is reduced. A second reason is that the poor aren't seen by most politicians as a solid voting bloc. There's no organization of the poor that can deliver votes to politicians. A third reason is that those poor people who do vote often cast their votes with other issues in mind. An anti-income-redistribution candidate might have a strong view on abortion as well, and for many the abortion view is the one that decides their vote.

Web Note 20.4
Macroeconomic Issues

A fourth reason is that elections require financing. Much of that financing comes from the rich. The money is used for advertising and publicity aimed at convincing the poor that it's actually in their best interests to vote for a person who supports the rich. People are often misled by that kind of biased publicity.

Reasonable-sounding arguments can be made to support just about any position, and the rich have the means to see that the arguments supporting their positions get the publicity. Of course, some of their arguments are also correct. The issues are usually sufficiently complicated that a trained economist must study them for a long time to determine which arguments make sense.

Income Redistribution Policies

The preceding discussion should have provided you with a general sense of the difficulty of redistributing income. Let's now consider briefly how income redistribution policies and programs have worked in the real world. In considering this, it is helpful to keep in mind that government has two direct methods and one indirect method to redistribute income. The direct methods are (1) *taxation* (policies that tax the rich more than the poor) and (2) *expenditures* (programs that help the poor more than the rich). The indirect method involves establishing and protecting property rights. Let's first consider direct methods.

Direct methods of redistribution are taxation and expenditures programs.

Taxation to Redistribute Income

The U.S. federal government gets its revenue from a variety of taxes. The three largest sources of revenue are the personal income tax, the corporate income tax, and the Social Security tax.

State and local governments get their revenue from income taxes, sales taxes, and property taxes. The rates vary among states.

Tax systems can be progressive, proportional (sometimes called *flat rate*), or regressive. A **progressive tax** is one in which *the average tax rate increases with income.* (A progressive income tax schedule might tax individuals at a rate of 15 percent for income up to $20,000; at 25 percent for income between $20,000 and $40,000; and at 35 percent for every dollar earned over $40,000.) It redistributes income from the rich to the poor. A **proportional tax** is one in which *the average rate of tax is constant regardless of income level.* Such a tax might be 25 percent of every dollar earned. It is neutral in regard to income distribution. A **regressive tax** is one in which *the average tax rate decreases as income increases*. It redistributes income from poor to rich. The United States has chosen a somewhat progressive income tax, while the Social Security tax is a proportional tax up to a specified earned income.

Q-8 A progressive tax is preferable to a proportional tax. True or false? Why?

Federal Income Taxes In the early 1940s, the federal personal income tax was made highly progressive, with a top tax rate of 90 percent on the highest incomes. The degree of progressivity went down significantly through various pieces of legislation after World War II until 1986, when the income tax system was amended to provide for an initial rate of 15 percent and a top rate of 28 percent. (The U.S. income tax also has an earned income tax credit where heads of households earning below a certain amount get a tax credit from government, reducing their taxes, and sometimes providing them with an income subsidy.)

The changes did not reduce the actual progressivity of the personal income tax as much as they seemed to because the 1986 reforms eliminated many of the loopholes in the U.S. Tax Code. Some loopholes had allowed rich people to legally reduce their reported incomes and to pay taxes on those lower incomes at lower rates. The top personal income tax rate on high-income individuals today is 35 percent.

Whereas the personal income tax is progressive, the Social Security tax is initially proportional. All individuals pay the same tax rate on wage income (7.65 percent for employer and 7.65 percent for employee; 15.3 percent for self-employed) up to a cap of about $110,000. Above that income cap, no Social Security tax is due (except for the Medicare portion, which has no cap on the amount to which it is applied). At this income cap, the Social Security tax becomes regressive: Higher-income individuals pay a lower percentage of their total income in Social Security taxes than do lower-income individuals. (They also receive relatively less in Social Security benefits, compared to what they put in. So, while the Social Security tax is regressive, taken as a whole the Social Security system is progressive.)

State and Local Taxes State and local governments get most of their income from the following sources:

1. Income taxes, which are generally somewhat progressive.
2. Sales taxes, which tend to be proportional (all people pay the same tax rate on what they spend) or slightly regressive. (Since poor people often spend a higher percentage of their incomes than rich people, poor people pay higher average sales taxes as a percentage of their incomes than rich people.)
3. Property taxes, which are taxes paid on the value of people's property (usually real estate, but sometimes also personal property like cars). Since the value of people's property is related (although imperfectly related) to income, the property tax is considered to be roughly proportional.

WWW Web Note 20.5 State Lotteries

When all the taxes paid by individuals to all levels of governments are combined, the conclusion that most researchers come to is that little income redistribution takes place on the tax side. The progressive taxes are offset by the regressive taxes, so the overall tax system is roughly proportional. That is, on average the tax rates individuals pay are roughly equal.

Expenditure Programs to Redistribute Income

Taxation has not proved to be an effective means of redistributing income. However, the government expenditure system has been quite effective. The federal government's expenditures that contribute to redistribution include the following.

Expenditure programs have been more successful than taxation for redistributing income.

Social Security The program that redistributes the most money is the **Social Security system,** *a social insurance program that provides financial benefits to the elderly and disabled and to their eligible dependents and/or survivors*. Social Security also has a component called **Medicare,** which is a *multibillion-dollar medical insurance system*.

The amount of an individual's Social Security retirement, disability, or survivors' monthly cash benefits depends on a very complex formula, which is skewed in favor of lower-income workers. The program is not a pension program that pays benefits in

Q-9 The U.S. Social Security system is only a retirement system. True or false?

proportion to the amount paid in. Many people will get much more than they paid in; some who never paid anything in will get a great deal; and others who paid in for years will get nothing. (No benefits are payable if you die before you retire and leave no survivors eligible for benefits due to your work.) On the whole, the program has been successful in keeping the elderly out of poverty. In addition, Social Security benefits have helped workers' survivors and the disabled.

Today, more than 55 million people receive cash Social Security benefits, many of whom also receive Medicare payments. Total benefits paid including Medicare, come to over $1 trillion each year.

Public Assistance **Public assistance** programs are *means-tested social programs targeted to the poor and providing financial, nutritional, medical, and housing assistance.* (These programs are more familiarly known as *welfare payments.*) Public assistance programs exist in every state of the union, although the amount paid varies greatly from state to state. The main kinds of public assistance are

Temporary Assistance for Needy Families (TANF). Provides temporary financial assistance to needy families with children under age 19.

Supplemental Nutritional Assistance Program (SNAP). Provides nutritional assistance in the form of coupons redeemable at most food stores.

Medicaid. Medical assistance for the poor, paid for by the individual states. It's different from, and usually more generous than, Medicare.

General assistance. State assistance to poor people when emergencies arise that aren't taken care of by any of the other programs.

By far the largest proportion of payments goes to needy families with dependent children, especially since these families are usually so poor that, in addition to qualifying for TANF, they meet the eligibility requirements for SNAP and Medicaid.

TANF was instituted by the Personal Responsibility and Work Opportunity Reconciliation Act of 1996 to replace Aid to Families with Dependent Children (AFDC). It has a number of provisions that distinguish it from earlier programs. One important provision is that it establishes a lifetime limit of 60 months (not necessarily consecutive) of benefits. The purpose of the law is to direct welfare recipients to work, and another provision in the law requires welfare recipients to take a job within two years. The law also gives states significant latitude in determining benefits and eligibility criteria. These changes are major ones; they raise many questions about job training and child care. The effects of this law are discussed in the box "From Welfare to Work."

Supplemental Security Income Hundreds of thousands more people would be receiving public assistance if it weren't for **Supplemental Security Income (SSI),** *a federal program that pays benefits, based on need, to the elderly, blind, and disabled.* Although SSI is administered through the Social Security offices, it is unlike Social Security benefits because eligibility for SSI payments is based solely on need. Again unlike Social Security, the recipients pay nothing toward the cost of the program. To be eligible, though, people must have very low incomes and almost no resources except a home, if they are fortunate enough to own one, a wedding ring and engagement ring, and an automobile. Today, over $40 billion is paid in SSI benefits each year.

Unemployment Compensation **Unemployment compensation** is *short-term financial assistance, regardless of need, to eligible individuals who are temporarily out of work.* It is limited financial assistance to people who are out of work through no fault of their own and have worked in a covered occupation for a substantial number of weeks in the period just before they became unemployed.

REAL-WORLD APPLICATION

From Welfare to Work

In an effort to reduce the negative incentive effects of welfare, in 1996 Congress passed the Personal Responsibility and Work Opportunity Reconciliation Act. The act required recipients of welfare assistance to work after two years on assistance and limited welfare assistance to a total of five years over a lifetime. Part of the act was also designed to offset the taxation implicit in moving from welfare to work, which could be as high as 90 percent or more, since under the old law welfare recipients who earned income above a certain level often lost almost all their welfare benefits.

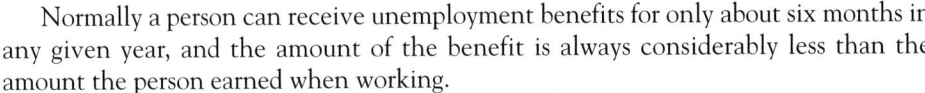

The act extended funding to the working poor; for example, it provided funding for child care to help mothers move into the workforce and extended Medicaid to include the first year of work. With the changes, the implicit tax on income was reduced to about 40 percent: For every dollar of additional income, people lost 40 cents of benefits. Congress also promised monetary rewards to states that were successful in moving people off the welfare rolls.

This act played an important role in reducing the number of people on welfare from its peak of 14 million in 1994 to about 4 million in 2008, in reducing the average stay on welfare from over eight to under four years, and in reducing the unemployment rate among single mothers.

The largest reduction occurred in the late 1990s and early 2000, when the economy was booming and one could expect the number of welfare recipients to fall anyway. But the reductions continued into the recessions.

Of course, the act also has some negative effects. Some people run out of benefits and are forced into deeper poverty. Observers are keeping a close eye on the figures and on the overall effect of the act, but the general feeling is that the act has significantly increased the incentives to get off, and stay off, welfare.

Normally a person can receive unemployment benefits for only about six months in any given year, and the amount of the benefit is always considerably less than the amount the person earned when working.

A person can't just quit a job and live on unemployment benefits. While receiving unemployment benefits, people are expected to actively search for work. Lower-income workers receive unemployment payments that are more nearly equal to their working wage than do higher-income workers, but there is no income eligibility test. Today, more than $55 billion is paid in unemployment benefits each year and this will likely increase.

Housing Programs Federal and state governments have many different programs to improve housing or to provide affordable housing. While many of these programs are designed to benefit low-income persons, there are also programs for moderate-income persons and lower-income persons (people whose incomes are lower than moderate but higher than low).

The federal agency overseeing most of these programs, the Department of Housing and Urban Development (HUD), has been criticized for abuse and mismanagement. Hundreds of millions of dollars that could have benefited the poor went instead to developers of housing and other projects, to consultants, and to others who skimmed off money before—or instead of—building or rehabilitating housing. In part because of these problems, federal funding for housing was steadily reduced during the 1980s. Today, about $40 billion is allocated to housing programs each year.

FIGURE 20-7 Distribution of Income before and after Taxes and Transfers

Although little redistribution takes place through the tax system, significant redistribution occurs through the transfer system, making the after-tax and transfer distribution of income more equal than the before-tax distribution of income.

Source: *Current Population Reports*, U.S. Bureau of the Census, 2008 (www.census.gov), and extrapolations by author.

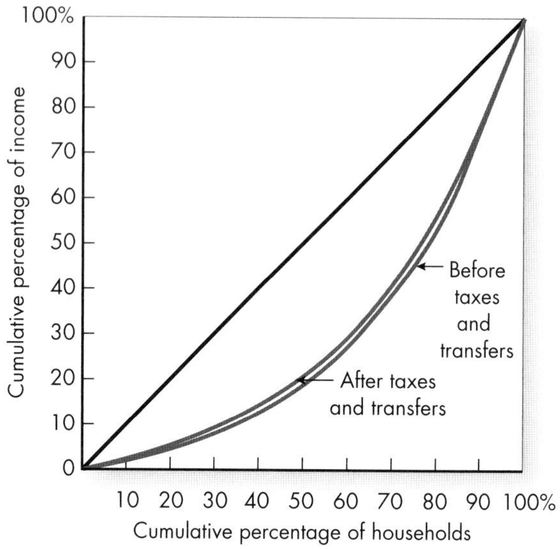

How Successful Have Income Redistribution Programs Been?

Most government redistribution works through its expenditure programs, not through taxes.

Figure 20-7 shows approximate Lorenz curves before and after including the effect of both taxes and government programs on the redistribution of income. As you can see, the after-transfer income is somewhat closer to being equally distributed. But because of the incentive effects of collecting and distributing the money, that redistribution has come at the cost of a reduction in the total amount of income earned by the society. The debate about whether the gain in equality of income is worth the cost in reduction of total income is likely to continue indefinitely.

While the direct methods of redistributing income get the most press and discussion, perhaps the most important redistribution decisions that the government makes involve an indirect method, the establishment and protection of property rights. Let's take an example: intellectual property rights. Intellectual property consists of things like a book you've written, a song you've composed, or a picture you've drawn. How these property rights are structured plays a fundamental role in determining the distribution of income.

Q-10 Why are property rights important in the determination of whether any particular income distribution is fair?

For example, if strict private property rights are given for, say, a design for a computer screen (e.g., a neat little trash can in the corners and windows of various files), any user other than the designer herself will have to pay for the right to use it. The designer (or the person who gets the legal right to the design) becomes very rich. If no property rights are given for the design, then no payment is made and income is much more equally distributed. Of course, without a promise of high returns to designing a computer screen device, fewer resources will be invested in finding the ideal design. While most people agree that some incentive is appropriate, there is no consensus on whether the incentives embodied in our current property rights structure are too large. I suspect that the trash can (recycling bin) design, while ingenious, would have been arrived at with a much smaller incentive.

The point of the above example is not that property rights in such ideas should not be given out. The point is that decisions on property rights issues have enormous distributional consequences that are often little discussed, even by economists. Ultimately, we can answer the question of whether income redistribution is fair only after we have answered the question of whether the initial property rights distribution is fair.

Conclusion

Much more could be said about the issues involved in income redistribution. But limitations of time and space pressure us to move on. I hope this chapter has convinced you that income redistribution is an important but difficult question. Specifically, I hope I have given you the sense that income distribution questions are integrally related to questions about the entire economic system. Supply and demand play a central role in the determination of the distribution of income, but they do so in an institutional and historical context. Thus, the analysis of income distribution must include that context as well as the analyst's ethical judgments about what is fair.

Summary

- The Lorenz curve is a measure of the distribution of income among families in a country. The farther the Lorenz curve is from the diagonal, the more unequally income is distributed.
- The official poverty measure is an absolute measure because it is based on the minimum food budget for a family. It is a relative measure because it is adjusted for average inflation.
- Economic and social mobility in the United States has decreased over the past decades.
- Income is less equally distributed in the United States than in some countries such as Sweden, but more equally distributed than in other countries such as Brazil. There is more income inequality among countries than income inequality within a country.
- Wealth is distributed less equally than income.
- Income differs substantially by class and by other socioeconomic characteristics such as age, race, and gender.
- Fairness is a philosophical question. People must judge a program's fairness for themselves.
- Income is difficult to redistribute because of incentive effects of taxes, avoidance and evasion effects of taxes, and incentive effects of redistribution programs.
- On the whole, the U.S. tax system is roughly proportional, so it is not very effective as a means of redistributing income.
- Government spending programs are more effective than tax policy in reducing income inequality in the United States.

Key Terms

income *(469)*
Lorenz curve *(461)*
Medicare *(477)*
poverty threshold *(464)*
progressive tax *(476)*
proportional tax *(476)*
public assistance *(478)*
regressive tax *(476)*
share distribution of income *(461)*
Social Security system *(477)*
socioeconomic distribution of income *(461)*
Supplemental Security Income (SSI) *(478)*
unemployment compensation *(478)*
wealth *(469)*

Questions and Exercises

connect ECONOMICS

1. The Lorenz curve for Bangladesh looks like this:

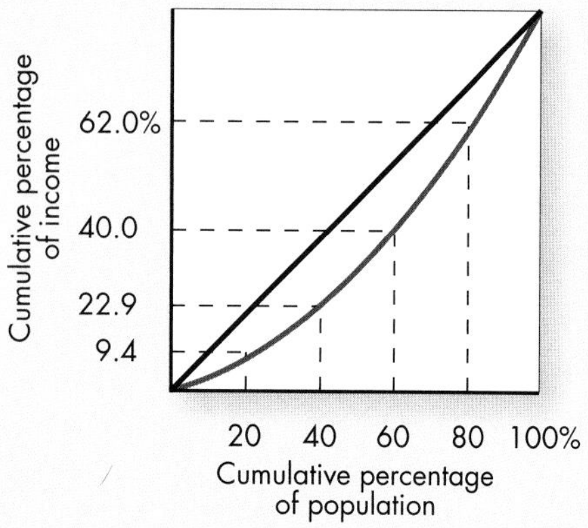

   How much income do individuals in the top income quintile in Bangladesh receive? LO1
2. If we were to draw a Lorenz curve for lawyers, what would it represent? LO1
3. Why are we concerned with the distribution of income between whites and blacks, but not between redheads and blonds? LO1
4. The accompanying table shows income distribution data for three countries.

	Percentage of Total Income		
Income Quintile	**India**	**Czech Republic**	**Mexico**
Lowest 20%	8.5%	10.5%	4.1%
Second quintile	12.1	13.9	7.8
Third quintile	15.8	16.9	12.5
Fourth quintile	21.1	21.3	20.2
Highest 20%	42.5	37.4	55.4

   a. Using this information, draw a Lorenz curve for each country.
   b. Which country has the most equal distribution of income?
   c. Which country has the least equal?
   d. By looking at the three Lorenz curves, can you tell which country has the most progressive tax system? Why or why not? LO1
5. Should poverty be defined absolutely or relatively? Why? LO2
6. Would the Lorenz curve among countries be more or less bowed out compared to the Lorenz curve for the United States? LO3
7. If a garbage collector earns more than an English teacher, does that mean something is wrong with the economy? Why or why not? (Difficult) LO4
8. Is the class system in the United States more like a pyramid, diamond, or pentagon? Why is this so? LO5
9. How does social mobility in the United States compare to that in Britain? Why do you think this is so? LO5
10. In Taxland, the first $10,000 earned per year is exempt from taxation. Between $10,000.01 and $30,000, the tax rate is 25 percent. Between $30,000.01 and $50,000, it's 30 percent. Above $50,000, it's 35 percent. You're earning $75,000 a year.
    a. How much in taxes will you have to pay?
    b. What is your average tax rate?
    c. What is your marginal tax rate? LO7
11. Some economists have proposed making the tax rate progressivity depend on the wage rate rather than the income level. Thus, an individual who works twice as long as another but who receives a lower wage would face a lower marginal tax rate.
    a. What effect would this change have on incentives to work?
    b. Would this system be fairer than our current system? Why or why not?
    c. If, simultaneously, the tax system were made regressive in hours worked so that individuals who work longer hours faced lower marginal tax rates, what effect would this change have on hours worked? LO7
12. In "Why Higher Real Wages May Reduce Altruism for the Poor," Ball State economist John B. Horowitz considers whether redistribution of income is a public good or a public bad. (Difficult)
    a. How might income redistribution be considered a public good?
    b. How might income redistribution be considered a public bad?
    c. What is the likely effect of higher real wages on whether income redistribution is perceived to be a public good or bad? LO7
13. Which have been more successful in redistributing income: tax or expenditure programs? LO8

Questions from Alternative Perspectives

1. Figure 20-7 shows the distribution of income before and after taxes and transfers. The top 20% of Americans had 49.7% of the income before taxes and transfers and 48.3% after taxes and transfers. The same figures for the bottom 20% are 3.4% and 4.3% respectively.
   a. How much do taxes and transfers "cost" the upper quintile?
   b. How much discretionary income should they be willing to invest to change this situation?
   c. How much discretionary income does the bottom quintile have to prevent such a change? (Institutionalist)
2. In the Old Testament, God promised riches to Israel if Israel kept God's commandments. But in the New Testament, Jesus says that it is easier for a camel to go through the eye of a needle than for a rich man to enter the kingdom of heaven.
   a. Considering the wealth distribution in Figure 20-5, what does this suggest about Americans?
   b. Should government do anything about it?
   c. What do the Old and New Testament teachings suggest about what private individuals ought to do? (Religious)
3. In 2008 the poverty level for a family of four was $21,200.
   a. If one-third of the total income of lower-income households is typically used for food, estimate the amount of money per day per person available for food for a person living at or below the poverty rate.
   b. How much does that leave for this family per month for everything else: rent, utilities, taxes, auto, medical, clothing, and education? (Radical)
4. Say you earn $200, and that the government takes $75 from you in taxes to give to someone else.
   a. How would you feel about that?
   b. What would that transfer likely do to your incentive to work?
   c. What would the government transfer of $75 likely do to the incentive to work of the person who receives the payment?
   d. Would the effect be different if you voluntarily gave $75 to someone else? (Austrian)
5. Anti-poverty programs in the United States since the mid 1990s have focused on welfare-to-work programs that compel welfare recipients to take paid jobs. Some economists argue that these programs place women who are not "ready for work" into jobs that are not "ready for mothers" and move them from the ranks of the welfare poor to the working poor.
   a. What policies would be necessary to make U.S. anti-poverty programs far more effective?
   b. How could public policy be used to make jobs more "mother-ready" and more likely to lift these women above the poverty line? (Feminist)

Issues to Ponder

1. Some economists argue that a class distinction should be made between managerial decision makers and other workers. Do you agree? Why or why not? (Difficult) LO4
2. List four conditions you believe should hold before you would argue that two individuals should get the same amount of income.
   a. How would you apply the conditions to your views on welfare?
   b. How would you apply the conditions to your views on how progressive the income tax should be?
   c. If the income tax were made progressive in wage rates (tax rates increase as wage rates increase) rather than progressive in income, would your conditions be better met? Why? LO6
3. Is it ever appropriate for society to:
   Let someone starve?
   Let someone be homeless?
   Forbid someone to eat chocolate? LO6
4. The dissident Russian writer A. Amalrik has written:

   > The Russian people . . . have . . . one idea that appears positive: the idea of *justice* . . . In practice, "justice" involves the desire that "nobody should live better than I do" . . . The idea of justice is motivated by hatred of everything that is outstanding, which we make no effort to imitate but, on the contrary, try to bring down to our level, by hatred of any sense of initiative, of any higher or more dynamic way of life than the life we live ourselves.

   What implications would such a worldview have for the economy? (Difficult) LO6
5. If you receive a paycheck, what percentage of it is withheld for taxes? What incentive effect does that have on your decision to work? LO7
6. "There are lies, damned lies, and statistics. Then, there are annual poverty figures." Both liberal and conservative economists believe U.S. poverty statistics are suspect. Here are some reasons:

(1) They do not take into account in-kind benefits such as food stamps and tax credits.
(2) They do not consider regional cost-of-living differences.
(3) They do not take into account unreported income.
(4) Food accounts for one-fourth of a family's budget, not one-third.
(5) Ownership of assets such as homes, cars, and appliances is not taken into account.

a. What would the effect of correcting each of these be on measured poverty?
b. Would making these changes be fair? LO2, LO7

7. "There are many more poor people in the United States than there are rich people. If the poor wanted to, they could exercise their power to redistribute as much money as they please to themselves. They don't do that, so they must see the income distribution system as fair." Discuss. (Difficult) LO8

Answers to Margin Questions

1. When drawing a Lorenz curve, you put the cumulative percentage of income on the vertical axis and the cumulative percentage of families (or population) on the horizontal axis. *(461)*
2. The U.S. definition of poverty is an absolute measure, but the way poverty is calculated means that some relativity is included in the definition. *(464)*
3. The United States has significantly more income inequality than Sweden and Japan, but significantly less than Brazil. *(468)*
4. In early capitalist society, the distributional fight was between workers and capitalists. In modern capitalist society, the distributional fight is more varied. For example, in the United States minorities are pitted against whites and males against females. *(472)*
5. No, it is not self-evident that greater equality of income would make society a better place to live. Unequal income distribution has its benefits. Still, most people would prefer a somewhat more equal distribution of income than what currently exists. *(473)*
6. What is fair is a very difficult concept. It depends on people's needs, people's wants, to what degree people are deserving, and other factors. Still, in the absence of any more information than is given in the question, I would divide the pie equally. *(473)*
7. No, one cannot reasonably assume other things remain constant. Redistributive programs have important side effects that can change the behavior of individuals and subvert the intent of the program. Three important side effects include substituting leisure for labor, a decrease in measured income, and attempts to appear more needy. *(475)*
8. As a general statement, "A progressive tax is preferable to a proportional tax" is false. A progressive tax may well be preferable, but that is a normative judgment (just as its opposite would be). Moreover, taxes have incentive effects that must be considered. *(476)*
9. False. The U.S. Social Security system includes many other aspects, such as disability benefits and survivors' benefits. *(477)*
10. The distribution of initial property rights underlies the initial distribution of income. Those with the property rights will reap the returns from those rights. Ultimately, we can answer the question whether income distribution is fair only after we have answered whether the initial property rights distribution is fair. *(480)*

Market Failure versus Government Failure

The business of government is to keep the government out of business—that is unless business needs government aid.

—*Will Rogers*

There is an ongoing (indeed unending) debate: Should the government intervene in markets such as health care or agriculture? The supply/demand framework you learned in the previous chapters was created to provide some insight into answering that question, and those chapters began exploring the issues. In this chapter we explore economic policy questions more deeply and develop a fuller understanding of some of the roles of government first presented in Chapter 3.

The economic analysis of policy is set in the economic framework, which can also be called the *invisible hand framework*. It says that if markets are perfectly competitive, they will lead individuals to make voluntary choices that are in the society's interest. It is as if individuals are guided by an invisible hand to do what society wants them to do.

AFTER READING THIS CHAPTER, YOU SHOULD BE ABLE TO:

1. Explain what an externality is and show how it affects the market outcome.
2. Describe three methods of dealing with externalities.
3. Define *public good* and explain the problem with determining the value of a public good to society.
4. Explain how informational problems can lead to market failure.
5. List five reasons why government's solution to a market failure could worsen the situation.

Market Failures

For the invisible hand to guide private actions toward the social good, a number of conditions must be met. When they are not met, economists say that there is a **market failure**—*a situation in which the invisible hand pushes in such a way that individual decisions do not lead to socially desirable outcomes*. In this chapter we consider three sources of market failures: externalities, public goods, and imperfect information.

Any time there is a market failure, it is possible that government intervention could improve the outcome. But it is important to remember that even if a market failure exists, it is not clear that government action will improve the result since the politics of implementing the solution often lead to further problems. These problems of government intervention are often called **government failures**—*when the government intervention in the market to improve the market failure actually makes the situation worse*. After discussing the three sources of market failures, we will discuss government failures. The economic policy debate can be best thought of as choosing which failure is likely to be the lesser of two evils.

ADDED DIMENSION

Pareto Optimality and the Perfectly Competitive Benchmark

Perfect competition serves as a benchmark for judging policies. A foundation for this benchmark is in the work of Stanford economist Kenneth Arrow, who showed that the market translates self-interest into society's interest. (Arrow was given a Nobel Prize in 1972 for this work.) Arrow's ideas are based on many assumptions that can only be touched on in an introductory book. I will, however, discuss one here—the interpretation of the term *society's welfare.* In the economic framework, society's welfare is interpreted as coming as close as one can to a *Pareto optimal position*—a position from which no person can be made better off without another being made worse off. (Pareto optimal policies will be discussed more in Chapter 23.)

Let's briefly consider what Arrow proved. He showed that if the market was perfectly competitive, and if there was a complete set of markets (a market for every possible good now and in the future), the invisible hand would guide the economy to a Pareto optimal position. If these assumptions hold true, the supply curve (which represents the marginal cost to the suppliers) would represent the marginal cost to society. Similarly, the demand curve (which represents the marginal benefit to consumers) would represent the marginal benefit to society. In a supply/demand equilibrium, not only would an individual be as well off as he or she possibly could be, given where he or she started from, but so too would society. A perfectly competitive market equilibrium would be a Pareto optimal position.

A number of criticisms exist to using perfect competition as a benchmark:

1. *The nirvana criticism:* A perfectly competitive equilibrium is highly unstable. It's usually in some person's interest to restrict entry by others, and, when a market is close to a competitive equilibrium, it is in few people's interest to stop such restrictions. Thus, perfect competition will never exist in the real world. Comparing reality to a situation that cannot occur (i.e., to nirvana) is unfair and unhelpful because it leads to attempts to achieve the unachievable. A better benchmark would be workable competition—a state of competition that one might reasonably hope could exist.
2. *The second-best criticism:* The conditions that allow us to conclude that perfect competition leads to a Pareto optimal position are so restrictive that they are never even approached in reality. If the economy deviates in hundreds of ways from perfect competition, how are we to know whether a movement toward more competition will improve people's welfare?
3. *The normative criticism:* Even if the previous two criticisms didn't exist, the perfect competition benchmark still isn't appropriate because there is nothing necessarily wonderful about Pareto optimality. A Pareto optimal position could be horrendous. For example, say one person has all the world's revenues and all the other people are starving. If that rich person would be made worse off by taking some money from him and giving it to the starving poor, that starting position would be Pareto optimal. By most people's normative criteria, it would also be a lousy place to remain.

Critics of the use of the perfect competition benchmark argue that society has a variety of goals. Pareto optimality may be one of them, but it's only one. They argue that economists should take into account all of society's goals—not just Pareto optimality—when determining a benchmark for judging policies.

Externalities

Web Note 21.1
The Invisible Hand

An externality is an effect of a decision on a third party not taken into account by the decision maker.

An important requirement for the invisible hand to guide markets in society's interest is that market transactions have no side effects on anyone not involved in the transactions. As I discussed in Chapter 3, such side effects are called **externalities**—*the effects of a decision on a third party that are not taken into account by the decision maker.* Externalities can be either positive or negative. Secondhand smoke and carbon monoxide emissions are examples of **negative externalities,** which occur *when the effects of a decision not taken into account by the decision maker are detrimental to others.* **Positive externalities** occur *when the effects of a decision not taken into account by the decision maker are beneficial to others.* An example is education. When you purchase a college education, it benefits not only you

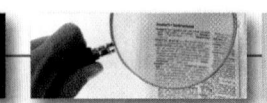

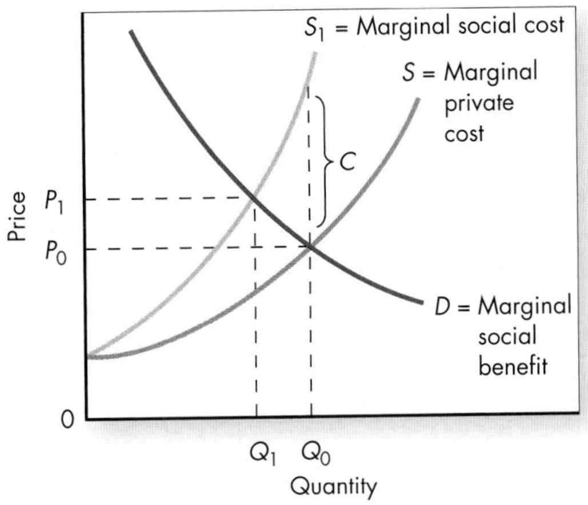

FIGURE 21-1 A Negative Externality

When there is a negative externality, the marginal private cost will be below the marginal social cost and the competitive price will be too low to maximize social welfare.

but others as well. Innovation is another example. The invention of the personal computer has had significant beneficial effects on society, which were not taken into account by the inventors. When there are externalities, the supply and/or demand curves no longer represent the marginal cost and marginal benefit curves to society.

A Negative Externality Example

Say that you and I agree that I'll produce steel for you. I'll build my steel plant on land I own, and start producing. We both believe our welfare will improve. But what about my plant's neighbors? The resulting smoke will pollute the air they breathe. The people involved in the market trade (you and I) are made better off, but people external to the trade are made worse off. Thus, there is a negative externality. My production of steel has a cost to society that neither you nor I take into account.

The effect of a negative externality is shown in Figure 21-1. The supply curve *S* represents the marginal private cost to society of producing steel. The demand curve *D* represents the marginal social benefit of consuming the steel. With no externalities, the marginal private costs and benefits represent the marginal social costs and benefits, so the supply/demand equilibrium (P_0, Q_0) represents where the marginal social benefit equals the marginal social cost. At that point society is as well off as possible.

When there are externalities, the marginal social cost differs from the marginal private cost.

But now consider what happens when production results in negative externalities. In that case people not involved in production also incur costs. This means that the supply curve no longer represents both the marginal private and marginal social costs of supplying the good. Marginal social cost is greater than the marginal private cost. This case can be represented by adding a curve in Figure 21-1 called the *marginal social cost curve*. The **marginal social cost** includes all the marginal costs that society bears—or *the marginal private costs of production plus the cost of the negative externalities associated with that production*.

Q-1 Why does the existence of an externality prevent the market from working properly?

Marginal social cost includes all the marginal costs that society bears.

Since in this case the externality represents an additional cost to society, the marginal social cost curve lies above the marginal private cost curve. The distance between the two curves represents the additional cost of the externality. For example, at quantity Q_0, the private marginal cost faced by the firm is P_0. The marginal cost from the externality at quantity Q_0 is shown by distance C. When the externality is not taken into account, the supply/demand equilibrium is at too high a quantity, Q_0, and at too low a price, P_0.

Negative Externalities and the Excise Tax Solution

Notice that the market solution results in a level of steel production that exceeds the level that equates the marginal social costs with the marginal social benefits. If the

FIGURE 21-2 A Positive Externality

When there is a positive externality, the marginal social benefit will be above the marginal private benefit and the market price will be too low to maximize social welfare.

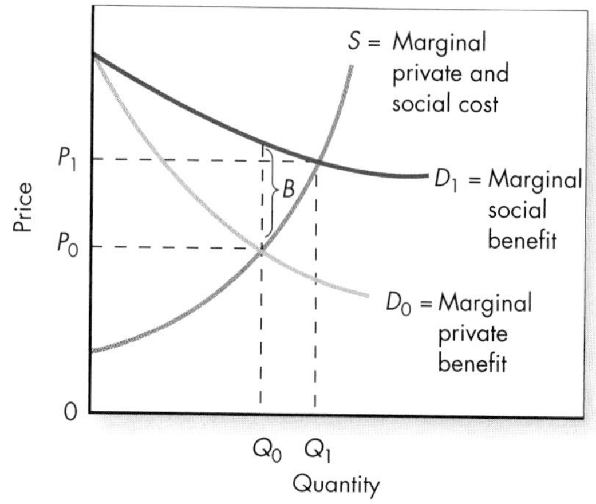

market is to maximize welfare, some type of government intervention may be needed to reduce production from Q_0 to Q_1 and raise price from P_0 to P_1.

A Positive Externality Example

Private trades can also benefit third parties not involved in the trade. These are positive externalities. Again, an example is education. Consider a person who is working and takes a class at night. He or she will bring the knowledge from class back to co-workers through day-to-day interaction on projects. The co-workers will be learning the material from the class indirectly. They are outside the initial decision to take the class, but they benefit nonetheless.

Q-2 If a positive externality exists, does that mean that the market works better than if no externality exists?

Positive externalities make the marginal private benefit below the marginal social benefit.

In the case of positive externalities, the market will not provide enough of the good. Let's see how. In Figure 21-2, we start again with the standard demand and supply curves. The supply curve S represents the marginal private cost of the course. The demand curve D_0 is the marginal private benefit to those who take the course. Since others not taking the course also benefit, the marginal social benefit, shown by D_1, is above the marginal private benefit. The **marginal social benefit** equals *the marginal private benefit of consuming a good plus the benefits of the positive externalities resulting from consuming that good.* The vertical distance between D_0 and D_1 is the additional benefit that others receive at each quantity. At quantity Q_0, the market equilibrium, the marginal benefit of the externality is shown by distance B. At this quantity, the marginal social benefit exceeds the marginal social cost. The market provides too little of the good. The optimal price and quantity for society are P_1 and Q_1, respectively. Again, some type of intervention to increase quantity may be warranted.

Alternative Methods of Dealing with Externalities

Externalities can be dealt with via
1. Direct regulation.
2. Incentive policies.
3. Voluntary solutions.

Ways to deal with externalities include (1) direct regulation, (2) incentive policies (tax incentive policies and market incentive policies), and (3) voluntary solutions.

Direct Regulation

In a program of **direct regulation,** *the amount of a good people are allowed to use is directly limited by the government.* Let's consider an example. Say we have two individuals, Ms. Thrifty, who uses 10 gallons of gasoline a day, and Mr. Big, who uses 20 gallons a day. Say we have decided that we want to reduce total daily gas consumption by 10 percent,

ADDED DIMENSION

Common Resources and the Tragedy of the Commons

Individuals tend to overuse commonly owned goods. Let's consider an example—say that grazing land is held in common. Individuals are free to bring their sheep to graze on the land. What is likely to happen? Each grazing sheep will reduce the amount of grass for other sheep. If individuals don't have to pay for grazing, when deciding how much to graze their sheep they will not take into account the cost to others of their sheep's grazing. The result may be overgrazing—killing the grass and destroying the grazing land. This is known as the *tragedy of the commons.* A more contemporary example of the tragedy of the commons is fishing. The sea is a common resource; no one owns it, and whenever people catch fish, they reduce the number of fish that others can catch. The result will likely be overfishing.

The tragedy of the commons is an example of the problems posed by externalities. Catching fish imposes a negative externality. Because of the negative effect on others, the social cost of catching a fish is greater than the private cost. Overfishing has been a problem in the United States and throughout the world. Thus, the tragedy of the commons is caused by individuals not taking into account the negative externalities of their actions.

Why doesn't the market solve the externality problem? Some economists argue that in the tragedy of the commons examples it would, if given a chance. The problem is a lack of property rights (lack of ownership). If rights to all goods were defined, the tragedy of the commons would disappear. In the fishing example, if someone owned the sea, he or she would charge individuals to fish. By charging for fishing rights, the owner would internalize the externality and thus avoid the tragedy of the commons.

or 3 gallons. The regulatory solution might require both individuals to reduce consumption by some specified amount. Likely direct regulatory strategies would be to require an equal quantity reduction (each consumer reducing consumption by 1.5 gallons) or an equal percentage reduction (each consumer reducing consumption by 10 percent).

Both of those strategies would reduce consumption, but neither would be **efficient** *(achieving a goal at the lowest cost in total resources without consideration as to who pays those costs)*. This is because direct regulation does not take into account that the costs of reducing consumption may differ among individuals. Say, for example, that Ms. Thrifty could almost costlessly reduce consumption by 3 gallons while Mr. Big would find it very costly to reduce consumption by even 0.5 gallon. In that case, either regulatory solution would be **inefficient** *(achieving a goal in a more costly manner than necessary)*. It would be less costly (more efficient) to have Ms. Thrifty undertake most of the reduction. A policy that would automatically make the person who has the lower cost of reduction *choose* (as opposed to being *required*) to undertake the most reduction would achieve the same level of reduction at a lower cost. In this case, the efficient policy would get Ms. Thrifty to choose to undertake the majority of the reduction.

Q-3 It is sometimes said that there is a trade-off between fairness and efficiency. Explain one way in which that is true and one way in which that is false.

Incentive Policies

Two types of incentive policies would each get Ms. Thrifty to undertake the larger share of reduction. One is to tax consumption; the other is to issue certificates to individuals who reduce consumption and to allow them to trade those certificates with others.

Economists tend to like incentive policies to deal with externalities.

Tax Incentive Policies Let's say that the government imposes a tax on gasoline consumption of 50 cents per gallon. This would be an example of a **tax incentive program** *(a program using a tax to create incentives for individuals to structure their activities*

FIGURE 21-3
Regulation through Taxation

If the government sets a tax sufficient to take into account a negative externality, individuals will respond by reducing the quantity of the pollution-causing activity supplied to a level that individuals would have supplied had they included the negative externality in their decision.

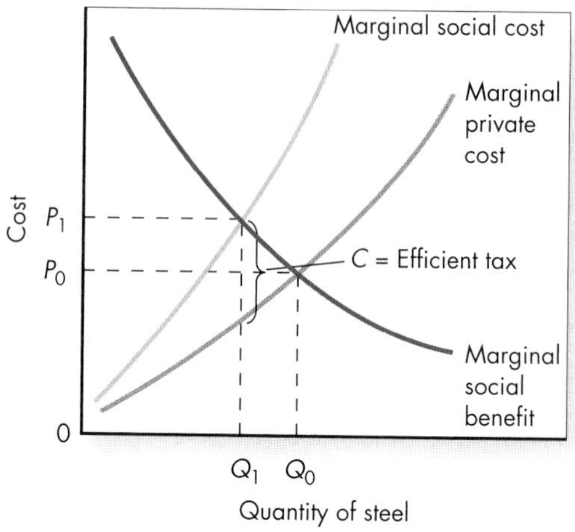

in a way that is consistent with the desired ends). Since Ms. Thrifty can almost costlessly reduce her gasoline consumption, she will likely respond to the tax by reducing gasoline consumption, say, by 2.75 gallons. She pays only $3.63 in tax but undertakes most of the conservation. Since Mr. Big finds it very costly to reduce his consumption of gasoline, he will likely respond by reducing gasoline consumption by very little, say by 0.25 gallon. He pays $9.88 in tax but does little of the conservation.

Q-4 In what sense is the tax incentive approach to externalities fair?

In this example, the tax has achieved the desired end in a more efficient manner than would the regulatory solution—the person for whom the reduction is least costly cuts consumption the most. Why? Because the incentive to reduce is embodied in the price, and individuals are forced to choose how much to change their consumption. The tax has made them internalize the externality. The solution also has a significant element of fairness about it. The person who conserves the most pays the least tax.

Let's now consider how the tax incentive solution will solve the problem in our earlier example of steel production. Figure 21-3 shows the situation. Say the government determines that the additional cost to society of producing steel equals C. If the government sets the pollution tax on steel production at C, the firm will reduce its output to Q_1 on its own. Such taxes on externalities are often called **effluent fees**—*charges imposed by government on the level of pollution created.* The efficient tax equals the additional cost imposed on society but not taken into account by the decision maker. With such a tax, the cost the suppliers face is the social cost of supplying the good. With the tax, the invisible hand guides the traders to equate the marginal social cost to the marginal social benefit and the equilibrium is socially optimal.

Market Incentive Policies A second incentive policy that gets individuals to internalize an externality is a **market incentive plan** *(a plan requiring market participants to certify that they have reduced total consumption—not necessarily their own individual consumption—by a specified amount).* Such a program would be close to the regulatory solution but involves a major difference. If individuals choose to reduce consumption by more than the required amount, they will be given a marketable certificate that they can sell to someone who has chosen to reduce consumption by less than the required amount. By buying that certificate, the person who has not personally reduced consumption by the requisite amount will have met the program's requirements. Let's see how the program would work with Mr. Big and Ms. Thrifty.

In our example, Mr. Big finds it very costly to reduce consumption while Ms. Thrifty finds it easy. So we can expect that Mr. Big won't reduce consumption much and will instead buy certificates from Ms. Thrifty, who will choose to undertake significant reduction in her consumption to generate the certificates, assuming she can sell them to Mr. Big for a high enough price to make that reduction worth her while. So, as was the case in the tax incentive program, Ms. Thrifty undertakes most of the conservation—but she reaps a financial benefit for it.

Obviously there are enormous questions about the administrative feasibility of these types of proposals, but what's important to understand here is not the specifics of the proposals but the way in which incentive policies are *more efficient* than the regulatory policy. As I stated before, *more efficient* means *less costly* in terms of resources, with no consideration paid to who is bearing those costs. Incorporating the incentive into a price and then letting individuals choose how to respond to that incentive lets those who find it least costly undertake most of the adjustment.

Incentive policies are more efficient than direct regulatory policies.

More and more, governments are exploring incentive policies for solving problems. Sin taxes (taxes on goods government believes to be harmful) are an example of the tax incentive approach. (These will be discussed further in Chapter 23.) Marketable permits for pollution and for CO_2 emissions are an example of the marketable certificate approach. You can probably see more examples discussed in the news.

Voluntary Reductions

A third alternative method of dealing with externalities is to make the reduction voluntary, leaving individuals free to choose whether to follow a socially optimal or a privately optimal path. Let's consider how a voluntary program might work in our Mr. Big and Ms. Thrifty example. Let's say that Ms. Thrifty has a social conscience and undertakes most of the reduction while Mr. Big has no social conscience and reduces consumption hardly at all. It seems that this is a reasonably efficient solution. But what if the costs were reversed and Mr. Big had the low cost of reduction and Ms. Thrifty had the high cost? Then the voluntary solution would not be so efficient. Of course, it could be argued that when people do something voluntarily, it makes them better off. So one could argue that even when Ms. Thrifty has a high cost of reduction and voluntarily undertakes most of the reduction, she also has a high benefit from reducing her consumption.

WWW Web Note 21.2
Free Riders and Union Shops

The largest problem with voluntary solutions is that a person's willingness to do things for the good of society generally depends on that person's belief that others will also be helping. If a socially conscious person comes to believe that a large number of other people won't contribute, he or she will often lose that social conscience: Why should I do what's good for society if others won't? This is an example of the **free rider problem** (*individuals' unwillingness to share in the cost of a public good*), which economists believe will often limit, and eventually undermine, social actions based on voluntary contributions. A small number of free riders will undermine the social consciousness of many in the society and eventually the voluntary policy will fail.

Q-5 What are two reasons to be dubious of solutions based on voluntary action that is not in people's self-interest?

Economists believe that a small number of free riders will undermine the social consciousness of many in the society and that eventually a voluntary policy will fail.

There are exceptions. During times of war and extreme crisis, voluntary programs are often successful. For example, during World War II the war effort was financed in part through successful voluntary programs. But generally the results of voluntary programs for long-term social problems that involve individuals significantly changing their actions haven't been positive.

The Optimal Policy

If a policy isn't optimal, resources are being wasted because the savings from reducing expenditures on a program will be worth more than the gains that will be lost from reducing the program.

An **optimal policy** is *one in which the marginal cost of undertaking the policy equals the marginal benefit of that policy*. If a policy isn't optimal (that is, the marginal cost exceeds the marginal benefit or the marginal benefit exceeds the marginal cost), resources are being wasted because the savings from reducing expenditures on a program will be worth more than the gains that would be lost from reducing the program, or the benefit from spending more on a program will exceed the cost of expanding the program.

Let's consider an example of this latter case. Say the marginal benefit of a program significantly exceeds its marginal cost. That would seem good. But that would mean that we could expand the program by decreasing some other program or activity whose marginal benefit doesn't exceed its marginal cost, with a net gain in benefits to society. To spend too little on a beneficial program is as inefficient as spending too much on a nonbeneficial program.

Some environmentalists want to rid the world of all pollution, while most economists want to reduce pollution to the point where the marginal cost of reducing pollution equals the marginal benefit.

This concept of optimality carries over to economists' view of most problems. For example, some environmentalists would like to completely rid the economy of pollution. Most economists believe that doing so is costly and that since it's costly, one would want to take into account those costs. That means that society should reduce pollution only to the point where the marginal cost of reducing pollution equals the marginal benefit. That point is called the *optimal level of pollution*—the amount of pollution at which the marginal benefit of reducing pollution equals the marginal cost. To reduce pollution below that level would make society as a whole worse off.

Public Goods

A public good is a good that is nonexclusive and nonrival.

A **public good** is *a good that is nonexclusive (no one can be excluded from its benefits) and nonrival (consumption by one does not preclude consumption by others)*. As I discussed in Chapter 3, in reality there is no such thing as a pure public good, but many of the goods that government provides—education, defense, roads, and legal systems—have public-good aspects to them. Probably the closest example we have of a pure public good is national defense. A single individual cannot protect himself or herself from a foreign invasion without protecting his or her neighbors as well. Protection for one person means that many others are also protected. Governments generally provide goods with significant public aspects to them because private businesses will not supply them, unless they transform the good into a mostly private good.

Web Note 21.3
Charging for Roads

What is and is not considered a public good depends on technology. Consider roads—at one point roads were often privately supplied since with horses and buggies the road owners could charge tolls relatively easily. Then, with the increased speed of the automobile, collecting tolls on most roads became too time-consuming. At that point the nonexclusive public-good aspect of roads became dominant—once a road was built, it was most efficiently supplied to others at a zero cost—and government became the provider of most roads. Today, with modern computer technology, sensors that monitor road use can be placed on roads and in cars. Charging for roads has once again become more feasible. In the future we may again see more private provision of roads. Some economists have even called for privatization of existing roads, and private roads are being built in California and in Bangkok, Thailand.

Market Demand for a Public Good

One of the reasons that pure public goods are sufficiently interesting to warrant a separate discussion is that the supply/demand model can be modified to neatly contrast the efficient supply of a private good with the efficient supply of a public good. The key to understanding the difference is to recognize that once a pure public good is supplied to one individual, it is simultaneously supplied to all, whereas a private good is supplied only to the individual who purchased it. For example, if the price of an apple is 50 cents, the efficient purchase rule is for individuals to buy apples until the marginal benefit of the last apple consumed is equal to 50 cents. The analysis focuses on the individual. If the equilibrium price is 50 cents, the marginal benefit of the last apple sold in the market is equal to 50 cents. That benefit is paid for by one individual and is enjoyed by one individual.

Now consider a public good. Say that the marginal benefit of an additional missile for national defense is 50 cents to one individual and 25 cents to another. In this case the value of providing one missile provides 75 cents (25 + 50) of total social benefit. With a public good the focus is on the group. The societal benefit in the case of a public good is the *sum* of the individual benefits (since each individual gets the benefit of the good). With private goods, we count only the benefit to the person buying the good since only one person gets it.

The above reasoning can be translated into supply and demand curves. The market demand curve represents the marginal benefit of a good to society. As we saw in Chapter 4, in the case of a private good, the market demand curve is the *horizontal sum* of the individual demand curves. The total amount of a private good supplied is split up among many buyers. While the market demand curve for a private good is constructed by adding all the quantities demanded at every price, the market demand curve in the case of public goods is the *vertical sum* of the individual demand curves at every quantity. The quantity of the good supplied is not split up; the full benefit of the total output is received by everyone.

With private goods you sum demand curves horizontally; with public goods you sum them vertically.

Figure 21-4 gives an example of a public good. In it we assume that society consists of only two individuals—A and B, with demand curves D_A and D_B. To arrive at the market demand curve for the public good, we vertically add the price that each individual is willing to pay for each unit since both receive a benefit when the good is supplied. Thus, at quantity 1 we add $0.60 to $0.50. We arrive at $1.10, the marginal benefit of providing the first missile. By adding together the willingness to pay by individuals A and B for quantities 2 and 3, we generate the market demand curve for missiles. Extending this example from two individuals to the economy as a whole, you can see that, even though the benefit of a public good is small to each person, the total benefit is large. With 300 million people in the United States, the benefit of that missile would be $150 million even if each person valued it on average at 50 cents.

Adding demand curves vertically is easy to do in textbooks, but not in practice. With private-good demand curves, individuals reveal their demand when they buy a good. If they don't buy it, it wasn't worth the price. Since individuals do not purchase public goods, their demand is not revealed by their actions. Government must guess at it. If a public good is to be financed by a tax on the citizens who benefit from it, individuals have an incentive to conceal their willingness to pay for it. This is why in the

Q-6 Why is it so difficult for government to decide the efficient quantity of a public good to provide?

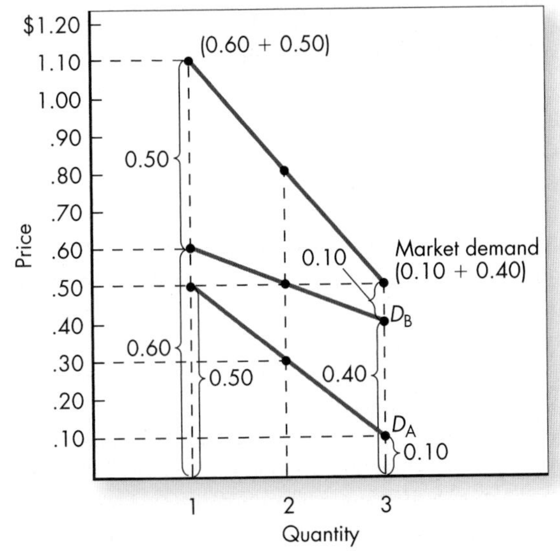

FIGURE 21-4
The Market Value of a Public Good

Since a public good is enjoyed by many people without diminishing its value to others, the market demand curve is constructed by adding the marginal benefit each individual receives from the public good at each quantity. For example, the value of the first unit to the market is $1.10, the sum of individual A's value ($0.50) and individual B's value ($0.60).

supply of public goods we see the free rider problem. The self-interested citizen wants to benefit from the public good without bearing the cost of providing it. Similarly, if people think they will not be taxed but will benefit from the public good, they have an incentive to exaggerate their willingness to pay.

Excludability and the Costs of Pricing

The public/private good differentiation is seldom clear-cut.

The public/private good differentiation is seldom clear-cut since many goods are somewhat public and somewhat private in nature, with the degree of publicness in large part determined by available technology. As technology changes, the degree of publicness of a good changes. For example, radio signals were previously classified as public goods because it was technologically impossible to exclude listeners, but when encoded satellite broadcasting was developed, exclusion became relatively easy. Today companies such as SIRIUS Satellite Radio supply radio broadcasts as private goods.

To capture the complicated nature of goods, economist Paul Romer has suggested that instead of categorizing goods as purely public or private, it is better to divide them by their degree of publicness and privateness, which means by their degree of rivalry in consumption, and their degree of excludability in their pricing. This division gives us the following categories:

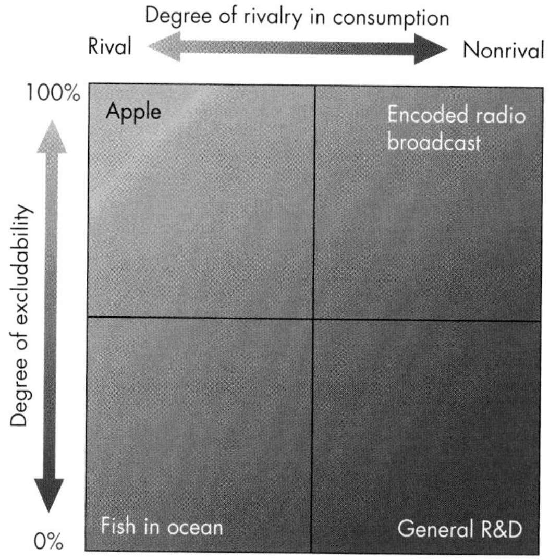

True private goods, such as an apple (if you eat it, no one else can, and you can easily exclude others from consuming it), which are both rival in consumption and 100 percent excludable, are in the upper-left corner; they are most efficiently supplied privately. True public goods, such as basic research and development, sometimes called the development of general-purpose technology (once an algebra is figured out, everyone can use it and one person using it does not eliminate its availability to others), which are nonrival in consumption and 0 percent excludable, are in the lower-right corner; they must be supplied publicly. Goods in other positions in the box can be provided either publicly or privately. How they are supplied depends on political decisions made by the government. An example of a debate about how to supply a good that is somewhat excludable is music. It is nonrival in consumption (after you've listened to a song, that song is still available to others to hear) but is excludable (those not owning CDs or concert tickets cannot listen), although the ease of excludability depends on the nature and level of enforcement of the property rights for music. For example, at one time Napster offered free music downloads, but because of pressure by the music industry, Napster now sells music downloads and pays royalties to those who own the songs. Because technology has changed with the development of digital recording and the Internet, the nature of supply of music has become contested, as the fights about Napster and other online sharing services demonstrate.

Informational Problems

The final case of market failure I want to address is caused by imperfect information. The perfectly competitive model assumes that individuals have perfect information about what they are buying. So, if they voluntarily buy a good, it is a reasonable presumption that they expect that they are making themselves better off by doing so. But what if the buyer doesn't have perfect information? Say someone convinces you that he is selling an expensive diamond and you buy it, only to find out later that it is actually just glass. Or alternatively, say someone convinces you her used car is a cherry (in perfect condition). You buy it only to discover later that it is a lemon (faulty) and won't run no matter what you do to it.

Real-world markets often involve deception, cheating, and inaccurate information. For example, car dealers know about defects in the cars they sell but do not always reveal those defects to consumers. Another example is when consumers who want health insurance do not reveal their health problems to the insurance company. In both cases, it is in the interest of the knowledgeable person not to reveal information that the other person or firm would need to know to make an informed decision about the transaction. Hence, imperfect information can be a cause of market failure.

Imperfect information can be a cause of market failure.

When there is a lack of information, or when buyers and sellers don't have equal information, markets in some goods may not work well. Let's consider the used-car example more carefully to make the point. Let's say that owners of used cars know everything about their cars, but buyers know nothing. If sellers are profit maximizers, they will reveal as little as possible about the cars' defects; they will reveal as much as they can about the cars' good qualities.

To make the example specific, let's say also that only two types of cars exist: "lemons" that are worth $4,000 and "cherries" that are worth $8,000. The market initially consists of equal quantities of lemons and cherries. Say also that the buyers cannot distinguish between lemons and cherries. What will happen? Individuals, knowing that they have a 50 percent chance of buying a lemon, may well offer around $6,000 (the average of $4,000 and $8,000). Given that price, individuals with cherries will be very hesitant to sell and individuals with lemons will be eager to sell. Eventually, buyers will recognize that the sellers of cherries have left the market. In the end only lemons will be offered for sale, and buyers will offer only $4,000 with the expectation that cars offered will be lemons. When the market for cherries—good used cars—has disappeared, the result is a market failure.

Such a market failure is called an **adverse selection problem**—*a problem that occurs when buyers and sellers have different amounts of information about the good for sale.* In the case of adverse selection, only lemons—those with the most problems—remain in the market. Take the example of medical insurance. Insurance providers need to make a profit. To do so, they set rates that reflect their estimate of the costs of providing health care. The problem is that individuals have better information about their health than do the insurance providers. Health insurers want a diverse group to spread out the costs, but they face a greater demand among those with the worst health problems. Seeing that their customers have more health problems than average, medical insurance providers raise the rates. Those who are in good health find those charges to be too high and reduce the quantity of health insurance they purchase. The providers are therefore left with a group with an even higher incidence of health problems and higher medical costs than the general population. Less than the desired amount of low-cost insurance exists for people in good health.

Adverse selection problems can occur when buyers and sellers have different amounts of information about the good for sale.

Q-7 How would you expect medical insurance rates to change if medical insurers could use information contained in DNA to predict the likelihood of major medical illnesses?

Signaling refers to an action taken by an informed party that reveals information to an uninformed party and thereby partially offsets adverse selection.

Informational problems can be partially resolved by signaling. **Signaling** refers to *an action taken by an informed party that reveals information to an uninformed party that offsets the false signal that caused the adverse selection problem in the first place*. Take the lemon problem with used cars. The adverse selection problem occurred because the individual's act of selling the used car provided a signal to the buyer that the car was a lemon. Lowering the offering price of a car would provide a stronger signal—buyers reasonably would equate low prices with low quality. But the false signal can be partially offset by a seller warranty—a guarantee to the buyer that the car is not a lemon. That's why many used cars come with warranties. The warranty offers a signal to the buyer that the car is not a lemon.

In other cases it is harder to offset a false signal. Consider the plight of an unemployed worker. This person may be an excellent worker who is willing to work for a low wage because she really needs the job. However, if she offers to work for a low wage, the firm may think that she must not be a very good worker since she is willing to work for that low wage. The knowledge that the firm may think that way may prevent her from offering to work at a low wage. So she remains unemployed even though, if there were full information, there is a wage at which she would like to work and at which the firm would like to hire her.

Workplace safety is another example of imperfect information causing market failure. Although businesses have an incentive to provide a safe working environment to limit costs, they may not choose a level of safety that would be preferred by employees. If the employer does not disclose unsafe working conditions, and those conditions cannot be easily identified by workers, there is again an informational problem. Employees may not be adequately compensated for the risks they face.

We would expect informational markets to develop that would resolve these information problems, and to some degree they do. For example, you can hire a firm to certify the quality of a car even if the seller does not offer a warranty. And students often intern at a company, which gives the company a chance to judge their quality. But because information often has significant public-good aspects, in many cases information markets do not develop fully, and those that do develop only partially resolve the problems.

Policies to Deal with Informational Problems

What should society do about informational problems that lead to market failures? One answer is to regulate the market and see that individuals provide the right information. Another is for the government to license individuals in the market, requiring those with licenses to reveal full information about the good being sold. Government has set up numerous regulatory commissions and passed laws that require full disclosure of information. The Federal Trade Commission, the Consumer Product Safety Commission, the Occupational Safety and Health Administration, the Food and Drug Administration, and state licensing boards are all examples of regulatory solutions designed to partially offset informational market failures.

But these regulatory solutions have problems of their own. The commissions and their regulations introduce restrictions that can slow down the economic process and prevent trades that people want to make. Consider as an example the Food and Drug Administration (FDA). It restricts what drugs may be sold until sufficient information about the drugs' effects can be disclosed. The FDA testing and approval process can take 5 to 10 years, is extraordinarily costly, and raises the price of drugs. The delays have caused some people to break the law by making the drugs available before they are approved.

Information problems may be a problem of the lack of a market.

A Market in Information Economists who lean away from government regulation suggest that the problem presented by the information examples above are not really a problem of market failure but instead a problem of the lack of a market. Information is valuable and is an economic product in its own right. Left on their own, markets will develop to provide the information that people need and are willing to pay for. (For example, a large number of consumer magazines provide such information.) In the car example, the buyer can hire a mechanic who can test the car with sophisticated diagnostic techniques and determine whether it is likely a cherry or a lemon. Firms can offer guarantees that will provide buyers with assurance that they can either return the car or have it fixed if the car is a lemon. There are many variations of such market solutions. If the government regulates information, these markets may not develop; people might rely on government instead of markets. Thus, the informational problem is not a problem of the market; it is a problem of government regulation.

Licensing of Doctors Let's consider another informational problem that contrasts the market approach with the regulatory approach: medical licensing.[1] Currently all doctors are required to be licensed to practice, but this was not always the case.

In the early 1800s, medical licenses were not required by law in the United States, so anyone who wanted to could set up shop as a physician. Today, however, it is illegal to practice medicine without a license. Licensing of doctors can be justified by information problems. Since individuals often don't have an accurate way of deciding whether a doctor is good, government intervention may be necessary. The information problem is reduced because licensing requires that all doctors have at least a minimum competency. People have the *information* that a doctor must be competent because they see the license framed and hanging on the doctor's office wall.

A small number of economists, of whom Milton Friedman is the best known, have proposed that licensure laws be eliminated, leaving the medical field unlicensed. They argue that licensure was instituted as much, or more, to restrict supply as it was to help the consumer. Specifically, critics of medical licensure raise these questions:

Some economists argue that licensure laws were established to restrict supply, not to help the consumer.

> Why, if licensed medical training is so great, do we even need formal restrictions to keep other types of medicine from being practiced?
>
> Whom do these restrictions benefit: the general public or the doctors who practice mainstream medicine?
>
> What have the long-run effects of licensure been?

Even the strongest critics of licensure agree that, in the case of doctors, the informational argument for government intervention is strong. But the question is whether licensure is the right form of government intervention. Why doesn't the government simply provide the public with information about doctors' training and about which treatments work and which don't? That would give the freest rein to *consumer sovereignty* (the right of the individual to make choices about what is consumed and produced). If people have the necessary information but still choose to treat cancer with laetrile, why should the government tell them they can't?

If the informational alternative is preferable to licensure, why didn't the government choose it? Friedman argues that government didn't follow that path because the licensing was done as much for the doctors as for the general public. Licensure has led to a monopoly position for doctors. They can restrict supply and increase price and thereby significantly increase their incomes.

Let's now take a closer look at the informational alternative that critics say would be preferable.

The Informational Alternative to Licensure The informational alternative is to allow anyone to practice medicine but to have the government certify doctors' backgrounds and qualifications. The government would require that doctors' backgrounds

[1]The arguments presented here about licensing doctors also apply to dentists, lawyers, college professors, cosmetologists (in some states, cosmetologists must be licensed), and other professional groups.

ADDED DIMENSION

Licensure and Surgery

Surgery should be the strongest case for licensure. Would you want an untrained butcher to operate on you? Of course not. But opponents of licensure point out that it's not at all clear how effectively licensure prevents butchery. Ask a doctor, "Would you send your child to any board-certified surgeon picked at random?" The honest answer you'd get is "No way. Some of them are butchers." How do they know that? Being around hospitals, they have access to information about various surgeons' success and failure rates; they've seen them operate and know whether or not they have manual dexterity.

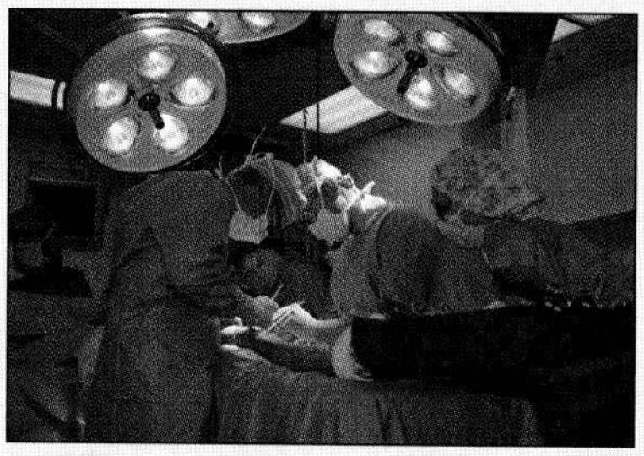

Advocates of the informational alternative suggest that you ask yourself, "What skill would you want in a surgeon?" A likely answer would be "Manual dexterity. Her fingers should be magic fingers." Does the existing system of licensure ensure that everyone who becomes a surgeon has magic fingers? No. To become licensed as a surgeon requires a grueling seven-year residency after four years of medical school, but manual dexterity, as such, is never explicitly tested or checked!

The informational alternative wouldn't necessarily eliminate the seven-year surgical residency. If the public believed that a seven-year residency was necessary to create skilled surgeons, many potential surgeons would choose that route. But there would be other ways to become a surgeon. For example, in high school, tests could be given for manual dexterity. Individuals with superb hand/eye coordination could go to a one-year technical college to train to be "heart technicians," who would work as part of a team doing heart surgery.

Clearly open-heart surgery is the extreme case, and most people will not be convinced that it can be performed by unlicensed medical personnel. But what about minor surgery? According to informational alternative advocates, many operations could be conducted more cheaply and better (since people with better manual dexterity would be doing the work) if restrictive licensing were ended. Or, if you don't accept the argument for human medical treatments, how about for veterinarians? For cosmetologists? For plumbers? Might the informational alternatives work in these professions?

be made public knowledge. Each doctor would have to post the following information prominently in his or her office:

1. Grades in college.
2. Grades in medical school.
3. Success rate for various procedures.
4. References.
5. Medical philosophy.
6. Charges and fees.

Q-8 Who would benefit and who would lose if an informational alternative to licensing doctors were used?

According to supporters of the informational alternative, these data would allow individuals to make informed decisions about their medical care. Like all informed decisions, they would be complicated. For instance, doctors who only take patients with minor problems can show high "success rates," while doctors who are actually more skilled but who take on problem patients may have to provide more extensive information so people can see why their success rates shouldn't be compared to those of the doctors who take just easy patients. But despite the problems, supporters of the informational alternative argue that it's better than the current situation.

Current licensure laws don't provide any of this information to the public. All a patient knows is that a doctor has managed to get through medical school and has passed the medical board exams (which are, after all, only sets of multiple-choice questions). The doctor may have done all this 30 years ago, possibly by the skin of his or her teeth, but, once licensed, a doctor is a doctor for life. (A well-known doctor joke is the following: What do you call the person with the lowest passing grade point average in medical school? Answer: Doctor.) Thus, the informational alternative would provide much more useful data to the public than the current licensing procedure does.

The informational alternative relies on people having the ability to assess the information provided. Supporters of licensing argue that people do not have that ability; supporters of the informational alternative argue that they do.

Government Failure and Market Failures

The above three types of market failure—externalities, public goods, and informational problems—give you a good sense of how markets can fail. They could be extended almost infinitely; all real-world markets in some way fail. But the point was to provide you not only with a sense of the way in which markets fail but also with a sense that economists know that markets fail and many of them support markets and oppose regulation anyway. Simply to point out a market failure is not necessarily to call for government to step in and try to rectify the situation. Why? The reason can be called *government failure*, which we defined above as happening when the government intervention in the market to improve the market failure actually makes the situation worse.

Q-9 Would an economist necessarily believe that we should simply let the market deal with a pollution problem?

Why are there government failures? Let's briefly list some important reasons:

1. *Government doesn't have an incentive to correct the problem.* Government reflects politics, which reflects individuals' interests in trying to gain more for themselves. Political pressures to benefit some group or another will often dominate over doing the general good.
2. *Governments don't have enough information to deal with the problem.* Regulating is a difficult business. To intervene effectively, even if it wants to, government must have good information, but just as the market often lacks adequate information, so does the government.
3. *Intervention in markets is almost always more complicated than it initially seems.* Almost all actions have unintended consequences. Government attempts to offset market failures can prevent the market from dealing with the problem more effectively. The difficulty is that generally the market's ways of dealing with problems work only in the long run. As government deals with the short-run problems, it eliminates the incentives that would have brought about a long-run market solution.

Web Note 21.4 Unintended Consequences

4. *The bureaucratic nature of government intervention does not allow fine-tuning.* When the problems change, the government solution often responds far more slowly. An example is the Interstate Commerce Commission, which continued to exist years after its regulatory job had been eliminated.

Q-10 If one accepts the three reasons for market failure, why might one still oppose government intervention?

5. *Government intervention leads to more government intervention.* Given the nature of the political process, opening the door in one area allows government to enter into other areas where intervention is harmful. Even in those cases where government action may seem to be likely to do some good, it might be best not to intervene, if that intervention will lead to additional government action in cases where it will not likely do good.

The above list is only a brief introduction to government failures. Much more could be said about each of them. But exploring them would take us away from economics and into political science. The important point to remember is that government failures exist and must be taken into account before making any policy recommendation. That's why real-world economic policy falls within the art of economics, and policy conclusions cannot be drawn from the models of positive economics.

REAL-WORLD APPLICATION

Global Warming and Economic Policy

An issue in which almost all the dimensions of economic policy analysis come into play is global warming. The issue is enormous, and a recent expert consensus estimate of the cost of global warming in terms of lost income was a 1 percent decline in global economic activity, which for the United States comes out to about $120 billion, or $400 per person. As discussed in the box in Chapter 1 on global warming, the framework within which the debate is taking place is the economic framework. Economists have done numerous studies of the costs and benefits of various policies, which have led to a consensus that global warming should be seen as an issue of market failure; that is, that the market places no price on emitting carbon-dioxide gas into the atmosphere even though emissions impose a cost on society.

The policy problems of dealing with global warming are formidable. The first is that there is a major free rider problem. Because there is no world government that can force countries to comply, any policy has to be voluntary, making it easy for one country to opt out (free ride). A second problem is that global warming is not a pure public bad. Some countries and areas within countries actually benefit from global warming. For example, significant global warming will extend the growing season in northern countries and make areas that previously were almost uninhabitable much more pleasant. The costs of global warming are highly concentrated in low-lying coastal areas. This diversity of costs makes arriving at a voluntary agreement much less likely.

A third problem is that the largest expected benefits to stopping global warming are in the future, while many of the costs are *now*, and people tend to discount future costs and benefits. A fourth problem is the lack of a clear cost/benefit analysis for various policy alternatives and the uncertainty of the success of various technologies. Cost estimates of various policies to become largely free of fossil fuel emissions by 2100 vary from 1 percent to 16 percent of total world output. (Were a cost-competitive fuel-cell-powered car or a fusion nuclear reactor developed, the use of fossil fuel would decrease significantly, and the cost estimate would be much less.)

All these problems suggest that the debate about global warming policy will likely be a lively one. Over the coming years, we can expect to see three types of policies implemented: (1) the lowest-cost/highest-benefit policies that are easy to implement such as more use of energy-efficient light bulbs, improved insulation standards on new buildings, and reduced standby power requirements on electronic devices; (2) the politically high-profile policies instituted on a state or country basis, rather than on a global basis, that don't really do much to solve the problem but that sound good in a sound bite; and (3) those policies that do not make much sense in an economic framework but that help certain firms and geographic areas, and that make sense within a political framework. Many economists believe that increased corn-based ethanol production is an example; the carbon-dioxide emissions from producing ethanol from corn are almost as great as the reduction in carbon-dioxide emissions resulting from the use of ethanol as a fuel, but the programs significantly help farmers, so they have political support.

Conclusion

As a textbook writer, I wish I could say that some conclusions can be drawn about whether the government should, or should not, enter into the economy. I certainly have views about particular instances (in case you haven't guessed, I'm a highly opinionated individual), but to lay out arguments and information that would convince a reasonable person to agree with me would take an entire book for each area in which government might intervene.

What I can do in this textbook is to stimulate your interest in discovering for yourself the information and the subtleties of the debates for and against government intervention. Just about every time you read, hear, or are asked the question "Should the government intervene in a market?" the answer is "It depends." If your first impulse is to give any answer other than that one, you may have trouble maintaining the appropriate objectivity when you start considering the costs and benefits of government intervention.

Should the government intervene in the market? It depends.

Summary

- Three sources of market failure are externalities, public goods, and imperfect information.
- An externality is the effect of a decision on a third party that is not taken into account by the decision maker. Positive externalities provide benefits to third parties. Negative externalities impose costs on third parties.
- The markets for goods with negative externalities produce too much of the good for too low of a price. The markets for goods with positive externalities produce too little of the good for too great a price.
- Economists generally prefer incentive-based programs to regulatory programs because incentive-based programs are more efficient. An example of an incentive-based program is to tax the producer of a good that results in a negative externality by the amount of the externality.
- Voluntary solutions are difficult to maintain for long periods of time because other people have an incentive to be free riders—to enjoy the benefits of others' volunteer efforts without putting forth effort themselves.
- An optimal policy is one in which the marginal cost of undertaking the policy equals its marginal benefit.
- Public goods are nonexclusive and nonrival. It is difficult to measure the benefits of public goods because people do not reveal their preferences by purchasing them in the marketplace.
- Theoretically, the market value of a public good can be calculated by summing the value that each individual places on every quantity. This is vertically summing individual demand curves.
- Individuals have an incentive to withhold information that will result in a lower price if one is a seller and a higher price if one is a consumer. Because of this incentive to withhold information, the markets for some goods disappear. Such market failures are known as adverse selection problems.
- Licensure and full disclosure are two solutions to the information problem.
- Government intervention may worsen the problem created by the market failure. Government failure occurs because (1) governments don't have an incentive to correct the problem, (2) governments don't have enough information to deal with the problem, (3) intervention is more complicated than it initially seems, (4) the bureaucratic nature of government precludes fine-tuning, and (5) government intervention often leads to more government intervention.

Key Terms

adverse selection problem *(495)*
direct regulation *(488)*
efficient *(489)*
effluent fees *(490)*
externality *(486)*
free rider problem *(491)*
government failure *(485)*
inefficient *(489)*
marginal social benefit *(488)*
marginal social cost *(487)*
market failure *(485)*
market incentive plan *(490)*
negative externality *(486)*
optimal policy *(491)*
positive externality *(486)*
public good *(492)*
signaling *(496)*
tax incentive program *(489)*

Questions and Exercises

connect ECONOMICS

1. State three reasons for a potentially beneficial role of government intervention. LO1, LO3, LO5
2. Is the marginal social benefit of a good that exhibits positive externalities greater or less than the private social benefit of that good? Why? LO1
3. Which is more efficient: a market incentive program or a direct regulatory program? Why? LO2
4. How would an economist likely respond to the statement "There is no such thing as an acceptable level of pollution"? LO2

5. Would a high tax on oil significantly reduce the amount of pollution coming from the use of oil? Why or why not? LO2
6. Would a high tax on oil significantly reduce the total amount of pollution in the environment? (Difficult) LO2
7. There's a gas shortage in Gasland. You're presented with two proposals that will achieve the same level of reduction in the use of gas. Proposal A would force everybody to reduce their gas consumption by 5 percent. Proposal B would impose a 50-cent tax on the consumption of a gallon of gas, which would also achieve a 5 percent reduction. Consumers of gas can be divided into two groups—one group whose demand is elastic and another group whose demand is in elastic.
   a. How will the proposals affect each group?
   b. Which group would support a regulatory policy?
   c. Which would support a tax policy? LO2
8. The marginal cost, marginal social cost, and demand for fish are represented by the curves in the graph below. Suppose that there are no restrictions on fishing.
   a. Assuming perfect competition, demonstrate graphically what the catch is going to be, and at what price will it be sold.
   b. What are the socially efficient price and output?
   c. Some sports fishers propose a ban on commercial fishing. As the community's economic adviser, you're asked to comment on it at a public forum. You answer from the perspective of an economist. LO2

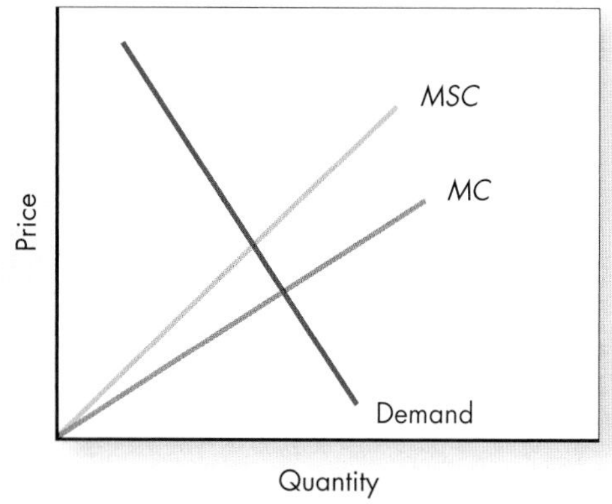

9. University of Texas professor Don Fullerton and Bucknell University professor Thomas C. Kinnaman studied the effects of Charlottesville, Virginia's change from charging a flat fee for garbage collection to charging $0.80 per 32-gallon bag and found the following results:
   The weight of garbage collected fell by 14 percent.
   The volume of garbage collected fell by 37 percent.
   The weight of recycling rose by 16 percent.
   a. Why did recycling increase and garbage collection decrease?
   b. Why did the weight of garbage fall by less than the volume of garbage collected?
   c. Demonstrate, using supply and demand curves, the effect of the change in pricing on the volume of garbage collected. LO2
10. List the public-good aspects (if any) of the following goods: safety, street names, and a steak dinner. LO3
11. Why are both excludability and nonrivalry important elements of public goods? LO3
12. Why are voluntary contributions to provide for public goods such as city parks unlikely to lead to an efficient quantity of parks in a city? LO3
13. Using the table below, which shows the demand for a public good in an economy consisting of two households, A and B, answer the following questions:

Price		$0.00	$0.50	$1.00	$1.50	$2.00	$2.50	$3.00
Quantity	A	12	10	8	6	4	2	0
demanded	B	4	3	2	1	0	0	0

   a. Graph the individual demand curves and the market demand curve.
   b. What would make you doubt that the table is an accurate reporting of the individual demand curves?
   c. If the marginal cost of providing one unit of the good is $2.00, what is the socially optimal amount of the public good?
   d. Given the free rider problem, is your answer to *c* most likely an underestimate or an overestimate? LO3
14. If you are willing to pay $1,000 for a used stereo that is a "cherry" and $200 for a used stereo that is a "lemon," how much will you be willing to offer to purchase a stereo if there is a 50 percent chance that the stereo is a lemon? If owners of cherry stereos want $700 for their cherries, how will your estimate of the chance of getting a cherry change? LO4
15. Give three examples of signaling in the real world. LO4
16. What is the adverse selection problem? LO4
17. If neither buyers nor sellers could distinguish between "lemons" and "cherries" in the used-car market, what would you expect to be the mix of lemons and cherries for sale? LO4
18. Automobile insurance companies charge lower rates to married individuals than they do to unmarried individuals. What economic reason is there for such a practice? Is it fair? LO4
19. An advanced degree is required to teach at most colleges. In what sense is this a form of restricting entry through licensure? LO4
20. Who would benefit and who would lose if an informational alternative to licensing doctors were introduced? LO4
21. A debate about dairy products concerns the labeling of milk produced from cows who have been injected with the hormone BST, which significantly increases milk production.

Since the FDA has determined that this synthetically produced copy of a milk hormone is indistinguishable from the hormone produced naturally by the cow, and also has determined that milk from cows treated with BST is indistinguishable from milk from untreated cows, some people have argued that no labeling requirement is necessary. Others argue that the consumer has a right to know.

a. Where do you think most dairy farmers stand on this labeling issue?
b. If consumers have a right to know, should labels inform them of other drugs, such as antibiotics, normally given to cows?
c. Do you think dairy farmers who support BST labeling also support the broader labeling law that would be needed if other drugs were included? Why? LO4

22. Economics professors Thomas Hopkins and Arthur Gosnell of the Rochester Institute of Technology estimated that in the year 2000, regulations cost the United States $662 billion, or about $5,700 per family.
    a. Do their findings mean that the United States had too many regulations?
    b. How would an economist decide which regulations to keep and which to do away with? LO5

Questions from Alternative Perspectives

1. The book titles this chapter "Market Failure versus Government Failure."
   a. Does the fact that the author spends most of the chapter discussing market failure rather than government failure suggest an ideological bias in the book?
   b. If so, how would you characterize that bias? (Austrian)
2. In the late 19th century, Washington Gladden said, "He who battles for the Christianization of society will find their strongest foe in the field of economics. Economics is indeed the dismal science because of the selfishness of its maxims and the inhumanity of its conclusions."
   a. Evaluate this statement.
   b. Is there a conflict between the ideology of the market and the precepts of Christianity?
   c. Would a society that emphasized a market mode of production benefit from having a moral framework that emphasized selflessness rather than selfishness? (Religious)
3. Institutional economists define economics as the study of how people use institutions to socially interact in the process of extracting materials from the biophysical world to produce and exchange goods and services to reproduce culture and better the human condition. If you accept this definition of economics, under what conditions is government intervention in the market acceptable? (Institutionalist)
4. Post-Keynesians suggest that contractual agreements might be a way to deal with asymmetric information.
   a. Name a business or consumer transaction where asymmetric information might occur.
   b. How could a contractual agreement overcome the problems of asymmetric information in that market?
   c. Would that contractual agreement arise without government intervention? (Post-Keynesian)
5. Water privatization in South Africa has been guided by what the World Bank calls the "cost recovery" approach: water should be made available to people only if the company providing it can recover its costs plus a profit. In 1995, private companies began taking over the provision of water in South Africa. Since then some cities have seen water prices increase fourfold, millions of people have had their water cut off, and outbreaks of cholera have returned for the first time in decades.
   a. Which of your textbook's list of market failures apply to the privatization of water utilities in South Africa?
   b. Is the failure so serious that it makes the private provision of water bad public policy?
   c. If not, why not? If so, what policies would make more economic sense? (Radical)

Issues to Ponder

1. More than half of 30 economists polled recently stated that the federal gasoline tax should be raised to $1 or higher. What do you suppose were their reasons? (Difficult) LO2
2. In his book *At the Hand of Man*, Raymond Bonner argues that Africa should promote hunting, charging large fees for permits to kill animals (for example, $7,500 for a permit to shoot an elephant). (Difficult)
   a. What are some arguments in favor of this proposal?
   b. What are some arguments against? LO2
3. California passed an air-quality law that required 3.75 percent of all the cars sold in the state to emit zero pollution by 1998, and required 10 percent of all cars sold in the state to meet this standard by 2003. (Difficult)
   a. What was the likely impact of this law?
   b. Can you think of any way in which this law might actually increase pollution rather than decrease it?
   c. How might an economist suggest modifying this law to better achieve economic efficiency? LO2

4. Economist Robert W. Turner suggested three market failures that could justify government provision of national parks. What three failures did he likely discuss and what is the cause of the failure? (Difficult) LO3
5. Should government eliminate the Food and Drug Administration's role in restricting which drugs may be marketed? Why or why not? (Difficult) LO4
6. Financial analysts are not currently required to be licensed. Should they be licensed? Why or why not? (Difficult) LO4
7. Recently scientists have identified a gene that accounts for 5 percent of thrill-seeking behavior. People with this gene are more likely to take more risks such as smoking and bungee jumping in search of the next thrill. Provide two arguments—one for and one against—requiring people to undergo testing to find out if they have this gene before a company agrees to provide life insurance. LO4
8. List five ways you are affected on a daily basis by government intervention in the market. For what reason might government be involved? Is that reason justified? LO5

Answers to Margin Questions

1. An externality is an effect of a decision not taken into account by the decision maker. When there are externalities, the private price no longer necessarily reflects the social price, and therefore the market may not work properly. *(487)*
2. No. The existence of a positive externality does not mean that the market works better than if no externality existed. It means that the market is not supplying a sufficient amount of the resource or activity, and insufficient supply can be as inefficient as an oversupply. *(488)*
3. Because efficiency does not take into account who pays the costs, there may be a trade-off between fairness and efficiency. For example, a tax on gasoline would be efficient, but because the poor tend to drive older, less fuel-efficient cars, they will end up paying more of the tax, which some may believe to be unfair. An example of a policy that might be seen as both fair and efficient is a gas tax designed to deter pollution. Consumers choose to reduce their gas use based on the new price, so the solution is efficient. The solution has an element of fairness in it since those causing the pollution are those paying more. *(489)*
4. The tax incentive approach to deal with externalities is fair in the following sense: Individuals whose actions result in more pollution pay more. Individuals whose actions result in less pollution pay less. In some broader sense this may not be fair if one takes into account the initial positions of those polluting. For example, the poor may have older cars that get fewer miles per gallon and have to pay a higher cost of pollution resulting from gasoline use. *(490)*
5. Voluntary actions that are not in people's self-interest may not work in large groups because individuals will rely on others to volunteer. There is also a potential lack of efficiency in voluntary solutions since the person who voluntarily reduces consumption may not be the person who faces the least cost of doing so. *(491)*
6. It is difficult for government to decide the efficient quantity of a public good because public goods are not purchased by individuals in markets. Individuals do not reveal the value they place on public goods. Individuals also face incentives to overstate the value they place on public goods if they do not have to pay for them, and to understate the value if they do have to share the cost. *(493)*
7. Since adverse selection is a problem in the medical insurance industry, with fuller information, I would expect that average medical rates would decline since the adverse selection problem would disappear. Medical insurers would be able to offer lower-cost insurance to people who are less likely to get sick and who perhaps choose not to be covered at today's high rates. *(495)*
8. If an informational alternative to licensing doctors were introduced, existing doctors would suffer a significant monetary loss, and students who would likely go on to medical school in existing institutions would face lower potential incomes when they entered practice. Those who benefit would likely be (1) those who did not want to go through an entire medical school schedule but were willing to learn a specialty that required far less education and in which they had a particular proclivity to do well and (2) consumers, who would get more for less. *(498)*
9. An economist would not necessarily believe that we should simply let the market deal with the pollution problem. Pollution clearly involves externalities. Where economists differ from many laypeople is in how to handle the problem. An economist is likely to look more carefully into the costs, try to build price incentives into whatever program is designed, and make the marginal private cost equal the marginal social cost. *(499)*
10. One can accept all three explanations for market failure and still oppose government intervention if one believes that government intervention will cause worse problems than the market failure causes. *(499)*

Politics and Economics: The Case of Agricultural Markets

American farmers have become welfare addicts, protected and assisted at every turn by a network of programs paid for by their fellow citizens. If Americans still believe in the virtue of self-reliance, they should tell Washington to get out of the way and let farmers practice it.

—*Stephen Chapman*

This Web chapter can be found at: www.mhhe.com/colander8e

Chapter Outline

AFTER READING THIS CHAPTER, YOU SHOULD BE ABLE TO:

1. Describe the competitive nature of agricultural markets.
2. Explain the good/bad paradox in farming.
3. State the general rule of political economy in a democracy.
4. Explain how a price support system works.
5. Explain, using supply and demand curves, the distributional consequences of four alternative methods of price support.
6. Discuss real-world pressures politicians face when designing agricultural policy.

CHAPTER 22

Behavioral Economics and Modern Economic Policy

Nobody's ever gone broke underestimating the intelligence of the general public.

—H. L. Mencken

When Dutch economist Aad Kieboom was put in charge of the men's restroom at Shiphol Airport, he instructed the builders to etch an image of a black housefly on each urinal. As we will see later in the chapter, that directive was an application of modern behavioral economic theory to policy. In this chapter, you will learn why it is, and many other ways in which behavioral economics changes the way economists approach policy.

I begin the chapter by putting the developments in behavioral economic policy in historical perspective, explaining why they developed. I then briefly review the policy implications of the traditional supply/demand models that have been the core of this book's presentation. Finally, I turn to the core of this chapter—the discussion of what might be called behavioral economic policy and how it differs from more traditional economic policy.

AFTER READING THIS CHAPTER, YOU SHOULD BE ABLE TO:

1. Define mechanism design and summarize its relationship to behavioral economics.
2. Define nudge and choice architecture and explain how they are related to behavioral economic policy.
3. Explain why a nudge policy meets a libertarian paternalism criterion.
4. Describe three types of choices where nudges can be useful.
5. State two types of nudge policies.
6. Distinguish between nudge and push policies.
7. Discuss the concerns many traditional economists have about nudge and push policies.

Behavioral Economic Policy in Perspective

Behavioral economics is that branch of modern economics that broadens the assumptions about behavior from rationality and self-interest to purposeful behavior and enlightened self-interest. As behavioral economists have broadened the building blocks of their models, they have also started to explore the implications of those broader building blocks for policy. Thus, today a **behavioral economic policy**—*economic policy based upon models using behavioral economic building blocks that take into account people's predictable irrational behavior*—is emerging that complements traditional economic policy.

Behavioral Economics and Economic Engineering

Behavioral economic policy has developed as part of a broader change in the way that economists see their role in policy making. As their understanding of markets has increased, modern economists have moved more heavily into what might be called **economic engineering**—*economics devoted not only to studying markets, but also to designing markets and other coordinating mechanisms.* Economic engineers don't just try to understand the way the economy works as economic scientists do. Economic engineers ask: Can they design mechanisms to better coordinate people's actions?

As modern economists have moved more toward engineering, they have begun to explore a broad range of mechanisms and institutions that solve coordination problems. These mechanisms and institutions are called **coordination mechanisms**—*methods of coordinating people's wants with other people's desires.* All markets are a type of coordination mechanism. There are auction markets, posted price markets, and markets where firms set prices. Each of these mechanisms coordinates wants in a slightly different way. What this means is that there is not a single market solution; there are hundreds of them. The economic policy debate is not about whether to have a market solution; the policy debate is what coordinating mechanism will best solve the problem at hand.

Q-1 How does economic engineering differ from economic science?

There is not a single market solution; there are hundreds of them.

Economists began studying coordinating mechanisms by studying markets with money prices. They soon discovered that coordinating mechanisms that don't involve money prices can be modeled as if they do involve prices. To study these coordinating mechanisms, they developed formal models based on **shadow prices**—*prices that aren't paid directly, but instead are paid in terms of opportunity cost borne by the demander, and thus determine his or her action indirectly.* In these shadow price models, every choice has an associated implicit shadow price, regardless of whether money is exchanged or not. Shadow price models convert opportunity costs to shadow prices.

Q-2 How does a shadow price differ from a normal price?

Shadow price analysis is extremely powerful. For example, it allows you to take morals and social pressure into account in your model. Thus, if you don't steal something when you could steal it, the explanation is that the shadow cost to you of doing so—of violating your moral code—is too high. Shadow price models allows you to indirectly measure the price of violating your morals.

Shadow price analysis allows you to take morals and social pressures into account in your models.

Let me give an example of the power of shadow price analysis. In his book *Freedomnomics: Why the Free Market Works*, University of Maryland economist John Lott gives an example of the number of batters hit by a ball when up at bat in the American and National Leagues. Starting in 1973, more batters were being hit in the American League than in the National League. The question was why. Lott developed a shadow price model that determined the cost to a pitcher of throwing a beanball (a pitch aimed at the batter's head). He pointed out that in 1973, the American League instituted the designated batter (pitchers were exempt from batting). The new rule meant that the pitcher no longer could be hit by a ball thrown by the opposing team's pitcher in retaliation. That rule change lowered the shadow price of throwing a beanball in his model for American League pitchers. The model gave him an explanation: the increase in beanballs in 1973 occurred because the cost of throwing a beanball fell for an American League pitcher. (Applying this insight to policy suggests that to reduce the number of beanballs, the league might raise the money price of pitching a beanball, perhaps by instituting a $10,000 fine for every hit batsman.) Shadow price analysis is central to the way in which economists think about the effect of incentives on an individual's actions and how institutions interact with incentives.

The introduction of models incorporating shadow price analysis has allowed economists to expand the scope of economics and study a wider range of social coordinating mechanisms, including a number of social problems far removed from traditional economic concerns. For example, a computer program that matches the classes you want to take with the classes that are available could be an example of a coordination mechanism based on shadow prices. The program would develop a shadow price for each course and then allocate the classes on the basis of a student's willingness to pay, as determined by the priorities he or she listed in his or her requested courses.

Shadow price analysis has allowed economists to expand the scope of economics.

Modern Economists as Reverse Engineers

Economists who use mechanism design engineering to develop policy use economic theory as a type of backward induction or reverse engineering process. Instead of building from scratch, taking an existing mechanism apart with the intention of improving it, they begin with the desired outcome and consider what coordinating mechanism will best achieve that outcome. Mechanism design economic engineers use laboratory experiments, field experiments, game theory models, computer simulations, and a variety of other tools to come up with coordinating mechanisms that achieve the desired ends. This branch of modern economics has been extraordinarily influential, and in 2007 the Nobel Prize for Economics went to three economists—Leonid Hurwicz, Eric Maskin, and Roger Myerson—who have done important work in the abstract theory of mechanism design.

Taking this engineering approach to economics also led to a change in the type of models modern economists needed to study markets. Because they were designing mechanisms that had to work, they needed models with assumptions that more precisely matched the institutions they were modeling. As opposed to studying just the simple supply/demand model, modern economists study whether the assumptions of their models match real-world market incentives. Often, they do not.

Modern economists study whether the assumptions of their models match real-world market incentives.

For example, the supply/demand model assumes that firms maximize profits. But real-world firms' decisions are made by individuals whose incentives may differ from the firm's incentives. When a decision maker's income is not the same as the firm's profit, as is generally the case, the firm's and the decision maker's incentives may be incompatible, and the individual is more likely to make decisions that don't maximize profits. For example, an employee may choose to fly first class with an airline that gives him more frequent flyer miles rather than fly on a low-cost airline, which would have saved the firm money. This behavior shows up as "irrationality" in the traditional supply/demand model because the assumptions don't match the institutional realities. Economists found these "irrationalities" caused by institutional factors throughout the economy.

All types of institutional realities impede the effectiveness of the incentives assumed in economists' models, which changes the way a system works most efficiently. Modern economists call these impediments *incentive compatibility problems*. An **incentive compatibility problem** is *a problem in which the incentive facing the decision maker does not match the incentive needed for the mechanism to achieve its desired end.*

Q-3 Does grading in courses involve an incentive compatibility problem?

Economists as Mechanism Design Engineers

Web Note 22.1
Nobel Mechanisms

Modern economists use their insights about incentive compatibility problems to design mechanisms that align incentives with desired ends. This has led to the development of a new branch of economics, called *mechanism design*, which is explicitly interested in designing mechanisms to achieve specific ends. **Mechanism design** involves *identifying a goal and then designing a mechanism such as a market, social system, or contract to achieve that end.*

The adoption of this mechanism design approach has transformed economic models into an enormously powerful tool for firms and governments. For example, when policy makers needed to figure out how to reduce CO_2 emissions, they turned to economists who designed cap-and-trade for CO_2 emissions. Similarly, when the British government wanted to allocate rights to the radio spectrum, they turned to economists who designed an auction mechanism.

The adoption of this mechanism design approach has transformed economic models into an enormously powerful tool for firms and governments.

Coordinating mechanisms don't have to be based on money prices. As mentioned above, economists have developed shadow prices that reflect value and costs of constraints in a market. For example, Harvard economist Al Roth used a shadow price model to design the National Residency Matching Program that matches medical

Markets as Information-Gathering Mechanisms

As economists have begun designing markets, they have discovered that they can take advantage of another useful function of markets—markets' ability to reveal people's collective wisdom. A price in a market represents the collective judgment of what people in the market are willing to pay for a good. Using that insight, economists reasoned: Why not create markets as a way of extracting information from people, that is, to design markets as an information-gathering mechanism? For example, say you are wondering who will win the general election. To make a prediction, economists at the University of Iowa designed an "election futures" market that allows people to "bet" on who is going to win. (A future is the promise to buy an item in the future at a specified price.) For example, you might have bought a *$100 John McCain future* for $45—the price of a $100 John McCain future on the day I wrote this. So on that day, people thought that John McCain was going to win the election sufficiently to pay $45 for the possibility of being paid $100. If John McCain had won the election, those who bought the future would have received $100. Because he lost they got nothing. Below is the price history in the market.

The goal of this market is not to provide an opportunity for people to bet. The goal is to predict what candidate is going to win the election. The prices of the futures reflect the collective wisdom of market participants—their predictions of the likelihood of a candidate winning. Thus, if a candidate's $100 future is selling for $20, most people think he is going to lose. You can check out the Iowa Election Futures market at www.biz.uiowa.edu/iem. Do these information markets work? Election futures markets such as this one have done much better at predicting the winners of elections than have the many public opinion polls.

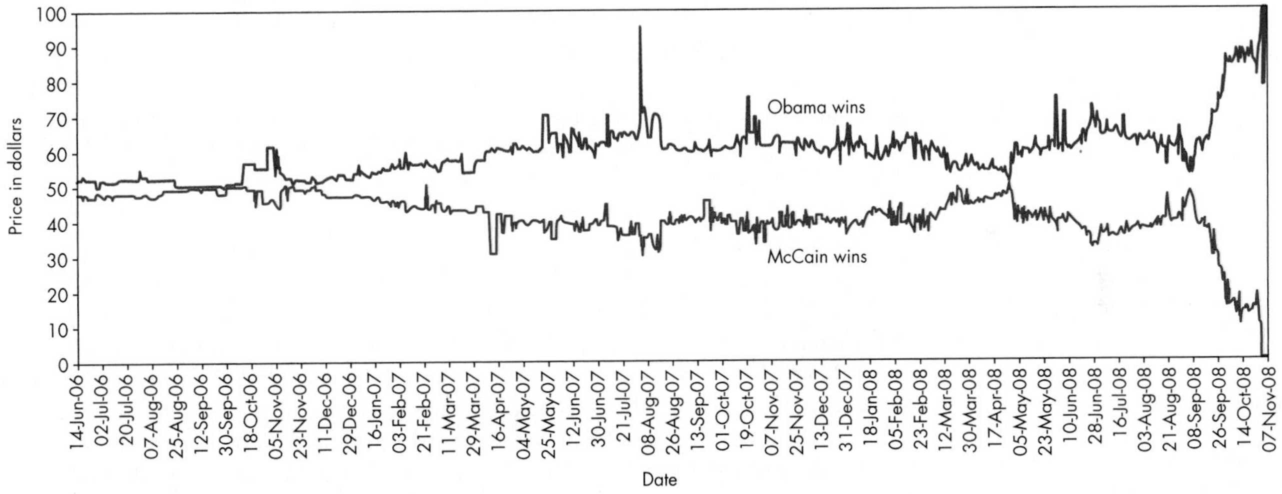

students to residency programs. Mechanism design economists also have played an important role in modifying some of the online dating services, and in creating the search algorithms used by GoogleSearch and YahooSearch. All are "coordinating mechanisms" that try to anticipate what the person wants and to match it with what is being offered. Through shadow price models, all types of allocating and coordinating mechanisms come under the purview of modern economics.

Web Note 22.2 The Prediction Market

Behavioral Economics and Mechanism Design

Q-4 Why did economists' work in mechanism design lead to a greater interest in behavioral economics?

Mechanism design is important to this chapter because economists' interest in behavioral economics grew out of this engineering approach to economics. As economists started working on real-world problems, they saw that coordination mechanisms did not always work as predicted even when they adjusted for institutional realities. The

Behavioral economic policies developed as a way of tweaking existing coordinating mechanisms to make them work better, given people's actual behavior.

reason was that their traditional assumptions about human behavior did not always fit reality. So mechanism design economists began to take into account people's predictable irrationalities when designing coordination mechanisms. In order to do that, they had to better understand how people's behavior deviated from the model's predicted behavior, which led to the emergence of behavioral economics. Behavioral economic policies developed as a way of tweaking existing coordinating mechanisms to make them work better, given people's actual behavior.

Let's consider an example of a policy that didn't work as expected and see what behavioral economists say it means for mechanism design. The example involves finding a solution for late pick-ups at a day care. It seems that a number of day care centers were having a problem getting parents to pick up their kids on time. To solve the problem, the centers followed the traditional economic solution: they imposed a fine for parents who picked up the kids late. The fine established a monetary price for picking up the kids late and was expected to decrease the number late pick-ups. However, that wasn't the result. Instead, the problem worsened; late pick-ups *rose*.

Why did that happen? Behavioral economists argued that the fine "commoditized" the choice. Once a social infraction, late pick-ups became a service parents could buy. Without a fine, the parents felt a moral obligation to pick up the kids on time. There was a high moral shadow price on picking up kids late. The introduction of a fine replaced the moral obligation with a market payment, so the relevant price went down, not up.

Behavioral economists argue that because people are social creatures, the coordinating mechanism that economists design must take into account much more than simple price incentives; it must also include social and moral incentives and the economist's models must include these additional elements as shadow prices. Failure to do so can worsen, rather than improve, the situation. Santa Fe behavioral economist Sam Bowles summarizes the implications behavioral economists drew from this and similar experiments when he argued that traditional economics incorrectly assumes that "policies that appeal to economic self-interest do not affect the salience (importance) of ethical, altruistic, and other social preferences."

The problem for behavioral mechanism design economists is to find the right combination of market, social, and moral incentives.

The interaction between markets and social and moral incentives is complicated. For example, Bowles also finds that individuals from more market-oriented societies tend to be more moral, which he explains by arguing that "fair-mindedness is essential to the exchange process and that in market-oriented societies individuals engaging in mutually beneficial exchanges with strangers represent models of successful behavior who are then copied by others." The problem for behavioral mechanism design economists is to find the right combination of market, social, and moral incentives that work to solve the particular problem at hand. Knowing what combination requires taking the existing practices and mores in each society and situation into account.

Policy Implications of Traditional Economics

The policy implication of the traditional model is that government should stay out of people's way and let them trade.

Now that I've given you the context for the development of behavioral economic policy, let's review the policy implications that follow from traditional assumptions to give us a starting point for our consideration of behavioral economic policy. In traditional economics, voluntary trade (without externalities) makes people involved in the trade better off. When people have made all the trades they can, they will be as well off as they can possibly be. If that weren't the case, they would make another trade. The policy implication of the traditional model is that government should stay out of people's way and let them trade, stepping in only to offset times when trades affect people not involved in the exchange, discouraging trades with negative externalities, and encouraging trades with positive externalities. The model directs economists toward *laissez-faire*—keep government out of the market, and let people do their own thing.

Of course, economists know that reality is more complicated and that the *theorems* (logical implications of a model, given all assumptions) about the benefits of trade that follow from the model do not immediately transfer to a *precept* (policy implication of the model as it relates to the real world) of laissez-faire. The precept of laissez-faire is based on more than the model; it is based on value judgments and judgments about how well the model fits reality. For most economists, that laissez-faire precept has lots of exceptions and includes a wide variety of ideas about policy.

These exceptions are, however, exceptions, and, for a traditional economist, the thrust of thinking like an economist means *first* to expect that the market will solve the problem, and *then*, if that doesn't seem be happening, to check why. If the reason why the market isn't working as the model predicted is important, then one modifies the policy precept. Thus, in his *Wealth of Nations*, Adam Smith listed a large number of areas where he believed government should regulate the economy even though his overall model led to laissez-faire.

Q-5 True or false: A traditional economist believes people are always rational.

Web Note 22.3 Irrationality and Cheating

Behavioral economics complicates the traditional story based on the supply/demand model because it gives up the underlying assumption that people are fully rational and self-interested. Without this assumption, voluntary trade doesn't necessarily make people better off. Instead of focusing economists' thinking on people's rational selves, behavioral economics focuses economists' thinking on people's *predictable irrationality* and designs policies that take people's predictable irrationality into account.

Behavioral economics focuses economists' thinking on people's *predictable irrationality* and designs policies that take people's predictable irrationality into account.

Choice Architecture and Behavioral Economic Policy

One of the findings of behavioral economics is that **choice architecture**—*the context in which decisions are presented*—impacts people's decisions. Traditional economic models assume that choice architecture doesn't matter; thus, for example, it assumes that the order in which choices are presented does not matter to a person's choice. If order does matter, then, in the traditional model, the person is being irrational, and if the effect shows up sufficiently so that it is predictable, he is being predictably irrational. If a traditional economist finds that people are predictably irrational, he or she will have to modify the policy implications of his or her theorems as he or she moves to policy precepts.

One of the findings of behavioral economics is that choice architecture impacts people's decisions.

Behavioral economists argue that modifying precepts after the fact to take predictable irrationality into account isn't enough. They argue that people are predictably irrational in so many areas that economists' models and policy recommendations have to include those predictable irrationalities in both models and policies. Behavioral economic policy—a policy designed to influence people's choice architecture in a way that directs people to make decisions that make them better off under the assumption that they are predictably irrational—does just that.

Two economists leading the charge in creating a separate behavioral economic policy are Chicago economists Richard Thaler and Cass Sunstein.[1] Their book *Nudge* gives a variety of examples of how choice architecture influences decisions and how to design choice architecture to influence behavior. Let's consider a simplification of one of their examples: Carolyn, the director of food services for a large city school system, must choose how to present the food to the students; she has two options:

1. Arrange the food so that the student chooses a healthy lunch, all things considered.
2. Arrange the food so that the students pick the same foods they would choose on their own.

[1]Much of the discussion in this chapter is based on Thaler and Sunstein's presentation, including the urinal description that opened the chapter.

Q-6 If an economist believes that choice architecture is important, is he or she more likely to be a traditional economist or a behavioral economist?

Thaler and Sunstein say that a traditional economist would likely choose option two, following the premise that free choice is best. But they argue that traditional economists cannot claim that option two reflects free choice because "what they would choose on their own" depends on how choices are presented. Thaler and Sunstein argue that a behavioral economist would choose option one. Option one gives the students free choice but nudges them to use that free choice to make a "better" selection. Students are still free not to choose healthy food but will be faced with an arrangement of food that will lead more of them to choose healthy food. Thaler and Sunstein call this a **nudge**—*a deliberate design of the choice architecture that alters people's behavior in predictably positive ways*.

Now that I've explained what a nudge is, let's return to the urinal at Amsterdam Airport. What was going on? It turns out that men are not very careful when they relieve themselves and can make quite a mess. They tend to splash a lot. But what Aad Kieboom noticed was that by changing the urinal slightly, the splashing can be reduced. It seems that if men see a fly when they are relieving themselves, they aim for it. If the image of the fly is placed slightly off center in the urinal, the choice architecture is right, and the mess is reduced considerably. His staff found that the "fly-in-the-urinal" reduced spillage by 80 percent.[2]

Nudges are not a new discovery. Private firms use nudges all the time to guide their customers to make choices that benefit the firm. Grocery stores position their highly profitable goods that you are likely to buy on impulse at just the right height and place to get the customer to buy them—think of the candy at the checkout counter. They also place higher-priced organic foods in a separate section (it reduces price comparison) and place milk at the back of the store (it requires people to walk past, and likely buy, other products along the way). Advertising is another way in which firms nudge their customers. Advertising frames a firm's product in a positive way that the firm's psychologists have found will lead people to develop a desire and need for that product. Advertising nudges seem to be successful since firms spend billions on advertising.

Nudge Policy and Libertarian Paternalism

Q-7 A policy designed to structure choices so that people make a certain choice is called what type of policy?

While the existence of nudges has been well known, what's new in behavioral economic policy suggested by Thaler and Sunstein is the argument that government should use nudges as a policy tool. (We will call the government use of nudges *nudge policy*.) In **nudge policy,** *government structures choices facing people so that they are free to choose what they want, but also more likely to choose what is best for them.*[3]

Libertarian paternalistic policy is a policy that leaves people free to choose, but nonetheless guides them toward a choice that a paternalistic observer would see as good for them.

Nudge policy advocates claim that nudge policy meets what they call a criterion of *libertarian paternalism*. By libertarian, they mean people are still free to choose. They argue that a nudge policy does not go against traditional economics since government is not interfering with people's freedom of choice. By paternalism, they mean people are likely to make better decisions (as judged by an outside beneficent decision maker). Thus, a **libertarian paternalistic policy** is *a policy that leaves people free to choose, but nonetheless guides them toward a choice that a paternalistic observer would see as good for them.* Thaler and Sunstein see their nudge policies as libertarian paternalistic policies. For example, in the spirit of libertarianism, a nudge policy would leave people free to smoke cigarettes, eat lots of candy, or not save for the future (all of which Thaler and Sunstein consider bad) if that's what people really want. But, in the spirit of paternalism, a nudge policy would frame people's choices to engage less often in these activities.

---

[2]There is now a fly-in-the-urinal decal company. You can see it on the Web at www.urinalfly.com.
[3]I will discuss the problem of deciding what is "best for them" below.

To give you a sense of how nudge policy would work, let's consider an example. Say you are presented with a retirement savings plan that allows you to save 10 percent of your income. If you choose to save 10 percent, your company will supplement your savings by another 10 percent. To get the company's 10 percent contribution, you have to check a box on the employee savings plan form. Given that choice, economists have found that, even though it seems like a very good deal, often 50 percent of the employees will choose to participate in the savings plan. For traditional economists, that would be the end of the story; they would conclude that 50 percent of the people decided that participating in the savings plan does not make them better off.

For behavioral economists, that is not the end of the story. They point out that people's choices depend on how the choices are framed and, in this case, it depends on what is the default option. What if, instead of having to check a box to *opt into* the savings plan, people had to check a box in order to *opt out* of the savings plan? When framed in this way, a larger percent of people will choose to participate and a smaller percent will decline. Behavioral economists ask: Which group is rational: the 50 percent that choose not to participate when they have to opt into the savings plan, or the larger percent that choose to participate when they have to opt out?

Behavioral economists point out that people's choices depend on how the choices are framed.

When Are Nudges Needed?

Thaler and Sunstein list various types of choices where they believe that nudges can be useful. Below we consider three.

Choices in Which Benefits and Costs Are Separated by Time Behavioral economists have found that people tend to make what behavioral economists consider less-than-optimal choices when the benefits and costs of those choices are separated by time. People tend to weight the immediate costs and benefits more, and future costs and benefits less, than if they were given time to reflect on the decision. Such choices present a possibility for policy nudges. Consider weight loss. Many people have a hard time losing weight. Losing weight requires facing an upfront cost (less food and more exercise) and delayed gain (slimmer physique). Many Americans agree that they are overweight and claim to want to lose weight, so designing their choices to make it easier to say no to eating excess food may be warranted. Similarly, saving requires consuming less now for a delayed benefit of consuming more later. Most people believe that they save too little, and when they look back, they wish that they had saved more. But, of course, by the time they decide they'd made a mistake, it's too late to fix it. So again, here is an opportunity for a useful nudge. Other examples are exercise and studying.

Reflecting back, most of us would have chosen to exercise or study more than we actually did. But when we were making the decision to exercise or study, somehow we just couldn't do it. The treadmill looked like so much work; the textbook (not this one, obviously) was so boring, and the TV show looked so good that we decided to watch it rather than study or exercise. All these are examples of choices in which the benefits and costs are separated by time, and that Thaler and Sunstein see open to nudges.

Complicated Choices with Many Dimensions Complicated choices are another type of choice that people are not good at making, and are therefore good candidates for a nudge. Say you are trying to decide about what type of loan to get for school. You look on the Web site and you find six or seven different options, some of which involve origination fees, some of which don't, some of which involve having your parents cosign the loan, others not, some of which have flexible rates (LIBOR + 2) and some of which have fixed interest rates, some of which involve immediate payback, others that involve payback starting six months after graduation. After spending hours struggling with them all, your mind swirls. Which one makes sense? Many students decide that there's no good way to figure it out; it's just too complicated. They could use a nudge—giving them some guidance about which is the likely best option. The nudge doesn't preclude them from choosing a different option, but if they can't figure it out, this is the option they are advised to choose.

Three types of choices where nudges may be useful are:

1. choices in which benefits and costs are separated by time,
2. complicated choices with many dimensions, and
3. infrequent choices.

Infrequent Choices An infrequent decision is a third type of decision in which nudge policies may be useful. Infrequent decisions provide little opportunity to practice making choices, evaluate feedback, or explore one's preferences. Making a particular decision for the first time is probably difficult, but if you make a similar set of decisions again and again, through trial and error, you will likely get better, and, eventually, you will get pretty good. Take food shopping: the first time you went to choose a melon, you probably had trouble. But after some practice—sometimes choosing a not-yet-ripe melon and other times hitting the mark—you have gotten pretty good at identifying the feel and smell of a good melon. Repetitive decisions such as these tend to be much more rational and capture what people actually want. Infrequent decisions—such as what college to go to, whom to marry, or what house to buy—are much more difficult.

To learn from frequently made decisions, a person needs feedback—information about the consequences of one's choices. Imagine how difficult it would be to learn how to play the piano on a keyboard that makes no sound. Hearing that wrong note provides immediate feedback on one's playing. Feedback means experiencing the consequences of making a decision.

Frequently made choices also give one a chance to learn about one's preferences or what the advantages of alternative decisions might be. How would you know if you like a caramel rumba frappucino until you've tasted one? Trying various flavors of frappucino and deciding which one we like is possible, but trying out lots of different mortgages is not. You have to choose a mortgage and predict the outcome based on little to no experience or information. Not surprisingly, people don't make especially good decisions about what type of mortgage to take out. Advocates of nudge policy argue that if people had had nudges telling them the risks of taking out a mortgage based on expected large increases in house prices, the recent subprime mortgage fiasco might have been less of a fiasco.

Two Types of Nudges

The nudges that Thaler and Sunstein propose can be classified as either advantageous default option nudges or information and encouragement nudges. Let's consider both briefly.

Advantageous Default Options Nudges The first is *advantageous default option policy*. We have already seen an example of how default options influence people's behavior in the savings example discussed earlier. When faced with a choice, people are predisposed to select the default option. By taking advantage of that tendency, economic policy makers can direct people to do what they think is better for them, while still leaving people free to make their own choice. Another example involves health insurance. If employees had to *opt out* of purchasing health insurance, they would be much more likely to buy it, which is presumably the more rational choice. A more controversial example of the default option involves organ donation. If, when people apply for driver's licenses, they had to request that their organs *not be donated*, Thaler and Sunstein argue that more organs would be available for transplant.

Information and Encouragement Nudges Another type of policy that Thaler and Sunstein recommend can be classified as *information and encouragement policy*. With these policies, government encourages people to make certain choices that government has decided are good for them. An example of an encouragement nudge would be for the government to actively inform people how their energy use compares to the average as a way to encourage people to conserve energy. For example, a number of households in San Marcos, California, were sent a letter telling them how their home energy use compared to the norm. In addition, the letters sent to those who used more-than-average energy were stamped with a frowning emoticon ☹ while the letter to those who had below-average energy use were stamped with a smiling emoticon ☺. The letters reduced energy usage by above-average energy users without affecting the below-average energy users. So the government got people to reduce their energy use without *requiring* energy conservation.

Two types of nudges are:
1. advantageous default option nudges and
2. information and encouragement nudges.

Information nudges come in many forms. One such nudge instituted by colleges to reduce alcohol consumption is advertising the actual drinking habits of college students. This sounds counterintuitive. Wouldn't advertising how much alcohol students drink, when it is illegal for most college students to do so, encourage drinking? Not so. Researchers found that the widespread perception is that college students drink excessively, and that that perception was leading college students to drink to fit in. Such behavior is often referred to as *herding*—behavior in which people mimic what they think other people are doing. The perception that college students drink excessively is inaccurate; students actually drink relatively moderate amounts of alcohol. At the University of Arizona (considered by many as a top party school), for example, the average student drinks one alcoholic beverage a week. By publicizing the fact that most college students don't drink excessively, the herding behavior pushing students towards drinking can be offset and colleges can nudge students to drink less.

Another form of information nudge is designed to guide a person through complicated decisions. The argument for such nudges can be seen with an example. If you are like me, you have a very hard time trying to understand your current cell phone bill. In fact, cell phone bills appear to be designed to confuse. When looking at my bill, I often have no idea how the cost relates to decisions I make about phone calls or whether some other pricing structure or alternative provider would be better. My state of confusion makes it all the harder to decide to change my plan.

Thaler and Sunstein argue that if firms send their customers a complete listing of all the ways they use the phone and all the fees that are charged in a way that can be compared to the pricing plans of other cell phone companies on a comparison Web site, individuals can make better decisions. They call such nudges RECAP (record, evaluate, and compare alternative prices) nudges.

The Problem of Deciding on and Implementing Nudges

Firms, because they aren't inherently paternalistic, don't necessarily have an incentive to implement the nudges that Thaler and Sunstein advocate. A profit-maximizing firm is out to maximize profit, not to make its customers and employees better off. Sometimes nudges both increase a firm's profits and make a firm's customers and employees better off. But the two goals don't always match. If government is going to consider nudge policies, some method must exist to decide (1) what nudges to implement and (2) how to get the nudge implemented. Should behavioral economists decide what nudges are appropriate? should businesses? or should government? If the decision maker is different than the one implementing the policy, then some method must exist to get the nudge implemented.

If the decision maker is different than the one implementing the policy, then some method must exist to get the nudge implemented.

The most likely decision maker will be the political process, which means government. The most likely group to implement many of the nudges that Thaler and Sunstein suggest will be private firms. This presents a problem for nudge policy since it

Q-8 If the government tells a company how to structure the bills it issues, is the policy a nudge policy?

Many nudges are mild forms of regulation.

isn't clear that, if it will reduce profits, business will want to implement the nudge in a way that will help the consumer. For example, the likely reason the cell phone bill is so complicated is not that firms don't know that customers would like the information to compare prices—it is *because* the complication makes it hard for customers to compare prices. Thaler and Sunstein recognize this, and accept that many of the nudges they seek to be implemented will require what they call "a very mild form of regulation," which for many economists, makes the nudge something more like a push.

Distinguishing a Nudge from a Push

In thinking about implementing nudge policies, I find it useful to separate the nudges suggested by behavioral economics into two categories: nudge policy and push policy. If government can institute the behavioral economic policy directly, or if a private firm chooses to implement a policy on its own, it's a nudge. However, if government has to develop a regulation and *requires* firms to implement a particular nudge, the nudge no longer meets the criteria of libertarian paternalism; the nudge is not a nudge, but a push. Thus, in my terminology, the RECAP policy discussed above, when imposed upon firms, is not a nudge; it is a push. Push policies restrict free choice by the firm for the greater good. A **push policy** is *a regulatory or tax policy to get firms or individuals to use "appropriate" nudges*. Such policies involve nudges for the person targeted by the policy but a push for the firm that has to implement the nudge. For example, a push policy might involve government requiring firms to present information in a certain way (as in RECAP), or requiring them to avoid certain actions they currently take.

A push policy is a regulatory or tax policy to get firms or individuals to use "appropriate" nudges.

Once one accepts the potential desirability of implementing the insights of behavioral economics through push policies, rather than just through nudge policies, the possibilities for behavioral economic policies increase enormously. For example, push policy might involve government intervening in the market to change incentives through taxation. It could also involve preventing firms from using many of the nudges that they currently use for their advantage. By that I mean that while government may not have yet used the insights of behavioral economics, private firms sure have, and many of the practices that they follow are designed to take advantage of them for their own profit, not necessarily to the benefit of the consumer. Firms use their knowledge that people gravitate toward the default option all the time.

For example, when ordering something on the Web, you will find that firms often ask whether you want to be included on their mailing list. Often, the box is checked already. To be excluded you have to uncheck the box. Firms can argue that you have a choice whether to be on the list or not. But they know that while you have a choice whether to be on the mailing list, far fewer people choose not to be on the list if the box were left unchecked. Government could require firms to frame the choice so that buyers have to check a box to be included in the mailing list.

Mailing options are another example. Amazon offers free mailing for orders over $25, which they advertise heavily. The default option is the "standard" mailing charge rather than the free mailing option. To get the free mailing, you have to override the default. Moreover, Amazon states that free shipping takes five to nine days rather than three to five days for standard mailing, even though the items are likely sent via the same mailing service. Government could require firms to set the default as the least-cost method of shipment and state shipping time based on actual shipping performance.

Another example of a firm taking advantage of the default option is the lure of free goods when subscribing for a service. For example, book clubs offer you seven books free in exchange for joining, leaving you free to drop out any time. It's a great deal if you drop out, but you can be sure that a sufficient number of people take the default option (staying in the plan), even though they may have wanted to drop out, to warrant book clubs making that offer. Here, government could make book clubs drop new subscribers unless they actively choose to continue beyond the free period. Each of these cases is an example of a push policy because government is regulating the behavior of firms.

The Behavioral and Traditional Economic Policy Frames

As you can see, adopting the behavioral economic framework opens up many ways in which government can usefully intervene in the market. Traditional economists say desires are inherent in each person. Behavioral economists say that desires are affected by context. In fact, one could argue that in order to allow people to express their true desires, all those nudges firms take to benefit themselves would have to be prevented, or countered, by government. For example, if advertising leads people to want things that don't make them happy, on behavioral economic policy grounds, it can be argued that government should implement an information nudge, providing "counter-advertising" that warns people about how firms are trying to change their desires. Countering all nudges by firms would involve a large regulatory presence by government.

Adopting the behavioral economic framework opens up many ways in which government can usefully intervene in the market.

Traditional economists say that having more makes you happier. Some behavioral economists suggest that having more is not what makes people happy. Often what makes them happy is having more *than other people*. Relative, not absolute, income matters. That proposition has potentially radical implication for economic policy. Specifically, it introduces the possibility that government can improve society's overall welfare by changing the way in which income is distributed.

The proposition that relative, not absolute, income matters has potentially radical implications for policy.

Cornell behavioral economist Robert Frank has pushed this argument the furthest in terms of implications for behavioral economic policy. He argues that after societies pass a certain threshold level of income, a threshold all western societies have passed, certain types of material goods don't matter a whole lot to our well being, and crowd out those goods that do matter. He argues that the problem in western economies is that "people don't spend their extra money in ways that yield significant and lasting increases in measured satisfaction." Instead they spend it on what institutionalist economist Thornstein Veblen called *conspicuous consumption goods*—goods that are bought to show off to the neighbors. Veblen even argued that the truly rich, the captains of industry, couldn't spend their money fast enough to show off, so they had to marry someone (a trophy wife) whose job it was to spend their money in a way that would show off their wealth.

Web Note 22.4
Keeping Up with the Joneses

Let's consider an example of how relative, not absolute, materialism matters. When we get that super duper, all-stainless-steel barbecue grill with Internet connection and built-in iPod speakers, we are better off. But when the neighbors get the same one, we slip back to being no better off. And if the neighbors get one with a built-in TV too, we are worse off (until we get one with a bigger built-in TV). Society ends up in a type of consumption war in which everyone is trying to outdo the other and no one is better off. (According to some, we might actually be worse off if the additional expenditures required additional work effort and less leisure.)

Frank argues that such consumption wars happen in many areas of our society. An example is houses—they get bigger and bigger, eventually turning into McMansions when much smaller houses would satisfy our needs. Cars are another example—they get bigger and bigger and turn into McHummers when a much less powerful car would do. He calls this push for goods to show off *luxury fever*.

Q-9 Do more conspicuous consumption goods make society better off?

At the same time that people are undertaking this conspicuous consumption, Frank argues that other types of goods—social goods that can be considered *inconspicuous consumption* (goods that are not physical but nevertheless experienced)—are being crowded out. For example, as more people drive bigger cars, traffic becomes congested,

ADDED DIMENSION

Karl Marx and Shove Policy

The arguments for push policy have been suggested by economists in the past. Perhaps the strongest advocate of the general ideas was Karl Marx. Marx argued that the market had a tendency to alienate people from their "true" selves. He argued that people are not born with a collection of inherent wants and desires, but instead develop a collection of wants and needs that reflect the institutions of society. For example, if firms need workers, society creates wants in people that will lead them to work. Thus, many of the wants that people have are created (artificial, not inherent (true) needs). For example, Marx argued that capitalist society created strong tendencies toward wanting materialistic goods. He argued that markets made people competitive, not cooperative; they alienated people from their true self. Markets made people, in the words of Marxist philosopher Herman Marcuse, one-dimensional people—people who only think of life in terms of material goods, and not in terms of spiritual and social goods.

Those arguments lead to strong policy conclusions that go far beyond nudges, or even pushes. Marx favored what might be called "shove" policy. To stop people from being one dimensional, and to help them escape from their material good fetishes, Marxists argued that we needed a revolution to overthrow the bourgeois capitalist government that legitimized capitalist institutions, and to replace it with a communist government committed to fulfilling the humans' true desires. He argued that eventually the communist government would wither away; once people's true desires were fulfilled, government would just no longer be necessary. People's true cooperative selves would overcome their competitive selves. These views led to the communist revolution, and are still held by a number of people throughout the world.

By almost all accounts, communism was not a success. Instead of fulfilling people's true desires, it created shortages and unfairness. Communist governments became seen as the oppressor, and people ultimately decided to overthrow the communist economies and replace them with market economies. This experience soured many economists, and other people, on government policies designed to fill people's "true" wants.

noise becomes excessive, the air becomes polluted, and social needs become shortchanged. His policy solution is to heavily tax those goods whose consumption value depends on showing off—thereby discouraging their consumption—and use the tax revenue to provide the social amenities that make society better off. He argues that we should structure the economy so that people work a lot less—say three days a week on average—and vacation a lot more. In *Luxury Fever* Frank argues that "reallocations of our time and money in these ways would result in healthier, longer, and more satisfying lives."

Concerns about Behavioral Economic Policies

Traditional economists have expressed serious misgivings about these behavioral economic policies.

As you can see, once one opens the gate to using behavioral economic insights, one can easily arrive at a number of policies that extend far beyond traditional economic precepts and nudges. Needless to say, traditional economists have expressed serious misgivings about these behavioral economic policies. In this section I present some of those concerns.

Very Few Policies Meet the Criterion of Libertarian Paternalism

The first concern has already been discussed; the possibility for true nudge policy that meets the libertarian paternalism criterion is very small. Many examples of nudges that advocates of libertarian paternalism give involve government regulation. For example, say the government believes that a particular default option, such as the saving option, will benefit people. If government passes a law that requires firms to make saving the default option, the policy does not meet the libertarian criterion, and thus is more than a nudge. Government is telling the firm what to do. Traditional economists argue that true nudge policies are too small a category to warrant a separate analysis.

Designing Helpful Policies Is Complicated

A second concern is that designing nudge policies quickly becomes complicated, requiring more information than government has. To see the difficulties that even a simple informational policy presents, consider requiring firms to label BST-free milk. (BST is a cow growth hormone.) That could be seen as simply an information policy, and thus not a strong nudge, despite the fact that labeling would be a government regulation. However, many economists oppose such labeling since most scientific tests have found that milk that comes from cows given the growth hormone BST is no different than milk that does not; they argue that people's concern about BST is itself predictably irrational—people cannot deal with complicated issues. Other economists argue that regardless of what science may conclude, if people believe that BST milk is bad for them, they should be given the information needed to avoid milk with BST; the regulation is simply providing feedback.

The problem is that placing the statement on the milk carton will likely raise people's concerns about the issue and lead some to choose higher-priced milk than they otherwise would. Should the government require such labeling or not, and if so, what other information should be included on the labels? Should people be informed of the antibiotic treatment cows receive, along with many other facts about how cow milk is produced? Where does one draw the line?

It Isn't Clear Government Knows Better

A third concern is that behavioral economic policies (whether true nudge policies or push policies) require government to decide, on the advice of behavioral economists, what is best for people, and what people truly want. For example, a "luxury tax," a policy that Frank and others advocate, involves determining what is a luxury and what is a necessity. Even though policies to tax luxuries may seem to resonate with the sense of frustration that many of us feel about perceived excesses of modern society, implementing such a policy requires the government to decide which goods make people truly happy and which goods don't. Doing that isn't easy. If people truly cared about relative, not absolute, income, people would be happy to give up some percentage of their income as long as everyone else did so as well. They are not.

Web Note 22.5 Questioning Nudge Policies

How can we be sure behavioral economists, or whoever is the decision maker about what nudges and pushes to implement, are right about what is best for people? Even if economists could agree that people do not always act in their own self-interest, it isn't clear government can determine what's in people's best interest either.

Even if economists could agree that people do not always act in their own self-interest, it isn't clear government can determine what's in people's best interest either.

Government Policy May Make the Situation Worse

A fourth concern is that nudge policy substantially increases the potential for *government failure*—where government, in dealing with a problem, actually makes the problem worse. Will government have the willpower to limit its nudges to the set that behavioral economists, or some other group, determine are appropriate? Or will they use nudges in other ways—perhaps to win an election, or to benefit one group over another? Just as traditional economists are concerned with government failure in implementing traditional economic policies to correct for externalities, traditional economists are concerned with government failure in implementing nudge policies.

Q-10 What are four concerns about behavioral economic policies?

Traditional economists argue that accepting behavioral economic policy will start the government sliding along a slippery slope.

Traditional economists argue that accepting behavioral economic policy will start the government sliding along a slippery slope. Since the government has a monopoly on power, somehow that monopoly has to be kept in check if it is to benefit the people, not members of the government or its friends. For that reason, early classical economists argued that government power had to be kept under control, even when the appropriate use of power could improve the situation, because one cannot assume that government will appropriately use its power. Because of the fear of an oppressive government, earlier economists felt that, for all its problems, the market with minimal government intervention was often the better alternative. Economics' laissez-faire set of policy precepts arose as part of a liberal tradition that was based upon certain inalienable rights of the individual that government could not violate. These arguments fit in political philosophy and are outside the confines of this text but they are the ones that a consideration of behavioral economic policy raises.

Conclusion: A Changing View of Economists: From Pro-market Advocates to Economic Engineers

In Chapter 1 I defined economic efficiency as achieving a goal as cheaply as possible and said that economists advise government in how to achieve economic efficiency. The traditional economic model made a shorthand adjustment to interpret the goal of society as designing the economy to maximize people's consumption. Markets tend to do that, and hence the traditional economic model tended to support markets.

Traditional economics justified its concentration on maximizing people's consumption by arguing that people knew what they wanted better than anyone else, and their actions revealed their desires. Consumer sovereignty was not to be questioned. Behavioral economics questions consumer sovereignty and thus opens up a Pandora's box of issues that the traditional economic model keeps out of sight.

Behavioral economics questions consumer sovereignty and thus opens up a Pandora's box of issues that the traditional economic model keeps out of sight.

Behavioral economics is part of a broader movement in modern economics where economists see themselves as mechanism design engineers. They solve problems by building coordination mechanisms that achieve predetermined goals. Traditional economists' models focus on economic incentives and people's tendency to respond to price incentives. Behavioral economists' models modify that by taking into account people's tendency to be predictably irrational. In doing this, behavioral economics opens up the policy discussion of economics from the traditional economic view that prices and incentives matter to a broader view that *everything matters;* for a behavioral economist, modern economic policy making involves complicated issues, and we need to take into account those complications when designing policy.

Who can argue with the truism that everything matters? Who better than a traditional economist using a behavioral economist's argument? Behavioral economics tells us that people are not good at making decisions when issues are complicated. Economic policy involves very complicated decisions, and the general population and policy makers need a nudge to get them to make good decisions. The traditional model gives them that nudge by concentrating on the most important aspects of choice—price incentives, and not distracting the analysis as behavioral economics does by concentrating on the many irrationalities that people exhibit. Furthermore, the traditional model protects individual liberty and prevents the state from trying to shape people's wants. By taking the focus away from that most important incentive, models based on behavioral economic insights fail to give people that nudge to concentrate on the most important element—price incentives—and, therefore, are likely to do more harm than good.

I leave it to you to decide which argument is right.

Summary

- Mechanism design is an engineering approach to economic problems in which one identifies a goal and then designs a mechanism such as a market, social system, or contract to achieve that goal.
- Behavioral economics is an outgrowth of the mechanism design approach to economics.
- Choice architecture is the context in which decisions are presented. A nudge is designed to influence choice architecture in a way that directs people to make choices that make them better off.
- Nudges are libertarian because people remain free to make choices. They are paternalistic because they change the structure of choices with the intention of influencing people's behavior in a way that improves their choices.
- Nudges can be useful for (1) choices where benefits and costs are separated by time, (2) complicated choices with many dimensions, and (3) infrequent choices.
- Two categories of nudge polices are (1) advantageous default option policies and (2) information and encouragement policies.
- A true nudge policy leaves everyone free to choose and does not have to be imposed through a regulation or taxation. Push policies are government policies requiring firms or individuals to use certain types of nudges. They do not meet the libertarian criterion.
- Behavioral economic policy is controversial. It is not clear that government can decide what is best for people or, even if they knew what was best, they would implement the policy. Government is subject to failure just as is the market.

Key Terms

behavioral economic policy *(506)*
choice architecture *(511)*
coordination mechanism *(507)*
economic engineering *(506)*
incentive compatibility problem *(508)*
libertarian paternalistic policy *(512)*
mechanism design *(508)*
nudge *(512)*
nudge policy *(512)*
push policy *(516)*
shadow price *(507)*

Questions and Exercises

connect ECONOMICS

1. What is a coordination mechanism? Give an example. LO1
2. True or false? For a market to have a coordination mechanism, money must be exchanged. Explain. LO1
3. Why were more batters being hit in the American League than in the National League starting in 1973? (Be sure your answer uses shadow prices.) LO1
4. To offset the effect of the designated batter system, what might the American League do to reduce the number of beanballs thrown? LO1
5. True or false? Only money prices affect incentives; shadow prices do not. Explain. LO1
6. What is the incentive compatibility problem? Give an example. LO1
7. What is the primary task of a mechanism design economist? LO1
8. How did mechanism design lead to behavioral economics? LO1
9. Can a model that includes just money price miss relevant prices? Why or why not? LO1
10. How is choice architecture related to behavioral economics and mechanism design? LO1
11. Behavioral economics is a new field in economics. Are nudges new too? LO2
12. What is a nudge policy? Give an example. LO2
13. How can a nudge be defined as libertarian? LO3
14. In what way is nudge policy paternalistic? LO3

15. Two people are given the choice to participate in a retirement program in which the firm matches contributions. Person A is given a form in which she must check a box to opt into the retirement program. Person B is given a form in which she must check a box to opt out of the retirement program. According to studies, which person is more likely to participate? Or are they equally likely to participate? Explain your answer. LO4
16. What are three types of choices in which nudges are useful? LO4
17. Why is a nudge useful for choices where benefits and costs are separated by time? LO4
18. Why, in the traditional model, is a nudge unnecessary but potentially helpful in the behavioral model? LO4
19. In which of the following cases might a nudge be helpful? Explain why or why not.
    a. Deciding what mortgage is affordable.
    b. Deciding whether to exercise or not on a particular day.
    c. Deciding whether to fill your gas tank.
    d. Deciding whom to marry. LO4
20. Classify the following nudges as either a "potentially advantageous default nudge," an "information or encouragement nudge," or "not a nudge."
    a. A firm redesigns its health enrollment form so that employees must explicitly choose to forgo health insurance.
    b. Your local city sends you an annual report of average water usage per resident with your actual usage along with tips for conserving water.
    c. Government raises the taxes on gasoline to reduce pollution.
    d. A consumer-advocacy group sets up a site with side-by-side comparison of auto-insurance cost based on estimated risk of drivers. LO5
21. What distinguishes a nudge from a push? LO6
22. Identify the following as either a nudge, a push, or neither.
    a. The cover of your state tax forms reports that 90 percent of residents pay taxes on time.
    b. If your friends gain weight, you are likely to gain weight too.
    c. Amazon is required by government to set the default mail option as standard.
    d. Government taxes in part to redistribute income.
    e. A health insurer issues participants credits for exercising and eating healthy foods that they can use to buy products. LO6
23. How is conspicuous consumption an example of the importance of relative materialism to one's happiness? LO6
24. How might conspicuous consumption lower total happiness? LO6
25. What are four reasons to be cautions about nudges? LO7

Questions from Alternative Perspectives

1. Behavioral economics seems to suggest that the "long-term self" rather than the "short-term self" is rational. How do we know that? (Austrian)
2. There is an implicit view in the chapter that if a policy meets the libertarian paternalistic goal, that it is a good policy. Is that necessarily the case? (Radical)
3. How does behavioral economics undermine the standard supply/demand model? (Institutionalist)
4. Behavioral economics acknowledges that cultural norms impact people's behavior, something that feminist economists have long included in their analysis. What risks does nudge policy pose for using cultural norms to affect behavior of those in society who have comparatively less power? (Feminist)

Issues to Ponder

1. What mechanism might be developed to determine whether it is appropriate for government to give a nudge? LO1
2. Do we as society focus too much on consumption, and, if so, how would one change that focus? LO2
3. Describe five nudges that firms currently use to get you to do what they want you to do. LO5

Answers to Margin Questions

1. Economic science tries to understand how the economy works; economic engineering tries to design mechanisms to better coordinate people's actions. *(507)*
2. A shadow price is an implicit price of an action whose value is measured in opportunity costs. It does not involve a payment to another person but is estimated by analyzing people's actions. *(507)*
3. Yes, it does. The goal of college is generally thought to be learning. Grading gives one an incentive to learn what is likely to be on the test, not what is necessarily the most useful or important knowledge. *(508)*
4. Economists' work in mechanism design led to a greater interest in behavioral economics because they discovered that people were predictably irrational, and that by taking that predictably irrationality into account, they could design more effective coordination mechanisms. *(509)*
5. False. They believe that people are sometimes irrational but are generally not irrational in a predictable way, and that if they are predictably irrational, that irrationality can be accounted for as an adjustment to the general model. *(511)*
6. He or she is more likely to be a behavioral economist. *(512)*
7. A policy designed to structure choices so that people make a certain choice is called a nudge policy. *(512)*
8. It depends. From the perspective of the firm, it definitely is not a nudge policy since the firm is being told what to do. It is a push policy. From the perspective of the individual, it can be seen as a nudge policy. *(516)*
9. Not necessarily. Increasing conspicuous consumption goods makes the owner feel better off but makes others feel worse off, and thus does not necessarily make society as a whole better off. *(517)*
10. Four concerns are: (1) There are very few true nudge policies; (2) Nudge policies quickly become complicated; (3) Governments do not necessarily know what is best; and (4) Nudge policies increase the potential for government failure. *(519)*

CHAPTER 23

Microeconomic Policy, Economic Reasoning, and Beyond

If an economist becomes certain of the solution of any problem, he can be equally certain that his solution is wrong.

—**H. A. Innis**

One important job of economists is to give advice to politicians and other policy makers on a variety of questions relating to social policy: How should unemployment be dealt with? How can society distribute income fairly? Should the government redistribute income? Would a program of equal pay for jobs of comparable worth (a pay equity program) make economic sense? Should the minimum wage be increased? These are tough questions.

In Chapters 21 and 22, I discussed the formal frameworks that modern economists use to think about such issues. In this chapter I consider economic reasoning in a broader context.

The reason for doing so is that economic reasoning and the supply/demand model are tools, not rules. To draw policy implications from it, the supply/demand model has to be placed in context. Used in the proper context, the supply/demand model is enormously strong, something no one should be without. Used out of context, it can lead to conclusions that don't seem right, and that maybe are not right. Consider the assembly-line chicken-production example in Chapter 13. Some of you may have felt that the assembly-line production of chickens was somehow not right—that the efficiency of the production process somehow did not outweigh the chickens' suffering. Yet the economic model, which focuses on efficiency, directs production toward that assembly line. This chapter considers when you might want to use economic reasoning, and when you might not.

The chapter is divided into two parts. The first part of the chapter extends the supply/demand model to a broader cost/benefit framework, tying together the discussion we had about economic reasoning in the introductory chapters with the chapters that developed the foundations of the supply/demand model. It shows you how economic reasoning is used in practice. The second part of the chapter turns economic reasoning back upon itself, considering not only the benefits (which are considerable) but also the costs of using economic reasoning. In doing so, I discuss how markets that are working perfectly may still lead to outcomes that are undesirable.

AFTER READING THIS CHAPTER, YOU SHOULD BE ABLE TO:

1. List three reasons why economists sometimes differ in their views on social policy.
2. Explain why liberal and conservative economists often agree in their views on social policy.
3. Explain the cost/benefit approach the typical economist takes to analyze regulations.
4. Describe three types of failure of market outcomes.
5. Explain why most economists are doubtful government can correct failure of market outcomes.

Economists' Differing Views about Social Policy

Economists' views on social policy differ widely because (1) they have different underlying values, (2) they interpret empirical evidence differently, and (3) they use different underlying models.

Economists have many different views on social policy because

1. Economists' suggestions for social policy are determined by their subjective value judgments (normative views) as well as by their objective economic analyses.
2. Policy proposals must be based on imprecise empirical evidence, so there's considerable room for differences of interpretation not only about economic issues but also about how political and social institutions work. Economic policy is an art, not a science.
3. Policy proposals are based on various models that focus on different aspects of a problem.

Web Note 23.1
The Clash of the Economists

All three reasons directly concern the role of ideology in economics. However, any policy proposal must embody both economic analysis and value judgments because the goals of policy reflect value judgments. When an economist makes a policy proposal, it's of this type: "If A, B, and C are your goals, then you should undertake policies D, E, and F to achieve those goals most efficiently." In making these policy suggestions, the economist's role is much the same as an engineer's: He or she is simply telling someone else how to achieve desired ends most efficiently. Ideally the economist is as objective as possible, telling someone how to achieve his or her goals (which need not be the economist's goals).

How Economists' Value Judgments Creep into Policy Proposals

Even though economists attempt to be as objective as possible, value judgments still creep into their analyses in three ways: interpretation of policy makers' values, interpretation of empirical evidence, and choice of economic models.

Interpretation of the Policy Maker's Values In practice, social goals are seldom so neat that they can be specified A, B, and C; they're vaguely understood and vaguely expressed. An economist will be told, for instance, "We want to make the poor better off" or "We want to see that middle-income people get better housing." It isn't clear what *poor, better off*, and *better housing* mean. Nor is it clear how judgments should be made when a policy will benefit some individuals at the expense of others, as real-world policies inevitably do.

Faced with this problem, some academic economists have argued that economists should recommend only **Pareto optimal policies**—*policies that benefit some people and hurt no one*. The policies are named in honor of the famous Italian economist Vilfredo Pareto, who first suggested that kind of criterion for judging social change.[1] It's hard to object to the notion of Pareto optimal policies because, by definition, they improve life for some people while hurting no one.

Pareto optimal policies are policies that benefit some people and hurt no one.

I'd give you an example of a real-world Pareto optimal policy if I could, but unfortunately I don't know of any. Every policy inevitably has some side effect of hurting, or at least seeming to hurt, somebody. In the real world, Pareto optimal policies don't exist. Any economist who has advised governments on real-world problems knows that all real-world policies make some people better off and some people worse off.

Q-1 If someone suggests that economists should focus only on Pareto optimal policies, how would you respond?

[1]Pareto, in his famous book *Mind and Society*, suggested this criterion as an analytic approach for theory, not as a criterion for real-world policy. He recognized the importance of the art of economics and that real-world policy has to be judged by much broader criteria than this.

But that doesn't mean that economists have no policy role. In their policy proposals, economists try to spell out the effects of a policy and whether the policy is consistent with the policy maker's value judgments. Doing so isn't easy because the policy maker's value judgments are often vague and must be interpreted by the economist. In that interpretation, the economist's own value judgments often slip in.

Interpretation of Empirical Evidence Value judgments creep into economic policy proposals through economists' interpretations of empirical evidence, which is almost always imprecise. For example, say an economist is assessing the elasticity of a product's demand in the relevant price range. She can't run an experiment to isolate prices and quantities demanded; instead she must look at events in which hundreds of other things changed, and do her best to identify what caused what. In selecting and interpreting empirical evidence, our values will likely show through, try as we might to be objective. People tend to focus on evidence that supports their position. Economists are trained to be as objective as they can be, but pure objectivity is impossible.

Let's consider the example of a debate in which some economists proposed that a large tax be imposed on sales of disposable diapers, citing studies that suggested disposable diapers made up between 15 and 30 percent of the garbage in landfills. Others objected, citing studies that showed disposable diapers made up only 1 or 2 percent of the refuse going into landfills. Such differences in empirical estimates are the norm, not the exception. Inevitably, if precise estimates are wanted, more studies are necessary. (In this case, the further studies showed that the lower estimates were correct.) But policy debates don't wait for further studies. Economists' value judgments influence which incomplete study policy makers choose to believe is more accurate.

Choice of Economic Models Similarly with the choice of models. A model, because it focuses on certain aspects of economic reality and not on others, necessarily reflects certain value judgments, so economists' choice of models must also reflect certain value judgments. Albert Einstein once said that theories should be as simple as possible, but not more so. To that we should add a maxim: Scientists should be as objective and as value-free as possible, but not more so.

Scientists should be as objective as possible, but not more so.

This book presents primarily mainstream economic models. This includes the standard supply/demand model and the new behavioral models. These models direct us to certain conclusions. Two other general models that some economists follow are a **Marxian (radical) model,** which is *a model that focuses on equitable distribution of power, rights, and income among social classes*, and a **public choice model,** which is *a model that focuses on economic incentives as applied to politicians*. These two models, by emphasizing different aspects of economic interrelationships, sometimes direct us to other conclusions.

Q-2 How does a radical analysis of labor markets differ from a mainstream analysis?

Let's consider an example. Mainstream economic analysis directs us to look at how the invisible hand achieves harmony and equilibrium through the market. Thus, when mainstream economists look at labor markets, they generally see supply and demand forces leading to equilibrium. When Marxist economists look at labor markets, their model focuses on the tensions among the social classes, and they generally see exploitation of workers by capitalists. When public choice economists look at labor markets, they see individuals using government to protect their monopolies. Their model focuses on political restrictions that provide rents to various groups. Each model captures different aspects of reality. That's why it's important to be as familiar with as many different models as possible.

Each model captures different aspects of reality. That's why it's important to be as familiar with as many different models as possible.

The Need for a Worldview

John Maynard Keynes, an economist who gained fame in the 1930s, once said that economists should be seen in the same light as dentists—as competent technicians. He was wrong, and his own experience contradicts that view. In dealing with real-world economic policy, Keynes was no mere technician. He had a definite worldview, which he shared with many of the policy makers he advised. An economist who is to play a role in forming policy must be willing to combine value judgments and technical knowledge. That worldview determines how and when the economic model will be applied.

Agreement among Economists about Social Policy

Despite their widely varying values, both liberal and conservative economists agree more often on policy prescriptions than most laypeople think they do. They're economists, after all, and their models focus on certain issues—specifically on incentives and individual choice. They believe economic incentives are important, and most economists tend to give significant weight to individuals' ability to choose reasonably. This leads economists, both liberal and conservative, to look at problems differently than other people do.

Liberal and conservative economists agree on many policy prescriptions because they use the same models, which focus on incentives and individual choice.

Many people think economists of all persuasions look at the world coldheartedly. In my view, that opinion isn't accurate, but it's understandable how people could reach it. Economists are taught to look at things in an "objective" way that takes into account a policy's long-run incentive effects as well as the short-run effects. Many of their policy proposals are based on these long-run incentive effects, which in the short run make the policy look coldhearted. The press and policy makers usually focus on short-run effects. Economists argue that they aren't being coldhearted at all, that they're simply being reasonable, and that following their advice will lead to less suffering than following others' advice will. This is not to say that all advice economists give will lead to significant benefits and less suffering in the long run. Some of it may be simply misguided.

The problem economists face is similar to the one parents face when they tell their children that they can't eat candy or must do their homework before they can play. Explaining how "being mean" is actually "being nice" to a six-year-old isn't easy.

Q-3 When can "being mean" actually be "being nice"?

A former colleague of mine, Abba Lerner, was well known for his strong liberal leanings. The government of Israel asked him what to do about unemployment. He went to Israel, studied the problem, and presented his advice: "Cut union wages." The government official responded, "But that's the same advice the conservative economist gave us." Lerner answered, "It's good advice, too." The Israeli Labor government then went and did the opposite; it raised wages, thus holding on to its union support in the short run.

Another example comes from a World Bank economist. She had to advise a hospital in a developing country to turn down the offer of a free dialysis machine because the marginal cost of the filters it would have to buy to use the machine significantly exceeded the costs of life-saving medicines that would save even more lives. Economic reasoning involves making such hard decisions.

The best way to see the consistency and the differences in economists' policy advice is to consider some examples. Let's start with a general consideration of economic views on government regulation.

Economists' Cost/Benefit Approach to Government Regulation

Say that 200 people die in a plane crash. Newspaper headlines trumpet the disaster while news magazines are filled with stories about how the accident might have been caused, citing speculation about poor maintenance and lack of government regulation.

Many regulations are formulated for political expediency and do not reflect cost/benefit considerations.

The publicity spreads the sense that "something must be done" to prevent such tragedies. Politicians quickly pick up on this, feeling that the public wants action. They introduce a bill outlawing faulty maintenance, denounce poor regulatory procedures, and demand an investigation of sleepy air controllers. In short, they strike out against likely causes of the accident and suggest improved regulations to help prevent any more such crashes.

Cost/benefit analysis is analysis in which one assigns a cost and benefit to alternatives, and draws a conclusion on the basis of those costs and benefits.

Economists differ in their views on government regulation of airlines and other businesses, but most find themselves opposing some of the supposedly problem-solving regulations proposed by politicians. They generally adopt a **cost/benefit approach** to problems—*assigning costs and benefits, and making decisions on the basis of the relevant costs and benefits*—that requires them to determine a quantitative cost and benefit for everything, including life. What's the value of a human life? All of us would like to answer, "Infinite. Each human life is beyond price." But if that's true, then in a cost/benefit framework, everything of value should be spent on preventing death. People should take no chances. They should drive at no more than 30 miles per hour with airbags, triple-cushioned bumpers, double roll bars—you get the picture.

Car crashes are evidence human life is not beyond price.

It might be possible for manufacturers to make a car in which no one would die as the result of an accident. But people don't want such cars. Many people don't buy the auto safety accessories that are already available, and many drivers ignore the present speed limit. Instead, many people want cars with style and speed.

The Value of Life

Far from regarding human life as priceless, people make decisions every day that reflect the valuations they place on their own lives. The table below presents a number of estimates of some of those decisions.

Basis for Calculation	Value of Human Life
Smoke detector purchases	$1,010,000–3,380,000
Automobile safety features	5,020,000–7,130,000
Bicycle helmets	1,580,000–5,680,000
Seat belt usage	1,320,000
Car seats	1,100,000

Sources: G. Blomquist, "Value of Life Saving: Implications of Consumption Activity," *Journal of Political Economy* 87, no. 3 (1979), pp. 540–58; R. Dardis, "The Value of Life: New Evidence from the Marketplace," *American Economic Review* 70, no. 5 (1980), pp. 1077–82; C. Garbacz, "Smoke Detector Effectiveness and the Value of Saving a Life," *Economics Letters* 31 (1989), pp. 281–86; P. S. Carlin and R. Sandy, "Estimating the Implicit Value of a Young Child's Life," *Southern Economic Journal* 58, no. 1 (1991), pp. 186–202; M. K. Dreyfus and W. K. Viscusi, "Rates of Time Preference and Consumer Valuations of Automobile Safety and Fuel Efficiency," *Journal of Law and Economics* 38, no. 1 (1995), pp. 79–105; R. R. Jenkins, N. Owens, and L. B. Wiggins, "Valuing Reduced Risks to Children: The Case of Bicycle Safety Helmets," *Contemporary Economic Policy* 19, no. 4 (2001), pp. 397–408. Updated to 2009 dollars by author.

These values are calculated by looking at people's revealed preferences (the choices people make when they must pay the costs). To find them, economists calculate how much people will pay to reduce the possibility of their death by a certain amount. If that's what people will pay to avoid death, the value of life can be calculated by multiplying the inverse of the reduction in the probability of death by the amount they pay. (What is relevant for these calculations is not the actual probabilities but the decision makers' estimate of the probabilities.)

REAL-WORLD APPLICATION

Economists in the Courtroom

Valuing life is more than just an academic exercise. These valuations play an important role in court cases on wrongful death in which one individual sues another for having caused a wrongful death. How do you put a value on the person's life? The courts have to do that—determine how much the defendant will have to pay the plaintiff if the court decides it was a "wrongful death." A court can't simply say that a life is priceless; it relies on economic expert witnesses to provide values.

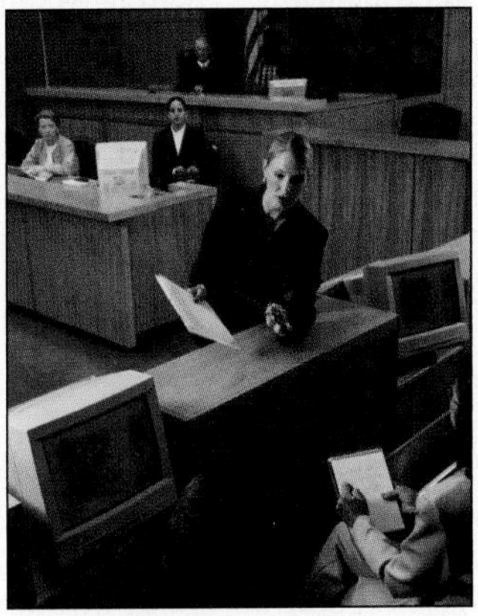

One way to value life is the method presented in the text—deduce how much people value life from their willingness to take risks. This sounds like a reasonable method, but it has problems that have been much discussed in the literature and in the courtroom. Some of these problems include: small risk values are irrelevant to large risk issues; the variance of estimates is too high to give a reasonable estimate; anonymous lives are irrelevant in specific cases; people's risk preferences differ; and people's decisions are not fully rational but reflect many other issues such as awareness of the problem and shock value. In fact, there is a whole branch of economics—forensic economics—that looks at such issues.

Another method economists use for valuing life is to calculate the lost earnings and pleasure that someone would have had in his or her remaining lifetime. But this method also has problems since it is difficult to specify either precisely. For example, is a depressed person's life worth less than a happy person's life? Is an investment banker's life worth more than a trainee's life? What is the appropriate discount rate to use to value earnings in different years? Courts have to sort through these many problems, and economists' testimony as expert witnesses often plays a key role in these cases.

For example, say someone will buy a smoke detector for \$25 but won't buy one if it costs more than \$25. Also say that the buyer believes that a smoke detector will reduce the chance of dying in a fire by 1/80,000. That means that to increase the likelihood of surviving a house fire by 1/80,000, the buyer will pay \$25. That also means that the buyer is implicitly valuing his or her life at roughly \$2,000,000 ($80,000 \times \$25 = \$2,000,000$).

Q-4 If the table in the text correctly describes the valuation individuals place on life with regard to smoke detector purchases and premium tire usage, how would you advise them to alter their behavior in order to maximize utility?

Alternatively, say that people will pay an extra \$60 for a set of premium tires that reduces the risk of death by 1/100,000. As opposed to having a 3/100,000 chance per year of dying in a skid on the highway, people driving cars with premium tires have a 2/100,000 chance of dying ($3/100,000 - 2/100,000 = 1/100,000$). Multiplying 100,000 (the inverse of the reduction in probability) by \$60, the extra cost of the set of premium tires, you find that people who buy these tires are implicitly valuing their lives at \$6,000,000.[2] Another way of determining the value that society places on life is to look at awards juries give for the loss of life. One study looking at such awards found that juries on average value life at about \$3.5 million.

No one can say whether people know what they're doing in making these valuations, although the inconsistencies in the valuations people place on their lives suggest that to some degree they don't, or that other considerations are entering into their decisions. But even given the inconsistencies, it's clear that people are placing a finite value on life. Most people are aware that in order to "live" they must take chances on losing their lives. Economists argue that individuals' revealed preferences are the best estimate that society can have of the value of life, and that in making policy society shouldn't pretend that life is beyond value.

Economists argue that individuals' revealed choices are the best estimate that society can have of the value of life, and that in making policy society shouldn't pretend that life is beyond value.

[2]For simplicity of exposition, I'm not considering risk preferences or other benefits of these decisions, such as lowering the chance of injury.

Web Note 23.2
The Value of Life

Placing a value on human life allows economists to evaluate the cost of a crash. Say each life is valued at $2 million. If 200 people die in that plane accident and a $200 million plane is destroyed, the cost of the crash is $600 million.

Right after the accident, or even long after the accident, tell a mother and father you're valuing the life of their dead daughter at $2 million and the plane at $200 million, and you'll see why economists have problems with getting their views across. Even if people can agree rationally that they implicitly place a value on their own lives, it's not something they want to deal with emotionally, especially after an accident. Using a cost/benefit approach, an economist must be willing to say, if that's the way the analysis turns out, "It's reasonable that my son died in this accident because the cost of preventing the accident by imposing stricter government regulations would have been greater than the benefit of preventing it."

Economists take the emotional heat for making such valuations. Their cost/benefit approach requires them to do so.

Comparing Costs and Benefits of Different Dimensions

After the marginal cost and marginal benefit data have been gathered and processed, one is ready to make an informed decision. Will the cost of a new regulation outweigh the benefit, or vice versa? Here again, economists find themselves in a difficult position in evaluating a regulation about airplane safety. Many of the costs of regulation are small but occur in large numbers. Every time you lament some "bureaucratic craziness" (such as a required weekly staff meeting or a form to be signed assuring something has been done), you're experiencing a cost. But when those costs are compared to the benefits of avoiding a major accident, the dimensions of comparison are often wrong.

Cost/benefit analysis sometimes leads one to uncomfortable results.

For example, say it is discovered that a loose bolt was the probable cause of the plane crash. A regulation requiring airline mechanics to check whether that bolt is tightened and, to ensure that they do so, requiring them to fill out a form each time the check is made might cost $1. How can we compare $1 to the $600 million cost of the crash? Such a regulation obviously makes sense from the perspective of gaining a $600 million benefit from $1 of cost.

But wait. Each plane might have 4,000 similar bolts, each of which is equally likely to cause an accident if it isn't tightened. If it makes sense to check that one bolt, it makes sense to check all 4,000. And the bolts must be checked on each of the 4,000 flights per day. All of this increases the cost of tightening bolts to $16 million per day. But the comparison shouldn't be between $16 million and $600 million. The comparison should be between the marginal cost ($16 million) and the marginal benefit, which depends on how much tightening bolts will contribute to preventing an accident.

Let's say that having the bolts checked daily reduces the probability of having an accident by 0.001. This means that the check will prevent one out of a thousand accidents that otherwise would have happened. The marginal benefit of checking a particular bolt isn't $600 million (which it would be if you knew a bolt was going to be loose), but is

$$0.001 \times \$600 \text{ million} = \$600{,}000$$

That $600,000 is the marginal benefit that must be compared to the marginal cost of $16 million.

Given these numbers, I leave it to you to decide: Does this hypothetical regulation make sense?

Putting Cost/Benefit Analysis in Perspective

Q-5 Why should you be very careful about any cost/benefit analysis?

The numbers in our plane crash example are hypothetical. The numbers used in real-world decision making are not hypothetical, but they are often ambiguous. Measuring costs, benefits, and probabilities is difficult, and economists often disagree on specific costs and benefits. Costs have many dimensions, some more quantifiable than others. Cost/benefit analysis is often biased toward quantifiable costs and away from nonquantifiable costs, or it involves enormous ambiguity as nonquantifiable costs are quantified.

Web Note 23.3
Applying Cost-Benefit Analysis

The subjectivity and ambiguity of costs are one reason why economists differ in their views of regulation. In considering any particular regulation, some economists will favor it and some will oppose it. But their reasoning process—comparing marginal costs and marginal benefits—is the same; they differ only on the estimates they calculate.

Cost/benefit analysis is often biased toward quantifiable costs.

The Problem of Other Things Changing

A major reason why economists come to different conclusions about policies involves the "other things equal" assumption discussed in Chapter 4. Supply/demand analysis assumes that all other things remain equal. But in a large number of issues it is obvious that other things do not remain equal. However, it is complicated to sort out how they change, and the sorting-out process is subject to much debate. The more macro the issue, the more other things change, and hence the more debate.

Let's consider the minimum wage example we discussed in earlier chapters. Suppose you can estimate the supply and demand elasticities for labor. Is that enough to enable you to estimate the number of people who will be made unemployed by a minimum wage? To answer that, ask yourself: Are other things likely to remain constant? The answer is: No; numerous things will change. Say the firm decides to replace these workers with machines. So it will buy some machines. But machines are made by other workers, and so the demand for workers in the machine-making industry will rise. So the decrease in employment in the first industry may be offset by an increase in employment elsewhere.

Q-6 When using marginal cost/marginal benefit analysis, do "other things remain constant"? Explain.

But there are issues on the other side too. For example, if other things change, workers who get the higher wage may not receive a net benefit. Say you had a firm that was paying a wage lower than the minimum wage but was providing lots of training, which was preparing people for much better jobs in the future. Now the minimum wage goes into effect. The firm keeps hiring workers, but it eliminates the training. Its workers actually could be worse off.

How important are such issues? That's a matter of empirical research, which is why empirical research is central to economics. Unfortunately, the data aren't very good, which is why there is so much debate about policy issues in economics.

There are many more examples of "other things changing," but the above should be sufficient to give you an idea of the problem.

The Cost/Benefit Approach in Context

Economics teaches people to be reasonable—sickeningly reasonable, some people would say. I hope that you have some sense of what I mean by that. The cost/benefit approach to problems (which pictures a world of individuals whose self-interested actions are limited only by competition) makes economists look for the self-interest behind individuals' actions, and for how competition can direct that self-interest into the public interest.

Economics teaches people to be "reasonable."

In an economist's framework,

- Well-intentioned policies often are prevented by individuals' self-interest-seeking activities.
- Policies that relieve immediate suffering often have long-run consequences that create more suffering.
- Politicians have more of an incentive to act fast—to look as if they're doing something—than to do something that makes sense from a cost/benefit point of view.

ADDED DIMENSION

Economic Efficiency and the Goals of Society

Economic efficiency means achieving a goal at the lowest possible cost. For the definition to be meaningful, the goal must be specified. Efficiency in the pursuit of efficiency is meaningless. Thus, when we talk about economic efficiency, we must have some goal in mind. In the supply/demand framework, we *assume* the goal is to maximize total utility given the income people have. Each of the three failures of market outcomes that we discuss in this section represents a situation in which the goals of society cannot be captured by a single measure—where society's goal is more complicated than to maximize total utility—and thus the assumed goal of efficiency (maximizing total utility) is not the only goal of society.

The marginal cost/marginal benefit story is embodied in the supply/demand framework.

The marginal cost/marginal benefit approach is telling a story. That story is embodied in the supply/demand framework. Supply represents the marginal costs of a trade, and demand represents the marginal benefits of a trade. Equilibrium is where quantity supplied equals quantity demanded—where marginal cost equals marginal benefit. That equilibrium maximizes the combination of consumer and producer surplus and leads to an efficient, or Pareto optimal, outcome. The argument for competitive markets within that supply/demand framework is that markets allow the society to achieve **economic efficiency**—*achieving a goal, in this case producing a specified amount of output, at the lowest possible cost.* Alternatively expressed, the story is that, given a set of resources, markets produce the greatest possible output. When the economy is efficient, it is on its production possibility curve, producing total output at its lowest opportunity cost.

The supply/demand framework is logical, satisfying, and (given its definitions and assumptions) extraordinarily useful. That's why we teach it. It gives students who understand it the ability to get to the heart of many policy problems. It tells them that every policy has a cost, every policy has a benefit, and if the assumptions are met, competition sees to it that the benefits to society are achieved at the lowest possible cost. Applied to policy issues, the framework gets you to face trade-offs that you would often rather avoid, and that you likely wouldn't see if you didn't use it. It is what "thinking like an economist" is all about.

Failure of Market Outcomes

Q-7 True or false? The goal of society is efficiency.

A good story emphasizes certain elements and deemphasizes others to make its point. When the moral of the story is applied, however, we have to be careful to consider all the relevant elements—especially those that the story didn't emphasize. That's why in the second part of this chapter I will discuss some implicit assumptions that the supply/demand framework pushes to the back of the analysis and that therefore often don't get addressed in principles courses. I classify these as failures of market outcomes. A **failure of market outcome** occurs *when, even though the market is functioning properly (there are no market failures), it is not achieving society's goals.*

Failure of market outcome occurs when, even though it is functioning properly, the market is not achieving society's goals.

Three separate types of failures of market outcomes will be considered:

1. *Failures due to distributional issues:* Whose surplus is the market maximizing?
2. *Failures due to rationality problems of individuals:* What if individuals don't know what is best for themselves?
3. *Failures due to violations of inalienable or at least partially inalienable rights of individuals:* Are there certain rights that should not be for sale?

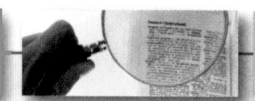

I'll discuss an example of each of the three failures of market outcomes and contrast them with market failures discussed in Chapter 21. Then I will conclude with a brief discussion of why, even though most economists recognize these failures of market outcomes, they still favor the use of markets for the large majority of goods that society produces.

Distribution

Say that the result of market forces is that some people don't earn enough income to be able to survive—the demand for their labor intersects the supply for their labor at a wage of 25 cents an hour. Also assume there are no market failures, as described in Chapter 21. (Information is perfect, trades have no negative externalities, and all goods are private goods.)

The market solution to a wage that is so low the worker can't survive is starvation—people who don't earn enough die. Not all low-wage workers must die, however. As some low-wage workers die, the supply of labor shifts back, raising the wage for the survivors. This process takes time, but eventually all remaining workers will receive a subsistence wage. This is the long-run market solution. Implicit within the supply/demand framework is a Darwinian "survival of the fittest" approach to social policy. Most people would regard the market solution—starvation—as an undesirable outcome. Even though the market is doing precisely what it is supposed to be doing—equating quantity supplied and quantity demanded—most people would not find the outcome acceptable.

Implicit within the supply/demand framework is a "survival of the fittest" approach to social policy.

Distribution of Total Surplus Let me now relate this distributional issue to the supply/demand framework by considering distribution of consumer and producer surplus. For most discussions of economic policy, an implicit assumption is that the goal of policy is to create as much total surplus as possible. In a world of only one good and one person, that goal would be clear. But with many goods and many people, what is meant by total surplus in terms of social welfare can be unclear. One reason is that society does not value all surplus equally. In the above starvation example, *the reason most people do not like the market outcome is that they care about not only the size of the total surplus but also how total surplus is distributed*. The supply/demand framework does not distinguish among those who get producer and consumer surplus, and thus avoids that distribution issue.

Examples of Distributional Issues Let's consider two real-world examples where distributional issues are likely to play a significant role in value judgments about the market outcome. Our economy produces $200-an-ounce olive oil, but it does not provide a minimum level of health care for all. This happens because income distribution is highly unequal. The high income of the wealthy means there is demand for $200-an-ounce bottles of olive oil. (It's all the rage in Silicon Valley.) Businesses establish production facilities to produce it (or any one of a million other luxury items), and it is sold on the market. Selling $200-an-ounce bottles of olive oil is efficient if one's goal is to maximize total consumer and producer surplus. However, given the distribution of income, it would be inefficient to produce health care for the poor. The poor just don't have sufficient income to demand it. Since they have little income, the poor are given little weight in the measure of consumer surplus.

A second example of where distribution of income likely makes a big difference in our normative judgments, and where we would likely not apply the consumer and producer surplus reasoning, concerns the demand for the AIDS drug cocktail. The cocktail can stop AIDS from killing people; thus, the desire for the AIDS cocktail among individuals with AIDS is high. The demand for the drug among those without AIDS is minimal.

In some African countries, almost 30 percent of the population has AIDS. Since consumer surplus reflects desire, one might think that in Africa the consumer surplus from the desire for the AIDS drug cocktail would be enormous. But it isn't. Most people in Africa have relatively little income; in fact, most have so little income that they cannot afford the cocktail at all if it were priced at the U.S. price. Since the price of the cocktail is above their total income, they get no consumer surplus from the cocktail at all in the supply/demand framework—it would be "inefficient" to supply it to them. In the supply/demand framework you can only have a demand for a good if you have the desire *and* the income to pay for it. So, despite the fact that it is inefficient to provide AIDS drugs to low-income Africans, the prices of AIDS drugs to African nations were significantly reduced. Distributional issues trumped efficiency issues.

For many goods, maximizing total surplus is a useful shorthand.

The point of these examples is not to convince you that the consumer surplus concept is useless. Far from it. For the majority of goods, it is a useful shorthand that demonstrates the power of competitive markets. The point of the examples is to show you the type of case where overriding the supply/demand framework in policy considerations may be socially desirable and efficient if society's goals include a particular distribution of consumer surplus. The sole purpose of society is not to maximize consumer and producer surplus. Society also has other goals. Once these other goals are taken into account, the competitive result may not be the one that is desired.

Societies integrate other goals into market economics by establishing social safety nets (programs such as welfare, unemployment insurance, and Medicaid). When individuals are below a certain income, what they receive does not depend solely on what they earn in the market. How high to set a given social safety net is a matter of debate, but favoring the market outcome in most cases is not inconsistent with favoring a social safety net in others.

Consumer Sovereignty and Rationality Problems

John Drunk drinks more than is good for him; he just has to have another drink. He buys liquor voluntarily, so that means buying it makes him better off, right? Not necessarily. Even when they have full information, individuals sometimes do not do what is in their own best interest. If they don't do what's best for themselves, then the market solution—let people enter freely into whatever trades they want to—is not necessarily the best solution. Again, the market is working, but the outcome may be a failure.

Q-8 A cocaine addict purchases an ounce of cocaine from a drug dealer. Since this was a trade both individuals freely entered, is society better off?

This problem is sometimes called *rationality failure of individuals*. The supply/demand framework starts with the proposition that individuals are completely **rational**—that *what individuals do is in their own best interest*. Reflecting on this, however, as we did in Chapter 10, we see that that is not always the case. Most of us are irrational at times; we sometimes can "want" something that we really "don't want." Think of smoking, chocolate, or any other of our many vices. We know those potato chips are bad for us, but they taste so good.

Even if we don't have serious addictions, we may have minor ones; often we don't know what we want and we are influenced by what people tell us we want. Businesses spend over $200 billion every year on advertising in the United States to convince us that we want certain things. Individuals can be convinced they want something that, if they thought further about it, they would not want. The fact that individuals don't know what they want can be a second reason for government intervention—getting people to want what is good for them.

Let's look at an example: The U.S. government has taken the position that if people could be induced to stop smoking, they would be better off. **Sin taxes**—*taxes that discourage activities society believes are harmful (sinful)*—are meant to do just this. Based on

ADDED DIMENSION

Elasticity and Taxation to Change Behavior

A good way to see how economists view the difference between the effect of a sin tax and the effect of a tax to raise revenue is to ask: Would a policy maker rather have an elastic or an inelastic demand curve for the good being taxed? If the purpose is to raise revenue while creating only a minimal amount of deadweight loss, an inelastic demand is preferable. If the purpose is to change behavior, as it is in the example of an alcohol-dependent individual, a more elastic demand curve is better because a relatively small tax can cause a relatively large reduction in purchases.

Consider an example of taxation to reduce consumption. If government believes that smoking is bad for people, it can decrease the amount people smoke by placing a tax on cigarettes. If the demand for cigarettes is inelastic, then the tax will not significantly decrease smoking; but if the demand is elastic, then it will. If demand is inelastic, government may choose alternative methods of affecting behavior, such as advertising campaigns. If the purpose of taxation is to raise taxes, an inelastic demand would be better; that's why most states rely on general sales taxes for revenue—such taxes allow them to raise revenue with relatively little effect on the efficiency of the market.

The following table provides a quick review of when a tax will be most effective, given a particular goal of government.

Goal of Government	Most Effective When
Raise revenue, limit efficiency loss	Demand or supply is inelastic
Change behavior	Demand or supply is elastic

the consumer surplus argument, a tax on smoking would create deadweight loss; it would reduce the combination of consumer and producer surplus. But in this case, government has decided that consumer surplus does not reflect individuals' welfare.

Web Note 23.4
Sin Taxes

Notice the difference between the argument for taxes to change behavior (sin taxes) and the argument for taxes to raise revenue discussed in Chapter 8. When government wants to raise revenue, it takes into account how much deadweight loss is created by the tax. With sin taxes, government is trying to discourage the use of the good that is being taxed and does not take into account deadweight loss. When society takes the position that individuals' demands in the marketplace do not reflect their true welfare, it is not at all clear that the market result is efficient. (See the box "Elasticity and Taxation to Change Behavior.")

Inalienable Rights

Nice Guy wants to save his son, who needs an operation that costs $300,000. He doesn't have that kind of money, but he knows that Slave Incorporated, a newly created company, has been offering $300,000 to the first person who agrees to become a slave for life. He enters into the contract, gets his money, and saves his son. Again, the market is working just as it is supposed to. There's no negative externality, and there's no information problem—Nice Guy knows what he's doing and Slave Inc. knows what it's doing. Both participants in the trade believe that it is making them better off.

Many people's view of the trade will likely be different; they would regard such a market outcome—an outcome that allows slavery—as a market outcome failure. That is why governments have developed laws that make such trades illegal.

Q-9 True or false? If someone chooses to sell himself into slavery, the individual, and thus society, is better off.

As Amartya Sen pointed out (and won a Nobel Prize for doing so), most societies regard certain rights as inalienable. By definition, inalienable rights cannot be sold or given away. There can be no weighing of costs and benefits. For example, the right to

REAL-WORLD APPLICATION

Where to Locate Polluting Industries

Larry Summers, an MIT-trained economist and former president of Harvard University, often carries economic reasoning to its logical conclusion, and talks about it in public, or at least lets it leak out to the public. These traits often get him in hot water. When Larry Summers was chief economist at the World Bank, he signed a memo that argued that the World Bank should encourage more migration of the dirty industries to the LDCs (less-developed countries). Part of the memo stated the following:

> The measurements of the costs of health-impairing pollution depend on the forgone earnings from increased morbidity and mortality. From this point of view a given amount of health-impairing pollution should be done in the country with the lowest cost, which will be the country with the lowest wages. I think the economic logic behind dumping a load of toxic waste in the lowest-wage country is impeccable and we should face up to that.

Based upon cost/benefit analysis and calculations of the "value of life," this reasoning follows, but it is not necessarily the correct reasoning, nor is it reasoning that most people will accept. Here is the response it provoked from Brazil's secretary of the Environment:

> Your reasoning is perfectly logical but totally insane . . . Your thoughts [provide] a concrete example of the unbelievable alienation, reductionist thinking, social ruthlessness and the arrogant ignorance of many conventional "economists" concerning the nature of the world we live in . . . If the World Bank keeps you as vice president it will lose all credibility. To me it would confirm what I often said . . . the best thing that could happen would be for the Bank to disappear.

I leave it to you to sort out which, if any, view is the correct one.

freedom is an inalienable right, so slavery is wrong, and any trade creating slavery should not be allowed, regardless of any issues of consumer and producer surplus.

Markets require the development of property rights.

The Need to Prioritize Rights To understand why market outcomes might be undesirable, we have to go back and consider markets in a broader perspective. Markets develop over time as individuals trade to make themselves better off. But markets don't just come into existence—they require the development of property rights for both suppliers and consumers. Each side must know what is being traded. So markets can exist only if there are property rights.

Property rights, in turn, are included in a broader set of rights that are part of society's constitution—the right to vote, the right to free speech, the right to the pursuit of happiness, the right to life. Property rights are subrights to the right to pursue happiness. If property rights conflict with other rights, society must make a judgment about which right has priority. Thus, within the written or unwritten constitution of a society, rights needs to be prioritized.

Examples of Inalienable Rights Let's consider a couple of examples. Say I come up to you with a gun and offer you this deal: Your money or your life. This can be viewed as a trade. Because I have the gun, I control whether you live or die. You control the money you have. If we make the "trade," you'll be better off because I don't shoot you and I'll be better off because I'll have more money. But it is not an acceptable trade because the right to your life was inalienable—no one but you owns it; I cannot claim to own it. So, even if the gun gave me the power over your life, it did not give me the right to it. Other moral prohibitions that are related to inalienable rights include those against prostitution, selling body parts, and selling babies.

Web Note 23.5
A Market for Body Parts

My point is not that the moral judgment our society has made about these rights is correct; they may or may not be correct. Nor is my point that such trades should not be subjected to the market. My point is that society must make these judgments. Such issues are moral questions and therefore do not have to stand up to the consumer and producer surplus arguments. If something is wrong, it is wrong; whether it is efficient is irrelevant.

Moral judgments must be made about where markets should exist, and someone might decide that the market should be allowed everywhere (that is the libertarian view), but such moral judgments can override consumer surplus arguments about markets achieving efficiency. Consider again the efficient-chicken-farming example discussed in Chapter 13. If you believe that it is immoral to treat chickens the way "efficient" farming requires them to be treated, then the fact that the farming is efficient may be irrelevant to you.

Moral judgments underlie all policy prescriptions.

Government Failure

Distributional issues, issues of rationality, and the existence of inalienable rights are representative of the types of problems that can arise in the market. For most economists these issues play a role in interpreting the policy results that follow from the economic model presented, even when there is no market failure. But it is important to remember that even these failures of market outcomes do not necessarily call for government action. The reason is government failure.

As I discussed in Chapter 21, if the failure is to be corrected, someone must formulate and enact the policy, and if we believe that government's attempt to correct it will do more harm than good, then we can still support the market as the lesser of two evils. For the government to correct the problem, it must

1. Recognize the problem.
2. Have *the will* to do something positive about the problem.
3. Have *the ability* to do something positive about the problem.

For the government to correct a problem, it must

1. Recognize the problem.
2. Have the will to deal with it.
3. Have the ability to deal with it.

Government seldom can do all three of these well. Often the result is that government action is directed at the wrong problem at the wrong time.

Probably the most vocal group of economists on the subject of government failure is *public choice economists*. This group, started by James Buchanan and Gordon Tullock, has pointed out that politicians are subject to the laws of supply and demand, like everyone else. Often the result of politics is that the redistribution that takes place does not go from rich to poor, but from one group of the middle class to another group of the middle class. Public choice economists argue that when the government enters the market, the incentives are not to achieve its goal in the least-cost manner; the incentives are to provide a policy that its voting constituency likes. The result is larger and larger government, with little benefit for society, and public choice economists advocate as little government intervention as possible regardless of whether there are market failures or failures of market outcomes.

Economic policy is, and must be, applied within a political context. This means that political elements must be taken into account. Politics enters into the determination of economic policy in two ways, one positive and one negative. Its positive contribution is that politicians take market failures and failures of market outcomes into account when formulating policy. Ultimately the political system decides what externalities should be adjusted for, what is a desirable distribution, what rights are above the market, and when people's revealed demand does not reflect their true demand. To the

Economic policy is, and must be, applied in a political context.

The Conventional Policy Wisdom among Economists

Where do economists come out on whether government can correct a failure of market outcomes? The easy answer is that they conclude that to make a policy decision, we must weight the costs of market failure against the costs of government failure. But those costs are often poorly specified and difficult to estimate. Thus, policy considerations require subjective judgments. Let me give you my interpretation of how economists fit these broader considerations into their analysis.

Most economists downplay the distribution issues for the majority of goods, and use distribution in their policy consideration only for the extreme examples, such as those I presented in the text. They believe that it is far better to be open about the distributional goals and to give money directly to individuals, rather than to hide the redistribution by changing the pricing structure through subsidizing goods. Let's take an example: The European Union's agricultural policy currently provides large amounts of price supports for European agricultural production. To keep farmers in business, the prices of agricultural goods are kept high. If the social decision were to keep farmers in business, most economists, however, would prefer to see the EU provide direct subsidies to farmers. Then the policy of redistribution is clear to everyone, and is far less costly in terms of both efficiency and implementation.

The "rights argument" plays a role in all economists' policy arguments. Almost all economists oppose selling citizenship. All oppose slavery. All see economic policy as being conducted within a constitutional setting, and that means that inalienable rights come before market efficiency.

There are, of course, areas of ambiguity—allowing the regulated sale of body parts from individuals who have died is one such area. Let's consider it. There is currently a shortage of organs for transplants. When someone dies, from a medical perspective his or her organs can usually be "harvested" and used by someone else—but only if the deceased had signed a donor card. If the family of the deceased donor were given $5,000 for burial expenses, some economists argue, the shortage of transplant organs would disappear and everyone would be better off—the family could give the deceased a much nicer funeral and people needing the organs could live. Our society is moving cautiously in that direction; in 1999 Pennsylvania approved a plan to give $300 in funeral expenses to the survivors of those who donate organs. (The plan was never implemented because it was determined to conflict with federal law.) My feeling is that economists are more open to such market solutions than the general public, but there is nothing in economics that requires such solutions.

The argument about problems arising from rationality issues is also accepted by most economists, but they downplay it for most nonaddictive goods. The reason is that while it is true that individuals may not know what they want, it is far less likely that the government will know better. Based on that view, on average, the acceptance of consumer sovereignty, and the market result, is probably warranted. Exceptions include children and some elderly. How to deal with addictive goods is still very much in debate among economists, and there is no conventional wisdom.

extent that the government's political decisions reflect the will of society, government is making a positive contribution.

Q-10 In what way does government positively contribute to economic policy? In what way does it negatively contribute to economic policy?

The negative contribution is that political decisions do not always reflect the will of society.[3] The political reality is that, in the short run, people are often governed by emotion, swayed by mass psychology, irrational, and interested in their own rather than the general good. Politicians and other policy makers know that; the laws and regulations they propose reflect such calculations. Politicians don't get elected and reelected

[3]By even discussing the "will of society" I am avoiding a very difficult problem in political philosophy of what that will is, and how it is to be determined. I leave it to your political science courses to discuss such issues.

by constantly saying that all choices have costs and benefits. What this means is that while policy makers listen to the academic economists from whom they ask advice, and with whom in private they frequently agree, in practice they often choose to ignore that advice.

Because government both adjusts for failures of market outcomes and is subject to short-run political pressures, the way in which economic reasoning influences policy can be subtle. Sometimes we see elaborate charades acted out: Politicians put forward bills that from a cost/benefit viewpoint don't make sense but that make the politicians look good. They hope the bills won't pass, but they also hope that presenting them will allow enough time to pass so that emotions can cool and a more reasonable bill can be put forward. Other times, compromise bills are proposed that incorporate as much cost/benefit policy as possible, but also appeal to voters' emotional sense. In short, economic policy made in the real world reflects a balancing of cost/benefit analysis and special interest desires.

Conclusion

Adam Smith, the creator of modern economics, was a philosopher; his economics was part of his philosophy. Before he wrote the *Wealth of Nations*, in which he set out his argument for markets, he wrote a book called *The Theory of Moral Sentiments*, in which he laid out his broader philosophy. That foundation, in turn, was part of the Scottish Enlightenment, which spelled out what was meant by a good society, and how they believed individuals' and society's rights should be considered. Any economic policy issue must be interpreted within such a broad philosophical framework. Clearly, an introductory course in economics cannot introduce you to these broader philosophical and political issues. But it can point out to you their importance, and that economic policy arguments must fit within that broader context.

This chapter was written to give you a sense of that broader context—economics provides the tools, not the rules, for policy. Cost/benefit analysis and the supply/demand framework are powerful tools for analyzing issues and coming up with policy conclusions. But to apply them successfully, they must be applied in context.

Economics provides the tools, not the rules, for policy.

Thomas Carlyle, who, as we saw in the introductory quotation to Chapter 4, argued that all you have to do is teach a parrot the words *supply* and *demand* to create an economist, was wrong. Economics involves the thoughtful use of economic insights and empirical evidence. If this chapter gave you a sense of the nature of that thoughtful application along with the core of economic reasoning, then it succeeded in its purpose.

Applying economics is much more than muttering "supply and demand." Economics involves the thoughtful use of economic insights and empirical evidence.

Summary

- Economists differ because of different underlying value judgments, because empirical evidence is subject to different interpretations, and because their underlying models differ.
- Value judgments inevitably work their way into policy advice, but good economists try to be objective.
- Economists tend to agree on certain issues because their training is similar. Economists use models that focus on economic incentives and rationality.
- The economic approach to analyzing issues is a cost/benefit approach. If the marginal benefits exceed the

marginal costs, do it. If the marginal costs exceed the marginal benefits, don't do it.

- People make choices every day that reveal the value that they place on their lives. The value of life is calculated by multiplying the inverse of the reduction in the probability of death by the amount individuals pay for that reduction.
- Collecting and interpreting empirical evidence is difficult, which contributes to disagreements among economists.
- Economics involves the thoughtful use of economic insights and empirical evidence.
- The cost/benefit approach and the supply/demand framework deemphasize the possibility that market outcomes may be undesirable to society.
- Three failures of market outcomes are failures due to distributional issues, failures due to rationality problems of individuals, and failures due to violations of inalienable rights.
- Although an implicit assumption in most policy discussions is that the goal of policy is to maximize consumer and producer surplus, society does care about how that total surplus is distributed.
- The supply/demand framework assumes that individuals are rational. Individuals are not always rational in practice. Their actions are swayed by addictions, advertising, and other pressures.
- Some rights, called inalienable rights, cannot be bought and sold. What rights are inalienable are moral judgments that do not have to stand up to the same cost/benefit framework.
- Economics provides the tools, not the rules, for policy.

Key Terms

cost/benefit approach *(528)*
economic efficiency *(532)*
failure of market outcome *(532)*
Marxian (radical) model *(526)*
Pareto optimal policy *(525)*
public choice model *(526)*
rational *(534)*
sin tax *(534)*

Questions and Exercises

1. Could anyone object to a Pareto optimal policy? Why? LO1
2. Would it be wrong for economists to propose only Pareto optimal policies? LO1
3. Would all economists oppose price controls? Why or why not? LO1, LO2
4. Should body organs be allowed to be bought or sold? Why or why not? LO3
5. Why might an economist propose a policy that has little chance of adoption? (Difficult) LO3
6. In the 1970s legislators had difficulty getting laws passed requiring people to wear seat belts. Now not only do most people wear seat belts, many cars have air bags too. Do people value their lives more now than in the 1970s? LO3
7. Economist Steven D. Levitt estimated that, on average, for each additional criminal locked up in the United States, 15 crimes are eliminated. In addition, although it costs about $30,000 a year to keep a prisoner incarcerated, the average prisoner would have caused $53,900 worth of damage to society per year if free. If this estimation is correct, does it make economic sense to build more prisons? LO3

8. The number of auto accidents per year is the equivalent of a 737-plane crash every day. In the book *Why Not?* Yale professors Barry Nabalof and Ian Ayres suggest that computers that record driver behavior (similar to the boxes in planes that record crashes) be installed in cars. In trials where such computers were installed in cars, crash rates fell by one-third.
   a. If these boxes cost $100 each, and their installation reduces the probability of a crash that costs an average of $30,000 in damage to persons and vehicles, do such boxes make sense?
   b. If they do make sense, what is a reason why they are not installed?
   c. In what cars will they likely be installed first?
   d. What will their installation likely do to driving habits? LO3
9. In the early 1990s, the 14- to 17-year-old population fell because of low birth rates in the mid-1970s. Simultaneously the combined decisions of aging baby boomers to have kids resulted in an increase in the number of babies and hence in an increase in the number of parents needing baby-sitters. What effect will these two events likely have on
   a. The number of times parents go out without their children?
   b. The price of baby-sitters?
   c. The average age of baby-sitters? LO3
10. If one uses a willingness-to-pay measure in which life is valued at what people are willing to pay to avoid risks that might lead to death, the value of a U.S. citizen's life is $2.6 million, a Swede's life is worth $1.2 million, and a Portuguese's life is worth $20,000 (according to an article in the *Journal of Transport Economics and Policy*).
   a. What policy implications does this value schedule have?
   b. Say you operate an airline. Should you spend more on safety precautions in the United States than you do in Portugal?
   c. Should safety standards be lower in Portugal and Sweden than in the United States? LO3
11. In "Valuing Reduced Risks to Children: The Case of Bicycle Safety Helmets," economists Robin R. Jenkins, Nicole Owens, and Lanelle Bembenek Wiggins estimate the value of the lives of children by using parents' willingness to purchase bicycle helmets. Wearing a helmet reduces the probability of death from bicycling by .0000041. The annualized cost of a helmet is $6.51.
   a. What economic concept is their study based on?
   b. Assuming helmets are worn 100 percent of the time, what is the value of life parents place on a child as revealed by their purchase of a bicycle helmet?
   c. What happens to the value-of-life estimate if parents expect their children to wear the helmets less than 100 percent of the time?
   d. What difficulties does such an analysis present? LO3
12. What are three ways in which a well-functioning market might result in undesirable results? LO4
13. Until recently, China had a strict one-child-per-family policy. For cultural reasons, families favor boys and there are now many more male than female children born in China. How is this likely to affect who pays the cost of dates in China in 15 to 20 years? Explain your response. LO4
14. According to economists Henry Saffer of Kean University, Frank J. Chaloupka of the University of Illinois at Chicago, and Dhaval Dave of CUNY Graduate Center, it costs $1,733 using the criminal justice system to deter one person from using drugs and $1,206 using treatment centers.
   a. Which of the two programs would you recommend?
   b. What additional information do you need to determine whether either is worth pursuing?
   c. The authors estimated that the social cost to society of a person using drugs is $897. Based on this information alone, should the government spend the money on drug control? LO4
15. As organ transplants become more successful, scientists are working on ways to transplant animal organs to humans. Pigs are the odds-on favorites as "donors" since their organs are about the same size as human organs.
   a. What would the development of such organ farms likely do to the price of pigs?
   b. If you were an economic adviser to the government, would you say that such a development would be Pareto optimal (for humans)?
   c. Currently, there is a black market in human organs. What would this development likely do to that market? LO1, LO4
16. Why are economists' views of politicians cynical? LO5
17. Michael Tanner and Stephen Moore of the Cato Institute recently calculated the hourly wage equivalent of welfare for a single mother with two children for each of the 50 United States. Their estimates ranged from $17.50 an hour for Hawaii to $5.33 in Mississippi. What do you suppose were their policy recommendations? What arguments can be made to oppose those prescriptions? (Difficult) LO5
18. Anthony Zielinski, a member of the Milwaukee Board of Supervisors, proposed that the county government sell the organs of dead welfare recipients to help pay off the welfare recipients' welfare costs and burial expenses. What was the likely effect of that proposal? Why? LO5

Questions from Alternative Perspectives

1. Even though a policy's stated goals may be laudable, its actual outcome can often cause serious problems.
   a. How much does it matter to an economist how closely a policy's goals match its outcome?
   b. How much does it matter to a politician? (Austrian)
2. In standard textbook economic analysis, institutions are often portrayed as creating market failures.
   a. Give an example of market failure caused by an institution not discussed in the text.
   b. What would a free market advocate likely say should be done about the failure?
   c. How would an Institutionalist likely respond? (Institutionalist)
3. The text deemphasizes the fact that people are social creatures who feel a need to conform to norms; Post-Keynesians emphasize them.
   a. Who shapes these social norms?
   b. Does society as a whole benefit from these norms?
   c. How does the existence of these norms affect the analysis presented in the text about the way markets work? (Post-Keynesian)
4. Critics have pointed out a number of flaws in cost/benefit analysis: It assigns a dollar value to things that are not commodities such as human life; it places a price on public goods that we consume collectively (such as air quality); it downgrades the importance of the future through its discount rates; and it ignores distributional issues and issues of fairness.
   a. How reliable do you consider cost/benefit analysis as a policy analysis tool?
   b. Does cost/benefit analysis work better in some situations and worse in others? (Be sure to give some examples and to explain your overall position.) (Radical)
5. In his paper "Why Did the Economist Cross the Road? The Hierarchical Logic of Ethical and Economic Reasoning," economist Andrew Yuengert of Pepperdine University argues that "economists often give truncated justifications for their activities as economists out of fear that 'ethical' considerations will render their conclusions unscientific."
   a. Do you agree with this view?
   b. How might the presentation of economics change if economists did not have that fear? (Religious)

Issues to Ponder

1. In cost/benefit terms, explain your decision to take an economics course. LO3
2. How much do you value your life in dollar terms? Are your decisions consistent with that valuation? LO3
3. If someone offered you $1 million for one of your kidneys, would you sell it? Why or why not? LO3
4. The technology is now developing so that road use can be priced by computer. A computer in the surface of the road picks up a signal from your car and automatically charges you for the use of the road.
   a. How could this technological change contribute to ending bottlenecks and rush-hour congestion? Demonstrate graphically.
   b. How will people likely try to get around the system?
   c. If people know when the prices will change, what will likely happen immediately before? How might this be avoided? LO3
5. According to U.S. government statistics, the cost of averting a premature death differs among various regulations. Car seat belt standards cost $100,000 per premature death avoided, while hazardous waste landfill disposal bans cost $4.2 trillion per premature death avoided. If these figures are correct, should neither, one, the other, or both of these regulations be implemented? LO3
6. Technology will soon exist such that individuals can choose the sex of their offspring. Assume that technology has now arrived and that 70 percent of the individuals choose male offspring.
   a. What effect will that have on social institutions such as families?
   b. What effect will it have on dowries—payments made by the bride's family to the groom—which are still used in a number of developing countries?
   c. Why might an economist suggest that if 70 percent male is the expectation, families would be wise to have daughters rather than sons? LO4
7. In a study of hospital births, the single most important prediction factor of the percentage of vaginal births as opposed to Caesarean (C-section) births was ownership status of hospitals—whether they were for-profit or nonprofit. (Difficult)
   a. Which had more C-sections, and why?
   b. What implications about the health care debate can you draw from the above results?
   c. How might the results change if the for-profit hospital received a fixed per-patient payment—as it would in a managed care system? LO5

Answers to Margin Questions

1. I would respond that in the real world, Pareto optimal policies don't exist, and all real-world policies designed to make someone better off will make someone worse off. In making real-world policy judgments, one cannot avoid the difficult distributional and broader questions. It is those more difficult questions, which are value-laden, that make economic policy an art rather than a science. *(525)*
2. A radical analysis of the labor market differs from the mainstream analysis in that it emphasizes the tensions among social classes. Thus, a radical analysis will likely see exploitation built into the institutional structure. Mainstream analysis is much more likely to take the institutional structure as given and not question it. *(526)*
3. Oftentimes being "mean" in the short run can actually involve being "nice" in the long run. The reason is that often policy effects that are beneficial in the long run have short-run costs, and people focusing on those short-run costs see the policy as "mean." *(527)*
4. To maximize utility, one would expect that the marginal value per dollar spent should be equal in all activities. Thus, if the table is correct, it would suggest that you should be far less concerned about premium tire usage and far more concerned about whether your house has smoke detectors or not. *(529)*
5. Costs and benefits are ambiguous. Economists often disagree enormously on specific costs and benefits, or the costs and benefits are difficult or impossible to quantify. Thus, you should be extremely careful about using a cost/benefit analysis as anything more than an aid to your analysis of the situation. *(530)*
6. Other things do not always remain constant. The more macro the issue, the more things are likely to change. These changes must be brought back into the analysis, which complicates things enormously. *(531)*
7. False. Efficiency is achieving a goal as cheaply as possible. Stating efficiency as a goal does not make sense. *(532)*
8. No. The cocaine addict may be responding to the cravings created from the addiction, and not from any rational desire for more cocaine. Society may not be better off. *(534)*
9. False. Society may find that personal freedom is an inalienable right. Selling such a right may make society worse off. *(535)*
10. Government makes a positive contribution by adjusting for market failures and failures of market outcomes. Government may make a negative contribution because government is swayed by short-run political pressures. *(538)*

PART III

Macroeconomics

The specific focus of macroeconomics is the study of unemployment, business cycles (fluctuations in the economy), growth, and inflation. While the macroeconomic theories studied have changed considerably over the past 65 years, the focus of macroeconomics on those problems has remained. Thus, we'll define macroeconomics as the study of the economy in the aggregate with specific focus on unemployment, inflation, business cycles, and growth.

The following chapters provide you with the background necessary to discuss the modern debate about these issues. Let's begin with a little history.

Macroeconomics emerged as a separate subject within economics in the 1930s, when the U.S. economy fell into the Great Depression. Businesses collapsed and unemployment rose until 25 percent of the workforce—millions of people—were out of work.

The Depression changed the way economics was taught and the way in which economic problems were conceived. Before the 1930s, economics was microeconomics (the study of partial-equilibrium supply and demand). After the 1930s, the study of the core of economic thinking was broken into two discrete areas: microeconomics, as before, and macroeconomics (the study of the economy in the aggregate).

Macroeconomic policy debates have centered on a struggle between two groups: Keynesian (pronounced KAIN-sian) economists and Classical economists. Should the government run a budget deficit or surplus? Should the government increase the money supply when a recession threatens? Should it decrease the money supply when inflation threatens? Can government prevent recessions? Keynesians generally answer one way; Classicals, another.

Classical economists generally oppose government intervention in the economy; they favor a laissez-faire policy.[1] Keynesians are more likely to favor government intervention in the economy. They feel a laissez-faire policy can sometimes lead to disaster. Both views represent reasonable economic positions. The differences between them are often subtle and result from their taking slightly different views of what government can do and slightly different perspectives on the economy.

In the 1980s the Classical and the Keynesian economic models that had developed didn't match the empirical evidence and were replaced by what came to be called dynamic stochastic general equilibrium models that tried to develop models from first principles or what were called micro foundations. Many macroeconomists felt that these new models made too many assumptions that didn't match reality to be useful in guiding policy, and most macro policy economists kept using the older policy models modified with insights from the newly developed micro-founded models. That is the approach I follow in this book.

The structure of Part III, Macroeconomics, is as follows: Section I, Macroeconomic Problems (Chapters 24 and 25), introduces the macroeconomic problems, terminology, and statistics used in tracking the economy's macroeconomic performance. Section II, The Macroeconomic Framework (Chapters 26–29), presents macroeconomic models, both the engineering models that economists use to guide policy and the new theoretical models that modern macroeconomists are working on. Section III, Finance, Money, and the Economy (Chapters 30–33), looks at how money and the financial system fit into the macro model, discusses monetary policy, and provides a discussion of the financial crisis that began in 2008. Section IV, Taxes, Budgets, and Fiscal Policy (Chapters 34 and 35), looks at the issues in fiscal policy and tax policy. Section V, International Policy Issues (Chapters 36–38), discusses policy within an international context.

---

[1] *Laissez-faire* (introduced to you in Chapter 2) is a French expression meaning "Leave things alone; let them go on without interference."

Economic Growth, Business Cycles, Unemployment, and Inflation

The Labor Picture in February

Unemployment rate

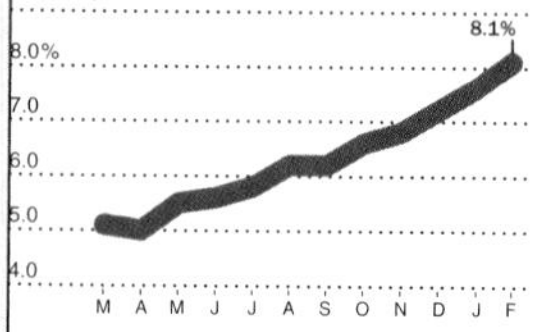

DEMOGRAPHICS

	FEB.	1-MONTH CHANGE	1-YEAR CHANGE
White	7.3%	+ 0.4 pts.	+ 2.9pts.
Black	13.4	+ 0.8	+ 5.0
Hispanic*	10.9	+ 1.2	+ 4.6
Asian	6.9†	+ 0.7†	+ 3.9†
Teenagers *(16-19)*	21.6	+ 0.8	+ 5.1

DURATION OF UNEMPLOYMENT
In weeks

	FEB.	1-MONTH CHANGE	1-YEAR CHANGE
Average	19.8	Unch.	+19.3%
Median	11.0	+ 6.8%	+31.0

Employment *Nonfarm payroll, 12-month change*

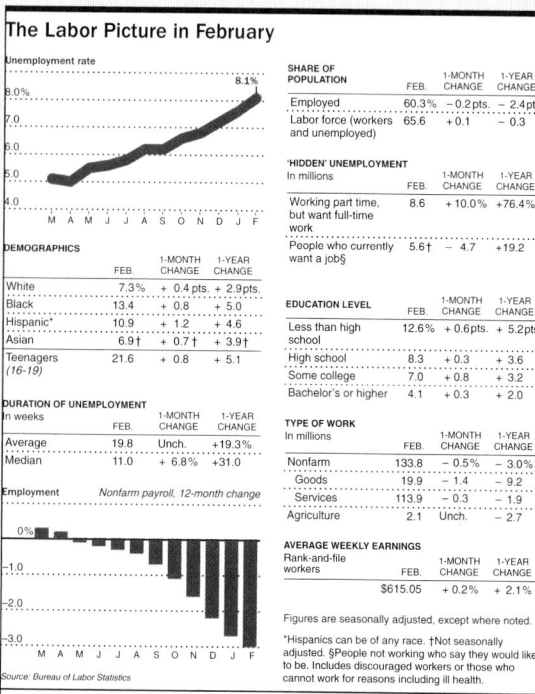

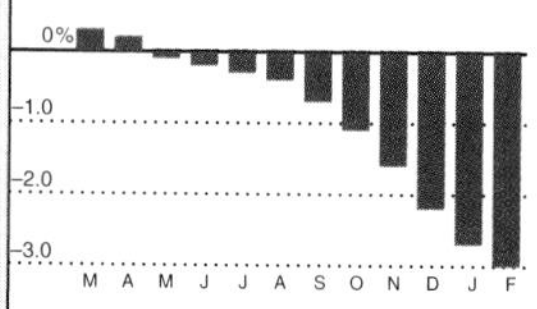

Source: Bureau of Labor Statistics

SHARE OF POPULATION

	FEB.	1-MONTH CHANGE	1-YEAR CHANGE
Employed	60.3%	– 0.2 pts.	– 2.4pts.
Labor force (workers and unemployed)	65.6	+ 0.1	– 0.3

'HIDDEN' UNEMPLOYMENT
In millions

	FEB.	1-MONTH CHANGE	1-YEAR CHANGE
Working part time, but want full-time work	8.6	+ 10.0%	+76.4%
People who currently want a job§	5.6†	– 4.7	+19.2

EDUCATION LEVEL	FEB.	1-MONTH CHANGE	1-YEAR CHANGE
Less than high school	12.6%	+ 0.6pts.	+ 5.2pts.
High school	8.3	+ 0.3	+ 3.6
Some college	7.0	+ 0.8	+ 3.2
Bachelor's or higher	4.1	+ 0.3	+ 2.0

TYPE OF WORK
In millions

	FEB.	1-MONTH CHANGE	1-YEAR CHANGE
Nonfarm	133.8	– 0.5%	– 3.0%
Goods	19.9	– 1.4	– 9.2
Services	113.9	– 0.3	– 1.9
Agriculture	2.1	Unch.	– 2.7

AVERAGE WEEKLY EARNINGS

Rank-and-file workers	FEB.	1-MONTH CHANGE	1-YEAR CHANGE
	$615.05	+ 0.2%	+ 2.1%

Figures are seasonally adjusted, except where noted.

*Hispanics can be of any race. †Not seasonally adjusted. §People not working who say they would like to be. Includes discouraged workers or those who cannot work for reasons including ill health.

The New York Times

Remember that there is nothing stable in human affairs; therefore avoid undue elation in prosperity, or undue depression in adversity.

—Socrates

AFTER READING THIS CHAPTER, YOU SHOULD BE ABLE TO:

1. Explain the difference between the long-run framework and the short-run framework.
2. Summarize some relevant statistics about growth, business cycles, unemployment, and inflation.
3. List four phases of the business cycle.
4. Explain how unemployment is measured and state some microeconomic categories of unemployment.
5. Relate the target rate of unemployment to potential income.
6. Define inflation and distinguish a real concept from a nominal concept.
7. State two important costs of inflation.

Open the pages of any major newspaper, or log onto CNN.com or a major network news source any day of the week, and you'll read about the economy: "Gas prices rose for the 10th straight week." "Consumer prices tumbled." "U.S. industrial output fell."

Like people, the economy has moods. Sometimes it's in wonderful shape—it's expansive; at other times, it's depressed. Like people whose moods are often associated with specific problems (headaches, sore back, itchy skin), the economy's moods are associated with various problems.

Macroeconomics is the study of the aggregate moods of the economy, with specific focus on issues associated with those moods—growth, business cycles, unemployment, and inflation. The macroeconomic theory we'll consider is designed to explain how supply and demand forces in the aggregate interact to create business cycles, unemployment, and inflation, and how they affect the level of growth in a country. The macroeconomic policy controversies we'll consider concern these four issues. So it's only appropriate that in this first macro chapter we consider an overview of these issues, their causes, their consequences, and the debate over what to do about them.[1]

Two Frameworks: The Long Run and the Short Run

In analyzing macroeconomic issues, economists generally use two frameworks: a short-run and a long-run framework. Issues of growth are generally considered in a long-run framework. Business cycles are generally considered in a short-run framework. Inflation and unemployment fall within both frameworks. Economists

[1]As I stated in the introduction to this part of the text, I present a consensus view of macroeconomics, although sometimes I distinguish between Keynesian and Classical approaches. I do so to keep the presentation at a level appropriate for a principles book. In reality, there is not always consensus among economists and many more distinctions can be made among economic viewpoints.

The Power of Compounding

A difference in growth rates of one percentage point may not seem like much, but over a number of years, the power of compounding can turn these small differences in growth rates into large differences in income levels. Consider Eastern European countries compared to Western European countries. In 1950, average per capita income was about $2,000 in Eastern European countries and about $4,500 in Western European countries. Over the next 60 years, income grew 2.1 percent a year in Eastern European countries and 2.6 percent a year in Western European countries. One-half percentage point may be small, but it meant that in those 60 years, income in Western European countries rose to $21,000, while income in Eastern European countries rose by much less to only $7,500.

The reason small differences in growth rates can mean huge differences in income levels is *compounding*. Compounding means that growth is based not only on the original level of income but also on the accumulation of previous-year increases in income. For example, say your income starts at $100 and grows at a rate of 10 percent each year; the first year your income grows by $10, to $110. The second year the same growth rate increases income by $11, to $121. The third year income grows by $12.10, which is still 10 percent but a larger dollar increase. After 50 years, that same 10 percent annual increase means income will be growing by over $1,000 a year.

use these two frameworks because the long-run forces that affect growth and the short-run forces that cause business cycles are different. Having two different frameworks allows us to consider these forces separately, making life easier for you.

What is the difference between the two frameworks? The long-run growth framework focuses on incentives for supply; that's why sometimes it is called *supply-side economics*. In the long run, policies that affect production or supply—such as incentives that promote work, capital accumulation, and technological change—are key. The short-run business cycle framework focuses on demand. That is why short-run macro analysis is sometimes called *demand-side economics*. Much of the policy discussion of short-run business cycles focuses on ways to increase or decrease components of aggregate expenditures, such as policies to get consumers and businesses to increase their spending.[2]

Q-1 From 2001 to 2002, employment in the United States declined by 122,500. The decline was in part due to a recession and in part due to U.S. firms outsourcing jobs to foreign countries. Is the decline in employment an issue best studied in the long-run framework or the short-run framework?

As an introduction to the central issues in macroeconomics, let's look briefly at growth, business cycles, unemployment, and inflation.

Growth

Generally the U.S. economy is growing or expanding. Economists measure growth with changes in **real gross domestic product (real GDP)**—*the market value of final goods and services produced in an economy, stated in the prices of a given year.* When people produce and sell their goods, they earn income, so when an economy is growing, both total output and total income are increasing. Such growth gives most people more income this year than they had last year. Since most of us prefer more to less, growth is easy to take.

Real GDP is GDP adjusted for price changes.

The U.S. Department of Commerce traced U.S. economic growth in output since about 1890 and discovered that, on average, output of goods and services grew about 3.5 percent per year. In the 1970s and 1980s, the growth was more like 2.5 percent. In the late 1990s and early 2000s, it was again 3.5 percent. This 2.5 to 3.5 percent growth

U.S. economic output has grown at an annual 2.5 to 3.5 percent rate.

[2]A short-run/long-run distinction helps make complicated issues somewhat clearer, but it obscures other issues such as: How long is the short run, and how do we move from the short run to the long run? Some economists argue that in the long run we are only in another short run, while others argue that since our actions are forward-looking, we are always in the long run.

rate is sometimes called the *secular growth trend*. The rate at which the actual output grows in any one year fluctuates, but on average the U.S. economy has been growing at that long-term trend. Since population has also been growing, per capita economic growth (growth per person) has been less than 2.5 to 3.5 percent.

Q-2 Say that output in the United States is $14 trillion, and there are 304 million people living in the United States. What is per capita output?

This brings us to another measure of growth—changes in per capita real output. **Per capita real output** is *real GDP divided by the total population*. Output per person is an important measure of growth because, even if total output is increasing, the population may be growing even faster, so per capita real output would be falling.

Global Experiences with Growth

Table 24-1 shows per capita growth for various areas of the world from 1820 to 2009. It tells us a number of important facts about growth:

1. Growth rates today are high by historical standards. For 130 years beginning in 1820, world output grew by only 0.9 percent per year. At that rate it took 82 years for world income to double. From 1950 until today, the world economy has grown at a much faster rate, approximately 2.1 percent per year, cutting the number of years it has taken income to double by more than half.
2. The range in growth rates among countries is wide. From 1820 to 1950, North America led, with 1.6 percent annual growth. From 1950 to 1990, however, Japan and Western Europe were among the fastest growing, partially due to the opportunities for growth lost during World War II and the replacement of productive capital destroyed in the war. Japan's growth acceleration is the most pronounced. Japan turned from investing in military might before World War II to investing in capital destroyed by the war. This acceleration meant that these countries were catching up to other high-growth areas of the world. Japan's average income in 1950 was around one-fifth of the average income in North America. By 1990 it had grown close to equal, although recently its economy slowed and it lost ground in the early 2000s. Another country that has been catching up is China. While income in China was actually lower in 1950 than in 1820, beginning in

TABLE 24-1 Average Annual per Capita Income, Various Regions

	Growth Rates			Income Levels (1990 international dollars)		
	1820–1950	1950–2009*	1820–2009*	1820	1950	2009*
The world	0.9	2.1	1.3	$ 675	$2,108	$ 7,300
Western Europe	1.1	2.6	1.5	1,202	4,578	21,200
North America	1.6	2.0	1.7	1,253	9,463	31,000
Japan	0.8	4.8	1.9	660	1,921	22,500
Eastern Europe	1.1	2.2	1.3	683	2,111	7,600
Former USSR	1.8	1.5	1.2	700	2,600	6,800
Latin America	1.0	1.6	1.2	691	2,503	6,500
China	−0.2	4.4	1.2	600	448	6,050
East Asia	0.3	3.5	1.7	500	668	5,300
Africa	0.6	1.1	0.7	420	1,307	1,700

*Author estimated updates from 2006 to 2009. Due to the global recession starting in 2007, economies grew very little during these years.

Source: Angus Maddison, *Historical Statistics for the World Economy*.

the last part of the 20th century and continuing into the 21st century, China's income has been one of the fastest growing in the world.

3. African countries have consistently grown below the average for the world. In 1820, Africa's per capita income was 40 percent less than the world average. The gap widened to 60 percent in 1950, and to 75 percent by 2009.

This two-century perspective of growth is useful, but by historical standards even two centuries is relatively short. Looking back even further shows us how high our current growth rates are. Before 1800 world income per capita grew about 0.03 percent a year. The growth trend that we now take for granted started only at the end of the 18th century, about the time that markets and democracies became the primary organizing structures of the economy and society. Thus, growth seems to be associated with the development of markets and democracy. Significant growth took off only as the market system developed, and it increased as markets increased in importance.

The growth trend we now take for granted started only at the end of the 18th century.

The Prospect for Future U.S. Growth

Past data are not necessarily a good predictor of future events, and while predictions are always dangerous, it is worthwhile asking: How may the future differ from the past, and what do those differences suggest about future U.S. economic growth? One big difference is the current economic development of the Indian and Chinese economies, which is similar to the growth experienced by other Asian countries, such as Korea and Thailand, in the 1980s. What's different about China and India is their size; combined, they have a population of 2.6 billion. As they develop into highly industrialized countries, the world economic landscape will change tremendously. Specifically, their development will likely place pressures on U.S. firms in both services and manufacturing industries either to become more competitive (by holding down wage increases or by developing more efficient production methods) or to move their production facilities abroad. It will also be accompanied by greater demand for natural resources. Some economists believe that China's and India's rise may be accompanied by slower growth in the United States, Western Europe, and other highly industrialized nations, as the growth dynamic gravitates to these Asian countries.

The Benefits and Costs of Growth

Web Note 24.1
Is Growth Good?

Economic growth (per capita) allows everyone in society, on average, to have more. Thus, it isn't surprising that most governments are generally searching for policies that will allow their economies to grow. Indeed, one reason market economies have been so successful is that they have consistently channeled individual efforts toward production and growth. Individuals feel a sense of accomplishment in making things grow and, if sufficient economic incentives and resources exist, individuals' actions can lead to a continually growing economy.

Politically, growth (or predictions of growth) allows governments to avoid hard distributional questions of who should get what part of our existing output: With growth there is more to go around for everyone. A growing economy generates jobs, so politicians who want to claim that their policies will create jobs generally predict those policies will create growth.

Politically, growth (or predictions of growth) allows governments to avoid hard questions.

Of course, material growth comes with costs: pollution, resource exhaustion, and destruction of natural habitat. These costs lead some people to believe that we would be better off in a society that deemphasized material growth. (That doesn't mean we shouldn't grow emotionally, spiritually, and intellectually; it simply means we should grow out of our material goods fetish.) Many people believe these environmental costs are important, and the result is often an environmental-economic growth stalemate.

To reconcile the two goals, some have argued that spending on the environment can create growth and jobs, so the two need not be incompatible. Unfortunately, this argument has a problem. It confuses growth and jobs with increased material consumption—what most people are worried about. As more material goods made available by growth are used for pollution control equipment, less is available for the growth of an average individual's personal consumption since the added material goods created by growth have already been used. What society gets, at best, from these expenditures is a better physical environment, not more of everything. Getting more of everything would violate the TANSTAAFL law.

This reasoning has implications for the debate about what policies to introduce to deal with global warming. Reducing global warming requires reducing carbon emissions, which means changing production methods away from methods that use carbon fuel. We can do it, but doing it will cost resources, and those resources will not be available for consumption goods. Of course, as economist Nicholas Stern argues, there is also a cost of not doing anything; he calculates that, if we do nothing, growth will be 20 percent less than it otherwise would be. If he is correct, there is a large cost of not doing anything. There is much debate about these issues and the relationship between global warming and economic growth is likely to be a hot topic of discussion over the coming years.

Business Cycles

A business cycle is the upward or downward movement of economic activity that occurs around the growth trend.

While the secular, or long-term, trend is a 2.5 to 3.5 percent increase in GDP, there are numerous fluctuations around that trend. Sometimes real GDP grows above the trend; at other times GDP falls below the trend. This phenomenon has given rise to the term *business cycle*. A **business cycle** is *the upward or downward movement of economic activity, or real GDP, that occurs around the growth trend*. Figure 24-1 graphs the fluctuations in GDP for the U.S. economy since 1860.

FIGURE 24-1 U.S. Business Cycles

Business cycles have always been a part of the U.S. economic scene. This figure suggests that until the severe recession that started in 2008, fluctuations in economic output have become less severe since 1945, although some economists dispute the data.

Source: *Historical Statistics of the United States, Colonial Times to 1970*, and U.S. Department of Commerce (www.doc.gov).

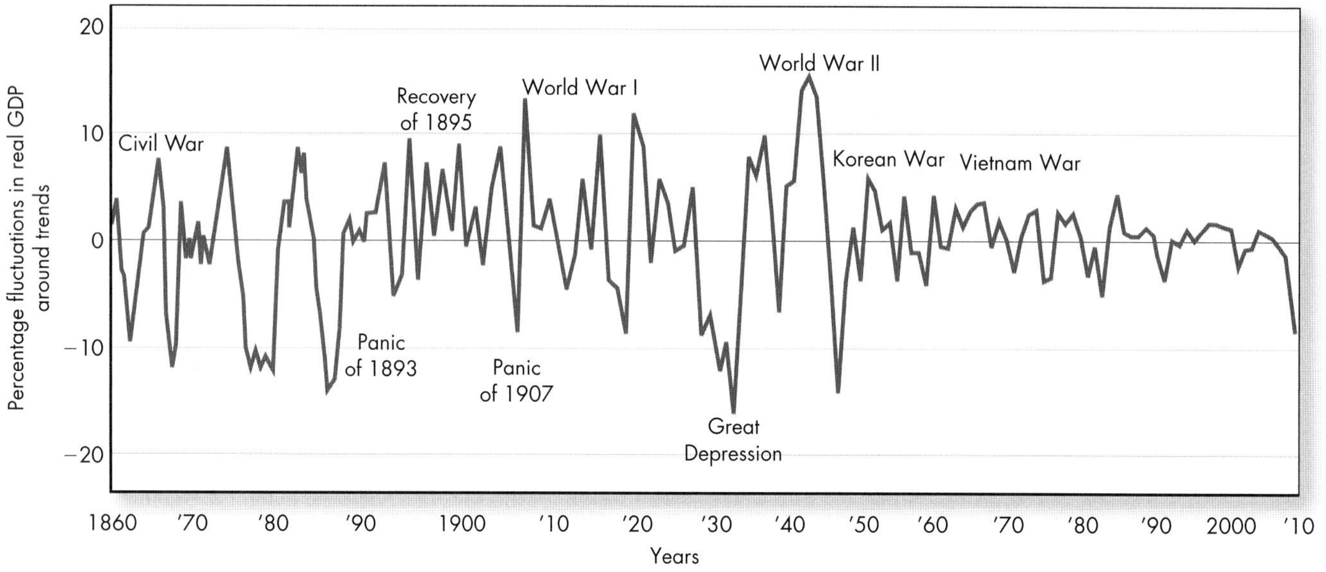

REAL-WORLD APPLICATION

NBER Dating of the Business Cycle

In December 2008, the six members of the NBER Business Cycle Dating Committee issued this statement:

> The NBER's Business Cycle Dating Committee has determined that a peak in business activity occurred in the U.S. economy in December 2007. The peak marks the end of an expansion that began in November 2001 and the beginning of a recession. The expansion lasted 73 months; the previous expansion of the 1990s lasted 120 months. A recession is a significant decline in economic activity spread across the economy, lasting more than a few months, normally visible in production, employment, real income, and other indicators.

National Bureau of Economic Research

Technically, an economy is in a recession only after it has been declared to be in a recession by a group of economists appointed by the National Bureau of Economic Research (NBER). Because real output is reported only quarterly and is sometimes revised substantially, the NBER Dating Committee looks at monthly data such as industrial production, employment, real income, sales, and sometimes even people's perceptions of what is happening in the economy to determine whether a recession has occurred. In 2001, for example, in the statement quoted above, the committee announced that a recession had begun in March even though, according to preliminary GDP figures, real output did not fall for two consecutive quarters. (Revised figures, which came out more than six months later, showed that GDP had actually started falling earlier and fell for three quarters.) The fact (1) that the NBER economists include many factors when determining a recession and (2) that they base their decision on preliminary data makes it difficult to provide an unambiguous definition of recession.

In 2008, the U.S. economy started falling into a recession that was much deeper than most previous recessions, and which some felt could turn into a depression. While technically it only became a recession when the NBER decided that it was a recession, by early 2008, it was clear to all that the United States was in a recession. People didn't need the NBER to tell them.

Until the late 1930s, economists took such cycles as facts of life. They had no convincing theory to explain why business cycles occurred, nor did they have policy suggestions to smooth them out. In fact, they felt that any attempt to smooth them through government intervention would make the situation worse.

Since the 1940s, however, many economists have not taken business cycles as facts of life. They have hotly debated the nature and causes of business cycles and of the underlying growth. In this book I distinguish two groups of macroeconomists: **Keynesians** (who *generally favor activist government policy*) and **Classicals** (who *generally favor laissez-faire or nonactivist policies*). Classical economists argue that fluctuations in economic activity are to be expected in a market economy. Indeed, they say, it would be strange if fluctuations did not occur when individuals are free to decide what they want to do. We should simply accept these fluctuations as we do the seasons of the year. Keynesian economists argue that fluctuations can and should be controlled. They argue that *expansions* (the part of the business cycle above the long-term trend) and *contractions* (the part of the cycle below the long-term trend) are symptoms of underlying problems of the economy, which should be dealt with by government actions. Classical economists respond that individuals will anticipate government's reaction, thereby undermining government's attempts to control cycles. Which of these two views is correct is still a matter of debate.

Keynesians generally favor activist government policy; Classicals generally favor laissez-faire policies.

The Phases of the Business Cycle

Much research has gone into measuring business cycles and setting official reference dates for the beginnings and ends of contractions and expansions. As a result of this research, business cycles have been divided into phases, and an explicit terminology has

FIGURE 24-2 Business Cycle Phases

Economists have many terms that describe the position of the economy on the business cycle. Some of them are given in this graph.

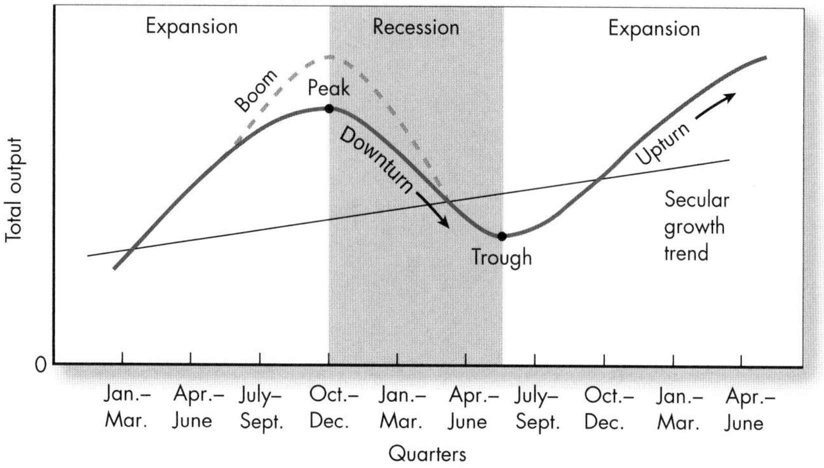

been developed. The National Bureau of Economic Research announces the government's official dates of contractions and expansions. In the postwar era (since mid-1945), the average business expansion has lasted about 57 months. A major expansion occurred from 1982 until mid-1990, when the U.S. economy fell into a recession. In mid-1991 it slowly came out of the recession, and began the longest expansion in U.S. history, which ended in March 2001. The recession ended in November 2001 and the economy expanded until December 2007 when the economy entered a deep recession.

Business cycles have varying durations and intensities, but economists have developed a terminology to describe all business cycles and just about any place within a given business cycle. Since the press often uses this terminology, it is helpful to go over it. I do so in reference to Figure 24-2, which gives a visual representation of a business cycle.

The four phases of the business cycle are
1. The peak.
2. The downturn.
3. The trough.
4. The upturn.

Let's start at the top. The top of a cycle is called the *peak*. A *boom* is a very high peak, representing a big jump in output. (That's when the economy is doing great. Most everyone who wants a job has one.) Eventually an expansion peaks. (At least, in the past, they always have.) A *downturn* describes the phenomenon of economic activity starting to fall from a peak. In a recession the economy isn't doing so great and many people are unemployed. A **recession** is generally considered to be *a decline in real output that persists for more than two consecutive quarters of a year.* The actual definition of a recession is more ambiguous than this generally accepted definition, as the box "NBER Dating of the Business Cycle" on the previous page points out.

A **depression** is *a large recession*. There is no formal line indicating when a recession becomes a depression. In general, a depression is much longer and more severe than a recession. This ambiguity allows some economists to joke, "When your neighbor is unemployed, it's a recession; when you're unemployed, it's a depression." If pushed for something more specific, I'd say that if unemployment exceeds 12 percent for more than a year, the economy is in a depression. The last time the United States was in a depression was in the 1930s, although in 2008 there was serious concern that the economy was entering a depression.

The bottom of a recession or depression is called the *trough*. As total output begins to expand, the economy comes out of the trough; economists say it's in an *upturn*, which may turn into an **expansion**—*an upturn that lasts at least two consecutive quarters of a year*. An expansion leads us back up to the peak. And so it goes.

This terminology is important because if you're going to talk about the state of the economy, you need the words to do it. Why are businesses so interested in the state of the economy? They want to be able to predict whether it's going into a contraction or an expansion. Making the right prediction can determine whether the business will be profitable or not. That's why economists spend a lot of time trying to predict the future course of the economy.

Why Do Business Cycles Occur?

Why do business cycles occur? Are they simply random events, a bit like static on a radio, or do they have some fundamental causes that make them predictable? And if they have causes, are those causes on the supply side or demand side of the economy? These questions will be addressed in the short-run chapters on business cycles. What we will see is that most economists believe that fluctuations of output around the growth trend are caused by changes in the demand for goods and services in the economy. We will also see that economists disagree whether these economic fluctuations can and should be reduced.

There is far less policy debate about depressions. The general view that something must and could be done to offset depressions emerged as the consensus during the Great Depression when, from 1929 to 1933, production of goods and services fell by 30 percent. The new consensus led to changes in the U.S. economy's structure, which included a more active role for government in reducing the severity of cyclical fluctuations. Both the financial structure and the government taxing and spending structure were changed, giving the government a more important role in stabilizing the economy.

If prolonged contractions are a type of cold the economy catches, the Great Depression of the 1930s was double pneumonia.

Look back at Figure 24-1 and compare the periods before and after World War II. (World War II began in 1941 and ended in 1945.) Notice that the downturns since 1945 have generally been less severe.

This change in the nature of business cycles can be better seen in the table below.

	Duration (in months)	
Business Cycles	**Pre–World War II (1854–1945)**	**Post–World War II (1945–2009)**
Number (trough to trough)	22	11
Average duration (trough to trough)	50	67
Length of longest cycle	99 (1870–79)	128 (1991–2001)
Length of shortest cycle	28 (1919–21)	28 (1980–82)
Average length of expansions	29	57
Length of shortest expansion	10 (1919–20)	12 (1980–81)
Length of longest expansion	80 (1938–45)	120 (1991–2001)
Average length of recessions	21	10
Length of shortest recession	7 (1918–19)	6 (1980)
Length of longest recession	65 (1873–79)	16+ (2007–)

Source: National Bureau of Economic Research (http://nber.org) and *Survey of Current Business* (www.bea.doc.gov).

Notice also that since the late 1940s cycle duration has increased but, more important, the average length of expansions has increased while the average length of contractions has decreased.

How to interpret this reduction is the subject of much controversy, as is the case with much economic evidence. Some economists argue that a large part of the reduction in the fluctuations' severity is statistical illusion. Others argue that the stronger government policy in trying to offset recessions has played a big role. If the severity of the fluctuations has been reduced (which most economists believe has happened), one reason is that changes in institutional structure were made as a result of the Great Depression. Still, others argue that the government policies had just bottled up underlying problems with the economy and created the possibility for a much larger recession.

Leading Indicators

Q-3 List three leading indicators.

Economists have developed a set of signs that indicate when a recession is about to occur and when the economy is in one. These signs are called *leading indicators*—indicators that tell us what's likely to happen 12 to 15 months from now, much as a barometer gives us a clue about tomorrow's weather. They include

1. Average workweek for production workers in manufacturing.
2. Average weekly initial claims for unemployment insurance.
3. Manufacturers' new orders for consumer goods and materials.
4. Vendor performance, measured as a percentage of companies reporting slower deliveries from suppliers.
5. Index of consumer expectations.
6. New orders for nondefense capital goods.
7. Number of new building permits issued for private housing units.
8. Stock prices—500 common stocks.
9. Interest rate spread—10-year government bond less federal funds rate.
10. Money supply, M2.

These leading indicators are followed carefully by economic reporters and form the grist of many newspaper articles suggesting that the economy is moving one way or another. There is even an index of leading economic indicators that combines all these measures into a single number. (You can find the most recent index at www.conferenceboard.org, the home page of The Conference Board.) Economists use leading indicators in making forecasts about the economy.

Notice that these measures are called *indicators*, not *predictors*. That's because they provide only rough approximations of what's likely to happen in the future. Take building permits (item 7) as an example. Building a house creates demand for goods and services and boosts output. Before building a house, you must apply for a building permit. Usually this occurs six to nine months before the actual start of construction. By looking at the number of building permits that have been issued, you can predict how much building is likely to begin in six months or so. But the prediction might be wrong since getting a building permit does not require someone to actually build. Economists also have *coincident indicators* that suggest what is currently happening in the economy and *lagging indicators* that suggest what has happened. Business economists—who spend much of their time and effort delving deeper into these indicators trying to see what they are really telling us, as opposed to what they seem to be telling us—joke that the leading indicators have predicted six of the past two recessions.

Unemployment

The unemployment rate is the percentage of people in the economy who are willing and able to work but who are not working.

Both business cycles and growth are directly related to unemployment in the U.S. economy. Unemployment occurs when people are looking for a job and cannot find one. The **unemployment rate** is *the percentage of people in the economy who are willing and able to work but who are not working.* When an economy is growing and is in an expansion, unemployment is usually falling; when an economy is in a recession, unemployment is usually rising, although often with a lag.

The relationship between the business cycle and unemployment is obvious to most people, but often the seemingly obvious hides important insights. Just why are the business cycle and growth related to unemployment? True, aggregate income must fall in a recession, but, logically, unemployment need not result. A different possibility is that unemployment doesn't rise, but that all people, on average, work less.

Unemployment has not always been a problem associated with business cycles. In preindustrial societies, households—from farms to cottage craftspeople—produced goods and services. The entire family contributed to farming, weaving, or blacksmithing. When times were good, the family enjoyed a higher level of income. When times weren't so good, they still worked, but accepted less income for the goods they produced. When economic activity fell, people's income earned per hour (their wage) fell. Low income was a problem; but since people didn't become unemployed, **cyclical unemployment** *(unemployment resulting from fluctuations in economic activity)* was not a problem.

While cyclical unemployment did not exist in preindustrial society, **structural unemployment** *(unemployment caused by the institutional structure of an economy or by economic restructuring making some skills obsolete)* did. For example, scribes in Europe had less work after the invention of the printing press in the 1400s. Some unemployment would likely result; that unemployment would be called *structural unemployment*. But structural unemployment wasn't much of a problem for government, or at least people did not consider it government's problem. The reason is that those in the family, or community, with income would share it with unemployed family members.

Q-4 True or false? In a recession, structural unemployment is expected to rise.

Unemployment as a Social Problem

The Industrial Revolution changed the nature of work and introduced unemployment as a problem for society. This is because the Industrial Revolution was accompanied by a shift to wage labor and to a division of responsibilities. Some individuals (capitalists) took on ownership of the means of production and *hired* others to work for them, paying them a wage per hour. This change in the nature of production marked a significant change in the nature of the unemployment problem.

First, it created the possibility of cyclical unemployment. With wages set at a certain level, when economic activity fell, workers' income per hour did not fall. Instead, factories would lay off or fire some workers. That isn't what happened on the farm; when a slack period occurred on the farm, the income per hour of all workers fell and few were laid off.

Second, the Industrial Revolution was accompanied by a change in how families dealt with unemployment. Whereas in preindustrial economies individuals or families took responsibility for their own slack periods, in a capitalist industrial society factory owners didn't take responsibility for their workers in slack periods. The pink slip (a common name for the notice workers get telling them they are laid off) and the problem of unemployment were born in the Industrial Revolution.

Without wage income, unemployed workers were in a pickle. They couldn't pay their rent, they couldn't eat, they couldn't put clothes on their backs. What was previously a family problem became a social problem. Not surprisingly, it was at that time—the late 1700s—that economists began paying more attention to the problem of unemployment.

When they initially recognized unemployment as a problem, economists and society still did not view it as a social problem. It was the individual's problem. If people were unemployed, it was their own fault; hunger, or at least the fear of hunger, and people's desire to maintain their lifestyle would drive them to find other jobs relatively quickly. Early capitalism had an unemployment solution: the fear of hunger.

Unemployment as Government's Problem

As capitalism evolved, the fear-of-hunger solution to unemployment became less acceptable. The government developed social welfare programs such as unemployment insurance and assistance to the poor. In the Employment Act of 1946, the U.S. government specifically took responsibility for unemployment. The act assigned

As capitalism evolved, capitalist societies no longer saw the fear of hunger as an acceptable answer to unemployment.

ADDED DIMENSION

From Full Employment to the Target Rate of Unemployment

As I emphasized in Chapter 1, good economists attempt to remain neutral and objective. It isn't always easy, especially since the language we use is often biased.

This problem has proved to be a difficult one for economists in their attempt to find an alternative to the concept of full employment. An early contender was the natural rate of unemployment. Economists have often used the word *natural* to describe economic concepts. For example, they've talked about "natural" rights and a "natural" rate of interest. The problem with this usage is that what's natural to one person isn't necessarily natural to another. The word *natural* often conveys a sense of "that's the way it should be." However, in describing as "natural" the rate of unemployment that an economy can achieve, economists weren't making any value judgments about whether 4.5–5 percent unemployment is what should, or should not, be. They simply were saying that, given the institutions in the economy, that is what is achievable. So a number of economists objected to the use of the word *natural.*

As an alternative, a number of economists started to use the term *nonaccelerating inflation rate of unemployment (NAIRU),* but even they agreed it was a horrendous term. And so many avoided its use and shifted to the relatively neutral term *target rate of unemployment.*

The target rate of unemployment is the rate that one believes is attainable without causing accelerating inflation. It is not determined theoretically; it is determined empirically. Economists look at what seems to be achievable and is historically normal, adjust that for structural and demographic changes they believe are occurring, and come up with the target rate of unemployment.

government the responsibility of creating *full employment*, an economic climate in which just about everyone who wants a job can have one. Government was responsible for offsetting cyclical fluctuations and thereby preventing cyclical unemployment, and somehow dealing with structural unemployment.

Initially government regarded 2 percent unemployment as a condition of full employment. The 2 percent was made up of **frictional unemployment** *(unemployment caused by people entering the job market and people quitting a job just long enough to look for and find another one)* and of a few "unemployables," such as alcoholics and drug addicts, along with a certain amount of necessary structural and seasonal unemployment resulting when the structure of the economy changed. Any unemployment higher than 2 percent was considered either unnecessary structural or cyclical unemployment and was now government's responsibility; frictional and necessary structural unemployment were still the individual's problem.

By the 1950s, government had given up its view that 2 percent unemployment was consistent with full employment. It raised its definition of full employment to 3 percent, then to 4 percent, then to 5 percent unemployment. In the 1970s and early 1980s, government raised it further, to 6.5 percent unemployment. At that point the term *full employment* fell out of favor (it's hard to call 6.5 percent unemployment "full employment"), and the terminology changed. The term I will use in this book is *target rate of unemployment*, although you should note that it is also sometimes called the *natural rate of unemployment* or the *NAIRU* (the nonaccelerating inflation rate of unemployment). As discussed in the accompanying box, these terms are interchangeable. The **target rate of unemployment** is *the lowest sustainable rate of unemployment that policy makers believe is achievable given existing demographics and the economy's institutional structure*. Since the late 1980s the appropriate target rate of unemployment has been a matter of debate, but most economists place it at somewhere around 5 percent unemployment.

The target rate of unemployment is the lowest sustainable rate of unemployment that policy makers believe is achievable under existing conditions.

REAL-WORLD APPLICATION

Categories of Unemployment

A good sense of the differing types of unemployment and the differing social views that unemployment embodies can be conveyed through three examples of unemployed individuals. As you read the following stories, ask yourself which category of unemployment each individual falls into.

Example 1

Joe has lost his steady job and collects unemployment insurance. He's had various jobs in the past and was laid off from his last one. He spent a few weeks on household projects, believing he would be called back by his most recent employer—but he wasn't. He's grown to like being on his own schedule. He's living on his unemployment insurance (while it lasts, which usually isn't more than six months), his savings, and money he picks up by being paid cash under the table working a few hours now and then at construction sites.

The Unemployment Compensation Office requires him to make at least an attempt to find work, and he's turned up a few prospects. However, some were back-breaking laboring jobs and one would have required him to move to a distant city, so he's avoiding accepting regular work. Joe knows the unemployment payments won't last forever. When they're used up, he plans to increase his under-the-table activity. Then, when he gets good and ready, he'll really look for a job.

Example 2

Flo is a middle-aged, small-town housewife. She worked before her marriage, but when she and her husband started their family, she quit her job to be a full-time housewife and mother. She never questioned her family values of hard work, independence, belief in free enterprise, and scorn of government handouts. When her youngest child left the nest, she decided to finish the college education she'd only just started when she married.

After getting her degree, she looked for a job, but found the market for middle-aged women with no recent experience to be depressed—and depressing. The state employment office where she sought listings recognized her abilities and gave her a temporary job in that very office. Because she was a "temp," however, she was the first to be laid off when the state legislature cut the local office budget—but she'd worked long enough to be eligible for unemployment insurance.

She hesitated about applying since handouts were against her principles. But while working there she'd seen plenty of people, including her friends, applying for benefits after work histories even slimmer than hers. She decided to take the benefits. While they lasted, she found family finances on almost as sound a footing as when she was working. Although she was bringing in less money, net family income didn't suffer much since she didn't have Social Security withheld nor did she have the commuting and clothing expenses of going to a daily job.

Example 3

Tom had a good job at a manufacturing plant where he'd worked up to a wage of $800 a week. Occasionally he was laid off, but only for a few weeks, and then he'd be called back. But then the work at the plant was outsourced. Tom, an older worker with comparatively high wages, was "let go."

Tom had a wife, three children, a car payment, and a mortgage. He looked for other work but couldn't find anything paying close to what he'd been getting. Tom used up his unemployment insurance and his savings. He sold the house and moved his family into a trailer. Finally he heard that there were a lot of jobs in Massachusetts, 800 miles away. He moved there, found a job, and began sending money home every week. Then the Massachusetts economy faltered. Tom was laid off again, and his unemployment insurance ran out again. He became depressed and, relying on his $300,000 life insurance policy, he figured he was worth more to his family dead than alive, so he killed himself.

As these three examples suggest, unemployment encompasses a wide range of cases. Unemployment is anything but a one-dimensional problem, so it's not surprising that people's views of how to deal with it differ.

Why the Target Rate of Unemployment Changed

Why has the target rate of unemployment changed over time? One reason is that, in the 1970s and early 1980s, a low inflation rate, which also was a government goal, seemed to be incompatible with a low unemployment rate. I'll talk about this incompatibility later when I discuss the problem of simultaneous inflation and unemployment. A second reason is demographics: Different age groups have different unemployment rates, and as the population's age structure changes, so does the target rate of unemployment.

A third reason is our economy's changing social and institutional structure. These social and institutional changes affected the nature of the unemployment problem. For example, women's role in the workforce has changed significantly in the past 50 years. In the 1950s, the traditional view was that "a woman's place is in the home." Usually only one family member—the man—had a job. If he lost his job, the family had no income. Since the 1970s, more and more women have entered the workforce so that today, in over 70 percent of all married-couple families, both husband and wife work. In a two-earner family, if one person loses a job, the family doesn't face immediate starvation. The other person's income carries the family over, allowing the one who lost a job to spend more time looking for another.

Government institutions also changed. As programs like unemployment insurance and public welfare were created to reduce suffering associated with unemployment, people's responses to unemployment changed. People today are more picky about what jobs they take than they were in the 1920s and 1930s. People don't just want any job; they want a *fulfilling* job with a decent wage. As people have become choosier about jobs, a debate has raged over the extent of government's responsibility for unemployment.

Whose Responsibility Is Unemployment?

Web Note 24.2
Unemployment and Entrepreneurship

Whether you consider someone unemployed depends on your sense of individual and societal responsibility. Classical economists generally believe individuals are responsible for finding jobs. They emphasize that an individual can always find *some* job at *some* wage, even if it's only selling apples on the street for 40 cents apiece. Given this view of individual responsibility, unemployment is impossible. If a person isn't working, that's his or her choice; the person simply isn't looking hard enough for a job. For an economist with this view, almost all unemployment is actually frictional unemployment.

Q-5 How are Keynesians and Classicals likely to differ in their views about what to do about outsourcing?

Keynesian economists tend to say society owes people jobs commensurate with their training or past job experience. They further argue that the jobs should be close enough to home so people don't have to move. Given this view, frictional unemployment is only a small part of total unemployment. Structural and cyclical unemployment are far more common.

In the 1960s the average rate of unemployment in Europe was considerably below the average rate of unemployment in the United States. In the 1990s and early 2000s in non-recessionary periods that reversed and the average unemployment rate in Europe has now significantly exceeded that in the United States. One of the reasons for this reversal is that Europe tried to create high-paying jobs, and it left a variety of taxes and social programs in place that discouraged the creation of low-paying jobs.

The United States, in contrast, actively promoted the creation of jobs of any type. The result has been a large growth of jobs in the United States, many of which are low-paying jobs. For example, an unemployed engineer in the United States might become a restaurant manager; in Europe, he would likely stay unemployed.

FIGURE 24-3 Unemployment Rate since 1900

The unemployment rate has always fluctuated, with the average around 5 or 6 percent. Since the 1930s, fluctuations have decreased. In the mid-1940s, the U.S. government started focusing on the unemployment rate as a goal. Initially, it chose 2 percent, but gradually that increased to somewhere around 5 percent.

Source: U.S. Bureau of Labor Statistics (www.bls.gov).

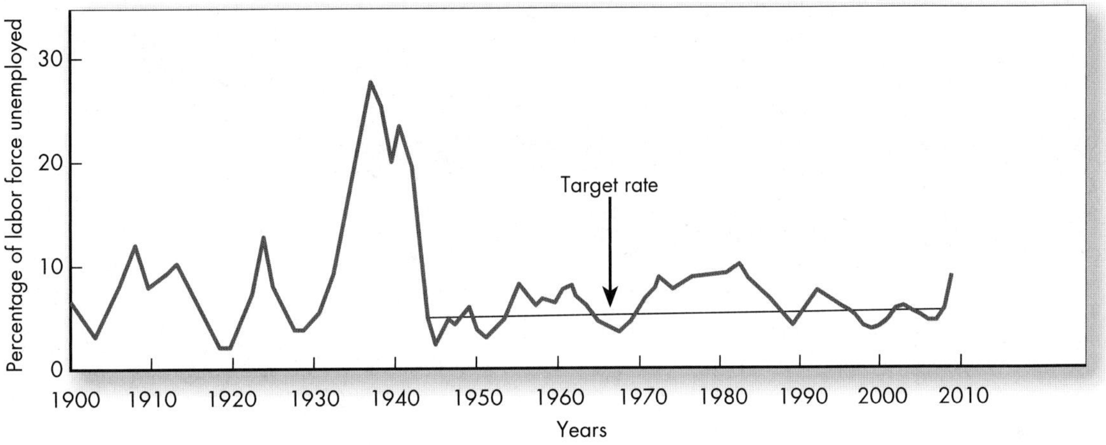

How Is Unemployment Measured?

When there's debate about what the unemployment problem is, it isn't surprising that there's also a debate about how to measure it. When talking about unemployment, economists usually refer to the "unemployment rate" published by the U.S. Department of Labor's Bureau of Labor Statistics. Fluctuations in the official unemployment rate since 1900 appear in Figure 24-3. In it you can see that during World War II (1941–45) unemployment fell from the high rates of the 1930s Depression to an extremely low rate, only 1.2 percent. You also can see that while the rate started back up in the 1950s, reaching 4 or 5 percent, it remained low until the 1970s, when the rate began gradually to rise again, peaking at 10.8 percent in 1983. In the 1990s and early 2000s, the unemployment rate has fluctuated from a high of 7.8 percent during the 1991 recession to a low of 3.8 percent in 2000. In 2009, the unemployment rate was about 9 percent.

Calculating the Unemployment Rate The U.S. unemployment rate is determined by dividing the number of people who are unemployed by the number of people in the **labor force**—*those people in an economy who are willing and able to work*—and multiplying by 100. For example, if the total unemployed stands at 12 million and the labor force stands at 150 million, the unemployment rate is

The unemployment rate is measured by dividing the number of unemployed individuals by the number of people in the civilian labor force and multiplying by 100.

$$\frac{12 \text{ million}}{150 \text{ million}} = 0.08 \times 100 = 8\%$$

To calculate the unemployment rate, we must measure both the labor force and the number of unemployed. To determine the labor force, start with the total civilian population and subtract all persons unavailable for work, such as inmates of institutions and people under 16 years of age. From that figure subtract the number of people not in the labor force, including homemakers, students, retirees, the voluntarily idle, and the

FIGURE 24-4 Unemployment/Employment Figures (in millions) in 2008

This exhibit shows you how the unemployment rate is calculated. Notice that the labor force is not the entire population.

Source: *Employment and Earnings 2009*. Bureau of Labor Statistics (www.bls.gov). Data may not add up due to rounding.

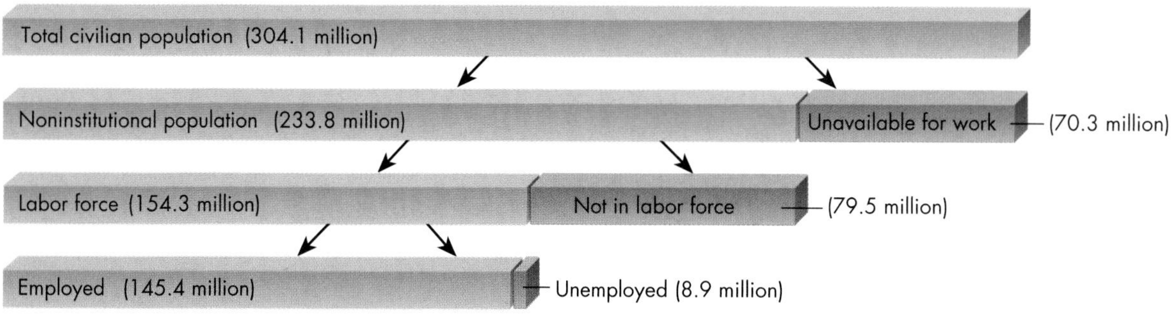

disabled. The result is the potential workforce, which is about 154 million people, or about 50 percent of the civilian population (see Figure 24-4). (The civilian population excludes about 2 million individuals who are in the armed forces.)

Q-6 During some months, the unemployment rate declines, but the number of unemployed rises. How can this happen?

The number of unemployed can be calculated by subtracting the number of employed from the labor force. The Bureau of Labor Statistics (BLS) defines people as *employed* if they work at a paid job (including part-time jobs) or if they are unpaid workers in an enterprise operated by a family member. The BLS's definition of *employed* includes all those who were temporarily absent from their jobs the week of the BLS survey because of illness, bad weather, vacation, labor-management dispute, or personal reasons, whether or not they were paid by their employers for the time off.

In 2008 the number of unemployed individuals was about 9 million. Dividing this number by the labor force (154.3 million) gives us an unemployment rate of 5.8 percent. In 2009, the number of unemployed and the unemployment rate rose considerably.

Web Note 24.3
Defining Unemployment

How Accurate Is the Official Unemployment Rate? The BLS measures unemployment using a number of assumptions that have been the source of debate. For example, should *discouraged workers*—people who do not look for a job because they feel they don't have a chance of finding one—be counted as unemployed? Some Keynesian economists believe these individuals should be considered unemployed. Moreover they question whether part-time workers who would prefer full-time work, the *underemployed*, should be classified as employed.

The Keynesian argument is that there is such a lack of decent jobs and of affordable transportation to get to the jobs that do exist that many people become very discouraged and have simply stopped looking for work. Because BLS statisticians define these people as voluntarily idle, and do not count them as unemployed, Keynesians argue that the BLS undercounts unemployment significantly.

Q-7 In what way is the very concept of unemployment dependent on the value judgments made by the individual?

The Classical argument about unemployment is that being without a job often is voluntary. People may say they are looking for a job when they're not really looking. Many are working "off the books"; others are simply vacationing. Some Classicals contend that the way the BLS measures unemployment exaggerates the number of those who are truly unemployed. They argue that many so-called unemployed are not actively seeking work.

To help overcome these problems, economists use supplemental measures to give them insight into the state of the labor market. These include the **labor force participation rate,** which *measures the labor force as a percentage of the total population at*

TABLE 24-2 Unemployment and Capacity Utilization Rates for Selected Countries (percentages)

	Capacity Utilization			Unemployment			Annual Growth in Real Output
	1975	1985	2008**	1975	1985	2008	1975–2008
United States	74.6	79.8	75	8.5	7.2	5.8	2.7
Japan	81.4	82.5	75	1.9	2.6	4.0	2.5
Germany***	76.9	79.6	76	3.4	8.2	7.1	1.7
United Kingdom	81.9	81.1	73	4.6	11.2	5.6	2.2
Canada	83.1	82.5	74	6.9	10.5	6.2	2.9
Mexico	85.0	92.0	79	*	*	3.7	3.3
Republic of Korea	86.4	74.6	74	*	10.9	3.2	6.7

*Unavailable.
**Capacity utilization rates are for most recent year available.
***For unified Germany: from 1989 to 2008.
Source: Angus Maddison, *Historical Statistics for the World Economy*.

least 16 years old, and the **employment–population ratio**—*the number of people who are working as a percentage of people available to work*.

Despite problems, the unemployment rate statistic still gives us useful information about changes in the economy. The measurement problems themselves change little from year to year, so you can ignore them when comparing unemployment from one year to another. Keynesian and Classical economists agree that a changing unemployment rate generally tells us something about the economy, especially if interpreted in the light of other statistics. That's why the unemployment rate is used as a measure of the state of the economy.

Despite problems, the unemployment rate statistic still gives us useful information about changes in the economy.

Unemployment and Potential Output

The unemployment rate gives a good indication of how much labor is available to increase production and thus provides a good idea of how fast the economy could grow. Capital is the second major input to production. Thus, the *capacity utilization rate*—the rate at which factories and machines are operating compared to the maximum sustainable rate at which they could be used—indicates how much capital is available for economic growth.

Table 24-2 shows the unemployment rates and the capacity utilization rates for selected countries over the last 30 years. Generally U.S. economists today feel that unemployment rates of about 4.5–5 percent and capacity utilization rates between 80 and 85 percent are about as much as we should expect from this economy. To push the economy beyond that would be like driving your car 110 miles an hour. True, the marks on your speedometer might go up to 130, but 90 is a more realistic top speed. Beyond 120 (assuming that's where your car is red-lined), the engine is likely to blow up (unless you have a Maserati).

Until recently, these expectations differ among countries. For example, in the early 2000s, Germany tended to have a higher achievable capacity utilization rate than the United States (85 percent for Germany; 80 percent for the United States) but its achievable unemployment rate was higher (closer to 8 percent unemployment compared to 4.5 to 5.0 percent unemployment in the United States) due to more restrictive labor market rules. Thus, as is the case with cars, maximum speeds can differ among economies, and can change over time.

Potential output is defined as the output that will be achieved at the target rate of unemployment and the target level of capacity utilization.

Economists translate the target unemployment rate and target capacity utilization rate into the target level of potential output, or simply potential output (or *potential income* because output creates income). **Potential output** is *the output that would materialize at the target rate of unemployment and the target rate of capacity utilization*. It is the rate of output beyond which prices would rise at ever-increasing rates; that is, the economy would experience accelerating inflation. Potential output grows at the secular (long-term) trend rate of 2.5 to 3.5 percent per year. When the economy is in a downturn or recession, actual output is below potential output. As you will see throughout the rest of the book, there is much debate about what are the appropriate target rates of unemployment, capacity utilization, and potential output.

Okun's rule of thumb states that a 1 percentage point change in the unemployment rate will be associated with a 2 percent change in output in the opposite direction.

To determine how changes in the unemployment rate are related to changes in output, we use **Okun's rule of thumb,** which states that *a 1 percentage point change in the unemployment rate will be associated with a 2 percent change in output in the opposite direction.*[3]

+1 percentage point change in unemployment → −2 percent change in output

For example, if unemployment rises from 6 percent to 7 percent, total output of $14 trillion will fall by 2 percent, or $280 billion, to $13.7 trillion. In terms of number of workers, a 1 percentage point increase in the unemployment rate means about 1.5 million additional people are out of work.

These figures are rough, but they give you a sense of the implications of a change. For example, say unemployment falls 0.2 percentage point, from 7.2 to 7.0 percent. That means about 300,000 more people have jobs and that output will be $56 billion higher than it otherwise would have been, if the increase holds for the entire year.

Notice I said "will be $56 billion higher than it otherwise would have been" rather than simply saying "will increase by $56 billion." That's because generally the economy is growing as a result of increases in productivity or increases in the number of people choosing to work. Changes in either of these can cause output and employment to grow, even if the unemployment rate doesn't change. We must point this out because in the 1980s the number of people choosing to work increased substantially, significantly increasing the labor participation rate. Then, in the early 2000s, as many large firms structurally adjusted their production methods to increase their productivity, unemployment sometimes rose even as output rose. Thus, when the labor participation rate and productivity change, an increase in unemployment doesn't necessarily mean a decrease in employment or a decrease in output.

Microeconomic Categories of Unemployment

In the decades after World War II, unemployment was seen primarily as cyclical unemployment, and the focus of macroeconomic policy was on how to eliminate that unemployment through a specific set of macroeconomic policies. Understanding those macroeconomic policies is important, but today it's not enough. Unemployment has many dimensions, so different types of unemployment are susceptible to different types of policies.

Some microeconomic categories of unemployment are: how people become unemployed, demographic unemployment, duration of unemployment, and unemployment by industry.

Today's view is that you don't use a sledgehammer to pound in finishing nails, and you don't use macro policies to deal with certain types of unemployment; instead you use micro policies. To determine where microeconomic policies are appropriate as a supplement to macroeconomic policies, economists break unemployment down into a

[3]The precise specification of Okun's rule of thumb has changed over time. Earlier estimates placed it at a 1 to 2.5 ratio.

FIGURE 24-5 Unemployment by Microeconomic Subcategories, 2008

Unemployment isn't all the same. This figure gives you a sense of some of the subcategories of unemployment.

Source: *Employment and Earnings 2009*, Bureau of Labor Statistics (www.bls.gov). Data may not add up due to rounding and definitional differences.

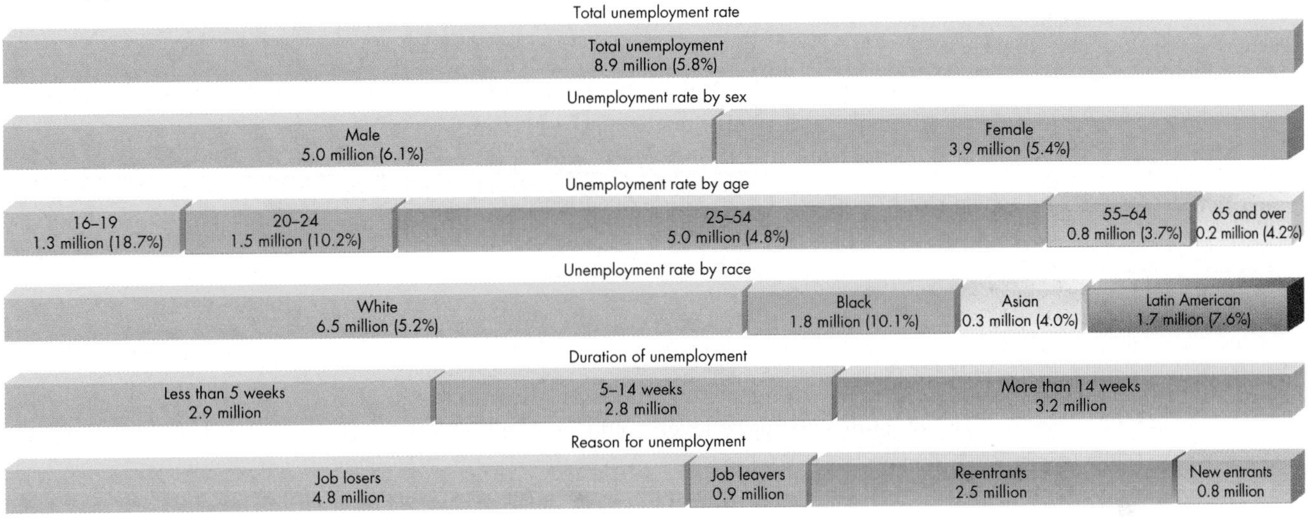

number of categories and analyze each category separately. These categories include how people become unemployed, demographic characteristics, duration of unemployment, and industry (see Figure 24-5).

Inflation

Inflation is *a continual rise in the price level.* The price level is an index of all prices in the economy. Even when inflation itself isn't a problem, the fear of inflation guides macroeconomic policy. Fear of inflation prevents governments from expanding the economy and reducing unemployment. It prevents governments from using macroeconomic policies to lower interest rates. It gets some political parties booted out of office and others elected.

Inflation is a continual rise in the price level.

A one-time rise in the price level is not inflation. Unfortunately, it's often hard to tell if a one-time rise in the price level is going to stop, so the distinction blurs in practice, but we must understand the distinction. If the price level goes up 10 percent in a month, but then remains constant, the economy doesn't have an inflation problem. Inflation is an *ongoing rise* in the price level.

In mid 2008, the economy experienced a price shock when the price of oil and commodities rose more than 40 percent. Since oil and commodities make up about 10 percent of the economy, that would mean that the price level would rise about 4 percent. If nothing else had changed, that would be the end of the story. However, it isn't. That price shock set in motion a set of price rises in most other goods, transferring the one-time price shock into inflationary pressure. Then, later in 2008, the global economy fell into a severe recession and the prices of commodities fell substantially, causing a negative price shock. That lowered inflationary pressures, but not by as much as the initial price shock had raised them.

FIGURE 24-6 Inflation since 1900

Until 1940, rises in the price level were followed by falls in the price level, keeping the price level relatively constant. Since the 1940s, inflation has generally been positive, which means that the price level has been continually rising.

Source: U.S. Department of Commerce (www.doc.gov).

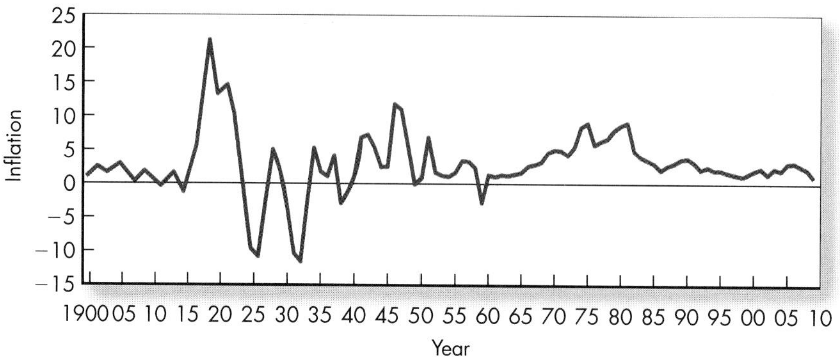

From 1800 until World War II, the U.S. inflation rate and price level fluctuated; sometimes the price level would rise, and sometimes the price level would fall—there would be deflation. Since World War II, the price level has continually risen, which means the inflation rate (the measure of the change in prices over time) has been positive, as can be seen in Figure 24-6. The rate fluctuates, but the movement of the price level has been consistently upward.

Deflation is a continual fall in the price level.

It is also possible to have **deflation**—*a continual fall in the price level*. Historically, we have seldom seen long periods of deflation, although in the late 1990s and early 2000s some countries, such as Japan, had deflation. It is important to note, however, that much of the concern about deflation is about asset deflation—a continual fall in the prices of assets such as houses and stocks—not goods and services deflation, which the standard price indices measure.

Measurement of Inflation

Web Note 24.4 Inflation Calculators

Since inflation is a sustained rise in the general price level, we must first determine what the general price level was at a given time by creating a **price index,** *a number that summarizes what happens to a weighted composite of prices of a selection of goods (often called a market basket of goods) over time*. An index converts prices relative to base year prices. Price indexes are important. Many people lament the high cost of goods and services today. They complain, for example, that an automobile that costs $15,000 today cost only $3,000 in the "good old days." But that comparison is meaningless because most prices have risen. Today, the average wage is more than five times what it was when cars cost only $3,000. To relate the two prices, we need a price index. There are a number of different measures of the price level. The most often used are the producer price index, the GDP deflator, and the consumer price index. Each has certain advantages and disadvantages.

Creating a Price Index Before introducing the official price indexes, let's work through the creation of a fictitious price index—the Colander price index—and calculate the associated inflation. I'll do so for 2009 and 2010, using 2009 as the base year. A price index is calculated by dividing the current price of a basket of goods by the base price of a basket of goods. The table below lists a market basket of goods I consume in a base year and their associated prices in 2009 and 2010. The market basket of goods is listed in column 1 and represents the quantity of each item purchased in the base year.

(1)	(2)	(3)	(4)	(5)
	Prices		Expenditures	
Basket of Goods	2009	2010	2009	2010
10 pairs jeans	$20.00/pr.	$25.00/pr.	$200	$250
12 flannel shirts	15.00/shirt	20.00/shirt	180	240
100 lbs. apples	0.80/lb.	1.05/lb.	80	105
80 lbs. oranges	1.00/lb.	1.00/lb.	80	80
Total expenditures			$540	$675

The price of the market basket in each year is the sum of the expenditures on each item—the quantity of each good purchased times its market price. The market basket remains the same in each year; only the prices change. The price of the market basket in 2009 is $540 and in 2010 is $675. To calculate the Colander price index, divide the 2010 price of the market basket by the price of the market basket in the base year and multiply it by 100. In this case 2009 is the base year, so the price index in 2010 is

$$\$675/\$540 \times 100 = 125$$

To make sure you are following this example, calculate the Colander price index in 2009.

The answer is 100. The base year index is always 100 since you are dividing base years by the base year prices and multiplying by 100.

Inflation in 2010, then, is the percent change in the price index. This is calculated in 2010 as the difference between the price indices in the two years (125 − 100 = 25) divided by the base index, 100, times 100.

$$\left(\frac{125 - 100}{100}\right) \times 100 = 25\%$$

But enough on price indexes in general. Let's now discuss the price indices most commonly used when talking about inflation.

Real-World Price Indexes The total output deflator, or **GDP deflator** (gross domestic product deflator), is *an index of the price level of aggregate output, or the average price of the components in total output (or GDP), relative to a base year.* (Recently, another price index, the chain-type price index for GDP, has become more popular; it is a GDP deflator with a constantly moving base year.) GDP is a measure of the total market value of aggregate production of goods and services produced in an economy in a year. (We'll discuss the calculation of GDP in more detail in the next chapter.) A deflator is an adjustment for "too much air." In this context, it is an adjustment for inflation—so that we know how much total output would have risen if there were no inflation.

The GDP deflator is an index of the price level of aggregate output or the average price of the components in GDP relative to a base year.

The GDP deflator is the inflation index economists generally favor because it includes the widest number of goods, and because the base period is adjusted yearly. Unfortunately, since it's difficult to compute, it's published only quarterly with a fairly substantial lag. That is, by the time the figures come out, the period the figures measure has been over for quite a while.

Published monthly, the **consumer price index (CPI)** *measures the prices of a fixed basket of consumer goods, weighted according to each component's share of an average consumer's expenditures.* It measures the price of a fixed basket of goods rather than

The consumer price index (CPI) is an index of inflation measuring prices of a fixed basket of consumer goods, weighted according to each component's share of an average consumer's expenditures.

FIGURE 24-7 Composition of CPI

The consumer price index is determined by looking at the prices of goods in the categories listed in this exhibit. These categories represent the rough percentages of people's expenditures.

Source: *CPI Detailed Reports*, Bureau of Labor Statistics (www.bls.gov).

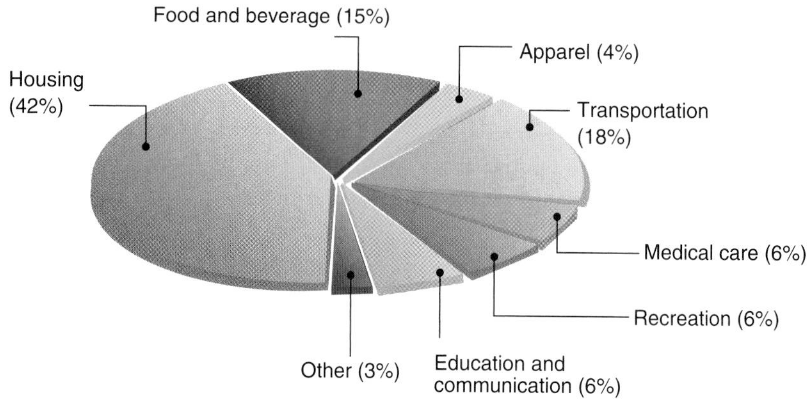

measuring the prices of all goods. It is the index of inflation most often used in news reports about the economy and is the index most relevant to consumers. Since different groups of consumers have different expenditures, there are different CPIs for different groups. One often-cited measure is the CPI for all urban consumers (the urban CPI)—about 87 percent of the U.S. population. The numbers that compose the urban CPI are collected at 87 urban areas and include prices from over 50,000 landlords or tenants and 23,000 business establishments.

Q-8 Say that health care costs make up 15 percent of total expenditures. Say they rise by 10 percent, while the other components of the price index remain constant. By how much does the price index rise?

Figure 24-7 shows the relative percentages of the basket's components. As you see, housing, transportation, and food make up the largest percentages of the CPI. To give you an idea of what effect the rise in price of a component of the CPI will have on the CPI as a whole, let's say food prices rise 10 percent in a year and all other prices remain constant. Since food is about 15 percent of the total, the CPI will rise $15\% \times 10\% = 1.5\%$. The CPI and GDP deflator indexes roughly equal each other when averaged over an entire year. (For more information on the CPI, go to www.bls.gov/cpi/cpifaq.htm.)

In the mid-1990s, many economists believed that the CPI overstated inflation by about 1 percentage point a year, and the Bureau of Labor Statistics implemented a number of changes that address some of those problems. In order to avoid some of the problems with the CPI, some policy makers have recently been focusing on another measure of consumer prices—the **personal consumption expenditure (PCE) deflator.** The PCE deflator is *a measure of prices of goods that consumers buy that allows yearly changes in the basket of goods that reflect actual consumer purchasing habits*. The measure smoothes out some of the problems associated with the CPI. Why are there different measures for consumer price changes? Indexes are simply composite measures; they cannot be perfect. (See the box "Measurement Problems with Price Indexes.")

The personal consumption expenditure (PCE) deflator allows yearly changes in the basket of goods.

CPI vs. PCE

The **producer price index (PPI)** *is an index of prices that measures average change in the selling prices received by domestic producers of goods and services over time*. This index measures price change from the perspective of the sellers, which may differ from the purchaser's price because of subsidies, taxes, and distribution costs and includes many goods that most consumers do not purchase. There are actually three different producer price indexes for goods at various stages of production—crude materials, intermediate goods, and finished goods. Even though the PPI doesn't directly measure the prices consumers pay, because it includes intermediate goods at early stages of production, it serves as an early predictor of consumer inflation since when costs go up, firms often raise their prices. (For more on the PPI, go to www.bls.gov/ppi/ppifaq.htm.)

ADDED DIMENSION

Measurement Problems with Price Indexes

You may have wondered about the fixed basket of goods used to calculate our fictitious price index and the CPI. The basket of goods was fixed in the base year. But buying habits change. The further in time that fixed basket is from the current basket, the worse any fixed-basket price index is at measuring inflation because of substitution and measurement problems.

- **Substitution problems.** Changes in prices change consumption patterns. In our fictitious price index example, the price of apples rose, but the price of oranges did not. It is likely that the basket of goods in 2009 included more oranges and fewer apples than in the base year basket, in which case total expenditures in 2009 would have been less and measured inflation would have been less. A fixed-basket price index does not take into account the fact that when the price of one good rises, consumers substitute a cheaper item and thus arrives at a higher rate of inflation than would a non–fixed basket price index.
- **Measurement problems**
  - **Quality.** A good today is seldom identical to a good yesterday. For example, a car in 1999 is assumed to be the same as a car in 2009. But by 2009, cars had much improved corrosion protection, and plastics were replacing metals. Adjustments must be made for these changes and they are seldom perfect. This makes it difficult to compare prices over time since the good is changing.
  - **New products.** A fixed basket of goods leaves no room for the introduction of new products. This would not be a problem if the prices of new products changed at about the same rate as prices of other goods in the basket, but in the 1970s this was not true. For years, the CPI did not include the price of computers, whose prices were declining at a 17 percent annual rate!
  - **Store measurement.** Ever since World War II, consumers have shifted consumption toward discount purchases. The Bureau of Labor Statistics, however, treats a product sold at a discount store as different from products sold at retail stores. Products sold at discount stores are assumed to be of lower quality. To the extent that they are not different, however, changes in the CPI arrive at a higher inflation rate than would an index that treats the products as equal.
  - **Nonmarket transactions.** The cost of housing is included in GDP. For nearly one-third of Americans, this cost is their monthly rent. But what about the remaining two-thirds of Americans who own their own homes? What is the cost of their housing? Remember opportunity costs from Chapter 1? The cost of living in one's own home is the rent you could have gotten for renting it to someone else. So, economists use market rental rates as an implicit rental rate for home ownership (called "owner's equivalent rent"). In the early 2000s, as housing prices rose, some people began buying two or three houses in the hopes of selling them for more in the future. That significantly increased the number of houses available for rent and held rents down. So although housing prices were soaring, the "owner's equivalent rent" was not, and that was holding measured inflation down. Then, starting in 2006 housing prices fell. Initially that left people with an unsold inventory of houses. So, rent stayed down. But once that inventory is reduced, we can expect rents to rise substantially, pushing measured inflation up.

These and other problems arise because of the choices with no "correct" answer that must be made when constructing a price index. The reality is that price indexes are far from perfect measures and, depending on the choices made, various indexes can differ by as much as 3 or 4 percentage points a year.

Real and Nominal Concepts

One important way in which inflation indexes are used is to separate changes in real output from changes in nominal output. Economists use the term *real* when talking about concepts that are adjusted for inflation. **Real output** is *the total amount of goods* *and services produced, adjusted for price-level changes*. It is the measure of output that would exist if the price level had remained constant. **Nominal output** is *the total amount of goods and services produced measured at current prices*. For example, say total output rises from $8 trillion to $10 trillion. Nominal output has risen by

$$\frac{\$10 \text{ trillion} - \$8 \text{ trillion}}{\$8 \text{ trillion}} = \frac{\$2 \text{ trillion}}{\$8 \text{ trillion}} \times 100 = 25\%$$

Q-9 Nominal output has increased from $10 trillion to $12 trillion. The GDP deflator has risen by 15 percent. By how much has real output risen?

Let's say, however, the price level has risen 20 percent, from 100 percent to 120 percent. The price index is 120. Because the price index has increased, real output (nominal output adjusted for inflation) hasn't risen by 25 percent; it has risen by less than the increase in nominal output. To determine how much less, we use a formula to adjust the nominal figures to account for inflation. This is called *deflating* the nominal figures. To deflate we divide the most recent nominal figure, $10 trillion, by the price index of 120 percent and multiply by 100:

$$\text{Real output} = \frac{\text{Nominal output}}{120} \times 100 = \frac{\$10 \text{ trillion}}{1.2} = \$8.3 \text{ trillion}$$

That $8.3 trillion is the measure of output that would have existed if the price level had not changed, that is, the measure of real output. Real output has increased from $8 trillion to $8.3 trillion, or by $300 billion.

% change in real output = % change in nominal output − Inflation

A way of finding out the percentage rise in real output without actually calculating real output is to use the formula

$$\% \text{ change in real output} = \% \text{ change in nominal output} - \text{Inflation}$$

In this example, the nominal output rose 25 percent and inflation rose 20 percent, so real output rose 5 percent.

When you consider price indexes, you mustn't lose sight of the forest for the trees. Keep in mind the general distinction between real and nominal output. The concepts *real* and *nominal* and the process of adjusting from nominal to real by dividing the nominal amount by a price index will come up again and again. So whenever you see the word *real*, remember:

The "real" amount is the nominal amount divided by the price index. It is the nominal amount adjusted for inflation.

> The "real" amount is the nominal amount divided by the price index. It is the nominal amount adjusted for inflation.

Economists' distinction between real and nominal concepts extends to other concepts besides output. They also distinguish real and nominal interest rates. A nominal interest rate is the interest rate you pay or receive. Say you have a student loan on which you pay 5 percent interest. That means the nominal interest rate is 5 percent. The real interest rate is the nominal interest rate adjusted for inflation. In the case of interest rates, to get the real interest rate, all we have to do is subtract the inflation rate from the nominal interest rate.

Real interest rate = Nominal interest rate − Inflation rate

$$\text{Real interest rate} = \text{Nominal interest rate} - \text{Inflation rate}$$

Real vs. Nominal

Thus, if the nominal interest rate is 5 percent and the inflation rate is 3 percent, the real interest rate is $5 - 3 = 2$ percent. The real interest rate is the amount that the loan is actually costing you because you will be paying it off with inflated dollars. To see this, let's consider an example. Say the nominal interest rate is 5 percent and the inflation rate is 5 percent. Your income is increasing at the same rate as the balance on your loan, including interest. The real interest rate is 0 percent; it is equivalent to getting an interest-free loan if there were no inflation since in terms of real spending power, you will be paying back precisely what you borrowed.

Expected and Unexpected Inflation

When an individual sets a price (for goods or labor), he or she is actually setting a relative price—relative to other prices in the economy. The money price is the good's nominal price. The laws of supply and demand affect relative prices, not nominal prices.

Now let's say that everyone suddenly expects the price level to rise 10 percent. Let's also say that all individual sellers want a ½ percent increase in their relative price. They're not greedy; they just want a little bit more than what they're currently getting. The relative price increase people want must be tacked onto the inflation they expect. In this case, they have to raise their money price by 10½ percent—10 percent to keep up and ½ percent to get ahead. Ten percent of the inflation is caused by expectations of inflation; ½ percent of the inflation is caused by pressures from suppliers wanting to increase profits. Thus, whether or not inflation is expected makes a big difference in individuals' behavior. That is why we make a distinction between expected and unexpected inflation. **Expected inflation** is *inflation people expect to occur*. **Unexpected inflation** is *inflation that surprises people*.

Since prices and wages are often set for periods of two months to three years ahead, whether inflation is expected can play an important role in the inflation process. In the early 1970s people didn't expect the high inflation rates that did occur. When inflation hit, people just tried to keep up with it. By the end of the 1970s, people expected more inflation than actually occurred and raised their prices—and, in doing so, caused the inflation rate to increase.

Expectations of inflation play an important role in any ongoing inflation. They can snowball a small inflationary pressure into an accelerating large inflation. Individuals keep raising their prices because they expect inflation, and inflation keeps on growing because individuals keep raising their prices. That's why expectations of inflation are of central concern to economic policy makers.

Costs of Inflation

Inflation has costs, but not the costs that most people associate with it. Specifically, inflation doesn't make the nation poorer. True, whenever prices go up somebody (the person paying the higher price) is worse off, but the person to whom the higher price is paid is better off. The two offset each other. So inflation does not make society on average any poorer. Inflation does, however, redistribute income from people who cannot or do not raise their prices to people who can and do raise their prices. Thus, inflation can have significant distributional or equity effects, which often create feelings of injustice about the economic system.

While inflation may not make the nation poorer, it does cause income to be redistributed, and it can reduce the amount of information that prices are supposed to convey.

A second cost of inflation is its effect on the information that prices convey to people. Consider an individual who laments the high cost of housing, pointing out that it has doubled in 10 years. But if inflation averaged 7 percent a year over the past 10 years, a doubling of housing prices should be expected. In fact, with 7 percent inflation, on average *all* prices double every 10 years. That means the individual's wages have probably also doubled, so he or she is no better off and no worse off than 10 years ago. The price of housing relative to other goods, which is the relevant price for making decisions, hasn't changed. When there's inflation, it's hard for people to know what is and what isn't a relative price change. People's minds aren't computers, so inflation reduces the amount of information that prices can convey and causes people to make choices that do not reflect relative prices.

Q-10 True or false? Inflation makes everyone in an economy worse off because everyone is paying higher prices.

Despite these costs, inflation is usually accepted by governments as long as it stays low, which for the United States currently means under 2½ to 3 percent. What scares economists are inflationary pressures above and beyond expectations of inflation. In that case, expectations of higher inflation can cause inflation to build up and compound itself. A 3 percent inflation becomes a 6 percent inflation, which in turn becomes a 12 percent inflation. Once inflation hits 5 percent or 6 percent, it's definitely no longer a little thing. Inflation of 10 percent or more is significant.

Expectations of inflation were very much on the minds of policy makers in mid-2008 when the economy experienced commodity price shocks that pushed the inflation rate to over 4 percent. If people had seen the price increase as a one-time event and accepted the decrease in their real income that it implied, it would not generate an ongoing inflation. But if the increase became built into expectations, it would have led to other price increases and resulted in accelerating inflation. That didn't occur since the economy fell into a severe recession in late 2008, which reversed the price increases in commodity prices, and replaced policy makers' concern about inflation with concern about preventing a depression.

Hyperinflation is exceptionally high inflation of, say, 100 percent or more per year.

While there is no precise definition, we may reasonably say that inflation has become **hyperinflation** *when inflation hits triple digits—100 percent or more per year.* The United States has been either relatively lucky or wise because it has not experienced hyperinflation since the Civil War (1861–65). Other countries, such as Brazil, Israel, and Argentina, have not been so lucky (or have not followed the same policies the United States has). These countries have frequently had hyperinflation. But even with inflation at these levels, economies have continued to operate and, in some cases, continued to do well.

Web Note 24.5
Hyperinflation

In hyperinflation people try to spend their money quickly, but they still use the money. Let's say the U.S. price level is increasing 1 percent a day, which is a yearly inflation rate of over 3,000 percent.[4] Is an expected decrease in value of 1 percent per day going to cause you to stop using dollars? Probably not, unless you have a good alternative. You will, however, avoid putting your money into a savings account unless that savings account somehow compensates you for the expected inflation (the expected fall in the value of the dollar), and you will try to ensure that your wage is adjusted for inflation. In hyperinflation, wages, the prices firms receive, and individual savings are all in some way adjusted for inflation. Hyperinflation leads to economic institutions with built-in expectations of inflation. For example, usually in a hyperinflation the government issues indexed bonds whose value keeps pace with inflation.

Once these adjustments have been made, substantial inflation will not destroy an economy, but it certainly is not good for it. Such inflation tends to break down confidence in the monetary system, the economy, and the government.

Conclusion

This chapter has talked about growth, unemployment, and inflation. The interrelationship among these three concepts centers on trade-offs between inflation on the one hand and growth and unemployment on the other. If the government could attack inflation without worrying about unemployment or growth, it probably would have solved the problem of inflation by now. Unfortunately, when the government tries to stop inflation, it often causes a recession—increasing unemployment and slowing growth. Similarly, reducing unemployment by stimulating growth tends to increase inflation. To the degree that inflation and unemployment are opposite sides of the coin, the opportunity

[4]Why over 3,000 percent and not 365 percent? Because of compounding. In the second day the increase is on the initial price level *and* the 1 percent rise in price level that occurred the first day. When you carry out this compounding for all 365 days, you get over 3,000 percent.

cost of reducing unemployment is inflation. The government must make a trade-off between low unemployment and slow growth on the one hand and inflation on the other. Opportunity costs must be faced in macro as well as in micro. The models you will learn in later chapters will help clarify the choices policy makers face.

Summary

- Economists use two frameworks to analyze macroeconomic problems. The long-run growth framework focuses on supply, while the short-run business-cycle framework focuses on demand.
- Growth is measured by the change in real gross domestic product (real GDP) and by the change in per capita real GDP. Per capita real GDP is real GDP divided by the total population.
- The secular trend growth rate of the economy is 2.5 to 3.5 percent. Fluctuations of real output around the secular trend growth rate are called *business cycles*.
- Phases of the business cycle include peak, trough, upturn, and downturn.
- Unemployment is calculated as the number of unemployed individuals divided by the labor force. Unemployment rises during a recession and falls during an expansion.
- The target rate of unemployment is the lowest sustainable rate of unemployment possible under existing institutions. It's associated with an economy's potential output. The lower the target rate of unemployment, the higher an economy's potential output.
- The microeconomic approach to unemployment subdivides unemployment into categories and looks at those individual components.
- A real concept is a nominal concept adjusted for inflation. Real output equals nominal output divided by the price index.
- Inflation is a continual rise in the price level. The CPI, the PPI, and the GDP deflator are all price indexes used to measure inflation.
- The GDP deflator is the broadest price index. It measures inflation of all goods produced in an economy. The CPI measures inflation faced by consumers. The PPI measures inflation faced by producers.
- Expectations of inflation can provide pressure for an inflation to continue even when other causes don't exist.
- Inflation redistributes income from people who do not raise their prices to people who do raise their prices. Inflation also reduces the information that prices convey.

Key Terms

Questions and Exercises

1. What are two ways in which long-term economic growth is measured? LO1
2. How does the U.S. per capita growth rate since 1950 compare to growth rates in other areas around the world? LO2
3. What is the difference between real output and potential output? LO2
4. The Bureau of Labor Statistics reported that in April 2009 the total labor force was 154,731,000 of a possible 235,272,000 working-age adults. The total number of unemployed was 13,724,000. From this information, calculate the following:
   a. Labor force participation rate.
   b. Unemployment rate.
   c. Employment–population ratio. LO2
5. Draw a representative business cycle, and label each of the four phases. LO3
6. The index of leading indicators has predicted all past recessions. Nonetheless it's not especially useful for predicting recessions. Explain. LO3
7. Distinguish between structural unemployment and cyclical unemployment. LO4
8. What type of unemployment is best studied within the long-run framework? LO4
9. What type of unemployment is best studied under the short-run framework? LO4
10. Does the unemployment rate underestimate or overestimate the unemployment problem? Explain. LO4
11. If unemployment rises by 2 percentage points, what will likely happen to output in the United States? (Use Okun's rule of thumb.) LO5
12. If nominal output is $250 and the price index is 150, what is real output? LO6
13. If nominal output rose 15 percent and the price index rose 2 percent, how much did real output increase? LO6
14. Answer the following questions about real output, nominal output, and inflation:
    a. The price level of a basket of goods in 2008 was $64. The price level of that same basket of goods in 2009 was $68. If 2008 is the base year, what was the price index in 2009?
    b. If nominal output is $300 billion and the price index is 115, what is real output?
    c. Inflation is 5 percent; real output rises 2 percent. What would you expect to happen to nominal output?
    d. Real output rose 3 percent and nominal output rose 7 percent. What happened to inflation? LO6
15. If nominal output rises from $13.5 billion to $14 billion and the GDP deflator rises from 100 to 105,
    a. What is the percentage increase in nominal output?
    b. What is the percentage increase in the price index?
    c. What has happened to real output?
    d. By how much would the price index have had to rise for real income to remain constant? LO6
16. Why are expectations central to understanding inflation? LO7
17. Inflation, on average, makes people neither richer nor poorer. Therefore it has no cost. True or false? Explain. LO7
18. Why would you expect that inflation would generally be associated with low unemployment? LO7

Questions from Alternative Perspectives

1. It is unfair, but true, that bad things happen. Unfortunately, to attempt to prevent unavoidable bad things can actually make things worse, not better. How might the above ideas be relevant to how society deals with business cycles? (Austrian)
2. Wesley Mitchell, a founder of Institutional economics, said that to understand the business cycle, a distinction must be made between making goods and making money. All societies make goods. In the modern money economy, those who control the production and distribution of goods will only allow economic activity to occur if they can "make money." He used this line of reasoning to conclude that what drives the business cycle are business expectations; production, and thus increased employment today, will only be allowed if business expects to sell those goods at a profit tomorrow. Is his proposition reasonable? Explain. (Institutionalist)
3. Since the Great Depression, the United States has been able to avoid severe economic downturns.
   a. What macroeconomic policies do you think have allowed us to avoid another Great Depression?
   b. Would you classify those policies as being Classical or Keynesian?
   c. Are such policies still relevant today? (Post-Keynesian)

4. The text presents the target rate of unemployment as being about 5 percent. William Vickrey, a Nobel Prize–winning economist, argued that the target unemployment rate should be seen as being between 1 percent and 2 percent. Only an unemployment rate that low, he argued, would produce genuine full employment that guaranteed job openings for all those looking for work. Achieving a low unemployment rate would, according to Vickrey, bring about "a major reduction in the illness of poverty, homelessness, sickness, and crime."
   a. What is the appropriate target unemployment rate?
   b. Explain your position.
   c. What policies would you recommend to counteract the human tragedy of unemployment? (Radical)
5. Studies have shown that women tend to pay more than men for things such as auto repairs, haircuts, and dry cleaning.
   a. Why do you think this is?
   b. How does this fact affect the usefulness of aggregate statistics such as the consumer price index (CPI)? (Feminist)

Issues to Ponder

1. In H. G. Wells's *Time Machine*, a late-Victorian time traveler arrives in England some time in the future to find a new race of people, the Eloi, in their idleness. Their idleness is, however, supported by another race, the Morlocks, underground slaves who produce the output. If technology were such that the Elois' lifestyle could be sustained by machines, not slaves, is it a lifestyle that would be desirable? What implications does the above discussion have for unemployment? (Difficult) LO2
2. If unemployment fell to 1.2 percent in World War II, why couldn't it be reduced to 1.2 percent today? (Difficult) LO4
3. In 1991, Japanese workers' average tenure with a firm was 10.9 years; in 1991 in the United States the average tenure of workers was 6.7 years.
   a. What are two possible explanations for these differences?
   b. Which system is better?
   c. In the mid-1990s, Japan experienced a recession while the United States' economy grew. What effect did this likely have on these ratios? (Difficult) LO4, LO5

Answers to Margin Questions

1. The change in employment is both a long-run and a short-run issue. It is a short-run issue because when the U.S. economy is in a recession, employment tends to decline. It is a long-run issue because outsourcing is the result of changes in the institutional structure of the global economy caused by reduced trade barriers and reduced communications costs. *(547)*
2. To calculate per capita output, divide real output ($14 trillion) by the total population (304 million). This equals $46,667. *(548)*
3. Three leading indicators are the average workweek, the layoff rate, and changes in the money supply. There are others. *(554)*
4. False. Structural unemployment is determined by the institutional structure of an economy, not fluctuations in economic activity. *(555)*
5. Keynesians are more likely to see outsourcing as a government problem and look for a government solution. Classicals are more likely to see it as an individual problem, part of the normal workings of the economy, and something that we must just accept. *(558)*
6. The unemployment rate is the number of unemployed divided by the labor force. The unemployment rate can fall while the number of unemployed rises if the labor force rises by a proportionately greater amount than the rise in the number of unemployed. *(560)*
7. Since people can always sell apples on the street, one can always get a job. So the value judgment is what type of job and at what wage society owes individuals jobs. *(560)*
8. The price index will rise by $0.15 \times 0.1 = 0.015 = 1.5\%$. *(566)*
9. Real output equals the nominal amount divided by the price index. Since the price index has risen by 15 percent, real output has risen to $10.435 trillion ($12 trillion divided by 1.15). Real output has risen by $435 billion. *(568)*
10. False. Inflation does not make everyone worse off because, although some people are paying higher prices, others are receiving higher prices. *(569)*

CHAPTER 25

Measuring the Aggregate Economy

The government is very keen on amassing statistics . . . They collect them, add them, raise them to the nth power, take the cube root and prepare wonderful diagrams. But you must never forget that every one of these figures comes in the first instance from the village watchman, who just puts down what he damn pleases.

—*Sir Josiah Stamp (head of Britain's revenue department in the late 19th century)*

AFTER READING THIS CHAPTER, YOU SHOULD BE ABLE TO:

1. Define GDP and list the four expenditure components of aggregate output.
2. Calculate GDP in a simple example, avoiding double counting.
3. Distinguish between "net" and "gross" and between "national" and "domestic."
4. List the four components of aggregate income.
5. Explain how profit is the key to the equality between aggregate income and aggregate production.
6. Distinguish between real GDP and nominal GDP.
7. Describe the shortcomings of using GDP.

Before you can talk about macroeconomics in depth, you need to be introduced to some terminology used in macroeconomics. That terminology can be divided into two parts. The first part deals with the macroeconomic statistics you are likely to see in the newspaper—GDP and its components. The second part discusses problems of using GDP figures. Among other things, it distinguishes between real and nominal (or money) concepts, which are used to differentiate and compare goods and services over time. These concepts play a central role in interpreting the movement in components of the national income accounts.

Aggregate Accounting

In the 1930s, it was impossible for macroeconomics to exist in the form we know it today because many concepts we now take for granted either had not yet been formulated or were so poorly formulated that it was useless to talk rigorously about them. This lack of terminology to describe the economy as a whole was consistent with the Classical economists' lack of interest in studying the aggregate economy in the 1930s; they preferred to focus on microeconomics.

With the advent of Keynesian macroeconomics in the mid-1930s, development of a terminology to describe the macroeconomy became crucial. Measurement is a necessary step toward rigor. A group of Keynesian economists set out to develop a terminology and to measure the concepts they defined so that people would have concrete terms to use when talking about macroeconomic problems. Their work (for which two of them, Simon Kuznets and Richard Stone, received the Nobel Prize) set up an *aggregate* accounting system—a set of rules and definitions for measuring economic activity in the economy as a whole. That aggregate accounting system often goes by the name *national income accounting*.

Aggregate accounting provides a way of measuring aggregate production and aggregate income. Both aggregate production and aggregate income can be broken down into subaggregates; aggregate accounting defines the relationship among these subaggregates.

This 17th-century engraving, "The Money Lender," shows that careful bookkeeping and accounting have been around for a long time.

Calculating GDP

The previous chapter introduced economists' primary measure of domestic output: real gross domestic product (real GDP). **Gross domestic product (GDP)** is *the total market value of all final goods and services produced in an economy in a one-year period*. GDP is probably the single most-used economic measure. When economists, journalists, and other analysts talk about the economy, they continually discuss GDP, how much it has increased or decreased, and what it's likely to do.

Gross domestic product (GDP) is the aggregate final output of residents and businesses in an economy in a one-year period.

Aggregate final output (GDP) consists of millions of different services and products: apples, oranges, computers, haircuts, financial advice, and so on. To arrive at total output, somehow we've got to add them all together into a composite measure. Say we produced 7 oranges plus 6 apples plus 12 computers. We have not produced 25 comapplorgs. You can't add apples and oranges and computers. You can only add like things (things that are measured in the same units). For example, 2 apples + 4 apples = 6 apples. If we want to add unlike things, we must convert them into like things. We do that by multiplying each good by its *price*. Economists call this *weighting the importance of each good by its price*. For example, if you have 4 pigs and 4 horses and you price pigs at $200 each and horses at $400 each, the horses are weighted as being twice as important as the pigs.

Multiplying the quantity of each good by its market price changes the terms in which we discuss each good from a quantity of a specific product to a *value* measure of that good. For example, when we multiply 6 apples by their price, 25 cents each, we get $1.50; $1.50 is a value measure. Once all goods are expressed in that value measure, they can be added together.

Once all goods are expressed in a value measure, they can be added together.

Take the example of 7 oranges and 6 apples. (For simplicity let's forget the computers, haircuts, and financial advice.) If the oranges cost 50 cents each, their total value is $3.50; if the apples cost 25 cents each, their total value is $1.50. Their values are expressed in identical measures, so we can add them together. When we do so, we don't get 13 orples; we get $5 worth of apples and oranges.

If we follow that same procedure with all the final goods and services produced in the economy in the entire year, multiplying the quantity produced by the market price per unit, we have all the goods and services an economy has produced expressed in units of value. If we then add up all these units of value, we have that year's gross domestic product.

The Components of GDP

GDP is usually divided into four categories depending on who buys the output, or by what are called *expenditure categories*. The four expenditure categories that comprise GDP are consumption, investment, government spending, and net exports.

Web Note 25.1
GDP Data

Consumption **Consumption** is *spending by households on goods and services*. Consumption includes such things as food, shampoo, televisions, furniture, and the services of doctors and lawyers. This is the production in the economy that consumers buy. When you buy a DVD, you are contributing to consumption expenditures.

Investment **Investment** is *spending for the purpose of additional production*. Investment includes business spending on factories and equipment for production, the change in business inventories, and purchases by households of new owner-occupied houses. Investment is output that is used to produce goods and services in the future. You should take note that when economists speak of investment as they discuss aggregate accounting, they don't mean the kind of activity taking place when individuals buy stocks rather than consuming—economists call such activity *saving*. So in economists' terminology when you buy a bond or stock rather than consuming, you are saving. When that savings is borrowed by businesses to buy factories, tractors, computers, or other goods or services that will increase their output, they are *investing*. The amount they spend on goods that will increase future output is what in aggregate accounting is called *investment*.

You might have been surprised to see the change in inventories and residential construction included in investment. Inventories are goods that have been produced, so they must be counted if one is going to include all produced goods, which is what GDP is designed to include, but they have not yet been purchased; inventories represent goods to be sold in the future. They are a type of investment by the firm. Residential construction is part of investment because most of the housing services from a new house will be provided in the future, not the present.

Government Spending **Government spending** is *goods and services that government buys*. Although government generally does not sell its "production" but provides it free, aggregate accounting rules count government production at the government's cost of providing that output. Thus, when the government buys the services of an analyst, or buys equipment for its space program, it is undertaking economic activity. These activities are classified as government expenditures.

In thinking about government expenditures, you should note that they include expenditures that involve production. Many government payments do not involve production, however, so the government's budget is much larger than government spending included in GDP. The most important category of government spending that is not included in GDP is **transfer payments**—*payments to individuals that do not involve production by those individuals*. Transfer payments include Social Security payments and unemployment insurance among others. These payments are not part of GDP since there is no production associated with them.

Net Exports **Net exports**—*spending on goods and services produced in the United States that foreigners buy (exports) minus goods and services produced abroad that U.S. citizens buy (imports)*. (In economics and business, the word "net" is used to distinguish two offsetting flows: exports, which represent a spending flow into the country, and imports, which represent a spending flow out of the country.) The reason we have to use the "net concept" for exports is that GDP measures production *within* the geographic borders of a country. Because exports represent spending by foreigners for goods and services produced within the United States, exports are added. But because imports represent spending on goods and services produced outside the United States, they are subtracted. Our interest is in spending on only those goods and services produced in the geographic confines of the United States.

Summarizing: GDP measures aggregate final production taking place in a country. This production can be subdivided into expenditure categories, and all production must fit into one of the four categories. A shorthand way of expressing this division of GDP into expenditure categories is

Q-1 Calculate GDP with the information below:

Consumption = 60
Investment = 20
Government spending = 20
Exports = 10
Imports = 15

$$\text{GDP} = \text{Consumption} + \text{Investment} + \text{Government spending} + \text{Net exports, or}$$
$$\text{GDP} = C + I + G + (X - M)$$

Since all production is categorized into one or another of these four divisions, by adding up these four categories, we get total production of U.S. goods and services.

TABLE 25-1 Expenditure Breakdown of GDP for Selected Countries

Country	GDP (U.S. $ in billions)	=	Consumption (% of GDP)	+	Investment (% of GDP)	+	Government Spending (% of GDP)	+	Exports (% of GDP)	−	Imports (−% of GDP)
United States	$14,265		$10,057		$1,996		$2,883		$1,861		−$2,883
			71%		14%		20%		13%		−20%
Belgium	376		51		23		23		89		−86
Czech Republic	248		47		38		20		70		−75
Germany	2,928		55		18		18		47		−41
Japan	4,294		55		25		18		18		−16
Mexico	1,480		66		26		10		28		−30
Poland	609		60		26		18		41		−45

Note: Percentages may not sum to 100 due to rounding. Data for United States and Germany are for 2008; 2007 for all others.
Source: *World Development Report*, 2009, The World Bank (www.worldbank.org), and *Survey of Current Business*, Bureau of Economic Analysis.

Table 25-1 gives the breakdown of GDP by expenditure category for selected countries. Notice that, in all countries, consumption expenditures is the largest component of production.

Two Things to Remember about GDP

In thinking about GDP, it is important to remember that (1) GDP represents a flow (an amount per year), not a stock (an amount at a particular moment of time); and (2) GDP refers to the market value of *final* output. Let's consider these statements separately.

Two important aspects to remember about GDP are
1. GDP represents a flow.
2. GDP represents the market value of final output.

GDP Is a Flow Concept Say a student just out of college tells you she earns $8,000. You'd probably think, "Wow! She's got a low-paying job!" That's because you implicitly assume she means $8,000 per year. If you later learned that she earns $8,000 per week, you'd quickly change your mind. The confusion occurred because how much you earn is a flow concept; it has meaning only when a time period is associated with it: so much per week, per month, per year. A stock concept is an amount at a given point in time. No time interval is associated with it. Your weight is a stock concept. You weigh 150 pounds; you don't weigh 150 pounds per week.

GDP is a flow concept, the amount of total final output a country produces per year. The *per year* is often left unstated, but is essential. GDP is usually reported quarterly (every three months), but it is reported on an *annualized basis,* meaning the U.S. Department of Commerce, which compiles GDP figures, uses quarterly figures to estimate total output for the whole year.

The store of wealth, in contrast, is a stock concept. The stock equivalent to national income accounts is the **wealth accounts**—*a balance sheet of an economy's stock of assets and liabilities*. Table 25-2 shows a summary account of U.S. net worth from the wealth accounts for the United States in 2008. These are stock measures; they exist at a moment of time. For example, on December 31, 2008, the accounting date for these accounts, U.S. private net worth was $51.4 trillion.

Q-2 How do wealth accounts differ from national income accounts?

In thinking about wealth, it is useful to distinguish between **real wealth,** which is *the value of the productive capacity of the assets of an economy measured by the goods and services it can produce now and in the future*, and **nominal wealth,** which is *the value of those assets measured at their current market prices*. Prices of assets can go up for two reasons. They may rise because the productive capacity of that asset has risen. Say the price of a company's stock goes up because the company has just invented a new product. Because of that

TABLE 25-2 U.S. National Wealth Accounts in 2008 (net worth)

	Dollars (in trillions)			Percentage of Component	
Private net worth	$51.4				120%
Tangible wealth		$24.8			
Owner-occupied real estate			$20.5	40	
Consumer durables			4.1	8	
Other			0.2	0	
Financial wealth		26.6			
Corporate equities			5.5	11	
Noncorporate equities			7.5	15	
Other (pension reserves, life insurance, etc.)			13.6	26	
Government net financial assets	−8.6				−17
Federal		−6.4		−12	
State and local		−2.2		−4	
Total net worth	42.8				100

Source: *Flow of Funds Accounts*, Board of Governors, Federal Reserve (www.federalreserve.gov). The value of the government's financial liabilities is greater than the value of its financial assets, which is why it shows up as a negative percentage.

new invention, the economy's ability to produce has increased and society is richer. Such asset price rises represent increases in real wealth.

Asset prices can also rise without an increase in productive capacity. In such cases we have a rise in nominal wealth but not real wealth. We will call these kinds of price increases **asset inflation**—*a rise in the price of assets unrelated to increases in their productive capacity*. Asset inflation does not involve a change in real assets—more buildings, factories, or changes in the productivity of the underlying assets. It is simply a higher price of assets. With asset inflation but no increase in real assets, the measured value of assets has increased, but the economy will not be able to produce more goods and services.

If we had a measure of asset inflation, we could adjust nominal wealth to find real wealth, just as we adjust nominal GDP for inflation to find real GDP. Unfortunately, because of the difficulties involved in determining whether or not the change in the price of an asset reflects changes in productive capacity of assets, we have no actual measure of asset inflation, which means we have no good measures for real wealth. We have to use very rough approximations. For example, when, say, real estate prices rise by 50 percent in five years when there is a 1 percent inflation in goods, but no significant change in population or in other relevant factors, then it is a reasonable presumption that society's real wealth in real estate has increased by very little. We can surmise that much of the 50 percent increase is likely due to asset inflation, not a change in real wealth. Even if we agree that there has been asset inflation, we still don't know whether the price of an asset is "too high." That's because we don't know whether the old price was too low, or whether the new price is now too high. We have to make judgments based on past trends.

Let's take an example. The 1990s and early 2000s were marked by significant increases in the prices of assets, especially housing. Some economists argued that prior to the price increases, housing had been undervalued, so that the increase in prices was just helping assets "catch up" to a level that reflected their productive capacity. They turned out to be wrong: the increase in housing prices came to a sudden end in 2008 when there was an 18 percent fall in nominal wealth—from $63 trillion in 2007 to $51 trillion in 2008. The fall in those asset prices did not reduce real wealth of society by anywhere near that amount, just as the rise didn't increase it. The reason is that few houses were destroyed by the fall in their prices. True, housing owners were made worse off. But they are not the entire picture. People who didn't own houses but were likely to buy one in the future (which includes many students) were made better off by an offsetting amount because the amount of work they will have to do to get a house in the future was reduced. The difference was that they didn't feel wealthier, even though they were, while the homeowners felt poorer.

GDP Measures Final Output As a student in my first economics class, I was asked how to calculate GDP. I said, "Add up the value of the goods and services produced by all the companies in the United States to arrive at GDP." I was wrong (which is why I remember it). Many goods produced by one firm are sold to other firms, which use those goods to make other goods. GDP doesn't measure total transactions in an economy; it measures **final output**—*goods and services purchased for their final use*. When one firm sells products to another firm for use in production of yet another good, the first firm's products aren't considered final output. They're **intermediate products**—*products used as input in the production of some other product*. To count intermediate goods as well as final goods as part of GDP would be to double count them. An example of an intermediate good would be wheat sold to a cereal company. If we counted both the wheat (the intermediate good) and the cereal (the final good) made from that wheat, the wheat would be double counted. Double counting would significantly overestimate final output.

If we did not eliminate intermediate goods, a change in organization would look like a change in output. Say a firm that produced steel merged with a firm that produced cars. Together they produce exactly what each did separately before the merger. Final output hasn't changed, nor has intermediate output. The only difference is that the intermediate output of steel is now internal to the firm. Using only each firm's sales of goods to final consumers (and not sales to other firms) as the measure of GDP means that changes in organization do not affect the measure of output.

Two Ways of Eliminating Intermediate Goods There are two ways to eliminate intermediate goods from the measure of GDP. One way is to calculate the final sales that make up GDP directly, either by measuring the expenditures on the products by final users or by measuring the production done specifically for final users. A second way to eliminate double counting is to follow the value added approach. **Value added** is *the increase in value that a firm contributes to a product or service*. It is calculated by subtracting intermediate goods (the cost of materials that a firm uses to produce a good or service) from the value of its sales. For instance, if a firm buys $100 worth of thread and $10,000 worth of cloth and uses them in making a thousand pairs of jeans that are sold for $20,000, the firm's value added is not $20,000; it is $9,900 ($20,000 in sales minus the $10,100 in intermediate goods that the firm bought).

To avoid double counting, you must eliminate intermediate goods, either by calculating only final output (expenditures approach) or by using the value added approach.

The table below provides another example.

Participants	I Cost of Materials	II Value of Sales	III Value Added	Row
Farmer	$ 0	$ 100	$100	1
Cone factory and ice cream maker	100	250	150	2
Middleperson (final sales)	250	400	150	3
Vendor	400	500	100	4
Totals	$750	$1,250	$500	5

It gives the cost of materials (intermediate goods) and the value of sales in the following scenario: Say we want to measure the contribution to GDP made by ice cream production of 200 ice cream cones at $2.50 each for total sales of $500. The vendor bought his cones and ice cream at a cost of $400 from a middleperson, who in turn paid the cone factory and ice cream maker a total of $250. The farmer who sold the cream to the factory got $100. Adding up all these transactions, we get $1,250, but that includes intermediate goods. Either by counting only the final value of the vendor's sales, $500, or by adding the value added at each stage of production (column III), we eliminate intermediate sales and arrive at the contribution of ice cream production to GDP of $500.

Value added is calculated by subtracting the cost of materials from the value of sales at each stage of production. The aggregate value added at each stage of production is, by definition, precisely equal to the value of final sales, since it excludes all intermediate products. In the table illustrating our example, the equality of the value added approach and the final sales approach can be seen by comparing the vendor's final sales of $500 (row 4, column II) with the $500 value added (row 5, column III).

Calculating GDP: Some Examples

Q-3 If a used-car dealer buys a car for $2,000 and resells it for $2,500, how much has been added to GDP?

To make sure you understand what value added is and what makes up GDP, let's consider some sample transactions and determine what value they add and whether they should be included in GDP. Let's first consider secondhand sales: When you sell your two-year-old car, how much value has been added? The answer is none. The sale involves no current output, so there's no value added. If, however, you sold the car to a used-car dealer for $2,000 and he or she resold it for $2,500, $500 of value has been added—the used-car dealer's efforts transferred the car from someone who didn't want it to someone who did. I point this out to remind you that GDP is not only a measure of the production of goods; it is a measure of the production of goods *and services*.

Now let's consider a financial transaction. Say you sell a bond (with a face value of $1,000) that you bought last year. You sell it for $1,250 and pay $100 commission to the dealer through whom you sell it. What value is added to final output? You might be tempted to say that $250 of value has been added, since the value of the bond has increased by $250. GDP, however, refers only to value that is added as the result of production or services, not to changes in the values of financial assets. Therefore, the price at which you buy or sell the bond is irrelevant to the question at hand. The only value that is added by the sale is the transfer of that bond from someone who doesn't want it to someone who does. Thus, the only value added as a result of economic activity is the dealer's commission, $100. The remaining $1,150 (the $1,250 you got from the bond minus the $100 commission you paid) is a transfer of an asset from one individual to another, but such transfers do not enter into GDP calculations. Only production of goods and services enters into GDP.

Q-4 How can the federal government have a $3.0 trillion budget but only have $1.1 trillion of that included in GDP?

Let's consider a different type of financial transaction: The federal government pays an individual Social Security benefits. What value is added? Clearly no production has taken place, but money has been transferred. As in the case of the bond, only the cost of transferring it—not the amount that gets transferred—is included in GDP. This is accomplished by including in GDP government expenditures on goods and services, but not the value of government transfer payments. Thus, Social Security payments, welfare payments, and veterans' benefits do not enter into calculations of GDP. That's why the government can have a $3.0 trillion budget but only $1.1 trillion ($3 trillion minus $1,900 billion of transfer payments) is included in GDP.

Finally, let's consider the work of a housespouse. (See the box "Is GDP Biased against Women?" for further discussion of this issue.) How much value does it add to economic

ADDED DIMENSION

Is GDP Biased against Women?

Although in the example in the book the housespouse is a man, the reality is that most housespouses are women. The fact that GDP doesn't include the work of housespouses is seen, by some, as a type of discrimination against women who work without pay at home since their work is not counted as part of the domestic product. One answer for why it is not counted is that housework does not involve a market transaction and hence could not be measured. That makes some sense, but it does not explain why the services houses provide to homeowners are estimated and included in GDP. Why can't housework also be estimated?

The answer is that it can be estimated, and my suspicion is that not including housespouses' services in GDP does represent the latent discrimination against women that was built into the culture in the 1930s when national income accounting was first developed. That latent discrimination against women was so deep that it wasn't even noticed. Anyone who has seen the movie *Rosie the Riveter,* which shows government programs to get women out from wartime employment and back into their role in the home, will have a good sense of the cultural views of people in the mid-1900s and earlier.

In thinking about whether GDP is biased against women, it is important to remember that the concepts we use are culturally determined and, over time, as cultural views change, the concepts no longer match our changed views. There is no escaping the fact that language is value-loaded. But so, too, is our attempt to point out the values in language. There are many other ways in which GDP reflects arbitrary choices and discrimination against groups. The major discussion of the fact that latent discrimination against women is embodied in GDP accounting itself reflects our current values, just as not including housespouses' work reflected earlier values.

activity in a year? Clearly if the housespouse is any good at what he or she does, a lot of value is added. Taking care of the house and children is hard work. Estimates of the yearly value of a housespouse's services range from $35,000 to $130,000, and some estimate that including housework in the national accounts would raise GDP more than 50 percent. Even though much value is added and hence, in principle, housespouse services should be part of GDP, by convention a housespouse contributes nothing to GDP. GDP measures only *market activities;* since housespouses are not paid, their value added is not included in GDP. This leads to some problems in measurement. For example, suppose a woman divorces her housespouse and then hires him to continue cleaning her house for $20,000 per year. That $20,000 value added, since it is now a market transaction, is included in GDP.

The housespouse example shows one of the problems with GDP. It also has other problems, but these are best left for intermediate courses. What's important for an introductory economics student to remember is that numerous decisions about how to handle various types of transactions had to be made to get a workable measure.

Some Complications

The above presentation of aggregate accounting makes it look as if aggregate accounting is quite simple—just measure consumption, investment, government spending, and net exports; add them together; and you have GDP. Conceptually, it is that simple, but, in practice, complicated conceptual decisions and accounting adjustments have to be made to ensure that all final production is included and that no double counting takes place. This leads to complicated accounting rules and alternative measures to account for different methods of measuring different concepts. Let me briefly introduce you to two of them.

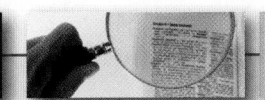

Gross and Net Concepts Notice that we use the term *gross* domestic product or GDP. Gross does not mean outrageous; it is a technical accounting term that distinguishes a concept that has not been adjusted for an offsetting flow. (Remember we used the term "net" in our discussion of the export component of GDP to distinguish a concept that is adjusted for an offsetting flow.) The complication is that during the production process, the machines and equipment wear out or simply become technologically obsolete. Economists call this wearing out process **depreciation**—*the decrease in an asset's value*. Depreciation is part of the cost of producing a good; it is the amount by which plants and equipment decrease in value as they grow older. Much of each year's investment involves expenditures to replace assets that have worn out. For example, as you drive your car, it wears out. A car with 80,000 miles on it is worth less than the same type of car with only 1,000 miles on it. The difference in value is attributed to depreciation.

Because some production is used to replace worn-out plant and equipment (depreciation), this production is not available for purchase for consumption, investment, or government spending. To account for this, economists have created another aggregate term that adjusts for depreciation. That term is *net domestic product*. **Net domestic product (NDP)** is *GDP less depreciation*.

NDP = GDP − Depreciation

NDP = GDP − Depreciation

Because depreciation affects capital available for production, depreciation shows up in the investment category of expenditures. Specifically, investment we have talked about so far is gross investment; **net investment** is *gross investment less depreciation*.

NDP takes depreciation into account. Since we want to measure output available for purchase, NDP is actually preferable to GDP as the expression of a country's domestic output. However, measuring true depreciation (the actual decrease in an asset's value) is difficult because asset values fluctuate. In fact, it's so difficult that, in the real world, accountants don't try to measure true depreciation, but instead use a number of conventional rules of thumb. In recognition of this reality, economists call the adjustment made to GDP to arrive at NDP the *capital consumption allowance* rather than *depreciation*. Since estimating depreciation is difficult, GDP rather than NDP is generally used in discussions of aggregate output.

National and Domestic Concepts A second complication of measuring aggregate output is whether the aggregate output that one is referring to is output produced within the borders of the country, or by the citizens and firms of the country.

Until 1992, the United States (unlike the rest of the world) used an accounting measure that focused on output produced by its firms and citizens. This was called *gross national product*. As economic issues have become internationalized, aggregate accounting has been affected. In 1992, the United States followed the rest of the world and switched to gross domestic product as its primary measure of aggregate output.

GDP is output produced within a country's borders; GNP is output produced by a country's citizens.

Whereas gross domestic product measures the economic activity that occurs within the geographic borders of a country, the economic activity of the citizens and businesses of a country is measured by **gross national product (GNP)**—*the aggregate final output of citizens and businesses of an economy in a one-year period*. So the economic activity of U.S. citizens working abroad is counted in U.S. GNP but isn't counted in U.S. GDP. Similarly for the foreign economic activity of U.S. companies. However, the production of a Mexican or German person or business working in the United States isn't counted in U.S. GNP but is counted in U.S. GDP. Thus, GDP describes the economic output within the physical borders of a country while GNP describes the economic output produced by the citizens of a country. To move from GDP to GNP we must add *net foreign factor income* to GDP. (That income reflects output of equal value.) **Net foreign factor income** is defined as *the income from foreign domestic factor sources minus foreign* *factor income earned domestically*. Put another way, we must add the foreign income of our citizens and subtract the income of residents who are not citizens.

$$GNP = GDP + \text{Net foreign factor income}$$

For many countries there's a significant difference between GNP and GDP. For example, consider Kuwait. Its citizens and companies have significant foreign income—income that far exceeds the income of the foreigners in Kuwait. This means that Kuwait's GNP (the output of its citizens) far exceeds its GDP (the output produced in Kuwait). For the United States, however, foreign output of U.S. businesses and people for the most part offsets the output of foreign businesses and people within the United States. Kuwait's net foreign factor income has been large and positive, while that of the United States has been minimal. Most discussions today focus on GDP since it is the primary measure presented in government statistics, but it is important to know GNP since aggregate income is normally measured on a national basis.

Q-5 Which is higher: Kuwait's GDP or its GNP? Why?

Calculating Aggregate Income

Aggregate accounting also calculates the aggregate income—the total income earned by citizens and firms of a country. This aggregate income is divided into the following four categories:

Compensation of Employees Employee compensation (the largest component of national income) consists of wages and salaries paid to individuals, along with fringe benefits and government taxes for Social Security and unemployment insurance.

Rents Rents are the income from property received by households. Rents received by firms are not included because a firm's rents are simply another source of income to the firm and hence are classified as profits. In most years, the rent component of national income is small since the depreciation owners take on buildings is close to the income they earn from those buildings.

Interest Interest is the income private businesses pay to households that have lent the businesses money, generally by purchasing bonds issued by the businesses. (Interest received by firms doesn't show up in this category for the same reason that rents received by firms don't show up in the *rent* category.) Interest payments by government and households aren't included in national income since by convention they're assumed not to flow from the production of goods and services.

Profits Profits are the amount that is left after compensation to employees, rents, and interest have been paid out. (The national income accounts use accounting profits that must be distinguished from economic profits, which are calculated on the basis of opportunity costs.)

Q-6 Calculate aggregate income with the information below:

Employee compensation = 140

Rents = 4

Interest = 12

Profits = 42

Table 25-3 shows these components for the United States and selected countries. It lists the aggregate income of countries and the components in absolute amounts and in percentages for the United States and in percentages for the remaining countries. As you can see, in all countries compensation of employees is the largest component of national income followed by profits. (One final word of caution: In each country statistics are collected using slightly different methods. This makes international comparison difficult.)

TABLE 25-3 Aggregate Income Breakdown for Selected Countries

(1) Country	(2) Aggregate Income (billions of $)	=	(3) Employee Compensation (% of total)	+	(4) Rents (% of total)	+	(5) Interest (% of total)	+	(6) Profits (% of total)
United States	$14,129		71%		1%		6%		22%
Japan	4,294		73		2		2		23
Germany	2,928		73		2		6		19
United Kingdom	2,213		62		4		3		30
Canada	1,270		68		8		6		18
Sweden	341		64		4		13		19

Note: Aggregate income in this table does not equal GDP in Table 25-1 because of statistical and conceptual adjustments. Percentages may not sum to 100 due to rounding. Data for the United States are for 2008. Most recent year available for all others.

Source: National Accounts, OECD, and individual country home pages.

Equality of Aggregate Income and Aggregate Production

By definition, whenever a good or service is produced (output), somebody receives an income for producing it. This means that aggregate income equals aggregate production, which can be expressed in the following identity:

$$\text{Aggregate income} \equiv \text{Aggregate production}^{1}$$

In establishing this identity, many accounting decisions need to be made to ensure complete equality. For example, since production figures are collected on a domestic basis (it measures what is produced in the geographic confines of the United States) while income figures are collected on a national basis (it measures what citizens and firms of the United States earn), it is necessary to make adjustments to equalize these. Similarly, taxes placed on corporations have to be accounted for to ensure that they are treated in a way that will maintain the equality. There are many more decisions, but at this introductory level, they are best left alone, so that the main point—that aggregate income—the value of the employee compensation, rents, interest, and profits—equals aggregate production—the value of goods produced—doesn't get lost in the complications.[2]

Profit is a residual that makes the income side equal the expenditure side.

How are these values kept exactly equal? The definition of profit is the key to the equality. Recall that *profit* is defined as what remains after all the firm's other income (employee compensation, rent, and interest) is paid out. For example, say a firm has a total output of $800 and that it paid $400 in wages, $200 in rent, and $100 in interest. The firm's profit is total output less these payments. Profit equals $800 − $700 = $100.

The accounting identity works even if a firm incurs a loss. Say that instead of paying $400 in wages, the firm paid $700, along with its other payments of $200 in rent and $100 in interest. Total output is still $800, but total payments are $1,000. Profits,

[1]An *identity* is a statement of equality that's true by definition. In algebra, an identity is sometimes written as a triple equal sign (≡). It is more equal than simply equal. How something can be more equal than equal is beyond me, too, but I'm no mathematician.

[2]In my previous classes, and in previous editions of this book, I've presented a number of these complications to my students in the belief that a bit of accounting suffering was good for their souls, and useful to know. (Besides, I had to learn them, so why shouldn't my students?) My students, along with some reviewers of the book, argued forcefully that the distinctions weren't central for students in introductory economics. Upon reflection, I agreed, so I eliminated them from the book. So you can thank my students for my not presenting them, and consult an intermediate macroeconomics text (mine preferably) if you want to go deeper into aggregate accounting issues.

still defined as total output minus payments, are negative: \$800 − \$1,000 = (−\$200). There's a loss of \$200. Adding that loss to other income [\$1,000 + (−\$200)] gives total income of \$800—which is identical to the firm's total output of \$800. It is no surprise that total output and total income, defined in this way, are equal.

The aggregate accounting identity (Total output = Total income) allows us to calculate GDP either by adding up all values of final outputs or by adding up the values of all earnings or income.

Using GDP Figures

The most important use of GDP figures is to compare one country's production with another country's and one year's production with another year's.

Web Note 25.2
Alternative Measures of Economic Growth

Comparing GDP among Countries

Most countries use somewhat similar measures to calculate GDP. Thus, we can compare various countries' GDP levels and get a sense of their economic size and power.

Per capita GDP is another measure often used to compare various nations' income. To arrive at per capita GDP, we divide GDP by the country's total population. Doing so gives us a sense of the relative standards of living of the people in various countries.

Some of the comparisons of these measures should give you cause to wonder. For example, at existing exchange rates Bangladesh has per capita GDP of about \$270, compared to U.S. per capita GDP of about \$45,000. How do people in Bangladesh live? In answering that question, remember that GDP measures market transactions. In poor countries, individuals often grow their own food (subsistence farming), build their own shelter, and make their own clothes. None of those activities are market activities, and while they're sometimes estimated and included in GDP, they often aren't estimated accurately. They certainly aren't estimated at the value of what these activities would cost in the United States. Also, remember that GDP is an aggregate measure that values activities at the market price in a society. The relative prices of the products and services a consumer buys often differ substantially among countries. In New York City, \$2,000 a month gets you only a small studio apartment. In Haiti, \$2,000 a month might get you a mansion with four servants. Thus, GDP can be a poor measure of the relative living standards.

Q-7 Why are GDP statistics not especially good for discussing the income of developing countries?

To avoid this problem in comparing per capita GDP, economists often calculate a different concept, *purchasing power parity*, which adjusts for the different relative prices among countries before making comparisons.

Just how much of a difference the two approaches can make can be seen in the case of China. In 1992, the International Monetary Fund (IMF) changed from calculating China's GDP using the exchange rate approach to calculating it using the purchasing power parity approach. Upon doing so, the IMF calculated that China's GDP grew over 400 percent in one year. Per capita income rose from about \$300 to well over \$1,000. When methods of calculation can make that much difference, one must use statistics very carefully.

Economic Welfare over Time

A second way in which the GDP concept is used is to compare one year with another. Using GDP figures to compare the economy's performance over time is much better than relying merely on our perceptions. Most of us have heard the phrase *the good old days*. Generally we hear it from our parents or grandparents, who are lamenting the state of the nation or economy. In comparing today to yesterday, they always seem to picture the past with greener grass, an easier life, and happier times. Compared to the good old days, today always comes out a poor second.

Using GDP figures to compare the economy's performance over time is much better than relying merely on our perceptions.

Our parents and grandparents may be right when they look back at particular events in their own lives, but if society were to follow such reasoning, it would conclude that all of history has been just one long downhill slide, worsening every year. In actuality, perceptions of the good old days are likely to be biased. It's easy to remember the nice things of yesterday while forgetting its harsh realities. Relying on past perception is not an especially helpful way of making accurate comparisons.

A preferable way is to rely on data that are not affected by emotion or other subjective perceptions. Looking at GDP over time provides a way of using data to make comparisons over time. For example, say we compare U.S. GDP in 1932 ($58 billion) to GDP in 2008 ($14.2 trillion). Would it be correct to conclude the economy had grown 228 times larger? No. As I discussed earlier, GDP figures aren't affected by emotions, but they are affected by inflation. To make comparisons over time, we can't confine ourselves to a simple look at what has happened to GDP. We must also look at what happened to prices.

Suppose prices of all goods and hence the price level go up 25 percent in one year, but outputs of all goods remain constant. GDP will have risen 25 percent, but will society be any better off? No. To compare GDP over time, you must distinguish between increases in GDP due to inflation and increases in GDP that represent real increases in production and income.

A real concept is a nominal concept adjusted for inflation.

Real and Nominal GDP

As stated earlier, to separate increases in GDP caused by inflation from increases in GDP that represent real increases in production and income, economists distinguish between **nominal GDP** *(GDP calculated at existing prices)* and **real GDP** *(nominal GDP adjusted for inflation)*. This distinction is sufficiently important to warrant repetition in this chapter. To calculate real GDP, we create a price index (a measure of how much the price level has risen from one year to the next), divide nominal GDP by that price index, and multiply by 100. That price index is the GDP deflator, introduced in the previous chapter.[3] Thus, we have

Real GDP is nominal GDP adjusted for inflation.

$$\text{Real GDP} = \frac{\text{Nominal GDP}}{\text{GDP deflator}} \times 100$$

Rearranging terms, we can provide a formula for calculating the GDP deflator if you know both nominal GDP and real GDP:

$$\text{GDP deflator} = \frac{\text{Nominal GDP}}{\text{Real GDP}} \times 100$$

To see how these formulas can be used, say the price level rises 10 percent (from a GDP deflator of 100 to a GDP deflator of 110) and nominal GDP rises from $10 trillion to $12 trillion. Part of that rise in nominal GDP represents the 10 percent rise in the price level. If you divide nominal GDP, $12 trillion, by the new GDP deflator, 110, and multiply by 100, you get $10.9 trillion (the amount GDP would have been if the price level had not risen).

Q-8 If real income has risen from $4 trillion to $4.2 trillion and the price level went up by 10 percent, by how much has nominal income risen?

$$\text{Real GDP} = \frac{\$12}{100} \times 100 = \$10.9$$

That $10.9 trillion is called real GDP. To decide whether production has increased or decreased over time, we simply compare the real incomes. In this example, real income

[3]Now you know why the total output deflator is called the *GDP deflator*. It is an index of the rise in prices of the goods and services that make up GDP.

has risen from $10 trillion to $10.9 trillion, so we can conclude that the real economy has grown by .9/10, or 9 percent.

To move from GDP deflators to the rate of inflation, you calculate the change in the deflator from one year to another, divide that change by the initial year's deflator, and multiply by 100. For example, if the initial deflator is 101 and the current deflator is 103, you can calculate the rate of inflation by dividing the difference, 2, by the initial deflator, 101, and multiplying by 100. Doing so gives an inflation rate of 1.98. For numbers close to 100, simply subtracting the two deflators (103 − 101 = 2) provides a reasonably good approximation to the rate of inflation.

The percentage change, or growth rate, of nominal and real GDP can be calculated by the same method; you calculate the difference between the figures for the two years, divide that difference by the initial year figure, and multiply by 100. For example, if nominal GDP rises from $13,807.5 billion in 2007 to $14,264.6 billion in 2008, the difference is $457.1 billion. Dividing that difference by the initial year's GDP, $13,807.5 billion, and multiplying by 100 gives a growth rate of 3.3 percent.

As I discussed in the last chapter, the growth rates of real GDP, nominal GDP, and inflation are related: Specifically:

% change in real GDP = % change in nominal GDP − Inflation.

% change in real GDP = % change in nominal GDP − Inflation

Doing that subtraction is what economists mean when they say that real GDP is equal to nominal GDP adjusted for inflation. We can see these relationships in the table below, which lists nominal GDP, the GDP deflator, and real GDP (base year 2000) for recent years and their percent changes from the previous year.

	Nominal GDP	GDP Deflator	Real GDP
2006 level in billions	$13,178.4	116.7	$11,294.8
2007 level in billions	$13,807.5	119.8	$11,523.9
% change from '06 to '07	4.8	2.7	2.1
2008 level in billions	$14,264.6	122.4	$11,652.7
% change from '07 to '08	3.3	2.2	1.1

Notice that you can arrive at the growth rate in real GDP by subtracting inflation from the percent change in nominal GDP. For example, in 2008 real GDP rose by 1.1 percent, which equals the growth of nominal GDP, 3.3%, minus inflation of 2.2%.

Real GDP is what is important to a society because it measures what is *really* produced. Considering nominal GDP instead of real GDP can distort what's really happening. Let's say the U.S. price level doubled tomorrow. Nominal GDP would also double, but would the United States be better off? No.

We'll use the distinction between real and nominal continually in this course, so to firm up the concepts in your mind, let's go through another example. Consider Iceland in 2007 and 2008, when nominal GDP rose from 1,301 billion krona to 1,465 billion krona while the GDP deflator rose from 140 to 157. Dividing nominal GDP in 2008 by the GDP deflator and multiplying by 100, we see that *real GDP* rose by only 0.3 percent. So nearly all of Iceland's growth was in prices.

Some Limitations of Aggregate Accounting

The quotation at this chapter's start pointed out that statistics can be misleading. I want to reiterate that here. Before you can work with statistics, you need to know how they are collected and the problems they have. If you don't, the results can be disastrous.

Limitations of aggregate accounting include the following:
1. Measurement problems exist.
2. GDP measures market activity, not welfare.
3. Subcategories are often interdependent.

Here's a possible scenario: A student who isn't careful looks at the data and discovers an almost perfect relationship between imports and investment in a Latin American country. Whenever capital goods imports go up, investment of capital goods goes up by an equal proportion. The student develops a thesis based on that insight, only to learn after submitting the thesis that no data on investment are available for that country. Instead of gathering actual data, the foreign country's statisticians estimate investment by assuming it to be a constant percentage of imports. Since many investment goods are imported, this is reasonable, but the estimate is not a reasonable basis for an economic policy. It would be back to the drawing board for the student.

If you ever work in business as an economist, statistics will be your life's blood. Much of what economists do is based on knowing, interpreting, and drawing inferences from statistics. Statistics must be treated carefully. They don't always measure what they seem to measure. Though U.S. national income accounting statistics are among the most accurate in the world, they still have serious limitations.

GDP Measures Market Activity, Not Welfare

The first, and most important, limitation to remember is that GDP measures neither happiness nor economic welfare. GDP measures economic (market) activity. Real GDP could rise and economic welfare could fall. For example, say some Martians came down and let loose a million Martian burglars in the United States just to see what would happen. GDP would be likely to rise as individuals bought guns and locks and spent millions of dollars on protecting their property and replacing stolen items. At the same time, however, welfare would fall.

Welfare is a complicated concept. The economy's goal should not be to increase output for the sake of increasing output, but to make people better off or at least happier. But a pure happiness measure is impossible. Economists have struggled with the concept of welfare and most have decided that the best they can do is to concentrate their analysis on economic activity, leaving others to consider how economic activity relates to happiness. I should warn you, however, that there is no neat correlation between increases in GDP and increases in happiness.

Measurement Errors

Q-9 How can measurement errors occur in adjusting GDP figures for inflation?

GDP figures are supposed to measure all market economic activity, but they do not. Illegal drug sales, under-the-counter sales of goods to avoid income and sales taxes, work performed and paid for in cash to avoid income tax, nonreported sales, and prostitution are all market activities, yet none of them is included in GDP figures. Estimates of the underground, nonmeasured economy range from 1.5 to 20 percent of GDP in the United States and as high as 70 percent in Nigeria. That is, if measured U.S. GDP is \$14 trillion, including the underground, nonmeasured activity would raise it to between \$14.2 trillion and \$16.8 trillion. If we were able to halt underground activity and direct those efforts to the above-ground economy, GDP would rise significantly. For instance, if we legalized prostitution and marijuana sales and quadrupled tax-collection mechanisms, GDP would rise. But that rise in GDP wouldn't necessarily make us better off. See the box "The Underground Economy and Illegal Immigration" for further discussion.

Web Note 25.3
The Underground Economy

Measurements of inflation can involve significant measurement errors.

A second type of measurement error occurs in adjusting GDP figures for inflation. Earlier I discussed problems using indexes. Measurement of inflation involves numerous arbitrary decisions including what base year to use, how to weight various prices, and how to adjust for changes in the quality of products. Let's take, for example, changes in the quality of products. If the price of a Toyota went up 5 percent

The Underground Economy and Illegal Immigration

In the text, we mentioned how the national income accounts fail to measure the underground economy and gave some examples of underground activities. One underground activity that has become increasingly important involves illegal immigration. Currently about 12 million people in the United States are undocumented workers, although the precise number isn't known since illegal immigrants aren't especially forthcoming when the government comes around to do a census study.

Most people in the United States are affected by this group. You can see them throughout the country in a variety of lower-level jobs such as maids, day laborers, construction workers, truckers, and farm laborers, among others. Many of these jobs are "on the books," which means that the undocumented workers have acquired a forged identity, with a Social Security number. They end up paying taxes and contributing to measured output even though they are illegal. Others work "off the books" and, like the many U.S. citizens who work off the books, their contribution to output does not show up in the national income accounts. Such "off the books" transactions occur when restaurants don't ring up cash sales or when waiters forget to declare tips on their tax returns—they reduce their tax payments and make it look as if they have less income and as if the economy has less production than actually exists.

How important is illegal immigration to the underground economy? While the standard measure is that there are about 12 million undocumented workers in the United States and that the underground economy is about 10 percent the size of the U.S. economy, some economists have estimated that the true number of undocumented workers is closer to 18 to 20 million, and that the underground economy is much larger than that 10 percent.

from 2009 ($20,000) to 2010 ($21,000), that's certainly a 5 percent rise in price. But what if the 2010 Toyota had a "new, improved" 16-valve engine? Can you say that the price of cars rose 5 percent, or should you adjust for the improvement in quality? And if you adjust, how do you adjust? The people who keep track of the price indexes used to measure inflation will be the first to tell you these questions have no one right answer. How that question, and a million other similar questions involved in measuring inflation, are answered can lead to significant differences in estimates of inflation and hence in estimates of real GDP growth.

One study for Canada argued inflation could be either 5.4 or 15 percent, depending on how the inflation index was calculated. Which inflation figure you chose would make a big difference in your estimate of how the economy was doing.

Misinterpretation of Subcategories

A third limitation of aggregate accounting concerns possible misinterpretation of the components. In setting up the accounts, a large number of arbitrary decisions had to be made: What to include in "investment"? What to include in "consumption"? How to treat government expenditures? The decisions made were, for the most part, reasonable, but they weren't the only ones that could have been made. Once made, however, they influence our interpretations of events. For example, when we see that investment rises, we normally think that our future productive capacity is rising, but remember that investment includes housing investment, which does not increase our future productive capacity. In fact, some types of consumption (say, purchases of personal computers by people who will become computer-literate and use their knowledge and skills to be

Q-10 How can some types of consumption increase our productive capacity by more than some types of investment?

more productive than they were before they owned computers) increase our productive capacity more than some types of investment.

Genuine Progress Indicator

Web Note 25.4
Measuring Welfare

The problems of aggregate accounting have led to a variety of measures of economic activity. One of the most interesting of these is the *genuine progress indicator (GPI)*, developed by Redefining Progress (www.redefiningprogress.org), which makes a variety of adjustments to GDP to better measure the progress of society rather than simply economic activity. The GPI makes adjustments to GDP for changes in other social goals. For example, if pollution worsens, the GPI falls even though the GDP remains constant. Each of these adjustments requires someone to value these other social goals, and there is significant debate about how social goals should be valued. Advocates of the GPI agree that such valuations are difficult, but they argue that avoiding any such valuation, as is done with the GDP, implicitly values other social goals, such as having no pollution, at zero. Since some index will be used as an indicator of the progress of the economy, it is better to have an index that includes all social goals rather than an index of only economic activity.

Measurement is necessary, and the GDP measurements and categories have made it possible to think and talk about the aggregate economy.

By pointing out these problems, economists are not suggesting that aggregate accounting statistics should be thrown out. Far from it; measurement is necessary, and the GDP measurements and categories have made it possible to think and talk about the aggregate economy. I wouldn't have devoted an entire chapter of this book to aggregate accounting if I didn't believe it was important. I am simply arguing that aggregate accounting concepts should be used with sophistication, that is, with an awareness of their weaknesses as well as their strengths.

Conclusion

Used with that awareness, aggregate accounting is a powerful tool; you wouldn't want to be an economist without it. For those of you who aren't planning to be economists, it's still a good idea for you to understand the concepts of national income accounting. If you do, the business section of the newspaper will seem less like Greek to you. You'll be a more informed citizen and will be better able to make up your own mind about macroeconomic debates.

Summary

- Aggregate accounting is a set of rules and definitions for measuring activity in the aggregate economy.
- GDP is the total market value of all final goods produced in an economy in one year. It's a flow, not a stock, measure of market activity.
- GDP is divided up into four types of expenditures:

  GDP = Consumption + Investment + Government spending + Net exports

- Intermediate goods can be eliminated from GDP in two ways:
  1. By measuring only final sales.
  2. By measuring only value added.
- Net domestic product is GDP less depreciation. NDP represents output available for purchase because production used to replace worn-out plant and equipment (depreciation) has been subtracted.

- GDP describes the economic output produced within the physical borders of an economy, while GNP describes the economic output produced by the citizens of a country.
- Aggregate income = Compensation to employees + Rent + Interest + Profit.
- Aggregate income equals aggregate production because whenever a good is produced, somebody receives income for producing it. Profit is key to that equality.
- Because GDP measures only market activities, GDP can be a poor measure of relative living standards among countries.
- To compare income over time, we must adjust for price-level changes. After adjusting for inflation, nominal measures are changed to "real" measures.

  % change in real GDP =
  % change in nominal GDP − Inflation
- $\text{Real GDP} = \dfrac{\text{Nominal GDP}}{\text{GDP deflator}} \times 100$
- GDP has its problems: GDP does not measure economic welfare; it does not include transactions in the underground economy; the price index used to calculate real GDP is problematic; subcategories of GDP are often interdependent.

Key Terms

asset inflation *(578)*
consumption *(575)*
depreciation *(582)*
final output *(579)*
government spending *(576)*
gross domestic product (GDP) *(575)*
gross national product (GNP) *(582)*
intermediate products *(579)*
investment *(575)*
net domestic product (NDP) *(582)*
net exports *(576)*
net foreign factor income *(582)*
net investment *(582)*
nominal GDP *(586)*
nominal wealth *(577)*
real GDP *(586)*
real wealth *(577)*
transfer payments *(576)*
value added *(579)*
wealth accounts *(577)*

Questions and Exercises

1. What expenditure category of production is largest for most countries? LO1
2. What's the relationship between a stock concept and a flow concept? Give an example that hasn't already been given in this chapter. LO1
3. State whether the following actions will increase or decrease GDP:
   a. The United States legalizes gay marriages.
   b. An individual sells her house on her own.
   c. An individual sells his house through a broker.
   d. Government increases Social Security payments.
   e. Stock prices rise by 20 percent.
   f. An unemployed worker gets a job. LO1
4. If you add up all the transactions in an economy, do you arrive at GDP, GNP, or something else? LO2
5. The United States is considering introducing a value-added tax. What tax rate on value added is needed to get the same revenue as is gotten from an income tax rate of 15 percent? LO2
6. There are three firms in an economy: A, B, and C. Firm A buys $250 worth of goods from firm B and $200 worth of goods from firm C, and produces 200 units of output, which it sells at $5 per unit. Firm B buys $100 worth of goods from firm A and $150 worth of goods from firm C, and produces 300 units of output, which it sells at $7 per unit. Firm C buys $50 worth of goods from firm A and nothing from firm B. It produces output worth $1,000. All other products are sold to consumers.
   a. Calculate GDP.
   b. If a value-added tax (a tax on the total value added of each firm) of 10 percent is introduced, how much revenue will the government get?

c. How much would government get if it introduced a 10 percent income tax?
d. How much would government get if it introduced a 10 percent sales tax on final output? LO2

7. If the government increases transfer payments, what happens to aggregate output? LO2
8. Economists normally talk about GDP even though they know NDP is a better measure of economic activity. Why? LO3
9. Which will be larger, gross domestic product or gross national product? LO3
10. You've been given the following data:

Net exports	$ 4
Net foreign factor income	2
Investment	185
Government spending	195
Consumption	500
Depreciation	59

From these data, calculate GDP, GNP and NDP. LO3

11. What is the largest component of aggregate income for most countries? LO4
12. Given the following data about the economy:

Profit	$ 268
Consumption	700
Investment	500
Government spending	300
Net exports	275
Rent	25
Depreciation	25
Net foreign factor income	3
Interest	150
Compensation to employees	1,329

a. Calculate aggregate output (GDP) and aggregate income.
b. Compare the two calculations in *a*. Why are they not precisely equal?
c. Calculate GNP.
d. Calculate NDP. LO1, LO3, LO4

13. You have been hired as a research assistant and are given the following data.

Compensation to employees	$329
Consumption	370
Exports	55
Net foreign factor income	3
Government spending	43
Investment	80
Imports	63
Interest	49
Profit	96
Rent	14
Net Investment	72

a. Calculate GNP, GDP, and aggregate income.
b. What is depreciation in this year?
c. What is NDP? LO1, LO3, LO4

14. What income category keeps aggregate output and aggregate income equal? LO5
15. What makes it difficult to compare GDP over time? How is the problem addressed? LO6
16. Below are nominal GDP and GDP deflators for four years.

Year	Nominal GDP in billions	GDP Deflator
2005	$12,421.9	113.0
2006	13,178.4	116.7
2007	13,807.5	119.8
2008	14,264.6	122.4

a. Calculate real GDP in each year.
b. Did the percentage change in nominal GDP exceed the percentage change in real GDP in any of the last three years listed?
c. In which year did society's welfare increase the most? LO6

Questions from Alternative Perspectives

1. Your textbook points out that GDP fails to recognize much of the work done in the home, largely by women. Most estimates assign that work great economic value. For instance, one measure, developed by the UN's International Training and Research Institute, calculates that counting unpaid household production would add 30–60 percent to the GDP of industrialized countries and far more for developing countries.

a. Why do you think that work done at home is left out, but housing services are not?
b. Does it make any difference to how women are treated and thought about that work done at home is not counted in GDP?
c. If you were valuing the services of a housespouse, how would you go about measuring the value of those services? (Feminist)

2. In "Christianity and Economics: A Review of the Recent Literature," economist John Tiemstra states, "taking good to mean self-perceived happiness derived from economic consumption adopts an ethic that is foreign to biblical Christianity." Your textbook cautions that GDP is not the same as welfare.
   a. What would you include in an index to measure the welfare of a society that takes into account Christian ethics?
   b. What would you purposefully not include in that index? (Religious)
3. Explain the sense in which GDP accounting is an institution (see the *Oxford Dictionary of the English Language* for a precise definition of an institution).
   a. How does GDP as an institution shape our understanding of the economic system?
   b. Who benefits from using GDP accounting as a measure of welfare? (Institutionalist)
4. In the expenditure approach of GDP, should G (government purchases) be taken into account within the calculation the same way C (consumption) and *I* (investment) are measured? If not, is there something inherently different about the nature of private and public expenditures? (Austrian)
5. The government spends far too much money collecting and organizing statistics. If those statistics were necessary, the private market would collect them.
   a. Explain the sense in which the above statement is true.
   b. Who do you think is the major supporter of government collection of data? (Austrian)
6. Unlike GDP, the "Genuine Progress Indicator" measures the costs as well as the benefits of economic growth by accounting for how production and consumption create social ills such as inequality and create environmental problems that threaten future generations, such as global warming and the depletion of natural resourses. GPI adjusts GDP downward to account for these costs, along with underemployment and the loss of leisure time. The result: the GPI rose from the 1950s through the early 1970s but has fallen since and today is still below its level in 1973.
   a. In your opinion, does gross national product per capita or the Genuine Progress Indicator provide a better measure of economic progress?
   b. Why? (Radical)

Issues to Ponder

1. Find consumption expenditures (as a percent of GDP) for the following countries. (Requires research.)
   a. Mexico
   b. Thailand
   c. Poland
   d. Nigeria
   e. Kuwait LO1
2. If the United States introduces universal child care, what will likely happen to GDP? What are the welfare implications? LO7
3. If society's goal is to make people happier, and higher GDP isn't closely associated with being happier, why do economists even talk about GDP? (Difficult) LO7

Answers to Margin Questions

1. GDP is the sum of consumption, investment, and government spending plus the total of exports minus imports, in this case 95. *(576)*
2. Wealth accounts measure stocks—a country's assets and liabilities at a point in time. Income accounts measure flows—a country's income and expenditures over a period of time. *(577)*
3. Only the value added by the sale would be added to GDP. In this case, the value added is the difference between the purchase price and the sale price, or $500. *(580)*
4. The government budget includes transfer payments, which are not included in GDP. Only those government expenditures that are for goods and services are included in GDP. *(580)*

5. GDP measures the output of the residents of a country—the output within its geographical borders. GNP measures the output of the citizens and businesses of a country. Kuwait is a very rich country whose residents have a high income, much of it from investments overseas. Thus, their GNP will be high. However, Kuwait also has large numbers of foreign workers who are not citizens and whose incomes would be included in GDP but not in GNP. In reality, Kuwait citizens' and businesses' foreign income exceeds foreign workers' and foreign companies' income within Kuwait, so Kuwait's GNP is greater than its GDP. *(583)*
6. Aggregate income is the sum of employee compensation, rents, interest, and profits, in this case 198. *(583)*
7. In developing countries, individuals often grow their own food and take part in many activities that are not measured by the GDP statistics. The income figures that one gets from the GDP statistics of developing countries do not include such activities and, thus, can be quite misleading. *(585)*
8. Nominal income must have risen $400 billion to slightly over $4.6 trillion so that, when it is adjusted for inflation, the real income will have risen to $4.2 trillion. *(586)*
9. Measurement errors occur in adjusting GDP figures for inflation because measuring inflation involves numerous arbitrary decisions such as choosing a base year, adjusting for quality changes in products, and weighting prices. *(588)*
10. Dividing goods into consumption and investment does not always capture the effect of the spending on productive capacity. For example, housing "investment" does little to expand the productive capacity. However, "consumption" of computers or books could expand the productive capacity significantly. *(589)*

Growth, Productivity, and the Wealth of Nations

Queen Elizabeth owned silk stockings. The capitalist achievement does not typically consist in providing more silk stockings for queens but in bringing them within the reach of factory girls in return for steadily decreasing amounts of effort.

—***Joseph Schumpeter***

Growth matters. In the long run, growth matters a lot. For example, if current growth rates continue, in less than 50 years China's economy will be larger than the U.S. economy. Given the importance of growth, it is not surprising that modern economics began with a study of growth. In *The Wealth of Nations*, Adam Smith noted that what was good about market economies was that they raised society's standard of living. He argued that people's natural tendency to exchange and specialize was the driving force behind growth. Specialization and trade, and the investment and capital that made these possible, were responsible for the wealth of nations.

As we discussed in an earlier chapter, through the 1920s, long-run growth remained an important focus of economics. Then, in the 1930s, the world economy fell into a serious depression. It was at that time that modern macroeconomics developed as a separate subject with a significant focus on short-run business cycles. It asked the questions "What causes depressions?" and "How does an economy get out of one?" Short-run macroeconomics became known as Keynesian economics, and remained the standard macroeconomics through the 1960s. Keynesian economics focuses on fluctuations around the growth trend and on whether those fluctuations influence that trend.

In the 1970s, as the memories of the Great Depression faded, the pendulum started to swing back again towards a focus on long-run growth and now, at the start of the 21st century, macroeconomists are taking a more balanced position that includes both long-run growth and short-run business cycles as the core content of macro. In this chapter I consider long-run growth, and in later chapters, I examine business cycles and policies to deal with them.

AFTER READING THIS CHAPTER, YOU SHOULD BE ABLE TO:

1. Define growth and relate it to living standards.
2. List five important sources of growth.
3. Distinguish diminishing marginal productivity from decreasing returns to scale.
4. Explain the convergence hypothesis and list four reasons why it has not taken place.
5. Distinguish Classical growth theory from new growth theory.

General Observations about Growth

Let's begin our consideration with some general observations about growth.

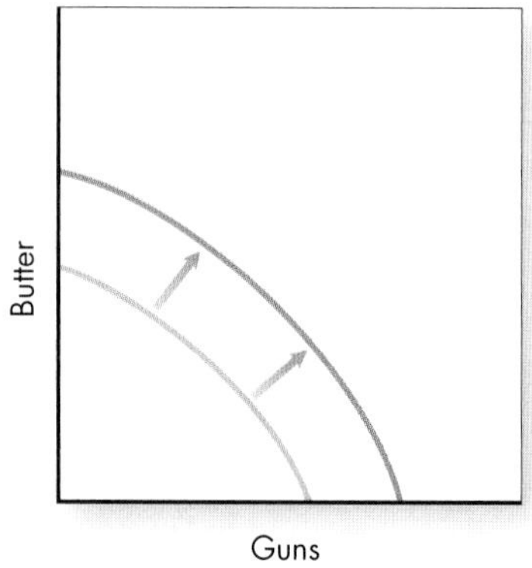

The analysis of growth focuses on forces that shift out the production possibility curve.

Growth and the Economy's Potential Output

Long-run growth occurs when the economy produces more goods and services from existing production processes and resources. The study of growth is the study of why that increase comes about. In discussing growth, economists use the term **potential output**—*the highest amount of output an economy can produce from existing production processes and resources.* Potential output conveys a sense of the growth that is possible. (Recall that *potential output* can also be called *potential income* because, in the aggregate, income and output are identical.) One way to think about growth and potential output is to relate them to the production possibility curve, presented in Chapter 2. That curve gave us a picture of the choices an economy faces given available resources. When an economy is at its potential output, it is operating on its production possibility curve. When an economy is below its potential output, it is operating inside its production possibility curve. The analysis of growth focuses on the forces that increase potential output; in other words, that shift out the production possibility curve.

Why do we use potential output in macro rather than the production possibility curve? Because macro focuses on aggregate output—GDP—and does not focus on the choices of dividing up GDP among alternative products as does micro and the production possibility curve. But the concept is the same. Potential output is a barrier beyond which an economy cannot expand without either increasing available factors of production or increasing **productivity** *(output per unit of input)*.

Q-1 How does long-run growth analysis justify its focus on supply?

Long-run growth analysis focuses on supply; it assumes demand is sufficient to buy whatever is supplied. That assumption is called **Say's law** *(supply creates its own demand)*, named after a French economist, Jean Baptiste Say, who first pointed it out. The reasoning behind Say's law is as follows: People work and supply goods to the market because they want other goods. The very fact that they supply goods means that they demand goods of equal value. According to Say's law, aggregate demand will always equal aggregate supply.

In the short run, economists consider potential output fixed; they focus on how to get the economy operating at its potential if, for some reason, it is not. In the long run, economists consider an economy's potential output changeable. Growth analysis is a consideration of why an economy's potential shifts out, and growth policy is aimed at increasing an economy's potential output.

The Importance of Growth for Living Standards

In 2004, Nobel Prize winner Robert Lucas wrote, "Of the tendencies that are harmful to sound economics, the most seductive, and in my opinion most poisonous, is to focus on questions of distribution . . . The potential for improving the lives of poor people by finding different ways of distributing current production is *nothing* [his italics] compared to the apparently limitless potential of increasing production." For Lucas, and many other economists, growth, not distribution or business cycles, is the most important macroeconomic issue.

Growth in income improves lives by fulfilling basic needs and making more goods available to more people.

All economists agree that growth makes an enormous difference for living standards. Take France and Argentina as examples. In the 1950s, per capita real income was about $5,000 in each country, but their growth rates differed. From 1950 to 2009, France's income grew at an average rate of 2.8 percent per year while Argentina's grew at an average rate of 1.2 percent per year. Because of the differences in growth rates, France's per capita income is now about $23,000 and Argentina's per capita income is about $10,000. The difference in income levels translates into very real differences in the quality of life. For example, in France 100 percent of the people have access to safe water; in Argentina 90 percent have such access. About one-third of households in Argentina have a computer; two-thirds do in France.

ADDED DIMENSION

Is Growth Good?

The discussion in the chapter emphasizes the generally held view among economists that growth is inherently good. It increases our incomes, thereby improving our standard of living. But that does not mean that all economists support unlimited growth. Growth has costs, and economics requires us to look at both costs and benefits. For example, growth may contribute to increased pollution—reducing the quality of the air we breathe and the water we drink, and endangering the variety of species in the world. In short, the wrong type of growth may produce undesirable side effects, including global warming and polluted rivers, land, and air.

New technology, upon which growth depends, also raises serious moral questions: Do we want to replace sexual reproduction with cloning? Will a brain implant be an improvement over 12 years of education? Will selecting your baby's genetic makeup be better than relying on nature? Just because growth *can* continue does not mean that it *should* continue. Moral judgments can be made against growth. For example, some argue that growth changes traditional cultures with beautiful handiwork, music, and dance into cultures of gadgets where people have lost touch with what is important. They argue that we have enough gadgets cluttering our lives and that it is time to start focusing on noneconomic priorities.

This moral argument against growth carries the most weight in highly developed countries—countries with per capita incomes of at least $20,000 a year. For developing countries, where per capita income can be as low as $150 per year, the reality is the choice between growth and poverty or even between growth and starvation. In these countries it is difficult to argue against growth.

One final comment: The benefits of growth do not have to be just higher incomes and more gadgets. They could also include more leisure activities and improved working conditions. In the 19th century, a 12-hour workday was common. Today the workday is eight hours, but had we been content with a lower income, the workday could now be two hours, with the remainder left for free time. We'd have less growth in GDP, but we'd have a lot more time to play.

Other examples are South Korea and Libya. In the 1950s, their incomes were also nearly identical, at $800 per person. Because of differing growth rates, Korea's per capita income has multiplied about 22 times, to about $18,000, while Libya's per capita income is about $2,700. Why? Because Libya has a 2 percent growth rate while South Korea has averaged an 5 percent annual growth rate. The moral of these stories: In the long run, growth rates matter a lot.

Small differences in growth rates can mean huge differences in income levels because of *compounding*. Compounding means that growth is based not only on the original level of income but also on the accumulation of previous-year increases in income. For example, say you start with $10,000. At a 7 percent interest rate that $10,000 after 10 years will be more than $20,000; after 20 years it will be more than $40,000; after 30 years it will be more than $80,000; and after 50 years it will be more than $320,000. So if you are worried about your retirement, it pays to start saving early at as high an interest rate as you can get. The longer you save, and the higher the interest rate you receive, the more you end up with.

Another way to see the effects of the difference in growth rates is to see how long it would take income to double at different growth rates. The Rule of 72 tells you that. The **Rule of 72** states: *The number of years it takes for a certain amount to double in value is equal to 72 divided by its annual rate of increase*. For example, if Argentina's income grows at a 1 percent annual rate, it will double in 72 years (72/1). If France's income grows at a 3 percent annual rate, it will double in only 24 years (72/3).

Q-2 If an economy is growing at 4 percent a year, how long will it take for its income to double?

$$\frac{72}{\text{(Rate of Growth)}} = \text{number of years to double}$$

Let's conclude our discussion by applying the Rule of 72 to the future growth of China and the United States and the comparison with which we started the chapter. Let's say that the current U.S. per capita income is $40,000 and that U.S. per capita income grows 1 percent per year; that means its per capita income will double every 72 years, so in 72 years its income will be $80,000 per capita. Let's say that

China's income is $2,000 per capita, but that it grows at 9 percent per year, which means that it doubles every 8 years. If that actually happens, within 40 years per capita income in China will surpass that in the United States and after 8 more years will be significantly higher. While such extrapolations are precarious, and it is highly unlikely that such different growth rates will continue, even a partial movement in that direction will involve significant changes in the world economic and political structure. That's why differential growth rates are so important.

Markets, Specialization, and Growth

Specialization and the division of labor that accompany markets increase productivity and growth.

Growth began when markets developed, and then, as markets expanded, growth accelerated. Why are markets so important to growth? To answer that question, let's go back to Adam Smith's argument for markets. Smith argued that markets allow **specialization** *(the concentration of individuals on certain aspects of production)* and **division of labor** *(the splitting up of a task to allow for specialization of production)*. According to Smith, markets create an interdependent economy in which individuals can take advantage of the benefits of specialization and trade for their other needs. In doing so, markets increase productivity—and, in turn, improve the standard of living.

You saw in Chapter 2 how comparative advantage and specialization increase productivity. If individuals concentrate on the production of goods for which their skills and other resources are suited, and trade for those goods for which they do not have a comparative advantage, everyone can end up with more of all goods. To see this even more clearly, consider what your life would be like without markets, trade, and specialization. You would have to grow all your food, build your own living space, and provide all your own transportation. Simply to exist under these conditions, you'd need a lot of skills, and it is unlikely that you'd become sufficiently adept in any one of them to provide yourself with anything other than the basics. You'd have all you can do to keep up.

Now consider your life today with specialization. Someone who specializes in dairy farming produces the milk you need. You don't need to know how it is produced, just where to buy it. How about transportation? You buy, not build, your car. It runs somehow—you're not quite sure how—but if it breaks down, you take it to a garage. And consider your education: Are you learning how to grow food or build a house? No, you are probably learning a specific skill that has little relevance to the production of most goods. But you'll most likely provide some good or service that will benefit the dairy farmer and auto mechanic. You get the picture—for most of the things you consume, you don't have the faintest idea who makes them or how they are made, nor do you need to know.

Economic Growth, Distribution, and Markets

Markets and growth are often seen as unfair with regard to the distribution of income. Is it fair that markets give some individuals so much (billions to Bill Gates), and others so little ($7.00 an hour to Joe Wall, who has a minimum wage job and two kids)? Such questions are legitimate and need to be asked. But in answering them we should also remember the quotation from Joseph Schumpeter that opened this chapter: Even if markets and growth do not provide equality, they tend to make everyone, even the poor, better off. The relevant question is: Would the poor be better off with or without markets and growth?

Even though growth isn't evenly distributed, it generally raises the incomes of the poor.

There are strong arguments, based on historical evidence, that people are better off with markets. Consider the number of hours an average person must work to buy certain goods at various periods in U.S. history. A century ago it took a worker 1 hour and 41 minutes to earn enough to buy a pair of stockings; today it takes only 18 minutes of work. Figure 26-1 gives a number of other examples. As you can see from the figure, growth has made average workers significantly better off; to get the same amount, they have to work far less now than they did in the past. Growth also has

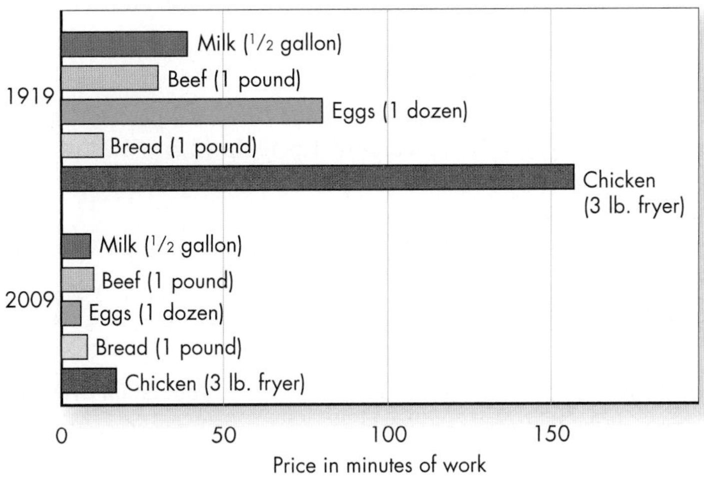

FIGURE 26-1 Cost of Goods in Hours of Work

Growth in the U.S. economy in the past century has reduced the number of hours the average person needs to work to buy consumer goods.

Source: Federal Reserve Bank of Dallas, *Time Well Spent* (1997 annual report). Updated by author.

made new products available. For example, before 1952 air conditioners were not available at any price.

The reality is that, judged from an *absolute* standard, the poor benefit enormously from the growth that markets foster. Markets, through competition, make the factors of production more productive and lower the cost of goods so that more goods are available to everyone. Today, the U.S. poverty level for a family of four is about $20,000. If we go back 100 years in U.S. history, and adjust for inflation, that $20,000 income would put a family in the upper middle class. Markets and growth have made that possible.

The above argument does not mean that the poor always benefit from growth; many of us judge our well-being by relative, not absolute, standards. Growth often reduces the share of income earned by the poorest proportion of society, making the poor *relatively* worse off. So, if one uses relative standards, one could say that the poor have become worse off over certain periods. Moreover, it is not at all clear that markets require the large differentials in pay that have accompanied growth in market economies. If such large differentials did not exist, and growth had been at the same rate, the poor would be even better off than they are.

Just because the poor benefit from growth does not mean they might not be better off if income were distributed more in their favor.

Per Capita Growth

When thinking about growth, it is important to distinguish between increases in total output and increases in per capita output, or total output divided by the total population. If there is **per capita growth,** the country is *producing more goods and services per person*. For example, say the real output of the economy is $4 billion and there are 1 million people. Each person, on average, has $4,000 to spend. Now say that output increases by 50 percent but that population also increases by 50 percent. In this case *output* has grown but *per capita output* has not; each person still has only $4,000 to spend. A number of countries have found themselves in such situations. Of the approximately 130 countries whose economies grew from 1990 to 2009, in about 10, the population grew even faster so that their per capita incomes fell. Take Kenya as an example. Its income grew at an annual rate of 2.2 percent, but its population grew at a higher 2.5 percent annual rate, meaning that per capita income fell an average 0.3 percent each year. Over this same time period, the U.S. economy grew an average 3.5 percent a year, but its population grew only 1.2 percent a year so that, on average, per capita income grew 2.3 percent a year.

If you know the percentage change in output and percentage change in population, you can approximate per capita growth:

Per capita growth = % change in output − % change in population

Q-3 Which country has experienced higher growth per capita: country A, whose economy is growing at a 4 percent rate and whose population is growing at a 3 percent rate, or country B, whose economy is growing at a 3 percent rate and whose population is growing at a 1 percent rate?

Let's consider two examples. In 2008, the Australian economy grew 2.2 percent but the population grew 1.2 percent. Per capita growth equaled 1 percent (2.2 − 1.2). In that same year in Poland, output rose 4.8 percent and the population declined 0.5 percent. Per capita income rose 5.3 percent (4.8 − −0.5).

Here are some additional examples showing per capita growth, real growth, and population growth for various countries in 2008:

Country	Per Capita GDP Growth	=	Real GDP Growth	−	Population Growth
Canada	−0.1		0.7		0.8
Denmark	0.0		0.3		0.3
Russia	6.5		6.0		−0.5
Sudan	3.2		5.3		2.1
Thailand	3.2		3.6		0.4
Venezuela	4.2		5.7		1.5

Source: CIA *World Factbook*, 2009.

Some economists have argued that per capita income is not what we should be focusing on; they suggest that it would be better to look at median income. (Remember, income and output are the same.) Per capita income measures the average, or *mean*, income. The *median* income, in contrast, is the income level that divides the population in equal halves. Half the people earn more and half the people earn less than the median income. In 2007, median income per household in the United States was $50,233. Half of all households earned less than $50,233, and half earned more.

Why focus on median income? Because it partially takes into account how income is distributed. If the growth in income goes to a small minority of individuals who already receive the majority of income, the mean will rise but the median will not. Let's consider an example where there is a large difference between the two measures. Say that the incomes of five people in a five-person economy are $20,000; $20,000; $30,000; $120,000; and $450,000. The median income is $30,000 (the middle income with two above and two below); the mean income is $128,000. Now say that the economy grows but that the two richest people get all the benefits, raising their incomes to $150,000 and $500,000, respectively. The median income remains $30,000; the mean income rises to $144,000. Unfortunately, statistics on median income are often not collected, so I will follow convention and focus on the mean, or per capita, income.

Q-4 How would increases in income have to be distributed for the median to remain constant and the mean income to rise?

Whether you're looking at per capita or median income, growth provides more goods and services for the people in an economy, allowing society to sidestep the more difficult issues of how those goods are distributed. That's why policy makers are interested in knowing what makes an economy grow.

The Sources of Growth

Economists generally single out five important sources of growth:

1. Growth-compatible institutions.
2. Capital accumulation—investment in productive capacity.

3. Available resources.
4. Technological development.
5. Entrepreneurship.

Let's consider each in turn.

Growth-Compatible Institutions

Throughout this book I have emphasized the importance of economic institutions and that having the right institutions is vitally necessary for growth. Consider China. Up until 1980 it grew at an average annual rate of 3 percent. After 1980, when it changed its institutional structure from a command-and-control to a more market-oriented economy, it started its rapid growth of 8.5 percent per year. Growth-compatible institutions—institutions that foster growth—must have incentives built into them that lead people to put forth effort and discourage people from spending a lot of their time in leisure pursuits or creating impediments for others to gain income for themselves.

Q-5 Why is private property a source of growth?

When individuals get much of the gains of growth themselves, they have incentives to work harder. That's why markets and private ownership of property play an important role in growth. In the former Soviet Union, individuals didn't gain much from their own initiative and, hence, often spent their time in pursuits other than those that would foster measured economic growth. Another growth-compatible institution is the corporation, a legal institution that gives owners limited liability and thereby encourages large enterprises (because people are more willing to invest their savings when their potential losses are limited).

Some developing countries follow a type of mercantilist policy in which government must approve any new economic activity. Some government officials get a large portion of their income from bribes offered to them by individuals who want to undertake economic activity. Such policies inhibit economic growth. Many regulations, even reasonable ones, also tend to inhibit economic growth because they inhibit entrepreneurial activities.

Peruvian economist Hernando DeSoto has given some vivid examples of how the lack of formal property rights limits development. He points out that because of regulations it takes an average of 500 working days to legalize a bakery in Cairo. He has many similar examples. Excessive regulations combined with bribery and corruption are important reasons why people don't legalize their businesses. In some ways, whether a business is legal or not is not of concern: both legal and illegal businesses provide goods. But legality impacts growth; illegal or semi-legal businesses must stay small to remain below the government's radar, and because the owners have no property rights, they do not have access to business loans to grow. Similarly, squatters only informally own their residence; their lack of formal ownership is a barrier to getting loans to improve their living space, which keeps them in the vicious cycle of poverty. DeSoto points out that the poor have informal control of trillions of dollars of assets but can't get loans on those assets to advance their economic futures in the normal market economy. The lack of property rights and the regulations doom the poor to remain in poverty.

Informal property rights limit borrowing by the poor, and hence limit growth.

The above argument is not an argument against all regulation; some regulation is necessary to ensure that growth is of a socially desirable type. The policy problem is in deciding between necessary and unnecessary regulation.

Investment and Accumulated Capital

A second important source of growth is capital and investment. In *Nickled and Dimed: On (Not) Getting By in America*, Barbara Ehrenreich explores how minimum wage workers manage to scrape by. What they don't have time or income for is saving—

putting together a nest egg to invest. Lacking savings, they often remain mired in poverty, just scraping by. The same argument holds for society as a whole; societies that can't afford to save will not grow either. Investment is absolutely necessary for growth. Somehow, the society as a whole has to manage to save (forgo consumption) if it wants to grow.

Some economists even argue that it is the savers, not the "givers," who are the beneficent people. University of Rochester economist Steven Landsburg makes the argument most explicitly. He argues that misers—the people who could deplete the world's resources but choose not to—are the true philanthropists. He writes that "nobody is more generous than the miser" and that when Scrooge gave up his miserly ways, the world was worse off, not better off. (As with all such provocative statements, the issues are complicated, and there is a deeper question about the justness of the institutional structure and whether that institutional structure could be changed to channel more income to the "nickled and dimed" while maintaining the level of saving. But those issues quickly go beyond the principles levels.)

Actually, it isn't saving that is important for growth; it's investment, and, for saving to be helpful, some method of translating saving into investment must exist in the society. Financial markets provide a method, which is why financial markets are an important aspect of macro. The role of financial markets in transferring savings into investment is captured in the loanable funds market shown in Figure 26-2.

Savings is the supply of loanable funds; it is an upward-sloping curve because, as the interest rate rises, more people are willing to save more. Investment is the demand for loanable funds; it is a downward-sloping curve because, as the interest rate falls, it pays businesses to borrow more and invest more. Notice in this market that the interest rate—the rate paid to borrow savings—is key; it equilibrates the supply and demand for loanable funds. When the supply of loanable funds (savings) increases, as shown in Figure 26-2(b), the interest rate falls from i_0 to i_1, and the quantity of loanable funds demanded (investment) increases from I_0 to I_1. Thus, societies interested in growth look carefully at the interest rate in the economy. (The interest rate that is important to this market is the real interest rate—the nominal interest rate minus the rate of inflation. This distinction will be discussed in depth below.)

Q-6 If the demand for loanable funds increases, what will likely happen to the interest rate?

FIGURE 26-2 (A AND B) The Loanable Funds Market

Savings is the supply of loanable funds; it is an upward-sloping curve. Investment is the demand for loanable funds; it is a downward-sloping curve. The interest rate equilibrates the supply and demand for loanable funds. When the supply of loanable funds (savings) increases as shown in (**b**), the interest rate falls from i_0 to i_1, and the quantity of loanable funds demanded (investment) increases from I_0 to I_1.

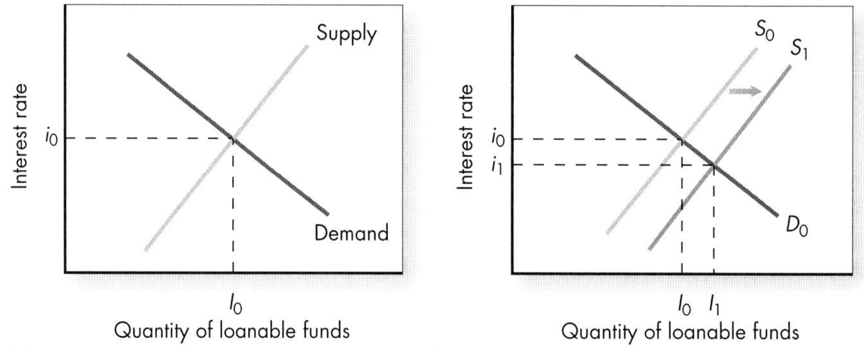

(a) **(b)**

Fifty years ago, capital accumulation (where capital was thought of as just *physical capital*) and investment were seen as the key elements in growth. Physical capital includes both private capital—buildings and machines available for production—and public capital—infrastructure such as highways and water supply. The *flow* of investment leads to the growth of the *stock* of capital. While physical capital is still considered a key element in growth, it is now generally recognized that the growth recipe is far more complicated. One of the reasons physical capital accumulation has been de-emphasized is that empirical evidence has suggested that capital accumulation doesn't necessarily lead to growth. For instance, the former Soviet Union invested a lot and accumulated lots of capital goods, but its economy didn't grow much because its capital was often internationally obsolete. Another reason is that products change, and buildings and machines useful in one time period may be useless in another (e.g., a six-year-old computer often is worthless). The value of the capital stock depends on its future expected earnings, which are very uncertain. Capital's role in growth is extraordinarily difficult to measure with accuracy.

A third reason for this de-emphasis on capital accumulation is that it has become clear that capital includes much more than machines. In addition to physical capital, modern economics includes **human capital** (*the skills that are embodied in workers through experience, education, and on-the-job training*, or, more simply, people's knowledge) and **social capital** (*the habitual way of doing things that guides people in how they approach production*) as types of capital. The importance of human capital is obvious: A skilled labor force is far more productive than an unskilled labor force. Social capital is embodied in institutions such as the government, the legal system, and the fabric of society. In a way, anything that contributes to growth can be called a type of capital, and anything that slows growth can be called a destroyer of capital. With the concept of capital including such a wide range of things, it is difficult to say what is not capital, which makes the concept of capital less useful.

There are three types of capital:
1. Physical capital.
2. Social capital.
3. Human capital.

Despite this modern de-emphasis on investment and physical capital, all economists agree that the right kind of investment at the right time is a central element of growth. If an economy is to grow, it must invest. The debate is about what kinds and what times are the right ones.

Web Note 26.1
Social Capital

Available Resources

If an economy is to grow, it will need resources. England grew in the late 1700s because it had iron and coal; the United States grew in the 20th century because it had a major supply of many natural resources, and it imported people, a resource it needed.

Of course, you have to be careful in thinking about what is considered a resource. A resource in one time period may not be a resource in another. For example, at one time oil was simply black gooey stuff that made land unusable. When people learned that the black gooey stuff could be burned as fuel, oil became a resource. What's considered a resource depends on technology. If solar technology is ever perfected, oil will go back to being black gooey stuff. So creativity can replace resources, and if you develop new technology fast enough, you can overcome almost any lack of existing resources. Even if a country doesn't have the physical resources it needs for growth, it can import them—as did Japan following World War II.

What is a resource depends on the production processes of an economy and technology.

The enormous growth of China has involved an increase in the demand for physical resources such as oil, iron ore, and copper—throughout the world. This has led both the United States and China to work toward securing continued access to sufficient physical resources in the future. China, in particular, is making deals with Latin American and African countries to lend them money with the proviso that they provide natural resources to China in the future.

Web Note 26.2
Oil Substitution

In 2007 and 2008 the large demand for resources pushed up the price of oil. Grain prices doubled and oil prices rose to more than $140 a barrel. Many noneconomists were predicting that the price of oil could only rise because oil was being used up. Economists were not so sure. They had seen such predictions before, and they had always been wrong. The reason is that the high price of oil brings about changes. Specifically, it reduces the quantity demanded and people figure out ways to skimp on using oil. Second, the high price creates incentives to develop alternatives. Here are just a few of the options being explored:

- Geothermal energy—the recoverable heat in rock under the United States equals 2,000 years' worth of energy.
- Algae-produced fuel—algae ponds are being created that create "cellulosic ethanol," giving an almost inexhaustible source of energy.
- Wind power—as windmills become more efficient, a larger percentage of energy can come from wind.
- Plug-in cars—electric cars use half the energy of gasoline engine cars.
- Fuel cells—hydrogen-powered fuel cells offer new ways to provide power.
- Sugarcane-based ethanol—this is far more efficient than corn-based ethanol.
- Nuclear—the potential for almost unlimited energy.

If all these options are out there, why aren't they being developed? The reason is that there is no guarantee that the oil price will stay high. At $150 a barrel for oil, they make sense; at $60 a barrel for oil, they aren't worth developing. Thus, when oil fell back to $60 a barrel in late 2008, many of these research programs were shelved.

Greater participation in the market is another means by which to increase available resources. In China at the end of the 20th century, for example, many individuals migrated into the southern provinces, which have free trade sectors. Before they migrated they were only marginally involved in the market economy. After they migrated they became employed in the market economy. This increased the labor available to the market, helping push up China's growth rate. In the United States beginning in the 1950s, the percentage of women entering the workforce increased, contributing to economic growth.

Increasing the labor force participation rate is not a totally costless way of increasing growth. We lose whatever people were doing before they joined the labor force (which was, presumably, something of value to society). Our aggregate income accounting figures, which are measures of market activity, simply do not measure such losses.

Technological Development

Growth isn't just getting more of the same thing. It's also getting some things that are different.

Advances in technology shift the production possibility curve out by making workers more productive. Technological advances increase their ability to produce more of the things they already produce but also allow them to produce new and different products. While in some ways growth involves more of the same, a much larger aspect of growth involves changes in **technology**—*the way we make goods and supply services*—and changes in the goods and services we buy. Think of what this generation buys—music downloads, cell phones, cars, computers, fast food—and compare that to what the preceding generation bought—LP records, cars that would now be considered obsolete, and tube and transistor radios. (When I was 11, I saved $30—the equivalent of over $100 now—so I could afford a six-transistor Motorola radio; personal computers didn't exist.)

Contrast today's goods with the goods the next generation might have available: video brain implants (little gadgets in your head to receive sound and full-vision broadcasts—you simply close your eyes and tune in whatever you want, if you've paid your cellular fee for that month); fuel-cell-powered cars (gas cars will be considered

REAL-WORLD APPLICATION

Growth and Terrorism

When talking about the costs of terrorism, many focus on the short-term effects—the tremendous cost in destruction of property and loss of life. But, according to a study by the Organization for Economic Coordination and Development, there are also long-term effects on growth, which may be less dramatic but even more costly. The study points out that the reaction to the terrorist attack of September 11, 2001,

- Caused significant increases in insurance premiums, increasing costs and making firms less likely to undertake new projects.
- Made it impossible to get insurance for a number of projects, stopping these projects altogether.
- Increased transportation costs because of increased security.

9/11

- Slowed international trade because of security, making it impossible to get goods when they were needed, forcing firms to hold more inventory and increasing costs.
- Caused firms to spend more on security, lowering productivity.

Each of these effects contributed to slower growth by reducing the sources of growth. The terrorist attacks acted like sand in the wheels of trade, reduced expenditures on capital, lowered productivity, and reduced start-ups by entrepreneurs. The end result was hundreds of billions of dollars of lost output. The cost will be especially great for many Islamic countries, making it difficult for these countries to tie into the global economy.

quaint but polluting); and instant food (little pills that fulfill all your nutritional needs, letting your video brain implant supply all the ambiance). Just imagine! You probably can get the picture, even without a video brain implant.

How does society get people to work on developments that may change the very nature of what we do and how we think? One way is through economic incentives; another is with institutions that foster creativity and bold thinking—such as this book; a third is through institutions that foster hard work. There are, of course, trade-offs. For example, the Japanese educational system, which fosters hard work and discipline, doesn't do as good a job at fostering creativity as the U.S. educational system, and vice versa.

Important advances in biotechnology, computers, and communications initially developed in the United States, and those developments helped fuel U.S. growth. Those new industries were much slower to develop in another important U.S. competitor, the European Union, which is one important reason why EU countries have grown far more slowly than has the United States in recent years.

Five sources of growth are
1. Growth-compatible institutions.
2. Capital accumulation.
3. Available resources.
4. Technological development.
5. Entrepreneurship.

Entrepreneurship

Entrepreneurship is the ability to get things done. That ability involves creativity, vision, willingness to accept risk, and a talent for translating that vision into reality. Entrepreneurs have been central to growth in the United States. They have created large companies, produced new products, and transformed the landscape of the economy. Examples of entrepreneurs include Thomas Edison, who revolutionized the generation and use of electricity in the late 1800s; Henry Ford, who revolutionized transportation in the early 1900s; and Bill Gates, who led Microsoft as it transformed and dominated the computer industry. When a country's population demonstrates entrepreneurship, it can overcome deficiencies in other ingredients that contribute to growth.

FIGURE 26-3 Sources of Real U.S. GDP Growth

Technology accounts for the majority of growth in the United States, followed closely by increases in labor.

Source: Edward E. Denison, *Trends in Economic Growth, 1928–82* (Washington, DC: The Brookings Institution, 1985), and author estimates.

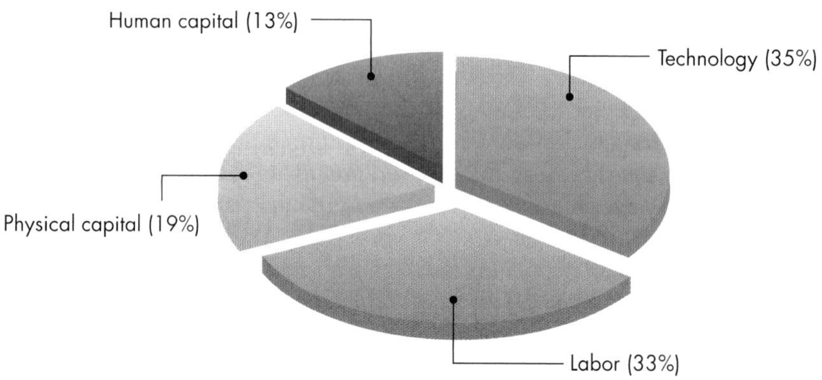

Turning the Sources of Growth into Growth

The five sources of growth cannot be taken as givens. Even if a country has all five ingredients, it may not have them in the right proportions. For instance, when Nicolas Appert discovered canning (storing food in a sealed container in such a way that it wouldn't spoil) in the early 19th century, the economic possibilities of society expanded enormously. But if, when the technological developments occurred, the savings at the time were not sufficient to finance the investment, the result would not have been growth. It is finding the right combination of the sources of growth that plays a central role in the growth of any economy.

Empirical Estimates of Factor Contribution to Growth

To determine the relative importance of the various causes of growth, economist Edward Denison empirically estimated the importance of each of the sources of growth for many countries, including the United States. These estimates, shown in Figure 26-3, suggest that increases in labor account for 33 percent, increases in physical capital account for 19 percent, increases in human capital account for 13 percent, and advances in technology account for the remaining 35 percent of growth. (Land does not appear in Denison's estimates; countries are assumed to be endowed with a given amount of land and natural resources.) While the specific percentages are at best rough, the importance of technology to growth is not. It is for that reason that modern economic thinking about growth has focused more and more on technology.

The Production Function and Theories of Growth

The production function shows the relationship between the quantity of inputs used in production and the quantity of output resulting from production.

To try to get a better handle on the sources of growth, economists have developed a number of theories of growth. These have centered around the **production function,** an abstraction that shows *the relationship between the quantity of inputs used in production and the quantity of output resulting from production*. The production function we shall use is the following:

$$\text{Output} = A \cdot f(\text{Labor, Capital, Land})$$

This production function has land, labor, and capital as factors of production, and an adjustment factor A to capture the effect of changes in technology. The adjustment factor is outside the production function since it can affect the production of all factors.

(The *f* stands for "function of.") The production function emphasizes the sources of growth: entrepreneurship is captured by labor, available resources by land, capital accumulation by capital, and technology and institutions by the production function itself and the adjustment factor, A.

Describing Production Functions

In talking about production functions, economists use a couple of important terms. The first describes what happens when all inputs increase equally—this is called *scale economies*. Scale economies describe what happens to output if all inputs increase by the same percentage. Say the amount of labor, land, and capital is doubled. What happens to output? If output also doubles, economists say that the production function exhibits **constant returns to scale,** which means that *output will rise by the same proportionate increase as all inputs*. With constant returns to scale, if all inputs rise by, say, 10 percent, output also will rise by 10 percent. When *output rises by a greater proportionate increase than all inputs*, there are **increasing returns to scale;** and when *output rises by a smaller proportionate increase than all inputs*, there are **decreasing returns to scale.**

The second term describes what happens *when more of one input is added without increasing any other inputs*. This case follows the **law of diminishing marginal productivity** *(increasing one input, keeping all others constant, will lead to smaller and smaller gains in output)*. The difference between decreasing returns to scale and diminishing marginal productivity is that decreasing returns to scale refers to what happens to output when *all* inputs increase by the same proportion. Diminishing marginal productivity refers to what happens to output when some inputs are increased, but the others are held constant. Generally, it is capital that is assumed fixed, and labor that is assumed variable. Returns to scale is a long-run concept—diminishing marginal productivity is a short-run concept.

Q-7 True or false? If you can increase production 10 percent by increasing all inputs 20 percent, the production process exhibits diminishing marginal productivity.

The law of diminishing marginal productivity applies to increases in any input, holding the others constant. As you put more and more laborers on a fixed plot of land, the increase in output contributed by each additional worker falls; eventually workers will get in each other's way and not only will the output per worker decline, but so too will total output. The same goes for capital. The first computer will help a secretary prepare documents more quickly. A second might help, too, but less so than the first. A third would clutter the office.

The Standard Theory of Growth—the Classical Growth Model

Classical economists recognized that all the above factors contributed to growth, but (as mentioned earlier in this chapter) their models of growth focused on capital accumulation. The **Classical growth model** is *a model of growth that focuses on the role of capital accumulation in the growth process*. The Classical economists' major policy conclusion was: The more capital an economy has, the faster it will grow. This focus on capital is what caused market economies to be called *capitalist economies*.

Since investment leads to the increase in capital, Classical economists focused their analysis, and their policy advice, on how to increase investment. The way to do that was for people to save:

$$\text{Saving} \rightarrow \text{Investment} \rightarrow \text{Increase in capital} \rightarrow \text{Growth}$$

Saving, investment, and capital are central to the Classical growth model.

According to the Classical growth model, if society wants its economy to grow, it has to save; the more saving, the better. Saving was good for both private individuals and governments. Thus, Classical economists objected to government deficits, which occur

ADDED DIMENSION

Demand, Keynesian Economics, and Growth

The presentation in this chapter is the generally accepted analysis of growth. It focuses on the supply-side sources of growth. But because empirical relationships in growth are so difficult to discern, groups of economists raise a variety of different issues. One such group, which has its origins in Keynesian ideas, argues that demand and supply are so interrelated in macro that demand has to be considered as a source of growth. The argument goes as follows: Firms produce only if they expect there to be demand for their product. If they expect demand to be growing, they will try new projects and in the process will learn by doing and develop new technology. Both of these activities shift the production function out and thereby create growth. So while it looks like a supply-side issue, it is the demand side that leads the supply side: By increasing demand, one can increase long-run supply.

True, they argue, increasing aggregate demand is only a short-run phenomenon, but since the long run is simply a set of successive short runs, the short run influences the long-run path that the economy follows. They are not separable, and, under the right conditions, demand-side policies should be considered as one way to increase supply. As Abba Lerner, one of the early Keynesian advocates of this view, has put it, *"In the long run we are simply in another short run."*

when government spends more than it collects in taxes. (This view of deficits and saving was directly challenged by Keynes in the 1930s, as we will see in the next chapter.)

Focus on Diminishing Marginal Productivity of Labor The early economists also focused on the law of diminishing marginal productivity. In the 1800s, when farming was the major activity of the economy, economists such as Thomas Malthus emphasized the limitations land placed on growth. They predicted that since land was relatively fixed, as the population grew, diminishing marginal productivity would set in. Figure 26-4 shows a production function exhibiting diminishing marginal productivity.

Since each additional worker adds less output to production than the individual before, the production function is bowed downward. Output rises as the number of laborers increases, but it does not keep pace with increases in labor. Because of diminishing marginal productivity, per capita income declines as the labor supply increases.

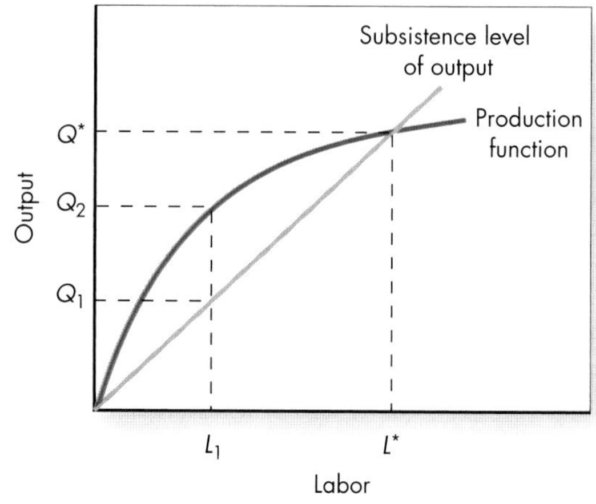

FIGURE 26-4
Classical Growth Theory

The classical theory of growth focused on diminishing marginal productivity of labor. Because of diminishing marginal productivity, per capita income declines as the labor supply increases, other inputs held constant. As output per person declines, at some point output available per person is no longer sufficient to feed the population.

As output per person declines, at some point output available is no longer sufficient to feed everyone.

In Figure 26-4, the straight line, labeled *subsistence level of output*, shows the minimum amount of output necessary to feed the labor force L. For example, at L_1 output is Q_2 and the minimum level of income for subsistence is Q_1. There is a surplus of $Q_2 - Q_1$. At L^* output is at its subsistence level. There is no surplus. Beyond L^* income falls below subsistence. If the population grows beyond L^*, some people would starve to death and the population would decline. Classical economists argued that the economy would be driven to point L^* in the long run because whenever there was a surplus of output, workers would have more children, increasing the labor supply. This belief, called the *iron law of wages*, combined with the diminishing marginal productivity led to the conclusion that in the long run there was no surplus and no growth. They called the long run the *stationary state*.

Q-8 If individuals suddenly needed less food to subsist, what would happen to labor and output, according to the Classical growth model?

Focus on Diminishing Marginal Productivity of Capital The Classical economists' predictions were wrong. Per capita output did not stagnate; it grew because of technological progress and increases in capital. Increases in technology and capital overwhelmed the law of diminishing marginal productivity and eventually economists no longer saw land as a constraint. Modern economists, such as Robert Solow, then changed the focus of the law of diminishing marginal productivity from land to capital. They argued that as capital grew faster than labor, capital would become less productive and lead to slower and slower growth; eventually the per capita growth of our economy would stagnate. The economy could still grow if labor increased at the same rate as capital, but output would not grow any faster than the growth of the population. That is, per capita income would not grow.

Technological progress and increases in capital have overwhelmed diminishing marginal productivity of labor.

The Convergence Debate

The Classical growth model also has strong implications about the future growth of the U.S. economy. It leads to the **convergence hypothesis**—*the hypothesis that per capita income in countries with similar institutional structures will gravitate toward the same level of income per person*. As countries get more capital and become richer, their growth rates would slow down. Thus, poorer countries with little capital (such as the Latin American countries) should grow faster than richer countries with lots of capital (such as the United States). Why? Because diminishing marginal productivity would be stronger for richer countries with lots of capital than for poorer countries with little capital. Eventually per capita incomes among countries should converge.

The convergence hypothesis states that per capita income in countries with similar institutional structures will gravitate toward the same level of income per person.

The convergence hypothesis suggests that because the United States currently has a higher per capita income, its economy should grow more slowly than the economies of developing countries with similar institutional structures. That's because the marginal product of capital is higher in the developing countries (which hence have lower costs of production), which leads to capital investment flows out of the United States and into developing countries. The argument for convergence is based on the law of one price introduced in Chapter 2: There will be pressure for equivalent factors of production, using equivalent capital and technology and operating in similar institutional structures, to be paid equally. If they are not, production will gravitate toward those countries with lower factor prices. The outsourcing of production to countries such as China and India is an example of the forces generated by the law of one price. If the convergence hypothesis is correct, these countries will continue growing faster than will the United States over the coming decades.

Q-9 Why would an economist likely predict that India and China will grow faster than the United States in the next decade?

These predictions of convergence have not come true as of the early 2000s for many countries. As we saw in an earlier chapter, growth rates have increased, not decreased, in the United States, and relative income levels of rich and poor countries have in many cases diverged, not converged. This difference between the observed reality and the predictions of the model caused economists to study the growth process empirically. Why doesn't the theory match the reality?

Economists have a number of explanations why convergence has not taken place, including lack of mobility of the factors of production, differing institutional structure, incomparable factors of production, and what are called technological agglomeration effects. Let's briefly consider each.

Lack of Factor Mobility The speed of convergence depends on factor and technological mobility. It is the transfer of capital and technology that causes convergence. These transfers occur because firms have an incentive to shift production of goods—say toys—to lower-cost countries such as China. As production facilities move, capital and technological know-how will shift from the United States to China. If, however, there are either perceived or real barriers to factor mobility—say China limits foreign ownership of domestically based firms—convergence will be slowed down.

Differing Institutional Structure The convergence hypothesis is relevant to countries with similar institutional structures. The more similar the institutional structures, the more likely it is that convergence will take place because firms are likely to move production to countries whose institutions are well-suited for the businesses' practices and culture. That's why Europe and Japan caught up quickly with the United States after World War II; they all had democratic governments, market-based economies, and stable political structures. These general institutional characteristics that are compatible sometimes go under the name *social capital*.

The debate about whether the economies of China and the United States are likely to converge is in large part due to the ambiguity about what are similar or equivalent institutional structures. China has recently adopted market-based institutions, but these are still new, and the political structure in China is not democratic; it remains under Communist party control. Is the Chinese institutional structure sufficiently similar to ours to fit the convergence hypothesis? Views on this differ, and hence views on how much convergence we can expect also differ.

Incomparable Factors of Production On the surface, the terms in the production function seem relatively straightforward, but in reality they involve enormous ambiguity. I will focus on one important ambiguity—precisely what we mean by *labor*. As an input in production, labor may seem rather simple—it is the number of hours worked. As a first approximation, that is what economists use as their measure of labor input. But labor is much more than that. The measure of labor needs to be adjusted to capture the skills, education, experience, and effort that laborers bring to production. These adjustments make measuring labor, and comparing the measurements among different countries, difficult.

Here's an example of the type of problem that develops: About the same number of people live in Bangladesh as in Japan, but the average worker in Japan has more education than the average worker in Bangladesh. Do we increase the labor measured in Japan to account for this difference? Generally, economists do so by separating labor into two components: standard labor (the actual number of workers or hours worked) and human capital (the skills that are embodied in workers through experience, education, and on-the-job training). Human capital gives us a measure for comparing the relative productivity of different workers. Thus, for example, when a society's workers become more educated, the country's human capital increases, even though labor hours may not increase.

Notice how modifying the definition of *labor* to emphasize human capital provides a possible answer for the Classical growth model's incorrect predictions. If labor skills can be continually increasing, there is no need for physical capital to exhibit diminishing marginal productivity. The labor force might be growing at 5 percent, and capital at 7 percent, but the human capital measure of labor also may be increasing at 2 percent, so no diminishing marginal productivity should be expected and per capita output will rise. A variation of this argument can be used to explain why incomes between poor and rich countries have not converged. If skills in rich countries are increasing at a faster rate than skills in poor countries, incomes would not be expected to converge.

Increases in human capital have allowed labor to keep pace with capital, allowing economies to avoid the diminishing productivity of capital.

Technological Agglomeration Effects An additional explanation for the failure of the Classical growth model to accurately predict our growth experience and the lack of convergence is **technological agglomeration**—*the geographic concentration of technological advances caused by the tendency of innovations to lead to further innovations in that industry and other industries*. Technology has developed, and is growing, faster in rich countries than in poor countries. If technology grows, it increases the productivity of all inputs and allows growth to continue. In terms of the production function, technology shifts the production function up, as shown in the margin, so that more can be produced at every quantity of labor. If technology grows faster than the diminishing marginal productivity of new capital, and grows faster over time, growth for all practical purposes has no limit. Technology overwhelms diminishing marginal productivity and growth rates increase over time: the economy gets richer and richer. Although the Classical model acknowledged the role of technology in growth, it took technology as given—determined outside the model. It did not explain what causes technology to grow.

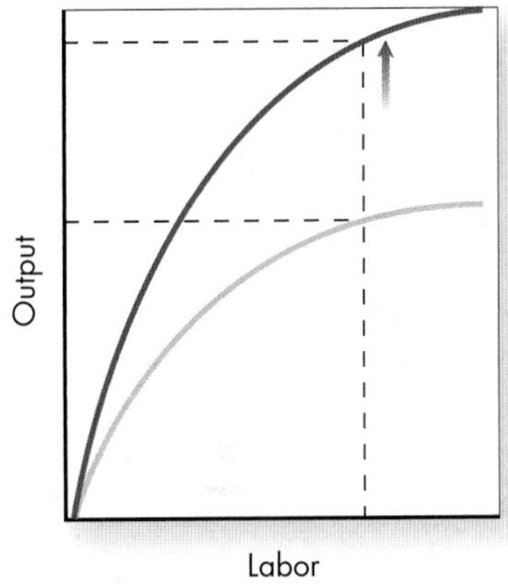

Technological growth shifts the production function up and the production possibility curve out.

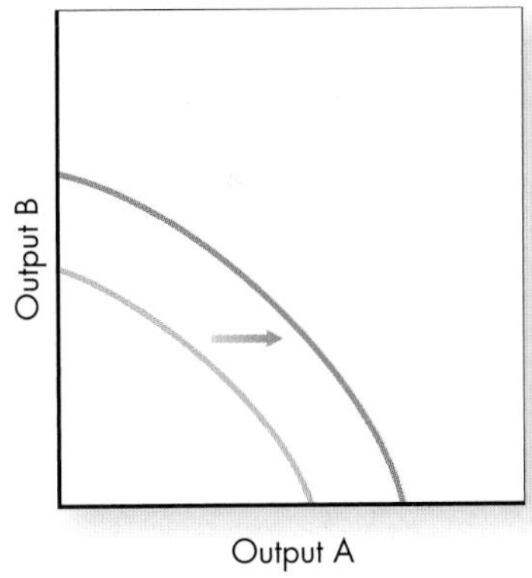

If technology increased equally in both developed and less-developed countries, these advances in technology would not affect the convergence hypothesis since it would shift both countries' production functions up. But it does not; technology tends to agglomerate, accelerating the advance of technology in developed countries, and only later spreading to less-developed countries. That's why the information technology revolution pushed up the U.S. growth rate over the past decade, slowing and even offsetting convergence.

As long as new technological advances occur faster in the rich developed countries than older technologies diffuse into less-developed countries, then convergence need not take place. So how well the United States does in the future depends in a significant part on how good we are at developing technologies for industries that do not yet exist. For example, if information technology jobs that are outsourced to India are replaced with even higher-paying fuel cell, nanotechnology, and biotechnical jobs in the United States, the U.S. future is pleasant. The U.S. growth rate could exceed rates in developing countries, even as we lose jobs through outsourcing.

What's of concern for the United States is that the pressures for convergence are also occurring in research and development. Developing countries are themselves trying to take the lead in developing new technologies. Should that occur, and the fuel cell, nanotechnology, and biotechnology jobs develop in India and China rather than in the United States, the positive agglomeration effects will occur there, and the speed of convergence would increase significantly.

New Growth Theory

Modern growth theory goes under the name *new growth theory*. Because technology is now recognized as an important ingredient in growth, modern growth theorists have made technology central to their analysis. They look for what makes technology grow. Thus, **new growth theory** is *a theory that emphasizes the role of technology rather than capital in the*

New growth theory emphasizes technology as the primary source of growth.

ADDED DIMENSION

Is the 21st Century the Age of Technology or One of Many Ages of Technology?

Sometimes newspapers write as if the importance of technology to the economy in the 21st century is a new phenomenon. It is not. Technology has been changing our society for the last two centuries, and it is not at all clear that the technological changes we are currently experiencing are any more revolutionary than those experienced by other generations in the last 200 years. For example, in terms of its impact on people's lives and communications in general, the Internet is small potatoes compared to the phone system.

One economist who recognized the importance of technology was Joseph Schumpeter. Schumpeter emphasized the role of the entrepreneur. He argued that entrepreneurs create major technological changes that drive the economy forward.

According to Schumpeter, the economy's growth depends on these entrepreneurs, and the industries they are in will be the leading industries, pulling the rest of the economy along after them. The accompanying figure lists five waves of technological innovation that have driven our economy. As you can see, in the late 1700s, steam power and iron manufacturing were the driving forces. In the 1860s, railroads were the dynamic industry. Later, electronics, automobiles, and chemicals drove our economy. In the 1980s through the early 21st century, computers and biotechnology have been the leading industries.

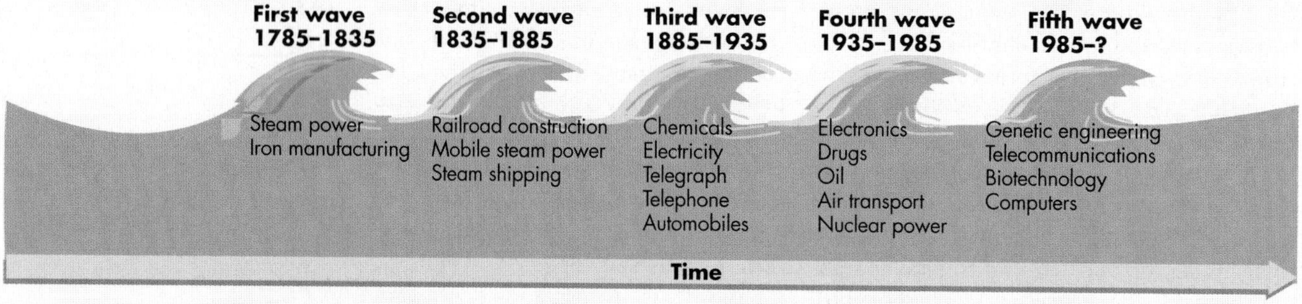

growth process. Increases in technology shift the production possibility curve out, and thus make the choices an economy faces a bit easier to make—they allow the society to get more of everything. Unlike Classical growth theory, which left technology outside of economic analysis, new growth theory focuses its analysis on technology. For new growth theorists the focus isn't on savings and capital; it is on technology:

Web Note 26.3
A New Growth Theorist

Technological advance → Investment → Further technological advance → Growth

Technology New growth theory's central argument is that increases in technology do not just happen. Technological advance is the result of what the economy does—it invests in research and development (e.g., drug companies researching new ways to fight disease); makes advances in pure science (e.g., the human genome project); and works out new ways to organize production (e.g., just-in-time inventory techniques). Thus, in a sense, investment in technology increases the technological stock of an economy just as investment in capital increases the capital stock of an economy. Investment in technology is called research and development; firms hire researchers to explore options. Some of those options pay off and others do not, but the net return of that investment in technology is an increase in technology.

If investment in technology is similar to investment in capital, why does new growth theory separate the two? The reason is twofold. First, increases in technology are not as directly linked to investment as are increases in capital. Increases in investment require increases in saving, that is, building the capital. Increases in technology can occur with little investment and saving if the proverbial light bulb goes off in someone's head and that person sees a new way of doing something.

Second, increases in technology often have enormous *positive spillover effects*, especially if the new technology involves common knowledge and is freely available to all. A technological gain in one sector of production gives people in other sectors of production new ideas on how to change what they are doing, which gives other people new ideas. Ideas spread like pool balls after the break. One hits another, and soon all the nearby balls have moved. Put in technical economic terms, technological change often has significant **positive externalities**—*positive effects on others not taken into account by the decision maker*. Through those externalities, what is called general purpose technological change can have a much larger effect on growth than can an increase in capital.

The common knowledge aspect of technology creates positive externalities, which new growth theory sees as the key to growth.

The positive externalities result from the *common knowledge* aspect of technology because the idea behind the technology can often be used by others without payment to the developer. Using the same assembly line for different car models is just one example of a technological advance that has become incorporated into common knowledge. Any car manufacturer can use it.

Basic research is not always freely available; it is often protected by **patents**—*legal protection of a technological innovation that gives the owner of the patent sole rights to its use and distribution for a limited time*. (If the development is an idea rather than a good, it can be copyrighted rather than patented, but the general concept is the same.) Patents turn innovations into private property. The Windows operating system is an example of a technology that is owned, and hence is not common knowledge. The ideas in technologies that are covered by patents, however, often have common knowledge elements. Once people have seen the new technology, they figure out sufficiently different ways of achieving the same end while avoiding violating the patent.

Learning by Doing As the new growth theory has analyzed technology, it has focused economic thinking on another aspect of economic processes—an individual's tendency to **learn by doing,** or to *improve the methods of production through experience*. As people do something, they become better and better at it, sometimes because of new technologies, and sometimes simply because they learned better ways to do it just from practice. Thus, as production increases, costs of production tend to decrease over time. The introduction of new technology is sometimes the result of learning by doing.

Learning by doing overcomes the law of diminishing marginal productivity because learning by doing increases the productivity of workers.

Learning by doing changes the laws of economics enormously. It suggests that production has positive externalities in learning. If these positive externalities overwhelm diminishing marginal productivity, as new growth theory suggests they do, the predictions about growth change. In the Classical theory, growth is limited by diminishing marginal productivity; in the new theory, growth potential is unlimited and can accelerate over time. It's a whole new world out there—one in which, holding wants constant, scarcity decreases over time.

We can see in Figure 26-5 new growth theory's predictions for future growth. All inputs are on the horizontal axis, and the production function exhibits increasing returns to scale. (As more of all inputs are added, the additional output per combination of inputs increases.) With this curve, per capita income can grow forever and the dismal science of economics becomes the optimistic science.

Technological Lock-In One of the questions new growth theory raises is: Does the economy always use the "best" technology available? Some say no and point to examples of technologies that have become entrenched in the market, or locked in to new products despite the availability of more efficient technologies. This is known as *technological lock-in*.

FIGURE 26-5 New Growth Theory

New growth theory focuses on increasing returns to scale. With increasing returns, increases in inputs lead to proportionately greater increases in output. For example, the initial increase of inputs from 0 to 10 results in a 5-unit increase in output. An increase in inputs from 10 to 20 results in a higher 10-unit increase in output. With increasing returns, output per person can rise forever.

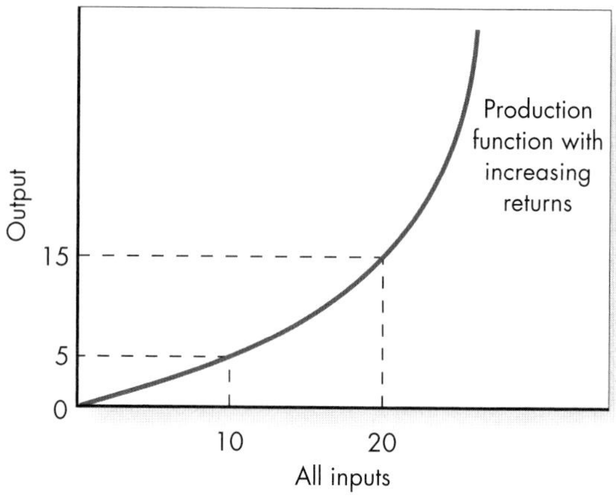

One proposed example of technological lock-in goes under the name QWERTY, which is the upper-left six keys on the standard computer keyboard. Economist Paul David argues that the design of this keyboard was chosen to slow people's typing down so that the keys in old-style mechanical typewriters would not lock up. He further argues that developments in word processing have since eliminated the problem the QWERTY keyboard was designed to solve (we don't use mechanical typewriters any more). But once people started choosing this keyboard, it was too costly for them to develop another.

This interpretation of history has been disputed by other economists, who argue that the QWERTY keyboard is not significantly less efficient than other keyboard arrangements and that, if it were, competition would have eliminated it. Sometimes this counterargument almost seems to state that the very fact that a technology exists means that it is the most efficient. Most economists do not go that far; they argue that even if the QWERTY keyboard is not a highly inefficient technology, other examples of lock-in exist: beta format videos were preferable to VHS, the Windows operating system is inferior to many alternatives, the English language doesn't compare to Esperanto, and English measurement systems are quite inefficient compared to metric.

Q-10 In what way does the Internet demonstrate network externalities?

One reason for technological lock-in is the existence of *network externalities*—an externality in which the use of a good by one individual makes that technology more valuable to other people. Telephones exhibit network externalities. A single telephone is pretty useless. Whom would you call? Two telephones are more useful, but as more and more people get telephones, the possible interactions (and the benefits of telephones) increase exponentially. Network externalities can make switching to a superior technology expensive or nearly impossible. The Windows operating system is another example of a product that exhibits network externalities, and makes it difficult for other operating systems to develop.

Growth Policies

Exactly what these theories mean for growth and growth policies is the subject of much debate among economists. But there is some agreement about general policies that are good for growth. These include

- Encouraging saving and investment.
- Formalizing property rights and reducing bureaucracy and corruption.

REAL-WORLD APPLICATION

Micro Credit

In 2006 the Nobel Peace Prize went to Mohammed Yunus, a U.S.-trained economist. He won the prize for developing a financial institution in one of the poorest countries of the world—Bangladesh—called the Grameen Bank that makes loans to poor village women at market interest rates. Even though the bank loaned to individuals with little or no collateral, the bank has had excellent payback ratios, far exceeding what most people thought possible.[1]

With a loan from the Grameen Bank (www.grameen-info.org), these women purchased the raw materials to weave baskets whose sale will provide a source of income.

How did he do it? Most banks in developing countries tend to focus on loans to well-off people with resources to serve as collateral. This leaves the traditional part of many developing countries' economies without an effective way to translate saving into investment, stranding many entrepreneurial individuals without ways to develop their ideas. Yunus reconsidered the fundamental role of banking in an economy: to make it possible for people with good ideas to develop those ideas by providing them with funds—and to devise a structure that allowed such lending to take place.

He saw that Western banking institutions did not fulfill that role for Bangladesh. By basing their lending decisions on the amount of collateral a borrower had, they essentially made it impossible for most people in Bangladesh to get loans. But Yunus also recognized that collateral served a useful purpose: It forced people to make the difficult decision about whether they really needed the loans, and to work hard to see that they could pay the loans back, even if the going got tough. If you eliminate collateral, something else must replace it.

Yunus's ingenious solution was the *borrowing circle*—a credit system that replaces traditional collateral with guarantees by friends of the borrower. Recognizing that social pressures were extremely strong in Bangladesh, Yunus offered to make loans to any woman who could find four friends who would agree to help her pay the loan back if necessary. If the borrower defaulted, the others could not borrow until the loan was repaid.

This simple concept worked. Today the Grameen Bank has more than 6.6 million borrowers and lends $60 million every month. The loans are taken out to buy such things as a cow or material to make a fishing net—not large items, but items to use in activities that generate bottom-up growth. Other microcredit banks—banks that make small loans to poor people using alternative forms of collateral—have developed similar plans.

Other countries have also replicated the microcredit approach pioneered by Grameen Bank and today there are more than 90 Grameen replicas across Asia, Africa, Latin America, Europe, and the United States. In the United States, microcredit banks focus on helping low-income people who are generally excluded from formal credit markets develop home-based businesses. Today, the idea of microfinance has spread to the Internet, making it possible for you to make a loan to, say, a baker in Afghanistan. Go to kiva.org to explore how.

While the concept of microfinance is extraordinarily simple, it made use of economic insights that simultaneously reflected an understanding of the cultural and social dimensions of the economy.

[1]Recently some observers have questioned whether the bank has overstated the payback ratios, but even if they are lower than reported, they are still higher than most people thought possible before the bank was created.

- Providing more of the right kind of education.
- Promoting policies that encourage technological innovation.
- Promoting policies that allow taking advantage of specialization.

Web Note 26.4
Loans that Change Lives

Most economists would agree that each of these is good for growth. Unfortunately, the devil is in the details, and the policy problem is translating these general policies into specific politically acceptable policies.

Conclusion

Growth happens, or at least it generally has happened in market economies. But that doesn't mean it happens on its own. While saying precisely why growth happens is beyond economists at this point, economists have identified important sources of growth. These include capital accumulation, available resources, growth-compatible institutions, technological development, and entrepreneurship. What economists haven't been able to determine yet is how they all fit together to bring about growth, and the general feeling is that there is no single way of putting them together—what works likely changes over time. This makes developing an actual growth policy prescription difficult, though no less important.

Summary

- Growth is an increase in the amount of goods and services an economy can produce when both labor and capital are fully employed.
- Growth increases potential output and shifts the production possibility curve out, allowing an economy to produce more goods.
- Per capita growth means producing more goods and services per person. It can be calculated by subtracting the percentage change in the population from the percentage change in output.
- Five sources of growth are (1) growth-compatible institutions, (2) capital accumulation, (3) available resources, (4) technological development, and (5) entrepreneurship.
- The loanable funds market translates savings into investment that is necessary for growth. The interest rate equilibrates saving and investment.
- The production function shows the relationship between the quantity of labor, capital, and land used in production and the quantity of output resulting from production.
- The law of diminishing marginal productivity states that increasing one input, keeping all others constant, will lead to smaller and smaller gains in output.
- Returns to scale describes what happens to output when all inputs increase proportionately.
- The convergence hypothesis is that per capita income in countries with similar institutional structures will converge.
- Convergence has not taken place because of the lack of factor mobility, differing institutional structures, incomparable factors of production, and technological agglomeration.
- The Classical growth model focuses on the role of capital accumulation in the growth process. The law of diminishing productivity limits growth of per capita income.
- New growth theory emphasizes the role of technology in the growth process. Increasing returns to scale means output per person can rise forever.
- Advances in technology, which account for 35 percent of growth, have overwhelmed the effects of diminishing returns.

Key Terms

Classical growth model *(607)*
constant returns to scale *(607)*
convergence hypothesis *(609)*
decreasing returns to scale *(607)*
division of labor *(598)*
human capital *(603)*
increasing returns to scale *(607)*
law of diminishing marginal productivity *(607)*
learn by doing *(613)*

new growth theory (611)
patent (613)
per capita growth (599)
positive externality (613)
potential output (596)
production function (606)
productivity (596)
Rule of 72 (597)
Say's law (596)
social capital (603)
specialization (598)
technological agglomeration (611)
technology (604)

Questions and Exercises

connect ECONOMICS

1. Who most likely worked longer to buy a dozen eggs: a person living in 2009 or a person living in 1910? Why? LO1
2. Per capita income is growing at different rates in the following countries: Nepal, 1.1 percent; Kenya, 1.7 percent; Singapore, 7.2 percent; Egypt, 3.9 percent. How long will it take for each country to double its income per person? LO1
3. Calculate real growth per capita in the following countries:
   a. Democratic Republic of Congo: population growth = 3.0 percent; real output growth = −1.8 percent.
   b. Estonia: population growth = −0.4 percent; real output growth = 4.2 percent.
   c. India: population growth = 2.0 percent; real output growth = 6 percent.
   d. United States: population growth = 0.5 percent; real output growth = 2.5 percent. LO1
4. What roles do specialization and division of labor play in economists' support of free trade? LO2
5. How can an increase in the U.S. saving rate lead to higher living standards? LO2
6. Demonstrate graphically how the loanable funds market translates savings into investment. What equilibrates saving and investment? LO2
7. Name three types of capital and explain the differences among them. LO2
8. In what ways do informal property rights limit growth? LO2
9. How does growth through technology differ from growth through the accumulation of physical capital? LO2
10. *Credentialism* occurs when a person's academic degrees become more important than his or her actual knowledge. How can credentialism hurt economic growth? LO2
11. Using the demand and supply of loanable funds, demonstrate the effect of the following on the interest rate. As a result, what would you expect to be the impact of the change on growth?
    a. Government increases spending.
    b. Businesses become more productive.
    c. The people as a whole save more. LO2
12. On what law of production did Thomas Malthus base his prediction that population growth would exceed growth in goods and services? LO3
13. Why hasn't Thomas Malthus's prediction come true? LO3
14. If output increases by 20 percent when one of two inputs increases by 20 percent, are there constant returns to scale? Why or why not? LO3
15. According to the convergence hypothesis, which country will grow faster: the United States or Bangladesh? Why? LO4
16. List four reasons why convergence might not occur. LO4
17. If individuals suddenly needed more food to subsist, what would the Classical growth model predict would happen to labor and output? Demonstrate graphically. LO5
18. How does new growth theory explain the lack of convergence? LO5
19. What are network externalities and how do they lead to growth? LO5
20. The graph below shows a production function and the subsistence level of output.
    a. Does the production function exhibit increasing or decreasing marginal productivity?
    b. Label a level of population at which the population is expected to grow. What is the surplus output at that population level?
    c. Label a level of population at which the population is expected to decline. Why is the population declining at this point?
    d. Label the population at which the economy is in long-run equilibrium. Why is this a long-run equilibrium? LO5

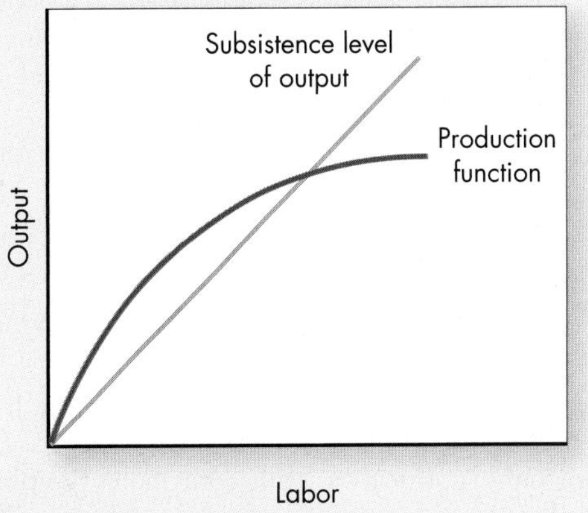

21. Explain how each of the following is expected to affect growth:
    a. Increase in technology.
    b. Positive externalities.
    c. Patents.
    d. Learning by doing.
    e. Technological lock-in. LO5

Questions from Alternative Perspectives

1. Capitalism was a derogatory term coined by Karl Marx to deride the riches of those who accumulated capital. He said that the accumulation of capital helps the rich get richer while simultaneously making the poor get poorer.
   a. Have the poor become poorer under capitalism?
   b. Based on the growth model presented in the text, what would you expect to happen to poor people's income when society accumulates capital? (Austrian)
2. Ecological economists believe that economic possibilities are constrained by natural laws (for example, the laws of thermodynamics, biological assimilation, and the limiting factor). Unlimited material growth from a finite resource base—spaceship earth—is therefore impossible. How many "earths" would it take for everyone to live like U.S. citizens? (To help answer this question, you might visit and take the test at http://redefiningprogress.org/footprint.) (Institutionalist)
3. Many Keynesians believe the best way to deal with growth is to have government promote an industrial policy that focuses on the development of technological change using tax credits, government research funding, and the transfer of technological knowledge from the military to the civilian sector.
   a. Would such a policy be consistent with the new growth theory?
   b. Would those believing in the Classical growth model support such a policy? (Post-Keynesian)
4. There is a furious debate among economists about the relationship between equality (or inequality) and economic growth. Based on the observation that developing countries often experience increasing inequality during their initial periods of rapid growth, some economists emphasize the role of inequality in establishing incentives to work, save, and invest. The experience of the East Asian economies that grew rapidly after reducing their levels of inequality (through land reform and other means) led other economists to argue that greater equality leads to faster economic growth. The reasons they cite are numerous: more political stability, greater access to credit, higher levels of spending on education, and wider land ownership.
   a. How do these arguments about the positive link between equality and economic growth fit with your textbook's list of the sources of economic growth?
   b. What do you think is the relationship between equality (or inequality) and economic growth? (Radical)
5. Christians believe that everything ultimately belongs to God. Is that belief consistent with economists' belief that property rights are necessary for growth? (Religious)

Issues to Ponder

1. a. If you suddenly found yourself living as a poor person in a developing country, what are some things that you now do that you would no longer be able to do? What new things would you have to do?
   b. Answer the questions again assuming that you are living in the United States 100 years ago. LO1
2. Have the poor benefited more or less from economic growth than the rich? LO1
3. What problem would a politician face when promoting policies to encourage saving? LO2
4. De Paul University Professor Ludovic Comeau Jr. hypothesizes that the length of time that a country has had a democratic political structure contributes positively to growth. In what way can a political structure be capital? LO2
5. Could the borrowing circle concept be easily adapted for use in the United States?
   a. Why or why not?
   b. What modifications would you suggest if it were to be adopted?
   c. Minorities in the United States often do not use banks. In what ways are U.S. minorities' problems similar to those of people in developing countries? (Requires reading "Real-World Application: Micro Credit" on page 615.) LO2

Answers to Margin Questions

1. The long-run growth analysis justifies its focus on supply by assuming that aggregate supply will create an equal level of aggregate demand. This is known as Say's law. *(596)*
2. Using the Rule of 72 (divide 72 by the growth rate of income), we can calculate that it will take 18 years for income to double when its growth rate is 4 percent a year. *(597)*
3. Country B is experiencing the higher growth in income per capita. To calculate this, subtract the population growth rates from the income growth rates for each country. Country A's per capita growth rate is 1 percent (4 − 3) and country B's per capita growth rate is 2 percent (3 − 1) *(600)*
4. The increases would have to be distributed so that no one whose income is below the median receives enough to bring his or her income above the median. *(600)*
5. Private property provides an incentive for people to produce by creating the possibility of benefiting from their efforts. *(601)*
6. With the demand for loanable funds shifting out, the interest rate will likely rise. *(602)*
7. False. A 20 percent increase in production that results from a 10 percent increase in all inputs means the production process exhibits decreasing *returns to scale*. A key part of the statement is that all inputs are changing. If one input were being kept fixed, the production function would be exhibiting diminishing marginal productivity. *(607)*
8. If individuals suddenly needed less food, the subsistence level line would rotate down. The number of laborers the economy could sustain would rise, and output would rise as well. *(609)*
9. An economist would likely predict that India and China will grow faster than the United States in the next decade because of the law of one price, which states that, assuming similar institutional structures, equivalent factors will be paid the same wage; until that happens, firms will have an incentive to transfer production to the lower-wage countries, leading to higher growth in those countries. *(609)*
10. The Internet connects hundreds of millions of people around the globe and reduces communication costs. The benefit of one person using the Internet is virtually nonexistent. The benefit of the Internet rises as more people use it because the higher usage increases the amount of information available on the Internet and increases the ability of each user to communicate. *(614)*

CHAPTER 27

The Aggregate Demand/Aggregate Supply Model

The Theory of Economics . . . is a method rather than a doctrine, an apparatus of the mind, a technique of thinking which helps its possessor to draw correct conclusions.

—J. M. *Keynes*

AFTER READING THIS CHAPTER, YOU SHOULD BE ABLE TO:

1. Discuss the historical development of macroeconomics.
2. Explain the shape of the aggregate demand curve and what factors shift the curve.
3. Explain the shape of the short-run aggregate supply curve and what factors shift the curve.
4. Explain the shape of the long-run aggregate supply curve.
5. Show the effects of shifts of the aggregate demand and aggregate supply curves on the price level and output in both the short run and long run.
6. Explain how dynamic feedback effects can destabilize the economy.
7. Discuss the limitations of the macro policy model.

The previous chapter's discussion of growth and markets focused on the positive side of markets: markets unleash individual incentives, increase supply, and bring about growth. But markets can run into serious problems—markets can create recessions, inflation, and unemployment. The United States in 2008 is a good example. In early 2008, economic growth was slowing even as inflation was picking up, leaving the government in a policy bind—should it try to increase growth or should it fight inflation? By September 2008, that policy bind was answered, although not in the way that policy makers had expected or hoped. The economy fell into a serious recession that many thought might lead to a depression. Faced with this serious recession, the U.S. government turned its attention away from concern about inflation, growth, and supply-side policies to recession and demand-side policies—both monetary and fiscal policy—that would keep the economy from going into a deep recession.

The tools that government has to deal with recessions, unemployment, and inflation—i.e., monetary and fiscal policies (policies that we will discuss in depth below)—affect the aggregate demand side of the economy. Thus, whereas the last chapter's policy focus was on production (the supply side) and individual incentives, this chapter and the next focus on expenditures (the demand side). As you will see, economists debate the effectiveness of monetary and fiscal policy. Some favor intervention; some don't. While the problems of a recession are serious, so too are the problems with government policies. The debate among economists is about whether the cure (intervention) is worse than the disease.

Even if the noninterventionist economists were to convince all other economists that government should not intervene with monetary and fiscal policy, the odds are that government would still intervene. As I've said before, the reality is that politicians make policy; they listen to economists only when they want to. And whenever the economy faces the threat of a recession, politicians' focus inevitably changes from long-run supply issues and growth to short-run demand issues and stabilization.

The Historical Development of Macro

An important reason for politicians' initial interest in short-run demand policies is the Great Depression of the 1930s, a deep recession that lasted for 10 years. Most of you think of the Great Depression only as something your grandparents and great-grandparents experienced. But it was a defining event that undermined people's faith in markets and was the beginning of macro's focus on the demand side of the economy. It is also where our story of macroeconomics begins.

Web Note 27.1
The Great Depression

During the Depression of the 1930s, output fell by 30 percent and unemployment rose to 25 percent. Not only was the deadbeat up the street unemployed but so were your brother, your mother, your uncle—the hardworking backbone of the country. These people wanted to work; if the market wasn't creating jobs for them, it was the market system that was at fault.

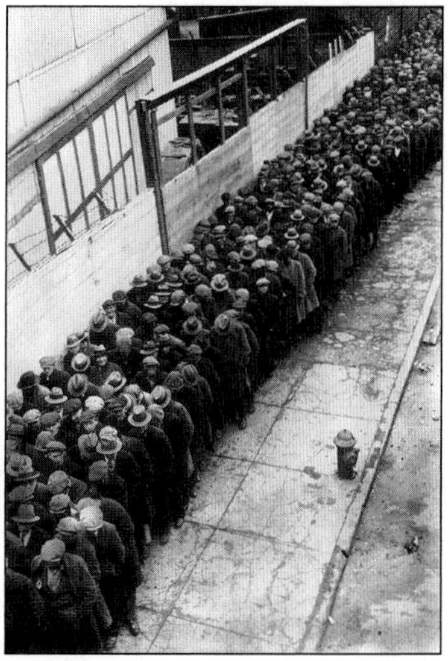

During the Depression, unemployment lines were enormously long.

From Classical to Keynesian Economics As I discussed in an earlier chapter, economists before the Depression focused on the long run and the problem of growth. Their policy recommendations were designed to lead to long-run growth, and they avoided discussing policies that would affect the economy in the short run. In the 1930s, macroeconomists started focusing their discussion of macroeconomic policy on short-run issues. To distinguish the two types of economics, the earlier economists who focused on long-run issues such as growth were called *Classical economists* and economists who focused on the short run were called *Keynesian economists*. Keynesian economists were named because a leading advocate of the short-run focus was John Maynard Keynes, the author of *The General Theory of Employment, Interest and Money*, and the originator of macroeconomics as a separate discipline from micro.

Classical Economists

Q-1 Distinguish a Classical economist from a Keynesian economist.

Classical economists believed in the market's ability to be self-regulating through the invisible hand (the pricing mechanism of the market). Short-run problems were seen as temporary glitches; the Classical framework said that the economy would always return to its potential output and its target (or natural) rate of unemployment in the long run. Thus, the essence of Classical economists' approach to problems was laissez-faire (leave the market alone).

Classical economists support laissez-faire policies.

As long as the economy was operating relatively smoothly, the Classical analysis of the aggregate economy met no serious opposition. But when the Great Depression hit and unemployment became a serious problem, most Classical economists avoided the issue (as most people tend to do when they don't have a good answer). When pushed by curious students to explain how the invisible hand, if it was so wonderful, could have allowed the Depression, Classical economists used microeconomic supply and demand arguments. They argued that labor unions and government policies kept prices and wages from falling. The problem, they said, was that the invisible hand was not being allowed to coordinate economic activity.

Their laissez-faire policy prescription followed from their analysis: Eliminate labor unions and change government policies that held wages too high. If government did so, the wage rate would fall, unemployment would be eliminated, and the Depression would end.

The Layperson's Explanation for Unemployment

Laypeople (average citizens) weren't pleased with this argument. (Remember, economists don't try to present pleasing arguments—only arguments they believe are correct.) But laypeople couldn't point to anything wrong with it. It made sense, but it wasn't satisfying. People thought, "Gee, Uncle Joe, who's unemployed, would take a job at half the going wage. But he can't find one—there just aren't enough jobs to go around at any wage." So most laypeople developed different explanations. One popular explanation of the Depression was that an oversupply of goods had glutted the market. All that was needed to eliminate unemployment was for government to hire the unemployed, even if only to dig ditches and fill them back up. The people who got the new jobs would spend their money, creating even more jobs. Pretty soon, the United States would be out of the Depression.

Classical economists argued against this lay view. They felt that money to hire people would have to be borrowed. Such borrowing would use money that would have financed private economic activity and jobs, and would thus reduce private economic activity even further. The net effect would be essentially zero. Their advice was simply to have faith in markets.

The Essence of Keynesian Economics

Keynes focused on the short run, not the long run.

As the Depression deepened, the Classical "have-faith" solution lost its support. Everyone was interested in the short run, not the long run. John Maynard Keynes put the concern most eloquently: "In the long run, we're all dead."

Keynes stopped asking whether the economy would eventually get out of the Depression on its own and started asking what short-run forces were causing the Depression and what society could do to counteract them. By taking this approach, he created the macroeconomic framework that focuses on short-run issues such as business cycles and how to stabilize output fluctuations.

Web Note 27.2
John Maynard Keynes

While Keynes's ideas had many dimensions, the essence was that as wages and the price level adjusted to sudden changes in expenditures (such as an unexpected decrease in investment demand), the economy could get stuck in a rut.

If, for some reason, people stopped buying—decreased their demand in the aggregate—firms would decrease production, causing people to be laid off; these people would, in turn, buy less—causing other firms to further decrease production, which would cause more workers to be laid off, and so on. Firms' supply decisions would be affected by consumers' buying decisions, and the economy would end up in a cumulative cycle of declining production that would end with the economy stuck at a low level of income. In developing this line of reasoning, Keynes provided a simple model of how unemployment could be caused by too little spending and how the economy could fall into a depression. The issue was not whether a more desirable equilibrium existed; it was whether a market economy, once it had fallen into a depression, and was caught in a cumulative downward cycle, could get out of it on its own in an acceptable period of time.

In making his argument, Keynes carefully distinguished the adjustment process for a single market (a micro issue) from the adjustment process for the aggregate economy (a macro issue), arguing that the effects differ significantly when everyone does something versus when only one person does it. You were introduced to this problem in Chapter 4 under the name *fallacy of composition*.

The problem is neatly seen by considering an analogy to a football game. If everyone is standing, and you sit down, you can't see. Everyone is better off standing. No one has an incentive to sit down. However, if somehow all individuals could be enticed to sit down, all individuals would be even better off. Sitting down is a public good—a good that benefits others but one that nobody on his or her own will do. Keynesians argued that, in times of recession, spending is a public good because it benefits everyone, so government should spend or find ways of inducing private individuals to spend. This difference between individual and economywide reactions to spending decisions creates a possibility for government to exercise control over aggregate expenditures and

Keynesians argued that, in times of recession, spending is a public good that benefits everyone.

ADDED DIMENSION

In the Long Run, We're All Dead

When Keynes said, "In the long run, we're all dead," he didn't mean that we can forget the long run. What he meant was that if the long run is so long that short-run forces do not let it come about, then for all practical purposes there is no long run. In that case, the short-run problem must be focused on.

Keynes believed that voters would not be satisfied waiting for market forces to bring about full employment. If something were not done in the short run to alleviate unemployment, he felt, voters would opt for fascism (as had the Germans) or communism (as had the Russians). He saw both alternatives as undesirable. For him, what would happen in the long run was academic.

Classicals, in contrast, argued that the short-run problems were not as bad as Keynes made them out to be and therefore should not be focused on to the exclusion of long-run problems.

Modern-day Classicals argue that while Keynes is dead, we are not, and the result of his short-run focus was long-run problems—specifically an inflationary bias in the economy. It is only by giving up Keynesian policies that we eliminate that bias.

Up until 2008, Keynesian ideas had lost favor, but when the financial crisis of 2008 hit, and the macroeconomy fell into a serious recession, Keynesian ideas came back into vogue.

thereby over aggregate output and income. *Government's attempt to control the aggregate level of spending in the economy* is called **aggregate demand management.**

Equilibrium Income Fluctuates The key idea of the Keynesian model is that the aggregate economy's short-run adjustment process could be destabilizing and actually lead the economy away from its potential income, at least temporarily. Specifically, Keynes argued that a falling price level could have a negative feedback effect on aggregate demand, reducing aggregate demand more than the lower price level increased the quantity of aggregate demand. If that happened, the macroeconomy could end up in a never-ending vicious downward cycle of falling output and prices. Keynesians argued that such cycles didn't happen because, institutionally, prices did not fluctuate much, and, in the short run, could be considered essentially fixed. A vicious cycle of decline could still develop, but it would not be accelerated or made worse by the effects of a declining price level on aggregate demand. In the short run equilibrium income is not fixed at the economy's long-run potential income; it fluctuates. Thus, for Keynes, there was a difference between **equilibrium income** *(the level of income toward which the economy gravitates in the short run because of the cumulative cycles of declining or increasing production)* and **potential income** *(the level of income that the economy technically is capable of producing without generating accelerating inflation)*. Keynes believed that at certain times the economy needed some help in reaching its potential income.

The key idea in Keynesian economics is that equilibrium income fluctuates and can differ from potential income.

He argued that market forces that are supposed to bring the economy back to long-run potential income don't work fast, and at times will not be strong enough to get the economy out of a recession; the economy could get stuck in a low-income, high-unemployment rut. As the economy adjusts to fluctuations of supply and demand in the aggregate, the equilibrium income toward which the economy would gravitate would change. The economy would not naturally gravitate to potential income in the short run.

The Paradox of Thrift Let's say that a large portion of the people in the economy suddenly decides to save more and consume less. Expenditures would decrease and saving would increase. If that saving is not immediately transferred into investment, and hence back into expenditures (as the Classicals assumed it would be), investment demand will not increase by enough to offset the fall in consumption demand, and total demand will fall. There will be excess supply. Faced with this excess supply, firms will likely cut back production, which will decrease income. People will be laid off. As people's incomes fall, both their consumption and saving will decrease. (When you're laid off, you don't save.) Eventually income will fall far enough so that once again saving and investment will be in equilibrium, but then the economy could be at an almost permanent recession, with ongoing unemployment. Keynesians believed that in this case the economy would need government's help to prop up aggregate expenditures. That is the essence of macro demand-side expansionary policy.

Keynesian economists advocated an activist demand management policy.

Notice that the Keynesian framework gives a quite different view of saving than did the growth framework in the last chapter. There, saving was seen as something good; more saving leads to more investment, which leads to more growth. In the Keynesian framework, there is a **paradox of thrift**—*an increase in saving can lead to a decrease in expenditures, decreasing output and causing a recession.*

Q-2 How does the short-run view of saving differ from the long-run view?

By the 1950s, Keynesian economics had been accepted by most economists, and was taught almost everywhere in the United States. The model that was meant to capture Keynesian economics was called the multiplier model. This model emphasized aggregate output fluctuations and explored why those output fluctuations generally would not lead to wild fluctuations in output—depressions—and instead lead to smaller fluctuations—recessions. Then, in the 1970s inflation became a serious issue for economies, which meant that the multiplier model, which assumed that the price level is fixed, was not very helpful. The standard model taught in macro shifted to the aggregate supply/aggregate demand (*AS/AD*) model. It is that *AS/AD* model that I introduce you to in this chapter.

It is important to remember two things about the *AS/AD* model. The first is that it is a pedagogical model—designed to give students and policy makers a framework to organize their thinking about the macroeconomy. It is a rough-and-ready framework, not a model developed from first principles. The second point is that in its standard presentation, the *AS/AD* model does not focus on problems that occur because of interactions between individuals—and thus does not highlight the dynamic feedback problems discussed above. These dynamic forces are especially important when aggregate demand declines significantly, as happened in 2008 and 2009. The multiplier model developed in the next chapter does a better job of highlighting those dynamic forces.

Both that *AS/AD* model and the multiplier model are exceedingly simple, but, combined, they give a sense of how economists think about the macroeconomy and give you a framework to think about the macroeconomy. They are the models used by most macro policy economists to discuss short-run fluctuations in output and unemployment.

The *AS/AD* Model

The *AS/AD* model consists of three curves. The curve describing the supply side of the aggregate economy in the short run is the short-run aggregate supply (*SAS*) curve, the curve describing the demand side of the economy is the aggregate demand curve, and the curve describing the highest sustainable level of output is the long-run aggregate supply (*LAS*) curve.

Knowing the difference between microeconomic supply and demand curves and macroeconomic aggregate demand and supply curves is very important.

The first thing to note about the *AS/AD* model is that it is fundamentally different from the microeconomic supply/demand model. In microeconomics the price of a single good is on the vertical axis and the quantity of a single good on the horizontal axis. The reasoning for the shapes of the micro supply and demand curves is based on the concepts of substitution and opportunity cost. In the macro *AS/AD* model, the price level of all goods, not just the price of one good, is on the vertical axis and aggregate output, not a single good, is on the horizontal axis. The shapes of the curves have nothing to do with opportunity cost or substitution.

The second thing to note about the *AS/AD* model is that it is a *historical model*. A historical model is a model that starts at a point in time and says what will likely happen when changes affect the economy. It does not try to explain how the economy got to its starting point; the macroeconomy is too complicated for that. Instead, the model starts from historically given price and output levels and, given the institutional structure of the economy, considers how changes in the economy are likely to affect those levels. What this means is that much of the discussion in this chapter is based on the economy's institutional realities and observed empirical regularities.

Let's now consider the three central components of the *AS/AD* model: the aggregate demand (*AD*) curve, the short-run aggregate supply (*SAS*) curve, and the long-run aggregate supply (*LAS*) curve.

The Aggregate Demand Curve

The **aggregate demand (AD) curve** is *a curve that shows how a change in the price level will change aggregate expenditures on all goods and services in an economy*. (Aggregate expenditures is the sum of consumption, investment, government expenditures, and net exports.) A standard *AD* curve is shown in Figure 27-1. Although the curve is called an aggregate demand curve, let me repeat that it is not the same as a microeconomic demand curve. The *AD* curve is more an equilibrium curve.[1] It shows the level of aggregate expenditures at every price level, implicitly taking into account some interactions among all producers and consumers in an economy.

Take the time to draw an *AD* curve, making sure to label the axes correctly.

Aggregate Demand

The Slope of the *AD* Curve

As you can see, the *AD* curve is downward-sloping. A good place to begin understanding why it is downward-sloping is to remember the composition of aggregate demand.

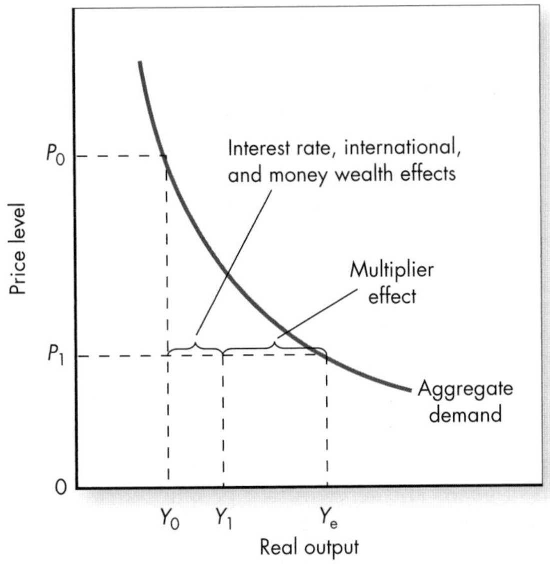

FIGURE 27-1
The Aggregate Demand Curve

The *AD* curve is a downward-sloping curve that looks like a typical demand curve, but it is important to remember that it is quite a different curve. The reason it slopes downward is not the substitution effect, but instead the interest rate effect, the international effect, and the money wealth effect. The multiplier effect strengthens each of these effects.

[1]In a number of articles and in previous editions, I tried to change the terminology so that students would not be misled into thinking that the *AD* curve was a normal demand curve. But my changes did not catch on.

As I discussed in the chapter on aggregate accounting, aggregate expenditures (demand) is the sum of consumption, investment, government spending, and net exports. The slope of the *AD* curve depends on how these components respond to changes in the price level.

In principle, we would expect the *AD* curve to be vertical. Why? Because one of the definitional assumptions of economics is that the price level is simply what is called a *numeraire*. The price level is simply a reference point, and the actual value of that numeraire should not matter. To see why, say that all prices (including wages) doubled. How would people's choices change? They wouldn't. Instead of earning $10 an hour, you would now earn $20 an hour. All the goods you buy would cost twice as much too, so you wouldn't be better off or worse off. Only the reference point has changed. Thus, as a first approximation, we would expect that you would buy the same amount of real goods at every price level. That would make the *AD* curve vertical.

Macroeconomists have examined this proposition and have developed a number of explanations for why a falling price level increases aggregate expenditures in normal times. These explanations make the standard *AD* curve downward-sloping rather than vertical. I'll discuss three of these standard effects: the interest-rate effect, the international effect, and the money wealth effect.

The Interest Rate Effect One explanation for why the aggregate demand curve slopes downward is called the **interest rate effect**—*the effect that a lower price level has on investment expenditures through the effect that a change in the price level has on interest rates*. The interest rate effect works as follows: a decrease in the price level will increase the purchasing power of the money in people's pockets and people will find they're holding more money than they need. So, they deposit the extra money at banks in some form, giving banks more money to loan out. As banks make more loans, interest rates will fall, which, in turn, will increase investment expenditures. Why? Because at lower interest rates businesses will undertake more investment projects. Since investment is one component of aggregate demand, the quantity of aggregate demand will increase when the price level falls.

The International Effect A second reason why aggregate quantity demanded increases with a fall in the price level is the **international effect,** which tells us that *as the price level falls (assuming the exchange rate does not change), net exports will rise*. As the price level in the United States falls, the price of U.S. goods relative to foreign goods goes down and U.S. goods become more competitive than foreign goods; thus, U.S. exports increase and U.S. imports decrease. Let's consider an example. In the mid-1990s, the Bulgarian currency was fixed to the German mark. Bulgaria's price level rose enormously, increasing the demand for German imports and reducing the quantity of aggregate demand in Bulgaria.

The Money Wealth Effect A third explanation why the *AD* curve isn't vertical is called the money wealth effect. To understand this effect consider Figure 27-1. Say we start out at price P_0 and output Y_0 in Figure 27-1. (Remember, as I said above, in a historical model we start at a given price and output and determine what would happen if the price level rises or falls from that level.) Now, say that the price level falls to P_1. How will this affect the total amount of goods and services that people demand? The **money wealth effect** (sometimes called the *real balance effect*) tells us that *a fall in the price level will make the holders of money richer, so they buy more*. In other words, if the price level falls, the dollar bill in your pocket will buy more than before because the purchasing power of the dollar rises. You are, in effect, richer and as you get richer, other things equal, you will buy more goods and services. Since consumption expenditures are a component of aggregate demand, aggregate expenditures will increase, which is shown graphically by a movement along the *AD* curve. (To differentiate such movements along the *AD* curve from a shift in the *AD* curve, I call movements due to changes in the price level "changes in the quantity of aggregate demand.") Most economists do not see the money wealth effect as strong; they do, however, accept the logic of the argument.

So, in Figure 27-1 when we include the international effect, the interest rate effect, and the money wealth effect, a fall in the price level from P_0 to P_1 causes the quantity of aggregate demand to increase to Y_1.

The Multiplier Effect The above three effects give us some explanation why the quantity of aggregate demand will increase with a fall in the price level. But the story about the slope of the aggregate demand curve doesn't end there. It also takes into account the **multiplier effect**—*the amplification of initial changes in expenditures*. It is important to recognize that when considering the demand curve in micro, we can reasonably assume that other things remain constant; in macro, other things change. Whereas the demand curve in micro includes only the initial change, the aggregate demand curve includes the repercussions that these initial changes have throughout the economy. What I mean by *repercussions* is that the initial changes in expenditures set in motion a process in the economy that amplifies these initial effects.

The slope of the *AD* curve is determined by the money wealth effect, the interest rate effect, the international effect, and the multiplier effect.

In micro other things can be assumed to remain constant, whereas in macro other things change.

To see how these repercussions will likely work in the real world, imagine that the price level in the United States rises. U.S. citizens will reduce their purchases of U.S. goods and increase their purchases of foreign goods. (That's the international effect.) U.S. firms will see the demand for their goods and services fall and will decrease their output. Profits will fall and people will be laid off. Both these effects will cause income to fall, and as income falls, people will demand still fewer goods and services. (If you're unemployed, you cut back your purchases.) Again production and income fall, which again leads to a drop in expenditures. This secondary cutback is an example of a repercussion. These repercussions *multiply* the initial effect that a change in the price level has on expenditures.

The multiplier effect amplifies the initial interest rate, international, and money wealth effects, thereby making the slope of the *AD* curve flatter than it would have been. You can see this in Figure 27-1. The three effects discussed above increase output from Y_0 to Y_1. The repercussions multiply that effect so that output increases to Y_e.

Economists have suggested other reasons why changes in the price level affect the quantity of aggregate demand, but these four should be sufficient to give you an initial understanding. Going through the same exercise that I did above for the interest rate, international, money wealth and multiplier effects for a fall (rather than a rise) in the price level is a useful exercise.

Let's conclude this section with an example that brings out the importance of the multiplier effect in determining the slope of the *AD* curve. Say that the multiplier effect amplifies the interest rate, international, and money wealth effects by a factor of 2 and that the interest rate, international, and money wealth effects reduce output by 4 when the price level rises from 100 to 110. What will be the slope of the *AD* curve? Since the multiplier effect is 2, the total decline in output will be $2 \times 4 = 8$, so the slope will be $-10/8$ or -1.25.

Q-3 Is it true or false that the slope of the *AD* curve is -1 if as the price level falls from 110 to 100, the international effect increases output by 10?

How Steep Is the AD Curve? While all economists agree about the logic of the interest rate effect, the international effect, and the money wealth effect, most also agree that for small changes in the price level, the net effect is relatively small. So, even after the effect has been expanded by the multiplier, the *AD* curve has a very steep slope.[2] Unfortunately, statistically separating out the effects determining the slope of the *AD*

[2]Of the three, the international effect is probably the strongest, but its strength depends on whether fluctuations in the exchange rate offset it; exchange rate determination will be discussed in depth in a later chapter.

There is much noise in the relationship between the price level and aggregate expenditures.

curve from shifts in the *AD* curve is difficult because there is much noise—random unexplained movements—in the relationship between the price level and aggregate expenditures. It is that noise on the aggregate level that makes the economy so hard to predict, and accounts for the description of economic forecasting as "driving a car blindfolded while following directions given by a person who is looking out of the back window." In order to make the graphs easy to follow, they show a flatter *AD* curve than probably exists in reality.

Dynamic Price Level Adjustment Feedback Effects

At times these dynamic effects can overwhelm the standard effects and make the aggregate economic unstable.

The interest rate, international, and money wealth effects, amplified by the multiplier effect, are all logically correct. But there are other forces in the economy that counteract these forces. At times these dynamic effects can overwhelm the standard effects and make the aggregate economy unstable, making expansions stronger and contractions larger. They can reduce or completely offset the stabilizing effects of a price-level adjustment in bringing about an aggregate equilibrium.

These forces are especially important when aggregate demand is declining and the price level needs to fall to bring about aggregate equilibrium. Here is the problem: Pressure for the price level to fall brings with it:[3]

- Expectations of falling aggregate demand.
- Lower asset prices, making society on average *feel* poorer, even though, theoretically, it is not *actually* poorer.
- Financial panics, triggered by a decline in the value of financial assets, causing individuals and banks, who relied on those financial assets as collateral in loans they have made, to require full payment on (to call in) those loans, which forces borrowers (mainly firms) to reduce production and lay off workers, decreasing aggregate demand further.

Each of these forces, which the standard model assumes away, works in an opposite direction to the standard effects that cause the quantity of aggregate demand to increase when the price level falls. If these dynamic forces are strong enough, aggregate demand will fall (shift to the left) when the price level falls. In fact, the price level doesn't even have to fall; there only has to be the pressure for the price level to fall. We will discuss these dynamic forces more in the chapter on the current financial crisis.

Shifts in the *AD* Curve

Next, let's consider what causes the *AD* curve to shift. A shift in the *AD* curve means that at every price level, total expenditures have changed. Anything other than the price level that changes the components of aggregate demand (consumption, investment, government spending, and net exports) will shift the *AD* curve. Five important shift factors of aggregate demand are foreign income, exchange rate fluctuations, the distribution of income, expectations, and government policies.

Foreign Income A country is not an island unto itself. U.S. economic output is closely tied to the income of its major world trading partners. When our trading partners go into a recession, the demand for U.S. goods, and hence U.S. exports, will fall, causing the U.S. *AD* curve to shift in to the left. Similarly, a rise in foreign income leads to an increase in U.S. exports and a rightward shift of the U.S. *AD* curve.

[3]These dynamic pressures are also at work in reverse when there are pressures for the price level to increase. But for increases, the pressures tend to reinforce the expansionary forces, and are usually seen as positive effects, especially when there is no fear of inflation.

Exchange Rates The currencies of various countries are connected through exchange rates. When a country's currency loses value relative to other currencies, its goods become more competitive compared to foreign goods. Foreign demand for domestic goods increases and domestic demand for foreign goods decreases as individuals shift their spending to domestic goods at home. Both these effects increase net exports and shift the *AD* curve to the right. By the same reasoning, when a country's currency gains value, the *AD* curve shifts in the opposite direction. You can see these effects on the U.S.-Canadian border. In the early 1990s, the Canadian dollar had a high value relative to the U.S. dollar. This caused many Canadians near the border to make buying trips to the United States. When the Canadian dollar fell in value, those buying trips decreased, and the Canadian *AD* curve shifted right.

Q-4 If a country's exchange rate rises, what happens to its *AD* curve?

Distribution of Income Some people save more than others, and everyone's spending habits differ. Thus, as income distribution changes, so too will aggregate demand. One of the most important distributional effects concerns the distribution of income between wages and profits. Workers receive wage income and are more likely to spend the income they receive; firms' profits are distributed to stockholders or are retained by the firm. Since stockholders in the United States tend to be wealthy, and the wealthy save a greater portion of their income than the poor do, a higher portion of income received as profits will likely be saved. Assuming all saving is not translated into investment, as the real wage decreases but total income remains constant, it is likely that consumption expenditures will fall and the aggregate demand curve will shift to the left. Similarly, as the real wage increases, it is likely that aggregate demand will shift to the right.

Expectations Another important shift factor of aggregate demand is expectations. Many different types of expectations can affect the *AD* curve. To give you an idea of the role of expectations, let's consider two expectational shift factors: expectations of future output and future prices. When businesspeople expect demand to be high in the future, they will want to increase their productive capacity; their investment demand, a component of aggregate demand, will increase. Thus, positive expectations about future demand will shift the *AD* curve to the right.

Expectations of higher future income increase expenditures and shift the *AD* curve out.

Similarly, when consumers expect the economy to do well, they will be less worried about saving for the future, and they will spend more now—the *AD* curve will shift to the right. Alternatively, if consumers expect the future to be gloomy, they will likely try to save for the future and will decrease their consumption expenditures. The *AD* curve will shift to the left.

Another type of expectation that shifts the *AD* curve concerns expectations of future prices. If you expect the prices of goods to rise in the future, it pays to buy goods now that you might want in the future—before their prices rise. The current price level hasn't changed, but aggregate quantity demanded at that price level has increased, indicating a shift of the *AD* curve to the right.

The effect of expectations of future price levels is seen more clearly in a hyperinflation. In most cases of hyperinflation, people rush out to spend their money quickly—to buy whatever they can to beat the price increase. So even though prices are rising, aggregate demand stays high because the rise in price creates an expectation of even higher prices, and thus the current high price is seen as a low price relative to the future. I said that an increase in expectations of inflation will "have a tendency to" rather than "definitely" shift the *AD* curve to the right because those expectations of inflation are interrelated with a variety of other expectations. For example, an expectation of a rise in the price of goods you buy could be accompanied by an expectation of a fall in income, and that fall in income would work in the opposite direction, decreasing aggregate demand.

Five important shift factors of *AD* are

1. Foreign income.
2. Exchange rates.
3. The distribution of income.
4. Expectations.
5. Monetary and fiscal policies.

This interrelation of various types of expectations makes it very difficult to specify precisely what effect certain types of expectations have on the *AD* curve. But it does not eliminate the importance of expectations as shift factors. It simply means that we often aren't sure what the net effect of a change in expectations on aggregate demand will be.

Monetary and Fiscal Policies One of the most important reasons why the aggregate demand curve has been so important in macro policy analysis is that often macro policy makers think that they can control it, at least to some degree. For example, if the government spends lots of money without increasing taxes, it shifts the *AD* curve to the right; if the government raises taxes significantly and holds spending constant, consumers will have less disposable income and will reduce their expenditures, shifting the *AD* curve to the left. Similarly, when the Federal Reserve Bank, the U.S. economy's central bank, expands the money supply, it can often lower interest rates, making it easier for both consumers and investors to borrow, increasing their spending, and thereby shifting the *AD* curve to the right. This deliberate increase in aggregate demand to influence the level of income in the economy is what most policy makers mean by the term *macro policy*. Expansionary macro policy shifts the *AD* curve to the right; contractionary macro policy shifts it to the left.

Deliberate shifting of the *AD* curve is what most policy makers mean by macro policy.

Multiplier Effects of Shift Factors As I emphasized when I introduced the *AD* curve, you cannot treat the *AD* curve like a micro demand curve. This comes out most clearly when considering shifts in the curve caused by shift factors. The aggregate demand curve may shift by more than the amount of the initial shift factor because of the multiplier effect. The explanation is the same as when I introduced the multiplier effect. When government increases its spending, firms increase production, which leads to higher income. A fraction of that increase in income is spent on more goods and services, shifting the *AD* curve even further to the right. This leads firms to increase production again; income and expenditures also rise. Each round, the increase gets smaller and smaller until the increase becomes negligible. In the end the *AD* curve will have shifted by a multiple of the initial shift. Just how large that multiple is depends on how much the change in income affects spending in each round. Thus, in Figure 27-2, when an initial shift factor of aggregate demand is 100 and the multiplier is 3, the *AD* curve will shift to the right by 300, three times the initial shift. The extra 200 shift is due to the multiplier effect.

Q-5 If government spending increases by 20, by how much does the *AD* curve shift out?

The *AD* curve holds all shift factors constant, so the slope of the *AD* curve reflects only the effects of a change in the price level (including multiplier effects).

FIGURE 27-2 Effect of a Shift Factor on the *AD* Curve

The *AD* curve shifts out by more than the initial change in expenditures. In this example, exports increase by 100. The multiplier magnifies this shift, and the *AD* curve shifts to the right by a multiple of 100, in this case by 300.

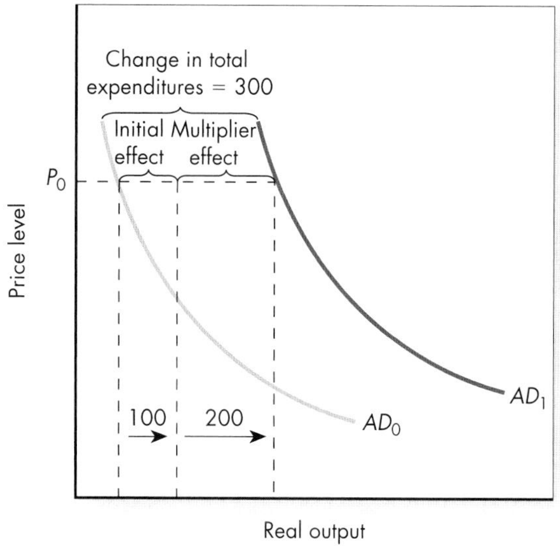

To see that you are following the argument, consider the following two shifts: (1) a fall in the U.S. exchange rate, increasing net exports by 50, and (2) an increase in government spending of 100. Explain how the *AD* curve will shift in each of these cases, and why that shift will be larger than the initial shift. If you are not sure about these explanations, review the multiplier effect discussion above.

The Short-Run Aggregate Supply Curve

The second component of the *AS/AD* model is the **short-run aggregate supply (SAS) curve**—*a curve that specifies how a shift in the aggregate demand curve affects the price level and real output in the short run, other things constant.* A standard SAS curve is shown in Figure 27-3.

The Slope of the SAS Curve

FIGURE 27-3 The Short-Run Aggregate Supply Curve

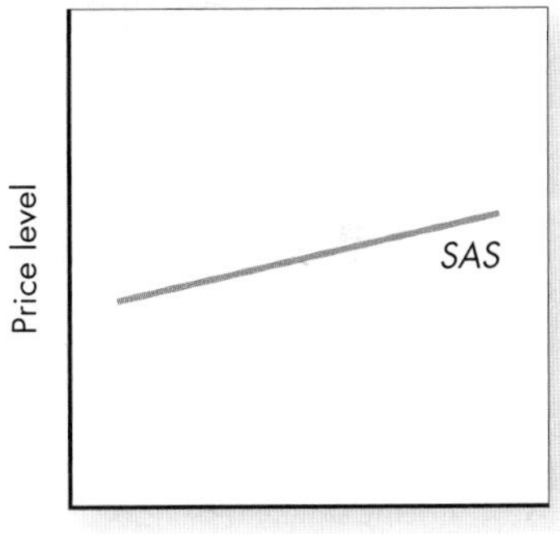

As you can see, the SAS curve is upward-sloping, which means that in the short run, other things constant, an increase in output is accompanied by a rise in the price level. That is, when aggregate demand increases, the price level—the composite of all prices—rises. The shape of the SAS curve reflects two different types of markets in our economy: auction markets (which are the markets represented by the supply/demand model) and posted-price markets (in which prices are set by the producers and change only infrequently).

In markets where prices are set by the interaction between buyers and sellers, none of whom have enough market power to set prices, there is little question why prices rise when demand increases as long as the supply curve for firms in the market is upward-sloping. But these auction markets make up only a small percentage of final goods markets. (They are much more common in markets for resources such as oil or farm products.) In most final goods markets, sellers set a price for their goods and buyers take these prices as given. These posted-price markets comprise 90 percent of the total final goods markets. In posted-price markets, firms set prices as a markup over costs. For example, if the markup is 40 percent and the cost of production is $10 per unit, the firm would set a price of $14.

Posted-price markets are often called **quantity-adjusting markets**—*markets in which firms respond to changes in demand primarily by changing production instead of changing their prices*. It would be wrong, however, to assume that prices in these markets are totally unresponsive to changes in demand. When demand increases, some firms will take the opportunity to raise their prices slightly, increasing their markup, and when demand falls, firms have a tendency to lower their prices slightly, decreasing their markup. This tendency to change markups as aggregate demand changes contributes to the upward slope of the SAS curve. So, the two reasons the SAS curve slopes upward are (1) upward-sloping supply curves in auction markets and (2) firms' tendency to increase their markup when demand increases.

The two reasons the *SAS* curve slopes upward are (1) upward-sloping supply curves in auction markets and (2) firms' tendency to increase their markup when demand increases.

One reason I did not give for the upward slope of the SAS curve is changes in cost of production. That's because along an SAS curve, all other things, including input prices, are assumed to remain constant. Increases in input prices shift the SAS curve.

Shifts in the SAS Curve

Notice that in the definition of the SAS curve, we have assumed that other things remain constant. As discussed above, this does not mean that other things *will* remain constant. It simply means that changes in other things, such as input prices, shift the SAS curve. For example, if input prices rise, the SAS curve shifts up; if input prices fall,

Changes in input prices cause a shift in the *SAS* curve.

ADDED DIMENSION

Why Are Prices Inflexible?

Why do firms adjust production instead of price? A number of reasons have been put forward by economists, and recently a group of economists, led by Princeton economist Alan Blinder, surveyed firms to find out which reasons firms believed were most important. The survey choices included strategic pricing, cost-based pricing rules, and implicit contracts.

1. **Strategic pricing.** About 90 percent of final-goods markets in the United States are markets in which a few major firms compete, each taking each other's reactions into account in their decisions. Although, under U.S. law, firms cannot get together and decide on a pricing strategy for the industry, they can informally coordinate their pricing procedures. If all firms can implicitly agree to hold their prices up when faced with decreased demand, they are not violating the law and will be better off than they would be if they acted in an uncoordinated fashion.

   They also won't increase prices when they experience an increase in demand because they fear that doing so will undermine the coordinated pricing strategy with other firms or they will lose market share when other firms don't raise prices.

   This is not to say that the U.S. economy is not competitive. Ask any businessperson and he or she will tell you that it is highly competitive. But firms now often compete on fronts other than price.
2. **Cost-based pricing rules.** Strategic pricing is maintained by firms' tendency to use cost-based pricing rules. In a cost-plus-markup pricing procedure, firms set prices based on the costs of production. For a majority of firms, the most important costs are labor costs, which tend to be fixed by long-term wage contracts between workers and employers. (Unions, for example, typically negotiate wage contracts for three-year periods.) Thus, costs do not change with changes in demand, and, following a cost-plus-markup strategy, neither do prices.
3. **Implicit contracts.** Most firms have ongoing relationships with their customers. That means that they don't want to antagonize them. They have found that one way to avoid antagonizing customers is not to take advantage of them even when they could. In the Blinder survey, firms felt that they had implicit contracts with their customers to raise prices only when their costs changed, or when market conditions changed substantially.

The combination of these reasons leads to a large segment of the economy in which the prices do not significantly change as demand changes. For that reason, we generally don't see big changes in the overall price level. Of course, if costs, especially labor costs, start rising significantly, then prices will rise too. To the degree that demand changes affect costs, prices will respond, but, as a first approximation, it is generally acceptable to say that the price level does not significantly move in response to demand. That's why the short-run aggregate supply curve is not very steep.

the *SAS* curve shifts down. So a change in input prices, such as wages, is a shift factor of aggregate supply. An important reason why wages change is expectations of inflation. If workers expect prices to be rising by 2 percent, they are likely to ask for at least a 2 percent rise in wages simply to keep up with inflation and maintain their real wage. If they expect the price level to fall by 2 percent, they are far more likely to be happy with their current wage. So the expectation of inflation is a shift factor that works through wages.

Another shift factor of aggregate supply is a change in the productivity of the factors of production such as labor. An increase in productivity, by reducing the amount of inputs required for a given amount of output, reduces input costs per unit of output and shifts the *SAS* curve down. A fall in productivity shifts the *SAS* curve up.

Two other shift factors are changes in import prices of final goods and changes in excise and sales taxes. Import prices are a shift factor because they are a component of an economy's price level. When import prices rise, the *SAS* curve shifts up; when import prices fall, the *SAS* curve shifts down. By raising the cost of goods, higher sales taxes shift the *SAS* curve up, and lower sales taxes shift the *SAS* curve down.

In summary, anything that changes factor costs will be a shift factor of supply. Such factors include

- Changes in input prices.
- Productivity.
- Import prices.
- Excise and sales taxes.

Economists spend a lot of time tracking these shift factors because they are central to whether the economy will have an inflation problem. Two of these—the wage component of input prices and labor productivity—are followed with special care because labor costs make up about two-thirds of total production costs.

The rule of thumb economists use when estimating how much the *SAS* curve will shift is that it will shift by the percentage change in wages and other factor prices minus changes in productivity. For example, if productivity rises by 3 percent and wages rise by 7 percent, we can expect the price level to rise by 4 percent for a given level of output. I show a shift up in the *SAS* curve in Figure 27-4. If wages and productivity rise by equal percentages, the price level would remain constant. If wages and other factor prices rise by less than the increase in productivity, the price level can fall, as recently happened in Japan. The relationship can be written as follows:

% change in the price level = % change in wages − % change in productivity

FIGURE 27-4
Input Price Rise and the *SAS* Curve

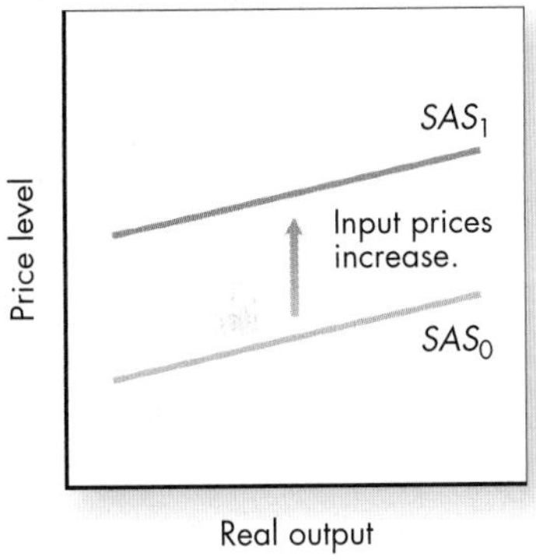

In the real world, we see shifts in the *SAS* curve in many areas. In 2007 and into mid-2008 oil prices more than doubled. That led to a sharp rise in the producer price index and a significant rise in factor prices, causing the *SAS* curve to shift up. Another example occurred in Argentina in early 2002 when the value of its currency, the peso, fell drastically. That caused the price of imports measured in pesos to increase substantially, which shifted its *SAS* curve up.

The Long-Run Aggregate Supply Curve

The final curve that makes up the *AS/AD* model is the **long-run aggregate supply (LAS) curve**—*a curve that shows the long-run relationship between output and the price level.* Whereas the *SAS* curve holds input prices constant, no prices are assumed held constant on the *LAS* curve. The position of the *LAS* curve is determined by potential output—the amount of goods and services an economy can produce when both labor and capital are fully employed. Figure 27-5(a) shows an *LAS* curve.

The *SAS* curve holds input prices constant; no prices are assumed held constant on the *LAS* curve.

Notice that the *LAS* curve is vertical. Since at potential output all resources are being fully utilized, a rise in the price level means that the prices of goods and factors of production, including wages, rise. Consider it this way: If all prices doubled, including your wage, your real income would not change. Since potential output is unaffected by the price level, the *LAS* curve is vertical.

A Range for Potential Output and the LAS Curve

The position of the *LAS* curve is determined by potential output. Because our estimates of potential output are inexact, precisely where to draw the *LAS* curve is generally

FIGURE 27-5 (A AND B) The Long-Run Aggregate Supply Curve

The long-run aggregate supply curve shows the output that an economy can produce when both labor and capital are fully employed. It is vertical because at potential output a rise in the price level means that all prices, including input prices, rise. Available resources do not rise and thus neither does potential output.

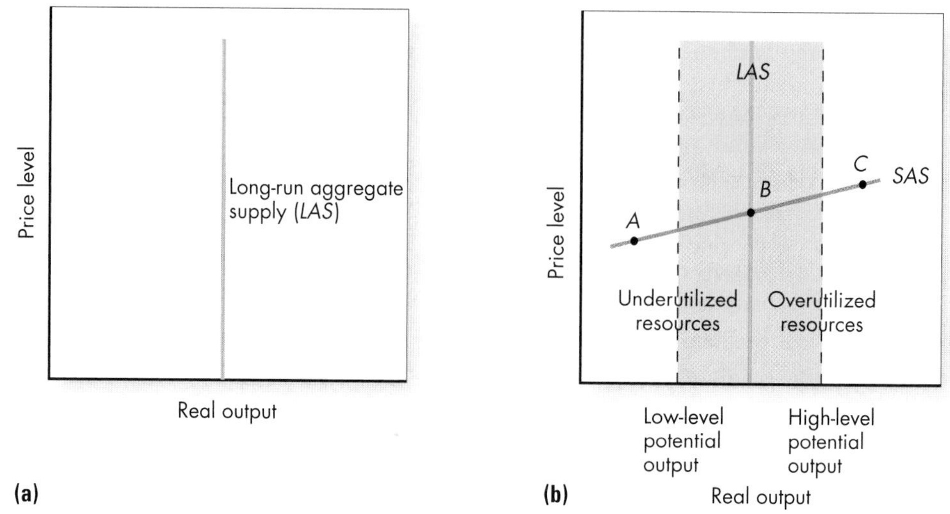

somewhat in debate. To understand policy debates, it is helpful to consider potential output to be a range of values. This range is bounded by a high level of potential output and a low level of potential output, as Figure 27-5(b) shows. The *LAS* curve can be thought of as being in the middle of that range.

Short-Run Aggregate Supply vs. Long-Run Aggregate Supply

This range is important because how close actual output (the position of the economy on the *SAS* curve) is to potential output is a key determinant of whether the *SAS* curve is expected to shift up or down. At points on the *SAS* curve to the left of the *LAS* curve (such as point *A*), resources are likely to be underutilized and we would expect factor prices to fall and, other things equal, the *SAS* curve to shift down. At points to the right of the *LAS* curve (such as point *C*), we would expect factor prices to be bid up and, other things equal, the *SAS* curve to shift up. Moreover, the further actual output is from potential output, the greater the pressure we would expect on factor prices to rise or fall. At the point of intersection between the *SAS* curve and the *LAS* curve (point *B*), other things equal, factor prices have no pressure to rise or fall.

In reality, whether factor prices will rise or fall in response to a change in demand is often in debate. That debate reflects the different estimates of potential output. Given the uncertainty of measured potential output, we would expect there to be a debate about whether the *SAS* curve will be shifting up or down. We will discuss these issues later. For now, all I want you to remember is that the *LAS* curve is an abstraction that reduces what is actually a range of potential output into a single value.

Shifts in the *LAS* Curve

Because the position of the *LAS* curve is determined by potential output, it shifts for the same reasons that potential output shifts. As discussed in the chapter about growth, those reasons are changes in capital, available resources, growth-compatible institutions, technology, and entrepreneurship. Increases in any of these increase potential output and shift the *LAS* curve out to the right. Decreases in any of these reduce potential output and shift the *LAS* curve in to the left. The position of the *LAS* curve plays an important role in determining long-run equilibrium and in determining whether policy should focus on long-run or short-run issues.

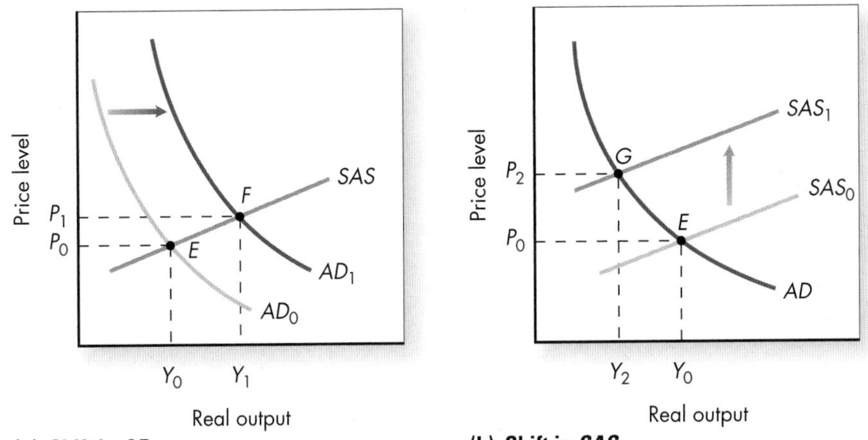

(a) Shift in *AD* **(b) Shift in *SAS***

FIGURE 27-6 (A AND B)
Equilibrium in the *AS/AD* Model

Short-run equilibrium is where the short-run aggregate supply and aggregate demand curves intersect. Point *E* in **(a)** is equilibrium; **(a)** also shows how a shift in the aggregate demand curve to the right changes equilibrium from *E* to *F*, increasing output from Y_0 to Y_1 and increasing price level from P_0 to P_1. In **(b)** a shift up in the short-run aggregate supply curve changes equilibrium from E to G.

Equilibrium in the Aggregate Economy

Now that we have introduced the *SAS*, *AD*, and *LAS* curves, we'll consider short-run and long-run equilibrium and how changes in the curves affect those equilibria. I start with the short run.

In the short run, equilibrium in the economy is where the short-run aggregate supply curve and the aggregate demand curve intersect. Thus, short-run equilibrium is shown by point *E* in Figure 27-6(a). If the *AD* curve shifts to the right, from AD_0 to AD_1, equilibrium will shift from point *E* to point *F*. The price level will rise to P_1 and output will increase to Y_1. A decrease in aggregate demand will shift output and the price level down.

Figure 27-6(b) shows the effect on equilibrium of a shift up in the *SAS* curve. Initially equilibrium is at point *E*. An upward shift in the *SAS* curve from SAS_0 to SAS_1 increases the price level from P_0 to P_2 and reduces equilibrium output from Y_0 to Y_2.

Macroeconomic Equilibrium

Long-run equilibrium is determined by the intersection of the *AD* curve and the *LAS* curve.

Long-run equilibrium is determined by the intersection of the *AD* curve and the *LAS* curve, as shown by point *E* in Figure 27-7(a). Since in the long run output is determined by the position of the *LAS* curve, which is at potential output Y_p, the aggregate demand curve can determine only the price level; it does not affect the level of real output. Thus, as shown in Figure 27-7(a), when aggregate demand increases from AD_0 to AD_1, the price level rises (from P_0 to P_1) but output does not change. When aggregate demand decreases, the price level falls and output remains at potential. In the long run, output is fixed and the price level is variable, so aggregate output is determined not by aggregate demand but by potential output. Aggregate demand determines the price level.

Integrating the Short-Run and Long-Run Frameworks

To complete our analysis, we have to relate the long run and short run. We start with the economy in both long-run and short-run equilibrium. As you can see in Figure 27-7(b), at point *E*, with output Y_p, and price level P_0, the economy is in both a long-run equilibrium and a short-run equilibrium, since at point *E* the *AD* curve and *SAS* curve intersect at the economy's *LAS* curve. That is the situation economists hope for—that aggregate demand grows at just the same rate as potential output, so that growth and unemployment are at their target rates, with no, or minimal, inflation. In the late 1990s, the U.S. economy was in just such a position—potential output was increasing at the same rate that aggregate demand was increasing; unemployment was low, as was inflation.

Q-6 If the *SAS*, *AD*, and *LAS* curves intersect at the same point and wages are constant, what is likely to happen to output and the price level?

FIGURE 27-7 (A AND B) Long-Run Equilibrium

Long-run equilibrium is where the *LAS* and *AD* curves intersect. Point *E* is long-run equilibrium. In (**a**) you can see how a shift in the aggregate demand curve changes equilibrium from *E* to *H*, increasing the price level from P_0 to P_1 but leaving output unchanged. The economy is in both short-run and long-run equilibrium when all three curves intersect in the same location. In (**b**) you can see the adjustment from recessionary and inflationary gaps to long-run equilibrium.

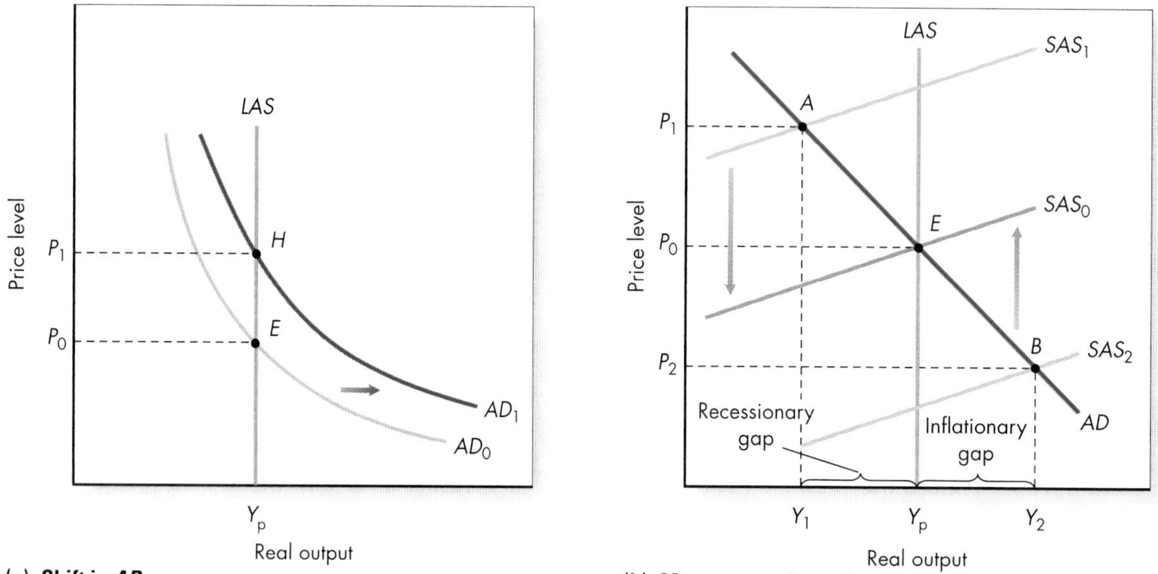

(a) Shift in *AD*

(b) Movement to Long-Run Equilibrium

The Recessionary Gap Alas, the economy is not always at that point *E*. An economy at point A in Figure 27-7(b) is in a situation where the quantity of aggregate demand is below potential output and not all the resources in the economy are being fully used. The distance $Y_p - Y_1$ shows the amount of output that is not being produced but could be. This distance is often referred to as a **recessionary gap,** *the amount by which equilibrium output is below potential output.*

Q-7 Demonstrate graphically both the short-run and long-run *AS/AD* equilibrium with a recessionary gap.

If the economy remains at this level of output for a long time, costs and wages would tend to fall because there would be an excess supply of factors of production. As costs and wages fall, the price level also falls. Assuming the standard price level effects are sufficiently strong, the short-run aggregate supply curve would shift down (from SAS_1 to SAS_0) until eventually the long-run and short-run equilibrium would be reached at point *E*. But generally in our economy that does not happen.[4] Long before that happens, either the economy picks up on its own or the government introduces policies to expand output. That's why we seldom see declines in the price level. If the government expands aggregate demand, or some other shift factor expands aggregate demand, the *AD* curve shifts to the right, eliminating the recessionary gap and keeping the price level constant.

When income exceeds potential output, there is an inflationary gap.

The Inflationary Gap An economy at point *B* in Figure 27-7(b) demonstrates a case where the short-run equilibrium is at a higher income than the economy's potential output. In this case, economists say that the economy has an **inflationary gap** shown

[4]If, as happened in the Great Depression in the 1930s and in Japan in the early 2000s, the economy stays below its potential output long enough, we would likely see the price level fall.

A REMINDER

A Review of the *AS/AD* Model

	What Shape Is It?	What Determines Its Shape?	What Shifts the Curve?
Aggregate demand	Downward-sloping: As the price level declines expenditures rise.	The interest rate effect, the international effect, the money wealth effect, and the multiplier effect.	Sudden changes in *C*, *I*, (*X*–*M*), or *G* caused by changes in foreign income, expectations about future income or prices, exchange rates, monetary policy, fiscal policy.
Short-run aggregate supply	Upward-sloping: The price level increases as output increases.	Firm behavior. Most firms change production instead of price when demand changes. Some firms will raise prices when output increases.	Increases in input prices shift the *SAS* curve up. Decreases in input prices shift the *SAS* curve down.
Long-run aggregate supply	Vertical: Changes in the price level have no effect on output.	Potential output is output that the economy can produce when labor and capital are fully utilized. It is not affected by prices.	Anything that increases potential output, such as increases in available resources and technological innovation.

by $Y_2 - Y_p$—*aggregate expenditures above potential output that exist at the current price level.* Output cannot remain at Y_2 for long because the economy's resources are being used beyond their potential. Factor prices will rise and the SAS curve will shift up from SAS_2 to SAS_0; the new equilibrium is at point *E*.

The Economy beyond Potential How can resources be used beyond their potential? By overutilizing them. Consider the resources you put into classwork. Suppose that your potential is a B+. If you stay up all night studying and cram in extra reading during mealtimes, you could earn an A. You can't keep up that effort for long. Eventually you'll get tired. The same is true for production. Extra shifts can be added and machinery can be run longer periods, but eventually the workers will become exhausted and the machinery will wear out. Output will have to return to its potential.

The result of this inflationary gap will be a bidding up of factor prices and a rise in costs for firms. When an economy is below potential, firms can hire additional factors of production without increasing production costs. Once the economy reaches its potential output, however, that is no longer possible. If a firm is to increase its factors of production, it must lure resources away from other firms. It will do so by offering higher wages and prices. But the firm facing a loss of its resources will likely respond by increasing its wages and other prices it pays to its employees and to other suppliers.

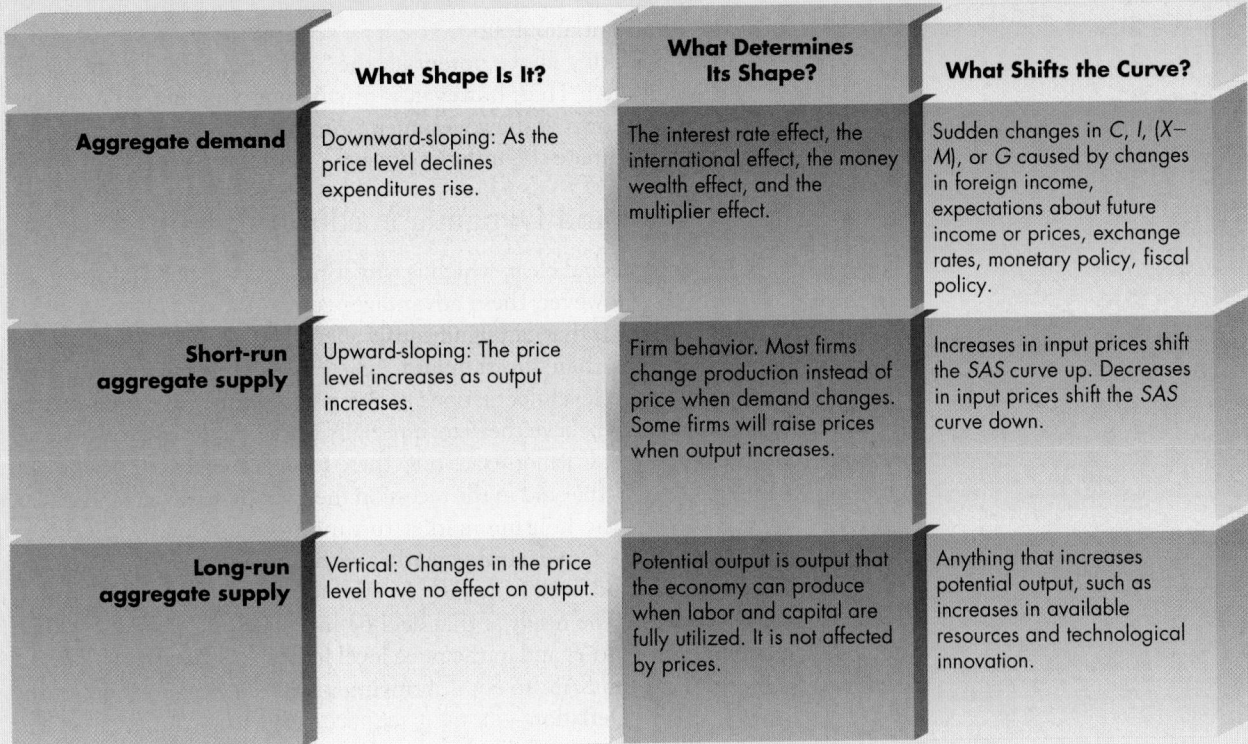

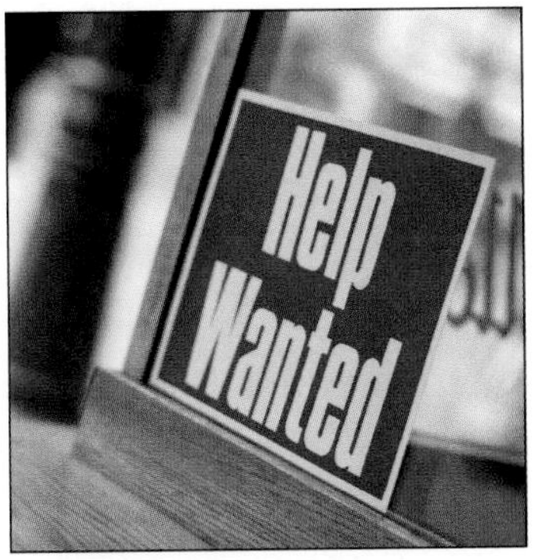

If aggregate expenditures are above potential output, then increased demand for labor would put upward pressure on wages and subsequently on the overall level of prices.

As firms compete for resources, their costs rise beyond increases in productivity, shifting up the *SAS* curve. This means that once an economy's potential output is reached, the price level tends to rise. In fact, economists sometimes look to see whether the price level has begun to rise before deciding where potential output is. Thus, in the late 1990s, economists kept increasing their estimates of potential output because the price level did not rise even as the economy approached, and exceeded, what they previously thought was its potential output.

If the economy is operating above potential, the *SAS* curve will shift up until the inflationary gap is eliminated. That, however, is usually not what happens. Either the economy slows down on its own or the government introduces aggregate demand policy to contract output and eliminate the inflationary gap.

The *AS/AD* Model and Dynamic Feedback Effects

The *AS/AD* model is simple and clear, which is why it has become the workhorse model of macro policy makers. However, these advantages come at a cost of assuming away many possible feedback effects that can significantly affect the macroeconomy and lead to quite different conclusions than the standard *AS/AD* model gives. Specifically, the *AS/AD* model presents price level fluctuations as being significantly more self-correcting than many macroeconomists believe they are, especially in response to decreases in aggregate demand. In Figure 27-8, I demonstrate how these feedback effects can cause serious problems for the economy, as they did in the recession the U.S. economy fell into in 2008.

The crisis began with the housing market turning from a booming market with housing prices rising quickly to a declining market with housing prices falling. This led to a fall in aggregate demand back from AD_0 to AD_1. Looking at the model in Figure 27-8, one would think that the result of that decline in aggregate demand would be an initial fall in output from Y_0 to Y_1 and in the price level from P_0 to P_1 (arrow *A*). The *SAS* curve would shift down from SAS_0 to SAS_1, bringing prices down to P_2 and the output level back to Y_0 (arrow *B*). **Deflation**—*the fall in the price level*—would move the economy along the aggregate demand curve and help bring the economy back to potential output. So the recession would be eliminated by deflation.

Unfortunately, a falling price level has other dynamic feedback effects on aggregate demand. For example, the pressures for falling prices might create expectations that aggregate output will fall further, which will lead people to cut back on spending and firms to cut back on production, shifting the *AD* curve back to AD_2 (arrow C) in Figure 27-8. Aggregate demand may shift back by more than the falling price level increased the

FIGURE 27-8
Feedback Effects and the *AS/AD* Model

The feedback effects of a declining price level on aggregate demand mean that as the *SAS* curve shifts down to return the economy to equilibrium, the aggregate demand curve shifts back to the left, leading the economy away from equilibrium.

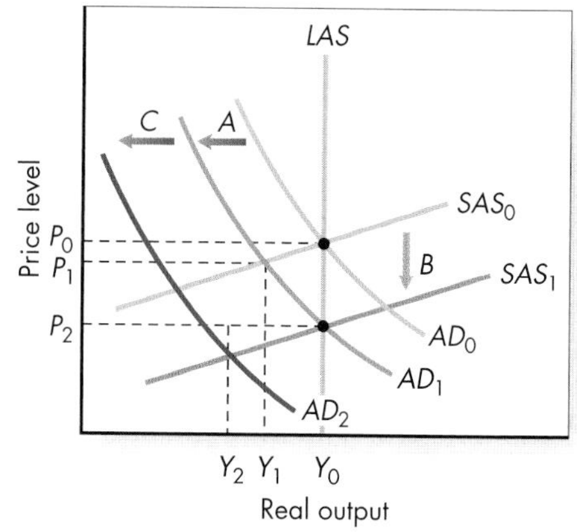

quantity of aggregate demand. The entire process may become a self-fulfilling vicious circle in which both prices and output continue to fall. (This was exactly the situation that the economy experienced in the 1930s when it fell into the Great Depression, and is the reason many macroeconomic policy makers were extremely worried in late 2008.)

Aggregate Demand Policy

A primary reason for government policy makers' interest in the *AS/AD* model is their ability to shift the *AD* curve with policy. As I mentioned above, they can do this with monetary or fiscal policy. Monetary policy involves the Federal Reserve Bank changing the money supply and interest rates. (Understanding the process requires a knowledge of the financial sector, which will be discussed at length in later chapters.) In this chapter I'll concentrate on **fiscal policy**—*the deliberate change in either government spending or taxes to stimulate or slow down the economy.* Fiscal policy is often discussed in terms of the government budget deficit (government expenditures less government revenue). If aggregate income is too low (actual income is below potential income), the appropriate fiscal policy is expansionary fiscal policy: increase the deficit by decreasing taxes or increasing government spending. Expansionary fiscal policy shifts the *AD* curve out to the right. If aggregate income is too high (actual income is above potential income), the appropriate fiscal policy is contractionary fiscal policy: decrease the deficit by increasing taxes or decreasing government spending. Contractionary fiscal policy shifts the *AD* curve to the left.

Fiscal policy is the deliberate change in either government spending or taxes to stimulate or slow down the economy.

Web Note 27.3
Fiscal Policy

Let's go through a couple of examples. Say the economy is in a recessionary gap at point *A* in Figure 27-9(a). To eliminate the recessionary gap, government needs to implement expansionary fiscal policy. The appropriate fiscal policy would be to cut taxes or increase government spending, letting the multiplier augment those effects so that the *AD* curve shifts out to AD_1. This would raise the price level slightly but would eliminate the recessionary gap. Alternatively, say the economy is in an inflationary gap at point *B* in Figure 27-9(b). To prevent the inflation caused by the upward shift of the *SAS* curve, the appropriate fiscal policy is to increase taxes or cut government spending. Either of these actions will shift the *AD* curve in to AD_2. This lowers the price level slightly and eliminates the inflationary gap. So the best way to picture fiscal policy is as a policy designed to shift the *AD* curve to keep output at potential.

Q-8 If politicians suddenly raise government expenditures, and the economy is well below potential output, what will happen to prices and real income?

Aggregate Demand Policy

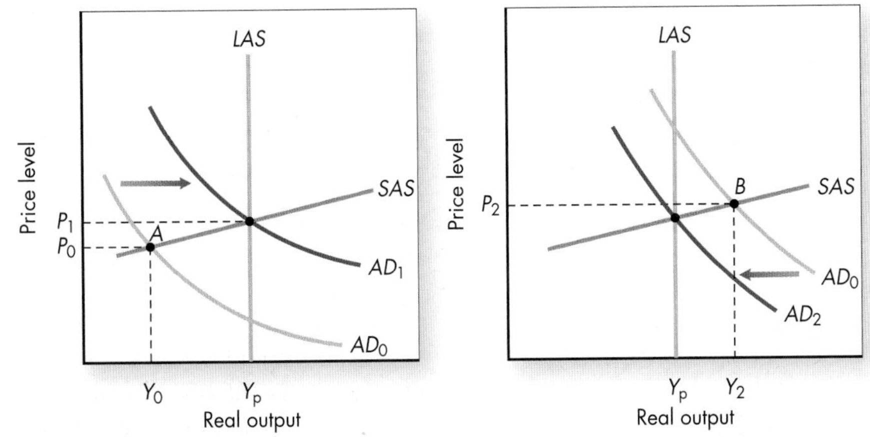

(a) Expansionary Fiscal Policy

(b) Contractionary Fiscal Policy

FIGURE 27-9 (A AND B)
Fiscal Policy

Expansionary fiscal policy can bring an economy out of a recessionary gap, as shown in **(a)**. If an economy is in an inflationary gap, contractionary fiscal policy can reduce real output to prevent inflation, as shown in **(b)**.

Some Additional Policy Examples

Now that we've been through the model, let's give you some practice with it by making you an adviser to the president. He comes to you for some advice. Unemployment is 12 percent and there is no inflation. History suggests that the economy is well below its potential output, so there is no need to worry about increasing factor prices. What policy would you recommend?

Pause for answer

The answer I hope you gave was expansionary fiscal policy, shifting the *AD* curve out to its potential income, as in Figure 27-10(a).

Now let's try a different scenario. Unemployment is 5 percent and it is believed that that 5 percent is the *target rate of unemployment*—the rate of unemployment that is consistent with potential output. But measures of consumer optimism suggest that a large rise in consumer expenditures is likely. What policy would you recommend?

Pause for answer

The answer I hope you gave is contractionary fiscal policy to counteract the expected rise in the *AD* curve before it occurs and prevent the economy from creating an inflationary gap. What would happen without that fiscal policy is shown in Figure 27-10(b). The economy is initially at point C, where the price level is P_0 and output is Y_p. In the absence of offsetting policy, the increase in expenditures along with the multiplier would move the economy to point *D* at a level of output (Y_1) above potential, creating an inflationary gap. If left alone, factor prices will rise, shifting the *SAS* curve up until it reaches SAS_1. The price level would rise to P_1 and the real output would return to Y_p, point *E*. But, of course, that didn't happen because you recommended a policy of cutting government spending or raising taxes so that the *AD* curve shifts back to AD_0, making the equilibrium at point C, not point *E*, and avoiding any rise in prices. The economy remains at potential output at a constant price level, P_0.

To give you an idea of how fiscal policy has worked in the real world, we'll look at two examples: the effect of wartime spending in the 1940s and the prolonged expansion of the mid-1990s to early 2000s.

Fiscal Policy in World War II In the 1940s the focus of U.S. policy switched from the Depression to fighting World War II. Fighting a war requires transferring civilian production to war production, so economists' attention turned to how to do so.

FIGURE 27-10 (A AND B)
Shifting *AD* and *SAS* Curves

In (**a**) you can see what happens when the economy is below potential and aggregate demand increases just enough to bring output to its potential. In (**b**) you can see what happens when the economy begins at potential and aggregate expenditures rise. Since the economy rises to above potential, input prices begin to rise and the SAS curve shifts up.

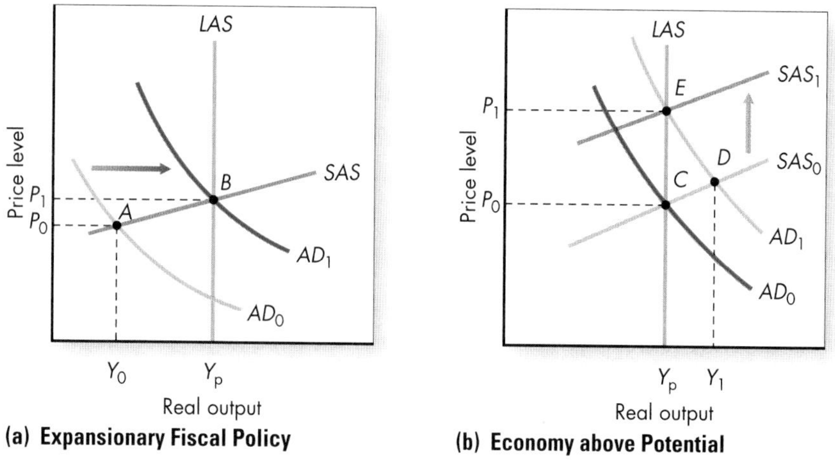

FIGURE 27-11 (A AND B) War Finance: Expansionary Fiscal Policy

During wars, government budget deficits have risen significantly. As they have, unemployment has fallen and GDP has risen enormously. You can see the effect in the table in (a), which presents the U.S. government budget deficit and unemployment rate during World War II. The graph in (b) shows that this is what would be predicted in the AS/AD model.

Source: *Historical Statistics of the United States: Colonial Times to 1970*.

Year	GDP (billions of 1958 dollars)	Deficit (billions of dollars)	Unemployment rate
1937	$ 90	$ −2.8	14.3%
1938	84	−1.0	19.0
1939	90	−2.9	17.2
1940	99	−2.7	14.6
1941	124	−4.8	9.9
1942	157	−19.4	4.7
1943	191	−53.8	1.9
1944	210	−46.1	1.2
1945	211	−45.0	1.9
1946	208	−18.2	3.9

(a) U.S. GDP, Budget Deficits, and Unemployment Rates

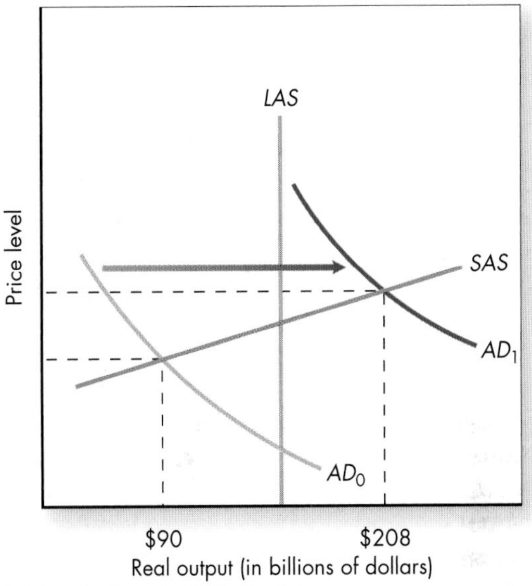

(b) Prediction of *AS/AD* Model

Taxes went up enormously, but government expenditures rose far more. The result can be seen in Figure 27-11(a), which tabulates GDP, the deficit (government expenditures less taxes), and unemployment data for the wartime time span 1937–1946. As you can see, the deficit increased greatly and real GDP rose by more than the increase in the deficit. Figure 27-11(b) shows the effect in the *AS/AD* model. The *AD* curve shifts to the right by more than the increase in the deficit. As predicted, the U.S. economy expanded enormously in response to the expansionary fiscal policy that accompanied the war. One thing should bother you about this episode: If the economy exceeded its potential output, shouldn't the short-run aggregate supply curve have started to shift up, causing a serious inflation problem? It didn't because the wartime expansion was accompanied by wage and price controls, which prevented significant price-level increases, and by rationing.

During the war, economic output expanded as far as anyone dared hope it could. This expansion was also accompanied by an expansionary monetary policy, so we must be careful about drawing too strong an inference about the effect of fiscal policy from the episode. (The importance of monetary policy will be discussed in a later chapter.)

WWW Web Note 27.4 War Bonds

It might seem from the example of World War II, when the U.S. economy expanded sharply, that wars are good for the economy. They certainly do bring about expansionary policy, increase GDP, and decrease unemployment. But remember, GDP is *not* welfare and a decrease in unemployment is not necessarily good. In World War II people went without many goods; production of guns and bombs increased, but production of butter decreased. Many people were killed or permanently disabled, which decreases unemployment but can hardly be called a good way to expand the economy.

U.S. Economic Expansion As a second example, let's consider the government budget picture in the early 2000s. In the late 1990s and early 2000s, the budget went from a large deficit to a large surplus, so it would seem as if government fiscal policy was slowing the economy down. But the economy was booming. There are two explanations for this seeming paradox. The first is that, yes, the surplus was slowing the economy, but the contractionary effect of the surplus was offset by significant increases in consumer and investment spending. The private saving rate actually fell to zero at times and consumption increased enormously. Had the government budget not been in surplus, the economy would have likely exceeded potential output and inflation would have accelerated.

The second explanation for the paradox is that much of the surplus was the result of the booming economy, not contractionary fiscal policy. In fact, much of the deficit reduction, and movement into budget surplus, resulted from unexpected increases in government revenue. When an economy is booming, as income rises, tax revenues rise and expenditures on income-support programs decline automatically. Much of the unexpected decline in the deficit was a result of tax revenue surprises.

Despite pressures in 2000 and 2001 by most economists to maintain the budget surplus (when tax revenues exceed expenditures), political pressures led to decreasing it, both by increasing government spending and by decreasing taxes. Then in mid-2001, the economy started to slow down. That slowdown was exacerbated by the terrorist attacks of September 11, following which investment and consumption fell, throwing the economy into a recession. Because of the recession, government had far less reason to run a surplus to slow the economy. In fact, the tax cut came at just the right time, keeping the recession very mild by helping hold up consumer spending. So here we have a case of expansionary fiscal policy working to prevent a recession. However, it is important to remember that the tax cuts were not proposed for their expansionary fiscal policy effects. Sometimes dumb luck is an important part of good economic policy.

Why Macro Policy Is More Complicated Than the *AS/AD* Model Makes It Look

Policy is more complicated than the *AS/AD* model makes it seem.

The *AS/AD* model makes the analysis of the aggregate economy look easy. All you do is determine where the economy is relative to its potential output and, based on that, choose the appropriate policy to shift the *AD* curve. Alas, it's much harder than that.

First, implementing fiscal policy—changing government spending and taxes—is a slow legislative process. Government spending and taxing decisions are generally made for political, not economic, reasons. Thus, there is no guarantee that government will do what economists say is necessary. And even if it does, the changes often cannot be completed in a timely fashion.

Q-9 Why is it so important for policy makers to know what potential output is?

A second problem is that we have no way of measuring potential output, so when we increase aggregate demand, we can't determine whether or not the *SAS* curve will be shifting up. Thus, the key to applying the policy is to know the location of the *LAS* curve, which is vertical at the economy's potential output. Unfortunately, we have no way of knowing that with certainty. Fortunately, we do have ways to get a rough idea of where it is.

Web Note 27.5
Unemployed Machines

Because inflation accelerates when an economy is operating above potential, one way of estimating potential output is to estimate the rate of unemployment below which inflation has begun to accelerate in the past. This is the target rate of unemployment. We can then estimate potential output by calculating output at the target rate of unemployment and adjusting for productivity growth. Unfortunately the target rate of unemployment fluctuates and is difficult to predict.

Q-10 If politicians suddenly raise government expenditures and the economy is above potential income, what will happen to prices and real income?

A third problem was mentioned above. There are many other possible interrelationships in the economy that the model does not take into account. One is the effect of falling asset prices and a falling price level on expectations of aggregate demand.

When there are pressures for the price level to fall, there are also generally strong pressures for asset prices to fall. This fall in asset prices has three effects on aggregate demand. First, while the fall in asset prices is in part caused by falling expectations about the growth potential of the economy, the causation can also go the other way: the decrease in asset prices can decrease expectations about the growth of the economy. The expectation of lower economic growth tends to shift the *AD* curve back to the left. Second, falling asset prices decrease people's perception of the value of their wealth, which decreases aggregate demand. Third, falling asset prices potentially undermine the stability of the financial system, which can make production impossible since the financial system is essential for production. This last effect undermines aggregate production and shifts the *SAS* curve to the left. Running an economy with a financial system that has stopped working is a bit like running an automobile without oil. It can bring an economy to a sudden halt.

Because of these effects, the aggregate economy can become dynamically unstable, in which a shock to the economy can set in motion a set of changes that will not be automatically self-correcting. Instead, falling output and asset prices lead to a vicious circle in which falling output and falling prices bring about further declines. The major concern of macro policy economists in 2008 and early 2009 was that the U.S. economy had fallen into precisely such a vicious circle.

In summary, there are two ways to think about the effectiveness of fiscal policy: in the model and in reality. Models are great, and simple models, such as the one I've presented in this book, that you can understand intuitively are even greater. Put in the numbers and out comes the answer. Questions based on such models make great exam questions. But don't think that policies that work in a model will necessarily work in the real world.

The effectiveness of fiscal policy in reality depends on the government's ability to perceive a problem and to react appropriately to it. The essence of fiscal policy is government changing its taxes and its spending to offset any fluctuation that would occur in other autonomous expenditures, thereby keeping the economy at its potential level of income. If the model is a correct description of the economy, and if the government can act fast enough and change its taxes and spending in a *countercyclical* way, recessions can be prevented. This type of management of the economy is called **countercyclical fiscal policy**—*fiscal policy in which the government offsets any change in aggregate expenditures that would create a business cycle*. The term **fine-tuning** is used to describe such *fiscal policy designed to keep the economy always at its target or potential level of income*. With fine-tuning, the government responds to problems before they happen, and the aggregate economy runs smoothly.

A countercyclical fiscal policy designed to keep the economy always at its target or potential level of income is called fine-tuning.

As I will discuss below, today almost all economists agree the government is not capable of fine-tuning the economy. The modern debate is whether it is up to any tuning of the economy at all. The reason is that the dynamic adjustment in the economy is extraordinarily complicated and that, once you take into account reasonable expectations of future policy, the formal analytical model (called the dynamic stochastic general equilibrium model) becomes hopelessly complex. Graduate students in economics get Ph.D.s for worrying about such hopeless complexities. At the introductory level, all we require is that you (1) know this simple *AS/AD* model and (2) remember that, in the real world, it cannot be used in a mechanistic manner; it must be used with judgment.

Almost all economists agree the government is not capable of fine-tuning the economy.

Conclusion

Let's conclude the chapter with a brief summary. In the 1930s macroeconomics developed as Classical economists' interest in growth and supply-side issues shifted to Keynesian economists' interest in business cycles and demand-side issues. To capture the issues about the effect of aggregate demand on the economy, economists developed the *AS/AD* model.

The *AS/AD* model summarizes the expected effects that shifts in aggregate supply and aggregate demand have on output and the price level. In the short run, outward shifts in the *AD* curve cause real output and the price level to rise. Inward shifts cause the opposite. If the economy is beyond potential output and the *LAS* curve, the *SAS* curve will shift up, causing the price level to increase and real output to decrease, until real output falls back to potential. The equilibrium is where aggregate demand intersects the *LAS* curve. In the model, the government can, through fiscal policy, shift the *AD* curve in or out, thereby achieving the desired level of real output, as long as that desired level does not exceed potential output.

Macro policy is more an art than a science.

Unfortunately, potential output is hard to estimate, and implementing fiscal policy in a timely fashion is difficult, making macroeconomic policy more an art than a science.

Summary

- Classical economists focus on the long run and use a laissez-faire approach.
- Keynesian economists focus on short-run fluctuations and use an activist government approach.
- The *AS/AD* model consists of the aggregate demand curve, the short-run aggregate supply curve, and the long-run aggregate supply curve.
- The aggregate demand curve slopes downward because of the interest rate effect, the international effect, the money wealth effect, and the multiplier effect.
- The short-run aggregate supply (*SAS*) curve is upward-sloping because, while for the most part firms in the United States adjust production to meet demand instead of changing price, some firms will raise prices when demand increases.
- The long-run aggregate supply (*LAS*) curve is vertical at potential output.
- The *LAS* curve shifts out when available resources, capital, labor, technology, and/or growth-compatible institutions increase.
- Short-run equilibrium is where the *SAS* and *AD* curves intersect. Long-run equilibrium is where the *AD* and *LAS* curves intersect.
- Aggregate demand management policy attempts to influence the level of output in the economy by influencing aggregate demand and relying on the multiplier to expand any policy-induced change in aggregate demand.
- Fiscal policy—the change in government spending or taxes—works by providing a deliberate countershock to offset unexpected shocks to the economy.
- A falling price level can have dynamic feedback effects on aggregate demand, perhaps more than offsetting the effect of the falling price level on the quantity of aggregate demand.
- Macroeconomic policy is difficult to conduct because implementing fiscal policy is a slow process and we don't really know where potential output is.
- We must estimate potential output by looking at past levels of potential output and by looking at where the price level begins to rise.

Key Terms

aggregate demand (*AD*) curve *(625)*
aggregate demand management *(623)*
countercyclical fiscal policy *(643)*
deflation *(638)*
equilibrium income *(623)*
fine-tuning *(643)*
fiscal policy *(639)*
inflationary gap *(636)*
interest rate effect *(626)*
international effect *(626)*
long-run aggregate supply (*LAS*) curve *(633)*
money wealth effect *(626)*
multiplier effect *(627)*
paradox of thrift *(624)*
potential income *(623)*
quantity-adjusting markets *(631)*
recessionary gap *(636)*
short-run aggregate supply (*SAS*) curve *(631)*

Questions and Exercises

connect ECONOMICS

1. Distinguish between a laissez-faire economist and an activist economist. LO1
2. Classicals saw the Depression as a political problem, not an economic problem. Why? LO1
3. Why, in principle, would one expect the *AD* curve to be vertical? LO2
4. What are five factors that cause the *AD* curve to shift? LO2
5. Explain how a rise in the price level affects aggregate quantity demanded with the:
   a. Interest rate effect.
   b. International effect.
   c. Money wealth effect. LO2
6. What will likely happen to the slope or position of the *AD* curve in the following circumstances?
   a. The exchange rate changes from fixed to flexible.
   b. A fall in the price level doesn't make people feel richer.
   c. A fall in the price level creates expectations of a further-falling price level.
   d. Income is redistributed from rich people to poor people.
   e. Autonomous exports increase by 20.
   f. Government spending decreases by 10. LO2
7. What dynamic feedback effects can offset the interest rate, international, and money wealth effects? LO2
8. What are two factors that cause the *SAS* curve to shift? LO3
9. What will likely happen to the *SAS* curve in each of the following instances?
   a. Productivity rises 3 percent; wages rise 4 percent.
   b. Productivity rises 3 percent; wages rise 1 percent.
   c. Productivity declines 1 percent; wages rise 1 percent.
   d. Productivity rises 2 percent; wages rise 2 percent. LO3
10. Why is the *LAS* curve vertical? LO4
11. What will happen to the position of the *SAS* curve and/or *LAS* curve in the following circumstances?
    a. Available factors of production increase.
    b. A civil war occurs.
    c. Wages that were fixed become flexible, and aggregate demand increases. LO3, LO4
12. If an economy is in short-run equilibrium that is below potential, what forces will bring the economy to long-run equilibrium? LO5
13. Moore's law states that every 18 months, the computing speed of a microchip doubles.
    a. What effect does this likely have on the economy?
    b. Explain your answer using the *AS/AD* model. LO5
14. Congratulations! You have been appointed an economic policy adviser to the United States. You are told that the economy is significantly below its potential output and that the following will happen next year: World income will fall significantly and the price of oil will rise significantly. (The United States is an oil importer.)
    a. What will happen to the price level and output? Using the *AS/AD* model, demonstrate your predictions graphically.
    b. What policy might you suggest to the government? LO5
15. What fiscal policy actions would you recommend in the following instances?
    a. The economy begins at potential output, but foreign economies slow dramatically.
    b. The economy has been operating above potential output and inflationary pressures rise.
    c. A new technology is invented that significantly raises potential output. LO5
16. Demonstrate graphically how a falling price level can destabilize an economy. LO6
17. Why is countercyclical fiscal policy difficult to implement? LO7
18. Why is knowing the level of potential output important to designing appropriate fiscal policy? LO7
19. In the late 1990s, a growing number of economists argued that world policy makers were focusing too much on fighting inflation. The economists also argued that the technical level of potential output had risen. Show their argument using the *AS/AD* model. LO7
20. Why is macro policy more difficult than the simple model suggests? LO7

Questions from Alternative Perspectives

1. Austrian economist Murray Rothbard has argued that government intervention during 1929 made what could have been a 1-year recession set off by the stock market crash into a 12-year depression. He believed that by creating confusing signals, government intervention kept investors from gaining knowledge of what investments to avoid.
   a. Is Rothbard's explanation of the Depression consistent with the *AS/AD* model?
   b. If one agrees with Rothbard, how would one's proposed policies to deal with recessions differ from those presented in the book? (Austrian)
2. In the 1950s, Michael Hubert King, an oil geologist, mathematically determined that when 50 percent of oil reserves have been extracted, annual oil output would inexorably decline. He looked at the rate of oil discovery in the United States and predicted that domestic oil production would peak in 1969. The peak occurred in 1970! Today global oil production is nearly at maximum production capacity, and it is likely that in the very near future the inexorable decline will begin globally.
   a. Use the *AS/AD* model and the production possibility curve to describe what will happen when oil production declines.
   b. What will this do to the question of "distribution," both within and between nations? (Institutionalist)
3. Consider the following economic principles held by Classical economists: (1) Short-run problems are temporary glitches that are solved by the market; (2) The economy always returns to its potential in the long run; and (3) Unemployment is the result of institutional barriers to the market.
   a. What are Keynes's criticisms of these economic principles?
   b. Why did he believe that they were wrong? (Post-Keynesian)
4. Draw an *AS/AD* diagram from the Keynesian viewpoint. Assume the initial equilibrium in your diagram is just at the level of potential output. Then reduce the level of aggregate demand in your diagram. Now stare at this diagram.
   a. Can you identify the excess capacity or depression in the diagram and what caused it?
   b. What should be done to return the economy to a full employment level of output?
   c. What does this exercise suggest about the distinction between economic theorizing (or positive economics) and policy recommendations (normative economics)?
   d. Is one more value laden than the other? (Radical)

Issues to Ponder

1. The opening quotation of the chapter refers to Keynes's view of theory.
   a. What do you think he meant by it?
   b. How does it relate to the emphasis on the "other things constant" assumption?
   c. Do you think Keynes's interest was mainly in positive economics, the art of economics, or normative economics? Why? LO1
2. If the economy were close to high potential output, would policy makers present their policy prescriptions to increase real output any differently than if the economy were far from potential output? Why? LO5
3. If the effective demand curve slopes upward, so that a fall in the price level causes a decrease in aggregate demand, how will your recommendation for fiscal policy be affected when the economy experiences a negative demand shock? LO6

Answers to Margin Questions

1. A Classical economist takes a laissez-faire approach, and believes the economy is self-regulating. A Keynesian economist takes an interventionist approach, and believes that equilibrium output can remain below potential output. *(621)*
2. In the short run, saving can lead to a decrease in expenditures and reduce equilibrium output. In the long run, saving leads to the accumulation of capital and an increase in potential output. In the long run, saving increases equilibrium output. *(624)*
3. False. The multiplier magnifies the initial effect. The rise in expenditures will be greater than 10, making the *AD* curve flatter than a slope of −1. *(627)*
4. A rise in a country's exchange rate will make domestic goods more expensive to foreigners and foreign goods less expensive to domestic residents. It will shift the *AD* curve in to the left because net exports will fall. *(629)*
5. The *AD* curve will shift out by more than 20 because of the multiplier. *(630)*

6. If the *AD*, *SAS*, and *LAS* curves intersect at the same point, the economy is in both long-run and short-run equilibrium. Nothing will happen to the price level and output. *(635)*
7. If there is a recessionary gap, the *SAS* and *AD* curves intersect to the left of potential output at a point such as *A* in the figure below. At that level of output there will be pressure for factor prices to fall, pushing the *SAS* curve down. Unless the *AD* curve shifts out (as it usually does), the *SAS* curve will shift down and output will rise until output equals potential output and the economy is in both long-run and short-run equilibrium at a point such as *B*. *(636)*

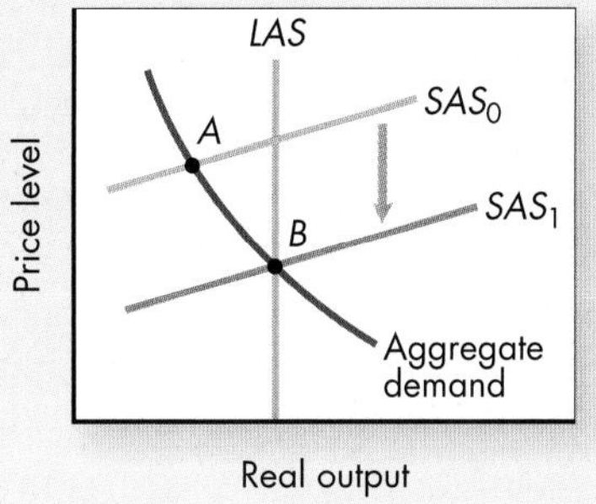

8. If the economy is well below potential, I would predict that output will rise and the price level will rise only slightly. *(639)*
9. Where the economy is relative to potential will determine whether the price level will rise (inflationary gap) or fall (recessionary gap) and determine the type of fiscal policy needed. *(642)*
10. If the economy is above potential output, I would predict that factor prices will rise, shifting the *SAS* curve up. The expansion in government expenditures will shift the *AD* curve out further, putting even more pressure on factor prices to rise. My answer, therefore, is that the price level will rise very quickly and real output will fall until it equals potential output. *(643)*

CHAPTER 28

The Multiplier Model

Keynes stirred the stale economic frog pond to its depth.

—*Gottfried Haberler*

The *AS/AD* model was not always the central model of macroeconomics. Up until the inflation of the 1970s, the **multiplier model**—*a model that emphasized the effect of fluctuations in aggregate demand, rather than the price level, on output*—was the central model. Until the 1970s, fluctuations in the price level didn't seem to bring about aggregate equilibrium.

Whereas the *AS/AD* model downplays the dynamic feedbacks that could bring about dynamic instability to the aggregate economy, the multiplier model built them into the analysis. It portrayed an aggregate economy that was what economists call locally unstable, but globally stable. In the multiplier model, output did not tend to gravitate toward a single equilibrium, but neither did it explode or implode uncontrollably so that no equilibrium developed. The economy would settle at a level of output within a reasonably close range of the initial equilibrium. In the multiplier model small shifts in aggregate demand would be amplified into larger shifts in real output; the economy would gravitate toward a new equilibrium that may be above or below its potential.

For small and moderate fluctuations in demand, the multiplier model proved to be pedagogically useful, but it was not especially useful as a practical model since it was not quantitatively precise. The model left out too many things, many of which led the economy back to potential output. Thus, for small fluctuations, most economists believe that the *AS/AD* model provides a better sense of how the macroeconomy operates in normal times when shifts in aggregate demand or supply tend to be self-correcting.

For large fluctuations in aggregate demand, however, such as occurred in the world economy in 2008, the multiplier model gives a better sense of what is happening since price level changes cannot be relied on to self-correct the aggregate economy. The multiplier model explains why economists were so worried about the economy falling into a depression in 2008, and thus it is an important model for all students to learn.

Swedish economist Axel Leijonhufvud has studied macroeconomic crises and argues that policy makers should work with two models of the aggregate economy—one for normal times and one for times of crisis. He argues that as long as the economy stays within a small corridor close to what is considered normal,

AFTER READING THIS CHAPTER, YOU SHOULD BE ABLE TO:

1. Explain the difference between induced and autonomous expenditures.
2. Show how the level of income is graphically determined in the multiplier model.
3. Use the multiplier equation to determine equilibrium income.
4. Explain how the multiplier process amplifies shifts in autonomous expenditures.
5. Demonstrate how fiscal policy can eliminate recessionary and inflationary gaps.
6. List seven reasons why the multiplier model might be misleading.

ADDED DIMENSION

Econometric Models

U.S. government agencies and virtually every major corporation in the United States subscribe to, or generate their own, forecasts of the economy. Such forecasts about interest rates, prices, investment, consumption, and government policy actions are essential to corporate decisions from whether to open a new factory to how much to pay employees. They are also essential to government decisions that impact the economy. If some day you work in government or in a firm, you will likely come across a report that forecasts the economy.

Economists forecast the future of the economy using *econometric* models, models that forecast a variety of *measures* of the economy. (The word "metric" means measure.) The models presented in this chapter are a major simplification of econometric models. Two well-known econometric models are the Fed (Federal Reserve Bank) econometric model and the DRI–WEFA model. In econometric models, economists find standard relationships among aspects of the macroeconomy and use those relationships to predict what will happen to inflation, unemployment, and growth under certain conditions. For example, when former President George W. Bush wanted to know the effect his proposed tax cut would have on the economy, he went to economists who entered the tax cut into their econometric models and estimated the effect. He went back to them when he wanted to know how the Iraq War spending would affect the economy. Using their econometric models, they estimated the effect.

While econometric models are much more complicated than the models presented in this text, they have the same structure: a short-run aggregate supply component with essentially fixed prices, an aggregate demand component, and a potential output component.

equilibrating forces dominate, and thus the standard *AS/AD* model can be used. But when demand or output fluctuates greatly and the economy is outside the normal corridor, the standard *AS/AD* model no longer incorporates the dynamics of the economy accurately. In such cases, some variant of the multiplier model becomes a better model. In this chapter I present that multiplier model.

We'll start our discussion of the multiplier model by looking separately at production decisions and expenditure decisions.

Aggregate Production

Aggregate production (AP) is *the total amount of final goods and services produced in every industry in an economy*. It is at the center of the multiplier model. As I noted in the chapter on measuring the aggregate economy, production creates an equal amount of income, so actual income and actual production are always equal; the terms can be used interchangeably.

Graphically, aggregate production in the multiplier model is represented by a 45° line on a graph, with real income measured in dollars on the horizontal axis and real production measured in dollars on the vertical axis, as in Figure 28-1. Given the definition of the axes, connecting all the points at which real production equals real income produces a 45° line through the origin. Since, by definition, production creates an amount of income equal to the amount of production or output, this 45° line can be thought of as an *aggregate production curve*, or, alternatively, the *aggregate income curve*. At all points on the aggregate production curve, income equals production. For example, consider point A in Figure 28-1, where real income (measured on the horizontal axis) is $4,000 and real production (measured on the vertical axis) is also $4,000. That identity between real

Graphically, aggregate production in the multiplier model is represented by a 45° line through the origin.

Q-1 What is true about the relationship between income and production on the aggregate production curve?

FIGURE 28-1
The Aggregate Production Curve

Since, by definition, real output equals real income, on each point of the aggregate production curve, income must equal production. This equality holds true only on the 45° line.

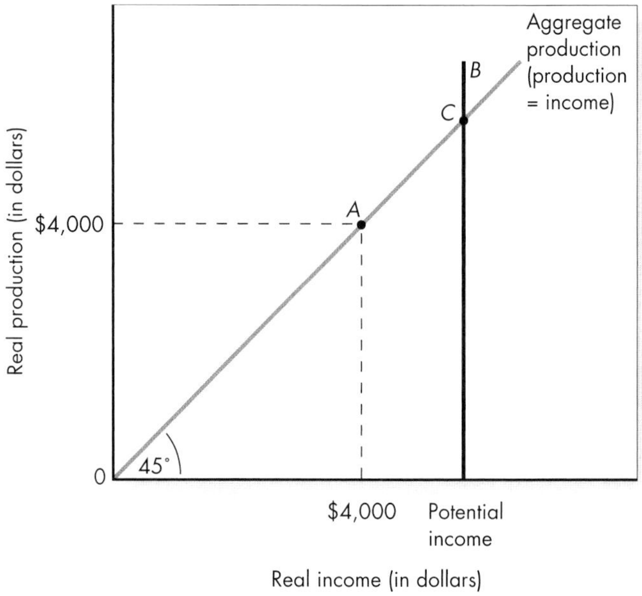

production and real income is true only on the 45° line. Output and income, however, cannot expand without limit. The model is most relevant when output is below its potential. Once production expands to the capacity constraint of the existing institutional structure—to potential income (line *B*)—any increase beyond that can only be temporary.

Aggregate Expenditures

Aggregate expenditures in an economy (*AE*) equal $C + I + G + (X - M)$.

The term **aggregate expenditures** refers to *the total amount of spending on final goods and services in the economy*. This amount consists of four main expenditure classifications: consumption (spending by consumers), investment (spending by business), spending by government, and net exports (the difference between U.S. exports and U.S. imports). These four components were presented in our earlier discussion of aggregate accounting, which isn't surprising since the aggregate accounts were designed around the multiplier model. In the multiplier model, we focus on the four components' relationship to income. The multiplier model asks the question "How does each of these change as income changes?" To keep the exposition as simple but as general as possible, we focus in this chapter on the aggregate relationship between all expenditure components combined and income, that is, on the relationship between aggregate expenditures and income. (In Appendix A at the end of this chapter, we present a disaggregated discussion.)

Autonomous and Induced Expenditures

Autonomous expenditures are expenditures that do not systematically vary with income.

For purposes of the multiplier model, all forms of expenditures are classified as either autonomous or induced. **Autonomous expenditures** are *expenditures that do not systematically vary with income*. **Induced expenditures** are *expenditures that change as income changes*. Say that each time income rises by 100, expenditures increase by 60. The induced expenditures would be 60.

This assumed empirical relationship between income and aggregate expenditures can be represented graphically with the aggregate expenditure (*AE*) curve. To keep

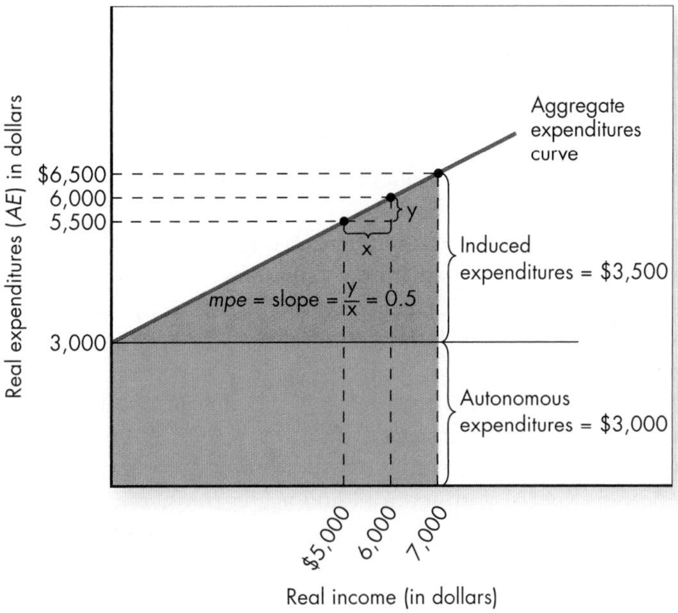

FIGURE 28-2 Aggregate Expenditures Curve

The *AE* curve depicted here has a slope of .5, the *mpe*, and an intercept of $3,000, the level of autonomous expenditures. The brown shaded area represents induced expenditures. Aggregate expenditures are the sum of these two components.

the analysis simple, the *AE* curve is usually estimated to be a linear relationship (a straight line) for incomes near current income. To make the graphical exposition easier, we will also assume that the linear relationship continues for all levels of income. This allows us to draw a linear aggregate expenditures curve such as the one shown in Figure 28-2.

Autonomous vs. Induced Expenditures

Notice that when income is $6,000, aggregate expenditures are also $6,000; but when income rises by $1,000 to $7,000, aggregate expenditures rise by $500 to $6,500. The reason is that only induced expenditures change as income changes. When income falls to $5,000, expenditures fall to $5,500. Along this *AE* curve, induced expenditures fall by $500 when income falls by $1,000.

To figure out autonomous expenditures, we have to extend the *AE* curve to the left, to the point where income is zero (where the *AE* curve intersects the vertical axis). Doing so, you can see that when income is zero, aggregate expenditures are $3,000. So, autonomous expenditures are $3,000. Consumption, investment, government spending, and net exports each has an autonomous component. Autonomous expenditures are the sum of all of them. It is the level of expenditures that would exist at zero income, assuming the *AE* curve is linear. (Again, it is important to recognize that this linear extension is just for expositional purposes. In reality, income is not expected to fall to zero, and the model is used to describe changes around the existing level of income.) The point to remember about autonomous expenditures is that they remain constant at all levels of income; therefore, a graph of autonomous expenditures is a straight, horizontal line as shown in Figure 28-2.

Autonomous expenditures are unrelated to income; induced expenditures are directly related to income.

To summarize, aggregate expenditures are comprised of two components: autonomous expenditures that do not vary with income and induced expenditures that vary with income. The gray shaded region in Figure 28-2 represents autonomous expendi tures; the brown shaded region represents induced expenditures. So, at income $7,000, aggregate expenditures of $6,500 are comprised of $3,000 of autonomous expenditures and $3,500 of induced expenditures.

Q-2 What is the difference between induced expenditures and autonomous expenditures?

$$mpe = \frac{\text{Change in expenditures}}{\text{Change in income}}$$

Q-3 If expenditures change by \$60 when income changes by \$100, what is the *mpe*?

The Marginal Propensity to Expend The slope of an aggregate expenditures curve is equal to the **marginal propensity to expend (*mpe*)**—*the ratio of the change in aggregate expenditures to a change in income*. (Remember, slope is the change in the value on the vertical axis divided by the change in the value on the horizontal axis, or rise over run.) The expenditures function I have drawn has a slope of .5, which means that for every \$1,000 increase in income, aggregate expenditures rise by \$500. If the *mpe* were .4, the slope of the *AE* curve would be .4 and aggregate expenditures would rise by \$400 for every \$1,000 increase in income.

The marginal propensity to expend is assumed to be greater than 0 and less than 1. Therefore, the aggregate expenditures curve will have a slope that is less than the 45-degree *AP* curve and greater than a horizontal line (such as autonomous expenditures). Economists estimate the slope of the *AE* curve by looking at how much aggregate expenditures have changed with a change in income around past income and then use that information to estimate the relationship for current levels of income.

The marginal propensity to expend is an aggregation of the various relationships between each component of aggregate expenditures (consumption, investment, government spending, exports, and imports) and aggregate income. There is a marginal propensity to consume, a marginal propensity to import, and, in more complicated models, a variety of other marginal propensities. (Appendix A at the end of the chapter provides a disaggregated presentation of these components.) But it is the aggregate of these—the *mpe*—that is the key to the multiplier model.

The marginal propensity to consume (*mpc*) is the most important component of the *mpe*.

While the presentation will focus on the aggregate *mpe*, let me briefly discuss its components. The most important determinant of the marginal propensity to expend is the marginal propensity to consume (*mpc*)—the change in consumption that occurs with a change in income.[1] It is less than 1 because individuals tend to save a portion of their income, so when income goes up by 100 their spending will go up by, say, only 80. In that case the marginal propensity to consume would be .8. If induced consumption were the only component, the marginal propensity to expend would be .8.

While the marginal propensity to consume is important to expenditures, other important, policy-relevant factors also affect how expenditures change with income. One of these factors is the income tax. As income rises, people pay higher income tax, which lowers how much additional income people have at their disposal to spend, which lowers the increase in their expenditures. Thinking back to the national income classifications, disposable income is less than GDP. So taxes reduce the size of the marginal propensity to expend from what it would have been if all income were available to households to spend. In the United States, taxes that vary with income are approximately 20 percent of total income. Another important determinant of the marginal propensity to expend is the marginal propensity to import—the change in imports that occurs with a change in income. With increasing globalization, individuals are spending a larger portion of their income on imports. That portion is not part of aggregate expenditures on domestic goods. Instead, it is part of the aggregate expenditures of other countries, so the fact that imports increase as income increases also reduces the size of the marginal propensity to expend. Americans spend about 15 percent of increases of their income on imports. In some countries, such as the Netherlands, that fraction can be as high as 50 or 60 percent.

---

[1]The importance of this component has led some to concentrate the multiplier model presented in principles books on consumption and the marginal propensity to consume. However, to keep the analysis simple, this focus generally requires them to assume that the other components do not vary with income. I focus on a broader concept—marginal propensity to expend—because it is more inclusive, requires less algebraic manipulation, and incorporates two other primary reasons why income may not get translated into expenditures. This allows us to talk more about policy and less about the model.

ADDED DIMENSION

History of the Multiplier Model

Policy fights in economics occur on many levels. Keynes fought on most of them. But it wasn't Keynes who convinced U.S. policy makers to accept his ideas. (Indeed, President Franklin D. Roosevelt met Keynes only once and thought he was a pompous academic.) Instead, it was Alvin Hansen, a textbook writer and policy adviser to government who was hired away from the University of Wisconsin by Harvard in the mid-1930s, who played the key role in getting Keynesian economic policies introduced into the United States.

The story of how Hansen converted to Keynes's ideas is somewhat mysterious. At the time, almost all economists were Classicals, and Hansen was no exception. (Otherwise it's doubtful Harvard would have recruited him.) But, somehow, on the train trip from Wisconsin to Massachusetts, Hansen metamorphosed from a Classical to a Keynesian. His graduate seminar at Harvard in the late 1930s and the 1940s became the U.S. breeding ground for Keynesian economics.

What made Hansen and other economists switch from Classical to Keynesian economics? It was the Depression; the Keynesian story explained it much better than did the Classical story, which centered on the real wage being too high.

Hansen quickly realized that talking about interdependencies of supply and demand decisions didn't work for policy makers and businesspeople. They wanted numbers—specifics—and Keynes's work had no specifics. So Alvin Hansen and his students, especially Paul Samuelson, set about to develop specifics. They developed the multiplier model of Keynesian economics.

The Aggregate Expenditures Function The relationship between aggregate expenditures and income that is depicted by the *AE* curve can be written mathematically as follows:

$$AE = \underbrace{AE_0}_{\text{autonomous}} + \underbrace{mpeY}_{\text{induced}}$$

It consists of the same two components that make up the *AE* curve: autonomous expenditures (the AE_0—the subscript zero tells you it is autonomous) and induced expenditures (the *mpeY*). The aggregate expenditures function depicted by the *AE* curve we've discussed so far and shown in Figure 28-2 is $AE = \$3{,}000 + .5Y$. Autonomous expenditures are \$3,000 and the *mpe* is .5. Just like the *AE* curve, the aggregate expenditures function takes into account all components of aggregate spending. Therefore, autonomous expenditures are the sum of the autonomous components of expenditures $[AE_0 = C_0 + I_0 + G_0 + (X_0 - M_0)]$ and induced expenditures are the sum of the induced components of expenditures. These induced expenditures are determined by the marginal propensity to consume, the marginal propensity to import, and taxes that vary with income.

$AE_0 = C_0 + I_0 + G_0 + (X_0 - M_0)$

In Figure 28-3, I graph three expenditures functions. A good exercise is to determine which of the *AE* curves (*a*, *b*, or *c*) is associated with which expenditures function described by the following situations:

- *Situation 1*. Autonomous consumption is 100; autonomous investment is 40; autonomous net exports are 30; autonomous spending by government is 20; and the marginal propensity to expend is .6.
- *Situation 2*. Autonomous consumption is 100; autonomous investment is 40; autonomous net exports are 30; autonomous spending by government is 30; and the marginal propensity to expend is .5.
- *Situation 3*. Autonomous expenditures are 140 and the marginal propensity to expend is .6.

The answers are 1-*b*, 2-*c*, and 3-*a*. There are a number of ways you could have associated each of these situations with the graphs. Since the marginal propensity to

FIGURE 28-3 (A, B, AND C) **Three Aggregate Expenditures Functions**

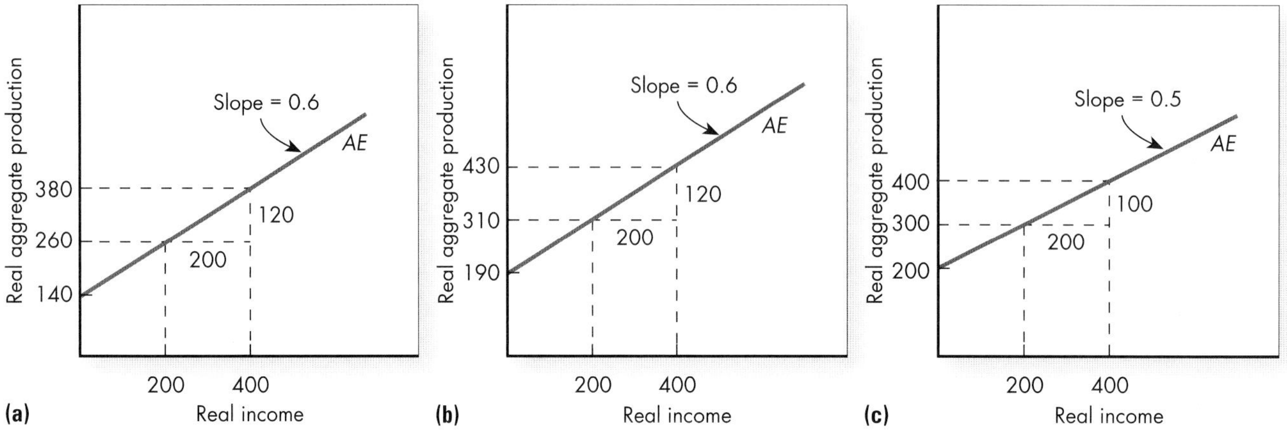

expend in Situation 2 was .5, its slope had to be .5. Thus, only graph *c* is consistent with it. Situations 1 and 3 have the same marginal propensity to expend, so we have to differentiate them by their autonomous expenditures component. Adding up autonomous expenditures in Situation 1 gives us 190, so the intercept (the level of expenditures at zero income) must be 190. That is the case for *b*. Checking, graph *a* has an intercept of 140, and a slope of .6, which means that it is consistent with Situation 3.

The aggregate expenditures function is important because once you have estimated an expenditures function for the economy, you can predict expenditures at any income. Say you have estimated an aggregate expenditures function to be $AE = 240 + .4Y$. If income is $500, you would estimate aggregate expenditures to be $440, that is, [240 + .4(500)]. Estimating aggregate expenditures is fundamental to predicting whether the economy will grow or fall into a recession.

Autonomous Shifts in the Expenditures Function A key element of the expenditures function for our purposes concerns changes in autonomous expenditures. These changes are usually classified by which of the four subcomponents of autonomous expenditures changed—autonomous consumption, autonomous investment, autonomous government spending, or autonomous net exports. All of these can change suddenly, and, when one or more do, the *AE* curve shifts up or down. For example, if autonomous consumption rises by $200, and autonomous investment falls by $80, autonomous expenditures will rise by $120 ($200 − $80).

Economists keep close tabs on these autonomous components as they develop their forecasts of the economy. For example, imagine that consumer confidence suddenly decreases, perhaps because of a terrorist threat. Consumers figure they had better save more to prepare themselves for the upcoming recession, so they cut back expenditures; autonomous consumption falls and the expenditures function shifts down. Alternatively, imagine that businesses come to believe that the economy will grow faster than they had expected. To prepare, they will increase investment, increasing autonomous investment and shifting the aggregate expenditures curve up.

Web Note 28.1
Keynes on Investment

I'll let you work these final two examples by yourself. The first is that the government enters into a major war, and the second is that the country's exchange rate suddenly falls, causing the price of the country's exports to fall and the price of imports to rise. If you answered that they both shift the expenditures function up, you've got the reasoning down.

The reason it is important to focus on shifts is that the multiplier model is a historical model. It can be used to analyze shifts in aggregate expenditures from a historically given income level, but not to determine income independent of the economy's historical position. Notice how I discussed the model in the examples—some shift in autonomous expenditures occurred and that shift led to a change in income from its existing level.

The multiplier model is a historical model most useful for analyzing shifts in autonomous expenditures.

As I mentioned above, while economists speak of what expenditures would be at zero income, or while we say the *mpe* is constant over all ranges of income, that is done simply to make the geometric portrayal of the model easier. What is actually assumed is that within the relevant range around existing income—say a 5 percent increase or decrease—the *mpe* remains constant, and the autonomous portion of the expenditures is the intercept that would occur if we extended the expenditures function.

Determining the Equilibrium Level of Aggregate Income

Now that we've developed the graphical framework for the multiplier model, we can put the aggregate production and aggregate expenditures together and see how the level of aggregate income is determined. We begin by considering the relationship between the aggregate expenditures curve and the aggregate production curve more carefully. We do so in Figure 28-4.

The aggregate production (*AP*) curve is a 45° line up until the economy reaches potential income. Its slope is 1, so at all points on the *AP* curve, aggregate expenditures equal aggregate income. It tells you the level of aggregate production and also the level of aggregate income since, by definition, real income equals real production when the price level does not change. Expenditures are shown by the *AE* curve. Planned expenditures (expenditures as calculated using the expenditures function) do not necessarily equal production or income. In equilibrium, however, planned expenditures must equal production.

To determine income graphically in the multiplier model, you find the income level at which aggregate expenditures equal planned aggregate production.

To see why that's the case, let's first say that production, and hence income, is \$14,000. As you can see, at income of \$14,000, planned expenditures are \$12,000. Aggregate production exceeds planned aggregate expenditures. Firms are producing more

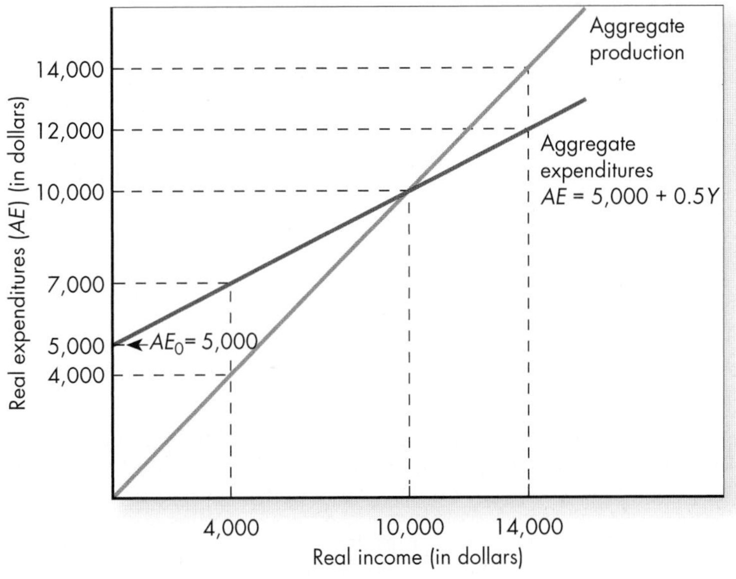

FIGURE 28-4 **Comparing *AE* to *AP* and Solving for Equilibrium Graphically**

Equilibrium in the multiplier model is determined where the *AE* and *AP* curves intersect. That equilibrium is at \$10,000. At income levels higher or lower than that, planned production will not equal planned expenditures.

Real Income	Planned Expenditures	Aggregate Production	Inventories
\$ 0	\$ 5,000	\$ 0	−\$5,000
4,000	7,000	4,000	−3,000
10,000	**10,000**	**10,000**	**0**
14,000	12,000	14,000	+2,000

goods than are bought, and inventories are rising by more than firms want. This is true for any income level above \$10,000. Similarly, at all income levels below \$10,000, aggregate production is less than planned aggregate expenditures and inventories are falling below levels desired by firms. For example, at a production level of \$4,000, planned aggregate expenditures are \$7,000. Inventories are falling by \$3,000.

The Keynesian Model

The only income level at which aggregate production equals planned aggregate expenditures is \$10,000. Since we know that, in equilibrium, planned aggregate expenditures must equal planned aggregate production, \$10,000 is the equilibrium level of income in the economy. It is the level of income at which neither producers nor consumers have any reason to change what they are doing. At any other level of income, since there is either a shortage or a surplus of goods, firms' inventory is greater than or less than desired, and they will have an incentive to change production. Thus, you can use the aggregate production curve and the aggregate expenditures curve to determine the level of income at which the economy will be in equilibrium.

The Multiplier Equation

The multiplier equation is an equation showing the relationship between autonomous expenditures and the equilibrium level of income: Y = Multiplier × Autonomous expenditures.

The expenditures multiplier is a number that tells us how much income will change in response to a change in autonomous expenditures: $[1/(1 - mpe)]$.

Another useful way to determine the level of income in the multiplier model is through the **multiplier equation,** *an equation that tells us that income equals the multiplier times autonomous expenditures.*[2]

$$Y = \text{Multiplier} \times \text{Autonomous expenditures}$$

The **expenditures multiplier** is *a number that tells us how much income will change in response to a change in autonomous expenditures.* To calculate the expenditures multiplier, you divide 1 by $(1 - mpe)$. Thus:

$$\text{Multiplier} = \frac{1}{(1 - mpe)}$$

Once you know the value of the marginal propensity to expend, you can calculate the expenditures multiplier by reducing $[1/(1 - mpe)]$ to a simple number. For example, if $mpe = .8$, the multiplier is

$$\frac{1}{(1 - .8)} = \frac{1}{.2} = 5$$

To determine equilibrium income using the multiplier equation, you determine the expenditures multiplier and multiply it by the level of autonomous expenditures.

Since the expenditures multiplier tells you the relationship between autonomous expenditures and income, once you know the multiplier and the level of autonomous expenditures, calculating the equilibrium level of income is easy. All you do is multiply autonomous expenditures by the multiplier. For example, using the autonomous expenditures of \$5,000 and a multiplier of 2, from Figure 28-4, we can calculate equilibrium income in the economy to be \$10,000. This is the same equilibrium income we got from the graphical exercise.

mpe and the Multiplier

Let's see how the equation works by considering another example. Say the *mpe* is .4. Subtracting .4 from 1 gives .6. Dividing 1 by .6 gives approximately 1.7. Say, also, that autonomous expenditures (AE_0) are \$750. The multiplier equation tells us to calculate income, multiply autonomous expenditures, \$750, by 1.7. Doing so gives $1.7 \times \$750 = \$1,275$.

The multiplier equation gives you a simple way to determine equilibrium income in the multiplier model. Five different marginal propensities to expend and the

[2]The multiplier equation does not come out of thin air. It comes from combining the set of equations underlying the graphical presentation of the multiplier model into the two brackets. The multiplier equation is derived in the box "Solving for Equilibrium Income Algebraically" on page 659.

multiplier associated with each (I round off to the nearest 10th) are shown in the table below.

mpe	Multiplier = 1/(1 − *mpe*)
.3	1.4
.4	1.7
.5	2
.75	4
.8	5

Q-4 If the *mpe* = .5, what is the expenditures multiplier?

Notice as *mpe* increases, the multiplier increases. The reason is that as the *mpe* gets larger, the induced effects of any initial shift in income also get larger. Knowing the multiplier associated with each marginal propensity to expend gives you an easy way to determine equilibrium income in the economy.

Let's look at one more example of the multiplier. Say that the *mpe* is .4 and that autonomous expenditures rise by $250 so they are $1,000 instead of $750. What is the level of equilibrium income? Multiplying autonomous expenditures, $1,000, by 1.7 tells us that equilibrium income is $1,700. With a multiplier of 1.7, income rises by $425 (250 × 1.7) as a result of the $250 increase in autonomous expenditures.

Q-5 If autonomous expenditures are $2,000 and the *mpe* = .4, what is the level of equilibrium income in the economy?

The Multiplier Process

Web Note 28.2
How Large a Multiplier?

Let's now look more carefully at the forces that are pushing the economy toward equilibrium. What happens when the macroeconomy is in disequilibrium—when the amount being injected into the economy does not equal the amount leaking from the economy? Put another way, what happens when aggregate production does not equal aggregate expenditures? Figure 28-5 shows us.

Let's first consider the economy at income level A, where aggregate production equals $7,000 and planned aggregate expenditures equal $5,500. Since production

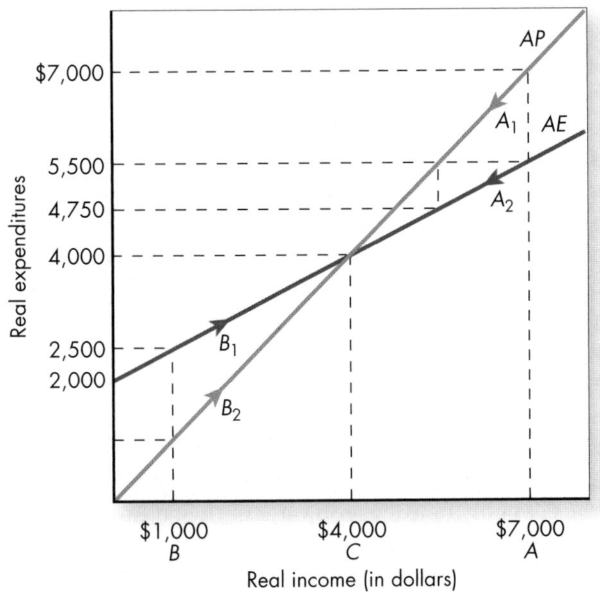

FIGURE 28-5
The Multiplier Process

At income levels A and B, the economy is in disequilibrium. Depending on which direction the disequilibrium goes, it generates increases or decreases in planned production and expenditures until the economy reaches income level C, where planned aggregate expenditures equal aggregate production.

exceeds planned expenditures by \$1,500 at income level A, firms can't sell all they produce; inventories pile up. In response, firms make an adjustment. They decrease aggregate production and hence income. As businesses slow production, the economy moves inward along the aggregate production curve, as shown by arrow A_1. As income falls, people's expenditures fall, and the gap between aggregate production and aggregate expenditures decreases. For example, say businesses decrease aggregate production to \$5,500. Aggregate income also falls to \$5,500, which causes aggregate expenditures to fall, as indicated by arrow A_2, to \$4,750. Production still exceeds planned expenditures, but the gap has been reduced by \$750, from \$1,500 to \$750.

Since a gap still remains, production and income keep falling. A good exercise is to go through two more steps. With each step, the economy moves closer to equilibrium.

Q-6 When inventories fall below planned inventories, what is likely happening to the economy?

Now let's consider the economy at income level *B* (\$1,000) and expenditures level \$2,500. Here production is *less* than planned expenditures. Firms find their inventory is running down. (Their investment in inventory is far less than they'd planned.) In response, they increase aggregate production and hence income. The economy starts to expand as aggregate production moves along arrow B_2 and aggregate expenditures move along arrow B_1. As individuals' income increases, their expenditures also increase, but by less than the increase in income, so the gap between aggregate expenditures and aggregate production decreases. But as long as expenditures exceed production, production and hence income keep rising.

Finally, let's consider the economy at income level C, \$4,000. At point C, production is \$4,000 and planned expenditures are \$4,000. Firms are selling all they produce, so they have no reason to change their production levels. The aggregate economy is in equilibrium. This discussion should give you insight into what's behind the arithmetic of those earlier models.

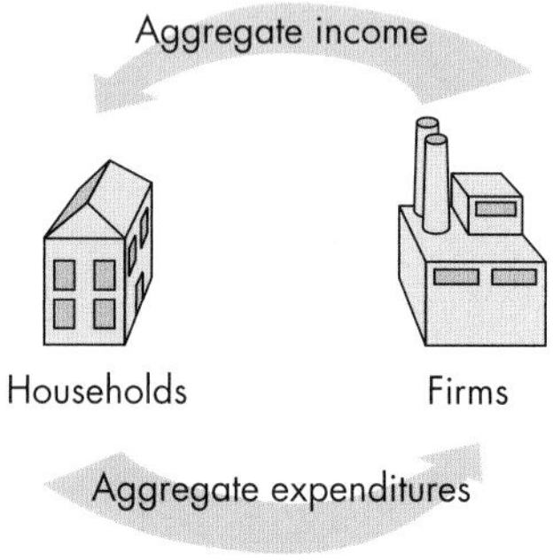

Circular flow diagram.

The Circular Flow Model and the Intuition behind the Multiplier Process

Now let's think about the intuition behind the multiplier. You know from the circular flow diagram that when all individuals spend all their income (which they derive from production), the aggregate economy is in equilibrium. The circular flow diagram in the margin shows the aggregate income definitional identity: aggregate income equals aggregate output. The flow of expenditures equals the flow of income (production). How, if not all income is spent (the *mpe* is less than 1), can expenditures equal income? The answer is that the withdrawals (income that is not spent on domestic goods) are offset by injections of autonomous expenditures.

When thinking about the multiplier process, I picture a leaking bathtub. Withdrawals are leaks out of the bathtub. Injections are people dumping buckets of water into the tub. When the water leaking out of the bathtub just equals the water being poured in, the level of water in the tub will remain constant; the bathtub will be in equilibrium. If the amount being poured in is either more or less than the amount leaking out, the level of the water in the bathtub will be either increasing or decreasing. Thus, equilibrium in the economy requires the withdrawals from the spending stream to equal injections into the spending stream. If they don't, the economy will not be in equilibrium and will be either expanding or contracting.

Web Note 28.3
Local Multipliers

To see this, let's consider what happens if injections and withdrawals are not equal. Say that withdrawals exceed injections (more water is leaking out than is being poured in). In that case, the income in the economy (the level of water in the bathtub) will be declining. As income declines, so will withdrawals. Income will continue to decline until the autonomous injections flowing in (the buckets of water) just equal the withdrawals flowing out (the water leaks).

ADDED DIMENSION

Solving for Equilibrium Income Algebraically

For those of you who are mathematically inclined, the multiplier equation can be derived by combining the equations presented in the text algebraically to arrive at the equation for income. Rewriting the expenditures relationship, we have

$$AE = AE_0 + mpeY$$

Aggregate production, by definition, equals aggregate income (Y) and, in equilibrium, aggregate income must equal the four components of aggregate expenditures. Beginning with the equilibrium condition, we have

$$Y = AE$$

Substituting the terms from the first equation, we have

$$Y = AE_0 + mpeY$$

We want to solve this equation for Y, so first we subtract $mpeY$ from both sides,

$$Y - mpeY = AE_0$$

We then factor out Y:

$$Y(1 - mpe) = AE_0$$

and finally we solve for Y by dividing both sides by $(1 - mpe)$:

$$Y = \left[\frac{1}{(1 - mpe)}\right] \times \left[AE_0\right]$$

This is the multiplier equation, and $\left[\frac{1}{(1 - mpe)}\right]$ is the multiplier.

The Multiplier Model in Action

Determining the equilibrium level of income using the multiplier is an important first step in understanding the multiplier analysis. The second step is to modify that analysis to answer a question that is of much more interest to policy makers: How much would a change in autonomous expenditures change the equilibrium level of income? This second step is important since it is precisely those sudden changes in autonomous expenditures that can cause a recession. That is why we discussed shifts in autonomous expenditures above.

It is because autonomous expenditures are subject to sudden shifts that I was careful to point out *autonomous* means "determined outside the model and not affected by income." Autonomous expenditures can, and do, shift for a variety of reasons. When they do, the multiplier process is continually being called into play.

Autonomous means "determined outside the model."

The Steps of the Multiplier Process

Any initial change in autonomous aggregate expenditures is amplified by the dynamic feedback effects in the multiplier process. Let's see how this works in the example in Figure 28-6, which will also serve as a review. Assume that trade negotiations between the United States and other countries have fallen apart and U.S. exports decrease by \$100. This is shown in the AE curve's downward shift from AE_1 to AE_2.

How far must income fall until equilibrium is reached? To answer that question, we need to know the initial change, $\Delta AE = -\$100$, and the size of the multiplier, $[1/(1 - mpe)]$. In this example, $mpe = .5$, so the multiplier is 2. That means the final decrease in income that brings about equilibrium is \$200 (two times as large as the initial shift of \$100).

Q-7 If exports fall by \$30 and the $mpe = .9$, what happens to equilibrium income?

Figure 28-6(b), a blowup of the circled area in Figure 28-6(a), shows the detailed steps of the multiplier process so you can see how it works. Initially, autonomous expenditures fall by \$100 (length A), causing firms to decrease production by \$100 (length B). But that decrease in income causes expenditures to decrease by another \$50 ($.5 \times$ \$100) (length C). Again firms respond by cutting production, this time by \$50 (length D). Again income falls (length E), causing production to fall (length F). The process continues again and again (the remaining steps) until equilibrium income falls by \$200,

FIGURE 28-6 (A AND B) Shifts in the Aggregate Expenditures Curve

Graph (**a**) shows the effect of a shift of the aggregate expenditures curve. When autonomous expenditures decrease by $100, the aggregate expenditures curve shifts downward from AE_1 to AE_2. In response, income falls by a multiple of the shift, in this case by $200.

Graph (**b**) shows the multiplier process under a microscope. In it the adjustment process is broken into discrete steps. For example, when income falls by $100 (length *B*), expenditures fall by $50 (length C). In response to that fall of expenditures, producers reduce output by $50, which decreases income by $50 (length *D*). The lower income causes expenditures to fall further (length *E*) and the process continues.

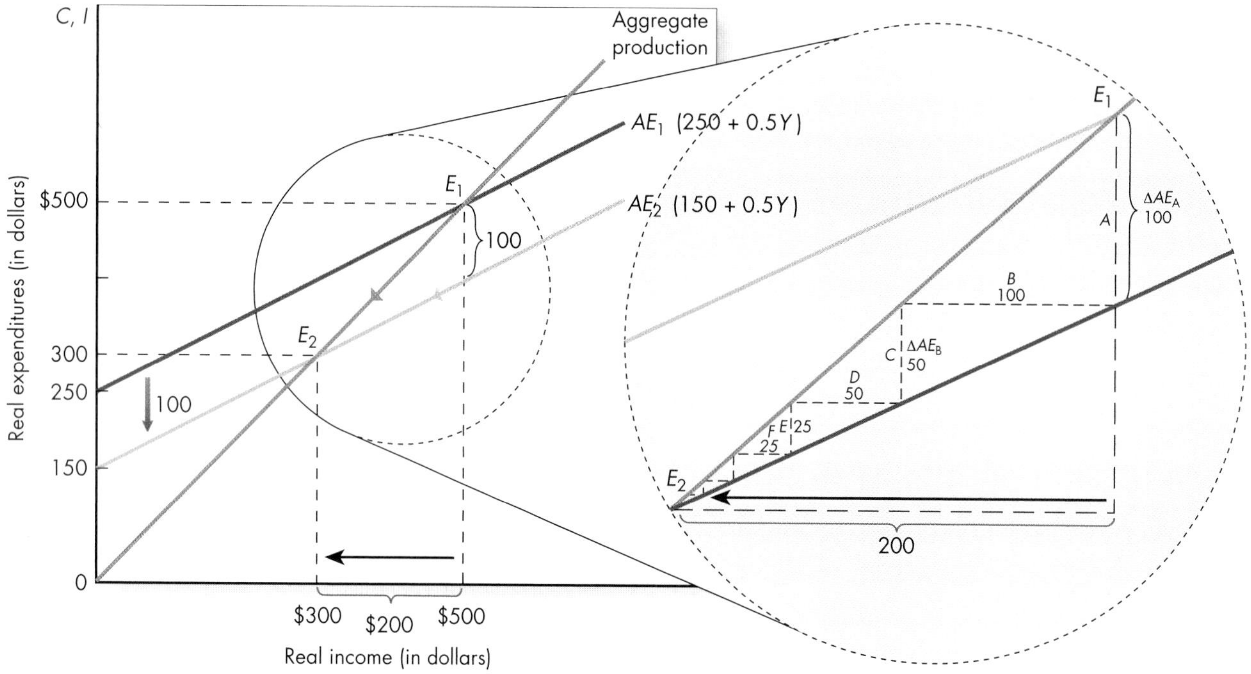

(a) The Adjustment Process **(b) Blowup of the Adjustment Process**

two times the amount of the initial change. The *mpe* tells how much closer at each step aggregate expenditures will be to aggregate production. You can see this adjustment process in Figure 28-7, which shows the first steps with multipliers of various sizes.

Examples of the Effect of Shifts in Aggregate Expenditures

There are many reasons for shifts in autonomous expenditures that can affect the economy: natural disasters, changes in investment caused by technological developments, shifts in government expenditures, large changes in the exchange rate, and so on. As I discussed above, in order to focus on these shift factors, autonomous expenditures are often broken up into their component parts: autonomous consumption (C_0), autonomous investment (I_0), autonomous government spending (G_0), and autonomous net exports ($X_0 - M_0$) (the difference between autonomous exports and autonomous imports). Changes in consumer sentiment affect C_0; major technological breakthroughs affect I_0; changes in government's spending decisions affect G_0; and changes in foreign income and exchange rates affect ($X_0 - M_0$).

Learning to work with the multiplier model requires practice, so in Figure 28-8 (a and b) I present two different expenditures functions and two different shifts in autonomous expenditures. Below each model is the equation representing how much aggregate income changes in terms of the multiplier and autonomous expenditures. As you see, the multiplier equation calculates the shift, while the graph determines it in a visual way. Now let's turn to some real-world examples.

FIGURE 28-7 **The First Five Steps of Four Multipliers**

The larger the marginal propensity to expend, the more steps are required before the shifts become small.

$mpe = .4$

Multiplier $= 1/(1 - 0.4) = 1.7$

$mpe = .5$

Multiplier $= 1/(1 - 0.5) = 2$

$mpe = .6$

Multiplier $= 1/(1 - 0.6) = 2.5$

$mpe = .8$

Multiplier $= 1/(1 - 0.8) = 5$

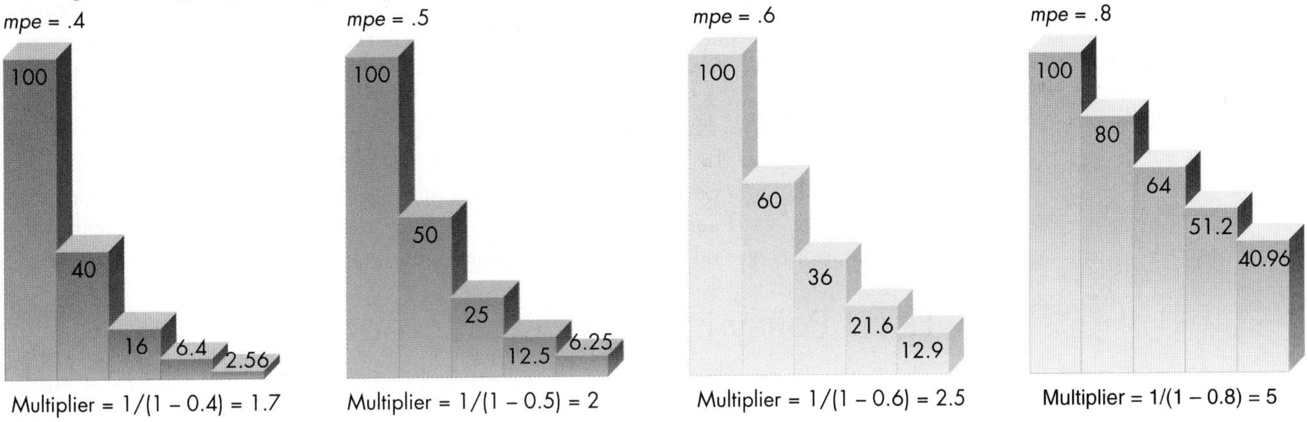

Japan in the 1990s A dramatic appreciation of the Japanese exchange rate in 1995 cut Japanese exports, decreasing aggregate expenditures so that aggregate production was greater than planned aggregate expenditures. Then, simultaneously, consumers became worried and autonomous consumption fell. Suppliers could not sell all that they produced.

FIGURE 28-8 (A AND B) **Two Different Expenditures Functions and Two Different Shifts in Autonomous Expenditures**

The steeper the slope of the *AE* curve, the greater the effect of a shift in the *AE* curve on equilibrium income. In (**a**) the slope of the *AE* curve is .75 and a shift of $30 of autonomous expenditures causes an increase in income of $120. In (**b**), the slope of the *AE* curve is .66 and a shift of $30 of autonomous expenditures causes a decrease in income of $90.

$$\Delta Y = \frac{1}{1 - .75}[\Delta AE_0]$$
$$= 4[\Delta AE_0] = 120$$

(a) **An Upward Shift of *AE***

$$\Delta Y = \frac{1}{1 - .66}[\Delta AE_0]$$
$$= 3[\Delta AE_0] = -90$$

(b) **A Downward Shift of *AE***

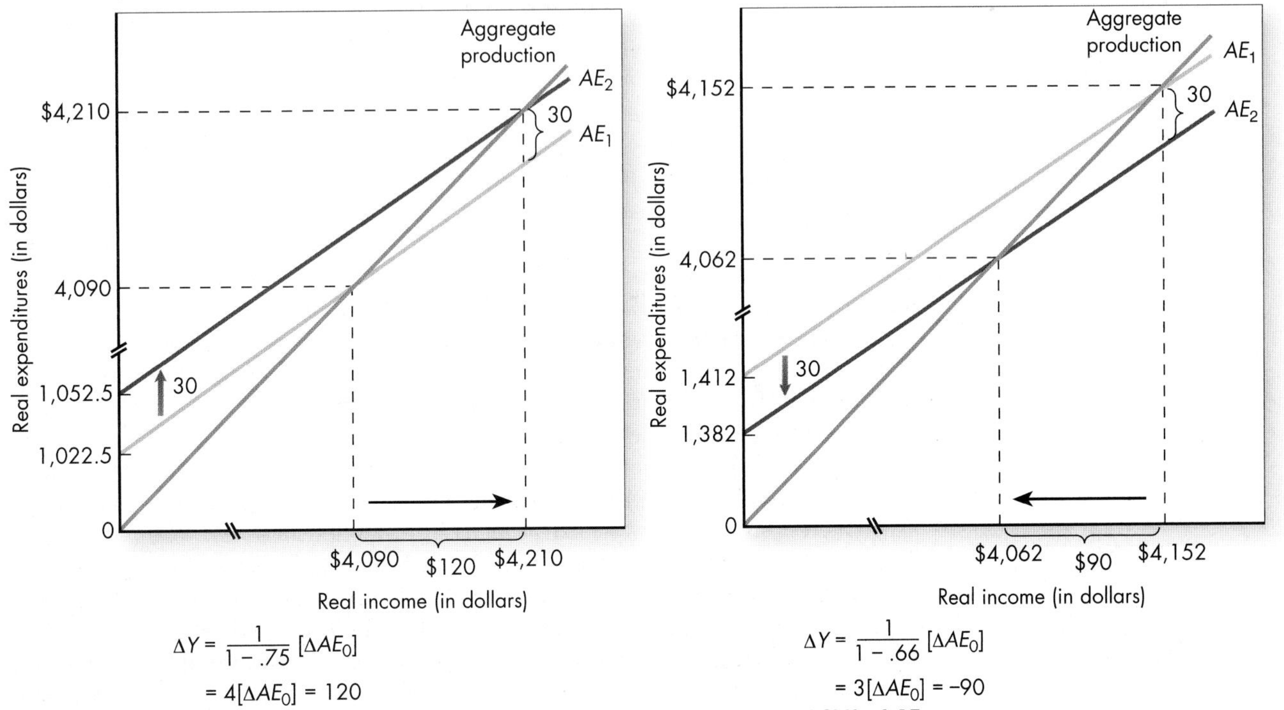

Their reaction was to lay off workers and decrease output. That response would have solved the problem if only one firm had been affected. But since all firms (or at least a large majority) were affected, the fallacy of composition came into play. As all producers responded in this fashion, aggregate income, and hence aggregate expenditures, also fell. The suppliers' cutback started what is sometimes called a vicious cycle. Aggregate expenditures and production spiraled downward, which is what the multiplier process explains.

The Worldwide Recession of 2008 Our second example is 2008 when the housing market in the United States collapsed, the financial market almost collapsed, and the stock market dropped precipitously. The result was a sudden large shift down in the *AE* curve, with aggregate output falling so much that many economists feared the world economy was falling into a depression.

Fiscal Policy in the Multiplier Model

The multiplier model is of such interest to policy makers not only because it allows them to predict the effects of shifts in autonomous expenditures but also because they believe that it allows them to control the level of output with countershifts of their own. By implementing policies affecting autonomous spending, governments can shift the *AE* curve up or down and, in the model at least, achieve the desired level of output.

Fighting Recession: Expansionary Fiscal Policy

To see how this is done, let's consider how government policy can get an economy out of a recession with fiscal policy. I consider this case in both the *AS/AD* model with a fixed price level and the multiplier model in Figure 28-9(a). The top panel shows fiscal policy in the multiplier model. The bottom part shows fiscal policy in the *AS/AD* model. Initially the economy is at equilibrium at income level $1,000, which is below potential income ($1,180). The economy is in a recessionary gap. This is what ideally happens: The government recognizes this recessionary gap in aggregate income of, say, $180 and responds with expansionary fiscal policy by increasing government expenditures by $60.

Assuming the price level is constant (the *SAS* curve is flat), the increased government spending shifts the *AE* curve from AE_1 upward to AE_2. Businesses that receive government contracts hire the workers who have been laid off by other firms and open new plants; output increases by the initial expenditure of $60. But the process doesn't stop there. At this point, the multiplier process sets in. As the newly employed workers spend more, other businesses find that their demand increases. They hire more workers, who spend an additional $40 (since their *mpe* = .67). This increases income further. The same process occurs again and again. By the time the process has ended, income has risen by $180 to $1,180, the potential level of income.

The effects are shown in the *AS/AD* model in the bottom part of Figure 28-9(a). The *AD* curve shifts to the right by three times the increase in government expenditures, or by $180. The initial shock shifts the *AD* curve to the right by $60; the $120 shift is due to the multiplier effects that the initial shift brings about.

How did the government economists know to increase spending by $60? By backward induction. They empirically estimated that the *mpe*—the slope of the aggregate expenditures curve—was .67, which meant that the multiplier was $1/(1 - .67) = 1/.33 = 3$. They divided the multiplier, 3, into the recessionary gap, $180, and determined that if they increased spending by $60, income would increase by $180.

If the *SAS* curve had been upward-sloping, and the price level had not remained constant, predicting the precise level of increase in real income would have been harder because the increase would have been split between a change in real income and a change in nominal income. The increase in real income would have been less than it

FIGURE 28-9 (A AND B) Fiscal Policy

In (**a**) if the economy is below its potential income level, the government can increase government spending to stimulate the economy. Doing so shifts the *AD* curve to the right and the *AE* curve shifts up. Income expands by a multiple of that increase. In (**b**) we see appropriate government policy for an inflationary gap. In the absence of any policy, shortages and accelerating inflation will occur. To prevent this, government must use contractionary fiscal policy, shifting the *AE* curve downward from AE_1 to AE_2 to reduce equilibrium income from $5,000 to $4,000. The bottom part of (**b**) shows this policy in the *AS/AD* model.

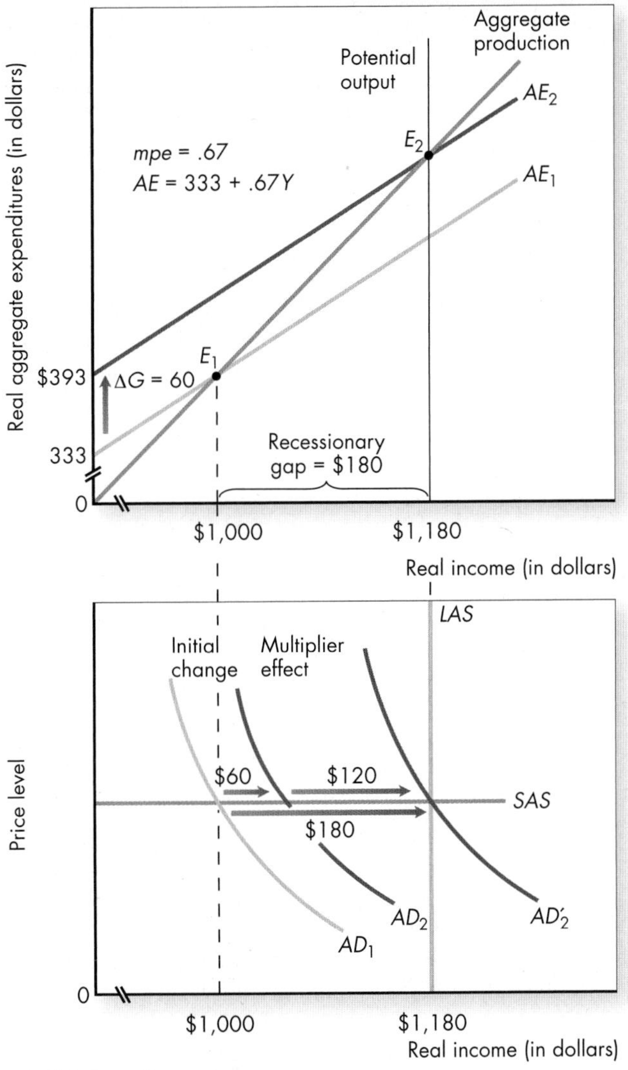

(a) Fighting a Recession

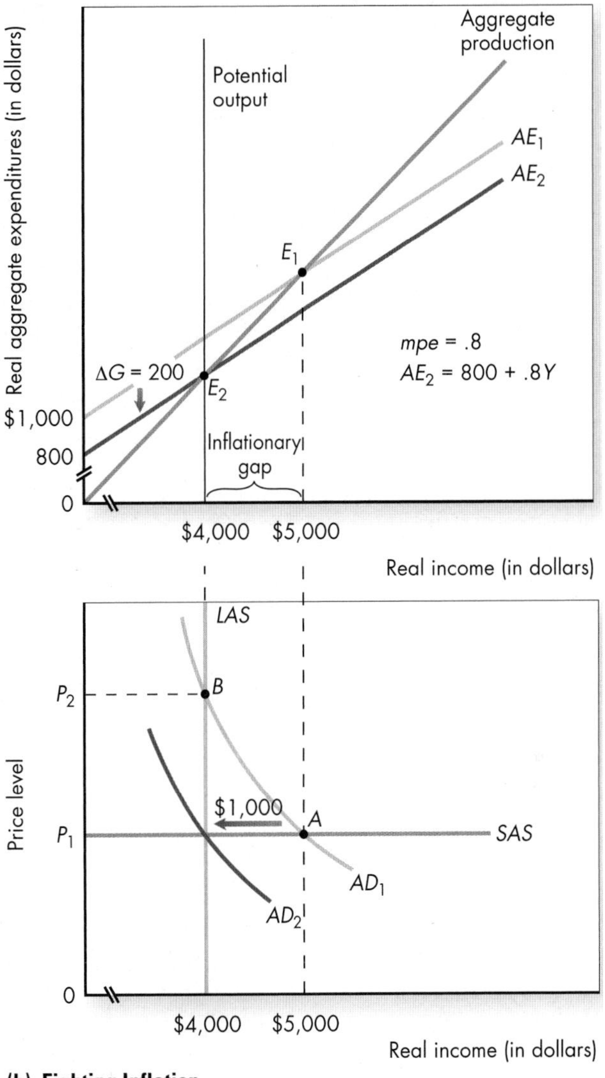

(b) Fighting Inflation

was with a flat *SAS* curve. The precise amount would depend on the degree of upward slope of the *SAS* curve.[3] The steeper the slope of the *SAS* curve, the less real income would have changed.

[3]You can determine the approximate percentage reduction in the multiplier effect on real income by writing the slope of the *SAS* curve as a fraction and then placing the numerator of that fraction over the sum of the numerator and the denominator. The result is the approximate decrease in the size of the multiplier effect on real income. For example, if the slope of the *SAS* curve is 1/10, the multiplier effect on real income will be reduced by about [1/(1 + 10)], or 1/11, from what it would have been had the *SAS* curve been horizontal.

ADDED DIMENSION

Keynes and Fiscal Policy

One of the themes of this book is that economic thought and policy are more complicated than an introductory book must necessarily make them seem. Fiscal policy is a good case in point. In the early 1930s, before Keynes wrote *The General Theory,* he was advocating public works programs and deficits (government spending in excess of tax revenues) as a way to get the British economy out of the Depression. He came upon what we now call the *Keynesian theory* as he tried to explain to Classical economists why he supported deficits. After arriving at his new theory, however, he spent little time advocating fiscal policy and, in fact, never mentions fiscal policy in *The General Theory.* The book's primary policy recommendation is the need to socialize investments—for the government to take over the investment decisions from private individuals. When one of his followers, Abba Lerner, advocated expansionary fiscal policy at a seminar Keynes attended, Keynes strongly objected, leading Evsey Domar, another Keynesian follower, to whisper to a friend, "Keynes should read *The General Theory.*"

What's going on here? There are many interpretations, but the one I find most convincing is the one presented by historian Peter Clarke. He argues that, while working on *The General Theory,* Keynes turned his interest from a policy revolution to a theoretical revolution. He believed he had found a serious flaw in Classical economic theory. The Classicals assumed that an economy in equilibrium was at full employment, but they did not show how the economy could move to that equilibrium from a disequilibrium. That's when Keynes's interest changed from a policy to a theoretical revolution.

His followers, such as Lerner, carried out the policy implications of his theory. Why did Keynes sometimes oppose these policy implications? Because he was also a student of politics and he recognized that economic theory can often lead to politically unacceptable policies. In a letter to a friend, he later said Lerner was right in his logic, but he hoped the opposition didn't discover what Lerner was saying. Keynes was more than an economist; he was a politician as well.

Fighting Inflation: Contractionary Fiscal Policy

Q-8 Demonstrate graphically the effect of contractionary fiscal policy.

Fiscal policy can also work in reverse, decreasing expenditures that are too high. Expenditures are "too high" when the economy temporarily exceeds its potential output. An economy operating above potential will generate accelerating inflation.

Figure 28-9(b) shows contractionary fiscal policy in the multiplier and *AS/AD* models. Potential income is \$4,000, but the equilibrium level of income is \$5,000. The difference between the two, \$1,000, is the inflationary gap. This inflationary gap causes upward pressure on wages and prices with no additional lasting increase in output. If the government wants to avoid inflation, it can use contractionary policy. By how much should government reduce government expenditures? To determine that, it has to calculate the multiplier. In this example, the marginal propensity to expend is assumed to be .8, which means that the multiplier would be 5. So a cut in autonomous expenditures of \$200 would shift the *AE* curve down by \$200 and decrease equilibrium income by \$1,000.

Q-9 The marginal propensity to expend is .33, and there is an inflationary gap of \$100. What fiscal policy would you recommend?

The bottom part of Figure 28-9(b) shows the effects of a \$200 cut in government expenditures in the *AS/AD* model. With a multiplier of 5, the *AD* curve shifts to the left by \$1,000. Because the *SAS* curve is flat, equilibrium output declines to \$4,000.

Using Taxes Rather Than Expenditures as the Tool of Fiscal Policy

As a brain teaser, you might try to figure out what you would have advised the government to do if it had wanted to increase taxes rather than decrease expenditures to get the economy out of the inflationary gap in Figure 28-9(b). By how much should it increase taxes? If you said by \$200 since the multiplier is 5, you're on the right wavelength, but not quite right. True, the multiplier, $1/(1 - mpe)$, is 5, but a change in taxes affects initial expenditures in a slightly different way than does a direct change in expenditures. Specifically, expenditures will not decrease by the full amount of the tax increase. The reason why is that people will likely reduce their saving in order to hold up their expenditures. Expenditures will initially fall by that portion of the decrease in their disposable income that consumers spend on U.S. goods, which, as I stated earlier, is measured by the consumer's marginal propensity to consume (*mpc*). For simplicity, let's assume that the marginal propensity to consume equals the marginal propensity to expend. Then, initially, the decrease in expenditures from the tax increase will be (.8 × \$200) = \$160, rather than \$200. To get the initial shift of \$200 from increasing taxes, the government must increase taxes by \$200/.8, or \$250. Then when people reduce spending by .8 of that, their expenditures will fall by \$200.

A change in taxes affects initial expenditures differently than a direct change in expenditures.

Limitations of the Multiplier Model

On the surface, the multiplier model makes a lot of intuitive sense. However, surface sense can often be misleading. The multiplier model leaves out many aspects of the aggregate economy and overemphasizes others. As I discussed in the chapter on thinking like a modern economist, models must be used with care. They focus on certain relationships and in doing so direct our focus away from other relationships. These other relationships are considered by the model to be exogenous noise.

The multiplier model both underestimates and overestimates the effects of changes in the economy. Specifically, when shifts in aggregate demand are small, the noise that tends to bring the economy back to its original equilibrium drowns out much of the multiplier effect predicted by the model. Therefore, the multiplier model overestimates the effects of shifting demand. That's why the multiplier model lost favor in the 1970s. When shifts in demand are large, as in 2008, the opposite occurs: the noise that destabilizes the economy overwhelms the model's predicted effect and the model instead underestimates the effect of shifting demand. The multiplier model portrayed the economy as globally stable in the sense that the aggregate economy would settle down to a new equilibrium. But, as I will discuss below, that is not necessarily the case.

So let me briefly list some of the limitations of the multiplier model.

The Multiplier Model Is Not a Complete Model of the Economy

The multiplier model provides a technical method of determining equilibrium income. But in reality the model doesn't do what it purports to do—determine equilibrium income from scratch. Why? Because it doesn't tell us where those autonomous expenditures come from or how we would go about measuring them.

At best, what we can measure, or at least estimate, are directions and rough sizes of autonomous demand shifts, and we can determine the direction and possible overadjustment the economy might make in response to those changes. If you think back to our initial discussion of the multiplier model, this is how I introduced it—as an explanation of forces affecting the adjustment process, not as a determinant of the final equilibrium independent of where the economy started. It is a historical, not an analytical, model. Without some additional information about where the economy started from, or what is the desired level of output, the multiplier model is incomplete.

At best, what we can estimate are directions and rough sizes of autonomous demand or supply shifts.

Shifts Are Sometimes Not as Great as the Model Suggests

A second problem with the multiplier model is that it leads people to overemphasize the shifts that would occur in aggregate expenditures in response to a shift in autonomous expenditures. Say people decide to save some more. You might think that it would lead to a fall in expenditures. But wait, that saving will go into the financial sector and be translated back into the expenditures sector as loans to other consumers or as loans to businesses funding investment. So if you take a broad view of aggregate expenditures, many of the shifts in expenditures are simply rearrangements from one group of expenditures to another.

Fluctuations Can Sometimes Be Greater Than the Model Suggests

The multiplier model allows changes in output to affect demand for output only through the income-expenditures interdependencies, making the size of the marginal propensity to expend central. Because the marginal propensity to expend is less than one (recall, the *mpe* is defined as being between zero and one), the model predicts that the fluctuations will be dampened. After the aggregate economy experiences a decrease in demand, it will settle down to a new equilibrium. But that need not be the case. If changes in output change the expectations of future output, or influence the demand for output through some other path, the result can be a model in which changes in demand are magnified, creating a global instability in the model that causes output to fall seemingly uncontrollably.

Let's consider an example of one such model called the **multiplier-accelerator model**—*a model in which changes in output are accelerated because changes in investment depend on changes in income (rather than on the level of income)*. In this model, when aggregate demand falls, output falls as in the standard multiplier model. But as output falls, unlike in the simple multiplier model, investment also falls since firms can see no reason to invest. (Why invest if there is no demand for your goods?) This new interconnection accelerates the fall in aggregate demand, and in output, possibly making the second shift larger than the first shift. Under certain conditions, output can be pushed into an uncontrollable freefall, unless something else changes.

There are many other possible accelerants of decreasing aggregate demand, all of which can create a push toward such an uncontrollable freefall. For example, expectations might be endogenous, in which case the fall in aggregate demand creates self-fulfilling expectations of further decreases in aggregate demand—the economy becomes worse because people expect it to become worse. It was precisely such conditions that the U.S. economy faced in 2008 and 2009. Because of the importance of these effects, which almost led the economy into a depression, I devote an entire later chapter to them.

The Price Level Will Often Change in Response to Shifts in Demand

One of the assumptions of the multiplier model is that the price level is fixed—that makes aggregate production a 45° line. But in reality the price level can change as aggregate demand changes because price markups and labor market conditions change. These changes in the price level make the model more complicated. Some adjustment must be made when the price level changes in response to changes in aggregate demand. That adjustment is usually made by shifting the *AE* curve up (in the case of a falling price level) or down (in the case of a rising price level) if the standard effects of price level changes on aggregate demand are considered. But if expectations are endogenous and feed back on aggregate demand, the price level changes can be destabilizing. These other paths through which changes in price level affect output make the effect of policy on real income uncertain. (These adjustments are discussed in Appendix B.)

People's Forward-Looking Expectations Make the Adjustment Process Much More Complicated

People's forward-looking expectations make the adjustment process much more complicated. The multiplier model presented here assumes that people respond to current changes in income. Most people, however, act on the basis of expectations of the future. Consider the assumed response of businesses to changes in expenditures. They lay off workers and cut production at the slightest fall in demand. In reality, their response is far more complicated. They may well see the fall as a temporary blip. They will allow their inventory to rise in the expectation that the next month another temporary blip will offset the previous fall. Business decisions about production are forward looking, and do not respond simply to current changes. As a contrast to the simple multiplier model, some modern economists have put forward a **rational expectations model** of the macroeconomy in which *all decisions are based on the expected equilibrium in the economy*. Some economists go so far as to argue that since people rationally expect the economy to achieve its potential income, it will do so. Other economists emphasize extrapolative expectations, which can cause the aggregate economy to explode or implode in boom and bust cycles.

Shifts in Expenditures Might Reflect Desired Shifts in Supply and Demand

There is an implicit assumption in the multiplier model that shifts in demand are not reflections of shifts in desired production or supply. Reality is much more complicated. Shifts can occur for many reasons, and many shifts can reflect desired shifts in aggregate production, which are accompanied by shifts in aggregate expenditures. An example of such a change occurred in Japan in the 1990s as Japan's industries lost their competitive edge to Korean, Chinese, and Taiwanese industries. The Japanese economy faltered, but the problem was not simply a fall in aggregate demand, and therefore the solution to it was not simply to increase aggregate demand. There was a simultaneous shift in aggregate supply that had to be dealt with.

Suppliers operate in the future—shifting supply, not to existing demand, but to expected demand, making the relationship between aggregate production and current aggregate demand far more complicated than it seems in the multiplier model. Expansion of this line of thought has led some economists, called *real-business-cycle economists*, to develop the **real-business-cycle theory** of the economy: *the theory that fluctuations in the economy reflect real phenomena—simultaneous shifts in supply and demand, not simply supply responses to demand shifts*. Supply drives the economy. Let's consider the expansion of the U.S. economy in the late 1990s. The *AS/AD* model would attribute that to a shift of the *AD* curve to the right, combined with a relatively fixed *SAS* curve that did not shift up as output expanded. The real-business-cycle theory would attribute that shift in income to businesses' decision to increase supply due to technological developments, and a subsequent increase in demand via Say's law.

Real-business-cycle theory suggests that fluctuations in the economy reflect real phenomena.

Expenditures Depend on Much More Than Current Income

Q-10 What effect would expenditures being dependent on permanent income have on the size of the multiplier?

Let's say your income goes down 10 percent. The multiplier model says that your expenditures will go down by some specific percentage of that. But will they? If you are rational, it seems reasonable to base your consumption on more than one year's income—say, instead, on your permanent or lifetime income. What happens to your income in a particular year has little effect on your lifetime income. If it is true that people base their spending primarily on lifetime income, not yearly income, the marginal propensity to consume out of changes in current income could be very low, approaching zero. In that case, the expenditures function would essentially be a flat line, and the multiplier would be 1. There would be no secondary effects of an initial shift in expenditures. This set of arguments is called the **permanent income hypothesis**—*the hypothesis that expenditures are determined by permanent or lifetime income*. It undermines the reasoning of much of the specific results of the simple multiplier model.

Conclusion

While each of the above criticisms has some validity, most macro policy makers still use some variation of the multiplier model as the basis for their policy decisions. They don't see it as a *mechanistic model*—a model that pictures the economy as representable by a mechanically determined, timeless model with a determinant equilibrium. Modern economists have come to the conclusion that there is no simple way to understand the aggregate economy. Any mechanistic interpretation of an aggregate model is doomed to fail. The hope of economists to have a model that would give them a specific numeric guide to policy has not been fulfilled.

The model is still useful if it is seen as an interpretive model or an aid in understanding complicated disequilibrium dynamics. The specific results of the multiplier model are a guide to common sense, enabling us to emphasize a particular important dynamic interdependency while keeping others in mind. With that addendum—that it is not meant to be taken literally but only as an aid to intuition—the simple multiplier model deals with the issues that concern today's highest-level macro theorists.

Summary

- The multiplier model focuses on the induced effect that a change in production has on expenditures, which affects production, and so on.
- The multiplier model is made up of the aggregate production and aggregate expenditures curves. In equilibrium, aggregate production must equal planned aggregate expenditures.
- The aggregate production (*AP*) curve is a line along which real income equals real production. It is a 45° line.
- Aggregate expenditures (*AE*) are made up of consumption, investment, government spending, and net exports:

$$AE = C + I + G + (X - M)$$

- Expenditures depend on the level of income; the marginal propensity to expend (*mpe*) tells us the change in expenditures that occurs with a change in income.
- The *AE* curve shows aggregate expenditures graphically. Its slope is the *mpe* and its *y*-intercept equals autonomous expenditures.
- Equilibrium output, or income, is where the *AP* and *AE* curves intersect.
- Equilibrium output can be calculated using the multiplier equation:

$$Y = \text{Multiplier} \times \text{Autonomous expenditures}$$

- The multiplier tells us how much a change in autonomous expenditures will change equilibrium income. The multiplier equals $1/(1 - mpe)$.
- When an economy is in equilibrium, withdrawals from the spending stream equal injections into the spending stream (autonomous expenditures).
- Shifts in autonomous expenditures can be the initial change that begins the multiplier process. The multiplier process expands that initial shift to a much larger decrease or increase in production and income.
- Expansionary fiscal policy, increasing government expenditures or decreasing taxes, is represented graphically as an upward shift of the aggregate expenditures curve or a rightward shift in the *AD* curve.

- Contractionary fiscal policy, decreasing government expenditures or increasing taxes, is represented graphically as a downward shift of the aggregate expenditures curve or a leftward shift in the *AD* curve.
- The multiplier model has limitations: (1) it is incomplete without information about where the economy started and what is the desired level of output, (2) it overemphasizes shifts that occur in aggregate expenditures, (3) it can both over- and underestimate the effects of changes in the economy, (4) it assumes that the price level is fixed when in reality it isn't, (5) it doesn't take expectations into account, (6) it ignores the possibility that shifts in expenditures are desired, and (7) it ignores the possibility that consumption is based on lifetime income, not annual income.
- Macroeconomic models cannot be applied mechanistically; they are only guides to common sense.

Key Terms

aggregate expenditures *(650)*
aggregate production (*AP*) *(649)*
autonomous expenditures *(650)*
expenditures multiplier *(656)*
induced expenditures *(650)*
marginal propensity to expend (*mpe*) *(652)*
multiplier-accelerator model *(666)*
multiplier equation *(656)*
multiplier model *(648)*
permanent income hypothesis *(668)*
rational expectations model *(667)*
real-business-cycle theory *(667)*

Questions and Exercises

Connect ECONOMICS

1. When is the multiplier model more appropriate: for small or large changes in aggregate demand? LO1
2. What are induced and autonomous expenditures at point A in the graph below? LO1

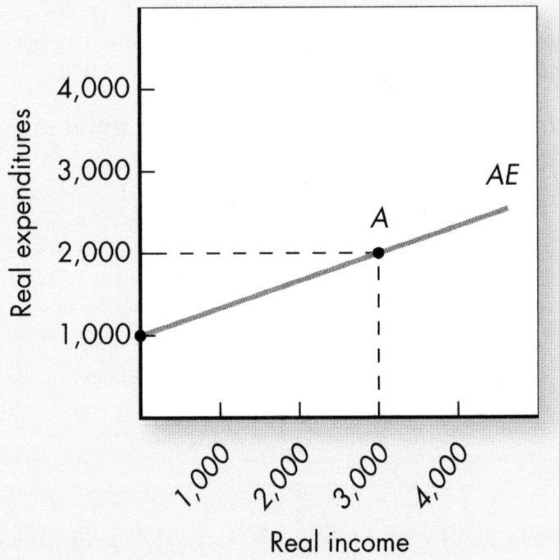

3. If planned expenditures are below actual production, what will happen to income? Explain the process by which this happens. LO2
4. Are inventories building up at levels of output above or below equilibrium output? Explain your answer. LO2
5. What happens to the aggregate expenditures curve when autonomous expenditures fall? LO2
6. What happens to equilibrium income when the marginal propensity to expend rises? LO2
7. What is equilibrium income if the aggregate expenditures function is $AE = 300 + .4Y$? LO3
8. The marginal propensity to expend is .8. Autonomous expenditures are $4,200. What is the level of equilibrium income in the economy? Demonstrate graphically. LO3
9. The marginal propensity to expend is .66 and autonomous expenditures have just fallen by $20.
   a. What will likely happen to equilibrium income?
   b. Demonstrate graphically. LO3
10. If withdrawals were instantaneously translated into expenditures, what would be the multiplier's size? What would be the level of autonomous expenditures? LO4
11. Congratulations. You've been appointed economic adviser to Happyland. Your research assistant says the country's *mpe* is .8 and autonomous expenditures have just risen by $20.
    a. What will happen to income?
    b. Your research assistant comes in and says he's sorry but the *mpe* wasn't .8; it was .5. How does your answer change?
    c. He runs in again and says exports have fallen by $10 and investment has risen by $10. How does your answer change?
    d. You now have to present your analysis to the president, who wants to see it all graphically. Naturally you oblige. LO2, LO3, LO4

12. Congratulations again. You've just been appointed economic adviser to Examland. The *mpe* is .6; autonomous investment is $1,000; autonomous government spending is $8,000; autonomous consumption is $10,000; and autonomous net exports are $1,000.
    a. What is the equilibrium level of income in the country?
    b. Autonomous net exports increase by $2,000. What will happen to income?
    c. What will happen to unemployment? (Remember Okun's rule of thumb.)
    d. You've just learned the *mpe* changed from .6 to .5. How will this information change your answers in *a*, *b*, and *c*? LO2, LO3, LO4
13. What forces could cause shocks to aggregate expenditures? LO5
14. The marginal propensity to expend is .5 and there is a recessionary gap of $200. What fiscal policy would you recommend? LO5
15. Why does cutting taxes by $100 have a smaller effect on GDP than increasing expenditures by $100? LO5
16. In 1992, as President George H. W. Bush was running (unsuccessfully) for reelection, the economy slowed down; then in late 1993, after President Bill Clinton's election, the economy picked up steam.
    a. Demonstrate graphically with the multiplier model a shift in the *AE* curve that would have caused the slowdown.
    b. Demonstrate graphically with the multiplier model a shift in the *AE* curve that would have caused the improvement. LO4, LO5
17. Congratulations yet again. You've just been appointed chairman to the Council of Economic Advisers in Textland. You must rely on your research assistant for the specific numbers. He says income is $50,000, *mpe* is .75, and the president wants to lower unemployment from 8 to 6 percent. (Remember Okun's rule of thumb.)
    a. Advise him.
    b. Your research assistant comes in and says "Sorry, I meant that the *mpe* is .67." You redo your calculations.
    c. You're just about to see the president when your research assistant comes running, saying, "Sorry, sorry, I meant that the *mpe* is .5." Redo your calculations. LO4, LO5
18. State what fiscal policy you would recommend to eliminate the inflationary or recessionary gap in the following scenarios:
    a. Recessionary gap of $800; *mpe* = .5.
    b. Inflationary gap of $1,500; *mpe* = .8.
    c. Real GDP = $10,200; potential GDP = $9,000; *mpe* = .2.
    d. Real GDP = $40,500; potential GDP = $42,000; *mpe* = .7. LO5
19. Congratulations one more time. You have been appointed chair of Economic Advisers in Fantasyland. Income is currently $600,000, unemployment is 5 percent, and there are signs of coming inflation. You rely on your research assistant for specific numbers. He tells you that potential income is $564,000 and the *mpe* is .5.
    a. The government wants to eliminate the inflationary gap by changing expenditures. What policy do you suggest?
    b. By how much will unemployment change after your policy has taken effect?
    c. Your research assistant comes in and says, "Sorry, I meant that the *mpe* is .8." Redo your calculations for parts *a* and *b*. LO5
20. Why is the circular flow diagram of the economy an only partially correct conception of the multiplier model? LO6
21. How do mechanistic models differ from interpretive models? LO6
22. How does the multiplier-accelerator model magnify changes in demand? LO6

Questions from Alternative Perspectives

1. Traffic engineer Hans Monderman has shown that traffic flows can be made safer and flow better if the number of road signs is reduced and, in many types of intersections, eliminated altogether. What relevance do his insights about traffic flows have for macroeconomic policy? (Austrian)
2. During the Great Depression, Norman Cousins made the following remark: "There are approximately 10,000,000 people out of work in the U.S. today. There are also 10,000,000 or more women married and single who are job holders. Simply fire the women, who should not be working anyway, and hire the men. Presto! No unemployment. No relief. No depression." How would you evaluate this statement? Is work a human right or a gender-based privilege? Do you think that men would have taken jobs that were traditionally considered "women's work" in the 1930s even if they were unemployed? (Feminist)
3. When the federal government uses expenditures to stimulate the economy, it changes not only the present

but the future as well. Use the *AS/AD* model and the production possibility curve to explore the probable near-term and long-term consequences of three alternative stimulus options: medical care for all Americans; an increased military presence across the Middle East to promote U.S. domestic tranquility; the development of oil-saving and climate-friendly energy alternatives. In your analysis be sure to include the effect of increased deficits on investment. (Institutionalist)

4. One remarkable thing about U.S. households is how little they save. The U.S. personal savings rate through the first five months of 2007 was negative. This negative savings rate seems to be the product of increased borrowing by poorer households, reduced savings by richer households, and the proliferation of low-wage jobs (which provide incomes too low from which to save). The flip side of the savings rate is the marginal propensity to consume. Rough estimates suggest that the *mpc* for the U.S. economy averaged about 90 percent between 1946 and 1990. But between 1991 and 2000, the *mpc* was 105 percent, and has been even higher since then. People are, on balance, consuming all their income and then some, and are up to their eyeballs in consumer debt.
   a. What do these data imply for a multiplier model?
   b. What do these data say about what has powered the U.S. economy from 2001 to 2008, and should the data have suggested that the expansion was unsustainable? (Radical)
5. Coaxing spending out of the private sector, especially investment spending, has never been an easy matter. What persuades investors to part with their money? Economist Stephen Fazzari provided one answer to that question in his study of 5,000 U.S. manufacturing firms. Fazzari found that interest rates exerted far less influence on investment decisions than either sales growth or a firm's available funds or financial conditions. What do Fazzari's findings suggest about the importance of Classical cost-side factors and Keynesian spending-side factors in the investment decisions of manufacturing firms? Also, what do Fazzari's findings suggest about what public policies might effectively promote investment? (Post-Keynesian)

Issues to Ponder

1. What is the current state of U.S. fiscal policy? Would you advise the United States to change its fiscal policy? Why? LO5
2. Mr. Whammo has just invented a magic pill. Take it and it transports you anywhere. Explain his invention's effects on the economy. LO5
3. Charlie Black, a GOP strategist, was once quoted as stating, "I can't tell you why this happens, but there's a lag time (before people tune into good economic news)." What is the effect of this delay in the adjustment of expectations by consumers on the dynamics of the multiplier model? LO6

Answers to Margin Questions

1. Income equals production on the aggregate production curve. *(649)*
2. Induced expenditures change as income changes. Autonomous expenditures are independent of income. *(651)*
3. The *mpe* is .6. *(652)*
4. The multiplier is 2 when the *mpe* = .5. *(657)*
5. The level of income is $3,333. *(657)*
6. When inventories fall below planned inventories, the economy is probably expanding; firms will likely increase production, which will cause expenditures to increase, which will further draw down inventories. *(658)*
7. Equilibrium income falls by $300. *(659)*
8. As you can see in the accompanying graph, contractionary fiscal policy shifts the *AD* curve to the left. The multiplier then takes over to shift the *AD* curve to the left by a multiple of the initial decline in aggregate expenditures. Assuming a flat *SAS* curve, income falls by a multiple of the initial shift. In the multiplier model, the *AE* curve shifts down and equilibrium income falls by a multiple of the decline in government expenditures. *(664)*

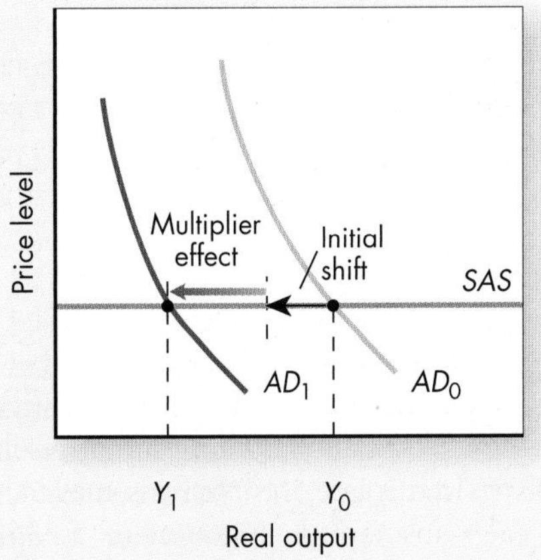

9. Since there is an inflationary gap, I would recommend contractionary fiscal policy. Since the multiplier is 1.5 (given the marginal propensity to expend of .33), I would recommend decreasing government spending by $66. *(664)*

10. If expenditures are dependent on permanent income, not current income, expenditures would not change as much with a change in current income and the multiplier would get smaller. *(667)*

APPENDIX A

An Algebraic Presentation of the Expanded Multiplier Model

In the chapter, I developed the basic multiplier model, focusing on the *mpe*. In this appendix, I briefly outline a fuller presentation in which consumption, taxes, and imports are related to income. That means that instead of having a single expenditures curve, we have a separate curve for each component of aggregate expenditures: consumption, investment, government spending, and net exports.

The Consumption Function Model

I begin with a model in which only consumption varies with income. The table below shows the components of the model as they are usually presented at the introductory level; Figure A28-1 graphs them.

(1) C +	(2) I +	(3) G +	(4) X − M =	(5) AE	(6) Y	(7) ΔAE	(8) ΔY	ROW
1,000	1,000	1,000	1,000	4,000	0			A
1,500	1,000	1,000	1,000	4,500	1,000	500	1,000	B
2,000	1,000	1,000	1,000	5,000	2,000	500	1,000	C
2,500	1,000	1,000	1,000	5,500	3,000	500	1,000	D
3,000	1,000	1,000	1,000	6,000	4,000	500	1,000	E
3,500	1,000	1,000	1,000	6,500	5,000	500	1,000	F
4,000	1,000	1,000	1,000	7,000	6,000	500	1,000	G
4,500	1,000	1,000	1,000	7,500	7,000	500	1,000	H
5,000	1,000	1,000	1,000	8,000	8,000	500	1,000	I
5,500	1,000	1,000	1,000	8,500	9,000	500	1,000	J
6,000	1,000	1,000	1,000	9,000	10,000	500	1,000	K
6,500	1,000	1,000	1,000	9,500	11,000	500	1,000	L
7,000	1,000	1,000	1,000	10,000	12,000	500	1,000	M

Notice that the only expenditure that is assumed to vary with income is consumption, which varies linearly with income and has a slope equal to the marginal propensity to consume (*mpc*)—the additional consumption that results from additional income. In this case, the *mpc* is assumed to be .5, so the slope of the consumption function is .5. All other expenditures are assumed to be autonomous. The summation of expenditures, aggregate expenditures, is in column 5.

FIGURE A28-1 Expenditure Components

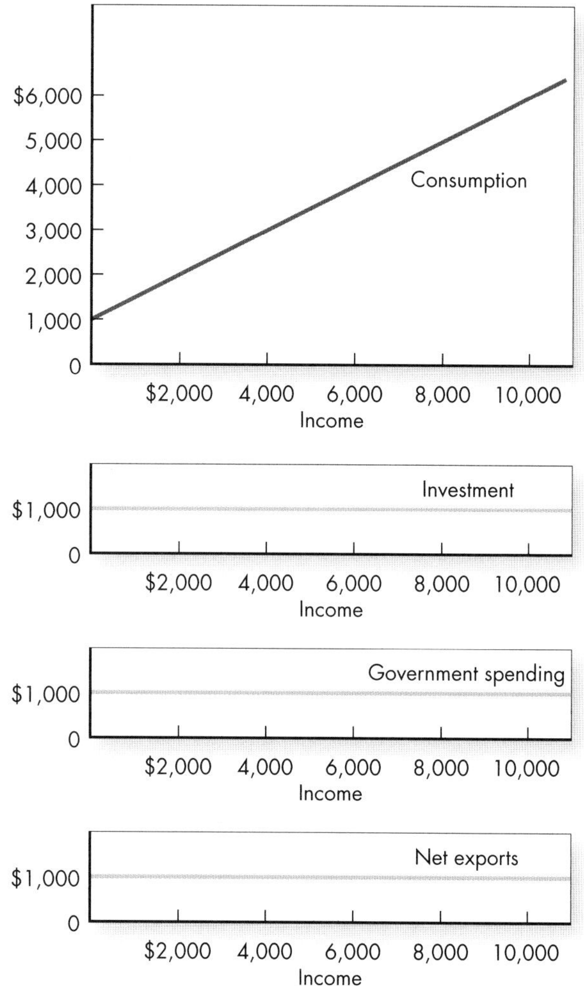

FIGURE A28-2 (A AND B) **Summation of Aggregate Expenditures**

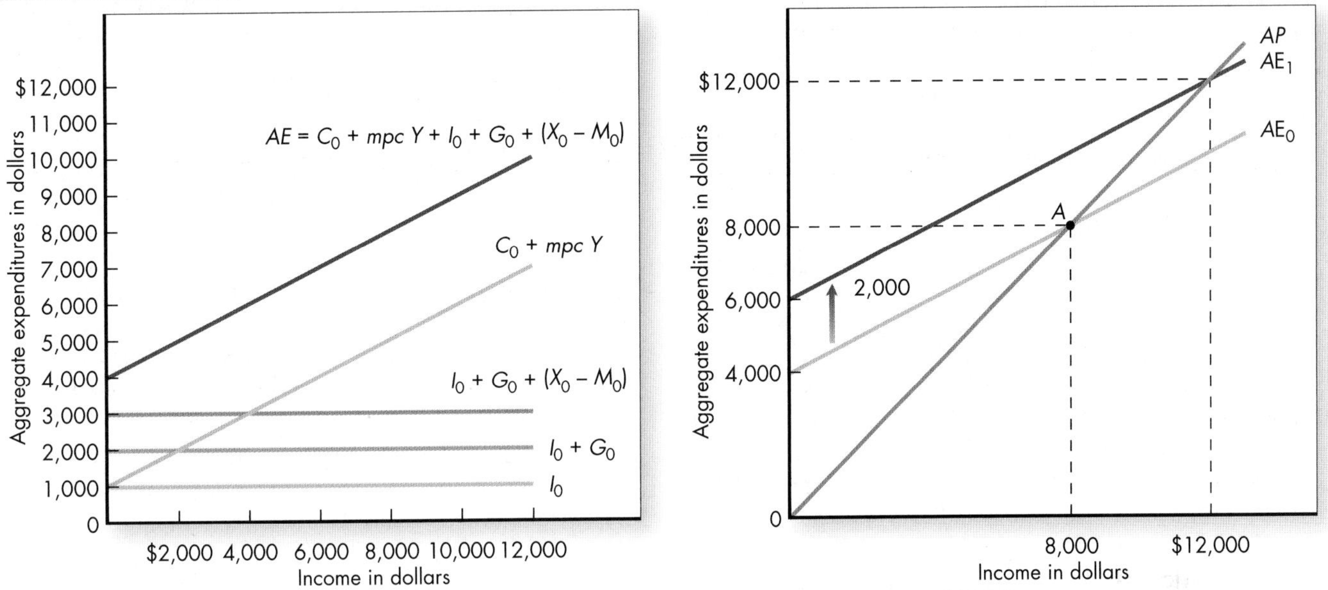

(a) Components of Aggregate Expenditures **(b) Increased Investment of $2,000**

To arrive at an aggregate expenditures function, we add up the curves vertically. I do this in Figure A28-2(a). Because we have assumed that consumption is the only expenditure that varies with income, the aggregate expenditures curve has the same slope as the consumption function. Notice that the aggregate expenditures curve crosses the vertical axis at a point that's the sum of all four autonomous expenditures: $C_0 + I_0 + G_0 + (X_0 - M_0) =$ $4,000. A good exercise to help you visualize the relationships involved is to compare the data in the columns with points on the graph to see how they correspond.

As was discussed in the text, aggregate equilibrium is where the aggregate expenditures function intersects the aggregate production curve—at point A in Figure A28-2(b). If any of the autonomous expenditures increase, the aggregate equilibrium will change. Say that autonomous investment increased by 2,000. That shifts up the *AE* curve by 2,000 and, as you can see, increases the equilibrium income by 4,000. Why by 4,000? Because of the multiplier discussed in the chapter. With only consumption varying with income, the marginal propensity to expend is determined by the marginal propensity to consume. Since in this case *mpe* = *mpc*, the multiplier is 1/(1 − *mpc*).

A More Complete Model

More generally, the various components of aggregate expenditures will depend on income in varying degrees, which will mean that the components each will have some slope—they will have both an induced and an autonomous component. The slope of the aggregate expenditures curve will be the composite of all these slopes. Presenting that case geometrically becomes quite messy, so we will switch to an algebraic presentation.

In this fuller presentation, we break up the *mpe* into its component parts so that there is an *mpc*, specified as *c* in the equations; a marginal propensity to import, specified as *m* in the equations; and a marginal tax rate, specified as *t* in the equations.

This more complete multiplier model consists of the following equations:

$$(1)\ C = C_0 + cY_d$$
$$(2)\ Y_d = Y - T + R$$
$$(3)\ I = I_0$$
$$(4)\ G = G_0$$
$$(5)\ R = R_0$$
$$(6)\ T = T_0 + tY$$
$$(7)\ X = X_0$$
$$(8)\ M = M_0 + mY$$
$$(9)\ C + I + G + (X - M) = Y$$

Equation (1) is the consumption function: C_0 is autonomous consumption; *c* is the marginal propensity to consume; cY_d is the *mpc* multiplied by disposable income.

Equation (2) defines disposable income as a function of income minus taxes plus government transfers, R.

Equation (3) is the investment function. I_0 is autonomous investment.

Equation (4) is the government expenditures function. G_0 is autonomous spending.

Equation (5) is the government transfer function. R_0 is autonomous transfer payments.

Equation (6) is the tax function. Taxes are composed of two parts. The autonomous component, T_0, is unaffected by income. The induced portion of taxes is tY. The tax rate is represented by t.

Equation (7) is the exogenous export function.

Equation (8) is the import function. Imports are composed of two parts. M_0 is the autonomous portion. The induced portion is mY. The marginal propensity to import is represented by m.

Equation (9) is the national income accounting identity: Total expenditures = income

To use this model meaningfully, we must combine all these equations into a single equation, called a *reduced-form equation*, which will neatly show the effect of various shifts on the equilibrium level of income. To do so we first substitute Equation (2) into Equation (1), giving us

$$\text{(1a) } C = C_0 + c(Y - T + R)$$

We then substitute (1a), (3), (4), (5), (6), (7), and (8) into Equation (9), giving

$$C_0 + c[Y - (T_0 + tY) + R_0] + I_0 + G_0 + [X_0 - (M_0 + mY)] = Y$$

Removing the parentheses:

$$C_0 + cY - cT_0 - ctY + cR_0 + I_0 + G_0 + X_0 - M_0 - mY = Y$$

Moving all of the Y terms to the right side:

$$C_0 - cT_0 + cR_0 + I_0 + G_0 + X_0 - M_0 = Y - cY + ctY + mY$$

Factoring out Y on the right side:

$$C_0 - cT_0 - cR_0 + I_0 + G_0 + X_0 - M_0 = Y(1 - c + ct + m)$$

Dividing by $(1 - c + ct + m)$ gives

$$[C_0 - cT_0 - cR_0 + I_0 + G_0 + X_0 - M_0] \times \left[\frac{1}{(1 - c + ct + m)}\right] = Y$$

$1/(1 - c + ct + m)$ is the multiplier for a simple multiplier model with endogenous taxes and endogenous imports.

We can relate this multiplier to the multiplier presented in the text $[1/(1 - mpe)]$ by recognizing that the marginal propensity to expend is

- Composed of the marginal propensity to consume, the marginal propensity to consume times the tax rate, and the marginal propensity to import and
- Equal to $c - ct - m$

Thus, $mpe = c - ct - m$. We can see that the two are the same by collecting terms and rewriting the multiplier as $1/[1 - (c - ct - m)]$. We can then replace the $c - ct - m$ with mpe. In the geometric case presented initially, the income tax, t, and the marginal propensity to import, m, were assumed to be zero, which reduces the multiplier to $1/(1 - c)$.

To see whether you follow the math, let's try a numerical example. Say you want to increase income (Y) by 100. Assume $c = .8$, $t = .2$, and $m = .14$. Substituting in these numbers, you find that the multiplier is 2. (The approximate multiplier for the United States is usually around 2.) Having calculated the multiplier, we can now determine how much to change autonomous expenditures to affect income. For example, to increase income by 100, we must increase autonomous expenditures by (100/2) = 50.

Questions and Exercises

1. You have just been made our nation's adviser. The president wants to increase output by 400 by decreasing taxes. Your research assistant tells you that the *mpc* is .8, and all other components of aggregate expenditures are determined outside the model. What policy would you suggest?
2. The president returns to you and tells you that instead of changing taxes, he wants to achieve the same result by increasing government expenditures. What policy would you recommend?

3. Your research assistant has a worried look on her face. "What's the problem?" you ask. "I goofed," she confesses. "I thought taxes were exogenous when actually there's a marginal tax rate of .1." Before she can utter another word, you say, "No problem. I'll simply recalculate my answers to questions 1 and 2 and change them before I send them in." What are your corrected answers?
4. She still has a pained expression. "What's wrong?" you ask. "You didn't let me finish," she says. "Not only was there a marginal tax rate of .1; there's also a marginal propensity to import of .2." Again you interrupt to make sure she doesn't feel guilty. Again you say, "No problem. I'll simply recalculate my answers to questions 1 and 2 to account for the new information." What are your new answers?
5. Explain, using the words *expenditures* and *leakages*, why making taxes and imports endogenous reduces the multiplier.
6. Suppose imports were a function of disposable income instead of income. What would be the new multiplier? How does it compare with the multiplier when imports were a function of income?

APPENDIX B

The Multiplier Model and the *AS/AD* Model

In the last chapter, I emphasized that the *AD* curve was quite different from a micro demand curve; it was an equilibrium curve—a curve that told us the relationship between different price levels and different equilibria in the goods market. It has traditionally been derived from the multiplier model, and thus it has implicitly accepted the dynamics of that model. To see how it is derived from the multiplier model, we must first recall how the *AE* curve shifts as the price level rises and falls.

In Figure B28-1(a) I draw three *AE* curves—one for each of the price levels P_1, P_2, and P_3, where $P_1 > P_2 > P_3$. How a change in the price level affects the *AE* curve can be explained by the money wealth, interest rate, and international effects. A rise in the price level will shift the *AE* curve down. Similarly, a fall in the price level will shift the *AE* curve up. (A much more detailed discussion of the relationship between the price level and expenditures can be found in the last chapter.)

The initial equilibrium is at point A. Notice that as the price level falls, aggregate expenditures rise. This initial increase causes induced expenditures to change. Production shifts because of these induced effects, increasing output further than the initial shift in aggregate expenditures and the initial increase in output to Y_1'. The new equilibrium output at P_2 is Y_2 (point B), and at P_3 the new equilibrium output is Y_3 (point C).

In Figure B28-1(b) I show the equilibrium price levels and outputs on a graph, with price level on the vertical axis and real output on the horizontal axis. That gives us points A, B, and C, which correspond to points A, B, and C in Figure B28-1(a). Drawing a line through these points gives us the aggregate demand curve: a curve that shows how a change in the price level will affect quantity of aggregate demand. Notice that the slope of the *AD* curve includes both the effect of the initial shift in aggregate expenditures from a change in the price level and the multiplier effects as production and expenditures move to equilibrium. The initial shift in aggregate expenditures is shown by point *B'*. If there were no multiplier effects, the *AD* curve would go through points *A* and *B'*.

The first thing to note when considering the two models is that the multiplier model assumes that the price level is constant, so it assumes that the aggregate supply curve is flat. This means that the multiplier model tells us precisely how much the *AD* curve will shift when autonomous expenditures shift by a specified amount. The difference between the shift in autonomous expenditures and the *AD* curve shift is due to the multiplier.

The relationship between a shift in autonomous expenditures in the *AS/AD* model and the multiplier model can be seen in Figure B28-1(c) and (d). These consider a fall in autonomous expenditures of \$20 when the multiplier is 2. In Figure B28-1(c) you can see that, in the multiplier model, a fall in expenditures of \$20 will cause income to fall by \$40, from \$4,052 to \$4,012.

Figure B28-1(d) shows that same adjustment in the *AS/AD* model. Initially expenditures fall by \$20, but the *AD* curve shifts back not by \$20, but by \$40—the initial shift multiplied by the multiplier. That's because the *AD* curves take into account the interdependent shifts between supply and demand decisions that are set in motion by the initial shift. Thus, we need the multiplier model, or some alternative model of induced effects, before we can draw an *AD* curve. (I make the qualification "or some other model" to emphasize that the interdependent shifts assumed in the multiplier model are not the only interdependent shifts that could occur. Had we assumed a different dynamic adjustment process, we would have had a different *AD* curve.)

FIGURE B28-1 (A–D) Relationship between the *AS/AD* Model and the *AP/AE* Model

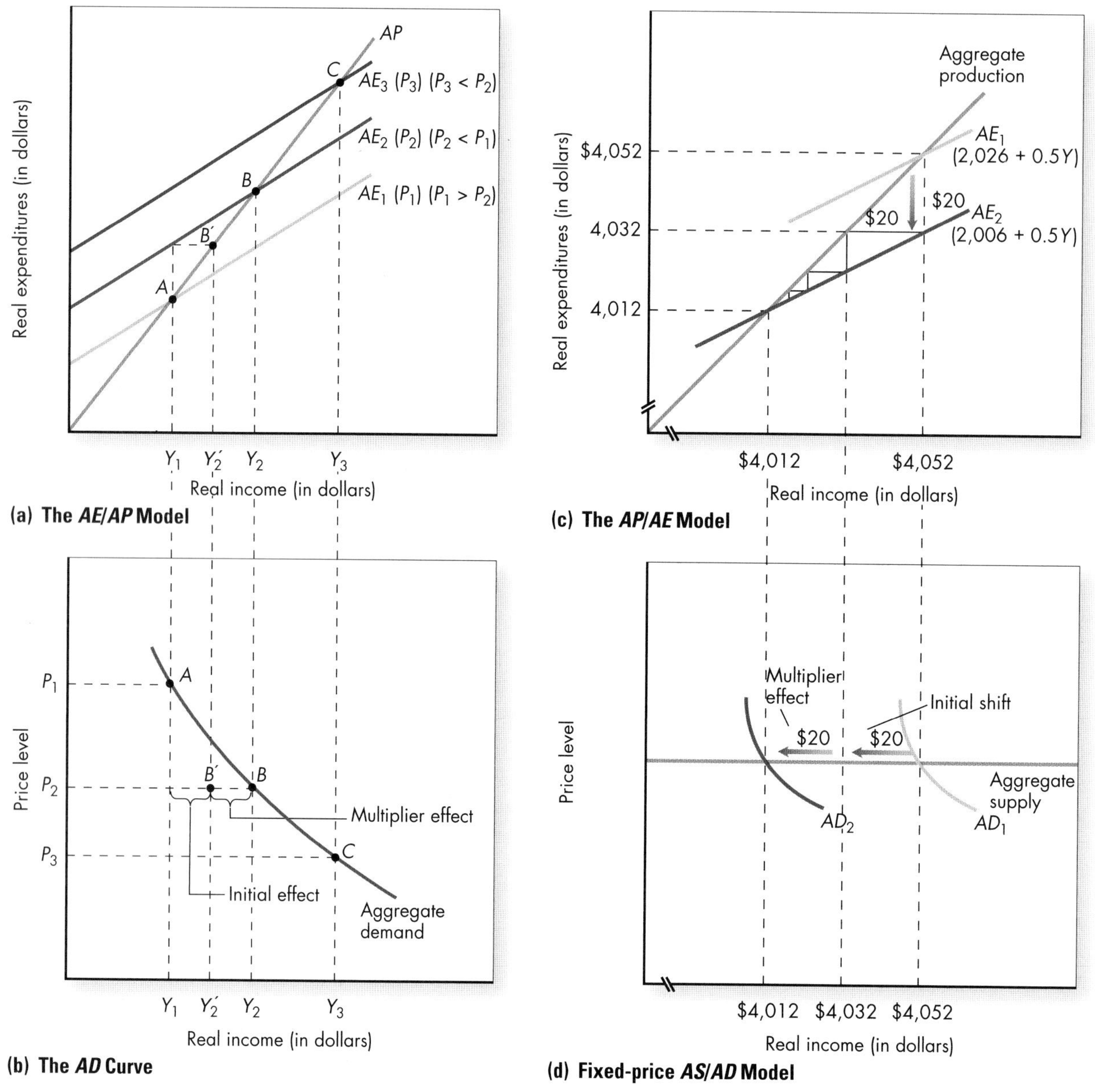

A good test of your understanding here is to ask yourself what happens in the long run if the economy is operating above its potential where prices are perfectly flexible. (In that case, the rise in aggregate demand is fully offset by a rise in the price level, and the *AE* curve shifts right back where it started.)

Much of the modern debate in macro concerns the dynamic adjustment process that the multiplier model is meant to describe. We won't go into that debate here since it quickly becomes very complicated, but I do want to point out to you that the multiplier model is not the end of the analysis; it is simply the beginning—one of the simplest cases of dynamic adjustment. The real-world dynamic adjustment is more complicated, which is one of the reasons why there is so much debate about macroeconomic issues.

Questions and Exercises

1. Demonstrate graphically the effect of an increase in autonomous expenditures when the *mpe* = .5 and the *SAS* curve is flat:
   a. In the multiplier model.
   b. In the *AS/AD* model.
   c. Do the same thing as in *a* and *b*, only this time assume that the *SAS* curve is upward-sloping.
2. State how the following information changes the slope of the *AD* curve.
   a. The effect of price level changes on autonomous expenditures is reduced.
   b. The size of the multiplier increases.
   c. Autonomous expenditures increase by $20.
   d. Falls in the price level disrupt financial markets, which offset the normally assumed effects of a change in the price level.

Thinking Like a Modern Macroeconomist

Maybe there is in human nature a deep-seated perverse pleasure in adopting and defending a wholly counterintuitive doctrine that leaves the uninitiated peasant wondering what planet he or she is on.

—Robert Solow

AFTER READING THIS CHAPTER, YOU SHOULD BE ABLE TO:

1. Distinguish between the standard macro model and the modern macro model.
2. Trace the development of the standard and modern models of the economy.
3. Discuss the advantages and disadvantages of the standard macro model.
4. Explain what assumption each of the letters in "DSGE" from the DSGE model represents.
5. State three policy implications of the dynamic stochastic general equilibrium (DSGE) model.
6. Summarize the complex systems approach to macro.

When I told my editor that I was going to write a chapter on thinking like a modern macroeconomist, she screamed. Why? Because she knows what modern macro is; it is a highly theoretical, highly mathematical set of models with no simple application to macro policy. Modern macro is all the things that the standard macroeconomics isn't.

To give you a sense of how technical modern macro is, consider this sentence from the introductory chapter of top modern economists Lars Ljungqvist and Thomas Sargent's recent graduate introductory macro text. In it they discuss the "spectral density matrix and the Fourier transform of the covariogram of a covariant stationary stochastic process." Yeah right—ain't no way anyone is going to dare to put that into an introductory economics text and hope to sell any.[1]

Most introductory textbook authors shelter you from such terminological thuggery, believing it will scare you half to death. But, as you've gathered, I'm not the usual introductory textbook author. I jump in where only fools tread, and I bring my readers with me. I do so not because I am a sadist, but rather because I am a teacher who wants my students to have a sense of modern macro, and I can't give you that sense without letting you know that it is highly technical.

Why It Is Important to Know about Modern Macro Theory

There are three reasons why I believe that you need to know about modern macro theory. The first is that if you're learning macro, you don't want to learn outdated arguments and theories. You might be left thinking that macroeconomists are

[1]Well, I just put it in—so see, editors, I dare. But to students reading this chapter, don't worry; I put it there just to show that I could. I don't expect you to memorize it; it's definitely not going to be on the test.

stupid, and that certainly isn't the case. Modern economists are bright—super bright—and macroeconomists are among the brightest of the bright. You deserve to be introduced to their models.

Modern economists are bright—super bright—and macroeconomists are among the brightest of the bright. You deserve to be introduced to their models.

A second reason is that modern macro models are fundamentally different from **standard macro models**—*the models (such as the AS/AD and multiplier models and their derivatives) used by most applied macroeconomists*. Modern macro models provide different frames of analysis than those standard macro models. (Remember back to Chapter 6 where I discussed the importance of framing.) Were modern macro models simply more technical versions of the standard macro models that I have presented to you in the last two chapters, there would be no need to present them. But they aren't. They are fundamentally different, and they provide you with a totally different frame for thinking about macro problems. That different frame provides important caveats about applying the standard macro model that led to the many addenda that I added to discussions of the policy implications of the two models I presented above. This chapter helps you understand where those caveats come from.

Q-1 Name two standard macroeconomic models.

A third reason why it is important to include a discussion of modern macro models is that these models are being used for policy decisions. For example, modern macroeconomists from the University of Minnesota, V. V. Chari and Patrick Kehoe write, "Over the last several decades, the United States and other countries have undertaken a variety of policy changes that are precisely what macroeconomic theory of the last 30 years [i.e., modern macroeconomics] suggests." They further state, "To what particular policies should policymakers commit themselves? For many macroeconomists considering this question, quantitative general equilibrium models [another name for modern macro models] have become the workhorse model, and they turn out to offer surprisingly sharp answers."

Most economists agree that the modern macro model demonstrates some logical problems with the standard macro models, which should make any user think long and hard before basing policy on them. Many economists are not so sure it does more than that. There is a lively ongoing debate in the economics profession about the extent to which modern macro models can be fruitfully used for policy analysis. Advocates argue that, at a minimum, the modern macro model provides an important counterbalance to the policy activism suggested by the standard macro models.

There is a lively ongoing debate in the economics profession about the extent to which modern macro models can be fruitfully used for policy analysis.

The chapter proceeds as follows. First, I review the distinction between *engineering models* and *scientific models* that I presented in Chapter 6, and relate that distinction to why modern and standard macro models differ. Second, I briefly review the history of macroeconomic thinking and explain why scientific economists moved away from using standard macro models, while applied policy economists stuck with them. Third, I provide a beginning student's guide to the dominant modern macro model (the dynamic stochastic general equilibrium model), explaining what I believe it captures and what it doesn't. And, finally, I discuss some work on the frontier of modern macro science that is working to reintegrate the scientific and engineering models, and how that work challenges the policy precepts of both the standard macro models and the dominant modern macro models.

Engineering Models and Scientific Models

As I've emphasized throughout this book, modern economic thinking involves reducing a question to a model, and then using that model to analyze a problem or a question. In Chapter 6, we saw the debate between traditional economists and behavioral economists about which model to use, and how different choices led to different policy focuses. In macro, we have all those same debates about modeling, but we also have another debate—whether we should be using what is essentially an **engineering model**—*a model with loose*

It is important to distinguish engineering models from scientific models.

formal foundations whose primary purpose is to guide thinking about policy, or a **deductive scientific model**—*a model with carefully specified formal foundations whose primary purpose is understanding for the sake of understanding*. Policy relevance is a nice sidelight of a scientific model, but it is not the primary focus.

Standard Models as Engineering Models and the Modern Model as a Scientific Model

Q-2 Is the standard macro model a scientific or engineering model?

The standard macro models that you learned in the past two chapters are the models used by most business and government macroeconomists. They are best seen as engineering models. They are very institutionally oriented models that provide a framework for discussing macro policy.

Modern macroeconomic scientists use deductive scientific models of the macroeconomy such as the dynamic stochastic general equilibrium (DSGE) model. (I will explain the DSGE model below.) Modern macroeconomists see their models as only indirectly relevant for policy. For example, when Robert Lucas, a Nobel Prize–winning modern macroeconomist at the University of Chicago, was asked what he would do if he were appointed to the Council of Economic Advisers, he said that he would resign.

That doesn't mean that modern macro scientific models don't have policy implications—they do. At a minimum they raise serious concerns about naïvely applying the simple standard engineering models that you learned in the last two chapters to policy, and they point out several important addenda to those standard models.

Some modern macroeconomists go further, however, and try to use their scientific models to provide specific policy advice. For example, some argue that modern macro models tell us definitively that discretionary monetary and fiscal policy won't work. While textbook authors (me included) bend over backwards to be neutral and present all sides (it's not that we're naturally fair—it's just that we don't want to lose sales), let me say now that such a definitive view is simply wrong. As the famous London School of Economics economist Lionel Robbins put it: "In the present state of knowledge, the man who can claim for economic science much exactitude is a quack." (Who said I wasn't opinionated?)

The different focuses of the standard macro model and modern macro model are reasonable.

The different focuses of the standard macro model and modern macro model are reasonable. Government and business economists need their models to be quickly applicable. They use a combination of empirical and deductive models that have evolved over time and provide a reasonable framework for talking about macro problems. The standard macro models are rough and ready models that seem to have worked in the past. The models are meant to be used by practitioners who care much more about *whether* a model works than *how* it works.

Modern macroeconomic scientists care first and foremost about the logic of their models: knowing that they work without knowing *how* and *why* just doesn't cut it for them. The scientific macro model is much more formal and precise than are engineering models. Whereas the engineering models include lots of hand waving and loose discussion appealing to intuition, the scientific model carefully spells out all the assumptions. Economists can argue about whether or not the assumptions are reasonable, but the logical implications of *making* those assumptions are clear. (Well . . . the models are extremely formal and complex, so the implications are really only clear to someone who has studied lots and lots of math!)

Engineering and Scientific Models Are Different Models

Ideally, the scientific and the engineering models would work in parallel, with the engineering models being simplified and less formal versions of the scientific models. In that case, it wouldn't be necessary to introduce you to the modern macro model—the standard macro model would have been your introduction. Unfortunately, that isn't the case in macro. The scientific models are completely different from the engineering models. This differentiation exists because modern macroeconomic scientists have come to believe that the standard macro models are fundamentally unscientific, so they've been working on developing more scientific alternatives. At the same time, most applied policy macroeconomists don't believe that these alternatives actually *work* for answering most policy questions, at least not yet. That's because, in order to be a model that can be solved, the current scientific model has had to leave out many complications, and most applied policy macroeconomists think that these complications play an important role in the workings of the economy.

From the Keynesian Revolution to Modern Macro Models

Let's now consider how we got to the development of these two vastly different kinds of macro models. As is discussed in previous chapters, macroeconomics began in the 1930s with the Keynesian model. Classical macroeconomists (all macroeconomists before the 1930s) didn't have a formal model of the macroeconomy; instead they had a number of informal models—the most important of which was the quantity theory of money that posited a relationship between the quantity of money in a country and the price level: the greater the amount of money, the higher the price level. These informal models were based on loose empirical regularities that they had discovered over time.

While Classical economists did not have a science of macroeconomics from which they could develop theorems, they did have a number of precepts about macro policy. These included

- The government should practice sound finance; the government should always balance the budget.
- The government should maintain a strong currency: The government should face restrictions that prevent it from printing too much money. Keeping the central bank independent and having a gold standard were seen as the best ways to do that.
- The government should be prepared for the central bank to be the lender of last resort; if you have a financial crisis, the central bank should make lots of credit available at a high interest rate.

Classical economic precepts included sound finance, maintaining a strong currency and the central bank being the lender of last resort.

These policy precepts guided Classical economists' advice about macro policy and were supported by general reasoning, but no formal model.

The Emergence of the Keynesian Model

The Great Depression of the 1930s challenged Classical economic precepts and led to the development of the Keynesian model and Keynesian (interpret "activist") precepts about policy, which replaced the Classical model. This development was called the Keynesian Revolution because it was based on the work of Cambridge University economist John Maynard Keynes. Through the 1950s learning macroeconomics meant learning the Keynesian model. The multiplier model in the last chapter developed from that early model.

Keynesian economics, as it initially developed, was based on an idea known as the *fallacy of composition*—what is true for the parts is not necessarily true for the aggregate. What this meant in terms of economics is that at least some features of the economy as a whole can't be understood just by understanding the behavior of individuals and firms.

For example, in the supply/demand model, supply and demand are assumed to be independent of each other. In the aggregate economy, the assumption could not hold—when aggregate supply changes, aggregate demand will change as well—the two are interdependent. Microeconomics and macroeconomics were seen as distinct, much like the difference between quantum physics of the subatomic level and the standard physics of large objects. That's why if you were taking economics 20 or more years ago, you could begin studying economics with either microeconomics or macroeconomics. They were different subjects with different models.

A Model without Microfoundations

The standard macro model began as a top-down model that emphasized the fallacy of composition.

Q-3 Are microfoundations needed for a macro model?

Appealing to the fallacy of composition, the standard macro model began as a top-down model that *started* with aggregate relationships, not with a deductive model of the aggregate economy built on the traditional building blocks of microeconomic reasoning. Put another way, it had no formal microfoundations, and macroeconomists didn't think it needed any—it was *macro*economic analysis.

There is nothing wrong with a macro model without microfoundations. As I will discuss below, the modern scientific complex system approach to macro is trying to develop precisely such a model. An economist would use a macro model rather than a micro-founded model because he or she believes there are so many complex interactions in the economy that these interactions cannot be captured in a solvable micro-founded model, and that the aggregate system is going to behave quite differently than could be usefully predicted from a micro analysis of the components. An example from weather might help you understand: Meteorologists use "macro" properties like the jet stream (fast-flowing, relatively narrow streams of air about 6–10 miles from the ground that typically flow east across the continental United States) and hurricane patterns to predict the weather. Trying to understand weather patterns by studying the micro-level motion of individual air molecules is simply not fruitful.

The early macroeconomists' vision of the aggregate economy was similar: macroeconomics, like the weather, is too complex to study from the bottom up. The subsequent history of macro can be viewed as a gradual but near-complete erosion of that vision.

The Movement Away from True Top-Down Macro Models Scientists don't like to admit that a problem is too complex for them to analyze, so even though using macro models without microfoundations isn't wrong in principle, macroeconomic theorists didn't like it, and they worked hard to combine the micro models and the macro models. And as they did, the vision that the macroeconomy was too complex to have microfoundations began to fade. Starting in the 1960s, macroeconomists expanded many of the Keynesian models into more complicated models with selective microfoundations. They focused less on the fallacy of composition, and the strict separation of micro and macro disappeared. Macroeconomists continued to use the same basic Keynesian models but began to believe that the models were based implicitly on microfoundations. The microfoundations were not fully understood, but macroeconomists believed they eventually would be.

Microeconomics made its way into macro models when macroeconomists of this period built various sectors—a monetary sector, a labor market sector, a consumption goods sector, and a household sector, each of which could be described by an equation—into a composite model of the macroeconomy.[2] Many of these macro

[2]It was at that time that it became standard to start the principles of macroeconomics course with a discussion of supply and demand and microeconomics, so that students had the tools to discuss the subsectors of the macro model.

models had over 300 equations. Engineering and scientific models at this time followed the same reasoning. The higher-level macro models were extensions of the simple multiplier model with more sectors, and more sophisticated analysis of what went on in those sectors.

Problems Begin to Surface These multisector macro models provided the basis for policy analysis at the time—they were engineering models. But they were increasingly based on, and fine-tuned with, formal statistical tools that integrated real data into their equations, and by the mid 1960s these macro models were being presented not as engineering models, but as fully scientific ones.

Unfortunately, the real-world data didn't fit the models as well as macroeconomists would have liked, and some of the fundamental behavioral relationships (microfoundations) that their Keynesian macro models assumed began to be called into question. For example, Keynesian models had been based on a particular relationship between current consumption and current income (the consumption function). When economists started studying and empirically measuring that relationship, however, they found that it was not anywhere near as close a relationship as they had assumed. They discovered, for example, that expectations, wealth, and expected future income also played important roles in determining consumption.

Q-4 True or false? The standard macro models were abandoned despite the fact that they fit the empirical facts well.

Consumption Depends on Lifetime Income To correct the problem, economists set out to develop models that would reflect rational behavior in the traditional microeconomic sense discussed in Chapter 6. These models made current consumption based on lifetime, not just on current, income. In these models, changes in current income did not change consumption much. For example, say you earn an extra 10 percent income this year. The standard macro model assumes you will increase consumption by some percentage of that increase in income—say 60 percent. But, in these new models, unless the increase in income is expected to continue, a 10 percent increase in income represents less than half a percent of one's lifetime income (depending on the person's age). So if people base their consumption on lifetime income, as "rational" people would do, they would not increase their consumption much at all in response to an increase in current income. Thus, if people are rational, the underlying reasoning with the standard macro models was faulty.

Questioning Theoretical Foundations As statistical techniques and computer power to use them developed, economists discovered that *most* of the close empirical relationships that earlier economists thought they had found were questionable. What they thought were empirically grounded relationships were, in fact, just common time trends between two variables. That is, over time, both increased and thus looked as if they were closely related, but in fact, when researchers analyzed the data with high-powered statistical techniques, they discovered that the variables were nowhere near as closely related as they first seemed.

The mounting empirical evidence that their models were imperfect forced economists to look more carefully at the theoretical foundations of their models. When they did so, they found that when they assumed individuals are rational in the traditional microeconomic sense and forward looking, the very *logic* of their macro models was flawed. They began to lose faith that these models *could* actually be micro founded, as they had tacitly assumed. As was the case with consumption, the relationships in the models assumed that people based their actions on current variables. Economists began to argue that rational individuals would base their actions on both current variables and expected variables.

This has important policy implications. Let's say, for instance, that the government runs expansionary fiscal and monetary policy when the economy experiences a recession. If people are rational, they will come to expect that government will run expansionary monetary and fiscal policy in the future, and will build that expectation into their behavior. So whereas with the standard macro model a decline in aggregate demand leads to a falling price level as people cut their prices when they cannot sell their goods, if people expect government to boost aggregate demand, they no longer cut their prices—government will create sufficient demand through expansionary policy. The expectation of government policy will build an inflationary bias in the structure of the economy, which is what happened during this time. In fact, in the 1970s, the term *stagflation*—the combination of high unemployment and high inflation—developed. The recession raised unemployment while government policies and the expectation of government intervention kept inflation high. The standard macro model could not explain stagflation.

If macroeconomists had been willing to accept that their models were *ad hoc* engineering models with no claim to being scientifically grounded, the standard macro models might have remained more popular. But macroeconomists of the time were unwilling to admit that, and the standard macro models lost favor among economic scientists. At that point, macroeconomists started working on a new model that avoided the problems of the standard macro model.

Microfoundations and New Classical Macroeconomics

Web Note 29.1
Recent Nobel
Prizes for Macro

The first big step in the shift away from the standard macroeconomics occurred in the late 1970s and early 1980s, when macroeconomists, led by Nobel Prize–winner Robert Lucas, showed formally that you couldn't derive the standard macro models from traditional micro building blocks, and therefore the macro models were not based on deductive reasoning (and weren't even internally logical). This led to the development of **New Classical macroeconomics**—*an approach to macroeconomics that studies macroeconomic questions using traditional microeconomic building blocks that emphasize rationality.* New Classical macroeconomics changed the frame within which macro models were considered. The fallacy of composition was completely discarded as New Classical macroeconomists concentrated on getting the logic of the model right. The DSGE model, which I describe below, is an example of a New Classical macro model.

New Classical macroeconomics is an approach to macroeconomics that studies macroeconomic questions using traditional microeconomic building blocks that emphasize rationality.

In many ways, New Classical macroeconomics was not macroeconomics at all—it was the microeconomics of an entire economy. By that I mean that New Classical macroeconomics is a complete departure from standard macro. Instead of making the flows of aggregates the centerpiece of their model, New Classical macroeconomists made the decision process of an individual, using traditional assumptions of rationality and self-interest, the centerpiece of the model. For a New Classical economist, macro was simply micro writ large.

In developing their macro model, the problem that the New Classical macroeconomists had to face was the same problem that the earlier macroeconomists had to face—the complexity of the aggregate economy. New Classicals, however, approached the problem in a fundamentally different way than did earlier macroeconomists. Instead of thinking of the macroeconomy as involving too many interactions to formally model from the bottom up, they simply abstracted from those interactions by focusing on the decisions that a *single individual*—known as a **representative agent**—would make over multiple time periods. They set their goal as developing a model of the aggregate economy built on the solid traditional microfoundations of rationality, foresight, and self-interest. It was this New Classical version of "macro as micro writ large" that led to the modern DSGE (dynamic stochastic general equilibrium) model.

Q-5 How does New Classical macroeconomics differ from Keynesian macroeconomics?

A Beginner's Guide to the DSGE Model

Probably the best way to introduce you to the DSGE model is with Nobel Prize–winner Robert Solow's description:

> [The DSGE model is] a model in which a single immortal consumer–worker–owner maximizes a perfectly conventional time-additive utility function over an infinite horizon, under perfect foresight or rational expectations, and in an institutional and technological environment that favors universal price-taking behavior.

That's a verbal translation of the DSGE model down from the highly mathematical way that it is normally presented to the level of what might be called normal "professorese." I agree; professorese still leaves it pretty incomprehensible to even the most conscientious beginning student. So I'll translate it into something a bit more understandable.

A Single Immortal Consumer–Worker–Owner

Web Note 29.2
DSGE Applications

The DSGE model reduces the macro problem down to the problem facing a single individual whom we assume lives forever. (We are actually not worried about him dying, but if we don't assume that he lives forever, the mathematics gets considerably more complicated.) Our representative individual is interested in consuming as much as he can and working as little as he can and is pondering how best to manage the trade-off between work and consumption over his lifetime.

Thus, for example, he is asking himself questions such as: How much do I want to consume now as opposed to later? When do I want to retire? Should I borrow money now so I can consume more now, taking into account that I will have to pay it back later? The fact that he is making decisions that will guide him through his entire lifetime rather than just decisions for a single point in time is where the **d**ynamic (in the **D**SGE) comes from; **dynamic** means *taking "time" explicitly into account*. Because the representative individual is looking forward and making decisions over time in the model, it is a dynamic model.

A Perfectly Conventional Time-Additive Utility Function

To talk about our representative individual's decision, we have to specify what he likes and what he doesn't like, and how he makes his decisions. Solow captures the assumption about the representative individual's likes and dislikes in the statement that the individual maximizes "a time-additive utility function." What that means is that our representative individual is a fairly conventional person who sees trade-offs in life—he is willing to give up some pleasure now to get more later, and vice versa. Moreover, the specifications of the pleasure or utility he gets from those activities are not interconnected in complicated ways; for example, his decisions about what to do today don't affect the choices he'll want to make tomorrow, except possibly through their effects on his wealth.

Perfect Foresight or Rational Expectations

The DSGE model also assumes that our representative individual is a very, very bright person, with a lightening-fast calculating mind. By that I mean that he is able to make all these decisions perfectly and instantaneously—his mind doesn't get boggled as mine often does when faced with complicated decisions. Moreover, he is taking into account *all* possibilities that might happen. That's where the perfect foresight and **rational expectations**—*expectations that turn out to be correct in reference to the model*—come from. He gets his decisions right, before he does anything. He makes no mistakes. This is what Solow means when he says the person has perfect foresight.

Rational expectations are expectations that turn out to be correct in reference to the model.

Actually, the concept of perfect foresight needs a bit of clarification: he doesn't know what will actually happen; instead he knows all the things that *might* happen and the probability with which each of them will happen. That's where the stochastic in the DSGE comes in. **Stochastic** means that *events happen with a certain probability that can be specified mathematically*. So our representative individual doesn't know what will happen, but he does know the probability that the various events will happen. (Think of throwing a die—you know that you will get a 1 through a 6 with a 1/6th chance of each.) Our representative individual figures out what to do for each of these possible outcomes (called contingent states), and for all the contingent states that are contingent on each of these. In fact, he has calculated his best strategy for every possible potential outcome that might occur. Doing so makes the stochastic model the analytic equivalent to a perfect foresight model (although it has a lot more variables), which is why Solow calls it a perfect foresight model.

Universal Price-Taking Behavior

To make his decisions, our representative individual has to know the structure of the markets. Will some firm create a monopoly and push up prices? How will the markets interact? To answer that question, we have to make assumptions about markets and here we see from Solow's description that there is almost "universal price-taking behavior." That means that almost all markets are assumed to be highly competitive, so that the forces of supply and demand are the primary determinants of price. All these markets are assumed to be in equilibrium. So the model is a **general equilibrium model,** which means that it is *a model of all the markets in the economy, not just a single market*. A general equilibrium model is one in which you include interrelationships among markets and do not hold "all other things constant" as you do in *partial equilibrium* supply/demand models. (That's where the general equilibrium in the DSGE comes in.)

Q-6 What does DSGE stand for?

Now these assumptions may seem highly restrictive, and they are. Macro scientists make them not because they think they perfectly, or even closely, describe reality, but because they are necessary if economists are going to be able to solve this macro model. Modern macroeconomists are working hard on extending the model—adding more than one representative individual, adding less than perfectly competitive markets, adding the possibility of more than one equilibrium, and many more variations. In the United States, most graduate macroeconomic dissertations are working on extending the DSGE model.

Policy Implications of the DSGE Model

One reason to study the DSGE model is that it provides insight into policy and the way people will likely react to policy. Let's consider three policy implications that modern macroeconomists have drawn from the DSGE model.

The Ricardian Equivalence Problem

Three policy implications of the DSGE model are (1) the Ricardian equivalences problem, (2) the time inconsistency/credibility problem, and (3) the Lucas critique problem.

The first policy implication is the **Ricardian equivalence problem**—*the problem that anything the government does to affect the economy will mostly be offset by countervailing actions by private individuals as they optimize over the future*. Say the government runs a deficit in order to expand the economy. Our representative individual will reason that the government will have to borrow to pay for the deficit, which will mean that he will have to pay higher taxes in the future in order to pay the loan back. Consider what that means for his decision. Since he has to pay higher taxes in the future, he will want to save more now, which will mean that he will consume less now. This means that the expansionary effect of the government deficit will be offset by the contractionary effect of the representative consumer decreasing consumption. The net effect is a wash and the supposed expansionary effect of fiscal policy evaporates.

WWW Web Note 29.3 Still Problematic

The Time-Inconsistency/Credibility Problem

The second policy implication of the DSGE model is the **time-inconsistency/credibility problem**—*the problem that the best government policy from today's point of view can turn out to be a policy the government wants to change in the future, and that rational individuals can anticipate this*. Consider, for example, the best government policy regarding prescription drugs. The best policy for a government that wants to encourage businesses to develop a new anti-cancer drug might be patent protection for new discoveries. But once an important new discovery has been made, the government's best policy changes: government will want to allow competition so the drug will be more affordable. That's the *time inconsistency* part of the problem. The *credibility* part of the problem is the observation that drug developers can anticipate that the government will have an incentive to renege on promises of patent protection. If the government cannot credibly commit to protect the patents, even when it doesn't want to later, the government may find it hard to encourage businesses to develop the drugs at all.

The same sorts of problems can arise with discretionary monetary policy to fight recessions. When the economy is falling into recession, standard macro precepts suggest running expansionary monetary policy. But let's think about the consequences of running expansionary monetary policy if our representative agent *expects* this to happen. He will build that expectation into his actions when deciding on his best dynamic plan of action. He will reason—whenever the economy goes into a recession, the government will step in and increase demand, making it unnecessary for me to lower my wage or price. The result will be that wages and prices won't fall in a recession and there is an inflationary bias built into the economy. Now here's the crunch. In order to prevent this inflationary bias from generating accelerating inflation, the Fed will have to run contractionary monetary policy.

Because of this inflationary bias, the best policy might be for the government *not* to fight recessions so strongly so that the representative agent will lower his wage or price during recessions, reducing the need for government to implement contractionary monetary policy, allowing it to maintain a lower natural rate of unemployment. But even though the best *policy rule* is to refrain from fighting recessions too strongly, the best *policy* if and when any *particular* recession comes is to renege on the rule and fight it just as hard as if there were no inflationary bias problems. In this case, government can lower unemployment without risking higher inflation. In other words, the *best* thing for a government to do is to successfully convince people that it *won't* fight recessions, and then, once they're convinced, fight recessions anyway. But this means that people are unlikely to be convinced in the first place!

One can get around the time-inconsistency problem by establishing credible rules—such as an explicit inflation target, or a "balanced budget rule" that guides policy rather than choosing the best policy on a case-by-case basis. Not surprisingly, the rules have become a central part of the discussions in modern macroeconomic policy.

The Lucas Critique Problem

The final problem that the DSGE model highlights is the **Lucas critique problem**—*the problem that because government policies can affect the behavior of individuals, historical data can lead to misleading predictions about the impact of a* new *policy*. Because the standard macro model is based on historical relationships among the data, this undermines the logic of the standard macroeconometric model.

Q-7 What are three policy problems that the DSGE model has highlighted?

The classic example of this problem has to do with inflation. Most economists now believe that *unexpectedly* high inflation can cause lower unemployment, but that (modestly) high inflation that is anticipated does not affect unemployment. Now imagine you didn't know this, and you were examining an economy in which the government had long been taking a "hands off" policy approach. In some years in this economy, just by random chance, inflation had been unexpectedly high, so that unemployment was low. In other years, inflation happened to be unexpectedly low, so unemployment was high.

If you were making a model of the relationship between inflation and unemployment by just looking at the historical pattern of data in this economy, your model would show that high inflation goes hand-in-hand with low unemployment. The model would "predict" that the government could lower unemployment by raising inflation. The problem with this model is that it does not take into account the possibility that individuals are rational. If individuals are rational, they will know that government is implementing such a policy and will expect higher inflation. The underlying relationship between inflation and unemployment, which could not be discerned from the data alone, requires that inflation be unexpected. Because the model doesn't take this into account, its prediction would be *wrong*. *Anticipated* inflation is unlikely to have much of an effect on unemployment.

The basic problem with macro models based on patterns in historical data is that unless the model correctly captures *why* the patterns exist, changes in policies can reveal shortcomings in the structural integrity of the model. This makes the models irrelevant for providing policy advice. Notice that the model above based on the data worked perfectly well until it was used to provide policy advice—but then it stopped working completely. Without the ability to provide policy advice, you might as well throw out all the applied policy macro models.

How Relevant Are the Problems?

As you can see, the DSGE model poses some significant challenges for the logic and policy implications of the standard macro model that you learned in the last two chapters. Those problems have been the subject of much discussion in economics over the past decade. Don't worry; I am not going to go through that discussion. Let me just say that advocates of the standard macro model have an answer for each of these problems. Essentially, the answer is that the standard macro model is an engineering model that requires care in application, and that in applying the models they take these problems into account.

The standard macro model is a highly imperfect and problematic model, and significant care must be taken in drawing any policy conclusions from it.

That's a reasonable argument for an engineering model, but it does not save the standard macro model as a scientific model. The standard macro model is a highly imperfect and problematic model, and significant care must be taken in drawing any policy conclusions from it. When I presented the models, I tried to do that. If you read the chapters carefully, you noticed that all three problems were discussed as potential difficulties with the model in those chapters. Almost all economists agree with these cautions.

Some DSGE advocates (macroeconomic theorists), however, go further than that and argue that the standard macro model is just plain wrong. That view is not universal, however, and my friends who are applied policy macroeconomists in business or government tell me that standard macro models are much more useful in understanding what's going on in the macroeconomy than are the modern scientific macro models. As you can see, there are some major differences of opinion among modern macroeconomists about which model to use and what macro theory is relevant.

You can probably tell where I stand from my discussion at the beginning of this chapter. While the DSGE model provides helpful cautions for the standard macro policy, as it currently exists, in my opinion, the DSGE model should not be used for direct policy analysis. But more and more macroeconomists are arguing that the DSGE model is relevant for policy, so it needs some discussion. Central banks are now starting to use DSGE models for direct policy analysis in an attempt to be "modern." I consider this use of the model a major mistake.

To give you a better sense of what the advocates of using the DSGE model for policy argue, let's consider some arguments of University of Minnesota economists V. V. Chari and Patrick Kehoe, who have been forceful advocates for using the DSGE model for policy advice. In an article in the Winter 2006 issue the *Journal of Economic Perspectives*, they write:

> Macroeconomics [by which they mean the DSGE model] is now firmly grounded in the principles of economic theory. These advances have not been restricted to the ivory tower [by which they mean graduate school macroeconomics professors]. Over the last several decades, the United States and other countries have undertaken a variety of policy changes that are precisely what macroeconomic theory of the last 30 years suggests. . .
>
> Examples of the effects of theory on the practice of policy include increased central bank independence and adoption of inflation targeting and other rules to guide monetary policy.

and

> Macroeconomic theory has had a profound and far reaching effect on the institutions and practices governing monetary policy and is beginning to have a similar effect on fiscal policy. The marginal social product of macroeconomic science is surely large and growing rapidly.

They draw the following implications from the DSGE model:

> . . . discretionary (macro) policy making has only costs and no benefits, so that if government policymakers can be made to commit to a policy rule, society should make them do so.

Is such a strong position justified and should we accept the "sharp answers" of the DSGE models? My view is definitely not, and the mistake that Chari and Kehoe make is not distinguishing theorems from precepts. One draws theorems—logical deductions that follow from the model, given all the assumptions of the model—from a model. To move from theorems to policy precepts you have to make a decision about how well the assumptions of the model fit reality.

For example, what happens if the economy isn't perfectly competitive (as it surely is not)? What happens if people cannot make infinitely fast calculations or aren't perfectly rational? What happens if the system does not have a single equilibrium but many equilibria? What happens if people's pleasure depends on complicated interrelationships over time, so that we can't use additive utility functions? And many, many more. Once one moves to precepts, most economists believe that the implications about policy that Chari and Kehoe draw from the model are incorrect. The DSGE model is just too far removed from anything resembling the real-world economy for anyone to draw definitive policy conclusions from it. It provides cautions and addenda, not policy conclusions.

The DSGE model is just too far removed from anything resembling the real-world economy for anyone to draw definitive policy conclusions from it.

Consider the bank crisis of 2008. Ben Bernanke, an advocate of inflation targeting and central bank independence—both policies that follow from the DSGE model—directly violated the precept of inflation targeting; he also asked Congress for a stronger connection between the central bank and the government than had existed before. Why? Because he felt that the crisis warranted it, and the precepts that followed from the DSGE model did not fit the circumstances. He was most worried about preventing a major depression. Most applied policy macroeconomists agreed with him.

All macroeconomists agree that views on macro policy have changed over the past decades, but most applied macroeconomists argue that events shaped that change more than developments in macro theory, and that the arguments for and against central bank independence, inflation targeting, and rules over discretion were well known long before the modern DSGE model developed. The primary contribution of modern macro theorists has been to translate well-known policy insights into formal mathematics, and remind economists of their importance.

The primary contribution of modern macro theorists has been to translate well-known policy insights into formal mathematics, and remind economists of their importance.

Modern Macroeconomic Policy and the Collapse of the Tacoma Narrows Bridge

Let me give you an example of when too heavy reliance on a formal scientific model can lead engineers astray. In the late 1930s, using the best science of the time, engineers built a bridge over the Tacoma Narrows in Washington. The formal scientific models of the bridge concluded that the bridge was solid and safe. Unfortunately, the modelers were not able to include something that we now call "aerodynamic flutter" that can cause tortional disturbance. (Don't ask.) This aerodynamic flutter meant that even mild winds caused the bridge to sway. When the bridge was built, people noticed that it swayed a bit and initially the bridge architects said the swaying presented no problem—their models said the bridge was solid and safe.

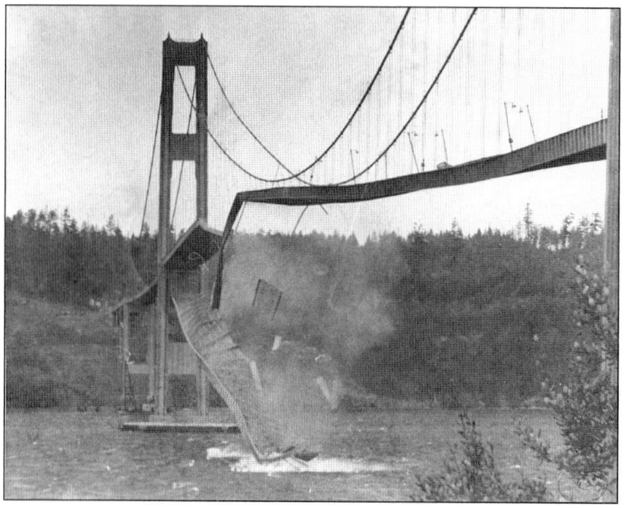

On November 7, 1940, they were proved wrong when the swaying increased, causing the bridge to sway like a blanket being lifted up and down on both sides. (You can see the collapse of the bridge on a variety of sites on the Web; it is worth seeing them, and thinking of the economy as you watch the bridge sway.) This footage is still shown to engineering, architecture, and physics students to teach them about the potential for interactive positive feedback effects to undermine a model's results that do not include them.

What's the collapse of a bridge got to do with modern macroeconomics? Something similar to aerodynamic flutter is one of many second- or third-order dynamic effects that can occur when individuals interact in the economy. It is the type of effect that the DSGE model cannot yet take into account. What applied policy macroeconomists worry about is that using a scientific model that does not take such effects into account could lead to a collapse of the economy similar to the collapse of the bridge. It happened before—in the 1930s.

The concerns about such a catastrophic collapse of the macroeconomy were especially strong in 2008, when the U.S. Federal Reserve Bank and the U.S. government intervened in the macroeconomy in ways that previously would have seemed impossible. (We will discuss this intervention in later chapters.) One of the reasons they intervened so quickly was that the chairman of the Federal Reserve was Ben Bernanke, an economic historian who had studied the Great Depression. He could see parallels between the U.S. economy in 2008 and the economy in the 1930s during the Great Depression. When he saw what was happening to financial markets in 2008, he got scared, not because of the scientific model, but because of his knowledge of economic history. It looked and felt like the economy was really swaying.

It was the Great Depression that led to the development of the standard macro model, a model that incorporates positive feedback effects. But as we discussed above, modern macroeconomists have shown that the standard model doesn't follow from traditional microeconomic assumptions. The modern DSGE macro model is more useful as the beginning of a scientific model, but it remains far too simple to use as a guide to policy. Its flaw is that in order to be a solvable analytic model, it has to assume away interactive effects of one individual's decision on others' decisions. That essentially rules out any of the multiplier effects that were central to the standard macro model by assumption, not by analysis.

Applied policy macroeconomists believe that in many instances, these interactive effects are central to the real-world problems that macroeconomies face, and can cause the type of dynamic feedback problems that brought down the Tacoma Narrows Bridge. This is why the fallacy of composition is central to the standard model. So the engineering approach justifies its difference from the formal scientific model by the presumed existence and importance of complex interaction effects that the scientific model does not yet incorporate.

Q-8 What does the Tacoma Narrows Bridge have to do with the fallacy of composition problem?

The Complexity Approach to Macro: The Future of Modern Macro

By now you are likely asking—if these interactive effects are so important, why *don't* modern scientific macroeconomic models deal with them? The first answer to that question is that doing so is really, really, hard, especially in the formal DSGE model. The second answer is that other macroeconomists are, in fact, working on developing new types of models that can deal with them. These models are called **complex systems macro models**—*macro models of the economy that take into account dynamic interactions of agents in the models, where agents have less than full information and can be less than infinitely rational*. Complex systems can only be understood by considering the interaction of the parts simultaneously with the analysis of the parts themselves. Economists have found that, because of these interactions, these complex system macro models can have **emergent properties**—*properties of the system that could not have been predicted from a deductive analysis starting from the components of the system*, thus justifying the basic macro approach of the standard macro models.

The Underlying Dynamic Assumptions of the Standard, DSGE, and Complex Systems Models

To give you a sense of how the complex systems model differs from the standard model and the DSGE model, let's consider a model that highlights the differences in assumptions about expectations in the various models. It is a variation on what is called the cobweb model, which played an important role in developing modern macro models. This very simple model is a standard supply/demand model with one difference—suppliers don't know what price they'll be able to sell their product for when they decide how much to supply. The model starts at equilibrium and then demand shifts out to the right. The implied assumptions of the standard model, the DSGE model, and the complex systems model can then be used to make predictions about what will happen.

The Standard Macro Model: Backward-Looking Expectations

Let's begin with the assumption of the standard macro model. In that model, individuals and firms predict the future using **historically based expectations**—*expectations*

FIGURE 29-1 (A AND B) **Backward-Looking Expectations**

With historically based expectations, a small gap in expected and actual prices can become larger and larger. This model of continually getting it wrong isn't particularly believable.

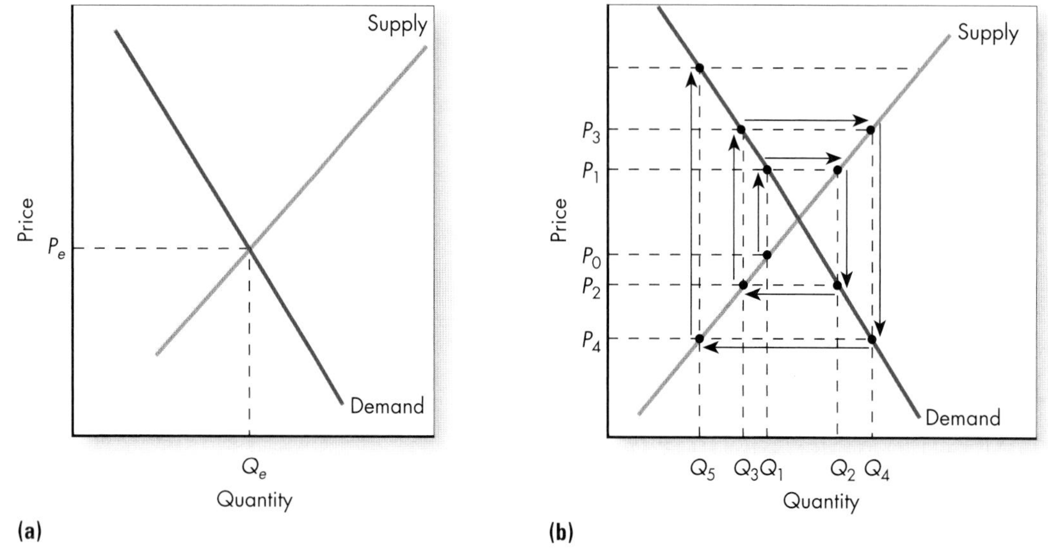

about the future that are based on past events. Let's keep the simplest type of historically based expectations and say suppliers expect the price today to be equal to whatever it was yesterday—that is, suppliers expect the most recent price to continue.[3]

Let's first see how this assumption works out if everything starts out in equilibrium and neither supply nor demand shifts. The situation is shown in Figure 29-1(a): suppliers expect price P_e and produce quantity Q_e. Because the quantity demanded at P_e is also Q_e, the market clears—the suppliers' price expectations are exactly correct.

Now suppose the market doesn't begin in equilibrium, as shown in Figure 29-1(b). Say that suppliers expected price P_0, which led them to supply quantity Q_1. The market price at which buyers are willing to buy Q_1 units is P_1. So instead of getting the price P_0 they expected, suppliers end up getting the higher price P_1. Suppliers *like* getting a higher price, but if they had correctly anticipated the higher price, they would have wanted to produce more than Q_1: if they had known the price was going to be P_1, they would have supplied Q_2 instead of Q_1.

Suppliers now face the problem of deciding what to produce for time period 2. Since suppliers are backward-looking (they assume that the price in the coming period is the price in the market during the last period), suppliers expect price P_1 to continue and *now* decide to supply Q_2. But as you can see in Figure 29-1(b), when Q_2 is supplied, the price falls to P_2, much lower than expected. Again, suppliers are unhappy—this time, they wish they had produced less.

Because price is so low and suppliers assume that the low price P_2 will prevail, many suppliers decide not to produce in the next period. Specifically, suppliers reduce their supply to Q_3. As you can see in Figure 29-1(b), in doing so they actually make the

[3]We can change the assumption to be a weighted combination of past prices, but it is far easier to assume that they base it only on the last price. The same issues carry through to more complicated variations of historically based expectations.

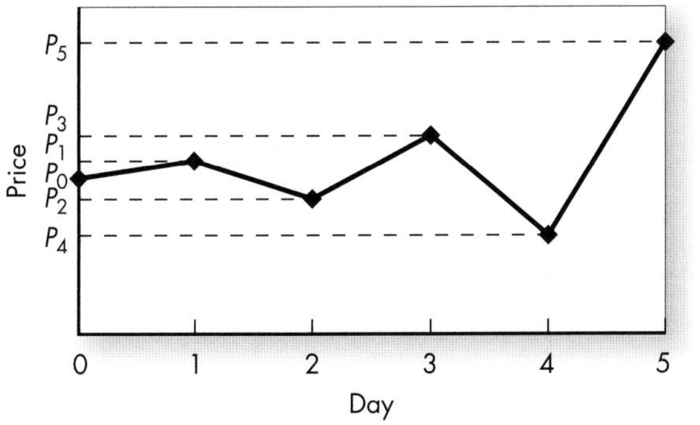

FIGURE 29-2
Price Dynamics with Backward-Looking Expectations
With backward-looking expectations, fluctuations in price can explode.

situation worse. The price suppliers get rises to P_3, which is even higher than P_1, the price at which the market began. Suppliers wish they had produced more than Q_3.

The price dynamics of the market are shown in Figure 29-2.

Given the assumptions about backward-looking expectations, this process of continually getting it wrong will persist and, given the nature of the supply and demand curves drawn, will lead to ever-greater fluctuations in price and quantity. Other possible outcomes, with different supply and demand curves, include fluctuations that dampen and eventually converge and persistent fluctuations that oscillate between the same values.

Of course, this model isn't terribly believable: suppliers never seem to learn from their mistakes, and never seem to notice that "too high" prices in this model are followed by "too low" prices. In other words, in this simplistic model, suppliers are just plain dumb.

Q-9 Why does the assumption of rationality cause problems for the standard cobweb model?

The standard macro models rely implicitly on similar sorts of assumptions involving "dumb" expectations. For example, the expansionary effect of tax cuts in the multiplier model is based on the assumption that people don't pause to think that lower taxes today will typically require higher taxes tomorrow. The DSGE model was developed to help free macroeconomic models from making the "people are dumb and don't learn" assumptions that the standard macro models implicitly embodied.

The DSGE Model: Rational Expectations

New Classical economists rightly strongly objected to these sorts of "dumb expectations" assumptions of the standard macro model—people would learn from their mistakes. The question was how to model this "learning" process. A group of economists got together to figure out how, including two future Nobel Prize winners, Franco Modigliani and Herbert Simon, and a third economist, John Muth. Muth proposed a very simple alternative assumption—people are smart and should expect the price predicted by the model. After all, all they had to do was to talk to an economist, and he or she would tell them what the equilibrium was. Muth called these expectations *rational expectations*.

Say the market had been in equilibrium with a price $P = 39$ for a long time when, all of a sudden, demand shifted out, raising the new equilibrium price to 40. Figure 29-3 shows the price dynamics for rational expectations.

When the demand shifted out (on day 50), the price instantaneously shifted to the new equilibrium. That's a really nice property if you are trying to analytically solve and model, and because it led to solvable models, rational expectations became the center stone for New Classical models, including the DSGE model. So in the DSGE model, all markets are assumed to immediately move to equilibrium—the adjustment to equilibrium is instantaneous.

FIGURE 29-3 Price Dynamics with Rational Expectations

With rational expectations—people expect the price predicted by the model—price adjusts to its new equilibrium immediately.

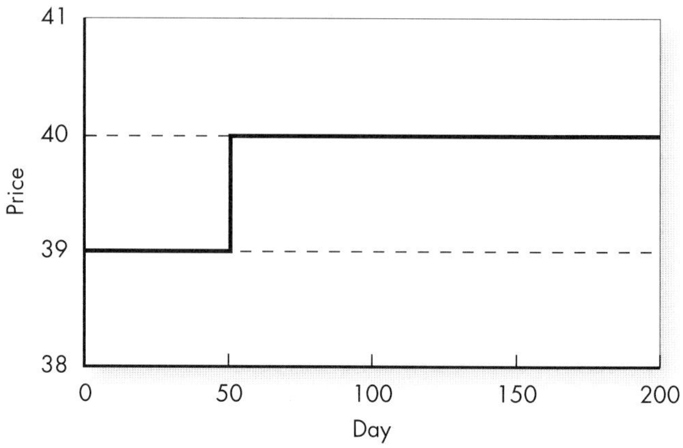

Complex Systems Models: Smart People with Less-Than-Perfect Foresight

Herbert Simon, who would go on to pioneer work in artificial intelligence, was unhappy with Muth's "rational expectations" solution—he said it made things too easy—and, more importantly, did not describe reality. He argued the economists didn't know precisely what the underlying model was, and thus we needed a model of how reasonably smart people interact when they don't know the precise underlying model. His work became the foundation for *complex systems models*. In these models, people are smart but do not have perfect foresight or infinite amounts of computing power, thus making the macroeconomy too complex to model. In a complex system, people don't know what the correct model is because the scientists don't know what the correct model is. They are both continually learning.

In a complex system, there is no "correct" model on which to base price expectation.

In a complex system, there is no "correct" model on which to base price expectation, so everyone has to make his or her best guess about what the price will be. The analysis focuses on how people make reasonable guesses. Modern complex systems macroeconomists have been struggling to create a reasonable guess model, and have found some interesting results, but everything is still very tentative. Specifically, economists have found that **learning procedures**—*the methods by which people learn about the system*—are central to the expectations process, and that people will likely use historical data to learn from in highly sophisticated ways.

Q-10 What are complexity economists' arguments against the rational expectations model?

They have found that people learn by discovering patterns in the past data and tentatively check to see if those patterns are likely to continue. To the degree that they believe that the pattern will persist, they will start basing their actions on the expected pattern. But there is a catch—in doing so they will often change the pattern. This will lead them to start looking for patterns of patterns, which means they will be learning how patterns change over time.

If they find such relationships, they will start basing their actions on patterns of changing patterns, but when they do, they will change the patterns of the change in patterns, which leads them to higher levels of pattern-matching analysis. Thus, the fluctuations in the aggregate economy are driven by people who are trying to find patterns of patterns of patterns . . . , and they get so caught up in those patterns that they are no longer concerned with the underlying realities of the economy.

For most historians of economic thought, that idea was precisely the idea that Keynes was trying to convey in his work that marked the beginning of macroeconomics. For

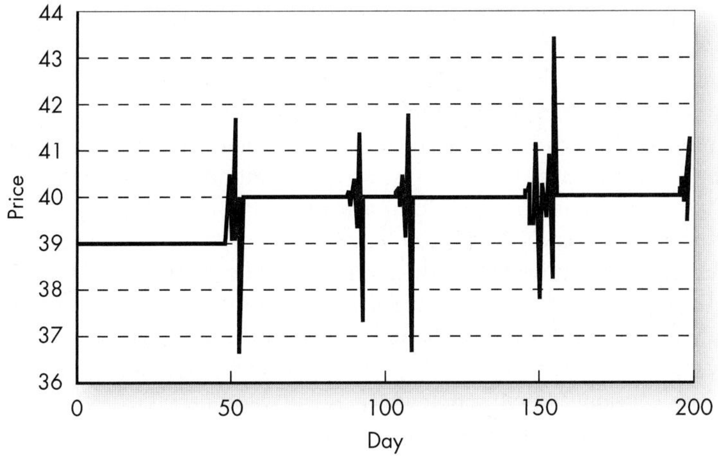

FIGURE 29-4 Price Dynamics in a Learning Model

In a learning model, prices are relatively stable but experience periodic fluctuations.

example, he made an analogy to a beauty contest with the way the market works. He wrote: "It is not a case of choosing those [faces] which, to the best of one's judgment, are really the prettiest, nor even those which average opinion genuinely thinks the prettiest. We have reached the third degree where we devote our intelligences to anticipating what average opinion expects the average opinion to be. And there are some, I believe, who practice the fourth, fifth and higher degrees."

He argued that as people's expectations become so interdependent, no one focuses on the fundamentals of the economy, and the result can be a serious depression such as happened in the Great Depression. The problem lies in the dynamics of the system. Many analysts believe that is precisely what happened in the recent credit crisis and housing bubble—where housing prices kept rising because more and more people started basing their expectations of future housing prices on patterns of ever-rising prices.

Let's consider the implications of one such learning model that combines the assumptions of the standard model and the DSGE model.[4] In this model, suppliers have to pay a small cost to make better predictions about the future price. To make things simple, we'll assume that if they pay the small cost, they'll be able to *perfectly* predict the future price—the assumption in the DSGE model. Alternatively, they can forgo paying that small cost and rely on their "naïve" predictions that last period's price will be the price in the next period—the assumption in the standard model.

Figure 29-4 plots the price dynamics that can emerge from this model in response to the same demand shock I showed for the standard and DSGE models above. As you can see, prices behave very oddly (technically speaking, prices behave *chaotically*) after the demand shock on day 50. In the early days after the demand shock, the prices bounce around a bit, but then they seem to settle down close to the new equilibrium price of 40. Prices stay close to equilibrium for a long time, until suddenly, *without any external shock,* prices begin to fluctuate wildly again. Again, prices settle down only to fluctuate wildly again. This chaotic pattern continues. What we see, in short, are extended periods where the market price is the price predicted by the DSGE model, but with cyclical—but aperiodic and unpredictable—periods of significant instability.

[4]This model was developed by William Brock and Cars Hommes in 1997. It appeared in the journal *Econometrica*.

What's going on here? The answer is that when prices remain close to the equilibrium price for a long time, suppliers think they have found a new pattern—prices stay roughly constant over time—and they figure that they won't waste the money to make better predictions telling them what they already know. They choose to "free ride" rather than pay the cost of predictions that are only marginally better than their naïve predictions. But when more and more people start relying on the pattern, the equilibrium becomes unstable and prices tend to spiral away from it—just like in the standard cobweb model.

When prices get sufficiently far from equilibrium, suppliers suffer sufficiently from their bad predictions that it becomes worthwhile to pay the cost of becoming better informed. These better expectations restabilize the market, just like in the DSGE model. What is interesting about this model is that the periods of instability occur at seemingly random times (and, in fact, the times *are* actually random in the formal sense).

Complexity economists argue that this type of price movement is typical in competitive markets in a complex economy where people independently form their expectations. Such random price movements make macro policy much more an art than a science.

Macroeconomics, Learning, and Behavioral Economics

The pressures for instability in markets become even greater when behavioral economic insights are added to the model. Modern complex systems macroeconomists rely heavily on insights from behavioral economics to provide the key to how people learn. In these models, they have found that people tend to **herd**—*to copy other successful behavior even though that successful behavior may have been just luck.* Herding can result in even larger fluctuations away from equilibrium, keeping the market from equilibrium for long periods of time.

Web Note 29.4
Herding Tendencies

People's tendency to herd is well documented in numerous experiments. For example, in one experiment, economist Matthew Salganik and his coauthors created an artificial music market from individuals who visited a popular Web site. They were given a list of songs from unknown bands and asked to download them and assign a rating to the songs. Half the participants were not given any information about what other people had chosen. The other half were shown how many times each song had been downloaded.

If people's choices were not influenced by others, then the two groups should have made approximately the same selection. If not, then people were basing their selection on what others had chosen. They found that people downloaded what others had downloaded, making the model a path-dependent tipping-point model I introduced in Chapter 6 and consistent with the standard macro model, rather than the DSGE macro model. This means that for music choices, one cannot use a unique equilibrium rational choice model, and that the choice by individuals in a group has to be analyzed in the context of the group. The same has been found to be true in many other cases—individuals in groups decide differently than do individuals outside groups. Translating that behavioral insight into macroeconomics provides a likely foundation for the standard macro models with their emphasis on the fallacy of composition.

Translating behavioral insights into macroeconomics provides a likely foundation for the standard macro models.

Agent-Based Computational Economic Models of the Macroeconomy

The problem with these multiple-level pattern-finding and learning models that are key to complex systems models is that they are almost always too complex to solve analytically. They are far more technically complicated than the dominant modern macro DSGE models, which are already highly technical. If we had to rely on analytic solutions to these models, it would be a long time before we get any reasonable results from them. However, because of increasing computational power, modern economists such as Iowa State economist Leigh Tesfatsion, George Mason economist Rob Axtell, and Brandeis economist Blake LeBaron believe that they may be able to gain insight into these complex systems models by creating computer models of miniature macroeconomies. They hope to be able to study real-world macroeconomies through their study of **agent-based computational economic (ACE) models**—*virtual computer macroeconomies of rational agents with less-than-perfect information*. Having created such virtual macroeconomies, they experiment with different learning patterns of the agents in the model. The hope is that useful insights can be drawn from these computer models *without* having to fully understand the underlying technical complications. (You can see a discussion of ACE modeling along with many examples at: www.econ.iastate.edu/tesfatsi/ace.htm.)

In these models, enormous price fluctuations occur as markets dynamically adjust. These fluctuations *are not* caused by people being dumb or not using all available information; people are assumed to be fully rational. Instead, the fluctuations are caused by people trying to learn in an environment that is continually changing. Everyone is trying to figure out what everyone else is doing when the process of figuring out changes the way the system works. One learning procedure that people use is to ask a trustworthy friend what he or she thinks will happen and to copy the strategy that others use, especially others that they consider especially bright. They also try to get whatever information they can about future demand and supply, but that is likely limited and often contradictory. Ultimately, they make some prediction, but they will not be too confident in that prediction. And there will be lots of different predictions out there. The people in these complex systems will rely on estimates of various groups, their knowledge of what has happened in the past, and their gut instincts—what Keynes called animal spirits. The resulting system can never be perfectly specified.

In complex systems models fluctuations are caused by people trying to learn in an environment that is continually changing.

The Limits of ACE Models

These complex systems models are really neat and likely are the future of modern macroeconomic theory. But were it not for some modern macroeconomists' attempts to apply the simpler DSGE macro model to reality (and to some policy makers actually listening to them), I wouldn't be presenting these models at all because the standard macro models that you have learned captured many of the insights found in complex systems models.

The standard macro models capture many of the insights found in complex systems models.

As impressive as these scientific complex systems macro models are, they are not especially useful to policy makers as direct guides to policy. They are primarily useful in letting policy makers know how little we actually know about the macroeconomy. Just about their only concrete result is to show that models that don't take these interactive effects into account may well miss important elements of the macroeconomy, and that when these elements are added, just about anything can happen. Applied macroeconomists already knew that.

Choosing the Right Model

Web Note 29.5
Reassessing Macro Models

The important question for policy makers is which of these many models of the macroeconomy to use. Will people on average get it right, as the DSGE model assumes? In other words, will the mistakes that people make cancel out? Those who make poor estimates will go out of business; those who make good estimates will win, and eventually only those who make good estimates will remain. If, on average, suppliers get it right, then the DSGE model may be a reasonable one to use. Or will suppliers get it wrong—creating bubbles and large deviations of the actual price from the fundamental price? There is no simple answer to this question.

To figure out which model to use, modern macroeconomists conduct experiments about how people respond in periods of uncertainty and do historical studies of what people have actually done. They have found that suppliers develop highly changeable rules of thumb that often, in normal times, get the prediction right, so that the DSGE rational expectations model is often a reasonable description of the macroeconomy. But they also have found that sometimes suppliers get it wrong—really wrong. In this case, there are serious problems for the market and the appropriate model can involve exploding cycles that occur when people are basing their decisions on past prices. In these cases, the standard macro model is more likely to be the appropriate model.

Researchers have found that it is easiest for people to get it right when markets are relatively stable, but are less likely to get it right when markets become slightly unstable. Moderate instability induces more instability. UCLA economist Axel Leijonhufvud, whose work I discussed earlier in the discussion of whether to use the *AS/AD* model or the multiplier model, has pushed this argument the furthest. He argues that there tends to be a corridor in which people's rules of thumb operate well and markets lead to reasonable macro results. When the market is in the corridor, the DSGE model is a reasonable one; the market will coordinate the economy. But when the economy moves outside the corridor—when it faces big shocks, especially ones that have not been experienced before—markets can have big problems and might not coordinate the economy; they might actually make it worse. In 2007, the U.S. economy was getting to the edge of the corridor and in 2008, it got outside it. The result was the swaying of the economy, and the fears that the economy was headed toward a type of Tacoma Narrows Bridge collapse.

So the answer that the complex systems approach comes to on whether people's expectations will stabilize an economy or not is that *it depends*. Sometimes they will and sometimes they won't. Unfortunately, that's not a lot of help to policy makers since they can't tell them when it will and when it won't.

Conclusion

So there we have it—a whirlwind tour of modern macroeconomic theory. What are you supposed to take away from it? First, that macroeconomics is complex and difficult; there are no easy answers. Second, all macro models have problems, and we must put together insights from all of them to come up with useful guides to policy. In terms of policy, the DSGE model has some important insights that you had better add as addenda to your standard macro models that you learned in previous chapters. These include:

As addenda to the standard model you should remember that (1) people are smart, (2) credibility is important, and (3) rules have advantages.

- People are smart, and your policy had better take that into account.
- Credibility is important.
- Rules have certain advantages over discretion.

Complex systems macro also has important insights to keep in mind too. These include:

- In complex situations, groups of individually rational smart people can sometimes act in ways that seem collectively quite irrational.
- All models may leave out important elements that can cause a complex system to collapse, so you should always look at reality as well as the model when conducting policy in a complex system.
- Macroeconomics is complex, and we have no definitive theory to guide us. Thus, policy must be made based on an educated common sense—not on any single theory. There are no unchanging rules of macro policy.

If you remember these, and modify your use of the standard macro models with these insights, you will have all you need to know about the implications of the DSGE and complex systems models for macro policy—at least for my course.

Summary

- The standard macro model is a top-down model of the economy based on historical relationships among variables. It is an engineering model suitable for policy.
- The modern macro model is a model built from microfoundations. It is a scientific model designed to understand how the economy works.
- The standard macro model is based on the fallacy of composition and while the interrelationships among variables in the economy are sometimes too difficult to understand, the standard macro model provides general guidance for policy makers that take these interrelationships into account.
- The standard macro model was developed as a result of the experience of the Great Depression. The modern models developed as economists had access to more data and computational power.
- The disadvantage of the standard macro model is that it assumes that people are not rational or forward thinking.
- The advantage of the DSGE model is that it considers that people are not stupid when making their decisions. The disadvantage is that it makes highly restrictive assumptions that do not hold in the real world.
- D stands for *dynamic*, S for *stochastic*, G for *general*, and E for *equilibrium*.
- Three policy prescriptions of the DSGE model are (1) people are smart, and your policy had better take that into account; (2) credibility is important; and (3) rules have certain advantages over discretion.
- The complex systems approach to macro assumes that people cannot predict the future with perfect accuracy (as does the DSGE model) nor does it assume that people rely only on historical information (as does the standard macro model). It assumes that people learn and that the process is complex.
- The differences between the three models are the following: The standard model assumes people base their expectations on history. The DSGE model assumes people can correctly predict future events. The complex systems models assume that people learn from past mistakes.
- Complex systems models are too complicated to solve mathematically. Agent-based computational models are microeconomies with agents who are given learning mechanisms. The results of the model emerge as the agents interact and make decisions.

Key Terms

agent-based computational economic models *(697)*
complex systems macro models *(691)*
deductive scientific model *(680)*
dynamic *(685)*
emergent properties *(691)*
engineering model *(679)*
general equilibrium model *(686)*
herd *(696)*
historically based expectations *(691)*
learning procedures *(694)*
Lucas critique problem *(687)*
New Classical macroeconomics *(684)*
rational expectations *(685)*
representative agent *(684)*
Ricardian equivalence problem *(686)*
standard macro models *(679)*
stochastic *(686)*
time-inconsistency/credibility problem *(687)*

Questions and Exercises

1. Are modern macro models better characterized as engineering models or deductive scientific models? Explain your answer. LO1
2. Are standard macro models better characterized as engineering models or deductive scientific models? Explain your answer. LO1
3. When did macroeconomics emerge as a separate discipline? Why did it happen at that time? LO2
4. What did early macroeconomists believe about the economy that justified a separate macroeconomics? LO2

5. How did the fact that the modeling of consumption within the standard model fell short of fitting real-world data lead to changes in the model in the 1960s? LO2
6. What changes did macroeconomists make to the consumption portion of the standard model in the 1960s to make it better fit real-world data? LO2
7. What is New Classical macroeconomics? LO2
8. What distinguishes New Classical macroeconomics from Keynesian economics? LO2
9. Explain the meaning of each of the letters in DSGE. LO4
10. What is the Ricardian equivalence problem? LO5
11. Why might a government want to establish credibility with regard to fighting inflation? LO5
12. Why might a government break its promise of fighting inflation? LO5
13. What is the time-inconsistency/credibility problem? LO5
14. What is the Lucas critique problem? LO5
15. Why does the author believe that it is problematic to draw precepts from the DSGE model? LO5
16. What does the collapse of the Tacoma Narrows Bridge have to do with modern macroeconomics? LO6
17. Demonstrate how historically based expectations can lead to increasingly greater fluctuations in prices. LO3
18. How is the complex systems approach to macroeconomics an improvement to both the standard and neoclassical macro models? LO6
19. Why is learning in the complex systems approach an ongoing process? LO6
20. How does the learning model by Brock and Hommes explain unexpected price fluctuations? LO6
21. How does herding lead to price fluctuations? LO6
22. How can instability create more instability? LO6

Questions from Alternative Perspectives

1. Consider the quotation in the chapter from Chari and Kehoe: "Discretionary [macro] policy has all costs and no benefits, so that if government can be made to commit to a policy rule, it should do so." Is it true that using expansionary fiscal policies in times of recession has had "all costs and no benefits?" Can you think of anyone who might disagree with this? (Radical)
2. The "general equilibrium" part of the DSGE model seems to suggest that there is a *unique* equilibrium for a given economy, and indeed, most modern scientific macro models have a single equilibrium. (In fact, the existence of a *unique* equilibrium is regarded as a desirable feature of such models, since that's when it gives the sharpest predictions.) Contrast this with the multiplier model, and explain why such a feature is likely to bias the model towards suggesting non-activist macroeconomic policies. (Post-Keynesian)
3. Consider the end of Robert Solow's quote describing the DSGE model: ". . . in an institutional framework that favors universal price taking behavior." Do you think this is an accurate description of the economy you live in? In particular:
   a. Are *you* a "price taker" in most of your economic interactions?
   b. Can you think of any institutions that are *not* well described as price takers?
   c. Do you think these institutions play an important role in the modern economy? (Institutionalist)
4. This chapter contained a quick-and-dirty history of macroeconomic thought. It started with Keynes, worked through Robert Lucas and the New Classicals, as well as modern DSGE theorists like V. V. Chari and Patrick Kehoe and one of their critics, Robert Solow. What do all of these scholars have in common, and do you think this is just a coincidence? (Feminist)
5. The "complex systems" approach to macroeconomics starts from the idea that the economy involves incredibly complex interactions between many individuals and institutions. One of its important insights is the idea of emergent properties—properties of the system that couldn't have been predicted from a deductive analysis starting from the components of the system. Does the complexity of the economy and the existence of emergent properties make you more or less confident in the ability of the government to successfully manage the economy? (Austrian)

Issues to Ponder

1. The book contrasts scientific and engineering models. Loosely speaking, a model is "scientific" if it is designed to *understand* how the economy works in the abstract, while engineering models are those that are designed to capture how the economy works in practice, even though we don't really understand why. Which do you think is more important? LO1

2. How is the "fallacy of composition" related to the difference between micro demand and supply curves and macro aggregate demand and supply curves? LO2
3. The three big "problems" identified by modern macroeconomics were the Lucas critique problem, the Ricardian equivalence problem, and the time inconsistency/credibility problem. How important do you believe these are? LO5

Answers to Margin Questions

1. Two standard macroeconomic models are the *AS/AD* model and the multiplier model. *(679)*
2. The standard macro model is an engineering model. *(680)*
3. No, there is nothing wrong with a macro model without microfoundations. Whether microfoundations are wanted, or needed, depends on the nature of the system being modeled and the use to which the model is being put. *(682)*
4. False. One of the reasons they were abandoned is that they did not fit the empirical data well when modern statistical techniques allowed a careful consideration of those data. *(683)*
5. New Classical macroeconomics uses a representative agent approach and assumes agents are fully rational; it uses a microfoundations approach. Keynesian macroeconomics uses a macro approach, does not rely on microfoundations, and does not necessarily assume that we can specify what rationality is. *(684)*
6. DSGE stands for dynamic stochastic general equilibrium. *(686)*
7. Three policy problems that the DSGE model has highlighted are the Ricardian equivalence problem, the time-inconsistency problem, and the Lucas critique problem. *(687)*
8. In designing the Tacoma Narrows Bridge, engineers did not take account of certain small feedback effects, assuming they would cancel each other out. They did not; the fallacy of composition problem is precisely this—in the aggregate, a system might operate quite differently than in a simple model that assumes away small feedback effects. *(691)*
9. The standard cobweb model assumes people are dumb in a way that does not make sense. Rational people will learn from their past mistakes. *(693)*
10. The rational expectations model assumes that people know the true model. In fact they don't, and there is no knowable single model. People are continually learning and economists need to use models that incorporate that learning. *(694)*

CHAPTER 30

The Financial Sector and the Economy

The peculiar essence of our banking system is an unprecedented trust between man and man; and when that trust is much weakened by hidden causes, a small accident may greatly hurt it, and a great accident for a moment may almost destroy it.

—Walter Bagehot

AFTER READING THIS CHAPTER, YOU SHOULD BE ABLE TO:

1. Explain why the financial sector is central to almost all macroeconomic debates.
2. Demonstrate graphically how the long-term interest rate is determined.
3. Explain what money is.
4. Enumerate the three functions of money.
5. State the alternative measures of money and their primary components.
6. Explain how banks create money.
7. Calculate both the simple money multiplier and the money multiplier.
8. Explain why people hold money and how the short-term interest rate is determined in the money market.

The financial sector is exciting (as suggested in this famous painting, "The Bulls and Bears in the Market"); it is also central to almost all macroeconomic debates. This central role is often not immediately obvious to students. In thinking about the economy, students often focus on the *real sector*—the market for the production and exchange of goods and services. In the real sector, real goods or services such as shoes, operas, automobiles, and textbooks are exchanged. That's an incomplete view of the economy. The *financial sector*—the market for the creation and exchange of financial assets such as money, stocks, and bonds—plays a central role in organizing and coordinating our economy; it makes modern economic society possible. A car won't run without oil; a modern economy won't operate without a financial sector.

As I've noted throughout this book, markets make specialization and trade possible and thereby make the economy far more efficient than it otherwise would be. But the efficient use of markets requires a financial sector that facilitates and lubricates those trades. Let's consider an example of how the financial sector facilitates trade. Say you walk into a store and buy a t-shirt. You shell out a 20-dollar bill and the salesperson hands you the t-shirt. Easy, right? Right—but why did the salesperson give you a t-shirt for a little piece of paper? The answer to that question is: Because the economy has a financial system that has convinced him that that piece of paper has value. To convince him (and you) of that requires an enormous structural system, called the financial sector, underlying the t-shirt transaction and all other transactions. That financial system makes the transaction possible; without it the economy as we know it would not exist.

The modern financial sector is highly sophisticated. It disperses credit throughout the economy in highly diverse ways. For example, when a bank makes you a loan, often that loan is securitized, which means that it is packaged with other loans (say 1,000 such similar loans) into a security, or bond, and sold to individuals. These bonds based on other loans are called *derivatives* because they are derived from another loan. An individual who buys that securitized bond in a sense owns 1/1,000 of your loan.

Sometimes these securitized bonds are packaged with different types of loans (say another 1,000) into second-order derivative bonds, so that now the person buying the new bond will own 1/100,000 of your loan along with a similar percentage of other loans. Why package loans? Because it spreads the risk of default, making owning the loans safer than they otherwise would be. Spreading the risk through securitization is a central feature of modern financial markets. The risk that securitizing loans cannot reduce is something called *systemic risk*—the risk that all or many of the loans all default together. As we will see in later chapters, the U.S. financial sector discovered that risk in 2008.

Why Is the Financial Sector Important to Macro?

In thinking about the financial sector's role, remember the following insight: *For every real transaction, there is a financial transaction that mirrors it.* For example, when you buy an apple, the person selling the apple is buying 50 cents from you by spending his apple. The financial transaction is the transfer of 50 cents; the real transaction is the transfer of the apple.

The financial sector is central to almost all macroeconomic debates because behind every real transaction, there is a financial transaction that mirrors it.

As long as the financial system is operating smoothly, you hardly know it's there; but should that system break down, the entire economy would be disrupted and would either stagnate or go into a recession or even into a depression. That's what almost happened in 2008 when people lost faith in the existing financial institutions, and the financial sector was coming to a grinding halt. It was much like running a car without oil. Oil is only a small percentage of the car, but I can tell you from sad experience that you can run a car without oil only for about 10 miles before the entire engine seizes up. In October 2008, there was serious concern that was about to happen to the U.S. economy, and that the economy would totally seize up because of a meltdown of the financial sector.

As I will discuss in Chapter 32, in response to concern about such a seizing up, the U.S. government undertook unprecedented actions to try to prevent that by "bailing out" banks and other financial institutions with hundreds of billions of dollars. To understand that bailout, you have to understand the role of the financial sector in the economy. That's why it is necessary to give you an overview of the financial sector as part of your foundation of macroeconomics. Thus, although in this book I don't have a separate section on the steel sector or even the computer sector of the economy, I do have a separate section on money, banking, and the financial sector of the economy.

Q-1 Joe, your study partner, says that since goods and services are produced only in the real sector, the financial sector is not important to the macroeconomy. How do you respond?

The financial sector—financial markets and institutions—has two roles. First, it facilitates trade, making it possible for normal business to happen—that's its role as a lubricant to the economy. The second, related, role of the financial sector is to transfer saving—outflows from the spending stream in hundreds of different forms—back into spending. Think of this role of the financial sector as a gigantic channeling device, something like that shown in Figure 30-1. If the financial sector expands the spending flow too much, you get inflationary pressures. If it contracts the spending flow too much, you get a recession. And if it transfers just the right amount, you get a smoothly running economy.

The financial sector channels saving back into spending.

Flows from the spending stream are channeled into the financial sector as saving when individuals buy **financial assets**—*assets such as stocks or bonds, whose benefit to the owner depends on the issuer of the asset meeting certain obligations*. These obligations by the issuer of the financial asset are called financial liabilities. For every financial asset, there is a corresponding financial liability. (Financial assets and liabilities are discussed in detail in Appendix A to this chapter.)

For every financial asset, there is a financial liability.

FIGURE 30-1 The Financial Sector as a Conduit for Savings

Financial institutions channel saving—outflows from the spending stream from various entities (government, households, and corporations)—back into the spending stream as loans to various entities (government, households, and corporations). To emphasize the fact that savings take many forms, a breakdown of the type of savings for one entity, households, is shown on the left. The same is done for loans on the right, but for corporations. Each of these loans can itself be broken down again and again until each particular loan is identified individually. The lending process is an individualistic process, and each loan is different in some way from each other loan.

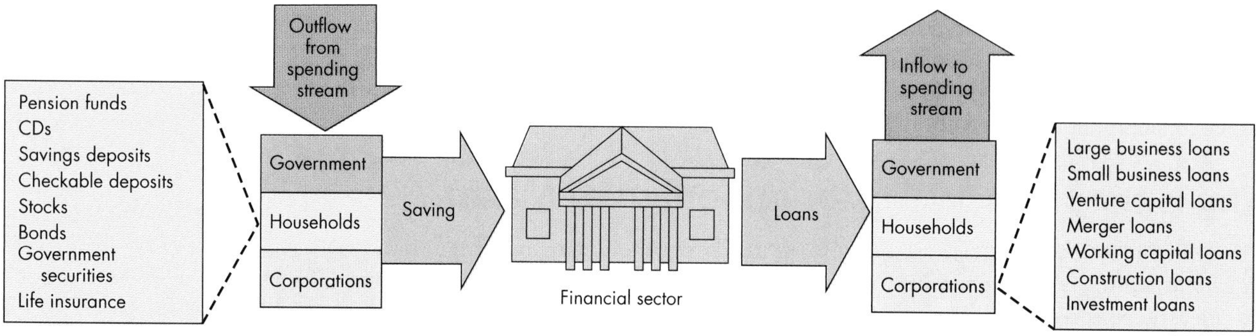

The Role of Interest Rates in the Financial Sector

Web Note 30.1
Interest Rates

Interest rates—*the prices that are charged or paid for the use of a financial asset*—are key variables in the financial sector. While there are many interest rates in the economy—mortgage interest rates, interest rates on credit cards, interest rates on government bills, interest rates on corporate bonds, and many more—for simplicity I will talk about interest rates as if there were just two: a short-term interest rate and a long-term interest rate.

The long-term interest rate is the price paid for the use of financial assets with long repayment periods. Examples are mortgages and government bonds. The market for these long-term financial assets is called the *loanable funds market.* The short-term interest rate is the price paid for the use of financial assets with shorter repayment periods such as savings deposits and checking accounts. These short-term financial assets are called *money*. So, the long-term interest rate is determined in the loanable funds market and the short-term interest rate is determined in the money market.

FIGURE 30-2
Market for Loanable Funds

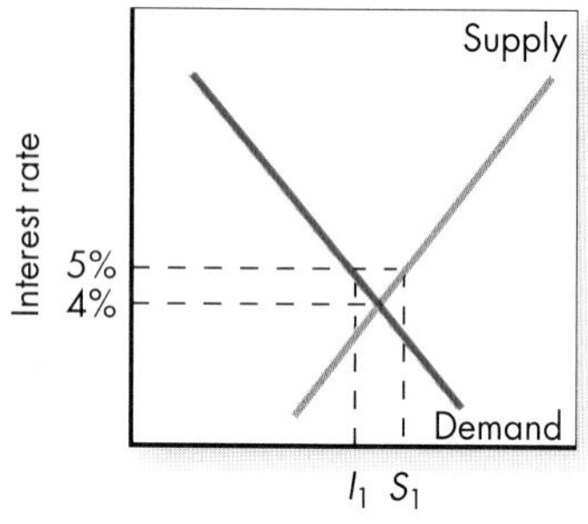

The long-term interest rate is determined in the market for loanable funds as shown in Figure 30-2. In it you can see that the quantity of loanable funds supplied (savings) is equal to the quantity of loanable funds demanded (investment) at an interest rate of 4 percent. If the interest rate for some reason does not equal 4 percent, say it is 5 percent, the quantity of savings (in this case S_1) will exceed the quantity of investment (in this case I_1), and all savings will not be channeled back into investment. The circular flow will be broken, and macroeconomic problems can develop.

To get at the problems that can develop, macroeconomics simplifies the flow of saving into two types of financial assets. One type works its way back into the system: bonds, loans, and stocks. These are translated back into investment by financial intermediaries. It is these financial assets to which the loanable funds market refers.[1] The other type of financial asset, when held by individuals, is not necessarily assumed to work its way back into the flow—we'll call this financial asset "money." Savings held as money are assumed not to work their way back into the loanable funds market and

[1]With a different interest rate for each different type of financial asset, you may be wondering which interest rate we are talking about. The answer is that we are talking about an average of the many different interest rates. Since that average interest rate is generally not easily calculable, often the interest rate on 10-year bonds is used as a proxy for the interest rate on all loanable funds.

hence those savings do not get translated into investment. This means that some savings escape the circular flow. Compared to the complicated maze of interconnected flows that exists in reality, this is an enormous simplification, but it captures a potentially serious problem and possible cause of fluctuations in the economy.

Q-2 Why are interest rates important to the economy?

The Definition and Functions of Money

Let's now turn our attention to money.

At this point you're probably saying, "I know what money is; it's currency—the dollar bills I carry around." In one sense you're right: currency is money. But in another sense you're wrong; currency is just one example of money. In fact, a number of short-term financial assets are included as money. To see why, let's consider the definition of money: **Money** is *a highly liquid financial asset that's generally accepted in exchange for other goods, is used as a reference in valuing other goods, and can be stored as wealth.*

Money is a financial asset that makes the real economy function smoothly by serving as a medium of exchange, a unit of account, and a store of wealth.

To be *liquid* means to be easily changeable into another asset or good. When you buy something with money, you are exchanging money for another asset. So any of your assets that are easily spendable are money. Social customs and standard practices are central to the liquidity of money. The reason you are willing to hold money is that you know someone else will accept it in trade for something else. Its value is determined by its general acceptability to others. If you don't believe that, try spending yuan (Chinese money) in the United States. If you try to buy dinner with 100 yuan, you will be told, "No way—give me money."

The U.S. Central Bank: The Fed

So is there any characteristic other than general acceptability that gives value to money? Consider the dollar bill that you know is money. Look at it. It states right on the bill that it is a Federal Reserve note, which means that it is an IOU (a liability) of the **Federal Reserve Bank (the Fed)**—*the U.S. central bank whose liabilities (Federal Reserve notes) serve as cash in the United States.* Individuals are willing to accept the Fed's IOUs in return for real goods and services, which means that Fed notes are money.

What, you ask, is a central bank? To answer that question, we had better first consider what a bank is. A **bank** is *a financial institution whose primary function is accepting deposits for, and lending money to, individuals and firms.* (There are more complicated definitions and many types of banks, but that will do for now; the issues are discussed more fully in Appendix A to this chapter.) If you have more currency than you want, you take it to the bank and it will "hold" the extra for you, giving you a piece of paper (or a computer entry) that says you have that much currency held here ("hold" is in quotation marks because the bank does not actually hold the currency). What the bank used to give you was a bank note, and what you used to bring in to the bank was gold, but those days are gone forever. These days what you bring is that Federal Reserve note described above, and what you get is a paper receipt and a computer entry in your checking or savings account. Individuals' deposits in these accounts serve the same purpose as does currency and are also considered money.

Which brings us back to the Federal Reserve Bank, the U.S. central bank. It is a bank that has the right to issue notes (IOUs). By law these Federal Reserve Bank notes are acceptable payment for people's taxes, and by convention these notes are acceptable payment to all people in the United States, and to many people outside the United States. IOUs of the Fed are what most of you think of as cash.

To understand why money is more than just cash, it is helpful to consider the functions of money in more detail. Having done so, we will consider which financial assets are included in various measures of money.

Functions of Money

Q-3 What are the three functions of money?

As I stated above, money is an asset that can be quickly exchanged for any other asset or good. Money serves three functions:

1. It serves as a medium of exchange.
2. It serves as a unit of account.
3. It serves as a store of wealth.

To get a better understanding of what money is, let's consider each of its functions in turn.

Money as a Medium of Exchange The easiest way to understand money's medium-of-exchange use is to imagine what an economy would be like without money. Say you want something to eat at a restaurant. Without money you'd have to barter with the restaurant owner for your meal. *Barter* is a direct exchange of goods and/or services. You might suggest bartering one of your papers or the shirt in the sack that you'd be forced to carry with you to trade for things you want. Not liking to carry big sacks around, you'd probably decide to fix your own meal and forgo eating out. Bartering is simply too difficult. Money makes many more trades possible because it does not require a double coincidence of wants by two individuals, as simple barter does.

The use of money as a medium of exchange makes it possible to trade real goods and services without bartering. Instead of carrying around a sack full of diverse goods, all you need to carry around is a billfold full of money. You go into the restaurant and pay for your meal with money; the restaurant owner can spend (trade) that money for anything she wants.

Money doesn't have to have any inherent value to function as a medium of exchange.

Money doesn't have to have any inherent value to function as a medium of exchange. All that's necessary is that everyone believes that other people will accept it in exchange for their goods. This neat social convention makes the economy function more smoothly.

Money as a Unit of Account A second use of money is as a unit of account, that is, a measure of value. Money prices are actually relative prices. A money price, say 25 cents, for a pencil conveys the information of a relative price—1 pencil = ¼ of 1 dollar—because money is both our unit of account and our medium of exchange. When you think of 25 cents, you think of ¼ of a dollar and of what a dollar will buy. The 25 cents a pencil costs only has meaning relative to the information you've stored in your mind about what money can buy. If a hamburger costs $1.50, you can compare hamburgers and pencils (1 pencil = ⅙ of a hamburger) without making the relative price calculations explicitly.

Having a unit of account makes life much easier. For example, say we had no unit of account and you had to remember the relative prices of all goods. For instance, with three goods you'd have to memorize that an airplane ticket to Miami costs 6 lobster dinners in Boston or 4 pairs of running shoes, which makes a pair of shoes worth 1½ lobster dinners.

Memorizing even a few relationships is hard enough, so it isn't surprising that societies began using a single unit of account. If you don't have a single unit of account, all combinations of 100 goods will require that you remember thousands of relative prices. If you have a single unit of account, you need know only 100 prices. A single unit of account saves our limited memories and helps us make reasonable decisions based on relative prices.

Money is used as a unit of account at a point in time, and it's also a unit of account *over time*. For example, money is a standard of deferred payments such as on college loans that many of you will be making after graduation. The value of those loan payments depends on how the money prices of all other goods change over time.

Money is a useful unit of account only as long as its value relative to other prices doesn't change too quickly.

Money is a useful unit of account only as long as its value relative to the average of all other prices doesn't change too quickly. For example, in hyperinflation all prices rise so much that our frame of reference for making relative price comparisons is lost. Is 25 cents for a pencil high or low? If the price level increased 33,000 percent (as it did in 1988 in Nicaragua) or over 100,000 percent (as it did in the early 2000s in Zimbabwe), 25 cents for a pencil would definitely be low, but would $100 be low? Without a lot of calculations we can't answer that question. A relatively stable unit of account makes it easy to answer.

In hyperinflation, all prices rise so much that our frame of reference is lost.

Given the advantages to society of having a unit of account, it's not surprising that a monetary unit of account develops even in societies with no central bank or government. For example, in a prisoner of war camp during World War II, prisoners had no money, so they used cigarettes as their unit of account. Everything traded was given a price in cigarettes. The exchange rates on December 1, 1944, were

1 bar of soap: 2 cigarettes

1 candy bar: 4 cigarettes

1 razor blade: 6 cigarettes

1 can of fruit: 8 cigarettes

1 can of cookies: 20 cigarettes

As you can see, all prices were in cigarettes. If candy bars rose to 6 cigarettes and the normal price was 4 cigarettes, you'd know the price of candy bars was high.

Money as a Store of Wealth When you save, you forgo consumption now so that you can consume in the future. To bridge the gap between now and the future, you must acquire a financial asset. This is true even if you squirrel away currency under the mattress. In that case, the financial asset you've acquired is simply the currency itself. Money is a financial asset. (It's simply a bond that pays no interest.) So a third use of money is as a store of wealth. As long as money is serving as a medium of exchange, it automatically also serves as a store of wealth. The restaurant owner can accept your money and hold it for as long as she wants before she spends it. (But had you paid her in fish, she'd be wise not to hold it more than a few hours.)

As long as money is serving as a medium of exchange, it automatically also serves as a store of wealth.

You might wonder why people would hold money that pays no interest. Put another way: Why do people hold a government bond that pays no interest? The reason is that money, by definition, is highly liquid—it is more easily translated into other goods than are other financial assets. Since money is also the medium of exchange, it can be spent instantaneously (as long as there's a shop open nearby). Our ability to spend money for goods makes money worthwhile to hold even if it doesn't pay interest.

Q-4 Why do people hold money rather than bonds when bonds pay higher interest than money?

Alternative Measures of Money

According to the definition of *money*, what people believe is money and what people will accept as money are determining factors in deciding whether a financial asset is money. Consequently, it's difficult to measure *money* unambiguously. A number of different financial assets serve some of the functions of money and thus have claims to being called *money*. To handle this ambiguity, economists have developed different measures of money and have called them M_1 and M_2. Each is a reasonable concept of money. Let's consider their components.

M_1

M_1 is a measure of the money supply; it consists of currency in the hands of the public plus checking accounts and traveler's checks.

M_1 consists of *currency in the hands of the public, checking account balances, and traveler's checks*. Clearly, currency in the hands of the public (the dollar bills and coins you carry around with you) is money, but how about your checking account deposits? The reason they're included in this measure of money is that just about anything you can do with currency, you can do with a check or debit card. You can store your wealth in your checking account; you can use a check or debit card as a medium of exchange (indeed, for some transactions you have no choice but to use a check), and your checking account balance is denominated in the same unit of account (dollars) as is currency. If it looks like money, acts like money, and functions as money, it's a good bet it's money. Indeed, checking account deposits are included in all measures of money.

The same arguments can be made about traveler's checks. (Some advertisements even claim that traveler's checks are better than money because you can get them replaced.) Currency, checking account deposits, and traveler's checks make up the components of M_1, the narrowest measure of money. Figure 30-3 presents the relative sizes of M_1's components.

M_2

M_2 is a measure of the money supply; it consists of M_1 plus other relatively liquid assets.

M_2 is made up of M_1 *plus savings deposits, small-denomination time deposits, and money market mutual fund shares*. The relative sizes of the components of M_2 are given in Figure 30-3.

The money in savings accounts (savings deposits) is counted as money because it is readily spendable—all you need do is go to the bank and draw it out. Small-denomination time deposits are also called *certificates of deposit* (*CDs*).

Q-5 Which would be a larger number, M_1 or M_2? Why?

M_2's components include more financial assets than M_1. All its components are highly liquid and play an important role in providing reserves and lending capacity for commercial banks. What makes the M_2 measure important is that economic research has shown that M_2 is the measure of money often most closely correlated with the price level and economic activity.

FIGURE 30-3 Components of M_2 and M_1

The two most-used measures of the money supply are M_1 and M_2. The two primary components of M_1 are currency in the hands of the public and checking accounts. M_2 includes all of M_1, plus savings deposits, time deposits, and money market mutual funds. Traveler's checks represent 0.3% of M_1.

Source: H.6 *Money Stock Measures*, 2009 (www.federalreserve.gov).

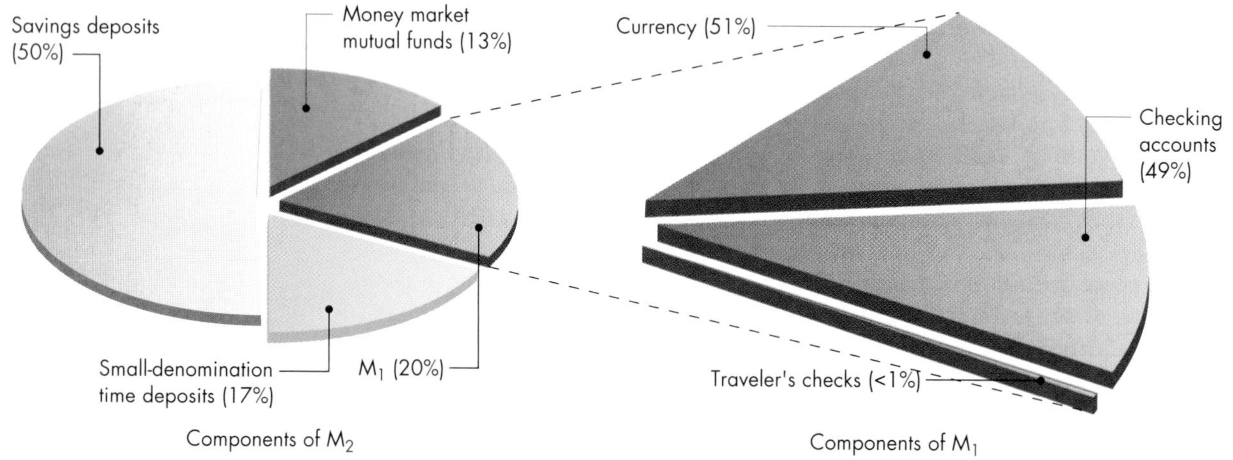

REAL-WORLD APPLICATION

Characteristics of a Good Money

The characteristics of a good money are that its supply be relatively constant, that it be limited in supply (sand wouldn't make good money), that it be difficult to counterfeit, that it be divisible (have you ever tried to spend half a horse?), that it be durable (raspberries wouldn't make good money), and that it be relatively small and light compared to its value (watermelon wouldn't make good money either). All these characteristics were reasonably (but not perfectly) embodied in gold. Many other goods have served as units of account (shells, wampum, rocks, cattle, horses, silver), but gold historically became the most important money, and in the 17th and 18th centuries gold was synonymous with money.

But gold has flaws as money. It's relatively heavy, easy to counterfeit with coins made only partly of gold, and, when new gold fields are discovered, subject to fluctuations in supply. These flaws led to gold's replacement by paper currency backed only by trust that the government would keep its commitment to limit its supply.

Paper money can be a good money if somehow people can trust the government to limit its supply and guarantee that its supply will be limited in the future. That trust has not always been well placed.

Most societies today supplement paper money such as dollar bills with electronic money that exists as debits and credit entries recorded on the computer. Both electronic money and paper money are vulnerable to fraud. Electronic money can be created by criminals who electronically change debit and credit entries, which is why banks spend billions of dollars on computer security and encryption technology each year. Paper money can be counterfeited. For example, in World War II, Germany planned to counterfeit a significant amount of British pounds and drop them in Britain to disrupt the British economy. It didn't succeed; by the time they had printed the notes, they didn't have the aircraft to fly them over and drop them in Britain.

Counterfeiting continues today. For example, you may have noticed that some of the currency you carry has changed its look in recent years. That's because counterfeiters with new technology could create almost perfect counterfeit copies of the older designs. In 1989, authorities found some counterfeit U.S. $100 bills that had the right mix of cotton and linen and that had been manufactured on the very expensive Intaglio press, the same kind of press used to print real dollar bills. They called these counterfeit notes "supernotes." To stop the counterfeiters of the supernotes, the United States redesigned the U.S. currency, adding additional security measures such as color-shifting ink, watermarks, a security thread, an ultraviolet glow, and microprinting. Counterfeiters will copy these newly designed bills, which means that it is likely that U.S. authorities will have to redesign U.S. paper currency about every 10 years in order to keep ahead of counterfeiters.

So far, counterfeiting is still relatively unimportant in the United States. But in some developing countries, merchants and even banks are hesitant to accept large-denomination U.S. currency, which means that counterfeiting in those countries is undermining the usefulness of the dollar as money.

Distinguishing between Money and Credit

You might have thought that credit cards would be included in one of the measures of *money*. But I didn't include them. In fact, credit cards are nowhere to be seen in a list of the components of money. Credit cards are not money. Credit cards aren't a financial liability of the bank that issues them. Instead, credit cards create a liability for their users (money owed to the company or bank that issued the card) and the banks have a financial asset as a result.

Credit cards are not money.

Let's consider how a credit card works. You go into a store and buy something with your credit card. You have a real asset—the item you bought. The store has a financial asset—an account receivable. The store sells that financial asset at a slight discount to the bank and gets cash in return. Either the bank collects cash when you pay off your financial liability

Money Laundering

The U.S. government has issued over $820 billion worth of cash. That's about $2,700 for every man, woman, and child. Now ask yourself how much cash you're carrying on you. Add to that the amounts banks and businesses keep, and divide that by the number of people in the United States. The number economists get when they do that calculation is way below the total amount of cash the United States has issued. So what happens to the extra cash?

Let's switch for a minute to a Miami safehouse being raided by drug enforcement officers. They find $50 million in cash. That's what most economists believe happens to much of the extra cash that remains in the United States. It goes underground. An underground economy lurks below the real economy. The underground economy consists of two components: (1) the production and distribution of illegal goods and services and (2) the legal economic activity that is not reported.

Illegal activity, such as selling illegal drugs and prostitution, generates huge amounts of cash. (Most people who buy an illegal good or service would prefer not to have the transaction appear on their monthly credit card statements.) This presents a problem for a big-time illegal business. It must explain to the Internal Revenue Service (IRS) where all its money came from. That's where money laundering comes in. Money laundering is simply making illegally gained income look as if it came from a legal business. Any business through which lots of cash moves is a good front for money laundering. Laundromats move lots of cash, which is where the term money laundering came from. The mob bought laundromats and claimed a much higher income from the laundromats than it actually received. The mob thus "laundered" the excess money. Today money laundering is much more sophisticated. It involves billions of dollars and international transactions in three or four different countries, but the purpose is the same: making illegally earned money look legal.

or, if you don't pay it off, the bank earns interest on its financial asset (often at a high rate, from 12 to 18 percent per year). Credit cards are essentially prearranged loans.

This distinction between credit and money should be kept in mind. Money is a financial asset of individuals and a financial liability of banks. Credit is savings made available to be borrowed. Credit is not an asset of the borrowing public.

Q-6 Are credit cards money?

Credit cards and credit impact the amount of money people hold. When preapproved loan credit is instantly available (as it is with a credit card), there's less need to hold money. (If you didn't have a credit card, you'd carry a lot more currency.) With credit immediately available, liquidity is less valuable to people. So credit and credit cards do make a difference in how much money people hold, but because they are not financial liabilities of banks, they are not money.

While credit cards are not money, a debit card serves the same function as a check—think of it as a computer checkbook—and hence is part of the monetary system. It allows you to spend money in your bank account (to debit your account) and thus makes your bank account more liquid. With a debit card, no loan is involved; you are spending your money.

The ease with which people can access credit has reduced the need to hold money, reducing the importance of money, and increasing the importance of credit, in the economy. If you can get an instant loan, why carry cash or hold money in a bank? Thus, in modern financial sectors, measures of access to credit and credit availability are as important as are measures of money. It was this availability of short-term credit that dried up in October 2008, threatening to seize up the U.S. economy.

Banks and the Creation of Money

Modern financial sectors are highly complex, with many different types of assets and liabilities. To make the financial sector understandable to students, it is useful to simplify and talk about a single financial institution—a bank—and a single concept—money—and to discuss how the amount of money can be expanded and contracted. That's what I do here. But you should remember that the discussion is simply an example of the way in which financial sectors expand and contract the amount of credit in the economy.

Banks are financial institutions that borrow from people (take in deposits) and use the money they borrow to make loans to other individuals. Banks make a profit by charging a higher interest on the money they lend out than they pay for the money they borrow. Individuals keep their money in banks, accepting lower interest rates, because doing so is safer and more convenient than the alternatives.

The Creation of Money

Banking is generally analyzed from the perspective of **asset management** (*how a bank handles its loans and other assets*) and **liability management** (*how a bank attracts deposits and what it pays for them*). When banks offer people "free checking" and special money market accounts paying 4 percent, they do so after carefully considering the costs of those liabilities to them.

It is important to think of banks as both borrowers and lenders.

To think of banks as borrowers as well as lenders may seem a bit unusual, but borrowing is what they do. When you own a savings account or a checking account, the bank is borrowing from you, paying you a zero (or low) interest rate. It then lends your money to other people at a higher interest rate.

How Banks Create Money

Banks are centrally important to macroeconomics because they create money. How do banks create money? The process is simple—so simple it seems almost magical to many.

Banks "create" money because a bank's liabilities are defined as money. So when a bank incurs liabilities, it creates money.

The key to understanding how banks create money is to remember the nature of financial assets: Financial assets can be created from nothing as long as an offsetting financial liability is simultaneously created. Since money is any financial asset that can be used as a medium of exchange, unit of account, and store of value, money can be created rather easily. The asset just needs to serve the functions of money. Seeing how dollar bills are created is the easiest way to begin examining the process. Whenever the Fed issues an IOU to you or someone else, it creates money.[2] Similarly, other banks create money by creating financial assets that serve the functions of money. As we saw when we considered the measures of money, bank checking accounts serve those functions, so they are money, just as currency is money. When a bank places the proceeds of a loan it makes to you in your checking account, it is creating money. You have a financial asset that did not previously exist.

The First Step in the Creation of Money To see how banks create money, let's consider what would happen if you were given a freshly printed $100 bill. Remember, the Fed created that $100 bill simply by printing it. The $100 bill is a $100 financial asset of yours and a financial liability of the Fed, which issued it.

About 95 percent of all bills printed each year replace worn-out notes. The remaining 5 percent represent new currency in circulation.

If the process of creating money stopped there, it wouldn't be particularly mysterious. But it doesn't stop there. Let's consider what happens next as you use that money.

The Second Step in the Creation of Money The second step in the creation of money involves the transfer of money from one form to another—from currency to

---

[2]As we'll see when we discuss the Fed in more detail, dollar bills aren't the Fed's only IOUs.

a bank deposit. Say you decide to put the $100 bill in your checking account. To make the analysis easier, let's assume that your bank is a branch of the country's only bank, Big Bank. All money deposited in branch banks goes into Big Bank. After you make your deposit, Big Bank is holding $100 in currency for you, and you have $100 more in your checking account. You can spend it whenever you want simply by writing a check. So Big Bank is performing a service for you (holding your money and keeping track of your expenditures) for free. Neat, huh? Big Bank must be run by a bunch of nice people.

But wait. You and I know that bankers, while they may be nice, aren't as nice as all that. There ain't no such thing as a free lunch. Let's see why the bank is being so nice.

Web Note 30.2
Gold

Banking and Goldsmiths To see why banks are so nice, let's go way back in history to when banks first developed.[3] At that time, gold was used for money and people carried around gold to make their payments. But because gold is rather heavy, it was difficult to use for big purchases. Moreover, carrying around a lot of gold left people vulnerable to being robbed by the likes of Robin Hood. So they looked for a place to store their gold until they needed some of it.

From Gold to Gold Receipts The natural place to store gold was the goldsmith shop, which already had a vault. For a small fee, the goldsmith shop would hold your gold, giving you a receipt for it. Whenever you needed your gold, you'd go to the goldsmith and exchange the receipt for gold.

Pretty soon most people kept their gold at the goldsmith's, and they began to wonder: Why go through the bother of getting my gold out to buy something when all that happens is that the seller takes the gold I pay and puts it right back into the goldsmith's vault? That's two extra trips.

Consequently, people began using the receipts the goldsmith gave them to certify that they had deposited $100 worth (or whatever) of gold in his vault. At that point, gold was no longer the only money—gold receipts were also money since they were accepted in exchange for goods. However, as long as the total amount in the gold receipts directly represented the total amount of gold, it was still reasonable to say, since the receipts were 100 percent backed by gold, that gold was the money supply.

Q-7 Most banks prefer to have many depositors rather than one big depositor. Why?

Gold Receipts Become Money Once this process of using the receipts rather than the gold became generally accepted, the goldsmith found that he had substantial amounts of gold in his vault. All that gold, just sitting there! On a normal day, only 1 percent of the gold was claimed by "depositors" and had to be given out. Usually on the same day an amount at least equal to that 1 percent came in from other depositors. What a waste! Gold sitting around doing nothing! So when a good friend came in, needing a loan, the goldsmith said, "Sure, I'll lend you some gold receipts as long as you pay me some interest." When the goldsmith made this loan, he created more gold receipts than he had covered in gold in his vault. He created money.

Pretty soon the goldsmith realized he could earn more from the interest he received on loans than he could earn from goldsmithing. So he stopped goldsmithing and went full-time into making loans of gold receipts. At that point, the number of gold receipts outstanding significantly exceeded the amount of gold in the goldsmith's vaults. But not to worry; since everyone was willing to accept gold receipts rather than gold, the goldsmith had plenty of gold for those few who wanted actual gold.

---

[3]The banking history reported here is, according to historians, apocryphal (more myth than reality). But it so nicely makes the point that I repeat it anyhow.

It was, however, no longer accurate to say that gold was the country's money or currency. Gold receipts were also money. They met the definition of *money*. These gold receipts were backed partially by gold and partially by people's trust that the goldsmiths would pay off their deposits on demand. The goldsmith shops had become banks.

Money is whatever meets the definition of money.

Banking Is Profitable The banking business was very profitable for goldsmiths. Soon other people started competing with them, offering to hold gold for free. After all, if they could store gold, they could make a profit on the loans to other people (with the first people's money). Some even offered to pay people to store their gold.

The goldsmith story is directly relevant to banks. People store their currency in banks and the banks issue receipts—checking accounts—that become a second form of money. When people place their currency in banks and use their receipts from the bank as money, those receipts also become money because they meet the definition of *money*: They serve as a medium of exchange, a unit of account, and a store of wealth. So money includes both currency that people hold and their deposits in the bank.

Which brings us back to why banks hold your currency for free. They do it not because they're nice, but because when you deposit currency in the bank, your deposit allows banks to make profitable loans they otherwise couldn't make.

The Money Multiplier

With that background, let's go back to your $100, which the bank is now holding for you. You have a checking account balance of $100 and the bank has $100 currency. As long as other people are willing to accept your check in payment for $100 worth of goods, your check is as good as money. In fact, it is money in the same way gold receipts were money. But when you deposit $100, no additional money has been created yet. The form of the money has simply been changed from currency to a checking account or demand deposit.

Now let's say Big Bank lends out 90 percent of the currency you deposit, keeping only 10 percent as **reserves**—*currency and deposits a bank keeps on hand or at the Fed or central bank, to manage the normal cash inflows and outflows*. This 10 percent is the **reserve ratio** (*the ratio of reserves to total deposits*). Banks are required by the Fed to hold a percentage of deposits; that percentage is called the required reserve ratio. Banks may also choose to hold an additional percentage, called the *excess reserve ratio*. The reserve ratio is the sum of the required reserve ratio and the excess reserve ratio. Thus, the reserve ratio is at least as large as the required reserve ratio, but it can be larger.

The reserve ratio is the ratio of currency (or deposits at the central bank) to deposits a bank keeps as a reserve against currency withdrawals.

So, like the goldsmith, Big Bank lends out $90 to someone who qualifies for a loan. That person the bank loaned the money to now has $90 currency and you have $100 in a demand deposit, so now there's $190 of money, rather than just $100 of money. The $10 in currency the bank holds in reserve isn't counted as money since the bank must keep it as reserves and may not use it as long as it's backing loans. Only currency held by the public, not currency held by banks, is counted as money. By making the loan, the bank has created $90 in money.

Of course, no one borrows money just to hold it. The borrower spends the money, say on a new sweater, and the sweater store owner now has the $90 in currency. The store owner doesn't want to hold it either. She'll deposit it back into the bank. Since there's only one bank, Big Bank discovers that the $90 it has loaned out is once again in its coffers. The money operates like a boomerang: Big Bank loans $90 out and gets the $90 back again.

The same process occurs again. The bank doesn't earn interest income by holding $90, so if the bank can find additional credible borrowers, it lends out $81, keeping $9 (10 percent of $90) more in reserve. The story repeats and repeats itself, with a slightly smaller amount coming back to the bank each time. At each step in the process, money (in the form of checking account deposits) is being created.

Determining How Many Demand Deposits Will Be Created What's the total amount of demand deposits that will ultimately be created from your \$100 when individuals hold no currency? To answer that question, we continue the process over and over: 100 + 90 + 81 + 72.9 + 65.6 + 59 + 53.1 + 47.8 + 43.0 + 38.7 + 34.9. Adding up these numbers gives us \$686. Adding up \$686 plus the numbers from the next 20 rounds gives us \$961.08.

As you can see, that's a lot of adding. Luckily there's an easier way. Economists have shown that you can determine the amount of money that will eventually be created by such a process by multiplying the initial \$100 in money that was printed by the Fed and deposited by $1/r$, where r is the reserve ratio (the percentage banks keep out of each round). In this case the reserve ratio is 10 percent.

Dividing,

$$\frac{1}{r} = \frac{1}{.10} = 10$$

so the amount of demand deposits that will ultimately exist at the end of the process is

$$(10 \times \$100) = \$1{,}000$$

The \$1,000 is in the form of checking account deposits (demand deposits). The entire \$100 in currency that you were given, and that started the whole process, is in the bank as reserves, which means that \$900 (\$1,000 − \$100) of money has been created by the process.

The simple money multiplier is the measure of the amount of money ultimately created per dollar deposited by the banking system. When people hold no currency, it equals $1/r$.

The higher the reserve ratio, the smaller the money multiplier.

Calculating the Money Multiplier We will call the ratio $1/r$ the **simple money multiplier**—*the measure of the amount of money ultimately created per dollar deposited in the banking system, when people hold no currency*. It tells us how much money will ultimately be created by the banking system from an initial inflow of money. In our example, $1/.10 = 10$. Had the bank kept out 20 percent each time, the money multiplier would have been $1/.20 = 5$. If the reserve ratio were 5 percent, the money multiplier would have been $1/.05 = 20$. The higher the reserve ratio, the smaller the money multiplier, and the less money will be created.

An Example of the Creation of Money To make sure you understand the process, let's consider an example. Say that the reserve ratio is 20 percent and that John Finder finds \$10,000 in currency, which he deposits in the bank. Thus, he has \$10,000 in his checking account and the bank has \$8,000 (\$10,000 − \$2,000 in reserves) to lend out. Once it lends that money to Fred Baker, there is \$8,000 of additional money in the economy. Fred Baker uses the money to buy a new oven from Mary Builder, who, in turn, deposits the money back into the banking system. Big Bank lends out \$6,400 (\$8,000 − \$1,600 in reserves).

Now the process occurs again. Table 30-1 shows the effects of the process for 5 rounds, starting with the initial \$10,000. Each time it lends the money out, the money returns like a boomerang and serves as reserves for more loans. After 5 rounds we reach a point where total demand deposits are \$33,616, and the bank has \$6,723 in reserves. This is approaching the \$50,000 we'd arrive at using the money multiplier:

$$\frac{1}{r}(\$10{,}000) = \frac{1}{.2}(\$10{,}000) = 5(\$10{,}000) = \$50{,}000$$

If we carried it out for more rounds, we'd actually reach what the formula predicted.

TABLE 30-1 The Money-Creating Process

In the money-creating process, the currency keeps coming back to the banking system like a boomerang. With a 20 percent reserve requirement, ultimately (1/.2) × \$10,000 = \$50,000 will be created. In this example, you can see that after 5 rounds, much of the creation of deposits will have taken place. As you carry out the analysis further, the money creation will approach the \$50,000 shown in the last line.

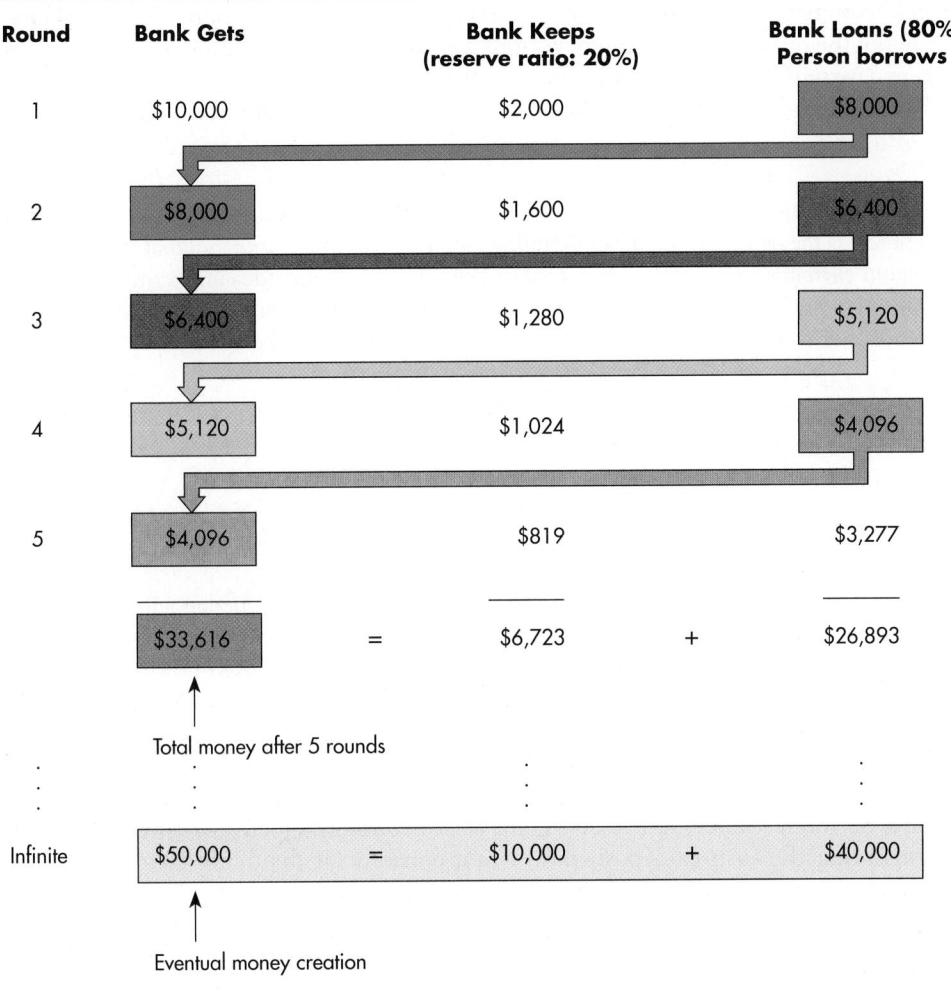

Round	Bank Gets		Bank Keeps (reserve ratio: 20%)		Bank Loans (80%) Person borrows
1	\$10,000		\$2,000		\$8,000
2	\$8,000		\$1,600		\$6,400
3	\$6,400		\$1,280		\$5,120
4	\$5,120		\$1,024		\$4,096
5	\$4,096		\$819		\$3,277
	\$33,616 (Total money after 5 rounds)	=	\$6,723	+	\$26,893
⋮	⋮		⋮		⋮
Infinite	\$50,000 (Eventual money creation)	=	\$10,000	+	\$40,000

Note that the process ends only when the bank holds all the currency in the economy, and the only money held by the public is in the form of demand deposits. Notice also that the total amount of money created depends on the amount banks hold in reserve. Specifically, an economy can support a supply of money equal to reserves times the money multiplier.

To see that you understand the process, say that banks suddenly get concerned about the safety of their loans, and they decide to keep **excess reserves**—*reserves held by banks in excess of what banks are required to hold*. What will happen to the money multiplier? If you answered that it will decrease, you've got it. Excess reserves decrease the money multiplier as much as required reserves do. I mention this example because this very thing happened in the banking system in 2008. Banks became concerned about the safety of their loans; they started holding large excess reserves, and the money multiplier decreased.

In summary, the process of money creation isn't difficult to understand as long as you remember that money is simply a bank's financial liability held by the public. Whenever banks create financial liabilities for themselves, they create financial assets for individuals, and those financial assets are money.

When people hold currency, the money multiplier is $(1 + c)/(r + c)$.

Q-8 If banks hold 20 percent of their deposits as reserves, and the ratio of money people hold as currency to deposits is 20 percent, what is the money multiplier?

Q-9 If people suddenly decide to hold more currency, what happens to the size of the money multiplier?

Calculating the Money Multiplier In the example, I assumed that only banks hold currency. The simple money multiplier reflects that assumption. In reality, banks are not the only holders of currency. Firms and individuals hold currency too, so in each round we must also make an adjustment in the multiplier for what people and firms hold. When firms and individuals hold currency, the **money multiplier** in the economy is

$$\frac{(1 + c)}{(r + c)}$$

where r is *the percentage of deposits banks hold in reserve* and c is *the ratio of money people hold in currency to the money they hold as deposits*.[4] Let's consider an example. Say the banks keep 10 percent in reserve and the ratio of individuals' currency holdings to their deposits is 25 percent. This means the money multiplier will be

$$\frac{1 + 0.25}{(0.1 + 0.25)} = \frac{1.25}{0.35} = 3.43$$

The more cash people hold, the smaller the money multiplier.

Endogenous Money and Credit

The discussion of the money multiplier so far is best seen as a pedagogical crutch for understanding the relationship between reserves and the money supply. The reason why is that the discussion makes it seem as though changes in high-powered money—reserves—cause changes in the total money supply (causation goes from reserves to the money supply). That's not how it works in practice. There are two reasons why. First, causation is mutual, by which I mean that the amount of reserves in the economy is often determined by what total money supply will achieve a certain interest rate. So interest rates, not reserves, are what economists focus on. The second reason is that the cash-to-deposit ratio is not constant; it fluctuates greatly so policy makers have no firm money multiplier on which to set reserves to achieve a specific supply of money.

This doesn't mean that the multiplier equation doesn't hold true. It is true by definition. What it means is that the multiplier is not operational in the sense that one can apply it to reserves to predict the money in the economy. As we will see in the next chapter, in today's economy the money supply tends to be endogenously determined. Policy makers work through the process using backward induction. They target an interest rate, then choose a money supply consistent with that interest rate, and finally find the level of reserves that is consistent with that money supply.

Faith as the Backing of Our Money Supply

Web Note 30.3
E-Currency

The creation of money and the money multiplier are easy to understand if you remember that money held in the form of a checking account (the financial asset created) is offset by an equal amount of financial liabilities of the bank. The bank owes its depositors the

[4]Notice that this becomes the simple money multiplier when $c = 0$; that is, when people do not hold currency.

ADDED DIMENSION

The Real-World Money Multiplier and Changing Banking Rules

Life keeps getting tougher. In the old days, economics students only had to learn the simple money multiplier. Recent reforms in the U.S. banking system have made that impossible. The Depository Institutions Deregulation Act of 1980 extended the reserve requirement to a wide variety of financial institutions besides banks, but it also lowered the reserve requirement for most deposits.

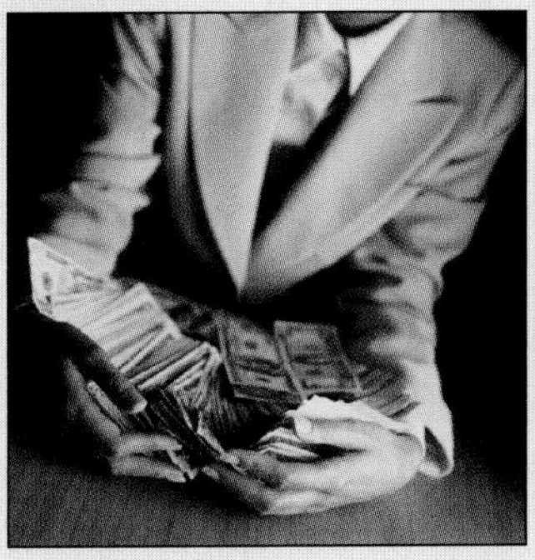

In the early 2000s, the average reserve requirement for all types of bank deposits was under 2 percent and, in normal times, banks held very few excess reserves. (The U.S. reserve requirement on checking accounts is between 3 and 10 percent. Great Britain has no reserve requirements.)

If you insert that low average ratio into the simple money multiplier, you get a multiplier of 50! The real-world money multiplier is much lower than that because of people's holding of currency; the ratio of money people hold as currency is over 50 percent. (For each person in the United States, there's over $2,700 in currency, although it is estimated that two-thirds of currency in circulation is held abroad. That still leaves about $900 for each person in the United States. Don't ask me where that currency is, but according to the data it's out there.) Thus, despite the fact that it makes calculating the real-world money multiplier a bit more difficult, these holdings must be included in the story. Otherwise you won't have a sense of how the real-world system works.

amount in their checking accounts. Its financial liabilities to depositors, in turn, are secured by the loans (the bank's financial assets) and by the financial liabilities of people to whom the loans were made. Promises to pay underlie any modern financial system.

The initial money in the story about the goldsmiths was gold, but it quickly became apparent that it was far more reasonable to use gold certificates as money. Therefore, gold certificates backed by gold soon replaced gold itself as the money supply. Then, as goldsmiths made more loans than they had gold, the gold certificates were no longer backed by gold. They were backed by promises to get gold if the person wanted gold in exchange for the gold certificate. Eventually the percentage of gold supposedly backing the money became so small that it was clear to everyone that the promises, not the gold, underlay the money supply.

The same holds true with banks. Initially, currency (Federal Reserve IOUs) was backed by gold, and banks' demand deposits were in turn backed by Federal Reserve IOUs. But by the 1930s the percentage of gold backing money grew so small that even the illusion of the money being backed by anything but promises was removed. All that backs the modern money supply are bank customers' promises to repay loans and the guarantee of the government to see that the banks' liabilities to individuals will be met.

All that backs the modern money supply are bank customers' promises to repay loans and government guarantees of banks' liabilities to individuals.

The Demand for Money and the Role of the Interest Rate

Now that we've discussed the nature of money, let's consider how money fits in with the financial flows discussed at the beginning of the chapter, and the potential problems that may develop in the macroeconomy as people shift their holdings between financial assets and money. To do that, we must first ask: Why do people hold money?

This is a relevant question because, by assumption, money doesn't pay any interest, whereas other financial assets do pay interest, so to hold money people are forgoing interest payments.[5]

Why People Hold Money

Q-10 What are three reasons people hold money?

The only reason people would be willing to hold money is if they get some benefit from doing so, so we need to examine that benefit. The first benefit is easy: money allows you to buy things. You can *spend* money; you can't spend bonds. You can change a financial asset into spendable money, but that takes time and effort. *The need to hold money for spending* is called the **transactions motive.** Second, you hold money for emergencies. For example, if your car breaks down, you'll need cash to get it towed. Knowing that there will always be unforeseen needs, you might carry $20 cash in addition to what you would otherwise carry. *Holding money for unexpected expenses and impulse buying* is called the **precautionary motive** for holding money. The third reason for holding money is called the speculative motive. The **speculative motive** is *holding cash to avoid holding financial assets whose prices are falling.* It comes about because the price of financial assets such as bonds varies in value as the interest rate fluctuates. For example, if you expect the price of a bond (or any financial asset) to fall, that bond is not something you would want to be holding because you will be losing money by holding it; you'd rather be holding money. Your money holdings might not be earning any interest, but at least their value isn't falling like the price of the asset. In a sense, you are speculating about what the future value of the bond will be. That's why it's called the speculative motive for holding money. You hold money rather than longer-term financial assets so you don't lose if asset prices fall. (Of course, if asset prices are expected to rise, then you want to reduce your holdings of money and increase your asset holdings.)

This 18th-century etching by Robert Goez, The Speculator, *captures a popular view of financial activities. It shows a man reduced to rags by bad speculation.*

Let's consider an example of bond price fluctuations. (Remember, bonds are often used as the reference asset for all financial assets when people provide loanable funds.) Say you have a one-year $1,000 bond that pays an interest rate of 4 percent a year, and that 4 percent is the interest rate in the economy. The bond sells for $1,000 and will provide $40 interest for the year. You're happy earning that 4 percent (that's the best you can do) so you buy the bond for $1,000. Now say that the day after you buy the bond, the interest rate in the economy rises to 6 percent. Because the price of the bond is inversely related to the interest rate in the economy, the price of that 4 percent $1,000 bond that you bought for $1,000 will fall, in this case to $981.13. (See the box "Interest Rates and the Price of Bonds" for a further explanation.) In one day, your bond has fallen in value by $18.87, an amount that far exceeds the interest you earned on the bond for that day. In this case, you would have preferred to have held cash instead of the bond because the cash would not have fallen in value. Holding cash in the expectation of falling bond prices is the speculative demand for money.

Most professional bond speculators, who often carry portfolios of millions and even billions of dollars of bonds, make their money on changes in the prices of bonds, not on the interest payments of bonds. The reason is that although the changes in annualized interest rates on any particular day are generally small—so small that they are measured in basis points, each of which is one one-hundredth of a percentage point—even those small changes in interest rates swamp the income made on the interest rate payments for the day.

Interest Rates and the Price of Bonds

[5]As discussed above, in today's economy, many components of money pay interest, but they pay a lower interest than do other financial assets. The analysis I present here applies to the differential rate of interest paid between money and longer-term financial assets; we assume zero interest on money simply to keep the presentation as simple as possible.

ADDED DIMENSION

Interest Rates and the Price of Bonds

In the example in the text, you may have thought that if the interest rate in the economy rose from 4 percent to 6 percent, and you had bought the bond paying 4 percent, that you would just sell it and buy the 6 percent bond. Would that you could, but that's not the way the bond market works. You only get your $1,000 back when the bond matures. If you wanted your money before that time, you would have to sell it to someone else, but the price of the 4 percent bond would have fallen as soon as the interest rate in the economy rose. More generally, we have the following relationship:

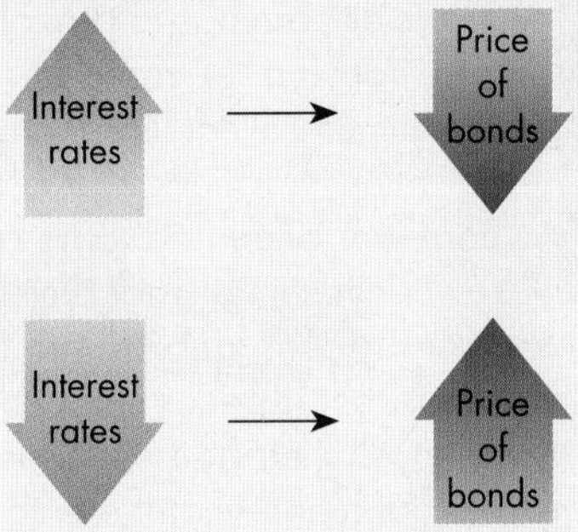

As an example, say that you buy a $1,000, one-year bond with a coupon rate (the fixed rate of interest paid on the bond) of 4 percent when the economy's interest rate is 4 percent. The price of that bond is determined by the formula:

$$P = \frac{(1000 + 40)}{1 + r}$$

where r is the interest rate in the economy and the numerator is the face value of the bond and the interest it pays. Since the bond's interest rate is the same as the interest rate for other savings instruments, you pay $1,000 for that bond. Now say that the economy's interest rate falls to 2 percent so that all new bonds being offered pay only 2 percent. That makes your bond especially desirable since it pays a higher interest rate. The price of the bond rises:

$$P = \frac{1040}{1.02} = 1{,}019.61$$

People would be willing to pay up to $1,019.61. Alternatively, if the economy's interest rate rises to 6 percent, as it did in the example in the text, your bond will be less desirable and people would be willing to pay only $981.13. In summary, when the interest rate falls, the price of existing bonds rises, and when the interest rate rises, the price of existing bonds falls.

The longer the length of the bond to maturity, the more the price varies with the change in the interest rate. (For a further discussion of this inverse relationship, see the present value discussion in Appendix A to this chapter.)

In the real world, interest rates fluctuate all the time, and bond investors are continually looking for clues about whether the interest rates are going to rise or fall. When they expect bond prices to rise, they get rid of their cash and buy bonds; when they expect bond prices to fall, they get out of bonds and into cash.

Taking all three of these motives—transactions, precautionary, and speculative—into account, you can see that it makes sense to hold some money even though it is costing you something in forgone interest to do so—and the lower the interest rate, the greater the quantity of money demanded.

Web Note 30.4
Stash Your Cash

Equilibrium in the Money Market

We can capture this demand for money relationship in the graph in Figure 30-4, which has the interest rate on the vertical axis and the quantity of money you want to hold on the horizontal axis.

Notice that the demand for money is downward-sloping. That's because, as the interest rate falls, the cost of holding money falls (that is, the interest you don't earn by holding money falls), so it makes sense to hold more money. When interest rates rise, bonds and other financial assets that pay that high interest rate become more attractive, so you hold more financial assets and less money.

REAL-WORLD APPLICATION

The Housing Bust of 2007

Throughout history, market economies have experienced financial panics, which result when what are called financial bubbles burst. There is debate in economics about what a financial bubble is, and whether a seeming financial bubble actually is one, but the general agreement is that if a rise in asset prices is "unsustainable," then it should be considered a bubble. Let's consider as an example of what is meant by "unsustainable" the recent housing price increase, where houses in some areas increased by more than 30 percent a year for four or five years. The beginning of the rise was grounded in supply and demand forces—demand was increasing, and since supply was relatively inelastic, prices rose. The people who were buying could afford to pay the mortgages and were buying to live in the houses. The price rise concerned some people who didn't yet own houses, and they didn't want to get left out. So they bought more expensive houses that they might not easily afford, but that they could continue to make payments on in a pinch. Had credit been limited to standard mortgages, the price rise in housing would have likely stopped there. But the financial industry began to give out *teaser mortgages*—mortgages that have low payments in the first couple of years, but which later become much more expensive. Many people took out these mortgages in the belief that they would either be able to refinance when the higher-rate mortgage kicked in or sell the house at a profit, and pay back the loan. So housing prices rose more, and the houses sold.

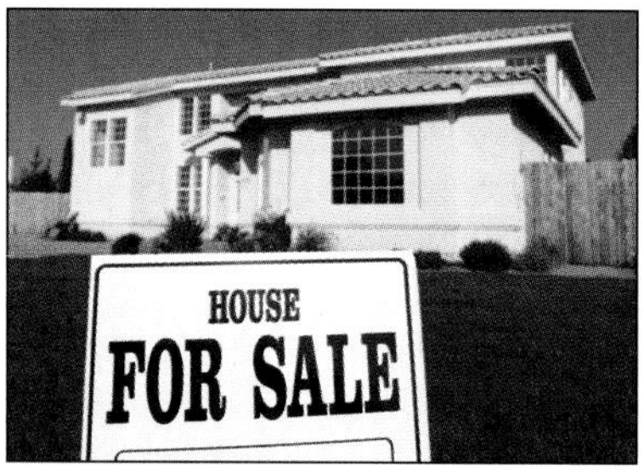

These price increases were potentially sustainable as long as the mortgages were only given to people who could pay them off with other assets, should housing prices not continue to rise. But then, a new type of mortgage—the subprime mortgage—developed, which granted mortgages to people who did not have the financial assets or earnings to pay off the loan unless housing prices rose. (They were sometimes called "liar loans" because to get them the mortgage broker and the borrower often had to lie about the borrower's income.) That development introduced some unsustainability into the situation. The reason is that if prices stopped rising, these buyers would have to sell their houses to meet their mortgage commitments. That meant that there could be a sudden large increase in the supply of houses to the market, which would depress prices. That's what started in 2007, leading to the financial crisis and recession in 2008 and 2009 that I will discuss in Chapter 32.

FIGURE 30-4 **The Money Market**

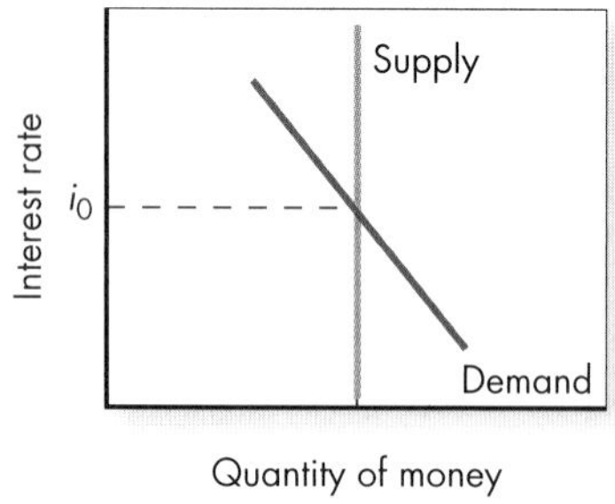

To complete our analysis of the financial sector, we need to add a supply of money to Figure 30-4. For simplicity, at this point, we assume the supply of money is set at some fixed level regardless of the interest rate. That is, we assume that the supply curve of money is vertical. (We will discuss the supply of money in much more detail in the next chapter.) The equilibrium interest rate will be where the demand for, and supply of, money intersect—in this case, at i_0. As we discussed in the beginning of the chapter, the interest rate determined in this market (the money market) is the short-term interest rate.

The Many Interest Rates in the Economy

As I stated at the beginning, the economy doesn't have just a single interest rate; it has many, just as there are many types of financial assets. (With recent developments in financial markets, the variety of financial assets grows every year.) Each of these financial assets will have an implicit interest rate associated with it (the implicit interest rate of an asset that pays no interest is the expected percentage change in the price of that asset, so if the asset price is expected to rise by 10 percent, its implicit interest rate is 10 percent). In such a multiple-asset market, which is what we have in the real world, the potential for the interest rate in the loanable funds market (which can be thought of as a composite market for all these varied financial assets) to differ from the interest rate in the market for a particular asset is large. The result can be what is sometimes called a financial asset market bubble.

Let's take an example: the housing market in the early 2000s. During that period, housing prices were rising 10–15 percent per year (more than 50 percent in some areas) and were expected to continue to rise. That meant that the implicit rate of interest paid by houses was 10–15 percent (minus the costs of buying and selling the house). The interest rate that one could borrow at—the mortgage rate—was about 5.5 percent, which meant that it made sense to borrow as much as one possibly could and buy as many houses or as big a house as one could. And that's what many people did. As they did, housing prices rose, and the expectations were confirmed, which led to more and more people buying houses for speculative purposes. The strong housing market, because it led to additional construction and expenditures related to house buying, pulled the real economy along and helped the real economy expand. As long as one expected the housing prices to rise at a higher rate than the interest rate at which one could borrow, the strategy of buying as many houses as one could made good sense.

In 2007, people lowered their expectations of housing price appreciation; some even expected housing prices to fall. So, many of those who had purchased houses with the intention of selling them at a higher price began to sell their houses more aggressively so that they could return to holding their financial assets in cash before housing prices really fell. The demand for housing decreased substantially, and the equilibrium price of housing available for sale fell. The result was a financial crisis that is sufficiently important that it gets an entire chapter devoted to it.

Conclusion

We'll stop our introduction to money and the financial sector there. As you can see, money is central to the operation of the macroeconomy. If money functions smoothly, it keeps the outflow from the expenditure stream (saving) and the flow back into the expenditure stream at a level that reflects people's desires. Money can be treated simply as a mirror of people's real desires. When money doesn't function smoothly, it can cause serious problems.

Summary

- The financial sector is the market where financial assets are created and exchanged. It channels flows out of the circular flow and back into the circular flow.
- Every financial asset has a corresponding financial liability.
- The economy has many interest rates. The long-term interest rate is determined in the market for loanable funds, while the short-term interest rate is determined in the money market.
- Money is a highly liquid financial asset that serves as a unit of account, a medium of exchange, and a store of wealth.
- There are various measures of money. The two most important are M_1 and M_2. M_1 consists of currency in the hands of the public, checking account balances, and traveler's checks. M_2 is M_1 plus savings deposits, small-denomination time deposits, and money market mutual fund shares.

- Since money is what people believe money to be, creating money out of thin air is easy. How banks create money out of thin air is easily understood if you remember that money is simply a financial liability of a bank. Banks create money by loaning out deposits.
- The simple money multiplier is $1/r$. It tells you the amount of money ultimately created per dollar deposited in the banking system.
- The money multiplier when people hold cash is $(1 + c)/(r + c)$.
- There are three reasons people hold money, referred to as (1) the transactions motive, (2) the precautionary motive, and (3) the speculative motive. The demand for money is inversely related to the interest rate paid on money.
- Financial asset market bubbles can cause problems for an economy.

Key Terms

asset management *(711)*
bank *(705)*
excess reserves *(715)*
Federal Reserve Bank (the Fed) *(705)*
financial assets *(703)*
interest rate *(704)*
liability management *(711)*
M_1 *(708)*
M_2 *(708)*
money *(705)*
money multiplier *(716)*
precautionary motive *(718)*
reserve ratio *(713)*
reserves *(713)*
simple money multiplier *(714)*
speculative motive *(718)*
transactions motive *(718)*

Questions and Exercises

connect ECONOMICS

1. If financial institutions don't produce any tangible real assets, why are they considered a vital part of the U.S. economy? LO1
2. What are loanable funds? LO2
3. In what market are long-term interest rates determined? LO2
4. In what market are short-term interest rates determined? LO2
5. Will there be too much or too little investment in the economy if the interest rate is higher than the rate that would equilibrate the supply and demand for loanable funds? LO2
6. Explain the effect of the following events on the interest rate in the loanable funds market. Demonstrate your answer graphically.
   a. Tax revenue is lower than expected and people expect cities to default on municipal bonds. They sell their bonds and hold cash instead.
   b. A significant number of people begin to use online banking services, allowing them to lower the average balance on their checking account.
   c. Economists begin to expect economic growth to pick up. In response, firms increase the amount they spend on capital goods. LO2
7. What are the three functions of money? LO3
8. If dollar bills (Federal Reserve notes) are backed by nothing but promises and are in real terms worthless, why do people accept them? LO3
9. For each of the following, state whether it is considered money in the United States. Explain why or why not.
   a. A check you write against deposits you have at Bank USA.
   b. Brazilian reals.
   c. The available credit you have on your MasterCard.
   d. Reserves held by banks at the Federal Reserve Bank.
   e. Federal Reserve notes in your wallet.
   f. Gold bullion.
   g. Grocery store coupons. LO3
10. What function is money serving when people compare the price of chicken to the price of beef? LO4
11. How does inflation affect money's function as a store of wealth? LO4
12. State whether the following is an example of the transactions, precautionary, or speculative motive for holding money:
    a. I like to have the flexibility of buying a few things for myself, such as a latte or a snack, every day, so I generally carry \$10 in my pocket.
    b. You never know when your car will break down, so I always keep \$50 in my pocket.

c. When the stock market is falling, money managers generally hold more in cash than when the stock market is rising.
d. Any household has bills that are due every month. LO4

13. What are two components of M_2 that are not components of M_1? LO5
14. Categorize the following as components of M_1, M_2, both, or neither.
    a. State and local government bonds.
    b. Checking accounts.
    c. Money market mutual funds.
    d. Currency.
    e. Stocks.
    f. Corporate bonds.
    g. Traveler's checks. LO5
15. State the immediate effect of each of the following actions on M_1 and M_2:
    a. Barry writes his plumber a check for $200. The plumber takes the check to the bank, keeps $50 in cash, and deposits the remainder in his savings account.
    b. Maureen deposits the $1,000 from her CD in a money market mutual fund.
    c. Sylvia withdraws $50 in cash from her savings account.
    d. Paulo cashes a $100 traveler's check that was issued in his Ohio bank at a New York bank. LO5
16. Why was character George Bailey in the film *It's a Wonderful Life* right when he stated on the day of a bank run that depositors could not withdraw all their money from the bank? LO6
17. U.S. paper currency is made with several features that are difficult to counterfeit including a security thread, color-shifting ink, microprinting, a portrait, a watermark, and a fine-line printing pattern. As duplication technology, however, continually improves and more and more counterfeits are circulated, what will happen to the following?
    a. The value of money circulated.
    b. The volume of cashless transactions.
    c. The amount of money the U.S. Treasury spends to introduce additional security measures. LO6
18. Write the equations for the simple money multiplier and the money multiplier. Which multiplier is most likely to be larger? LO7
19. True or false? Policy makers in practice use the money multiplier to determine the amount of reserves needed to achieve the desired money supply. Explain. LO7
20. If the U.S. government were to raise the reserve requirement to 100 percent, what would likely happen to the interest rate banks pay on deposits? Why? LO7
21. While Jon is walking to school one morning, a helicopter flying overhead drops a $100 bill. Not knowing how to return it, Jon keeps the money and deposits it in his bank. (No one in this economy holds currency.) If the bank keeps 5 percent of its money in reserves:
    a. How much money can the bank initially lend out?
    b. After this initial transaction, by how much is the money in the economy changed?
    c. What's the money multiplier?
    d. How much money will eventually be created by the banking system from Jon's $100? LO6, LO7
22. Calculate the money multipliers below:
    a. Assuming individuals hold no currency, calculate the simple money multiplier for each of the following: 5%, 10%, 20%, 25%, 50%, 75%, 100%.
    b. Assuming the currency to deposit ratio is 20 percent, recalculate the money multipliers in *a*. LO7
23. If people expect interest rates to rise in the future, how will they change the quantity of money they demand? Explain your answer. LO8
24. Do interest rates and prices of bonds vary inversely or directly with one another? Explain your answer. LO8
25. Why is the demand for money downward-sloping? LO8
26. If the interest rate equilibrates the loanable funds market, but is too high to equilibrate the money market, what will happen to the price of financial assets? LO8
27. Explain the effect of the following events on the interest rate in the money market. Demonstrate your answer graphically.
    a. The supply of money increases.
    b. A significant number of people begin to use credit cards for daily transactions, reducing the amount of money they hold.
    c. Bond traders expect bond prices to rise, and therefore reduce their cash holdings. LO8

Questions from Alternative Perspectives

1. The U.S. government has a monopoly on U.S. dollars.
   a. Could money be supplied privately?
   b. Has money ever been supplied privately? If so, how do you suppose people knew its value? (Austrian)
2. The Federal Reserve's Board of Governors is arguably the most powerful policy-making body in the United States.
   a. Since its inception, how many women have served on the Board of Governors?
   b. What do almost all of the current members of the Board of Governors have in common? www.federalreserve. gov/bios/boardmembership.htm (Feminist)

3. In Institutional economists' view, money not only serves as a medium of exchange, a unit of account, and a store of wealth, it also operates as an idea that shapes human understanding and interaction. Construct a list of examples during a day's interactions where money operates as an idea whereby people interact or attempt to understand a situation. For example, a friend might say, "Sherry is dating Herbert; she can do better than that!" (Institutionalist)
4. The chapter talks about the role that depositors and banks play in the "creation" of money.
   a. Do you think this role is consistent with the view that the money supply is only determined exogenously by the central bank?
   b. How could depositors and banks endogenously determine the money supply? (Post-Keynesian)
5. While *sharia* (interest) is banned in Islam, profit-sharing is not. An Islamically sound banking practice could be a system in which depositors deposited money under a principle of profit-sharing and the bank provided funds on the same principle with a mark-up as payment for their financial services.
   a. How does this system differ from a system based on interest?
   b. How might the system of interest be exploitative and a system based on profit-sharing not be exploitative? (Religious)

Issues to Ponder

1. Money is to the economy as oil is to an engine. Explain. LO3
2. About 30 U.S. localities circulate their own currency with names like "Ithaca Hours" and "Dillo Hours." Doing so is perfectly legal (although by law they are subject to a 10 percent federal tax, which currently the government is not collecting). These currencies are used as payment for rent, wages, goods, and so on. Are these currencies money? Explain. LO3
3. Economist Michael Bryan reports that on the island of Palau, the Yapese used stone disks as their currency. The number of stones in front of a person's house denoted how rich he or she was.
   a. Would you expect these stones to be used for small transactions?
   b. An Irish-American trader, David O'Keefe, was shipwrecked on the island, and thereafter returned to the island with a boatload of stones. If they were identical to the existing stones, what would that do to the value of the stones?
   c. If O'Keefe's stones could be distinguished from the existing stones, how would that change your answer to *b*?
   d. An anthropologist described the stones as "a memory of contributions"—the more stones a person has, the more that person has contributed to the community. Could the same description be used to describe our money? LO3

Answers to Margin Questions

1. I would respond by saying that the financial sector is central to the macroeconomy. It facilitates the trades that occur in the real sector. *(703)*
2. Savings that escape the circular flow can cause fluctuations in the economy. Interest rates help translate the flow of saving into investment, which make their way back into the spending stream. *(705)*
3. The three functions of money are (1) medium of exchange, (2) unit of account, and (3) store of wealth. *(706)*
4. Money provides liquidity and ease of payment. People hold money rather than bonds to get this liquidity and hold down transaction costs. *(707)*
5. M_2 would be the larger number since it includes all of the components of M_1 plus additional components. *(708)*
6. Credit cards are not money. Credit cards are a method by which people borrow. *(710)*
7. Banks operate on the fact that they will have some money flowing in and some money flowing out at all times. When the number of withdrawals and deposits is large, on average, they will offset one another, allowing banks to make loans on the "float," the average amount that they are holding. If there is one big depositor at a bank, this is less likely to happen, and the bank must hold larger reserves in case that big depositor withdraws that money. *(712)*
8. The money multiplier is $(1 + c)/(r + c)$, which is equal to $1.2/0.4 = 3$. *(716)*
9. The real-world money multiplier would decrease since individuals holding cash make the denominator of the money multiplier larger. *(716)*
10. People hold money to spend (transactions motive), for unexpected expenses and impulse buying (precautionary motive), and to avoid holding financial assets whose prices are falling (speculative motive). *(718)*

APPENDIX A

A Closer Look at Financial Assets and Liabilities

Financial Assets and Financial Liabilities

To understand the financial sector and its relation to the real sector, you must understand how financial assets and liabilities work and how they affect the real economy.

An *asset* is something that provides its owner with expected future benefits. There are two types of assets: real assets and financial assets. Real assets are assets whose services provide direct benefits to their owners, either now or in the future. A house is a real asset—you can live in it. A machine is a real asset—you can produce goods with it.

Financial assets are *assets, such as stocks or bonds, whose benefit to the owner depends on the issuer of the asset meeting certain obligations.* **Financial liabilities** are *liabilities incurred by the issuer of a financial asset to stand behind the issued asset.* It's important to remember that *every financial asset has a corresponding financial liability*; it's that financial liability that gives the financial asset its value. In the case of bonds, for example, a company's agreement to pay interest and repay the principal gives bonds their value. If the company goes bankrupt and reneges on its liability to pay interest and repay the principal, the asset becomes worthless. The corresponding liability gives the financial asset its value.

For example, a **stock** is *a financial asset that conveys ownership rights in a corporation.* It is a liability of the firm; it gives the holder ownership rights that are spelled out in the financial asset. An equity liability such as a stock usually conveys a general right to dividends, but only if the company's board of directors decides to pay them.

A debt liability conveys no ownership right. It's a type of loan. An example of a debt liability is a bond that a firm issues. A **bond** is *a promise to pay certain amounts of money at specified times in the future.* A bond is a liability of the firm but an asset of the individual who holds the bond. A debt liability such as a bond usually conveys legal rights to interest payments and repayment of principal.

Real assets are created by real economic activity. For example, a house or a machine must be built. Financial assets are created whenever somebody takes on a financial liability or establishes an ownership claim. For example, say I promise to pay you $1 billion in the future. You now have a financial asset and I have a financial liability. Understanding that financial assets can be created by a simple agreement of two people is fundamentally important to understanding how the financial sector works.

Valuing Stocks and Bonds

A financial asset's worth comes from the stream of income it will pay in the future. With financial assets such as bonds, that stream of income can be calculated rather precisely. With stocks, where the stream of income is a percentage of the firm's profits, which fluctuate significantly, the stream of future income is uncertain and valuations depend significantly on expectations.

Let's start by considering some generally held beliefs among economists and financial experts. The first is that an average share of stock in a company in a mature industry sells for somewhere between 15 and 20 times its normal profits. The second is that bond prices rise as market interest rates fall, and fall as market interest rates rise. The first step in understanding where the beliefs come from is to recognize that $1 today is not equal to $1 next year. Why? Because if I have $1 today, I can invest it and earn interest (say 10 percent per year), and next year I will have $1.10, not $1. So if the annual interest rate is 10 percent, $1.10 next year is worth $1 today; alternatively, $1 next year is worth roughly 91 cents today. A dollar two years in the future is worth even less today, and dollars 30 years in the future are worth very little today.

Present value is *a method of translating a flow of future income or savings into its current worth.* For example, say a smooth-talking, high-pressure salesperson is wining and dining you. "Isn't that amazing?" the salesman says. "My company will pay $10 a year not only to you, but also to your great-great-great-grandchildren, and more, for 500 years—thousands of dollars in all. And I will sell this annuity—this promise to pay money at periodic intervals in the future—to you for a payment to me now of only $800, but you must act fast. After tonight the price will rise to $2,000."

Do you buy it? My rhetoric suggests that the answer should be no—but can you explain why? And what price *would* you be willing to pay?

To decide how much an annuity is worth, you need some way of valuing that $10 per year. *You can't simply add up the $10 five hundred times.* Doing so is wrong. Instead you must *discount* all future dollars by the interest rate in the economy. Discounting is required because a dollar in the future is not worth a dollar now.

If you have $1 now, you can take that dollar, put it in the bank, and in a year you will have that dollar plus interest. If the interest rate you can get from the bank is 5 percent, that

TABLE A30-1 (A AND B) **Sample Present Value and Annuity Tables**

	Interest Rate						
Year	3%	4%	6%	9%	12%	15%	18%
1	$0.97	$0.96	$0.94	$0.92	$0.89	$0.87	$0.85
2	0.94	0.92	0.89	0.84	0.80	0.76	0.72
3	0.92	0.89	0.84	0.77	0.71	0.66	0.61
4	0.89	0.85	0.79	0.71	0.64	0.57	0.52
5	0.86	0.82	0.75	0.65	0.57	0.50	0.44
6	0.84	0.79	0.70	0.60	0.51	0.43	0.37
7	0.81	0.76	0.67	0.55	0.45	0.38	0.31
8	0.79	0.73	0.63	0.50	0.40	0.33	0.27
9	0.77	0.70	0.59	0.46	0.36	0.28	0.23
10	0.74	0.68	0.56	0.42	0.32	0.25	0.19
15	0.64	0.56	0.42	0.27	0.18	0.12	0.08
20	0.55	0.46	0.31	0.18	0.10	0.06	0.04
30	0.41	0.31	0.17	0.08	0.03	0.02	0.01
40	0.31	0.21	0.10	0.03	0.01	0.00	0.00
50	0.23	0.14	0.05	0.01	0.00	0.00	0.00

(a) Present Value Table (value now of $1 to be received *x* years in the future)
The present value table converts a future amount into a present amount.

	Interest Rate						
Number of Years	3%	4%	6%	9%	12%	15%	18%
1	$ 0.97	$ 0.96	$ 0.94	$ 0.92	$0.89	$0.87	$0.85
2	1.91	1.89	1.83	1.76	1.69	1.63	1.57
3	2.83	2.78	2.67	2.53	2.40	2.28	2.17
4	3.72	3.63	3.47	3.24	3.04	2.85	2.69
5	4.58	4.45	4.21	3.89	3.60	3.35	3.13
6	5.42	5.24	4.92	4.49	4.11	3.78	3.50
7	6.23	6.00	5.58	5.03	4.56	4.16	3.81
8	7.02	6.73	6.21	5.53	4.97	4.49	4.08
9	7.79	7.44	6.80	6.00	5.33	4.77	4.30
10	8.53	8.11	7.36	6.42	5.65	5.02	4.49
15	11.94	11.12	9.71	8.06	6.81	5.85	5.09
20	14.88	13.59	11.47	9.13	7.47	6.26	5.35
30	19.60	17.29	13.76	10.27	8.06	6.57	5.52
40	23.11	19.79	15.05	10.76	8.24	6.64	5.55
50	25.73	21.48	15.76	10.96	8.30	6.66	5.55

(b) Annuity Table (value now of $1 per year to be received for *x* years)
The annuity table converts a known stream of income into a present amount.

dollar will grow to $1.05 a year from now. That means if the interest rate is 5%, if you have 95 cents now, in a year it will be worth nearly a dollar tomorrow ($0.9975 = $0.95 + 5% × $0.95 to be exact). Reversing the reasoning, $1 on year in the future is worth a little bit more than 95 cents today. So the present value of $1 one year in the future at a 5 percent interest rate is 95 cents.

A dollar *two* years from now is worth even less today. Carry out that same reasoning and you'll find that if the interest rate is 5 percent, $1 two years from now is worth approximately 90 cents today. Why? Because you could take 90 cents now, put it in the bank at 5 percent interest, and in two years have almost $1.

The Present Value Formula

Carrying out such reasoning for every case would be a real pain. But luckily, there's a formula and a table that can be used to determine the present value (PV) of future income. The formula is

$$PV = A_1/(1 + i) + A_2/(1 + i)^2 + \cdots + A_n/(1 + i)^n$$

where

A_n = the amount of money received *n* periods in the future

i = the interest rate in the economy (assumed constant)

Solving this formula for any time period longer than one or two years is complicated. To deal with it, people either use a business calculator or a present value table such as the one in Table A30-1.

Table A30-1(a) gives the present value of a single dollar at some time in the future at various interest rates. Notice a couple of things about the chart. First, the further into the future one goes, the lower the present value. Second, the higher the interest rate, the lower the present value. At a 12 percent interest rate, $1 fifty years from now has a present value of essentially zero.

Table A30-1(b) is an annuity table; it tells us how much a constant stream of income for a specific number of years is worth. Notice that as the interest rate rises, the value of an annuity falls. At an 18 percent interest rate, $1 per year for 50 years has a present value of $5.55. To get the value of amounts other than $1, simply multiply the entry in the table by the amount. For example, $10 per year for 50 years at 18 percent interest is 10 × $5.55 or $55.50.

As you can see, the interest rate in the economy is a key to present value. *You must know the interest rate t^ know the value of money over time.* The higher the current (and assumed constant) interest rate, the more a given amount of money in the present will be worth in the future. Or,

REAL-WORLD APPLICATION

The Press and Present Value

The failure to understand the concept of present value often shows up in the popular press. Here are three examples.

Headline: **COURT SETTLEMENT IS $40,000,000.**

Inside story: The money will be paid out over a 40-year period.

Actual value: $11,925,000 (8 percent interest rate).

Headline: **DISABLED WIDOW WINS $25 MILLION LOTTERY**

Inside story: The money will be paid over 20 years.

Actual value: $13,254,499 (8 percent interest rate).

Headline: **BOND ISSUE TO COST TAXPAYERS $68 MILLION**

Inside story: The $68 million is the total of interest and principal payments. The interest is paid yearly; the principal won't be paid back to the bond purchasers until 30 years from now.

Actual value: $20,000,000 (8 percent interest rate).

Such stories are common. Be on the lookout for them as you read the newspaper or watch the evening news.

alternatively, the higher the current interest rate, the less a given amount of money in the future will be worth in the present.

Some Rules of Thumb for Determining Present Value

Sometimes you don't have a present value table or a business calculator handy. For those times, there are a few rules of thumb and simplified formulas for which you don't need either a present value table or a calculator. Let's consider two of them: the infinite annuity rule and the Rule of 72.

The Annuity Rule To find the present value of an annuity that will pay $1 for an infinite number of years in the future when the interest rate is 5 percent, we simply divide $1 by 5 percent (.05). Doing so gives us $20. So at 5 percent, $1 a year paid to you forever has a present value of $20. The **annuity rule** is that *the present value of any annuity is the annual income it yields divided by the interest rate*. Our general annuity rule for any annuity is expressed as

$$PV = X/i$$

That is, the present value of an infinite flow in income, X, is that income divided by the interest rate, i.

Most of the time, people don't offer to sell you annuities for the infinite future. A typical annuity runs for 30, 40, or 50 years. However, the annuity rule is still useful. As you can see from the present value table, in 30 years at a 9 percent interest rate, the present value of $1 isn't much (it's 8 cents), so we can use this infinite flow formula as an approximation of long-lasting, but less than infinite, flows of future income. We simply subtract a little bit from what we get with our formula. The longer the time period, the less we subtract. For example, say you are wondering what $200 a year for 40 years is worth when the interest rate is 8 percent. Dividing $200 by .08 gives $2,500, so we know the annuity must be worth a bit less than $2,500. (It's actually worth $2,411.)

The annuity rule allows us to answer the question posed at the beginning of this section: How much is $10 a year for 500 years worth right now? The answer is that it depends on the interest rate you could earn on a specified amount of money now. If the interest rate is 10 percent, the maximum you should be willing to pay for that 500-year $10 annuity is $100:

$$\$10/.10 = \$100$$

If the interest rate is 5 percent, the most you should pay is $200 ($10/.05 = $200). So now you know why you should have said no to that supersalesman who offered it to you for $800.

The Rule of 72 A second rule of thumb for determining present values of shorter time periods is the **Rule of 72,** which states:

> *The number of years it takes for a certain amount to double in value is equal to 72 divided by the rate of interest.*

Say, for example, that the interest rate is 4 percent. How long will it take for your $100 to become $200? Dividing 72 by 4 gives 18, so the answer is 18 years. Conversely, at a 4 percent interest rate the present value of $200 18 years in the future is about $100. (Actually it's $102.67.)

ADDED DIMENSION

Do Financial Assets Make Society Richer?

Financial assets are neat. You can call them into existence simply by getting someone to accept your IOU. *Remember, every financial asset has a corresponding financial liability equal to it.* So when individuals in a country increase their financial assets by $1 trillion, they are also increasing their financial liabilities by $1 trillion. An optimist would say a country is rich. A pessimist would say it's poor. An economist would say that financial assets and financial liabilities are simply opposite sides of the ledger and don't indicate whether a country is rich or poor. You have to go beyond financial assets and liabilities.

To find out whether a country is rich or poor, you must look at its *real assets.* If financial assets increase the economy's efficiency and thereby increase the amount of real assets, they make society better off. This is most economists' view of financial assets. If, however, they decrease the efficiency of the economy (as some economists have suggested some financial assets do because they focus productive effort on financial gamesmanship), financial assets make society worse off.

The same correspondence between a financial asset and its liability exists when a financial asset's value changes. Say stock prices fall significantly. Is society poorer? The answer is: It depends on the reason for the change. Let's say there is no known reason. Then, while the people who own the stock are poorer, the people who might want to buy stock in the future are richer since the price of assets has fallen. So in a pure accounting sense, society is neither richer nor poorer when the prices of stocks rise or fall for no reason.

But there are ways in which changes in the value of financial assets might signify that society is richer or poorer. For example, the changes in the values of financial assets might *reflect* (rather than cause) real changes. If suddenly a company finds a cure for cancer, its stock prices will rise and society will be richer. But the rise in the price of the stock doesn't cause society to be richer. It reflects the discovery that made society richer. Society would be richer because of the discovery even if the stock's price didn't rise.

There's significant debate about how well the stock market reflects real changes in the economy. Classical economists believe it closely reflects real changes; Keynesian economists believe it doesn't. But both sides agree that the changes in the real economy, not the changes in the price of financial assets, underlie what makes an economy richer or poorer.

Alternatively, say that you will receive $1,000 in 10 years. Is it worth paying $500 for that amount now if the interest rate is 9 percent? Using the rule of 72, we know that at a 9 percent interest rate it will take about eight years for $500 to double:

$$72/9 = 8$$

so the future value of $500 in 10 years is more than $1,000. It's probably about $1,200. (Actually it's $1,184.) So if the interest rate in the economy is 9 percent, it's not worth paying $500 now in order to get that $1,000 in 10 years. By investing that same $500 today at 9 percent, you can have $1,184 in 10 years.

The Importance of Present Value

Many business decisions require such present value calculations. In almost any business, you'll be looking at flows of income in the future and comparing them to present costs or to other flows of money in the future.

Generally, however, when most people calculate present value, they don't use any of the formulas. They go to their computer, press in the numbers to calculate the present value, and watch while the computer displays the results.

Let's now use our knowledge of present value to explain the two observations at the beginning of this section: (1) an average share of stock sells for between 15 and 20 times its normal profits and (2) bond prices and interest rates are inversely related. Since all financial assets can be broken down into promises to pay certain amounts at certain times in the future, we can determine their value with the present value formula. If the asset is a bond, it consists of a stream of income payments over a number of years and the repayment of the face value of the bond. Each year's interest payment and the eventual repayment of the face value must be calculated separately, and then the results must be added together.

If the financial asset is a share of stock, the valuation is a bit less clear since a stock does not guarantee the payment of anything definite—just a share of the profits. No profits, no payment. So, with stocks, expectations of profits are of central importance. Let's consider an example:

Say a share of stock is earning $1 per share per year and is expected to continue to earn that long into the future. Using the annuity rule and an interest rate of 6.5 percent, the present value of that future stream of expected earnings is about 1/.065, or a bit more than $15. Assuming profits are expected to grow slightly, that would mean that the stock should sell for somewhere around $20, or 20 times its profit per share, which is the explanation to economists' view that an average stock sells for about 15 times normal profits.

To see the answer to the second—bond prices and interest rates are inversely related—say the interest rate rises to 10 percent. Then the value of the stock or bond that is earning a fixed amount—in this case $1 per share—will go down to $10. Interest rate up, value of stock or bond down. This is the explanation of the second observation.

There is nothing immutable in the above reasoning. For example, if promises to pay aren't trustworthy, you don't put the amount that's promised into your calculation; you put in the amount you actually expect to receive. That's why when a company or a country looks as if it's going to default on loans or stop paying dividends, the value of its bonds and stock will fall considerably. For example, in the early 2000s, many people thought Argentina would default on its bonds. That expectation caused the price of Argentinean bonds to fall and interest rates to rise more than 30 percentage points.

Of course, the expectations could go in the opposite direction. Say that the interest rate is 10 percent, and that you expect a company's annual profit, which is now $1 per share, to grow by 10 percent per year. In that case, since expected profit growth is as high as the interest rate, the current value of the stock is infinite. It is such expectations of future profit growth that fueled the Internet stock craze and caused the valuation of firms with no current profits (indeed, many were experiencing significant losses) at multiples of sales of 300 or more. Financial valuations based on such optimistic expectations are the reason most economists considered the stock market in Internet stocks to be significantly overvalued in the late 1990s and correctly predicted the fall in prices that occurred in 2001 and 2002.

Key Terms

annuity rule *(727)*
bond *(725)*
financial assets *(725)*
financial liabilities *(725)*
present value *(725)*
Rule of 72 *(727)*
stock *(725)*

Questions and Exercises

1. If the government prints new $1,000 bills and gives them to all introductory students who are using the Colander text, who incurs a financial liability and who gains a financial asset?
2. Is the currency in your pocketbook or wallet a real or a financial asset? Why?
3. Joe, your study partner, has just said that, in economic terminology, when he buys a bond he is investing. Is he correct? Why?
4. Joan, your study partner, has just made the following statement: "A loan is a loan and therefore cannot be an asset." Is she correct? Why or why not?
5. How much is $50 to be received 50 years from now worth if the interest rate is 6 percent? (Use Table A30-1.)
6. How much is $50 to be received 50 years from now worth if the interest rate is 9 percent? (Use Table A30-1.)
7. Your employer offers you a choice of two bonus packages: $1,400 today or $2,000 five years from now. Assuming a 6 percent rate of interest, which is the better value? Assuming an interest rate of 10 percent, which is the better value?
8. Suppose the price of a one-year bond with a $100 face value that pays 10 percent interest is $98.
   a. Are market interest rates likely to be above or below 10 percent? Explain.
   b. What is the bond's yield or return?
   c. If market interest rates fell, what would happen to the price of the bond?
9. Explain in words why the present value of $100 to be received in 10 years would decline as the interest rate rises.
10. A 6 percent bond will pay you $1,060 one year from now. The interest rate in the economy is 10 percent. How much is that bond worth now?

11. You are to receive $100 a year for the next 40 years. How much is it worth now if the current interest rate in the economy is 6 percent? (Use Table A30-1.)
12. You are to receive $200 in 30 years. About how much is it worth now? (The interest rate is 3 percent.)
13. A salesperson calls you up and offers you $200 a year for life. If the interest rate is 9 percent, how much should you be willing to pay for that annuity?
14. The same salesperson offers you a lump sum of $20,000 in 10 years. How much should you be willing to pay? (The interest rate is still 9 percent.)
15. What is the present value of a cash flow of $100 per year forever (a perpetuity), assuming:
    The interest rate is 10 percent.
    The interest rate is 5 percent.
    The interest rate is 20 percent.
    a. Working with those same three interest rates, what are the future values of $100 today in one year? How about in two years?
    b. Working with those same three interest rates, how long will it take you to double your money?
16. State whether you agree or disagree with the following statements:
    a. If stock market prices go up, the economy is richer.
    b. A real asset worth $1 million is more valuable to an individual than a financial asset worth $1 million.
    c. Financial assets have no value to society since each has a corresponding liability.
    d. The United States has much more land than does Japan. Therefore, the value of all U.S. land should significantly exceed the value of land in Japan.
    e. U.S. GDP exceeds Japan's GDP; therefore, the stock market valuation of U.S.-based companies should exceed that of Japan-based companies.

Monetary Policy

There have been three great inventions since the beginning of time: fire, the wheel and central banking.

—Will Rogers

When Ben Bernanke speaks, people listen. That's because he's chairman of the U.S. central bank—the Federal Reserve Bank (the Fed)—and it is the Fed that is in charge of maintaining the financial health of the economy. Thus, when the financial sector almost seized up in fall of 2008, the Fed stepped in and undertook policies to try to prevent it from collapsing. Those policies were part of its "lender of last resort" function in times of financial crisis. It isn't only in financial crises that the Fed is important. In normal times, it is responsible for the country's monetary policy, and in this chapter I discuss the Fed's role and monetary policy in normal conditions. (In the next chapter I discuss the Fed's role in a financial crisis.) **Monetary policy** is *a policy of influencing the economy through changes in the banking system's reserves that influence the money supply and credit availability in the economy.* Unlike fiscal policy, which is controlled by the government directly, monetary policy is controlled by the U.S. central bank, the Federal Reserve Bank (the Fed).

AFTER READING THIS CHAPTER, YOU SHOULD BE ABLE TO:

1. Explain how monetary policy works in the *AS/AD* model.
2. Summarize the structure and duties of the Fed.
3. Describe how the Fed changes the supply of money primarily through open market operations.
4. Define the Federal funds rate and discuss how the Fed uses it as an intermediate target.
5. State the Taylor rule and explain its relevance to monetary policy.
6. Define the yield curve and explain how its shape reflects the limit of the Fed's ability to control the economy.

How Monetary Policy Works in the Models

Monetary policy works through its influence on credit conditions and the interest rate in the economy. As shown in Figure 31-1(a), expansionary monetary policy shifts the *AD* curve out to the right and contractionary monetary policy shifts it in to the left. Changes in nominal income will be split between changes in real income and changes in the price level.

If the economy is significantly above potential output, once long-run equilibrium is reached, monetary policy affects only nominal income and the price level, as shown in Figure 31-1(b). Real output remains unchanged. Suppose the economy begins at potential output Y_P (point *A*), and expansionary monetary policy shifts the *AD* curve from AD_0 to AD_1. Because the economy is beyond potential, rising factor cost pressures very quickly shift the *SAS* curve up from SAS_0 to SAS_1. Once the long-run equilibrium has been reached, the price level rises from P_0 to P_1 and real output returns to potential output (point *B*). So, beyond potential output, expansionary monetary policy does not affect real output.

The general rule is: Expansionary monetary policy increases nominal income. Its effect on real income depends on how the price level responds:

$$\%\Delta\text{Real income} = \%\Delta\text{Nominal income} - \%\Delta\text{Price level}$$

FIGURE 31-1 (A AND B) The Effect of Monetary Policy in the *AS/AD* Model

Expansionary monetary policy shifts the *AD* curve to the right; contractionary monetary policy shifts the *AD* curve to the left. In (**a**) we see how monetary policy affects both real output and the price level. If the economy is at or above potential, as in (**b**), expansionary monetary policy will cause input costs to rise, which will eventually shift the *SAS* curve up enough so that real output remains unchanged. The only long-run effect of expansionary monetary policy when the economy is above potential is to increase the price level.

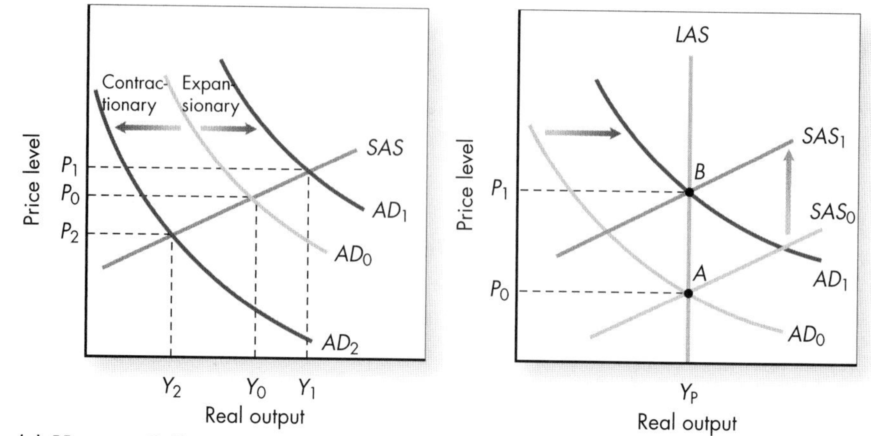

(a) Monetary Policy

(b) Expansionary Monetary Policy beyond Potential Output

Thus, if nominal income rises by 5 percent and the price level rises by 2 percent, real income will rise by 3 percent.

In this chapter I explore how monetary policy changes aggregate expenditures, shifting the aggregate demand curve out to the right or in to the left. The effect of monetary policy on aggregate demand is not direct; rather it affects aggregate demand indirectly through the short-term and long-term interest rates. To see the indirect effect, consider Figure 31-2. Figure 31-2(a) shows the supply and demand for money graph that I presented in the last chapter. Recall that the interest rate in the money market is determined by the supply of money and the demand for money. The demand for money comes from people's desire to hold money, which is affected by the short-term interest rate. The Fed undertakes monetary policy by changing the supply of money. When it conducts expansionary monetary policy, it increases the supply of money from M_0 to M_1. In response, the interest rate in the money market falls from i_0 to i_1. That increase in the supply of money leads to a parallel increase in the supply of loanable funds, shown in Figure 31-2(b), which lowers the interest rate that firms pay to borrow.

That lower interest rate for loanable funds increases the quantity of loanable funds demanded, which increases investment. Since investment is a component of aggregate demand, that increase in investment shifts out the aggregate demand curve, as we saw in Figure 31-1(a).

Expansionary monetary policy is monetary policy aimed at reducing interest rates and raising the level of aggregate demand.

Summarizing, **expansionary monetary policy** is *a policy that increases the money supply and decreases the interest rate*. It tends to *increase* both investment and output.

Contractionary monetary policy is monetary policy aimed at increasing interest rates and thereby restraining aggregate demand.

Contractionary monetary policy works in the opposite direction. **Contractionary monetary policy** is *a policy that decreases the money supply and increases the interest rate*. It tends to *decrease* both investment and output.

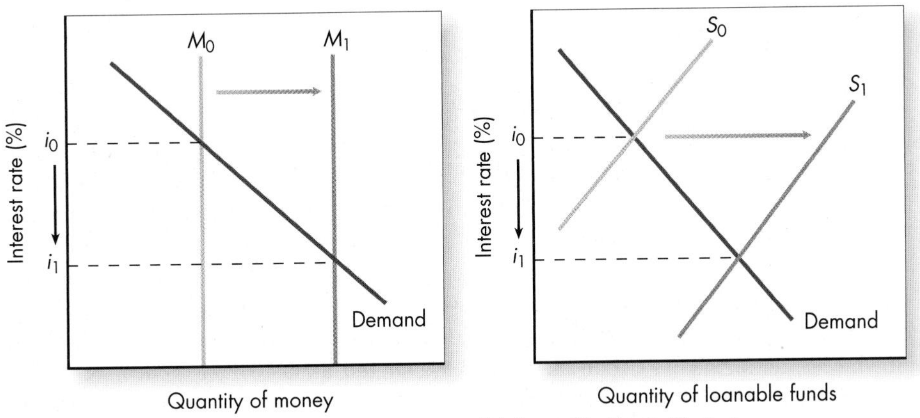

(a) Money Market **(b) Loanable Funds Market**

FIGURE 31-2 (A AND B) Monetary Policy and the Money Market

Monetary policy affects the interest rate in the money market. When conducting expansionary monetary policy, the Fed increases the money supply from M_0 to M_1 as shown in (**a**). The increase in the supply of money leads to a parallel increase in the supply of loanable funds as shown in (**b**). The decline in interest rates increases investment spending, which shifts the aggregate demand curve out to the right.

How Monetary Policy Works in Practice

Models make it all look so easy. Would that it were so easy. The reality of monetary policy is much messier and more complicated, and in this section, I discuss some of the institutional details that make monetary policy so complicated. I begin with a short summary of structure and workings of the Federal Reserve Bank of the United States—generally called, "the Fed."

Q-1 Demonstrate the effect of expansionary monetary policy in the *AS/AD* model.

Monetary Policy and the Fed

Monetary policy is conducted by a country's **central bank**—*a type of banker's bank whose financial obligations underlie an economy's money supply*. The central bank in the United States is the Fed. If commercial banks (the banks you and I use) need to borrow money, they go to the central bank. If there's a financial panic and a run on banks, the central bank is there to make loans to the banks until the panic goes away. Since its IOUs (I owe you's) are cash, the Fed can create money simply by issuing an IOU. It is this ability to create money that gives the central bank the power to control monetary policy. (A central bank also serves as a financial adviser to government. As is often the case with financial advisers, the government sometimes doesn't like the advice and doesn't follow it.)

It is the central bank's ability to create money that gives it the power to control monetary policy.

In many countries, such as Great Britain, the central bank is a part of the government, just as this country's Department of the Treasury and the Department of Commerce are part of the U.S. government. In the United States, the central bank is not part of the government in the same way. The box "Central Banks in Other Countries" on page 734 gives you an idea of some differences.

Web Note 31.1
Other Central Banks

Structure of the Fed The Fed is not just one bank; it is composed of 12 regional banks along with the main Federal Reserve Bank whose headquarters are in Washington, D.C. The Fed is governed by a seven-member Board of Governors. Members of the Board of Governors, together with the president of the New York Fed and a rotating group of four presidents of the other regional banks, are voting members of the **Federal Open Market Committee (FOMC),** *the Fed's chief body that decides monetary policy*. All 12 regional bank presidents attend, and can speak at, FOMC meetings. The financial press and business community follow their discussions closely. There are even Fed watchers whose sole occupation is to follow what the Fed is doing and to tell people what it will likely do.

Q-2 What group of the Fed decides monetary policy?

REAL-WORLD APPLICATION

Central Banks in Other Countries

In the United States, the central bank is the Fed, and much of this chapter is about its structure. But the Fed is only one of many central banks in the world. Let's briefly introduce you to some of the others.

The People's Bank of China

The People's Bank of China (PBOC) was established in 1948, shortly after the communist victory and the establishment of the People's Republic of China, by nationalizing all Chinese banks and incorporating them into a single bank. (The former Chinese central bank, named the Central Bank of China, was relocated to Taipei in 1949 and is the central bank for Taiwan.) From 1949 to 1978, the PBOC was the only bank in the People's Republic of China.

In the 1980s the commercial banking functions of the PBOC were split off into state-owned independent banks, and the PBOC began focusing on central bank functions such as monetary policy and regulation of the financial sector. In 1995, it was restructured and consciously modeled after the U.S. Fed. It opened nine regional branches and focused its operations on foreign reserve issues, monetary policy, and financial regulation.

People's Bank of China

European Central Bank

In the late 1990s a number of European Union countries formed a monetary union, creating a common currency called the euro, and a new central bank called the European Central Bank (ECB), whose structure is still evolving. As of 2009, the governing council had 22 members, including the heads of the 16 countries that had adopted the euro as their currency.

The primary objective of the ECB is different from the Fed's; the ECB is focused solely on maintaining price stability, as was the former German central bank, the Bundesbank, after which it was modeled. Some economists have considered the ECB an expansion of the Bundesbank for the entire EU.

Most economists hold a wait-and-see attitude about the bank. They point out that the ECB is a new bank and it will take time for its operating procedures to become established. We can expect significant political infighting as the various countries attempt to influence the decisions of the ECB to favor them.

The Bank of England

The Bank of England is sometimes called the Old Lady of Threadneedle Street (because it's located on that street, and the British like such quaint characterizations). It does not use a required reserve mechanism. Instead, individual banks determine their own needed reserves, so any reserves they have would, in a sense, be excess reserves. Needless to say, bank reserves are much lower in England than they are in the United States.

How does the Old Lady control the money supply? Until recently, with the equivalent of open market operations and with informal directives to banks, what might be called "tea control." Since England has only a few large banks, the Old Lady passed on the word at tea as to which direction she thought the money supply should be going and the banks complied. Alas for sentimentalists, "tea control" is fading in England, as are many quaint English ways.

The Bank of Japan

Like the People's Bank of China, the Bank of Japan is quite similar to the Fed. It uses primarily open market operations to control the money supply. Reserve requirements are similar to the Fed's, but because it allows banks a longer period in which to do their averaging, and Japan does not have the many small banks that the United States does—banks that often hold excess reserves—excess reserves are much lower in Japan than in the United States. The Japanese financial system exhibits more interdependence between the central bank, commercial banks, and industry than does the U.S. system, which means that Japanese companies get more of their funding from commercial banks, which in turn borrow more from the Bank of Japan than U.S. commercial banks borrow from the Fed. The financial position of many Japanese commercial banks was questionable over the past decade, and the Bank of Japan worked with the banks to restructure loans without causing a breakdown of the financial system.

Clearly, there's more to be said about each of these central banks, but this brief introduction should give you a sense of both the similarities and the diversities among the central banks of the world.

The president of the United States appoints each governor for a term of 14 years, although most governors choose not to complete their terms. The president also designates one of the governors to be the chairperson of the Fed (in 2009, this was Ben Bernanke) for a four-year term. A chairperson can serve multiple terms, and the Fed chairperson is sometimes referred to as the second most powerful person in Washington (the most powerful being the president of the United States).

Web Note 31.2
The Fed

The Fed's general structure reflects its political history. Figure 31-3 demonstrates that structure. Notice in Figure 31-3(a) that most of the 12 regional Fed banks are in

FIGURE 31-3 (A AND B) **The Federal Reserve System**

The Federal Reserve System is composed of 12 regional banks. It is run by the Board of Governors. The Federal Open Market Committee (FOMC) is the most important policy-making body.

Source: The Federal Reserve System (www.federalreserve.gov).

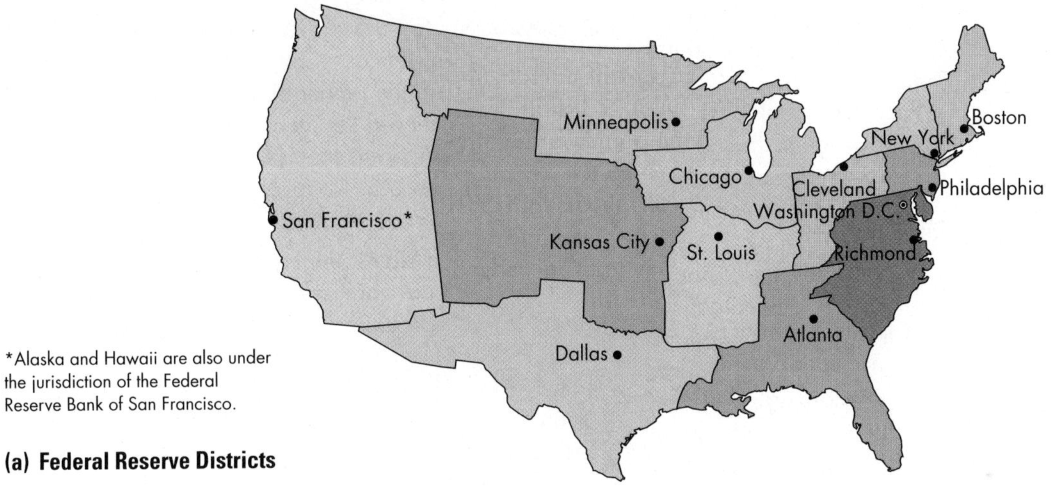

(a) Federal Reserve Districts

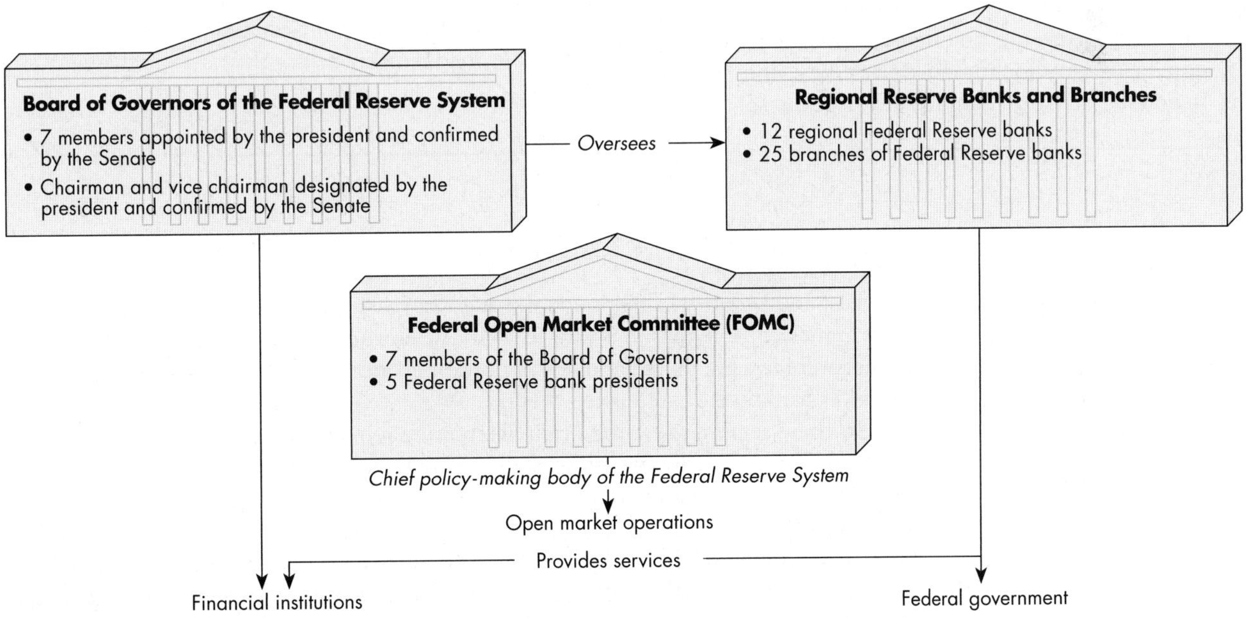

(b) Federal Reserve Structure

ADDED DIMENSION

How Independent Should the Central Bank Be?

The Fed is relatively independent, but not all central banks are. One of the big debates in the early 2000s concerned how independent the central bank should be. Advocates of central bank independence argued that independence allows central banks to make the hard political decisions that a government influenced by political pressures cannot make. Increasing interest rates hurts—it slows down the economy and causes unemployment. But if the economy is above its sustainable level, it needs to be slowed down, or inflation will accelerate. As former Fed chairman William Martin said, "The job of the Federal Reserve is to take away the punch bowl just when the party is getting good." Independence, such as exists with the U.S. central bank, gives the Fed the ability to do that.

In some developing countries, the central bank is part of the government—and economists have found that when that is the case, the punch bowl tends to remain out longer. The result is that the money supply is more expansionary, and there tend to be higher levels of inflation.

There are many dimensions of independence—one is *goal independence* and another is *policy instrument independence*. Goal independence is having the freedom to determine what ultimate goals, such as low unemployment or low inflation, take priority. Policy instrument independence is having the freedom to determine how to achieve those goals. Many economists point out that goal independence is not necessarily a good thing. In a democracy goals are determined in the political process, and in a well-functioning democracy, the central bank is accountable for achieving the goals set by the political process, and does not set the goals itself. Once the goals are set, then one can talk about policy instrument independence.

Alan Blinder, former vice chairman of the Fed, put it this way:

> The independence of the Fed means, to me, two things. First, that we have very broad latitude to pursue our goals as we see fit; we decide what to do in pursuit of those goals.
>
> Second, it means that once our monetary policy decisions are made, they cannot be reversed by anybody in the U.S. government—except under extreme circumstances. (Congress would have to pass a law limiting the power of the Fed.) But although we are free to choose the means by which we achieve our goals, the goals themselves are given to us by statute, by the U.S. Congress. And that is how it should be in a democracy.

In the United States, the Fed has policy instrument independence, but not goal independence. By federal law, the goals of the Federal Reserve Bank are "maximum employment," "stable prices," and "moderate long-term interest rates." Those are different goals than the goals of the European Central Bank (ECB); the ECB's goal is only "stable prices." These different goals, however, become almost identical if one believes, as a number of economists do, that the only way to achieve maximum employment and moderate long-term interest rates is by achieving stable prices.

the East and Midwest. The South and West have only three banks: Atlanta, Dallas, and San Francisco. The reason is that in 1913, when the Fed was established, the West and South were less populated and less important economically than the rest of the country, so fewer banks were established there.

As these regions grew, the original structure remained because no one wanted to go through the political wrangling that restructuring would bring about. Instead, the southern and western regional Feds established a number of branches to handle their banking needs.

Even though each of the 12 geographic districts has a separate regional Federal Reserve bank, these regional banks have little direct power over the banking system. District banks and their branch banks handle administrative matters and gather information about business and banking conditions in their geographic regions for the Fed.

Duties of the Fed In legislation establishing the Fed, Congress gave it six explicit functions:

1. Conducting monetary policy (influencing the supply of money and credit in the economy).
2. Supervising and regulating financial institutions.
3. Serving as a lender of last resort to financial institutions.
4. Providing banking services to the U.S. government.
5. Issuing coin and currency.
6. Providing financial services (such as check clearing) to commercial banks, savings and loan associations, savings banks, and credit unions.

In normal times, the most important of these functions is monetary policy. In times of financial crisis, the "lender of last resort" function is the most important. In this chapter I focus on monetary policy in normal times. In the next chapter when I discuss the Fed's reaction to the financial crisis of 2008 and 2009, I will focus more on the "lender of last resort" function.

The Conduct of Monetary Policy

WWW Web Note 31.3
The FOMC

You've already seen that monetary policy shifts the *AD* curve. Let's now consider how it does so in practice. To do so, we need to look more specifically at the institutional structure of the banking system and the role of the Fed in that institutional structure.

Think back to our discussion of the banking system in the last chapter. Banks take in deposits, make loans, and buy other financial assets, keeping a certain percentage of reserves for those transactions. Those reserves are IOUs of the Fed—either vault cash held by banks or deposits at the Fed. *Vault cash, deposits at the Fed, plus currency in circulation* make up the **monetary base.** The monetary base held at banks serves as legal reserves of the banking system. By controlling the monetary base, the Fed can influence the amount of money in the economy and the activities of banks. The money supply is determined directly by the monetary base (the amount of IOUs that the Fed has outstanding), and, indirectly, by the amount of credit that banks extend.

Allowable reserves are either banks' vault cash or deposits at the Fed.

Open Market Operations The primary way that the Fed changes the amount of reserves in the system is through **open market operations**—*the Fed's buying and selling of government securities* (the only type of asset that, until recently, the Fed held in any appreciable quantity). These open market operations are the primary tool of monetary policy in normal times.

The Fed's buying and selling of government securities is called open market operations.

When the Fed buys Treasury bills, Treasury bonds or any other assets, it pays for them with IOUs that serve as reserves for banks. These IOUs don't have to be a written piece of paper. They may simply be a computer entry credited to a bank's account at the Fed.

Because the IOUs that the Fed uses to buy a government security serve as reserves to the banking system, with the simple act of buying a Treasury bond and paying for it with its IOU, the Fed can increase the money supply (since this creates reserves for the bank). To increase the money supply, the Fed goes to the bond market, buys a bond, and pays for it with its IOU. The individual or firm that sold the bond now has an IOU of the Fed. When the individual or firm deposits the IOU in a bank—presto!—the reserves of the banking system are increased. If the Fed buys bonds, it increases the monetary base. The total money supply rises by the increase in the monetary base times the money multiplier.

REAL-WORLD APPLICATION

Inside an FOMC Meeting

Let's go inside one of the eight regular Federal Open Market Committee (FOMC) meetings to gain some insight into how the Fed actually conducts monetary policy. The meeting consists of FOMC members and top Fed staff sitting around a large table debating what should be done. There's been enormous preparation for the meeting. The economists on the Federal Reserve staff have tracked the economy, and have made economic forecasts. Based on their studies, they've briefed the FOMC members, and the high-level staff get to sit in on the meeting. (Getting to sit in on the meeting is seen as a real perk of the job.)

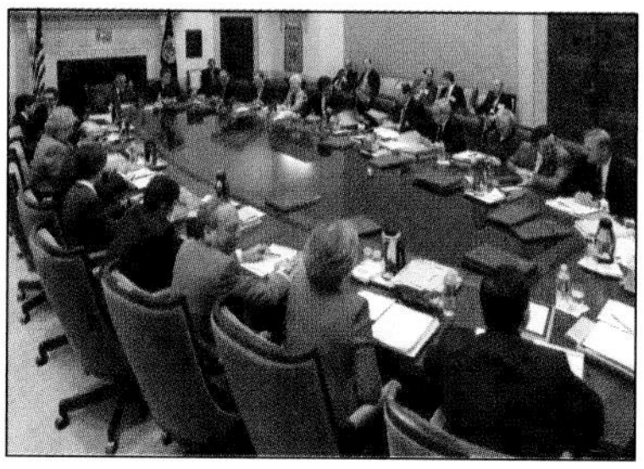

The information they've put together is gathered in three books, which are distinguished by colors. The Beige Book is prepared by each of the 12 regional Federal Reserve banks and summarizes regional business conditions based on local surveys and conversations with local business people. The Green Book is prepared by the staff of the Federal Reserve in Washington, D.C.; it presents a two-year forecast of the U.S. economy as a whole. The Blue Book, also prepared by the Fed staff in Washington, analyzes three possible monetary policy options. This Blue Book is the central policy document, and one of the three options it presents will be selected by the FOMC.

The meeting begins with a summary of monetary policy actions since the committee last met, followed by a forecast of the economy. The Fed governors and regional bank presidents also present their forecasts. Once current economic conditions and forecasts are discussed, the director of monetary affairs presents the three monetary policy proposals in the Blue Book. Then there is open discussion of the various policy proposals. The committee meeting ends with a vote on what policy to follow, along with a policy directive on what open market operations to execute. At that point, the FOMC also makes a public announcement regarding current policy actions as well as what future actions they may take. For example, on March 21, 2007, the FOMC issued the following statement:

> The Federal Open Market Committee decided today to keep its target for the federal funds rate at 5¼ percent. Recent indicators have been mixed and the adjustment in the housing sector is ongoing. Nevertheless, the economy seems likely to continue to expand at a moderate pace over coming quarters. Recent readings on core inflation have been somewhat elevated. Although inflation pressures seem likely to moderate over time, the high level of resource utilization has the potential to sustain those pressures. In these circumstances, the Committee's predominant policy concern remains the risk that inflation will fail to moderate as expected. Future policy adjustments will depend on the evolution of the outlook for both inflation and economic growth, as implied by incoming information.

The announcement was made at about 2:15 PM and within the next hour, the interest rate in the economy fell and the stock market shot up, with the Dow Jones Industrial Average rising 1.3 percent as you can see in the graph below.

MINUTE-BY-MINUTE

Dow Jones Industrial Average

Yesterday's close: **12447.52, up 1.3%**

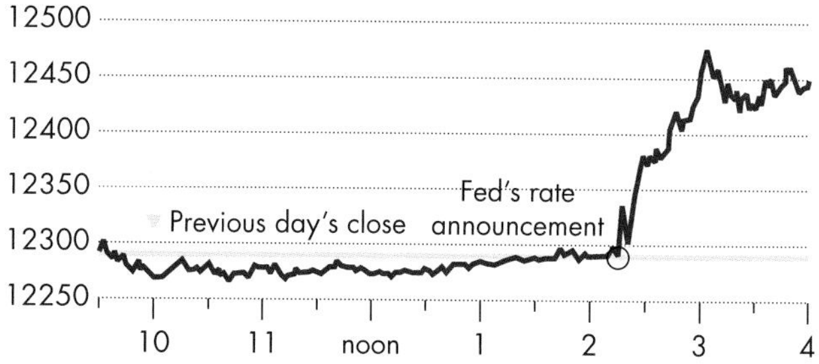

Source: WSJ Market Data Group

Why did this happen? The statement did not announce a change of interest rates. It said only that future policy adjustments are uncertain. What caused the change was what was *not* said in the statement. Previous statements had said that the Fed was leaning toward raising interest rates. This one did not, which led many in the stock market to believe that the Fed might lower interest rates in the future. Since traders saw that as good for the stock market, they bought stocks, pushing their prices up.

When the Fed sells Treasury bonds, it collects back some of its IOUs, reducing banking system reserves and decreasing the money supply. Thus,

To expand the money supply, the Fed buys bonds.

To contract the money supply, the Fed sells bonds.

Q-3 When the Fed buys bonds, is it expanding or contracting the money supply?

Understanding open market operations is essential to understanding monetary policy as it is actually practiced in the United States. So let's go through some examples.

Open market operations involve the purchase or sale of federal government securities (bonds). When the Fed buys bonds, it deposits the funds in federal government accounts at a bank. Bank cash reserves rise. Banks don't like to hold excess reserves, so they lend out the excess, thereby expanding the deposit base of the economy. The money supply rises. Thus, an open market purchase is an example of *expansionary monetary policy* (monetary policy that tends to reduce interest rates and raise income) since it raises the money supply (as long as the banks strive to minimize their excess reserves).

Tools of Monetary Policy

An open market sale has the opposite effect. Here, the Fed sells bonds. In return for the bond, the Fed receives a check drawn against a bank. The bank's reserve assets are reduced (since the Fed "cashes" the check and takes the money away from the bank), and the money supply falls. That's an example of *contractionary monetary policy* (monetary policy that tends to raise interest rates and lower income).

The Reserve Requirement and the Money Supply As I discussed in the previous chapter, the total amount of money created from a given amount of currency depends on the percentage of deposits that a bank keeps in reserves (the bank's reserve ratio). By law, the Fed controls the minimum percentage of deposits banks keep in reserves by controlling the reserve requirement of all U.S. banks. That minimum is called the **reserve requirement**—*the percentage the Federal Reserve Bank sets as the minimum amount of reserves a bank must have*.

For checking accounts (also called *demand deposits*), the amount banks keep in reserves depends partly on the Federal Reserve requirements and partly on how much banks feel they need for safety (the cash they need to keep on hand at any time to give to depositors who claim some of their deposits in the form of cash). The amount most banks need for safety is much smaller than what the Fed requires. For them, it's the Fed's reserve requirement that determines the amount they hold as reserves.

Banks hold as little in reserves as possible.

Banks typically hold as little in reserves as possible. Why? Because reserves earn little interest for a bank (although that may change in the future). And we all know that banks are in business to earn profits. How much is as little as possible? That depends on the type of liabilities the bank has. In the early 2000s, required reserves for large banks for their checking accounts were about 10 percent. The reserve requirement for all other accounts was zero, making the reserve requirement for total liabilities somewhat under 2 percent.

In 2008, total reserves were about $45 billion and required reserves were about $43 billion. This means excess reserves (reserves in excess of requirements) were about $2 billion. In 2009, banks significantly increased their excess reserves.

The total money supply, which includes checking account deposits in banks, depends upon the reserve requirement. Thus, by changing the reserve requirements, the Fed can increase or decrease the money supply. If the Fed increases the reserve requirement, it contracts the money supply; banks have to keep more reserves so they have less money to lend out; the decreased money multiplier contracts the money supply. If the Fed decreases the reserve requirement, it expands the money supply; banks have more money to lend out; the increased money multiplier further expands the money supply.

The money multiplier is $(1 + c)/(r + c)$.

The total effect on the money supply of changing the reserve requirement can be determined by thinking back to the money multiplier, which, as you saw in the previous chapter, equals $(1 + c)/(r + c)$ where r is the percentage of each dollar that banks hold

ADDED DIMENSION

Using the Money Multiplier in Practice

The money multiplier has been a staple of the macro principles course since its inception, and it remains an important concept in understanding how the monetary base is related to the aggregate supply of money in the economy. But recent changes in the financial system have made the operational use of the multiplier less important. For the most part, central banks don't determine how much to change the monetary base to get a desired change in the money supply using an assumed fixed multiplier. Instead, they adjust the monetary base to target either a desired amount of bank credit in the economy or a short-term interest rate.

The money multiplier relationship continues to be true by definition, but it is not the operational concept that it once was. The reasons include the decrease in the reserve requirement (in many countries, required reserves are zero); financial innovations that have increased the ways in which individuals can hold money; the increase in the amount of cash that individuals hold; and the decline in the stability of the relationship between the money supply and output. Each of these makes it harder to use the money multiplier as an operational variable, which is why much of the monetary policy discussion today focuses more on the interest rate than on the money supply.

in reserves and c is the ratio of people's cash to deposits. When banks hold no excess reserves and face a reserve requirement of 15 percent, and people's cash-to-deposit ratio is 35 percent, the approximate money multiplier will be 1.35/0.5 = 2.7, so $1 million in reserves will support a total $2.7 million money supply. Let's say that the cash-to-deposit ratio is about 0.4 ($c = 0.4$), the average reserve requirement for demand deposits is about 0.1 ($r = 0.1$), and banks hold little in the way of excess reserves. That would make the money multiplier for demand deposits and currency (M_1):

Q-4 If the cash-to-deposit ratio is 0.2 and the reserve requirement is 0.1, what happens to the money supply when the Fed sells $100 of bonds?

$$\frac{1 + 0.4}{(0.1 + 0.4)} = \frac{1.4}{0.5} = 2.8$$

A $100 increase in the monetary base will support a $280 increase in the money supply. For other deposits the reserve requirement is zero, so the money multiplier is larger for those.

What does a bank do if it comes up short of reserves? It can borrow from another bank that has excess reserves in what's called the Federal funds market. (The rate of interest at which these reserves can be borrowed is called the *Fed funds rate*. As I will discuss below, this Fed funds rate is a significant indicator of monetary policy.)

Another option that the bank has if it is short of reserves is to stop making new loans and to keep as reserves the proceeds of loans that are paid off. Still another option is to sell Treasury bonds to get the needed reserves. (Banks often hold some of their assets in Treasury bonds so that they can get additional reserves relatively easily if they need them.) Treasury bonds are sometimes called *secondary reserves*. They do not count as bank reserves—only IOUs of the Fed count as reserves. But Treasury bonds can be easily sold and transferred into cash, which does count as reserves. Banks use all these options.

It is important to note that while these options are open to the individual banks, they are not open to the entire system of banks. The total amount of reserves is controlled by the Fed, and if the entire banking system is short of reserves, the banking system will have to figure out a way of either reducing the need for reserves or borrowing reserves from the Fed.

Borrowing from the Fed and the Discount Rate As I stated at the beginning of the chapter, a central bank is a banker's bank, and if the entire banking system is short of reserves, banks can go to the Federal Reserve and take out a loan. The **discount rate** is *the rate of interest the Fed charges for loans it makes to banks*. An increase in the discount rate makes it more expensive for banks to borrow from the Fed. A discount rate decrease makes it less expensive for banks to borrow.

Up until 2002, the Fed set the discount rate slightly lower than the cost of reserves for banks from other sources, relying on moral suasion to stop banks from borrowing unless they really needed to. Beginning in 2003, the Fed changed this policy and now it sets the discount rate slightly higher than the banks' other costs of funds. An increase in the discount rate discourages banks from borrowing and contracts the money supply; a decrease in the discount rate encourages the banks to borrow and increases the money supply.

The Fed Funds Market

To get an even better sense of the way monetary policy works, let's look at it from the perspective of a bank. The bank will review its books, determine how much in reserves it needs to meet its reserve requirement, and see if it has excess reserves or a shortage of reserves.

Say your bank didn't make as many loans as it expected to, so it has a surplus of reserves (excess reserves). Say also that another bank has made a few loans it didn't expect to make, so it has a shortage of reserves. The bank with surplus reserves can lend money to the bank with a shortage, and it can lend it overnight as **Fed funds**—*loans of excess reserves banks make to one another.* At the end of a day, a bank will look at its balances and see whether it has a shortage or surplus of reserves. If it has a surplus, it will call a Federal funds dealer to learn the **Federal funds rate**—*the interest rate banks charge one another for Fed funds.* Say the rate is 6 percent. The bank will then agree to lend its excess reserves overnight to the other bank for the daily equivalent of 6 percent per year. It's all simply done electronically, so there's no need actually to transfer funds. In the morning the money (plus overnight interest) is returned. The one-day interest rate is low, but when you're dealing with millions or billions, it adds up.

The Federal funds rate is the interest rate banks charge one another for overnight reserve loans.

The **Federal funds market,** *the market in which banks lend and borrow reserves,* is highly efficient. The Fed can reduce reserves, and thereby increase the Fed funds rate, by selling bonds. Alternatively, when the Fed buys bonds, it increases reserves, causing the Fed funds rate to fall. Generally, large city banks are borrowers of Fed funds; small country banks are lenders of Fed funds.

Figure 31-4 shows the Fed funds rate and the discount rate since 1990. Notice also that the Fed funds rate tended to be slightly above the discount rate until 2003, when

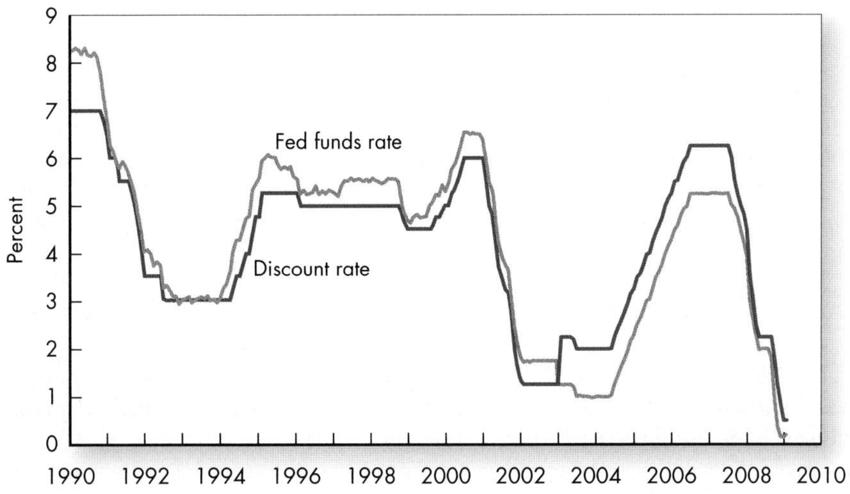

FIGURE 31-4

The Fed Funds Rate and the Discount Rate

The Federal Reserve Bank follows expansionary or contractionary monetary policy by targeting a lower or higher Fed funds rate. The discount rate generally follows the Fed funds rate closely. Before 2003, it was kept lower than the Fed funds rate. Since 2003, the discount rate has been set slightly above the Fed funds rate target.

REAL-WORLD APPLICATION

Will the Reserve Requirement Be Eliminated?

In 2006, President Bush signed the Financial Services Regulatory Relief Act of 2006 to improve the efficiency of the banking system. The Act allows the Fed to reduce the reserve ratio to zero and to pay interest on reserves that banks maintain at the Fed. In November of 2008, the Fed started paying interest on reserves, but because the change occurred while the Fed was dealing with the financial panic of 2008, and was accompanied by numerous other changes in Fed polices (changes that I will discuss below) as it played its "lender of last resort" role, it will likely be years before economists can assess the implication of paying interest on reserves in normal times.

If the Fed also reduces the reserve requirements to zero, it will be following the practices of central banks of other industrialized nations such as Canada, the United Kingdom, New Zealand, and Japan. The reason for the change is that financial institutions have changed. More and more financial transactions take place outside the banking system, and distinguishing banks from other financial institutions has become harder and harder.

In practice, the change will make all reserves excess reserves, and make the interest rate paid on reserve balances a key element in the determination of reserves and hence of the money supply. Thus, the Fed will be able to affect reserves through the discount rate, open market operations, and the interest rate paid on reserves.

The transition to the new system will likely involve some changes in the amount of reserves held by banks, but it is unlikely to have a significant effect on the actual conduct of monetary policy. In practice, central banks conduct monetary policy largely by targeting short-term interest rates through open market operations. If the system changes, the Fed will establish a relationship between the discount rate (the rate the Fed charges banks for lending reserves), the interest rate on reserves, and the targeted Fed funds rate. Which of these will become the lead indicator of Fed policy will depend on the relative differentials that the Fed chooses for these interest rates.

the Fed changed its operating procedures and began setting the discount rate slightly above the Fed funds rate. As you can see, in 2001 and 2002 the Fed funds rate fell from 6 to 1.25 percent as the Fed followed an expansionary monetary policy. In mid-2004 the Fed began to raise the Fed funds rate. Then, in 2008, the financial crisis led the Fed to lower the Fed funds rate to almost zero.

Offensive and Defensive Actions Economists keep a close eye on the Federal funds rate in determining the state of monetary policy. It has become an important intermediate target of the Fed in determining what monetary policy to conduct. Remember, the Fed sets minimum reserve requirements, but the actual amount of reserves available to banks is influenced by the amount of cash people hold and excess reserves that banks may choose to hold. That changes daily. For example, say there's a storm, and businesses don't make it to the bank with their cash. Bank reserves will fall even though the Fed didn't do anything. The Fed can, and does, offset such changes—by buying and selling bonds. Such actions are called *defensive actions*. They are designed to maintain the current monetary policy. These defensive actions are to be contrasted with *offensive actions*, which are actions meant to make monetary policy have expansionary or contractionary effects on the economy.

Q-5 There's been a big storm and cash held by individuals has increased. Should the Fed buy or sell bonds? Why?

The Fed Funds Rate as an Operating Target How does the Fed decide whether its buying and selling of bonds is having the desired effect? It has to look at other targets—and in recent years the Federal funds rate has been the operating target of the Fed. Thus, the Fed determines whether monetary policy is tight or loose depending on what is happening to the Federal funds rate. In practice, it targets a range for that rate, and buys and sells bonds to keep the Federal funds rate within that range. If the Federal funds rate rises above the Fed's target range, it buys bonds, which increases

Monetary policy affects interest rates such as the Federal funds rate. The Fed looks at the Federal funds rate to determine whether monetary policy is tight or loose.

reserves and lowers the Federal funds rate. If the Federal funds rate falls below the Fed's target range, it sells bonds, which decreases reserves and raises the Federal funds rate.

The Complex Nature of Monetary Policy

While the Fed focuses on the Fed funds rate as its operating target, it also has its eye on its ultimate targets: stable prices, acceptable employment, sustainable growth, and moderate long-term interest rates. But those ultimate targets are only indirectly affected by changes in the Fed funds rate, so the Fed watches what are called *intermediate targets:* consumer confidence, stock prices, interest rate spreads, housing starts, and a host of others. Intermediate targets are not always good guides for the Fed's ultimate targets. The Federal Reserve Bank of San Francisco once had an exhibit of an electronic video game in its lobby.[1] The object of the game was to hit a moving target with a dart from a moving arm. With both the arm and the target moving, most visitors missed the target.

The game was there to demonstrate the difficulties of implementing monetary policy. Monetary policy "shoots from a moving arm." Ultimately, policy actions of the Fed influence output and inflation, but the influence is not direct, and many other factors also influence output and inflation.

Web Note 31.4
A Moving Arm

In reality, the Fed's problem is even more complicated than the video game suggests. A more telling game would be one modeled after a Rube Goldberg cartoon. If you hit the first moving target, it releases a second dart when hit. That second dart is supposed to hit a second moving target, which in turn releases a third dart aimed at yet another moving target. Given the complicated path that monetary policy follows, it should not be surprising that the Fed often misses its ultimate targets. Small wonder that the Fed often doesn't have the precise effect it wants.

The following diagram summarizes the tools and targets of the Fed:

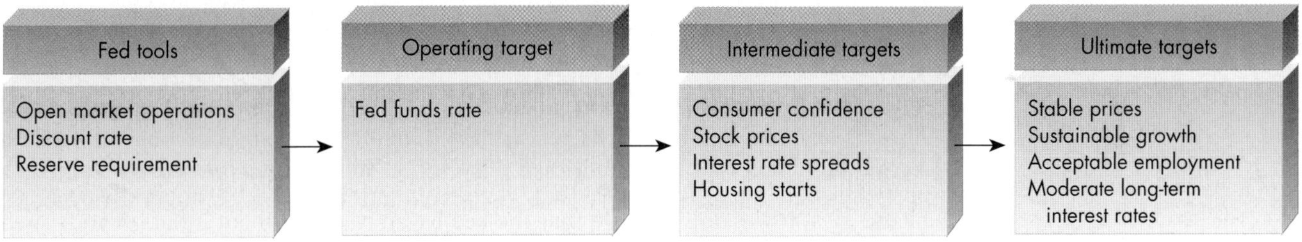

The Taylor Rule

U.S. Treasury economist John Taylor has summarized a rule that, in the late 1990s and early 2000s, described Fed policy relatively well. The rule, which has become known as the **Taylor rule,** can be stated as follows: *Set the Fed funds rate at 2 percent plus current inflation if the economy is at desired output and desired inflation. If the inflation rate is higher than desired, increase the Fed funds rate by 0.5 times the difference between desired and actual inflation. Similarly, if output is higher than desired, increase the Fed funds rate by 0.5 times the percentage deviation.*

Formally the Taylor rule is:

Fed funds rate = 2 percent + Current inflation
+ 0.5 × (actual inflation less desired inflation)
+ 0.5 × (percent deviation of aggregate output from potential)

Q-6 If inflation is 1 percent, the Fed wants 2 percent inflation, and output is 2 percent below potential, what would the Taylor rule predict for a Fed funds rate target?

[1]Because of security concerns, central bank lobbies are now generally off limits to the public and this exhibit is no longer accessible.

Let's consider some examples. Say that inflation is 2.5 percent, the Fed's target rate of inflation is 2 percent, and the aggregate output exceeds potential output by 1 percent. That means that the Fed would set the Fed funds rate at 5.25 percent (2 + 2.5 + 0.5(2.5 − 2) + 0.5(1)). The first row in the table below shows the calculations. The second row shows another example with different numbers.

Federal Funds Rate	=	2 Percent	+	Current Inflation	+	0.5(Actual less targeted inflation)	+	0.5(Deviation from potential output)
5.25	=	2	+	2.5	+	0.5(2.5 − 2)	+	0.5(1)
4.5	=	2	+	2	+	0.5(2 − 2)	+	0.5(1)

FIGURE 31-5 Federal Fund Rate and the Taylor Rule

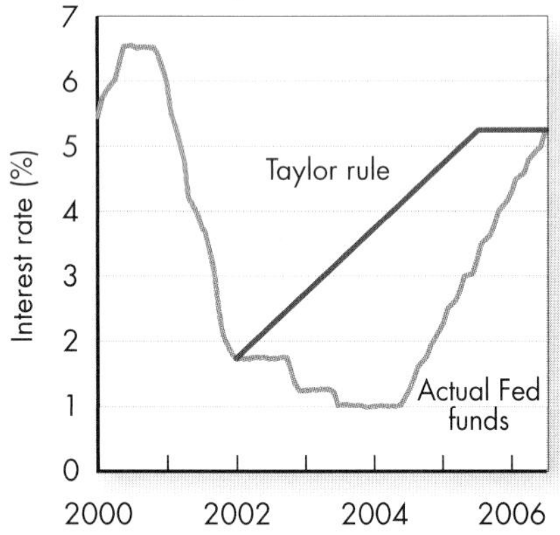

Web Note 31.5
Taylor Rule

The Fed does not always slavishly follow the Taylor rule. For example, in late 2000 and early 2001, the economy was 1 percent over potential output by most estimates and inflation was 2 percent, which was equal to the target rate. The Taylor rule predicted that the Fed would set the Fed funds rate at 4.5 percent. (See the calculations in row 2 of the table.) Instead, it targeted a 6 percent rate because it was especially concerned about the economy overheating. Then right after September 11, the Fed became concerned about the economy going into a severe recession and it lowered the Fed funds rate significantly—close to zero—even though little else had changed. It maintained that low interest rate from 2002 to 2006 compared to what the Taylor rule would suggest, as can be seen in Figure 31-5. They chose to do this because inflation did not seem to be a problem—the fear was deflation, not inflation—and because they wanted to avoid a recession that many economists were predicting.

The problem was that, while there was not inflation in goods, asset prices were rising quickly, which many saw as financial bubbles. One of the most important bubbles was in the housing market. Critics of Fed policy argued that these financial bubbles were being fueled by the low interest rates and the availability of credit encouraged by a historically low Fed funds rate. As you can see in Figure 31-5, it was only in 2006 that the Fed began to worry about inflation and raised the interest rate up to where the Taylor rule suggested it should be, and it was in 2006 that the housing bubble started to burst. Thus, many economists argue that Fed policy was an important contributor to the housing bubble.

The higher interest rates of 2006 and 2007 did not last, and, as the economy seemed to be falling into a recession and financial crisis, the Fed again deviated from the Taylor rule. Consider early 2008, when inflation was about 3.5 percent, which was about 2 percent above the Fed's target, and the economy was close to its potential income. According to the Taylor rule, the Feds fund rate should have been 7.5 percent. The actual Fed funds rate was 5.5 percent. By the end of 2008, the Fed's Fed funds target rate was down to 0.2 percent and the Fed was doing whatever it could to increase the money supply in other than standard ways. We will discuss this episode in the next chapter. Here I want to note that this is a good example of how the Fed uses models. It has a model for normal times, and it has another model for crises. The art of monetary policy is deciding which type of situation the economy is in.

Controlling the Interest Rate Notice how the Taylor rule focuses the discussion of monetary policy on the interest rate (specifically, the Fed funds rate), not the money supply. On the surface, this may seem inconsistent with the discussions of monetary policy that focused on the money supply, but it is not. It is simply a difference in focus.

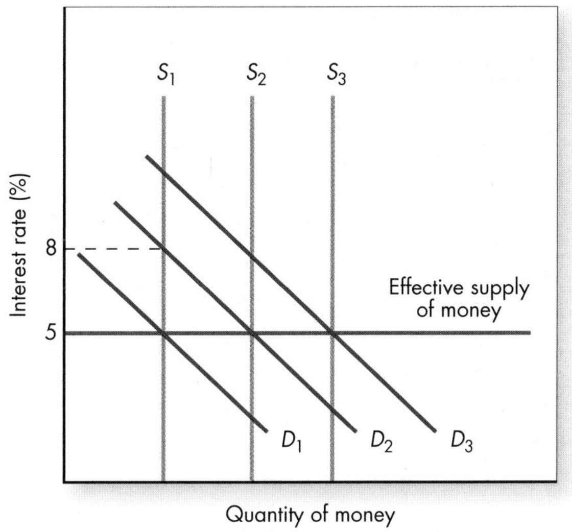

FIGURE 31-6 The Effective Supply Curve for Money

When the Fed chooses a monetary rule that targets the interest rate, it creates an effective supply curve of money that is flat at the target rate. To create a flat effective supply of money, the Fed adjusts the supply of money to changes in the demand for money at the targeted rate.

The Fed does control the amount of money in the economy, but it uses that control to target an interest rate, not to control the money supply. Specifically, as the demand for money shifts, the Fed adjusts the money supply (through open market operations) so that the market equilibrates at the targeted interest rate. Essentially, the Fed is choosing a monetary rule that creates an *effective supply curve of money* that is perfectly flat at the target interest rate. How it does so is shown in Figure 31-6.

Say that we start with an interest rate of 5 percent, a money supply of S_1, and a money demand of D_1. Then, the demand for money rises to D_2. If the Fed held the money supply constant, the interest rate would rise to 8 percent. However, if in response to the increase in demand the Fed automatically raises the money supply to S_2, the interest rate remains at 5 percent. Similarly, if money demand rises to D_3, the Fed increases the money supply to S_3. As long as the Fed is willing to change the money supply to whatever level is necessary to achieve the targeted interest rate, it can determine the interest rate in the money market.

The Fed targets the interest rate by adjusting the money supply so that its targeted interest rate will equalize the supply and demand for money.

Q-7 How does the Fed create a flat effective money supply curve?

Limits to the Fed's Control of the Interest Rate The above discussion makes it sound as if the Fed can control the interest rate, and it can, if by interest rate we mean the short-term interest rate. But, as we discussed in the last chapter, the economy has more than one interest rate. The long-term interest rate in the economy is determined in the *loanable funds market*, not the money market. As long as the short-term interest rate and the long-term interest rate move in tandem, then the Fed can also control the long-term interest rate. Unfortunately, they do not always move in tandem, and that has made the study of the relationship between the short-term and long-term rates an important part of discussions of monetary policy. Economists carefully follow this relationship in a graph called the **yield curve**—*a curve that shows the relationship between interest rates and bonds' time to maturity*. I show two alternative yield curves in Figure 31-7. As you can see, as you move out along the yield curve, bonds' time to maturity increases. Figure 31-7(a) demonstrates what is called a standard yield curve. It is a yield curve in which the short-term rates are lower than the long-term rate. Thus, if you invest in a one-year bond, you would earn 4 percent interest, and if you invest in a 30-year bond, you would earn 6 percent interest. This is considered a standard yield curve because long-term bonds are riskier than short-term bonds, so it is reasonable that they generally have a slightly higher interest rate.

The yield curve is a curve that shows the relationship between interest rates and bonds' time to maturity.

FIGURE 31-7 (A AND B) The Yield Curve

The standard yield curve shown in (**a**) is upward-sloping: as the time to maturity increases, so does the interest rate. An inverted yield curve shown in (**b**) is downward-sloping: as the time to maturity increases, the interest rate decreases.

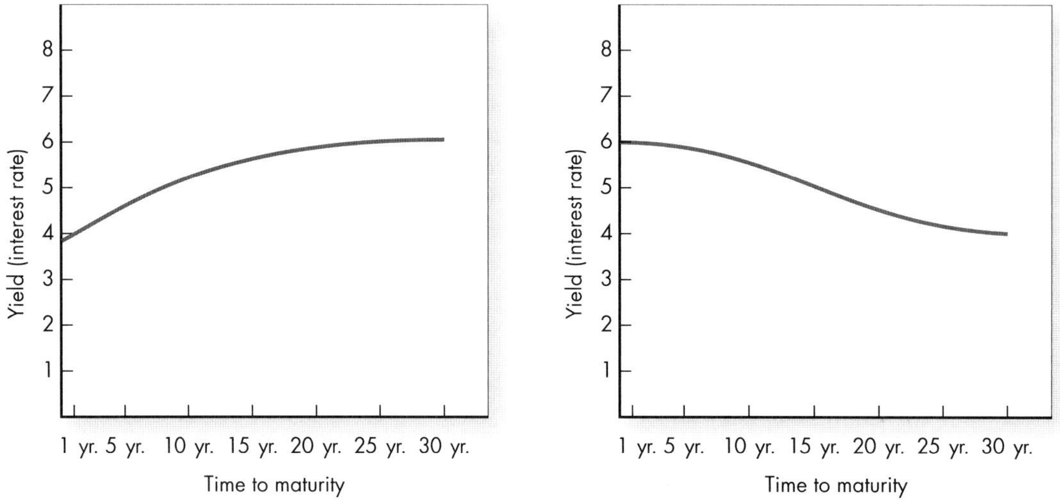

(a) Yield Curve **(b) Inverted Yield Curve**

That relationship between short-term and long-term interest rates does not always hold. Figure 31-7(b) shows what is called an **inverted yield curve**—*a yield curve in which the short-term rate is higher than the long-term rate.* In the graph, you can see that a one-year bond pays 6 percent interest and a 30-year bond pays a lower, 4 percent, interest rate.

Why is the shape of the yield curve important? Because the standard discussion of monetary policy is based on the assumption that when the Fed pushes up the short-term rate, the long-term rate moves up as well. If the long-term rate doesn't move with the short-term rate, then investment won't respond, and monetary policy won't have any significant effect. Think of the issue as one of pushing a pea along a plate with a noodle. If the noodle is dry, you can do it easily, but if the noodle is wet, when you move one end, the other end doesn't move, and it is much more difficult.

As financial markets have become more liquid, and as technological changes in financial markets have provided firms with many alternative sources of credit, the Fed has found that its ability to control the long-term rate has lessened, and that monetary policy is becoming more and more like controlling the economy with a wet noodle rather than a dry noodle. When it uses contractionary monetary policy, as opposed to shifting the entire yield curve up the policy simply causes an inverted yield curve. That's why policy makers pay close attention to the yield curve.

The monetary influence is not gone; economists have found that if the Fed is willing to push the short-term rate high enough, it is able to pull the long-term rate with it, but the Fed's control of the long-term rate is more like the control parents have over their kids—they can influence (and hope) but cannot control.

Quantitative Easing

Another limitation on the Fed's conduct of monetary policy is a technical one. The Fed cannot lower the nominal interest rate below zero, which places a limit on how much expansionary pressure the Fed can create using normal monetary policy. As we will see in the next chapter, however, when faced with a financial crisis, the Fed has other tools to stimulate the economy. These other tools are called *quantitative easing tools*. **Quantitative easing tools** are *tools that increase the money supply but that do not affect the Fed funds rate*. One example of quantitative easing is for the Fed to buy bonds even when the Fed funds rate is zero. Even though it doesn't lower the Fed funds rate, it does increase reserves in the system and may make banks more comfortable to increase lending. Another example of quantitative easing is for the Fed to buy assets other than bonds, such as money market funds, corporate bonds, or mortgage-backed securities, paying for them with its reserves. Buying these assets can lower their interest rates directly and thus affect the economy even when the Fed funds rate is zero. (You can see quantitative easing as monetary policy designed to lower the far end of the entire yield curve, and not just the short-term end of the yield curve.) As I will discuss in the next chapter, in the 2008 financial crisis the Fed used a large number of quantitative easing tools in its attempt to prevent a financial meltdown.

Maintaining Policy Credibility

Policy makers are very concerned about establishing policy credibility. The reason why is that they believe that it is necessary to prevent inflationary expectations from becoming built into the system. They fear that if inflationary expectations become built into the system, the long-term interest rate, which is the rate that primarily influences investment, will be pushed up, making the yield curve steeper and requiring even stronger contractionary monetary policy to eliminate the inflation. To see why the long-term rate will rise if inflationary expectations become built into the system, it is important to remember that the long-term interest rate has two components: a real interest rate component and an inflationary expectations component, which means that you must distinguish the real interest rate from the nominal interest rate.

You learned about this real/nominal interest rate distinction in an earlier chapter. Recall, **nominal interest rates** are *the rates you actually see and pay*. When a bank pays 7 percent interest, that 7 percent is a nominal interest rate. What affects the economy is the real interest rate. **Real interest rates** are *nominal interest rates adjusted for expected inflation*.

For example, say you get 7 percent interest from the bank, but the price level goes up 7 percent. At the end of the year you have $107 instead of $100, but you're no better off than before because the price level has risen—on average, things cost 7 percent more. What you would have paid $100 for last year now costs $107. (That's the definition of *inflation*.) Had the price level remained constant, and had you received 0 percent interest, you'd be in the equivalent position of receiving 7 percent interest on your $100 when the price level rises by 7 percent. That 0 percent is the *real interest rate*. It is the interest rate you receive after adjusting for inflation.

The real interest rate cannot be observed because it depends on expected inflation. To calculate the real interest rate, you must subtract what you believe to be the expected rate of inflation from the nominal interest rate:

Real interest rate = Nominal interest rate − Expected inflation rate[2]

[2]This is an equation that works best for small amounts of inflation.

A REMINDER

Some Limits of Fed Control

- In much of the discussion of the macro model, economists assume a single interest rate, which suggests the Fed has more control over the economy than it actually does.
- The long-term and short-term interest rates can differ, with the money market determining the short-term interest rate and the loanable funds market determining the long-term interest rate.
- The Fed's primary influence is in the money market and hence on the short-term interest rate. Its influence on the long-term interest rate is less direct.
- The yield curve is generally upward-sloping, but when the Fed attempts to contract the money supply, it can become inverted, or downward-sloping. Similarly, if the Fed tries to expand the money supply, the yield curve will generally become steeper.

Q-8 What is the difference between a standard yield curve and an inverted yield curve?

Q-9 If the nominal interest rate is 10 percent and expected inflation is 3 percent, what is the real interest rate?

For example, if the nominal interest rate is 7 percent and expected inflation is 4 percent, the real interest rate is 3 percent. The relationship between real and nominal interest rates is important both for your study of economics and for your own personal finances.

Q-10 How does the distinction between nominal and real interest rates add uncertainty to the effect of monetary policy on the economy?

What does this distinction between nominal and real interest rates mean for monetary policy? It adds yet another uncertainty to the effect of monetary policy. In the *AS/AD* model, we assumed that expansionary monetary policy lowers the interest rate and contractionary monetary policy increases the interest rate. However, if the expansionary monetary policy leads to expectations of increased inflation, expansionary monetary policy can increase nominal interest rates (the ones you see) and leave real interest rates (the ones that affect borrowing decisions) unchanged. Why? Because of expectations of increasing inflation. Lenders will want to be compensated for the inflation (which will decrease the value of the money they receive back) and will push the nominal interest rate up to get the desired real rate of interest.

Monetary Policy Regimes The distinction between nominal and real interest rates and the possible effect of monetary policy on expectations of inflation has led most economists to conclude that a monetary regime, not a monetary policy, is the best approach to policy. A **monetary regime** is *a predetermined statement of the policy that will be followed in various situations*. A monetary policy, in contrast, is a response to events; it is chosen without a predetermined framework.

Monetary regimes are now favored because rules can help generate the expectations that even though in certain instances the Fed is increasing the money supply, that increase is not a signal that monetary expansion and inflation are imminent. The monetary regime that the Fed currently uses involves feedback rules that center on the Federal funds rate. If inflation is above its target, the Fed raises the Federal funds rate (by selling bonds, thereby decreasing the money supply) in an attempt to slow inflation down. If inflation is below its target, and if the economy is going into a recession, the Fed lowers the Fed funds rate (by buying bonds, thereby increasing the money supply). The Taylor rule discussed above is a quantification of this general feedback rule.

A REMINDER

Conventional Wisdom about Monetary Policy

Expansionary	Contractionary
Advantages 1. Interest rates may fall. 2. Economy may grow. 3. Decreases unemployment.	**Advantages** 1. Helps fight inflation. 2. Trade deficit may decrease. 3. Capital inflow.
Disadvantages 1. Inflation may worsen. 2. Capital outflow. 3. Trade deficit may increase.	**Disadvantages** 1. Risks recession. 2. Increases unemployment. 3. Slows growth. 4. May help cause short-run political problems. 5. Interest rates may rise.

Problems with Monetary Policy Regimes Establishing an explicit monetary policy regime to hold down expectations of inflation is not without its problems. Inevitably, special circumstances arise where it makes sense to deviate from the regime. The problem is analogous to the problem faced by parents. All parenting manuals tell parents to maintain credibility and to set fair and firm rules. Most parents attempt to do so. But as all, or at least most, parents know, sometimes exceptions are necessary. Not all contingencies can be planned for. So I suspect that both parents and monetary policy makers will consistently emphasize their firm rules and state that they will follow them no matter what, but that inevitably they will trade some credibility for some short-term gain, or in the belief that the initial rule did not take into account the particular situation that arose.

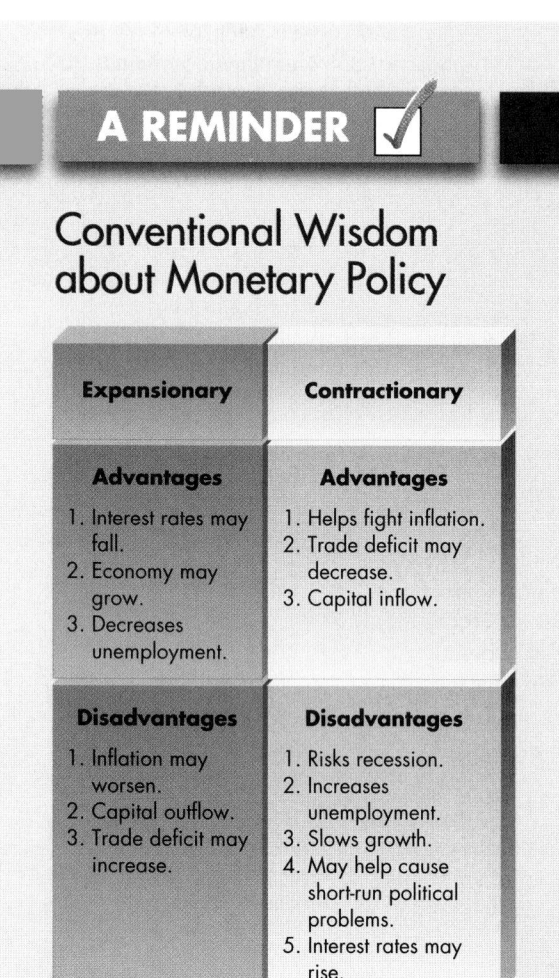

To make its commitment to a monetary regime clear to the public, even as it deviates slightly from that commitment in specific instances, the Fed has been trying, over the past decade, to increase the degree of *transparency* that accompanies its monetary policy decisions. Specifically, the Fed is releasing the minutes of its FOMC meetings much sooner after the meetings adjourn than it did in the past, and is going out of its way to explain its decisions. The hope is that the greater degree of transparency will demonstrate the Fed's general resolve to fight inflation, and show that any possible deviation from that resolve can be explained by special circumstances.

Conclusion

The above discussion should give you a good sense that conducting monetary policy is not a piece of cake. It takes not only a sense of the theory but also a feel for the economy. (See the box "Conventional Wisdom about Monetary Policy" for a summary of the standard view of monetary policy.) In short, the conduct of monetary policy is not a science. It does not allow the Fed to steer the economy as it might steer a car. It does work well enough to allow the Fed to *influence* the economy—much as an expert rodeo rider rides a bronco bull.

The Fed can influence, not steer, the economy.

Summary

- Monetary policy is the policy of influencing the economy through changes in the banking system's reserves that affect the money supply.
- In the *AS/AD* model, contractionary monetary policy works as follows:

$$M\downarrow \rightarrow i\uparrow \rightarrow I\downarrow \rightarrow Y\downarrow$$

- Expansionary monetary policy works as follows:

$$M\uparrow \rightarrow i\downarrow \rightarrow I\uparrow \rightarrow Y\uparrow$$

- The Federal Open Market Committee (FOMC) makes the actual decisions about monetary policy.
- The Fed is a central bank; it conducts monetary policy for the United States and regulates financial institutions.
- The Fed changes the money supply through open market operations:

  To expand the money supply, the Fed buys bonds.
  To contract the money supply, the Fed sells bonds.

- When the Fed buys bonds, the price of bonds rises and interest rates fall. When the Fed sells bonds, the price of bonds falls and interest rates rise.
- A change in reserves changes the money supply by the change in reserves times the money multiplier.
- The Federal funds rate is the rate at which one bank lends reserves to another bank. It is the Fed's primary operating target.
- The Taylor rule is a feedback rule that states: Set the Fed funds rate at 2 plus current inflation plus one-half the difference between actual and desired inflation plus one-half the percent difference between actual and potential output.
- The yield curve shows the relationship between interest rates and bonds' time to maturity.
- The Fed's direct control is on short-term interest rates; its effect on long-term interest rates is indirect. Fed policy intended to shift the yield curve might instead change its shape, and therefore not have the intended impact on investment.
- Nominal interest rates are the interest rates we see and pay. Real interest rates are nominal interest rates adjusted for expected inflation: Real interest rate = Nominal interest rate − Expected inflation.
- Because monetary policy can affect inflation expectations as well as nominal interest rates, the effect of monetary policy on interest rates can be uncertain. This uncertainty has led the Fed to follow monetary regimes.

Key Terms

central bank *(733)*
contractionary monetary policy *(733)*
discount rate *(740)*
expansionary monetary policy *(733)*
Fed funds *(741)*
Federal funds market *(741)*
Federal funds rate *(741)*
Federal Open Market Committee (FOMC) *(733)*
inverted yield curve *(746)*
monetary base *(737)*
monetary policy *(731)*
monetary regime *(748)*
nominal interest rate *(747)*
open market operations *(737)*
quantitative easing tools *(747)*
real interest rate *(747)*
reserve requirement *(739)*
Taylor rule *(743)*
yield curve *(745)*

Questions and Exercises

1. Say that investment increases by 20 for each interest rate drop of 1 percent. Say also that the expenditures multiplier is 3. If the money multiplier is 4, and each 5 unit change in the money supply changes the interest rate by 1 percent, what open market policy would you recommend to increase income by 240? LO1, LO4
2. Demonstrate the effect of contractionary monetary policy in the *AS/AD* model. LO1
3. Demonstrate the effect of expansionary monetary policy in the money and loanable funds markets. LO1
4. Demonstrate the effect of expansionary monetary policy in the *AS/AD* model when the economy is
   a. Below potential output.
   b. Significantly above potential output. LO1
5. Is the Fed a private or a public agency? LO2
6. Why are there few regional Fed banks in the western part of the United States? LO2
7. What are the six explicit functions of the Fed? LO2
8. How does the Fed use open market operations to increase the money supply? LO3
9. Write the formula for the money multiplier. If the Fed eliminated the reserve requirement, what would happen to the money multiplier and the supply of money? LO3
10. If a bank is unable to borrow reserves from the Fed funds market to meet its reserve requirement, where else might it borrow reserves? What is the name of the rate it pays to borrow these reserves? LO3
11. What happens to interest rates and the price of bonds when the Fed buys bonds? LO3
12. If the Federal Reserve announces a change in the direction of monetary policy, is it describing an offensive or defensive action? Explain your answer. LO3
13. Why would a bank hold Treasury bills as secondary reserves when it could simply hold primary reserves—cash? LO3
14. The Fed wants to increase the money supply (which is currently 4,000) by 200. The money multiplier is 3 and people hold no cash. For each 1 percentage point the discount rate falls, banks borrow an additional 20. Explain how the Fed can achieve its goals using the following tools:
    a. Change the reserve requirement.
    b. Change the discount rate.
    c. Use open market operations. LO3
15. Suppose the Fed decides it needs to pursue an expansionary policy. Assume people hold no cash, the reserve requirement is 20 percent, and there are no excess reserves. Show how the Fed would increase the money supply by $2 million through open market operations. LO3
16. Suppose the Fed decides that it needs to pursue a contractionary policy. It wants to decrease the money supply by $2 million. Assume people hold 20 percent of their money in the form of cash balances, the reserve requirement is 20 percent, and there are no excess reserves. Show how the Fed would decrease the money supply by $2 million through open market operations. LO3
17. Some individuals have suggested raising the required reserve ratio for banks to 100 percent.
    a. What would the money multiplier be if this change were made?
    b. What effect would such a change have on the money supply?
    c. How could that effect be offset? LO3
18. Congratulations! You have been approved adviser to the Federal Reserve Bank.
    a. The Federal Open Market Committee decides that it must increase the money supply by 60. Committee members tell you the reserve ratio is 0.1 and the cash-to-deposit ratio is 0.3. They ask you what directive they should give to the open market desk. You tell them, being as specific as possible, using the money multiplier.
    b. They ask you for two other ways they could have achieved the same end. You tell them.
    c. Based on the *AS/AD* model, tell them what you think the effect on the price level of your policy will be. LO3
19. What is meant by the *Federal funds rate*? LO4
20. Why is the Fed funds rate the interest rate that the Fed most directly controls? LO4

21. What is the relationship between tools, operating targets, intermediate targets, and ultimate targets? LO4
22. What are examples of tools, operating targets, and ultimate targets? LO4
23. The "Check 21" Act, which allows banks to transfer check images instead of paper checks, speeds up check processing. What is the likely effect on:
    a. Float (duplicate money because a check has been deposited but not yet deducted from the payer's account).
    b. Variability of float.
    c. Defensive Fed actions. LO4
24. The table below gives the Fed funds rate target at the end of each year shown.

Year	Federal Funds Target Rate
2005	5.00%
2006	5.25
2007	4.25
2008	0.25

    Using these figures, describe how the monetary policy directions changed from 2005 through 2008. LO5
25. Target inflation is 2 percent; actual inflation is 3 percent. Output equals potential output. What does the Taylor rule predict will be the Fed funds rate? LO5
26. State the Taylor rule. What does the rule predict will happen to the Fed funds rate in each of the following situations?
    a. Inflation is 2 percent, the inflation target is 3 percent, and output is 2 percent below potential.
    b. Inflation is 4 percent, the inflation target is 2 percent, and output is 3 percent above potential.
    c. Inflation is 4 percent, the inflation target is 3 percent, and output is 2 percent below potential. LO5
27. What would the Fed have to do in the following instances to keep the interest rate constant? Demonstrate graphically.
    a. A significant number of people begin to use credit cards for daily transactions, reducing the amount of money they hold.
    b. Bond traders expect bond prices to fall, and therefore increase their cash holdings. LO5
28. What is the shape of the effective supply curve for money? LO6
29. Why does the effective supply curve for money have the shape it does? LO6
30. If the nominal interest rate is 6 percent and inflation is 5 percent, what's the real interest rate? LO6
31. What is an inverted yield curve? LO6
32. Are you more likely to see an inverted yield curve when the Fed is implementing contractionary or expansionary monetary policy? LO6
33. Why would policy makers pay attention to the shape of the yield curve? LO6
34. Does it matter to policy makers how people form expectations? LO6
35. How does a policy regime differ from a policy? LO6
36. How might an inflation target policy impair the ability of the Fed? LO6
37. How are transparency and credibility related? LO6
38. What are two quantitative easing tools? LO6
39. Fill in the blanks in the following table: LO6

	Real Interest Rate	Nominal Interest Rate	Expected Inflation
a.	5	?	2
b.	?	3	4
c.	3	6	?
d.	?	5	1

Questions from Alternative Perspectives

1. Fisher Black, an economist who designed a famous options pricing model, argued that because of developments in financial markets, central banks would soon have no ability to control the economy with monetary policy, and that the price level would be indeterminant rather than determined by the money supply. What do you think his argument was? (Austrian)
2. The quotation at the beginning of this chapter, and those for almost all the chapters, is from a man not a woman.
    a. Does this suggest anything about the author's viewpoint or about the economics profession?
    b. Should we be concerned about the lack of quotations from women? (Feminist)
3. Monetary policy is difficult when interest rates are low. For example, in the early 2000s the Bank of Japan lowered the interest rate to 0.01 percent with little effect on investment.
    a. Why is it difficult for monetary policy to be effective when interest rates are very low?
    b. How might institutions be changed to make monetary policy effective under these circumstances? (Institutionalist)

4. Monetarists believe that money is neutral in that it has no real effect on interest rates, output, or employment. Keynes, alternatively, believed that money is not neutral in both the short and long run. For Keynesians, money supply can affect real decision making, providing liquidity when firms need it. How would a belief in the non-neutrality of money affect the policy discussion in the book? (Post-Keynesian)
5. As radical economists see it, when it comes to making monetary policy, the Fed consistently puts the interests of bondholders ahead of people seeking work. It regularly moves to protect the value of their stocks and bonds by keeping inflation low even at the expense of maintaining employment growth.
   a. In your opinion, does the Fed use monetary policy to direct the economy to everyone's benefit?
   b. Should the Fed serve the interests of the holders of financial assets or the interests of workers? (Radical)

Issues to Ponder

1. "The effects of open market operations are somewhat like a stone cast in a pond." After the splash, discuss the first three ripples. LO1, LO3
2. You can lead a horse to water, but you can't make it drink. How might this adage be relevant to expansionary (as opposed to contractionary) monetary policy? LO6
3. In November 2008 the central bank began to pay interest on reserves held at the bank.
   a. What effect would you expect this to have on excess reserves?
   b. Did banks generally favor or oppose this action?
   c. Would central banks generally favor or oppose this action?
   d. What effect did this probably have on interest rates paid by banks? LO3

Answers to Margin Questions

1. Expansionary monetary policy makes more money available to banks for lending. Banks lower their interest rates to attract more borrowers. With lower interest rates, businesses will borrow more money and increase investment expenditures. The multiplier shifts the *AD* curve to the right by a multiple of the increase in investment expenditures. Real output increases to Y_1, and the price level rises to P_1. What ultimately happens to output and the price level depends on where the economy is relative to potential. *(733)*

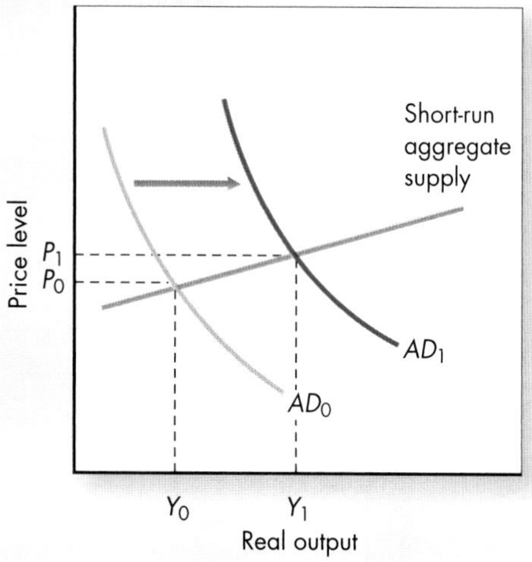

2. The Federal Open Market Committee (FOMC) decides on monetary policy *(733)*.
3. When the Fed buys bonds, it is expanding the money supply. *(739)*
4. The money multiplier in this case is 4, so the money supply declines by $400. *(740)*
5. The Fed should buy bonds to offset the unintended decline in reserves. *(742)*
6. The Taylor rule predicts a Fed funds rate target of 1.5 percent. *(743)*
7. The Fed adjusts the money supply so that the targeted interest rate equilibrates the demand and supply for money. When demand increases, the Fed increases supply to maintain the interest rate target. It does the opposite when demand decreases. *(745)*
8. In a standard yield curve, bonds with greater time to maturity pay higher interest rates. In an inverted yield curve, bonds with greater time to maturity pay *lower* interest rates. *(747)*
9. The real interest rate is 7 percent, the nominal interest rate (10) less expected inflation (3). *(747)*
10. Because expansionary monetary policy can lead to expectations of higher inflation, expansionary monetary policy can lead to higher nominal interest rates. Because real interest rates cannot be observed directly, interest rates are not always a good guide for the direction of monetary policy. *(748)*

Financial Crises, Panics, and Macroeconomic Policy

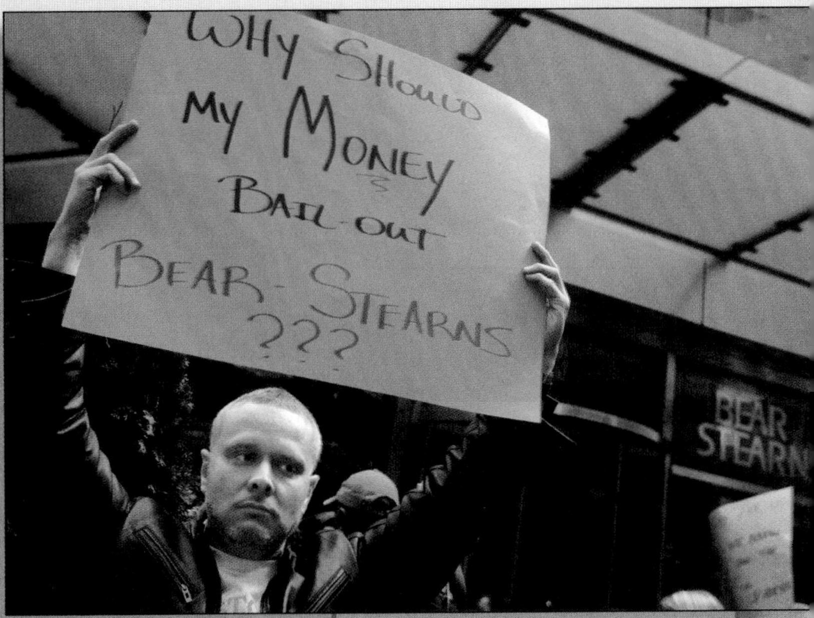

Economics is a science of thinking in terms of models joined to the art of choosing models which are relevant to the contemporary world.

—J. M. Keynes

In 2008, the world financial system seized up. Banks went bankrupt, the stock market dropped precipitously, and the U.S. economy fell into a serious recession. Government took extraordinary steps—buying up banks, buying up financial assets, guaranteeing deposits, and guaranteeing loans to try and calm the crisis. The expenditures went into the trillions of dollars. In this chapter I discuss what happened, why it happened, and what can be done to see that it doesn't happen again.

AFTER READING THIS CHAPTER, YOU SHOULD BE ABLE TO:

1. Explain why economists worry more about the collapse of the financial sector than the collapse of other sectors.
2. List the three stages of a financial crisis.
3. Discuss how herding and leverage can lead to a bubble.
4. Explain how extrapolative expectations can lead to bubbles and depressions.
5. Distinguish between nonsystemic and systemic risk.
6. Describe the three stages by which an economy gets out of a financial crisis.
7. Explain the importance of the moral hazard problem, the law of diminishing control, and the bad precedent problem.

Why Are Financial Panics Scary?

Why so much fear about a credit crisis? And why so much effort to keep financial companies afloat? The financial sector got itself into this mess—why not just let the Wall Street bigwigs go bankrupt? After all, the financial sector is not all that big—we worry far less about the automobile or computer sectors being too big to fail. The answer is simple: We worry about the financial sector not because it is big, but because all the other sectors rely on a functioning financial sector. The failures of other big sectors would be painful, but they would not bring all other sectors crashing down with them like a financial sector collapse would. That's why one of the roles of a central bank is to be a *lender of last resort*.

Think about what would happen if *your* credit dried up—say even though you're every bit as trustworthy as before, you suddenly find you can no longer borrow money (which means *no* credit cards). Some things might still work just fine—you could just use cash at the local grocery store. Some things would be harder. If you didn't have credit, you'd have to pay all your bills in advance. (And to do this by check you'd still need a well-functioning financial system.) Some things would be downright impossible; forget about buying anything on the Internet. Paying for college? No problem . . . if you've already saved up enough to pay up front and in full.

The situation is even worse for companies. While they might not use credit cards, just like you borrow for your short-term needs, they borrow short-term to buy the raw materials for production and to pay their workers. If that credit line disappears, many—perhaps most—companies would essentially be forced to close, leaving their workers out of a job. That's why a severe financial crisis can bring the entire real economy to a halt.

So when credit freezes up, the real economy can quickly freeze up. It's not like the slow effect of a contractionary demand shock. It is fast, like a heart attack, rather than a slow sickness. As I discussed in the previous chapter, you should think of credit as financial oil. While oil is a relatively minor part of a working engine, it is absolutely essential. The fear in October 2008 was that the financial crisis on Wall Street would spread from Wall Street (the financial sector) to Main Street (the real sector), creating not a recession but a depression.

The Great Depression

Probably the best place to start to understand the events and government policies of 2008 and 2009 is with some history—starting with 1929 to be precise, right before the beginning of the Great Depression of the 1930s. Why start there? Because it is the last time the United States experienced anything like this type of a financial crisis.

That's not to say that we're headed for a second Great Depression. The economy today is unlikely to get nearly that bad, in part because we've learned a lot since then about how to respond to financial crises. Most economists are quick to note that another Great Depression is extremely unlikely. Still, getting an historical perspective on the matter is valuable. Just before the Great Depression in early 1929, hardly anyone worried about a financial crisis or an economic depression either.

Crashes are made up of a combination of small events, each of which makes the economy worse.

Without the benefit of hindsight it is hard to know what series of unfortunate events will lead an economy into a depression. *Crashes are made up of a combination of small events*, each of which makes the economy worse. At each step along the path, recovery looks possible, even probable, leading many to believe that the economy will recover and a major crash will be avoided. Generally it does. But in a major crash, things just keep going wrong. It's like betting on red in roulette and the wheel coming up black over and over again. That's what happened in the 1930s, and that's what we hope is not happening in the present crisis.

The Stock Market Crash of 1929

Times had been good throughout the "roaring 1920s." As stock prices soared, people made money in the stock market hand over fist. Sure, going forward, many expected a little less "roar," but almost nobody predicted what happened in September and October of 1929. In those two months, stock prices fell by nearly 50 percent.

Q-1 True or false? If stock prices fall by 50 percent, that fall makes society poorer by 50 percent.

You may be thinking that the stock market crash caused the Great Depression. After all, when the stock market fell by 50 percent, people who owned stock lost 50 percent of the wealth they held in stocks. But note that, for society as a whole, this was only a fall in nominal wealth, not real wealth. People still had to eat. They still wanted to buy goods. No factories were destroyed by the crash; the productive capacity still existed to produce those goods.

So, through 1933, most economists expected the economy to recover on its own. "Prosperity is just around the corner" was a favorite quip. While, with hindsight, this belief may look naïve, it was not so unreasonable at the time. Stock prices had fallen before, many times, and each time the market had righted itself fairly quickly. Things didn't look any different in the early 1930s. It took another unlucky "black ball"—a financial meltdown—to spin the economy into a depression.

The Financial Meltdown of the 1930s

The 1930s financial meltdown was only indirectly related to the stock market crash. The real problem arose because people had borrowed from banks to invest in the stock market boom of the 1920s. When the stock market crashed, banks began to have trouble collecting on those loans. People with deposits at banks got scared; they lost faith that the banks would have their money when they wanted to withdraw it. And some banks didn't. But nobody really knew which banks could cover withdrawals and which ones were at risk of defaulting. So if a rumor began to fly about a bank failing . . . well, that's all it took for people to flock to withdraw all the money they had deposited before the bank closed. (In the 1930s bank deposits were not insured by the government as they are today, so if you didn't get to the bank before it shut, you'd lose all of your deposits.) There was what is known as a bank run. These *bank runs* caused many perfectly sound banks to fail. To have money available as a precaution against these sorts of runs, and to cover their bad loans, banks started hoarding, rather than lending, money. Since firms couldn't get loans, they stopped investing (buying productive capital). As they stopped investing, unemployment increased. As unemployment increased, people bought less, leading firms to cut back production even more. The financial system wasn't working any more, and the recession started turning into a depression.

The financial crisis exploded in 1933, four years after the crash of the stock market, when a whole series of banks appeared to be on the brink of failure. Fear swept over the United States—the type of fear that can become self-fulfilling. If everyone thinks that the system is about to collapse, then everyone withdraws their cash and the system *does*, in fact, collapse. It was at the point of near financial collapse that the U.S. government acted, taking drastic action to prevent an even greater financial breakdown. The drastic actions stopped further economic decline, but by 1933 much damage was already done, and the economy didn't recover from the depression until World War II.

Web Note 32.1
Comparative Crises

Understanding the 2008 Financial Crisis

Now, let's consider the 2008 financial crisis. Unlike in the 1930s, when the government took years to act, in 2008 the government acted immediately. Only months after the financial crisis began, the Fed put aside its standard cautious approach to monetary policy and undertook a wide variety of unprecedented actions to prevent the financial crisis from worsening. Similarly, the Treasury dropped all its standard practices and "bailed out" financial firms, and Congress instituted strong expansionary fiscal policy. The hope was that such actions would be enough to prevent the financial meltdown that would turn a serious recession into a second Great Depression (and that the negative side effects of these "bailouts" would not undermine the long-run health of the U.S. economy).

Even though every financial crisis is different, all generally occur in stages—and 2008 is no exception. The first stage is generally the inflation of a **bubble**—*unsustainable rapidly rising prices of some type of financial asset* (such as stocks or houses). Price increases in a bubble are unsustainable because they do not reflect an increase in the real productive value of the asset. In the 1920s for the Great Depression, the underlying cause was a stock market bubble, and in the early 2000s, it was a housing market bubble. Second, the bubble bursts, causing a recession. Third, the effects of the bursting bubble threaten the entire financial system. Fourth, people cut spending. And fifth, firms cut back even more, creating a downward spiral that can turn a recession into a depression. The government's massive response to the 2008 crisis was an attempt to prevent this downward spiral.

The first stage of a financial crisis is generally the inflation of a bubble.

The best place to start in understanding the crisis the U.S. economy experienced in 2008—and why the government's response was so rapid—is to consider in greater detail the earlier stages of the crisis.

Thinking like a Modern Economist

Tulipmania, the South Sea Bubble, and Behavioral Economics

Bubbles have been a fixture in economies for centuries. Two of the most famous financial bubbles are Tulipmania and the South Sea Bubble.

The height of Tulipmania occurred in Holland between November 1636 and February 1637. It centered on, you guessed it, tulips—a relatively newly introduced and popular flower. Over three months, tulip bulb prices are estimated to have risen by several thousand percent, all without any tulips actually changing hands—tulips don't even *grow* between November and February. Instead, speculators tried to make money by buying and reselling *promises* to deliver tulip bulbs the following May, after they had flowered. Contracts for some particularly rare bulbs were reportedly trading for prices equivalent to 20 years of a typical workman's wages, and for a full 12 acres of land. Trading was purely speculative; people bought tulip contracts with the full intention of "flipping" them for a profit well before May. The bubble burst in February when people realized that at the current prices, no one would be willing to pay the outrageous prices for an actual *tulip*.

Another financial bubble was the South Sea bubble of the early 1700s. The South Sea bubble started when rumors spread that the South Sea Company—a company granted a monopoly on trade with South American colonies by the British government—would be enormously profitable. When the stock price of the South Sea Company doubled, others noticed and wanted to get in on the profit, pushing the price up further. The price of its stock rose almost tenfold between January and August of 1720. (The rise was helped along by various shady dealings between the company and members of the British Parliament.)

How could people afford to buy this stock at such high prices? They borrowed, and were allowed to leverage their purchases. (Pay me 10 percent now and the remaining 90 percent next week.) As long as the stock price was rising, that wasn't a problem. When it was time to pay the remaining 90 percent, the stockholder could sell the stock at a higher price, repay the loan, and pocket the difference.

But then, suddenly, the rumors reversed. The stock prices started falling and everyone called in their loans. To pay their loans people tried to sell stock that no one wanted to buy; stock prices plummeted and the bubble burst even more quickly than it had formed.

Behavioral economics and standard economics explain these bubbles differently. Standard economics works hard to provide a rational explanation for financial bubbles. It has a theory of what might be called rational bubbles. For example, some economists have argued that the high prices of tulips and of South Sea Company stock were plausible in light of the scarcity and novelty of certain bulbs and imperfect information about the profitability of trade with the Americas. If bubbles are rational, they should be considered an unavoidable aspect of modern society. Modern behavioral economists disagree. They argue that bubbles form precisely because people *aren't* fully rational—they are subject to herd mentality. That is, they are predictably irrational. This difference is important because if behavioral economists are right, then there *is* a potential role for policy to reduce the severity and occurrence of bubbles.

Stage 1: The Bubble Forms

Through the middle of the first decade of 2000, times were good. While the economy experienced a recession in 2001, it was brief and economic growth resumed. Loose lending standards allowed more and more families to borrow to buy houses, and the value of their houses was increasing rapidly, making homeowners feel richer and richer.

In 2006, housing prices started to level off, and many talked about the prices settling into a permanently high plateau. But by 2007 housing prices began to fall precipitously, and it became clear that the boom in housing prices in the early 2000s was a financial bubble, much like the stock market bubble of the 1920s.

The 1920s stock market bubble and the 2000s housing bubble were both formed from two ingredients: **herding**—*the human tendency to follow the crowd*—and **leverage**—*borrowing to make financial investments*. Combining these two can create a bubble where prices rise above their underlying real values.

Q-2 What are two central ingredients of a bubble?

When prices are higher than their true underlying values, they're bound to come down eventually. And when they're built on leverage, when they do, they're bound to come down *quickly*. But it is important to recognize that while a bubble is happening, it is almost impossible to say for sure whether the bubble is *really* a bubble or whether the increase in prices reflects a structural change in the economy. Throughout both the 1920s and the 2000s, many smart people were convinced that the high prices reflected true underlying values. Unfortunately, it seems that bubbles can only be recognized for sure after the fact.

While it is happening, it is almost impossible to say for sure whether the bubble is really a bubble.

Herding: Extrapolative Expectations To understand what happens in a bubble, let's think about it within a supply/demand model. The key to a bubble is **extrapolative expectations**—*expectations that a trend will continue*. It works like this: Initially, the market experiences a shock, which causes prices to rise. In a standard supply/demand model, the initial rise in price is the end of the story. The rise in prices brings the market back into equilibrium. But in a bubble model, the initial rise in price causes expectations of a further price increase. This causes the demand curve to shift out to the right, which leads prices to rise further, fulfilling expectations, and leading to expectations of even more price increases. Expectations feed back on themselves, and prices rapidly spiral upwards.

Rise in price → Expectations of a further rise in price → Rise in demand at the current price → Rise in price → Expectations of a further rise in price . . . and so on

Let's see how this happens graphically in Figure 32-1. Figure 32-1 illustrates the importance of the "other things constant" assumption in the usual supply/demand model. It traces out what happens when demand shifts out from D_0 to D_1. At the

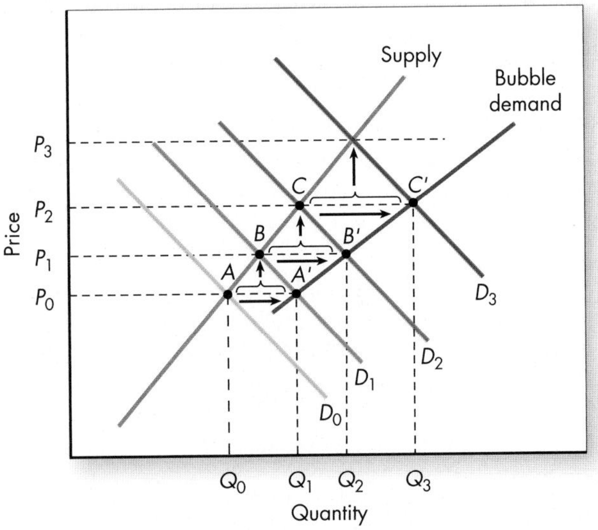

FIGURE 32-1 Supply/Demand Forces in a Bubble

If expectations of asset prices are extrapolative, people will expect a price increase will continue, shifting demand to the right, which confirms that expectation. An effective upward-sloping bubble demand can result.

original equilibrium price P_0, this new higher demand causes a shortage of $Q_1 - Q_0$. In the normal supply/demand model, with "other things constant," this causes price and quantity supplied to increase and quantity demanded to decrease, bringing us to a new equilibrium at point B, where the price is P_1.

If price expectations are extrapolative, we *can't* assume that other things are constant, the rise in prices from P_0 to P_1 leads people to expect further price increases. This shifts the demand out to D_2 and increases the quantity demanded at P_1 to Q_2. Thus, we have a shortage represented by the distance $B' - B$, which is greater than the initial shortage represented by the distance $A' - A$. The rise in price has actually moved the market *further* from equilibrium! Further price adjustments move us still further away in this manner: The larger shortage $B' - B$ causes prices to rise to P_2, which causes demand to shift further out to D_3 and even larger shortage $C' - C$, and so forth.

With extrapolative expectations, shortages become worse as time progresses because the more the price rises, the more people expect it to keep rising, and so the more people want the good. If we connect the quantity demanded at each price, we find that the market operates *as if* the demand curve is upward-sloping—even though each "other-things-constant" demand curve is "really" downward-sloping. (Demand curves that suspend the assumption of "other things constant" are called *effective* demand curves or, in this case, an effective *bubble* demand curve.)

Q-3 If there are extrapolative expectations, how does the effective demand curve differ from the "other things constant" demand curve?

Inflating a bubble depends on the ability of demanders to finance the increase in demand.

Leverage Inflating a bubble depends on the ability of demanders to finance the increase in demand. If the government doesn't increase the money supply, the only method of financing is through an increase in credit. That is, people must be able to leverage their purchases. The process through which leverage creates credit is similar to the money creation process—except here the multiplier process doesn't create money; it creates credit and financial instruments that serve some of the same functions as money. That creation process allows the endogenous expectations (expectations determined within the model) of rising prices to be met, and price increases to continue.

To understand the power of leverage, consider the decision of a person buying a stock in 1928. He would buy a share of stock at \$2 and it would rise to \$3, which meant that he made a 50 percent return. While a 50 percent return is pretty good, ingenious types figured out a way to use leverage to do even better. For example, what if instead of buying a single \$2 stock, a person borrowed \$198 at 10 percent interest and bought 100 shares for \$200? When the stock price went up to \$3, he could sell his stock for \$300, pay back the \$198 he borrowed plus \$19.80 in interest, and be left with a profit of \$80.20—about a 4,000 percent return! That's the power of leverage.[1] When you can expect returns like that, you want to get as much money into the stock market as possible.

Q-4 If you invest \$100 in a stock, borrowing 90 percent of the \$100 at 10 percent interest, and the stock price rises by 20 percent, what is the return on your investment?

Borrowing on the hope of future price increases is risky since those price increases aren't guaranteed; leveraging allows people to take enormous risks. The problem is that leveraging can lead to herding behavior. When people around you see how much you are earning, they want to profit too. Everyone buys more stocks, which increases the risk that the society is taking enormously.

Leveraging allows people to take enormous risks.

1920s: Leverage in the Stock Market In the 1920s lots of people started using the power of leverage to buy stocks whose prices they expected to rise so that they could sell them later at an enormous profit. They borrowed as much as they could. New ways to borrow money sprang up: People found that they could borrow from

---

[1]Notice that for leverage to work, you don't need to be buying stocks. You could be buying houses, mortgages, bonds, paintings, baseball cards, antiques—you name it. As long as the price is rising more than the rate of interest you can borrow at, you can get rich using leverage.

banks, using their stock as collateral (an asset that the lender gets if you don't make your payment on the loan). Stock brokers—individuals who buy and sell stock—got loans from banks so they could help their customers borrow even more. Want to buy 100 shares, but only have enough for 20? No problem, the broker would lend you the difference. This was known as buying "on margin" and people applauded this financial innovation as reflecting the magic of the market. Times were good—you danced the Charleston, you drank at the local speakeasy, and you made an easy killing in the stock market.[2]

2000s: Leverage in the Housing Market Times were similarly good in the early 2000s in the United States. Housing prices were rising nationally; *Flip That House* and other similar TV shows showcased people making tens of thousands of dollars by buying a house with very little or no down payment, and watching its price rise. It seemed like you could get rich quick just by owning a house. Low interest rates and innovative mortgages (mortgages with zero amount down, and no serious concern about whether the person's income was large enough to make the payments) made it easy for some people to handle larger and larger mortgages on bigger and more expensive houses and others who previously couldn't qualify for a mortgage to obtain them.

Homeownership rates rose to historical highs of nearly 70 percent and housing prices were rising rapidly. The feeling was that you simply couldn't lose on buying a house as an investment. As long as house prices kept rising, flipping houses, and stretching into a mortgage, made sense. To take advantage of the riches to be made in the housing market, many people became extremely leveraged. Some bought five or six houses, which they couldn't afford but which they planned to sell before they had to pay the mortgage back. All these actions increased the risk of significant problems occurring in the economy if housing prices didn't continue to rise, and left the economy vulnerable to the housing bubble bursting.

But that's not all. Leverage by homeowners was nothing compared with the leverage built on top of the housing market in the financial sector. Investment banks and hedge funds had figured out how to create securities whose values were *linked* to the performance of these mortgages. These securities were leveraging the already leveraged mortgages, creating a type of double—and in many cases even triple or quadruple—leverage, allowing investors to make money even faster on rising house prices. A full description of all of the action underlying this sort of leverage would be a textbook in and of itself—so I'll just try to give you a quick-and-dirty understanding of how it all worked.

Securitization of Mortgages Prior to the turn of the 21st century, the mortgage market was relatively boring. Local banks (and other mortgage originators) made well-documented loans to safe borrowers. Sometimes these banks kept the mortgages themselves. Other times they sold the mortgage to someone else. The market for these already-issued mortgages, known as the *secondary mortgage market*, was dominated by two companies: Fannie Mae and Freddie Mac.[3]

---

[2]In the 1920s one group, however, wasn't doing so well—agriculture. During World War I agriculture had done fantastically, with the United States having to feed not only the United States, but also Europe. Grain prices were high. Then, as European agriculture got back on its feet, agricultural prices fell, and the more farmers produced, the more prices fell. Moreover, Europe fell into a depression long before the United States, which meant that though they might have wanted to buy U.S. food, they couldn't afford it. Combine that with a severe drought, and farms were hurting throughout most of the 1920s. For city folk, the low food prices were a boon.

[3]Fannie and Freddie were originally established as government enterprises in the 1930s. They were privatized in 1968 but continued to be considered "government-sponsored enterprises" since they received explicit and implicit benefits (and policy mandates) from the federal government.

Fannie and Freddie bought conforming mortgages (ones that met certain "safe" guidelines). Typically, they then wrapped thousands of mortgages from all over the country together and sold "slices" of the income from the mortgages in the bundle. These slices are known as **mortgage-backed securities**—*financial assets whose flow of income comes from a combination of mortgages.* This process of bundling together and slicing up mortgages into new financial instruments is known as *securitization.* This is what we discussed in Chapter 30 when we talked about mortgages being combined with other mortgages into *derivative bonds.*

The process of bundling together and slicing up of mortgages into new financial instruments is known as *securitization.*

Q-5 What are two advantages that securitization provides?

This securitization had two big advantages for local banks (and other mortgage originators): *diversification* and *liquidity.* **Diversification** is *the act of combining different financial instruments, whose prices are not expected to move together, in an effort to reduce risk.* **Liquidity** measures *one's ability to convert an asset into cash.* Diversification increases liquidity. Here's why. If a bank made and held only local loans, the bank would face the risk that if the local economy declined, many of the people they had loaned money to would simultaneously default. If instead it sold the mortgages to Fannie Mae, and used the money from the sale to buy mortgage-backed securities, it would be better diversified. It would effectively own little pieces of mortgages from all around the country, reducing its exposure to any local downturn. It would also have more liquidity because there was a well-functioning nationwide market for mortgage-backed securities. If it needed quick cash, it could always simply sell its diversified securities; it was much harder to sell a single mortgage quickly.

Fannie and Freddie were limited by law from buying many of the less-safe mortgages that were issued in the 2000s. But investment banks had the bright idea to do what Fannie and Freddie did with the riskier mortgages: combine a whole bunch of riskier mortgages together and sell slices of the bundle as mortgage-backed securities. Sure, the mortgages were individually riskier, but banks and investors figured that as long as lots of them were bundled together, the downside risk was limited. And besides, as long as housing prices kept rising, these securities weren't risky at all. Since supposedly "expert" credit rating agencies had rated these securities as highly safe assets, most felt that there was little reason for concern.

It was the magic of the market all over again. Mortgage originators (financial institutions that approve, make, and process mortgage loans) got paid to write new mortgages, which they securitized and sold to investors (which meant they didn't have to worry as much about how safe the loans really were). And investors were happy to buy them since credit-rating agencies (who were making money rating these securities) said they were almost completely safe. With the Fed maintaining a low short-term interest rate, it was a perfect recipe for making money through leverage. Firms borrowed at the cheap short-term interest rates and invested in the higher-yielding mortgage-backed securities. Until 2003 the typical leverage in big investment banks to buy these securities was 12-1 (one needed only 1/12th of the value of the security to purchase it); after 2003, 30-1 leverage became the norm.[4]

Derivatives and Credit Default Swaps All sorts of new securities arose and acquired fancy names—derivatives, CDOs, exotics (see the box "The Alphabet Soup of Modern Finance"). Financial institutions became big blenders—combining all types of loans, mixing them together, and then pulling out a new blended derivative security that was precisely what people wanted for an optimally diversified portfolio. These

[4]In retrospect, if investment banks had borrowed long term instead of short term, they probably could have weathered the subsequent downturn. But, thanks in part to Fed policy in the early 2000s, short-term interest rates were very low, so that's where the opportunities for *serious* leverage were.

REAL-WORLD APPLICATION

The Alphabet Soup of Modern Finance

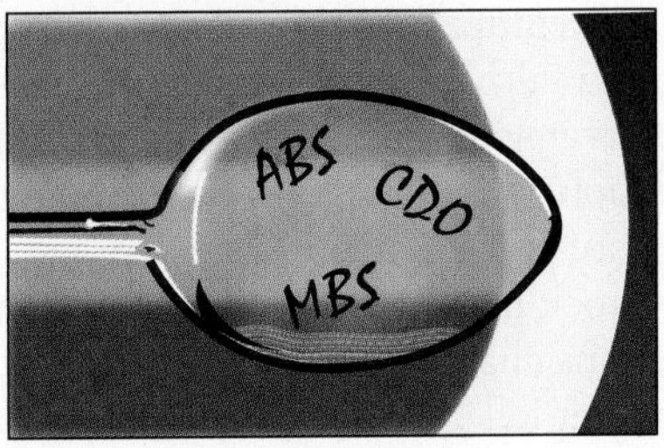

During the housing bubble, a bewildering number of words and acronyms arose to describe the various securities that were created and traded. Here's a brief primer on the most common terms.

- *Derivatives.* Any financial asset whose value depends on the value of some other asset.
- *MBS: Mortgage-Backed Securities.* Derivatives that provide income based on the revenue from an underlying bundle of mortgages.
- *ABS/CDO: Asset-Backed Securities/Collateralized Debt Obligations.* Derivatives that provide income based on revenue from some other underlying bundle of income-providing assets, such as credit cards, auto loans, or even bundles of different MBSs.
- *Exotics.* Nonstandard derivatives designed especially for a particular company with a particular diversification need.
- *CDS: Credit Default Swaps.* Derivatives that provide "insurance" against the risk that a company will go bankrupt. Designed originally to provide a company's bond holder with a guarantee that the bond will still make payments even if the issuing company defaults.
- *SIV: Structured Investment Vehicles.* Subsidiaries of banks designed to invest in MBSs, ABSs, and CDSs. Designed to allow banks to skirt regulations that limited their leverage by keeping assets "off the books" of the parent bank.

derivative securities helped firms diversify their portfolios, making firms feel safer. They didn't have their assets in one basket, but in thousands of baskets. Sure, this blending made it hard, and sometimes impossible, to tell what made up these securities, but that didn't matter as long as people generally trusted that securities of this sort would provide a return and could be sold if necessary.

This financial wizardry allowed companies to earn fabulous profits. They paid their employees accordingly. Students only one or two years out of college could earn $250,000 to $500,000 a year, and investment banking was the number one job aspiration for many top students.

Insurance companies like AIG were in on the action too: They made lots of money selling default insurance designed to protect investors from the default of the company they had bought their securities from. This insurance—known as a credit default option or swap—was new and hard to value, but, at least on the books, insurance providers were making lots of money. (In fact, there was multiple insurance on these derivative securities because firms sold derivatives of derivatives. The entire credit default swap market was $40 trillion a year.) Credit default insurance gave participants in the derivatives market a sense that they were covered no matter what happened. This sense of safety encouraged investors to expand leverage even more. The bottom line: A bubble in the derivatives market developed on top of the housing bubble.

Initially, this bubble led to economic expansion—it was like drinking two cans of Red Bull before breakfast each morning. Homeowners felt richer and increased their spending. Financial companies and insurance companies were practically printing their own money by creating new securities, and insurance providers were making a killing selling insurance on them. Incomes rose, spending was strong, and times were good. Just like in the 1920s, the bubble kept inflating.

Stage 2: The Bubble Bursts

A bubble bursts when people suddenly realize that an increase in perceived financial wealth is an illusion.

Above I stated that a bubble inflates when leverage, herding, and extrapolative expectations cause asset prices to rise rapidly, creating a wonderful circle of perceived increases in wealth. A bubble bursts when people suddenly realize that this increase in perceived wealth is all an illusion. As everyone rushes to get into safe assets, herding and (de)leveraging work in the opposite direction—and it all happens much faster than the inflation of the bubble. The economy can swing wildly, like the Tacoma Narrows Bridge discussed in Chapter 29.

The stock market boom of the 1920s was built on optimistic expectations. Those expectations changed—and changed quickly—in the fall of 1929. In September, the stock market fell 17 percent. People started to get worried, but in October the market bounced back somewhat, rising about 8 percent; things seemed to be getting better. In mid-October, one of the most famous economists of the day, Yale economist Irving Fisher, famously proclaimed, "Stock prices have reached what looks like a permanently high plateau." He invested his and his wife's money in the stock market.

Then came the "the black days": Black Thursday, Black Monday, and Black Tuesday (though they only acquired the name "black" after the fact). On Black Thursday, October 24, 1929, for no apparent reason, stock prices started to fall and more people started to panic, trying to sell, sell, sell at any price. Banks got together to try to stop the fall, publicly buying stock to show how safe the market was. But it didn't work; on October 28th the market plunged another 13 percent—and then another 12 percent the next day.

As stocks began to fall, lenders started to worry about getting paid back, and they started to call in their loans. The first ones to call the loans were the stockbrokers with whom people had taken margin accounts—buying 100 shares but only paying for 20—with the others bought on margin. With falling prices, the leverage that had made margin accounts so appealing started working in reverse: People were forced to sell their stock to pay back their loans, which put further downward pressure on stock prices, and forced yet more margin calls. Deleveraging began. Banks started to worry; they had loaned money to the stockbrokers, who looked like they might not be able to get their money back. So banks started calling in *their* loans to brokers and others. That created even more deleveraging and forced even more selling. That's why there was a *crash*. When the fall happened, it was *fast*.

Let's now briefly consider late 2007, when it was clear that the housing bubble was beginning to deflate. Compared with the stock market crash of 1929, the decline in house prices was slow. Housing markets just don't move as quickly as markets for other financial assets. But there was a *big* crash in the market for the derivative securities that had been *built* on the housing market. What had looked like safe and profitable assets turned to be a house of cards. When the bottom card—the market for actual *houses*—was disturbed, the whole structure fell apart. That wobbling takes us into the third stage of the crisis—which I'll come back to and talk about in more detail in just a bit.

What's important to note for now is that as housing prices fell, about a year before it looked like the whole financial system might melt down, economists, like economists in the early 1930s, weren't generally worried. Most of them felt that the economy could handle the bursting of the housing bubble. The productive capacity of the economy hadn't changed, so the real foundations for the economy still looked firm.

Until a bubble bursts you cannot be sure it was a bubble.

The bottom line on bubbles is that until they burst, you cannot be sure you are in one. And when a bubble bursts, while lots of people will lose money, and the economy will likely be pushed into a recession, bursting bubbles don't destroy real wealth, only financial wealth, so they generally don't throw the economy into a depression. The real problem with a bursting bubble is that it opens up the possibility of something far worse: a financial meltdown—and *that* can cause a depression.

Stage 3: Financial Meltdown and Possible Depression

Web Note 32.2
Bubble Analysis

A financial meltdown results when a bursting bubble undermines confidence in the entire financial sector. Financial companies fail left and right and cease to provide the "oil" needed for the economic engine. Not only does the excess leveraging disappear; the leveraging needed in the normal functioning of a market economy ends as well. As credit disappears, the economy seizes up and consumer and investor confidence evaporates. As we'll see below, when an economy seizes up, the effectiveness of the standard monetary and fiscal policy tools is also compromised, making the problems extremely difficult to cure. In the worst of all possible scenarios, people lose faith not just in the financial system, but in the political system too. If the problem gets that bad, the government can't sell its bonds and the entire political and economic system is threatened with collapse.

Things never got this bad in the 1930s, but they still got pretty bad. Monetary policy—the only game in town up to that point in history—was no longer working. Though the Fed *tried* to use expansionary monetary policy by significantly increasing the monetary base, it was unsuccessful. People—justifiably afraid of bank runs—simply stopped keeping their money in banks. The cash-to-deposit ratio rose substantially, decreasing the money multiplier and therefore the total money supply, even as the Fed poured reserves into the financial system. Firms stopped investing, first because they couldn't get loans from banks—who were afraid to loan money out as they hoarded it to protect against bank runs—and, second, because the economy was in such bad shape, investment made no sense. Firms didn't expect to be able to sell much, so why invest?

Q-6 Why might standard expansionary monetary policy not expand the economy?

As firms stopped investing, unemployment increased. As unemployment increased, people bought less, and firms cut back production even more. The Keynesian multiplier kicked in with a vengeance. The multiplier effect slowing the economy was further strengthened by the expectational accelerator discussed in Chapter 28. When the expectational accelerator kicks in, the downward spiral becomes self-fulfilling and can lead the economy into a vicious circle that ends in a depression. That's what happened in the 1930s. The recession that began in 1929 deepened and by 1933, GDP had fallen by 33 percent from its 1929 peak—and it looked like the economy might get even worse.

AS/AD with an Expectational Accelerator: A Model of a Depression To see how an "expectational accelerator" can lead to a depression, let's consider how all the factors come together and destabilize the aggregate economy in the *AS/AD* model. We already saw in Figure 32-1 how extrapolative expectations can destabilize a supply/demand market. When a bursting bubble is large and pervasive enough, the same thing can happen in the aggregate economy.

In Figure 32-1, extrapolative expectations of rising prices led to increases in demand, so the market behaved as if the effective demand curve was upward-sloping. Similarly, in the depression model depicted in Figure 32-2, extrapolative expectations about falling real output led to contractions in investment and consumption. Coupled with the wealth illusion that accompanies the bursting of a bubble (when people mistake falling nominal wealth for falling real wealth), these destabilizing forces combine to give an internal downward-shifting dynamic to the *AD* curve that produces an upward-sloping "effective" *AD* curve. The economy is pushed into a downward spiral from which it is difficult to escape.

In Figure 32-2, the problem starts with a small shift back in the *AD* curve from AD_0 to AD_1. This causes excess aggregate supply (an aggregate demand shortage) of

FIGURE 32-2 A Depression Model

Extrapolative expectations about falling real output can lead to a cycle of shrinking aggregate demand, and an upward-sloping effective aggregate demand curve.

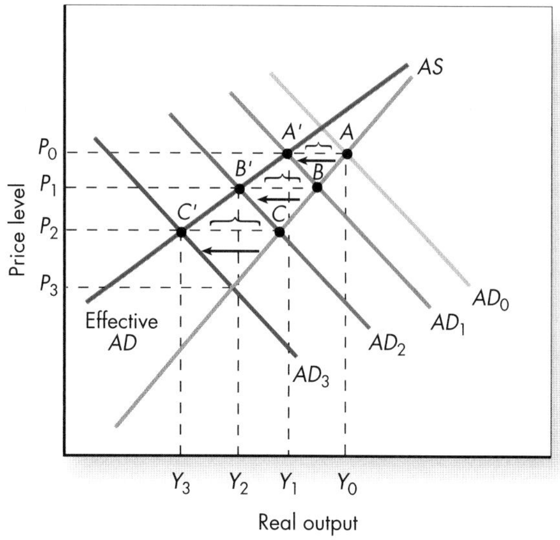

In a depression model endogenously changing expectations prevent equilibrium from being reached.

$Y_1 - Y_0$. In the standard model, that shortage would be resolved by a fall in the price level to P_1 and a fall in output, making the new equilibrium at point *B*. However, in a depression model, which includes the expectational accelerator, endogenously changing expectations prevent that equilibrium from being reached. Instead, that adjustment process causes people to expect output and the price level to fall further. If the fall in the price level is accompanied by a fall in asset prices (such as housing prices), which it generally is, holders of assets feel poorer, which leads them to spend less. Simultaneously, the fall in output leads people to fear an even greater future decline, a fear that reduces investment and consumers' willingness to spend.

These changing expectations shift the *AD* curve back further from AD_1 to AD_2. So at price level P_1, the aggregate demand shortage is now represented by the distance $B' - B$, which is larger than the initial shortage $A' - A$. The fall in the price level and the fall in output have worsened, instead of improving, the situation. That fall in the price level and in output confirms expectations, and causes expectations of even greater declines in output and the price level. If the process continues, the aggregate demand curve shifts further to the left to AD_3, the price level falls to P_2, and aggregate income falls to Y_3, and the economy finds itself in freefall. If we connect points A', B', and C', we see that we have an effective aggregate demand curve that slopes *up* instead of *down*.

The scary thing about a depression model is that the downward spiral has no bottom until something else changes the dynamics of the system.

What makes the depression model different from the standard model? Other things that are assumed to remain constant in the normal *AS*/*AD* analysis—such as expectations—do not remain constant in the depression model. Each *AD* curve in the model has its normal downward slope, but endogenously changing expectations cause it to keep shifting down to the left. These continual shifts overwhelm the money wealth, interest rate, and international effects that are assumed in the standard model to stabilize the economy. The economy becomes unstable, and it behaves *as if* the *AD* curve slopes the wrong way. The scary thing about this depression model is that, unlike in the case in the multiplier model, the downward spiral has no bottom until something *else* changes the dynamics of the system.

REAL-WORLD APPLICATION

Black Swans: What's Normal?

In a 50-trading-day period between mid-September and mid-November of 2008, stock markets were extremely volatile. On 25 of those days, the Wilshire 5000 (the broadest available stock market index) closed at least 4 percent up or down from the previous day's close. According to the models used by banks and other financial institutions, these kinds of fluctuations were impossible. After all, during the past 25 years, movements of 4 percent or more had only happened about once per year, or about once in every 250 trading days. These models were based on this historical reality and, extrapolating this trend, the models predicted only about a one-in-five chance over a 50-trading-day period of even a *single* day with a greater than 4 percent swing. The probability of as many as 25 swings of this size in a 50-trading-day period . . . well, if the historical rate had held up, this would have been less likely than getting heads on a coin toss *over 150 times in a row,* which is the same thing as saying: basically never. Clearly, the banks' models were wrong: Something changed in 2008 that caused the historical pattern to break down.

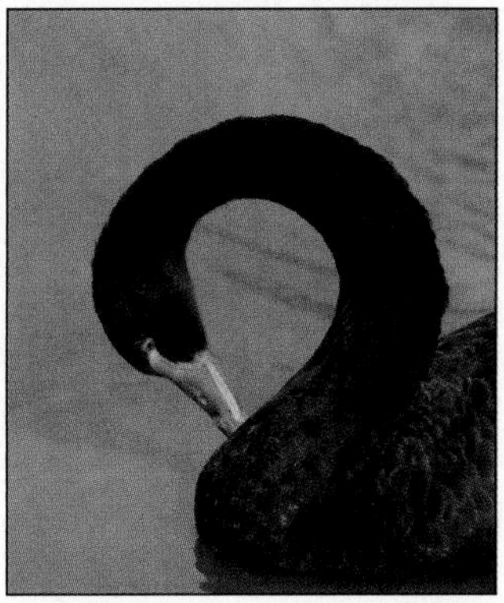

Events that diverge so drastically from normal historical patterns are known as "black swans." (They are so named because, for a long time, people believed that *all swans are white* . . . until a black swan was discovered, proving them wrong!) Ignoring the possibility of black swans—like the sudden increase in stock market volatility, or the simultaneous collapse of housing markets nationwide—led lenders in the early 2000s to worry much less about systemic risk crisis than, in retrospect, they probably should have. Based on *historical* norms, it was reasonable to think that they did not have to worry about systemic risk—or at least that's what their models told them. Using the historical record to predict the future is useful . . . but as experience shows, and our supply/demand model with extrapolative expectations demonstrates, doing so can also be misleading and dangerous. Models that extrapolate from the past will *always* miss the black swans, which appear precisely when things start to follow a different pattern. But if one doesn't use models based on historical data, what models can one use? The answer is unclear, which is why macroeconomic policy remains an art based on judgment, not a science based on firm models.

Why the Financial Crisis of 2008 Was Really Scary It was fear that the economy was described by the above depression model that so concerned economists in the 2008 crisis, especially because the bursting of the housing bubble had eerily similar parallels to what happened in the Great Depression. The crisis began when market conditions deteriorated in 2007. Housing prices leveled off and began to fall, and many families who had bought homes on the expectation of rising prices found they could not make their mortgage payments. Mortgage defaults began to rise. The derivative bonds built on these mortgages, which were bought by people, banks, pension funds, and college endowments, suddenly looked riskier. But even at this point, many people weren't worried since the large investment banks that had created the derivative bonds promised to stand by them. Moreover, they had backed up their promises by buying insurance to protect against default risk. So even as late as early 2008, people recognized that while there were reasons to be concerned about housing and financial markets, they still felt okay because they thought they were covered for those risks.

The problem was that insurance providers could only reliably provide insurance against **nonsystemic risks**—*risks of one event that are offset by another event elsewhere*. For example, holding a mortgage-backed security containing slices of mortgages from all over the country protects you against any particular local downturns. No one, neither

Q-7 What types of risks cannot be insured against?

government nor firms, can insure against **systemic risks**—*the risks of a problem happening to all parts of the economy simultaneously*. Mortgage-backed securities cannot protect you from a *national* housing market collapse. Systemic risks cannot be insured against because there is nothing against which to balance the risks. (Think of the problem as buying insurance against worldwide nuclear war. If it happens, even if you live, who will be around to pay you, and what would you spend the money on?) This problem, while fully understood by economists in theory, wasn't seriously considered as relevant in this case because systemic collapse was viewed as extremely unlikely. The national housing market had never before collapsed in the United States.

People are often slow to perceive systemic risks.

People are often slow to perceive systemic risks because individuals don't realize that their experience is shared by others. Systemic risks occur when a combination of hundreds of risks that normally offset each other begin to start moving together, as when the Tacoma Narrows Bridge collapsed, as discussed in Chapter 29. In the case of mortgage-backed securities, all the risks seemed to be covered, except for what appeared to be almost unthinkable, one-in-a-million risks. Unfortunately, the risks were interconnected (when one company went under, it pulled others with it), increasing general risk enormously, something that risk models did not take into account. This meant that when investment firm Lehman Brothers, which had been assumed infallible, failed, all the other firms that had relied on Lehman Brothers guaranteeing their loans also were in danger of failing. As that happened, the entire financial system started to sway, and we found ourselves in the worst financial crisis since the Great Depression.

How Do Economies Get Out of a Financial Crisis?

Now that we've reviewed what a financial crisis is and how economies can get into one, let's consider how they can get back out. The first thing we will note is that when the financial system collapses, and the economy falls into a deep recession or depression—or looks like it might be about to—the government is almost compelled to step in and help out. The strongest free market advocates might argue against more dramatic government interventions (though there is near-universal agreement that the Fed needs to at least serve as a lender of last resort). But the simple fact is that they're unlikely to win the political debate when a crisis actually hits. So the policy question is: What can a government do when a financial crisis has thrown the economy into a severe recession or even a depression?

Q-8 What are three stages of dealing with a financial crisis?

Economists' answer to this question is very similar to the answer a doctor would give to a patient who has a heart attack. First, stabilize the patient. We will call this the *triage* stage. In 2008 this involved a $700 billion financial bailout of banks in an attempt to prevent the entire financial system from collapsing. This bailout is similar to what a heart attack patient would get from an EMT at the scene of an accident or while in the ambulance on the way to the hospital. Financial triage often requires nonstandard policy. After, and if, you have stabilized the patient, you can turn to the *treatment* stage. This involves expansionary monetary and fiscal policy with all the nuances that go along with such policies. The third stage of treatment for a heart attack is the *rehabilitation* stage—setting up a physical regimen of exercise and diet that will prevent the patient from having future heart attacks. The process is similar for an economy. In this rehabilitation stage, one needs to develop new regulatory rules that prevent, or at least significantly reduce, the likelihood of future harmful economic bubbles.

These phases are better understood now than they were in the Great Depression. Let's begin with a brief summary of how the U.S. government dealt with the Great Depression, and how their actions fit into the three-stage response scheme of (1) triage,

(2) treatment, and (3) rehabilitation. I'll then talk about how the response to 2008 is proceeding and is likely to proceed going forward.

How the Government Responded to the Great Depression

On March 6, 1933—four years after the start of the Great Depression—newly inaugurated President Franklin D. Roosevelt and Congress took a series of completely unprecedented steps to try and shore up the financial system and get financial oil back in the economic engine. Among other things, they declared a national bank holiday, temporarily closing all banks so that no one could withdraw their deposits. This was *financial triage*—doing whatever it takes to prevent a complete and immediate collapse of financial markets. And it was reasonably successful: Runs on banks slowed considerably. But the economy was still extremely weak, and individuals and firms were still fearful of a future collapse.

Ineffective Monetary Policy in a Financial Crisis Even if triage is successful, the economy will still be weak, and the government will need to move into the second stage of its response: *treatment* of this weakness and malaise. Nowadays, we think of this treatment as consisting of *large* doses of the standard sort of expansionary monetary and fiscal policies you learned about in earlier chapters. But in the 1930s, monetary policy was the only game in town; the potential usefulness of fiscal stimulus was not yet well understood. Furthermore, although the government *did* try to employ expansionary monetary policy by dramatically expanding the monetary base, it had at best limited success. As I discussed above, the hoarding of cash by individuals and banks undermined the effectiveness of monetary policy. This is often called a **liquidity trap**—*a situation where people only want to hold liquid assets, and they would hold them even if they had to pay money to hold them.* When there is a liquidity trap, standard expansionary monetary policy of the sort you learned about in previous chapters does not work. The government increases the money supply, but it doesn't increase lending. It is like money trying to push a string.

Limited Fiscal Stimulus in the 1930s Depression It is often incorrectly believed that the set of government programs collectively known as the New Deal represented significant expansionary fiscal policies. In truth it did not. In fact, the prevailing wisdom about the government's role at the time—fully bought into by President Roosevelt—was that avoiding a deficit should be a priority. This severely limited the fiscal stimulus government tried to apply. (Besides, in the 1930s government expenditures as a percentage of GDP were much smaller than they are today, so they had less of an influence on the economy.) This is not to say the New Deal wasn't important. It is simply to say that it is probably best not thought of as a standard fiscal stimulus (it was way too small), but instead as an attempt to prevent the "expectational accelerator" from making the economy even worse by convincing workers that the government was on their side and doing whatever it could.

Since fiscal expansion was limited, and monetary expansion was ineffective, the "treatment" phase was quite modest in the Great Depression, and, not surprisingly, the economy stayed weak. It was only when the need to arm the country for World War II overrode concerns about the deficit in the late 1930s that a major fiscal expansion took place, and ultimately pulled the economy out of recession. In fact, the success of this wartime fiscal expansion in getting the economy back on track convinced many that fiscal stimulus has a key role to play in the treatment phase of responses to financial crises.

Establishing New Financial Regulation The third and final stage of response is the *rehabilitation stage*. In the 1930s, the government took great pains to set up systems and regulatory structures that could help prevent the financial markets from freezing up again in the future. Government set up rules for banks, what they could and could not do, and also set up a system of **deposit insurance**—*a system under which the federal government promised to stand by an individual's bank deposits*—and thereby help prevent future bank runs.

The moral hazard problem is a problem that arises when people don't have to bear the negative consequences of their actions.

Deposit insurance meant government-backed bank deposits, and thereby prevented bank runs. But in doing so, it also created a **moral hazard problem**—*a problem that arises when people don't have to bear the negative consequences of their actions*. Specifically, with deposit insurance, people can put their money into a bank that offers high interest rates and makes excessively risky loans without worrying they will lose their deposit. To offset that moral hazard problem, when the government established deposit insurance, it (1) established strict regulations of banks; (2) separated banks from other financial institutions; and (3) designed systems so that necessary financial transactions, which could not be allowed to fail, stayed within banks. These were included in a number of financial laws passed in the 1930s, the most important of which was known as the **Glass-Steagall Act**—*an act of Congress passed in 1933 that established deposit insurance and implemented a number of banking regulations.*

So after the depression, the United States had a highly regulated commercial banking system. The point of the regulations was to make commercial banking boring, and therefore safe. People called commercial banking the "3-6-3 business"—borrow at 3 percent, lend at 6 percent, and be on the golf course by 3:00 p.m. These regulations were implemented as a result of the Depression, in the belief that the government could never again let banks go under—they were too important to fail. And if they were too important to fail, they have to be regulated to mitigate moral hazard problems.

How the Government Responded to the 2008 Crisis

Let's now consider how the three stages of the response to the crises in 2008 were similar to, and differed from, the response in the 1930s.

Financial Triage in 2008 In both the 1930s and 2008 government engaged in financial triage, but it was much stronger and quicker in 2008. In part this was because of the lessons learned in the 1930s. But the interconnectedness of the modern financial system (through the blending of derivative securities) also made the problem potentially more serious in 2008 than in the 1930s.

Web Note 32.3
Quantitative Easing

When financial markets seemed to be seizing up in 2008, the Fed and the U.S. government took unprecedented actions to try to prevent a modern version of the "bank run" that had thrown the U.S. economy into a depression in the 1930s. Ben Bernanke, the chairman of the Fed, was an economic historian who had studied the 1930s and saw the parallels. Fearing the worst, he put aside "textbook" theory and started financial triage, doing whatever he could to provide liquidity to the system.

Generally, the actions can be divided into three general groupings: loans, guarantees of loans and financial instruments, and investments in financial institutions. Under these new policies, the government went far beyond standard monetary policy. It loaned billions to banks and insurance companies; it introduced **quantitative easing**—*nonstandard monetary policy designed to expand credit in the economy*. In 2008–09 this involved loaning out over a trillion dollars directly to the private sector through novel mechanisms. It also involved accepting lower-quality assets as collateral, opening its lending facilities to noncommercial banks, and directly purchasing short-term bonds from money market mutual funds. In addition, Congress passed legislation authorizing the Troubled Asset

Relief Program (or TARP), which permitted the Treasury to spend up to $700 billion to buy distressed assets and recapitalize financial institutions by investing directly in them.

All these triage actions were undertaken to prevent a complete meltdown of the U.S. financial system. Some felt it was too much; others felt it was too little. Both positions could be defended. The important point for this argument is that all these policies were emergency, or triage, policies, and have to be seen as such. Their goal was very short-run—to prevent a financial meltdown. One could get political consensus on them because a financial meltdown would throw the economy into a depression. If, when you are reading this, the economy is not in a depression, then they did their job.

As I stated above, even if the financial triage policy is a success, it can and generally will create other problems—some of which I'll come back to below. In any case, the economy will still be weak and heading into a serious recession (rather than the depression that would have happened in the absence of the triage policy). The economic downturn motivates the second stage of financial crisis response—treating the economy to get it out of the recession.

Fiscal and Monetary Stimulus in 2008 Some of the 2008 financial triage steps described above can also be thought of as the beginning of the treatment stage. In particular, Fed chairman Ben Bernanke and the Fed basically pulled out all the stops on the use of standard expansionary monetary policy. The Fed funds target rate was slashed to near zero and lending was expanded dramatically—essentially making monetary policy as expansionary as it could get. As in the 1930s—or in any major financial crisis—standard monetary policy can have only a limited impact on the economy. That's why the Fed introduced quantitative easing and nonstandard monetary policy, flooding the system with as much liquidity as it could.

The area where the policy response in 2008 differed most from the experience in the Great Depression was in the size of the fiscal expansion. In the 1930s, the government focused on balancing the budget. In 2008, policy makers were much less concerned about the deficit and the government ran strongly expansionary fiscal policy. In early 2008, it passed a small fiscal stimulus package and in early 2009, it passed a much larger $800 billion fiscal stimulus. This is the legacy of Keynesian macroeconomics, and shows how the policy model discussed in Chapters 27 and 28 influenced policy makers' views. While most economists supported some type of fiscal stimulus, there were also serious concerns about the size of the deficit that stimulus was causing because, ultimately, the government will have to deal with the growing debt.

Q-9 Did fiscal policy in the 1930s differ from fiscal policy in 2008?

Other countries moved quickly to pass fiscal stimulus packages as well. China started a $600 billion public works program and the European Union implemented a fiscal stimulus of more than $250 billion. Moreover, all countries made it clear that if their economies fell further into recession, they would expand their expansionary fiscal policies.

The Problem of Rehabilitation: Facing Withdrawal Pains

Assuming the economy has survived the initial triage, and that the government has done what it can to treat the economic downturn, the government next has to turn to the third stage—establishing an institutional structure that will prevent such things from happening in the future. This is the hardest of the three stages—how do you rehabilitate the economy? Rehabilitation involves both offsetting all the damage government has done in the triage and treatment stages and redesigning the system to see that the conditions that caused the problem are resolved. It is in this rehabilitation stage where the hard economic decisions have to be made and the "no free lunch" principle has to be dealt with.

The rehabilitation stage is the hardest of the three stages.

REAL-WORLD APPLICATION

Moral Hazard and Bailouts in the Backcountry

Many people choose to ski or ride in the backcountry, hiking (or helicoptering, or snowcatting) mountains that aren't owned by traditional resorts. It's supposed to be quite a rush, and it's a great way to ensure that you get fresh powder. But every year a few people have unfortunate accidents. If a skier is buried in an avalanche, or a snowboarder has hit a tree and needs rapid evacuation, all efforts are made to save him (yes, it's usually a him)—often at great expense to taxpayers.

The basic principle of the market says that with the freedom to backcountry ski should come the responsibility to pay for any costs of your own rescue—taxpayers shouldn't be on the hook for costs incurred by some reckless kid who wanted a thrill. But the simple fact is that many backcountry skiers and riders are young and (relatively) poor: They simply won't be able to pay for it, and taxpayers *will* be on the hook. Much as taxpayers might like to scare people away from the backcountry with *threats* of "no rescue" for people with no ability to pay, when push comes to shove, if someone is dying on the mountain and can be rescued, they're *going* to be rescued—and they know it, too. What is to be done?

There's no right answer to that question. But if rescues get sufficiently expensive, there is good reason to regulate backcountry skiing, say by banning it outright, or by requiring a backcountry ski license—or imposing jail time for violators.

Financial regulation is similar: The financial sector is so key to the economy that it's virtually certain to be bailed out after a major crisis, and it knows it. The question then becomes: What are the best regulations to prevent the costs of bailing it out from being too high?

The problem arises because when government is trying to save the economy from a collapse, it undertakes policies such as bailouts and creates enormous deficits with negative long-run consequences. It is like putting a patient on OxyContin—it eases the pain and helps him make it through the day, but it can leave him addicted. The same happens with economies. Most economists feel that in triage, bailouts to save the financial system are necessary. But they also recognize that those bailouts lead others to want bailouts, and can create an economy addicted to bailouts. Bailing out either directly in the triage stage or with monetary and fiscal stimulus policies in the treatment stage leads to two problems for the rehabilitation stage. The first is the **bad precedent problem**—*the problem that if you give a bailout to one, all want it*—and the second is the *moral hazard problem* discussed above—the problem that occurs when people don't have to bear the negative consequences of their actions.

Let consider two examples of the type problems that the triage policy creates. Let's first consider an example of the *bad precedent* problem. Soon after the financial bailout, the three U.S. automobile manufacturers came to the government asking for a bailout; their cars weren't selling and they were at risk of going bankrupt. They argued: You gave a bailout to Wall Street—the financial sector—why not also to Main Street—the manufacturing sector? Viewed in the proper light, this "why not us too" argument had little merit. The financial system was necessary to keep the entire economy functioning. It was too central to be allowed to fail.

Q-10 How can one justify bailouts for the financial sector and oppose bailouts for the automobile sector?

In contrast, most economists felt that losing the "big three" U.S.-based auto manufacturers would hurt, but wouldn't take the rest of the economy down with it. To put it in terms of the three stages of response to a financial crisis: Saving the financial sector is the whole point of the financial triage stage. Saving the auto industry is something different entirely. Perhaps it should be done, but if so, the automobile bailout should be viewed as part of the *treatment* stage—perhaps because saving the auto industry would be a particularly effective way of providing fiscal stimulus, or perhaps because having an automobile industry will be necessary for long-term growth of the U.S. economy.

Unfortunately, making U.S. automobile firms globally competitive in a sustainable manner is going to be very difficult. The automakers' long-run competitors are Asian firms such as the Indian firm Tata or the Chinese firm Chery. Their production costs are on the order of 40 percent less than those of existing U.S. or Japanese manufacturers! If U.S. auto firms are to be long-run competitive in an open global economy, they must meet that global competition, which will likely require cuts in costs far beyond what the government was pushing for. And if they don't, there will be calls for further bailouts because of the bad precedent set by a bailout now.

An example of the moral hazard problem that bailouts can cause in the rehabilitation stage can be seen by considering the effects of subsidizing loans for homeowners facing foreclosure. Suppose that, in 2006, you had prudently decided not to buy a house because you believed that houses were already significantly overpriced. Your foolish friend, on the other hand, bought into the "house prices always rise" myth and decided to buy a big McMansion that he could not really afford. You were prudent and your friend was foolish, and he's under water on his house and facing foreclosure. Now suppose the government comes along and bails him out. What's the outcome? He ends up with a nice house and you end up with nothing. Who's foolish now? The belief that the government will bail people and firms out when they make stupid decisions helped create the crisis in the first place, and any bailout now will likely lead people to expect a bailout in the future. They will then choose to follow risky strategies, potentially creating even larger problems in the future. So the bailout rewards precisely the wrong type of behavior, and hence creates a moral hazard problem for future decisions.

Bailouts reward precisely the wrong type of behavior, and hence create a moral hazard problem.

The above arguments have many variations; I can't go through them all here, but these two should give you a sense of the types of problems that the bailouts in the triage and stimulus stages present for the long run. They have major long-run costs and, in most economists' minds, can only be justified in the triage and treatment stages if they were absolutely necessary to keep the economy from imploding.

Establishing Appropriate Financial Regulatory Rules

As the government is dealing with offsetting the addictive effects of the triage and treatment policies, it must also figure out how to change the rules of the game so that such crises don't happen again. That will not be easy. First, politics, not what's good for the economy, is likely to guide regulations. Second, even if the government establishes the appropriate regulation for 2010, those regulations will likely no longer be appropriate 5 or 10 years in the future. The reason why can be called the **law of diminishing control,** which holds that *whenever a regulatory system is set up, individuals or firms being regulated will figure out ways to circumvent those regulations*. The result is that any regulation will become less effective over time.

The law of diminishing control is that whenever a regulatory system is set up, individuals or firms being regulated will figure out ways to circumvent those regulations.

That's what happened with the earlier Glass-Steagall regulations that the government set up in the wake of the 1930s depression; those regulations gradually lost their effectiveness. While the regulations contained risk by keeping the "core" of the banking system within a well-regulated commercial banking sector, they did not contain risk in the broader financial sector, and the riskier investments simply moved over to that broader financial sector. But over the 1970s and 1980s, the commercial bank business model was undermined as non-commercial banking institutions found ways to take over some of the key aspects of commercial banking's traditional turf. For example, savings banks began issuing what were called NOW (negotiable order of withdrawal) accounts to get around a government regulation that prohibited banks from paying interest on checking accounts. NOW accounts allow savings banks to pay high interest on savings deposits and allow customers to negotiate withdrawals (let people pay for their goods with these NOW accounts). These withdrawals looked almost identical to checks from a commercial bank. But since they were legally considered to be savings accounts, they avoided regulations prohibiting interest on checking accounts. Money flowed out of commercial banks—which were not allowed to pay interest on their accounts—and into savings banks. Other financial institutions developed products like money market accounts and mutual fund accounts, which also let depositors write checks on their holdings of bonds and even stocks.

Commercial banks' central role in the economy was further eroded as nonbank financial firms developed new ways to bypass commercial banks and borrow money directly from the public. For example, they started issuing their own short-term bonds, known as *commercial paper*. These were typically arranged by investment banks, who sold them directly to investors, bypassing banks entirely.

As these new financial instruments developed, regulated commercial banks lost business to unregulated financial institutions. Thus, what had been a protective umbrella over the necessary financial system covered a smaller and smaller portion of the entire system. The commercial banking system was still regulated, but the "financial oil" increasingly flowed through the less regulated parts of the financial infrastructure.

This shift was compounded by the fact that financial markets were becoming global, and the U.S. regulations only controlled U.S. financial institutions. This reduced the ability of the United States to strictly regulate many financial institutions, who could legitimately threaten to move to those countries that offered the least regulation. (Think of it as a child of divorced parents, who plays one parent off the other to get the least regulation.)

Another reason regulation becomes less effective over time is that if regulation is successful, people begin to forget that it was ever necessary and will lobby to dismantle the regulations. For example, in the 1930s the financial crisis changed the population's view of the market and government. It moved them to favor regulation. But as decades passed and societal memories of the Great Depression faded, so did that view. Regulation and regulators were increasingly viewed by many as an undesirable hindrance of the free market and all its magic. This meant that relatively low-paid regulators were faced with the nearly impossible task of balancing the pressures from changing technologies making the old regulations obsolete, with the need to get *some* regulation within an atmosphere that saw regulation as preventing our economy from growing.

An inherent problem of regulation is the "too-big-to-fail problem."

An inherent problem of regulation is the "too big to fail problem," which is another example of the moral hazard problem. If individuals in the financial sector recognize the financial sector's importance to the economy and know that the government will be forced to bail them out, it changes their behavior, just like your kids' behavior changes when they know you'll bail them out. They do stupid things. The problem with kids, and with large banks, is that when you threaten them that you aren't going to bail them out, the threat isn't credible. It takes resolve that I, and most governments, don't have. (Note to my children—my wife has that resolve.) Unless one has that resolve, any threat is not going to be credible, which means that kids and businesses (of soft parents and soft governments) will continue to do stupid things—they won't take the full consequences of their actions into account.

General Principles of Regulation

The basic principle of the market is that along with freedom to undertake activities in the market comes responsibility for one's actions.

In the rehabilitation stage after a financial crisis, the government must somehow get the market part of the economy to face the basic principle of the market: Along with freedom to undertake activities in the market comes responsibility for one's actions.

If firms (or kids) are not, and cannot be made, responsible for the negative consequences of their actions, there is a role for regulations to restrict the set of actions firms are permitted to take. Regulation is necessary if a bailout is in the cards. (As I tell my kids—the golden rule of economics is: Him who pays the bills makes the rules.)

The golden rule of economics is: Him who pays the bills makes the rules.

The question policy makers face in trying to design the rules and regulations for our economy in the future is: Can a government influenced by special interests institute the right type of regulation? Economists come to different answers on this question, which is why they have different views of regulation.

Let's close our discussion of regulation and the rehabilitation stage with three general precepts about dealing with financial crises that most economists would sign on to. They are:

- Set as few bad precedents as possible. In the triage and treatment stages, you may undertake policies to keep the economy alive that create long-run problems. Recognize that, and try to offset them as best you can.
- Deal with moral hazard. If a firm or individual is to be unregulated, it should be subject to the consequences of its actions. This leads to a corollary: If a firm or individual is considered too big to fail, it has to be regulated. Notice that this rule does not say that government should or should not regulate. It just says that it has to be consistent.
- Deal with the law of diminishing control. Regulation has to be considered a process, not a one-time decision. The economy is a dynamic changing entity, subject to the law of diminishing control, which means that when technology changes, rules must change. Expect that, and if government has regulations, have a method of changing those regulations to adapt to the changing situation.

Conclusion

The financial crisis provides a good sense of the way in which economic models should be applied in reality. Models cannot be applied mechanically, without attention to the specifics. Are things that the model assumed constant staying constant? If not, how does that change the model? Is it time to focus on standard precepts, or is it time to throw all the standard precepts out because the situation has changed?

The way in which models are to be used is probably best captured in continuation of the quotation from Keynes that began the chapter:

> Economics is a science of thinking in terms of models joined to the art of choosing models which are relevant to the contemporary world. It is compelled to be this, because, unlike the typical natural science, the material to which it is applied is, in too many respects, not homogeneous through time. The object of a model is to segregate the semi-permanent or relatively constant factors from those which are transitory or fluctuating so as to develop a logical way of thinking about the latter, and of understanding the time sequences to which they give rise in particular cases.

In this quotation, Keynes made the importance of judgment clear. His point, and the point that I have tried to emphasize throughout this book, is that economics provides no mechanical answer to problems. This means that an economist must choose among many models, explaining how on the one hand this might happen, but how, on the other hand, something else might happen. In a debate, one of Keynes' critics is reported to have challenged Keynes' tendency to change his mind as he applied different models to problems. In this, possibly apocryphal, story, Keynes shut him up by saying, "When the facts change, I change. What do you do, sir?"

Summary

- The financial sector provides the credit that all other sectors need for both day-to-day and long-term needs. If the financial sector were to collapse, all other sectors would crash along with it.
- The stages of a financial crisis are (1) a bubble forms, (2) the bubble bursts, and (3) the financial sector collapses. A depression may follow.
- The two ingredients of a bubble are herding and leveraging. Herding creates the run up in prices. Leveraging increases people's ability to herd, which further increases prices.
- When the market experiences a shock that leads to higher prices, extrapolative price expectations can lead to an upward-sloping effective demand curve and a bubble.
- Herding and leverage also work in reverse, but with greater speed. As prices decline, lenders call in loans, which makes people sell their assets, which leads to greater declines in prices.
- In a depression model with extrapolative expectations, there can be an upward-sloping effective demand curve.
- Nonsystemic risk is a risk that is caused by the occurrence of one local event. Nonsystemic risks can be covered by an offsetting event elsewhere. Systemic risk is a risk of an event that affects the entire system and cannot be offset.
- The three stages of responding to a financial crisis are (1) triage, (2) treatment, and (3) rehabilitation.
- Triage and treatment of financial crises typically have bad side effects like the bad precedent and moral hazard problems.
- The law of diminishing control is the observation that after a regulation is implemented, as time progresses, it becomes less and less effective because firms find ways around the regulations.

Key Terms

bad precedent problem *(770)*
bubble *(755)*
deposit insurance *(768)*
diversification *(760)*
extrapolative expectations *(757)*
Glass-Steagall Act *(768)*
herding *(757)*
law of diminishing control *(771)*
leverage *(757)*
liquidity *(760)*
liquidity trap *(767)*
moral hazard problem *(768)*
mortgage-backed securities *(760)*
nonsystemic risk *(765)*
quantitative easing *(768)*
systemic risk *(766)*

Questions and Exercises

connect ECONOMICS

1. Why are policy makers more concerned about the financial market than other markets such as the automobile or computer markets? LO1
2. Why is trust important to the functioning of the economy? LO1
3. True or false? The 1929 stock market crash is the single cause of the Great Depression. Explain. LO2
4. How did depositors' loss of trust in banks contribute to the depression? LO2
5. What are the two ingredients that caused the stock market bubble in 1920 and early 2000s? LO3
6. What is the shape of the effective demand curve in a market with a bubble? LO4
7. How do extrapolative expectations contribute to the shape of the demand curve in a market with a bubble? LO4
8. What is leveraging? LO4
9. How is the effect of leveraging on stock prices like the process of money creation? LO4
10. What does it mean to securitize a loan? LO5
11. How do mortgage-backed securities provide both diversification and liquidity? LO5

12. How does leverage work in reverse to hasten the bursting of a bubble? LO4
13. How does a decline in aggregate demand in the depression model lead to a spiraling decline in the price level and output? LO4
14. What are the three stages of dealing with a financial crisis? LO6
15. What policy actions are involved in each of the three stages of dealing with a financial crisis? LO6
16. What are three financial triage actions government took in response to the financial crisis in 2008? LO6
17. What is the moral hazard problem and what does it have to do with banking? LO6
18. What is the law of diminishing control? LO7
19. What is the bad precedent problem in relation to financial bubbles? LO7
20. What is the "too big to fail" problem? LO7

Questions from Alternative Perspectives

1. To what extent are government interventions and the anticipation of such interventions responsible for the crisis of 2008? (Austrian)
2. While there were economic "hiccups" between the Great Depression and the crisis of 2008, there were no major financial crises and reasonably steady economic growth for over six decades—the longest crisis-free spell in U.S. history. What institutions did the Great Depression change that might have contributed to this long crisis-free spell? (Institutionalist)
3. Who generally benefits from a bubble and who is usually most hurt when a bubble bursts? (Radical)
4. Post-Keynesians such as Hyman Minsky had been warning of a financial crisis such as the one we recently experienced for years. Why do you think they weren't listened to? (Post-Keynesian)
5. In what way might a recession or a depression actually make society better off? (Religious)

Issues to Ponder

1. How can economists support a bailout package when they recognize that the bailout will create a moral hazard problem? LO7
2. If you have a son whom you have forbidden to drink and drive, threatening to throw him out of the house, if he does actually drink and drive, do you throw him out of the house? LO7
3. In what sense is the financial crisis a result of deregulation? LO7

Answers to Margin Questions

1. False. This is not necessarily true. It can reflect a decline in nominal wealth, not real wealth. (754)
2. Two central ingredients of a bubble are herding and leverage. (757)
3. With extrapolative expectations, the demand curve shifts due to the adjustment process. This means that the effective demand curve will be flatter than the "other things constant" demand curve and it may even be upward-sloping if the extrapolative expectations are powerful enough. (758)
4. You will earn $11 on an investment of $10, which makes your rate of return 110 percent. (758)
5. Two advantages of securitization are diversification and liquidity. (760)
6. Standard expansionary monetary policy might not expand the economy if banks simply hold extra reserves because they don't feel safe lending out the money. (763)
7. Systemic risks cannot be insured against. (766)
8. The three stages of dealing with a financial crisis are triage, treatment, and rehabilitation. (766)
9. Yes, it was used much more in 2008. (769)
10. Financial sectors can be justified because of the financial sector's central role in the economy. If it fails, other sectors will fail as well; it is like oil to a gasoline engine. The automobile sector is important, but it does not have that same central role. (770)

Inflation and the Phillips Curve

The first few months or years of inflation, like the first few drinks, seem just fine. Everyone has more money to spend and prices aren't rising quite as fast as the money that's available. The hangover comes when prices start to catch up.

—**Milton Friedman**

Politicians tend to get reelected when the economy is doing well. Thus, it should not surprise you that political pressures exert a strong bias toward lowering taxes and increasing spending, and expanding the money supply. What prevents politicians and the Fed from implementing expansionary policies is inflation, or at least the fear of generating an accelerating inflation. It is for that reason that inflation and its relationship to unemployment and growth come to center stage in any discussion of macro policy. Hence this chapter. It extends our earlier consideration of inflation and considers the trade-offs between inflation, unemployment, and growth.

AFTER READING THIS CHAPTER, YOU SHOULD BE ABLE TO:

1. State some of the distributional effects of inflation.
2. Explain how inflation expectations are formed.
3. Outline the quantity theory of money and its theory of inflation.
4. Outline the institutionalist theory of inflation.
5. Differentiate between long-run and short-run Phillips curves.
6. Explain the different views on the relationship between inflation and growth.

Some Basics about Inflation

I introduced you to inflation in an earlier chapter. There, you saw the definition of *inflation* (a continuous rise in the price level) and how inflation is measured (with price indexes). I also explained that expectations of inflation can become built into individuals' behavior and economic institutions and cause a small inflation to accelerate, and that inflation creates feelings of injustice and destroys the informational value of prices and the market. (If any of those concepts seem a bit vague to you, a review might be a good idea.) I now build on that information to give you more insight into inflation.

The Distributional Effects of Inflation

Who wins and who loses in an inflation? The answer to that is simple: The winners are people who can raise their wages or prices and still keep their jobs or sell their goods. The losers are people who can't raise their wages or prices or who lose their jobs because their wage is too high. Consider a worker who has entered a contract to receive 4 percent annual wage increases for three years. If the worker expected inflation to be 2 percent at the time of the agreement, she was expecting her real wage to rise 2 percent each year. If instead inflation is 6 percent, her real wage will *fall* 2 percent. The worker loses, but the firm gains because it can charge 4 percent more for its products than it anticipated. The worker's wage was fixed by contract, but the firm could raise its prices. On average, winners and losers balance out; inflation does not make the population richer or poorer. Most people, however, worry about their own position, not what happens to the average person.

Q-1 True or false? Inflation makes an economy poorer. Explain your answer.

Lenders and borrowers, because they often enter into fixed nominal contracts, are also affected by inflation. If lenders make loans at 5 percent interest and expect inflation to be 2 percent, they plan to earn a 3 percent real rate of return on their loan. If, however, inflation turns out to be 4 percent, lenders will only earn a 1 percent real rate of return, and borrowers, who were expecting to pay a real interest rate of 3 percent, end up paying only 1 percent. Lenders will lose; borrowers will gain. In other words, unexpected inflation redistributes income from lenders to borrowers.

Unexpected inflation redistributes income from lenders to borrowers.

The composition of the group winning or losing from inflation changes over time. For example, before 1975, people on Social Security and pensions lost out during inflation since Social Security and pensions were, on the whole, fixed in nominal terms. Inflation lowered recipients' real income. Starting in 1975 Social Security payments and many pensions were changed to adjust automatically for changes in the cost of living, so Social Security recipients are no longer losers. Their real income is independent of inflation. (Actually, because of the adjustment method, some say that Social Security recipients actually now gain from inflation since the adjustment more than compensates them for the rise in the price level.)

What we can say about the distributional consequences of inflation is that people who don't expect inflation or who are tied to fixed nominal contracts will likely lose during an inflationary period. However, if these people are rational, they probably won't let it happen again; they'll be prepared for a subsequent inflation. That is, they will change their expectations of inflation.

Expectations of Inflation

Expectations of inflation play a key role in the inflationary process. When expectations of inflation are high, people tend to raise their wages and prices, causing inflation. So, in fact, expectations can become self-fulfilling. Because of the importance of expectations in perpetuating, and perhaps even in creating, inflation, economists have looked carefully at how individuals form expectations. Almost all economists believe that the expectations that people have of inflation are in some sense rational, by which I mean they are based on the best information available, given the cost of that information. But economists differ on what is meant by rational and thus on how those expectations are formed. Some economists argue that rational people will expect the same inflation that is predicted by the economists' model. That is, they form **rational expectations**—*the expectations that the economists' model predicts*. If inflation was, say, 2 percent last year and is 4 percent this year, but the economists' model predicts 0 percent inflation for the coming year, individuals will rationally expect 0 percent inflation.

WWW Web Note 33.1 Forecasting Inflation

Other economists argue that rational expectations cannot be defined in terms of economists' models. These economists instead focus on the process by which people develop their expectations. One way people form expectations is to look at conditions that already exist, or have recently existed. Such expectations are called **adaptive expectations**—*expectations based in some way on the past*. Thus, if inflation was 2 percent last year and 4 percent this year, the prediction for inflation will be somewhere around 3 percent. Adaptive expectations aren't the only type that people use. Sometimes they use **extrapolative expectations**—*expectations that a trend will continue*. For example, say that inflation was 2 percent last year and 4 percent this year; extrapolative expectations

ADDED DIMENSION

Deflation

The low inflation of the early 2000s brought fear of a new problem—deflation (a sustained fall in the price level). Deflation is the opposite of inflation and is associated with a number of problems in the economy. One problem is that it may prevent the central bank from lowering the real interest rate as much as it wants to, since with deflation the real interest rate is the sum of the nominal interest rate and the rate of deflation. Thus, if the nominal interest rate is 2 percent and the rate of deflation is 3 percent, the real interest rate is 5 percent. But because people can always hold money rather than bonds, the nominal interest rate cannot fall below 0 percent. Since in a deflationary economy the real interest rate is higher than the nominal interest rate, deflation places a limit on how low the Fed can push the real interest rate. For example, the Fed cannot achieve a goal of 1 percent for real interest rates when the rate of deflation is 3 percent. Even if it lowers the nominal interest rate to 0 percent—the lowest level it can—the Fed cannot reduce the real rate of interest below 3 percent—the rate of deflation. This means that monetary policy might not be able to lower interest rates enough to stimulate the economy as much as desired.

Another problem of deflation is that it is often associated with large falls in asset prices—specifically stock and real estate prices. Declines in these asset prices can cause serious problems for an economy for two reasons. First, as people see their wealth evaporating, they may cut their current spending, which can decrease aggregate demand and slow the economy. Second, since these assets often serve as collateral for loans, large falls in asset prices can make many financial institutions' liabilities exceed their assets, causing them to become insolvent. Thus, deflation can undermine a country's financial system. This happened in the early 2000s in Japan, making it difficult for the Japanese government to stimulate its economy. It left the Japanese government wondering how to save its banking system from a large-scale default because such a default would totally undermine any recovery efforts. The same thing happened to the United States in late 2008.

Q-2 Name three different types of expectations.

would predict 6 percent inflation next year. These are only three of the many reasonable ways people form expectations. Because there is no one economic model that predicts the economy perfectly, there is no way of specifying one rational expectation; there are only reasonable expectations. Individuals use various ways of forming expectations, often shifting suddenly from one way to another.

Since expectations play a key role in policy, shifts in the process of forming expectations can change the way the economy operates. It was precisely such a shift in the formation of expectations that played a key role in the late 1990s, when the economy expanded significantly without generating inflation. Sometime in the early 1990s in the United States, individuals stopped expecting high inflation (which, at the time, meant inflation greater than about 6 percent) and began expecting low inflation (which, at the time, meant inflation lower than 2 percent), and those expectations became self-fulfilling. The United States continued to have relatively low inflation through the early 2000s.[1] In early 2008, oil and food prices jumped, and many people expected inflation to increase. However, in late 2008, the economy fell into a serious recession, and oil and food prices fell, quelling fear of immediate inflation. But fear remained that when the economy comes out of the recession, oil and food prices would rise once again.

[1]The meaning of the terms "high inflation" and "low inflation" can change over time as people's beliefs about what is "normal inflation" change. This means that the terms high and low, which we will use throughout the chapter, must be interpreted in the context of the time and country being talked about. In the United States in 2008, inflation under 2 percent was still considered low, but because inflation had been within the lower range for a few years, what was considered "high inflation" had changed; in 2008 inflation over 4 percent was considered high. In developing countries, where inflation has often exceeded 50 percent, "high" and "low" inflation have quite different meanings from "high" and "low" inflations in developed countries; for example, 15 percent inflation could be considered low in a developing country.

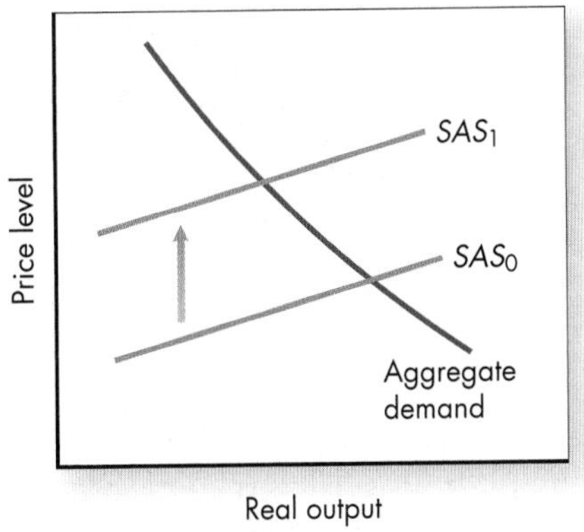

FIGURE 33-1
Nominal Wages, Productivity, and Inflation
When nominal wages increase by more than the growth of productivity, the SAS curve shifts up, resulting in inflation. When nominal wages increase by less than the growth of productivity, the SAS curve shifts down, resulting in deflation.

Productivity, Inflation, and Wages

Two key measures that policy makers use to determine whether inflation may be coming are changes in productivity and changes in wages. Together these measures determine whether or not the short-run aggregate supply curve will be shifting up. The rule of thumb is that wages can increase by the amount that productivity increases without generating any inflationary pressure:

$$\text{Inflation} = \text{Nominal wage increase} - \text{Productivity growth}$$

Inflation = Nominal wage increase − Productivity growth

For example, if productivity is increasing at 2 percent, as it has been in the early 2000s, wages can go up by 2 percent without generating any inflationary pressure. Let's consider another example—the mid-1970s, when productivity growth slowed to 1 percent while wages went up by 6 percent. Inflation was 6 percent − 1 percent = 5 percent.

You probably recognize this relationship from an earlier chapter. This is the same relationship that explains how the short-run aggregate supply curve shifts. When nominal wages increase by more than the growth of productivity, the SAS curve shifts up as shown in Figure 33-1, resulting in inflation. When nominal wages increase by less than the growth of productivity, the SAS curve shifts down, resulting in deflation (a sustained fall in the price level).

Theories of Inflation

Economists hold two slightly different theories of inflation: the quantity theory and the institutional theory. The quantity theory emphasizes the connection between money and inflation; the institutional theory emphasizes the relationship between market structure and price-setting institutions and inflation. The two theories overlap significantly, but because they come to different policy conclusions, it is helpful to consider them separately.

The Quantity Theory of Money and Inflation

The quantity theory of money can be summed up in one sentence: *Inflation is always and everywhere a monetary phenomenon.* If the money supply rises, the price level will rise. If the money supply doesn't rise, the price level won't rise. Forget all the other stuff—it just obscures the connection between money and inflation.

In the quantity theory model, inflation is caused by growth in the money supply. It focuses on the equation of exchange:
$MV = PQ$

The Equation of Exchange The quantity theory of money centers on the **equation of exchange,** *an equation stating that the quantity of money times the velocity of money equals the price level times the quantity of real goods sold.* This equation is

$$MV = PQ$$

where:

M = Quantity of money
V = Velocity of money
P = Price level
Q = Quantity of real goods sold

The Quantity Theory of Money

Q is the real output of the economy (real GDP) and P is the price level, so PQ is the economy's nominal output (nominal GDP). V, the **velocity of money,** is *the number of times per year, on average, a dollar goes around to generate a dollar's worth of income.* Put another way, velocity is the amount of income per year generated by a dollar of money. Since $MV = PQ$, MV also equals nominal output. Thus, if there's \$100 of money in the economy and velocity is 20, nominal GDP is \$2,000. We can calculate V by dividing nominal GDP by the money supply. Let's take the United States as an example. In the United States in 2009, nominal GDP was approximately \$14 trillion and M was approximately \$1,500 billion (using M_1), so velocity (GDP/M) was about 9, meaning each dollar in the economy circulated enough to support approximately \$9 in total income.

Velocity Is Constant The equation of exchange is a tautology, meaning it is true by definition. What changes it from a tautology to the quantity theory are three assumptions. The first assumption is that velocity remains constant (or changes at a predictable rate). Money is spent only so fast; how fast is determined by the economy's institutional structure, such as how close individuals live to stores, how people are paid (weekly, biweekly, or monthly), and what sources of credit are available. (Can you go to the store and buy something on credit, that is, without handing over cash?) This institutional structure changes slowly, quantity theorists argue, so velocity won't fluctuate very much. Next year, velocity will be approximately the same as this year.

If velocity can be predicted, the quantity theory can be used to predict how much nominal GDP will grow if we know how much the money supply grows. For example, if the money supply goes up 6 percent and velocity is predicted to be constant, the quantity theory of money predicts that nominal GDP will go up by 6 percent.

Something that is determined outside the model is called autonomous.

Real Output Is Independent of the Money Supply The second assumption is that Q is independent of the money supply. That is, Q is autonomous, meaning real output is determined by forces outside those forces in the quantity theory. If Q grows, it is because of factors that affect the real economy. Thus, policy analysis about the real economy based on the quantity theory focuses on the real economy—the supply side of the economy, not the demand side.

Three assumptions of quantity theory:

1. Velocity is constant.
2. Real output is independent of money supply.
3. Causation goes from money to prices.

This assumption makes analyzing the economy a lot easier than if the financial and real sectors are interrelated and if real economic activity is influenced by financial changes. It separates two puzzles: how the real economy works and how the price level and financial sector work. Instead of having two different jigsaw puzzles all mixed up, each puzzle can be worked separately. The quantity theory doesn't say there aren't interconnections between the real and financial sectors, but it does say that most of these interconnections involve short-run considerations. The quantity theory is primarily concerned with the long run.

Q-3 What's the difference between the equation of exchange and the quantity theory of money?

Causation Goes from Money to Prices With both V (velocity) and Q (quantity of output) unaffected by changes in M (money supply), the only thing that can change is P (price level). Given the two assumptions so far, either prices or money could be the

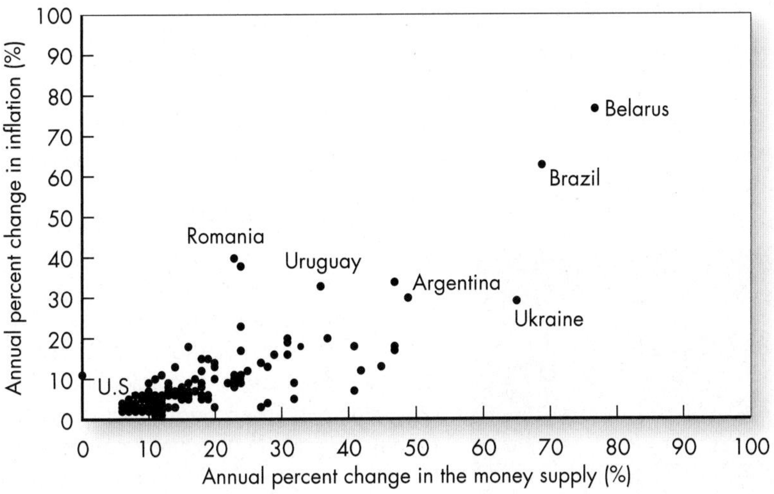

FIGURE 33-2
Inflation and Money Growth, 1960–2007

The empirical evidence that supports the quantity theory of money is most convincing in countries that experience significant inflation. Belarus and Brazil are examples where high money growth has accompanied high rates of inflation.

Source: Federal Reserve Bank of Minneapolis. Update by David Altig, Federal Reserve Bank of Atlanta.

driving force. The quantity theory makes the additional assumption that causation goes from money to prices.

With these three assumptions, the equation of exchange becomes the quantity theory of money:

$$M\overline{V} \rightarrow P\overline{Q}$$

In its simplest terms, the **quantity theory of money** says that *the price level varies in response to changes in the quantity of money*. Another way to write the quantity theory of money is: $\%\Delta M \rightarrow \%\Delta P$. If the money supply goes up 20 percent, prices go up 20 percent. If the money supply goes down 5 percent, the price level goes down 5 percent.

Q-4 According to the quantity theory of money, what should the Fed do to lower inflation?

Examples of Money's Role in Inflation As you can see in Figure 33-2, which plots inflation against the money supply for 110 countries from 1960 to 2007, there is a relationship between money supply growth and inflation. The connection between growth in the money supply and inflation is especially evident for large inflations such as in Belarus, Brazil, and Argentina. For example, in Belarus inflation and money supply growth were both growing at about 80 percent per year. Russia in the 1990s, when the Russian government was forced to print enormous amounts of money to pay its bills, is another example. As a result, in both cases inflation blew up into hyperinflation.

In Figure 33-2, you can also see a large cluster of countries where inflation is below 10 percent. When inflation is 10 percent or below, the relationship in the short run between money and inflation isn't so clear. Consider the United States. Beginning in the mid-1970s, both inflation and money supply rose, with inflation exceeding 8 percent in some years. Inflation remained high for about six years and people began to expect that the high inflation would continue. However, in late 1979 and the early 1980s, the Fed began to fight inflation by decreasing the growth of the money supply significantly. But initially inflation did not decline; instead, unemployment jumped from 7 to 10 percent and inflation remained high. So the short-run connection between inflation and money did not exist. Eventually inflation did fall—to 4 percent in 1984 and to below 2 percent in the early 2000s—even though the money supply kept growing quite fast. It was only in early 2008 when inflation increased to more than 4 percent that people got worried that inflation would return. Their worry quickly subsided as the economy fell into a severe recession in late fall 2008.

ADDED DIMENSION

The Keeper of the Classical Faith: Milton Friedman

One of the most important economists of the 20th century is Milton Friedman, who died in 2006 at the age of 94. In macroeconomics, Friedman is best known for his support of the quantity theory.

By most accounts, Friedman was a headstrong student. He didn't simply accept the truths his teachers laid out. If he didn't agree, he argued strongly for his own belief. He was very bright, and his ideas were generally logical and convincing. He needed to be both persistent and intelligent to maintain and promote his views in spite of strong opposition.

Nobel Prize Winner Milton Friedman

Throughout the Keynesian years of the 1950s and 1960s, Friedman stood up and argued for the quantity theory, keeping it alive. During this period, Classical economics was called *monetarism,* and because Friedman was such a strong advocate of the quantity theory, he was considered the leader of the monetarists.

Friedman argued that fiscal policy simply didn't work. It led to expansions in the size of government. He also opposed an activist monetary policy. The effects of monetary policy, he said, were too variable for it to be useful in guiding the economy. He called for a steady growth in the money supply, and argued consistently for a laissez-faire policy by government.

Friedman has made his mark in both microeconomics and macroeconomics. In the 1970s, his ideas caught hold and helped spawn a renewal of the quantity theory. He was awarded the Nobel Prize in economics in 1976.

The quantity theory view that printing money causes inflation is seen in this 18th-century satirical drawing.

Germany is another example. In the early 1990s, the German central bank felt Germany's inflation was too high. It cut the growth of the money supply considerably. The German economy fell into recession and remained in that recession through 1996. Again, inflation eventually did fall, but not until the late 1990s. Experiences like this are why economists emphasize that *there can be a long and variable lag in the connection between money growth and inflation.* For inflations below 10 percent, then, the policy maker's conventional wisdom is that, in the short run, a change in money supply growth initially affects output and only later, possibly, does it affect inflation.

Why Central Banks Increase the Money Supply If the connection between large increases in the money supply and inflation is so well known, you may well be wondering why some central banks continue to increase the money supply at such high rates. Consider Zimbabwe, which has had inflation well above 1,000 percent through much of the early 2000s and over 2,000,000 percent in 2008. Why doesn't the central bank simply stop increasing the money supply? The answer lies in the political structure of the country and the failure of the government to control spending. The Zimbabwe government is running huge budget deficits. To pay for the goods it is buying, it has to issue bonds, but no one wants to buy the bonds. If the government cannot sell its bonds, it will be in default, which would result in what many believe would be a complete breakdown of the economy. So the central bank of Zimbabwe has chosen to buy the bonds, which it does by printing money. So the underlying cause of the inflation in Zimbabwe is really the government budget deficit, which forces the central bank to buy the bonds to finance the deficit, which in turn leads to hyperinflation.

Financing the deficit by expansionary monetary policy is not costless. The inflation that results from the increases in the money supply works as a type of tax on individuals and is often called an **inflation tax** *(an implicit tax on the holders of cash and the holders of any obligations specified in nominal terms)*. Inflation is considered a tax because it reduces the value of cash and other nominal obligations.

REAL-WORLD APPLICATION

A New Inflation Equation?

The quantity theory has not done such a good job of predicting inflation in recent years, which has sent economists out searching for the reasons why. One reason is that financial innovations have caused the velocity of money to change in ways that cannot be easily predicted, making it impossible to predict inflation based on money supply growth. A second reason is globalization, which has changed the nature of competitive institutions. To take account of that globalization, researchers at the Federal Reserve Bank of Dallas have developed a new variation of the quantity theory that considers how globalization affects the relationship between money and inflation, and output growth. They find that inflation varies inversely with output growth not only in the domestic economy, but also with output growth of the global economy. This means that even if the domestic money supply increases and domestic output doesn't grow much, if global output is increasing significantly, then the result will not be significant domestic inflation.

The relative importance of domestic and global output depends on country size, consumers' preference for domestic goods, ease of substitution of domestic for foreign goods, and the ability of a country to redeploy its workers who face global competition. Dallas Fed researchers argue that "had we understood the links between foreign output growth, trade, and inflation, we might have contemplated the booming 1990s with less anxiety about inflation."

The revised equation is still a work in progress, but it shows the way that economists work—they continually test their models against the empirical evidence, and when the models and evidence don't match, they work on modifying the models in a reasonable way to make them match.

The point of this example is that central banks know that issuing large quantities of money will cause inflation. What they don't know, and what the policy discussions are about, is whether it's worse to have the inflation or the unpleasant alternatives of a recession, or perhaps even a breakdown of the entire economy. Thus, the debate about monetary policy is not about whether the inflation is caused by the issuance of too much money, but whether countries' budget deficits can be ended.

Q-5 Why do some central banks issue large quantities of money if they know that doing so will cause inflation?

The Institutional Theory of Inflation

The alternative to the quantity theory is the institutional theory of inflation. Supporters of the institutional theory of inflation accept much of the quantity theory—money and inflation do move together. Where they differ is in what they see as the cause and the effect. According to the quantity theory of money, changes in the money supply cause changes in the price level. The direction of causation goes from left to right:

$$MV \rightarrow PQ$$

Q-6 Use the equation of exchange to demonstrate the difference between the quantity theory and the institutional theory of inflation.

Institutional theorists see it the other way around. Increases in prices force government to increase the money supply or cause unemployment. The direction of causation goes from right to left:

$$MV \leftarrow PQ$$

According to the institutional theory of inflation, the source of inflation is in the price-setting process of firms. When setting prices, firms and individuals find it easier to raise prices than to lower them and do not take into account the effect of their pricing decisions on the price level.

The institutional theory of inflation focuses on the institutional and structural aspects of an economy, as well as the money supply, as important causes of inflation.

Put slightly differently, the institutional theory sees the nominal wage- and price-setting process as generating inflation. As one group pushes up its nominal wage or

REAL-WORLD APPLICATION

Inflation Targeting

One of the big debates about Fed policy concerns whether the Fed should preannounce a policy about what it will do if inflation is at different levels. Such announcements are known as inflation targeting. With inflation targeting, the Fed commits itself to tightening the money supply and raising interest rates if inflation exceeds a certain level. Advocates of inflation targeting argue that it provides better assurances for investors that the central bank will fight inflation, and thus holds inflationary expectations down. They point to the success of countries such as New Zealand, which introduced inflation targeting in 1989 when a law was passed that required the Reserve Bank of New Zealand to keep consumer price inflation between 0 and 3 percent a year, a target agreed on by the government and the central bank. After averaging 10 percent a year in the 1980s, New Zealand's inflation rate fell in the early 1990s and averaged below 3 percent per year thereafter.

Advocates of inflation targeting argue that this experience, and ones like it, show that inflation targeting helps central banks establish credibility in their resolve to fight inflation. Critics of inflation targeting argue that explicit inflation targeting has problems. Inflation is hard to measure, and sometimes the price level goes up because of reasons that have little to do with forces creating sustainable pressure for inflation. According to critics, having an inflation target could force the central bank to raise interest rates and cut money supply growth when there was no need to do so because it is too hard for the bank to distinguish the differences between sustainable and temporary inflation pressures. They argue that it is better to have an *implicit inflation target,* which can be adjusted slightly for the particular situation, which allows the bank to establish credibility, while at the same time giving it a bit of "wiggle room" to take account of particular situations. To date, the Fed has followed the critics, and has not adopted an explicit inflation target, but it has an implicit target, which is to keep inflation below about 2.5 percent.

In 2007 and 2008, inflation exceeded its implicit inflation target, which would suggest that the Fed should have tightened monetary policy. But it didn't have an explicit inflation target, which allowed it to loosen monetary policy based on its concern about the economy's reaction to the subprime mortgage financial crisis. Had the Fed been committed to an explicit target, it would not have had that option; it would have had to tighten monetary policy, regardless of the effect on the financial crisis and output.

Institutional theorists see the nominal wage- and price-setting process as generating inflation.

price, another group responds by doing the same. More groups follow until, finally, the first group finds that its relative wage or price hasn't increased. Then the entire process starts again. Once the nominal wage and price levels have risen, government has two options: It can either ratify the increase by increasing the money supply, thereby accepting the inflation, or it can refuse to ratify it. If it refuses to ratify it, firms will not be able to sell all they want at the higher price and will cut production and lay off workers (firms generally don't lower nominal wages). Unemployment will rise.

Supporters of the institutional theory of inflation argue that in most sectors of the economy, competition works slowly. Social pressures, as well as the invisible hand, influence wages and prices. The result is that even when there is substantial unemployment and considerable excess supply of goods, existing workers can still put an upward push on nominal wages, and existing firms can put an upward push on nominal prices.

Q-7 How would a quantity theorist likely respond to an insider/outsider model of inflation?

To get a better picture of how existing workers can push up wages despite substantial unemployment, let's consider the **insider/outsider model,** *an institutionalist story of inflation where insiders bid up wages and outsiders are unemployed.* Insiders are current business owners and workers who have good jobs with excellent long-run prospects. Outsiders are everyone else. Insiders receive above-equilibrium wages, profits, and rents. If the world were competitive, their wages, profits, and rents would be pushed down to the equilibrium level. To prevent this from happening, according to the insider/outsider model, insiders develop sociological and institutional barriers that prevent outsiders from competing away those above-equilibrium wages, profits, and rents. Such barriers include unions, laws restricting the firing of workers, and brand recognition. Because of those barriers, outsiders (often minorities) must take low-paying dead-end jobs or attempt to undertake marginal businesses that pay little return for many hours worked. Even when outsiders do find better jobs or business opportunities, they are first to be fired and their businesses are the first to suffer in a recession. Thus, outsiders have much higher unemployment rates than insiders. For example, in the United States, blacks tend to be outsiders; black unemployment rates have consistently been twice as high as white unemployment rates for the same age groups.

Institutionalists believe that, under current conditions, the costs of unemployment are borne more heavily by minorities and other outsiders.

In short, the institutional theories of inflation emphasize that our economy is only partially competitive. The invisible hand is often thwarted by social and political forces. Such partially competitive economies are often characterized by insiders' monopolies. Insiders get the jobs and are paid monopoly wage levels. Outsiders are not employed at those higher wages. Imperfect competition allows workers (and firms) to raise nominal wages (and prices) even as unemployment (and excess supply of goods) exists. Then, as other insiders do likewise, the price level rises. This increase in the price level lowers workers' real wages. In response, workers further raise their nominal wages to protect their real wages. The result is an ongoing chase in which the insiders protect their real wages, while outsiders (the unemployed) suffer. (If the ideas of nominal and real are unclear to you, a review of earlier chapters may be in order.)

WWW Web Note 33.2
WWII Income Policies

Demand-Pull and Cost-Push Inflation

Quantity and institutional theories of inflation are sometimes differentiated as demand-pull inflation and cost-push inflation. When the majority of industries are at close to capacity and they experience increases in demand, we say there's demand-pull pressure. The inflation that results is called **demand-pull inflation**—*inflation that occurs when the economy is at or above potential output*. Demand-pull inflation is generally characterized by shortages of goods and shortages of workers. Because there's excess demand, firms know that if they raise their prices, they'll still be able to sell their goods and workers know if they raise their wages, they will still be employed.

When significant proportions of markets (or one very important market, such as the labor market or the oil market) experience price rises not related to demand pressure, we say that there is cost-push pressure. The resulting inflation is **cost-push inflation**—*inflation that occurs when the economy is below potential output*. In cost-push inflation, because there is no excess demand (there may actually be excess supply), firms that raise their prices are not sure demand will be sufficient to sell off their goods and workers are not sure that after raising their wage they will all be employed. But the ones who actually do the pushing are fairly sure they won't be the ones who can't sell off their goods or the ones fired. A classic cost-push example occurred in the 1970s when the Organization of Petroleum Exporting Countries raised its price on oil, triggering cost-push inflation.

Notice that in much of the discussion of inflation I did not use these distinctions. The reason is that although demand-pull and cost-push pressures can be catalysts for starting inflation, they are not causes of continued inflation. The reality is that in an ongoing inflation, cost-push or demand-pull forces become intertwined. As Alfred Marshall (the 19th century English economist who originated supply and demand analysis) said, it is impossible to separate the roles of supply and demand in influencing price, just as it is impossible to say which blade of the scissors is cutting a sheet of paper.

In an ongoing inflation, cost-push and demand-pull forces become intertwined.

Inflation and Unemployment: The Phillips Curve

Now that we've been through two main theories of inflation, let's talk about anti-inflation policy—how do policy makers keep inflation down? One obvious policy is to keep aggregate demand low—hold down growth of the money supply and run

FIGURE 33-3 Addressing Inflation with Monetary Policy

When aggregate demand and short-run aggregate supply intersect at a level of output that is greater than potential output, inflationary pressures rise. Government can either keep output high and have low unemployment but higher inflation or lower aggregate demand to keep inflation low but accept higher unemployment. This illustrates the trade-off some policy makers believe exists between inflation and unemployment.

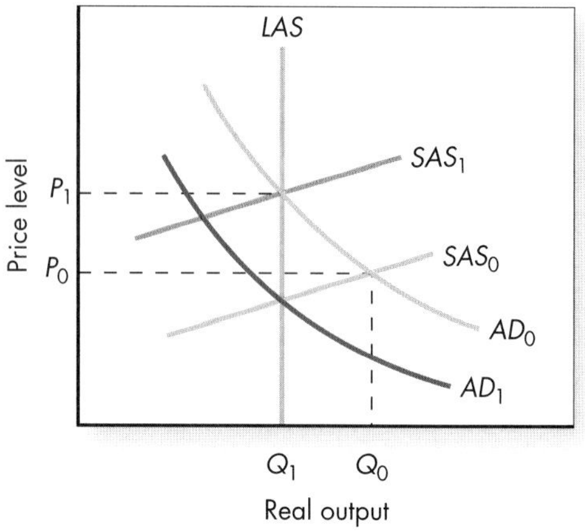

contractionary fiscal policy. This policy can be seen in our standard *AS/AD* model. Figure 33-3 shows a situation where with aggregate demand at AD_0 and aggregate supply at SAS_0, the quantity of aggregate demand exceeds potential output, a situation with inflationary pressures.

Short-run equilibrium is at a price level of P_0 and output Q_0, which means that output exceeds potential output. This creates upward pressure on the price level toward P_1. To hold down inflationary pressures, the government must shift the *AD* curve back to AD_1. But governments are also under pressure to hold output high, and the government likely doesn't realize that output is above potential. Often, the only way government can know for sure is that inflation starts increasing. So, government can either keep aggregate demand high at AD_0 (and keep output high and unemployment low but accept higher inflation) or lower aggregate demand to AD_1 to keep inflation low but accept lower output and higher unemployment.

Since higher output and lower unemployment are often associated with higher inflation, some policy makers have suggested that there is a trade-off between inflation and unemployment.

Web Note 33.3
Back in Vogue

That trade-off can be represented graphically, as shown in Figure 33-4(a). The **short-run Phillips curve** is *a downward-sloping curve showing the relationship between inflation and unemployment when expectations of inflation are constant*. In a Phillips curve diagram, unemployment is measured on the horizontal axis; inflation is on the vertical axis. The Phillips curve shows us the possible short-run combinations of those two phenomena. It tells us that when unemployment is low, say 4 percent, inflation tends to be high, say 4 percent (point A in Figure 33-4(a)). It also tells us that if we want to lower inflation, say to 1 percent, we must be willing to accept high unemployment, say 7 percent (point *B* in Figure 33-4(a)).

History of the Phillips Curve

The Phillips curve began as an empirical relationship and was discovered by, you guessed it, an economist named Phillips. In the 1950s and 1960s, when unemployment was high, inflation was low; when unemployment was low, inflation was high. Figure 33-4(b) shows this empirical relationship for the United States for the years 1954–1968, when the short-run Phillips curve became part of how economists looked at the economy.

Because the short-run Phillips curve seemed to represent a relatively stable trade-off, in the 1960s the short-run Phillips curve began to play a central role in discussions

FIGURE 33-4 (A AND B) The Phillips Curve Trade-Off

Analyzing the empirical relationship between unemployment and inflation from 1954 to 1968—shown in (**b**)—led economists to believe there was the relatively stable Phillips curve that, for policy choices, could be represented by the smooth Phillips curve in (**a**).

Source: Economic Report of the President.

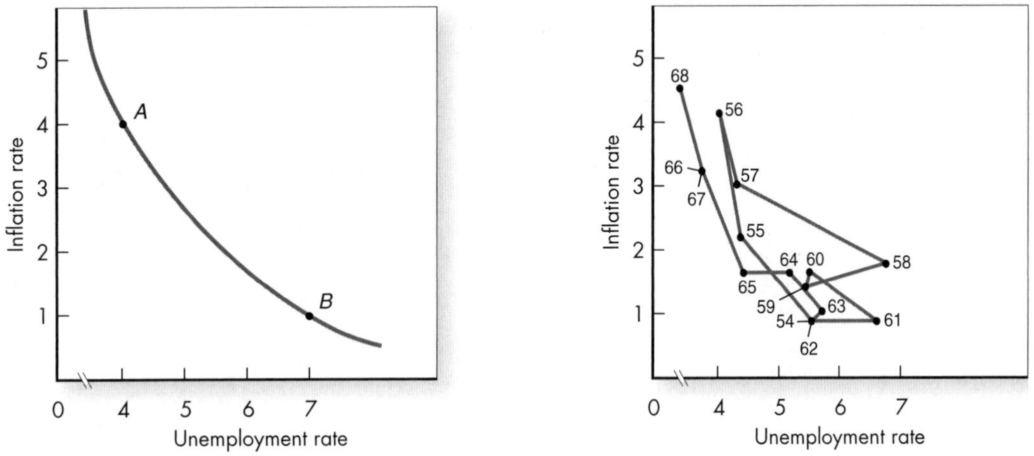

(a) The Hypothesized Phillips Curve **(b) The Rise of the Phillips Curve (1954–1968)**

of macroeconomic policy. Republicans (often advised by supporters of the quantity theory) generally favored contractionary monetary and fiscal policy, which maintained high unemployment and low inflation (a point like *B* in Figure 33-4(a)). Democrats (often advised by supporters of the institutional theory) generally favored expansionary monetary and fiscal policies, which brought about low unemployment but high inflation (a point like A in Figure 33-4(a)).

In the early 1970s, however, the empirical short-run Phillips curve relationship seemed to break down. The data no longer seemed to show a trade-off between unemployment and inflation. Instead, when unemployment was high, inflation was also high. This phenomenon is termed **stagflation**—*the combination of high and accelerating inflation and high unemployment*. Since that time, the Phillips curve has been ephemeral—sometimes seeming as if it were reappearing, and then disappearing again.

The Long-Run and Short-Run Phillips Curves

Economists have explained this constantly changing relationship between inflation and unemployment by incorporating expectations of inflation into the analysis. They argue that actual inflation depends both on supply and demand forces and on how much inflation people expect. If people expect a lot of inflation, they will ask for higher nominal wage and price increases. To incorporate expectations into the Phillips curve it is necessary to distinguish between a short-run Phillips curve and a long-run Phillips curve.

At all points on the short-run Phillips curve, expectations of inflation (the rise in the price level that the average person expects) are fixed. Thus, on the short-run Phillips curve, expectations of inflation can differ from actual inflation. *At all points on the long-run Phillips curve, expectations of inflation are equal to actual inflation.* The **long-run Phillips curve** is thought to be *a vertical curve at the unemployment rate consistent with potential output*. (See the vertical curve in the margin.) It shows the trade-off (or complete lack thereof) when expectations of inflation equal actual inflation. Economists argue

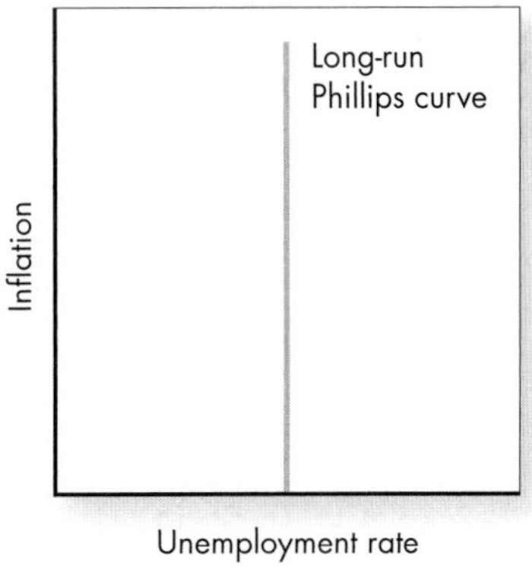

The long-run Phillips curve is vertical; it shows the lack of a trade-off between inflation and unemployment when expectations of inflation equal actual inflation. Expectations of inflation do not change along a short-run Phillips curve.

FIGURE 33-5 (A AND B) **Inflation Expectations and the Phillips Curve**

Both (**a**) and (**b**) show how an increase in aggregate demand can increase output initially. Eventually, however, the economy will return to potential output but with a higher rate of inflation. The economy begins at point A. Initially, the aggregate demand curve moves from AD_0 to AD_1, pushing output above its potential in (**a**). As firms compete for labor, wages increase. To cover increasing costs, firms raise their prices. The combination of lower unemployment and higher inflation is shown by point *B* in (**b**). As workers realize that inflation is not 0 percent, but rather 4 percent, they will ask for further wage increases. Ultimately this process shifts the *SAS* curve to SAS_2 and the short-run Phillips curve to PC_1 (along which expected inflation equals 4 percent) and the economy to point C. The economy is once again in equilibrium. Unemployment has returned to 5.5 percent, but inflation is now 4 percent.

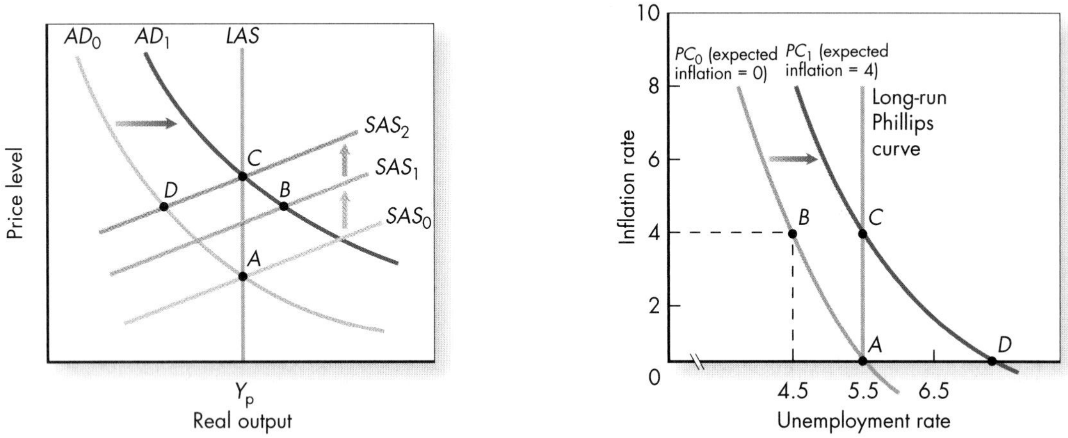

(a) Inflation and the *AS/AD* Model **(b) Inflation and the Phillips Curve**

Q-8 Draw the long-run Phillips curve. Why does it have its shape?

The Long-Run and Short-Run Phillips Curves

that expectations of inflation explain why the short-run Phillips curve relationship broke down in the 1970s.

Let's consider how expectations of inflation can explain high inflation and high unemployment in reference to both our *AS/AD* model and the Phillips curve model. Say the economy starts out with a rate of unemployment consistent with potential output. So there is no inflation, and the economy is at its potential output. (Wages can still be going up by the rate of productivity growth, say it's 3 percent, but the price level is not rising.) Further assume that individuals are expecting zero inflation; that is, if they get a 3 percent wage increase, they expect their real income to rise by 3 percent. This starting point is represented by point A in Figure 33-5(a) and (b).

In Figure 33-5(a) you can see that short-run aggregate supply and aggregate demand intersect at potential income at point A. Since the economy is in both short-run and long-run equilibrium, there are no forces moving the economy away from point A in the *AS/AD* model. Point A in Figure 33-5(b) is also on both the long-run and short-run Phillips curve. This means that point A is a sustainable combination of inflation and unemployment—the situation can continue indefinitely. The only sustainable combination of inflation and unemployment rates on the short-run Phillips curve is where it intersects the long-run Phillips curve because that is the only unemployment rate consistent with the economy's potential income.

Moving Off the Long-Run Phillips Curve Now let's say that the government decides to increase aggregate demand, shifting the *AD* curve from AD_0 to AD_1. This pushes output above its potential, Y_p, as in Figure 33-5(a). That will increase the demand for labor, and that competition for labor will push wages up by more than the increase in productivity as firms compete for the small pool of unemployed workers. Say wages rise by 7 percent. Initially that increase is enough to satisfy workers who are still assumed to expect zero inflation. But notice that, unless potential output increases, there is a problem—their expectation will not be met. Since productivity is still rising by only 3 percent while wages are rising by 7 percent, the higher wage costs force firms to raise their prices by 4 percent, shifting the *SAS* curve up from SAS_0 to SAS_1. The economy moves to point *B*. This same point *B* is shown in the Phillips curve diagram where the economy is still on the short-run Phillips curve. Unemployment falls from 5.5 to 4.5 percent and inflation rises from 0 to 4 percent. But point *B* is not on the long-run Phillips curve and actual inflation exceeds expected inflation.

Moving Back onto the Long-Run Phillips Curve Since expectations of inflation differ from actual inflation, point *B* is not a sustainable position. Since it is beyond potential income, Y_p, the *SAS* curve will continue to shift up. Eventually workers realize that their real wages aren't increasing by 7 percent; they are rising by only 3 percent. As workers come to expect the 4 percent inflation, they ask for higher wages to compensate for that inflation. The short-run Phillips curve will shift up from PC_0 to PC_1 since each short-run Phillips curve represents the trade-off for a given level of inflationary expectation. As wages increase, the *SAS* curve shifts up to SAS_2. As the price level rises, the dollars that people hold are worth less, causing the quantity of aggregate demand to decline and the economy to move to point *C*. Output returns to its potential, unemployment returns to its target rate, and the economy returns to a long-run equilibrium at point *C* on the long-run Phillips curve. Unemployment is once again at its target rate, but inflation, and expectations of inflation, are now 4 percent.

The general relationship is the following: Any time unemployment is lower than the target level of unemployment consistent with potential output, inflation and expectations of inflation will be increasing. That means that the short-run Phillips curve will be shifting up. The short-run Phillips curve will continue to shift up until output is no longer above potential. Thus, any level of inflation is consistent with the target level of unemployment if the cause of that inflation is expectations of inflation. Economists used these expectations of inflation to explain the experience in the 1970s. The economy had been pushed beyond its potential, which had caused inflation to accelerate. (This explanation was supplemented with discussions of supply-side inflationary pressures caused by the large rise in oil prices that occurred at that time.)

Stagflation and the Phillips Curve

The problem with point C is that although the economy is back at potential output, inflationary expectations are built into people's price-setting behavior. That expectational inflation can be eliminated only if aggregate demand falls, pushing the economy to a higher level of unemployment that exceeds the target rate. That is how economists explained the stagflation in the late 1970s and early 1980s. To end stagflation, the government attempted to push down the inflation through contractionary aggregate demand policy. The lower aggregate demand (shifting aggregate demand back from AD_1 to AD_0) pushed the economy to a position such as point *D* in Figure 33-5. At point *D*, unemployment exceeds the target rate. The higher unemployment puts downward pressure on wages and prices, shifting the short-run Phillips curve down.

As you can see, the long-run Phillips curve tells us whether there will be upward pressure on the price level (when the economy is to the left of the long-run Phillips curve, and unemployment is below the target rate) or downward pressure on the price level (when the economy is to the right of the long-run Phillips curve, and unemployment is above the target rate).

Q-9 If the economy is at point *A* on the Phillips curve below, what prediction would you make for unemployment and inflation?

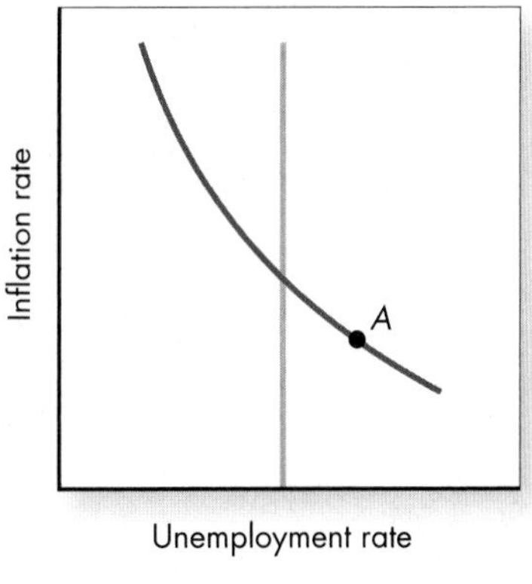

The Relationship between Inflation and Growth

The on-going debates about macro policy can be understood by thinking back to our discussion of low and high potential output and their relation to inflationary pressure. A graph of these is shown in Figure 33-6(a). Economists generally agree that below low potential output there will be no inflationary, and possibly some deflationary, pressures. They also agree that above high potential output there will be significant inflationary pressures. The degree of inflationary pressure between these two extremes is ambiguous. Since no one knows precisely where potential output is, there is usually a debate within this range.

The government wants to choose as high an output level as possible yet keep inflation low and prevent it from accelerating. At what point it can do that is the subject of much debate. Supporters of the institutional theory of inflation tend to argue that it is best to err on the high side, with policy aiming for high potential output as in Figure 33-5(a). Economists who focus on the quantity theory tend to argue that it is best to err on the low side, with policy aiming at low potential output.

Quantity Theory and the Inflation/Growth Trade-Off

I suspect many of you will agree that erring on the high side in terms of real output makes the most sense. If that were the entire trade-off, such a reaction is probably right. But supporters of the quantity theory point out a problem with that reasoning, which might be called the "little bit pregnant problem." At the beginning of a pregnancy, it's true you are only a little bit pregnant, but that "little bit" has initiated a set of cellular changes that will fundamentally alter your life. Supporters of the quantity theory say it is the same with a small rise in the price level: You can't have a "little bit" of inflation. That little bit is setting in motion a series of events that will make the inflation grow and grow, unless the government gives up its attempt to achieve a high rate of output. Their solution to prevent inflation is abstinence—just say no to any rise in the price level.

Q-10 Why do quantity theorists believe that government should err on the side of lower output and a lower chance of inflation?

Those who support the quantity theory argue that erring on the low side pays off—it stops any chance of inflation. It establishes credibility of the Fed's resolve not to increase the money supply. If some inflation is allowed and the Fed loses credibility, that inflation undermines the long-run growth prospects of the economy, and hence causes

FIGURE 33-6 (A AND B)
The Inflation/Growth Trade-Off

Quantity theorists are much more likely to err on the side of preventing inflation, arguing that an ongoing inflation will begin at low potential output. They emphasize the trade-off shown in (b). Institutionalists are more likely to argue that the inflation threshold is at high potential output.

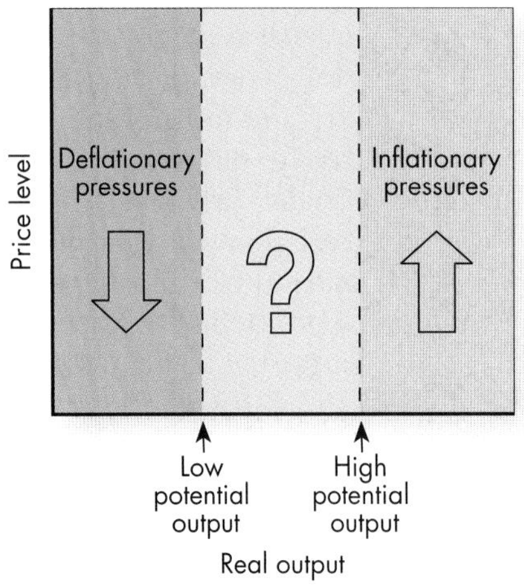

(a) Inflationary Pressures

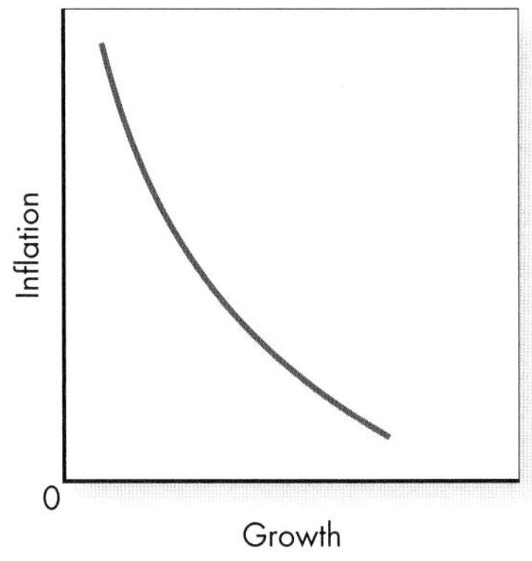

(b) Growth/Inflation Trade-Off

future levels of potential income to be lower than they otherwise would be. Put another way, inflation undermines long-run growth; abstinence creates the environment for long-run growth. Thus, for quantity theorists, while there is no long-run trade-off between inflation and unemployment, there is a long-run trade-off between inflation and growth: High inflation leads to lower growth.

Low inflation leads to higher growth for a variety of reasons. Low inflation reduces price uncertainty, making it easier for businesses to invest in future production. Businesses can more easily enter into long-term contracts when inflation is low, which lowers the cost of doing business. Low inflation also makes using money much easier. When inflation is high, people spend more time trying to avoid the costs of inflation, which diverts their energies away from productive activities that would lead to growth.

The hypothesized relationship between inflation and growth is shown in Figure 33-6(b). For quantity theorists, even if there is a short-run relationship between inflation and unemployment, it is precarious for government to try to take advantage of it, because doing so can undermine the long-run growth potential of the economy. For quantity theorists, government policy creating an environment of price-level stability is the policy most likely to lead to high rates of growth. They suggest that the reason for the success of the economy in the late 1990s and early 2000s was that people believed that the Fed would fight inflation should it appear.

Deflation

If inflation is bad for growth, it might seem that **deflation**—*a continual fall in the price level*—might be good for growth. But, based on experience, that definitely is not the case. Deflation is almost always associated with recessions and fears of depression. One of the reasons is that deflation in goods and services is generally associated with *asset price deflation*—falls in the price of assets such as stocks and houses. Such asset price declines generally bring about wealth illusion, which for a deflation means that society perceives itself on average as poorer because the holders of the assets feel poorer, but the nonholders of the assets do not feel richer even though, in an accounting sense, they are. Thus, as we discussed in earlier chapters, government generally tries to prevent deflation and the accompanying recession and decline in growth by increasing money supply whenever deflation threatens.

Deflation is a continual fall in the price level.

Institutional Theory and the Inflation/Growth Trade-Off

Other economists, mainly supporters of the institutional theory of inflation, are less sure about this negative relationship between inflation and growth. They agree that price-level rises have the potential of generating inflation, and that high accelerating inflation undermines growth, but they do not agree that all price-level increases start an inflationary process. The lower unemployment rate accompanying the inflation is so nice, and if the government is really careful—I mean really, really careful—it can avoid reaching the point where the little bit of rise in price level starts the monster of inflation growing within the economy. And besides, if inflation gets started, the government has some medicine that will rid the economy of the inflation relatively easily.

The real-world difference between the two views can be seen in the debate about monetary policy in the early 2000s, when the unemployment rate fell to around 4 percent. Until then, potential income had been estimated at an unemployment rate of 5.5 to 6 percent. So it seemed as if the economy was operating significantly beyond low-level potential output. But inflation remained low, at about 2–3 percent. Economists who focus on the quantity theory argued that inflation was just around the corner, and that unless the government instituted contractionary aggregate demand policy, the seeds of inflation would be sown. Other economists argued that institutional changes

Web Note 33.4
The Fed and Growth

in the labor market had reduced the inflation threat and that more expansionary policy was called for. The Fed followed a path between the two. Initially, inflation did not rise, but instead fell as the economy slowed and unemployment rose. It was at that point that, for some economists, the policy concern changed from inflation to deflation. Whether inflation would have risen had growth continued was unclear. Then in 2004, inflation began to reappear, and some economists complained that the Fed had been too expansionary. Inflation of about 2–3 percent continued through 2008, when, because of oil and food price shocks, inflation picked up. In response, the Fed implemented contractionary monetary policy, pushing the interest rate up. But then, because of the recession, the Fed switched to strongly expansionary monetary policy and put its concern about inflation on the back burner.

Conclusion

The quantity and institutional theories of inflation, growth, and unemployment reflect two consistent but different worldviews. The institutional theorists see a world in which sociological and institutional factors interact with market forces, keeping the economy in a perpetual disequilibrium when considered in an economic framework. The quantity theorists see a world in which market forces predominate and institutional and sociological factors are insignificant. The overall economy is in continual equilibrium. These two theories carry over to economists' analyses of the central policy issue facing most governments as they decide on their monetary and fiscal policies: the trade-off between inflation and unemployment and growth. These different worldviews are an important reason why there are disagreements about policy, and the debate will likely continue for a long time.

Summary

- The winners in inflation are people who can raise their wages or prices and still keep their jobs or sell their goods. The losers are people who can't raise their wages or prices. On average, winners and losers balance out.
- People form expectations in many ways. Three ways are to base expectations on economic models, on an average of the past, and on a trend.
- A basic rule of thumb to predict inflation is: Inflation equals nominal wage increases minus productivity growth.
- The equation of exchange is $MV = PQ$; it becomes the quantity theory when velocity is constant, real output is independent of the money supply, and causation goes from money to prices. The quantity theory says that the price level varies in direct response to changes in the quantity of money. That is,

  $\%\Delta M \rightarrow \%\Delta P$
- Central banks sometimes print money knowing that it will lead to inflation because the alternative might be a breakdown of the economy.
- The institutional theory of inflation sees the source of inflation in the wage-and-price-setting institutions; it sees the direction of causation going from price increases to money increases.
- The long-run Phillips curve allows expectations of inflation to change; it is generally seen as vertical.
- The short-run Phillips curve holds expectations constant. It is generally seen as downward-sloping and shifts up when expectations of inflation rise and shifts down when expectations of inflation fall.
- Quantity theorists see a long-run trade-off between inflation and growth; the higher inflation, the lower the growth rate. Institutional theorists are less sure about this trade-off.

Key Terms

adaptive expectations *(777)*
cost-push inflation *(785)*
deflation *(791)*
demand-pull inflation *(785)*
equation of exchange *(780)*
extrapolative expectations *(777)*
inflation tax *(782)*
insider/outsider model *(784)*
long-run Phillips curve *(787)*
quantity theory of money *(781)*
rational expectations *(777)*
short-run Phillips curve *(786)*
stagflation *(787)*
velocity of money *(780)*

Questions and Exercises

connect ECONOMICS

1. Why do lenders tend to lose out in an unexpected inflation? LO1
2. Under what conditions would lenders not lose out in inflation? LO1
3. If you base your expectations of inflation on what has happened in the past, what kind of expectations are you demonstrating? LO2
4. If productivity growth is 3 percent and wage increases are 5 percent, what would you predict inflation would be? LO2
5. What three assumptions turn the equation of exchange into the quantity theory of money? LO3
6. What does the quantity theory predict will happen to inflation if the money supply rises 10 percent? LO3
7. Why did the relationship between growth in the money supply and inflation break down in the 1990s? LO3
8. For what countries is the connection between the growth in the money supply and inflation still evident? What accounts for this? LO3
9. If governments are aware that increases in the money supply cause inflation, why do some countries increase the money supply by significant amounts anyway? LO3
10. What is the inflation tax? Who pays it? LO3
11. Who is more likely to support monetary rules—a quantity theorist or an institutionalist? Explain your answer. LO3
12. Assume the money supply is $500, the velocity of money is 8, and the price level is $2. Using the quantity theory of money:
    a. Determine the level of real output.
    b. Determine the level of nominal output.
    c. Assuming velocity remains constant, what will happen if the money supply rises 20 percent?
    d. If the government established price controls and also raised the money supply 20 percent, what would happen? LO3
13. What is the direction of causation between money and prices according to the institutional theory of inflation? LO4
14. What is the insider/outsider theory of inflation? Would quantity or institutional theorists likely believe this theory? LO4
15. Draw a short-run Phillips curve. What does it say about the relationship between inflation and unemployment? LO5
16. Draw a long-run Phillips curve. What does it say about the relationship between inflation and unemployment? LO5
17. If people's expectations of inflation didn't change, would the economy move from a short-run to a long-run Phillips curve? LO5
18. In the mid-1990s and through the early 2000s, Japan's annual money supply growth rate fell to 1–2 percent from an average annual rate of 10–11 percent in the late 1980s. What effect did this decline likely have on
    a. Japanese real output?
    b. Japanese unemployment?
    c. Japanese inflation? LO5
19. Congratulations. You've just been appointed finance minister of Inflationland. Inflation has been ongoing for the past five years at 5 percent. The target rate of unemployment, 5 percent, is also the actual rate.
    a. Demonstrate the economy's likely position on both short-run and long-run Phillips curves.
    b. The president tells you she wants to be reelected. Devise a monetary policy strategy for her that might help her accomplish her goal.
    c. Demonstrate that strategy graphically, including the likely long-run consequences. LO5
20. European Community Bank (ECB) governing council member Erkki Liikanen was quoted in a 2004 *Wall Street Journal* article as saying, "The stronger we get the

productivity growth . . . the more room we will get in monetary policy (to keep interest rates low)."
   a. Demonstrate his argument using the *AS/AD* model.
   b. Demonstrate his argument using the Phillips curve model. LO5

21. What is the reasoning behind the view that there is a trade-off between inflation and growth? LO6

Questions from Alternative Perspectives

1. According to the quantity theory of money, the government controls inflation through the supply of money.
   a. Does that mean that the government can stop inflation if it wants to do so?
   b. What reasons might government have not to stop inflation? (Austrian)
2. The Book of Leviticus states, "You shall do no injustice in judgment, in measurement of length, weight, or volume. You shall have just balances, just weights, a just ephah, a just hin. I am the Lord your God, who brought you out of the land of Egypt." When the Israelites began using shekels for money, a just weight meant that the silver coin had a particular weight and therefore an intrinsic value.
   a. If U.S. currency is not backed by gold, how do we know the dollar is a "just weight"?
   b. How is inflation an injustice in measurement?
   c. Who bears the injustice of inflation? (Religious)
3. When it comes to understanding inflation, and even other aspects of the business cycle, ecological economists will often emphasize the role of energy, and especially oil, in shaping macroeconomic outcomes. In this chapter, you were briefly introduced to the analytical concepts of demand-pull and cost-push inflation. To decide how important oil prices are in shaping macroeconomic outcomes such as inflation, do the following:
   a. Graph the average annual CPI inflation rate from 1970–2000s (www.bls.gov has the data); graph the world price of oil over the same time period (www.eia.doe.gov/emeu/cabs/chron.html has these data); overlay the graphs (this is sometimes called "tear drop analysis") and move them forward and backward a bit to create leads and lags. What kind of a pattern do you see?
   b. Use the *AD/AS* model to analyze the impact of an oil shock on the economy.
   c. What is the necessary consequence of using fiscal policy to stimulate the economy after a supply-side oil shock? What conclusions do you draw from the analysis? (Institutionalist)
4. This chapter discusses causes of inflation.
   a. Do you believe the cause of inflation is to be found in the institutional structure of wage- and price-setting institutions or in excess demand for goods and services?
   b. If you believe inflation is caused by wage- and price-setting institutions, what type of policy would Keynesian and Classical economists recommend?
   c. If you believe that inflation is caused by excess demand, would their policy recommendations be the same? (Post-Keynesian)
5. Radicals see the trade-off between inflation and unemployment as one that pits inflation-phobic investors—out to protect the value of their assets and the corporate profits in which they invest—against workers who are out for employment and wage growth. Lower unemployment rates and more jobs bolster the bargaining power of workers, pushing up wages, which either leads to inflation or eats into corporate profit margins. The trade-off changed in the 1990s as globalization put workers in no position to push for higher wages even as unemployment rates declined. Compare this explanation of change in the trade-off between unemployment and inflation during the 1990s with the one in your textbook.
   a. Where do they agree and where do they differ?
   b. Which do you find more convincing? (Radical)

Issues to Ponder

1. People's perception of inflation often differs from actual inflation.
   a. List five goods that you buy relatively frequently.
   b. Looking in old newspapers (found in the library on microfiche), locate sales prices for these goods since 1950, finding one price every five years or so. Determine the average annual price rise for each good from 1950 to today.
   c. Compare that price with the rise in the consumer price index. LO2
2. In the early 1990s, Argentina stopped increasing the money supply and fixed the exchange rate of the Argentine austral at 10,000 to the dollar. It then renamed the Argentine currency the "peso" and cut off four zeros so that one peso equaled one dollar. Inflation slowed

substantially. After this was done, the following observations were made. Explain why these observations did not surprise economists. (Difficult)

a. The golf courses were far less crowded.
b. The price of goods in dollar-equivalent pesos in Buenos Aires, the capital of the country, was significantly above that in New York City.
c. Consumer prices—primarily services—rose relative to other goods.
d. Luxury auto dealers were shutting down. LO3

3. Grade inflation is widespread. In 1990, 81 percent of the students who took the SATs had an A or B average, but 40 percent of them scored less than 390 on the verbal SAT. Students' grades are increasing but what they are learning is decreasing. Some economists argue that grade inflation should be dealt with in the same way that price inflation should be dealt with—by creating a fixed standard and requiring all grades to be specified relative to that standard. One way to accomplish this is to index the grades professors give: specify on the grade report both the student's grade and the class average, and deflate (or inflate) the grade to some common standard. Discuss the advantages and disadvantages of such a proposal. (Difficult) LO3, LO4
4. What would Alfred Marshall likely say about the cost-push/demand-pull distinction? LO4
5. The Phillips curve is just a figment of economists' imagination. True or false? LO5
6. Wayne Angell, a former Fed governor, stated in an editorial, "The Federal Reserve should get back on track getting inflation rates so low that inflation would no longer be a determining factor in household and business investment decisions." Mr. Angell believes inflation lowers long-term growth. (Difficult)

a. Is Wayne Angell most likely a quantity theorist or institutionalist? Explain your answer.
b. How does inflation affect household decisions and, consequently, growth? LO6

Answers to Margin Questions

1. False. Inflation does not make an economy poorer. It redistributes income from those who do not raise their prices to those who do raise their prices. *(777)*
2. Three types of expectations are rational expectations, adaptive expectations, and extrapolative expectations. *(778)*
3. The equation of exchange, $MV = PQ$, is a tautology. What changes it to the quantity theory are three assumptions about the variables, specifically that velocity remains constant, that real output is determined separately, and that the causation flows from money to prices. With these assumptions added, the equation of exchange implies that changes in the money supply are reflected in changes in the price level—which is what the quantity theory of money says. *(780)*
4. According to the quantity theory of money, the Fed should decrease the growth of the money supply to lower inflation. *(781)*
5. Some central banks issue large quantities of money for a number of reasons. One reason is that, in their estimation, the benefit of doing so (avoiding a breakdown of the government and perhaps the entire economy) exceeds the cost (starting an inflation). Another reason is that some central banks lack the independence to maintain low inflation as a goal. *(783)*
6. According to the quantity theory, the direction of causation goes from money to prices ($MV \rightarrow PQ$)—increases in the money supply lead to increases in the price level. According to institutional theory, the direction of causation goes from prices to money ($MV \leftarrow PQ$)—increases in the price level are ratified by government, which increases the money supply. *(783)*
7. A quantity theorist would likely say that the insider/outsider model of inflation tends to obscure the central cause of inflation—increases in the money supply. *(784)*
8. As you can see in the graph below, the long-run Phillips curve is perfectly vertical. That is, inflation is independent of the unemployment rate. Its shape is dependent on the assumption that people's expectations of inflation completely adjust to inflation in the long run, and that adjustment is not institutionally constrained. *(788)*

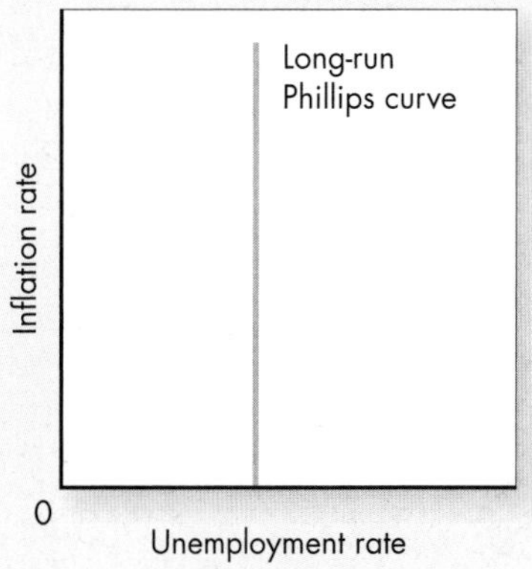

9. If the economy is at point *A* on the Phillips curve below, inflation is below expected inflation and unemployment is higher than the target rate of unemployment. If this were the only information I had about the economy, I would expect unemployment to fall. Inflation remains the same, but inflation expectations fall. *(789)*

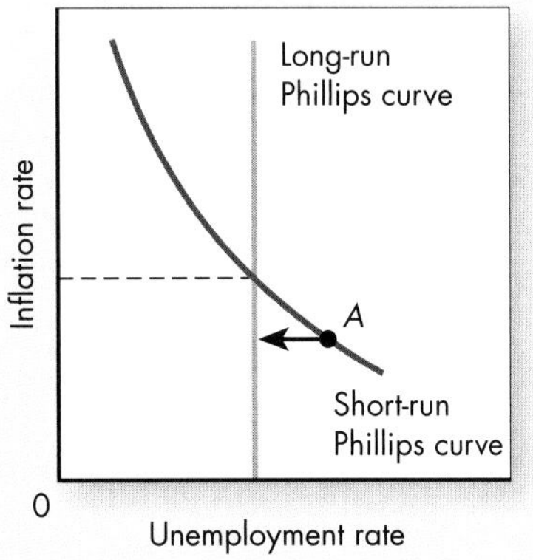

10. Quantity theorists believe that government should err on the side of low output and a lower chance of inflation because any amount of inflation sets into motion a series of changes in the economy that will likely lead to higher inflation. *(790)*

CHAPTER 34

Deficits and Debt

Any government, like any family, can for a year spend a little more than it earns. But you and I know that a continuance of that habit means the poorhouse.

—Franklin D. Roosevelt

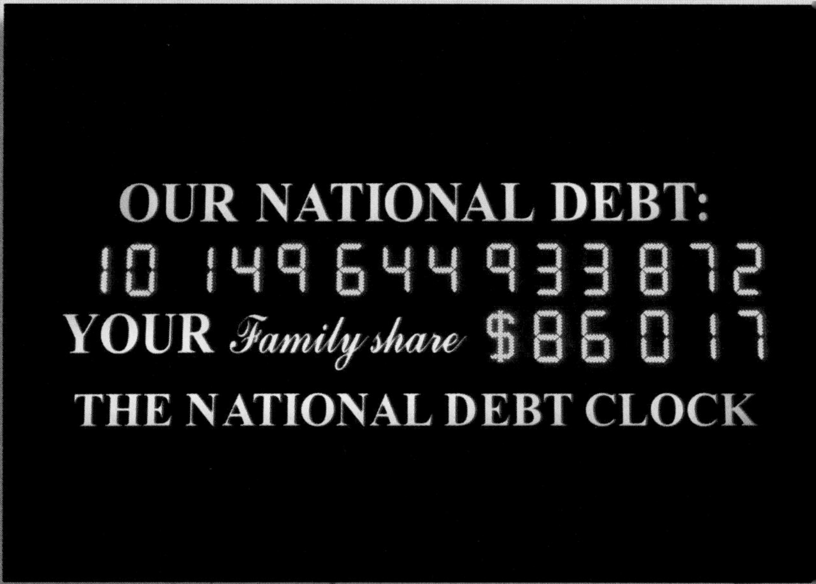

AFTER READING THIS CHAPTER, YOU SHOULD BE ABLE TO:

1. Define the terms *deficit, surplus,* and *debt.*
2. Distinguish between a passive deficit and a structural deficit.
3. Differentiate between real and nominal deficits and surpluses.
4. Explain why the debt needs to be judged relative to assets.
5. Describe the historical record for the U.S. deficit and debt.

In 2009 the United States was running a large budget deficit, as it had for the past seven years. Those deficits were a substantial change from the U.S. budget surpluses that the U.S. government had run from 1998 to 2001, during which time economists had predicted future budget surpluses that cumulatively would exceed $5.9 trillion over the next 15 years. How can the budget picture change so fast? And what do such changes mean for the economy? This chapter considers these and other questions from an economist's perspective in order to give you some deeper insight into policy debates that you will likely hear about in the news media.

Let's begin by reviewing what economic theory has to say about deficits and surpluses. In the long-run framework, surpluses are good because they provide additional saving for an economy and deficits are bad because they reduce saving, growth, and income. In the short-run framework, the view of deficits and surpluses depends on the state of the economy relative to its potential. If the economy is operating below its potential output, deficits are good and surpluses are bad because deficits increase expenditures, moving output closer to potential.

Combining the two frameworks gives us the following policy directive: Whenever possible, run surpluses, or at least a balanced budget, to help stimulate long-run growth. That recommendation is made even stronger when the economy is booming—that is, when it is above its level of potential income. Should the economy fall into a recession, however, policy makers must choose between the different policies suggested by the long-run and short-run frameworks.

Now let's consider what policies the government actually followed. Let's start by considering the beginning of 2000, when the U.S. economy was booming, unemployment was at historic lows, and there was general agreement that the economy was at or beyond its potential output. If ever there was a time to let government build up a surplus and cut debt, it was then; that was the policy both the short- and long-run economic frameworks recommended. What policy did the government follow? It increased spending and cut taxes—precisely the opposite of what economic theory suggested was needed.

Q-1 How can deficits be both good and bad for an economy?

In 2001, the situation changed and the economy fell into a mild recession. When the World Trade Center and the Pentagon were attacked on September 11, many feared that the mild recession, which had begun March 2001, would become a severe recession and possibly a depression because consumers would lose confidence in the economy. Suddenly, that earlier tax cut didn't look so bad in economists' short-run framework, and the tax cut played a role in making the recession of 2001 the shortest on record.

So what's going on here? The answer is complicated. To explain it, we need some background on accounting issues that pertain to deficits, some specifics about the demography and institutions of the United States, and some knowledge of politics as it relates to surpluses, deficits, and debt. This chapter is intended to provide you with that background.

Defining Deficits and Surpluses

The definitions of *deficit*, *surplus*, and *debt* are simple, but this simplicity hides important aspects that will help you understand current debates about deficits and debt. Thus, it's necessary to look carefully at some ambiguities in the definitions.

A deficit is a shortfall of incoming revenues under payments. A surplus is an excess of revenues over payments.

A **deficit** is *a shortfall of revenues under payments*. A **surplus** is *an excess of revenues over payments;* both are flow concepts. If your income (revenue) is $20,000 per year and your expenditures (payments) are $30,000 per year, you are running a deficit. This definition tells us that a government budget deficit occurs when government expenditures exceed government revenues. The table below shows federal government total expenditures, total revenue, and the difference between the two for various years since 1980.

(Billions of Dollars)	1980	1990	2000	2005	2008	2009*
Revenues	517.1	1,032.1	2,025.5	2,153.9	2,523.6	2,159
Expenditures	590.9	1,253.1	1,789.2	2,472.2	2,978.5	4,004
(−) Deficit/(+) surplus	−73.8	−221.0	236.2	−318.3	−454.8	−1,845

Source: Congressional Budget Office, *The Economic and Budget Outlook*, January 2009 (www.cbo.gov).
*Estimated.

The federal government ran deficits through the 1980s and most of the 1990s. It began to run surpluses in 1998, and returned to running deficits in 2002. In 2009 the federal deficit grew enormously.

Financing the Deficit

The government finances its deficits by selling bonds to private individuals and to the central bank.

Just like private individuals, the government must pay for the goods and services it buys. This means that whenever the government runs a deficit, it has to finance that deficit. It does so by selling *bonds*—promises to pay back the money in the future—to private individuals and to the central bank. There's a whole division of the U.S. Treasury devoted to managing the government's borrowing needs.

Q-2 How does the U.S. government finance its deficit spending?

The United States is fortunate to have people who want to buy its bonds. Some developing countries have few people who want to buy their bonds (lend them money) and therefore have trouble financing their deficits. However, countries have an option that individuals don't have. Their central banks can loan them the money (buy their bonds). Since the central bank's IOUs are money, the loans can be made simply by printing money; in principle, therefore, the central bank has a potentially unlimited source of funds. But, as we saw in earlier chapters, printing too much money can lead to serious inflation problems, which have negative effects on the economy. So, whenever possible, governments try not to use the "print money" option to finance their deficits.

Arbitrariness of Defining Deficits and Surpluses

Whether or not you have a deficit or surplus depends on what you count as a revenue and what you count as an expenditure. These decisions can make an enormous difference in whether you have a surplus or deficit. For example, consider the problem of a firm with annual revenues of $8,000 but no expenses except a $10,000 machine expected to last five years. Should the firm charge the $10,000 to this year's expenditures? Should it split the $10,000 evenly among the five years? Or should it use some other approach? Which method the firm chooses makes a big difference in whether its current budget will be in surplus or deficit.

Accounting is central to the debate about whether we should be concerned about a deficit. Say, for example, that the government promises to pay an individual $1,000 ten years from now. How should government treat that promise? Since the obligation is incurred now, should government count as a current expense an amount that, if saved, would allow it to pay that $1,000 later? Or should government not count the amount as an expenditure until it actually pays out the money? The **Social Security system**—*a social insurance program that provides financial benefits to the elderly and disabled and to their eligible dependents and/or survivors*—is based on promises to pay, and thus the accounting procedures used for Social Security play an important role in how big the government's budget deficit actually is.

Many Right Definitions

Many accounting questions must be answered before we can determine the size of a budget deficit. Some have no right or wrong answer. For others, the answers vary according to the wording of the question. For still others, an economist's "right way" is an accountant's "wrong way." In short, there are many ways to measure expenditures and receipts, so there are many ways to measure surpluses and deficits.

There are many ways to measure expenditures and receipts, so there are many ways to measure deficits and surpluses.

To say that there are many ways to measure deficits is not to say that all ways are correct. Pretending to have income that you don't have is wrong by all standards. Similarly, inconsistent accounting practices—such as measuring an income flow sometimes one way and sometimes another—are wrong. Standard accounting practices rule out a number of "creative" but improper approaches to measuring deficits. But even eliminating these, there remain numerous reasonable ways of defining deficits, which accounts for some of the debate.

Deficits and Surpluses as Summary Measures

The point of the previous discussion is that a deficit is simply a summary measure of a budget. As a summary, a surplus or deficit figure reduces a complicated set of accounting relationships to one figure. To understand what that summary measure is telling us, you've got to understand the accounting procedures used to calculate it. Only then can you make an informed judgment about whether a deficit is something to worry about. What's important is not whether a budget is in surplus or deficit but whether the economy is healthy.

Deficit and surplus figures are simply summary measures of the financial health of the economy. To understand the summary, you must understand the methods that were used to calculate it.

Structural and Passive Deficits and Surpluses

The discussion of fiscal policy in earlier chapters emphasized the effect of the deficit on total income. But when thinking about such policies, it is important to remember that many government revenues and expenditures depend on the level of income in the economy. For example, say that the multiplier is 2 and the government is running expansionary policy. Say that that government increases its spending by $100 (increasing the budget deficit by $100), which causes income to rise by $200. If the tax rate is 20 percent, tax revenues will increase by $40 and the net effect of the policy will be to increase the budget deficit by $60, not $100. So as income changes, the deficit changes.

One implication of this feedback effect of changes in income on the deficit is the need to distinguish a deficit caused by a recessionary fall in income and a deficit brought about by government policy actions. Economists' method of distinguishing these is to differentiate between structural deficits and passive deficits.

To differentiate between a budget deficit being used as a policy instrument to affect the economy and a budget deficit that is the result of income deviating from its potential, economists ask the question: "Would the economy have a budget deficit if it were at its potential level of income?" If it would, that portion of the budget deficit is said to be a **structural deficit**—*the part of a budget deficit that would exist even if the economy were at its potential level of income.* In contrast, if an economy is operating below its potential, the actual deficit will be larger than the structural deficit. In such an economy, that part of the total budget deficit is a **passive deficit**—*the part of the deficit that exists because the economy is operating below its potential level of output.* The passive deficit is also known as the cyclical deficit. When an economy is operating above its potential, it has a passive surplus.

The structural deficit is the deficit that remains when the cyclical elements of the deficit have been removed.

The actual deficit is always made up of the structural deficit and the passive, or cyclical, deficit.

$$\text{Actual deficit} = \text{Structural deficit} + \text{Passive deficit}$$

This distinction has policy importance because economists believe that an economy can eliminate a passive budget deficit through growth in income, whereas it can't grow out of a structural deficit. Because the economy can't grow out of them, structural budget deficits are of more concern to policy makers than are passive budget deficits.

Q-3 An economy's actual income is $1 trillion; its potential income is also $1 trillion. Its actual deficit is $100 billion. What is its passive deficit?

Let me give an example. Say potential income is $14 trillion and actual income is $13.8 trillion, a shortfall of $200 billion. Say also that the actual budget deficit is $250 billion and the marginal tax rate is 25 percent. If the economy were at its potential income, tax revenue would be $50 billion higher and the deficit would be $200 billion. That $200 billion is the structural deficit. The $50 billion (25 percent multiplied by the $200 billion shortfall) is the passive portion of the deficit.

As you can see from this example, assuming government spending doesn't change with income, you can calculate the passive deficit in the following way:

Passive deficit = Tax rate × (Potential output − Actual output)

Structural deficit = Actual deficit − Passive deficit

$$\text{Passive deficit} = \text{Tax rate} \times (\text{Potential output} - \text{Actual output})$$

Once you know the passive deficit, you can also calculate the structural deficit:

$$\text{Structural deficit} = \text{Actual deficit} - \text{Passive deficit}$$

Often there is significant debate about what an economy's potential income level is, and hence there is disagreement about what percentage of a deficit is structural and what percentage is passive. Nonetheless, the distinction is often used and is important to remember. For example, the passive/structural distinction plays a key role in explaining the sudden movement from predictions of surpluses to predictions of deficits that I discussed in the opening part of this chapter. The 2001 recession decreased the passive surplus because, as income fell, tax revenues fell. The terrorist attacks in late 2001 also caused economists to lower their predictions of potential output, which lowered the estimate of the structural surplus. These changes alone reduced trillions of dollars in the predicted surplus. Take these changes, combine them with the tax cut that had previously been passed by Congress, and with the expected increases in government expenditures associated with the war on terror, and—*poof*—the expected $5.9 trillion surplus disappeared and turned into a large expected deficit.

Nominal and Real Deficits and Surpluses

Another distinction that economists make when discussing the budget deficit and surplus picture is the real/nominal distinction. A **nominal deficit** is *the deficit determined by looking at the difference between expenditures and receipts.*[1] It's what most people think of when they think of the budget deficit; it's the value that is generally reported. The **real deficit** is *the nominal deficit adjusted for inflation.* To understand this distinction, it is important to recognize that inflation wipes out debt (accumulated deficits less accumulated surpluses). How much does it wipe out? Consider an example: If inflation is 4 percent per year, the real value of all assets denominated in dollars is declining by 4 percent each year. If you had $100, that $100 will be worth 4 percent less at the end of the year—the equivalent of $96 without inflation. By the same reasoning, when there's 4 percent inflation, the value of the debt is declining 4 percent each year. If a country has a debt of $2 trillion, 4 percent inflation will eliminate $80 billion of the real value of the debt each year.

Q-4 Explain how inflation can wipe out debt.

The larger the debt and the larger the inflation, the more debt will be eliminated by inflation. For example, with 10 percent inflation and a $2 trillion debt, $200 billion of the debt will be eliminated by inflation each year. With 10 percent inflation and a $4 trillion debt, $400 billion of the debt would be eliminated.

Inflation reduces the value of the debt. That reduction is taken into account when the real deficit is calculated.

If inflation is wiping out debt, and the deficit is equal to the increases in debt from one year to the next, inflation also affects the deficit. Economists take this into account by differentiating nominal deficits from real deficits.

We can calculate the real deficit by subtracting the decrease in the value of the government's total outstanding debts due to inflation. Specifically:[2]

$$\text{Real deficit} = \text{Nominal deficit} - (\text{Inflation} \times \text{Total debt})$$

Real deficit = Nominal deficit − (Inflation × Total debt)

Let's consider an example. Say that the nominal deficit is $280 billion, inflation is 4 percent, and total debt is $3 trillion. Substituting into the formula gives us a real deficit of $160 billion [$280 billion − (0.04 × $3 trillion) = $280 billion − $120 billion = $160 billion].

This insight into debt is directly relevant to the budget situation in the United States. For example, back in 1990, the nominal U.S. deficit was about $221 billion, while the real deficit was about one-third of that—$79 billion; in 2008 the U.S. government deficit was about $455 billion; there was 2.2 percent inflation and a total debt of about $10.7 trillion. That means the real deficit was $220 billion.[3] The table below shows the U.S. nominal and real deficits and surpluses for selected years.

Q-5 The nominal deficit is $40 billion, inflation is 2 percent, and the total debt is $4 trillion. What is the real deficit?

(Billions of Dollars)	1980	1990	2000	2005	2008
Nominal (−)deficit/(+)surplus	−74	−221	+236	−318	−455
Plus Inflation × Total debt	86	142	125	270	235
Government debt	930	3,233	5,674	8,170	10,700
Inflation (%)	9.3	4.4	2.2	3.3	2.2
Equals Real (−)deficit/(+)surplus	+12	−79	+361	−48	−220

Source: *The Economic and Budget Outlook*, Congressional Budget Office, January 2007 (www.cbo.gov); and *The Economic Report of the President*, 2009.

[1]In this section I will discuss deficits only. Since a surplus is a negative deficit, the discussion can be easily translated into a discussion of surpluses.

[2]This is an approximation for low rates of inflation. When inflation becomes large, total debt is multiplied by Inflation/(1 + Inflation), rather than just by inflation.

[3]Because a surplus is the opposite of a deficit, you must add inflation times total debt to the nominal surplus to arrive at the real surplus.

Because the United States has had both debt and inflation for the years shown, the real deficits are smaller than the nominal deficits and the real surpluses are greater than the nominal surpluses.

The lowering of the real deficit by inflation is not costless to the government. Persistent inflation becomes built into expectations and causes higher interest rates. When inflationary expectations were low, as they were in the 1950s, the U.S. government paid 3 or 4 percent on its bonds that financed the debt. In 1990, when inflationary expectations were high, the government paid 8 or 9 percent interest, which is about 5 percentage points more than it paid in the 1950s. With its $3.2 trillion debt, this meant that the United States was paying about $160 billion more in interest than it would have had to pay if no inflation had been expected and the nominal interest rate had been 3 rather than 8 percent. That reduced the amount it could spend on current services by $160 billion. In other words, $160 billion of the 1990 nominal U.S. deficit existed because of the rise in interest payments necessary to compensate bondholders for the expected inflation. As inflationary expectations and nominal interest rates fell through the 1990s and early 2000s, the difference between the real and nominal deficit (surplus) decreased, but the inflation that remained left bondholders requiring a small inflation premium, meaning that interest rates paid by government were higher than they otherwise would have been.

The Definition of Debt and Assets

Debt is accumulated deficits minus accumulated surpluses. Whereas *deficit* is a flow concept, *debt* is a stock concept.

Debt is *accumulated deficits minus accumulated surpluses*. Whereas deficits and surpluses are flow measures (they are defined for a period of time), debt is a stock measure (it is defined at a point in time). For example, say you've spent $30,000 a year for 10 years and have had annual income of $20,000 for 10 years. So you've had a deficit of $10,000 per year—a flow. At the end of 10 years, you will have accumulated a debt of $100,000 (10 × $10,000 = $100,000)—a stock. (Spending more than you have in income means that you need to borrow the extra $10,000 per year from someone, so in later years much of your expenditure will be for interest on your previous debt.) If a country has been running more surpluses than deficits, the accumulated surpluses minus accumulated deficits are counted as part of its assets.

Q-6 Distinguish between *deficit* and *debt*.

Debt Management

Web Note 34.1
Public Debt 101

The U.S. government, through its Treasury Department, must continually refinance the bonds that are coming due by selling new bonds, as well as sell new bonds when running a deficit. This makes for a very active market in U.S. government bonds, and the interest rate paid on government bonds is a closely watched statistic in the economy. If the government runs a surplus, it can either retire some of its previously issued bonds by buying them back or simply not replace the previously issued bonds when they come due.

To judge a country's debt, we must view its debt in relation to its assets.

The Need to Judge Debt Relative to Assets Debt is also a summary measure of a country's financial situation. As a summary measure, debt has even more problems than deficit. Unlike a deficit, which is the difference between outflows and inflows, and hence provides both sides of the ledger, debt by itself is only half of a picture. The other half of the picture is assets. For a country, assets include its skilled workforce, its natural resources, its factories, its housing stock, and its holdings of foreign assets. For a government, assets include not only the buildings and land it owns but also, and more important, a portion of the assets of the people in the country, since government gets a portion of all earnings of those assets in tax revenue.

REAL-WORLD APPLICATION

Social Security and the U.S. Deficit

If you listen to *Car Talk* on PBS, you know that Tom and Ray Magliozzi often leave readers with a puzzler. In economics we also have puzzlers, and here's one of them for you to ponder. If debt is accumulated deficits, then the change in the debt in a particular year should be the size of the deficit or surplus. So if the U.S. debt is $9,229 billion as it was in 2007, and the deficit in 2008 is $455 billion, then the U.S. debt in 2008 should be 455 + 9,229 = $9,684 billion. When we look at the data however, we see that debt in 2008 was $10,700 billion. Why is this?

Car Talk makes you wait a week for the answer, but we don't have a week, so here's the answer. The deficit that the government reports is the deficit on what is called the unified budget, which is comprised of "off-budget" accounts (government trust funds, including the Social Security system) and "on-budget" accounts (most other government tax revenues and expenditures). The debt the government reports, however, does not include other government accounts, such as the Social Security system account, which at the time were running surpluses. The only asset that Social Security can hold is government bonds. So it is buying government debt (bonds) with its surplus revenues, building up a trust fund of assets to pay benefits to future retirees. In effect, the government on-budget account owes the Social Security and other trust funds $4.1 trillion.

So the answer to the puzzler is that the reported government debt is on the on-budget accounts only while the reported deficit is on the unified account. Since the government is reporting different concepts, there is no reason that the debt in one year plus the deficit should equal the debt in the following year unless the Social Security and other government trust accounts are in balance. Of course, the larger debt reported is offset by the assets in the trust fund, but as I will discuss that in the appendix to this chapter, this method of accounting should leave you wondering how much trust you should have in the Social Security trust fund.

To get an idea of why the addition of assets is necessary to complete the debt picture, consider two governments: one has debt of $3 trillion and assets of $50 trillion; the other has only $1 trillion in debt but only $1 trillion in assets. Which is in a better financial position? The government with the $3 trillion debt is because its debt is significantly exceeded by its assets. The point is simple: To judge a country's debt, we must view its debt in relation to all its assets.

Q-7 Why is debt only half the picture of a country's financial situation?

This need to judge debt relative to assets adds an important caveat to the long-run position that government budget deficits are bad. When the government runs a deficit, it might be spending on projects that increase its assets. If the assets are valued at more than their costs, then the deficit is making the society better off. Government investment can be as productive as private investment or even more productive.

To distinguish between expenditures that are building up assets and those that are not, many businesses have separate capital and expenditures budgets. When they run deficits in their capital account, we do not say that they are spending recklessly; we say that they are investing in the future, and generally we applaud that investment. We say they are running a deficit only in reference to their expenditures budget. While the U.S. government budget separates out investment from noninvestment expenditures, it does not have a separate capital account; it reports a consolidated budget, so it does not take into account the asset accumulation or the depreciation of its assets in determining its deficit.

Why aren't government finances generally discussed in relation to separate current and capital budgets? Because with government expenditures it is extraordinarily difficult to determine what an investment is. Business's investments will earn income that allows the business to pay off those investments. Most government goods earn no income; they are supplied free to individuals and are paid for by taxes. Impossible-to-answer questions arise such as: Are expenditures on new teachers an investment in better knowledge? Or: Are expenditures on a poverty program an investment in a better

ADDED DIMENSION

Generational Accounting

As I have emphasized in the text, different accounting procedures shed light on slightly different issues. Each provides a different perspective of the financial situation, and the combination of them provides you with a full understanding of the issues. One accounting procedure that some economists use is generational accounting. Generational accounting shows government deficits in terms of each generation's net lifetime tax payments and benefits received. Economists such as Larry Kotlikoff and Alan Auerbach have shown that our current system of taxation and transfers results in an intergenerational transfer of resources from younger to older generations. With the older generation becoming larger as the baby boomers age, these transfers are likely to put a severe strain on the tax system and the political foundations of our tax and transfer policies over the next couple of decades.

social environment? There are no unambiguous answers to these and similar questions; government accountants believe it is best to avoid such questions altogether.

Assets and debt are subject to varying definitions.

Arbitrariness in Defining Debt and Assets Like income and revenues, assets and debt are subject to varying definitions. Say, for example, that an 18-year-old is due to inherit $1 million at age 21. Should that expected future asset be counted as an asset now? Or say that the government buys an aircraft for $1 billion and discovers that it doesn't fly. What value should the government place on that aircraft? Or say that a country owes $1 billion, due to be paid 10 years from now, but inflation is ongoing at 20 percent per year. The inflation will reduce the value of the debt when it comes due by so much that its current real value will be $162 million—the approximate present value of $1 billion in 10 years with 20 percent inflation. It will be like paying about $162 million today. Should the country list the debt as a $1 billion debt or a $162 million debt?

As was the case with income, revenues, and deficits, there's no single answer to how assets and debts should be valued. So even after you take assets into account, you still have to be careful when deciding whether or not to be concerned about debt.

The government holds about 45 percent of its own debt.

The arbitrariness of the debt figure can be seen by considering the holdings of U.S. debt more carefully. In 2008, the U.S. government had a total of $10.7 trillion in debt, but the actual amount held by people and organizations outside the federal government is much less than that, as shown in Figure 34-1. There you can see that 45 percent of the debt is internal to the government (including the Fed's holdings)—one branch of

FIGURE 34-1
Ownership of U.S. Government Debt

This pie chart shows that the debt is held by U.S. citizens, foreign citizens, financial institutions, and other government entities including state and local governments.

Source: *Treasury Bulletin*, U.S. Department of the Treasury, December 2008 (www.fms.treas.gov).

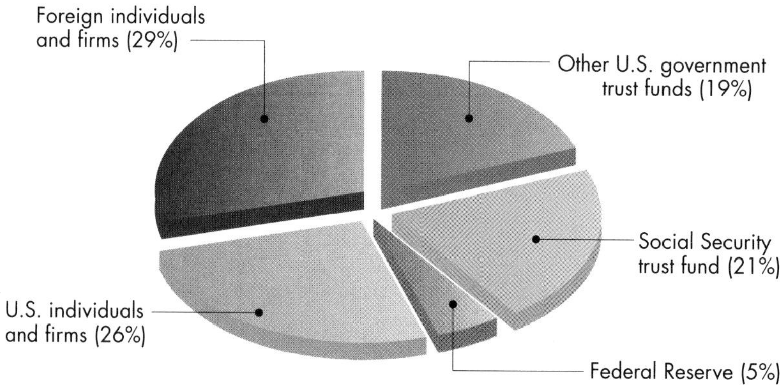

the federal government owes another branch of the government the debt. It is an asset of one part of government and a debt of another part. When we net out these offsetting debts and assets, the total federal debt decreases from about $10.7 trillion to $5.8 trillion. Of that $5.8 trillion, about 47 percent is held by U.S. individuals and firms and about 53 percent is held by foreign individuals and firms.

Many of the bonds to finance the current deficit are being bought by the Social Security trust fund, a fund managed by the Social Security Administration in order to meet its future obligations. By law, the Social Security trust fund must be held in the form of nonmarketable government bonds. This means that one agency of government (the Social Security Administration) is buying the bonds of another agency (the Treasury Department). Until about 2016, when the Social Security system's outlays are predicted to exceed its revenues, the percentage of debt held by government agencies will continue to increase. In 2008, the Social Security trust fund owned 21 percent of the debt. By 2012, the fund is expected to own 50 percent of the debt. (The Social Security system will be discussed in more detail in the appendix to this chapter.)

Difference between Individual and Government Debt

The final point I want to make concerns the quotation from the beginning of the chapter, by Franklin D. Roosevelt, about deficit spending leading to the poorhouse. Roosevelt may have been a great president, but based on that comment, he probably would have failed his economics course. All debt is not the same. In particular, government debt is different from an individual's debt. There are three reasons for this.

First, government is ongoing. Government never has to pay back its debt. An individual's life span is limited; when a person dies, there's inevitably an accounting of assets and debt to determine whether anything is left to go to heirs. Before any part of a person's estate is passed on, all debts must be paid. The government, however, doesn't ever have to settle its accounts.

Second, government has an option that individuals don't have for paying off a debt. Specifically, it can pay off a debt by creating money. As long as people will accept a country's currency, a country can always exchange money (non-interest-bearing debt) for bonds (interest-bearing debt).

Third, total government debt includes **internal debt** *(government debt owed to other governmental agencies or to its own citizens)*. Paying interest on the internal debt involves a redistribution among citizens of the country, but it does not involve a net reduction in income of the average citizen. For example, say that a country has $3 trillion in internal debt. Say also that the government pays $150 billion in interest on its debt each year. That means the government must collect $150 billion in taxes, so people are $150 billion poorer; but it pays out $150 billion in interest to them, so, on average, people in the country are neither richer nor poorer because of the debt. **External debt** *(government debt owed to individuals in foreign countries)* is more like an individual's debt. Paying interest on external debt involves a net reduction in domestic income. U.S. taxpayers will be poorer; foreign holders of U.S. bonds will be richer.

Three reasons government debt is different from individual debt are

1. The government lives forever; people don't.
2. The government can print money to pay its debt; people can't.
3. Government owes much of its debt to itself—to its own citizens.

Q-8 Why do economists distinguish between internal and external debt?

WWW Web Note 34.2 External Debts

U.S. Government Deficits and Debt: The Historical Record

Now that we have been through the basics of deficits and debt, let's look at the historical record. From World War II until recently, the U.S. government ran almost continual deficits. From the 1950s to the early 1970s, the government budget balance fluctuated between small $3 billion surpluses to $25 billion deficits. Beginning in the mid-1970s,

FIGURE 34-2 (A AND B) U.S. Budget Deficits and Debt Relative to GDP

The size of the deficits and the size of the debt look somewhat different when considered relative to the GDP. Notice specifically how the total debt-to-GDP ratio declined substantially from the 1950s to the 1980s and how it increased in the 1980s and early 1990s. It declined in the late 1990s and early 2000s, but then rose substantially in 2008 and 2009. [In Figure 34-2(a), deficits are stated as negative values.]

Source: *The Economic and Budget Outlook*, Congressional Budget Office, 2009 (www.cbo.gov); U.S. Bureau of the Census, *Historical Statistics*, and estimates.

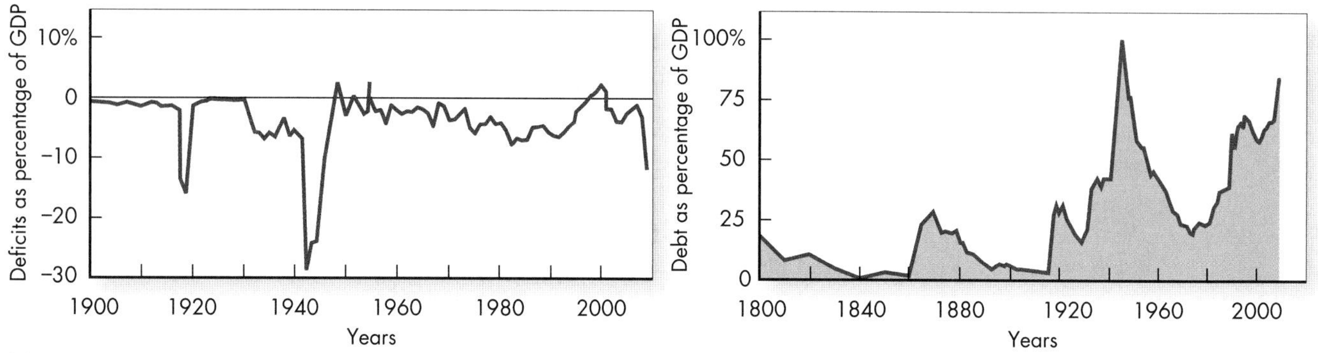

(a) Budget Deficits as Percentage of GDP **(b) Debt as Percentage of GDP**

deficits grew considerably, from $53 billion in 1975 to $290 billion in 1992, before declining in the mid-1990s, disappearing in 1998, but then reappearing in 2002. Over most of that time, total debt has increased. It doubled in the 30 years from 1946 to 1975 and grew more quickly beginning in the mid-1970s, rising by a multiple of 30 to $10.7 trillion by 2008. Most economists, however, are much more concerned with deficits and debt relative to GDP than with the absolute figures.

Figure 34-2 graphs the budget deficit and debt as a percentage of GDP. From this perspective, as you can see in Figure 34-2(a), deficits as a percentage of GDP did not rise significantly in the 1970s and the 1980s, as they did when we considered them in absolute terms. And it's the same with debt. As you can see in Figure 34-2(b), debt, relative to GDP, has not been continually increasing. Instead, from the end of World War II to the 1970s, and from 1988 to 1990, the debt/GDP ratio actually decreased. In the mid-1990s it stabilized at somewhat under 70 percent of GDP, and in the late 1990s and early 2000s it fell to about 60 percent. Then, it started to rise again to 75 percent in 2008 and is expected to rise significantly more in 2009.

Deficits and debt relative to GDP provide measures of a country's ability to pay off a deficit and service its debt.

Economists prefer the "relative to GDP" measure because it better measures the government's ability to handle the deficit; a nation's ability to pay off a debt depends on its productive capacity (the asset side of the picture). GDP serves the same function for government as income does for an individual. It provides a measure of how much debt, and how large a deficit, government can handle. So when GDP grows, so does the debt the government can reasonably carry.

The Debt Burden

Most of the decrease in the debt-to-GDP ratio in U.S. history occurred through growth in GDP. Growth in GDP can occur in two ways: through inflation (a rise in nominal but not real GDP) or through real growth. Both ways reduce the problem of the debt. As I discussed above, inflation wipes out the value of existing debt; with inflation, there can be large nominal budget deficits but a small real deficit.

Q-9 What annual deficit could a $5 billion economy growing at a real annual rate of 5 percent have without changing its debt/GDP ratio?

When an economy experiences real growth, the ability of the government to incur debt is increased; the economy becomes richer and, being richer, can handle more debt. As

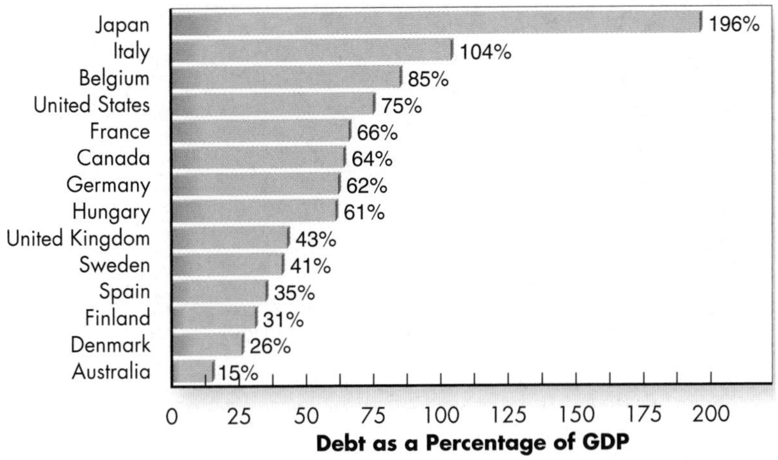

FIGURE 34-3 U.S. Debt Compared to Foreign Countries' Debt

The U.S. debt does not appear so large when compared to the debts of some other countries in the early 2000s.

Source: *World Economic Outlook*, International Monetary Fund (www.imf.org), and individual country Web pages, www.econstats.com.

noted in an earlier chapter, real growth in the United States has averaged about 2.5 to 3.5 percent per year, which means that U.S. debt can grow at a rate of 2.5 to 3.5 percent without increasing the debt/GDP ratio. But for debt to grow, government must run a deficit, so a constant debt/GDP ratio in a growing economy is consistent with a continual deficit.

How much of a deficit are we talking about? U.S. federal government debt in 2008 was about $10.7 trillion and GDP was about $14 trillion, so the government debt/GDP ratio was about 75 percent. A real growth rate of 2.5 percent means that real GDP is growing at about $350 billion per year. That means that government can run a deficit of $263 billion a year without increasing the debt/GDP ratio. Of course, for those who believe that the total U.S. government debt is already too large relative to GDP, this argument (that the debt/GDP ratio is remaining constant) is unsatisfying. They'd prefer the debt/GDP ratio to fall.

U.S. Debt Relative to Other Countries

When judged relative to other countries, the United States does not have an especially large debt burden, as can be seen in Figure 34-3. Notice that the U.S. debt is only 75 percent of GDP. If it were 106 percent, as it is in Italy, the U.S. debt would be approximately $4 trillion higher than it is. This international comparison, combined with the fact that much of the U.S. debt is held by other government agencies, suggests that the U.S. government can have trillions of dollars more in debt before there is significant need for concern.

Interest Rates and Debt Burden

Considering debt relative to GDP is still not quite sufficient to give an accurate picture of the debt burden. How much of a burden a given amount of debt imposes depends on the interest rate that must be paid on that debt. The annual **debt service** is *the interest rate on debt times the total debt*.

In 2008, the U.S. government paid out approximately $250 billion in interest. A larger debt would require even higher interest payments. The interest payment is government revenue that can't be spent on defense or welfare; it's a payment for past expenditures. Ultimately, the interest payments are the burden of the debt. That's what people mean when they say a deficit is burdening future generations.

FIGURE 34-4
Federal Interest Payments Relative to GDP

Interest payments as a percentage of GDP remained relatively constant until the 1970s, after which they rose significantly due to high interest rates and large increases in debt. In the late 1990s, they fell as interest rates fell and surpluses reduced the total debt and started to rise slightly in the early 2000s.

Source: *The Economic and Budget Outlook*, Congressional Budget Office, 2009 (www.cbo.gov).

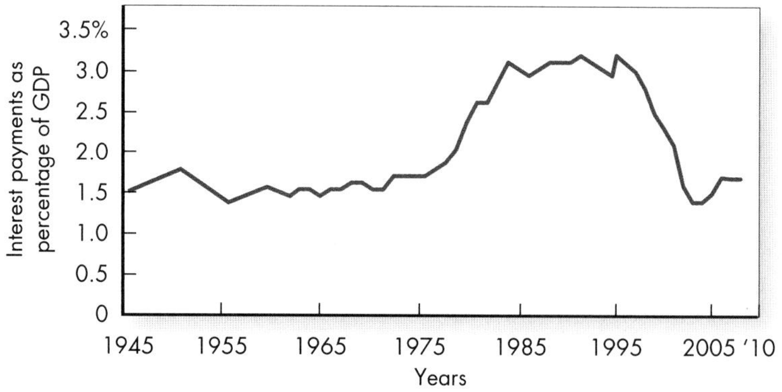

Over the past 50 years, the interest rate has fluctuated considerably; when it has risen, the debt service has increased; when it has fallen, debt service has decreased. Figure 34-4 shows the federal interest payments relative to GDP. This ratio increased substantially in World War II and then again in the 1970s and early 1980s. In the mid 1990s it declined, but in the early 2000s it began to rise again and is currently between 1.5 and 2 percent. As long as the government has a debt, it will make interest payments.

The United States can afford its current debt in the sense that it can afford to pay the interest on that debt. In fact, as I discussed above, it could afford a much higher debt/GDP ratio since U.S. government bonds are still considered one of the safest assets in the world. No one is worried about the U.S. government's defaulting; that's why we stated above that the U.S. debt can be increased by trillions of dollars without problems.

A REMINDER

Four Important Points about Deficits and Debt

1. Deficits are summary measures of the state of the economy. They are dependent on the accounting procedures used.
2. It is the health of the economy, not the deficit, with which we should be concerned.
3. Deficits and debt should be viewed relative to GDP to determine their importance.
4. Real deficit = Nominal deficit − (Inflation × Debt).

Projections for the Deficit

As mentioned earlier in the chapter, as recently as 2000, projections were for continual budget surpluses and a paying down of the debt. In 2001 Congress passed the Economic Growth and Tax Relief Reconciliation Act, which cut taxes significantly. Simultaneously, economic growth slowed and, with the war on terrorism, government expenditures increased significantly. Together, these factors reduced revenues and raised expenditures, turning the surpluses into deficits in 2002.

In 2003 and 2004, Congress cut taxes further and the war in Iraq lasted far longer and was far more costly than expected, leading to continued deficits that were declining as a percentage of GDP. However, in 2008, the U.S. economy experienced a severe financial crisis, which led to what is expected to be the deepest recession since World War II. In response to the financial crisis and the freezing up of credit markets, congress created a $700 billion fund to prevent large financial institutions from collapsing. The government used this fund to buy financial assets, which while not expenditures on goods, still showed up as government budget expenditures and raised the deficit. In addition to these expenditures, in early 2009 the government passed a $800 billion stimulus package of tax cuts and expenditure increases to fight the recession. These two policies, combined with the automatic stabilizers set in motion by the recession, increased the 2009 budget deficit to over $1.8 trillion,

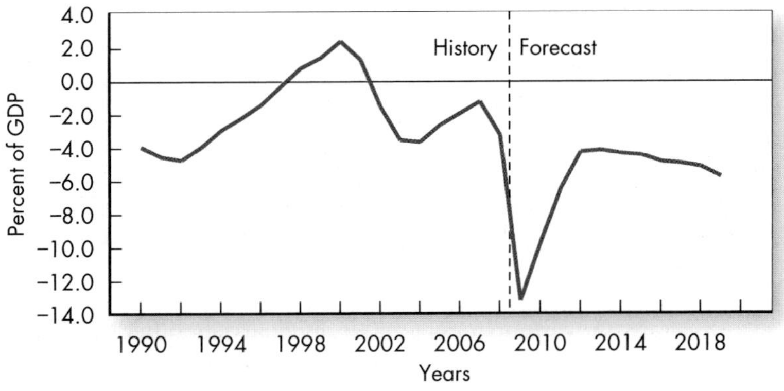

FIGURE 34-5
Projections for the Budget Deficit

In the late 1990s, the deficit as a percentage of GDP declined, and in early 2000, it moved into surplus. Tax cuts and spending increases soon pushed it into deficit at about 3 percent of GDP. The financial crisis and recession in 2008–2009 led to a large increase in the deficit to well over 10 percent of GDP, and large structural deficits are expected to continue even if the economy recovers, which is what these estimates assume.

Source: Congressional Budget Office Budget Projections, January 2009.

which, as you can see in Figure 34-5 is 13 percent of GDP, the largest deficit in both absolute and percentage terms since World War II.

As a percent of GDP, deficits are predicted to decrease over the coming years as the economy comes out of the recession and grows. But assuming taxes and spending continue as planned, even with this expected recovery and growth, a large unsustainable structural deficit will remain. The reason is that structural deficits do not disappear through growth and recovery but must be dealt with structurally. This means that in the coming years, U.S. taxes must be raised or government expenditures must be cut if the deficit is to be cut to be less than 5 percent of GDP. If that is not done, the deficits will continue to be high throughout the next decade, adding almost $10 trillion to the U.S. debt. Adding that much government debt is worrisome; it raises the prospect that U.S. government debt will become less desirable for individuals to hold. If that happens, the U.S. government will have to pay higher interest rates that include a risk premium on its debt. Thus, while the U.S. political system has avoided facing up to the "no free lunch" precept in the past, it is unlikely to be able to not face up to it in the future. It is not a prospect that politicians look forward to.

Q-10 How did the Economic Growth and Tax Relief Reconciliation Act of 2001 contribute to the return of deficits?

Conclusion

This has been a relatively short chapter, but the points in it are important. Deficits, debts, and surpluses are all accounting measures. Whether a budget is in surplus or deficit is not especially important. What is important is the health of the economy. The economic framework tells us that if the economy is in a recession, you shouldn't worry much about deficits—they can actually be good for the economy. If you are in an expansion, surpluses make much more sense. It is the state of the economy that we need to consider when making decisions about whether deficits or surpluses are good.

Economics also tells us that there are limits to how much real output one can transfer with financial assets over time. In each time period, the real aggregate demand must equal the real aggregate supply; otherwise inflation or deflation will result. When demographic changes cause real supply and demand to differ substantially, as they will begin to do in the 2020s, there will be a real problem that financial transfers cannot solve. The *AS/AD* model tells us that that "real" problem must have a "real" solution. Politically we are unlikely to hear much discussion of such solutions, which is why the future economic health of the United States can be precarious even if the U.S. budget is in surplus.

Summary

- A deficit is a shortfall of revenues under payments. A surplus is the excess of revenues over payments. Debt is accumulated deficits minus accumulated surpluses.
- Budget deficits and surpluses should be judged in light of economic and political conditions.
- Deficits and surpluses are summary measures of a budget. Whether a budget deficit is a problem depends on the budgeting procedures that measure it.
- A passive deficit is that part of the deficit that exists because the economy is below or above potential:

  Passive deficit =
  Tax rate × (Potential output − Actual output)
- A structural deficit is that part of a budget deficit that would exist even if the economy were at its potential level of income.

  Structural deficit = Actual deficit − Passive deficit
- A real deficit is a nominal deficit adjusted for the effect of inflation:

  Real deficit = Nominal deficit − (Inflation × Debt)
- A country's debt must be judged in relation to its assets. What is counted as a debt and as an asset can be arbitrary.
- Government debt and individual debt differ in three major ways: (1) government is ongoing and never needs to repay its debt, (2) government can pay off its debt by printing money, and (3) most of government debt is internal—owed to its own citizens.
- Deficits, surpluses, and debt should be viewed relative to GDP because this ratio better measures the government's ability to handle the deficit and pay off the debt. Compared to many countries, the United States has a low debt-to-GDP ratio.
- The Economic Growth and Tax Relief Reconciliation Act of 2001, an economic slowdown, and the war on terrorism contributed to a return to budget deficits in 2002.

Key Terms

debt *(802)*
debt service *(807)*
deficit *(798)*
external debt *(805)*
internal debt *(805)*
nominal deficit *(801)*
passive deficit *(800)*
real deficit *(801)*
Social Security system *(799)*
structural deficit *(800)*
surplus *(798)*

Questions and Exercises

1. "Budget deficits should be avoided, even if the economy is below potential, because they reduce saving and lead to lower growth." Does this policy directive follow from the short-run or the long-run framework? Explain your answer. LO1
2. What are the two ways government can finance a budget deficit? LO1
3. Your income is $40,000 per year; your expenditures are $45,000. You spend $10,000 of that $45,000 for tuition. Is your budget in deficit or surplus? Why? LO1
4. Canada's debt was $630 billion at the end of 2003. Using the information below (in billions of Canadian dollars), fill in the blanks for Canada's budget balance and debt for the following years: LO1

	Revenues	Expenditures	Debt
2004	$203	$202	$___
2005	215	___	626
2006	227	221	___
2007	___	230	619
2008	258	243	___

5. If the structural budget deficit is $100 billion and the actual deficit is $300 billion, what is the size of the passive or cyclical deficit? LO2
6. If the actual budget deficit is $100 billion, the economy is operating $250 billion above its potential, and the marginal tax rate is 20 percent, what are the structural deficit and the passive deficit? LO2
7. Say the marginal tax rate is 30 percent and that government expenditures do not change with output. Say also that the economy is at potential output and that the deficit is $200 billion.
   a. What is the size of the passive deficit?
   b. What is the size of the structural deficit?
   c. How would your answers to *a* and *b* change if the deficit were still $200 billion but the output were $200 billion below potential?
   d. How would your answers to *a* and *b* change if the deficit were still $200 billion but output were $100 billion above potential?
   e. Which is likely of more concern to policy makers: a passive or a structural deficit? LO2
8. Calculate the real deficit or surplus in the following cases:
   a. Inflation is 10 percent. Debt is $3 trillion. Nominal deficit is $220 billion.
   b. Inflation is 2 percent. Debt is $1 trillion. Nominal deficit is $50 billion.
   c. Inflation is −4 percent. (Price levels are falling.) Debt is $500 billion. Nominal deficit is $30 billion.
   d. Inflation is 3 percent. Debt is $2 trillion. Nominal surplus is $100 billion. LO3
9. Inflation is 20 percent. Debt is $2 trillion. The nominal deficit is $300 billion. What is the real deficit? LO3
10. How would your answer to question 9 differ if you knew that expected inflation was 15 percent? LO3
11. Assume a country's nominal GDP is $600 billion, government expenditures less debt service are $145 billion, and revenue is $160 billion. The nominal debt is $360 billion. Inflation is 3 percent and interest rates are 6 percent.
    a. Calculate debt service payments.
    b. Calculate the nominal deficit.
    c. Calculate the real deficit. LO3
12. List three ways in which individual debt differs from government debt. LO4
13. If all of the government's debt were internal, would financing that debt make the nation poorer? LO4
14. Why is debt service an important measure of whether debt is a problem? LO4
15. Assume that a country's real growth is 2 percent per year, while its real deficit is rising 5 percent a year.
    a. Can the country continue to afford such deficits indefinitely?
    b. What problems might it face in the future? LO4

Questions from Alternative Perspectives

1. International issues aside, what limits government's ability to undertake monetary or fiscal policy? (Austrian)
2. To help understand the distributional consequences of the tax cuts advocated by many conservative politicians, answer the following:
   a. What income groups have the largest marginal propensity to consume: high or low income?
   b. If your goal were to minimize the deficit cost of a tax stimulus, who should receive the tax cuts? Who received the tax cuts?
   c. What will the tax cut do, relatively speaking, to the debt?
   d. Is there a pattern here? (Institutionalist)
3. After President George W. Bush's election in 2000, he proposed cutting taxes.
   a. Would you consider that proposal Keynesian, Classical, or a combination of the two?
   b. From your response, how should President Bush have dealt with the U.S. deficit to be consistent with the school of thought that you chose? (Post-Keynesian)
4. If future economic growth rates average as little as 2.4 percent—far slower than the 3.0 percent average growth rate the U.S. economy posted over the last 75 years—the Social Security system will remain solvent long into the foreseeable future. A shortfall of 0.4 percent of GDP as projected by the CBO could be paid for merely by repealing the Bush tax cuts that go to the richest 1 percent of taxpayers. Those tax giveaways to the best off in our society will cost 0.6 percent of GDP if they are made permanent.
   a. How does that position differ from your textbook's position that the real problem with Social Security is not its solvency but the future mismatch between real production and real expenditures?
   b. What do both these positions suggest about the effectiveness of proposals to divert Social Security funds into private accounts? (Radical)
5. Over 40 countries in the world now report what has been called a "women's budget," analyzing public expenditures and revenue from a gender perspective.
   a. What might be an example of a gender effect on the expenditure side of the budget?
   b. On the revenue side?
   c. Why are these effects important to consider? (Feminist)

Issues to Ponder

1. Two economists are debating whether the target rate of unemployment is 4 percent or 6 percent. Mr. A believes it's 4 percent; Ms. B believes it's 6 percent. One says the structural deficit is $40 billion; the other says it's $20 billion. Which one says which? Why? (Difficult) LO2
2. "The debt should be of concern." What additional information do you need to undertake a reasonable discussion of this statement? LO4
3. You've been hired by Creative Accountants, economic consultants. Your assignment is to make suggestions about how to structure a government's accounts so that the current deficit looks as small as possible. Specifically, they want to know how to treat the following: (Difficult)
   a. Government pensions.
   b. Sale of land.
   c. Social Security taxes.
   d. Proceeds of a program to allow people to prepay taxes for a 10 percent discount.
   e. Expenditures on F-52 bombers. LO4
4. How can a government that isn't running a deficit still get itself into financial trouble? LO4

Answers to Margin Questions

1. Deficits can be good when an economy is operating below its potential because they increase aggregate demand and total output. Deficits can be bad in the long run if they lead to lower investment because lower investment will lead to lower growth. *(798)*
2. The U.S. government sells bonds to finance deficit spending. *(798)*
3. Since the economy is at its potential income, its passive deficit is zero. All of its budget deficit is a structural deficit. *(800)*
4. Inflation reduces the value of the dollars with which the debt will be repaid and hence, in real terms, wipes out a portion of the debt. *(801)*
5. The real deficit equals the nominal deficit minus inflation times the total debt. Inflation times the total debt in this case equals $80 billion (0.02 × $4 trillion). Since the nominal deficit is $40 billion, the real deficit is actually a surplus of $40 billion ($40 billion − $80 billion = −$40 billion). *(801)*
6. Deficit is a flow concept, the difference between income and expenditures. Debt—accumulated deficits minus accumulated surpluses—is a stock concept. *(802)*
7. To get a full picture of a country's financial situation, you have to look at assets as well as debt since a large debt for a country with large assets poses no problem. *(803)*
8. Paying interest on internal debt redistributes income among citizens in a country. Paying interest on external debt is a reduction in domestic income. *(805)*
9. A $5 billion economy growing at a real annual rate of 5 percent could have an annual deficit of $250 million (0.05 × $5 billion) and not increase its debt/GDP ratio. *(806)*
10. The act contributed to the return of deficits by lowering tax revenues and increasing government spending. *(809)*

APPENDIX A

Social Security, Medicare, and Lockboxes

One of the debates about how concerned we should be about deficits involves the Social Security system. To understand this debate about Social Security and deficits, it is important to recognize that the United States uses a **cash flow accounting system**—*an accounting system entering expenses and revenues only when cash is received or paid out*. When it spends or collects money, these outflows or inflows show up on the budget. When the government doesn't have a cash inflow or outflow, nothing shows up on the budget. Thus, in 2004, when the government created a drug benefit for future retirees, the government incurred enormous future obligations; those obligations didn't show up as part of the deficit.

Currently the Social Security system is running a large surplus in its portion of the budget. According to one projection, however, Social Security will be legally required to pay out benefits to retirees that far exceed its revenue. Some politicians have argued that to safeguard the current revenue needed to pay these future obligations, we should create a "lockbox" in which current Social Security revenue would be locked up for future retirees. (In reality there would be no physical lockbox; the word is a metaphor for an accounting rule that would require the government to dedicate the surpluses in the Social Security portion of the budget to pay down the debt held by the public.)

While this proposal has certain attractive attributes, they are not those most people identify with the lockbox concept. The proposal would only indirectly help future Social Security recipients. To see how, let's consider the Social Security system more carefully.

The Social Security system began with the passage of the Federal Insurance Contribution Act (FICA) in 1935; FICA requires employees and firms to pay taxes and, in return, gives the employees a pension after they retire.

A Pay-as-You-Go System

The Social Security system was set up as a **pay-as-you-go system** where *the payments to current beneficiaries are funded through current payroll taxes*. This means that the Social Security system is an unfunded pension system. A *funded pension system* is a system where the contributions paid by workers plus interest are used to fund those workers' pensions. An *unfunded pension system*, however, is not necessarily unsound. In an ongoing system, there will always be revenue coming in and payments going out. There are always current workers to support a system that pays the aged. The benefit of the unfunded system is that it allows initial payments to individuals to exceed what they paid in. As long as the population's age distribution, the annual death rate, the number of people working, and productivity do not change much, an unfunded system runs smoothly.

The Effect of the Baby Boom

An unfunded system does, however, present a potential problem if the amount paid in differs from the amount paid out. To see this, say we have only three groups of people: workers, the retired elderly, and the very young (who aren't yet working). Now suddenly we start a pension program. We use the money that we collect from the workers to pay pensions to the elderly retired people, who have paid nothing in because they retired before the system started up. In short, this group gets benefits without having paid anything into the system. In the

This lithograph, titled "Legislative assault (on the budget)," appeared in a French newspaper in 1835.

FIGURE A34-1 Projection of Workers Compared with Social Security Retirees

The number of workers per retiree has declined considerably since 1945, and it will continue to decline in future decades.

Note: Working-age persons are aged 20–64, and retirement-age persons are aged 65 and over.

Source: Social Security Administration.

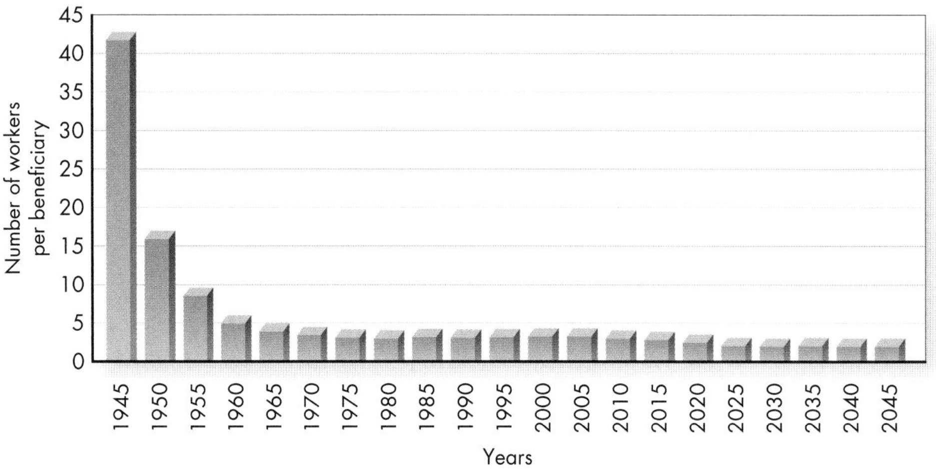

next generation, the elderly die, the workers become elderly, and the young become workers. The new group of elderly gets paid by the new workers. As long as the three groups remain at equivalent relative sizes, the process works neatly—each generation will get paid when its time comes.

But what happens when there's a "baby boom"—when one group has an unusually large number of children in a short period of time? In this case, the sizes of the generations are significantly different. Initially things work out wonderfully. The baby boomers become workers, and there are lots of them relative to the elderly. There's plenty of money coming in and comparatively little going out. This allows for an increase in payments to the elderly, a decrease in the taxes paid in by the working group, an increase in the trust fund, or some combination of the three.

In the next generation, the baby-boom workers become elderly. Then, assuming the baby boomers have fewer children than their own parents had, the number of people collecting benefits becomes larger but the number of workers contributing to the system becomes smaller. In this case, payments per beneficiary must decrease, real contributions per worker coming in must increase, or some combination of the two must occur. None of these alternatives is particularly pleasant.

This example doesn't come out of nowhere. It represents the current situation in the U.S. Social Security system. From 1946 through the late 1960s, there was a baby boom, and these baby boomers are currently in the labor force. They'll start retiring in large numbers in the early 2010s and, when they do, the number of workers per retiree will decrease, so that around 2020 there will be about 2.5 workers per retiree instead of more than 15 workers per retiree as in the 1950s. Figure A34-1 shows these unpleasant projections.

The Social Security Trust Fund

In the 1970s and 1980s, economists pointed out that this problem would be occurring. In response, in 1983 the government passed an amendment to the Social Security Act of 1935. The age of eligibility was raised slightly, Social Security tax rates (FICA) were raised, and Social Security payments became subject to taxation for some beneficiaries. These measures were designed to create surpluses in the coming years.

Currently, were it not for surpluses in the Social Security system, the budget deficit would be much larger. For example, as discussed in the text, in 2008 the Social Security system had a $180 billion surplus. Without this surplus and the surplus on other off-budget accounts, the government budget would have had a $638 billion deficit rather than a $450 billion deficit.

That portion of the surplus is not available for spending; it is earmarked for the Social Security trust fund, which holds special bonds issued by government that cannot be bought and sold on the bond market. The 1983 act was designed to produce surpluses that could be placed into a trust fund to make the payments coming due in the 2020 to 2040 period without requiring huge tax increases or massive borrowing then. The lockbox proposals are designed to ensure that those surpluses held in the trust fund would be available. In the early 2000s, the Social

Security Administration estimated that surpluses would continue until about 2020. At that time, outlays will begin to exceed revenue, and by about 2040, the Social Security trust fund will be used up and the system will have to either begin borrowing, increase revenue, or reduce benefits. This doesn't mean the system is in crisis; it is far from a crisis, but it does mean that some adjustments need to be made.

The Social Security system is not the only government spending program that will experience significant funding problems in the future. The Medicare program will face more serious problems; since the elderly use significantly more medical services than younger individuals, these expenses will be substantial. The problem of future funding of the system was exacerbated in 2004 when the government expanded the Medicare program to include partial coverage of drugs for the elderly. Since the elderly are heavy users of drugs, the cost of this coverage is likely to spiral as baby boomers retire. This Medicare program is far closer to crisis than is the Social Security program. It has been estimated that in 2030, 60 or even 65 percent of the government budget will be spent on Social Security and Medicare, compared to the current 35 percent.

The bottom line is that the U.S. budget, considered separately from the Social Security budget, is having to borrow much more than the amount of its current official deficit. Its borrowing offsets the saving represented by the trust fund, which exists to pay future Social Security claims.

Why should a student care about these issues? Because there is no such thing as a free lunch, and someone is going to have to pay. When the baby boomers retire but continue consuming, those who are students today but will be workers in the future (that's you) are the ones who will pay.

The Real Problem and the Real Solution

While the conventional wisdom is for government to run a surplus when the economy is booming, it does not suggest that the trust fund will provide the complete answer to the Social Security funding problem. Even if we had a fully funded trust fund, it would not solve the Social Security problem. The reason is that the trust fund is simply a financial solution; the actual solution must be a "real" solution—a solution that deals with the supply and demand of real resources, not with nominal amounts.

To understand why this is the case, it is helpful to think of the problem in terms of the *AS/AD* model, which tells us that, in equilibrium, real aggregate demand must

FIGURE A34-2 The Real Problem

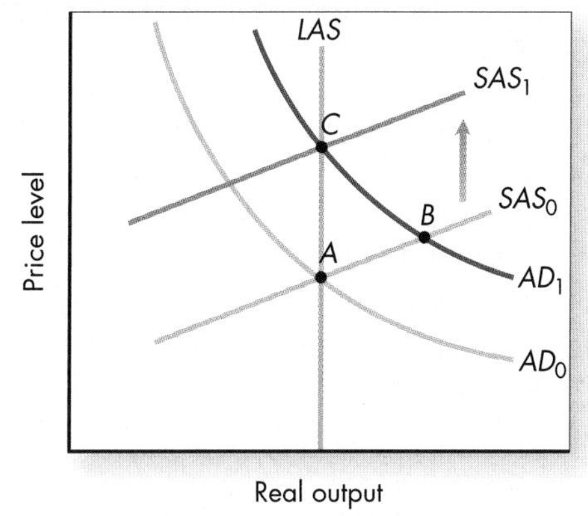

equal real aggregate supply—the amount of real goods available to consume must equal the amount of real goods for sale, as is true at point A in Figure A34-2. Herein lies the problem. When baby boomers, such as myself, retire in between 2010 and 2030, we will stop producing real goods, *but we will continue consuming* real goods. And given our medical needs, we will likely consume quite heavily—medicine, travel, and all that good stuff. Real goods must be provided to us. Our Social Security and Medicare payments, our other pensions, and our savings will give us significant nominal income to spend. In terms of the *AS/AD* model, the *AD* curve will shift to the right from AD_0 to AD_1. If that shift is not matched by a shift of the *LAS* curve, the quantity of aggregate demand will exceed the quantity of aggregate supply and the result will be inflation. That is, there will be pressure for the *SAS* curve to shift up and for inflation to rise. The problem is that someone has to produce the goods that we're spending on. That's where you and your fellow workers come in. Put bluntly, starting in 2010, you must produce not only enough real goods for yourself and your family but also enough for the retired baby boomers. Put another way, *the real output per worker must increase, but the real consumption of workers must not increase* as much if the increasing number of retired baby boomers are to have real goods to consume.

The Trust Fund Illusion

If this real problem—the need to match aggregate supply and aggregate demand—exists whether or not the Social Security trust fund exists, what does the trust fund do? The answer is "not much" directly, but it does have a positive indirect effect. The trust fund, like the lockbox policy meant to protect the trust fund, is an accounting illusion. When the United States created the Social Security system, it created obligations to individuals. What the trust fund does is to back that obligation with government bonds—an obligation of the government to pay a certain amount in the future. It backs one government obligation with another.

As I emphasized in the beginning of this chapter, the concepts of *deficit* and *surplus* are creatures of the accounting system used. Placing money into the Social Security trust fund essentially changes an unbooked obligation into a booked obligation. Given the political fear of deficits, this change may lead government to spend less now, and to keep taxes higher now, than it otherwise would. To the degree the government does this, the trust fund decreases the debt in private hands, making the interest burden of the debt less than it otherwise would have been. The holders of debt will not have the interest payments to spend on real goods in the future, making more real goods available for consumption in the future. So, the trust fund might help, even if it does not completely solve the problem.

Politics and Economic Policy[1]

Politics generally mixes illusions with reality, and both Republicans and Democrats have avoided discussing real solutions—solutions that match real production with real expenditures. They either want to assume that the Social Security trust fund will solve the problem, or they want to obfuscate (hide) the problem with rhetoric that doesn't really explain what the problem is. The real solution requires them to deal with the "real" problem that there is no free lunch.

Privatizing Social Security

One proposal being put forward is to privatize at least part of Social Security, creating what its advocates call an "ownership society." This may or may not be a good idea, but it will not solve the Social Security funding problem that the United States is facing. The reason is that the Social Security system is in large part a pay-as-you-go system. If younger people pull out of the system and move to private accounts, someone must pay the retirees who have been promised benefits. That can be done through either more government borrowing (the politically most-likely solution) or higher taxes. Privatization that does not reduce benefits or increase contributions does not solve the problem.

So what policy does provide a real solution? Any policy that brings the real forces of aggregate demand and aggregate supply into equilibrium. The matching of real production with real expenditures could be accomplished if you and your fellow workers save a large portion of your income rather than consume it; if you increase your productivity without increasing your pay; if the government taxes you more heavily starting in 2010, so you don't have income to spend; if Social Security recipients choose to save rather than spend their income; or if even more foreign saving flows in than has already been flowing into the United States. Policies that lead to these results will alleviate the problem.

All real policies achieve one of two ends: They increase future workers' contributions to real production more than they increase their consumption, or they reduce the real amount I and my fellow baby boomers spend when we retire. There are a number of ways such reductions can be accomplished, none of them politically attractive, which is why they are not much talked about. If not accomplished through policy, the spending reduction will be accomplished through inflation.

One policy is to increase taxes on workers. Another is to cut benefits once baby boomers start retiring. One way to cut benefits is to make Social Security "means tested," so that high-income individuals do not receive as much as they were promised. Another way to cut benefits is to increase the standard retirement age to 72. (It's now 65 to 68.)[2] This increase could be justified by the fact that the elderly live longer and are in better health now than in the past. Since many of us baby boomers will die off between 65 and 72, the savings would be considerable. Moreover, with the delayed Social Security benefits, many of us would work longer, increasing the number of people working and decreasing the number of people consuming without producing.

Neither of these benefit-cutting policies would affect the current budget picture, but both would significantly improve the U.S. economic picture because future real commitments would be decreased. I doubt that either of these policies will be considered, but they are the type of policies that will deal with the "real" macro problem facing the United States in the future.

---

[1]This section reflects my particular view, so treat it as a stimulant for thought, not as the correct view. Your teacher, who grades your exam, will tell you the "correct" view.

[2]Government pension systems were started by the 19th-century German leader Otto von Bismarck. He reportedly chose 65 as the retirement age because his advisers told him that vital statistics for the country showed most people died before age 65.

Key Terms

cash flow accounting system *(812)*

pay-as-you-go system *(813)*

Questions and Exercises

1. How did the Social Security system contribute to the surpluses of the late 1990s?
2. How can a baby boom cause problems for an unfunded pension system?
3. What are two solutions to the "real" problem posed by the growing number of retiring baby boomers beginning in 2020?
4. Why won't a fully funded Social Security trust fund solve the real problem the U.S. economy will face as more and more baby boomers retire?

CHAPTER 35

The Modern Fiscal Policy Dilemma

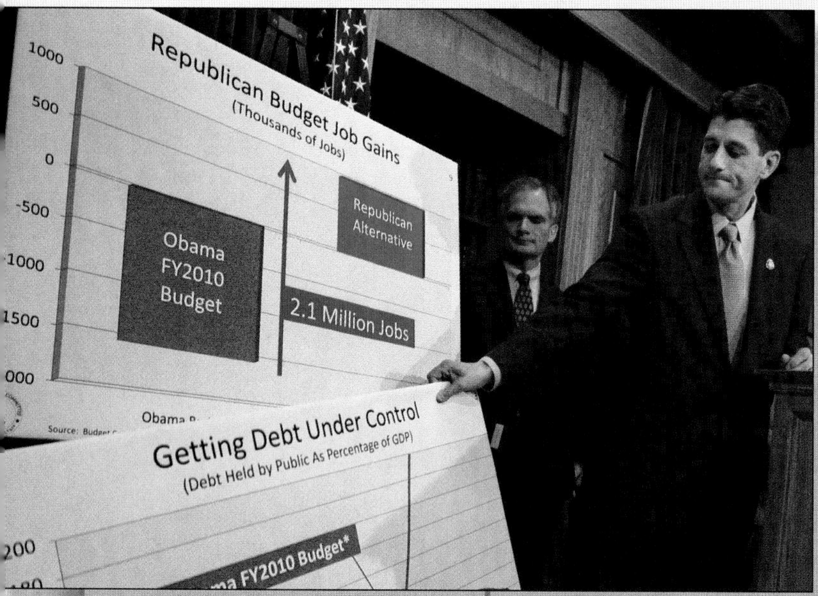

An economist's lag may be a politician's catastrophe.

—*George Schultz*

AFTER READING THIS CHAPTER, YOU SHOULD BE ABLE TO:

1. Explain the logic of the Ricardian equivalence theorem.
2. Distinguish sound finance from functional finance.
3. List six assumptions of the *AS*/*AD* model that lead to potential problems with the use of fiscal policy.
4. Explain how automatic stabilizers work.

Modern economies face a serious major policy dilemma. In a serious recession, such as the one that the world economies entered into in 2008, almost all economists agree that governments need to run expansionary fiscal policy—that is, deficits. That follows from the standard macro policy models. In the long run, however, governments need to maintain a solid financial situation, which means that they need to balance their budgets, or perhaps even run surpluses to offset some of the past deficits they built up trying to prevent recessions. The reason is not that deficits are inherently bad. The reason is that deficits reduce government's future borrowing capacity; if governments build up "too large" debt, they will likely find it harder to sell their debt in the future.[1] A government that cannot easily sell its debt will either go bankrupt or have to resort to inflationary finance, with the central bank financing the government by printing money. Neither is good for any economy.

So the modern fiscal policy dilemma is that when faced with the economy falling into a depression, governments need to run large deficits, but they can only do that for limited periods without undermining their long-run financial integrity. This chapter addresses that dilemma. In this chapter I do two things. First, I provide a brief discussion of the evolution of economists' thinking about fiscal policy, and how we arrived at the modern fiscal policy precepts that guide our thinking about modern fiscal policy. And second, I relate those precepts to the fiscal policy problems that an economy on the verge of a serious recession faces, such as the United States faced in 2009.

Classical Economics and Sound Finance

Let's begin by looking at how economists' views of public finance and fiscal policy have changed over time. Before the 1930s, economists generally supported a policy that was described as "sound finance." **Sound finance** was *a view of fiscal policy*

[1]The problem is deciding what is a too large debt. As we discussed in the last chapter, there is no simple way of specifying what is "too large." But the bigger the government's debt is, the closer it is getting to "too large." As a very rough rule of thumb, many economists use 100 percent of GDP as a benchmark for when debt is definitely getting "too large."

that the government budget should always be balanced except in wartime. Economists held this view based on a combination of political and economic grounds, but primarily on political grounds. (Before 1930, economic analysis and political analysis were not as separate as they are today, and it is hard to separate out positions held on political as opposed to economic grounds.) The reason politics was important is that the Classical liberal tradition, which was the dominant tradition of economists at the time, viewed government with suspicion, so any policy that would make it easier to increase government spending during peacetime was seen as undesirable.

Ricardian Equivalence Theorem: Deficits Don't Matter

Although the theoretical economists believed in the principle of sound finance, they also recognized that pure economic arguments for balancing the budget were weak or nonexistent. For example, David Ricardo, one of the most famous economists in the 19th century, pointed out that, in a purely theoretical sense, government spending financed by selling government bonds (the government running a budget deficit) was no different from government spending financed by taxes (the government running a balanced budget). The reason was that if the government ran deficits, it would have to increase taxes in the future both to pay the interest on the bonds and to repay the bonds when they came due. Those future taxes would make the taxpayers poorer in the same way that paying taxes now would make them poorer. Assuming people can borrow and save, and thereby shift spending between now and the future, people would save more now to pay for those future taxes. So, there is no reason why financing spending with a deficit should affect the aggregate level of income differently than financing spending with taxes. The difference between the two is simply a matter of who does the borrowing. It followed that a government deficit would not lead to an expansion of output in the economy. This *theoretical proposition that deficits do not affect the level of output in the economy because individuals increase their savings to account for expected future tax payments to repay the deficit* has become known as the **Ricardian equivalence theorem,** to which you were introduced in an earlier chapter.

Q-1 Does the Ricardian equivalence theorem lead to a policy of sound finance?

Web Note 35.1
When Do Deficits Matter?

Despite economists' recognition of the logical truth of the Ricardian equivalence theorem, most economists, including Ricardo, felt that, in practice, deficits could affect output and that it mattered a lot, politically, whether government financed its spending by bonds (ran deficits) or by taxes (balanced the budget). Based on their political ideology, economists of the time strongly pushed government to finance its spending with taxes, not bonds. Hence, their principle of sound finance. The reason they supported the principle of sound finance was because they felt that, politically, requiring government to follow the principle of sound finance made increasing government spending more difficult, and brought home to the politicians the central economic lesson that there is no free lunch. They argued that adhering to a policy of sound finance forced government to face the costs of a spending decision simultaneously with the benefits of that spending decision, something that bond finance—financing government spending by borrowing—did not do.

Because of their advocacy of sound finance, through the 1930s, fiscal policy—the deliberate running of a deficit or surplus to guide the level of aggregate output in the economy—was not part of the economist's lexicon. Although economists of the time recognized that government spending could impact the level of output in the economy, they felt that, except in wartime, the long-run fiscal integrity of the government that sound finance led to should override such concerns. So through the 1930s economists' answer to the exam question about what government should do if there was a recession was that the government should maintain a balanced budget.

Q-2 What would a pre-1930s Classical economist recommend government do if there is a recession?

The Sound-Finance Precept

The precept of sound finance was not absolute. For example, in the 1920s in Europe, and in the 1930s in the United States, the world economies fell into a sustained depression from which there seemed to be no escape. In response, major economists of the time such as A. C. Pigou, F. Knight, and J. M. Keynes started questioning the sound-finance principles for the short run. The reason was that they felt that the depressed state of the economy had created a vicious cycle in which the expectations of a continued depression kept investment spending low, which kept total spending low, and that low spending led to low output and high unemployment. They believed that the market would get out of the depression eventually, but as the depression continued, they came to believe that "eventually" was longer than was politically acceptable.

Given this collapse of economic expectations, many economists of the time favored giving up the principle of sound finance, at least temporarily, and using government spending to stimulate the economy. For example, numerous economists favored government public works programs such as the Federal Emergency Relief Program, which provided funds for unemployed workers, and the Works Progress Administration (WPA), which built roads and bridges. So, faced with a serious depression, economists were quite willing to support spending on these programs without tax increases, which essentially meant that they were willing to support deficit financing to stimulate the economy.

Their arguments for deficit spending were based on simple commonsense reasoning, not any complex underlying models (remember, their reasoning told them that, theoretically, Ricardian equivalence held, and deficits wouldn't expand the economy). But their theory also told them that depressions, such as the one in which the economy was stuck in the 1930s, shouldn't happen either. Given the depression that the economy was stuck in, they were willing to entertain the notion that it was possible that if the government spent more than it collected in taxes—ran a deficit—the economy would be jump-started: income would increase; the recipients of that increased income would spend more, creating a virtuous circle that ultimately would help pull the economy out of the recession. At least it was worth a try.

At the time, economists debated how much of the government spending stimulus would be offset by increased savings as bonds were sold to finance the deficit. But despite theoretical concerns, policy-making economists of the time generally felt that expansionary fiscal policy—government spending exceeding government tax revenues—could be of some use in helping pull an economy out of a severe recession. So, in the 1930s, economists' answer to the exam question, what to do if the economy is in a recession, changed from "do nothing" to a more nuanced answer. If the recession is small, maintain a policy of sound finance, but if it is a very bad recession—a depression—then consider trying to stimulate the economy with some government programs and deficit financing. But such deficit financing was a last resort that was inappropriate to small or moderate recessions.

Q-3 What would an economist who believes in nuanced sound finance recommend government do if there is a recession?

Keynesian Economics and Functional Finance

The textbook presentation of the economist's view of public finance and fiscal policy changed significantly in the late 1940s, as the ideas of J. M. Keynes' *The General Theory* worked their way into the principles of economics texts. Keynes' book was enormously important; it set in motion a series of events that influenced the way in which economists looked at the aggregate economy for about 50 years, and that still have some lingering effects on both the textbook presentation and applied policy. In fact, it was that book that created the field of macroeconomics and led to fiscal policy being seen as a method of controlling the level of income in the economy, rather than as just a practical policy that might be helpful in serious depressions.

Actually, what became known as Keynesian economics does not all follow from Keynes' work; *The General Theory* is a theoretical book, which is open to many interpretations about policy. The book does not mention fiscal policy as a policy tool; Keynes' support of fiscal policy as a practical tool predated his writing of *The General Theory* and was not dependent on it.[2] Instead, what became known as Keynesian economics was developed by his students together with a group of economists who were influenced by those students. In terms of what shows up in the textbook presentations, the ideas of one of those students, Abba Lerner, stands out. Lerner's book, *The Economics of Control*, spelled out what he called a *functional finance* view of public finance and fiscal policy. That functional finance view became the principles textbook view when Nobel Prize–winning economist Paul Samuelson incorporated it into his famous textbook, which established the template for all texts that followed.

Functional Finance

Q-4 How does functional finance differ from sound finance?

Functional finance held that, *as a theoretical proposition, governments should make spending and taxing decisions on the basis of their effect on the economy, not on the basis of some moralistic principle that budgets should be balanced.* Under functional finance, if spending in the economy was too low, the government should run a deficit; if spending was too high, the government should run a surplus.

To explain why functional finance was preferred to sound finance, Lerner gave the following famous analogy.

> Imagine yourself in a Buck Rogers interplanetary adventure, looking at a highway in a City of Tomorrow. The highway is wide and straight, and its edges are turned up so that it is almost impossible for a car to run off the road. What appears to be a runaway car is speeding along the road and veering off to one side. As it approaches the rising edge of the highway, its front wheels are turned so that it gets back onto the road and goes off at an angle, making for the other side, where the wheels are turned again. This happens many times, the car zigzagging but keeping on the highway until it is out of sight. You are wondering how long it will take for it to crash, when another car appears which behaves in the same fashion. When it comes near you, it stops with a jerk. A door is opened, and an occupant asks whether you would like a lift. You look into the car and before you can control yourself you cry out, "Why, there's no steering wheel." Want a ride?

For Lerner, the aggregate economy was subject to wild fluctuations and it needed a steering wheel to guide it. Fiscal policy was that steering wheel. Notice that the total focus here is on the government steering the economy; there is no discussion of politics or whether the recession is a major one or a minor one as there was in the nuanced view of sound finance. Lerner's functional finance had no nuances about policy.

Functional finance nicely fits the *AS/AD* model you learned in Chapter 27 and the multiplier model in Chapter 28. In these models, there was a desired level of output—potential output—but the economy fluctuated around it. However, by using its fiscal (and monetary) policy steering wheel, the government could increase or decrease either expenditures or taxes, thereby shifting the *AD* curve to the right or left to steer the

---

[2]Although the book was primarily about theory, Keynes never followed up on his theoretical arguments; he was an adviser to the British government and, with World War II and the economic problems following the war, that advising took up most of his time, and then after the war he had a heart attack that left him out of the debate about his work.

economy to the desired level of output. (A good review exercise is to go through various changes in government spending and taxes in the *AS/AD* model.)

In functional finance, if there is a recession, the government should run a deficit.

So in functional finance, the economist's answer to the question, what to do if there is a recession, is to run a deficit to return the economy to its potential output. Policy followed directly from the model.

Functional Finance in Practice

Lerner's stark presentation of functional finance did not last long as a guiding principle for practical macro public finance and fiscal policy. The reason was that the model made a number of assumptions that, in practice, did not hold, and the model did not deal with the difficult practical problems of implementing fiscal policy. These problems don't mean that functional finance models are wrong; they simply mean that for fiscal policy to work, the policy conclusions drawn from the model must be modified to reflect the real-world problems. Let's consider how the reality might not fit the model. The multiplier model assumes

Six assumptions of the multiplier model that could lead to problems with fiscal policy are

1. Financing the deficit doesn't have any offsetting effects.
2. The government knows what the situation is.
3. The government knows the economy's potential income level.
4. The government has flexibility in changing spending and taxes.
5. The size of the government debt doesn't matter.
6. Fiscal policy doesn't negatively affect other government goals.

1. Financing the deficit doesn't have any offsetting effects. (In reality, it often does.)
2. The government knows what the situation is—for instance, the size of the *mpe*, and other exogenous variables. (In reality, the government must estimate them.)
3. The government knows the economy's potential income level—the highest level of income that doesn't cause accelerating inflation. (In reality, the government may not know what this level is.)
4. The government has flexibility in changing spending and taxes. (In reality, government cannot change them quickly.)
5. The size of the government debt doesn't matter. (In reality, the size of the government debt often does matter.)
6. Fiscal policy doesn't negatively affect other government goals. (In reality, it often does.)

Let's consider each assumption a bit further.

1. Financing the Deficit Doesn't Have Any Offsetting Effects One of the limitations of the functional finance approach embodied in the *AS/AD* and multiplier models is that they assume that financing the deficit has no offsetting effects on income. Some economists argue that that is not the case, that the government financing of deficit spending will offset the deficit's expansionary effect.

The *AS/AD* and multiplier models assume that saving and investment can be unequal, and that the government can increase its expenditures without at the same time causing a decrease in private expenditures. Some economists object to that assumption. They believe the interest rate equilibrates saving and investment. They argue that when the government borrows to finance the deficit, that borrowing will increase interest rates and crowd out private investment.

Crowding out is the offsetting effect on private expenditures caused by the government's sale of bonds to finance expansionary fiscal policy.

Interest rate **crowding out**—*the offsetting of a change in government expenditures by a change in private expenditures in the opposite direction*—occurs as follows: When the government runs a budget deficit, it must sell bonds (that is, it must borrow) to finance that deficit. To get people to buy and hold the bonds, the government must make them attractive. That means the interest rate the bonds pay must be higher than it otherwise would have been. This tends to push up the interest rate in the economy, which makes it more expensive for private businesses to borrow, so they reduce their borrowing and their investment. That private investment is crowded out by expansionary fiscal policy. Hence the name *crowding out*. Increased government spending crowds out private spending.

FIGURE 35-1 (A AND B) Crowding Out

An increase in government spending will expand income, but it will also cause interest rates to rise, as is shown in (**a**), thereby causing investment to decrease, which will tend to decrease income, as is shown in (**b**). This is called *interest rate crowding out*. The net effect of fiscal policy depends on the degree of crowding out that takes place.

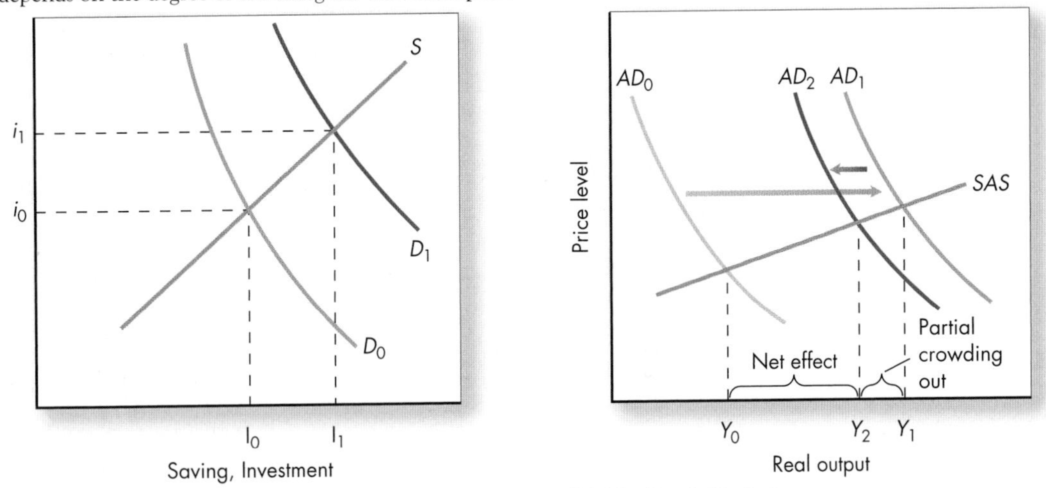

(a) Loanable Funds Market **(b) The Goods Market**

Figure 35-1(a) shows the supply and demand for loanable funds. Since any increase in government spending not financed by taxes has to be financed by bonds, deficit spending increases the demand for loanable funds; the demand for loanable funds increases from D_0 to D_1 and the interest rate rises from i_0 to i_1. That rise in interest rate will cause investment to decrease, which will offset the shift of aggregate demand in response to a deficit. Figure 35-1(b) shows the effect of this offset in the *AS/AD* model. Initially, income in the economy is Y_0 and government has decided to expand income to Y_1 by increasing its spending. If financing government spending were not an issue, expansionary fiscal policy would shift the *AD* curve to the right by a multiple of the increase in government spending, increasing income from Y_0 to Y_1. However, as we saw in Figure 35-1(a), financing is an issue. Financing the deficit increases interest rates and decreases investment. This shifts the *AD* curve to the left to AD_2. Income falls back to Y_2. How much it shifts back is a matter of debate; it depends upon how responsive the interest rate is to shifts in the demand for loanable funds and how responsive investment is to changes in the interest rate.

Q-5 If interest rates had no effect on investment or consumption, how much crowding out would occur?

Because of crowding out, the net expansionary effect of fiscal policy is smaller than it otherwise would have been. Some economists argue that crowding out can totally offset the expansionary effect of fiscal policy, so the net effect is zero, or even negative, since they consider private spending more productive than government spending. This is the view taken by some of those who focus on the supply-side effects of fiscal policy. Larger deficits decrease the pool of savings available for investment by raising interest rates. The result is that potential output does not increase as much as it otherwise would, and thus deficits lead to slower growth.

The crowding out effect also works in reverse with contractionary fiscal policy. Say the government runs a budget surplus. That surplus will slow the economy since it shifts the *AD* curve back to the left. But it also means the U.S. Treasury (the U.S. government department that issues bonds to finance the deficit) can buy back some of its outstanding bonds, which, as we discussed in earlier chapters, will have a tendency to

Q-6 Demonstrate graphically what would happen if government expenditures policy stimulated private investment.

push bond prices up and interest rates down. Lower interest rates will stimulate investment, which in turn will have an offsetting expansionary effect on the economy. So when we include financing the deficit in our consideration of fiscal policy, the shift in *AD* from the surplus is partially offset.

How large this financing offset to fiscal policy will be is a matter of debate. The empirical evidence about the degree of crowding out is mixed and has not resolved the debate. Both sides see some crowding out occurring as the debt is financed by selling bonds. The closer to the potential income level the economy is, the more crowding out is likely to occur.

Even as the U.S. government ran large budget deficits in the early 2000s, the U.S. interest rate did not rise substantially. Some economists consequently downplayed the importance of crowding out. Other economists argued that crowding out did not occur because foreign governments and private sources were willing to finance the U.S. deficit by purchasing U.S. bonds. The increase in the supply of savings from foreign sources held the U.S. interest rate down. However, they point out that eventually foreigners will find other places to invest and will be less willing to buy U.S. bonds, and when they do, the U.S. interest rate could rise substantially if the U.S. budget deficits persist.

2. The Government Knows What the Situation Is The numbers we use to demonstrate fiscal policy in the *AS/AD* model were chosen arbitrarily. In reality, the numbers used in models must be estimated or based on preliminary figures subject to revision. Most economic data are published quarterly, and it usually takes six to nine months of data to indicate, with any degree of confidence, the state of the economy and which way it is heading. Thus, we could be halfway into a recession before we even know it is happening. For example, data revisions showed GDP fell for three consecutive quarters in 2001, whereas the preliminary figures had shown only a one-quarter decline. (Data are already three months old when published; then we need two or three quarters of such data before we have enough information to work with.)

In an attempt to deal with this problem, the government relies on large macroeconomic models and leading indicators to predict what the economy will be like six months or a year from now. As part of the input to these complex models, the government must predict economic factors that determine the size of the multiplier. These predictions are imprecise, so the forecasts are imprecise. Economic forecasting is still an art, not a science.

Economists' data problems limit the use of fiscal policy for fine-tuning. There's little sense in recommending expansionary or contractionary policy until you know what policy is called for.

Web Note 35.2
What's the Speed Limit?

3. The Government Knows the Economy's Potential Income Level The problem of not knowing the level of potential income is related to the problem we just discussed. The target rate of unemployment and the potential level of income are not easy concepts to define. At one time it was thought 3 percent unemployment meant full employment. Some time later it was generally thought that 6.5 percent unemployment meant full employment. About that time economists stopped calling the potential level of income the *full-employment* level of income.

Any variation in potential income can make an enormous difference in the policy prescription that could be recommended. To see how big a difference, let's translate a 1 percent change in unemployment into a change in income. According to *Okun's rule of thumb* (defined in an earlier chapter as the general rule of thumb economists use to translate changes in the unemployment rate into changes in income), a 1 percentage point fall in the unemployment rate is associated with a 2 percent increase in income.

Thus, in 2009 with income at about \$14 trillion, a 1 percentage point fall in the unemployment rate would have increased income by about \$280 billion.

Now let's say that one economist believes 5.5 percent is the long-run achievable target rate of unemployment, while another believes it's 4 percent. That's a 1.5 percentage point difference. Since a 1 percent decrease in the unemployment rate means an increase of \$280 billion in national income, their views of the income level we should target differ by over \$420 billion (1.5 × \$280 = \$420). Yet both views are reasonable. Looking at the same economy (the same data), one economist may call for expansionary fiscal policy while the other may call for contractionary fiscal policy.

In practice, differences in estimates of potential income often lead to different policy recommendations. Empirical estimates suggest that the size of the multiplier is somewhere between 1.5 and 2.5. Let's say it's 2.0. That means autonomous expenditures must be predicted to increase or decrease by more than \$210 billion before an economist who believes the target rate of unemployment is 4 percent would agree with the same policy recommendation put forward by an economist who believes the rate is 5.5 percent. Since almost all fluctuations in autonomous investment and autonomous consumption are less than this amount, there's no generally agreed-on policy prescription for most fluctuations. Some economists will call for expansionary policy; some will call for contractionary policy; and the government decision makers won't have any clear-cut policy to follow.

Differences in estimates of potential income often lead to different policy recommendations.

You might wonder why the range of potential income estimates is so large. Why not simply see whether the economy has inflation at the existing rate of unemployment and income level? Would that it were so easy. Inflation is a complicated process. Seeds of inflation are often sown years before inflation results. The main problem is that establishing a close link between the level of economic activity and inflation is a complicated statistical challenge to economists, one that has not yet been satisfactorily met. That leads to enormous debate as to what the causes are.

Q-7 Why don't economists have an accurate measure of potential income?

Almost all economists believe that outside some range (perhaps 3.5 percent unemployment on the low side and 10 percent on the high side), too much spending causes inflation and too little spending causes a recession. That 3.5 to 10 percentage point range is so large that, in most cases, the U.S. economy is in an ambiguous state where some economists are calling for expansionary policy and others are calling for contractionary policy.

In most cases, the U.S. economy is in an ambiguous state where some economists are calling for expansionary policy and others are calling for contractionary policy.

Once the economy reaches the edge of the range of potential income or falls outside it, the economists' policy prescription becomes clearer. For example, in the Depression, when this multiplier model was developed, unemployment was 25 percent—well outside the range. Should the economy ever go into such a depression again, economists' policy prescriptions will be clear. The call will be for expansionary fiscal policy. Most times the economy is within the ambiguous range, so there are disagreements among economists.

4. The Government Has Flexibility in Changing Spending and Taxes For argument's sake, let's say economists agree that contractionary policy is needed and that's what they advise the government. Will the government implement it? And, if so, will it implement contractionary fiscal policy at the right time? The answer to both questions is: probably not. There are also problems with implementing economists' calls for expansionary fiscal policy. Even if economists are unanimous in calling for expansionary fiscal policy, putting fiscal policy in place takes time and has serious implementation problems.

Numerous political and institutional realities in the United States today make it a difficult task to implement fiscal policy. Government spending and taxes cannot be changed instantaneously. The budget process begins more than a year and a half before the government's fiscal year begins. Former President George W. Bush's plans for tax

Fighting the Vietnam War Inflation

In the chapter I described a 2001 case study in which fiscal policy worked the way it was supposed to through luck. Usually that isn't the case, and many times fiscal policy's effect comes at the wrong time and affects the economy in the wrong way. For example, one time that economists were united in their views on appropriate fiscal policy was during the Vietnam War, from the early 1960s until 1975, when the economy was pushed to its limits. About 1965, President Lyndon B. Johnson's economic advisers started to argue strongly that a tax increase was needed to slow the economy and decrease inflationary pressures. President Johnson wouldn't hear of it. He felt a tax increase would be political suicide. Finally in mid-1968, after Johnson had decided not to run for reelection, a temporary income tax increase was passed. By then, however, many economists felt that the seeds of the 1970s inflation had already been sown.

The Vietnam War led to inflationary pressures.

relief that culminated in the Economic Growth and Tax Relief Reconciliation Act of 2001 were written months before the economy went into recession and many more months before the September 11, 2001, terrorist attacks, which deepened the recession. When the tax relief was first implemented, it looked to most economists as if it would be too expansionary and that it was not needed. That's why initially President Bush emphasized its supply-side effects. However, as I mentioned above, in this case the timing of the reductions in taxes was just about right. It helped boost consumer spending in a slowing economy and played an important demand-side role, even though countercyclical policy was not the motivation for passing the act.

Another difficulty is that nearly two-thirds of the government budget is mandated by government programs such as Medicare and Social Security and by interest payments on government debt. Even the remaining one-third, called discretionary spending, is difficult to change. Defense programs are generally multiyear spending commitments. Discretionary spending also includes appropriations to fund established government agencies such as the Department of Agriculture, the Department of Transportation, and the Internal Revenue Service. Changing their budgets is politically difficult.

Politicians face intense political pressures; their other goals may conflict with the goals of fiscal policy. For example, few members of Congress who hope to be reelected would vote to raise taxes in an election year. Similarly, few members would vote to slash defense spending when military contractors are a major source of employment in their districts, even when there's little to defend against. Squabbles between Congress and the president may delay initiating appropriate fiscal policy for months, even years. By the time the fiscal policy is implemented, what may have once been the right fiscal policy may have ceased to be right, and some other policy may have become right.

Real-world fiscal policy is similar to steering a car with a five-second delay from turning the steering wheel to turning the wheels.

Imagine trying to steer a car at 60 miles an hour when there's a five-second delay between the time you turn the steering wheel and the time the car's wheels turn. Imagining that situation will give you a good sense of how fiscal policy works in the real world.

5. The Size of the Government Debt Doesn't Matter There is no inherent reason why adopting activist policies should have caused the government to run deficits year after year and hence to incur ever-increasing debt—accumulated deficits less accumulated surpluses. Activist functional finance policy is consistent with running deficits some years and surpluses other years. In practice, the introduction of activist functional finance policy has been accompanied by many deficits and few surpluses, and by a large increase in government debt.

There are two reasons why activist government policies have led to an increase in government debt. First, early activist economists favored large increases in government spending as well as favoring the government's using fiscal policy. These early activist economists employed the multiplier model to justify increasing spending without increasing taxes. A second reason is political. Politically it's much easier for government to increase spending and decrease taxes than to decrease spending and increase taxes. Due to political pressure, expansionary fiscal policy has predominated over contractionary fiscal policy.

Whether debt is a problem is an important and complicated issue, as we saw in the last chapter. All you need remember is that if one believes that the debt is harmful, then there might be a reason not to conduct expansionary fiscal policy, even when the model calls for it.

6. Fiscal Policy Doesn't Negatively Affect Other Government Goals A society has many goals; achieving potential income is only one of them. So it's not surprising that those goals often conflict. When the government runs expansionary fiscal policy, the trade deficit tends to increase. As the economy expands and income rises, exports remain constant but imports rise. If a nation's international considerations do not allow a balance of trade deficit to become larger, as is true in many countries, those governments cannot run expansionary fiscal policies—unless they can somehow prevent this balance of trade deficit from becoming larger.

Summary of the Problems So where do these six problems leave fiscal policy? While they don't eliminate its usefulness, they severely restrict it. Fiscal policy is a sledgehammer, not an instrument for fine-tuning. When the economy seems to be headed into a depression, the appropriate fiscal policy is clear. This was the case in 2008 and 2009. Similarly, when the economy has a hyperinflation, the appropriate policy is clear. But in less extreme cases, there will be debate on what the appropriate fiscal policy is—a debate economic theory can't answer conclusively.

Fiscal policy is a sledgehammer, not an instrument for fine-tuning.

Integrating these practical problems in running deficits has led modern economists to a much more nuanced view of deficit finance than found in the functional finance view. The modern view held by applied macro policy economists is that deficits can have stimulative effects on aggregate output, but they also agree with earlier Classical economists that there are political reasons for having balanced budgets, and not for relying on governments to control spending and taxes to achieve the desired level of output. As a tool, except in a potential depression, discretionary fiscal policy is not very helpful. But that does not mean that modern macro policy economists have discarded fiscal policy altogether. Instead of advocating standard discretionary fiscal policy in which government responds to fluctuations in income with changes in government spending and taxes, modern economists advocate building fiscal policy into institutions.

Building Fiscal Policies into Institutions

Economists quickly recognized the political problems with instituting discretionary countercyclical fiscal policy. To avoid these problems, they suggested policies that built fiscal policy into U.S. institutions so that it wouldn't require any political decisions.

An automatic stabilizer is any government program or policy that will counteract the business cycle without any new government action.

They called a built-in fiscal policy an **automatic stabilizer**—*a government program or policy that will counteract the business cycle without any new government action*. Automatic stabilizers include welfare payments, unemployment insurance, and the income tax system.

Web Note 35.3 Economy on Auto-Pilot?

How Automatic Stabilizers Work

Automatic Stabilizers

To see how automatic stabilizers work, consider the unemployment insurance system. When the economy is slowing down or is in a recession, the unemployment rate will rise. When people lose their jobs, they will reduce their consumption, starting the multiplier process, which decreases income. Unemployment insurance immediately helps offset the decrease in individuals' incomes as the government pays benefits to the unemployed. Thus, government spending increases, and part of the fall in income is stopped without any explicit act by the government. Automatic stabilizers also work in reverse. When income increases, government spending declines automatically.

Another automatic stabilizer is our income tax system. Tax revenue fluctuates as income fluctuates. When the economy expands, tax revenues rise, slowing the economy; when the economy contracts, tax revenues decline, providing a stimulus to the economy. Let's go through the reasoning why. When the economy is strong, people have more income and thus pay higher taxes. This increase in tax revenue reduces consumption expenditures from what they would have been and moderates the economy's growth. When the economy goes into a recession, the opposite occurs.

State Government Finance and Procyclical Fiscal Policy

Automatic stabilizers are sometimes offset by other institutional structures that work as a type of automatic *destabilizer*. Examples of such destabilizers are states' constitutional provisions to maintain balanced budgets. These provisions mean that whenever a recession hits, states are faced with declining tax revenue. To maintain balanced budgets, the states must cut spending, increase tax rates, or both. For example, during the 2001 and 2008 recessions, state governments struggled to balance their budgets by cutting expenditures on education, transportation, health care, and a variety of other programs while raising income and sales taxes. These actions deepened the recession. Similarly, during the 10-year expansion in the 1990s, state revenue rose; and states increased spending and decreased tax rates. The expansionary effect of these changes further increased total income. The result is what economists call **procyclical fiscal policy**—*changes in government spending and taxes that increase the cyclical fluctuations in the economy instead of reducing them*.

Countercyclical vs. Procyclical Policies

The procyclical nature of state government spending demonstrated itself in 2008 when the U.S. economy fell into a deep recession. In order to keep their budgets balanced, state governments began implementing massive spending cutbacks and tax increases, both of which worsened the recession. These cutbacks were reduced somewhat by temporary federal government assistance, but it was unclear how long that assistance could continue since the federal government was running massive unsustainable deficits.

To reduce the procyclical nature of state financing, economists have suggested states establish *rainy-day funds*—reserves kept in good times, to be used to offset declines in revenue during recessions. Large rainy-day funds (which some economists have called rainy-season funds) would decrease the destabilizing aspect of state government spending.

But politics usually keep rainy-day funds small; the funds are targets that are just too tempting for spending proposals or tax cuts.

An alternative way of building countercyclical policies into institutions would be for states to use a five-year rolling-average budgeting procedure (with a built-in underlying trend rate of increase) as the budget they are required to balance. With a rolling-average budget, revenues available for spending would be determined from a growth-adjusted average of revenues for the past five years. When revenues increase substantially in a year, the surplus available to be spent would build up only slowly and would therefore be much less politically tempting to raid. When revenues fall, the measured deficit would grow much more slowly, and the constitutional budget-balancing requirements would be much less procyclical.

Balancing a rolling-average budget, rather than the current-year budget, would counterbalance the balanced-budget requirement and would remove much of the procyclical aspect of current state budgeting procedures. In fact, if the federal government started using a similar five-year rolling-average budget, it too could build a more reasonable fiscal policy into its accounting procedures and reduce the need for discretionary stimulus packages.

The Negative Side of Automatic Stabilizers

Q-8 What effect do automatic stabilizers have on the size of the multiplier?

Automatic stabilizers may seem like the solution to the economic woes we have discussed, but they, too, have their shortcomings. One problem is that when the economy is first starting to climb out of a recession, automatic stabilizers will slow the process, rather than help it along, for the same reason they slow the contractionary process. As income increases, automatic stabilizers increase government taxes and decrease government spending, and as they do, the discretionary policy's expansionary effects are decreased.

Despite these problems, most economists believe that automatic stabilizers have played an important role in reducing normal fluctuations in our economy. They point to the kind of data we see in Figure 35-2, which up until 2008 showed a significant decrease in fluctuations in the economy. Other economists aren't so sure; they argue both that the apparent decrease in fluctuations is an optical illusion and that there was a building up of problems that led to the financial crisis that began in 2008. As usual,

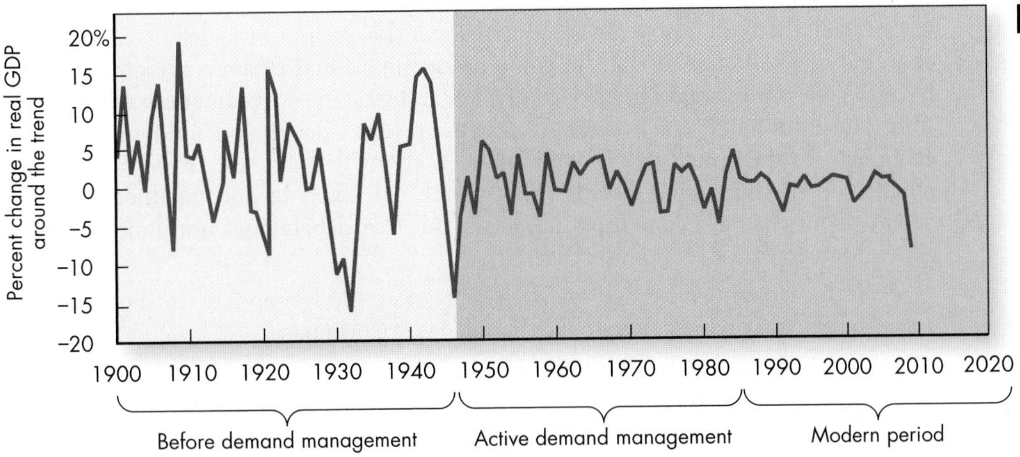

FIGURE 35-2 Decrease in Fluctuations in the Economy

Compared to the early 1900s, fluctuations in the economy have decreased; this suggests that policy makers have done something right.

Source: Federal Reserve Historical Charts, Economic Report of the President (www.doc.gov), and author estimates.

economic data are sufficiently ambiguous to give both sides strong arguments. The jury is still out.

Modern Macro Policy Precepts

Q-9 What should government do if there is a recession? (modern economists' answer)

Taking all the qualifications into account, the modern macro policy precept is a blend of functional and sound finance. Modern economists' answer to the question, "What should the government do about a recession?" is generally: Do nothing in terms of specific tax or spending policy, but let the automatic stabilizers in the economy do the adjustment. The reason for not undertaking specific policies is not because of a lack of concern about recession, but because, theoretically, it is unclear what effect a deficit would have and, practically and politically, it is very difficult to implement the control via fiscal policy at the right time. The "do nothing" approach reflects the sound finance precept. There is a substantial exception, however. That exception is that if the economy seems to be falling into a severe recession or depression, then the majority of economists believe that government should run expansionary fiscal policy.

Fiscal Policy in 2009 and Beyond

The U.S. economy found itself entering a severe recession in 2008. In response to the significant decreases in private aggregate demand, governments throughout the world cut taxes and increased spending, running large deficits—that is, using expansionary fiscal policy. (A good exercise is to demonstrate these policies with the *AS/AD* model and the multiplier model.) As I discussed in Chapter 32, the U.S. government instituted a $700 billion bailout plan to buy up assets that the banking system could not. It also formally guaranteed numerous bonds and money market funds, creating huge additional obligations for government, which could eventually cost trillions of dollars. In addition, it instituted an $800 billion stimulus package that consisted of both tax cuts and spending increases, and, with the automatic stabilizers kicking in because of the recession, the total deficit in 2009 will approach $2 trillion. In short, the government ran very, very expansionary fiscal policy, trying to offset the leftward shift of the *AD* curve. This was a policy with which the large majority of economists were on board. This was not fine-tuning, with major concerns about the deficits crowding out private investment, or about the level of potential output. In 2008 almost all macro policy economists agreed that the United States, and likely the world economy, was headed toward a serious recession or depression, and that it was the government's role to try to prevent it.

As united as macro policy economists were in 2008 that expansionary fiscal policy was needed, there was also serious concern about the extent of the deficits. All macroeconomists also believed that, at some point, functional finance principles would have to give way to sound finance principles, and that the government would have to shift gears from functional finance—trying to prevent a depression and jump-start the economy—to the principles of sound finance—trying to make sure the U.S. economy remains on solid financial footing. That switch will likely be accompanied by much debate about the right time to switch gears. But that debate does not undermine the general agreement of economists that:

Q-10 What is the appropriate policy for an economy headed toward:
- A depression?
- A hyperinflation?
- Normal times?

- If the economy is headed toward a depression, the appropriate fiscal policy is functional finance; fiscal policy should be expansionary,
- If the economy is headed toward hyperinflation, the appropriate fiscal policy is functional finance; fiscal policy should be contractionary; government should be running surpluses and paying off debt.
- If the economy is in normal times, the appropriate fiscal policy is sound finance; balance the budget.

REAL-WORLD APPLICATION

Incentive and Supply-Side Effects of Public Finance

The various political parties' views of public finance have changed significantly over the past 50 years. In the 1950s and early 1960s, the political parties' views on deficit finance were clear. The Democrats were Keynesian; they were the party of the deficits. Republicans were Classical; they were the party of sound finance. Consistent with these positions, Democrats pushed for increases in government programs and government spending, in part justifying these programs as a way to increase the size of the government budget and thereby increase effectiveness of fiscal policy as a tool of stabilization.

The push by Democrats for increased spending was partly offset by Republicans who pushed for tax decreases, but that push was often overwhelmed by their support of sound finance. Ultimately, Republicans found that they had to compromise on their support for sound finance and accept some level of deficits because of the political difficulty of cutting government programs once they were started. During this time, the relative size of the government increased, and government ran almost continual deficits. However, these deficits were not especially large relative to GDP, and no serious economist felt that these deficits were raising questions about the long-run financial viability of the government.

Just about the time that the New Classical revolution was taking hold in the early 1980s, Republicans were giving up their support for a balanced budget. Instead of supporting a balanced budget, they began to support cutting taxes whenever possible. Part of the justification for that position was the New Classical policy view of deficits and the Ricardian equivalence theorem. Supply-side economics emphasized the incentive effects of tax cuts, which they argued would lead to growth in output and hence would increase tax revenue. Some even argued the tax cuts would more than finance themselves, increasing, not decreasing, total tax revenues. The lay-public name for these views was *supply-side economics*. Most economists are hesitant about such claims. While all economists believe that incentive effects are important in the long run, most believe that the short-run incentive effects are relatively small.

That does not mean the Republican view could not be supported. Most economists felt that the reasoning for the Republican view on public finance was subtler and more political than the view presented in supply-side economics. Essentially, the Republican view could be supported if one believed that government spending was enormously inefficient and needed to be kept down, and that political forces would work to spend whatever money was available. If these views were true, it means that a budget surplus, or even a deficit that does not exceed a certain level of GDP that would alarm the public, is an invitation for increased government spending. These two propositions led Republicans to eliminate their support of sound finance and a balanced budget. The new Republican supply-side position became one of "always cut taxes" and "never raise taxes." This might be called the "starve the beast" approach to public finance. It is a public finance policy designed to reduce government spending in whatever way possible. To achieve that end, Republicans favor cutting taxes whenever they can to "starve the beast" and prevent the growth in any government program. In this view, any policy that does that, and tax cuts are one such policy, is a good policy.

This Republican position came into being with the Reagan era; George Bush the Elder violated it and his loss to Clinton in the 1992 election was attributed to that violation, making the "tax-cut" philosophy deeply entrenched in the Republican view. This left a few fiscally conservative Democrats, and a few maverick Republicans, as the few reluctant supporters of sound finance, and made large fiscal deficits the norm.

Conclusion

The above discussion of fiscal policy may make it look as if economic policy is highly subjective. That isn't true. While economic policy is not a cut-and-dried topic, neither is it totally subjective. As Keynes once said, economics is a method rather than a doctrine, an apparatus of the mind, a technique of thinking that helps the possessor to draw correct conclusions. The operative word there is *method*, not *doctrine*.

In economics you don't learn correct economic policy; what you learn is a method for thinking about economic policy that others have found useful. That method is to learn some models and then to judiciously apply them to a variety of situations. The modern macro policy precepts summarized in this chapter are examples of that judicious application.

Summary

- Sound finance is a view that the government budget should always be balanced except in wartime.
- The Ricardian equivalence theorem states that it doesn't matter whether government spending is financed by taxes or deficits; neither would affect the economy.
- Although proponents of sound finance believed the logic of the Ricardian equivalence theorem, they believed that, in reality, deficit spending could affect the economy. Still, because of political and moral issues, proponents of sound finance promoted balanced budgets.
- Functional finance is the theoretical proposition that governments should make spending and taxing decisions based on their effect on the economy, not moralistic principles.
- Six problems that make functional finance difficult to implement are:
  1. Interest rate crowding out.
  2. The government knowing what the situation is.
  3. The government knowing the economy's potential income.
  4. Government's inability to respond quickly enough.
  5. The size of government debt not mattering.
  6. Conflicting goals.
- Activist fiscal policy is now built into U.S. economic institutions through automatic stabilizers.
- Economists agree that if the economy is headed toward a depression or hyperinflation, follow the precepts of functional finance—expansionary fiscal policy to offset a depression and contractionary fiscal policy to offset hyperinflation. If the economy is experiencing moderate fluctuations, follow the precepts of sound finance—balance the budget.

Key Terms

automatic stabilizer *(828)*
crowding out *(822)*
functional finance *(821)*
procyclical fiscal policy *(828)*
Ricardian equivalence theorem *(819)*
sound finance *(818)*

Questions and Exercises

connect ECONOMICS

1. According to the Ricardian equivalence theorem, what is the effect of deficit spending on each of the following:
   a. The interest rate and private investment. Demonstrate your answer using the supply and demand for loanable funds.
   b. Output in the economy. Demonstrate your answer with the *AS/AD* model. LO1
2. According to the Ricardian equivalence theorem, why is government spending offset by a reduction in private spending? LO1
3. Why does sound finance not depend on the Ricardian equivalence theorem? LO2
4. What is functional finance? LO2

5. Why is functional finance difficult to implement? LO2
6. According to crowding out, how is government spending offset by a reduction in private spending? LO2
7. If interest rates have no effect on investment, how much crowding out will occur? LO2
8. Explain the place of activist fiscal policy in directing the economy according to each of the following points of view:
   a. Sound finance.
   b. Functional finance. LO2
9. How does the budget process make fiscal policy difficult to implement? LO3
10. Use the *AS/AD* model to explain why most presidents advocate government spending programs when running for reelection. LO3
11. Use the *AS/AD* model to explain the maxim in politics that if you are going to increase taxes, the time to do it is right after your election, when reelection is far off. LO3
12. Demonstrate the effect of the following on output and the price level in the *AS/AD* model and on the interest rate and investment in using the supply and demand for loanable funds:
    a. Full crowding out.
    b. Partial crowding out.
    c. Full crowding out and private investment is more productive than government investment. LO3
13. The government has just increased taxes.
    a. Demonstrate the effect on the price level and output in the standard model.
    b. How would your answer to *a* differ if there were partial crowding out?
    c. How would your answer to *a* differ if there were complete crowding out? LO3
14. Suppose one economist believes the target rate of unemployment is 4.5 percent while another believes it is 5.5 percent. Using Okun's rule of thumb, by how much would you expect their estimates of potential GDP to differ in a $10 trillion economy? LO3
15. How are state balanced-budget requirements procyclical? LO4
16. How do automatic stabilizers work? LO4
17. How can automatic stabilizers slow an economic recovery? LO4
18. A tax cut has just been announced. Congressman Growth states that its effect will be on the supply side. Congressman Stable states that its effect will be on the demand side.
    a. Demonstrate graphically the effect of the tax cut on the price level and output in the standard *AS/AD* model.
    b. Which of the two congressmen's views better fits the model?
    c. Demonstrate graphically the effect of the tax cut on the price level and output if the other congressman is correct.
    d. In the short run, which of the two congressmen is more likely correct?
    e. How might the existence of significant crowding out change your answer to *d*? *Review question*

Questions from Alternative Perspectives

1. It is often argued that savings should be encouraged. If one believes in the free market, does encouraging savings make sense? Why or why not? (Austrian)
2. During the Depression, unemployment rose to 25 percent. The *AS/AD* model presented in the book suggests that a fall in the price level would have solved the problem. Keynesians are not so convinced and believe that a fall in the price level would have lowered income, which would have shifted aggregate demand back further.
   a. Demonstrate the standard argument graphically.
   b. How does it deal (or not deal) with that interconnection between a fall in the price level and aggregate demand? (Post-Keynesian)
3. In this chapter you learned the importance of automatic stabilizers. At the state level, "rainy day" funds play a crucial role in maintaining services when state revenues decrease during a recession. While this may appear to be a rational institution, institutions are social constructs and what appears rational depends upon individual belief systems. The existence of a rainy-day fund can be interpreted as definitive proof of excess taxation and, in states that allow voter referendums, this fund can be eliminated by a majority vote. What vested interests—those seeking something for nothing—benefit from such decisions? (Institutionalist)
4. The economy has often been far from full employment.
   a. What would it take to run a regime of continuous full employment?
   b. How would the establishment of a full employment regime alter the relations between workers and capitalists?
   c. Is such a regime politically feasible? (Radical)
5. Any policy has both advantages and disadvantages, implying that policy makers must weigh both the advantages and disadvantages when deciding what policy to follow.
   a. Does society share absolute, objective values that guide the weighing of the alternatives?
   b. What role should religious beliefs play in establishing these values? (Religious)

Issues to Ponder

1. Congratulations! You've just been appointed chairman of the Council of Economic Advisers in Textland. The *mpe* is .8. There is a recessionary gap of $400.
   a. The government wants to eliminate the gap by changing expenditures. What policy would you suggest?
   b. Your research assistant comes running in and tells you that instead of changing expenditures, the government wants to achieve the same result by decreasing taxes. What policy would you recommend now? (Requires reading and using the math in Appendix A of the chapter "The Multiplier Model.")
   c. Your research assistant has a worried look on her face. "What's the problem?" you ask. "I goofed," she confesses. "I thought taxes were exogenous when actually there's a marginal tax rate of .2." Before she can utter another word, you say, "No problem, I'll simply recalculate my answers to parts *a* and *b* and change them before I send them in." What are your corrected answers? (Requires reading Appendix A of the chapter "The Multiplier Model.")
   d. She still has a pained expression, "What's wrong?" you ask. "You didn't let me finish," she says. "Not only was there a marginal tax rate of .2; there's also a marginal propensity to import of .2." Again you interrupt to make sure she doesn't feel guilty. Again you say, "No problem," and recalculate your answers to parts *a* and *b* to account for the new information. What are your new answers? (Requires reading Appendix A of the chapter "The Multiplier Model.")
   e. That pained look is still there, but this time you don't interrupt. You let her finish. She says, "And they want to see the answers graphically." You do the right thing. *Review question*
2. When Professor Robert Gordon lowered his estimate of the target unemployment rate from 6 percent to 5.5 percent in early 1995, he quipped, "I've just created 600,000 jobs."
   a. What events in the 1990s most likely motivated his revision of the target unemployment rate?
   b. Show the effect this revision would have on the *AS/AD* model.
   c. The unemployment rate at the time of the revision was 5.5 percent. Income was $7.3 trillion. Within 18 months the unemployment rate had fallen to 5 percent without signs of accelerating inflation. How much higher would the level of potential income have been in 1995 if the target unemployment rate were 5 percent rather than 5.5 percent?
3. President Bill Clinton's policy in 1993 was designed to reduce the deficit but increase employment.
   a. Why would such a policy not fit well in the multiplier model?
   b. Explain in words how such a policy might achieve the desired effect.
   c. Graphically demonstrate your answer in *b*.
   d. What data would you look at to see if your explanation in *b* and *c* is appropriate? *Review question*

Answers to Margin Questions

1. No; the Ricardian equivalence theorem states that the method of financing a deficit does not matter; sound finance argues that it does matter and that deficits should not be run. *(819)*
2. Pre-1930 economists believed that government should maintain a balanced budget even if there was a recession. *(819)*
3. An economist who believes in nuanced sound finance would say that government should maintain a balanced budget for a small recession, but if there were a large recession or depression, they should be open to running deficits. *(820)*
4. They are fundamentally different; sound finance states that you should always balance the government budget; functional finance states that you should use the government budget balance as a steering wheel to control the economy, and that the state of the economy should determine whether you have a deficit or surplus. *(821)*
5. If interest rates did not affect investment or consumption expenditures, there would be no crowding out. *(823)*

6. If government spending stimulated private spending, the phenomenon of what might be called *crowding in* might occur. The increase in government spending would shift the *AD* from AD_0 to AD_1 as in the accompanying diagram. The resulting increase in income would cause a further increase in investment, shifting the aggregate demand curve out further to AD_2. Income would increase from Y_0 to Y_2—by more than what the simple *AS/AD* model would predict. *(824)*

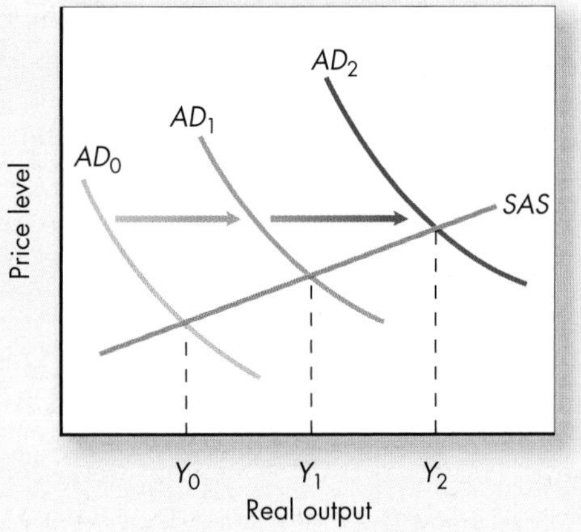

7. Potential income is not a measurable number. It is a conceptual number that must be estimated based on observable information about such phenomena as inflation, productivity, and unemployment. Estimating potential income is a challenge. *(825)*
8. Automatic stabilizers tend to decrease the size of the multiplier, decreasing the fluctuations in the economy. *(829)*
9. The modern economists' answer to what to do if there is a recession is, generally, do nothing in terms of specific tax or spending policy, but let the automatic stabilizers in the economy do the adjustment for you. *(830)*
10. Use functional finance when an economy is headed toward a depression or hyperinflation. In normal times, use sound finance. *(830)*

CHAPTER 36

International Financial Policy

A foreign exchange dealer's office during a busy spell is the nearest thing to Bedlam I have struck.

—***Harold Wincott***

In 2009 a euro that had cost 80 cents a number of years earlier cost about $1.35, and there were expectations that the value of the dollar might fall further. The dollar had, however, fallen far less against the Chinese yuan because the Chinese government was holding the value of its currency down. Earlier, in 2001, Argentina went through five presidents in two weeks as it struggled to adjust from a fixed to a flexible exchange rate, and in the late 1990s the international financial system almost broke down as Asian currency values fell substantially.

To understand what's happening in these events, you must understand exchange rates and the balance of payments. This chapter gives you that understanding. The chapter starts with an in-depth consideration of the balance of payments, showing how it relates to the trade balance and exchange rates. That discussion is then tied to a consideration of the supply of and demand for currencies and how monetary and fiscal policy affect exchange rates. Finally I discuss exchange rate policy in some depth and present the arguments for and against various exchange rate regimes.

AFTER READING THIS CHAPTER, YOU SHOULD BE ABLE TO:

1. Describe the balance of payments and the trade balance, and relate them to the supply and demand for currencies.
2. List four important fundamental determinants of exchange rates.
3. Explain how a country influences its exchange rate by using monetary or fiscal policy.
4. Explain how a country stabilizes or fixes an exchange rate.
5. Define purchasing power parity and real exchange rate.
6. Differentiate fixed, flexible, and partially flexible exchange rates, and discuss the advantages and disadvantages of each.
7. Discuss the advantages and disadvantages of a common currency.

The Balance of Payments

The best door into an in-depth discussion of exchange rates and international financial considerations is a discussion of **balance of payments** *(a country's record of all transactions between its residents and the residents of all foreign nations)*.[1] These include a country's buying and selling of goods and services (imports and exports) and interest and profit payments from previous investments, together with all the capital inflows and outflows. Table 36-1 presents the 1987 and 2008 balance of payments accounts for the United States. These accounts record all payments made by foreigners to U.S. citizens and all payments made by U.S. citizens to foreigners in those years.

[1]Balance of payments records are not very good. Because of measurement difficulties, many transactions go unrecorded and many numbers must be estimated, leaving a potential for large errors.

TABLE 36-1 The Balance of Payments Account, 1987 and 2008

	1987 (billions of dollars)		2008 (billions of dollars)	
1. Current account				
2. Merchandise				
3. Exports	+250		+1,291	
4. Imports	−410		−2,112	
5. Balance of merchandise trade		−160		−821
6. Services				
7. Exports	+ 99		+ 544	
8. Imports	− 91		− 405	
9. Balance on services		+ 8		+139
10. Balance of trade		−152		−682
11. Net investment income	+ 14		+ 128	
12. Net transfers	− 23		− 119	
13. Invest. trans. balance		− 9		+ 9
14. Balance on current account		**−161**		**−673**
15. Financial and capital account				
16. Capital balance		1		− 3
17. Private financial account				
18. Foreign-owned assets in the U.S.	+203		+ 178	
19. U.S.-owned assets abroad	− 90		+ 482	
20. Balance on private financial account		+113		+660
21. Government financial account				
22. Foreign government financial bal.	+ 45		+ 421	
23. U.S. government financial bal.	+ 10		− 534	
24. Balance on government financial acct.		+ 55		−113
25. Balance on financial and capital account		**+169**		**+544**
26. Statistical Discrepancy		− 8		+129
27. Total		**0**		**0**

Goods the United States exports must be paid for in dollars so, in order to buy U.S. exports, foreigners must exchange their currencies for dollars. Exports involve a flow of payments into the United States, so in the balance of payments accounts they have a plus sign. Similarly, U.S. imports must be paid for in foreign currency; they involve a flow of dollars out of the United States, and thus they have a minus sign. Notice that the bottom line of the balance of payments is $0. By definition, the bottom line (which includes all supplies and demands for currencies, including those of the government) must add up to zero.

The balance of payments is a country's record of all transactions between its residents and the residents of all foreign countries.

As you can see in Table 36-1, the balance of payments account is broken down into the current account and the financial and capital account. The **current account** (lines 1–14) is *the part of the balance of payments account in which all short-term flows of payments are listed.* It includes exports and imports, which are what we normally mean when we talk about the trade balance. The **financial and capital account** (lines 15–25) is *the part of the balance of payments account in which all long-term flows of payments are listed.* If a U.S. citizen buys a German stock, or if a Japanese company buys a U.S. company, the transaction shows up on this account.

The current account is the part of the balance of payments account that lists all short-term flows of payments.

The financial and capital account is the part of the balance of payments account that lists all long-term flows of payments.

The U.S. government can influence the exchange rate (the rate at which one currency trades for another) by buying and selling **official reserves**—*government holdings* *of foreign currencies*—or by buying and selling other international reserves, such as gold. Such buying and selling is recorded in the government financial balance (line 23)—the part of the balance of payments account that records the amount of its own currency or foreign currencies that a nation buys or sells. Foreign governments can also influence the U.S. exchange rate by buying and selling reserves. Such buying and selling is recorded in the foreign government financial balance (line 22).

To get a better idea of what's included in these accounts, let's consider each of them more carefully.

The Current Account

Looking at Table 36-1, you can see that the current account is composed of the merchandise (or goods) account (lines 2–5), the services account (lines 6–9), the net investment income account (line 11), and the net transfers account (line 12).

Web Note 36.1
Balance or Inbalance?

Starting with the merchandise account, notice that in 1987 the United States imported $410 billion worth of goods and exported $250 billion worth of goods. *The difference between the value of goods exported and the value of goods imported* is called the **balance of merchandise trade.** Looking at line 5, you can see that the United States had a balance of merchandise trade deficit of $160 billion in 1987 and $821 billion in 2008.

The merchandise trade balance is often discussed in the press as a summary of how the United States is doing in the international markets. It's not a good summary. Trade in services is just as important as trade in merchandise, so economists pay more attention to the combined balance of goods and services.

The balance of trade is the difference between the value of goods and services exported and imported.

Thus, the **balance of trade**—*the difference between the value of goods and services exported and imported*—(line 10) becomes a key statistic for economists. Notice that in both 1987 and 2008 most of the U.S. trade deficit resulted from an imbalance in the merchandise account. The services account worked in the opposite direction. It was slightly positive in 1987; in 2008 the services account reduced the trade deficit by $139 billion. Such services include tourist expenditures and insurance payments by foreigners to U.S. firms. For instance, when you travel in Japan, you spend yen, which you must buy with dollars; this is an outflow of payments, which is a negative contribution to the services account.

Q-1 If you, a U.S. citizen, are traveling abroad, where will your expenditures show up in the balance of payments accounts?

There is no reason that in a particular year the goods and services sent into a country must equal the goods and services sent out, even if the current account is in equilibrium, because the current account also includes payments from past investments and net transfers. When you invest, you expect to make a return on that investment. The payments to foreign owners of U.S. capital assets are a negative contribution to the U.S. balance of payments. The payment to U.S. owners of foreign capital assets is a positive contribution to the U.S. balance of payments. These payments on investment income are a type of holdover from past trade and services imbalances. So even though they relate to investments, they show up on the current account.

Payments on investment income show up on the current account.

The final component on the current account is net transfers, which include foreign aid, gifts, and other payments to individuals not exchanged for goods or services. If you send a $1,000 bond to your aunt in Mexico, it shows up with a minus sign here.

Adding up the pluses and minuses on the current account, we arrive at line 14, the current account balance. Notice that in 1987 the United States ran a $161 billion deficit on the current account, and in 2008 the United States had a deficit of $673 billion (line 14). That means that, in the current account, the supply of dollars greatly exceeded the demand for dollars. If the current account represented the total supply of and demand for dollars, the value of the dollar would have fallen. But it doesn't represent the total. There are also the financial account and statistical discrepancies.

The Financial and Capital Account

The financial and capital account measures the flow of payments between countries for financial assets such as stocks, bonds, and ownership rights to real estate. It is broken into two subcategories: (1) the capital account, which includes debt forgiveness, migrant's transfers, and transfers related to the sale of fixed assets; and (2) the financial account, which includes trade in assets such as business firms, bonds, stocks, and ownership right to real estate.[2] As you can see, the capital account transactions are rather small on balance. As you can also see in Table 36-1, in both years there was a significant inflow of financial assets into the United States in excess of outflows of assets from the United States. In 1987, financial inflows (payments by foreigners for U.S. real and financial assets) were $169 billion more than financial outflows (payments by U.S. citizens for foreign assets). In 2008, inflows exceeded outflows by $544 billion.

To buy these U.S. assets, foreigners needed dollars, so these net financial inflows represent a demand for dollars. In 1987 and 2008, the demand for dollars to buy real and financial assets offset the excess supply of dollars on the current account. Because of the importance of financial flows, when you think about what's likely to happen to a currency's value, it's important to remember both the demand for dollars to buy goods and services and the demand for dollars to buy assets.

In thinking about what determines a currency's value, it's important to remember both the demand for dollars to buy goods and services and the demand for dollars to buy assets.

If we added up the current account balance and the financial account balance, the two would not completely balance because of measurement errors. Line 26 takes care of that problem; it is the sum of all the above items with the sign reversed, and thus is a measure of the statistical discrepancy in the figures. In 1987 there was a small −$8 billion discrepancy, and in 2008 there was a +$129 billion discrepancy. These discrepancies arise because many international transactions, especially on the capital account, go unrecorded and hence must be estimated. Including line 26, the net balance of payments, including all government payments, is always zero.

When economists say that a country is running a balance of payments deficit or surplus, they are excluding its government's financial transactions (line 23). Thus, if line 23 is positive, the United States is running a balance of payments deficit and, if it is negative, it is running a balance of payments surplus. Government financial transactions represent its buying and selling of currencies. Foreign governments also may be buying up U.S. currency, which they did substantially in 2008, as you can see by the large positive entry on line 22. These foreign countries are increasing their holding of U.S. dollars, and their purchases of U.S. dollars allow the U.S. balance of payments accounts to remain in equilibrium even as private quantities supplied and demanded for these currencies differ.

While the current and financial accounts offset each other, there is a difference between the long-run effects of the demand for dollars to buy currently produced goods and services and the demand for dollars to buy assets. Assets earn profits or interest, so when foreigners buy U.S. assets, they earn income from those assets just for owning them. The net investment income from foreigners' previous asset purchases shows up on line 11 of the current account. It's the difference between the income U.S. citizens receive from their foreign assets and the income foreigners receive from their U.S. assets. If assets earned equal returns, we would expect that when foreigners own more U.S. capital assets than U.S. citizens own foreign capital assets, net investment income should be negative. And when U.S. citizens own more foreign capital assets than

[2]The separation of the financial and capital accounts is a recent change; earlier, both were simply called the capital account.

foreigners own U.S. capital assets, net investment income should be positive. Why is this? Because net investment income is simply the difference between the returns on U.S. citizens' assets held abroad and foreign citizens' assets held in the United States.

Since the 1980s, the inflow of capital into the United States has greatly exceeded the outflow of capital from the United States. As a result, the United States has become a net debtor nation; the amount foreigners own in the United States now exceeds the amount U.S. citizens own abroad by well over $1 trillion. So we would expect that U.S. investment income would be highly negative. But looking at line 11 of Table 36-1, we see that was not the case. The reason? Foreigners' returns have been low, and many of the foreign assets owned by U.S. citizens abroad are undervalued. For example, the Japanese bought a lot of U.S. real estate at very high prices and have been losing money on those investments. While this trend has continued much longer than expected, we cannot expect it to continue forever.

Q-2 How can net investment income be positive if a country is a net debtor nation?

Exchange Rates

Web Note 36.2
Exchange Rate Data

Supply and demand are two central forces of economics, so it shouldn't be surprising that our initial discussion of the determination of exchange rates uses supply and demand curves. As I stated above, an exchange rate is the rate at which one country's currency can be traded for another country's currency. The exchange rate is determined in what is called the **forex market** *(foreign exchange market)*. In the forex markets, traders buy and sell currencies, taking orders from banks, which in turn take orders for currencies from individuals and companies that want to exchange one currency for another. It is a very busy market with nearly $2 trillion traded every day.

The exchange rate will tell you the price of a foreign currency. Below is an exchange rate table from March 24, 2009. It tells you how much a dollar was worth in terms of other currencies on that day.

Exchange Rates, March 24, 2009

	U.S. $ Equivalent	Currency per U.S. $
Argentina (peso)	0.2712	3.6873
Canada (dollar)	0.8160	1.2252
China (renminbi)	0.1465	6.8278
Denmark (krone)	0.1832	5.4585
Israel (shekel)	0.2474	4.0420
Japan (yen)	0.0102	97.8400
Pakistan (rupee)	0.1246	80.2570
Philippines (peso)	0.0207	48.2160
Russia (ruble)	0.0301	33.1680
Saudi Arabia (riyal)	0.2666	3.7509
U.K. (pound)	1.4716	0.6795
European Union (euro)	1.3517	0.7398

The second column reports the U.S. dollar equivalent. It tells you the price of foreign currencies in terms of dollars. For example, one Argentinean peso costs about 27 cents. You also can look at exchange rates from the viewpoint of the foreign currency. For example, how many pesos are needed to buy one U.S. dollar? The third column tells you that one U.S. dollar costs 3.69 pesos.

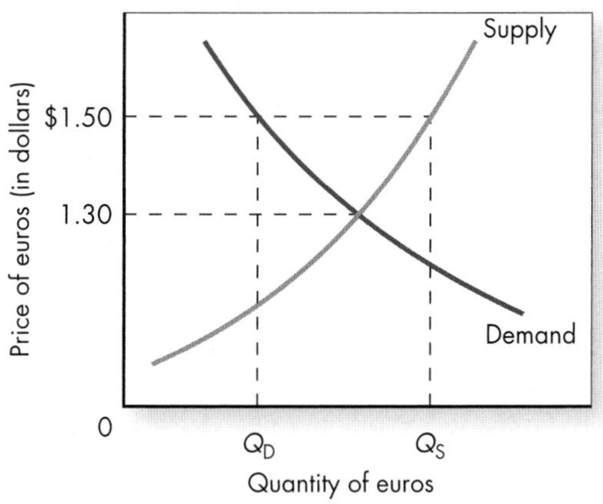

FIGURE 36-1 The Supply of and Demand for Euros

As long as you keep quantities and prices *of what* straight, the standard, or fundamental, analysis of the determination of exchange rates is easy. Just remember that if you're talking about the supply of and demand for euros, the price will be measured in dollars and the quantity will be in euros.

As you learned in Chapter 5, people exchange currencies to buy goods or assets in other countries. For example, an American who wants to buy stock of a company that trades on the EU stock exchange first needs to buy euros with dollars. If the stock costs 150 euros, he will need to buy 150 euros. With an exchange rate of $1.30 for 1 euro, he will need to pay $195 to buy 150 euros ($1.30 × 150). Only then can he buy the stock.

Let's now turn to the graphs. At first glance, the graphical analysis of foreign exchange rates seems simple: You have an upward-sloping supply curve and a downward-sloping demand curve. But what goes on the axes? Obviously price and quantity, but what price? And what quantity? Because you are talking about the prices of currencies relative to each other, you have to specify which currencies you are using.

In Figure 36-1, I present the supply of and demand for euros in terms of dollars. Notice that the quantity of euros goes on the horizontal axis and the dollar price of euros goes on the vertical axis. When you are comparing currencies of only two countries, the supply of one currency equals the demand for the other currency. To demand one currency, you must supply another. In this figure, I am assuming that there are only two trading partners: the United States and the European Union. This means that the supply of euros is equivalent to the demand for dollars. The Europeans who want to buy U.S. goods or assets supply euros to buy dollars. Let's consider an example. Say a European wants to buy an IBM computer made in the United States. She has euros, but IBM wants dollars. So, to buy the computer, she or IBM must somehow exchange euros for dollars. She is *supplying* euros in order to *demand* dollars.

To demand one currency, you must supply another currency.

The supply curve of euros is upward-sloping because the more dollars European citizens get for their euros, the cheaper U.S. goods and assets are for them and the greater the quantity of euros they want to supply for those goods. Say, for example, that the dollar price of one euro rises from $1.30 to $1.35. That means that the price of a dollar to a European has fallen from 0.78 euro to 0.74 euro. For a European, a good that cost $100 now falls in price from 78 euros to 74 euros. U.S. goods are cheaper, so the Europeans buy more U.S. goods and more dollars, which means they supply more euros.

Q-3 Show graphically the effect on the price of euros of an increase in the demand for dollars by Europeans.

The demand for euros comes from Americans who want to buy European goods or assets. The demand curve is downward-sloping because the lower the dollar price of euros, the more euros U.S. citizens want to buy, using the same reasoning I just described.

The market is in equilibrium when the quantity supplied equals the quantity demanded. In my example, equilibrium occurs at a dollar price of $1.30 for one euro. If the price of euros is above or below $1.30, quantity supplied won't equal the quantity demanded and there will be pressure for the exchange rate to move to equilibrium. Say, for example, that the price is $1.50. The quantity of euros supplied will be greater than the quantity demanded. People who want to sell euros won't be able to sell them. To find buyers, they will offer to sell their euros for less. As they do, the price of euros falls.

Exchange Rates and the Balance of Payments

The total balance of payments (including government financial flows) is always in equilibrium, so we know that the quantity of a currency supplied always equals the quantity demanded. That does not mean, however, that foreign or domestic governments did not buy or sell currencies to maintain that equilibrium. If a government wants to keep its exchange rate higher than what would be supported by the market, the government must remove the excess supply of its currency. Its purchase of domestic currency would be recorded as a positive entry in the government financial account. Without that entry, the balance of payments would be in deficit. Thus, in Figure 36-1, when the price of euros is $1.50, the quantity of euros supplied exceeds the quantity demanded, so without the government's purchase of euros, Europe is running a balance of payments deficit. When the price of euros is below $1.30, the quantity of euros demanded exceeds the quantity supplied, so excluding government sale of euros, Europe is running a balance of payments surplus.

A deficit in the balance of payments means that the private quantity supplied of a currency exceeds the private quantity demanded. A surplus in the balance of payments means the opposite.

Fundamental Forces Determining Exchange Rates

Exchange rate analysis is usually broken down into fundamental analysis and short-run analysis. In this section, I discuss fundamental analysis—a consideration of the fundamental forces that determine the supply of and demand for currencies, and hence cause them to shift. These fundamental forces include a country's income, a country's prices, the interest rate in a country, and the country's trade policy. That means that changes in a country's income, changes in a country's prices, changes in interest rates, and changes in trade policy can cause the supply of and demand for a currency to shift. Let's consider how they do so.

Changes in a Country's Income The demand for imports depends on the income in a country. When a country's income falls, demand for imports falls. Hence, demand for foreign currency to buy those imports falls, which means that the supply of the country's currency to buy the foreign currency falls. That's why, in my presentation of the *AS*/*AD* model, I said that imports depend on income.

How important is this relationship? Very important. For example, in the early 2000s, strong economic growth in the United States relative to its primary trading partners led to increased imports, which increased the supply of U.S. dollars. The increase in the supply tended to lower the price of the dollar relative to foreign currencies.

Changes in a Country's Prices The United States' demand for imports and foreign countries' demand for U.S. exports depend on prices of U.S. goods compared to prices of foreign competing goods. If the United States has more inflation than other countries, foreign goods will become cheaper, U.S. demand for foreign currencies will tend to increase, and foreign demand for dollars will tend to decrease. This rise in U.S. inflation will shift the dollar supply outward and the dollar demand inward.

Four important fundamental determinants of exchange rates are income, prices, interest rates, and trade policy.

Changes in Interest Rates People like to invest their savings in assets that will yield the highest return. Other things equal, a rise in U.S. interest rates relative to those abroad will increase demand for U.S. assets. As a result, demand for dollars will increase, while simultaneously the supply of dollars will decrease as fewer Americans sell their dollars to buy foreign assets. A fall in the U.S. interest rate or a rise in foreign interest rates will have the opposite effect.

Changes in Trade Policy The demand for imports is affected by a government's trade policy. An increase in trade restrictions, such as the 30 percent tariff President George W. Bush imposed on imported steel in 2002, increases the price of imports, reducing the quantity of imports demanded. Consequently, the demand for foreign currency to buy those imports declines so that the supply of a country's currency falls. A number of other countries threatened to impose retaliatory tariffs on American goods, which they were allowed to do under WTO rules. These retaliatory tariffs would have reduced U.S. exports and reduced the demand for the U.S. dollar. To avoid these retaliatory tariffs, President Bush repealed the tariffs on steel in late 2003.

Some Examples To make sure that you've understood the analysis, let's consider some examples. First, the U.S. economy goes into recession with interest rates remaining constant—what will likely happen to exchange rates? Second, the Mexican economy has runaway inflation—what will likely happen to exchange rates? And third, the interest rate on yen-denominated assets increases—what will likely happen to the exchange rate? If you answered: The value of the dollar will rise, the value of the peso will fall, and the value of the yen will rise, you're following the argument. If those weren't your answers, a review is in order.

Indirect Methods of Influencing Exchange Rates

The government can influence the price of its currency either directly through market intervention or indirectly through monetary and fiscal policy. Let's begin with the indirect method of monetary and fiscal policy.

Monetary Policy's Effect on Exchange Rates

Monetary policy affects exchange rates in three primary ways: (1) through its effect on the interest rate, (2) through its effect on income, and (3) through its effect on price levels and inflation.

The Effect on Exchange Rates via Interest Rates Expansionary monetary policy pushes down the U.S. interest rate, which decreases the financial inflow into the United States, decreasing the demand for dollars, pushing down the value of the dollar, and decreasing the U.S. exchange rate. Contractionary monetary policy does the opposite. It raises the U.S. interest rate, which tends to bring in financial capital flows from abroad, increasing the demand for dollars, increasing the value of the dollar, and increasing the U.S. exchange rate. This interest rate effect is the dominant short-run effect, and it often overwhelms the other effects.

Q-4 What effect does the lowering of a country's interest rates have on exchange rates?

The interest rate effect on exchange rates is the dominant short-run effect.

To see why these effects take place, consider a person in Japan in the early 2000s, when the Japanese interest rate was close to 0 percent. He or she reasoned, "Why should I earn 0 percent return in Japan? I'll save (buy some financial assets) in the United States where I'll earn 3 percent." If the U.S. interest rate goes up due to contraction in the money supply, other things equal, the advantage of holding one's financial assets in the United States will become even greater and more people will want to save here. People in Japan hold yen, not dollars, so in order to save in the United States they must buy dollars. Thus, a rise in U.S. interest rates increases demand for dollars and, in terms of yen, pushes up the U.S. exchange rate. This example illustrates that it is relative interest rates that govern the flow of financial assets.

REAL-WORLD APPLICATION

Iceland's Monetary Woes

In 2006, the Icelandic inflation rate exceeded its target inflation rate, and investors became worried. The financial press began to issue comments such as this: "The negative outlook has been triggered by a material deterioration in Iceland's macro-prudential risk indicators, accompanied by an unsustainable current account deficit and soaring net external indebtedness." A group of developed countries, the Organisation for Economic Co-operation and Development (OECD), warned that that failure to bring inflation down could damage the country's international credibility, and that "[i]n the absence of swift and vigorous policy action, financial market stability could be at risk."

In response to these and other warnings, foreign exchange traders began selling króna, the Icelandic currency. The króna's value started to decline, which led the Icelandic Central Bank to tighten the money supply and raise interest rates. In 2006 the Icelandic Central Bank issued the following statement:

> Economic developments since the end of March indicate that a considerable increase in the policy rate may be required to maintain sufficiently tight monetary conditions. Rising inflation expectations have caused the real policy rate to decline. Furthermore, the depreciation of the króna has eased conditions in the traded goods sector. The current policy rate hike is intended to respond to these developments. Attaining the inflation target within an acceptable period of time is the firm intention of the Central Bank.

The Central Bank of Iceland continued raising interest rates by substantial amounts, to 12 percent and then to 13.5 percent, stating that "further rises were unavoidable." In mid-2007, the interest rate was about 15 percent while inflation had decreased to less than 6 percent.

That temporarily resolved the short-run problem, but it did not resolve the longer-run problem of massive external indebtedness of all Icelandic banks. In 2008, when the global credit crisis hit the world economy, that indebtedness caused all the Icelandic banks to fail, and the Icelandic government had nowhere near the money needed to support them. This led to a freezing up of the exchange markets for Icelandic currencies, and an appeal from Iceland for loans to help reestablish a viable banking system.

Countries are continually taking into account the effect of monetary policy on exchange rates. For example, in the mid-1990s, Taiwan kept its money supply tight, raising its interest rates to keep the new Taiwan dollar high. In 1997 Taiwan cut reserve ratios; interest rates fell and the value of the new Taiwan dollar fell.

The Effect on Exchange Rates via Income Monetary policy also affects income in a country. As money supply rises, income expands; when money supply falls, income contracts.[3] This effect on income provides another way in which the money supply affects the exchange rate. As we saw earlier, when income rises, imports rise while exports are unaffected. To buy foreign products, U.S. citizens need foreign currency, which they must buy with dollars. So when U.S. imports rise, the supply of dollars to the foreign exchange market increases as U.S. citizens sell dollars to buy foreign currencies to pay for those imports. This decreases the dollar exchange rate. This effect

[3]When there's inflation, it's the rate of money supply growth relative to the rate of inflation that's important. If inflation is 10 percent and money supply growth is 10 percent, the rate of increase in the real money supply is zero. If money supply growth falls to, say, 5 percent while inflation stays at 10 percent, there will be a contractionary effect on the real economy.

through income and imports provides a second path through which monetary policy affects the exchange rate: Expansionary monetary policy causes U.S. income to rise, imports to rise, and the U.S. exchange rate to fall via the income path. Contractionary monetary policy causes U.S. income to fall, imports to fall, and the U.S. exchange rate to rise via the income path.

The Effect on Exchange Rates via Price Levels A third way in which monetary policy can affect exchange rates is through its effect on prices in a country. Expansionary monetary policy pushes the U.S. price level up. As the U.S. price level rises relative to foreign prices, U.S. exports become more expensive, and goods the United States imports become relatively cheaper, decreasing U.S. competitiveness. This increases demand for foreign currencies and decreases demand for dollars. Thus, via the price path, expansionary monetary policy pushes down the dollar's value for the same reason that an expansion in income pushes it down.

Q-5 What effect would contractionary monetary policy have on a country's exchange rates?

Contractionary monetary policy puts downward pressure on the U.S. price level and slows down any existing inflation. As the U.S. price level falls relative to foreign prices, U.S. exports become more competitive and the goods the United States imports, relatively more expensive. Thus, contractionary monetary policy pushes up the value of the dollar via the price path.

The Net Effect of Monetary Policy on Exchange Rates Notice that all these effects of monetary policy on exchange rates are in the same direction. Expansionary monetary policy pushes a country's exchange rate down; contractionary monetary policy pushes a country's exchange rate up. Summarizing these effects, we have the following relationships for expansionary and contractionary monetary policy:

Monetary policy affects exchange rates through the interest rate path, the income path, and the price level path, as shown in the accompanying diagram.

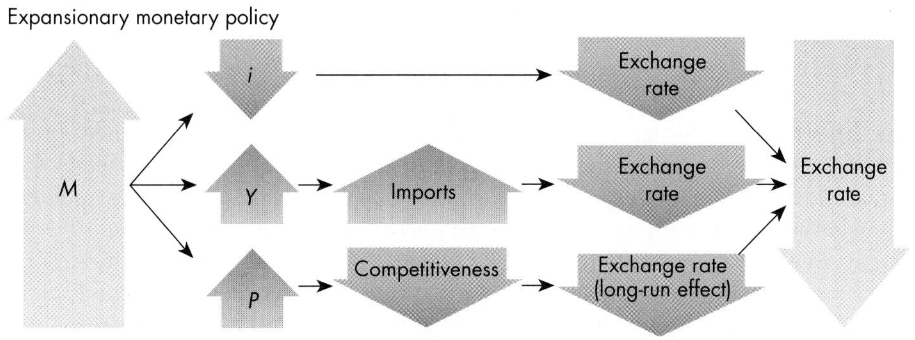

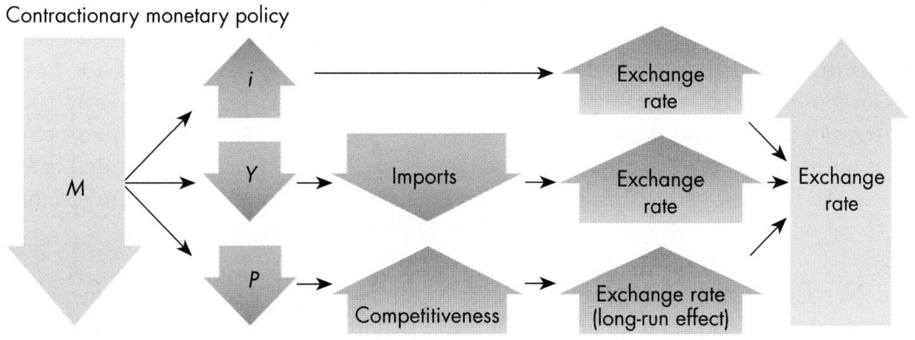

Expansionary monetary policy lowers exchange rates. It decreases the relative value of a country's currency.

Contractionary monetary policy increases exchange rates. It increases the relative value of a country's currency.

There are, of course, many provisos to the relationship between monetary policy and the exchange rate. For example, as the exchange rate falls, the price of imports goes up and there is some inflationary pressure from that rise in price and hence some pressure for the price level to rise as well as fall. Monetary policy affects exchange rates in subtle ways, but if an economist had to give a quick answer to what effect monetary policy would have on exchange rates, it would be

> Expansionary monetary policy lowers exchange rates. It decreases the relative value of a country's currency.
>
> Contractionary monetary policy increases exchange rates. It increases the relative value of a country's currency.

Fiscal Policy's Effect on Exchange Rates The effect of fiscal policy on exchange rates is not so clear. The reason why can be seen by considering its effects on income, the price level, and interest rates.

The Effect on Exchange Rates via Income Expansionary fiscal policy expands income and therefore increases imports, increasing the trade deficit and lowering the exchange rate. Contractionary fiscal policy contracts income, thereby decreasing imports and increasing the exchange rate. These effects of expansionary and contractionary fiscal policies via the income path are similar to the effects of monetary policy, so if it's not intuitively clear to you why the effect is what it is, it may be worthwhile to review the slightly more complete discussion of monetary policy's effect presented previously.

The Effect on Exchange Rates via Price Levels Let's turn to the effect of fiscal policy on exchange rates through prices. Expansionary fiscal policy increases aggregate demand and increases prices of a country's exports; hence, it decreases the competitiveness of a country's exports, which pushes down the exchange rate. Contractionary fiscal policy works in the opposite direction. These are the same effects that monetary policy had. And, as was the case with monetary policy, the price path is a long-run effect.

The Effect on Exchange Rates via Interest Rates Fiscal policy's effect on the exchange rate via the interest rate path is different from monetary policy's effect. Let's first consider the effect of expansionary fiscal policy. Whereas expansionary monetary policy lowers the interest rate, expansionary fiscal policy raises interest rates because the government sells bonds to finance that budget deficit. The higher U.S. interest rate causes foreign capital to flow into the United States, which pushes up the U.S. exchange rate. Therefore, expansionary fiscal policy's effect on exchange rates via the interest rate effect is to push up a country's exchange rate.

Contractionary fiscal policy decreases interest rates since it reduces the bond financing of that deficit. Lower U.S. interest rates cause capital to flow out of the United States, which pushes down the U.S. exchange rate. Thus, the U.S. government budget surplus in the late 1990s put downward pressure on the interest rate and downward pressure on the exchange rate value of the dollar, while the deficits in the early 2000s put upward pressure on the interest rate and exchange rate. That upward pressure on the interest rates was offset, however, by large flows of capital into the United States not for the interest rate return, but for safety reasons, as many investors were attempting to get out of other assets and into U.S. government bonds.

Q-6 What is the net effect of expansionary fiscal policy on the exchange rate?

The Net Effect of Fiscal Policy on Exchange Rates Of these three effects, the interest rate effect and the income effect are both short-run effects. These two work in opposite directions, so the net effect of fiscal policy on the exchange rate is, in general, ambiguous, although in specific instances either the interest rate effect or the income effect may swamp the other. The following diagram summarizes these three effects.

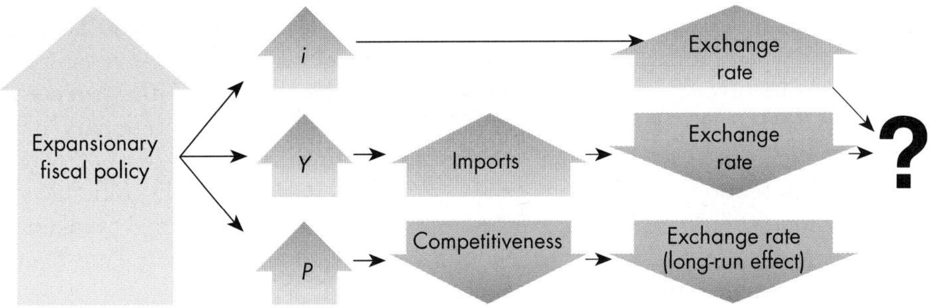

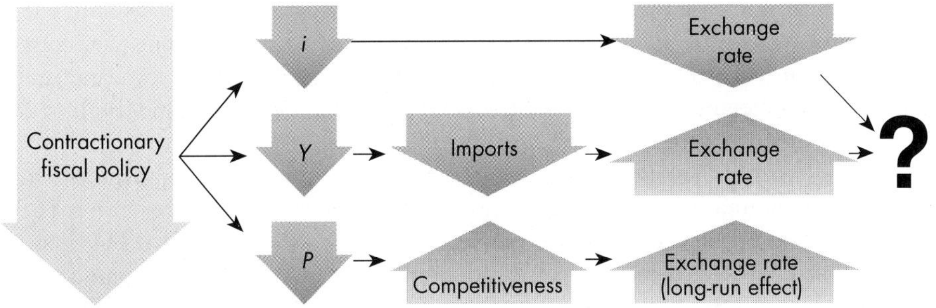

Fiscal policy affects exchange rates through the income path, the interest rate path, and the price level path, as shown in the accompanying diagram.

As you can see, it's unclear what the effect of expansionary or contractionary fiscal policy will be on exchange rates.

Direct Methods of Influencing Exchange Rates

The supply/demand analysis may have made it look like exchange rates are driven by fundamentals. Unfortunately, that is not the case. In day-to-day trading, fundamentals can be overwhelmed by expectations of how a currency will change in value. The supply and demand curves for currencies can shift around rapidly in response to rumors, expectations, and expectations of expectations. As they shift, they bring about large fluctuations in exchange rates that make trading difficult and have significant real effects on economic activity.

Let me outline just one potential problem. Say you expect the price of the currency to fall one-half of 1 percent tomorrow. What should you do? The correct answer is: Sell that currency quickly. Why? One-half of 1 percent may not sound like much, but, annualized, it is equivalent to a rate of interest per year of 617 percent. Based on that expectation, if you're into making money (and you're really sure about the fall), you will sell all of that currency that you hold, and borrow all you can so you can sell some more. You can make big money if you guess small changes in exchange rates correctly. (Of course, if you're wrong, you can lose big money.) This means that if the market generally believes the exchange rates will move, those expectations will tend to be self-fulfilling. Self-fulfilling expectations undermine the argument in favor of letting markets determine exchange rates: When expectations rule, the exchange rate may not reflect actual demands and supplies of goods. Instead, the exchange rate can reflect expectations and rumors. The resulting fluctuations serve no real purpose, and cause problems for international trade and the country's economy. Let's consider an example.

Q-7 Why don't most governments leave determination of the exchange rate to the market?

Suppose that a firm decides to build a plant in the United States because costs in the United States are low. But suppose also that the value of the dollar then rises significantly; the firm's costs rise significantly too, making it uncompetitive. When currencies fluctuate, companies find it harder to make good decisions on where to produce.

In a real-world example, from July to September 1997, the value of the Thai baht fell nearly 40 percent. Goodyear (Thailand), which had been one of the five most profitable companies on the Stock Exchange of Thailand, suddenly faced a 20 percent rise in the costs of raw materials because it paid for those raw materials in dollars. It also faced a decline in tire prices because the demand for tires had fallen 20 to 40 percent when the Thai economy contracted. Within just two months, a highly profitable venture had become unprofitable. Other firms were closing shop because they were unable to pay the interest on loans that were denominated in dollars. In summary, large fluctuations make real trade difficult and cause serious real consequences.

The problems caused by fluctuating exchange rates have led to calls for government to intervene and either stabilize or fix its exchange rate directly by buying or selling its currency. It can increase the value of its currency by buying its currency, assuming it has international reserves to buy it with. Alternatively, it can decrease the value of its currency by selling its currency. This ability of a country to buy and sell its currency means that, assuming it has sufficient reserves, a country can fix its currency at a specific level.

A country fixes the exchange rate by standing ready to buy and sell its currency anytime the exchange rate is not at the fixed exchange rate.

A country can maintain a fixed exchange rate above its market price only as long as it has the reserves.

Currency Support Let's consider currency support. Suppose that, given the interaction of private supply and demand forces, the equilibrium value of the euro is $1.30 a euro, but the European Union wants to maintain a value of $1.50 a euro. This is shown in Figure 36-2. At $1.50 a euro, quantity supplied exceeds quantity demanded. The European Union must buy the surplus, $Q_2 - Q_1$, using official reserves (foreign currency holdings). In doing so, it shifts the total demand for euros to D_1, making the equilibrium market exchange rate (including the European government's demand for euros) equal to $1.50. This process is called **currency support**—the *buying of a currency by a government to maintain its value at above its long-run equilibrium value*. It is a direct exchange rate policy. If a government has sufficient official reserves, or if it can convince other governments to lend it reserves, it can fix the exchange rate at the rate it wants, no matter what the private level of supply and demand is. In reality, governments have no such power to support currencies in the long run since their reserves are limited. For example, in 2002 the Argentinean government tried to keep its currency fixed to the

FIGURE 36-2 A Demonstration of Direct Exchange Rate Policy

If the government chooses to hold the exchange rate at $1.50, when the equilibrium is $1.30, there is an excess supply given by $Q_2 - Q_1$. The government purchases this excess (using official reserves) and closes the difference, thus maintaining equilibrium.

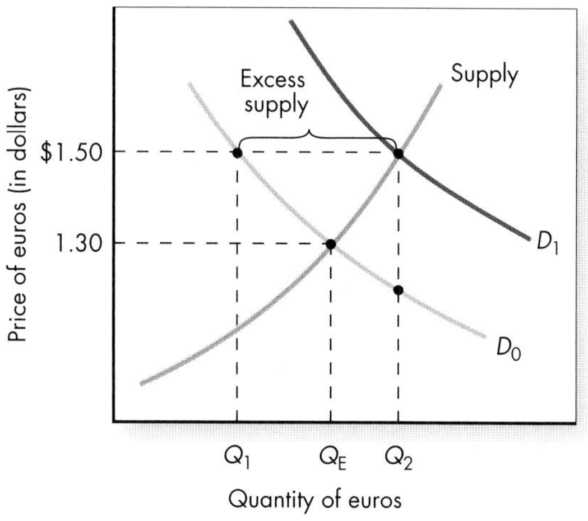

U.S. dollar, but it ran out of foreign reserves and was forced to let its currency decline in value.

A country has more power to prevent the value of its currency from rising since it can create its own money. Thus, throughout the early 2000s, China used yuan to buy large amounts of dollars, thereby preventing the value of the yuan from rising relative to the dollar.

Currency Stabilization A more viable long-run exchange rate policy is **currency stabilization**—the *buying and selling of a currency by the government to offset temporary fluctuations in supply and demand for currencies*. In currency stabilization, the government is not trying to change the long-run equilibrium; it is simply trying to keep the exchange rate at that long-run equilibrium. The government sometimes buys and sometimes sells currency, so it is far less likely to run out of reserves.

Successful currency stabilization requires the government to choose the correct long-run equilibrium exchange rate. A policy of stabilization can become a policy of support if the government chooses too high a long-run equilibrium. Unfortunately, government has no way of knowing for sure what the long-run equilibrium exchange rate is, so how much stabilizing it can do depends on its access to reserves. If it has sufficient reserves, the government buys up sufficient quantities of its currency to make up the difference.

Once the government has dried up the sources of borrowing foreign currencies, if it wants to hold its exchange rate above the private equilibrium exchange rate, it must move to indirect methods of monetary and fiscal policy to affect private supplies and demands for its currency.

The same argument about running out of reserves cannot be made for a country that wants to maintain a below-market exchange rate. Since a government can create all the domestic currency it wants, it's easier for the European Union to push the value of its currency down by selling euros than it is for the government to hold it up by buying euros. By the same token, it's easier for another country (say, Japan) to push the value of the euro up (by pushing the value of the yen down). Thus, if the two governments can decide which way they want their exchange rates to move, they have a large incentive to cooperate. Of course, cooperation requires an agreement on the goals, and often countries' goals conflict. One role of the various international economic organizations is to provide a forum for reaching agreement on exchange rate goals and a vehicle through which cooperation can take place.

Q-8 In general, would it be easier for the United States to push the value of the dollar down or up? Why?

Notice that, in principle, any trader could establish a fixed exchange rate by guaranteeing to buy or sell a currency at a given rate. Any "fix," however, is only as good as the guarantee, and to fix an exchange rate would require many more resources than an individual trader has; only governments have sufficient resources to fix an exchange rate, and often even governments run out of resources.

In reality, given the small level of official reserves compared to the enormous level of private trading, significant amounts of stabilization are impossible. Instead, governments use *strategic currency stabilization*—buying and selling at strategic moments to affect expectations of traders, and hence to affect their supply and demand. Such issues are discussed in depth in international finance courses.

Strategic currency stabilization is the process of buying and selling at strategic moments to affect the expectations of traders, and hence affect their supply and demand.

Stabilizing Fluctuations versus Deviating from Long-Run Equilibrium The key to whether or not exchange rate intervention is a viable option involves the long-run equilibrium exchange rate. Direct exchange rate policy can succeed if the problem is one of stabilization. If, however, the problem is long run, or if the government estimates the wrong equilibrium, eventually the government will run out of official reserves. Here's the rub: While in theory it is important to make the distinction, in practice it is difficult to do so. The government can only guess at the long-run equilibrium

REAL-WORLD APPLICATION

Determining the Causes of Fluctuations in the Dollar's Value

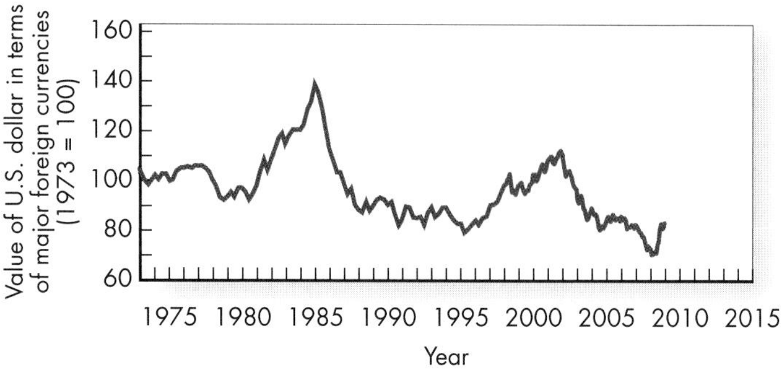

Source: Board of Governors, Federal Reserve System (www.federalreserve.gov).

As you can see on the graph, the dollar's value has fluctuated considerably since 1973. A good exercise to see if you understand movements in the value of the dollar is to try to choose which factors caused the fluctuation.

Let's start with the relatively small fluctuations in 1973 and 1974. These probably reflected expectational bubbles—in which speculators were more concerned with short-run fluctuations than long-run fundamentals—while the dollar's low value in 1979 and 1980 reflected high inflation, relatively low real interest rates, and the booming U.S. economy during this period.

The rise of the dollar in the early 1980s reflected higher real U.S. interest rates and the falling U.S. inflation rate, although the rise was much more than expected and probably reflected speculation, as did the sudden fall in the dollar's value in 1985. Similarly, the fluctuations in the late 1980s and early 1990s reflected both changing interest rates in the United States and changing foreign interest rates, as well as changing relative inflation rates.

In the late 1990s, the value of the dollar rose substantially. Part of the explanation for this lies in the weakness of the Japanese economy, which led the Japanese central bank to increase the Japanese money supply, thereby lowering the Japanese interest rate. That weakness also was reflected in the fall in the prices of Japanese stocks. That fall led investors to shift out of Japanese stocks and into U.S. stocks, thereby increasing the demand for the dollar, and pushing up the U.S. effective exchange rate. Since the early 2000s, the value of the dollar has generally been declining as its trade deficit has expanded.

As you can see, after the fact we economists are pretty good at explaining the movements in the exchange rates. Alas, before the fact we aren't so good because often speculative activities make the timing of the movements unpredictable.

rate since no definitive empirical measure of this rate exists. The long-run equilibrium must be estimated. If that estimate is wrong, a sustainable stabilization policy becomes an unsustainable deviation from long-run equilibrium policy. Thus, a central issue in exchange rate intervention policy is estimating the long-run equilibrium exchange rate.

Purchasing Power Parity and Real Exchange Rates

Purchasing power parity is one way economists have of estimating the long-run equilibrium rate. **Purchasing power parity (PPP)** is *a method of calculating exchange rates that attempts to value currencies at rates such that each currency will buy an equal basket of goods*. It is based on the idea that the exchange of currencies reflects the exchange of real goods. If you are able to exchange a basket of goods from country X for an equivalent basket of goods from country Z, you should also be able to exchange the amount of currency from country X that is needed to purchase country X's basket of goods for the amount of currency from country Z that is needed to purchase country Z's basket of goods. For example, say that the yen is valued at 100 yen to $1. Say also that you can buy the same basket of goods for 1,000 yen that you can buy for $7. In that case, the purchasing power parity exchange rate would be 143 yen to $1 (1,000/7 = 143) compared to an actual exchange rate of 100 yen to $1. An economist would say that at 100 to the dollar the yen is overvalued—with 100 yen you could not purchase a basket of goods equivalent to the basket of goods you could purchase with $1.

TABLE 36-2 Actual and Purchasing Power Parity Exchange Rates for 2008

Country	Actual Exchange Rate (currency per dollar)	PPP Exchange Rate (currency per dollar)	Under (−)/ Over (+) valuation
Switzerland	1.0816	1.680	+55%
United Kingdom	0.54	0.651	+21
Japan	103.39	117.128	+13
United States	1	1	0
Brazil	1.8327	1.468	−20
Russia	33.523	18.890	−44
China	6.9477	3.694	−47
Mozambique	26,840	12,579	−53
India	43.39	16.142	−63
Uganda	2,076	654	−68

Source: *World Economic Outlook Database*, 2008. International Monetary Fund (www.imf.org).

Table 36-2 shows various calculations for purchasing power parity for a variety of countries. The second column shows the 2008 actual exchange rates. The third column shows purchasing power parity exchange rates. The fourth column shows the difference between the two, or the 2008 distortion in the exchange rates (if you believe the PPP exchange rates are the correct ones).

Purchasing power parity is a method of calculating exchange rates such that various currencies will each buy an equal basket of goods and services.

Criticisms of the Purchasing Power Parity Method

For many economists, estimating exchange rates using PPP has serious problems. If the currency is overvalued and will eventually fall, why don't traders use that information and sell that currency now, making it fall now? After all, they are out after a profit. So if there is open trading in a currency, any expected change in the exchange rate will affect exchange rates now. If traders don't sell now when there are expectations that a currency's overvaluation will eventually make its value fall, they must believe there is some reason that its value won't, in fact, fall.

Web Note 36.3
The Big Mac Index

Critics argue that the difficulty with PPP exchange rates is the complex nature of trade and consumption. They point out that the PPP will change as the basket of goods changes. This means that there is no one PPP measure. They also point out that, since all PPP measures leave out asset demand for a currency, the measures are missing an important element of the demand. Critics ask: Is there any reason to assume that in the long run the asset demand for a currency is less important than the goods demand for a currency? Because the asset demand for a currency is important, critics of PPP argue that there is little reason to assume that the short-run actual exchange rate will ever adjust to the PPP exchange rates. And if that rate doesn't adjust, then PPP does not provide a good estimate of the equilibrium rate. These critics further contend that the existing exchange rate is the best estimate of the long-run equilibrium exchange rate.

Purchasing power parity exchange rates may or may not be appropriate long-run exchange rates.

Real Exchange Rates

Regardless of one's view of the usefulness of purchasing power parity, the concept gets at the importance of prices in the determination of exchange rates. Say, for example, that the price level in the United States goes up by 10 percent while the price level in Europe stays constant. In such a situation, we would expect some change in the exchange rate—the most likely effect would be that the U.S. dollar falls by 10 percent relative to the euro. To capture the distinction between changes in exchange rates caused by changes in price

A real exchange rate is an exchange rate adjusted for differential inflation or differential changes in the price level.

levels and changes in exchange rates caused by other things, economists differentiate between nominal and real exchange rates. A **real exchange rate** is *an exchange rate adjusted for differential inflation or differential changes in the price level.* A nominal exchange rate is the exchange rate you see in the papers—it is the rate you'd get when exchanging currencies.

Let's consider the above example: The U.S. price level rises by 10 percent, the European price level remains constant, and the nominal U.S. exchange rate falls by 10 percent. In that case, the real exchange rate will have remained constant. More generally, the change in the real exchange rate (foreign/domestic or in this case euro/$) can be approximately calculated by adding the difference in the rates of inflation between the two countries (domestic inflation − foreign inflation) to the percentage change in the nominal exchange rate.

Q-9 If U.S. inflation is 2 percent, the European Union's inflation rate is 4 percent, and the nominal U.S. dollar exchange rate rises by 3 percent relative to the euro, what happens to the real exchange rate of the dollar?

$$\%\Delta \text{ real exchange rate} = \%\Delta \text{ nominal exchange rate} + [\text{Domestic inflation} - \text{Foreign inflation}]$$

For example, say the U.S. price level had risen only by 8 percent and Europe's had remained constant, but the U.S. nominal exchange rate had fallen by 10 percent. In that case, we would say that the real U.S. exchange rate had fallen by 2 percent.

$$\%\Delta \text{ real exchange rate} = -10 + (8 - 0) = -2 \text{ percent}$$

Advantages and Disadvantages of Alternative Exchange Rate Systems

The problems of stabilizing exchange rates have led to an ongoing debate about whether a fixed exchange rate, a flexible exchange rate, or a combination of the two is best. This debate nicely captures the macro issues relevant to exchange rate stabilization, so in this section I consider that debate. First, a brief overview of the three alternative regimes:

Three exchange rate regimes are
1. Fixed exchange rate: The government chooses an exchange rate and offers to buy and sell currencies at that rate.
2. Flexible exchange rate: Determination of exchange rates is left totally up to the market.
3. Partially flexible exchange rate: The government sometimes affects the exchange rate and sometimes leaves it to the market.

Fixed exchange rate: *When the government chooses a particular exchange rate and offers to buy and sell its currency at that price.* For example, suppose the U.S. government says it will buy euros at $1.30 per euro and sell dollars at 0.78 euro per dollar. In that case, we say that the United States has a fixed exchange rate of 0.78 euro to the dollar.

Flexible exchange rate: *When the government does not enter into foreign exchange markets at all, but leaves the determination of exchange rates totally up to currency traders.* The price of its currency is allowed to rise and fall as market forces dictate.

Partially flexible exchange rate: *When the government sometimes buys or sells currencies to influence the exchange rate, while at other times letting private market forces operate.* A partially flexible exchange rate is sometimes called a dirty float because it isn't purely market-determined or government-determined.

Fixed Exchange Rates

The advantages of a fixed exchange rate system are

1. Fixed exchange rates provide international monetary stability.
2. Fixed exchange rates force governments to make adjustments to meet their international problems.

The disadvantages of a fixed exchange rate system are

1. Fixed exchange rates can become unfixed. When they're expected to become unfixed, they create enormous monetary instability.
2. Fixed exchange rates force governments to make adjustments to meet their international problems. (Yes, this is a disadvantage as well as an advantage.)

Let's consider each in turn.

Fixed Exchange Rates and Exchange Rate Stability The advantage of fixed exchange rates is that firms know what exchange rates will be, making trade easier. However, to maintain fixed exchange rates, the government must choose an exchange rate and have sufficient official reserves to support that rate. If the rate it chooses is too high, its exports lag and the country continually loses official reserves. If the rate it chooses is too low, it is paying more for its imports than it needs to and is building up official reserves.

Fixed exchange rates provide international monetary stability and force governments to make adjustments to meet their international problems. (This is *also* a disadvantage.) If they become unfixed, they create monetary instability.

The difficulty is that as soon as the country gets close to its official reserves limit, foreign exchange traders begin to expect a drop in the value of the currency, and they try to get out of that currency because anyone holding that currency when it falls will lose money. For example, in December 1997, when traders found out that South Korea had only $10 billion in reserves instead of the official government announcement of $30 billion, they sold the Korean won and its value dropped. False rumors of an expected depreciation or decrease in a country's fixed exchange rate can become true by causing a "run on a currency," as all traders sell that currency. Thus, at times fixed exchange rates can become highly unstable because expectation of a change in the exchange rate can force the change to occur. As opposed to small movements in currency values, under a fixed rate regime these movements occur in large, sudden jumps.

Fixed Exchange Rates and Policy Independence Maintaining a fixed exchange rate places limitations on a central bank's actions. In a country with fixed exchange rates, the central bank must ensure that the international quantities of its currency supplied and demanded are equal at the existing exchange rate.

Say, for example, that the United States and the Bahamas have fixed exchange rates: $1 B = $1 U.S. The Bahamian central bank decides to run an expansionary monetary policy, lowering the interest rate and stimulating the Bahamian economy. The lower interest rates will cause financial capital to flow out of the country, and the higher income will increase imports. Demand for Bahamian dollars will fall. To prop up its dollar and to maintain the fixed exchange rate, the Bahamian government will have to buy its own currency. It can do so only as long as it has sufficient official reserves of other countries' currencies.

Because most countries' official reserves are limited, a country with fixed exchange rates is limited in its ability to conduct expansionary monetary and fiscal policies. It loses its freedom to stimulate the economy in response to a recession. That's why, when a serious recession hits, many countries are forced to abandon fixed exchange rates. They run out of official reserves, and choose expansionary monetary policy to achieve their domestic goals over contractionary monetary policy to achieve their international goals.

Flexible Exchange Rates

The advantages and disadvantages of a flexible exchange rate (exchange rates totally determined by private market forces) are the reverse of those of fixed exchange rates. The advantages are

1. Flexible exchange rates provide for orderly incremental adjustment of exchange rates rather than large, sudden jumps.
2. Flexible exchange rates allow government to be flexible in conducting domestic monetary and fiscal policies.

The disadvantages are

1. Flexible exchange rates allow speculation to cause large jumps in exchange rates, which do not reflect market fundamentals.
2. Flexible exchange rates allow government to be flexible in conducting domestic monetary and fiscal policies. (This is a disadvantage as well as an advantage.)

Let's consider each in turn.

Flexible Exchange Rates and Exchange Rate Stability Advocates of flexible exchange rates argue as follows: Why not treat currency markets like any other market and let private market forces determine a currency's value? There is no fixed price for TVs; why should there be a fixed price for currencies? The opponents' answer is based on the central role that international financial considerations play in an economy and the strange shapes and large shifts that occur in the short-run supply and demand curves for currencies.

When expectations shift supply and demand curves around all the time, there's no guarantee that the exchange rate will be determined by long-run fundamental forces. The economy will go through real gyrations because of speculators' expectations about other speculators. Thus, the argument against flexible exchange rates is that they allow far too much fluctuation in exchange rates, making trade difficult.

Flexible exchange rate regimes provide for orderly incremental adjustment of exchange rates rather than large sudden jumps, and allow governments to be flexible in conducting domestic monetary and fiscal policies. (This is also a disadvantage.)

Flexible Exchange Rates and Policy Independence The policy independence arguments for and against flexible exchange rates are the reverse of those given for fixed exchange rates. Individuals who believe that national governments should not have flexibility in setting monetary policy argue that flexible exchange rates don't impose the discipline on policy that fixed exchange rates do. Say, for example, that a country's goods are uncompetitive. Under a fixed exchange rate system, the country would have to contract its money supply and deal with the underlying uncompetitiveness of its goods. Under a flexible exchange rate system, the country can maintain an expansionary monetary policy, allowing inflation simply by permitting the value of its currency to fall.

Advocates of policy flexibility argue that it makes no sense for a country to go through a recession when it doesn't have to; flexible exchange rates allow countries more flexibility in dealing with their problems. True, policy flexibility may lead to inflation, but inflation is better than a recession.

Partially Flexible Exchange Rates

Faced with the dilemma of choosing between these two unpleasant policies, most countries have opted for a policy in between: partially flexible exchange rates. With such a policy, they try to get the advantages of both fixed and flexible exchange rates.

When policy makers believe there is a fundamental misalignment in a country's exchange rate, they will allow private forces to determine it—they allow the exchange rate to be flexible. When they believe that the currency's value is falling because of speculation, or that too large an adjustment in the currency is taking place, and that that adjustment won't achieve their balance of payments goals, they step in and fix the exchange rate, either supporting or pushing down their currency's value. Countries that follow a currency stabilization policy have partially flexible exchange rates.

Partially flexible exchange rate regimes combine the advantages and disadvantages of fixed and flexible exchange rates.

If policy makers are correct, this system of partial flexibility works smoothly and has the advantages of both fixed and flexible exchange rates. If policy makers are incorrect, however, a partially flexible system has the disadvantages of both fixed and flexible systems.

Which View Is Right?

Q-10 Does government intervention stabilize exchange rates?

Which view is correct is much in debate. Most foreign exchange traders I know tell me that the possibility of government intervention increases the amount of private speculation in the system. In the private investors' view, their own assessments of what exchange rates should be are better than those of policy makers. If private investors knew the government would not enter in, private speculators would focus on fundamentals and would stabilize short-run exchange rates. When private speculators know government might enter into the market, they don't focus on fundamentals; instead they continually try to outguess government policy makers. When that happens, private speculation doesn't stabilize; it destabilizes exchange rates as private traders try to guess what the government thinks.

Fixed vs. Flexible vs. Partially Flexible Exchange Rates

Many of my economics colleagues who work for the Fed aren't convinced by private investors' arguments. They maintain that some government intervention helps stabilize currency markets. I don't know which group is right—private foreign exchange traders or economists at the Fed. But to decide, it is necessary to go beyond the arguments and consider how the various exchange rate regimes have worked in practice. Appendix A to this chapter gives you an introduction into the history of exchange rate regimes.

The Euro: A Common Currency for Europe

If you think of countries with a fixed exchange rate as being in a marriage, you can think of a common currency as in a marriage for life, from which it is almost impossible to escape. In 2002 12 European nations consummated their fixed exchange rate regime established under the EU's plan for monetary union and adopted the euro as their common currency. Other countries have joined since; those countries using the euro as their currency are shown in Figure 36-3 with the euro symbol (€). (Additional members of the EU are considering joining in the near future.) They adopted the euro for a number of reasons, some political and some economic; but regardless of why they did it, the euro will have significant effects on international finance and trade over the next decade.

Web Note 36.4
Multinational Money

First, let's consider the advantages the EU countries get from adopting a common currency. The first advantage is that, politically, a common currency ties the countries closely together. World Wars I and II started from fights among European countries. An important motive behind the increasing integration of Europe—from initial creation of a common market, to the establishment of the European Union with reduced border controls, to the establishment of the monetary union—has been to prevent large-scale war from ever happening again. Many feel that political reasons drove the countries toward union.

Three economic advantages of a common currency are that it

1. eliminates the cost of exchanging currencies,
2. facilitates price comparisons, and
3. creates a larger market.

There are, however, also economic reasons. One is to eliminate the cost of exchanging currencies when trading among members, and thereby provide an incentive to increase trade within the EU countries. A second is price transparency. With the adoption of a single currency, consumers and businesses can more easily see price differentials, resulting in greater competition. For example, instead of having to compare a pair of German shoes priced at 60 marks with an Italian pair priced at 48,000 lire, a consumer just needs to compare 30 euros with 25 euros. A third advantage is that the common currency makes it more likely that companies will think of Europe as a single market. Producing for that market would give European consumers more clout and make Europe, as well as the United States, the reference market when new goods are planned. It would also allow European firms to take advantage of economies of scale when producing for the European market. Finally, planners hoped that the importance of the euro would lead individuals throughout the world to hold their assets in euros rather than in dollars. That would mean lower interest rates for Europe relative to what they would have been, and the possibility that the euro will be used as an international reserve currency along with the dollar. An international reserve currency is a currency in which people and firms hold their savings. This means that the EU could create euros and exchange them for other currencies to buy products without increasing the money supply and risking inflation. (For the EU, it would be like getting an interest-free loan.) Because the U.S. dollar has been the world's reserve currency, the United States has been getting those interest-free loans, which is one of the reasons it's been able to run continual large trade deficits. If the euro partially replaces the dollar

FIGURE 36-3 Map of EU Countries

Members of the European Union as of 2009 included Austria, Belgium, Bulgaria, Cyprus, Czech Republic, Denmark, Estonia, Finland, France, Germany, Greece, Hungary, Ireland, Italy, Latvia, Lithuania, Luxembourg, Malta, The Netherlands, Poland, Portugal, Romania, Slovakia, Slovenia, Spain, Sweden, and the United Kingdom. Those countries that also share a common currency are marked with a €, the symbol of the euro.

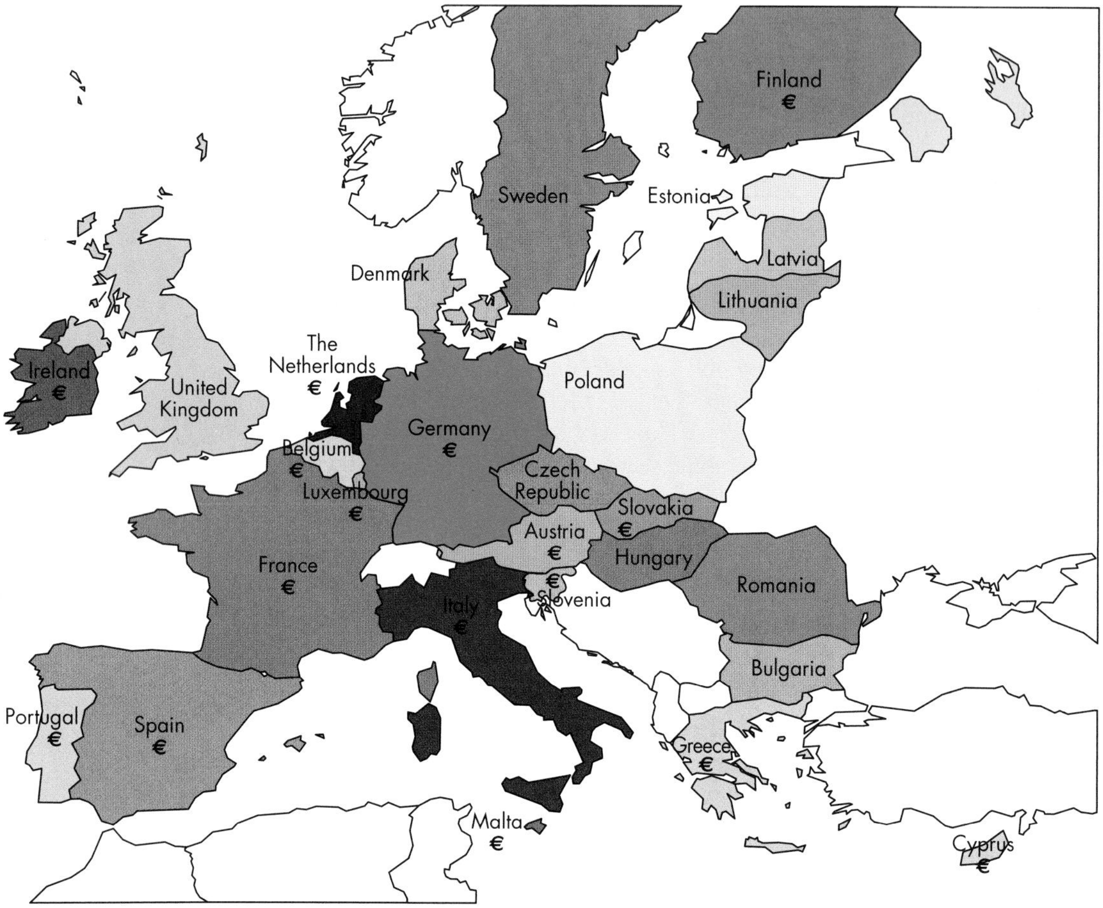

A major disadvantage of a common currency is the loss of independent monetary policy for member countries.

as the world reserve currency, there will likely be a large fall in demand for the dollar and a decrease in its relative value.

One major disadvantage of the common currency area is that members of the EU will no longer have independent monetary policies. So if an external shock hurts one region worse than another, the region hit hard cannot increase the money supply to offset the effect on output. For example, in 2004 to 2006, Ireland's economy was growing quickly while Germany's economy was contracting, but the two countries shared the same interest rate and monetary policy. A common currency also presents nationalism problems. A country's currency is a symbol to people of their country, and giving it up means losing part of their identity. Loss of nationalism is one reason Britain has been reluctant to adopt the euro.

The initial adoption of the euro has gone relatively smoothly, although realization of its advantages is still in the future. It will be an experiment that will be followed carefully over the next decade.

Conclusion

This chapter began with a quotation suggesting that a foreign exchange dealer's office can be the nearest thing to bedlam that there is. Seeing some order within that bedlam is not easy, but understanding the balance of payments and its relation to the determination of exchange rates is a good first step. And it is a necessary step. With international transportation and communication becoming easier and faster and other countries' economies growing, the U.S. economy will become more interdependent with the global economy in the upcoming decades, making understanding these issues more and more necessary to understanding macroeconomics.

Summary

- The balance of payments is made up of the current account and the financial and capital account.
- Exchange rates in a perfectly flexible exchange rate system are determined by the supply of and demand for a currency.
- An increase in a country's income increases the demand for foreign currency and leads to a decline in the value of the country's own currency.
- An increase in a country's price level reduces the demand for one's currency and increases the demand for foreign currency and leads to a decline in the value of one's own currency.
- A decrease in a country's interest rates reduces the demand for that country's currency and increases the demand for foreign currency, leading to a decline in the value of one's own currency.
- Increased trade restrictions on imports reduce the demand for foreign currencies, leading to an increase in the value of one's own currency.
- To raise the price of its currency, a country can either increase private demand through contractionary monetary policy or decrease private supply through contractionary monetary policy.
- Expansionary monetary policy, through its effect on interest rates, income, and the price level, tends to lower a country's exchange rate.
- Fiscal policy has an ambiguous effect on a country's exchange rate.
- A country can stabilize or fix its exchange rate by either directly buying and selling its own currency or adjusting its monetary and fiscal policy to achieve its exchange rate goal.
- It is easier technically for a country to bring the value of its currency down than it is to support its currency.
- It is extraordinarily difficult to correctly estimate the long-run equilibrium exchange rate; one method of doing so is the purchasing power parity approach.
- Fixed exchange rates provide international monetary stability but can create enormous monetary instability if they become unfixed. Fixed exchange rates force governments to make adjustments to meet their international problems.
- Flexible exchange rates allow exchange rates to make incremental changes, but are also subject to large jumps in value as a result of speculation. Flexible exchange rates give governments flexibility in conducting domestic monetary and fiscal policy.
- A real exchange rate is an exchange rate adjusted for differences in inflation:

  $$\%\Delta \text{ real exchange rate} = \%\Delta \text{ nominal exchange rate} + [\text{Domestic inflation} - \text{Foreign inflation}]$$

- A common currency creates strong political ties, reduces the cost of trade, facilitates price comparisons, and creates a larger single market. A common currency also makes it impossible to have an independent monetary policy. The 13 countries that share the euro gave up their own national currencies and gave up independent monetary policies.

Key Terms

balance of merchandise trade *(838)*
balance of payments *(836)*
balance of trade *(838)*
currency stabilization *(849)*
currency support *(848)*
current account *(837)*
financial and capital account *(837)*
fixed exchange rate *(852)*
flexible exchange rate *(852)*
forex market *(840)*
official reserves *(837)*
partially flexible exchange rate *(852)*
purchasing power parity (PPP) *(850)*
real exchange rate *(852)*

Questions and Exercises

connect ECONOMICS

1. If a country is running a balance of trade deficit, will its current account be in deficit? Why? LO1
2. When someone sends 100 British pounds to a friend in the United States, will this transaction show up on the financial and capital account or current account? Why? LO1
3. Support the following statement: "It is best to offset a capital and financial account surplus with a current account deficit." LO1
4. Support the following statement: "It is best to offset a capital and financial account deficit with a current account surplus." LO1
5. Will the following be suppliers or demanders of U.S. dollars in foreign exchange markets?
   a. A U.S. tourist in Latin America.
   b. A German foreign exchange trader who believes that the dollar exchange rate will fall.
   c. A U.S. foreign exchange trader who believes that the dollar exchange rate will fall.
   d. A Costa Rican tourist in the United States.
   e. A Russian capitalist who wants to protect his wealth from expropriation.
   f. A British investor in the United States. LO1
6. State whether the following will show up on the current account or the capital and financial account:
   a. IBM's exports of computers to Japan.
   b. IBM's hiring of a British merchant bank as a consultant.
   c. A foreign national living in the United States repatriates money.
   d. Ford Motor Company's profit in Hungary.
   e. Ford Motor Company uses that Hungarian profit to build a new plant in Hungary. LO1
7. In the early 2000s, China was running a large current account surplus.
   a. What did this suggest about its financial and capital account?
   b. China's private balance of payments was in surplus. What does this suggest about its exchange rate regime?
   c. What actions was the Chinese central bank likely undertaking in the foreign exchange markets? Demonstrate the situation with supply and demand graphs.
   d. If the Chinese central bank pulled out of the forex market, what would likely happen to the yuan?
   e. In May 2004, inflation picked up in China; what effect did that likely have on the value of the yuan? LO2
8. Draw the fundamental analysis of the supply and demand for the British pound in terms of dollars. Show what will happen to the exchange rate with those curves in response to each of the following events:
   a. The U.K. price level rises.
   b. The United States reduces tariffs.
   c. The U.K. economy experiences a boom.
   d. The U.K. interest rates rise. LO2
9. The government of Never-Never Land, after much deliberation, finally decides to switch to a fixed exchange rate policy. It does this because the value of its currency, the neverback, is so high that the trade deficit is enormous. The finance minister fixes the rate at \$10 a neverback, which is lower than the equilibrium rate of \$20 a neverback.
   a. What trade or traditional macro policy options could accomplish this lower exchange rate?
   b. Using the laws of supply and demand, show graphically how possible equilibria are reached. LO2
10. You've been hired as an economic adviser to Yamaichi Foreign Exchange Traders. What buy or sell recommendations for U.S. dollars would you make in response to the following news?
   a. Faster economic growth in the EU.
   b. Expectations of higher interest rates in the United States.
   c. The U.S. interest rate rises, but less than expected.
   d. Expected loosening of U.S. monetary policy.
   e. Higher inflationary predictions for the United States.
   f. The U.S. government imposes new trade restrictions on imports. LO2
11. In Figure 36-2, a foreign government chooses to maintain an equilibrium market exchange rate of U.S. \$1.30 per

unit of its own currency. Discuss the implications of the government trying to maintain a higher fixed rate—say at $1.50. LO3

12. From 2001 through 2008, the U.S. trade gap widened, spurred by a surge of imports. What was likely happening to income in the U.S. economy? LO3
13. Draw the schematics to show the effect of expansionary monetary policy on the exchange rate. LO3
14. What effect on the U.S. trade deficit and exchange rate would result if Japan ran an expansionary monetary policy? LO3
15. What would be the effect on the U.S. exchange rate if Japan ran a contractionary fiscal policy? LO3
16. If expansionary monetary policy immediately increases inflationary expectations and the price level, how might the effect of monetary policy on the exchange rate be different than that presented in this chapter? LO3
17. What effect will a combination of expansionary fiscal policy and contractionary monetary policy have on the exchange rate? LO3
18. Ms. Economist always tries to travel to a country where the purchasing power parity exchange rate is lower than the market exchange rate. Why? LO5
19. If U.S. inflation is 4 percent and Japan's inflation is 1 percent, and the nominal U.S. dollar exchange rate falls by 3 percent relative to the yen, what happens to the real exchange rate? LO5
20. A *Wall Street Journal* article, "As Fear of Deficits Falls, Some See a Larger Threat," describes the following threat of a high U.S. budget deficit:

    [T]he investors who finance our deficits by buying Treasury bonds and bills, especially the foreigners who buy a larger share of them than ever, will question our ability to repay them, and balk at lending more—triggering a big drop in the dollar and much higher interest rates.

    a. Why would a drop in foreign confidence in the U.S. ability to repay debt lead to a drop in the dollar and much higher interest rates?
    b. In what way are higher interest rates and a lower value of the dollar bad for the U.S. economy? LO5
21. Which is preferable: a fixed or a flexible exchange rate? Why? LO6
22. If currency traders expect the government to devalue a currency, what will they likely do? Why? LO6
23. A country eliminates all tariffs. Would you expect the value of its currency to rise or fall? Explain your answer. LO6
24. In mid-1994 the value of the dollar fell sufficiently to warrant coordinated intervention among 17 countries. Still, the dollar went on falling. One economist stated, "[The intervention] was clearly a failure . . . It's a good indication something else has to be done." Why would the United States and foreign countries want to keep up the value of the dollar? LO6
25. What are three advantages of the euro for Europe? LO7
26. What are two disadvantages of the euro for Europe? LO7

Questions from Alternative Perspectives

1. If all currencies were on a gold standard, there would be no exchange rates between currencies and we would not face the difficulties presented by fluctuating exchange rates.
    a. What would be the benefit of having all currencies on a gold standard?
    b. What would be the cost? (Austrian)
2. According to Gary North in *Priorities and Dominion: An Economic Commentary on Matthew*, in the book of Matthew, Jesus teaches about the rate of exchange between earthly wealth and eternal wealth.
    a. Would Jesus argue for a high or low exchange rate for earthly riches? Explain your answer.
    b. Do wealthy people believe the exchange rate is high or low?
    c. Do you believe the perceived exchange rate falls or rises as one approaches death? (Religious)
3. Most traders in currencies are men.
    a. Why is this?
    b. Why has it remained even though there is supposed to be no discrimination in employment?
    c. The language of traders is often quite coarse; does this fact provide a possible answer to both *a* and *b*?
    d. Did you think of it before you read *c*? (Feminist)
4. Nobel Prize–winning economist James Tobin has suggested that a method of decreasing unwanted sudden capital flows among countries would be to place a small tax on such flows. Post-Keynesian economist Paul Davidson argued against doing so because it won't solve the problem, suggesting that it is like using a pebble when a boulder is needed. What might Davidson's argument be? (Hint: It is related to the role of expectations.) (Post-Keynesian)
5. Most economists favor lowering barriers to trade. But even among mainstream economists there is far less support for financial liberalization—the removal of government regulation of financial and capital

markets—than for trade liberalization. "It is a seductive idea," says free-trader Jagdish Bhagwati, "but the claims of enormous benefit from free capital mobility are not persuasive." In addition, capital market liberalization entails substantial risks because it strips away the regulations intended to control the flow of short-term loans and contracts in and out of a country. The IMF, on the other hand, remains an unabashed supporter of free financial markets, arguing that they are a precondition for a developing country attracting long-term foreign investment.

a. Who has it right?
b. Is financial liberalization a good or bad policy, especially for developing countries? (Radical)

Issues to Ponder

1. In the early 1980s, the U.S. economy fell into a recession (the government faced the problem of both a high federal deficit and a high trade deficit, called the twin deficits), and the dollar was very strong. Can you provide an explanation for this sequence of events? (Difficult) LO1
2. During the 1995–96 Republican presidential primaries, Patrick Buchanan wrote an editorial in *The Wall Street Journal* beginning, "Since the Nixon era the dollar has fallen 75 percent against the yen, 60 percent against the mark." What trade policies do you suppose he was promoting? He went on to outline a series of tariffs. Agree or disagree with his policies. (Difficult) LO3
3. In an op-ed article, Paul Volcker, former chairman of the Board of Governors of the Federal Reserve, asked the following question: "Is it really worth spending money in the exchange markets, modifying monetary policy, and taking care to balance the budget just to save another percentage or two [of value of exchange rates]?" What's your answer to this question? (Difficult) LO3
4. If you were the finance minister of Never-Never Land, how would you estimate the long-run exchange rate of your currency, the neverback? Defend your choice as well as discuss its possible failings. (Difficult) LO5
5. Dr. Dollar Bill believes price stability is the main goal of central bank policy. Is the doctor more likely to prefer fixed or flexible exchange rates? Why? (Difficult) LO6
6. One of the basic laws of economics is the law of one price. It says that given certain assumptions one would expect that if free trade is allowed, the prices of goods in multiple countries should converge. This law underlies purchasing power parity.
   a. What are the three assumptions likely to be?
   b. Should the law of one price hold for labor also? Why or why not?
   c. Should it hold for capital more so or less so than for labor? Why or why not? LO5
7. Should Canada, the United States, and Mexico adopt a common currency? Why or why not? LO7

Answers to Margin Questions

1. The expenditures of a U.S. citizen traveling abroad will show up as a debit on the services account. As tourism or traveling, it is a service. *(838)*
2. Net investment income is the return a country gets on its foreign investment minus the return foreigners get on their investment within a country. A country is a net debtor nation if the value of foreign investment within a country exceeds the value of its investment abroad. A country can be a net debtor nation and still have its net investment income positive if its foreign investment is undervalued at market values (valuation is generally done at book value), or if its foreign investment earns a higher rate of return than foreigners' investment within that country. *(840)*
3. An increase in the demand for dollars is the equivalent of an increase in the supply of euros, so an increase in the demand for dollars pushes down the price of euros in terms of dollars, as in the following diagram. *(841)*

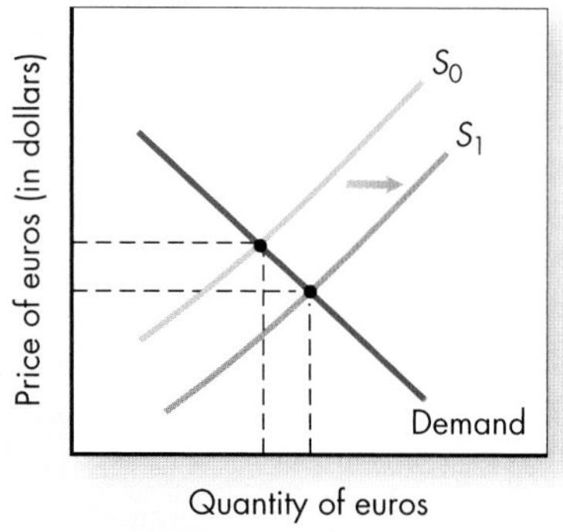

4. A fall in a country's interest rate will push down its exchange rate. *(843)*
5. Contractionary monetary policy pushes up the interest rate, decreases income and hence imports, and has a tendency to decrease inflation. Therefore, through these

paths, contractionary monetary policy will tend to increase the exchange rate. *(845)*

6. The net effect of expansionary fiscal policy on exchange rates is uncertain. Through the interest rate effect it pushes up the exchange rate, but through the income and price level effects it pushes down the exchange rate. *(846)*
7. In the short run, normal market forces have a limited, and possibly even perverse, effect on exchange rates, which is why most governments don't leave determination of exchange rates to the market. *(847)*
8. In general, it would be easier for the United States to push the value of the dollar down because doing so involves the United States buying up foreign currencies, which it can pay for simply by printing more dollars. To push the dollar up requires foreign reserves. *(849)*
9. The real exchange rate of the dollar relative to the euro rises 1 percent.

   %Δ real exchange rate = %Δ nominal exchange rate + [Domestic inflation − Foreign inflation] = 3 + (2 − 4) = 1. *(852)*
10. There is much debate about whether government intervention stabilizes exchange rates—private traders tend to believe it does not; government economists tend to believe that it does. *(854)*

APPENDIX A

History of Exchange Rate Systems

A good way to give you an idea of how the various exchange rate systems work is to present a brief history of international exchange rate systems.

The Gold Standard: A Fixed Exchange Rate System

Governments played a major role in determining exchange rates until the 1930s. Beginning with the Paris Conference of 1867 and lasting until 1933 (except for the period around World War I), most of the world economies had a system of relatively fixed exchange rates under what was called a **gold standard**—*a system of fixed exchange rates in which the value of currencies was fixed relative to the value of gold and gold was used as the primary reserve asset.*

Under a gold standard, the amount of money a country issued had to be directly tied to gold, either because gold coin served as the currency in a country (as it did in the United States before 1914) or because countries were required by law to have a certain percentage of gold backing their currencies. Gold served as currency or backed all currencies. Each country participating in a gold standard agreed to fix the price of its currency relative to gold. That meant a country would agree to pay a specified amount of gold on demand to anyone who wanted to exchange that country's currency for gold. To do so, each country had to maintain a stockpile of gold. When a country fixed the price of its currency relative to gold, it fixed its currency's price in relation to other currencies as a result of the process of arbitrage.

Under the gold standard, a country made up the difference between the quantity supplied and the quantity demanded of its currency by buying or selling gold to hold the price of its currency fixed in terms of gold. How much a country would need to buy and sell depended on its balance of payments deficit or surplus. If the country ran a surplus in the balance of payments, it was required to sell its currency—that is, buy gold—to stop the value of its currency from rising. If a country ran a deficit, it was required to buy its currency—that is, sell gold—to stop the value of its currency from falling.

The gold standard enabled governments to prevent short-run instability of the exchange rate. If there was a speculative run on its currency, the government would buy its currency with gold, thereby preventing the exchange rate from falling.

But for the gold standard to work, there had to be a method of long-run adjustment; otherwise countries would have run out of gold and would no longer have been able to fulfill their obligations under the gold standard. The **gold specie flow mechanism** was *the long-run adjustment mechanism that maintained the gold standard.* Here's how it worked: Since gold served as official reserves to a country's currency, a balance of payments deficit (and hence a downward pressure on the exchange rate) would result in a flow of gold out of the country and hence a decrease in the country's money supply. That decrease in the money supply would contract the economy, decreasing imports, lowering the country's price level, and increasing the interest rate, all of which would work toward eliminating the balance of payments deficit.

Similarly a country with a balance of payments surplus would experience an inflow of gold. That flow would increase the country's money supply, increasing income (and hence imports), increasing the price level (making imports cheaper and exports more expensive), and lowering the interest rate (increasing capital outflows). These would work toward eliminating the balance of payments surplus.

Thus, the gold standard determined a country's monetary policy and forced it to adjust any international balance of payments disequilibrium. Adjustments to a balance of payments deficit were often politically unpopular; they often led to recessions, which, because the money supply was directly tied to gold, the government couldn't try to offset with expansionary monetary policy.

The gold specie flow mechanism was called into play in the United States in late 1931 when the Federal Reserve, in response to a shrinking U.S. gold supply, decreased the amount of money in the U.S. economy, deepening the depression that had begun in 1929. The government's domestic goals and responsibilities conflicted with its international goals and responsibilities.

That conflict, which was rooted in the after-effects of World War I and the Depression, led to partial abandonment of the gold standard in 1933. At that time the United States made it illegal for individual U.S. citizens to own gold. Except for gold used for ornamental and certain medical and industrial purposes, all privately owned gold had to be sold to the government. Dollar bills were no longer backed by gold in the sense that U.S. citizens could exchange dollars for a prespecified amount of gold. Instead, dollar bills were backed by silver, which meant that any U.S. citizen could change dollars for a prespecified amount of silver. In the late 1960s, that changed also. Since that time, for U.S. residents, dollars have been backed only by trust in the soundness of the U.S. economy.

Gold continued to serve, at least partially, as international backing for U.S. currency. That is, other countries could still exchange dollars for gold. However, in 1971, in response to another conflict between international and domestic goals, the United States totally cut off the relationship between dollars and gold. After that, a dollar could be redeemed only for another dollar, whether it was a U.S. citizen or a foreign government who wanted to redeem the dollar.

The Bretton Woods System: A Fixed Exchange Rate System

As World War II was coming to an end, the United States and its allies met to establish a new international economic order. After much wrangling, they agreed upon a system called the **Bretton Woods system,** *an agreement about fixed exchange rates that governed international financial relationships from the period after the end of World War II until 1971.* It was named after the resort in New Hampshire where the meeting that set up the system was held.

The Bretton Woods system established the International Monetary Fund (IMF) to oversee the international economic order. The IMF was empowered to arrange short-term loans between countries. The Bretton Woods system also established the World Bank, which was empowered to make longer-term loans to developing countries. Today the World Bank and IMF continue their central roles in international financial affairs.

The Bretton Woods system was based on mutual agreements about what countries would do when experiencing balance of payments surpluses or deficits. It was essentially a fixed exchange rate system. For example, under the Bretton Woods system, the exchange rate of the dollar for the British pound was set at slightly over $4 to the pound.

The Bretton Woods system was not based on a gold standard. When countries experienced a balance of payments surplus or deficit, they did not necessarily buy or sell gold to stabilize the price of their currency. Instead they bought and sold other currencies. To ensure that participating countries would have sufficient reserves, they established a stabilization fund from which a country could obtain a short-term loan. It was hoped that this stabilization fund would be sufficient to handle all short-run adjustments that did not reflect fundamental imbalances.

In those cases where a misalignment of exchange rates was determined to be fundamental, the countries involved agreed that they would adjust their exchange rates. The IMF was empowered to oversee an orderly adjustment. It could authorize a country to make a one-time adjustment of up to 10 percent without obtaining formal approval from the IMF's board of directors. After a country had used its one-time adjustment, formal approval was necessary for any change greater than 1 percent.

The Bretton Woods system reflected the underlying political and economic realities of the post–World War II period in which it was set up. European economies were devastated; the U.S. economy was strong. To rebuild, Europe was going to have to import U.S. equipment and borrow large amounts from the United States. There was serious concern over how high the value of the dollar would rise and how low the value of European currencies would fall in a free market exchange. The establishment of fixed exchange rates set limits on currencies' relative movements; the exchange rates that were chosen helped provide for the rebuilding of Europe.

In addition, the Bretton Woods system provided mechanisms for long-term loans from the United States to Europe that could help sustain those fixed exchange rates. The loans also eliminated the possibility of competitive depreciation of currencies, in which each country tries to stimulate its exports by lowering the relative value of its currency.

One difficulty with the Bretton Woods system was a shortage of official reserves and international liquidity. To offset that shortage, the IMF was empowered to create *a type of international money* called **special drawing rights (SDRs).** But SDRs never became established as an international currency and the U.S. dollar kept serving as official reserves for individuals and countries. To get the dollars to foreigners, the United States had to run a deficit in its current account. Since countries could exchange the dollar for gold at a fixed price, the use of dollars as a reserve currency meant that, under the Bretton Woods system, the world was on a gold standard once removed.

The number of dollars held by foreigners grew enormously in the 1960s. By the early 1970s, those dollars far exceeded in value the amount of gold the United States had. Most countries accepted this situation; even though they could legally demand gold for their dollars, they did not. But Charles de Gaulle, the nationalistic president of France, wasn't pleased with the U.S. domination of international affairs at that time. He believed Europe deserved a much more prominent position. He demanded gold for the dollars held by the French central bank, knowing that the United States didn't have enough gold to meet his demand. As a result of his and other countries' demands, on August 15, 1971, the United States ended its policy of exchanging gold for dollars at $35 per ounce. With that change, the Bretton Woods system was dead.

The Present U.S. System: A Partially Flexible Exchange Rate System

International monetary affairs were much in the news in the early 1970s as countries groped for a new exchange rate system. The makeshift system finally agreed on involved partially flexible exchange rates. Most Western countries' exchange rates are allowed to fluctuate, although at various times governments buy or sell their own currencies to affect the exchange rate.

Under the present partially flexible exchange rate system, countries must continually decide when a balance of payments surplus or deficit is a temporary phenomenon and when it is a signal of a fundamental imbalance. If they believe the situation is temporary, they enter into the foreign exchange market to hold their exchange rate at what they believe is an appropriate level. If, however, they believe that the balance of payments imbalance is a fundamental one, they let the exchange rate rise or fall.

While most Western countries' exchange rates are partially flexible, certain countries have agreed to fixed exchange rates of their currencies in relation to rates of a group of certain other currencies. For example, a group of European Union countries adopted irreversible fixed exchange rates among their currencies, by electing to have one currency—the euro, which was introduced in 2002. Other currencies are fixed relative to the dollar (not by the United States but by the other countries).

Deciding what is, and what is not, a fundamental imbalance is complicated, and such decisions are considered at numerous international conferences held under the auspices of the IMF or governments. A number of organizations such as the Group of Eight focus much discussion on this issue. Often the various countries meet and agree, formally or informally, on acceptable ranges of exchange rates. Thus, while the present system is one of partially flexible exchange rates, the range of flexibility is limited.

Key Terms

- Bretton Woods system *(862)*
- gold specie flow mechanism *(861)*
- gold standard *(861)*
- special drawing rights (SDRs) *(863)*

CHAPTER 37

Macro Policy in a Global Setting

"We design them here, but the labor is cheaper in Hell."

The actual rate of exchange is largely governed by the expected behavior of the country's monetary authority.

—*Dennis Robertson*

In 2006, the U.S. exchange rate fell, the U.S. trade deficit reached an all-time high, and newspapers were full of stories of outsourcing and loss of American jobs. In 2008, the global monetary crisis overshadowed these longer-run issues, as countries worried about preventing a collapse of their financial systems. While these longer-run issues were put aside, they did not go away. They are still with us and are likely to be much in the news throughout the coming years. In this chapter, we pull together what we have learned about monetary and fiscal policy, comparative advantage, trade deficits, and exchange rates, and talk about macro policy in a global setting. To begin, we need to discuss our international macro goals.

AFTER READING THIS CHAPTER, YOU SHOULD BE ABLE TO:

1. Discuss why there is significant debate about what U.S. international goals should be.
2. Describe the paths through which monetary policy affects the trade balance.
3. Explain the paths through which fiscal policy affects the trade balance.
4. Summarize the reasons why governments try to coordinate their monetary and fiscal policies.
5. State the potential problem of internationalizing a country's debt.
6. Explain how restoring U.S. competitiveness will likely affect U.S. policy in the future.

The Ambiguous International Goals of Macroeconomic Policy

Macroeconomic international goals are less straightforward than domestic goals. There is general agreement about the domestic goals of macroeconomic policy: We want low inflation, low unemployment, and high growth. There's far less agreement on what a country's international goals should be.

Most economists agree that the international goal of U.S. macroeconomic policy is to maintain the U.S. position in the world economy. But there's enormous debate about what achieving that goal means. Do we want a high or a low exchange rate? Do we want a balance of trade surplus? Or would it be better to have a balance of trade deficit? Or should we not even pay attention to the balance of trade? Let's consider the exchange rate goal first.

The Exchange Rate Goal

The U.S. exchange rate has fluctuated significantly over the past 30 years. There is a debate over whether a country should have a high or a low exchange rate. A high exchange rate for the dollar makes foreign currencies cheaper, lowering the price of imports. Lowering import prices places competitive pressure on U.S. firms and helps to hold down inflation. All of this benefits U.S. residents' living standard. But a high exchange rate encourages imports and discourages exports. In doing so, it can cause a balance of trade deficit that can exert a contractionary effect on the economy by decreasing aggregate demand for U.S. output. So a high exchange rate also has a cost to U.S. residents.

A low exchange rate has the opposite effect. It makes imports more expensive and exports cheaper, and it can contribute to inflationary pressure. But, by encouraging exports and discouraging imports, it can cause a balance of trade surplus and exert an expansionary effect on the economy.

Many economists argue that a country should have no exchange rate policy because exchange rates are market-determined prices that are best left to the market. These economists question whether the government should even worry about the effect of monetary policy and fiscal policy on exchange rates. According to them, government should simply accept whatever exchange rate exists and not consider it in its conduct of monetary and fiscal policies.

FIGURE 37-1 The Trade Balance

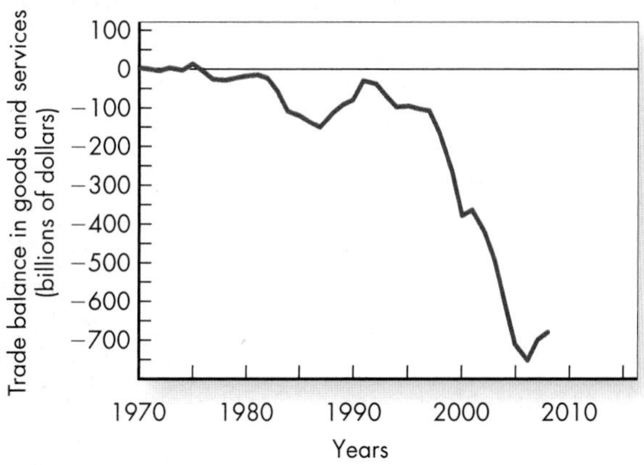

The Trade Balance Goal

Figure 37-1 shows the U.S. trade balance over the past 40 years. You can see that the United States has consistently run a trade deficit over that period, and that that trade deficit has generally increased. A deficit in the trade balance (the difference between imports and exports) means that, as a country, we're consuming more than we're producing. Imports exceed exports, so we're consuming more than we could if we didn't run a deficit. A surplus in the trade balance means that exports exceed imports—we're producing more than we're consuming. Since consuming more than we otherwise could is kind of nice, it might seem that a trade deficit is preferred to a trade surplus.

Q-1 What effect does a low exchange rate have on a country's exports and imports?

Exchange rates have conflicting effects and, depending on the state of the economy, there are arguments for both high and low exchange rates.

But wait. A trade deficit isn't without costs, and a trade surplus isn't without benefits. We pay for a trade deficit by selling off U.S. assets to foreigners—by selling U.S. companies, factories, land, and buildings to foreigners, or selling them financial assets such as U.S. dollars, stocks, and bonds. All the future interest and profits on these assets will go to foreigners, not U.S. citizens. That means eventually, sometime in the future, we will have to produce more than we consume so we can pay them *their* profit and interest on *their* assets. Thus, while in the short run a trade deficit allows more current consumption, in the long run it presents potential problems.

The trade balance is the difference between a country's exports and imports.

As long as a country can borrow, or sell assets, a country can have a trade deficit. But if a country runs a trade deficit year after year, eventually the long run will arrive and the country will run out of assets to sell and run out of other countries from whom to borrow. When that happens, the trade deficit problem must be faced.

Running a trade deficit is good in the short run but presents problems in the long run.

The debate about whether a trade deficit should be of concern to policy makers involves whether these long-run effects should be anticipated and faced before they happen.

Opinions differ greatly. Some say not to worry—just accept what's happening. These "not-to-worry" economists argue that the trade deficit will end when U.S. citizens don't want to borrow from foreigners anymore and foreigners don't want to buy any more of our assets. They argue that the inflow of financial capital (money coming into the United States to buy our assets) from foreigners is financing new investment that will make the U.S. economy strong enough in the long run to reverse the trade deficit

Q-2 Why do some people argue that we should not worry about a trade deficit?

REAL-WORLD APPLICATION

The U.S. Trade Deficit and the Value of the Dollar

The continued U.S. trade deficit from the 1970s into the early 2000s has confounded many analysts. Why has it remained so high? Why are other countries willing to give the United States many more real goods and services than they require in return? The answer is that they want to buy U.S. assets. There are a number of reasons why. First, the value of U.S. assets has increased. For example, Japan's stock market and real estate markets were falling while the U.S. stock market was rising, which gave Japanese investors a strong incentive to invest in the United States. Second, the United States is considered a safe haven—a solid economy that is safer than any other. If you want safety, you buy U.S. government bonds. Third, Japan and China have been buying large amounts of dollars in order to prevent the value of the dollar from falling relative to their currencies. At some point, however, the demand for U.S. assets is expected to end and the U.S. trade deficit will have to fall. In 2006 and 2007, the value of the dollar fell substantially relative to many other currencies, but then in 2008 it rose as the financial crisis made safety, not the return on investment, the overriding factor in individuals' decisions about where to hold their assets.

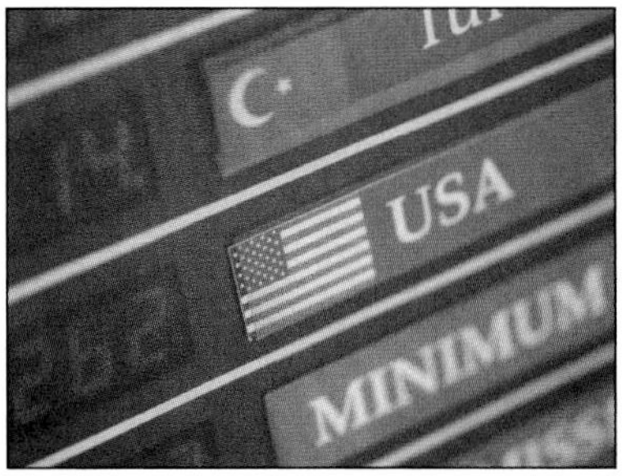

If a majority of economic analysts are correct, once the financial crisis ends, we should see a continued fall in the price of the dollar, which will lower the relative price of U.S. exports and increase the cost of imports. Because people don't want to hold assets in currencies whose values are falling, this fall could be much more sudden than policy makers would like, creating serious questions about whether they can do anything to prevent it.

without serious disruption to the U.S. economy. So why deal with the trade deficit now, when it will take care of itself in the future?

Others argue that, yes, the trade deficit will eventually take care of itself, but the accompanying economic distress will be great. By dealing with the problem now, the United States can avoid a highly unpleasant solution in the future.

Both views are reasonable, which is why there's no consensus on what a country's trade balance goal should be.

International versus Domestic Goals

Domestic goals generally dominate international goals.

In the real world, when there's debate about a goal, that goal is generally less likely to guide policy than goals about which there's general agreement. Since there's general agreement about our country's domestic goals (low inflation, low unemployment, and high growth), domestic goals generally dominate the U.S. political agenda.

Even if a country's international goals weren't uncertain, domestic goals would likely dominate the political agenda. The reason is that inflation, unemployment, and growth affect a country's citizens directly. Trade deficits and exchange rates affect them indirectly—and in politics, indirect effects take a back seat.

Web Note 37.1
Putting Exchange Rates First

Often a country responds to an international goal only when the international community forces it to do so. For example, in the 1980s when Brazil couldn't borrow any more money from other countries, it reluctantly made resolving its trade deficit a key goal. Similarly, when other countries threatened to limit Japanese imports, Japan took steps to increase the value of the yen and decrease its trade surplus. Currently China is facing international pressure to let its exchange rate rise. When a country is forced to face certain economic facts, international goals can become its primary goals. As countries become more economically integrated, these pressures from other countries become more important.

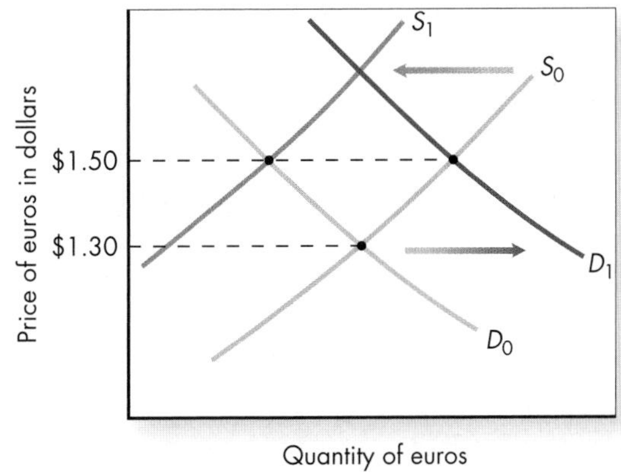

FIGURE 37-2 Targeting an Exchange Rate with Monetary and Fiscal Policy

To increase the exchange rate value of the euro, the European Central Bank (ECB) could run contractionary monetary policy to increase interest rates and increase the private demand for euros or induce a recession and decrease the private supply of euros, or a combination of the two.

Balancing the Exchange Rate Goal with Domestic Goals

In the last chapter we talked about monetary and fiscal policy's effect on the exchange rate. In it we saw that while fiscal policy's effect on exchange rates was ambiguous, monetary policy had a predictable effect: Expansionary monetary policy tended to push the exchange rate down; contractionary monetary policy tended to push the exchange rate up.[1] What this means is that in principle, the government can control the exchange rate with monetary policy. The problem with doing so is that monetary policy also affects the domestic economy—contractionary monetary policy decreases income and jobs. Contractionary monetary policy is not a policy that countries generally want to follow.

The way in which monetary policy affects the exchange rate is by affecting the supply and demand for the country's currency. To review this, let's consider the case of Europe that we examined in the previous chapter. That case is shown in Figure 37-2. Europe's problem here is that it wants the exchange rate for the euro to be $1.50, not $1.30. The EU has three options for raising the value of the euro: decrease the private supply of euros (shifting the supply curve in from S_0 to S_1), increase the private demand for euros (shifting the demand curve out from D_0 to D_1), or use some combination of the two. Let's see how it could accomplish its goal with monetary or fiscal policy.

Q-3 If a country wants to fix its exchange rate at a rate that is higher than the market rate, what monetary or fiscal policy must it use?

To increase the demand for euros, the EU must create policies that increase the private foreign demand for EU assets, or for EU goods and services. In the short run, the European Central Bank (ECB) can increase the interest rate by running contractionary monetary policy. A higher interest rate increases the foreign demand for the EU's interest-bearing assets. The problem with this approach is that to maintain an exchange rate at a certain level, a country must give up any attempt to target its interest rate to achieve domestic goals. To put it another way: A country can achieve an interest rate target or an exchange rate target, but generally it cannot achieve both at the same time.

Contractionary monetary policy also slows down the domestic economy and induces a recession. This recession decreases the demand for imports and thereby decreases the private supply of euros. Governments are usually loath to use this contractionary policy because politically induced recessions are not popular. It is because of the constraints that fixed exchange rates, or any policy designed to hold its exchange rate up, place

Q-4 If a country runs a contractionary monetary policy, what effect will that likely have on its exchange rate?

[1]We don't discuss fiscal policy as a control policy for exchange rates because fiscal policy has an ambiguous effect on the exchange rate, as the interest rate effect of fiscal policy pushes the exchange rate one way and the income effect pushes it another. (See the previous chapter if you are not clear on this effect.)

on domestic monetary and fiscal policy that many countries choose flexible, or at least partially flexible, exchange rate regimes.

Monetary and Fiscal Policy and the Trade Deficit

Since a major policy issue for the United States in the coming years is likely to be its large trade deficit, and the pressures that will likely decrease that deficit, let's now turn to a consideration of how monetary and fiscal policy affect the trade deficit. We begin with monetary policy.

Monetary Policy's Effect on the Trade Balance

When a country's international trade balance is negative (in deficit), the country is importing more than it is exporting. When a country's international trade balance is positive (in surplus), the country is exporting more than it is importing.

Monetary policy affects the trade balance primarily through its effect on income. Specifically, expansionary monetary policy increases income. When income rises, imports rise, while exports are unaffected. As imports rise, the trade balance shifts in the direction of deficit. So expansionary monetary policy shifts the trade balance toward a deficit.

Q-5 What effect will contractionary monetary policy have on the trade balance?

Contractionary policy works in the opposite direction. It decreases income. When income falls, imports fall (while exports are unaffected), so the trade balance shifts in the direction of surplus. Thus, expansionary monetary policy increases the trade deficit; contractionary monetary policy decreases the trade deficit.

Monetary policy will also affect the trade balance in a variety of other ways—for example, through its effect on the price level and the exchange rate. These other effects tend to be more long-run effects and tend to offset one another. So we will not consider them here. While many complications can enter the trade balance picture, most economists would summarize monetary policy's short-run effect on the trade balance as follows:

Expansionary monetary policy makes a trade deficit larger.

Contractionary monetary policy makes a trade deficit smaller.

Expansionary monetary policy makes a trade deficit larger.

Contractionary monetary policy makes a trade deficit smaller.

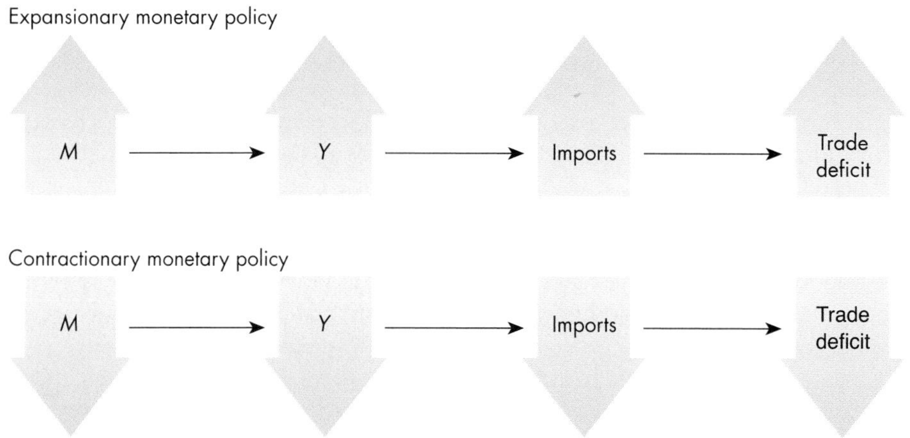

Fiscal Policy's Effect on the Trade Balance

Fiscal policy, like monetary policy, works on the trade deficit primarily through its effects on income. (Again, there are other paths by which fiscal policy affects the trade deficit, but this one is the largest since changes in income are quickly reflected in a change in imports.) So if asked for a quick answer, economists would say that contractionary fiscal policy decreases a trade deficit.

Summarizing the effects of expansionary and contractionary fiscal policy schematically, we have

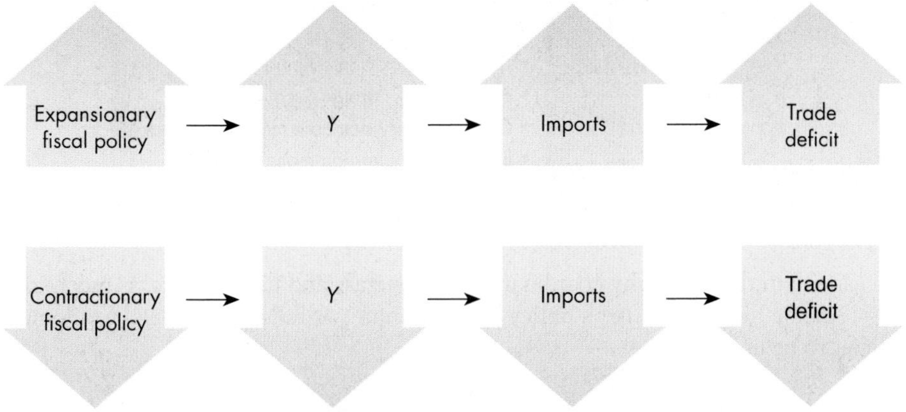

Q-6 What is the effect of expansionary fiscal policy on the trade deficit?

Contractionary fiscal policy decreases a trade deficit.

International Phenomena and Domestic Goals

Web Note 37.2 Coordinating Policies

So far, we've focused on the effect of monetary and fiscal policies on international goals. But often the effect is the other way around: International phenomena change and have significant influences on the domestic economy and on the ability to achieve domestic goals.

For example, say that Japan ran contractionary monetary policy. That would increase the Japanese exchange rate and increase Japan's trade surplus, which means it would decrease the U.S. exchange rate and increase the U.S. trade deficit, both of which would affect U.S. domestic goals.

Alternatively, let's consider how the current situation is likely to play out for the United States in the coming decade. Currently, the United States is running a large trade deficit, which will be difficult to sustain. If the United States chooses to reduce that trade deficit with monetary or fiscal policy, it will have to run contractionary monetary and fiscal policy, keeping the economy from growing as fast as it otherwise would. That is not a politically attractive option, which is an important reason why the United States has not chosen to deal with the trade deficit with monetary or fiscal policy.

Q-7 If other countries stop buying large amounts of dollar-denominated assets, what will likely happen to the value of the dollar?

But what if other countries stop buying the large amount of dollar-denominated assets that they are currently buying? The dollar exchange rate will fall, possibly precipitously, unless the trade deficit is reduced. In the long run, that fall in the exchange rate will improve the competitiveness of the U.S. economy, decrease imports, and increase exports. But in the short run, the dollar's decline will place the U.S. economy in a bind since it will push up prices of imports, creating inflationary pressure, and make Americans worse off. Too fast of a decline will likely create severe financial problems that can reverberate through the economy. Thus, the U.S. government will feel pressure to cut some of the trade deficit with contractionary monetary and fiscal policy, policies imposed on the United States by its international position.

International Goals and Policy Alternatives

The table on the next page provides a summary of how alternative policy actions achieve international goals.

International Goal	Policy Alternatives
Lower exchange rate	• Contractionary foreign monetary policy • Expansionary domestic monetary policy
Lower trade deficit	• Contractionary domestic fiscal policy • Expansionary foreign fiscal policy • Contractionary domestic monetary policy • Expansionary foreign monetary policy

You can see in the table why coordination of monetary and fiscal policies is much in the news, since a foreign country's policy can eliminate, or reduce, the need for domestic policies to be undertaken.

International Monetary and Fiscal Coordination

Governments try to coordinate their monetary and fiscal policies because their economies are interdependent.

Unless forced to do so because of international pressures, most countries don't let international goals guide their macroeconomic policy. But for every effect that monetary and fiscal policies have on a country's exchange rates and trade balance, there's an equal and opposite effect on the combination of other countries' exchange rates and trade balances. When one country's exchange rate goes up, by definition another country's exchange rate must go down. Similarly, when one country's balance of trade is in surplus, another's must be in deficit. This interconnection means that other countries' fiscal and monetary policies affect the United States, while U.S. fiscal and monetary policies affect other countries, so pressure to coordinate policies is considerable.

Web Note 37.3
Interconnection

Coordination Is a Two-Way Street

Q-8 If domestic problems call for expansionary monetary policy and international problems call for contractionary monetary policy, what policy will a country likely adopt?

Policy coordination—*the integration of a country's policies to take account of their global effects*—of course, works both ways. If other countries are to take the U.S. economy's needs into account, the United States must take other countries' needs into account in determining its goals. Say, for example, the U.S. economy is going into a recession. This domestic problem calls for expansionary monetary policy. But expansionary monetary policy will increase U.S. income and U.S. imports and lower the value of the dollar. Say that, internationally, the United States has agreed that it must work toward eliminating the U.S. trade deficit in the short run. Does it forsake its domestic goals? Or does it forsake its international commitment?

Each country will likely do what's best for the world economy as long as it's also best for itself.

There's no one right answer to those questions. It depends on political judgments (how long until the next election?), judgments about what foreign countries can do if the United States doesn't meet its international commitments, and similar judgments by foreign countries about the United States.

Despite the complications, the above discussion gives you an understanding of many events that may have previously seemed incomprehensible. To show you the relevance of what I have said above about international considerations, let's look at two situations.

Let's consider the example of Argentina in the early 2000s. In the early 1990s, Argentina established a fixed exchange rate between the peso and the U.S. dollar and promised to maintain that exchange rate under all circumstances. Numerous international investors relied on that promise. In the late 1990s, the Argentinean economy went into recession and domestic political pressures called for expansionary aggregate demand policy. Maintaining the fixed exchange rate required contractionary aggregate demand policy. The internal political pressures won, and Argentina abandoned its fixed exchange rate in early 2002.

The second concerns Japan in 1993 and early 1994. Japan was experiencing a recession, in part because its tight monetary policy had pushed up interest rates and hence pushed up the exchange rate for the yen. Other countries, especially the United States and European countries, put enormous pressure on Japan to run expansionary fiscal policy, which would keep the relative value of the yen high but simultaneously increase Japanese income, and hence Japanese demand for imports. In response, Japan ran expansionary fiscal policy and this helped to keep the value of the yen higher than it otherwise would have been. Soon thereafter, Japan simultaneously ran expansionary monetary policy, thereby lowering the interest rate and the exchange rate. There are many more examples, but these two should give you a good sense of the relevance of the issues.

A REMINDER

Monetary and Fiscal Policy's Effect on International Goals

The effect of expansionary monetary and fiscal policy on international goals in the short run is summarized in the diagram. In the short run, expansionary monetary policy tends to increase a trade deficit and decrease the exchange rate. Expansionary fiscal policy tends to increase the trade deficit. Its effect on the exchange rate is ambiguous. The effects of contractionary policy work in the opposite direction.

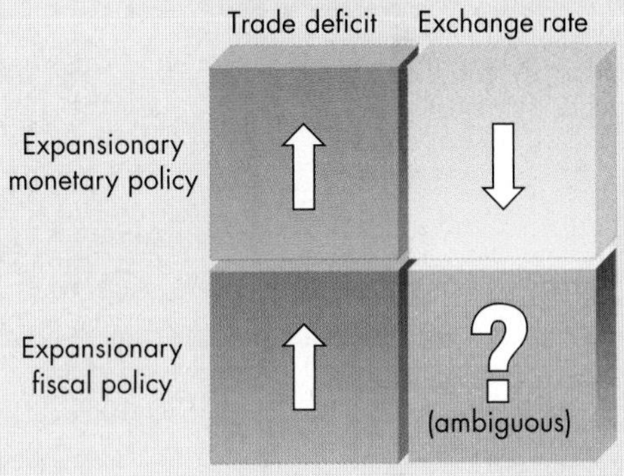

Crowding Out and International Considerations

Let's reconsider the issue of crowding out that we considered in an earlier chapter, only this time we'll take into account international considerations. Say a government is running a budget deficit and the central bank has decided it won't increase the money supply to help finance the deficit. (This happened in the 1980s with the Fed and the U.S. government.) What will be the result?

The basic idea of crowding out is that the budget deficit will cause the interest rate to go up. But wait. There's another way to avoid the crowding out that results from financing the deficit: Foreigners could buy the debt at the existing interest rate. This is called *internationalizing the debt,* and that is what happened to the U.S. economy in recent years.

There have been massive inflows to the United States of financial capital from abroad. These inflows held down the U.S. interest rate even as the federal government ran large budget deficits. Thus, large U.S. budget deficits didn't push up interest rates because foreigners, not U.S. citizens, were buying U.S. debt.

Q-9 How does internationalizing the debt reduce crowding out?

While internationalizing a country's debt may help in the short run, in the long run it presents potential problems since foreign ownership of a country's debts means the country must pay interest to those foreign countries and that debt may come due.

But, as we discussed, internationalization of the U.S. debt is not costless. While it helps in the short run, it presents problems in the long run. Today more than 50 percent of privately held U.S. government debt is held by foreigners. Foreign ownership of U.S. debt means that the United States must pay foreigners interest each year on that debt. To do so, the United States must export more than it imports, which means that the United States must consume less than it produces at some time in the future to pay for the trade deficits it's running now. As you can see, the issues quickly become complicated.

Globalization, Macro Policy, and the U.S. Economy

We began this book stating that the United States operates in a global economy and that policy today must consider global issues. As a conclusion to the chapter, let's pull our various discussions together and review the likely problems that international considerations are creating for the U.S. economy over the coming decades. I start with some general points about the relationship of international issues to macro policy.

International Issues and Macro Policy

The first point is that the more globally connected a country is, the less flexibility it has with its monetary and fiscal policy. Global issues restrict the use of monetary and fiscal policy to achieve domestic goals. How much they do so, and the manner in which they do so, depend on the country's exchange rate regime, which leads to our second point: How fast a country must respond to international pressure depends on the exchange rate regime it follows. If an economy sets fixed exchange rates, its monetary and fiscal policies are much more restricted than they are with flexible exchange rates. The reason is that the amount of currency stabilization that can be achieved with direct intervention is generally quite small since a country's foreign reserves are limited. When this is the case, to keep its currency fixed at the desirable level, it must adjust the economy to the exchange rate. Specifically, it must undertake policies that will change either the private supply of its currency or the private demand for its currency. It can do so by traditional macro policy—monetary and fiscal policy—influencing the economy, or by trade policy to affect the level of exports and imports. This means that if monetary and fiscal policies are being used to achieve exchange rate goals, they cannot also be used to achieve domestic goals.

Q-10 If a country has a fixed exchange rate, does it have more or less flexibility in choosing its monetary and fiscal policy to achieve domestic goals?

The second point is that with flexible exchange rates, countries have more freedom with monetary and fiscal policy, but then they have to accept whatever happens to their exchange rate, and there are often strong political forces that do not want to do that. That is the position in which the United States will find itself if foreigners significantly reduce their demand for U.S. assets.

The third point is that an alternative to using monetary and fiscal policy to guide the economy toward meeting its international goals is trade policy designed to affect the level of exports and imports. As discussed in a previous chapter, specific use of tariffs and quotas is limited by international conventions, but indirect policies to affect imports and exports are used all the time. For example, U.S. tax laws can be designed to make it more costly for companies to produce abroad. Implicit subsidies can be given for exports and implicit constraints can be placed on imports. We can expect such programs to continue and to expand in the coming decade as the United States attempts to reduce its trade deficit by means other than a fall in the exchange rate of the dollar, which is the alternative path to reducing its trade deficit.

The fourth point is that macro policy is short-run policy, which must be conducted within a longer-range setting of the country's overall **competitiveness**—*the ability of a country to sell its goods to other countries*. That longer-range setting for the United States in the coming decade is not likely to be conducive to expansionary macro policy, which is a change from the past. Following World War II, the long-run setting did allow expansionary macro policy. The United States had a strong competitive position and a trade surplus even though the value of the dollar was high. (During that time, the United States had a fixed exchange rate; see Appendix A of the previous chapter for a brief history of the period.)

In the 1970s, economic development and investment abroad reduced U.S. competitiveness. Fortunately for the United States, foreign individuals and countries had an enormous demand for U.S. assets. (The capital and financial account surplus discussed in the last chapter reflects that demand.) Had foreign individuals and countries not wanted to increase their holdings of U.S. assets, the long-run setting for macro policy would have been far less conducive to expansionary macro policy. The trade deficit would have lowered the value of the dollar, which would have offset the declining U.S. competitiveness. If this had happened, however, and the United States had also wanted to hold the value of the dollar up, U.S. monetary and fiscal policy would have had to have been contractionary.

Because foreign individuals and countries have been willing to increase their holdings of dollars through the early 2000s, international issues have not limited U.S. macro policy. Thus, the U.S. has been able to run highly expansionary fiscal policies and large government budget deficits without causing U.S. interest rates to rise because inflows of foreign financial assets bought the bonds to finance the deficit.

Restoring International Trade Balance to the U.S. Economy

Web Note 37.4
Trade Policy Agenda

When we think about the likely future direction of the U.S. economy, we have to integrate the theory of comparative advantage into our discussion because it provides the long-run setting within which short-run policy is conducted. The theory of comparative advantage focuses on the case where trade is balanced—where the comparative advantages of both countries in various goods are balanced. If that is not the case, economic theory assumes something will adjust to bring them into balance.[2] But when the demand for a country's assets is large, those adjustments do not have to take place. That's what happened to the United States. The large demand for U.S. assets allowed U.S. production in a variety of goods and services to lose their competitiveness. U.S. comparative advantage was not in produced goods but in assets; the demand for its assets meant that the United States did not need a demand for its goods and services. Thinking only in terms of goods and services, at current exchange rates, the United States doesn't have a comparative advantage in as many different goods and services as do other countries. That's what it means to be running a trade deficit.

As long as other countries are willing to accept U.S. currency or U.S. assets in payment for the goods that they produce, the United States can continue to run a trade deficit at the current exchange rate.

As long as other countries are willing to accept U.S. currency or U.S. assets in payment for the goods that they produce, the United States can continue to run a trade deficit at the current exchange rate. We've seen the beginning of the downward pressure on the value of the dollar, but as of 2009, the dollar has not fallen much against the Chinese yuan or Indian rupee because their central banks have bought dollars to stop their own currencies from appreciating. (A good review of the last chapter is to discuss, using supply and demand curves, how the Central Bank of China is preventing the appreciation of the yuan.) In fact, in 2008, the downward pressure on the dollar abated, and the dollar actually rose in value relative to a number of other currencies, as the global financial crisis led people to search for the safest asset, which many still believed to be U.S. treasury bonds. But that is likely to be only a temporary situation.

At some point, foreigners will likely stop wanting to accumulate more U.S. currency or assets and foreign government support will likely slow. When this happens, assuming nothing else changes, the dollar will depreciate, especially relative to the rupee and yuan, until the United States regains comparative advantage in enough goods to create a balance in the balance of payments without the inflow of foreign financial assets. Until that happens, we can expect further outsourcing of U.S. jobs and weak U.S. economic growth.

The fall in the value of the dollar is not absolutely certain. Many events could temporarily change the situation. For example, political uncertainty in China or India could slow the process enormously, and even possibly reverse it. Similarly, large inflation in China or India would serve the same purpose as a rise in their

[2]When David Ricardo first developed the comparative advantage argument, he discussed how, if there were trade imbalances between the two countries, those imbalances would be quickly eliminated by changes in the two countries' price levels as money followed from the deficit country to the surplus country. When he was writing, countries based their currencies on gold, and it was probably a reasonable assumption. Today, capital markets are much more developed, and capital flows in the opposite direction can offset the need for quick adjustment based on imbalances of trade.

Global economies are interconnected; if the U.S. economy were to collapse, so would other world economies.

exchange rates, and eliminate the need for the value of the dollar to fall. Even if those events don't happen, a sudden collapse of the U.S. exchange rate is not likely to be in the cards because the collapse of the U.S. economy that would accompany it is not in the interest of other countries. Global economies are interconnected; if the U.S. economy were to collapse, so would other world economies. Thus, we can expect foreign governments to step in to support the dollar and slow its fall if the private demand for U.S. assets decreases. Just as the United States does not want its currency to fall too precipitously, China and India do not want their currencies to rise too quickly. This suggests that international pressures on U.S. macro policy will keep U.S. growth slower than what it otherwise would be, and place continual downward pressure on U.S. wages for workers producing an expanding number of tradable goods.

A Conclusion

It's time to conclude the chapter and our consideration of global macro policy. Both have been just an introduction. You shouldn't think of them as any more than that. In no way has this brief chapter exhausted the international topics relevant to macro policy. But the chapter has, I hope, made you aware of the international dimensions of our economic goals—and of the problems that international issues pose for macro policy—and the book has made you aware of the central insights of economics. That awareness is absolutely necessary if you are to understand the ongoing debates about economic policy.

Summary

- The international goals of a country are often in dispute.
- Domestic goals generally dominate international goals, but countries often respond to an international goal when forced to do so by other countries.
- Expansionary monetary policy, through its effect on income, increases a country's trade deficit.
- Contractionary fiscal policy tends to decrease a country's trade deficit.
- For every effect that monetary and fiscal policies have on a country's exchange rate and trade balance, there is an equal and opposite effect on the combination of foreign countries' exchange rates and trade balances. Therefore, countries try to coordinate their policies.
- International financial inflows can reduce crowding out.
- Internationalizing a country's debt means that at some time in the future the country must consume less than it produces.
- The United States has lost its competitiveness in the production of many goods. Unless foreigners continue to demand U.S. assets, the U.S. trade deficit will put downward pressure on the dollar and U.S. policy makers will face implementing contractionary policies and/or trade restrictions.

Key Terms

competitiveness *(872)*

policy coordination *(870)*

Questions and Exercises

1. Why might a sudden large drop in the value of the dollar put pressure on the United States to run contractionary monetary and fiscal policy? LO1
2. If the value of the dollar is expected to fall:
   a. Would you rather be holding dollars or other currencies?
   b. Would the same argument you used to answer *a* also hold for the Chinese government?
   c. Why might the Chinese government buy dollars even though it expects the value of the dollar to fall? LO1
3. What effect on the U.S. trade deficit would result if China and Japan ran an expansionary monetary policy? LO2
4. What would be the effect on the U.S. trade deficit if China and Japan ran a contractionary fiscal policy? LO2
5. Draw the schematics to show the effect of expansionary monetary policy on the trade deficit. LO2
6. You observe that over the past decade a country's trade deficit has risen.
   a. What monetary or fiscal policies might have led to such a result?
   b. You also observe that interest rates have steadily risen along with a rise in the exchange rate. What policies would lead to this result?
   c. Could another explanation be that people in other countries wanted to hold lots of that country's debt? LO2
7. Congratulations! You have been appointed an adviser to the IMF. A country that has run trade deficits for many years now has difficulty servicing its accumulated international debt and wants to borrow from the IMF to meet its obligations. The IMF requires that the country set a target trade surplus.
   a. What monetary and fiscal policies would you suggest the IMF require of that country?
   b. What would be the likely effect of that plan on the country's domestic inflation and growth?
   c. How do you think the country's government will respond to your proposals? Why? LO2
8. Congratulations! You've been hired as an economic adviser to a country that has perfectly flexible exchange rates. State what monetary and fiscal policy you might suggest in each of the following situations, and explain why you would suggest those policies.
   a. You want to lower the interest rate, decrease inflationary pressures, and lower the trade deficit.
   b. You want to lower the interest rate, decrease inflationary pressures, and lower a trade surplus.
   c. You want to lower the interest rate, decrease unemployment, and lower the trade deficit.
   d. You want to raise the interest rate, decrease unemployment, and lower the trade deficit. LO2
9. Is the United States justified in complaining about Japan's and China's use of an export-led growth policy? Why? LO3
10. In the 1990s, Japan's economic recession was much in the news.
    a. What would you suspect was happening to its trade balance during this time?
    b. What policies would you guess other countries (such as those in the Group of Eight) were pressuring Japan to implement? LO3
11. According to a study done at J.P. Morgan, as world trade has increased from about 12 percent of world output in the 1970s to about 25 percent of world output in the early 2000s, global differences in growth rates has been decreasing, from around 3 percent in the 1970s to about 1 percent in the early 2000s.
    a. If that is true, would one expect more or less stabilization coming from trade with other countries?
    b. What does this convergence of growth rates suggest about the possibility of a global recession?
    c. If a global recession occurred, what policy recommendation would you put forward? LO4
12. How does internationalizing the debt reduce crowding out? LO5
13. What are the costs of internationalizing the debt? LO5
14. What would likely happen to exchange rates if one country has a comparative advantage in production of most goods and the financial and capital account was balanced? (Difficult) LO6

Questions from Alternative Perspectives

1. In developed countries, it is highly questionable whether an activist monetary and fiscal policy is of any use. Why is it even more questionable in developing countries? (Austrian)
2. Your text talks about how the United States has been consuming more than it has been producing for more than 30 years, making it the largest debtor nation in the world. Deuteronomy 28:43–44 warns against such

indebtedness to foreigners. "Aliens residing among you shall ascend above you higher and higher, while you shall descend lower and lower. They shall lend to you but you shall not lend to them; they shall be the head and you shall be the tail."

a. Is the trade deficit bad even if it can continue indefinitely?
b. Are there biblical ethics against living beyond one's means that suggests any trade deficit is bad?
c. In what way is the Deuteronomist's saying true for America today? (Religious)

3. In 2002, the U.S. federal budget deficit (how much greater government spending was than taxes) was about 2.6 percent of GDP. That year the trade deficit (how much imports surpassed exports) was even larger, about 4.1 percent of GDP. Also in 2002, investment in the U.S. economy exceeded U.S. private savings by about 1.5 percent of GDP.
   a. What is the relationship among these three balances?
   b. What do they tell us about who financed the U.S. budget deficit in 2002?
   c. And what do they suggest about the extent of crowding out of private investment in the U.S. economy in 2002? (Institutionalist)
4. The U.S. trade deficit reached $681 billion, or 4.8 percent of GDP, in 2008. Some economists argue that this gap is truly frightening because the current account deficit is the amount of money the United States must attract from abroad. If foreign investors stop buying U.S. bonds and stocks, then skyrocketing interest rates, plummeting stock values, and an economic downturn will surely follow. Others see the gaping current account deficit as a sign of economic vitality. The flipside of a large trade deficit is, after all, a surplus of capital flowing into your country.
   a. Is the U.S. current account deficit a sign of impending disaster or a sign of economic health or something in between?
   b. How has this unprecedented shortfall affected the U.S. economy and how will it affect our economic future? (Post-Keynesian)
5. What has happened to world income inequality is a matter of sharp dispute. Many analysts claim that world incomes converged in the second half of the twentieth century, leading to a sharp reduction in world inequality. Many others report that the gap between the poorest and the richest people and countries has continued to widen over the last two decades. When a friend of mine who writes about global inequality sorted through these studies, he came to this conclusion: "The wide range of different results of respected studies of world inequality in the last two decades casts doubt on the idea that world inequality has sharply and unambiguously declined or increased during the epoch of neoliberalism." Assuming my friend has read them correctly and fairly, what do these studies imply about the convergence hypothesis and about the globalization process? (Radical)

Issues to Ponder

1. Look up the current U.S. exchange rate relative to the yen. Would you suggest raising it or lowering it? Why? (Difficult) LO1
2. Look up the current U.S. trade balance. Would you suggest raising it or lowering it? Why? (Difficult) LO1

Answers to Margin Questions

1. A low exchange rate value of a country's currency will tend to stimulate exports and curtail imports. *(865)*
2. A trade deficit means a country is consuming more than it is producing. Consuming more than you produce is pleasant. It also means that capital is flowing into the country, which can be used for investment. So why worry? *(865)*
3. To increase the value of its currency, a country can increase the private demand for its currency by implementing contractionary monetary policy or it could decrease private supply of its currency by implementing contractionary monetary and fiscal policy. *(867)*
4. Contractionary monetary policy will likely lead to an increase in its exchange rate. *(867)*
5. Contractionary monetary policy will tend to decrease income, decreasing imports and decreasing the trade deficit. *(868)*
6. The effect of expansionary fiscal policy on the trade deficit is to increase the trade deficit. *(869)*
7. If other countries stop buying dollar-denominated assets, the value of the dollar will likely fall. *(869)*
8. Generally, when domestic policies and international policies conflict, a country will choose to deal with its domestic problems. Thus, it will likely use expansionary monetary policy if domestic problems call for that. *(870)*
9. Because foreigners buy U.S. bonds that finance the U.S. debt, the demand for bonds is higher than it otherwise would be and the interest rate is lower than it otherwise would be. *(871)*
10. If a country has a fixed exchange rate, it has less flexibility in choosing its monetary and fiscal policies to achieve domestic goals. *(872)*

Macro Policies in Developing Countries

Rise up, study the economic forces which oppress you . . . They have emerged from the hand of man just as the gods emerged from his brain. You can control them.

—*Paul LaFargue*

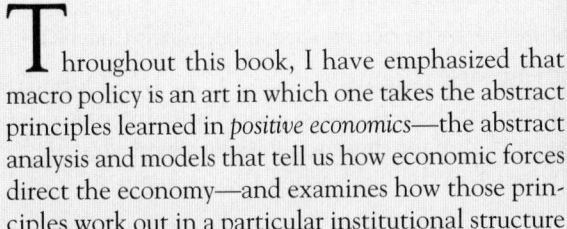

Throughout this book, I have emphasized that macro policy is an art in which one takes the abstract principles learned in *positive economics*—the abstract analysis and models that tell us how economic forces direct the economy—and examines how those principles work out in a particular institutional structure to achieve goals determined in *normative economics*—the branch of economics that considers what goals we should be aiming for. In this chapter, we see another aspect of that art.

Most of this book has emphasized the macroeconomics of Western industrialized economies, the United States in particular. That means I have focused on their goals and their institutions. In this chapter, I shift focus and discuss the macroeconomic problems of developing economies.

AFTER READING THIS CHAPTER, YOU SHOULD BE ABLE TO:

1. State some comparative statistics on rich and poor countries.
2. Differentiate the normative goals of developing and developed countries.
3. Explain why economies at different stages in development have different institutional needs.
4. Explain what is meant by the term *dual economy.*
5. Distinguish between a regime change and a policy change.
6. Explain why the central bank issuing too much money is not a sufficient explanation of inflation for developing countries.
7. Distinguish various types of convertibility.
8. List seven obstacles facing developing countries.

Developing Countries in Perspective

There are nearly 6.6 billion people in the world. Of these, 5 billion (about 75 percent) live in developing, rather than developed, countries. Per capita income in developing countries is around $500 per year; in the United States, per capita income is about $40,000.

These averages understate the differences between the poorest country and the richest. Consider the African country of Chad—definitely one of the world's poorest. Its per capita income is about $250 per year—less than 1/100 of the per capita income in the United States. Moreover, income in Chad goes primarily to the rich, so Chad's poor have per capita income of significantly less than $250.

How does a person live on that $250 per year, as many people in the world do? To begin with, that person can't

Go out for Big Macs.

Use Joy perfume (or any type of perfume).

Wear designer clothes.

ADDED DIMENSION

What to Call Developing Countries

In this chapter, following common usage, I call low-income countries *developing countries.* They have not always been called *developing.* In the 1950s they were called *backward,* but it was eventually realized that *backward* carried with it significant negative value judgments. Then these countries were called *underdeveloped,* but it was eventually realized that *underdeveloped* also suggested significant negative value judgments. More recently they have been called *developing,* but eventually everyone will realize that *developing* implies significant negative value judgments. After all, in what sense are these countries "developing" any more than the United States? All countries are evolving or developing countries. Many so-called developing countries have highly refined cultures, which they don't want to lose; they may want to develop economically but not at the cost of cultural change.

What should one call these countries? That remains to be seen, but whatever one calls them, bear in mind that language can conceal value judgments.

And that person must

Eat grain—usually rice or corn—for all meals, every day.

Mix fat from meat—not meat itself—with the rice on special occasions (maybe).

Live in one room with 9 or 10 other people.

Work hard from childhood to old age (if there is an old age). Those too old to work in the fields stay at home and care for those too young to work in the fields. (But children go out to work in the fields when they're about six years old.)

Go hungry because no matter how many family members can work in the fields, probably the work and soil don't yield enough to provide the workers with an adequate number of calories per day.

In a poor person's household, it's likely that a couple of the older children have gone into the city to find work that pays money wages. If they were lucky and found jobs, they can send money home each month. That money may be the only cash income their family back in the village has. The family uses the money to buy a few tools and cooking utensils.

The preceding is, of course, only one among billions of different stories. Even Americans and Europeans who are classified as poor find it hard to contemplate what life is really like in a truly poor country.

Don't Judge Society by Its Income Alone

Poor people in developing countries survive and often find pleasure in their hard lives. In many poor countries, there are far fewer suicides than in the United States. For example, the U.S. suicide rate for men is approximately 18 per 100,000 people. In Costa Rica it's 9.7; in Mexico it's 5.4; and in Peru it's 0.6. Who has time for suicide? You're too busy surviving. There's little ambiguity and few questions about the meaning of life. Living! That's what life's all about. There's no "Mom, what am I going to do today?" You know what you're going to do: survive if you can. And survival is satisfying.

Often economically poor societies have cultures that provide individuals with a deep sense of fulfillment and satisfaction.

Often these economically poor societies have elaborate cultural rituals and networks of intense personal relationships that provide individuals with a deep sense of fulfillment and satisfaction.

Are people in these societies as happy as Americans are? If your immediate answer is no, be careful to understand the difficulty of making such a judgment. The answer isn't clear-cut. For us to say, "My God! What a failure their system is!" is wrong. It's an inappropriate value judgment about the relative worth of cultures. All too often Americans have gone into another country to try to make people better off but have ended up making them worse off.

An economy is part and parcel of a culture. You can't judge just an economy; you must judge the entire culture. Some developing countries have cultures that, in many people's view, are preferable to ours. If one increases a country's income but takes away its culture in doing so, its people arguably may be worse off.

An economy is part and parcel of a culture.

That said, if we asked people in developing countries if they believe that they would be better off if they had more income, most would definitely answer yes!

Even culturally sensitive people agree that economic growth within the context of a developing country's culture would be a good thing, if only because those countries exist simultaneously with market economies. Given market societies' expansionary tendencies, without economic growth, cultures in economically poor countries would simply be overrun and destroyed by the cultures of market societies. Their land would be taken, their agricultural patterns would be changed, their traditional means of subsistence would be destroyed, and their cultures would be obliterated. So, generally, the choice isn't between development and preservation of the existing culture (and its accompanying ancient ways to which the poor have adjusted). Rather, the choice is between development (with its attendant wrenching cultural transitions) and continuing poverty and slower, but still painful, cultural transitions.

Q-1 In what way is economic development the only choice for developing countries?

Some Comparative Statistics on Rich and Poor Nations

The low average income in poor countries has its effects on people's lives. Life expectancy is about 60 years in most very economically poor countries (compared to about 80 years in the United States). In economically poor countries, most people drink contaminated water, consume about half the number of calories the World Health Organization has determined is minimal for good health, and do physical labor (often of the kind done by machine in developed countries). Table 38-1 compares developing countries, middle-income countries, and developed countries.

As with all statistics, care must be taken in interpreting the figures in Table 38-1. For example, the income comparisons were all made on the basis of current exchange rates. But relative prices between rich and poor countries often differ substantially; the cost of goods relative to total income tends to be much lower for people in developing countries than for those in developed countries.

To allow for these differences, some economists have looked at the domestic purchasing power of money in various countries and have adjusted the comparisons accordingly. Rather than comparing incomes by using exchange rates, they use **purchasing power parity (PPP)**—*a method of comparing income by looking at the domestic purchasing power of money in different countries*. That is, purchasing power parity equalizes the cost of an identical basket of goods among countries. Using purchasing power parity, the World Bank found that income differences among countries are cut by half. In other words, when one uses the World Bank's PPP method of comparison, it's as if the people in developing countries had much more income than they had when their incomes were compared using market exchange rates.

Purchasing power parity exchange rates are calculated by determining what a specified basket of consumer goods will cost in various countries.

A similar adjustment can be made with the life expectancy rates. A major reason for the lower life expectancies in developing countries is their high infant mortality rates. Once children survive infancy, however, their life expectancies are much closer to those

TABLE 38-1 **Statistics on Selected Developing, Middle-Income, and Developed Countries**

Country	Physicians (per 1,000)	Daily Calorie Supply	Life Expectancy	Infant Mortality (per 1,000)	Labor Force in Agriculture (%)	Labor Force in Industry (%)	Adult Literacy Rate	Land and Mobile Phones (per 1,000)	GDP per Capita ($)
Developing									
Bangladesh	0.26	2,205	64	59	63%	11%	43%	37	$ 470
Ethiopia	0.03	1,857	52	81	80	7	43	8	220
Haiti	0.25	2,086	60	60	66	9	53	64	560
Middle-Income									
Brazil	2.06	3,050	72	23	20	14	89	587	5,910
Iran	0.45	3,085	71	36	25	31	77	270	3,470
Republic of Korea	3.29	3,058	78	4	7	25	98	1,168	19,690
Thailand	0.37	2,467	70	18	43	20	93	365	3,400
Developed									
Japan	2.00	2,761	82	3	4	28	99	1,176	37,670
Sweden	3.28	3,185	81	3	1	28	99	1,743	46,060
United States	2.30	3,774	78	6	1	20	99	1,223	46,040

Sources: *World Development Report*, 2009, The World Bank (www.worldbank.org); *CIA World Factbook*, 2008. Because of reporting lags, some data are for earlier years. GDP is calculated with the Atlas method.

of children in developed countries. Say life expectancy at birth is 50 years and that 10 percent of all infants die within their first year. As a person grows older, at each birthday the person's life expectancy is higher. So if a child lives to the age of 3 years, then at that point the child has an actual life expectancy of close to 60 years, rather than 50 years.

Growth versus Development

Growth occurs because of an increase in inputs, given a production function; development occurs through a change in the production function.

Economists use the term *developing*, rather than *growing*, to emphasize that the goals of these countries involve more than simply an increase in output; these countries are changing their underlying institutions. Put another way, these economies are changing their production functions; they are not increasing inputs given a production function. Thus, *development* refers to an increase in productive capacity and output brought about by a change in the underlying institutions, and *growth* refers to an increase in output brought about by an increase in inputs.

Q-2 Why does restructuring in developed countries suggest that the distinction between growth and development can be overdone?

The distinction can be overdone. Institutions, and hence production functions, in developed as well as in developing countries are continually changing, and output changes are a combination of changes in production functions and increases in inputs. For example, in the 1990s and early 2000s, the major Western economies have been **restructuring** their economies—*changing the underlying economic institutions*—as they work to compete better in the world economy. As they restructure, they change their methods of production, their laws, and their social support programs. Thus, in some ways, they are doing precisely what developing countries are doing—developing rather than just growing. Despite the ambiguity, the distinction between growth and development can be a useful one if you remember that the two blend into each other.

While the lessons of abstract theory do not change when we shift our attention to developing economies, the institutions and goals change enormously.

The reason economists separate out developing economies is that these economies have (1) different institutional structures and (2) a different weighting of goals than do Western developed economies. These two differences—in institutional structure and in goals—change the way in which the lessons of abstract theory are applied and discussed.

Differing Goals

When discussing macro policy within Western developed economies, I did not dwell on questions of normative goals of macroeconomics. Instead, I used generally accepted goals in the United States as the goals of macro policy—achieving low inflation, low unemployment, and an acceptable growth rate—with a few caveats. You may have noticed that the discussion focused more on what might be called stability goals—achieving low unemployment and low inflation—than it did on the acceptable growth rate goal. I chose that focus because growth in Western developed countries is desired because it holds unemployment down, and because it avoids difficult distributional questions, as much as it is desired for its own sake. Our economy has sufficient productive capacity to provide its citizens, on average, with a relatively high standard of living. The problem facing Western societies is as much seeing that all members of those societies share in that high standard of living as it is raising the standard.

There are differences in normative goals between developing and developed countries because their wealth differs. Developing countries face basic economic needs whereas developed countries' economic needs are considered by most people to be normatively less pressing.

In the developing countries, the weighting of goals is different. Growth and development are primary goals. When people are starving and the economy isn't fulfilling people's **basic needs**—*adequate food, clothing, and shelter*—a main focus of macro policy will be on how to increase the economy's growth rate through development so that the economy can fulfill those basic needs.

Differing Institutions

Developing countries differ from developed countries not only in their goals but also in their macroeconomic institutions. These macroeconomic institutions are qualitatively different from institutions in developed countries. Their governments are different; their financial institutions—the institutions that translate savings into investment—are different; their fiscal institutions—the institutions through which government collects taxes and spends its money—are different; and their social and cultural institutions are different. Because of these differences, the way in which we discuss macroeconomic policy is different.

Economies at different stages of development have different institutional needs because the problems they face are different.

One of the differences concerns very basic market institutions—such as Western-style property rights and contract law. In certain groups of developing countries, most notably sub-Saharan Africa, these basic market institutions don't exist; instead, communal property rights and tradition structure economic relationships. How can one talk about market forces in such economies?[1] On a more mundane level, consider the issue of monetary policy. Talking about monetary policy via open market operations (the buying and selling of bonds by the central bank) is not all that helpful when there is no market for government bonds, as is the case in many developing countries.

Let's now consider some specific institutional differences more carefully.

Political Differences and Laissez-Faire Views of how activist macroeconomic policy should be are necessarily contingent on the political system an economy has. One of the scarcest commodities in developing countries is socially minded leaders. Not that developed countries have any overabundance of them, but most developed countries have at least a tradition of politicians seeming to be fair and open-minded, and a set of institutionalized checks and balances that limit leaders using government for their personal benefit. In many developing countries, those institutionalized checks and balances on governmental leaders often do not exist.

In many developing countries, institutional checks and balances on government leaders often do not exist.

Let's consider a few examples. First, let's look at Saudi Arabia, which, while economically rich, maintains many of the institutions of a developing country. It is an

[1]One can, of course, talk about economic forces. But, as discussed in Chapter 1, economic forces become market forces only in a market institutional setting.

absolute monarchy in which the royal family is the ultimate power. Say a member of that family comes to the bank and wants a loan that, on economic grounds, doesn't make sense. What do you think the bank loan officer will do? Grant the loan, if the banker is smart. Thus, despite the wealth of the country, it isn't surprising that many economists believe the Saudi banking system reflects that political structure—and may find itself in serious trouble if oil prices fall significantly.

A second example is Nigeria, which had enormous possibilities for economic growth in the 1980s because of its oil riches. It didn't develop. Instead, politicians fought over the spoils, and bribes became a major source of their income. Corruption was rampant, and the Nigerian economy went nowhere. I will stop there, but, unfortunately, there are many other examples.

Because of the structure of government in many developing countries, many economists who, in Western developed economies, favor activist government policies may well favor Classical laissez-faire policies for the same reasons that early Classical economists did—because they have a profound distrust of the governments. That distrust, however, must have limits. As I discussed in Chapter 3, even a laissez-faire policy requires some government role in setting the rules. So there is no escaping the need for socially minded leaders.

The Dual Economy A second institutional difference between developed and developing countries is the dual nature of developing countries' economies. Whereas it often makes sense to talk about a Western economy as a single economy, it does not for most developing countries. A developing country's economy is generally characterized by a **dual economy**—*the existence of two sectors: a traditional sector and an internationally oriented modern market sector.*[2]

The term dual economy refers to the existence of the two sectors in most developing countries: a traditional sector and an internationally oriented modern market sector.

Q-3 What is meant by the term *dual economy?*

Often, the largest percentage of the population participates in the traditional economy. It is a local currency, or no currency, sector in which traditional ways of doing things take precedence. The second sector—the internationally oriented modern market sector—is often indistinguishable from a Western economy. Activities in the modern sector are often conducted in foreign currencies, rather than domestic currencies, and contracts are often governed by international law. This dual economy aspect of developing countries creates a number of dilemmas for policy makers and affects the way they think about macroeconomic problems.

Web Note 38.1
The Modern Sector

For example, take the problem of unemployment. Many developing countries have a large subsistence-farming economy. Subsistence farmers aren't technically unemployed, but often there are so many people on the land that, in economic terms, their contribution to output is minimal or even negative, so for policy purposes one can consider the quantity of labor that will be supplied at the going wage unlimited. But to call these people unemployed is problematic. These subsistence farmers are simply outside the market economy. In such cases, one would hardly want, or be able, to talk of an unemployment problem in the same way we talk in the United States.

Fiscal Structure of Developing Economies A third institutional difference concerns developing countries' fiscal systems. To undertake discretionary fiscal policy—running a deficit or surplus to affect the aggregate economy—the government must be able to determine expenditures and tax rates, with a particular eye toward the difference between the two. As discussed in an earlier chapter, discretionary fiscal policy is difficult for Western developed countries to undertake; it is almost impossible for developing economies.

[2]I discuss these two sectors as if they were separate, but in reality they are interrelated. Portions of the economy devoted to the tourist trade span both sectors, as do some manufacturing industries. Still, there is sufficient independence of the two sectors that it is reasonable to treat them as separate.

In the traditional sector of many developing countries, barter or cash transactions predominate, and such transactions are especially difficult to tax. Often, the governments in these economies don't have the institutional structures with which to collect taxes (or, when they have the institutional structure, it is undermined by fraud and evasion), so their taxing options are limited; that's why they often use tariffs as a primary source of revenue.

Often developing countries do not have the institutional structures with which to collect taxes.

Similar problems exist with government expenditures. Many expenditures of developing countries are mandated by political considerations—if the government doesn't make them, it will likely be voted out of office. Within such a setting, to talk about activist fiscal policy—choosing a deficit for its macroeconomic implications—even if it might otherwise be relevant, is not much help since the budget deficit is not a choice variable, but instead is a result of other political decisions.

Many government expenditures in developing countries are mandated by political considerations.

The political constraints facing developing countries can, of course, be overstated. The reality is that developing countries do institute new fiscal regimes. Take, for example, Mexico. In the early 1980s, Mexico's fiscal problems seemed impossible to solve, but in the late 1980s and early 1990s, Carlos de Salinas, a U.S.-trained economist, introduced a fiscal austerity program and an economic liberalization program that lowered Mexico's budget deficit and significantly reduced its inflation. But such changes are better called a **regime change**—*a change in the entire atmosphere within which the government and the economy interrelate*—rather than a **policy change**—*a change in one aspect of government's actions, such as monetary policy or fiscal policy*. Regimes can change suddenly. For example, in Mexico soon after President Salinas left office, his brother was implicated in a murder and drug scandal. Foreign investors became worried and pulled money out of Mexico. The peso fell, inflation and interest rates rose, and the Mexican economy fell into a serious recession. In one day, the regime of confidence had changed to a regime of uncertainty and confusion, full of questions about what policy actions the Mexican government would take.

A regime change is a change in the entire atmosphere within which the government and the economy interrelate; a policy change is a change in one aspect of government's actions.

Financial Institutions of Developing Economies

I spent two chapters discussing the complex financial systems of developed countries because you had to understand those financial systems in order to understand macro policy. While some parts of that discussion carry over to developing countries, other parts don't since financial systems in developing countries are often quite different than those in developed countries.

The primary difference arises from the dual nature of developing countries' economies. In the traditional part of developing economies, the financial sector is embryonic; trades are made by barter, or with direct payment of money; trades requiring more sophisticated financial markets, such as mortgages to finance houses, just don't exist.

The primary difference between financial institutions in developing countries and developed countries arises from the dual nature of developing countries' economies.

In the modern international part of developing economies, that isn't the case. Developing countries' international financial sectors are sometimes as sophisticated as Western financial institutions. A currency trading room in Ecuador or Nigeria looks similar to one in New York, London, or Frankfurt. That modern financial sector is integrated into the international economy (with pay rates that often approach or match those of the West). This dual nature of developing countries' financial sectors constrains the practice of monetary policy and changes the regulatory and control functions of central banks.

The above is one of many institutional examples of differences that exist and that change the nature of the macro problem. What's important is not so much the specifics of the example but, rather, the general point it brings home. Economies at different stages of development have different institutional, and policy, needs. Institutions with the same names in different countries can have quite different roles. Such institutions can differ in subtle ways, making it important to have specific knowledge of a country's institutions before one can understand its economy and meaningfully talk about policy.

It is important to have specific knowledge of a country's institutions before one can understand its economy and meaningfully talk about policy.

REAL-WORLD APPLICATION

A Real, Real-World Application: The Traditional Economy Meets the Internet

San Juana Hernandez, of Acuna, Mexico, wanted to borrow some money to paint her grocery store and order some more goods to stock. Marco Apaza, of La Paz, Bolivia, needed some money to expand his sporting goods wholesale business and to build an addition on his parents' home, where he lives, so that he has a bit more room. They needed only small amounts—under $1,000 each. In the traditional economy, the possibilities for loans didn't exist; banks generally don't make the type of small loans that they needed, and there were no good methods of providing the loans. But both got their loans, in part because I loaned them some of the money. How did I do it from up here in Vermont? I went to the Web site Kiva.org, found their loan request (along with thousands of others), and sent some money via PayPal. Kiva.org combined my money with that of another 40 or so people, and made the loan to them.

This innovative program, which is a modern variation on the micro credit programs discussed in earlier chapters, allows a type of international micro credit, in which individuals throughout the world can make loans to individuals in developing countries. The people go to a microfinance agency in their home city, which checks them out to see that they are legitimate borrowers, and which then posts their loan request on the Kiva Web site. Individuals with money to lend can go to the Web site and choose to make loans to whomever they want. There is no guarantee that the loans will be paid back, but the experience to date about repayments has been, as it has with most micro credit lending, very good. Such programs show that technology can help break down the barrier between the traditional and the market sector.

Monetary Policy in Developing Countries

Now that I've discussed some of the ways in which financial institutions differ in developing countries, let's consider some issues of central banking and monetary policy for those economies.

Central Banks Are Less Independent

The first thing to note about central banking in developing countries is that its primary goal is often different than a central bank's primary goal in developed countries. The reason is that, while all central banks have a number of goals, at the top of them all is the goal of keeping the economy running. In normal times western central banks have the luxury of assuming away the problem of keeping the economy running—inertia, institutions, and history hold western industrial economies together, and keep them running. Central banks in developing countries can't make that assumption.

Central banks in developing countries generally have far less independence than do central banks in developed countries.

What this means in practice is that central banks in developing countries generally have far less independence than do central banks in developed countries. With a political and fiscal system that generates large deficits and that cannot exist without these deficits, the thought of an independent monetary policy goes out the window.

Q-4 If everyone knows that the cause of inflation in developing countries is the creation of too much money, why don't these countries stop inflation?

A second difference concerns the institutional implementation of monetary policy. In a developing country, a broad-based domestic government bond market often does not exist. So if the government runs a deficit and is financing it domestically, the central bank usually must buy the bonds, which means that it must increase the money supply. As you know, increasing the money supply leads to higher inflation. And developing countries on the whole have experienced high inflation, as Figure 38-1 shows. Central banks recognize that increasing the money supply will cause inflation, but

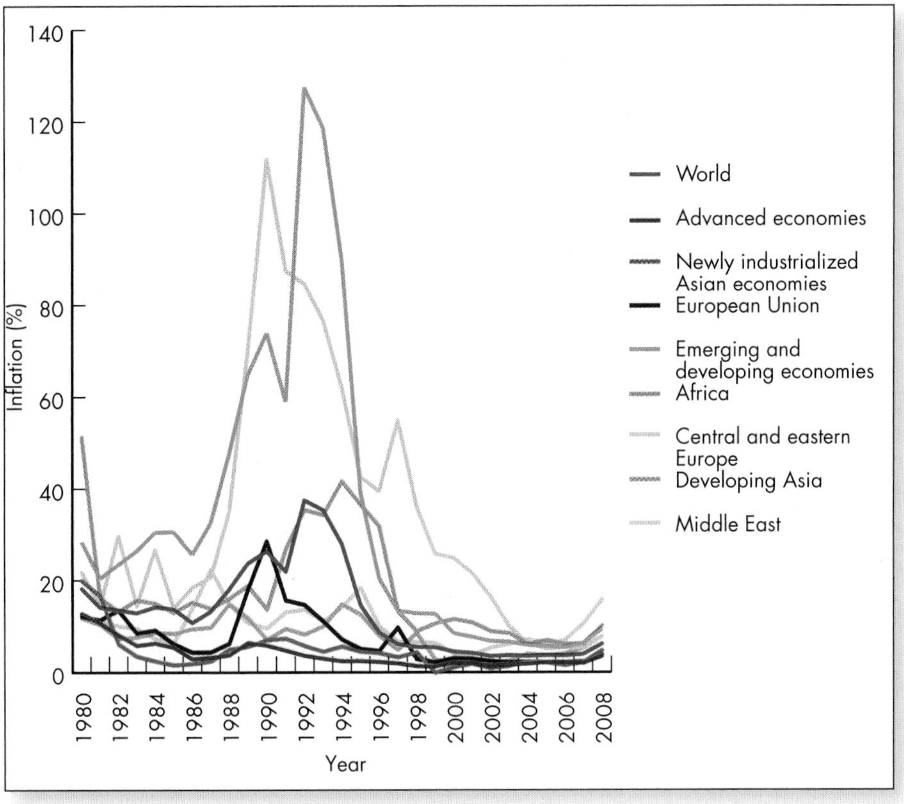

FIGURE 38-1 CPI Inflation, Selected Country Groupings.

On the whole, developing emerging countries have experienced higher inflation. In the early 2000s, however, inflation has been relatively low for most countries.

Source: *World Economic Outlook Database*, International Monetary Fund, www.imf.org.

often central banks feel as if they have no choice because of the political consequences of not issuing the money.

Central banks recognize that printing too much money causes inflation, but often feel compelled to do so for political reasons.

As I discussed above, often, in developing countries, the government's sources of tax revenue are limited, and the low level of income in the economy makes the tax base small. A government attempting to collect significantly more taxes might risk being overthrown. Similarly, its ability to cut expenditures is limited. If it cuts expenditures, it will almost certainly be overthrown. With new tax sources unavailable and with no ability to cut expenditures, the government uses its only other option to meet its obligations—it issues debt. And, if the central bank agrees with the conclusion that the government is correct in its assessment that it has no choice, then if the central bank doesn't want the government to be overthrown, it has no choice but to monetize that debt (print money to pay that debt). Sometimes the central bank's choices are even more limited; dictatorships simply tell the central bank to provide the needed money, or be eliminated.

The Importance of an Independent Central Bank

Issuing money to finance budget deficits may be a short-term solution, but it is not a long-term solution. It is an accounting identity that real resources consumed by the economy must equal the real resources produced or imported. If the government deficit doesn't increase output, the real resources the government is getting because the central bank is monetizing its debt must come from somewhere else. Where do those real resources come from? From the *inflation tax*—an implicit tax on the holders of cash and the holders of any obligations specified in nominal terms. Inflation works as a type of tax on these individuals.

Inflation works as a tax on holders of obligations specified in nominal terms.

Faced with the prospect of a collapse of government, the central banks generally choose to keep the governments operating (which isn't surprising since they are often branches of the government). To do that, they increase the money supply enormously, causing hyperinflation in many of these countries. These hyperinflations soon take on a life of their own. The expectation of accelerating inflation creates even more inflationary pressure as individuals try to spend any money they have quickly, before the prices go up. This increases velocity, nominal demand for goods, and inflationary pressures.

Q-5 In an inflation, who else, besides government, gets revenue from an inflation tax?

One problem with using an inflation tax is that in an inflation, the government is not the only recipient of revenue; any issuer of fixed-interest-rate debt denominated in domestic currency also gains. And the holder of any fixed-interest-rate debt denominated in domestic currency loses. This income redistribution caused by an inflation can temporarily stimulate real output, but it can also undermine the country's financial institutions.

The point of the above discussion is that the central banks know that issuing large quantities of money will cause inflation. What they don't know, and what the policy discussions are about, is which is worse: the inflation or the unpleasant alternatives. Should the central bank bail out the government? There are legitimate questions about whether countries' budget deficits are absolutely necessary or not. It is those assessments in which the debate about developing countries' inflation exists; the debate is not about whether the inflation is caused by the issuance of too much money.

The fact that inflation is only a temporary solution doesn't stop developing countries' leaders from using it.

Opponents of any type of bailout point out that any "inflation solution" is only a temporary solution that, if used, will require ever-increasing amounts of inflation to remain effective. Proponents of bailouts agree with this argument but argue that inflation buys a bit more time, and the alternative is the breakdown of the government and the economy. Because of the unpleasant alternative, the fact that inflation is only a temporary solution doesn't stop developing countries' leaders from using it. They don't have time for the luxury of long-run solutions and are often simply looking for policies that will hold their governments together for a month at a time.

Focus on the International Sector and the Exchange Rate Constraint

Another difference between the monetary policies of developed and developing countries concerns the policy options they consider for dealing with foreign exchange markets. Developed countries are generally committed to full exchange rate convertibility. With full exchange rate convertibility, individuals can exchange their currency for any other country's currency without significant government restrictions.

Developing countries often do not have fully convertible currencies. Individuals and firms in these countries face restrictions on their ability to exchange currencies—sometimes general restrictions and sometimes restrictions that depend on the purpose for which they wish to use the foreign exchange.

Various Types of Convertibility Since convertibility plays such a central role in developing countries' macro policies, let's review the various types of convertibility. The United States has **full convertibility**—*individuals may change dollars into any currency they want for whatever legal purpose they want.* (There are, however, reporting laws about movements of currency.) Most Western developed countries have full convertibility.

Q-6 Distinguish between convertibility on the current account from full convertibility.

A second type of convertibility is **convertibility on the current account**—*a system that allows people to exchange currencies freely to buy goods and services, but not to buy assets in other countries.* The third type of convertibility is **limited capital account convertibility**—*a system that allows full current account convertibility and partial capital account convertibility.* There are various levels of restrictions on what types of assets one can exchange, so there are many types of limited capital account convertibility.

Almost no developing country has full convertibility.

Almost no developing country allows full convertibility. Why? One reason is that they want to force their residents to keep their savings, and to do their investing, in their home country, not abroad. Why don't their citizens want to do that? Because when there is a chance of a change in governments—and government seizure of assets as there often is in developing countries—rich individuals generally prefer to have a significant portion of their assets abroad, away from the hands of their government.

These limits on exchange rate convertibility explain a general phenomenon found in most developing countries—the fact that much of the international part of the dual economy in developing countries is "dollarized"—contracts are framed, and accounting is handled, in dollars, not in the home country's currency. Dollarization exists almost completely in the international sectors of countries that have nonconvertible currencies, and largely in the international sectors of countries where the currency is convertible on the current account but not on the capital account. This dollarization exists because of nonconvertibility, or the fear of nonconvertibility. Thus, ironically, nonconvertibility increases the focus on dollarized contracts in the international sector, and puts that sector beyond effective control by the central bank.

Nonconvertibility does not halt international trade—it merely complicates it since it adds another layer of uncertainty and bureaucracy to the trading process. Each firm that is conducting international trade must see that it will have sufficient foreign exchange to carry on its business. Developing governments will often want to encourage this international trade, while preventing outflows of their currencies for other purposes.

Nonconvertibility does not halt international trade; it merely makes it more difficult.

When developing countries have partially convertible exchange rates, exchange rate policy—buying and selling foreign currencies in order to help stabilize the exchange rate—often is an important central bank function. This is such an important function because trade in most of these countries' currencies is *thin*—there is not a large number of traders or trades. When trading is thin, large fluctuations in exchange rates are possible in response to a change in a few traders' needs. Even the uncertainties of the weather can affect traders. Say an expected oil tanker is kept from landing in port because of bad weather. The financial exchange—paying for that oil—that would have taken place upon landing does not take place, and the supply/demand conditions for a country's currency could change substantially. In response, the value of the country's currency could rise or fall dramatically unless it were stabilized. The central bank often helps provide exchange rate stabilization.

Conditionality and the Balance of Payments Constraint In designing their policies, developing countries often rely on advice from the International Monetary Fund (IMF). One reason is that the IMF has economists who have much experience with these issues. A second reason is that, for these countries, the IMF is a major source of temporary loans that they need to stabilize their currencies.

These loans usually come with conditions that the country meet certain domestic monetary and fiscal stabilization goals. Specifically, these goals are that government deficits be lowered and money supply growth be limited. Because of these requirements, IMF's loan policy is often called **conditionality**—*the making of loans that are subject to specific conditions*. These goals have been criticized by economists such as Joseph Stiglitz, who argues that the contractionary monetary and fiscal policies often required by conditionality tend to be procyclical and only worsen the recession. The IMF responds that in a developing country, the long-run fiscal and monetary goals must take precedence to establish a basis for development.

The basis for most IMF loans is conditionality.

Even a partially flexible exchange rate regime presents the country with the **balance of payments constraint**—*limitations on expansionary domestic macroeconomic policy due to a shortage of international reserves*. Attempts to expand the domestic economy with expansionary monetary policy continually push the economy to its balance of payments constraint. To meet both its domestic goals and international balance of payments constraints, many developing countries turn to loans from the IMF, not only for the exchange rate stabilization reasons discussed above but also for a more expansionary macro policy than otherwise would be possible. Because of the IMF's control of these

The balance of payments constraint consists of limitations on expansionary domestic macro policy due to a shortage of international reserves.

loans, macro policy in developing countries is often conducted with one eye toward the IMF, and sometimes with a complete bow.

The Need for Creativity

The above discussion may have made it seem as if conducting domestic macro policy in developing countries is almost hopelessly dominated by domestic political concerns and international constraints. If by macro policy one means using traditional monetary and fiscal policy tools as they are used in standard ways, that's true. But macro policy, interpreted broadly, is much more than using those tools. It is the development of new institutions that expand the possibilities for growth. It is creating a new production function, not operating within an existing one. Macro policy, writ large to include the development of new institutions, can have enormous effects. To undertake such policies requires an understanding of the role of institutions, the specific nature of the problem in one's country, and creativity.

Obstacles to Economic Development

What stops countries from developing economically? Economists have discovered no magic potion that will make a country develop. We can't say, "Here are steps 1, 2, 3, 4. If you follow them you'll grow, but if you don't follow them you won't grow."

Web Note 38.2
Development Economists

What makes it so hard for developing countries to devise a successful development program is that social, political, and economic problems blend into one another and cannot be considered separately. The institutional structure that we take for granted in the United States often doesn't exist in those countries. For example economists' analysis of production assumes that a stable government exists that can enforce contracts and supply basic services. In most developing countries, that assumption can't be made. Governments are often anything but stable; overnight, a coup d'état can bring a new government into power, with a whole new system of rules under which businesses have to operate. Imagine trying to figure out a reasonable study strategy if every week you had a new teacher who emphasized different things and gave totally different types of tests from last week's teacher. Firms in developing countries face similar problems.

While economists can't say, "Here's what you have to do in order to grow," we have been able to identify some general obstacles that all developing countries seem to face:

Seven problems facing developing countries are
1. Political instability.
2. Corruption.
3. Lack of appropriate institutions.
4. Lack of investment.
5. Inappropriate education.
6. Overpopulation.
7. Health and disease.

1. Political instability.
2. Corruption.
3. Lack of appropriate institutions.
4. Lack of investment.
5. Inappropriate education.
6. Overpopulation.
7. Health and disease.

I consider each in turn.

Political Instability

A student's parents once asked me why their son was doing poorly in my economics class. My answer was that he could not read well and he could hardly write. Until he could master those basics, there was no use talking about how he could better learn economics.

Roughly the same reasoning can be applied to the problem of political instability in developing countries. Unless a country achieves political stability (acceptance within a country of a stable system of government), it's not going to develop economically, no matter what it does.

All successful development strategies require a stable government. A mercantilist or a socialist development strategy requires an elaborate government presence. A market-based strategy requires a much smaller government role, but even with markets, a stable environment is needed for a market to function and for contracts to be made with confidence.

All successful development strategies require a stable government.

Many developing countries don't have that stability. Politically they haven't established a tradition of orderly governmental transition. Coups d'état or armed insurrections always remain possible.

One example is Somalia. There, a civil war among competing groups in 1990 led to famine and enormous hardship, which provoked the sympathy of the world. But attempts by the UN and the United States to establish a stable government by sending troops there caused as many, or more, problems than they resolved, and in 1995 the United States withdrew its troops. Today Somalia continues to lack a unified central government. Political instability exists in most developing countries, but it is strongest in Africa, which in large part accounts for Africa's low rate of economic growth relative to that of the other geographic areas.

Even countries whose governments aren't regularly toppled face threats of overthrow, and those threats are sufficient to prevent individual economic activity. To function, an economy needs some rules—any rules—that will last.

Q-7 Why does political instability present an economic problem for developing countries?

The lack of stability is often exacerbated by social and cultural differences among groups within a country. Political boundaries often reflect arbitrary decisions made by former colonial rulers, not the traditional cultural and tribal boundaries that form the real-life divisions. The result is lack of consensus among the population as a whole as well as intertribal suspicion and even warfare.

For example, Nigeria is a federation established under British colonial rule. It comprises three ethnic regions: the northern, Hausa Fulan, region; the western, Yoruba, region; and the eastern, Ibo, region. These three regions are culturally distinct and so are in continual political and military conflict. Nigeria has experienced an endless cycle of military coups, attempts at civilian rule, and threats of secession by the numerically smaller eastern region. Had each region been allowed to remain separate, economic development might have been possible; but because the British lumped the regions together and called them a country, economic development is next to impossible.

The Influence of Political Instability on Development Do these political considerations affect economic questions? You bet. As I will discuss shortly, any development plan requires financial investment from somewhere—either external or internal. Political instability closes off both sources of investment funds.

Any serious potential investor takes political instability into account. Foreign companies considering investment in a developing country hire political specialists who analyze the degree of risk involved. Where the risk is too great, foreign companies simply don't invest.

Political instability also limits internal investment. Income distribution in many developing countries is highly skewed. There are a few very rich people and an enormous number of very poor people, while the middle class is often small.

Whatever one's view of the fairness of such income inequality, it has a potential advantage for society. Members of the wealthy elite in developing countries have income to spare, and their savings are a potential source of investment funds. But when there is political instability, that potential isn't realized. Fearing that their wealth may be taken from them, the rich often channel their investment out of their own country so that, should they need to flee a revolution, they'll still be able to live comfortably. Well-off people in developing countries provide major inflows of investment into the United States and other Western countries.

Q-8 Income inequality leads to higher levels of savings by the rich and therefore has significant advantages for developing countries. True or false? Explain your answer.

Political Instability and Unequal Distribution of Income The highly skewed distribution of income in most developing countries contributes in another way to political instability. It means that the poor majority has little vested interest in maintaining the current system. A coup? Why not? What have they got to lose? The economic prospects for many people in developing countries are so bleak that they are quite willing to join or at least support a guerrilla insurgency that promises to set up a new, better system. The resulting instability makes development almost impossible.

Corruption

When rights to conduct business are controlled and allocated by the government, economic development can be hindered.

Bribery, graft, and corruption are ways of life in most developing countries. In Egypt it's called *baksheesh* (meaning "gift of money"); in Mexico it's called *la mordida* ("the bite"). If you want to park in a parking spot in Mexico City, you'd better pay the policeman, or your car will get a ticket. If you want to take a photograph of the monument to Ramses II in front of the Cairo railroad station, you'd better slip the traffic officer a few bucks, or else you may get run over.

Web Note 38.3 Transparency

Without a well-developed institutional setting and a public morality that condemns corruption, economic forces function in a variety of areas that people in developed countries would consider inappropriate. In any country, the government has the right to allow imports, to allow development, to determine where you can park your car, to say whether you can take photographs of public buildings, to decide who wins a lawsuit, and so forth. In developing countries, however, those rights can be, and often are, sold. The litigant who pays the judge the most wins. How about the right to import? Want to import a new machine? That will be 20 percent of the cost, please.

Such graft and corruption quickly become institutionalized to the degree that all parties involved feel they have little choice but to take part. Government officials say that graft and bribery are built into their pay structure, so unless they take bribes, they won't have enough income to live on. Businesspeople say that if they want to stay in business, they have to pay bribes. Similarly, workers must bribe business in order to get a job, and labor leaders must be bribed not to cause trouble for business.

Societies decide what is right and wrong; economists don't.

I'm not claiming that such payments are wrong. Societies decide what is right and wrong; economists don't. The term *bribery* in English has a pejorative connotation. In many other languages, the terms people use for this type of activity don't have such negative connotations.

Q-9 In what way do bribes limit development?

But I am claiming that such payments—with the implied threat that failure to pay will have adverse consequences—make it more difficult for a society's economy to grow. Knowing that those payments must be made prevents many people from undertaking actions that might lead to growth. For example, a friend of mine wanted to build a group of apartments in the Bahamas, but when he discovered the payoffs he'd have to make to various people, he abandoned the whole idea.

Limiting an activity makes the right to undertake that limited activity valuable to the person doing the limiting. When bribery is an acceptable practice, it creates strong incentives to limit an ever-increasing number of activities—including many activities that could make a country grow.

Lack of Appropriate Institutions

Almost all economists agree that, to develop, a country should establish markets. Markets require the establishment of property rights. In a recent book, *The Mystery of Capital,* Hernando DeSoto argued that developing countries' main problem is that their assets, such as houses, do not have the legal standing to be used as collateral or to be bought and sold easily, so markets cannot work. Unfortunately, establishing property rights is a difficult political process. That is the problem of a number of African countries: how to establish property rights with an undeveloped political process.

Creating markets is not enough. The markets must be meshed with the cultural and social fabric of the society. Thus, questions of economic development inevitably involve much more than supply and demand. They involve broader questions about the cultural and social institutions in a society.

Markets do not just exist; they are created, and their existence is meshed with the cultural and social fabric of the society.

Let me give an example of cultural characteristics not conducive to development. Anyone who has traveled in developing countries knows that many of these countries operate on what they call "_______ time," where the "_______" is the name of the particular country one is in. What is meant by "_______ time" is that in that country, things get done when they get done, and it is socially inappropriate to push for things to get done at specific times. Deadlines are demeaning (many students operate on "_______ time").

As a self-actualizing mentality, "_______ time" may be high-level mental development, but in an interdependent economic setting, "_______ time" doesn't fit. Economic development requires qualities such as extreme punctuality and a strong sense of individual responsibility. People who believe their being two minutes late will make the world come to an end fit far better with a high-production country than do people who are more laid back. The need to take such cultural issues into account explains why development economics tends to be far less theoretical and far more country- and region-specific than other branches of economics.

As a self-actualizing mentality, "_______ time" may be a high-level mental development, but in an interdependent economic setting, "_______ time" doesn't fit.

Lack of Investment

Even if a country can overcome the political, social, and institutional constraints on development, there are also economic constraints. If a country is to grow, it must somehow invest, and funds for investment must come from savings. These savings can be either brought in from abroad (as private investment or foreign government aid) or generated internally (as domestic savings). Each source of investment capital has its problems.

Investment Funded by Domestic Savings In order to save, a person must first have enough to live on. With per capita incomes of $250 per year, poor people in developing countries don't have a whole lot left over to put into savings. Instead, you rely on your kids, if they live, to take care of you in your old age. As for the rich, the threat of political instability often makes them put their money into savings abroad, as I discussed before. For the developing country, it's as if the rich didn't save. In fact, it's even worse because when they save abroad, the rich don't even spend the money at home as do poor people, so the rich generate less in the way of short-run income multiplier effects in their home country than do the poor.

With per capita incomes of as low as $250 per year, poor people in developing countries don't have a lot left over to put into savings.

That leaves the middle class (small as it is) as the one hope these countries have for domestic savings. For them, the problem is: Where can they put their savings? Often these countries have an underdeveloped financial sector; there's no neighborhood bank, no venture capital fund, no government-secured savings vehicle. The only savings vehicle available may be the government savings bond. But savings bonds finance the government deficit, which supports the government bureaucracy, which is limiting activities that could lead to growth. Few middle-class people invest in those government bonds. After all, what will a government bond be worth after the next revolution? Nothing!

Some governments have taxed individuals (a type of forced savings) and channeled that money back into investment. But again, politics and corruption are likely to interfere. Instead of going into legitimate productive investment, the savings—in the form of "consulting fees," outright payoffs, or "sweetheart contracts"—go to friends of those in power. Before you get up on your high horse and say, "How do the people allow that to happen?" think of the United States, where it's much easier to prevent

REAL-WORLD APPLICATION

The Doha Round and Development Aid

Say you are a cotton farmer in Africa. Since your labor costs are much lower than U.S. labor costs, you figure you can compete, even though U.S. technology and capital far exceed yours. Taking technology and labor into account, you figure you have a 20 percent cost advantage, so that even taking into account higher shipping costs, your cotton is cost competitive. Unfortunately for you, that cost advantage disappears because U.S. cotton farmers have a benefit that you don't have—they get substantial subsidies from the U.S. government, which allows them to outcompete you. It isn't only in cotton, and it isn't only in the United States that the subsidies undermine your ability to compete on the world market. Farmers get help in a large number of agricultural goods, and the European and Japanese governments also give their farmers large subsidies. African and other developing nations argue that these subsidies undermine their ability to compete, and to develop. They argue that they don't want foreign aid as much as they want a level playing field so that they can compete.

It was precisely such arguments that led the World Trade Organization to organize the Doha round of trade negotiations. It was designed to reduce tariffs and other trade barriers that developing countries place on developed countries' goods, and in return reduce subsidies and other assistance that developed countries give to their own agricultural production. These trade negotiations started in 2001 and in mid-2009 were still ongoing as political pressures in developed countries made governments unable to reduce farm subsidies that the developing countries argued were needed to create a level playing field in trade of agricultural goods.

such activities but where scandals in government spending are still uncovered with depressing regularity.

Investment Funded from Abroad The other way to generate funds for investment is from external savings, either foreign aid or foreign investment.

Foreign Aid The easiest way to finance development is with **foreign aid** *(funds that developed countries lend or give to developing countries)*. The problem is that foreign aid generally comes with strings attached; funds are earmarked for specific purposes. For example, most foreign aid is military aid; helping a country prepare to fight a war isn't a good way to help it develop.

As you can see in the table below, the United States gives about \$23 billion (about \$80 per U.S. citizen) per year in foreign aid.

Country	Development Aid 2008 (millions of U.S. dollars)	Percent of GDP
Sweden	\$ 4,730	0.98%
United Kingdom	11,409	0.43
Austria	1,681	0.42
France	10,957	0.39
Germany	13,910	0.38
Canada	4,725	0.32
Italy	4,444	0.20
Japan	9,362	0.18
United States	26,008	0.18

Source: OECD DAC *Chairman's Report* (www.oecd.org).

For the 5.5 billion people in developing countries, total foreign aid from all countries comes to about $20 per person. That isn't going to finance a lot of economic development, especially when much of the money is earmarked for military purposes.

Total foreign aid from all countries comes to about $20 per person in developing countries.

Foreign Investment If a global or multinational company believes that a country has a motivated, cheap workforce; a stable government supportive of business; and sufficient **infrastructure investment**—*investment in the underlying structure of the economy,* such as transportation or power facilities—it has a strong incentive to invest in the country. That's a lot of ifs, and generally the poorest countries don't measure up. What they have to offer instead are raw materials that the global corporation can develop.

Countries at the upper end of the group of developing countries (such as Mexico and Brazil) may meet all these requirements, but large amounts of foreign investment often result in political problems as citizens of these countries complain about imperialist exploitation, outside control, and significant outflows of profits. Developing countries have tried to meet such complaints by insisting that foreign investment come in the form of joint development projects under local control, but that cuts down the amount that foreign firms are willing to invest.

When the infrastructure doesn't exist, as is the case in the poorest developing countries, few firms will invest in that country, no matter how cheap the labor or how stable the government. Firms require infrastructure investment such as transportation facilities, energy availability, and housing and amenities for their employees before they will consider investing in a country. And they don't want to pay to establish this infrastructure themselves.

Competition for Investment among Developing Countries The world is made up of about 30 highly industrial countries and about 160 other countries at various stages of development. Global companies have a choice of where to locate, and often developing countries compete to get the development located in their country. In their efforts to get the development, they may offer tax rebates, free land, guarantees of labor peace, or loose regulatory environments within which firms can operate.

This competition can be keen, and can result in many of the benefits of development being transferred from the developing country to the global company and ultimately to the Western consumer since competition from other firms will force the global company to pass on the benefits in the form of lower prices.

Competition for global company investment often leads to the benefits of that investment being passed on to the Western consumer.

An example of the results of such competition can be seen in the production of chemicals. Say a company is planning to build a new plant to produce chemicals. Where does it locate? Considering the wide-ranging environmental restrictions in the United States and Western Europe, a chemical company will likely look toward a developing country that will give it loose regulation. If one country will not come through, the chemical firm will point out that it can locate elsewhere. Concern about Mexico's relatively loose environmental regulatory environment was one of the sticking points of U.S. approval of NAFTA.

Focal Points and Takeoff The scope of competition among developing countries can be overstated. Most companies do not consider all developing countries as potential production and investment sites. To decide to produce in a developing country requires a knowledge of that country—its legal structure, its political structure, and its infrastructure. Gaining this information involves a substantial initial investment, so most companies tend to focus on a few developing countries about which they have specific knowledge, or that they know other companies have chosen as development sites. (If company X chose it, it must meet the appropriate criteria.)

Because of this informational requirement, developing countries that have been successful in attracting investment often get further investment. Eventually they reach a

REAL-WORLD APPLICATION

Millennium Development Goals

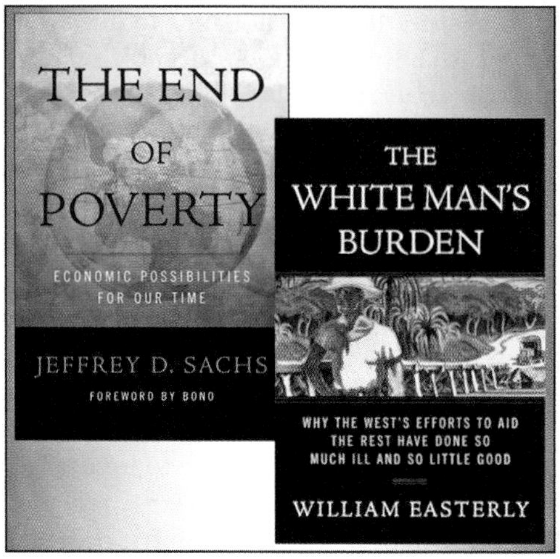

In 2000, leaders from around the world gathered at the United Nations and adopted the UN Millennium Declaration that set specific goals to combat poverty, hunger, disease, illiteracy, environmental degradation, and discrimination against women to be achieved by 2015. The goals have come to be known as the Millennium Development Goals. They include

1. Cut extreme poverty and hunger in half.
2. Achieve universal primary education.
3. Empower women and promote equality between women and men.
4. Reduce under-five mortality by two-thirds.
5. Reduce material mortality by three-quarters.
6. Reverse the spread of disease, especially HIV/AIDS and malaria.
7. Ensure environmental sustainability.
8. Create a global partnership for development, with targets for aid, trade, and debt relief.

No one would argue about the desirability of achieving these goals, but economists have debated how to achieve them. Economist Jeffrey Sachs wrote a book called *The End of Poverty* where he argues that extreme poverty, defined as living on less than $1 a day, can be eliminated by 2025 by doubling foreign aid and using that aid to address the multiplicity of problems extremely poor countries face, from the very simple problem of lacking mosquito nets to prevent malaria to more complicated issues of drinkable water. Sachs argues that we can eliminate extreme poverty and disease if we just try.

Not all economists agree with Sachs about what should be done about the problem. Economist William Easterly wrote a book called *The White Man's Burden* where he argues that extreme poverty is caused by a complicated interplay of politics, society, technology, geography, and economic systems; therefore, the cures are also necessarily complicated. He argues that we have doubled foreign aid in the past with no measurable result, and that Sachs' "End of Poverty program" will lead to little success. Easterly is not opposed to eradicating poverty, but he promotes a slower piecemeal approach that will (1) allow policy makers and economists to evaluate the success of specific programs, (2) hold institutions accountable for how funds are spent, and (3) be based on a good understanding of which programs work.

So, have the UN Millennium Declaration and Sachs' "End of Poverty program" been successful? Success has been slow and not universal across countries. For example, from 1990 to 2004, the proportion of the world's population living in extreme poverty dropped from 29 to 18 percent. But most of this was in southeastern Asia and Oceania, which had already experienced economic growth. Extreme poverty fell very little in sub-Saharan Africa and Latin America.

stage called **economic takeoff**—*a stage when the development process becomes self-sustaining*. Other developing countries fall by the wayside. This means that economic development is not evenly spread over developing countries, but rather is concentrated in a few.

Inappropriate Education

The right education is a necessary component of any successful development strategy. The wrong education is an enormous burden.

The right education is a necessary component of any successful development strategy. The wrong education is an enormous burden. Developing countries tend to have too much of the wrong education and too little of the right education.

Often educational systems in developing countries resemble Western educational systems. The reason is partly the colonial heritage of developing countries and partly what might be described as an emulation factor. The West defines what an educated person is, and developing countries want their citizens to be seen as educated. An educated person should be able to discuss the ideas of Vladimir Nabokov, the poetry of Lord Byron, the intricacies of chaos theory, the latest developments in fusion technology, the nuances of the modern Keynesian/Classical debate, and the dissociative properties of Andy Warhol's paintings. So saith Western scholars; so be it.

But, put bluntly, that type of education is almost irrelevant to economic growth and may be a serious detriment to growth. Basic skills—reading, writing, and arithmetic, taught widely—are likely to be more conducive to growth than is high-level education. When education doesn't match the needs of the society, the degrees—the credentials—become more important than the knowledge learned. The best jobs go to those with the highest degrees, not because the individuals holding the degrees are better able to do the job, but simply because they hold the credentials. **Credentialism,** in which *the degrees, or credentials, become more important than the knowledge learned,* serves to preserve the monopoly position of those who manage to get the degree.

If access to education is competitive, credentialism has its advantages. Even irrelevant education, as long as it is difficult, serves a screening or selection role. Those individuals who work hardest at getting an education advance and get the good jobs. Since selecting hardworking individuals is difficult, even irrelevant education serves this selection role.

But developing countries' current educational practices may be worse than irrelevant. Their educational systems often reflect Western culture, not their own cultures. The best students qualify for scholarships abroad, and their education in a different tradition makes it difficult for them to return home.

In my studies in Europe and the United States, I've come to know a large number of the best and the brightest students from developing countries. They're superb students and they do well in school. But as they near graduation, most of them face an enormously difficult choice. They can return to their home country—to material shortages, to enormous challenges for which they have little training, and to an illiterate society whose traditional values are sometimes hostile to the values these new graduates have learned. Or they can stay in the West, find jobs relevant to their training, enjoy an abundance of material goods, and associate with people to whom they've now learned to relate. Which would you choose?

The choice many of them make results in a **brain drain** (*the outflow of the best and brightest students from developing countries to developed countries*). Many of these good students don't return to the developing country. Those that do go home take jobs as government officials, expecting high salaries and material comforts far beyond what their society can afford. Instead of becoming the dynamic entrepreneurs of growth, they become impediments to growth.

Many good students from developing countries who study abroad don't return to the developing country.

There are, of course, many counterexamples to the arguments presented here. Many developing countries try to design their education system to fit their culture. And many of the dynamic, selfless leaders who make it possible for the country to develop do return home. As with most issues, there are both positive and negative attributes to the way something is done. I emphasize the problems with educational systems in developing economies because the positive attributes of education are generally accepted. Without education, development is impossible. The question is how that education should be structured.

Q-10 How could too much education cause problems for development?

Overpopulation

Two ways a country can increase per capita income are

1. Decrease the number of people in the country (without decreasing the total income in the country).
2. Increase the income (without increasing the population).

In each case, the qualifier is important because income and population are related in complicated ways: People earn income; without people there would be no income. But often the more people there are, the less income per person there is because the resources of the country become strained.

A country's population can never be higher than can be supported by the natural resources that it has, or can import. But that doesn't mean that overpopulation can't be an obstacle to development. Nature has its own ways of reducing populations that are too large: Starvation and disease are the direct opposite to development. That control system works in nature, and it would work with human societies. The problem is that we don't like it.

Web Note 38.4
Population and Development

Thomas Carlyle gave economics the name *the dismal science* as he was verbally sparring about a number of issues with economists of his period. The name stuck with economics in large part because of the writings of Thomas Malthus, who in the early 1800s said that society's prospects are dismal because population tends to outrun the means of subsistence. (Population grows geometrically—that is, at an increasing rate; the means of subsistence grow arithmetically—that is, at a constant rate.) The view was cemented into economic thinking in the law of diminishing marginal productivity: As more and more people are added to a fixed amount of land, the output per worker gets smaller and smaller.

Many developing economies have not avoided the Malthusian fate because diminishing marginal productivity has exceeded technological change.

Through technological progress, most Western economies have avoided the fate predicted by Malthus because growth in output has exceeded growth in population. In contrast, many developing economies have not avoided the Malthusian fate because diminishing marginal productivity has exceeded technological change, and limited economic growth isn't enough to offset the increase in population. The result is a constant or falling output per person.

That doesn't mean that developing countries haven't grown economically. They have. But population growth makes per capita output growth small or negative.

Population grows for a number of reasons, including

1. As public health measures are improved, infant mortality rates and death rates for the population as a whole both decline.
2. As people earn more income, they believe they can afford to have more children.
3. In rural areas, children are useful in working the fields.

What to do? Should the government reduce the population growth rate? If it should, how can it do so? Various measures have been tried: advertising campaigns, free condoms, forced sterilization, and economic incentives. For example, in China the government has tried imposing severe economic penalties on couples who have more than one child, while providing material incentives such as a free television set to couples who agreed not to have more than one child.

China's vigorous population control campaign has had a number of effects. First, it created so much anger at the government that in rural areas the campaign was dropped. Second, it led to the killing of many female babies because, if couples were to have only one baby, strong cultural and economic pressures existed to ensure that the baby was a male. Third, it led to an enormous loss of privacy. Dates of women's menstrual periods were posted in factories and officials would remind them at appropriate times that they should take precautions against getting pregnant. Only a very strong government could impose such a plan.

Even successful population control programs have their problems.

Even successful population control programs have their problems. In Singapore a population control campaign was so successful among educated women that the government became concerned that its "population quality" was suffering. It began a selective campaign to encourage college-educated women to have children. They issued "love tips" to men (since some college-educated women complained that their male companions were nerds and had no idea how to be romantic) and offered special monetary bonuses to college-educated women who gave birth to children. As you might imagine, the campaign provoked a backlash, and it was eventually dropped by the government.

Individuals differ substantially in their assessment of the morality of these programs, but even if one believes that population control is an appropriate government concern, it does not seem that such programs will be successful, by themselves, in limiting population growth.

Health and Disease

Web Note 38.5
Fighting Disease

Before a country can hope to develop, it must have a reasonably healthy population. If you are sick, it's hard to think, to work, or even to do standard daily tasks like growing food. In many developing countries, large portions of the population are undernourished or sick. Disease hits young children particularly hard. Millions of children die from pneumonia, diarrhea, malaria, and measles, all of which, because of the children's general malnutrition, are often aggravated by intestinal worms. Older individuals suffer from HIV/AIDS, tuberculosis, and malaria. For example, more than 30 million people now have AIDS in Africa, and about one-third of today's 15-year-olds in Africa will likely die of AIDS.

These diseases make it difficult for people to work, or even to take care of their kids, and create a vicious cycle. You're sick, you can't work, and so you and your family become victims of malnutrition. You get even more prone to disease, and less able to work and contribute to development. Thus, maintaining public health is more than a humanitarian issue; it is a key development issue.

What to do? Most of these diseases can be alleviated with drugs, but developing the infrastructure to provide these drugs is often difficult or impossible, even when the money for the drugs becomes available. Thus, one must not only get the drugs but also create the cultural and physical environment in which those drugs can be effective. Drug companies have little incentive to work on developing low-cost medicines to treat diseases in developing countries because the people there don't have much money to pay for them, so the return would be low. Instead, pharmaceutical companies focus their research on providing high-priced drugs to be sold in rich countries. Drug companies created anti-AIDS drugs, but their focus was on markets in wealthy developed countries. Only later, and under significant social and political pressure, did they start offering treatment for AIDS at low cost to developing countries.

Mission Impossible

Economic development is a complicated problem because it is entwined with cultural and social issues.

At this point in my course, I inevitably throw my hands up and admit that I don't know what makes it possible for a country to develop. Nor, judging from what I have read, do the development experts. The good ones (that is, the ones I agree with) admit that they don't know; others (that is, the ones I don't agree with) simply don't know that they don't know.

My gut feeling is that there are no definitive general answers that apply to all developing countries. The appropriate answer varies with each country and each situation. Each proposed solution to the development problem has a right time and a right place. Only by having a complete sense of a country, its history, and its cultural, social, and political norms can one decide whether it's the right time and place for this or that policy.

Summary

- While policies in developed countries focus on stability, developing countries struggle to provide basic needs.
- Development refers to an increase in productive capacity and output brought about by a change in underlying institutions, while growth refers to an increase in output brought about by an increase in inputs.
- Many developing economies have serious political problems that make it impossible for government to take an active, positive role in the economy.
- Many developing countries have dual economies—one a traditional, nonmarket economy and the other an internationalized market economy.
- Many developing countries need a change in the entire atmosphere within which the government and economy relate. They need regime changes rather than policy changes.
- Although developing countries know that printing too much money leads to inflation, their choices are limited. Some central banks lack independence and for others the only alternative is the collapse of government.
- Most monetary policies in developing countries focus on the international sector and are continually dealing with the balance of payments constraint.
- Most developing countries have some type of limited convertibility to limit the outflow of saving.
- Macro policies in developing countries are more concerned with institutional policies and regime changes than are macro policies in developed countries.
- Seven obstacles to economic development are political instability, corruption, lack of appropriate institutions, lack of investment, inappropriate education, overpopulation, and poor health and disease.

Key Terms

balance of payments constraint *(887)*
basic needs *(881)*
brain drain *(895)*
conditionality *(887)*
convertibility on the current account *(886)*
credentialism *(895)*
dual economy *(882)*
economic takeoff *(894)*
foreign aid *(892)*
full convertibility *(886)*
infrastructure investment *(893)*
limited capital account convertibility *(886)*
policy change *(883)*
purchasing power parity (PPP) *(879)*
regime change *(883)*
restructuring *(880)*

Questions and Exercises

connect ECONOMICS

1. How does the exchange rate method of comparing incomes differ from the purchasing power method of comparing incomes? LO1
2. What is the difference between development and growth? LO2
3. What are three ways in which the institutions of developing countries differ from those in developed countries? LO3
4. Why might an economist favor activist policies in developed countries and laissez-faire policies in developing countries? LO3
5. In the 1990s, Germany passed a law requiring businesses to take back and recycle all forms of packaging. A large group of businesses formed a company to collect and recycle these packages. Its costs are 4.5 cents per pound for glass, 9.5 cents per pound for paper, and 74 cents per pound for plastic. This accounts for a recycling cost of about \$100 per ton for glass and \$2,000 per ton for plastic; the average recycling cost of paper is \$500 per ton. A developing country has offered to create a giant landfill and accept Germany's waste at a cost of \$400 per ton, which includes \$50 per ton sorting and transport costs and a \$350-per-ton fee to be paid to the developing country.
   a. Should Germany accept this proposal?
   b. Will the proposal benefit the developing country? LO1, LO2, LO3

6. What is meant by "the dual economy"? LO4
7. How does a regime change differ from a policy change? LO5
8. What is the inflation tax? LO6
9. Why doesn't the fact that the "inflation solution" is only a temporary solution stop many developing countries from using it? LO6
10. What is conditionality, and how does it relate to the balance of payments constraint? LO7
11. Why are investment and savings so low in developing countries? LO8
12. If developing countries are so unstable and offer such a risky environment for investment, why do foreigners invest any money in them at all? LO8
13. Should developing countries send their students abroad for an education? LO8
14. How does corruption limit investment and economic growth? LO8
15. According to the Peruvian economist Hernando de Soto, in the 1980s, getting a deed for property in Peru involved 207 bureaucratic steps, took 43 months, and cost 10 weeks' worth of the official minimum wage.
    a. What problems would that create for economic development?
    b. What problems would the lack of titling create for public utilities? LO8

Questions from Alternative Perspectives

1. Christians are called to be Christ-like, a "light to lighten the nations" (Luke 2:32).
    a. In light of the basic biblical norms of justice, righteousness, and stewardship, how should a nation decide how much development aid to provide developing countries?
    b. Is it within Christian norms to make that aid conditional? (Hint: Consider the biblical concept of forgiveness, which includes repentance and the restoration of right relationships.) (Religious)
2. When thinking about development, it is often presented as an analytic exercise, but development policies have very real consequences.
    a. Who is responsible for economies that fail to develop?
    b. Who will primarily suffer the consequences from a failure at economic development?
    c. If your answers to *a* and *b* differ, how might that difference affect the development policies chosen? How does this difference possibly affect the choice of development policies? (Institutionalist)
3. In an earlier chapter, the book described the Grameen bank as an example of a successful micro credit reform.
    a. Why do many of the micro credit policies focus on women rather than men?
    b. Does your answer in *a* suggest anything about other policies that might help developing countries develop? (Feminist)
4. Islam considers the interest on loans to be an instrument of oppression of the poor by the wealthy. That is why interest is banned by the Qur'an. In 2003, member countries of the Islamic Development Bank owed \$883 billion in external debt and paid \$14 billion in interest.
    a. How could loans be an instrument of oppression?
    b. How could loans be an instrument of development?
    c. The Islamic Development Bank makes loans that remain within Islamic law. What do you suppose are the conditions for those loans? (You might want to look at its Web site at www.isdb.org for help.) (Religious)
5. The brief argument for globalization goes something like this. Countries that trade a lot grow quickly and poverty rates decline in rapidly growing countries. Therefore, globalization promotes rapid growth and alleviates poverty and is far superior to economic isolation. Radicals believe that the globalization debate is not about economic isolation vs. integration into the world economy; rather, the real debate is about what policies allow a developing economy to successfully engage with the world economy. The advocates' case tells us about a country's degree of engagement with the world economy but not the manner of that engagement. From the radical perspective, knowing that international trade and faster economic growth rates are positively correlated hardly constitutes an endorsement of the neo-liberal policy of lower barriers for trade and the movement of international capital.
    a. How should a developing economy engage with the global economy: through free trade and financial liberalization policies?
    b. Would the strategies promoted by the opponents of globalization—more national control and limits on the movement of foreign and domestic capital—be better polices for engaging with the world economy? (Radical)

Issues to Ponder

1. If you suddenly found yourself living as a poor person in a developing country, what are some things that you now do that you would no longer be able to do? What new things would you have to do? LO1
2. What is wrong with saying that people in developing countries are worse off than people in the United States? LO1
3. Does the fact that suicide rates are lower in developing countries than in the United States imply that Americans would be better off living in a developing country? Why? LO1
4. Spend one day living like someone in a developing country. Eat almost nothing and work lifting stones for 10 hours. Then, that same evening, study this chapter and contemplate the bootstrap strategy of development. LO1
5. Interview a foreign student in your class or school. Ask about each of the seven obstacles to economic development and how his or her country is trying to overcome them. LO2
6. It has been argued that development economics has no general theory; it is instead the application of common sense to real-world problems.
   a. Do you agree or disagree with that statement? Why?
   b. Why do you think this argument about the lack of generality of theories is made for developing countries more than it is made for developed countries? LO2
7. Choose any developing country and answer the following questions about it:
   a. What is its level of per capita income?
   b. What is its growth potential?
   c. What is the exchange rate of its currency in relation to the U.S. dollar?
   d. What policy suggestions might you make to the country? LO1, LO2, LO3
8. Why do governments in developing countries often seem more arbitrary and oppressive than governments in developed countries? LO3
9. If you were a foreign investor thinking of making an investment in a developing country, what are some things that you would be concerned about? LO8
10. Should a country control the size and makeup of its population? Why? LO8
11. A United Nations study reported that more than 300 million low-income women owned businesses in developing countries, but only 5 million had access to credit other than from money lenders. How might the UN alleviate this obstacle to growth? What other obstacles might exist for women entrepreneurs in developing nations? (Difficult) LO8
12. Say that you have been hired to design an education system for a developing country.
    a. What skills would you want it to emphasize?
    b. How might it differ from an ideal educational system here in the United States?
    c. How much of the U.S. educational system involves credentialism, and how much involves the learning of relevant skills? LO8

Answers to Margin Questions

1. Given market societies' expansionary tendencies, the cultures in economically poor countries that do not grow would simply be overrun and destroyed by cultures of market societies. This means that the choice is not between development and preservation of existing culture; rather, the choice is between economic development with its attendant wrenching cultural transitions and continued poverty with exploitation by developed countries and its attendant wrenching cultural transitions. *(879)*
2. Restructuring in developed countries suggests that the distinction between growth and development can be overdone since it is an example of developed countries' growth occurring through changing institutions—development—rather than through increasing inputs—growth. *(880)*
3. *Dual economy* refers to a developing country's tendency to have two economies that have little interaction: one a traditional nonmarket economy and the other an internationally oriented modern market economy. *(882)*
4. While everyone agrees that inflation in developing countries is caused by the central bank issuing too much money, the real policy question concerns what the political consequences of not issuing too much money may be. Sometimes the cure for inflation can be worse than the problem. *(884)*

5. In an inflation, any issuers of fixed-interest-rate debt denominated in the domestic currency gain from the holders of these debts. *(886)*
6. Full convertibility includes convertibility on the capital account as well as on the current account. It means that people are allowed to buy foreign financial assets—to save abroad. Convertibility on the current account means that people are allowed to buy foreign currencies to buy foreign goods, but not necessarily to buy foreign financial assets. *(886)*
7. In order for a market to operate, a set of rules—any rules—is needed. Lack of stability undermines the existence of any rules and leads to a failure of cooperation among people. *(889)*
8. It depends, but the answer is probably false. Often the wealthy elite in a developing country fear that if they invest in their country, their money will be taken away, so they often invest out of their country—meaning that the benefits of their savings go to other countries, not to the investors' own developing country. *(889)*
9. The more it costs to undertake economic activities, the fewer economic activities individuals undertake. *(890)*
10. Education is absolutely necessary for development, but it is most helpful if it is the right type of education—focusing on basic skills such as reading, writing, and arithmetic. When education focuses on abstract issues, determined by different cultures and having little relevance to the country's problems, "too much" education can lead to a brain drain and a diversion of people's talent away from the central development issues. *(895)*

Glossary

A

Abduction A method of anlysis that uses a combination of inductive methods and deductive methods.
Acquisition A transaction in which a company buys another company and the purchaser has the right of direct control over the resulting operation (but does not always exercise that right).
Adaptive Expectations Expectations based in some way on the past.
Adverse Selection Problem A problem that occurs when buyers and sellers have different amounts of information about the good for sale.
Agent-Based Computational Economic (ACE) Model A culture dish approach to the study of economic phenomena in which agents are allowed to interact in a computationally constructed environment and the researcher observes the results of that interaction.
Aggregate Demand (*AD*) Curve A curve that shows how a change in the price level will change aggregate expenditures on all goods and services in an economy.
Aggregate Demand Management Government's attempt to control the aggregate level of spending in the economy.
Aggregate Expenditures The total amount of spending on final goods and services in the economy; consumption (spending by consumers), investment (spending by business), spending by government, and net foreign spending on U.S. goods (the difference between U.S. exports and U.S. imports).
Aggregate Production (*AP*) The total amount of goods and services produced in every industry in an economy.
Annuity Rule The present value of any annuity is the annual income it yields divided by the interest rate.
Antitrust Policy The government's policy toward the competitive process.
Art of Economics The application of the knowledge learned in positive economics to the achievement of the goals one has determined in normative economics.
Asset Inflation A rise in the price of assets unrelated to increases in their productive capacity.
Asset Management How a bank handles its loans and other assets.
Automatic Stabilizer Any government program or policy that will counteract the business cycle without any new government action.
Autonomous Expenditures Expenditures that do not systematically vary with income.
Average Fixed Cost Fixed cost divided by quantity produced.
Average Product Output per worker.
Average Total Cost Total cost divided by the quantity produced.
Average Variable Cost Variable cost divided by quantity produced.

B

Backward Induction You begin with a desired outcome and then determine the decisions that lead you to that outcome.
Bad Precedent Problem The problem that if you give a bailout to one, all want it.
Balance of Merchandise Trade The difference between the value of goods exported and the value of goods imported.
Balance of Payments A country's record of all transactions between its residents and the residents of all foreign nations.
Balance of Payments Constraint Limitations on expansionary domestic macroeconomic policy due to a shortage of international reserves.
Balance of Trade The difference between the value of the goods and services a country imports and the value of the goods and services it exports.
Bank A financial institution whose primary function is accepting deposits for, and lending money to, individuals and firms.
Bar Graph A graph where the area under each point is filled in to look like a bar.
Barriers to Entry Social, political, or economic impediments that prevent firms from entering a market.
Basic Needs Adequate food, clothing, and shelter.
Behavioral Economic Policy Economic policy based upon models using behavioral economic building blocks that take into account people's predictable irrational behavior.
Behavioral Economics Microeconomic analysis that uses a broader set of building blocks than rationality and self-interest used in traditional economics. Also: The study of economic choice that is based on realistic psychological foundations.
Bilateral Monopoly A market with only a single seller and a single buyer.
Bond A promise to pay a certain amount of money plus interest in the future.
Brain Drain The outflow of the best and brightest students from developing countries to developed countries.
Bretton Woods System An agreement about fixed exchange rates that governed international financial relationships from the period after the end of World War II until 1971.

Budget Constraint A curve that shows us the various combinations of goods an individual can buy with a given amount of money.

Business A private producing unit in our society.

Business Cycle The upward or downward movement of economic activity, or real GDP, that occurs around the growth trend.

Butterfly Effect Model A model in which a small change causes a large effect.

Bubble Unsustainable rapidly rising prices of some type of financial asset.

C

Capitalism An economic system based on the market in which the ownership of the means of production resides with a small group of individuals called capitalists.

Cartel A combination of firms that acts as if it were a single firm.

Cartel Model of Oligopoly A model that assumes that oligopolies act as if they were monopolists that have assigned output quotas to individual member firms of the oligopoly so that total output is consistent with joint profit maximization.

Cash Flow Accounting System An accounting system entering expenses and revenues only when cash is received or paid out.

Central Bank A type of bankers' bank whose financial obligations underlie an economy's money supply.

Cheap Talk Communication that occurs before the game is played that carries no cost and is backed up only by trust, and not any enforceable agreement.

Choice Architecture The context in which decisions are presented.

Classical Growth Model A model of growth that focuses on the role of capital accumulation in the growth process.

Classicals Macroeconomists who generally favor laissez-faire or nonactivist policies.

Clayton Antitrust Act A U.S. law that made four specific monopolistic practices illegal: price discrimination, tie-in contracts, interlocking directorships, and buying stock in a competitor's company in order to reduce competition.

Closed Shop A firm where unions control the hiring.

Coefficient of Determination A measure of the proportion of the variability in the data that is accounted for by the statistical model.

Comparable Worth Laws Laws mandating comparable pay for comparable work.

Comparative Advantage The ability to be better suited to the production of one good than to the production of another good.

Competitiveness The ability of a country to sell its goods to other countries.

Complements Goods that are used in conjunction with other goods.

Complex Systems Macro Models Macro models of the economy that take into account dynamic interactions of agents in the models, where agents have less than full information and can be less than infinitely rational.

Concentration Ratio The value of sales by the top firms of an industry stated as a percentage of total industry sales.

Conditionality The making of loans that are subject to specific conditions.

Conglomerate Merger The merging of relatively unrelated businesses.

Conspicuous Consumption The consumption of goods not for one's direct pleasure, but simply to show off to others.

Constant Returns to Scale A situation in which long-run average total costs do not change with an increase in output. Also: Output will rise by the same proportionate increase as all inputs.

Consumer Price Index (CPI) A measure of prices of a fixed basket of consumer goods, weighted according to each component's share of an average consumer's expenditures.

Consumer Sovereignty The principle that the consumer's wishes determine what's produced.

Consumer Surplus The difference between what consumers would have been willing to pay and what they actually pay. Also, the value the consumer gets from buying a product less its price.

Consumption Spending by households on goods and services.

Contestable Market Model A model of oligopoly in which barriers to entry and barriers to exit, not the structure of the market, determine a firm's price and output decisions.

Contractionary Monetary Policy Monetary policy that decreases the money supply and increases interest rates.

Contractual Legal System The set of laws that govern economic behavior.

Convergence Hypothesis The hypothesis that per capita income in countries with similar institutional structures will gravitate toward the same level.

Convertibility on the Current Account An exchange rate system that allows people to exchange currencies freely to buy goods and services, but not to buy assets in other countries.

Cooperative Game A game in which players can form coalitions and can enforce the will of the coalition on its members.

Coordinate System A two-dimensional space in which one point represents two numbers.

Coordination Mechanisms Methods of coordinating people's wants with other people's desires.
Corporate Takeover An action in which another firm or a group of individuals issues a tender offer (that is, offers to buy up the stock of a company) to gain control and to install its own managers.
Corporation A business that is treated as a person, legally owned by its stockholders. Its stockholders are not liable for the actions of the corporate "person."
Cost Minimization Condition A situation where the ratio of marginal product to the price of an input is equal for all inputs.
Cost/Benefit Approach Assigning costs and benefits, and making decisions on the basis of the relevant costs and benefits.
Cost-Push Inflation Inflation that occurs when the economy is below potential output.
Countercyclical Fiscal Policy Fiscal policy in which the government offsets any change in aggregate expenditures that would create a business cycle.
Credentialism When the academic degrees, or credentials, become more important than the knowledge learned.
Cross-Price Elasticity of Demand The percentage change in demand divided by the percentage change in the price of a related good.
Crowding Out The offsetting of a change in government expenditures by a change in private expenditures in the opposite direction.
Currency Stabilization Buying and selling of a currency by the government to offset temporary fluctuations in supply and demand for currencies.
Currency Support Buying of a currency by a government to maintain its value at above its long-run equilibrium value.
Current Account The part of the balance of payments account in which all short-term flows of payments are listed.
Cyclical Unemployment Unemployment resulting from fluctuations in economic activity.

D

Deacquisition One company's sale of either parts of another company it has bought or parts of itself.
Deadweight Loss The loss of consumer and producer surplus from a tax.
Debt Accumulated deficits minus accumulated surpluses.
Debt Service The interest rate on debt times the total debt.
Decreasing Returns to Scale A situation when output rises by a smaller proportionate increase than all inputs.
Deficit A shortfall of revenues under payments.
Deflation A continual fall in the price level.
Deduction A method of reasoning in which one deduces a theory based on a set of almost self-evident principles. Also, the fall in the price level.
Deductive Scientific Model A model with carefully specified formal foundations whose primary purpose is understanding for the sake of understanding.
Demand A schedule of quantities of a good that will be bought per unit of time at various prices, other things constant.
Demand Curve The graphic representation of the relationship between price and quantity demanded.
Demand-Pull Inflation Inflation that occurs when the economy is at or above potential output.
Demerit Good or Activity A good or activity that government believes is bad for people even though they choose to use the good or engage in the activity.
Deposit Insurance A system under which the federal government promised to stand by an individual's bank deposits.
Depreciation A measure of the decline in value of an asset that occurs over time through use. Also: A decrease in the value of a currency.
Depression A large recession.
Derived Demand The demand for factors of production by firms, which depends on consumers' demands.
Derived Demand Curve for Labor A curve that shows the maximum amount of labor, measured in labor hours, that a firm will hire.
Direct Regulation A program in which the amount of a good people are allowed to use is directly limited by the government.
Direct Relationship A relationship in which when one variable goes up, the other goes up too.
Discount Rate The rate of interest the Fed charges for loans it makes to banks.
Diseconomies of Scale Situation when the long-run average total costs increase as output increases.
Diversification The act of combining different financial instruments, whose prices are not expected to move together, in an effort to reduce risk.
Division of Labor The splitting up of a task to allow for specialization of production.
Dominant Strategy A strategy that is preferred by a player regardless of the opponent's move.
Dual Economy The existence of two sectors: a traditional sector and an internationally oriented modern market sector.
Duopoly An oligopoly with only two firms.
Dynamic Taking "time" explicitly into account.
Dynamic Efficiency A market's ability to promote cost-reducing or product-enhancing technological change.

E

E-commerce Buying and selling over the Internet.
Econometrics The statistical analysis of economic data.
Economic Decision Rule If the marginal benefits of doing something exceed the marginal costs, do it. If the marginal costs of doing something exceed the marginal benefits, don't do it.
Economic Efficiency Achieving a goal at the lowest possible cost.
Economic Engineering Economics devoted not only to studying markets, but also to designing markets and other coordinating mechanisms.
Economic Force The necessary reaction to scarcity.
Economic Model A framework that places the generalized insights of a theory in a more specific contextual setting.
Economic Policy An action (or inaction) taken by government to influence economic actions.
Economic Principle A commonly held economic insight stated as a law or general assumption.
Economic Profit Explicit and implicit revenue minus explicit and implicit cost. Also, a return on entrepreneurship above and beyond normal profits.
Economic Takeoff A stage when the development process becomes self-sustaining.
Economically Efficient A method of production that produces a given level of output at the lowest possible cost.
Economics The study of how human beings coordinate their wants and desires, given the decision-making mechanisms, social customs, and political realities of the society.
Economies of Scale Situation when long-run average total costs decrease as output increases.
Economies of Scope Situation when the costs of producing products are interdependent so that it's less costly for a firm to produce a good when it's already producing another.
Efficiency Achieving a goal as cheaply as possible. Also: Using as few inputs as possible.
Efficiency Wages Wages paid above the going-market wage to keep workers happy and productive.
Efficient Achieving a goal at the lowest cost in total resources without consideration as to who pays those costs.
Effluent Fees Charges imposed by government on the level of pollution created.
Elastic The percentage change in quantity is greater than the percentage change in price ($E > 1$).
Embargo A total restriction on the import or export of a good.
Emergent Properties Properties of the system that could not have been predicted from a deductive analysis starting from the components of the system.
Empirical Model A model that statistically discovers a pattern in the data.
Employment–Population Ratio The number of people who are working as a percentage of people available to work.
Endowment Effects People value something more just because they have it.
Engineering Model A model with loose formal foundations whose primary purpose is to guide thinking about policy.
Enlightened Self-Interest People care about other people as well as themselves.
Entrepreneur An individual who sees an opportunity to sell an item at a price higher than the average cost of producing it.
Entrepreneurship The ability to organize and get something done. Also: Labor services that involve high degrees of organizational skills, concern, oversight responsibility, and creativity.
Equation of Exchange An equation stating that the quantity of money times the velocity of money equals the price level times the quantity of real goods sold.
Equilibrium A concept in which opposing dynamic forces cancel each other out.
Equilibrium Income The level of income toward whichz-the economy gravitates in the short run because of the cumulative cycles of declining or increasing production.
Equilibrium Price The price toward which the invisible hand drives the market.
Equilibrium Quantity The amount bought and sold at the equilibrium price.
Euro The currency used by 16 members of the European Union.
European Commission (EC) The executive group of the European Union that guides action and safeguards the European Union nations; also called Commission of the European Communities. The EU's antitrust agency.
Excess Demand Situation when quantity demanded is greater than quantity supplied.
Excess Reserves Reserves held by banks in excess of what banks are required to hold.
Excess Supply Situation when quantity supplied is greater than quantity demanded.
Exchange Rate The price of one country's currency in terms of another currency.
Excise Tax A tax that is levied on a specific good.
Expansion An upturn that lasts for at least two consecutive quarters of a year.
Expansionary Monetary Policy Monetary policy that increases the money supply and decreases the interest rate.
Expected Inflation Inflation people expect to occur.
Expenditures Multiplier A number that tells how much income will change in response to a change in autonomous expenditures.

Experimental Economics A branch of economics that studies the economy through controlled laboratory experiments.
External Debt Government debt owed to individuals in foreign countries.
Externality An effect of a decision on a third party not taken into account by the decision maker.
Extrapolative Expectations Expectations that a trend will continue.

F

Failure of Market Outcome A situation in which, even though the market is functioning properly (there are no market failures), it is not achieving society's goals.
Fallacy of Composition The false assumption that what is true for a part will also be true for the whole.
Fed Funds Loans of excess reserves banks make to one another.
Federal Funds Market The market in which banks lend and borrow reserves.
Federal Funds Rate The interest rate banks charge one another for Fed funds.
Federal Open Market Committee (FOMC) The Fed's chief body that decides monetary policy.
Federal Reserve Bank (the Fed) The U.S. central bank whose liabilities (Federal Reserve notes) serve as cash in the United States.
Federal Trade Commission Act A U.S. law that made it illegal for firms to use "unfair methods of competition" and to engage in "unfair or deceptive acts or practices."
Feudalism An economic system in which traditions rule.
Final Output Goods and services purchased for their final use.
Financial and Capital Account The part of the balance of payments account in which all long-term flows of payments are listed.
Financial Assets Assets such as stocks or bonds, whose benefit to the owner depends on the issuer of the asset meeting certain obligations.
Financial Liabilities Liabilities incurred by the issuer of a financial asset to stand behind the issued asset.
Fine-Tuning Fiscal policy designed to keep the economy always at its target or potential level of income.
Firm An economic institution that transforms factors of production into goods and services.
Fiscal Policy The deliberate change in either government spending or taxes to stimulate or slow down the economy. Also, the changing of taxes and spending to affect the level of output in the economy.
Fixed Costs Costs that are spent and cannot be changed in the period of time under consideration.
Fixed Exchange Rate When the government chooses a particular exchange rate and offers to buy and sell its currency at that price.
Flexible Exchange Rate When the government does not enter into foreign exchange markets at all, but leaves the determination of exchange rates totally up to market forces.
Foreign Aid Funds that developed countries lend or give to developing countries.
Forex Market The foreign exchange market.
Framing Effect The tendency of people to base their choices on how the choice is presented.
Free Rider A person who participates in something for free because others have paid for it.
Free Rider Problem Individuals' unwillingness to share in the cost of a public good.
Free Trade Association A group of countries that have reduced or eliminated trade barriers among themselves.
Frictional Unemployment Unemployment caused by people entering the job market and people quitting a job just long enough to look for and find another one.
Full Convertibility An exchange rate system in which individuals may change dollars into any currency they want for whatever legal purpose they want.
Functional Finance A theoretical proposition that governments should make spending and taxing decisions on the basis of their effect on the economy, not on the basis of some moralistic principle that budgets should be balanced.

G

Game Theory Formal economic reasoning applied to situations in which decisions are interdependent.
Game Theory Model A model in which one analyzes the strategic interaction of individuals when they take into account the likely response of other people to their actions.
GDP Deflator An index of the price level of aggregate output, or the average price of the components of GDP, relative to a base year.
General Agreement on Tariffs and Trade (GATT) A regular international conference to reduce trade barriers held from 1947 to 1995. It has been replaced by the World Trade Organization (WTO).
General Equilibrium Model A model of all the markets in the economy, not just a single market.
General Rule of Political Economy When small groups are helped by a government action and large groups are hurt by that same action, the small group tends to lobby far more effectively than the large group.
Glass-Steagall Act An act of Congress passed in 1933 that established deposit insurance and implemented a number of banking regulations.

Global Corporation A corporation with substantial operations on both the production and sales sides in more than one country.
Globalization The increasing integration of economies, cultures, and institutions across the world.
Gold Specie Flow Mechanism The long-run adjustment mechanism that maintained the gold standard.
Gold Standard The system of fixed exchange rates in which the value of currencies was fixed relative to the value of gold and gold was used as the primary reserve asset.
Good/Bad Paradox The phenomenon of doing poorly because you're doing well.
Government Failure A situation in which the government intervention in the market to improve market failure actually makes the situation worse.
Government Spending Goods and services that government buys.
Grandfather To pass a law affecting a specific group but providing that those in the group before the law was passed are exempt from some provisions of the law.
Graph A picture of points in a coordinate system in which points denote relationships between numbers.
Gross Domestic Product (GDP) The total market value of all final goods and services produced in an economy in a one-year period.
Gross National Product (GNP) The aggregate final output of citizens and businesses of an economy in a one-year period.

H

Herd To copy other successful behavior even though that successful behavior may have been just luck.
Herding The human tendency to follow the crowds.
Herfindahl Index An index of market concentration calculated by adding the squared value of the individual market shares of all firms in the industry.
Heuristic Model A model that is expressed informally in words.
Historically Based Expectations Expectations about the future that are based on past events.
Horizontal Merger The combining of two companies in the same industry.
Hostile Takeover A merger in which the firm being taken over doesn't want to be taken over.
Households Groups of individuals living together and making joint decisions.
Human Capital The skills that are embodied in workers through experience, education, and on-the-job training, or, more simply, people's knowledge.
Hyperinflation Inflation that hits triple digits—100 percent or more per year.

I

Implicit Collusion A type of collusion in which multiple firms make the same pricing decisions even though they have not explicitly consulted with one another.
Incentive Compatibility Problem A problem in which the incentive facing the decision maker does not match the incentive needed for the mechanism to achieve its desired ends.
Incentive-Compatible Contract A contract in which the incentives of each of the two parties to the contract are made to correspond as closely as possible.
Incentive Effect How much a person will change his or her hours worked in response to a change in the wage rate.
Income Payments received plus or minus changes in the value of a person's assets in a specified time period.
Income Effect The reduction in quantity demanded because price increases make us poorer.
Income Elasticity of Demand The percentage change in demand divided by the percentage change in income.
Increasing Returns to Scale A situation when output rises by a greater proportionate increase than all inputs.
Indifference Curve A curve that shows combinations of goods among which an individual is indifferent.
Indivisible Setup Cost The cost of an indivisible input for which a certain minimum amount of production must be undertaken before the input becomes economically feasible to use.
Induced Expenditures Expenditures that change as income changes.
Induction A method of reasoning in which one develops general principles by looking for patterns in the data.
Industrial Policy A formal policy that government takes toward business.
Industrial Revolution A time when technology and machines rapidly modernized industrial production and mass-produced goods replaced handmade goods.
Inefficiency Getting less output from inputs that, if devoted to some other activity, would produce more output.
Inefficient Achieving a goal in a more costly manner than necessary.
Inelastic The percentage change in quantity is less than the percentage change in price ($E < 1$).
Infant Industry Argument The argument that with initial protection, an industry will be able to become competitive.
Inferior Good Good whose consumption decreases when income increases.
Inflation A continual rise in the price level.
Inflation Tax An implicit tax on the holders of cash and the holders of any obligations specified in nominal terms.
Inflationary Gap A difference between equilibrium income and potential income when equilibrium income

exceeds potential income. That is, aggregate expenditures above potential output that exist at the current price level.

Infrastructure Investment Investment in the underlying structure of the economy.

Inherent Comparative Advantage Comparative advantage that is based on factors that are relatively unchangeable.

Input What is put into a production process to achieve an output.

Insider/Outsider Model An institutionalist story of inflation where insiders bid up wages and outsiders are unemployed.

Institutions The formal and informal rules that constrain human behavior.

Interest The income paid to savers—individuals who produce now but don't consume now.

Interest Rate The price paid for the use of a financial asset.

Interest Rate Effect The effect that a lower price level has on investment expenditures through the effect that a change in the price level has on interest rates.

Intermediate Products Products used as inputs in the production of some other product.

Internal Debt Government debt owed to other governmental agencies or to its own citizens.

International Effect As the price level falls (assuming the exchange rate does not change), net exports will rise.

Interpolation Assumption The assumption that the relationship between variables is the same between points as it is at the points.

Inverse Relationship A relationship between two variables in which when one goes up, the other goes down.

Inverted Yield Curve A yield curve in which the short-term rate is higher than the long-term rate.

Investment Spending for the purpose of additional production.

Invisible Hand The price mechanism; the rise and fall of prices that guides our actions in a market.

Invisible Hand Theorem A market economy, through the price mechanism, will tend to allocate resources efficiently.

Isocost Line A line that represents alternative combinations of factors of production that have the same costs.

Isoquant Curve A curve that represents combinations of factors of production that result in equal amounts of output.

Isoquant Map A set of isoquant curves that show technically efficient combinations of inputs that can produce different levels of output.

J

Judgment by Performance To judge the competitiveness of markets by the performance (behavior) of firms in that market.

Judgment by Structure To judge the competitiveness of markets by the structure of the industry.

K

Keynesians Macroeconomists who generally favor activist government policy.

L

Labor Force Those people in an economy who are willing and able to work.

Labor Force Participation Rate The percentage of the total population at least 16 years old who either work or are actively looking for work.

Labor Market The factor market in which individuals supply labor services for wages to other individuals and to firms that need (demand) labor services.

Labor Productivity The average output per worker.

Laissez-Faire An economic policy of leaving coordination of individuals' actions to the market.

Land Bank Program A program in which government supports prices by giving farmers economic incentives to reduce supply.

Law of Demand Quantity demanded rises as price falls, other things constant. Also can be stated as: Quantity demanded falls as price rises, other things constant.

Law of Diminishing Control Whenever a regulatory system is set up, individuals or firms being regulated will figure out ways to circumvent those regulations.

Law of Diminishing Marginal Productivity As more and more of a variable input are added to an existing fixed input, eventually the additional output one gets from that additional input is going to fall. Also, increasing one input, keeping all others constant, will lead to smaller and smaller gains in output.

Law of Diminishing Marginal Rate of Substitution As you get more and more of a good, if some of that good is taken away, then the marginal addition of another good you need to remain on the same indifference curve gets less and less.

Law of One Price The wages of workers in one country will not differ significantly from the wages of (equal) workers in another institutionally similar country.

Law of Supply Quantity supplied rises as price rises, other things constant. Also can be stated as: Quantity supplied falls as price falls, other things constant.

Lazy Monopolist A monopolist that does not push for efficiency, but merely enjoys the position it is already in.

Learning by Doing As we do something, we learn what works and what doesn't, and over time we become more proficient at it. Also: To improve the methods of production through experience.

Learning Procedures The methods by which people learn about the system.
Leverage Borrowing to make financial investments.
Liability Management How a bank attracts deposits and what it pays for them.
Libertarian Paternalistic Policy A policy that leaves people free to choose, but nonetheless guides them toward a choice that a paternalistic observer would see as good for them.
Limited Capital Account Convertibility An exchange rate system that allows full current account convertibility and partial capital account convertibility.
Limited Liability The liability of a stockholder (owner) in a corporation; it is limited to the amount the stockholder has invested in the company.
Line Graph A graph where the data are connected by a continuous line.
Linear Curve A curve that is drawn as a straight line.
Liquidity One's ability to convert an asset into cash.
Liquidity Trap A situation where people only want to hold liquid assets, and they would hold them even if they had to pay money to hold them.
Long-Run Aggregate Supply (*LAS*) Curve A curve that shows the long-run relationship between output and the price level.
Long-Run Decision A decision in which a firm chooses among all possible production techniques.
Long-Run Phillips Curve A vertical curve at the unemployment rate consistent with potential output. (It shows the trade-off [or complete lack thereof] when expectations of inflation equal actual inflation.)
Lorenz Curve A geometric representation of the share distribution of income among families in a given country at a given time.
Lucas Critique Problem The problem that because government policies can affect the behavior of individuals, historical data can lead to misleading predictions about the impact of a *new* policy.
Luxury A good that has an income elasticity greater than 1.

M

M_1 Currency in the hands of the public, checking account balances, and traveler's checks.
M_2 M_1 plus savings deposits, small-denomination time deposits, and money market mutual fund shares, along with some esoteric financial instruments.
Macroeconomic Externality An externality that affects the levels of unemployment, inflation, or growth in the economy as a whole.
Macroeconomics The study of the economy as a whole, which includes inflation, unemployment, business cycles, and growth.
Marginal Benefit Additional benefit above the benefits already derived.
Marginal Cost Additional cost over and above the costs already incurred. Also: Increase (decrease) in total cost from increasing (or decreasing) the level of output by one unit. Also: The change in total cost associated with a change in quantity.
Marginal Factor Cost The additional cost to a firm of hiring another worker.
Marginal Physical Product (*MPP*) The additional units of output that hiring an additional worker will bring about.
Marginal Product The additional output that will be forthcoming from an additional worker, other inputs constant.
Marginal Productivity Theory Factors are paid their marginal revenue product (what they contribute at the margin to revenue).
Marginal Propensity to Expend (*mpe*) The ratio of the change in aggregate expenditures to a change in income.
Marginal Rate of Substitution The rate at which one good must be added when the other is taken away to keep the individual indifferent between the two combinations. Also: The rate at which one factor must be added to compensate for the loss of another factor to keep output constant.
Marginal Revenue (*MR*) The change in total revenue associated with a change in quantity.
Marginal Revenue Product (*MRP*) The marginal revenue a firm expects to earn from selling an additional worker's output.
Marginal Social Benefit The marginal private benefit of consuming a good plus the benefits of the positive externalities resulting from consuming that good.
Marginal Social Cost The marginal private costs of production plus the cost of the negative externalities associated with that production.
Marginal Utility The satisfaction one gets from consuming one additional unit of a product above and beyond what one has consumed up to that point.
Market Demand Curve The horizontal sum of all individual demand curves.
Market Economy An economic system based on private property and the market in which, in principle, individuals decide how, what, and for whom to produce.
Market Failure A situation in which the invisible hand pushes in such a way that individual decisions do not lead to socially desirable outcomes.
Market Force An economic force that is given relatively free rein by society to work through the market.
Market Incentive Plan A plan requiring market participants to certify that they have reduced total consumption—not necessarily their own individual consumption—by a specified amount.

Market Niche An area in which competition is not working.

Market Structure The physical characteristics of the market within which firms interact.

Market Supply Curve The horizontal sum of all individual supply curves. Also: Horizontal sum of all the firms' marginal cost curves, taking account of any changes in input prices that might occur.

Marxian (Radical) Model A model that focuses on equitable distribution of power, rights, and income among social classes.

Mechanism Design Identifying a goal and then designing a mechanism such as a market, social system, or contract to achieve that end.

Medicare A multibillion-dollar medical insurance system.

Mercantilism An economic system in which government determines the what, how, and for whom decisions by doling out the rights to undertake certain economic activities.

Merger The act of combining two firms.

Merit Good or Activity A good or activity that government believes is good for you, even though you may not choose to consume the good or engage in the activity.

Microeconomics The study of individual choice, and how that choice is influenced by economic forces.

Minimum Efficient Level of Production The amount of production that spreads setup costs out sufficiently for a firm to undertake production profitably.

Minimum Wage Law A law specifying the lowest wage a firm can legally pay an employee.

Mixed Strategy A strategy of choosing randomly among moves.

Model A simplified representation of the problem or question that captures the essential issues.

Modern Economists Economists who are willing to use a wider range of models than did earlier economists.

Monetary Base Vault cash, deposits at the Fed, plus currency in circulation.

Monetary Policy A policy of influencing the economy through changes in the banking system's reserves that influence the money supply and credit availability in the economy.

Monetary Regime A predetermined statement of the policy that will be followed in various situations.

Money A highly liquid financial asset that's generally accepted in exchange for other goods, is used as a reference in valuing other goods, and can be stored as wealth.

Money Multiplier $(1 + c)/(r + c)$, where r is the percentage of deposits banks hold in reserve and c is the ratio of money people hold in currency to the money they hold as deposits.

Money Wealth Effect A fall in the price level will make the holders of money richer, so they buy more.

Monitoring Costs Costs incurred by the organizer of production in seeing to it that the employees do what they're supposed to do.

Monitoring Problem The need to oversee employees to ensure that their actions are in the best interest of the firm.

Monopolistic Competition A market structure in which many firms sell differentiated products; there are few barriers to entry.

Monopoly A market structure in which one firm makes up the entire market.

Monopoly Power The ability of individuals or firms currently in business to prevent other individuals or firms from entering the same kind of business.

Monopsony A market in which a single firm is the only buyer.

Moral Hazard Problem A problem that arises when people don't have to bear the negative consequences of their actions.

Mortgage-Backed Securities Financial assets whose flow of income comes from a combination of mortgages.

Most-Favored Nation A country that will be charged as low a tariff on its exports as any other country.

Movement along a Demand Curve The graphical representation of the effect of a change in price on the quantity demanded.

Movement along a Supply Curve The graphical representation of the effect of a change in price on the quantity supplied.

Multiplier-Accelerator Model A model in which changes in output are accelerated because changes in investment depend on changes in income (rather than on the level of income).

Multiplier Effect The amplification of initial changes in expenditures.

Multiplier Equation An equation that tells us that income equals the multiplier times autonomous expenditures.

Multiplier Model A model that emphasizes the effect of fluctuations in aggregate demand, rather than the price level, on output.

N

Nash Equilibrium A set of strategies for each player in the game in which no player can improve his or her payoff by changing strategy unilaterally.

Natural Experiment A naturally occurring event that approximates a controlled experiment where something has changed in one place but has not changed somewhere else. That is, an event created by nature that can serve as an experiment.

Natural Monopoly An industry in which a single firm can produce at a lower cost than can two or more firms. Also:

An industry in which significant economies of scale make the existence of more than one firm inefficient.

Necessity A good that has an income elasticity less than 1.

Negative Externality The adverse effect of a decision on others not taken into account by the decision maker. When the effects of a decision not taken into account by the decision maker are detrimental to others.

Net Domestic Product (NDP) The sum of consumption expenditures, government expenditures, net exports, and investment less depreciation. That is, GDP less depreciation.

Net Exports Spending on goods and services produced in the United States that foreigners buy (exports) minus goods and services produced abroad that U.S. citizens buy (imports).

Net Foreign Factor Income Income from foreign domestic factor sources minus foreign factor income earned domestically.

Net Investment Gross investment less depreciation.

Network Externality The phenomenon that the greater use of a product increases the benefit of that product to everyone.

New Classical Macroeconomics An approach to macroeconomics that studies macroeconomic questions using traditional microeconomic building blocks that emphasize rationality.

New Growth Theory A theory that emphasizes the role of technology rather than capital in the growth process.

Nominal Deficit The deficit determined by looking at the difference between expenditures and receipts.

Nominal GDP GDP calculated at existing prices.

Nominal Interest Rate The interest rate you actually see and pay when borrowing, or receive when lending.

Nominal Output The total amount of goods and services measured at current prices.

Nominal Wealth The value of the assets of an economy measured at their current market prices.

Noncooperative Game A game in which each player is out for him- or herself and agreements are either not possible or not enforceable.

Nonlinear Curve A curve that is drawn as a curved line.

Nonrecourse Loan Program A program in which government "buys" goods in the form of collateral on defaulting loans.

Nonsystemic Risk Risks of one event that are offset by another event elsewhere.

Normal Good Good whose consumption increases with an increase in income.

Normal Profit The amount the owners of business would have received in the next-best alternative. Also, payments to entrepreneurs as the return on their risk taking.

Normative Economics The study of what the goals of the economy should be.

North American Industry Classification System (NAICS) An industry classification that categorizes industries by type of economic activity and groups firms with like production processes.

Nudge A deliberate design of the choice architecture that alters people's behavior in predictably positive ways.

Nudge Policy Policy in which government structures choices facing people so that they are free to choose what they want, but also more likely to choose what is best for them.

O

Official Reserves Government holdings of foreign currencies.

Okun's Rule of Thumb (sometimes called Okun's Law) A 1 percentage-point change in the unemployment rate will be associated with a 2 percent change in output in the opposite direction.

Oligopoly A market structure in which there are only a few firms and firms explicitly take other firms' likely response into account; there are often significant barriers to entry.

Open Market Operations The Fed's buying and selling of government securities.

Opportunity Cost The benefit you might have gained from choosing the next-best alternative.

Optimal Policy A policy in which the marginal cost of undertaking the policy equals the marginal benefit of that policy.

Output A result of a productive activity.

Outsourcing The relocation of production once done in the United States to foreign countries.

P

Paradox of Thrift An increase in saving can lead to a decrease in expenditures, decreasing output and causing a recession.

Pareto Optimal Policy A policy that benefits some people and hurts no one.

Partially Flexible Exchange Rate When the government sometimes buys or sells currencies to influence the exchange rate, while at other times the government simply accepts the exchange rate determined by supply and demand forces, that is, letting private market forces operate.

Partnership A business with two or more owners.

Passive Deficit The part of the deficit that exists because the economy is operating below its potential level of output.

Patent The legal protection of a technical innovation that gives the person holding it sole right to use that innovation. (Note: A patent is good for only a limited time.)

Path-Dependent Model A model in which the path to equilibrium affects the equilibrium.

Pay-as-You-Go System A system in which payments to current beneficiaries are funded through current payroll taxes.

Payoff Matrix A table that shows the outcome of every choice by every player, given the possible choices of all other players.

Per Capita Growth Producing more goods and services per person.

Per Capita Real Output Real GDP divided by the total population.

Perfectly Competitive Market A market in which economic forces operate unimpeded.

Perfectly Elastic Quantity responds enormously to changes in price ($E = \infty$).

Perfectly Inelastic Quantity does not respond at all to changes in price ($E = 0$).

Permanent Income Hypothesis A proposition that expenditures are determined by permanent or lifetime income.

Personal Consumption Expenditure (PCE) Deflator A measure of prices of goods that consumers buy that allows yearly changes in the basket of goods that reflect actual consumer purchasing habits.

Pie Chart A circle divided into "pie pieces," where the undivided pie represents the total amount and the pie pieces reflect the percentage of the whole pie that the various components make up.

Policy Change A change in one aspect of government's actions, such as monetary policy or fiscal policy.

Policy Coordination The integration of a country's policies to take account of their global effects.

Positive Economics The study of what is, and how the economy works.

Positive Externality The positive effect of a decision on others not taken into account by the decision maker. Also, when the effects of a decision not taken into account by the decision maker are beneficial to others.

Potential Income The level of income that the economy technically is capable of producing without generating accelerating inflation.

Potential Output Output that would materialize at the target rate of unemployment and the target rate of capacity utilization. Also, the highest amount of output an economy can produce from existing production processes and resources.

Poverty Threshold The income below which a family is considered to live in poverty.

Precautionary Motive Holding money for unexpected expenses and impulse buying.

Precepts Policy rules that conclude that a particular course of action is preferable.

Precommitment Strategy A strategy in which people consciously place limitations on their future actions, thereby limiting their choices.

Present Value A method of translating a flow of future income or savings into its current worth.

Price Ceiling A government-imposed limit on how high a price can be charged. In other words, a government-set price below the market equilibrium price.

Price-Discriminate To charge different prices to different individuals or groups of individuals.

Price Elasticity of Demand The percentage change in quantity demanded divided by the percentage change in price.

Price Elasticity of Supply The percentage change in quantity supplied divided by the percentage change in price.

Price Floor A government-imposed limit on how low a price can be charged. In other words, a government-set price above equilibrium price.

Price Index A number set at 100 in the base year that summarizes what happens to a weighted composite of prices of a selection of goods (often called a market basket of goods) over time.

Price Stabilization Program A program designed to eliminate short-run fluctuations in prices, while allowing prices to follow their long-run trend line.

Price Support Program A program designed to maintain prices at higher levels than the market prices.

Price Taker A firm or individual who takes the price determined by supply and demand as given.

Principle of Diminishing Marginal Utility As you consume more of a good, after some point, the marginal utility received from each additional unit of a good decreases with each additional unit consumed, other things equal.

Principle of Increasing Marginal Opportunity Cost In order to get more of something, one must give up ever increasing quantities of something else.

Principle of Rational Choice Spend your money on those goods that give you the most marginal utility (*MU*) per dollar.

Prisoner's Dilemma A well-known game that demonstrates the difficulty of cooperative behavior in certain circumstances.

Private Good A good that, when consumed by one individual, cannot be consumed by another individual.

Private Property Right Control a private individual or firm has over an asset.

Procyclical Fiscal Policy Changes in government spending and taxes that increase the cyclical fluctuations in the economy instead of reducing them.

Producer Price Index (PPI) An index of prices that measures average change in the selling prices received by domestic producers of goods and services over time.

Producer Surplus Price the producer sells a product for less the cost of producing it.

Production The transformation of factors into goods and services.

Production Function The relationship between the inputs (factors of production) and outputs.
Production Possibility Curve (PPC) A curve measuring the maximum combination of outputs that can be obtained from a given number of inputs.
Production Possibility Table A table that lists a choice's opportunity costs by summarizing what alternative outputs can be achieved with given inputs.
Production Table A table showing the output resulting from various combinations of factors of production or inputs.
Productive Efficiency Achieving as much output as possible from a given amount of inputs or resources.
Productivity Output per unit of input.
Profit What's left over from total revenues after all the appropriate costs have been subtracted. That is, Total revenue − Total cost. Also, a return on entrepreneurial activity and risk taking.
Profit-Maximizing Condition $MR = MC = P$.
Progressive Tax A tax whose rates increase as a person's income increases.
Property Rights The rights given to people to use specified property as they see fit.
Proportional Tax A tax whose rates are constant at all income levels, no matter what a taxpayer's total annual income is.
Public Assistance Means-tested social programs targeted to the poor and providing financial, nutritional, medical, and housing assistance.
Public Choice Economist An economist who integrates an economic analysis of politics with an analysis of the economy.
Public Choice Model A model that focuses on economic incentives as applied to politicians.
Public Good A good that if supplied to one person must be supplied to all and whose consumption by one individual does not prevent its consumption by another individual. That is, a good that is nonexclusive and nonrival.
Purchasing Power Parity (PPP) A method of calculating exchange rates that attempts to value currencies at rates such that each currency will buy an equal basket of goods. Also, a method of comparing income by looking at the domestic purchasing power in different countries.
Purposeful Behavior Behavior reflecting reasoned but not necessarily rational judgment.
Push Policy A regulatory or tax policy to get firms or individuals to use "appropriate" nudges.

Q

Quantitative Easing Nonstandard monetary policy designed to expand credit in the economy.
Quantitative Easing Tools Tools that increase the money supply but that do not affect the Fed funds rate.
Quantity-Adjusting Markets Markets in which firms respond to changes in demand primarily by changing production instead of changing their prices.
Quantity Demanded A specific amount that will be demanded per unit of time at a specific price, other things constant.
Quantity Supplied A specific amount that will be supplied at a specific price, other things constant.
Quantity Theory of Money A theory that the price level varies in response to changes in the quantity of money.
Quasi Rent Any payment to a resource above the amount that the resource would receive in its next-best use.
Quota A quantity limit placed on imports.

R

Rational An adjective used to describe behavior individuals undertake in their own best interest.
Rational Expectations Expectations that the economists' model predicts. Also: Forward-looking expectations that use available information. Also: Expectations that turn out to be correct.
Rational Expectations Model A model in which all decisions are based on the expected equilibrium in the economy.
Real-Business-Cycle Theory A theory that fluctuations in the economy reflect real phenomena—simultaneous shifts in supply and demand, not simply supply responses to demand shifts.
Real Deficit The nominal deficit adjusted for inflation.
Real Exchange Rate The nominal exchange rate adjusted for differential inflation or differential changes in the price level.
Real Gross Domestic Product (real GDP) The market value of final goods and services produced in an economy, stated in the prices of a given year. Also: Nominal GDP adjusted for inflation.
Real Interest Rate Nominal interest rate adjusted for expected inflation.
Real Output The total amount of goods and services produced, adjusted for price-level changes.
Real Wealth The value of the productive capacity of the assets of an economy measured by the goods and services it can produce now and in the future.
Recession A decline in real output that persists for more than two consecutive quarters of a year.
Recessionary Gap The amount by which equilibrium output is below potential output.
Regime Change A change in the entire atmosphere within which the government and the economy interrelate.
Regression Model An empirical model in which one statistically relates one set of variables to another.

Regressive Tax A tax whose rates decrease as income rises.
Regulatory Trade Restrictions Government-imposed procedural rules that limit imports.
Rent The income from a factor of production that is in fixed supply.
Rent Control A price ceiling on rents, set by government.
Rent Seeking The restricting of supply in order to increase the price suppliers receive.
Rent-Seeking Activity Activity designed to transfer surplus from one group to another.
Representative Agent A single individual.
Reserve Ratio The ratio of reserves to total deposits.
Reserve Requirement The percentage the Federal Reserve Bank sets as the minimum amount of reserves a bank must have.
Reserves Currency and deposits a bank keeps on hand or at the Fed or central bank, enough to manage the normal cash inflows and outflows.
Restructuring Changing the underlying economic institutions.
Reverse Engineering The process of a firm buying other firms' products, disassembling them, figuring out what's special about them, and then copying them within the limits of the law.
Ricardian Equivalence Problem The problem that anything the government does to affect the economy will mostly be offset by countervailing actions by private individuals as they optimize over the future.
Ricardian Equivalence Theory The theoretical proposition that deficits do not affect the level of output in the economy because individuals increase their savings to account for expected future tax payments to repay the deficit.
Rule of 72 The number of years it takes for a certain amount to double in value is equal to 72 divided by its annual rate of interest.

S

Say's Law A law that states that supply creates its own demand.
Scarcity The goods available are too few to satisfy individuals' desires.
Screening Question A question structured in a way to reveal strategic information about the person who answers.
Self-Confirming Equilibrium An equilibrium in a model in which people's beliefs become self-fulfilling.
Sequential Game A game where players make decisions one after another, so one player responds to the known decisions of other players.
Shadow Price A price that isn't paid directly, but instead is paid in terms of opportunity cost borne by the demander, and thus determines his or her action indirectly.
Share Distribution of Income The relative division of total income among income groups.
Sherman Antitrust Act A U.S. law designed to regulate the competitive process.
Shift in Demand The graphical representation of the effect of anything other than price on demand.
Shift in Supply The graphical representation of the effect of a change in a factor other than price on supply.
Short-Run Aggregate Supply (*SAS*) Curve A curve that specifies how a shift in the aggregate demand curve affects the price level and real output in the short run, other things constant.
Short-Run Decision A decision in which the firm is constrained in regard to what production decisions it can make.
Short-Run Phillips Curve A downward-sloping curve showing the relationship between inflation and unemployment when expectations of inflation are constant.
Shutdown Point The point below which the firm will be better off if it temporarily shuts down than it will if it stays in business.
Signaling An action taken by an informed party that reveals information to an uninformed party and thereby partially offsets adverse selection.
Simple Money Multiplier The measure of the amount of money ultimately created per dollar deposited in the banking system, when people hold no currency.
Simultaneous Move Game A game where players make their decisions at the same time as other players without knowing what choice the other players have made.
Sin Tax A tax that discourages activities society believes are harmful (sinful).
Slope The change in the value on the vertical axis divided by the change in the value on the horizontal axis.
Social Capital The habitual way of doing things that guides people in how they approach production.
Social Security System A social insurance program that provides financial benefits to the elderly and disabled and to their eligible dependents and/or survivors.
Socialism An economic system based on individuals' goodwill toward others, not on their own self-interest, and in which, in principle, society decides what, how, and for whom to produce.
Socioeconomic Distribution of Income The allocation of income among relevant socioeconomic groupings.
Sole Proprietorship A business that has only one owner.
Sound Finance A view of fiscal policy that the government budget should always be balanced except in wartime.
Sovereign Wealth Funds Investments funds held by governments.
Special Drawing Rights (SDRs) A type of international money.

Specialization The concentration of individuals in certain aspects of production.
Speculative Motive Holding cash to avoid holding financial assets whose prices are falling.
Stagflation The combination of high and accelerating inflation and high unemployment.
Standard Macro Models The models (such as the *AS/AD* and multiplier models and their derivatives) used by most applied macroeconomists.
Status Quo Bias An individual's actions are very much influenced by what the current situation is, even when that reasonably does not seem to be very important to the decision.
Stochastic Events happen with a certain probability that can be specified mathematically.
Stock A financial asset that conveys ownership rights in a corporation. Also, certificate of ownership in a company.
Strategic Bargaining Demanding a larger share of the gains from trade than you can reasonably expect.
Strategic Decision Making Taking explicit account of a rival's expected response to a decision you are making.
Strategic Trade Policy Threatening to implement tariffs to bring about a reduction in tariffs or some other concession from the other country.
Structural Deficit The part of a budget deficit that would exist even if the economy were at its potential level of income.
Structural Unemployment Unemployment caused by the institutional structure of an economy or by economic restructuring making some skills obsolete.
Substitute A good that can be used in place of another good.
Substitution Effect The reduction in quantity demanded because relative price has risen.
Sunk Cost Cost that has already been incurred and cannot be recovered.
Supplemental Security Income (SSI) A federal program that pays benefits, based on need, to the elderly, blind, and disabled.
Supply A schedule of quantities a seller is willing to sell per unit of time at various prices, other things constant.
Supply Curve A graphical representation of the relationship between price and quantity supplied.
Surplus An excess of revenues over payments.
Systemic Risks The risks of a problem happening to all parts of the economy simultaneously.

T

Takeover The purchase of one firm by a shell firm that then takes direct control of all the purchased firm's operations.
Target Rate of Unemployment The lowest sustainable rate of unemployment that policy makers believe is achievable given existing demographics and the economy's institutional structure.
Tariff An excise tax on an imported (internationally traded) good.
Tax Incentive Program A program using a tax to create incentives for individuals to structure their activities in a way that is consistent with the desired ends.
Taylor Rule The rule is: Set the Fed funds rate at 2 percent plus current inflation if the economy is at desired output and desired inflation. If the inflation rate is higher than desired, increase the Fed funds rate by 0.5 times the difference between desired and actual inflation. Similarly, if output is higher than desired, increase the Fed funds rate by 0.5 times the percentage deviation.
Team Spirit The feelings of friendship and being part of a team that bring out people's best efforts.
Technical Efficiency A situation in which as few inputs as possible are used to produce a given output.
Technological Agglomeration The geographic concentration of technological advances caused by the tendency of innovations to lead to further innovations in that industry and other industries.
Technological Change An increase in the range of production techniques that leads to more efficient ways of producing goods as well as the production of new and better goods.
Technological Development The discovery of new or improved products or methods of production.
Technological Lock-In The prior use of a technology makes the adoption of subsequent technologies difficult.
Technology The way we make goods and supply services.
Theorems Propositions that are logically true based on the assumptions in a model.
Third-Party-Payer Market A market in which the person who receives the good differs from the person paying for the good.
Time-Inconsistency/Credibility Problem The problem that the best government policy from today's point of view can turn out to be a policy the government wants to change in the future, and that rational individuals can anticipate this.
Total Cost The explicit payments to the factors of production plus the opportunity cost of the factors provided by the owners of the firm.
Total Revenue The amount a firm receives for selling its product or service plus any increase in the value of the assets owned by the firm.
Total Utility The total satisfaction one gets from consuming a product.
Trade Adjustment Assistance Programs Programs designed to compensate losers for reductions in trade restrictions.

Traditional Economists Economists who study the logical implications of rationality and self-interest in relatively simple algebraic or graphical models such as the supply and demand model.
Transactions Motive The need to hold money for spending.
Transfer Payments Payments to individuals by government that do not involve production by those individuals.
Transferable Comparative Advantage Comparative advantage based on factors that can change relatively easily.

U

Ultimatum Game A game in which the person only gets the money if the other person accepts the offer. If the second person does not accept, they both get nothing.
Unemployment Compensation Short-term financial assistance, regardless of need, to eligible individuals who are temporarily out of work.
Unemployment Rate The percentage of people in the economy who are willing and able to work but who are not working.
Unexpected Inflation Inflation that surprises people.
Union Shop A firm in which all workers must join the union.
Unit Elastic The percentage change in quantity is equal to the percentage change in price ($E = 1$).
Utility The pleasure or satisfaction that one expects to get from consuming a good or service.
Utility-Maximizing Rule Utility is maximized when the ratios of the marginal utility to price of two goods are equal.

V

Value Added The increase in value that a firm contributes to a product or service.
Value of Marginal Product (VMP) An additional worker's marginal physical product multiplied by the price at which the firm could sell that additional product.
Variable Costs Costs that change as output changes.
Velocity of Money The number of times per year, on average, a dollar goes around to generate a dollar's worth of income.
Vertical Merger A combination of two companies that are involved in different phases of producing a product.
Vickrey Auction A sealed-bid auction where the highest bidder wins but pays the price bid by the next-highest bidder.

W

Wealth The value of the things individuals own less the value of what they owe.
Wealth Accounts A balance sheet of an economy's stock of assets and liabilities.
Welfare Loss Triangle A geometric representation of the welfare cost in terms of misallocated resources caused by a deviation from a supply/demand equilibrium.
World Trade Organization (WTO) An organization committed to getting countries to agree not to impose new tariffs or other trade restrictions except under certain limited conditions. See also *General Agreement on Tariffs and Trade*.

X

X-inefficiency The underperformance of a firm that has a monopoly position. The firm operates far less efficiently than it could technically.

Y

Yield Curve A curve that shows the relationship between interest rates and bonds' time to maturity.

Z

Zoning Laws Laws that set limits on the use of one's property.

A

Ads (noun) Short for "advertisements."
Ain't (verb) An ungrammatical form of "isn't," sometimes used to emphasize a point although the speaker knows that "isn't" is the correct form.
All the Rage (descriptive phrase) Extremely popular, but the popularity is likely to be transitory.
American League (name of an organization) An association of baseball teams. The United States has two baseball associations—the other is the National League.
Andy Warhol (proper name) American artist who flourished in the period 1960–1980. He was immensely popular and successful with art critics and the intelligentsia, but, above all, he gained worldwide recognition in the same way and of the same quality as movie stars and sports athletes do. His renown has continued even after his death.
Armada (proper noun) Historic term for the Spanish navy. Now obsolete.
Automatic Pilot (noun) To be on automatic pilot is to be acting without thinking.

B

Baby Boom (noun) Any period when more than the statistically predicted number of babies are born. Originally referred to a specific group: those born in the years 1945–1964.
Baby Boomers (descriptive phrase) Americans born in the years 1945 through 1964. An enormous and influential group of people whose large number is attributed to the "boom" in babies that occurred when military personnel, many of whom had been away from home for four or five years, were discharged from military service after the end of World War II.
Back Burner (complex noun) To put something on the back burner means to assign the object or thought to a subsidiary or unimportant role. Comes from cooking stoves fueled by wood, where the back burners received less heat and therefore were warm but not hot and handy for keeping something warm while you did something else.
Back to the Drawing Board (descriptive phrase) To start all over again after having your plan or project turn out to be useless.
Backfire (verb) To injure a person or entity who intended to inflict injury.
Bailed Out (descriptive phrase) To be rescued. It has other colloquial meanings as well, but they do not appear in this book.
Bailout (noun) The action of having been bailed out. (See "Bailed Out")
Bait and Switch (compound noun; can also be two verbs) Something that has been advertised as a quality item at a bargain price, but when you go to the store, there are none available, but there are plenty of items that are "nearly the same" except they are at much higher price.
Balloon (verb) To expand enormously and suddenly.
Bases on Balls (descriptive phrase) A strategy in the game of baseball. If a pitcher throws a long enough succession of defective throws, the batter gets to run—or walk—to the first base without having hit any balls.
Bean (noun) A person's head; also a person's mind or intellectual ability. ("Bean" is American slang for "head.")
Beanball (noun) A ball thrown with the intention of hitting the opponent on the head.
Bear Market (noun) Stock market dominated by people who are not buying (i.e., are hibernating). Opposite of a bull market, where people are charging ahead vigorously to buy.
Bedlam (noun) Chaotic and apparently disorganized activity. Today the word is not capitalized. A few hundred years ago in England, the noun meant the Hospital of St. Mary's of Bethlehem, an insane asylum. The hospital was not in Bethlehem; it was in London. "Bedlam" was the way "Bethlehem" was pronounced by the English.
Beluga Caviar (noun) The best, most expensive, caviar.
Benchmark (noun) A point of reference from which measurement of any sort may be made.
Better Mousetrap (noun) Comes from the proverb, "Invent a better mousetrap and the world will beat a path to your door."
Bidding (or Bid) (verb sometimes used as a noun) Has two different meanings. (1) Making an offer, or a series of offers, to compete with others who are making offers. Also the offer itself. (2) Ordering or asking a person to take a specified action.
Big Bucks (noun) Really, really large sum of money.
Big Mac (proper noun) Brand name of a kind of hamburger sold at McDonald's restaurants.
Bigwig (noun) An important person. Comes from fashion at various times and places in history, for important people, such as judges, who wear an outrageously big wig. You can see this today on British TV where the judges in British courtrooms wear very big wigs.
Bind (noun) To "be in a bind" means to be in a situation where one is forced to make a difficult decision one does not want to make—where any decision seems as if it would be wrong, or at least undesirable, where all choices appear bad, but a decision is necessary.
Blow It (verb; past tense: blew it) To do a poor job, to miss an opportunity, to perform unsatisfactorily.

Blow Off (verb) To treat as inconsequential; to deal superficially with something.
Blowout (noun) Serious release of pent-up emotions or of control over one's actions.
Boggled (adjective) All mixed up; confused almost to the point of hopelessness.
Booming (adjective) Being extraordinarily and quickly successful.
Boost (verb and noun) To give a sudden impetus, or boost, to something or someone.
Boston Red Sox (compound noun) A U.S. baseball team.
Botched Up (adjective) Operated badly; spoiled.
Bottleneck (noun) Situation in which no action can be taken because a large number of people or actions are confronted by a very small opening or opportunity.
Brainteaser (noun) Question or puzzle that intrigues the brain, thus "teasing" it to answer the question or solve the puzzle.
Brief (noun) Formal written document prepared by a lawyer supporting a legal argument or case. More generally, any careful argument or strongly held opinion, written or oral.
Bring Home (verb) To emphasize or convince.
Broke (adjective) (1) To "go broke" or to "be broke" is to become insolvent, to lose all one's money and assets. (2) Usually not as bad as to have gone broke—just to be (hopefully) temporarily out of money or short of funds.
Bronco Bull A bull ridden in a rodeo. The rider's objective is to stay on the bull until he wrestles it to the ground or is thrown off. (See also "Rodeo.")
Buck Rogers (proper name) American comic strip character popular in the first three-quarters of the 20th century.
Bucks (noun) American slang for "dollars."
Buffalo (adjective, as used in this book) "Buffalo chicken wings" are a variety of tempting food developed in, and hence associated with, the city of Buffalo. (Not all chicken wings are Buffalo chicken wings.)
Bus Person (noun) Has no relation to transportation. It's a term for the person who clears the tables in a restaurant.
Busch Stadium (name of a stadium) Anheuser-Busch is a firm that produces widely-consumed brands of beer. Its home offices are in St. Louis. It bought naming rights to Busch Stadium in St. Louis, MO.
Bust (noun) (as in "housing bust") A sudden decline in the price of an asset. (Opposite of boom.)

C

Cachet (noun) Prestige, distinction, high quality. This word is borrowed from French and is pronounced "ca-SHAY."
Call (verb) In sports refereeing, one meaning of "to call" is for the referee to announce his or her decision on a specific point.
Calvin Coolidge (proper name) President of the United States 1923–1928.
Carriage Maker (noun) Person or firm that makes carriages, a type of horse-drawn conveyance almost never seen any more except in films. Members of the British royal family ride in carriages on important ceremonial occasions, such as weddings.
Catch (noun) An event that stops or impedes an action. (Note: "Catch" can be either a noun or a verb. Its many definitions take up 5 or 6 column inches in a dictionary.) A proviso; an unexpected complication.
Caveat (noun) In English, this noun means "caution" or "warning." It comes from Latin, where it is a whole little sentence: "Let him beware."
Cellophane (noun) A transparent wrapping material. It differs from plastic wrap in that it is made of cellulose, not plastic.
Center Stage (noun) A dominant position.
Central Park West (proper noun) A fashionable and expensive street in New York City.
CEO (noun) Abbreviation of "chief executive officer."
Charade (noun) A pretense, usually designed to convince someone that you are doing something that you are definitely not doing.
Charleston (noun) A social dance requiring two people. It was popular in the 1920s and 1930s.
Chit (noun) Type of IOU (see IOU) or coupon with a designated value that can be turned in toward the purchase or acquisition of some item.
Chump Change (noun) Insignificant amount of money earned by or paid to a person who is not alert enough to realize that more money could rather easily be earned.
Clear-cut (adjective) Precisely defined.
Clip Coupons (verb) To cut coupons out of newspapers and magazines. The coupons give you a discount on the price of the item when you present the item and the coupon at the cashier's counter in a store. It can also mean collecting interest on bonds. (In earlier times, bonds had coupons attached. The holders clipped them and sent them in to the bond issuer to collect the bond's interest.)
Clout (noun) Influence or power.
Coffer (noun) A box or trunk used to hold valuable items; hence, "coffers" has come to mean a vault or other safe storage place to hold money or other valuable items.
Coin Flip (noun) The decision made by flipping, or tossing, a coin after agreeing, with others, or with oneself, to choose one of two alternatives based on which side of the coin is facing up after the flip. (Also see "flipside.")
Coined (verb) Invented or originated.
Coldhearted (adjective) Without any sympathy; aloof; inhuman.
Come Through (verb) Satisfy someone's demands or expectations.

Come Up Short (descriptive phrase) To be deficient.
Cookie Monster (proper noun) Character in the television show *Sesame Street*. (Also see "Elmo.")
Co-opted (adjective) Overwhelmed.
Cornrows (noun) Hair style in which hair is braided in shallow, narrow rows over the entire head.
Corvette (noun) A type of expensive sports car.
Costco (proper noun) Name of a chain of big stores selling groceries and other items at a sharp discount. Usually the items are packaged in large quantities—for example, 50-pound bags of flour.
Couch (verb) To construct and present an argument.
Crack (noun) A strong form of cocaine.
Cry over Spilt Milk (verb) To indulge in useless complaint or regret. Note that there is a departure from standard English spelling in this phrase, which uses the spelling "spilt" instead of "spilled." Either is correct, but "spilt" is seldom used. (Another such variation is the rare "spelt" for usual "spelled.")
Cut and Dried (descriptive phrase) Simple, obvious, and settled.

D

Deadbeat (noun) Lazy person who has no ambition, no money, and no prospects.
Deadweight (noun) Literally, the unrelieved weight of any inert mass (think of carrying a sack of bricks); hence, any oppressive burden.
Decent (adjective) One of its specialized meanings is "of high quality."
Doodle (noun and verb) Idle scribbles, usually nonrepresentational and usually made while actively thinking about something else, such as during a phone conversation or sitting in a class.
Doritos (proper noun) Brand name of a type of snack in chip form. The label lists its principal ingredient as corn, but it contains at least 30 other ingredients, many of them chemical.
Down Pat (descriptive phrase) To have something down pat is to know it precisely, accurately, and without needing to think about it.
Draw a Walk (descriptive phrase) In the game of baseball, the ability to cause the pitcher to throw a series of defective pitches to the batter, thus allowing the batter to advance to first base without having actually hit a ball.
Drop in the Bucket (noun) Insignificant quantity compared to the total amount available.
Drug Lunch (noun) The prescription drug company's salesman takes members of the medical staff to lunch and pays for their meals. This is one way to be sure that the medical facility prescribes that company's drug.
Dyed-in-the-Wool (adjective) Irretrievably convinced of the value of a particular course of action or of the truth of an opinion. Literally, wool that is dyed after it is shorn from the sheep but before it is spun into thread.

E

Elmo (proper noun) Character in the television show *Sesame Street*. (Also see "Cookie Monster.")
'Em (pronoun) Careless way of pronouncing "them." Written out, it reproduces the sound the speaker is making.
Energizer Bunny (noun) Character in a television commercial for Energizer batteries. Just as the batteries are alleged to do, the Energizer bunny keeps going and going.
Esperanto (noun) An artificial language invented in the 1880s, intended to be "universal." It is based on words from the principal European languages, and the theory was that all speakers of these European languages would effortlessly understand Esperanto. It never had a big following and today is almost unknown.
Establishment (noun and adjective) Noun: the prevailing theory or practice. Adjective: something that is used by people whose views prevail over other people's views.
Eureka Moment (noun) "Eureka" is Greek for "I have found it!" Means having a sudden insight. Aristophanes is said to have cried out "Eureka," jumped out of his bath, and run down the street crying "Eureka!" when it struck him suddenly that the weight of water displaced by a submerged body is the same as the weight of the body being displaced.

F

Fake (verb) To fake is to pretend or deceive; to try to make people believe that you know what you're doing or talking about when you don't know or aren't sure.
Fire (verb) To discharge an employee permanently. It's different from "laying off" an employee, an action taken when a temporary situation makes the employee superfluous, but the employer expects to take the employee back when the temporary situation is over.
Fit to a T (verb) Suit perfectly.
Fix (verb) To prepare, as in "fixing a meal." This is only one of the multiplicity of meanings of this verb.
Fleeting (adverb) This word's usage is elegant and correct, but rare. It means transitory or short-lived.
Flipside (noun) The other side of a two-sided object or of a two-sided argument or situation. Origin: In the days before tape and DVD, we used to have large disks, made of vinyl or other material, upon which music was recorded, using both sides of the disk.
Flop (noun) A dismal failure.
Follow Suit (verb) To do the same thing you see others do. Comes from card games where if a card of a certain suit

is played, the other players must play a card of that suit, if they have one.
Follow the Flag (verb) To be committed to doing business only with firms that produce in your own country or in your "colonies"—that is, territories that belong to your country.
Follow the Leader (noun) Name of a children's game. Metaphorically, it means to do what others are doing, usually without giving it much thought.
Forest for the Trees (descriptive phrase) To be so focused on details that you don't see the overall situation.
Form Follows Function (description) A phrase borrowed from architecture, where it means that the architect determines what a building is to be used for, and then designs the building to meet the demands of that use, or function.
Free Lunch (descriptive phrase) Something you get without paying for it in any way. Usually applied negatively: There is no "free lunch."
Front (noun and verb) Activity undertaken to divert attention from what it is.
Funky (adjective) Eccentric in style or manner.

G

Gadget (noun) Generic term for any small, often novel, mechanical or electronic device or contrivance, usually designed for a specific purpose. For instance, the small wheel with serrated rim and an attached handle used to divide a pizza pie into slices is a gadget.
Gas-Guzzling (adjective) Describes motor vehicles that use a non-economical or excessive amount of gasoline.
Gee (expletive) Emphatic expression signaling surprise or enthusiasm.
Get Across (verb) To convince.
Get You Down (descriptive phrase) Make you depressed about something or make you dismiss something altogether. (Do not confuse with "get it down," which means to understand fully.)
G.I. Joe (noun) A toy in the form of a boy (as "Barbie" is a girl). The original meaning was "government issue"—i.e., an item such as a uniform issued by the U.S. government to a member of the U.S. armed forces, and, by extension, the person to whom the item was issued.
Giveaways (noun) Something, usually valuable, that you confer without receiving anything tangible in return. In this book, it refers to Congress enacting tax cuts that are insignificant to all but people who are already rich.
Glitch (noun) Trivial difficulty.
GM (noun) The General Motors automobile company.
Go-between (noun) A person or firm that carries out the contact between two people or firms who are not able, or do not wish, to communicate directly with each other.
Go-Cart (noun) A small engine-powered vehicle that is used for racing and recreation.
Gold Mine (noun) Metaphorically, any activity that results in making you a lot of money.
Goldilocks (fictional character) In a children's story, Goldilocks is a beautiful little girl with blonde curls who emerges unharmed from an encounter with three bears because she is so good and charming.
Good and Ready (descriptive phrase) Really, really ready.
Good Cop/Bad Cop (noun) Alternating mood shifts. It comes from the alleged practice of having two police officers interview a suspect—one officer is kind and coaxing while the other is mean and nasty. This is supposed to make the suspect feel that the nice cop is a safe person to confide in.
Good Offices (descriptive phrase) An expression common in 18th-century England, meaning "services."
Gooey (adjective) Sticky or slimy.
Goofed (verb) Past tense of the verb *goof*, meaning to make a careless mistake.
GOP This acronym stands for "Grand Old Party." The GOP is the Republican political party.
Got It Made (descriptive phrase) Succeeded.
Greek (noun) See "Like Greek."
Grind (noun) Slang for necessary intense effort that may be painful but will likely benefit your understanding.
Groucho Marx (proper name) A famous U.S. comedian (1885–1977).
Gung-ho (adjective) Full of energy and eager to take action.
Guns and Butter (descriptive phrase) Metaphor describing the dilemma whether to devote resources to war or to peace.
Guzzle, Guzzler (verb and noun) Verb: to consume something greedily, wastefully, and rapidly. Noun: an object (or a person) that guzzles.

H

Haggling (noun) Bargaining, usually in a petty and confrontational manner.
Half Out of Their Mind (descriptive phrase) Very upset and not in a reasonable frame of mind.(This is not as bad as "Completely out of their mind.")
Handout (noun) Unearned offering (as distinct from a gift); charity.
Handy (adjective) Convenient.
Hangover (noun) The queasy feeling, usually accompanied by a headache, that can afflict a person who has gotten drunk. The feeling can last for hours after the person is no longer actually drunk.

Hard Liquor (noun) Alcoholic beverages with a high content of pure alcohol. Beer and wine are not "hard liquor," but most other alcoholic drinks are.
Hard Up (adjective) Seriously worried.
Hassle (noun and verb) Noun: unreasonable obstacle. Verb: to place unreasonable obstacles or arguments in the way of someone.
Hawking (adjective) Selling aggressively and widely.
Heat (noun) Anger, blame, outrage, and pressure to change.
Hefty (adjective) Large; substantial.
Hero Sandwich (noun) A type of very large sandwich.
High Horse, Getting on Your (descriptive phrase) Adopting a superior attitude; looking down (from your high horse) on other people's opinions or actions.
Highfalutin (adjective) American slang term meaning pretentious, self-important, supercilious.
Hitting the Mark (expression) Achieving your purpose.
Hog Bellies (noun) Commercial term for the part of a pig that becomes bacon and pork chops. (Also called *pork bellies*.)
Holds Its Own (descriptive phrase) Refuses to give up, even in the face of adversity or opposition.
Home Free (descriptive phrase) Safe and successful.
Hook (noun) Strategy to engage your attention.
Hot Air (descriptive phrase) An empty promise. Also, bragging.
Hot Dog (noun) A type of sausage.
Hot Potatoes (noun) Slang term for anything that everyone wants to avoid confronting.
How Come (expression) Why? That is, "How has it come about that . . . ?"

I

"In" (preposition sometimes used as an adjective) Placed within quotation marks to show it is used with a special meaning. Here it is used as an adjective, to indicate "fashionable or popular, usually just for a short period." To be "in" means to be associated with highly desirable people (the "in" people).
Incidentals (noun) Blanket term covering the world of small items a person uses on a daily basis as the need happens to arise—that is, needed per incident occurring. Examples are aspirin, combs, and picture postcards.
IOU (noun) A nickname applied to a formal acknowledgment of a debt, such as a U.S. Treasury bond. Also an informal but written acknowledgment of a debt. Pronounce the letters and you will hear "I owe you."
iPod (proper name) A compact digital music player designed by Apple Computer.
Iron Curtain (noun) Imaginary but daunting line between Western Europe and adjacent communist countries. After the political abandonment of Communism in these countries, the Curtain no longer exists.
It'll (contraction) "It will."
Ivory Tower (adjective/noun) Aloofness from life. Comes from a fairy tale about a princess who lived in an ivory tower where she had everything she needed and absolutely nothing to disturb her.

J

Jarring (adjective) Extremely surprising and unexpected occurrence, usually slightly unpleasant.
Jet Blue (proper name) A low-cost U.S. airline, which is actively entering new markets.
Jolt (noun) A sudden blow.
Jumpstart (verb and noun) Verb: to give a sudden, sharp impetus to an object or person in order to elicit an immediate response. Noun: the action that elicits an immediate response. A small portable cable device, called "a jumper,"can be carried in your car for emergency use if a battery goes dead.
Junk Food (noun) Food that tastes good but has little nutritional value and lots of calories. It is sometimes cheap, sometimes expensive, and it's quick and easy to buy and eat.
Just Say No (admonition) Flatly refuse. This phrase became common in the 1980s after Nancy Reagan, the wife of the then-president of the United States, popularized it in a campaign against the use of addictive drugs.

K

Ketchup (noun) Spicy, thick tomato sauce used on, among other foods, hot dogs.
Kick In (verb) To activate; to start or begin. (Can also mean "to contribute to.")
Kickback (noun) A firm's giving part of the price it has received for its product or service back to the firm or individual who authorized the purchase of that product or service. In effect, it is a type of bribe or blackmail demanded or expected by a purchaser's agent.
Klutz (noun) An awkward, incompetent person.
Knockoff (noun) A cheap imitation.

L

Laetrile (noun) Substance derived from peach pits, thought by some people to be a cure for cancer.
Lag Time (noun) The time between when you perform an action and the time you see results from having performed the action.
Laid Back (adjective) Casual; calm; free from worry and feelings of pressure.

Late Victorian (adjective or noun) Embodying some concept typical of the late period of Queen Victoria. Also, a person from that period or who acts like someone from that period. (Queen Victoria was queen of England from 1837 to 1901.)
Lay Off (verb) To discharge a worker temporarily.
Leads (noun) Persons or institutions that you think will be interested in whatever you have to sell. Also, the information you have that makes you think someone or something is worth pursuing.
Left the Nest (descriptive phrase) To have left one's parental home, usually because one has grown up and become self-sufficient.
Lemon (noun) Slang term for an object that is irreparably faulty. It's usually something for which you have paid a substantial amount of money and by whose performance you feel cheated.
Levi's (noun) Popular brand of jeans.
Like Greek (descriptive phrase) Incomprehensible (because, in the United States, classical Greek is considered to be a language that almost no one learns).
Limbo (noun) To be "in limbo" is to be in a place or situation from which there is no escape.
Lion's Share (noun) By far the best part of a bargain.
Lobby (verb and noun) Verb: to attempt by organized effort to influence legislation. Noun: an organized group formed to influence legislation. A lobbyist is a member of a lobby.
Lord Tennyson (proper name) Alfred Tennyson, 19th-century English poet who wrote a poem, *Ulysses*, about the nobility of effort ("To strive, to seek, to find and not to yield").
Losing Ground (verb) Regressing.
Lousy (adjective) Incompetent or distasteful.

M

Make It (verb) To succeed in doing something; for instance, "make it to the bank" means to get to the bank before it closes.
Mall (noun) Short for "shopping mall." A variety of stores grouped on one piece of land, with ample parking for all the mall's shoppers and often with many amenities such as covered walkways, playgrounds for children, fountains, and so on.
MasterCard (proper noun) Brand name of a widely issued credit card.
Mazuma (noun) U.S. slang term for money. It was used in the first half of the 20th century but is now rare, to say the least.
MBA (noun) An academic degree: master of business administration.
Medicaid (proper noun) Health insurance program for low-income people. It is administered jointly by the U.S. government and the individual states.
Medicare (proper noun) U.S. government health insurance program for people who are disabled or age 65 and over. There is no means test.
Messed Up (adjective) Damaged or badly managed.
Mind Your Own Business (admonition) Don't meddle in other people's affairs; don't ask intrusive questions.
Mind Your Ps and Qs (expression) Pay close attention to distinctions. It comes from the similarity of the small printed letters "p" and "q" where the only visual distinction is the location of the downstroke. Also, the letters are right next to each other in our alphabet.
Mob (noun) Organized criminal activity. Also, the group to which organized criminals belong.
Moot (adjective) Irrelevant because the issue in question has already been decided.
Mother of Necessity A witty remark that reverses the terms of a famous saying, "Necessity is the mother of invention."
Mousetrap (noun) Producing a better mousetrap is part of the saying, "Make a better mousetrap and the world will beat a path to your door." Metaphorically, producing a better mousetrap stands for doing anything better than it has previously been done.

N

NA (abbreviation) "Not available."
NASDAQ (also sometimes spelled "Nasdaq") (noun) Stock market operated by the National Association of Securities Dealers. The "AQ" stands for "Automated Quotations."
NATO (noun) North American Treaty Organization. Western alliance for joint economic and military cooperation. It includes the United States, Canada, and several European nations.
National League (name of an organization) An association of U.S. baseball teams. The United States has two baseball associations—the other is the American League.
Nature of the Beast (descriptive phrase) Character of whatever you are describing (need not have anything to do with a "beast").
Nerd (noun) An insignificant and uninteresting person or a person so absorbed in a subject that he or she thinks of nothing else and is therefore boring.
Nicholas Apert (proper name) Nineteenth-century French experimenter who discovered how to preserve food by canning or bottling it.
Nickel and Dimed (adjective) Worried over every expenditure, even of tiny sums like nickels and dimes; also having the last tiny sum of money extracted.

Nirvana (noun) This word is adopted from Buddhism. Its religious meaning is complicated, but it is used colloquially to mean salvation, paradise, harmony, perfection.
No Way (exclamation) Emphatic expression denoting refusal, denial, or extreme disapproval.
Nobel Prize (adjective/noun) A prestigious money prize awarded annually from a fund set up in 1901 by the will of Alfred Nobel, the inventor of dynamite. The prizes are in several categories: physics, chemistry, physiology and medicine, literature, and economics. Nobel also established the Nobel Peace Prize, distinguished by the word, "peace."
Not to Worry (admonition; also, when hyphenated, used as an adjective) Don't worry; or it's nothing to worry about.
Nudge (noun and verb) Noun: a little push. Verb: to give a little push.

O

Oakland Athletics (adjective/noun) A U.S. major league baseball team.
Off the Books (descriptive phrase) Not officially recorded (and hence it's an untaxed transaction).
Off-the-Cuff (adjective) A quick, unthinking answer for which the speaker has no valid authority (comes from the alleged practice of writing an abbreviated answer on the cuff of your shirt, to be glanced at during an examination).
Oliver Wendell Holmes (proper name) A justice of the U.S. Supreme Court, famous for his wit, his wisdom, his literary ability, his advocacy of civil rights, and his long life (1841–1935).
On Her (His) Own (descriptive phrase) By herself (himself); without any help.
On Their Toes (descriptive phrase) Alert; ready for any eventuality.
Op-Ed (adjective) Describes an article that appears on the "op-ed" page of a newspaper, which is **OP**posite the **ED**itorial page.

P

Pain, Real (noun) This real pain is not a real pain; rather, it is something—anything—that gives you a lot of trouble and that you dislike intensely. For instance, some people think balancing a checkbook is a real pain.
Pandora's Box (complex noun) An allusion to a Greek myth. To release a cloud of troubles. Pandora, a figure in Greek mythology, was given a box but told not to open it. She could not resist, and she opened it. It was filled with all the problems of the universe, which escaped to plague us forever.
Park Avenue (noun) An expensive and fashionable street in New York City.
Part and Parcel (noun) An integral element of a concept, action, or item.
Pass the Buck (descriptive phrase) Evade responsibility by forcing someone else to make the relevant decision.
Payola (noun) A slang term, meaning a bribe, either of money or a favor, given to someone to do something that is to your advantage—something that the person would not do for you unless he or she received a payola.
Peanuts (noun) Slang for a small amount, usually money but sometimes anything with a small value.
Pecking Order (noun) Hierarchy.
Peer Pressure (descriptive phrase) Push to do what everyone else in your particular group is doing.
Penny-Pincher (noun) Person who is unusually careful with money, sometimes to the point of being stingy.
Perks (noun) Short for "perquisites."
Philharmonic (adjective) A philharmonic orchestra is an orchestra that specializes in classical music. Sometimes used as a noun, as in "I heard the Philharmonic."
Phoenix from the Ashes (descriptive phrase) Metaphor for coming to life after having been thought to be dead. In ancient Greek mythology, the phoenix was a bird said to (really) rise from the ashes after a fire. (Phoenix, Arizona, was so named because of the hot climate that prevails there.)
Pick Up Steam (verb) As steam pressure increases, the speed of a steam engine increases. When this happens, we say the engine has "picked up steam."
Pickle (noun) Dilemma.
Picky (adjective) Indulging in fine distinctions when making a decision.
Pie (noun) Metaphor for the total amount of a specific item that exists.
Piece of Cake (descriptive phrase) Simple; easy to achieve without much effort or thought.
Piecemeal (adverb) To do something bit by bit instead of all at once.
Pinch (noun, used as part of a phrase) "In a pinch" means in a tough spot; in an emergency; in a situation calling for improvisation.
Pitcher (noun) In the game of baseball, the player who throws—or "pitches"—the ball to the player who is waiting to strike it.
Pitt, (Sir) William (historical figure) Chief financial officer and prime minister of Britain in the 1780s. He is usually designated "the younger" to distinguish him from his father, who was also a high British government official.
Poof! (exclamation) Spoken emphatically to mean that something has suddenly and inexplicably disappeared.
Poorhouse (noun) Public institution where impoverished individuals were housed. These institutions were purposely dreary and unpleasant. They no longer officially exist, but they have a modern manifestation: shelters for the homeless.

Pop-Tart (noun) Brand name of a type of junk food. It's a sweet filling enclosed in pastry that you pop into the toaster and when the pastry is hot, it pops out of the toaster.
Populist (noun and adjective) Noun: a member of a political party that purports to represent the rank and file of the people. Adjective: a political party, a group, or an individual that purports to represent rank-and-file opinion.
Pound (noun) Unit of British currency.
Powers That Be (expression) People or institutions that have power such that there is nothing one can do to influence those people or institutions—or at least nothing easy.
Practice Makes Perfect (expression) The grammar of this phrase is illogical but the meaning is clear.
Premium Tires All Round (descriptive phrase) Premium tires are tires of superior quality. When all the tires on your vehicle are premium tires, you have them "all round."
Presto! (exclamation) Immediately.
Proxy (noun) A stockholder can give a "proxy" to the firm. It is an authorization that permits the firm's officials to vote for the proposition that the stockholder directs them to vote for. By extension, proxy means a substitute.
Ps and Qs See under *Mind*.
Pub (noun) Short for "public house," a commercial establishment where alcoholic drinks are served, usually with refreshments and occasionally with light meals.

Q

Quack (noun) An imposter; an ignorant practitioner.
Queen Elizabeth (proper noun) Here the author means Queen Elizabeth the first (reigned in England from 1558 to 1603).
Quip (noun and verb) Noun: a jocular remark. Verb: to make a jocular remark.
Quote (noun) Seller's statement of what he or she will charge for a good or service.

R

R&D (noun) Research and development.
Rainy Day (noun) Period when you (hopefully) temporarily have an income shortage.
Rainy Day Fund (descriptive phrase) Money set aside when you are doing well financially—that is, in a financially sunny period—to use in case you have a period when you are doing less well financially—that is, when you run into a financially rainy period.
Raise Your Eyebrows (verb) To express surprise, usually by a facial expression rather than vocally.
Red Flag (noun) A red flag warns you to be very alert to a danger or perceived danger. (Ships in port that are loading fuel or ammunition raise a red flag to signal danger.)
Red-Handed (adjective) Indisputably guilty. Comes from being found at a murder or injury scene with the blood of the victim on one's hands.
Red-Lined (adjective) On a motor vehicle's tachometer, a red line that warns at what speed an engine's capacity is being strained.
Relief (noun) This term was an informal one, applied specifically to the financial assistance people in the United States received from the government during the Great Depression (1929 until about 1941). It arose because of a government program administered by the Works Progress Administration (WPA), formed to create jobs, and hence to employ people who otherwise would have been unemployed.
Renege (verb) Go back on; fail to keep an agreement. Also, in a card game, to fail to play the suit you have contracted to play.
Resort (noun) An expensive hotel with extensive grounds, swimming pools, and many attractive activities.
Right On! (exclamation) Expression of vigorous, often revolutionary, approval and encouragement.
Ring Up (verb) Before the introduction of computer-type machines that record each payment a retail customer makes—say at the supermarket or a restaurant—a "cash register" was used. When you pressed the keys representing the amount offered by the customer, a drawer sprang open and a bell rang.
Ritzy (adjective) Very expensive, fashionable, and ostentatious. Comes from the entrepreneur Caesar Ritz, a Swiss developer of expensive hotels, active in the first quarter of the 20th century. Upscale, fancy. Has overtones of ostentation.
Robin Hood (proper name) Semifictional English adventurer of the 12th or 13th century. He "stole from the rich and gave to the poor."
Rock Bottom (noun) To reach the absolute limit of one's endurance or resources.
Rodeo (noun) Entertainment where a person rides a bull that is wildly trying to throw the rider off. Horses are often exhibited similarly.
Rolodex File (noun) Manual—as opposed to electronic—device for organizing names, addresses, phone numbers, and e-numbers.
Rough-and-Ready (expression) Quick decision made because it's easy. It is a type of compromise or improvisation.
Rube Goldberg (proper name) A famous cartoonist whose cartoons depicted complicated methods of doing simple things.
Rule of Thumb (complex noun) Judgment based on practical experience rather than on scientific knowledge. Comes from habit of using the space between the tip to the first joint of your thumb as being about an inch—good enough for the task at hand but not precise.

S

Sacred Cow (noun) An institution or practice that social and/or political forces dictate is absolutely protected from change of any kind.
Saks (proper name) A midsize department store that sells expensive, fashionable items. There are very few stores in the Saks chain, and Saks stores are considered exclusive.
Savvy (adjective) Slang term meaning very knowledgeable. Adaptation of the French verb *savoir*, meaning "to know."
Scab (noun) Person who takes a job, or continues in a job, even though workers at that firm are on strike.
Scalp (verb) To buy a ticket legally and then resell it at a very high profit to an individual who wants it very badly but can't buy it legally because all the tickets have already been sold to others.
Scraps (noun) Little pieces of leftover food. Also, little pieces of anything that is left over: for example, steel that is salvaged from a wrecked car.
Scrooge (proper name) Character in Charles Dickens' *A Christmas Carol*, an English story written in the mid-1850s. He was unbelievably miserly and disagreeable (but in the story he reformed).
Sears Catalog (noun) Sears, Roebuck and Co. is a large chain of stores that sells a wide variety of goods. Before shopping malls, interstate highways, and the Internet, Sears used to have a huge mailing list to which it sent enormous catalogs. A person receiving such a catalog would have information about, and access to, thousands of items, many of which the person might not have known existed before the catalog provided the prospect.
Seizes Up (verb) To come to a sudden and complete stop that you cannot easily repair or alleviate.
Set Up Shop (verb) To go into business.
Shady (adjective) Questionable, a little bit or more than a little bit dishonest.
Shell Out (verb) To pay money, often somewhat more than you want to pay for the item in question.
Shivering in Their Sandals (descriptive phrase) Adaptation of standard English idiom *shivering in their shoes*, which means being afraid.
Shoo-in (noun) Highly probable (as in "you are a shoo-in" to get an A).
Shorthand (noun) Any of several systems of abbreviated writing or writing that substitutes symbols for words and phrases. Shorthand was widely used in business until the introduction of mechanical and electronic devices for transmitting the human voice gradually made shorthand obsolete. Today it means to summarize very briefly or to substitute a short word or phrase for a long description.
Show-off (noun) To be blatant and vulgar in displaying a possession or accomplishment. The person who is a show-off is displaying conspicuous consumption.
Show Up (verb) To put in an appearance, to arrive.
Shy Away (verb) To decisively refrain from something. (Comes from the world of horses, who are said to "shy at" things that startle them.)
Silk Stockings (noun) Silk stockings for women denoted luxury and extravagance, almost like caviar or pearls. With the development of nylon in 1940, silk stockings for anyone, let alone the queens or factory girls mentioned in this book, joined the dinosaurs in oblivion.
Sixpence (noun) A British coin that is no longer in use. It represented six British pennies; its U.S. equivalent in the 2000s would be about a nickel.
Skin of One's Teeth (descriptive phrase) To succeed by the skin of one's teeth means to just barely succeed. A micromeasure less and one would not have succeeded.
Skyrocket (verb and noun) Verb: to rise suddenly and rapidly. Noun: the type of fireworks that shoot into the sky and explode suddenly in a shower of brilliant sparks.
Slow as Molasses (descriptive phrase) Very slow. Molasses is a thick, sweet syrup made from sugar cane (known as "treacle" in the United Kingdom) that pours with agonizing slowness from its container.
Small Potatoes (noun) An expression meaning insignificant or trivial.
Smoke Screen (noun) Metaphorically, anything used intentionally to hide one's true intentions.
Smoking Gun (noun) This term has come to stand for any indisputable evidence of guilt or misdeeds.
Snitch (verb) To engage in petty theft. (This verb has another meaning, which is to betray a person by divulging a secret about that person. If you do that, you are not only snitching, you are a snitch.)
Snowball (verb) To increase rapidly, like a ball of wet snow that grows and grows when it is rolled rapidly in more wet snow.
Soft Drink (noun) Nonalcoholic beverage.
Sourpuss (noun) Dour; sulky; humorless. Derives from *sour*, which is self-explanatory, and *puss*, a slang word for "face."
Speakeasy (noun) A bar—a place to drink alcoholic beverages—that is operating illegally without a license. They were common in the United States during Prohibition, a period (1919–1933) when the sale and/or consumption of alcoholic beverages were prohibited by an amendment to the U.S. Constitution and lifted when that Constitutional amendment was revoked.
Spending a Penny (descriptive phrase) Spending any money at all. Do not confuse with usage in England, where the phrase means to go to the bathroom.

Spoils (noun) Rewards or advantages gained through illegal or unethical activity.
Squash (verb) To crush or ruin.
Squirrel Away (verb) To hide or conceal in a handy but secret place (as a squirrel stores nuts).
***Star Trek* (title)** Famous U.S. TV series about life in outer space.
Stay on Their Toes (idiom) To be alert.
Steady (noun) A person to whom you are romantically committed and with whom you spend a lot of time, especially in social activities.
Stealth Gains (noun) Gains that occur unbeknownst to you.
Sticky (adjective) Resistant to change, as if glued on.
Strings Attached (descriptive phrase) A gift that comes with strings attached comes with certain conditions set forth by the donor.
Strongarm (adjective) Repressive and violent.
Sucker (noun) A gullible person.
Super Bowl (noun) Important football game played annually that attracts millions of viewers (most of them see the game on TV).
Swap (verb and noun) Verb: to trade one thing for another. Noun: the trade itself.
Sweetheart Contract (noun) A contract where one party to the contract is given all, or almost all, the advantage; specifically, a contract between an employer and the workers' union where the employer gains the advantage and the contract on the workers' side has been arranged by a union official who secretly gives up advantages for the workers in return for significant advantage for the official.
Switch Gears (verb/noun) Change your strategy.

T

Tables Were Turned (descriptive phrase) The advantage of one side over the other reverses so that now the winner is the loser and the loser is the winner.
Tacky (adjective) In very poor taste.
Take a Flier (expression) To take a chance; to undertake a risky action in the hope that you will be lucky.
Take the Heat (verb) To accept all criticism of one's action or inaction, whether or not one is actually the person that should be blamed.
Take Title (verb) Legal term meaning to acquire ownership.
Tea Control (noun) A method of resolving differences by informal but powerful social mechanisms, such as inviting your opponents to tea and settling matters while passing teacups and plates of cake around.
Temp (noun) Worker whose job is temporary and who accepts the job with that understanding.
Tidy (adjective) Neat, advantageous, profitable. "A tidy sum" is a really nice amount of money that you may not have expected to acquire.
Time-and-a-Half (noun) In labor law, 150 percent of the normal hourly wage.
Tombstone Ad (noun) Newspaper advertisement announcing the completion of a stock or bond offering.
Ton (noun) A ton weighs 2,000 pounds and an English ton (often spelled "tonne") weighs 2,240 pounds. In this book, the term is used most frequently to mean simply "a large quantity."
Tough (adjective) Very difficult.
Trendy (adjective) A phenomenon that is slightly ahead of traditional ways and indicates a trend. Something trendy may turn into something traditional, or it may fade away without ever becoming mainstream.
Trophy Spouse (noun) A spouse (usually the wife) who is young, beautiful, and perhaps famous and/or rich who has been married to an older—sometimes much older—very successful and rich person, usually after divorcing one or more previous spouses. The trophy spouse is just that—a trophy. (See "show-off.")
Truck (verb) To exchange one thing for another. This was Adam Smith's definition in 1776 and it is still one of the meanings of the verb.
Truth (noun) When capitalized (other than at the start of a sentence), true beyond any doubt (as opposed to "truth"—the best truth we have at the moment).
Tune In (verb) To become familiar with.
Turf (noun) Territory, especially the figurative territory of a firm.
Turn of the Century (expression) The few years at the end of an expiring century and the beginning of a new century. For example: 1998–2002.
Turn Up One's Nose (verb) To reject.
Twinkies (noun) Brand name of an inexpensive small cake.

U

Under-the-Counter (adjective) Secret or concealed by an unscrupulous person. Also see *under the table* below.
Under the Table (descriptive phrase) To accept money surreptitiously in order to avoid paying taxes on it or to conceal the income for other reasons. Also, to proffer such money to avoid having it known that you are making a particular deal.
Union Jack (noun) Nickname for the British flag.
Up at Bat (expression) From the sport of baseball. A player (the "batter") who is in the position ("home plate") where a player from the opposing team (the "pitcher") will throw the ball to him. The player to whom the ball is

thrown is "up at bat." Thus, to be up at bat can mean being ready to meet an impending emergency or other situation.

Up in Arms (adjective) Furious and loudly protesting. Comes from the use of *arms* to stand for *firearms*.

V

Vanity License Plate (descriptive phrase) One-of-a-kind motor vehicle license plate issued to your individual specification. It might have your name, your profession, or any individual set of letters and numbers you choose that will fit on the plate.

Vignette (noun) Short little story that uses a few words to illustrate or reinforce a point.

Village Watchman (descriptive phrase) Before modern communication technology, in small communities local news was gathered and reported by an official, the village watchman or town crier, who walked around collecting facts and gossip.

Vinyl Records (adjective) Device for listening to recorded material. They were circular disks—some 8 inches in diameter, some 12 inches in diameter. Made of "vinyl," disks had a hole in the center and were placed over a small spike on a turntable.

W–X

Wadget (noun) Term used by economists to stand for any manufactured good except goods designated as widgets, which see.

Wal-Mart (proper name) A very large store that sells thousands of inexpensive items. There are thousands of Wal-Marts in the United States and the company has expanded into foreign markets.

Wampum (noun) String of beads made of polished shells, formerly used by North American Indians as money.

Wash (noun) Process or event that neutralizes an "either/or" situation; in fact, eliminates the argument or erases the event.

Whatever (noun) Designates an unspecified generic item or action when the speaker wants to let you know that it doesn't matter whether you know the exact item or place.

Wheaties (proper noun) Name of a brand of dry breakfast cereal.

White Elephant (noun) Property requiring expensive care but yielding little profit; trinket without value to most people but esteemed by a few. There are real white elephants, which are albinos. They are rare and therefore expensive and high-maintenance.

White Knight (noun) A company that comes to the rescue of another company. The term comes from the game of chess—some chess sets have white pieces and black pieces—and from the children's book, *Alice Through the Looking Glass*, where the story is structured as a game of chess and a chess piece, the white knight, tries to rescue Alice.

Whiz (noun) An expert.

Whopper (proper noun) Brand name of a kind of hamburger sold at Burger King restaurants.

Widget (noun) The opposite of a wadget, which see.

Wild About (descriptive phrase) Extremely enthusiastic about undertaking a particular action or admiring a particular object or person.

Wind Up (descriptive phrase) To discover that you have reached a particular conclusion or destination.

With-It (adjective) Current in one's knowledge.

Wodget (noun) A made-up term for a produced good. Variation of widget, which see.

Workhorse (noun) Common everyday method of accomplishing a task—nothing fancy. A "workhorse" in actuality is a strong horse of no particular beauty or attraction but is useful for pulling heavy loads in situations where using a machine is impractical.

Working Off the Books (descriptive phrase) Being paid wages or fees that are not reported to the tax or other authorities by either the payer or the payee.

World Series (complex noun) At the end of the baseball season the two opposing teams left after the season's contests have eliminated all the other teams meet each other. The winner in this "World Series" wins the season.

World War I (proper noun) 1914–1918. The United States did not enter until 1917.

World War II (proper noun) 1938–1945. The United States did not enter until 1941.

Wound Up (past tense of verb *wind up*) To have found oneself in a particular situation after having taken particular actions.

Writ Large (adjective) Strongly emphasized; defined broadly. ("Writ" is an obsolete form of the word "written.")

Writing on the Wall (descriptive phrase) To see the writing on the wall is to realize that a situation is inevitably going to end badly. It comes from the Biblical story that Nebuchadnezzar, king of Babylon, saw a fatal prediction written on a wall.

Y

You Bet! (exclamation) Expression meaning "It certainly is!" or "Absolutely!"

Z

Zune (proper name) A compact digital music player designed by Microsoft to compete with the iPod.

Photo Credits

ABOUT THE AUTHOR

page vii: Tad Merrick.

CHAPTER 1

page 4: © Hulton-Deutsch Collection/Corbis; **page 9:** Bleichroeder Print Collection, Baker Library, Harvard Business School; **page 11:** © Rachel Epstein/PhotoEdit; **page 14:** © Bettmann/Corbis; **page 16:** © Steve Cole/Getty Images/DAL; **page 19:** © AP Photo/Alden Pellett.

CHAPTER 2

page 25: © Royalty-Free/Corbis/DAL; **page 34:** (a) © PhotoDisc/Getty Images/RF; (b) © Jon Riley/Getty Images/RF; **page 38:** © Michael Newman/PhotoEdit; **page 39:** © AFP/Getty Images; **page 40:** Image courtesy of the Foresight Institute and the Institute for Molecular Manufacturing (IMM), www.imm.org.

CHAPTER 3

page 55: © Marianna Day Massey/ZUMA/Corbis; **page 58:** © AP Photo; **page 69:** © Digital Vision/Getty Images/RF.

CHAPTER 4

page 83: © Mike Ditz/2007 Transtock.com; **page 92:** © Royalty-Free/Corbis/DAL; **page 95:** © The McGraw-Hill Companies, Inc./Gary He, photographer/DAL.

CHAPTER 5

page 106: © National Oceanic and Atmospheric Administration/Department of Commerce; **page 114:** © Rachel Epstein/PhotoEdit.

CHAPTER 6

page 127: Book cover of *Freakonomics* by Steven D. Levitt and Stephen J. Dubner, William Morrow Publishers. Photo © Roberts Publishing Services; **page 131:** Book cover of *Predictably Irrational* by Dan Ariely, HarperCollins Publishers. Photo © Roberts Publishing Services; **page 131:** © PhotoAlto/PictureQuest/DAL; **page 132:** Image from Robert Bloomfield's Metanomics™. Used by permission; **page 133:** © Brand X Pictures/PunchStock/DAL; **page 134:** Book cover of *The Armchair Economist* by Steven E. Landsburg, The Free Press, Division of Simon & Schuster, Inc. Photo © Roberts Publishing Services; **page 136:** Book cover of *More Sex Is Safer Sex: The Unconventional Wisdom of Economics* by Steven E. Landsburg, The Free Press, Division of Simon & Schuster, Inc. Photo © Roberts Publishing Services; **page 137:** Prada shoes product, © PRADA 2008; **page 138:** Book cover of *The Economic Naturalist* by Robert H. Frank, Basic Books. Photo © Roberts Publishing Services; **page 139:** © Nice One Productions/Corbis/RF; **page 142:** Original image from an anonymous German postcard, circa 1888, public domain.

CHAPTER 7

page 154: © AP Photo/Rick Maiman; **page 158:** © Erica S. Leeds/DAL; **page 162:** © Tony Freeman/PhotoEdit; **page 169:** © AP Photo/Neil Redmond.

CHAPTER 8

page 179: George Cruikshank, Plucking a Goose, c. 1824. Pen and brown ink. Collection Grunwald Center for the Graphic Arts. Richard Volger Cruikshank Collection, Hammer Museum, Los Angeles. Photography by Robert Wedemeyer; **page 182:** © Royalty-Free/Corbis/DAL; **page 186:** © BananaStock/JupiterImages/DAL; **page 197:** Courtesy of David Colander.

CHAPTER 9

page 198: © Mike Nelson/AFP/Getty Images; **page 216:** © C. Sherburne/PhotoLink/DAL; **page 219:** © Paul Conklin/PhotoEdit.

CHAPTER 10

page 230: *Top Left:* © Ryan McVay/Getty Images/DAL; **page 230:** *Top Right:* © Ryan McVay/Getty Images/DAL; **page 230:** *Bottom Left:* © Brand X Pictures/PunchStock/DAL; **page 230:** *Bottom Right:* © Royalty-Free/Corbis/DAL; **page 232:** © Chris Hondros/Getty Images; **page 242:** © Royalty-Free/Corbis/DAL; **page 242:** © age fotostock/SuperStock.

CHAPTER 11

page 255: © Twentieth Century Fox/Photofest; **page 264:** © Twentieth Century Fox/Photofest; **page 266:** © Bill Inashita/CBS Archive via Getty Images.

CHAPTER 12

page 276: © The McGraw-Hill Companies, Inc./John Flournoy, photographer/DAL; **page 279:** © GeoStock/Getty Images/DAL; **page 279:** © Neil Beer/Getty Images/DAL; **page 279:** © PRNewsFoto/AK Steel/AP Images; **page 279:** © PRNewsFoto/The HON Company/AP Images; **page 290:** "Book Cover" from HORTON HATCHES THE EGG by Dr. Seuss, TM & Copyright © by Dr. Seuss Enterprises, L.P. 1940, renewed 1968. Used by permission of Random House Children's Books, a Division of Random House, Inc.

CHAPTER 13

page 295: © Royalty-Free/Corbis/DAL; **page 297:** © PRNewsFoto/Mazda North American Operations/AP Images; **page 299:** © Kent Knudson/PhotoLink/DAL; **page 302:** © David Young-Wolff/PhotoEdit; **page 304:** © Bettmann/Corbis; **page •••:** © PhotoDisc/Getty Images/DAL; **page 306:** © Digital Vision/PunchStock/DAL.

CHAPTER 14

page 317: © JP Laffont/Sygma/Corbis; **page 319:** Courtesy of Priceline.com. Used with permission; **page 327:** © Dynamic Graphics/PictureQuest/RF; **page 331:** © Bob Krist/Corbis; **page 334:** © Spencer Grant/PhotoEdit.

CHAPTER 15

page 340: © Nancy P. Alexander/PhotoEdit; **page 341:** No Credit; **page 348:** © Vincent Hobbs/SuperStock; **page 352:** Used with permission from Ralph Anspach and University Games.

CHAPTER 16

page 361: © AP Photo/Carlos Osorio.

CHAPTER 17

page 384: © AP Photo/John Froschauer; **page 386:** © Bob Daemmrich/Corbis; **page 387:** © Roy McMahon/Corbis/RF/DAL; **page 395:** © The McGraw-Hill Companies, Inc./Jill Braaten, photographer/DAL.

CHAPTER 18

page 404: © AP Photo/Tyler Mallory; **page 405:** © Bettman /Corbis; **page 409:** © David McNew/Getty Images; **page 411:** © Koichi Kamoshida/Getty Images; **page 414:** Microsoft product shot(s) reprinted with permission from Microsoft Corporation; **page 421:** © AP Photo/Pat Sullivan.

CHAPTER 19

page 430: © Ryan McVay/Getty Images/DAL; **page 446:** © Bettman/Corbis.

CHAPTER 19W

page 459 and page 19W-1: © Jack Star/PhotoLink/Getty Images/DAL; **page 19W-11:** Bleichroeder Print Collection, Baker Library, Harvard Business School.

CHAPTER 20

page 460: *Left:* © Hola Images/Getty Images/RF; **page 460:** *Right:* © Digital Vision/PunchStock/DAL; **page 479:** © Jack Star/PhotoLink/Getty Images/DAL.

CHAPTER 21

page 485: © Alex Wong/Getty Images; **page 489:** © PhotoLink/Getty Images/DAL; **page 498:** © Royalty-Free/Corbis/DAL; **page 500:** © Carl De Souza/AFP/Getty Images.

CHAPTER 21W

page 505 and page 21W-1: Photo by Lynn Betts, courtesy of USDA Natural Resources Conservation Service/DAL; **page 21W-2:** © Business Wire, General Mills/AP Images; **page 21W-4:** Courtesy of U.S. Department of Agriculture; **page 21W-11:** © Scenics of America/ PhotoLink/DAL.

CHAPTER 22

page 506: © Roberts Publishing Services; **page 509:** © AP Photo/Jim Bourg.

CHAPTER 23

page 524: © AP Photo/Ron Edmonds; **page 528:** © Royalty-Free/Corbis/DAL; **page 529:** © Royalty-Free/Corbis/DAL; **page 536:** © Louie Psihoyos/Science Faction; **page 538:** Courtesy of UNOS.

CHAPTER 24

page 546: © New York Times Graphics; **page 551:** Courtesy of Nation Bureau of Economic Research, Inc; **page 557:** © Andy Sacks/Getty Images.

CHAPTER 25

page 574: Image Source White/Getty Images/RF; **page 575:** Bleichroeder Print Collection, Baker Library, Harvard Business School; **page 589:** © David McNew/Getty Images.

CHAPTER 26

page 595: © Medioimages/Getty Images/DAL; **page 605:** © AP Photo/Amy Sancetta; **page 615:** © John Van Hasselt/Corbis.

CHAPTER 27

page 620: © AP Photo/Beth A. Keiser; **page 621:** © Bettman/Corbis; **page 637:** © PhotoDisc/Getty Images/RF.

CHAPTER 28

page 648: © Science Museum/Science & Society Picture Library, London; **page 649:** © Anthony Ise/Getty Images/DAL.

CHAPTER 29

page 678: © PaloAlto/PictureQuest/DAL; **page 690:** © AP Photo.

CHAPTER 30

page 702: © Collection of the New-York Historical Society, accession number 1971.104; **page 709:** © C. Sherburne/Photo Link/DAL; **page 710:** © PhotoLink/Getty Images/DAL; **page 711:** © AP Photo/Doug Mills; **page 717:** © PhotoDisc/Getty Images/DAL; **page 718:** Bleichroeder Print Collection, Baker Library, Harvard Business School; **page 720:** © Brand X Pictures/DAL.

CHAPTER 31

page 731: © AP Photo/J. Scott Applewhite; **page 734:** © Yuan Xuejun/The Image Works; **page 738:** Federal Reserve Photo—Britt Leckman.

CHAPTER 32

page 753: © Chris Hondros/Getty Images; **page 756:** Public domain image was scanned from reprint of 1841/1852 editions of Extraordinary Popular Delusions and the Madness of Crowds by Charles Mackay, LLD; **page 765:** © Joel Sartore/Getty Images; **page 770:** © Royalty-Free/Corbis/DAL.

CHAPTER 33

page 776: © Bettman /Corbis; **page 782:** © Time & Life Pictures/Getty Images; **page 782:** Bleichroeder Print Collection, Baker Library, Harvard Business School; **page 783:** Courtesy of the Federal Reserve Bank of Dallas.

CHAPTER 34

page 797: © AP Photo/Kathy Willens; **page 813:** Bleichroeder Print Collection, Baker Library, Harvard Business School.

CHAPTER 35

page 818: © AP Photo/J. Scott Applewhite; **page 826:** Photo courtesy of U.S. Army Center of Military History/NARA/Signal Corps. Photo # CC045191; **page 831:** © Denis Scott/Corbis.

CHAPTER 36

page 836: © AP Photo/Sang Tan; **page 844:** © Stockbyte/Getty Images/RF.

CHAPTER 37

page 864: © The New Yorker Collection 2004 Drew Dernavich from cartoonbank.com. All Rights Reserved; **page 866:** © Daisuke Morita/Getty Images/DAL.

CHAPTER 38

page 879: © Dr. Parvinder/DAL; **page 884:** Courtesy of Kiva.org; **page 892:** © AP Photo/str; **page 894:** Book covers of *The End of Poverty* by Jeffrey D. Sachs, The Penguin Press and *The White Man's Burden* by William Easterly, The Penguin Press. Photo © Roberts Publishing Services.

Index

Page numbers followed by n refer to notes.

C

D

M

Q

R

S

Hours and Earnings in Private Nonagricultural Industries, 1959–2008[1]

[Monthly data seasonally adjusted]

Year	Average Weekly Hours			Average Hourly Earnings			Average Weekly Earnings, Total Private			
		Manufacturing		Total Private		Manufacturing (current dollars)	Level		Percent Change from Year Earlier	
	Total Private	Total	Overtime	Current Dollars	1982 Dollars[2]		Current Dollars	1982 Dollars[2]	Current Dollars	1982 Dollars[2]
1959	39.0	40.3	2.7	$ 2.02	$6.69	$ 2.08	$ 78.78	$260.86	4.9	4.2
1960	38.6	39.8	2.5	2.09	6.79	2.15	80.67	261.92	2.4	0.4
1965	38.6	41.2	3.6	2.63	8.04	2.49	101.52	310.46	4.2	2.6
1970	37.0	39.8	2.9	3.40	8.46	3.23	125.80	312.94	4.2	−1.3
1975	36.0	39.5	2.6	4.73	8.48	4.71	170.28	305.16	5.6	−3.1
1980	35.2	39.7	2.8	6.84	7.99	7.15	240.77	281.27	6.8	−5.9
1985	34.9	40.5	3.3	8.73	7.91	9.40	304.68	276.23	2.4	−1.1
1990	34.3	40.5	3.8	10.19	7.66	10.78	349.29	262.43	3.3	−1.8
1995	34.3	41.3	4.7	11.64	7.53	12.34	399.53	258.43	2.3	−0.6
1996	34.3	41.3	4.8	12.03	7.57	12.75	412.74	259.58	3.3	0.4
1997	34.5	41.7	5.1	12.49	7.68	13.14	431.86	265.60	4.5	2.2
1998	34.5	41.4	4.8	13.00	7.89	13.45	448.56	272.18	3.9	2.5
1999	34.3	41.4	4.8	13.47	8.00	13.85	463.15	275.03	3.3	1.0
2000	34.3	41.3	4.7	14.00	8.03	14.32	481.01	275.97	3.9	0.3
2001	34.0	40.3	4.0	14.53	8.11	14.76	493.79	275.71	2.7	0.0
2002	33.9	40.5	4.2	14.95	8.24	15.29	506.72	279.18	2.6	1.3
2003	33.7	40.4	4.2	15.35	8.27	15.74	518.16	279.13	2.3	0.0
2004	33.7	40.8	4.6	15.69	8.24	16.14	529.09	277.88	2.1	−0.5
2005	33.8	40.7	4.6	16.13	8.18	16.56	544.33	276.17	2.9	−0.6
2006	33.9	41.1	4.4	16.76	8.24	16.81	567.87	279.19	4.3	1.1
2007	33.9	41.2	4.2	17.43	8.33	17.26	590.04	281.97	3.9	1.0
2008	33.6	40.8	3.7	18.08	8.30	17.74	607.99	279.14	3.0	−1.0

[1]For production or nonsupervisory workers; total includes private industry groups.

[2]Current dollars divided by the consumer price index for urban wage earners and clerical workers on a 1982 = 100 base.

Source: Department of Labor, Bureau of Labor Statistics.

Industrial Production and Consumer Prices, Percent Change, 1980–2008

Year	Industrial Production				Consumer Prices			
	United States	Canada	Japan	European Union	United States	Canada	Japan	European Union
1980	−2.8	−3.1	4.6	0.0	13.5	10.0	7.7	13.4
1985	1.0	5.1	3.7	3.0	3.6	4.1	2.1	6.1
1990	0.8	−2.8	4.3	3.5	5.4	4.8	3.1	5.9
1991	−1.7	−3.5	1.7	0.2	4.2	5.6	3.2	5.2
1992	2.6	1.3	−5.6	−1.3	3.0	1.5	1.7	4.5
1993	3.3	4.9	−3.4	−3.6	3.0	1.8	1.4	3.6
1994	5.3	6.2	1.2	4.9	2.6	0.2	0.6	3.1
1995	4.8	4.6	3.2	3.1	2.8	2.2	−0.1	3.1
1996	4.3	1.3	2.3	0.2	3.0	1.6	0.1	2.5
1997	7.3	5.6	3.5	3.6	2.3	−0.3	1.8	2.1
1998	5.8	3.5	−6.5	3.2	1.6	2.9	0.6	1.8
1999	4.5	5.9	0.3	1.6	2.2	1.7	−0.3	1.3
2000	4.5	8.6	5.5	4.5	3.4	2.7	−0.7	2.3
2001	−3.5	−3.9	−6.4	−0.1	2.8	2.5	−0.7	2.4
2002	0.0	1.5	−1.1	−0.8	1.6	2.2	−0.9	2.2
2003	1.1	1.6	2.8	0.6	2.3	2.8	−0.3	2.1
2004	2.5	0.2	5.4	2.2	2.8	1.9	0.0	2.1
2005	3.2	1.8	1.1	1.1	3.9	2.2	−0.4	2.2
2006	4.6	0.0	4.8	4.8	3.2	2.0	0.3	2.2
2007	1.5	0.0	1.1	3.7	2.8	2.2	0.0	2.4
2008	−2.3	−4.7	−1.6	−1.8	3.8	2.3	1.4	3.6

Source: Bureau of Labor Statistics, Federal Reserve, Eurostat, METI.